Encyclopedia
of the
American Constitution

Editorial Board

Encyclopedia
of the
American Constitution

LEONARD W. LEVY, Editor-in-Chief
Claremont Graduate School, Claremont, California

KENNETH L. KARST, Associate Editor
University of California, Los Angeles

DENNIS J. MAHONEY, Assistant Editor
Claremont Graduate School, Claremont, California

MACMILLAN PUBLISHING COMPANY
A Division of Macmillan, Inc.
NEW YORK

Collier Macmillan Publishers
LONDON

Macmillan Publishing Company
A Division of Macmillan, Inc.
866 Third Avenue, New York, NY 10022

Collier Macmillan Canada, Inc.

Printed in the United States of America

printing number
1   2   3   4   5   6   7   8   9   10

Library of Congress Catalog in Publication Data

Encyclopedia of the American Constitution.

Includes index.
1. United States—Constitutional Law—Dictionaries.
I. Levy, Leonard Williams, 1923–   II. Karst,
Kenneth L.   III. Mahoney, Dennis J.
KF4548.E53 1986   342.73′023′03   86–3038
ISBN 0–02–918610–2   347.3022303

STAFF:

Charles E. Smith, *Publisher*

Elly Dickason, *Project Editor*

Morton I. Rosenberg, *Production Manager*

Joan Greenfield, *Designer*

C

(Continued)

CONSTITUTIONALISM

Constitutionalism is a term not altogether congenial to American lawyers. It seems to share the characteristics of other "isms": it is neither clearly prescriptive nor clearly descriptive; its contours are difficult to discern; its historical roots are diverse and uncertain. Legal realist WALTON H. HAMILTON, who wrote on the subject for the *Encyclopedia of the Social Sciences*, began his article in an ironic vein: "Constitutionalism is the name given to the trust which men repose in the power of words engrossed on parchment to keep a government in order."

Historians, on the other hand, employ the concept with some confidence in its meaning. American historians tend to use it as a shorthand reference to the constitutional thought of the founding period. European historians have a somewhat harder time. Given a largely UNWRITTEN CONSTITUTION and the SOVEREIGNTY of Parliament, what does it mean to refer to British constitutionalism? What is the significance of Dicey's distinction between the "conventions of the constitution" and the "law of the constitution"? How meaningful is the distinction? As Dicey noted: "Whatever may be the advantages of a so-called unwritten constitution, its existence imposes special difficulties on teachers bound to expound its provisions." French authors view constitutionalism as an important element of the French Revolution, but run into difficulties as they contemplate the fact that, since the constitution of 1791, France has had fifteen of them—and by no means all democratic. German historians tend to restrict the use of the term *Konstitu-*

tionalismus to the Central European constitutional monarchies of the nineteenth century, though German-language equivalents for constitutionalism (*Verfassungsstaat, Verfassungsbegriff*) are frequently encountered in the literature. The German constitutionalist trauma is, of course, the ease with which the Weimar constitution, in its time viewed as one of the most progressive in the world, could be brought to collapse at the hands of determined enemies who then managed to organize arbitrariness in the form of law.

Constitutionalism has both descriptive and prescriptive connotations. Used descriptively, it refers chiefly to the historical struggle for constitutional recognition of the people's right to "consent" and certain other rights, freedoms, and privileges. This struggle extends roughly from the seventeenth century to the present day. Its beginnings coincide with the "enlightenment" of the seventeenth and eighteenth centuries. Used prescriptively, especially in the United States, its meaning incorporates those features of government seen as the essential elements of the American Constitution. Thus F. A. Hayek called constitutionalism the American contribution to the RULE OF LAW.

Constitutionalism obviously presupposes the concept of a CONSTITUTION. A Swiss authority of some influence in the American revolution, EMERICH DE VATTEL, in his famous 1758 treatise, *The Law of Nations or the Principles of Natural Law,* provided a definition: "The FUNDAMENTAL LAW which determines the manner in which the public authority is to be exercised is what forms the *constitution of the State.* In it can be seen the organization by means of which the Nation acts as a political body; how and

473

by whom the people are to be governed; and what are the rights and duties of those who govern. This constitution is nothing else at bottom than the establishment of the system, according to which a Nation proposed to work in common to obtain the advantages for which a political society is formed."

This rather neutral definition has to be read against the background of Vattel's theory of natural law. Vattel recognized the right of the majority to reform its government and, most important, excluded fundamental laws from the reach of legislators, "unless they are expressly empowered by the nation to change them." Moreover, Vattel believed that the ends of civil society were "to procure for its citizens the necessities, the comforts, and the pleasures of life, and in general their happiness; to secure to each the peaceful enjoyment of his property and a sure means of obtaining justice; and finally to defend the whole body against all external violence."

Later in the eighteenth century strong prescriptive elements became part of the very definition of a constitution. Two examples are equally famous. On October 21, 1776, the town of Concord, Massachusetts, resolved "that a Constitution in its Proper Idea intends a System of Principles Established to Secure the Subject in the Possession and enjoyment of their Rights and Privileges, against any Encroachment of the Governing Part." (See CONCORD RESOLUTION.) Article 16 of the French Declaration of the Rights of Man of 1789 put it even more bluntly: "A society in which the guarantee of rights is not assured nor the SEPARATION OF POWERS provided for, has no constitution."

Although it would be impractical to make such substantive features a necessary part of one's definition of a written or unwritten constitution, a proper understanding of constitutionalism as a historical phenomenon depends on them. Constitutionalism does not refer simply to having a constitution but to having a particular kind of constitution, however difficult it may be to specify its content. This assertion holds true even in the case of the interplay of old forces (monarchies and estates) with new forces (the middle class in particular) which characterized the emergence of constitutional monarchies in Central Europe during the nineteenth century. Seen from a constitutionalist perspective, many of the German constitutional monarchies were influenced by concepts that had much in common with constitutionalist thought. The most important of these concepts was the *Rechtsstaat:* a state based on "reason" and a strict regulation of government by law.

The concepts of a constitution and of fundamental laws have not had a constant meaning over time. Since the eighteenth century (though not before), it has become customary to translate Aristotle's word *politeia* as "constitution": "A constitution is the arrangement of the offices in a *polis,* but especially of the highest office." This definition precedes Aristotle's differentiation among six forms of government—those for the common good (monarchy, aristocracy, and "polity") and their perversions, which serve individual interests (tyranny, oligarchy, and democracy). Aristotle thus introduced substantive, not merely formal, criteria into his teachings about constitutional arrangements.

Cicero is usually credited with first giving the Latin term *constitutio* something like its modern meaning. About a mixed form of government, he said in *De Re Publica:* "This constitution has a great measure of equability without which men can hardly remain free for any length of time." Indeed, Roman law was characterized by constitutional notions. The constitution of the Roman republic, putting other substantive arrangements aside, was marked by the power of the plebs to pass on laws which bound the entire Roman people. While this republican prerogative of the plebs was later replaced by Senate lawmaking and eventually by the emperor's legislative monopoly, its status is perhaps best illustrated by Augustus's repeated refusal, on "constitutional" grounds, to accept extraordinary powers to renew law and morals. Though this Augustan reticence may have been a triumph of form over substance, "triumphs" of this kind have frequently illustrated how constitutional notions have become deeply entrenched.

In subsequent Roman usage the term *constitutio* came to identify imperial legislation that preempted all other law. The understanding of *constitutio* as signifying important legislation was retained during the Middle Ages in the Holy Roman Empire, in the church, and throughout Europe. A well-known English example is the Constitution of Clarendon issued by Henry II in 1164.

In England, the modern use of constitution as referring to the nature, government, and fundamental laws of a state dates from the early seventeenth century. In the House of Commons, in 1610, James Whitelock argued that the imposition of taxes by James I was "against the natural frame and constitution of the policy of this kingdom, which is ius publicum regni, and so subverteth the fundamental law of the realm and induceth a new form of State and government."

In Europe, perception that some laws were more fundamental than others were well established before the eighteenth century. MAGNA CARTA (1215), the PETITION OF RIGHT (1628), and the HABEAS CORPUS

Act (1679) are the best known English illustrations of this point. In addition, by their coronation oaths English kings obliged themselves "to hold and keep the laws and righteous customs which the community of [the] realm shall have chosen." Even if the law could not reach the king, the king was viewed as under the law (and, of course, under God). The bounds of the king's discretion were defined by the ancient laws and customs of England or, put differently, the COMMON LAW. By the seventeenth century, EDWARD COKE was even prepared to claim that acts of Parliament were subject to review under the common law (and natural law).

Though the status of French kings was considerably more mysterious and legal constraints on them were far fewer than in England, they too were viewed as subject to fundamental laws. The French Protestant political theorists of the sixteenth century expressed far-reaching views on the matter. François Hotman subtitled the XXVth chapter of the third edition of his *Francogallia* (1586): "The king of France does not have unlimited domain in his kingdom but is circumscribed by settled and specific law."

Beginning in the seventeenth century, the struggle over the limits of power, the ends of government, and the limits of obedience was frequently expressed in terms of social contract theory. Johannes Althusius, Hugo Grotius, JOHN LOCKE, and Jean-Jacques Rousseau all influenced the civil struggles of their age. Although the differences among these writers are profound, all of them stipulate a SOCIAL COMPACT as the foundation for the constitutional arrangements of the state. While such a contract is not necessarily based on an assumption of popular sovereignty, a social contract without the assumed or actual consent of "the people" or their representatives is unthinkable. Once this notion spread widely, it was difficult to maintain the divine right of kings, and it became almost irresistible to relocate sovereignty in the people—Thomas Hobbes notwithstanding.

One must not confuse the concept of a social contract with that of a constitution. For the "contractarians," constitutions follow from the social contract; they are not identical with it. Although the social contract is mostly a logical stipulation, at times the contract seems real enough, embodying or justifying specific constitutional arrangements. The Glorious Revolution in England, the American Revolution, the French Revolution—all appealed to the social contract.

The Glorious Revolution, like the English Civil War before it, was seen in contractarian terms. The Convention Parliament of 1689 resolved that James II "having endeavored to subvert the constitution of the kingdom by breaking the original contract between king and people . . . has abdicated the government and the throne is hereby vacant." The Declaration of Rights of 1689 was part of Parliament's contract with William and Mary and, later that year, was incorporated into the act of Parliament known as the BILL OF RIGHTS. After reciting Parliament's grievances against the absolutist tendencies of James II, the Bill of Rights prohibited the suspension of the laws by regal authority; provided for the election and privileges of Parliament (including a prohibition of prerogative taxation); and dealt with the right to petition, excessive bail, and the jury system.

Although this catalogue of constitutional concerns is modest by contemporary standards, the Bill of Rights, in conjunction with other British traditions and the "mixed government" confirmed by the Glorious Revolution, led MONTESQUIEU to celebrate England as the one nation in the world "that has for the direct end of its constitution political liberty." Montesquieu concluded his chapter on "The Constitution of England" in *The Spirit of the Laws* with the wry comment that it was not his task to examine whether the English actually enjoyed this liberty. "Sufficient it is for my purpose to observe, that it is established by their laws; and I inquire no further." When Montesquieu's book was published in 1748, some questions about constitutional liberty in England might indeed have been examined. For instance, the right to vote was extremely restricted and even that small electorate was not consulted when, by the Septennial Act of 1716, Parliament extended its own duration by another four years. For the American colonists who fought more against the British Parliament than against their monarch, this example of the "sovereignty of Parliament" marked the limit of British constitutionalism. As JAMES MADISON wrote in THE FEDERALIST #53, citing the Septennial Act: "Where no constitution paramount to the government, either existed or could be obtained, no constitutional security similar to that established in the United States, was to be attempted."

American constitutionalism during the colonial and revolutionary periods included the notions of a constitution as superior to legislation and the notion of a written constitution. As concerns the "writing" of constitutions, Gerald Stourzh has remarked, for the period after 1776, that Americans clearly differentiated "between the functions of constitution-*making* (with an additional differentiation between drafting and ratifying functions), of *amending* constitutions, and of *legislating* within the framework of the constitution."

One formal element in the American colonies was bound to have a profound impact on American constitutionalism, especially its choice of written constitutions as the means for anchoring the organization of their governments and the protection of their rights and privileges. COLONIAL CHARTERS, fundamental orders, and other written documents were used in the establishment of the colonies. These contracts between rulers and ruled provided for the government of the colonies, secured property rights, and even extended the guaranteed liberties and privileges of the English constitution. The 1629 CHARTER OF MASSACHUSETTS BAY is an important early example.

Pennsylvania, however, provides the most vivid illustration of the essential features and conundrums of American constitutionalism. In England, in 1682, a "frame of government of the province of Pensilvania" was agreed to by the Governor, WILLIAM PENN, and "divers freemen" of the province. It was a revision of an earlier plan drawn up by Penn which he had called "Fundamental Constitutions of Pennsylvania." The frame of government was replaced by a new frame as early as 1683. Its place was taken in 1701 by the Pennsylvania Charter of Privileges, granted by Penn during his second visit to the province and formally approved by the General Assembly. (See PENNSYLVANIA COLONIAL CHARTERS.) Though the focus here is on the Charter of Privileges, William Penn's preface to the Frame of Government deserves quotation: "*Any government is free to the people under it* (whatever be the frame) *where the laws rule, and the people are a party to those laws,* and more than this is tyranny, oligarchy, or confusion." Having invoked the notions of government of laws and popular consent, Penn went on, however, to warn against excessive optimism about the RULE OF LAW: "Governments, like clocks, go from the motion men give them; and as governments are made and moved by men, so by them they are ruined too." It is difficult to imagine a better reflection on the challenges faced by the American constitution makers of the eighteenth century.

The Pennsylvania Charter of Privileges of 1701 was a remarkable constitutional document. First of all, the charter itself was adopted in a constitutional manner, according to the provisions for amending the Frame of Government. Second, it began, not with the organization of government, but with an issue of fundamental rights: it guaranteed the freedom of conscience and made all Christians eligible for public office. Third, the charter provided for a unicameral representative assembly to be elected annually by the freemen with the right to initiate LEGISLATION and with all parliamentary powers and privileges "according to the Rights of the free-born Subjects of *England,* and as is usual in any of the King's Plantations in *America.*" Fourth, far ahead of its time, it gave to all "criminals" "the same Privileges of Witness and Council as their Prosecutors." Fifth, it guaranteed the "ordinary Course of Justice" in all disputes concerning property. Sixth, the proprietor committed himself and his heirs not to breach the liberties of the charter; anything done to the contrary should "be held of no Force or Effect." Seventh, the liberties, privileges, and benefits granted by the charter were to be enjoyed, "any Law made and passed by this General Assembly, to the Contrary hereof, notwithstanding." Eighth, the charter could be amended only by a vote of "*Six* Parts of *Seven*" of the Assembly and the consent of the governor. Ninth, the guarantee of liberty of conscience was placed even beyond the power of constitutional amendment "because the Happiness of Mankind depends so much upon the Enjoying of Liberty of their Consciences."

This colonial charter, granted by a feudal landowner, embodies the most significant elements of American constitutionalism as it emerged in the course of the century—the concept of consent and the concept of a written constitution sharply differentiated from ordinary legislation and with provisions for its amendment and a bill of rights, however rudimentary. Indeed, by placing the liberty of conscience beyond the amending power it posed the ultimate conundrum of constitutionalism—the possibility of unconstitutional constitutional amendments.

The concept of consent had direct consequences for questioning the powers of Parliament over America and for the American understanding of REPRESENTATION. In terms of constitutionalism, the most important part of the long list of grievances against George III with which the DECLARATION OF INDEPENDENCE began (following the model of the Declaration of Rights of 1689) was the passage which stated that the king had "combined with others to subject us to a JURISDICTION foreign to our constitutions, and unacknowledged by our laws; giving his assent to their acts of pretended legislation." The nation began with an assertion of the right to consent.

In the decades of constitution-making following independence the main organizational task of American constitutionalism was to spell out in detail the implications of popular sovereignty for the structure of government. What, for instance, should follow from the famous formulation in the VIRGINIA DECLARATION OF RIGHTS, of June 12, 1776, "that all power is vested in, and consequently derived from, the people; the magistrates are their trustees and servants, and at all times amenable to them"? Four subjects were of overriding importance: the franchise; the separation of powers; the amending process; and the protection of individual rights.

Political status in the colonies had mostly depended on property ownership, and the Revolution had not done away with these requirements. The federal CONSTITUTIONAL CONVENTION of 1787 could not agree on who should have the right to vote. Sovereignty of the people did not mean all the people. But who should have the right to vote was discussed frequently and with great seriousness. The voters of the Massachusetts town of Northampton, for instance, concluded in 1780 that restricting the franchise for the Massachusetts house to freeholders and other men of property was inconsistent with the concepts and principles of native equality and freedom, the social compact, personal equality, and no TAXATION WITHOUT REPRESENTATION. Their objections pertained only to elections to the house; indeed, they were based on the notion that in a bicameral legislature one chamber should represent property, the other persons. A few more decades had to elapse before property and taxpaying qualifications disappeared. The franchise was expanded in all Western societies in the course of the nineteenth century. The earliest and most inclusive expansion, however, came in the United States—although even here the vote was withheld from women, AMERICAN INDIANS, slaves, and, as a rule, free blacks.

The colonists widely believed that their governments were "mixed" in accord with the British model. A London compendium from 1755 said of the colonial governments: "By the governor, representing the King, the colonies are monarchical; by a Council they are aristocratical; by a house of representatives, or delegates from the people, they are democratical." While this was more an "ideal type" than an accurate description of the constitutional facts, the post-Revolution problem for those who had grown up within the tradition of mixed or balanced government was how to institute it under radically changed conditions. The question was not really whether to have balanced government, though some advocates of "simple" government existed.

The separation of powers doctrine, as put forward most influentially by Montesquieu, sought to limit power by separating factions and, to some extent, associating them with the executive and legislative functions of government. To Montesquieu the separation of powers was a necessary if not a sufficient condition of liberty. By 1776 the American constitutional prob-

lem had become not the separation of "powers" but the distribution of power flowing from a single source—the people.

Though the Americans continued to view the separation of powers as necessary to liberty and therefore indispensable to constitutionalism, they faced a formidable challenge in attempting to implement the concept. The towns of Essex County, Massachusetts, wrote "the Essex Result," a veritable dissertation on the subject in voicing their objections to the proposed Massachusetts constitution of 1778, which they considered insufficiently mindful of the separation of powers. They propounded the principle "that the legislative, judicial, and executive powers are to be lodged in different hands, that each branch is to be independent, and further, to be so balanced, and be able to exert such checks upon the others, as will preserve it from dependence on, or an union with them."

Practical problems were inevitable. The different powers of government do not imply clearly differentiated functions; they will necessarily be closely intertwined—especially if one adds the notion, urged in the Essex Result, of CHECKS AND BALANCES. In the major state constitutions enacted in 1776 and immediately after, the legislative branch usually dominated, but the constitutions distinguished conceptually between legislative, executive, and judicial functions. They made members of one branch ineligible to serve in the others, and they gave some measure of autonomy to the judiciary. However, with respect to such crucial features as the structure and election of the executive and the power of appointments, they differed radically one from the other.

As successful revolutionaries, the Americans faced a difficult political task. They needed to justify the power of the people to change their government and at the same time to assure the stability of the new order based on popular sovereignty. If, as a practical matter, consent meant consent by a majority, was that majority not also at liberty to change the states' new constitutions? If not, why not? Vattel had struggled valiantly to develop a satisfactory framework for thinking about constitutional change, though without much success. His argument in *The Law of Nations* that the legislative power could not amend the constitution is hardly a model of tight reasoning. Concluding his essay, Vattel observed: "However, in discussing changes in a constitution, we are here speaking only of the right; the expediency of such changes belongs to the field of politics. We content ourselves with the general remark that it is a delicate operation and one full of danger to make great changes in the State; and since frequent changes are hurtful in themselves, a Nation ought to be very circumspect in this matter and never be inclined to make innovations, except for the most urgent reasons or from necessity."

In America, THOMAS JEFFERSON was the foremost theorist of constitutional change. He believed that each generation has "a right to choose for itself the form of government it believes most promotive of its happiness. . . ." The same man who provided us with this theory of constitutional change wanted to be remembered in his epitaph for the VIRGINIA STATUTE OF RELIGIOUS LIBERTY (1786), which ended with a proviso that sought to secure the statute forever: we "do declare, that the rights hereby asserted are of the NATURAL RIGHTS of mankind, and that if any act shall be hereafter passed to repeal the present or to narrow its operation, such act will be an infringement of natural right."

In a way, the matter was simple. Jefferson and many of his fellow citizens were for change, stability, and inalienable rights all at the same time. These disparate aims were somewhat reconciled in practice by having the constitutions provide for their own amendment and for bills of rights. This course had important practical implications: it legitimized the concept of constitutional change and thus dramatically reduced the need for revolutions; and it advised the majority that it had no power to regulate at will the structure of government or basic rights of individuals. Enlightened America was anything but unanimous on the status of specific rights. Not every state constitution had a bill of rights; those that did almost always included the liberty of conscience, FREEDOM OF PRESS, trial by jury, and protection of property. Some of the rights, as Penn and Jefferson suggested, were considered so fundamental that their amendment would conflict with the very nature of constitutional government.

The CONSTITUTIONAL CONVENTION OF 1787 and the main features of the federal constitution, after a decade of state constitutions, further defined American constitutionalism. The Constitution precariously provided for a mode of RATIFICATION hardly in accord with the ARTICLES OF CONFEDERATION. Among the ironies of history is the fact that the Constitutional Convention's preference for the convention method of ratification (rather than ratification by all state legislatures as required by the Articles) resulted in attaching to the Constitution, in 1791, a BILL OF RIGHTS, which the Framers of Philadelphia had considered unnecessary.

The most important aspect of the Constitution was its implementation of the goal "to form a more perfect Union." Carl J. Friedrich characterized the claim that FEDERALISM is an American invention a defensible overstatement. The Constitution's effort to delineate clearly the powers of the federal government as against those of the states is remarkable indeed. Its main accomplishment was not to get bogged down by the metaphysics of sovereignty and to enable the federal government to legislate and tax in a manner binding the people directly, without using the states as intermediaries. This structure of "dual sovereignty" assured the viability of the federal government and, at least well into the twentieth century, the viability of the states. It underwent one substantial modification. When the "perpetual" nature of the Union was challenged over the issue of SLAVERY, constitutional amendments were enacted at the end of the Civil War for the primary purpose of securing equal rights to recently emancipated black citizens. These amendments eventually legitimized a great expansion of federal influence on the law of the states in the interest of greater equality for blacks and other minorities.

The constitutional organization of the federal government is delineated by the organization of the constitutional text. The PREAMBLE speaks of the people of the United States as ordaining and establishing the Constitution. The first (and presumably most important) article deals with the election and LEGISLATIVE POWERS OF CONGRESS. Article II vests the executive power in a President. Article III concerns the JUDICIAL POWER and its jurisdiction. Although this organization seems to provide us with a rather pure example of the separation of powers, the Constitution combines elements of separate and independent powers (such as an independent judiciary or a President not dependent on Congress for his term of office) with a thorough mixing of powers, best summarized by the concept of checks and balances.

Superficially, the legislative and executive branches seem to be assigned separate functions: lawmaking and law executing. The judicial branch, through dispute-settling, performs one part of the executive function under special conditions and special procedures. In reality, however, both the executive and the judiciary engage in lawmaking through interpretation and rule-making. The executive intrudes into the legislative function by exercising the VETO POWER. Congress, on the other hand, performs executive functions through legislative oversight, appropriations decisions, and confirming appointments. One might better forgo the Framers' own characterization of the system as one of separation of powers. American constitutionalism indulged itself in heaping checks upon checks so that the love of power of officials occupying the various branches of government could be harnessed.

On one of the most important of these checks and the most distinctly American contribution to constitutionalist doctrine, the Constitution of 1787 was silent. Nowhere does the constitutional text grant the power of JUDICIAL REVIEW of legislation. On the basis of the debates in the Constitutional Convention one can make a strong case that some of the most influential Framers thought that judicial review was implied, but this is not the same as saying that the Constitution implies it. How then did the American judiciary end up as the guardian of the Constitution?

There had been instances of courts exercising the power of judicial review as well as public debate of the issue in the new states. The case for judicial review was based on a peculiarly American amalgam of various strands of constitutionalism. First, there was the notion of a constitution as fundamental law. If Lord Coke could claim the common law as a basis for reviewing acts of Parliament, how much more plausible the claim that judges were bound to obey a fundamental charter viewed as supreme law. Second, if the constitutions derived their authority from the sovereignty of the people, and if legislators and other government officials were simply the people's trustees and servants, it was no great leap to reason that judges had to obey the will of the whole people as expressed in the constitution. Third, the special procedures for constitutional amendment typically denied the legislatures the power to amend by ordinary legislation, which suggested that attempts of that kind should go unenforced. Fourth, those constitutions containing bills of rights reenforced the notion of a constitution as superior law with the aim of protecting the rights of individuals against tyrannical majorities. Fifth, in the case of the federal constitution there was the added need to assure its status as supreme law throughout the Union. The arguments for and practice of judicial review of state legislation served to consolidate the understanding of the American Constitution as the supreme law of the land to which all government actors were subject.

Chief Justice JOHN MARSHALL in MARBURY V. MADISON (1803) to the contrary notwithstanding, the issue of judicial review was an intricate one. No simple constitutionalist syllogism could be constructed that invariably led one to conclude that judges had the power of judicial review. The amalgam, however, proved powerful under the conditions prevailing in the United States. When the Supreme Court went ahead and in effect appointed itself and the other judges guardians of the Constitution (in the case of the Supreme Court, eventually to become the preeminent guardian), the people, by and large, acquiesced.

The American institution of judicial review has influenced developments abroad. Various forms of constitutional review exist in Austria, Germany, India, Italy, Japan, and, now, even France—to name the most important. While their historical roots are many and their institutional characteristics diverse, the American model was highly visible when they came into being. One of the most instructive contemporary instances is that of the Court of Justice of the European Community. Starting with the need of assuring the uniformity of Community law throughout the member nations, the Court of Justice has transformed the treaties underlying the European Community (especially the Treaty of Rome) into the constitution of the community. These are radical developments. The constitutionalization of the Treaty of Rome has led to the introduction of judicial review, or what one might more appropriately call Community review, even into countries that have not previously recognized the power of their courts to pass on the constitutionality of legislation.

As constitutionalism does not refer to having a constitution but to structural and substantive limitations on government, it would be a gargantuan task to determine its incidence in a world full of written constitutions, of which many do not mean what they say, while others do not accomplish what they mean. The need to distinguish between form and substance would necessitate impossibly vast empirical assessments. The distinction between form and substance would also make desirable a detailed examination of the legal situation in countries, such as Great Britain, that meet most substantive requirements of constitutionalism without a written constitution, an entrenched bill of rights, or the power of judicial review.

Constitutionalism matured in the context of the liberal democracies with their emphasis on civil and political rights and their attempts clearly to define the public and the private sphere. The rights guaranteed, with the exception of certain rights to participate in the exercise of governmental power, were rights of the citizen against infringement by government of his own sphere, or "defensive" rights (German constitutional law has coined the term *Abwehrrechte* for this category). The eighteenth- and nineteenth-century constitutions do not contain social rights aimed at guaranteeing citizens a fair measure of well-being. A notable aspect of the Weimar constitution was its effort to formulate rights that would guarantee everyone a worthwhile existence. As the concept of CITIZENSHIP expanded from the formal equality of sharing legal capacities to the substantive equality of sharing goods, the contemporary welfare state became clearly committed to some undefined (and probably undefinable) minimum of such substantive equality. The predominant means for accomplishing such goals has been legislation rather than constitutionalization. Certain legislation of this kind has been viewed by some as in actual conflict with the constitutionalist scheme. This alleged conflict has, in turn, led to substantial efforts in the United States and other countries to reinterpret the liberal constitutions as not only permitting but demanding government intervention on behalf of the underprivileged.

In conjunction with these difficulties, but by no means restricted to them, American constitutional scholarship engages in periodic debates about methods of CONSTITUTIONAL INTERPRETATION. Much of the discussion reinvents the interpretive wheels of earlier generations. Its main focus is the degree of fidelity which may be owed the words of the Constitution and the intentions of its Framers. Some contemporary writing argues that the Constitution can incorporate contemporary value preferences of a highly subjective kind. The tension is between the need to expound an essentially unaltered eighteenth-century Constitution in a manner consistent with "the progress of the human mind," on the one hand, and the danger of dissolving the Constitution in the process. The dispute is further complicated by endless varieties of highly refined theories concerning the proper scope of judicial review.

Over its two hundred years the American Constitution has been assigned the role of a national ideology. It has performed this role for a people that has grown from a few million to almost 250 million citizens of very diverse background. While the historical disinclination to amend the Constitution by means other than judicial review may help account for its durability, it has also subjected the Constitution to considerable strain. As the secular equivalent of the Bible, as Walton Hamilton observed, "it became the great storehouse of verbal conflict, and rival truths were derived by the same inexorable logic from the same infallible source." More often than not, Americans invoke constitutional principles in order to understand and resolve conflicts. This fact attests to the extraordinary vitality of American constitutionalism. It may also endanger its viability. Too frequent crossings of the line between "constitution as ideology" and "ideology as constitution" will blur the line. The American concept of the legitimacy of government is closely tied to the Constitution. Its limitless manipulation may endanger the very legitimacy that has been the great accomplishment of American constitutionalism.

GERHARD CASPER

Bibliography
ADAMS, WILLI PAUL 1980 *The First American Constitutions.* Chapel Hill: University of North Carolina Press.
BAILYN, BERNARD 1967 *The Ideological Origins of the American Revolution.* Cambridge, Mass.: Belknap Press.
COOKE, JACOB E., ed. 1961 *The Federalist.* Middletown, Conn.: Wesleyan University Press.
DICEY, A. V. (1885)1959 *Introduction to the Study of the Law of the Constitution.* London: Macmillan.
FRANKLIN, JULIAN H., ed. 1969 *Constitutionalism and Resistance in the Sixteenth Century.* Indianapolis: Bobbs-Merrill.
FRIEDRICH, CARL J. 1941 *Constitutional Government and Democracy.* Boston: Little, Brown.
FRIEDRICH, CARL J. 1967 *The Impact of American Constitutionalism Abroad.* Boston: Boston University Press.
HAMILTON, WALTON H. 1931 Constitutionalism. Pages 255–258 in Edwin R. A. Seligman et al. (eds.), *Encyclopedia of the Social Sciences.* New York: Macmillan.
MAITLAND, F. W. 1926 *The Constitutional History of England.* Cambridge: At the University Press.
McILWAIN, CHARLES HOWARD (1940)1947 *Constitutionalism: Ancient and Modern.* Ithaca, N.Y.: Cornell University Press.
PENNOCK, J. RONALD and CHAPMAN, JOHN W., eds. 1979 *Constitutionalism.* New York: New York University Press.
PERRY, RICHARD L., ed. 1972 *Sources of Our Liberties.* New York: New York University Press.
STOURZH, GERALD 1977 The American Revolution, Modern Constitutionalism, and the Protection of Human Rights. Pages 162–176 in Kenneth Thompson et al. (eds.), *Truth and Tragedy: A Tribute to Hans J. Morgenthau.* Washington, D.C.: New Republic Book Co.
WOOD, GORDON S. 1969 *The Creation of the American Republic 1776–1787.* New York: Norton.
WORMUTH, FRANCIS D. 1949 *The Origins of Modern Constitutionalism.* New York: Harper.

CONSTITUTIONALISM AND THE AMERICAN FOUNDING

Between 1776 and 1789 the American people constituted themselves a nation by creating republican governments in the thirteen former English colonies and then, in the CONSTITUTIONAL CONVENTION OF 1787, by transforming the Union of confederated states into a genuine law-giving government. The novelty of this achievement was epitomized in the seal of the new nation, which, by incorporating the phrase "Novus Ordo Seclorum," announced "a new order of the ages." Yet in founding political societies Americans pursued a goal that had occupied Western man since antiquity: the establishment of government power capable of maintaining the stability and order necessary to realize the purposes of community, yet so defined and structured as to prevent tyranny. This age-old quest for the forms, procedures, and institutional arrangements most suitable for limiting power and implementing a community's conception of political right and justice, we know as CONSTITUTIONALISM.

Constitutionalism takes as its purpose resolution of the conflict that characterizes political life and makes government necessary, through procedures and institutions that seek to limit government and create spheres of individual and community freedom. Based on the paradoxical idea that the power to make law and to rule can be at once sovereign and effective, yet also defined, reasonable, and responsible, constitutionalism contains an inherent tension that sets it against utopianism and anarchism, which deny the reality of power, and against absolutism and totalitarianism, which tolerate no limitations on power. Nevertheless, although constitutionalists can in retrospect be seen as sharing common assumptions, differences among them have sometimes led to irreconcilable conflict. One such division occurred in the eighteenth century when the American people separated from the English and adopted a new type of constitutional theory and practice for the conduct of their political life.

Perhaps the most obvious feature of American constitutionalism was its apparent dependence upon legally binding written instruments prescribing the organization of government and fixing primary principles and rules to guide its operation. Texts had of course long been used in law, government, and politics, and the English constitution comprised written elements. Americans' resort to documentary, positive law techniques of government was so much more systematic and complete than any previous undertaking, however, as to amount to constitutional innovation. Following the American example, peoples everywhere in the modern world have adopted the practice of forming governments by writing constitutions. But Americans in the founding era did more than invent a new approach to the old problem of limited government. Their constitution-making was informed with a new purpose—the liberal purpose of protecting the NATURAL RIGHTS of individuals. American charters of FUNDAMENTAL LAW were not simply ordinances of government; they were also constitutions of liberty. The meaning of liberty, especially the relation between the individual and the community that was central to any practical definition of it, was a deeply controversial issue that divided Americans in state and national constitution-making. The adoption of the federal Constitution in 1787, however, marked a decisive shift toward protection of individuals in the pursuit of their interests, and away from enforcement of community consensus aimed at making citizens virtuous and moral as the central purpose of constitutional government in America.

American constitutionalism is thus concerned with organizational and procedural matters, on the one hand, and with substantive questions of political purpose, on the other. Most constitutional politics in the United States deals with the former concern, as groups and individuals assert or deny the existence of proper governmental power or challenge methods used to employ it. Nevertheless, constitutionalism is ultimately normative and purposive. Every state may be said to have a constitution, in the sense of an institutional structure and established procedures for conducting political affairs. But not every state is a constitutional state. In the Western political tradition constitutional government exists where certain forms and procedures limit the exercise of power. American constitutionalism goes farther by pursuing not only the negative goal of preventing tyranny but also the positive end of promoting individual liberty, both in the passive sense of protection against government power and in the active sense of participation in the decisions of the political community. Viewed in this light, American constitutionalism raises basic questions of political purpose that connect it with the mainstream of Western political philosophy.

In the history of constitutionalism the great problem has not been to create power but to define and limit it. The Western constitutional tradition has employed two methods toward this end. The first is the theory and practice of arranging the internal structure of government so that power is distributed and balanced. A second method of constitutionalism has been to subject government to legal limitations, or the RULE OF LAW.

English constitutionalism in the period of American colonization comprised both strands of the constitutional tradition. The common law courts in the early seventeenth century insisted on the superiority of law to the royal prerogative. Sir EDWARD COKE gave famous expression to the idea of a higher law controlling government in asserting that " 'sovereign power' is no parliamentary word. . . . MAGNA CARTA is such a fellow, that he will have no sovereign." Coke also said that "when an act of Parliament is against common right and reason, or repugnant, or impossible to be performed, the common law will control it and adjudge such act to be void." Parliament itself, however, subsequently claimed supremacy in lawmaking, and vindication of its authority in the Glorious Revolution of 1688 effectively precluded development of the rule of law into a politically relevant form of HIGHER LAW constitutionalism. An internally balanced institutional structure, expressed in the revised and revitalized theory of mixed government in the eighteenth century, became the principal model of constitutional government in England.

Essentially descriptive in its connotation, the English constitution was the structure of institutions, laws, conventions, and practices through which political issues were brought to resolution and carried out in acts of government. Yet the constitution was also prescriptive or normative, or at least it was supposed to be. More specifically, as MONTESQUIEU, WILLIAM BLACKSTONE, and other eighteenth-century writers affirmed, the end of the English constitution was civil and political liberty. From the standpoint of modern constitutionalism the legislative supremacy that contemporaries regarded as the foundation of English liberty was incompatible with effective restraints on governments. Nevertheless, Parliament was believed to be under a moral obligation to protect the rights and liberties of Englishmen, and the sanctions of natural law were still seen as effective restraints. Moreover, political accountability to public opinion through elections operated as a limitation on government. Englishmen thus continued to see their constitution as fixed and fundamental, notwithstanding legislative SOVEREIGNTY.

American constitutionalism began in the seventeenth century when English settlers founded political societies and institutions of government in North America. Two things stand out in this early constitutional experience. First, the formation of government was to a considerable extent based on written instruments. In corporate and proprietary colonies the founding documents were COLONIAL CHARTERS granted by the crown conferring enumerated powers on a particular person or group within a designated geographical area for specific purposes. Under these charters the colonists adopted further agreements, organic acts, ordinances, combinations, and frames of government giving more precise form to political institutions. In religiously motivated colonies government was more clearly the result of mutual pledging and association under civil-religious covenants. American colonists thus used constitutionlike instruments to create political community, define fundamental

values and interests, specify basic rights, and organize governmental institutions.

The second outstanding fact in early American constitutional history was substantial community control over local affairs. To be sure, the colonies employed the forms and practices of English government and generally emulated the metropolitan political culture. Their institutions at the provincial and local level were patterned after English models, and the theory of mixed government and the balanced constitution was accepted as valid. Yet discordant tendencies pointed to a distinctive course of constitutional development. The fact that in most colonies the power of the governor depended on royal authority while the power of the assembly rested on a popular base, as well as frequent conflict of interest between them, made separation and division of power a political reality discrepant with the theory of mixed government. Furthermore, popularly elected assemblies responsive to growing constituencies and enjoying de facto local sovereignty under written charters introduced a republican element into American politics.

As English subjects, Americans believed they lived under a free and fixed English constitution. Long before the Revolution they expressed this view in the course of conflicts with imperial officials. Numerous writers asserted that the constitution was a SOCIAL COMPACT between the people and their rulers; that the legislature could not alter the fundamental laws from which government derived its form, powers, and very existence; that government must exercise power within limits prescribed by a compact with the people. Moreover, the compact chosen to organize and direct government, as a colonial sermon of 1768 put it, must coincide with "the moral fitness of things, by which alone the natural rights of mankind can be secured." Disputing the descriptive English constitution that included parliamentary sovereignty, Americans were coming to think of a constitution as normative rules limiting the exercise of power for the purpose of protecting the people's liberty, property, and happiness.

In declaring their independence from England, Americans in a sense reenacted the founding experience of the seventeenth century. They took what their history and political circumstances determined to be the logical step of writing constitutions to organize their political communities. Before issuing the DECLARATION OF INDEPENDENCE, Congress recommended that the colonies adopt governments that "in the opinion of representatives of the people, best conduce to the happiness and safety of their constituents in particular, and America in general." Although some argued that the people acting in convention should form the government, political exigencies and Whig political theory conferred legitimacy on legislatures which, in all but two instances, were responsible for writing or adopting the first state constitutions.

The most distinctive feature of the state constitutions, their documentary character, followed the decision to form new governments as a matter of course. Given the long tradition of founding documents in America, it seemed obvious that the purposes of political community and limitations on government could be better achieved by writing a constitution than by relying on an unstipulated, imprecise constitution like England's, which did not limit government and was not really a constitution after all. Although consisting in part of written documents, the English constitution was too subjective, ultimately existing in men's minds and premised on the idea that "thinking makes it so." Americans insisted that the principles and rules essential to organizing power and preserving liberty be separated from the government and objectively fixed in positive form. Old in the tendency it reflected, though new in its comprehensive application, American constitutionalism rested on the idea that "saying it makes it so," or at least the hope that putting something in writing so it can be authoritatively consulted makes it easier to achieve specified ends.

The state constitutions stood in a direct line of descent from colonial documents that created political communities and established institutions of government. One type of founding document (compact or covenant) signified mutual promise and consent by which individuals formed a political community and identified basic values, rights, and interests. A second type of document (ordinance or frame) specified governmental institutions. Half the state constitutions written between 1776 and 1789 were described as compacts and contained bills of rights that defined basic community values. In the other constitutions the design of government received principal attention. All the constitutions reflected tendencies of previous political development; none created institutions on a completely clean slate. This fact appeared more clearly in documents that were mainly concerned with establishing a framework of government. In these more modern documents, which anticipated the course of American constitutional development, community consensus yielded in importance to protection of individual rights as the main purpose of constitution-making.

Republicanism was the political philosophy of the American Revolution. Although lacking in precise meaning, the concept is most accurately defined as government resting on the consent of the people and directed by the public will expressed through representative institutions. In the perspective of Western political thought republican philosophy was formulated in the seventeenth century to defend liberty against absolutism. The state constitutions were republican insofar as they limited government by prescribing public decision-making procedures that prevented government officials from aggrandizing power for private benefit rather than for the public good. The constitutions were liberal also in confirming and extending the right of political participation that according to republican philosophy constituted true liberty for individuals. In many respects, however, state constitutionalism in the revolutionary era was a doctrine of community power and control that restricted individual rights in a way that would now be seen as illiberal.

Under the state constitutions the most important power in modern government—the power to make law and to compel obedience—was lodged in the legislature. Unimpeded by internal governmental checks under the extreme version of the SEPARATION OF POWERS that prevailed in the first phase of state making, and sustained by presumptive identity with POPULAR SOVEREIGNTY as the source of political authority after the rejection of monarchy, legislatures acted forcefully to promote public virtue and the common good. Requirements of public virtue frequently took the form of restrictions on individual liberty through sumptuary laws and statutes regulating the transfer and use of property. Bills of rights that were part of state constitutions had little effect on curbing legislative power because they were treated as hortatory rather than legally binding. In the name of popular sovereignty and patriotism, state legislatures fashioned a constitutionalism of unity and power in government.

The concentrated power of republican virtue acting through institutions of community control was a useful and perhaps necessary expedient in the wartime emergency. In the doctrines of state sovereignty and the POLICE POWER revolutionary republicanism entered into the American constitutional tradition, and has offered a compelling model of constitutional government throughout our history to reformers and radicals on both the left and the right. However, the actions of the state legislatures too plainly contradicted the constitutional meaning of the Revolution to become accepted as the principal or exclusive expression of American constitutionalism. That meaning was nowhere better stated than by the MASSACHUSETTS CIRCULAR LETTER of 1768, which declared: ". . . in all free States the Constitution is fixed; & as the supreme Legislative derives its Power & Authority from the Constitution, it cannot overleap the Bounds of it, without destroying its own foundation." Yet this was precisely what was happening in the American republics.

The state constitutions may have been fundamental law in the sense of ordaining a framework of government, but they were not fundamental in the sense of controlling legislative power. In all but two states the constitution was written by the legislature and could be altered or abolished by that body. More than language of urging and admonition, contained in many of the constitutions, was needed to transform them into effective restraints on the actual exercise of power. Nor was the technique of internal institutional balance effectively employed to limit the state legislatures.

Attempts to restrict state legislative power in the 1780s broadened and reformed American constitutionalism. Writing and amending of constitutions by popularly elected conventions clarified the distinction between legislative law and fundamental law. Massachusetts in 1780 and New Hampshire in 1784 wrote their constitutions in conventions and required them to be ratified by the people in special elections. In theory this was the most effective way to make the constitution an antecedent higher law secure against legislative alteration. Further restriction of legislative power resulted from changes in the internal structure of government. Executive officers were given greater powers as CHECKS AND BALANCES—that is, a partial and limited sharing or mixing of functional powers among the departments—were introduced in some states as modification of the separation of powers. BICAMERALISM, a carry-over from colonial government, was recognized as a means of making legislative action more deliberate. And courts began to play a more prominent political role by treating constitutions as higher law in relation to legislative enactments.

So strong was the tradition of community self-government under legislative sovereignty, however, that it could not easily be dislodged as the main reliance of constitutionalism. Certainly little could be done to alter it by isolated efforts in the several states. Effective reform, if that was what was needed, could only come from an interstate collaboration working through the state system created by the colonies when they declared their independence. Heretofore peripheral to republican political development, the Union of the states in the Confederation became the focus of constitutional change.

The CONTINENTAL CONGRESS had been formed by the colonies in 1774 as a coordinating and advisory body to protect American interests and eventually to pursue the cause of national independence. Exigencies of war and common concerns among the states had given Congress political power, which it had exercised through informal rules and practices that were codified in the ARTICLES OF CONFEDERATION. Considered from a constitutional perspective as a limiting grant of power, the Articles were inadequate because, although they gave Congress ostensible power to do many things, they did not confer the lawmaking authority that is essential to government. Congress could at best make resolutions and recommendations, which in practice amounted to requests that the states could ignore. The Articles were unconstitutionlike in consequence of having been written by Congress and ratified by the states, rather than based in any direct way on popular authority. They were also unconstitutionlike with respect to institutional structure. Whether considered analogous to a legislative or executive body, Congress was the sole governmentlike organ, and only an evolving departmental system saved it from complete incompetence.

As an alliance or league of friendship, the Articles were a successful founding instrument. Yet in the form given it in the Articles, the confederation was incapable of addressing in a constructive manner the defects in American government revealed in the actions of the states. The confederation provided a field of political action, however, on which the reform of republican constitutionalism could take place. The practical impossibility of amending the Articles so as to strengthen Congress having been demonstrated, and the insecurity of liberty and property in the states apparently increasing, proponents of constitutional reform made a desperate move—the calling of a convention of the states at Philadelphia in May 1787—into an enduring achievement of statesmanship and constitutional invention.

Perhaps most significant, the Framers gave institutional expression to the idea that a constitution, in order to function as a limiting grant of power, must be higher as well as fundamental law. In addition to originating or organizing power, it must be maintained separate from and paramount to government. In a formal sense the Constitution as a founding document was superficially similar to the state constitutions. A preamble explained the reasons for the document, proclaimed the existence of a people and political community, defined specific purposes, and ordained a framework of government. In reality, however, the Framers departed from the model of the state constitutions. It was unnecessary to return to the fundamentals of the social compact and the purposes of republican government, as state constitution writers to varying degrees were inclined to do. The authors of the Constitution observed that they were not addressing the natural rights of man not yet gathered in society but natural rights modified by society and interwoven with the rights of the states. They knew that the nation whose existence they were recognizing was loosely related in its constituent parts and united by few principles and interests. It was far from the kind of cohesive, integrated community that the states by contrast seemed to be, and most unlike the nation-states of Europe. Hence the Framers briefly addressed in the PREAMBLE those few basic unifying purposes and values—liberty, justice, domestic peace, military defense, the general welfare—and gave virtually the entire document to stipulating the institutions and procedures of government. As fundamental law the Constitution thus was less a social compact for a coherent, like-minded community and more a contractlike specification of the powers, duties, rights, and responsibilities among the diverse polities and peoples that constituted the American Union.

Far more effectively than writers of earlier founding instruments, the Framers made the Constitution a paramount, controlling law. In a practical sense this was merely a question of law enforcement. Creating a real government to operate directly on individuals throughout a vast jurisdiction raised a new and potentially difficult compliance issue, but this received little attention at the Convention. It was the old compliance problem of the states that stood in the way of making the Constitution binding and effective. At first the delegates considered a congressional veto on state legislation to deal with this issue, but this was rejected as impracticable and was replaced by the SUPREMACY CLAUSE. This clause expressed the paramountcy of the federal Constitution over the states, and by inference, over national legislative law as well. Not explicitly stated, but implied in the judicial article, was the idea that the superior force of the Constitution depended on its application and interpretation by the courts.

The higher law character of the Constitution was further affirmed and institutionalized in the method of its drafting and in provisions for its ratification and amendment. Although delegates to the Philadelphia Convention were appointed by the state legislatures rather than elected by the people, the Constitution was a more genuine expression of the will of the people than were the Articles of Confederation, which were written by Congress. The Framers' apprehension about unlimited popular rule does not gainsay their commitment to the republican idea that government derives its just powers from the consent of the governed. Consistent with this commitment, institutions of direct popular consent that were still exceptional at the state level were incorporated into the national constitution. Ratification would be decided by conventions in the states, presumably popularly elected. Amendment of the Constitution could occur through popular approval, in state legislatures or special conventions, of proposals recommended by Congress or by a convention to be called by Congress on the application of two-thirds of the state legislatures. The superiority of the Constitution to legislative law was enhanced by this provision for amendment, as an utterly fixed and inflexible political law would become irrelevant to the task of governing an expanding society. If the Constitution required change, however, the people would have to amend it. Thus were popular sovereignty and the higher law tradition incorporated into American constitutionalism.

To make the Constitution paramount law in operational fact, however, it was not enough to assert its supremacy and assume that the people's innate law-abidingness would give it effect. This was to rely on "paper barriers," concerning the efficacy of which there was much skepticism among the Framers. It was necessary also to structure the organs of government so that power would be internally checked and limited. Although the Framers' objective was to create coercive authority where none existed, they rejected concentrated sovereign power as a constitutional principle. Delegated, divided, reciprocally limiting power formed the motif of their institutional design.

Unlike the state constitutions, which organized the inherent plenary power of the community, the Constitution delegated specific powers to the general government. The contrast was most significant in the plan of the legislative department, to which the state constitutions assigned the LEGISLATIVE POWER and which the federal constitutions defined by the ENUMERATED POWERS. Stable and energetic government seeming to require a strong executive and independent judiciary, the Constitution made grants of power of a more general nature to these branches, which under the separation of powers were counterweights to the lawmaking department. The separation principle by itself, however, as the state experience showed, was not a sufficient limitation on legislative power. Accordingly, checks and balances, by which each branch was given a partial and limited agency in the others' power (for example, executive participation in legislation through the VETO POWER or legislative judging in the IMPEACHMENT process) built further restraints into the Constitution.

The structure of the Union, of course, presented the most urgent question of institutional arrangements affecting the constitutional reality of a supreme political law. A division of power was already evident in the plan of the Articles of Confederation; what was needed was to transform the Union's political authority into a genuine power to impose lawful requirements on its constituent parts. This was achieved by reconstituting the Confederation as a compound republic, based on both the people and the states. Once this was accomplished, the pertinent fact for the paramountcy of the Constitution was the division of sovereignty. By giving the central government power over objects of general concern and allowing the states to retain almost all of their authority over local matters, the Framers divided sovereignty, thereby effectively eliminating it from the constitutional order. Arguments were certain to arise about the nature and extent of the powers of the several governments in the American state system, but the effect of such controversy would be to focus attention on the Constitution as the authoritative source of answers to questions about the rights of constituent members.

The Constitution was both fundamental and higher law because it expressed the will of the people, the ultimate source of authority in America. But it would truly limit power only if it was superior to the people themselves as a political entity, as well as to the legislative law. At the time some theorists of popular sovereignty argued that the people could alter their government at will, exercising the right of peaceful revolution and disregarding legalities of form and procedure, even as the Framers did in drafting and securing RATIFICATION OF THE CONSTITUTION against the express requirements of the Articles of Confederation. However we view their action, the authors of the Constitution rejected the notion of unlimited popular sovereignty. They provided restraints on the people in the form of a limited number of offices, long terms of office, indirect elections, large electoral districts, and separated and balanced departments of government. Although these provisions have often been viewed as antidemocratic and in conflict with republican theory, they are more accurately seen as modifying the popular form of government adopted during the Revolution. The Framers' intent, as JAMES MADI-

son wrote in THE FEDERALIST #10, was to supply "a republican remedy for the diseases most incident to republican government." And it should not be forgotten that despite careful distribution and balancing of authority, Congress remained potentially the most powerful branch of the government, most responsive to the people and possessed of the lawmaking power.

Making the Constitution effective as a permanent higher law involved matters of form, procedure, and institutional structure. Yet as procedural issues carry substantive implications, and means sometimes become ends in themselves, it is also necessary to ask what a constitution is for. To prevent tyranny, the constitutionalist goal, is to create a space in which differences among people become manifest, in which politics can appear and questions of purpose arise. If running a constitution always reflects political concerns, making a constitution is all the more a form of political action that derives from or partakes of political philosophy.

Americans were emphatic in declaring liberty to be the purpose of their constitutions. Moreover, if the purpose of politics is to protect men's natural rights, then American constitutions were liberal in purpose. Yet the concept of liberty, universally embraced as a political good, can be defined in different ways. And while recognition of natural rights gave modern politics a new purpose, it is equally true that virtue and moral excellence did not disappear from political discourse. These considerations give rise to two conceptions of political freedom in the constitutionalism of the founding period. The first is the liberty of self-governing political communities that were thought to have an obligation to make men virtuous and on which individuals depended for their happiness and well-being. The second rests on the primacy of natural rights and generally asserts individual liberty over community consensus as the purpose of government.

Although these conceptions of liberty stand in theoretical opposition to each other, they coexisted in the revolutionary era. After protesting imperial policies in the language of English constitutional rights, Americans justified national independence by appealing to universal natural rights. Wartime exigencies required decisive political action, however, which was based on the right of local communities to control individuals for the sake of the common good. States interfered with the liberty and property of individuals by controlling markets, restricting personal consumption, awarding monopoly privileges, and limiting imports and exports. They also regulated the speech and press freedoms of persons suspected of disloyalty to the patriot cause. In many ways revolutionary republicanism subordinated the rights of individual citizens to those of the community, defining true liberty as the pursuit of public happiness through political action.

Reacting against state encroachments on liberty and property, the constitution makers of 1787 emphasized protection of individual rights rather than promotion of virtue and community consensus as the purpose of government. Rather than an unattainable ideal of public virtue in ordinary citizens, they appealed to enlightened self-interest as the social reality on which the Constitution would rest. The Framers recognized factional conflict as a limiting condition for creating a constitution, yet also as an opportunity for broadening and redefining republican government. Alongside the communitarian ideal, which remained strong in many states, they created a new constitutional model in the complex and powerful government of the extended republic, based partly on the people yet so structured and limited that individual liberty, property, and pursuit of personal interests would be substantially protected against local legislative interference. This is not to say that mere private enrichment at the expense of the community good or general welfare was the end of the Constitution. The concepts of virtue and the public interest remained integral to political thought and discourse. But virtue assumed a new meaning as the prudent and rational pursuit of private commercial activity. Instead of telling people how to live in accordance with a particular conception of political right or religious truth, the Framers would promote ends believed beneficial to all of society—peace, economic growth, and intellectual advancement—by accommodating social competition and upholding citizens' natural rights against invasion by the organized power of the community, whether local, state, or national.

The Founding Fathers often appear antidemocratic because they created a strong central government, removed from direct popular and local community control, which they expected to be managed by an aristocratic elite. Notwithstanding its foundation in popular sovereignty and protection of individual liberty and rights, the Constitution contradicted rule by local communities guided by republican civic virtue as the real meaning of the Revolution. Although the Revolution stood for government by consent, there is no sound reason for regarding revolutionary state making as the single true expression of the republican principle. Essential parts of that principle were that government should operate through laws to which all were subordinate, both citizens and government officials, and that legislative law should be controlled by the higher law of the constitution. This was the meaning of the rule of law in the United States, and its more complete realization in the Constitution of 1787 signified climax and fulfillment of the Revolution.

The Framers' purpose must also be considered in relation to the threat of national disintegration, either from internal discord or foreign encroachment. The weakness of Congress in discharging its responsibilities was surely an impediment to protecting American interests, and an embarrassment to patriotic men. Yet the problem in 1787 was not the threat of total rupture of the Union attended by actual warfare among the states; the problem was the character of American politics and government, or the nature and tendency of republican government. Republicanism was the defining idea of the nation, and without it America would no longer have existed. The country was growing in the 1780s as population expanded, economic development occurred, and westward settlement continued. Yet the state system of 1776 was incapable of adequately accommodating and guiding this development. The states were too strong for the good of republican principles, the Union not strong enough. By restructuring the state system, by reconstituting the Union on the basis of a republican constitution that crystallized tendencies in congressional–state relations in the 1780s, the Framers sought to reform American government to the end of securing the republican ideals of the Revolution.

A constitution must recognize and conform to a people's principal characteristics and nature. Considered from this point of view the achievement of the Founding Fathers is undeniable. They created a complex government of delegated and dispersed, yet articulated and balanced, powers based on the principle of consent. Confirmation of that principle was in turn required by the Constitution in the cooperation and concurrence among the branches of government that were necessary for the conduct of public business. Made for an open, acquisitive, individualistic, competitive, and pluralistic society, the Constitution ordered the diverse constituent elements of American politics. More than merely a neutral procedural instrument for registering the play of social forces, it was a statement of ends and means for maintaining the principles that defined Americans as a national people. The Framers made a liberal constitution for a liberal society.

The Constitution was not only formally ratified but also quickly accorded full political legitimacy. The state constitutions, although not merely pretextual or façade documents, were not invoked and applied in the actual conduct of government as the United States Constitution was. And the new federal instrument was more than accepted: it rapidly became an object of veneration. The Constitution took a deep and abiding hold on the American political mind because it reflected a sober regard for the propensities of ordinary human nature and the realities of republican society; created powerful institutions capable of attracting men of talent, ambition, and enlarged civic outlook; and introduced changes in the conduct of public affairs that most people saw as improvements and that caused them to form an interest in the government it created.

The Constitution stipulated institutions, rules, and procedures embodying and symbolizing the principles of republican liberty, national unity, and balance and limitation of power. It was a fixed, objective document that could be consulted and applied, not a formless assemblage of principles, statutes, and decisions carried about in men's minds and dependent on social internalization for its effect. Yet the Constitution's principles and provisions were general and ambiguous enough to allow varying interpretations. Liberty, union, and reciprocally limiting power meant different things to different people, as did the rules and institutional arrangements expressing and embodying them. At a superficial level this circumstance produced conflict, but at a deeper level the effect was unifying. For groups and individuals were encouraged to pursue political goals within the framework of rules and requirements established by the Constitution. Thus the document became permanent and binding. Only the most extreme groups (radical abolitionists and slaveholders in the nineteenth century, totalitarian parties in the twentieth) have repudiated the Constitution as a framework for political action.

The Constitution possessed force and effect because it was useful and relevant to political life. Responsive to the social environment, it had instrumental value. At the same time, repeated reference to the document as the source and symbol of legitimate authority confirmed its intrinsic value, apart from the practical results of specific controversies. People believed, in other words, that it was important to follow the Constitution for its own sake or for the common good, rather than for a particular political reason. The intrinsic value of the Constitution lay not only in the wisdom and reasonableness of its principles in relation to the nature of American society but also in the form those principles were given in a written instrument. The effect of the Constitution as binding political law has much to do with its textual character.

The Framers addressed this issue in discussing "parchment barriers." The state constitutions were evidence that written stipulations were no guarantee of performance, especially when it came to limiting legislative power. Madison in particular said that it was not enough to erect parchment barriers in the form of constitutional provisions stating that the legislative department must confine itself to lawmaking. It was further necessary to arrange the interior structure of government so the constituent parts would limit each other. Personal motives of ambition and interest, Madison reasoned, when linked with constitutional offices would lead men to resist encroachments from other departments. These were the "auxiliary precautions" (supplementing accountability to the people) that would oblige government to control itself. Madison was saying that pluralistic differences in opinion and interest are necessary to make the prescriptions of the text function effectively.

Nevertheless, American constitutionalism insists that the text of the fundamental law be given its due. Madison's auxiliary precautions are in fact rules written into the document. Although the written text may not be sufficient, it is necessary to achieve the purposes of constitutionalism, or so it has seemed most of the time to most Americans. In the Constitutional Convention RUFUS KING said that he was aware that an express guarantee of STATES' RIGHTS, which he favored, would be regarded as "a mere paper security." But "if fundamental articles of compact are not sufficient defence against physical power," King declared, "neither will there be any safety against it if there be no compact."

Reference to the constitutional text has been a fixed feature of American politics. Its significance and effect have been variously estimated. A long tradition of criticism holds that the document has failed to limit government, especially the federal government in relation to the states. Others argue that constant invoking of the Constitution has trivialized politics by translating policy debate into legalistic squabbles that discourage dealing with issues on their merits. Reformers seeking a more programmatic politics have lamented that the Constitution by fragmenting power prevents responsible party government. And still others contend that the Constitution has worked precisely as intended: to eliminate genuine political action and make citizens passive subjects interested in private economic pursuits rather than public happiness and civic virtue.

These criticisms misunderstand the nature of constitutional politics and hence the binding and configurative effect of the Constitution. If politics is concerned with the end or purpose of political community, the proper role of government, the relationship between the individual and society, then it is difficult to see how the Constitution can be said to have brought an end to politics or prevented political action. As an expression of modern liberalism, however, the Constitution did signify a change in the nature of politics. To elevate natural rights into constitutionally protected CIVIL RIGHTS, as the Framers did, was to discourage an older politics based on the pursuit of glory, honor, conquest, and political or religious truth, as well as a newer ideological politics born of modern revolution. The Framers' constitutionalism was a way of organizing political life that paradoxically placed certain principles, rules, and procedures beyond politics, according them the status of fundamental and paramount law. Premised on the idea that citizens could pursue private interests while preserving community, it was intended to limit the scope and intensity of politics, preventing a total absorption of society that would impose tyranny in the name of ruler, party, people, or community.

Starting in the 1790s and continuing with remarkable continuity to the present day, public policy advocates have charted courses of action with reference to the Constitution. Using constitutional language firmly embedded in political rhetoric, such as DUE PROCESS OF LAW, EQUAL PROTECTION OF THE LAW, separation of powers, and so forth, they invoke its principles and values to justify their goals, argue over the meaning of its requirements, and align themselves with its manifest tenor as explicated in constitutional law and legislation. Political leaders do this not because they are unwaveringly committed to a specific constitutional principle; in different circumstances they might advocate a different principle. The decisive fact is the high public status accorded the Constitution: policymakers and political actors know that the people take the Constitution seriously, regard it as supreme law, believe that it is powerful because it embodies sound principles of government and society's basic values, and, indeed, venerate it. Aware of this popular prejudice in favor of the Constitution, and seeking the approval of public opinion, political groups and individuals are constrained to act in conformity with its provisions. Thus the Constitution as binding political law shapes the form and content of policies and events.

The constraining effect of the Constitution might nevertheless be questioned, for it will appear obvious that while some requirements are unequivocally clear (for example, the minimum age of the President), many provisions are ambiguous and imprecise in meaning. Confronted with this fact, many scholars have concluded that there is no single, true meaning of the Constitution, but rather that there are several possible readings of it, none of which possesses exclusive legitimacy. Some contend there is no real Constitution against which arguments about it can be evaluated, only different assertions as to what the Constitution is at any given time, or as to what we want it to be. Expressed in the oft-cited statement that the Constitution is what the Supreme Court says it is, this view, carried to its logical conclusion, would mean that the American Constitution is a developing, evolving, growing thing that is changed by the actions of judges, lawmakers, and executive officers. In that case the Constitution ceases to be a fixed, prescriptive, paramount law.

Politically and historically realistic as this analysis appears, it has never been accepted as legitimate in constitutional theory or in the conduct of constitutional politics. From the standpoint of the people and their representatives, the Constitution, in both its procedural requirements and its essential principles, has a true, fixed, ascertainable meaning. This popular understanding has existed from the beginning of constitutional politics in the debate over ratification, and it will probably continue until the popular belief, that the Constitution as a document says what it means and means what it says, is eroded or superseded by a more sophisticated view of the character of texts and political language. There is still a strong tendency in public opinion to think that written constitutions, in THOMAS JEFFERSON's words, "furnish a text to which those who are watchful may again rally and recall the people: they fix too for the people principles for their political creed."

The importance of the constitutional text in American government has been raised anew in recent years in the controversy over original intent jurisprudence. Many legal scholars have expressed doubt about the wisdom and legitimacy of consulting the original intent of the Constitution or of its authors in settling constitutional disputes. The words of the text, it is argued, apart from anything that its authors may have written or said about its meaning, must be considered as expressing the original intent. And the text must be read and understood according to the accepted meaning of words in the interpreter's own time, place, and historical situation. Some dispose of original intent more directly by asserting that constitutional interpretation need not be bound by the constitutional text, but may be based on fundamental social values and conceptions of justice and moral progress that judges are specially qualified to understand and apply. Either way, the Constitution is assured of its status as a "living document" adaptable to changing social conditions.

Although there may be sound reasons for disconnecting constitutional politics from original intent, from a historical standpoint it seems clear that neither the Framers nor the people over 200 years have taken so narrow a view of the meaning and relevance of original intent. The purpose of making a fixed, objective constitution was to decide the most important basic questions about politics and government once and for all—or until the people changed their mind and amended the document. The idea was to bind future generations in fundamental ways. This purpose would be defeated if those who later ran the Constitution were free to substitute their own definitions of its key terms. Yet the fact remains that constitutional principles and rules have been reinterpreted and redefined, in apparent contradiction of the Framers' intent, in decisions and statutes that have been accepted as politically legitimate. The Supreme Court has, in a sense, acted as a continuing constitutional convention.

Although the Founding Fathers intended the Constitution to be permanent and binding, the language of the document cannot realistically or reasonably, in a categorical sense, be frozen in its eighteenth-century meaning. It is the Constitution's essential purposes and its fundamental principles and procedures that were not intended to change. The question to be asked is whether fundamental principles and values—the values of individual liberty, national union, distributed and balanced power, the consent of the people—can be defined in an authoritative text and thereby realized in public law and policy to the satisfaction of the political community. American political history generally provides an affirmative answer to this question. But it is important to remember that an overriding imperative in American politics, law, and government has been to reconcile public policy with constitutional principles and rules as embodied in the text, and in accordance with the Framers' intentions. Moreover, original intent has not been viewed in a narrowly positivistic manner. The text was thought to have a definite and lasting meaning; and speeches, writings, and letters of the authors of the Constitution have always been thought pertinent to the task of elucidating its meaning. Whatever the practical effect of dismissal of the text and repudiation of original intent would be, such a step would alter the historic character of American constitutionalism.

Diverse in ethnic, religious, cultural, and social characteristics, Americans were united in 1776 by the political principles set forth in the Declaration of Independence. Inchoate though it was, the new nation was defined by these principles—liberty, equality, government by consent, the pursuit of happiness as an individual right—which in various ways were written into the state constitutions. By establishing a republican government for the nation, the Framers of the Constitution confirmed these principles, completing the Revolution and making it permanent. Since then American politics has derived from and been shaped by the Constitution, and has periodically been renewed by popular movements resulting in electoral realignments that have included a return to the first principles of the Founding as an essential element.

Understanding this attachment to the constitutional text has often been difficult for scholars and intellectuals, who tend to disparage it as "constitution worship." Perhaps reverence for the Constitution expresses not so much a naive literalism, however, as an awareness of the act of foundation as a source of authority. Considered in this perspective the constitutional text stands for the Founding, and the principles written into the document symbolically represent values evident in the actions of the Framers. The Founding required rational discussion, deliberation, compromise, and choice; consent, concurrence, and mutual pledging. These procedural values are embodied in constitutional provisions that require government under a fixed institutional structure and by deliberative processes that depend on compromise and concurrence, in accordance with substantive principles of natural rights, consent, and limited and balanced power.

HERMAN BELZ

Bibliography

CORWIN, EDWARD S. 1955 The "Higher Law" Background of American Constitutional Law. Ithaca, N.Y.: Cornell University Press.

FRIEDRICH, CARL J. 1968 Constitutional Government and Democracy. Cambridge, Mass.: Harvard University Press.

GOUGH, J. W. 1955 Fundamental Law in English Constitutional History. Oxford: Oxford University Press.

LIENESCH, MICHAEL 1980 The Constitutional Tradition: History, Political Action, and Progress in American Political Thought. Journal of Politics 42:2–30.

LUTZ, DONALD 1980 From Covenant to Constitution in American Political History. Publius 10:101–133.

MCILWAIN, CHARLES H. (1940)1947 Constitutionalism: Ancient and Modern. Ithaca, N.Y.: Cornell University Press.

VILE, M. J. C. 1967 Constitutionalism and the Separation of Powers. New York: Oxford University Press.

WRIGHT, BENJAMIN F. 1958 Consensus and Continuity: 1776–1787. New York: Norton.

CONSTITUTIONAL REASON OF STATE

Reason of state is one of the illimitable silences of the Constitution. Derived directly from Niccolò Machiavelli and JOHN LOCKE (who called it the "prerogative"), it is "the doctrine that whatever is required to insure the survival of the state must be done by the individuals responsible for it, no matter how repugnant such an act may be to them in their private capacity as decent and moral men." Not labeled "reason of state" by the Supreme Court, the doctrine often travels under the banner of NATIONAL SECURITY or the "interests of society."

National survival is the ultimate value protected by the doctrine. But more is covered; it is used whenever an important interest of the state is jeopardized, as perceived by those who wield effective control over the state's apparatus (government). Wartime use is the most obvious, stated classically by ABRAHAM LINCOLN in 1861: "Is there in all republics this inherent and fatal weakness? Must a government of necessity be too *strong* for the liberties of its people, or too *weak* to maintain its own existence?" Other instances in which reason of state has been the validating principle include the treatment of American Indians, wars of conquest (such as the Mexican War), economic depressions, and the control of dissident groups. Justification for both the Korean and Vietnam "wars" rests on the doctrine. (See KOREAN WAR.)

The basic constitutional problem is to distinguish between the circumstances fit for republican (that is, democratic) rule and those suited for personal rule. With rare exceptions—the principal ones are the *Steel Seizure Case* (YOUNGSTOWN SHEET AND TUBE V. SAWYER, 1952) and UNITED STATES V. UNITED STATES DISTRICT COURT (1972)—the Supreme Court has deferred to the political branches of government. The President normally is the moving force, with Congress usually acquiescing in executive actions designed to meet perceived emergencies. The PRIZE CASES (1863) were the leading early judicial statement approving the doctrine. (See also JAPANESE AMERICAN CASES.)

To the extent that the doctrine of reason of state finds acceptance, the theory of LIMITED GOVERNMENT recedes. Government in the United States has always been relative to circumstances, precisely as strong as conditions necessitated. The Constitution, accordingly, has been updated by successive generations of Americans, often at least tacitly employing reason of state principles.

No criteria exist by which to determine whether reason of state has been validly invoked. The Supreme Court has thus far failed to define such synonymous terms as "national security" and "society." By employing a BALANCING TEST, the Justices rule for society—for the state—whenever the vital interests of the state are considered to be in danger. In so doing, the Court never divulges how it determines what the interests of society are or the weights to be given to them. Reason of state, therefore, often amounts to government by fiat, but with the legitimizing imprimatur of the Supreme Court.

The BILL OF RIGHTS was an effort to limit the application of reason of state. However, Supreme Court interpretations have converted many of those seemingly absolute commands into mere hortatory admonitions to act reasonably in the circumstances. For example, the FIRST AMENDMENT's prescription that "no law" should abridge freedom of speech or press has been interpreted into relative standards. Reason of state thus has been resurrected by the Supreme Court after the constitutional Framers tried to hem it in.

Every nation employs a variation of reason of state, whether or not it has a written constitution. France, for example, expressly provides for EMERGENCY POWERS in Article 16 of the constitution of the Fifth Republic. The United States has accomplished the same result without an express constitutional provision or even a stated constitutional principle.

If, as many assert, the United States has entered a period of great danger, one in which its constitutional institutions will be sorely tested, reason of state will doubtless often be invoked—probably tacitly—as emergencies and crises arise. The doctrine can and will be employed to justify presidential use of violence without congressional authorization, as Presidents have almost routinely done in the past. It is the ultimate basis for expansion of presidential powers in many directions.

The Constitution was written at a propitious time in history, a time when a coalescence of factors—geography, natural resources, freedom from external pressures, a small population, capital and cheap labor from Europe—provided a favorable milieu for the FUNDAMENTAL LAW and its structure of government to flourish. Today, Americans face polar opposites—a shrinking planet, dwindling resources, total immersion in FOREIGN AFFAIRS, a burgeoning population, a slowing of productivity and of economic growth. Crisis government, accordingly, is becoming the norm. More and more, government will call upon emergency powers—upon reason of state—in efforts to cope. The large meaning is that a new fundamental law is emerging, one that can be called the "Constitution of Control." It exists as another layer on the palimpsest that is the Constitution of 1787.

ARTHUR S. MILLER

Bibliography

FRIEDRICH, CARL J. 1957 *Constitutional Reason of State.* Providence, R.I.: Brown University.

MILLER, ARTHUR SELWYN 1981 *Democratic Dictatorship: The Emergent Constitution of Control.* Westport, Conn.: Greenwood Press.

ROSSITER, CLINTON 1948 *Constitutional Dictatorship: Crisis Government in the Modern Democracies.* Princeton, N.J.: Princeton University Press.

CONTEMPT POWER
(Judicial)

The Constitution nowhere mentions contempt of court. The courts' powers in this area flow instead from a COMMON LAW tradition of debated antiquity and legitimacy. Contempt power has, however, become entangled with the Constitution in two respects: first, courts have had to explain how they came to exercise a power that in some respects seems antithetical to constitutional values; second, the Constitution has been held to limit some aspects of the courts' exercise of contempt power.

Contempt is the disobedience of a court's order or interference with its processes. Most judicial decrees are not orders to do or refrain from doing some act. Contempt would not arise, for example, from the simple failure to pay a money judgment. Some judgments, however, directly order a party to perform or refrain from performing some act. A court might order a party to transfer land, to integrate a school system, to cease polluting a stream, to answer questions put by the other side, or to refrain from obstructive behavior in the courtroom.

Having disobeyed such an order, one might be charged with a crime (since many jurisdictions make such acts criminal) or with contempt. Either charge might result in a fine or jail sentence, but the accompanying process might differ. For some categories of contempt the contemnor may suffer punishment without many of the rights normally attaching to criminal trials: to be represented by counsel, to prepare for trial, to present testimony, to cross-examine witnesses, or to have a TRIAL BY JURY. The list is extreme and would not apply to all of the often confusing categories of contempt developed by the courts, but it illustrates the potentially drastic nature of the power.

Courts employ such "criminal" contempt sanctions to redress judicial dignity, but individual litigants may also use contempt sanctions to gain the benefit of court orders. A party seeking to compel obedience to an INJUNCTION entered at his request may ask a court for a "civil" contempt sanction. Such a sanction typically orders the contemnor to jail or to the payment of a progressively mounting fine until he "purges" himself of the contempt by obeying the injunction in question. Though an accused civil contemnor enjoys the rights of counsel, testimony, and cross-examination, his hearing has none of the protections accorded criminal defendants, for the courts have held that this is a "civil" rather than a "criminal" proceeding in spite of the risk of imprisonment. Nor is the duration of the imprisonment or the size of the fine subject to any limitation save the discretion of the judge and the contemnor's continuing ability to perform the act required of him.

Justifying the use of apparently criminal penalties without protections constitutionally accorded criminal defendants, the courts have relied on claims of history, necessity, and categorization. The claim of history has rested on the propositions that at the time the Constitution was framed courts had long exercised contempt powers and that the Framers did not intend to alter them. Those claims have been challenged but are still made. The claim of necessity still urges the need for orderly adjudicatory proceedings and enforceable orders. The argument rests on the hypothesis that, were the usual restrictions of the BILL OF RIGHTS to apply to contempt proceedings, the courts would be unable to function. The argument from categorization involves simply the assertion that because neither civil nor criminal contempts involve "crimes," the portions of the Bill of Rights applicable to crimes do not apply. In the case of imprisonment for civil contempt this argument is bolstered by the circumstance that the contemnor has the power at any time to obtain his release by complying with the order—a power not enjoyed by a convicted criminal.

Though the courts' exercise of contempt power has thus been remarkable for the absence of constitutional constraints, some limits do exist. First, state and federal legislatures have statutorily required greater protections that the Constitution mandates. Second, the Supreme Court has imposed some constitutional limits: in criminal contempts the judge must find the defendant guilty beyond a reasonable doubt; in "indirect" contempts (those not committed before a judge or involving judicial officers) the contemnor is, in addition, accorded the rights of counsel, testimony, and cross-examination. Even in cases of direct contempt the contemnor may have a trial by jury if the judge proposes to inflict a serious penalty. Yet even in enunciating these protections, the Court has steadfastly insisted that the judge has a wide power to impose sentence on the spot for contemptuous behavior in the courtroom.

Judicial use of contempt power involves a collision between two *desiderata:* that of having tribunals able to conduct their proceedings and enforce their orders; and that of having persons whose freedom stands in jeopardy enjoy the protections of the Bill of Rights. Thus far the courts have concluded that in many situations the first goal necessitates subordinating the second.

STEPHEN C. YEAZELL

Bibliography
GOLDFARB, RONALD L. 1963 *The Contempt Power.* New York: Columbia University Press.

CONTEMPT POWER, LEGISLATIVE

See: Legislative Contempt Power

CONTINENTAL CONGRESS

On September 5, 1774, delegates from the colonies convened in Philadelphia in a "Continental" Congress, so called to differentiate it from local or provincial congresses. The FIRST CONTINENTAL CONGRESS adopted a Declaration and Resolves to protest British measures and promote American rights; it also adopted the ASSOCIATION. The Congress dissolved on October 24, 1774, having decided that the colonies should meet again if necessary on May 10, 1775. By that time, the colonies and Great Britain were at war. The Second Continental Congress adopted a Declaration of the Causes and Necessity of Taking Up Arms on July 6, 1775, and the DECLARATION OF INDEPENDENCE a year later. The Congress appointed GEORGE WASHINGTON as commander-in-chief of its armies, directed the war, managed FOREIGN AFFAIRS, and adopted a plan of union designated as the ARTICLES OF CONFEDERATION. After the thirteenth state ratified the Articles in 1781, the official governing body of the United States became known as "the Congress of the Confederation," but it was a continuation of the Continental Congress and was not reconstituted until 1789, when a Congress elected under the Constitution of the United States took office.

LEONARD W. LEVY

Bibliography
BURNETT, EDMUND C. 1941 *The Continental Congress.* New York: Macmillan.

CONTRACEPTION

See: Birth Control; *Griswold v. Connecticut;* Reproductive Autonomy

CONTRACT CLAUSE

In a flashing aperçu Sir Henry Maine observed that "the movement of progressive societies has hitherto been a movement from Status to Contract." In feudal systems a person acquired a fixed, social status by birth, one's legal rights and duties being determined thereby for life. The decline of feudalism was a fading away of the status system in favor of personal rights and duties based largely on contractual relationships. Obligations imposed by ancestry gave way to obligations voluntarily undertaken. Generally thereafter a person's place in society depended upon success or failure in covenants with respect, for example, to wages, raw materials, farm and industrial goods, or artistic talent. In such a setting it is crucial that agreements be dependable—not merely to promote the individual's security and mobility but for the good of a society that relies for its sustenance upon a vast network of voluntary, contractual relationships. Thus Article I, section 10, of the Constitution, reflecting in part unfortunate experience under the ARTICLES OF CONFEDERATION, forbids *inter alia* state laws "impairing the OBLIGATION OF CONTRACTS." In THE FEDERALIST #44, JAMES MADISON observed that such laws "are contrary to the first principles of the SOCIAL COMPACT and to every principle of sound legislation." In his view "the sober people of America" were "weary of fluctuating" legislative policy, and wanted reform that would "inspire a general prudence and industry, and give a regular course to the business of society."

Indeed the sanctity of contracts was deemed so vital to personal security that in fifty-five years following the Supreme Court's first contract clause decision (FLETCHER V. PECK, 1810), twenty-two states put such provisions in their own constitutions. With one exception each of them was included in the state's bill of rights. Prior to 1810 four states had already done this. All of them protected contracts generally (per *Fletcher*), not merely private contracts as in the NORTHWEST ORDIANCE. Plainly in JOHN MARSHALL'S day and long thereafter his Court's broad view of the contract clause was widely accepted—along with FREEDOM OF PRESS, FREEDOM OF RELIGION, and FAIR TRIALS—as one of those restrictions on government "which serve to protect the most valuable rights of the citizen."

Obviously those who thus equated property rights and civil liberty were—like the Founding Fathers and the MARSHALL COURT—disciples of JOHN LOCKE. He had taught that property and liberty go hand in hand; that neither thrives without the other; that to protect them both as indispensable to life itself is the reason for government. Generations later, in a radically changed economic setting, some Americans came to believe that property hampers liberty. Inevitably then (having forgotten Locke) they would misunderstand both the founders and our early judges—Lockians all. Thus the Progressive movement convinced itself and its heirs that the Marshall Court had erred in holding the contract clause applicable to state, that is, public, covenants and that in so holding the judges had revealed a pro-property bias. Both of these views—derived largely from *Fletcher* and *Dartmouth College v. Woodward* (1819)—seem erroneous. The first rests on the strange idea that unambiguous language of the Constitution means not what it plainly says, but rather something else, because of the supposed intent of its authors. (Of course authors' intent may be a proper key to the meaning of ambiguous terminology, but that is a very different matter.)

Had the CONSTITUTIONAL CONVENTION OF 1787 wanted the clause to cover only private agreements, that is, those between individuals, it need only have said so. The Continental Congress had done just that in the Northwest Ordinance: ". . . no law ought ever to be made, or to have force in the said territory, that shall in any manner whatever, interfere with or affect private contracts. . . ." Six weeks later, RUFUS KING moved to include its private contract approach in the Constitution. Following a brief discussion of possible ramifications of such a provision, it was dropped. A few days later, at the suggestion of the Committee of Style, the Constitutional Convention adopted the contract clause, which refers comprehensively to "contracts" without qualification. Nothing in our record of the proceedings explains the change of mind or the change of terminology. But this is certain: not a word there or in *The Federalist* even hints that the founders were concerned only with private covenants—that they thought a state should be free to violate its own agreements. ALEXANDER HAMILTON would later observe: "It is . . . impossible to reconcile the idea of a [state] promise which obliges, with

a power to make a law which can vary the effect of it." Hamilton, of course, had been a member of the Constitutional Convention.

Long before John Marshall became a judge, Justice JAMES WILSON, in CHISHOLM V. GEORGIA (1793), had asked rhetorically: "What good purpose could this constitutional provision secure if a state might pass a law impairing the obligation of its own contracts, and be amendable, for such a violation of right, to no controlling judiciary power?" This from one who had been perhaps the second most important leader of the Constitutional Convention. Justice WILLIAM PATERSON, too, had been influential at the Convention. Years before *Fletcher* in a similar case, VAN HORNE'S LESSEE V. DORRANCE (1795), he had held that a state could not impair its own contractual obligations. So did the highest court of Massachusetts in *Derby v. Blake* (1799) and in *Wales v. Stetson* (1806). *Fletcher* was not without significant judicial precedent.

The argument that the contract clause does not mean what it says rests essentially on the proposition that the crucial contract problem in late eighteenth-century America was erosion of private contract obligations by DEBTORS' RELIEF LEGISLATION. No doubt this was a vexing and well-known difficulty. Yet surely it is no *ipso facto* basis for excluding related problems plainly covered by explicit constitutional language. State negligence with respect to state obligations was after all a matter of experience. Even if it were known that the Framers intended the written words to embrace only private contracts, judges could not properly adopt that view. For those who ratified can hardly be said to have ratified something other than the words of the document. To hold otherwise is to undermine the basic premise of a written constitution. As the Marshall Court put it in orthodox manner in *Dartmouth*: "This case being within the words of the Contract Clause, must be within its operation likewise, unless there be something in the literal construction so obviously absurd or mischievous, or repugnant to the general spirit of the instrument, as to justify those who expound the constitution in making it an exception. . . ." No such basis for an exception having been discovered, the Supreme Court ever since has found the contract clause applicable as written to contracts generally, whether public or private.

A related problem in *Fletcher* concerned the scope of the term "contract." The Georgia legislature had sold and granted to speculators millions of acres of public land. A subsequent legislature had repealed the grant on the ground that it had been obtained by bribery. Meanwhile part of the land had been conveyed to innocent third-party purchasers. The issue in *Fletcher* was whether the initial grant entailed obligations protected against impairment by the contract clause. The Court responded affirmatively. Of course, in modern usage a grant is not a contract, but that does not solve the problem. For it is quite clear that in the late eighteenth century the term "contract" had far broader connotations than it does today. As Dean ROSCOE POUND has explained:

Contract was then used, and was used as late as Parsons on Contracts in 1853 to mean [what] might be called "legal transaction." . . . Not merely contract as we now understand it, but trust, will, conveyance, and grant of a franchise are included. . . . The writers on natural law considered that there was a natural legal duty not to derogate from one's grant. . . . This is the explanation of *Fletcher*, . . . and no doubt is what the [contract clause] meant to those who wrote it into the Constitution. ["The Charles River Bridge Case," *Massachusetts Law Quarterly* 27:19–20.]

In sum, in the context of the times a grant included an executory, contractual obligation of the grantor not to violate the terms of his grant.

On this and the public contract aspect of Marshall's opinions one finds no criticism or disagreement in a random selection of twelve legal treatises published before 1870, including THOMAS M. COOLEY's famous *Constitutional Limitations* (1868). Twelve years later, however, Cooley's *General Principles of Constitutional Law* (1880) took a somewhat critical stand. The change apparently reflected attacks upon the Marshall Court by C. M. Hill, R. Hutchinson, and J. M. Shirley writing separately in the *American Law Review* and the *Southern Law Review* from 1874 to 1879. In due course the Progressives would pick up these charges that the Marshall Court had erred, and they would add that "the great Chief Justice" was in fact "a stalwart . . . reactionary," a servant of property interests. It seems no coincidence that the Hill-Hutchinson-Shirley attacks germinated in an era (1865–1873) when nearly sixty percent of laws challenged under the contract clause were held invalid—an all-time high. Many such cases of course "favored" business interests and thus tended to offend Progressives. The result was that John Marshall became for them a villain.

Fletcher, of course, upheld the property claims of innocent, third-party purchasers. The alternative would have been to sustain the property claims of the innocent people of Georgia. Either way the judges would be deciding in favor of some, and against other, property interests. Either way innocent people would suffer. One fails to see how *Fletcher* can be said to reveal a property bias. Was there, however, bias of another sort in deciding for the ultimate buyers rather than for the initial owners? Far from exceptional, the choice was informed by a long settled (and still prevailing) rule of Anglo-American EQUITY jurisprudence. Although a fraudulent purchaser takes a good title *at law*, it is subject to cancellation by a chancery decree. Thus in a clash between a cheating buyer and his innocent victim the latter prevails. But *Fletcher* involved a clash between the innocent victim and an equally innocent, subsequent purchaser for value. With the equities thus in balance and the social interest in security of transactions on the side of the purchaser in possession, the chancellor does not intervene (the victim's recourse being an action for damages against the fraudulent party). In short, Marshall and his Court read the contract clause in the light of a long familiar rule of equity.

In the *Dartmouth* case, a group of philanthropists had received a public charter to create a college in New Hampshire. Later the state tried to take over and govern the school contrary to the charter provisions. Marshall's Court, following *Fletcher*, held that the charter was a contract which the state was not free to violate. Viewed narrowly the case was won by the college trustees, but they had no beneficial interest in the college property. They won on behalf of the donor-philanthropists (presumably deceased) and generations of future students.

The Progressive response is that the *Dartmouth* decision was a crafty gambit purposefully designed for an ulterior purpose: protection of corporation charters from legislative interference. That it was highly successful is demonstrated, we are told, by the enormous growth of corporate enterprise thereafter. This is make-believe. Justice JOSEPH STORY in *Dartmouth* pointed out that no state need grant irrevocable or nonamendable charters—that the power to amend or revoke may be reserved. Damage resulting from failure to do so can hardly be held a fault of the judges. In fact reservation of power to alter corporate charters became widespread after *Dartmouth* and was not unknown before. (See RESERVED POLICE POWER.)

Fletcher and *Dartmouth* are not pro-property, but rather pro-transaction, cases. They mean that when judges find no clearly overriding public interest such as they found in GIBBONS V. OGDEN (1824) they will not disturb the contractual arrangements, that is, the *transactions*, by which women and men conduct their affairs—be they philanthropists (*Dartmouth*) or land speculators and farmers (*Fletcher*). As Marshall put it, "the intercourse between man and man would be very seriously obstructed, if this principle be overturned." Incidentally, by killing New York's restrictive steamboat law *Gibbons* too promoted transactional freedom.

An inclination toward unfettered private activity was deep in the temper of the times. Americans were on the make. They had escaped the old-world fetters: king, feudal aristocracy, and established church. They were the "new men." A vast geographical frontier invited initiative and ingenuity. The standard of living was low, but natural resources were plentiful. These conditions put a high premium on private, developmental effort. Such was the setting in which contract clauses found their way into bills of rights along with other basic protections then deemed indispensable to personal freedom and social well-being.

If the Marshall Court found that the Constitution forbade reneging on state obligations, it also recognized that public agreements raised special problems justifying a special rule of strict construction. In PROVIDENCE BANK v. BILLINGS (1830) Rhode Island had chartered the Providence Bank "in the usual form" with no reference of stipulation concerning taxation. Later, when the state enacted a bank tax, Providence Bank argued that a power (taxation) which might be used to destroy its charter was foreclosed by implication. The Court demurred: "as the whole community is interested in retaining [the power to tax] undiminished, that community has a right to insist that its abandonment ought not to be presumed, in a case in which the deliberate purpose to abandon it does not appear." Obviously the mere grant of a corporate charter for an ordinary banking operation could not rationally be held to imply an immunity from routine, nondiscriminatory taxation.

Marshall's Jacksonian successors under Chief Justice ROGER B. TANEY followed the established path with two modifications: a temporary enlargement of the rule of strict construction, and a decision that a state may not by covenant fetter its power of EMINENT DOMAIN. The former occurred in CHARLES RIVER BRIDGE CO. v. WARREN BRIDGE CO. (1837). Massachusetts had authorized private investors to build, operate, and maintain a public drawbridge in exchange for toll rights for a period of forty (later extended to seventy) years. Before that period expired the state authorized a competing, in effect toll-free, bridge only yards away from the original facility. Was the state free thus to jeopardize the revenue of the first bridge, or did the forty-year provision implicitly preclude such interference? It must have been clear at the outset to all concerned that investors would not provide, maintain, and operate for forty years a public facility, if the state were free at any time to disrupt their only source of compensation. Surely in these circumstances the Marshall rule of strict construction was satisfied; the state's "deliberate purpose" to permit unimpeded toll collection for the period in question seems obvious.

The Taney Court did not repudiate—indeed it purported to follow—the *Providence Bank* rule of strict construction. In fact, it simply ignored the "deliberate purpose" aspect of that rule, and substituted an incompatible principle derived from English precedents: "nothing passes by implication in public grants." (Thus did Harvard College lose part of its endowment.) Justices Story and SMITH THOMPSON dissented on implied agreement grounds. Justice JOHN MCLEAN agreed with them on the merits, but thought the Court lacked JURISDICTION. In substance *Charles River* was a 4–3 decision—although five of the Justices had been appointed by President ANDREW JACKSON, the other two by his Jeffersonian predecessors.

The majority position—exalting form over substance—would have permitted construction of an adjacent, toll-free bridge immediately after construction of the first one. Yet surely no court would so decide. If this be true, the Taney rule against implied agreements must be untenable. The Court seems rarely to have used it, having returned long ago to the Marshall approach. See, for example, NORTHWESTERN FERTILIZING CO. v. HYDE PARK (1878): "Nothing is to be taken as conceded but what is given in unmistakable terms, *or by an implication equally clear*" (emphasis added). The major upshot of the Taney Court's stricter rule of construction was that those who covenanted with a state took care to secure elaborately explicit commitments.

Charles River Bridge exudes liberalism, stressing as it does the social interest in progress. Property rights, the Court proclaimed, must not impede developing technology. Old turnpike charters, for example, should be construed "strictly" lest they block new railroads. But no such clash of old and new was at issue before the Court. The real problem was that after some forty years the Massachusetts legislature had come to believe the tolls were no longer justified—the bridge having long since paid for itself. A severely split Court decided not the real, but a hypothetical, case—demonstrating once again that the framing of the issue largely determines the outcome of a controversy.

The other innovation of the Taney era came in *West River Bridge Co. v. Dix* (1848). Vermont had granted exclusive bridge rights. This did not prevent it from confiscating the grantees' bridge during the life of the grant—subject of course to JUST COMPENSATION. The Court's rationale was that all contracts are subject to HIGHER LAW conditions. "Such a condition is the right of eminent domain." The indispensable power of taxation, however, is not such a "condition" and thus may be limited by state covenants, as the Court held in PIQUA BRANCH OF THE STATE BANK V. KNOOP (1854). Surely the distinction rests not on "higher law"—whatever that meant to the Court in the *Piqua* opinion—but upon the just compensation requirement in the one situation but not in the other, and the fact that there are many taxpayers and many ways to secure public revenue, but only one recourse when a specific piece of private property stands in the way of the public welfare.

The WAITE COURT followed a similar approach in generously defining the so-called STATE POLICE POWER. Thus a charter to operate a lottery does not bar enforcement of a later antilottery law. "All agree that the legislature can not bargain away the police power," the Court declared in STONE V. MISSISSIPPI (1880). Of course neither the state in question, nor any other, has ever undertaken to "bargain away" its POLICE POWER. The DOCTRINE as enunciated in *Stone* is at best a truism providing no standard for judgment. Had it been used in *Dartmouth*, the school would have lost its case and its independence. In fact, as Gerald Gunther has remarked, the *Stone* police power rule has been used mainly in cases "involving prohibitions of matters widely regarded as 'evil' ": for example, lotteries and intoxicating beverages, in an era when "Court invalidations of state laws impairing corporate charter privileges reached its highest frequency." (See INALIENABLE POLICE POWER.)

The epidemic of railroad fever that began in the Midwest in the 1850s was a prolific source of contract clause litigation. Many towns, cities, counties, and states issued railroad-aid bonds at an overall face value exceeding half a billion dollars. The purpose was to induce railroad companies to build lines convenient to the various bond issuers. Some of the desired construction never materialized. Many, perhaps all, of the railroad companies were overcapitalized. Stock watering was common. Some public and company officials were less than honest. These developments produced widespread resentment which some communities may have used for selfish purposes. In any case, what Henry Adams called the "mortgaged generation" (1865–1895) tried in one form or another to evade or repudiate much of its bond obligation. These circumstances are reflected in the path-breaking case of GELPCKE V. DUBUQUE (1864). After several decisions upholding the authority of cities to issue railroad-aid bonds, the Iowa Supreme Court, reinterpreting state law, reversed itself. On review the nation's highest Court upheld the claims of the adversely affected bondholders. In doing so it intimated that the state court's shift of position, retroactively altering the position of investors, was incompatible with contract clause principles. Popularly elected state judges apparently were more responsive to public sentiment than were appointed members of the federal Supreme Court. Ten years later *Pine Grove Township v. Talcott* (1874) brought the most extreme application of *Gelpcke* doctrine: to situations in which the state judiciary held bond issues invalid without overruling any prior decisions. The Supreme Court's rationale was that similar bond issues had been upheld in many other states before issuance of the bonds in question.

The contract clause intimations in *Gelpcke* and *Pine Grove* became an explicit basis of decision in *Douglass v. Pike* (1880). Much later the Court said that state court decisions did not produce contract obligations, and that neither *Gelpcke* nor its numerous offspring had in fact held otherwise. (*Tidal Oil Co. v. Flanagan*, 1924.)

Along with these bond cases another numerically important group involved the old problem of tax exemption. Without foregetting Marshall's *Providence Bank* rule of strict construction, the Court blocked a series of state efforts to annul pledges of corporate tax immunity.

After 1890 the contract clause as applied to state covenants gradually declined in favor or a more comprehensive, new device called SUBSTANTIVE (economic) DUE PROCESS—a gross perversion of the FOURTEENTH AMENDMENT. Years later, after the demise of that perversion, two cases suggested a possible renaissance of the contract clause. In UNITED STATES TRUST CO. V. NEW JERSEY (1977), the Court expounded a new principle of "particular" (more careful) scrutiny for cases involving public covenants "because the State's self-interest is at stake." New Jersey had issued transportation-system bonds pledging it would not substantially divert to other transportation needs the reserves and revenues securing them. Later it repealed this pledge. State courts upheld the repeal as a police power measure designed to promote additional transportation facilities. The Supreme Court reversed. No longer willing to defer to state determination of such issues, it ruled that judges must decide whether the contract impairment is "reasonable and necessary to serve an important public purpose." In this case it found that the state's needs could be served by less drastic means. In a bitter dissent Justices WILLIAM J. BRENNAN, BYRON R. WHITE, and THURGOOD MARSHALL insisted that for a century the "central principle" had been this: "unusual deference to [state and local] law-making authority." They could not accept a departure "from the virtually unbroken line of our cases" holding that "lawful" exercises of the police power are "paramount to private rights held under contract." The question remains, however, whether a particular exercise of power is lawful.

We turn now from public to private contract problems. No doubt the contract clause was inspired largely by debtor's relief laws, for example, measures authorizing postponed repayment of debts, installment payments, or payment in goods (often at a discount). In the Supreme Court's first encounter with this private contract problem it struck down a New York law discharging debts upon surrender of the debtor's property however inadequate to meet his obligations. Chief Justice Marshall's opinion for a unanimous Court in STURGES V. CROWNINSHIELD (1819) is noteworthy for two points: the "mere existence" of the national BANKRUPTCY POWER does not preclude state insolvency legislation; and, while a state may not impair contract obligations, it may alter the legal sanctions (remedies, such as imprisonment for debt) for enforcement of such obligations. Eight years later OGDEN V. SAUNDERS (1827) construed *Sturges* to prohibit only retrospective application of insolvency measures. Prospective application was deemed a different matter. The Court's rationale was that a debtor relief act in existence at the time of a contract became part of the contract; later enforcement thus would not constitute an impairment. On this basis, however, a retroactive insolvency law could also be upheld. After all, a state's power to adopt future insolvency measures may equally be deemed part of every contract. In his only recorded constitutional dissent "the great Chief Justice" along with Justices GABRIEL DUVALL and Story objected: the 4–3 majority had reduced a safeguard for contract rights to no more than a prohibition on "retrospectivity." Later, we shall see, even this restriction faded away.

Marshall's dissenting view in *Ogden* finds support in two separate votes in the Constitutional Convention. The contract clause of the Northwest Ordinance applied only to "private contracts . . . previously formed." In "copying" it, the Founders (as we have seen) dropped the limiting word "private." *They also dropped the limiting term "previously formed."* Later, on September 15, the Convention reaffirmed this position by rejecting George Mason's motion to insert the word "previous" after the words "obligation of" in the contract clause. Thus on two occasions the convention *rejected* the limitation that *Ogden v. Saunders* read into the Constitution.

The *Sturges* distinction between impairment of ob-

ligations and alteration of remedies threatened in later years to undermine the contract clause. Thus BRONSON V. KINZIE (1843), a leading Taney Court decision, taught that the allowable scope of remedial changes depends on their "reasonableness," provided "no substantial right" is impaired. As Justice BENJAMIN N. CARDOZO wrote with characteristic restraint in *Worthen Co. v. Kavanaugh* (1935), the dividing line "is at times obscure." The leading modern case, HOME BUILDING AND LOAN ASSOCIATION V. BLAISDELL (1934), upheld a Minnesota "mortgage moratorium" law that extended the time of payment of mortgage loans, thus saving many homeowners, farmers, and businesses from foreclosure. The Court used the remedy and police power gambits to escape the *Sturges-Ogden* rule against retroactivity. The significance of the case is this: it is the culmination early in the Great Depression of a long, step-by-step process that replaced the absolute approach of the Constitution with a judicial balancing or "reasonableness" approach in private contract cases. Yet all agree these are the cases that above all else produced the unqualified language of the contract clause. Such absolutism does not mean that the founders were hard-hearted, preferring creditors to debtors. It means merely that, giving debtor-relief authority to Congress via the bankruptcy power, they opted for uniform, national treatment of the ubiquitous debtor/creditor tension.

Notwithstanding *Blaisdell* the "old Court" thereafter struck down several insolvency measures. One of them was LOUISVILLE JOINT STOCK LAND BANK V. RADFORD (1935). In effect it read the contract clause into the Fifth Amendment to invalidate a federal mortgage moratorium law (a matter of reverse INCORPORATION). Then with the advent of the Roosevelt Court in 1937 (until *United States Trust* in 1977) the contract clause all but vanished as a safeguard for contractual obligations—public or private. The only exceptions are *Indiana ex rel. Anderson v. Brand* (1938), protecting teacher tenure claims, and *Wood v. Lovett* (1941), protecting a tax-sale purchaser against repeal of a law that cured possible defects in his title. *Wood* is particularly interesting because it rests on the *Fletcher* principle that a state land grant entails an implied contractual obligation not to repudiate the grant in question. Then came ALLIED STRUCTURAL STEEL CO. V. SPANNAUS (1978). There an employer had adopted an employee pension agreement. The state tried to alter it by enlarging the employer's obligations retroactively. Finding the alternation too "severe" to be upheld, the Court observed: "If the Contract Clause is to retain any meaning at all . . . it must be understood to impose *some* limits upon the power of a State to abridge existing contractual relationships, even in the exercise of its otherwise legitimate police power." As in *United States Trust,* Justices Brennan, White, and Marshall dissented bitterly. Stressing again their view of minimal (or no) protection of economic interests vis-à-vis the police power, they added this: the contract clause at most prevents diminution, not enlargement, of contractual obligations.

All of these cases from *Fletcher* to *Spannaus* entail a common theme: the precept of reasonable expectations. To what extent, if any, is government free to disturb those formal pledges on which men and women acting in good faith have planned their lives? A healthy legal system accommodates changing social needs. When ours was a rich and vigorous, yet underdeveloped, nation with a low overall standard of living, our law encouraged capital formation, transactional freedom, and respect for contract obligations. The "design"—not always and everywhere fully perceived—was to encourage production in the interest of a more comfortable life for everyone. Given the propensity of successful institutions to press beyond the limits of their logic, such encouragement may take grotesque forms, for example, the judicial abuses called DUAL FEDERALISM and substantive due process. If eventually a "backward" nation becomes highly developed, emphasis seemingly shifts from economic rights to "personal rights," from production to welfare, as in the United States beginning in the 1930s. If such a shift results in overreaction, threatening the source of the "golden eggs," emphasis may focus again on production along with protection for property and contractual rights, as in *New Jersey Trust* and *Spannaus.*

WALLACE MENDELSON

Bibliography

HALE, ROBERT L. 1944 The Supreme Court and the Contract Clause. *Harvard Law Review* 57:512–557, 621–674, 852–892.

HURST, WILLARD 1956 *Law and the Conditions of Freedom.* Madison: University of Wisconsin Press.

SCHWARTZ, BERNARD 1980 Old Wine in Old Bottles? The Renaissance of the Contract Clause. *Supreme Court Review* 1979:95–121.

WRIGHT, BENJAMIN F. 1938 *The Contract Clause of the Constitution.* Cambridge, Mass.: Harvard University Press.

CONTRACT THEORY

See: Social Compact Theory

COOLEY, THOMAS M.
(1824–1898)

Thomas McIntyre Cooley was a distinguished law teacher, state judge, first chairman of the Interstate Commerce Commission, and author of the influential 1868 *Treatise on the Constitutional Limitations Which Rest upon the Legislative Power of the States of the American Union.* Born in western New York to a family with a Jeffersonian "bias," Cooley absorbed an anticorporate equal-rights ideology, fearful of "class legislation" that aided the few at the expense of many.

In 1843 Cooley went west to Michigan and combined activities in law, journalism, politics, and poetry. He helped organize the Free Soil Party in the state and in 1856 became a Republican. Narrowing his concerns to the law, he rapidly attained professional recognition. Appointed Compiler of the state's laws in 1857 and Reporter to the Supreme Court in 1858, he was selected in 1859 as a professor at the newly opened University of Michigan Law Department. In 1864 he was elected to the Michigan Supreme Court.

Cooley tempered his preoccupation with the law with historical and political values and naturally turned to constitutional questions. To Francis Thorpe's 1889 query on books for a constitutional law library he replied that "constitutional law is so inseparably connected with constitutional history and that is so vital a part of general history that I should not know where to draw the line."

Historical, COMMON LAW, and Jacksonian sensibilities were the presuppositions of Cooley's 1868 treatise, although his aim was merely to write "a convenient guidebook of elementary constitutional principles." The book was that; it had gone through six editions by 1890 and had a broader circulation, a greater sale, and more frequent citations than any other law book published in the second half of the nineteenth century.

The treatise was useful because no one prior to Cooley had systematically analyzed the cases and principles dealing with constitutional limitations on state legislative power. Chapters on constitutional protection to personal liberty, to liberty of speech, and to RELIGIOUS LIBERTY were supplemented with chapters on municipal government, EMINENT DOMAIN, taxation, and the POLICE POWER. Chapter Eleven, "Of the Protection to Property by the Law of the Land" attracted the most attention, for here Cooley discussed DUE PROCESS OF LAW and gave it a significant substantive definition. Cooley said that legislative restraints on property should be tested by "those principles of civil liberty and constitutional defense which have become established in our system of law, and not by any rules that pertain to forms of procedure only." His test of due process was historical: the "established principles" and "settled usuages" of the common law protected property rights.

Cooley's definition of due process was used in the briefs of corporation lawyers who also distorted his comprehensive definition of the liberty protected by the FOURTEENTH AMENDMENT as embracing "all our liberties—personal, civil, and political" to a FREEDOM OF CONTRACT doctrine. Twentieth-century commentators have often accepted these briefs, misinterpreting Cooley as a zealous advocate of the judicial protection of property rights. To Cooley, however, due process did not necessarily mean judicial process nor did individual property rights mean corporate property rights. His views on judicial self-restraint were summarized in his treatise comment that judges "cannot run a race of opinions upon points of right, reason, or expediency with the law-making power." And Cooley repeated Justice LEMUEL SHAW'S views on a strong police power.

When Cooley was writing his treatise he was lecturing students on "the struggle between corporations and the rights of the people," condemning the decision in DARTMOUTH COLLEGE V. WOODWARD (1819), issuing opinions criticizing special privileges for corporations, and using the principle of equal rights and the maxims of "no taxation except for a PUBLIC PURPOSE" and of "due process of law" to declare tax aid to railroad corporations unconstitutional.

Cooley anxiously observed the growth of corporate capitalism in post-Civil War America. Deploring the national sentiment "to become immediately rich and great," he worried over the conflict of labor and capital and felt "that *class legislation* has been making the rich richer and the poor poorer," adding that "property is never so much in danger of becoming master as when capital unjustly manipulates the legislation of the country." These remarks in an 1879 lecture at Johns Hopkins University have been overlooked, as has a similar warning in an 1884 article on "Labor and Capital Before the Law" that when constitutional protection to property especially benefits those who have possessions, "the Constitution itself may come to be regarded by considerable classes as an instrument whose office it is to protect the rich in the advantages they have secured over the poor, and one that should be hated for that reason."

In court decisions Cooley evidenced older Jefferso-

nian values, upholding free public education, the FREEDOM OF THE PRESS, the rights of local self-government, and the necessity for judicial self-restraint. But the changing America of the late nineteenth century diminished earlier Jeffersonian hopes. In a melancholic mood in 1883 he admitted that "the political philosophy of Burke never grows stale and is for all times and all people."

By the 1880s Cooley had a national reputation, earned by judicial duties and constant lecturing, editing, and writing, including editions of SIR WILLIAM BLACKSTONE and JOSEPH STORY and treatises on torts and taxation. Aspirations for a United States Supreme Court appointment were dashed in 1881 when railroad interests, Cooley thought, successfully lobbied for STANLEY MATTHEWS. But Cooley had given up on Republicans, and in 1886 wondered whether the Party "possesses any good reason for existence." He admired GROVER CLEVELAND and accepted his offer of the chairmanship of the Interstate Commerce Commission. Regulating the American railway system was a task beyond Cooley's declining powers, and the effort led to a breakdown that left him a semi-invalid after 1890.

An 1889 comment to the South Dakota Constitutional Convention reveals that Cooley had modified older beliefs in constitutional limitations to legislative power: "Even in the millennium people will be studying ways whereby—by means of corporate power—they can circumvent their neighbors. Don't do that to any such extent as to prevent the legislative power hereafter from meeting all the evils that may be within the reach of proper legislation."

ALAN R. JONES

Bibliography

JONES, ALAN R. 1986 *The Constitutional Conservatism of Thomas McIntyre Cooley: A Study in the History of Ideas.* New York: Garland Publishing.

TWISS, BENJAMIN 1942 *Lawyers and the Constitution: How Laissez-Faire Came to the Constitution.* Princeton, N.J.: Princeton University Press.

COOLEY v. BOARD OF WARDENS OF PORT OF PHILADELPHIA
12 Howard 299 (1851)

The chaos in judicial interpretation that characterized the TANEY COURT'S COMMERCE CLAUSE cases was ended in *Cooley,* the most important decision on the subject between GIBBONS V. OGDEN (1824) and

UNITED STATES V. E. C. KNIGHT CO. (1895). The Taney Court finally found a doctrinal formula that allowed a majority to coalesce around a single line of reasoning for the first time since the days of the MARSHALL COURT. That formula was the DOCTRINE of SELECTIVE EXCLUSIVENESS, announced for the majority by Justice BENJAMIN R. CURTIS. The doctrine was a compromise, combining aspects of the doctrines of CONCURRENT POWERS over commerce and EXCLUSIVE POWERS, but three Justices of the eight who participated rejected the compromise. Justices JOHN MCLEAN and JAMES M. WAYNE, whom Curtis privately called "high-toned Federalists," persisted in their nationalist view, expressed in dissent, that congressional powers over INTERSTATE and FOREIGN COMMERCE were always exclusive, while PETER V. DANIEL, an intransigent states-rightist, concurred in the majority's result on the ground that congressional power over commerce was never exclusive.

At issue in *Cooley* was the constitutionality of a Pennsylvania statute requiring ships of a certain size entering or leaving the port of Philadelphia to employ local pilots in local waters. Cooley, claiming that the state act unconstitutionally regulated foreign commerce, refused to pay the pilotage fee. The fact that the first Congress had provided that the states could enact pilotage laws did not alter Cooley's claim. Curtis for the Court acknowledged that if the grant of commerce powers to Congress had divested the states of a power to legislate, the act of Congress could not confer that power on the states. The problem was whether the power of Congress in this case was exclusive.

Commerce, Curtis declared, embraces a vast field of many different subjects. Some subjects imperatively demand a single uniform rule for the whole nation, while others, like pilotage, demand diverse local rules to cope with varying local situations. The power of Congress was therefore selectively exclusive. If the subject required a single uniform rule, the states could not regulate that subject even in the absence of congressional legislation. In such a case congressional powers would be exclusive. Such was the nationalist half of the doctrine. The other half, by which the Court sustained the state act, maintained that the states did possess concurrent powers over commerce if the subject required diversity of regulation. Thus Congress's power was exclusive or concurrent depending on the nature of the subject to be regulated. "It is the opinion of a majority of the court," Curtis declared, "that the mere grant to Congress of the power to regulate commerce, did not deprive the

States of power to regulate pilots, and that although Congress has legislated on this subject, its legislation manifests an intention . . . to leave its regulation to the several States."

The Court's doctrine of selective exclusiveness gave it a point of departure for analyzing commerce clause issues. The doctrine, however, had to be interpreted. It did not even suggest how the Court could determine which subjects required national legislation, thus excluding state action, and which required diverse local regulations. The doctrine could be manipulated by Justices who employed nationalist doctrine to invalidate state enactments.

LEONARD W. LEVY

Bibliography

SWISHER, CARL BRENT 1974 *History of the Supreme Court.* Vol. 5:404–407. New York: Macmillan.

COOLEY RULE

See: *Cooley v. Board of Wardens;* Selective Exclusiveness

COOLIDGE, CALVIN
(1872–1933)

John Calvin Coolidge, the thirtieth President of the United States, succeeded WARREN G. HARDING upon Harding's death in August 1923 and served until 1929. The heart of his legislative program was a series of tax reductions for individual taxpayers in all brackets, economy in government, and a balanced BUDGET.

The chief legislative controversy of the 1920s concerned the McNary-Haugen bills, which Coolidge vetoed in 1927 and 1928. These bills, proposed in response to a prolonged agricultural recession, would have authorized the federal government to buy and sell farm products in an effort to raise their prices. Coolidge opposed the bills as unworkable and as an unconstitutional expansion of the commerce power. The Congress, he argued, was limited to those powers granted to it or implied as incidental to the express powers. In language anticipating the opposition to the New Deal, Coolidge cautioned against the dangers of bureaucracy. He also observed that the people of the United States could reallocate the constitutional powers of the federal government and the states by means of the AMENDING PROCESS. Coolidge supported national legislation to regulate child labor, but he believed that a constitutional amendment would be required first to grant such power to the federal government.

Coolidge's only appointment to the Supreme Court was of his Amherst College classmate, Attorney General HARLAN FISKE STONE.

THOMAS B. SILVER

Bibliography
SILVER, THOMAS B. 1983 *Coolidge and the Historians.* Durham, N.C.: Carolina Academic Press.

COOLIDGE, UNITED STATES v.

See: Federal Common Law

COOLIDGE v. NEW HAMPSHIRE
403 U.S. 443 (1971)

In *Coolidge v. New Hampshire,* police officers, acting pursuant to a SEARCH WARRANT issued by the state attorney general, seized and later searched an automobile parked in the driveway of a murder suspect's home. The Supreme Court ruled the warrant invalid because a prosecutor could not be regarded as a neutral and detached magistrate. The automobile seizure was too far removed in time and space from the suspect's arrest to be considered incident to that arrest, was not grounded in any EXIGENT CIRCUMSTANCES to qualify for an AUTOMOBILE SEARCH or PLAIN VIEW exception nor was the discovery of the automobile inadvertent. Later decisions have confined *Coolidge* to its facts, emphasizing the automobile's location on a private driveway and the fact that the automobile was not contraband, stolen, or itself dangerous.

STEVEN SHIFFRIN

COOPER, THOMAS
(1759–1839)

Dr. Thomas Cooper, an English radical who settled in the United States in 1794, was an intellectual jack-of-all-trades, master of most, and the author of treatises on philosophy, law, religion, government, political economy, and various sciences. When he was a Jeffersonian editor, he was convicted of violating the SEDITION ACT OF 1798. His *Political Essays* and the report of his trial advocated a radically broad theory of FREEDOM OF THE PRESS. Later a Pennsylvania judge, he was removed from office and soured on liberalism, although his friend THOMAS JEFFERSON called him the "greatest man in America, in the powers of mind and in acquired information." When Cooper was president of what later became the University of South Carolina, he revised the state statutes and wrote *On the Constitution* (1826), which spoke for SLAVERY, state SOVEREIGNTY, and NULLIFICATION.

LEONARD W. LEVY

COOPER v. AARON
358 U.S. 1 (1958)

For several years after its decision in BROWN V. BOARD OF EDUCATION (1954–1955), the Supreme Court gave little guidance or support to the lower courts charged with supervising the DESEGREGATION of the public schools. In this case, however, the Court was confronted with direct defiance of *Brown* by a state's highest officials, and it met that challenge head-on.

Even before the *Brown* remedial opinion in 1955, the school board of Little Rock, Arkansas, had approved a plan for gradual desegregation of the local schools, and the federal district court had upheld the plan. Just before the opening of the fall 1957 term, the state governor, Orval Faubus, ordered the state's National Guard to keep black children out of Little Rock's Central High School. The attorney general of the United States obtained an injunction against the governor's action, and the children entered the school. A hostile crowd gathered, and the children were removed by the police. President DWIGHT D. EISENHOWER was thus prodded into his first significant act supporting desegregation; he sent Army troops to Central High to protect the children, and eight black students attended the school for the full academic year.

In February 1958, the school board asked the district court, in *Cooper v. Aaron,* for a delay of two and one-half years in the implementation of its plan, and in June the court agreed, commenting on the "chaos, bedlam and turmoil" at Central High. In August the federal court of appeals reversed, calling for implementation of the plan on schedule. The Supreme Court, in an unusual move, accelerated the hearing to September 11, and the next day it issued a brief order affirming the decision of the court of appeals. Later the Court published its full opinion, signed by all nine Justices to emphasize their continued unamimous support of *Brown.*

The opinion dealt quickly with the uncomplicated merits of the case, saying that law and order were not to be achieved at the expense of the constitutional rights of black children. The Court then added a response to the assertion by the Arkansas governor and legislature that the state was not required to abide by *Brown,* because *Brown* itself was an unconstitutional assumption of judicial power.

The response scored two easy points first: the Constitution, under the SUPREMACY CLAUSE, is "the supreme Law of the Land," and MARBURY V. MADISON (1803) had held that it was the province of the judiciary to "say what the law is." The Court's next step, however, was not self-evident: *Marbury* meant that the federal courts are supreme in expounding the Constitution; thus *Brown* was the supreme law of the land, binding state officers. This view, which carried the assertion of judicial power further than *Marbury* had taken it, has been repeated by the Court several times since the *Cooper* decision.

Cooper's importance, however, was not so much doctrinal as political. It reaffirmed principle at a crucial time. The televised pictures of black children being escorted into school through a crowd of hostile whites galvanized northern opinion. The 1960 election brought to office a president committed to a strong civil rights program—although it took his death to enact that program into law.

KENNETH L. KARST

(SEE ALSO: *John F. Kennedy; Civil Rights Act of 1964.*)

COOPERATIVE FEDERALISM

The theory of cooperative federalism postulates that the relationship between the national government and the states is one in which: governmental functions typically are undertaken jointly by federal and state (including local) agencies, rather than exclusively by one or the other; a sharing of power characterizes an integrated system instead of an exclusive SOVEREIGNTY at either level of government; and power tends not to concentrate at either level, or in any one agency, because the fragmented and shared nature of responsibilities gives citizens and interest groups "access" to many centers of influence.

Cooperative federalism is a modern phenomenon. Its main features—sharing of policy responsibilities and financial resources, interdependence of administration, overlapping of functions—are associated mainly with the FEDERAL GRANT-IN-AID programs. Collaboration, grants-in-aid from the national government to the states, bypassing of the states through establishment of grant programs aiding local or special-district governments directly, and development of auditing procedures and conditional grant requirements all have characterized cooperative federalism in the period after 1933.

Numerous analysts who celebrate these developments as signifying that old-style FEDERALISM is "dead," displaced by "intergovernmental relations," argue that the tension, pretensions at autonomy, and the notion of separateness of responsibilities that characterized governance in the pre-New Deal periods of constitutional development no longer form part of the reality of the federal system. Some scholars argue that relative power distribution is no longer a relevant issue. Forgotten is the elementary notion that "sharing" does not necessarily mean equality. Characteristically, in the modern grant-in-aid programs, the national government has not only raised and distributed the revenues, it has also designed the programs and established the goals, quite apart from overseeing administration.

Fascination with the alleged "non-centralization of power," which is seen to result from cooperative federalism, also can obscure the evidence of the vast additions of discretionary power in the national executive branch since 1933. Presidents from both parties have contributed to the growth of the "Imperial Presidency," and the process of centralization of power that has gone forward in this century has been profoundly influenced by this development.

The decision in MASSACHUSETTS V. MELLON (1923) established the juridical foundation of modern grant-in-aid constitutional theory. The Court there dismissed the complaint of Massachusetts that state prerogatives were improperly invaded by conditional grant programs (in that instance, the maternity-aid program of national grants). The interpretation of the TENTH AMENDMENT as "but a truism," in UNITED STATES V. DARBY (1941), further advanced the constitutional basis for cooperative federalism in action. Subsequently the Court upheld the principle of making grants conditional, even in *Oklahoma v. United States Civil Service Commission* (1947), when the federal legislation required adherence to HATCH ACT restraints on political activity by state officials. A contrary note was sounded by the Court in NATIONAL LEAGUE OF CITIES V. USERY (1976), in which the

Court asserted that "Congress may not exercise power in a fashion that impairs the states' integrity of their ability to function effectively in a federal system." Yet this assertion was made as the Court invalidated only a regulatory measure affecting hours and wages of local government employees, not a grant-in-aid or collaborative program. In GARCIA V. SAN ANTONIO TRANSIT AUTHORITY (1985) the Court overruled *Usery*, the majority declaring that case-by-case development since 1976 had failed to produce any principled basis for identifying " 'fundamental' elements of state sovereignty." The Court specifically cited the history of federal grants-in-aid as evidence that cooperative federalism and the political process gave adequate protection to the interests of the states.

HARRY N. SCHEIBER

Bibliography

CORWIN, EDWARD 1941 *Constitutional Revolution, Ltd.* Claremont, Calif.: Claremont Colleges.

COPPAGE v. KANSAS
236 U.S. 1 (1915)

In ADAIR V. UNITED STATES (1908), the Supreme Court had held that the section of the ERDMAN ACT that outlawed YELLOW DOG CONTRACTS was outside Congress's power to regulate INTERSTATE COMMERCE. Now, facing a question "not distinguishable in principle," a 6–3 Court struck down a Kansas statute banning yellow dog contracts. Justice MAHLON PITNEY for the majority, finding no reason to depart from *Adair*, reaffirmed the doctrine of FREEDOM OF CONTRACT. That "fundamental and vital" freedom fused rights of liberty and property so that any "arbitrary interference with that freedom of contract would impair those rights." Only a "legitimate" exercise of STATE POLICE POWER could limit it, and the majority could see no relation between the avowed purpose of the statute and the state's responsibility to protect the safety, morals, and health of its citizens. Indeed, "an interference with the normal exercise of personal liberty and property rights is the primary object of the statute." Concluding that it deprived employers and employees of the right to contract freely on their own terms, the majority voided the statute as a violation of SUBSTANTIVE DUE PROCESS guaranteed by the FOURTEENTH AMENDMENT.

In a brief dissent, Justice OLIVER WENDELL HOLMES reiterated the position he had stated in LOCHNER V. NEW YORK (1905). He saw nothing in the Constitution forbidding the Kansas statute, and

he declined to substitute the courts' judgment for the legislature's on this policy question. In a lengthier dissent joined by Justice CHARLES EVANS HUGHES, Justice WILLIAM R. DAY, who had voted with the majority in *Adair*, asserted that Kansas had enacted the statute to promote the general welfare, thereby validly limiting the freedom of contract.

DAVID GORDON

COPYRIGHT

The Framers of the Constitution delegated to the national government authority to enact copyright laws. The copyright power, together with the PATENT power, is found in Article I, section 8, clause 8, which empowers Congress "to promote the progress of science and useful arts, by securing for limited times to authors and inventors the exclusive right to their respective writings and discoveries." Because there is no record of any debate on this clause at the CONSTITUTIONAL CONVENTION OF 1787, and mention of it in THE FEDERALIST is perfunctory, the meaning of the clause must be found in case law.

The phrase "to promote the progress of science" states what the Supreme Court, in *Mazer v. Stein* (1954), described as "the economic philosophy behind the clause," which is "the conviction that encouragement of individual effort by personal gain is the best way to advance public welfare through the talents of authors. . . ." Most courts, however, would deny that the introductory phrase permits the denial of copyright to any particular work on the ground that it does not contribute to such "progress." In fact, a United States Court of Appeals held in 1979 that obscene content does not invalidate copyright.

The words "by securing" came into contention in *Wheaton v. Peters* (1834), the first important copyright case decided by the Supreme Court, and a case involving two of the Court's own reporters. The plaintiff there argued that the federal copyright statute merely added additional remedies to a right that already existed at COMMON LAW. To bolster this position, he argued that the word "secure" meant to protect, insure, save, and ascertain, not to create. The Court rejected this contention, holding that the federal statute had created a new right, but that the author had not complied with the act's conditions.

Because the clause contains the words, "for limited times," a federal copyright statute that purported to grant copyright protection in perpetuity would clearly be unconstitutional. So too would a term that is nominally "limited" but is in fact the equivalent of perpetual protection (for example, a one thousand year term). The term currently provided for newly created works, the life of the author plus fifty years, conforms with the "limited times" requirement.

Only "authors" may be granted copyright in the first instance, although, once granted, copyright is transferable by an author to others. The term "authors" in the Constitution gives rise to the "originality" requirement in the law of copyright, which excludes from copyright protection material copied from others. An author is no less an author because others have anticipated his work, as long as he did not copy from such others. This Judge Frank contrasted with an "inventor" under the patent power, who must by definition produce something "novel," that is, not anticipated in the prior art. By reason of the phrase "exclusive right," it is clear that Congress has the power to grant to authors the "exclusive right" to exploit their works. But Congress is under no compulsion to exercise its full powers under the Constitution. If it may withhold copyright protection altogether from a given category of works, it may also grant something less than exclusive rights. The phrase "to their respective writings" means that only "writings" may be the subject of copyright. But the concept of a "writing" for copyright purposes has been liberally construed. The Court has held that photographic portraits and sound recordings constitute a "writing." Indeed, in *Goldstein v. California* (1973), the Court defined "writings" as "any physical rendering of the fruits of creative intellectual or aesthetic labor." A work that has not been physically fixed is ineligible for copyright protection.

In *Goldstein* the Court held that the copyright power is not exclusive, so that, subject to the SUPREMACY CLAUSE, the states retain concurrent power to enact copyright laws. Until adoption of the current Copyright Act in 1978 this reserved state power was significant, because most unpublished works were protected by so-called common law (or state law) copyright. However, under the current Copyright Act this area of state law has been largely preempted, so that most works, published or unpublished, are protected, if at all, under the federal act.

In recent years the courts have begun to question whether, and to what extent, the copyright laws are subject to the FREEDOM OF SPEECH and FREEDOM OF THE PRESS guarantees of the FIRST AMENDMENT. If the First Amendment were literally applied it would invalidate the Copyright Act, since the act clearly abridges the freedom of speech and press of those who would engage in copyright infringement by copying from others. Nothing in the First Amend-

ment limits the freedom protected thereunder to speech that is original with the speaker. Nor does the fact that the Constitution also grants to Congress the power to enact copyright laws render the First Amendment inapplicable. The First Amendment and the remainder of the BILL OF RIGHTS limit only those powers that have otherwise been confided to the federal government. If it did not modify such powers, it would have no meaning at all. The conflict between these two socially useful, yet antithetical, interests is, of course, capable of resolution. The Ninth Circuit held in *Krofft v. McDonald's Corp.* (1977), and the Supreme Court implicitly agreed in *Zacchini v. Scripps-Howard Broadcasting Co.* (1977), that "ideas" lie in the domain of the First Amendment, so that copyright may not be claimed therein, but that the form of "expression" of ideas may be the subject of copyright, notwithstanding the First Amendment.

MELVILLE B. NIMMER

Bibliography
NIMMER, MELVILLE B. 1978 *Copyright.* 4 Vols. Albany, N.Y.: Matthew Bender & Co.

CORFIELD v. CORYELL
4 Wash. C.C. 371 (1823), 6 Fed. Case 546 (No. 3,230)

The importance of Justice BUSHROD WASHINGTON's circuit opinion derives from the fact that it contains the only exposition of Article IV, section 2, prior to the adoption of the FOURTEENTH AMENDMENT, that also uses the phrase PRIVILEGES AND IMMUNITIES. The clause in Article IV declares: "The Citizens of each state shall be entitled to all Privileges and Immunities of Citizens in the several states." *Corfield* arose because the plaintiff's vessel had been condemned under a state law forbidding nonresidents to take shell fish from state waters; in his TRESPASS action, the plaintiff relied upon the privileges and immunities clause. Washington declared, however, that the clause protected only the "fundamental" rights of CITIZENSHIP, such as the protection of government, the enjoyment of life, liberty, and property, the right to move about freely, the right to claim the benefit of the writ of HABEAS CORPUS, the right to sue, and the right to vote if qualified. This category did not include the right to exploit the state's oyster beds.

LEONARD W. LEVY

(SEE ALSO: *Slaughterhouse Cases, 1873.*)

CORNELIUS v. NAACP LEGAL DEFENSE AND EDUCATIONAL FUND, INC.
473 U.S.   (1985)

This decision demonstrated how cumbersome the Supreme Court's analysis of PUBLIC FORUM issues has become since its decision in PERRY EDUCATION ASSOCIATION V. PERRY LOCAL EDUCATORS' ASSOCIATION (1983).

A 1983 EXECUTIVE ORDER limited the Combined Federal Campaign (CFC), a charity drive among federal employees, to charities that provide direct health and welfare services, and expressly excluded legal defense and advocacy groups. Seven such groups sued in federal district court, challenging their exclusion as a violation of the FIRST AMENDMENT. That court agreed, and issued an INJUNCTION forbidding exclusion of the groups from CFC. The court of appeals affirmed, but the Supreme Court reversed, 4–3, in an opinion by Justice SANDRA DAY O'CONNOR.

The Court held that the government had not designated either the federal workplace or CFC in particular as a public forum, in the sense of the *Perry* opinion. Rather, each of these was a "nonpublic forum"—a government operation in which communications could be limited to those promoting the operation's mission. CFC's purpose was to provide a means for government employees to lessen the government's burden in meeting human health and welfare needs, by making their own contributions to those ends. It was not necessary, in excluding the plaintiffs from CFC, to show that their solicitations would be incompatible with the goals of CFC; the relevant standard was the reasonableness of the exclusion. The President could reasonably conclude that money raised for direct provision of food or shelter was more beneficial than money raised for litigation or advocacy on behalf of the needy. Furthermore, the government could properly avoid the appearance of political favoritism by excluding all such groups. Those organizations had alternative means for raising funds from government employees, including direct mail advertising and in-person solicitation outside the workplace.

The Court, recognizing that other groups not in the business of direct provision of health and welfare services had been allowed to participate in CFC, remanded the case for determination whether the government had excluded the plaintiff groups for the purpose of suppressing their particular viewpoints.

Justice HARRY A. BLACKMUN, joined by Justice WILLIAM J. BRENNAN, dissented, arguing that any governmental exclusion of a class of speakers from any forum must be justified by a showing that the would-be speakers' intended use of the forum was incompatible with the relevant governmental operation. Here no such incompatibility had been shown, he said. Justice JOHN PAUL STEVENS, also dissenting, expressed skepticism about the value of a DOCTRINE founded on a series of categories of forum. In this case, he said, the government's own arguments supported "the inference of bias" against the excluded groups.

KENNETH L. KARST

CORONADO COAL COMPANY v. UNITED MINE WORKERS

See: *United Mine Workers v. Coronado Coal Company*

CORPORATIONS AND THE CONSTITUTION

The United States is the organizational or the corporate society par excellence. Seen sociologically, numerous societal entities of a corporate nature exist. From the perspective of constitutional law, only the business corporation has the status of being a PERSON. Those enterprises are social organizations midway between the state and the individual, owing their existence to the latter's need for organization and the former's reluctance to supply it. They are part of the greatest silence of the Constitution—the nature and operation of the economy. Except for a few nebulous provisions in Article I, plus the OBLIGATION OF CONTRACTS clause and the property provisions of the Fifth Amendment, all is left to inference. Neither business corporations nor unions nor any other private organization (for example, universities, farmers' legions, veterans' leagues, and the like) are mentioned.

As a consequence, corporate organizations fit uneasily into constitutional theory. As collectivities, they are the principal units of today's political pluralism. The giant corporations dominate the economy, both domestically and internationally. It was not always so. As late as 1800, only about 300 business corporations existed. Industrialization, coupled with massive governmental aid (pursuant to ALEXANDER HAMILTON's principles), so burgeoned corporate growth that during the 1850s more were formed than ever before.

After the Civil War, the "trusts"—the forerunners of today's corporate giants—flowered.

The large corporations do not fit into democratic theory. Centers of economic and thus of political power, some are so mighty as to challenge the SOVEREIGNTY of the state. Constitutional decisions of the Supreme Court have formed a major part of the legal basis for that dominating position. DARTMOUTH COLLEGE V. WOODWARD (1819) set the tone. Chief Justice JOHN MARSHALL read the CONTRACT CLAUSE to nullify New Hampshire's attempt to alter Dartmouth's charter, originally granted by the English crown. In well-known language, Marshall called the corporation "an artificial being, invisible, intangible, and existing only in contemplation of law." He thus made it clear that corporations, although collectivities, were private entities, and by labeling them "artificial beings" he paved the way for the Court in 1886 to declare that corporations are PERSONS protected by the FOURTEENTH AMENDMENT. (Also in 1819, Marshall ruled that Congress had IMPLIED POWER to form corporations when "NECESSARY AND PROPER" to carry out its expressly granted powers. The decision, McCULLOCH V. MARYLAND, is also noteworthy for its theory of BROAD CONSTRUCTION of the Constitution.)

As constitutional persons, corporations were able to invoke the DUE PROCESS clauses to fend off adverse regulations. By inventing the concept of SUBSTANTIVE (or economic) DUE PROCESS, the Supreme Court helped to defang the Granger, Populist, and nascent labor movements. FREEDOM OF CONTRACT was read into the Constitution; laissez-faire economics became constitutional DOCTRINE. By that one development the Court catapulted JUDICIAL REVIEW into a powerful instrument of governance.

LOCHNER V. NEW YORK (1905) is the best known economic due process decision. Over a famous dissent by Justice OLIVER WENDELL HOLMES, the Court invalidated a statute regulating the hours of workers in bakeries, because both the company's and the workers' freedoms to contract were improperly invaded. So many similar decisions were rendered that by 1924 John R. Commons called the Court "the first authoritative faculty of political economy in the world's history."

That practice was altered by the Great Depression: in 1937 the Court grudgingly conceded that economic policy was a province of federal legislation. The turning point came in WEST COAST HOTEL CORP. V. PARRISH (1937) and the WAGNER ACT CASES (*National Labor Relations Board v. Jones & Laughlin Steel Corp.*, 1937). The latter decision in practical effect "constitutionalized" political pluralism. FERGUSON V. SKRUPA (1963) illustrates the modern, and doubtless permanent, attitude of the Court toward ECONOMIC REGULATION.

Noneconomic regulation is a different matter. In FIRST NATIONAL BANK OF BOSTON V. BELLOTTI (1978) the Court invalidated a Massachusetts statute prohibiting corporations from spending money to influence elections. Corporate managers now have an unabridgeable right not only to spend their personal funds to further their political views but to use the money of others (in legal theory, corporations are owned by the stockholders). Although fictional persons, corporations by judicial legislation are attaining many of the rights of natural persons.

Neither political theorists nor economists have produced a satisfactory theory of conscious economic cooperation and its effect on the constitutional order. The Supreme Court refuses to recognize the corporation for what it is—a private government that, save in label, differs little from public government. Americans are governed as much—perhaps more—by corporations as they are by the official organs of government. Corporations, moreover, have such an influence upon the governmental structure that a version of corporatism is in process of creation.

Corporations were originally considered to be arms of the state—divisions of society established to get some of the public's business done. Today, paradoxically, they are both associations of individuals and constitutional persons. As such, they challenge orthodox constitutional theory. Their governmental character could be acknowledged by the Supreme Court; but the Justices have usually refused to do so. However, SMITH V. ALLWRIGHT (1944) did apply constitutional norms to a corporate body (albeit not a chartered corporation)—the Democratic party; and in MARSH V. ALABAMA (1946) a business corporation operating a "company town" was subjected to the limits of the FIRST AMENDMENT.

The giant corporations have assets that overshadow those of most of the states (and, indeed, most nation-states). They have created a national economic system that makes a decentralized political order impractical. Traditional concepts of FEDERALISM have consequently had to give way to notions of nationalism. In recent decades, many corporations have become transnational and they are creating an international economic order. They thus challenge the political order of the nation-state much as their predecessors altered the original federal system.

Corporate bodies, whether business or otherwise,

have become so socially significant that in one perspective they have replaced the individual (the natural person) as the basic unit of society. The modern corporation has created societies with structural foundations different from those of the past. Constitutional theory must therefore adapt itself to the corporation on three levels: federalism (in many respects corporations are in effect the most important units of local government); nationalism (where the transnational corporation challenges the sovereignty of the nation-state); and individualism (the natural person must become adapted to living in a hierarchic, bureaucratic society). To date, little scholarly activity has addressed any of these levels.

ARTHUR S. MILLER

Bibliography

COLEMAN, JAMES S. 1974 *Power and the Structure of Society.* New York: W. W. Norton.
COMMONS, JOHN R. 1924 *Legal Foundations of Capitalism.* Madison: University of Wisconsin Press.
MILLER, ARTHUR SELWYN 1976 *The Modern Corporate State: Private Governments and the Constitution.* Westport, Conn.: Greenwood Press.

CORRIGAN v. BUCKLEY
271 U.S. 323 (1926)

Reviewing a RESTRICTIVE COVENANT case from the DISTRICT OF COLUMBIA, the Supreme Court unanimously held that it presented no substantial constitutional question. The Court dismissed Fifth and FOURTEENTH AMENDMENT claims because they referred to government and state, not individual, actions. (Surprisingly, the Court failed to mention that the Fourteenth did not apply in the District.) Although these amendments provide for equal rights, they did not in any manner prohibit or invalidate contracts entered into by private individuals in respect to the control and disposition of their own property. The Court therefore dismissed the case for want of JURISDICTION.

DAVID GORDON

(SEE ALSO: *State Action; Shelley v. Kraemer, 1948.*)

CORWIN, EDWARD S.
(1878–1963)

Edward S. Corwin, McCormick Professor of Jurisprudence at Princeton University, succeeded the nineteenth-century titans JAMES KENT, JOSEPH STORY, and THOMAS M. COOLEY. Corwin's understanding of constitutional and political thought distinguished him from these lawyers and judges, who exemplified Edmund Burke's maxim that the study of law sharpens the mind by narrowing it. Matchless learning in government and history made him an eminent COMMENTATOR ON THE CONSTITUTION.

Corwin's *Liberty against Government* (1948) was a major defense of liberty as the fundamental American principle. *The Twilight of the Supreme Court* (1934) upheld the New Deal with an idea of national power that left presidential and congressional power without statable limits. Corwin later more persuasively and moderately pondered the New Deal's extension of governmental power in relationship to the Founders' intention. In UNITED STATES V. DARBY (1941) Chief Justice HARLAN FISKE STONE had cited Chief Justice JOHN MARSHALL'S definition of congressional power over INTERSTATE COMMERCE in GIBBONS V. OGDEN (1824) and Marshall's interpretation of NECESSARY AND PROPER in MCCULLOCH V. MARYLAND (1819). Corwin persuasively denied that Marshall would have consented to be "thus conscripted in the service of the New Deal": "Liberty, the spacious liberty of an expanding nation, not social equality, was the lodestar of his political philosophy." Corwin's bow to the "great Chief Justice" Marshall showed that Corwin, too, championed liberty.

Public law, said Corwin, is the "law that governs government itself"; political theory is the branch that explains the moral source of the law's authority. Corwin identified his topics and accomplishments in public law as the origins and development of the idea of liberty against government, "the most important theme of American constitutional legal history"; JUDICIAL REVIEW in historical perspective; DUAL FEDERALISM; and the Presidency.

The Constitution and What It Means Today (1920, 1958), his best known work, combined scholarship and simplicity. Popular education for Corwin kept the Constitution from becoming a "craft mystery," whether one of bench and bar or of behaviorism. Corwin's most important work was *The President: Office and Powers* (1957), which concluded that the autonomous and self-directing idea of the Presidency had triumphed. Decades before the WATERGATE crimes he prophetically challenged the excesses of presidential power with the idea of liberty against government. The most important condition of the people's moderation in liberty was religious instruction. Corwin's *Constitution of Powers in a Secular State* (1951) opposed Supreme Court decisions against religious instruction in the public schools, arguing that the American people understand democracy as a system of ethical principles "grounded in religion." Hence, religion in effect should habituate Americans to virtue; virtue should guide the use of liberty.

Corwin's preeminence arose in part from his emphasis on fundamentals, restoration of natural law, explanations of doctrine, grasp of the perennial themes of American politics and history, and understanding of the enduring principles that prop the Constitution. In teaching future scholars, Corwin had, according to Alpheus T. Mason, the gift "of reaching within each person, of discovering something firm and worthwhile, of encouraging him to stand on it." As Corwin himself put it, "a noble emulation is the true source of excellence."

RICHARD LOSS

Bibliography

LOSS, RICHARD 1977 Edward S. Corwin: The Constitution of the Dominant Presidency. *Presidential Studies Quarterly* 7:53–65.
———, ed. 1981 *Corwin on the Constitution*, Volume I, *The Foundations of American Constitutional and Political Thought, the Powers of Congress, and the President's Power of Removal.* Ithaca, N.Y.: Cornell University Press.
STEVENS, RICHARD G. 1980 The Constitution and What It Meant to Corwin. *Political Science Reviewer* 10:1–53.

CORWIN AMENDMENT
(1861)

On 2 March 1861, in a futile attempt to prevent the secession of the slaveholding states, Congress proposed, and sent to the states for ratification, a constitutional amendment designed to protect SLAVERY in the states where it existed. The amendment, written by Representative Thomas Corwin of Ohio, would have prohibited any future constitutional amendment authorizing Congress to abolish or interfere with the "domestic institutions" of any state. Although the amendment went on specifically to include the institution of "persons held to service or labor," it is not clear what other domestic institutions, if any, might have been protected.

The Corwin Amendment was proposed after President-elect ABRAHAM LINCOLN rejected the CRITTENDEN compromise proposals, which would have permitted slavery in some federal territories. Its intended effect was that, although slavery would survive in the existing slave states, there would never be any new slave states admitted to the union, and slaveholders

would be an ever diminishing minority. In any case, the Corwin Amendment was largely a symbolic gesture of conciliation, as six southern states had already seceded by the time it was proposed. The legislatures of only two states (Ohio and Maryland) voted to ratify the Corwin Amendment.

DENNIS J. MAHONEY

Bibliography

HYMAN, HAROLD M. 1967 The Narrow Escape from the Compromise of 1860: Secession and the Constitution. Pages 149–166 in Harold M. Hyman and Leonard W. Levy, eds., *Freedom and Reform.* New York: Harper & Row.

COUNSEL, RIGHT TO BE REPRESENTED BY

See: Right to Counsel

COUNSELMAN v. HITCHCOCK
142 U.S. 547 (1892)

The first Supreme Court decision on immunity statutes, *Counselman* remained the leading case until it was distinguished away in KASTIGAR V. UNITED STATES (1972). Appellant refused to testify before a federal GRAND JURY on the ground that he might incriminate himself, though he had been granted USE IMMUNITY under an 1887 act of Congress guaranteeing that his evidence would not be used against him criminally, except in a prosecution for perjury. *Counselman* thus raised the question whether a grant of use immunity could supplant the Fifth Amendment right of a person not to be a witness against himself in a criminal case. The government contended that an investigation before a grand jury was not a criminal case, which could arise only after an INDICTMENT should be returned, but that in any instance, Counselman had received immunity in return for his testimony.

Justice SAMUEL BLATCHFORD for a unanimous Court declared that it is "impossible" that the clause of the Fifth Amendment could mean only what it says, for it is not limited to situations in which one is compelled to be a witness against himself in a "criminal case." The object of the clause is to insure that no person should be compelled as a witness "in any investigation" to testify to anything that might tend to show he had committed a crime. "The privilege is limited to criminal matters, but it is as broad as the mischief against which it seeks to guard," and therefore it applied to grand jury proceedings that might result in a prosecution. Clearly, said Blatchford, a statute cannot abridge a constitutional privilege nor replace one, "unless it is so broad as to have the same extent in scope and effect." The statute did not even do what it purported to do; it did not bar use of the compelled testimony, for its fruits could be used against the witness by searching out any leads, originating with his testimony, to other evidence that could convict him. No statute leaving the witness subject to prosecution after answering incriminating questions can have the effect of supplanting the constitutional provision. The 1887 act of Congress was unconstitutional because it was not a "full substitute" for that provision.

Thus the Court introduced the extraordinary doctrine that a statute could be a substitute for a provision of the Constitution, after having said that a statute could not "replace" such a provision. But the statute, to be constitutional, must serve "co-extensively" with the right it replaces. The Court laid down the standard for TRANSACTIONAL IMMUNITY: to be valid the statute "must afford absolute immunity against future prosecution for the offense to which the question relates."

LEONARD W. LEVY

(SEE ALSO: *Right Against Self-Incrimination*).

COURT MARTIAL

See: Military Justice and the Constitution

COURT OF CLAIMS

See: Claims Court of the United States

COURT OF CUSTOMS AND PATENT APPEALS

The Court of Customs Appeals was established by Congress in 1909 to hear appeals from the Board of General Appraisers, a body that itself heard appeals from decisions by customs collectors. (In 1926 the Board became the United States Customs Court, and in 1980 that court was converted into the United States COURT OF INTERNATIONAL TRADE.) In 1929 Congress renamed the court and expanded its jurisdiction. The new Court of Customs and Patent Appeals (CCPA) heard, in addition, appeals from the Patent Office in both patent and trademark cases.

In 1958 Congress declared the CCPA to be a CONSTITUTIONAL COURT, created under Article III. In *Glidden Co. v. Zdanok* (1962) the Supreme Court held, 5–2, that the CCPA was, indeed, an Article III court, despite its statutory authorization to do some nonjudicial business. There was no opinion of the Court, and the theories supporting the decision were in conflict. Justice JOHN MARSHALL HARLAN, for three Justices, concluded that the CCPA had been an Article III court since 1930, when Congress had granted its members life tenure during good behavior. Justice TOM C. CLARK, for the other two majority Justices, said that the 1958 declaration of Congress had converted the CCPA into a constitutional court. Justice WILLIAM O. DOUGLAS, joined by Justice HUGO L. BLACK, dissented, arguing that the court remained a LEGISLATIVE COURT despite the congressional declaration. Thus, while a majority rejected each theory argued in support of the decision, the result was acceptance of the CCPA's Article III status.

In the FEDERAL COURTS IMPROVEMENT ACT (1982) Congress abolished the CCPA, transferring its JURISDICTION to a newly established UNITED STATES COURT OF APPEALS FOR THE FEDERAL CIRCUIT.

KENNETH L. KARST

COURT OF INTERNATIONAL TRADE

In 1926 Congress converted the Board of General Appraisers, which had been hearing APPEALS from decisions of customs collectors, into the United States Customs Court. In 1956, Congress declared that the court was established under Article III. Because the court's business is strictly "judicial" and its members are appointed for life during good behavior, it is probably a CONSTITUTIONAL COURT on the same reasoning that was applied to the COURT OF CUSTOMS AND PATENT APPEALS (CCPA).

In 1980 Congress changed the Customs Court's name to the United States Court of International Trade and extended its JURISDICTION to include additional noncustoms matters relating to international trade. Its decisions, formerly reviewed by the CCPA, today are reviewed by the UNITED STATES COURT OF APPEALS FOR THE FEDERAL CIRCUIT.

KENNETH L. KARST

COURT OF MILITARY APPEALS

In the Uniform Code of Military Justice, enacted in the aftermath of World War II, Congress established the Court of Military Appeals (COMA). A civilian body, whose three judges serve for fifteen-year terms, COMA reviews questions of law arising in certain serious court-martial cases. COMA, which heard its first case in 1951, has never been part of the federal judiciary. The whole military justice system, COMA included, is part of the governance of the armed forces. Since 1983, however, many of COMA's decisions have been reviewable by the Supreme Court on petition for CERTIORARI. Whether or not such a review has taken place, a person in custody as a result of a court-martial decision can apply for HABEAS CORPUS in a federal district court. (See MILITARY JUSTICE AND THE CONSTITUTION.)

Like many another judicial or military institution, COMA has sought to expand its jurisdiction. It has developed a notion of its own "inherent powers," which it has used to nudge the military justice system toward increasing resemblance to the civilian system of criminal justice, notably by tightening the requirements of procedural fairness. Although some military officers have strongly criticized COMA's "constitutionalizing" innovations, most proposals for statutory restoration of the old order have died in congressional committees.

KENNETH L. KARST

Bibliography

WILLIS JOHN T. 1972 The Constitution, the United States Court of Military Appeals and the Future. *Military Law Review* 57:27–97.
———— 1972 The United States Court of Military Appeals: Its Origin, Operation and Future. *Military Law Review* 55:39–93.

COURT REORGANIZATION

See: Judicial System

COURTS, RELATIONSHIP OF STATE AND FEDERAL

See: Judicial System

COURTS OF APPEAL

See: United States Courts of Appeal

COX v. LOUISIANA
379 U.S. 536 (1965)
379 U.S. 559 (1965)

Some black students were jailed in a courthouse for PICKETING segregated lunch counters. About 2,000 other black students marched there and, in accor-

dance with police instructions, lined a sidewalk 101 feet away. Whites gathered. Cox made a speech that elicited some grumbling from whites; the police ordered the demonstration broken up; the students were dispersed.

Justice ARTHUR GOLDBERG writing for the Supreme Court reversed Cox's BREACH OF THE PEACE conviction, finding that Cox's actions threatened no violence and that the police could have handled any threat from the whites. The Court also held the breach of peace statute unconstitutionally vague and overbroad as construed by the state supreme court to define breach as "to arouse from a state of repose . . . to disquiet."

In striking down Cox's conviction for obstruction of public passages because the statute's actual administration had vested discretion in city officials to forbid some parades and allow others, the Court emphasized that violation of nondiscriminatory traffic laws would not be protected by the FIRST AMENDMENT. The court reversed Cox's conviction for picketing near a courthouse because the police, by directing the demonstrators to a particular sidewalk, had led them to believe that it was not near the courthouse within the terms of the statute so that a subsequent conviction created a "sort of entrapment," in violation of DUE PROCESS. Nevertheless, in dictum it invoked the old doctrine that picketing was subject to reasonable regulation as "speech plus" and supported the authority of a state legislature to forbid picketing near a courthouse because of its danger to the administration of justice.

Although *Cox* is often cited as a case establishing the concept of a PUBLIC FORUM, the Court went out of its way to say "We have no occasion . . . to consider the constitutionality of the . . . non-discriminatory application of a statute forbidding all access to streets and other public facilities for parades and meetings."

MARTIN SHAPIRO

COX v. NEW HAMPSHIRE
312 U.S. 569 (1941)

In this seminal decision, Chief Justice CHARLES EVANS HUGHES, writing for a unanimous Supreme Court, synthesized a series of cases involving speeches, parades, and meetings in parks and on streets. He held that there was a "right of assembly . . . and . . . discussion of public questions immemorially associated with resort to public places," but that such a right was limited by the authority of local government to make reasonable regulations governing "the time, place and manner" of such speech, if the regulations did not involve "unfair discrimination" among speakers. The Court upheld a state law requiring parade licenses issued by local governments on the grounds that, as construed by the state supreme court, it authorized only such reasonable and nondiscriminatory regulations. *Cox* is one of the building blocks in the creation of the doctrine of the PUBLIC FORUM.

This case took on renewed importance in the context of the CIVIL RIGHTS demonstrations of the 1960s. The crucial problem under the *Cox* test is often whether a law purporting to be a neutral regulation of traffic and noise control is actually a façade behind which local authorities seek to deny a public forum to speakers whose speech they dislike.

MARTIN SHAPIRO

COX BROADCASTING CORP. v. COHN
420 U.S. 469 (1975)

In *Cox Broadcasting Corp. v. Cohn* the Supreme Court held that broadcasting the name of a rape victim, derived from public court documents open to public inspection, could not constitutionally be made the basis for civil liability. The Court left open the questions whether liability could be imposed for a similar broadcast if the name had been obtained in an improper fashion, or if the name had not been directly derived from the public record, or if the name had not appeared in a public record open to public inspection, or if the public record were inaccurate.

STEVEN SHIFFRIN

COYLE v. SMITH
221 U.S. 559 (1911)

This decision construed the guarantee of a REPUBLICAN FORM OF GOVERNMENT in a case involving a state's admission to the Union. The enabling act admitting Oklahoma specified the location of the state capital, a condition which the Oklahoma legislature soon violated. The Supreme Court struck down the limitation as outside the limits of Congress's power over admission.

DAVID GORDON

CRAIG v. BOREN
429 U.S. 190 (1976)

It is ironic that the leading modern decision setting the STANDARD OF REVIEW for claims of SEX DISCRIMINATION involved discrimination against men, concerning an interest of supreme triviality. Oklahoma allowed women to buy 3.2 percent beer upon reaching the age of eighteen; men, however, had to be twenty-one. A young male would-be buyer and a female beer seller challenged the law's validity. The young man became twenty-one before the Supreme Court's decision; his challenge was thus rejected for MOOTNESS. The Court held that the seller had STANDING to raise the young man's constitutional claims, and further held, 8–1, that the law denied EQUAL PROTECTION OF THE LAWS. Justice WILLIAM H. REHNQUIST dissented.

Speaking through Justice WILLIAM J. BRENNAN, the Court held that classifications based on gender were invalid unless they served "important governmental objectives" and were "substantially related to achievement of those objectives." This intermediate standard was a compromise between the two views of the majority in FRONTIERO V. RICHARDSON (1973) as to the level of judicial scrutiny of both legislative objectives and legislative means. Under the RATIONAL BASIS standard of review, the objective need be only legitimate, and the means (in equal protection language, the classification) only rationally related to its achievement. At the opposite end of the continuum of standards of review, STRICT SCRUTINY demands a legislative objective that is a COMPELLING STATE INTEREST, and means that are necessary to achieving that objective. The *Craig* standard appears to have been deliberately designed to fall between these two levels of judicial scrutiny of legislation.

In the years since *Craig*, the Supreme Court has often invalidated classifications based on sex but typically has not challenged the importance of legislative objectives. Instead, the Court generally holds that a sex classification is not "substantially related" to a legislative goal. In *Craig* itself, the Court admitted that traffic safety, the state's objective, was important, but said maleness was an inappropriate "proxy for drinking and driving."

Justice JOHN PAUL STEVENS, concurring, doubted the utility of multitiered levels of judicial scrutiny in equal protection cases, and commented that men, as a class, have not suffered "pervasive discrimination." The classification was objectionable, however, because it was "based on the accident of birth," and perpetuated "a stereotyped attitude" of young men and women. Because the state's traffic safety justification failed, the law was invalid.

KENNETH L. KARST

CRAIG v. MISSOURI
4 Peters 410 (1830)

Craig defined BILLS OF CREDIT, which no state may issue without violating Article I, section 10, of the Constitution. By a 4–3 vote the Supreme Court ruled that bills of credit mean any paper medium intended to circulate as money on the authority of a state, even if not designated as legal tender in payment of debts. Missouri, lacking currency, authorized state loan offices to issue loan certificates, on collateral, to private citizens, in amounts ranging from fifty cents to ten dollars; the certificates could be used for payment of taxes and official salaries. Chief Justice JOHN MARSHALL's opinion invalidating the state act, though constitutionally correct, ignored economic realities: many states desperately needed a circulating medium. Senator THOMAS H. BENTON, for Missouri, defending its certificate law before the Court, thunderingly defended state sovereignty. The disastrous consequences of *Craig* provoked denunciations of the court and yet another movement in Congress to repeal section 25 of the JUDICIARY ACT OF 1789, the grant of APPELLATE JURISDICTION under which the Court had reversed state court judgments and held state acts unconstitutional. The repeal movement failed, but a solid South ominously opposed the Court.

LEONARD W. LEVY

(SEE ALSO: *Briscoe v. Bank of Kentucky, 1837.*)

CRAMER v. UNITED STATES
325 U.S. 1 (1945)

On the night of June 12, 1942, several specially trained saboteurs were put ashore from a German submarine near Amagansett, New York, with orders to disperse throughout the United States and to sabotage the American war effort. Anthony Cramer, a naturalized American citizen of German background, befriended two of the saboteurs, met with them, and was suspected of assisting them in their mission. However, the only overt acts to which two witnesses could testify were two meetings between Cramer and one of the saboteurs, who was an old friend of Cramer's. The prosecution was unable to produce the testimony of two witnesses concerning what took place at the meetings or to establish that Cramer gave information, encouragement, shelter, or supplies to the saboteurs. Cramer was tried for and convicted of TREASON, and he appealed his conviction to the Supreme Court.

The *Cramer* case marked the first time that the Supreme Court passed on the meaning of the treason clause of Article III, section 2, of the Constitution. Justice ROBERT H. JACKSON, for a 5–4 Court, held that the overt acts testified to by two witnesses must be sufficient, in their setting, to sustain a finding that actual aid and comfort was given to an enemy of the United States. Although there was other EVIDENCE of Cramer's Nazi sympathies and of his assistance to the saboteur, the overt acts—the meetings—were not in themselves treasonable, and the conviction could not stand.

DENNIS J. MAHONEY

(SEE ALSO: *Haupt v. United States; Ex Parte Quirin.*)

Bibliography
BELKNAP, MICHAL R. 1980 The Supreme Court Goes to War: The Meaning and Implications of the Nazi Saboteur Case. *Military Law Review* 89:59–95.

CRANCH, WILLIAM
(1779–1855)

President JOHN ADAMS in March 1801 commissioned his nephew, William Cranch, assistant judge of the newly created Circuit Court for the DISTRICT OF COLUMBIA. President THOMAS JEFFERSON in 1806 surprised Cranch, a loyal Federalist, by elevating him to chief judge, a post he filled until his death, half a century later.

Cranch simultaneously undertook the unofficial position of reporter of the decisions of the Supreme Court of the United States. His nine volumes of reports, for which he derived compensation at public sale, covered the period from the August Term, 1801, to the February Term, 1815. The role of the law reporter in Cranch's time commanded professional respect and even glamour. These reports, which added luster to the judge's reputation, received favorable comment, even from Jeffersonian opponents.

Cranch's first major constitutional opinion, *United States v. Bollman et al.* (1807), stressed the independence and power of the federal judiciary, themes that pervaded his other major opinions. President Jefferson in early 1807 had sought a bench warrant for the arrest of Erik Bollman and Samuel Swartwout on charges of TREASON in the Burr Conspiracy. Cranch dissented from the decision by the court's other two judges to issue the warrant. He took exception to the English doctrine of constructive treason. He also rejected the proposition that an executive communication from the President, without either an oath or affirmation, established sufficient probability of treasonous activity.

Three decades later Cranch spoke for a unanimous court in upholding the power of the judiciary to intervene in executive affairs. *United States ex rel. Stokes v. Kendall* (1837) stemmed from an alleged debt due Stokes and others for services they claimed to have rendered to the Post Office. When Postmaster General Amos Kendall refused to pay, despite congressional direction to do so, Stokes sought a WRIT OF MANDAMUS. Although no circuit court had ever issued such a writ against the executive branch, Cranch held that his court could do so. He found that the judicial power could properly issue a writ to command performance of a purely ministerial function by the head of an executive department.

Cranch remained a thoroughgoing Federalist long after that party ceased to exist. His opinions powerfully affirmed the role of the federal judiciary. His most important legacy was the establishment of the Circuit Court and its successors in the District of Columbia as the major forums in which to adjudicate causes involving executive departments and agencies.

KERMIT L. HALL

Bibliography

CARNE, WILLIAM F. 1901 Life and Times of William Cranch, Judge of the District Circuit Court, 1801–1855. *Records of the Columbia Historical Society* 5:294–310.

CRAWFORD v. BOARD OF EDUCATION
458 U.S. 527 (1982)
WASHINGTON v. SEATTLE SCHOOL DISTRICT NO. 1
458 U.S. 457 (1982)

By statewide votes, both Washington and California sought to limit the use of SCHOOL BUSING for purposes of DESEGREGATION. A 1978 Washington INITIATIVE effectively prohibited school boards from assigning children to public schools outside their residential neighborhoods for purposes of racial integration. A 1979 amendment to the California Constitution prohibited state courts from ordering school busing unless busing would be available in a federal court as a remedy for a violation of the FOURTEENTH AMENDMENT. The Supreme Court sustained the California measure, 8–1, but held the Washington measure invalid, 5–4.

In the *Seattle* case, Justice HARRY A. BLACKMUN wrote for the majority. Following the precedent of HUNTER V. ERICKSON (1969), he concluded that the Washington law placed a special burden on racial minorities, using an issue's racial nature to define the local decision-making structure. For the dissenters, Justice LEWIS F. POWELL argued that the Washington law had not altered the political process at all, but had merely adopted a neighborhood school policy—something a local school board itself remained free to do, within the limits of the Fourteenth Amendment.

Justice Powell wrote for the Court in the *Crawford* case. The California courts had previously read the state constitution to forbid DE FACTO as well as DE JURE school SEGREGATION. There was, however, no "ratchet" principle in the Fourteenth Amendment; the state could constitutionally adopt federal EQUAL PROTECTION standards. The amendment, Powell said, was not adopted with a racially discriminatory purpose; it chiefly reflected a choice for the neighborhood school policy. Justice THURGOOD MARSHALL, dissenting, considered the two cases indistinguishable. Indeed, the opinions of Justice Powell in the two cases bear marked similarities; yet, if *Hunter* be taken as the critical precedent, the distinction is supportable. A line is none the worse for being thin.

KENNETH L. KARST

CRIMINAL CONSPIRACY

The modern crime of conspiracy punishes the act of agreement with another to do something unlawful, and the vagueness and breadth of its scope are the legacies of seventeenth-century English judges who invented its COMMON LAW progenitor. Constitutional DOCTRINE has not shaped the boundaries of this crime; it is, indeed, the other way around. Most paradoxically, the crime has served both as a tool for the suppression of FIRST AMENDMENT freedoms and as a weapon for the defense of rights to racial equality. Like all political issues, the definition of "unlawful" conspiracies fluctuates with the moral hemlines of history.

In the eighteenth century, the English crime came to encompass the agreement to do any "immoral" acts, even noncriminal ones. This became an element of American conspiracy law as well, and one of its early critics was Chief Justice LEMUEL SHAW of the Massachusetts Supreme Judicial Court. In COMMON-WEALTH V. HUNT (1842) Shaw put an end to conspiracy prosecutions of laborers who organized to seek such noncriminal goals as higher wages or a CLOSED SHOP. Criminal goals, of course, remained punishable, and trade union conspiracy prosecutions died out in the 1890s only because they were replaced by judicial resort to the labor INJUNCTION. Statutes prohibiting noncriminal conspiracies remained on the books, but their demise was hastened by state court decisions holding them void for VAGUENESS or violative of the EX POST FACTO clause.

Federal conspiracy prosecutions commenced in 1867 with the enactment of a Federal Criminal Code provision prohibiting conspiracies to defraud the United States. The rise of organized crime during Prohibition provided the impetus for the expansion of federal conspiracy offenses; the Racketeer Influenced and Corrupt Organizations Act of 1970 is an exemplar of their sweeping scope. In 1925, Judge LEARNED HAND labeled conspiracy "the darling in the prosecutor's nursery," because of the progovernment features that mark conspiracy trials. HEARSAY statements of co-conspirators are admissible in evidence, and conspiratorial membership may be inferred solely from conduct showing a desire to further the conspiracy's goals. In *Pinkerton v. United States* (1946) the Court held conspirators liable for every crime committed by co-conspirators, including those of participants whose existence was unknown but foreseeable. The DOUBLE JEOPARDY clause does not bar separate, consecutive sentences for these offenses and the conspiracy itself. VENUE will lie anywhere an act is committed in furtherance of the conspiracy, often effectively nullifying the SIXTH AMENDMENT right to be tried where a crime is committed. Conspirators may be tried en masse, and fringe participants thus become tainted with the culpability of the ringleaders.

It is small wonder that in *Krulewitch v. United States* (1949) Justice ROBERT H. JACKSON declared that the "elastic, sprawling and pervasive" nature of the crime of conspiracy poses a "serious threat to fairness" in the administration of justice. Yet while many commentators call for limitations on the crime, DUE PROCESS arguments meet with recurrent failure in the courts. This amoeboid offense remains entrenched in state and federal law and in legislative proposals for criminal code reform.

Conspiracy was a potent weapon for the prosecution of political dissidents during World War I, and these cases brought the Supreme Court to its first important encounter with the First Amendment's guarantees of FREEDOM OF SPEECH and FREEDOM OF THE PRESS. The ESPIONAGE ACT of 1917 prohibited conspiracies to obstruct the draft or cause insubordination in the armed services, and in SCHENCK V. UNITED STATES (1919) and FROHWERK V. UNITED STATES (1919) a unanimous Court affirmed the conspiracy convictions of dissidents who had circulated antidraft publications. In *Schenck*, Justice OLIVER WENDELL HOLMES declared that only a CLEAR AND PRESENT DANGER of a conspiracy's success would justify conviction, but this formula was not an important limitation in these cases, where the danger was assumed. Justices Holmes and LOUIS D. BRANDEIS later argued for greater speech protections, but their pleas went unheeded for a generation. Conspiracy convictions of eleven national Communist party leaders were affirmed in DENNIS V. UNITED STATES (1951), even though the danger posed by their conspiracy to advocate the overthrow of the government was evidenced only by the party's structure and tenets. The doctrinal thaw came in 1957, with Justice JOHN MARSHALL HARLAN's opinion in YATES V. UNITED STATES portending the formula of BRANDENBURG V. OHIO (1969). *Brandenburg* allows prosecution for speech crimes—including conspiracy to advocate—only when advocacy of imminent, illegal action is likely to incite such action.

Brandenburg's weakness as a limit on conspiracy prosecutions is that it only guarantees defendants the benefit of appellate court scrutiny of jury verdicts. It provides no more than an indirect caution for legislative reliance on conspiracy statutes or prosecutorial decisions to seek indictments. Protection of speech interests rests ultimately in the court of public opinion, and the VIETNAM WAR era dissidents found an uncertain haven there. The "Chicago Seven" protesters at the 1968 Democratic National Convention were acquitted of conspiring to travel interstate with intent to incite a riot, but they were convicted of other INCITEMENT offenses. Benjamin Spock and William Sloane Coffin were convicted of conspiring to counsel draft evasion, based on their support of a DRAFT CARD BURNING rally in Boston. After appellate court reversals in *United States v. Dellinger* (1972) and *United States v. Spock* (1969), reprosecution was halted only because the government decided to give up trying. The CHILLING EFFECT of such prosecutions is irremediable, and judicial vindication of speech rights often becomes a matter of better late than never.

The concept of conspiracy can serve CIVIL LIBERTIES as aptly as it defeats them. After the Civil War,

Congress prohibited conspiracies "to injure, oppress, threaten or intimidate" any citizen's free exercise of constitutional rights, and also provided a civil action for DAMAGES against conspirators. Narrow judicial construction of these rights defeated their enforcement in the era of UNITED STATES V. HARRIS (1883) and the CIVIL RIGHTS CASES (1883). But Justice WILLIAM O. DOUGLAS's opinion in SCREWS V. UNITED STATES (1945) revived prosecutions of state officials, while UNITED STATES V. GUEST (1966) brought similar vindication against private individuals, and GRIFFIN V. BRECKENRIDGE (1971) opened the damage remedy door. Debate continues over the scope of rights protected by these remedies. But conspiracy's contribution toward curbing civil rights violators remains as notable as its role in rounding up racketeers.

CATHERINE HANCOCK

Bibliography

FILVAROFF, DAVID B. 1972 Conspiracy and the First Amendment. *University of Pennsylvania Law Review* 121:189–253.
JOHNSON, PHILLIP E. 1973 The Unnecessary Crime of Conspiracy. *California Law Review* 61:1137–1188.

CRIMINAL JUSTICE ACT
78 Stat. 552 (1964)

By the Criminal Justice Act Congress provided that counsel must be furnished at public expense for INDIGENT defendants in federal criminal cases. The act requires each district court to formulate a plan for furnishing counsel, subject to supervision by the circuit judicial council and the Judicial Conference of the United States. The act provides that counsel shall be furnished from the defendant's first appearance before a court or magistrate through the APPEAL process, and authorizes reimbursement for such expenses as investigations and expert testimony.

DENNIS J. MAHONEY

(SEE ALSO: *Right to Counsel.*)

CRIMINAL PROCEDURE

"It was a great day for the human race," Charles E. Merriam wrote in *Systematic Politics* (1945), "when the idea dawned that every man is a human being, an end in himself, with a claim for the development of his own personality, and that human beings had a dignity and a worth, respect for which is the firm basis of human association." This idea is the predicate for that branch of American constitutional law which is concerned with criminal procedure, for this body of law is deliberately weighted in favor of persons accused of crime. This pronounced tilt of the law is based on the assumption that it is vitally necessary to protect the dignity inherent in all human beings, regardless of their station in society.

The commitment of the Constitution to protect in some emphatic way the rights of criminal defendants is reflected in the fact that such protection is a principal theme of the federal BILL OF RIGHTS. Similar protections appear in the bills of rights that form parts of all state CONSTITUTIONS. Even before the ratification of the Bill of Rights in 1791, however, the Constitution in its original form did not ignore the subject altogether. Thus, the privilege of the writ of HABEAS CORPUS was guaranteed, and both BILLS OF ATTAINDER (legislative convictions for crime) and EX POST FACTO laws (laws making criminal acts that were innocent when done) were forbidden (Article I, sections 9 and 10). TRIAL BY JURY "for all crimes" was also guaranteed (Article III, section 2), and the offense of TREASON was defined with meticulous care to prevent abuse of a charge often made on flimsy grounds in moments of great political excitement (Article III, section 3).

The Bill of Rights filled in many more details by spelling out a long list of guarantees designed to protect criminal defendants: freedom from "unreasonable SEARCHES AND SEIZURES" (FOURTH AMENDMENT), INDICTMENT by GRAND JURY, freedom from DOUBLE JEOPARDY, the RIGHT AGAINST SELF-INCRIMINATION, the right to DUE PROCESS OF LAW (Fifth Amendment), the right to a speedy and PUBLIC TRIAL by an impartial local jury, the right to notice of charges, the right to confront adverse witnesses (*i.e.*, cross-examination), the right to have the assistance of counsel (SIXTH AMENDMENT), and freedom from excessive BAIL and from the infliction of CRUEL AND UNUSUAL PUNISHMENT (Eighth Amendment). In addition, section 1 of the FOURTEENTH AMENDMENT, with its provision that no state shall "deprive any person of life, liberty, or property, without due process of law," eventually opened the door to considerable supervision of criminal justice in the states by the federal courts.

This commitment to the safeguarding of the rights of defendants in criminal cases was deeply rooted in the COMMON LAW system which the earliest settlers brought with them from England. In ancient Anglo-Saxon and Norman times, questions of guilt or innocence were determined by such ritualistic devices as trial by battle or ordeal, or by compurgation (oath-taking), which were largely appeals to God to work a miracle establishing the defendant's innocence. Actually, private vengeance, taking the form of private war or blood feuds, was the principal check on criminal conduct. But by the time the first colonies were established in America, the basic procedures characteristic of modern jurisprudence had taken form. The essence of modern adjudication is the discovery of innocence or guilt through the presentation of proofs and reasoned argument.

Furthermore, it is important that under common law a person accused of crime carries with him the presumption of innocence, which means that the defendant is not obliged to prove his innocence, but rather that the BURDEN OF PROOF is on the prosecution to prove guilt. In addition, jurors must be instructed by the presiding judge that they may convict only if they find that guilt has been established "beyond a REASONABLE DOUBT," which is the greatest quantum of proof known to the law. In most civil litigation a preponderance of evidence suffices to support a verdict. Thus, in a landmark English case, *Woolmington v. D.P.P.* (1935), the House of Lords ruled clearly wrong an instruction of the trial judge to the effect that since the accused had shot his wife, the law presumed him to be guilty of murder unless he could satisfy the jury that death was due to an accident. "No matter what the charge or where the trial," Lord Sankey declared, "the principle that the prosecution must prove the guilt of the prisoner is part of the common law of England and no attempt to whittle it down can be entertained."

The common law rules relating to the presumption of innocence and the burden of proof are part of the law prevailing in every American state. For example, following the completion of a modern, revised criminal code in Wisconsin, the legislature adopted a statute that declared: "No provision of the criminal code shall be construed as changing the existing law with respect to presumption of innocence or burden of proof." These principles are also firmly rooted in federal jurisprudence. As Justice FELIX FRANKFURTER, dissenting in *Leland v. Oregon* (1952), wrote, "From the time that the law which we have inherited has emerged from dark and barbaric times, the conception of justice which has dominated our criminal law has refused to put an accused at the hazard of punishment if he fails to remove every reasonable doubt of his innocence in the minds of jurors. It is the duty of the Government to establish his guilt beyond a reasonable doubt." Similarly, the Supreme Court has ruled that the standard of proof beyond a reasonable

doubt in criminal cases is a due process requirement binding upon the state courts. It is, Justice WILLIAM J. BRENNAN asserted in IN RE WINSHIP (1970), "a prime instrument for reducing the risk of convictions resting on factual error. The standard provides concrete substance for the presumption of innocence. . . ." According to the Supreme Court, the states are required to prove beyond a reasonable doubt all elements of the crime with which the defendant was charged, and the jury must be so instructed. An instruction is improper if it has the effect of reducing substantially the prosecution's burden of proof or of requiring the defendant to establish his innocence beyond a reasonable doubt.

The solicitude of American constitutional law for the rights of the accused is so great that the American system has been described as a defendant's law, in contrast with inquisitorial systems of other countries which give the prosecution many advantages not available in the United States. American public law on this important subject rests upon the recognition of several important considerations that are not the product of abstract theorizing or mere sentimentalism but rather the result of historical experience over centuries of time. For one thing, it is an unquestionably legitimate, indeed essential, function of government to apprehend, try, and punish convicted criminals. But it is also the duty of those public officials who operate the criminal justice system to avoid violating the law themselves in their zeal to combat crime. Of course, our society has a serious crime problem which government cannot and should not ignore, but it has long been recognized that at some point the price of law enforcement may be exorbitant. As Justice Frankfurter observed in *Feldman v. United States Oil Refining Co.* (1944), "The effective enforcement of a well designed penal code is of course indispensable for social security," but he went on to say: "The Bill of Rights was added to the original constitution in the conviction that too high a price may be paid even for the unhampered enforcement of the criminal law and that, in its attainment, other social objects of a free society should not be sacrificed."

Surely, one of the indispensable objectives of a free society is to avoid the disorganizing consequences of lawlessness by public officials. Thus Justice OLIVER WENDELL HOLMES observed in his celebrated dissenting opinion in the Supreme Court's first WIRETAPPING case, OLMSTEAD V. UNITED STATES (1928), that "we must consider two objects of desire, both of which we cannot have, and make up our minds which to choose. It is desirable that criminals should be detected and to that end that all available evidence should be used. It is also desirable that the government should not itself foster and pay for other crimes, when they are the means by which the evidence is to be obtained. . . . We have to choose, and for my part I think is a less evil that some criminals should escape than that the Government should play an ignoble part." In a separate dissenting opinion in the same case, Justice LOUIS D. BRANDEIS warned that government forcefully teaches by example, that crime is contagious, and that "if the Government becomes a lawbreaker, it breeds contempt for law; it invites every man to become a law unto himself; it invites anarchy." To permit the government to commit crimes, he asserted, in order to convict criminals, "would bring terrible retribution."

Without question, if unrestrained by law, the police could apprehend and prosecutors could secure the conviction of far more lawbreakers than they now manage to catch and convict. For example, if the police had a free hand to break into any dwelling or other building and to rummage around as they please, looking for stolen goods or other contraband, such as controlled substances, unquestionably they would solve more crimes and put more thieves, burglars, drug peddlers, and other criminal characters in jail. But the price would be prohibitively high, since it would entail the destruction of a cherished aspect of privacy. Similarly, if the police were completely free to torture suspects, more confessions would be secured, and the conviction rate would rise significantly, but again, other values must be weighed in the balance. These values include avoiding the risk of convicting innocent people who cannot endure the pain and avoiding the danger of encouraging unprofessional, brutal police conduct which employs uncivilized methods shocking to the conscience. Obviously, choices must be made between the desire to catch and punish lawbreakers and our concern for maintaining the legal amenities of a civilized society. The search for a tolerable balance between these competing objectives is what much of our constitutional law is all about. As Justice WILLIAM O. DOUGLAS remarked, in *An Almanac of Liberty* (1954), "a degree of inefficiency is a price we necessarily pay for a civilized, decent society. The free state offers what a police state denies—the privacy of the home, the dignity and peace of mind of the individual." Aside from the fact that one hundred percent law enforcement would make the building of additional jails the highest priority of the country, it simply cannot be achieved without devoting resources far beyond what we can afford, considering all the other important functions for which government is responsible, and without resorting to methods that are almost universally deplored in civilized countries.

The various rights secured for the accused by our constitutional law are not technicalities; due process of law is at the center of our concept of justice. The overall purpose of our legal system is not so much to secure convictions as to render justice. Our rules of constitutional law are not only designed to protect people who are in trouble with the law but also to assure us that those who are engaged in the often exciting business of law enforcement will observe those time-tested rules which in large measure constitute the essence of fair procedure. "Let it not be overlooked," Justice ROBERT H. JACKSON, dissenting in SHAUGHNESSY V. UNITED STATES (1953), wrote, "that due process of law is not for the sole benefit of the accused. It is the best insurance for the Government itself against those blunders which leave lasting stains on a system of justice. . . ."

There are additional compelling reasons that explain and support our legal system's concern for protecting the rights of persons accused of crime. For one thing, a criminal case is essentially a contest between an individual and a government, that is to say, between parties of vastly unequal strength. This disparity in the strength of the parties is especially visible in the modern age of powerful governments. The teaching of experience the world over is that inequality tends to beget injustice, and where the parties are so unequal, a determined effort must be made to redress the imbalance of power. Thus, the accused is entitled to seek a reversal of a conviction in an appellate court, but the prosecution may not get an acquittal reversed, for the double jeopardy principle forbids it. In this respect, the scales of justice are tipped in favor of the weaker party.

In addition, our concern for the defendant's rights rests upon an understanding that for most people it is a very serious matter indeed to be accused by the government of having committed a crime. The possible consequences range from loss of employment to disruption of family life, injury to reputation, and, ultimately, loss of personal liberty. It follows that one accused of crime is likely to be in such deep trouble that he or she must have every opportunity to combat the charges, as fully, as quickly, and as decisively, as possible. Many rights—bail, a public and SPEEDY TRIAL, CONFRONTATION of accusers, and assistance of counsel—facilitate an early and effective defense, or at the very least, make one possible.

Furthermore, one of the major purposes of assuring a full measure of due process of law is to promote the sense of community by giving all of us the feeling that even guilty persons have been treated fairly. As Justice Douglas observed in BRADY V. MARYLAND (1963), "Society wins not only when the guilty are convicted but when criminal trials are fair; our system of the administration of criminal justice suffers when any accused is treated unfairly." As Justice Brennan said in FURMAN V. GEORGIA (1972), "Even the vilest criminal remains a human being possessed of common human dignity."

In a larger sense, our body of procedural law in the criminal field seeks to combat abuse of the POLICE POWER of the state. Police brutality is the hallmark of totalitarian and dictatorial systems of government. The twentieth century has been well schooled in the fearful menace of the midnight knock on the door, the ransacking of private dwellings by the police without legal warrant, the use of torture to break the will, and the ultimate indignity of incarceration in brutal concentration camps. For these compelling reasons our constitutional law was deliberately formulated to prevent the unrestrained exercise of police power.

Indeed, if one looks closely at the elements of the constitutional right to a FAIR TRIAL it becomes clear that for every rule there is a persuasive reason. The basic rights of the accused are responses to our concrete historical experience. Why, for example, does American constitutional law assure defendants representation by counsel? The answer was explained with convincing clarity by Justice GEORGE SUTHERLAND in POWELL V. ALABAMA (1932):

The right to be heard would be, in many cases, of little avail if it did not comprehend the right to be heard by counsel. Even the intelligent and educated layman has small and sometimes no skill in the science of law. If charged with crime, he is incapable, generally, of determining for himself whether the indictment is good or bad. He is unfamiliar with the rules of evidence. Left without the aid of counsel he may be put on trial without a proper charge, and convicted upon incompetent evidence, or evidence irrelevant to the issue or otherwise inadmissible. He lacks both the skill and knowledge adequately to prepare his defense, even though he has a perfect one. He requires the guiding hand of counsel at every step in the proceedings against him.

In GIDEON V. WAINWRIGHT (1963), the case that extended the RIGHT TO COUNSEL in state courts to all persons charged with felonies, Justice HUGO L. BLACK argued that it was an obvious truth that a person too poor to hire a lawyer cannot be assured a fair trial. He pointed out that government spends vast sums of money to engage the services of lawyers to prosecute, and that few defendants who can afford them fail to hire the best lawyers they can find to present their defenses, from which it follows that "lawyers in criminal courts are necessities, not luxuries."

To cite another example, in all American jurisdictions, state and federal, double jeopardy—which means essentially putting a person on trial twice for the same offense—is forbidden. Once a defendant has been tried and acquitted, he may not be put on trial a second time, even though the prosecution has found fresh relevant evidence not previously available to it or has discovered that serious legal errors were made at the trial. As explained by Justice Black in GREEN V. UNITED STATES (1957): "The underlying idea, one that is deeply ingrained in at least the Anglo-American system of jurisprudence, is that the State with all its resources and power should not be allowed to make repeated attempts to convict an individual for an alleged offense, thereby subjecting him to embarrassment, expense, and ordeal and compelling him to live in a continuing state of anxiety and insecurity, as well as enhancing the possibility that even though innocent he may be found guilty."

There are equally persuasive reasons for the guarantee of trial by jury. Justice BYRON R. WHITE noted, in the landmark case of DUNCAN V. LOUISIANA (1968), that the right of trial by jury is "an inestimable safeguard against the corrupt or overzealous prosecutor and against the compliant, biased, or eccentric judge." The jury, one of the distinctive features of Anglo-American jurisprudence, is the result of several centuries of concrete experience; it has changed in the past, in many different ways, and it is still a dynamic institution. The authors of the Constitution were thoroughly familiar with the jury system and made careful provision for it in the original document, before the Bill of Rights filled in additional details. Thus, our criminal law procedure has always reflected a reluctance to entrust prosecutors and judges with unchecked powers over life and liberty.

Similarly, there are compelling reasons why American constitutional law protects the individual against UNREASONABLE SEARCHES AND SEIZURES, the main reason being the desire to protect the RIGHT OF PRIVACY. This "right to be left alone," as Justice Brandeis asserted in his notable dissenting opinion in *Olmstead*, is "the most comprehensive of rights and the right most valued by civilized man." Fresh from his Nuremberg experience, Justice Robert Jackson wrote, in a spirited dissent in BRINEGAR V. UNITED STATES (1949), that the Fourth Amendment rights "are not mere second-class rights but belong in the catalog of indispensable freedoms. Among deprivation of rights, none is so effective in cowing a population, crushing the spirit of the individual and putting terror in every heart. Uncontrolled search and seizure is one of the first and most effective weapons in the arsenal of every arbitrary government." Justice Jackson also pointed out that because police officers are themselves the chief invaders of this right, the responsibility for protection against unreasonable searches and seizures has fallen on the courts.

An ancient teaching of English and American law is that to compel a person to convict himself or herself of a crime by being coerced into giving unwilling testimony is inadmissible. Our criminal jurisprudence makes the assumption that everyone is innocent until proved guilty beyond a reasonable doubt on the basis of competent evidence; the prosecution has the duty to prove guilt. Because the accused is not required to establish his innocence, it follows that he cannot be required to supply testimony that would lead to a conviction. The Fifth Amendment's guarantee against compulsory self-incrimination is thus neither an alien nor a novel doctrine but rather, as Justice Douglas wrote in *An Almanac of Liberty*, "one of the great landmarks in man's struggle to be free of tyranny, to be decent and civilized. It is our way of escape from the use of torture. It is part of our respect for the dignity of man."

The rights of the accused in American criminal procedure are not static but respond to changing social values and moral concepts. This dynamism is reflected in the judicial interpretation of the Eighth Amendment's prohibition of cruel and unusual punishment. Thus Chief Justice EARL WARREN wrote in TROP V. DULLES (1958): "The Amendment must draw its meaning from the evolving standards of decency that mark the progress of a maturing society." Similarly, in FURMAN V. GEORGIA, the Supreme Court for the first time held that the death penalty is unconstitutional under certain circumstances, Justice THURGOOD MARSHALL observing that "a penalty that was permissible at one time in our Nation's history is not necessarily permissible today." The court similarly made new law when it ruled in ESTELLE V. GAMBLE (1976) that deliberate indifference of a jailer to the medical needs of prisoners constituted an "unnecessary and wanton infliction of pain" proscribed by the Eighth Amendment. Similarly, the right to be free from unreasonable searches or seizures had to be given a progressively broadened scope as we moved into the age of electronic gadgetry. Given the dynamic character of American life, flexibility of interpretation was inevitable if a living Constitution was to retain its vitality, and the broad and generous character of constitutional language contributed to that flexibility.

Many policy questions relating to criminal procedure must be understood in the context of the federal character of the American system of government. Certain important powers are delegated by the Constitution to the national government, and except as the states are limited by that Constitution—which is the supreme law of the land—the TENTH AMENDMENT confirms that the states retain power over all other matters. One of the most important residual powers of the states is the power to define and punish crimes. Although Congress was not expressly empowered to enact a general code of criminal statutes, it was assumed from the beginning that the national government could enforce its laws by imposing criminal sanctions. The doctrine of IMPLIED POWERS provided the necessary doctrinal underpinning. For example, the delegated power to tax includes by implication the power to punish persons who commit tax frauds. The federal criminal code has expanded steadily since 1789 and is today a lengthy document. Even so, most criminal laws are state laws, and a very large majority of persons in jail are incarcerated in state institutions. That the criminal law in all its facets is mainly state law is a well-understood fact of American life. In a special message to Congress in 1968, President LYNDON B. JOHNSON pointed out that crime "is essentially a local matter. Police operations—if they are to be effective and responsible—must likewise remain basically local. This is the fundamental premise of our constitutional structure and of our heritage of liberty." It follows, said the President, that "the Federal Government must never assume the role of the Nation's policeman."

Decisions of state courts are not reviewable by the Supreme Court if they involve only issues of state law, as to which the highest state court speaks the last word. For example, a 1967 case involved an appeal from the Texas courts regarding the state's habitual-criminal statute. Under this statute, the trial jury is fully informed of previous criminal convictions and the state is not obliged to have a two-stage trial, one devoted to the pending charge and a second to a consideration of the previous convictions. On appeal, the Supreme Court ruled in SPENCER V. TEXAS that as a matter of national constitutional law the state is not required to provide a two-stage trial. Declining to interfere, the Court held that this matter is controlled by state procedural law; the Court is not "a rule-making organ for the promulgation of state rules of procedure."

There are, in fact, two avenues available to seek federal judicial review of the decisions of state courts in criminal cases. First of all, if a convicted defendant has taken whatever appeals are available to him under state law in the state courts and if he has sought review of a substantial federal (as distinguished from state law) question, then the Supreme Court has JURISDICTION to review the judgment on direct review if it chooses to do so. Second, one who is in custody following conviction in a state court and has exhausted his available postconviction state remedies may, in a proper case, assert his federal legal claim by applying to a federal district court for a writ of habeas corpus. Accordingly, whether through direct review by the Supreme Court or through habeas corpus proceedings, federal courts often correct state courts where federal rights have been denied. But federal courts do not sit merely to correct errors alleged to have occurred in state courts. As the Supreme Court said in *Herb v. Pitcairn* (1945), "Our only power over state judgments is to correct them to the extent that they incorrectly adjudge federal rights."

The key question, then, is: what is a federal right? A short answer is: any right arising under the Constitution of the United States, statutes of Congress, or treaties. But the provisions of the Constitution relating to basic rights are stated in vague and general language that does not in terms apply to the states. Indeed the Court held in a landmark case, BARRON V. BALTIMORE (1833), that the Bill of Rights did not apply to the states. This holding was based on the proposition that the Bill of Rights was intended only to supply additional protection from violations by the new, untested national government, and that wherever the states were limited by the constitution, the language to this effect was always explicit. Prior to the Civil War, federal court review of state criminal convictions under the Bill of Rights was not possible.

A major change in our whole system of government began in 1868 with the adoption of the Fourteenth Amendment, which provides that no state shall "deprive any person of life, liberty, or property, without due process of law." Not until 1923, however, did the Supreme Court undertake to employ this clause as a limit on state criminal procedure. In the leading case of MOORE V. DEMPSEY, the Court held that a conviction in a trial dominated by a mob was a violation of due process and could be remedied by a federal court through issuance of a writ of habeas corpus. In such a proceeding the federal court must make an independent evaluation of the facts, even though the state's highest appellate court has upheld the correctness of the conviction. The Supreme Court, too, on direct review, began to reverse state convictions as violations of due process. In 1932 the Court ruled that the Sixth Amendment right to representation by counsel, at least in capital cases, is an indispensable element of a fair trial which is guaranteed by the Fourteenth Amendment's due process clause. Later decisions extended the constitutional right to counsel in state courts to include any offense punishable by imprisonment for any period of time. Other decisions, most of which were made after World War II by the WARREN COURT, applied to the states, as due process requirements, most of the other provisions of the Bill of Rights which are designed to protect persons accused of crime. For example, in MAPP V. OHIO (1961) the Court extended to the states the EXCLUSIONARY RULE, long applicable in federal prosecutions by reason of the Fourth Amendment. Henceforth state courts, too, would be required to exclude from criminal trials all evidence secured as a result of unreasonable searches and seizures. Similarly, a state violates due process if it subjects a person to compulsory self-incrimination (MALLOY V. HOGAN, 1964), if it denies trial by jury at least where nonpetty offenses are involved (DUNCAN V. LOUISIANA, 1968), or if it subjects a defendant to the hazards of double jeopardy (BENTON V. MARYLAND, 1969). In fact, by 1970 all of the criminal procedure provisions of the Bill of Rights were made applicable to the states by way of Fourteenth Amendment due process, except the Fifth Amendment guarantee of indictment by grand jury and the Eighth Amendment prohibition of excessive bail. The bail guarantee very likely will be incorporated into the Fourteenth Amendment when the issue comes to the Supreme Court in the proper form. All the other rights of the accused guaranteed by the Bill of Rights are now regarded as elements of Fourteenth Amendment due process, enforceable against the states through federal judicial process. In the words of the Court, they are "fundamental principles of liberty and justice," or are "basic in our system of jurisprudence," or are "FUNDAMENTAL RIGHTS essential to a fair trial," or are "the very essence of a scheme of ordered liberty." (See INCORPORATION DOCTRINE.)

Not only does Fourteenth Amendment due process now incorporate most of the Bill of Rights, it also has an independent force wholly outside of the Bill of Rights. For example, in the famous case of *Mooney v. Holohan* (1935), the Court ruled that a state has denied the accused due process of law if the prosecution has deceived the court and jury by presenting testimony known to be perjured. Similarly, in *Jackson v. Virginia* (1979), the Court ruled that a state court conviction can pass the test of Fourteenth Amendment due process only if a rational trier of fact could find that each essential element of the crime had been established "beyond a reasonable doubt."

The expansion of the list of federally enforceable constitutional rights available to defendants in state courts has come a long way in enlarging both the review powers of the Supreme Court and the habeas corpus jurisdiction of the federal district courts. The federal courts are establishing more and more standards in the area of criminal justice which the states are obliged to observe.

In operating the criminal justice system, government must make some hard choices, since basic objectives undergirding that system often conflict. On the one hand, there is the due process model, preferred by the courts, which stresses our concern for maintaining the legal amenities of a civilized community. This process, adversarial and judicial in character, seeks to protect the dignity and autonomy of the individual. On the other hand, there is the crime control model, preferred by most law enforcement officials, which emphasizes the need to apprehend, try, and punish lawbreakers. The principal procedural objective is the quick, efficient, and reliable handling of persons accused of crime. The method is essentially administrative and managerial in character, operating, especially in respect to MISDEMEANORS, on assembly-line principles. Accordingly, many law enforcement officials are critical of what they see as the Supreme Court's tenderness on the subject of defendants' rights, arguing that change has been too rapid and too far-reaching. Impatience has even been expressed by a few Justices of the Court itself. An experienced California trial judge, Macklin Fleming, has gone so far as to accuse the Court of pursuing the unattainable objective of "perfect justice." It is difficult, perhaps impossible, to locate the exactly right balance between the due process model and the crime control model. But in seeking to achieve a tolerable balance the Supreme Court has moved with considerable caution, deciding one case at a time, and always within the mainstream of American culture and its dominant legal traditions.

DAVID FELLMAN

Bibliography

CASPER, JONATHAN D. 1972 *American Criminal Justice: The Defendant's Perspective.* Englewood Cliffs, N.J.: Prentice-Hall.

CORTNER, RICHARD C. 1980 *The Supreme Court and the Second Bill of Rights.* Madison: University of Wisconsin Press.

FELLMAN, DAVID 1976 *The Defendant's Rights Today.* Madison: University of Wisconsin Press.

FLEMING, MACKLIN 1974 *The Price of Perfect Justice.* New York: Basic Books.

FRIENDLY, HENRY J. 1967 The Bill of Rights as a Code of Criminal Procedure, in *Benchmarks.* Chicago: University of Chicago Press.

GOLDSTEIN, ABRAHAM S. 1960 The State and the Accused: Balance of Advantage in Criminal Procedure. *Yale Law Journal* 69:1149–1199.

PACKER, HERBERT L. 1964 Two Models of the Criminal Process. *University of Pennsylvania Law Review* 113:1–68.

CRIMINAL SYNDICALISM LAWS

Criminal syndicalism statutes were but one of several kinds of statutes punishing manifestations of unpopular thought and expression for their probable bad tendency enacted during and just after World War I by many midwestern and western states. The laws were a response to the economic unrest of the postwar period, specifically to the doctrines and activities of the Industrial Workers of the World (IWW), and to the antiradical hysteria prompted by the Russian Revolution of 1917. Twenty-two states and territories enacted—and eight other states considered but rejected—criminal syndicalism statutes between 1917 and 1920. Attempts to enact a federal criminal syndicalism law in 1919 and 1920 came to nothing, but the Smith Act of 1940 was patterned after the earlier model.

The Idaho statute, the first of its kind and a model for those adopted by other states, defined criminal syndicalism as "the doctrine which advocates crime, sabotage, violence or other unlawful methods of terrorism as a means of accomplishing industrial or political reform." Offenses punished as FELONIES under such statutes included oral or written advocacy of criminal syndicalism; justifying commission of or attempts to commit criminal syndicalism; printing or displaying written or printed matter advocating or advising criminal syndicalism; organizing or being or becoming a member of any organization organized or assembled to teach or advocate criminal syndicalism, or even presence at such an assembly. Though most citizens and state legislators believed that these statutes were directed solely against the use or advocacy of force and violence, in practice they jeopardized FREEDOM OF SPEECH, because they were used to punish those who expressed or even held opinions offensive to the majority of the community.

Criminal syndicalism statutes almost uniformly survived constitutional challenges in the state courts. In WHITNEY V. CALIFORNIA (1927) the United States Supreme Court upheld the California Criminal Syndicalism Act; Justice LOUIS D. BRANDEIS's eloquent opinion, concurring only in the result, set forth the most sophisticated formulation of the theoretical foundations and practical applications of the CLEAR AND PRESENT DANGER test previously formulated in other FIRST AMENDMENT cases. In *Fiske v. Kansas* (1927), the first decision overturning a conviction under a criminal syndicalism statute, the Supreme Court merely invalidated the statute's application, holding that the state had not shown that the defendant had advocated any but lawful methods to achieve the goals of the IWW. In DE JONGE V. OREGON (1937) a unanimous Court struck down the application of the Oregon Criminal Syndicalism Act to defendants who had merely attended a peaceful meeting of the Communist party; the Oregon legislature later repealed the statute. The labor troubles of the 1930s prompted efforts to strengthen existing criminal syndicalism laws, but these came to nothing, and several states followed Oregon's example in repealing their criminal syndicalism statutes. State criminal syndicalism statutes fell into disuse after the 1930s; in BRANDENBERG V. OHIO (1969) the Supreme Court declared the Ohio Criminal Syndicalism Act unconstitutional on its face, overruling *Whitney*, adopting the principles of Justice Brandeis's concurring opinion, and making successful prosecutions under criminal syndicalism statutes virtually impossible.

RICHARD B. BERNSTEIN

Bibliography

CHAFEE, ZECHARIAH, JR. 1941 *Free Speech in the United States.* Cambridge, Mass.: Harvard University Press.

DOWELL, ELDRIDGE FOSTER 1939 *A History of Criminal Syndicalism Legislation in the United States.* Baltimore: Johns Hopkins University Studies in Historical and Political Science, Series 57, No. 1.

CRITTENDEN, JOHN J.
(1787–1863)

A Kentucky lawyer, John Jordan Crittenden was a United States attorney general (1841, 1850–1853) and senator (1817–1819, 1835–1841, 1842–1848, 1855–1861). In late 1828 President JOHN QUINCY ADAMS nominated him to the Supreme Court, but the Senate's Democratic majority killed the appointment. A border state Whig, Crittenden always supported compromise on slavery. Thus, as President Millard Fill-

more's attorney general, Crittenden vigorously enforced the 1850 fugitive slave law. But he also opposed ANNEXATION OF TEXAS, the Mexican War, the KANSAS-NEBRASKA ACT, and Kansas statehood, because these issues raised the politically disruptive question of SLAVERY IN THE TERRITORIES. In December 1860 Crittenden proposed four resolutions and six constitutional amendments to settle the SECESSION crisis. The resolutions condemned the northern PERSONAL LIBERTY LAWS and reasserted the constitutionality of the fugitive slave laws. The amendments—one of which declared the others "unrepealable"—would have compensated masters for unrecovered fugitive slaves and given permanent protection to slavery where it already existed and in all existing territories or those "hereafter acquired" which were south of the MISSOURI COMPROMISE line. Crittenden's only concession to northern sentiments was to propose the permanent prohibition of slavery north of the Missouri Compromise line; however, many Northerners read "hereafter acquired" as an invitation for proslavery filibustering in Latin America. Furthermore, Republicans opposed any western extension of slavery. Southern extremists, on the other hand, wanted secession, and not compromise. Thus, only the amendment permanently protecting slavery in the existing states was approved by Congress. From 1861 to 1863 Crittenden worked to prevent Kentucky's secession and limit the war to preserving the Union. Thus, he opposed the EMANCIPATION PROCLAMATION, the CONFISCATION ACTS, the use of black troops, West Virginia statehood, and other administration policies.

PAUL FINKELMAN

Bibliography

KIRWAN, ALBERT D. 1962 *John J. Crittenden: The Struggle for the Union.* Lexington: University of Kentucky Press.

CROLY, HERBERT
(1869–1930)

New York journalist and social critic Herbert David Croly was the leading intellectual of the Progressive movement. Croly's *The Promise of American Life* (1909) became the programmatic handbook of the reformers: in it he advocated strengthening the federal government as the special protector of working people and the creation of a "welfare state." His inspiration was the nationalism of ALEXANDER HAMILTON rather than the individualism of THOMAS JEFFERSON. Croly believed that the process of government should be separated from politics and placed in the hands of experts. Croly advised President WOODROW WILSON, but his greatest influence on public affairs was as editor of *The New Republic*.

DENNIS J. MAHONEY

CROSS-EXAMINATION, RIGHT OF

See: Confrontation, Right of

CROSSKEY, WILLIAM W.
(1894–1968)

William Winslow Crosskey's reputation as a constitutional historian rests upon his *Politics and the Constitution in the History of the United States* (1953, 1960), a learned, controversial reinterpretation of the framing of the Constitution. Crosskey, a professor of law at the University of Chicago, argued that the Framers of the Constitution sought to create a unitary system of government with virtually unlimited legislative powers, that Congress would have supreme authority within the constitutional system, and that the power of JUDICIAL REVIEW was intended merely as a means for the judiciary to defend itself against encroachments by the other branches of government. Crosskey began with two premises: first, that the words of the Constitution should be understood according to the meanings they had in common usage in 1787; and, second, that the source relied upon by most historians to determine the intent of the Framers, JAMES MADISON's *Notes of the Debates in the Federal Convention of 1787*, had been deliberately distorted by Madison to support the "limited-powers" interpretation of the Constitution favored by Jeffersonian Republicans. Crosskey's third volume, completed posthumously by William W. Jeffrey, Jr., and published in 1980, asserted that nationalist sentiments and ideas pervaded the political climate in the United States from the Revolution to the opening of the CONSTITUTIONAL CONVENTION of 1787.

RICHARD B. BERNSTEIN

CRUEL AND UNUSUAL PUNISHMENT

The Eighth Amendment provides that "excessive BAIL shall not be required . . . nor cruel and unusual punishment inflicted." Similar provisions now exist in virtually all state constitutions. Even if they did not, the federal constitutional prohibition has been held in *Robinson v. California* (1962) to be binding on the states through the FOURTEENTH AMENDMENT's DUE PROCESS CLAUSE.

A legal prohibition against cruel and unusual punishment appears to have originated in the English BILL OF RIGHTS in 1688. Its purpose then was to curtail the shockingly barbarous punishments that were so common during that period.

How the prohibition was to be applied to American society, with its different values and legal system, remained unclear a century after the enactment of the American BILL OF RIGHTS. In the late nineteenth and early twentieth centuries, the Supreme Court did occasionally interpret the cruel and unusual punishment language, mostly as it related to the means for executing CAPITAL PUNISHMENT. However, not until the 1970s did the Supreme Court begin to give extensive consideration to the scope and meaning of the prohibition apart from capital punishment. The Court did not decide until 1977, for example, whether the cruel and unusual punishment clause applied to persons who had not been convicted of crime. INGRAHAM V. WRIGHT (1977) raised the question whether the corporal punishment of school children constituted cruel and unusual punishment. The Court held that it did not, stating that the Eighth Amendment provision is applicable only to persons convicted and incarcerated for crimes. In the Court's view, the prohibition was not necessary to protect children in public institutions, as other protections were available. Since *Ingraham*, the Supreme Court has also held that the Eighth Amendment is inapplicable to persons detained for treatment or detention and not punishment, such as persons committed to mental institutions (*Youngblood v. Romero*, 1982) or detained awaiting trial (*Bell v. Wolfish*, 1979). Any protection against improper punishments in such situations derives from due process of law and not the Eighth Amendment prohibition against cruel and unusual punishment.

Since the late 1970s, in a number of cases involving noncapital sentences and the treatment of prison inmates, the Court has generally given a narrow interpretation of the cruel and unusual punishment clause.

Prior to Supreme Court review of the issue, several federal and state courts had held that a sentence could be invalid on cruel and unusual punishment grounds if its length was disproportionate to the offense. Courts used several measures to determine whether a particular sentence violated the Eight Amendment: the nature of the crime, and particularly whether violence was involved; comparison of the individual sentence or statutory sentencing scheme with sentences or schemes for similar crimes in other jurisdictions; and comparison of the individual sentence or statutory sentencing scheme for the particular crime with those for other similar or more serious crimes in the same jurisdiction. Thus a federal court of appeals struck down a life sentence imposed on an offender under a Texas statute authorizing a life sentence for a person convicted of felonies on three separate occasions. In this case, the three felonies included: fraudulently using a credit card to obtain $80.00 worth of services; passing a forged check for $28.36; and obtaining $120.75 by false pretenses. The three convictions occurred over a nine-year period. In RUMMEL V. ESTELLE the Supreme Court reversed; the 5–4 majority refused to apply the comparative measures used by lower courts. Instead, it gave great weight to legislative judgments on criminal sentences and to the deterrence of habitual offenders. The fact that Rummel was eligible for early release on parole apparently eased the majority's decision. After *Rummel*, it was uncertain what circumstances might justify judicial intervention on cruel and unusual punishment grounds in cases not involving habitual offender statutes. In *Hutto v. Davis* (1982), in a PER CURIAM opinion, the Court, over three dissents, held that a forty-year sentence for possession of nine ounces of marijuana did not constitute cruel and unusual punishment. The Court reiterated the *Rummel* majority's view that federal courts should be "reluctan[t] to review legislatively mandated terms of imprisonment" and that "successful challenges to the proportionality of particular sentences" should be "exceedingly rare."

In 1983, in SOLEM V. HELM, however, the Supreme Court invalidated a life sentence without possibility of parole for a person convicted under a recidivist statute. The immediate charge involved passing a check for one hundred dollars written on a nonexistent account; all his prior felony convictions were for nonviolent crimes against property. The Court, in a 5–4 decision, applied a proportionality test in applying the cruel and unusual punishment clause. Even after this decision, it appears that the burden of attacking a sentence of a term of years on disproportionality grounds, at least in the federal courts, will be difficult to carry. Some state supreme courts have been more willing to use state constitutional counterparts to the Eighth Amendment to strike down terms that seem excessive relative to the crime committed.

In earlier cases, the Supreme Court did reverse some sentences involving issues other than their length. In TROP V. DULLES (1958), for example, the Court concluded that depriving a person of nationality for conviction by court-martial of wartime desertion constituted cruel and unusual punishment. Also, in WEEMS V. UNITED STATES (1909), the Court held that the crime of being an accessory to the falsification of a public document could not justify a twelve-to-twenty-year sentence at hard labor with chains and a permanent deprivation of civil rights.

The Supreme Court has also applied the Eighth Amendment to reverse the punishment of a person simply because of his status or condition. In *Robinson v. California* (1962) the Court held that punishing a person for being a drug addict constitutes cruel and unusual punishment. The Court refused, however, to apply this same reasoning six years later when it was asked to invalidate an alcoholic's conviction of public drunkenness in *Powell v. Texas* (1968).

In summary, the Supreme Court has rarely relied on the federal prohibition against cruel and unusual punishment to overturn a criminal sentence. The Court has also applied the prohibition sparingly to challenges by prisoners to prison conditions, even though courts have frequently found these conditions to be shocking.

Without question, most prisons throughout the country are archaic, overcrowded, filthy, and understaffed, and provide few worthwhile vocational or recreational activities for prisoners. Because the prison population is growing dramatically at a time when resources to maintain it are shrinking proportionately, prison conditions are deteriorating. In several cases in the late 1970s and early 1980s, the Supreme Court attempted to articulate standards for applying the prohibition against cruel and unusual punishment to challenges against prison conditions. In *Rhodes v. Chapman* (1981) the Court summarized these standards as follows: "Today the Eighth Amendment prohibits punishments which, although not physically barbarous, involve the unnecessary and wanton infliction of pain, or are grossly disproportionate to the severity of the crime. Among unnecessary and wanton infliction of pain are those that are totally without penological justification." The Court has not yet applied these standards to the intentional physical abuse of prisoners. It has, however, cited with approval a court of appeals decision, *Jackson v. Bishop* (1968), which proscribed the whipping of prisoners.

Holt v. Finney (1978) confronted the Supreme Court with its first Eighth Amendment challenge to prison conditions. The lower courts had declared that the general conditions of the Arkansas state prison system constituted cruel and unusual punishment. Among the conditions challenged were: administration of much of the prisons' activities by inmate trustees; dangerous barracks; overcrowded and filthy conditions in isolation or punishment cells and the poor diet of prisoners in these cells; and lack of any rehabilitation programs. The lower courts entered sweeping orders requiring major improvements in the prisons. Among these improvements were restrictions on the numbers of prisoners placed in isolation cells, a requirement that bunks be placed in these cells, a discontinuation of the "grue" diet, and a limit of thirty days in an isolation cell. The state appealed the thirty-day limitation. In a cautious opinion, the Supreme Court upheld the lower court's conclusion. Although it held that confinement in punitive isolation is not a per se violation of the Eighth Amendment, the Court stated that such confinement may become a violation depending on the conditions of isolation. If violations do occur, the Court said, remedies may include a limit on the time to be spent in isolation; the thirty-day restriction of the lower court seemed supportable in this case.

The Supreme Court reached a different result in a constitutional challenge to overcrowding in an Ohio prison. In *Rhodes v. Chapman* (1981) the issue was "double-bunking" prisoners in cells originally designed for single inmates. The courts below had found this practice to violate the Eighth Amendment because prisoners were serving long sentences; the prison was thirty-eight percent over capacity; decency required more living space; prisoners spent much of their time in their cells; and double-bunking was a regular practice, not a temporary condition.

The Supreme Court reversed, holding that there was no evidence that double-bunking in this case "inflicted unnecessary or wanton pain or [was] grossly disproportionate to the severity of crimes warranting punishment." The Court found that double-bunking did not lead to "deprivation of essential food, medical care, or sanitation" or to increased violence among inmates. In the Court's view, the Constitution "does not mandate comfortable prisons," and judges should be reluctant to intervene in prison condition cases unless the conditions were "deplorable" or "sordid": "In discharging [their] oversight responsibility, however, [federal] courts cannot assume that State legislatures and prison officials are insensitive to the requirements of the Constitution or to the perplexing sociological problems of how best to achieve the penal function in the criminal justice system."

In another opinion, *Estelle v. Gamble* (1976), the Supreme Court established some minimum requirements for the provision of health care in prisons. Stating that the government must provide medical care to those whom it punishes by incarceration, the Court held that "deliberate indifference to the serious medical needs of prisoners constitutes unnecessary and wanton infliction of pain proscribed by the Eighth Amendment." The Court placed several limits on successful claims, however. For example, an inadvertent failure to provide adequate medical care would not constitute "unnecessary and wanton infliction of pain." Nor would an accident, simple negligence, or a disagreement as to treatment options.

Thus, although the Supreme Court had indicated that the Eighth Amendment does protect prisoners from deplorable conditions, for the most part the Court has not shared the view of many lower courts or of prison experts as to what conditions are deplorable.

The Supreme Court has yet to consider a number of other important questions, such as the factors that must be weighed in assessing challenges to the conditions of a prison as a whole; the constitutional limits on behavior modification programs, including drug usage programs; and the minimum requirements for providing a secure environment for prisoners. Precedent suggests that the Supreme Court will be as cautious in addressing these and other related prison condition issues as it has been in confronting other asserted impositions of cruel and unusual punishment.

SHELDON KRANTZ

(SEE ALSO: *Institutional Litigation.*)

Bibliography

GRANNUCCI, ANTHONY F. 1969 Nor Cruel and Unusual Punishment Inflicted: The Original Meaning. *California Law Review* 57:839–865.

JOINT COMMITTEE ON THE LEGAL STATUS OF PRISONERS 1977 American Bar Association Standards Relating to the Legal Status of Prisoners. *American Criminal Law Review* 14:377–629.

KRANTZ, SHELDON 1983 *Corrections and Prisoners' Rights in a Nutshell*, 2nd ed. St. Paul, Minn.: West Publishing Co.

SHERMAN, MICHAEL and HAWKINS, GORDON 1981 *Imprisonment in America: Choosing the Future.* Chicago: University of Chicago Press.

UNIFORM LAW COMMISSION 1978 *Model Sentencing and Convictions Act.* New York: National Conference of Commissioners on Uniform State Laws.

UNITED NATIONS ECONOMIC AND SOCIAL COUNCIL 1957 *Minimum Rules for the Treatment of Prisoners.* New York: United Nations Publications.

CRUIKSHANK, UNITED STATES v.
92 U.S. 542 (1876)

Cruikshank paralyzed the federal government's attempt to protect black citizens by punishing violators of their CIVIL RIGHTS and, in effect, shaped the Constitution to the advantage of the Ku Klux Klan. The case arose out of a federal prosecution of nightriders responsible for the Colfax Massacre of 1873 in Grant Parish, Louisiana. Several hundred armed whites besieged a courthouse where hundreds of blacks were holding a public assembly; the attackers burned down the building and murdered about 100 people. The United States tried Cruikshank and others involved in the massacre and convicted three for violating section six of the FORCE ACT OF 1870. That act, which survives as section 241 of Title 18 of the United States Code, is a general conspiracy statute making it a federal crime, then punishable by a $5,000 fine and up to ten years in prison, for two or more persons to conspire to injure or intimidate any citizen with the intent of hindering his free exercise of any right or privilege guaranteed him by the Constitution or laws of the United States.

In a unanimous opinion by Chief Justice MORRISON R. WAITE, the Court ignored the statute and focused on the INDICTMENT to ascertain whether the rights Cruikshank and others interfered with were granted or secured by the United States. Reasserting the theory of dual CITIZENSHIP advanced in the SLAUGHTER-HOUSE CASES (1873), Waite concluded that the United States cannot grant or secure rights not under its JURISDICTION. Examining in turn each right named in the indictment as having been deprived, Waite found that they were all "left under the protection of the States." None was a federal right. The right to peaceably assemble predated the Constitution and remained "subject to state jurisdiction." The United States could neither infringe it nor protect it, for it was not an attribute of United States citizenship. So too the right to bear arms. The right to be secure in one's person, life, and liberty was protected by the FOURTEENTH AMENDMENT against state deprivation, but for protection of that right, sovereignty "rests alone with the States." The amendment, said Waite, "adds nothing to the rights of one citizen as against another." Thus the violence here conducted by private persons could not be reached by Congress, which was limited to assuring that the states do not violate the amendment's prohibitions. As for the right to vote, the FIFTEENTH AMENDMENT merely protected against discrimination based on race. The Constitution did not confer the right to vote on anyone; that right was not, Waite said, an attribute of national citizenship.

By such reasoning the Court held that the indictment did not show that the conspirators had hindered or prevented the enjoyment of any right granted or secured by the Constitution. Accordingly, no conviction based on the indictment could be sustained, and the Court ordered the defendants discharged. The conspiracy statute remained impotent until revived in recent times by the Department of Justice, but the Court did not sustain a conviction under the statute until 1966 (UNITED STATES V. PRICE; UNITED STATES V. GUEST), when the Court vitiated *Cruikshank*.

LEONARD W. LEVY

Bibliography

MAGRATH, C. PETER 1963 *Morrison R. Waite*. Pages 120–134. New York: Macmillan.

CRUZ v. BETO

See: Religious Liberty

CULTS (RELIGIOUS) AND THE CONSTITUTION

The term "cult," currently used to designate a particular unpopular and feared new religious group often claiming a personal relationship between its leader and the Divinity, is not found explicitly in the original Constitution, the FIRST AMENDMENT's free exercise or establishment clause, or the FOURTEENTH AMENDMENT's EQUAL PROTECTION clause. Among the most prominent of these groups in recent times have been the Unification Church, the Worldwide Church of God, Inc., the Church of Scientology, and the International Society for Krishna Consciousness.

Cults, which have experienced varying degrees of discrimination and persecution by law enforcement officials, have consistently claimed that the Constitution does not sanction legal distinctions between them on the one hand and long-established and respected faiths on the other. They note, too, that historically most of the now well-established and fully respected faiths, including Baptists, Roman Catholics, Jews, Mormons, Christian Scientists, and Jehovah's Witnesses, have been subjected to governmental discrimination before achieving acceptability and equal treatment.

The claim to equal treatment was upheld in LARSON V. VALENTE (1982) where the Supreme Court held unconstitutional a Minnesota statute, enforced against the Unification Church, that imposed special registration and reporting requirements upon religious groups that received more than half of their income from nonmembers, a provision the Court found to have been aimed at unpopular cults. This provision, the Court said, constituted precisely the sort of official denominational preference and discrimination forbidden by the establishment clause in the absence of a compelling interest not otherwise amenable to protection. Moreover, the statute also violated the clause by authorizing excessive governmental entanglement with and politicizing of religion.

Compelling registration is only one comparatively mild sanction imposed by government upon religious cults. Although that term had not yet become popular in 1944, when *United States v. Ballard* was decided by the Supreme Court, that decision ruled unconstitutional a mail fraud conviction of "I Am" members who obtained donations by representing that their leader was divinely appointed with supernatural powers to heal the incurably ill. To allow a jury to determine the truth or falsity of religious doctrines, the Court said, would render vulnerable representations concerning the miracles of the New Testament, the divinity of Christ, life after death, and the power of prayer. The First Amendment permits only a determination whether the defendants themselves actually believed that what they recounted was true, not whether it was actually true.

Other devices applied against cults include denial of tax exemption, dissolution of the corporate structure and seizure of assets (as in CHURCH OF JESUS CHRIST OF LATTER DAY SAINTS V. UNITED STATES, 1890), and prosecution for disturbance of the peace (as in CANTWELL V. CONNECTICUT, 1940, involving Jehovah's Witnesses).

Whatever may have been the Court's response in earlier times, today it accords cults the same constitutional protection accorded to long-standing and commonly accepted faiths.

LEO PFEFFER

Bibliography

New York University Review of Law and Social Change 1979–1980 Volume 9, #1: *Proceedings of Conference on Alternative Religions, Government Control and the First Amendment.*

CUMBERLAND ROAD BILL

See: Internal Improvements

CUMMINGS, HOMER S.
(1870–1956)

A prominent Connecticut Democrat, Homer S. Cummings served as attorney general under President FRANKLIN D. ROOSEVELT from 1933 to 1939, defending much of the New Deal legislation in the Supreme Court. He broke with recent practice when he personally argued the GOLD CLAUSE CASES (1935), and the Court reiterated much of his argument in its opinions. Cummings strongly supported Roosevelt's court packing plan as "clearly constitutional" and privately suggested a constitutional amendment requiring justices to retire at seventy. With Carl McFarland, he wrote *Federal Justice* (1937), a history of the Department of Justice based on previously neglected manuscript materials. Cummings instituted reform of federal criminal and administrative procedures, helping secure adoption of the FEDERAL RULES OF CIVIL PROCEDURE in 1938.

DAVID GORDON

CUMMINGS v. MISSOURI

See: Test Oath Cases

CURTIS, BENJAMIN R.
(1809–1874)

Benjamin Robbins Curtis of Massachusetts generally rates high marks for his six-year tenure on the Supreme Court. His bold dissent in DRED SCOTT V. SANDFORD (1857), followed by his dramatic resignation, largely accounts for his reputation. Yet Curtis's contributions to the development of constitutional law transcend that one case.

Curtis's prominence in the *Dred Scott* case is ironic, considering the fact that he received his appointment in 1851 because he was a northern Whig, acceptable to southern slave interests. By that time, he already was a leading figure in Boston legal circles. He had been selected in 1846 to succeed Justice JOSEPH STORY as an overseer (trustee) of Harvard College, and he was highly regarded for his promotion of procedure and litigation reforms. In 1851 he represented the Boston school board against the desegregationists in ROBERTS V. CITY OF BOSTON. But most important, Curtis had also endorsed Senator DANIEL WEBSTER's efforts in the COMPROMISE OF 1850, had advocated strict enforcement of the new Fugitive Slave Act, and had fought abolitionists and free-soilers, even opposing CHARLES SUMNER's successful Senate campaign in 1851. Shortly afterward, President MILLARD FILLMORE, following Webster's recommendation, nominated Curtis to succeed Justice LEVI WOODBURY. The only criticism came from the abolitionist press. Southern politicians, however, were satisfied and the Democratic Senate quickly confirmed the appointment.

Curtis's first major opinion, in COOLEY V. BOARD OF WARDENS (1851), reflected both his legal skills and his willingness to follow the middle ground of his patron, Daniel Webster. The case involved the limiting effects of the COMMERCE CLAUSE on state regulation, a subject that had divided the TANEY COURT since 1837. Southerners feared congressional regulation of interstate traffic in slaves, and consequently sought to interpret the commerce power narrowly. In *Cooley* Curtis acknowledged broad congressional authority over foreign and INTERSTATE COMMERCE, but the case challenged the validity not of congressional action but of local pilotage regulations for the port of Philadelphia. Curtis devised a compromise between the EXCLUSIVE POWER and CONCURRENT POWER views. His doctrine of SELECTIVE EXCLUSIVENESS recognized exclusive congressional power over subjects demanding uniform national regulation, but invited state regulation, in cases where Congress had not acted, of subjects admitting of diverse local regulation.

Curtis again demonstrated a shrewd practicality coupled with an ability to make law responsive to new conditions when he upheld federal regulations of steamboat operations. In *Steamboat New World v. King* (1854) Curtis applied the emerging law of negligence to the rapidly expanding technology of steamboating. In addition, he confirmed that federal admiralty jurisdiction applied to all inland, navigable waters. A year before the *Dred Scott* controversy over the content of the Fifth Amendment's DUE PROCESS clause, Curtis had discussed the subject in MURRAY'S LESSEE V. HOBOKEN LAND AND IMPROVEMENT COMPANY (1856) and had followed a traditional procedural interpretation of the clause.

The understanding of Curtis's role in *Dred Scott* has shifted with historiographical tides. When it was fashionable to view the Civil War as a "reconcilable conflict," Curtis was seen as a *provocateur;* but when the *Dred Scott* decision is seen as Chief Justice ROGER TANEY's attempt to make the nation safe for slavery,

Curtis's opinion emerges as a calm, reasoned historical and legal brief properly explicating national authority to regulate SLAVERY IN THE TERRITORIES. Curtis's opinion differed from Taney's conclusions in nearly every respect. He demonstrated historically that blacks could be American citizens, and hence could sue in the federal courts. Equally important, he offered constitutional language and long-standing historical precedent to justify congressional regulation of slavery in the territories. Curtis's comments on the need for judicial restraint were pointed: "To engraft on any instrument a substantive exception not found in it must be admitted to be a matter attended with great difficulty. . . . To allow this to be done with the Constitution, upon reasons purely political, renders its judicial interpretation impossible because judicial tribunals . . . cannot decide upon political considerations."

Curtis resigned a few months after the *Dred Scott* decision. He was dissatisfied with his circuit duties and his inadequate salary, and the *Dred Scott* imbroglio convinced him that he and his colleagues could no longer work together effectively and harmoniously.

During the Civil War, Curtis emerged as an outspoken critic of Lincoln's unprecedented exercise of PRESIDENTIAL POWERS. In good Whig fashion, he leveled constitutional attacks on Lincoln for suspending the writ of HABEAS CORPUS and for issuing the EMANCIPATION PROCLAMATION. Yet, following the war, he endorsed the sentiments of the National Union Convention in 1866 and advocated exclusive presidential control of reconstruction. Two years later, he joined WILLIAM M. EVARTS and others to represent President ANDREW JOHNSON in his IMPEACHMENT trial. Curtis's defense of the President argued that Johnson was not an "acting President," as some claimed, and that the TENURE OF OFFICE ACT unduly interfered with the President's constitutional prerogative to remove executive officers—an argument the Supreme Court came to accept half a century later. Finally, he offered a ringing affirmation of the FIRST AMENDMENT to defend Johnson against the charge that he had "improperly" spoken of Congress.

In his last years, Curtis had a lucrative law practice and argued more than fifty cases before the Supreme Court. Most noteworthy were his briefs in behalf of federal regulation of the insurance industry in PAUL V. VIRGINIA (1869) and his defense of the legal tender laws in HEPBURN V. GRISWOLD (1870).

Curtis's all too brief career on the Supreme Court must exclude him from a short list of truly great jurists. But he displayed uncommon skills, especially a talent for closely reasoned and logical arguments. His defense and understanding of the Constitution, on and off the bench, mark contributions that have been affirmed by the passage of time.

STANLEY I. KUTLER

Bibliography

CURTIS, GEORGE TICKNOR and CURTIS, BENJAMIN R., EDS. 1879 *Life and Writings of Benjamin Robbins Curtis.* Boston: Little, Brown.

FEHRENBACHER, DON E. 1978 *The Dred Scott Case: Its Significance in American Law and Politics.* New York: Oxford University Press.

LEACH, RICHARD H. 1952 Benjamin Robbins Curtis: Judicial Misfit. *New England Quarterly* 25:507–523.

CURTIS, GEORGE T.
(1812–1894)

A leading Boston attorney, George Ticknor Curtis ordered the rendition to slavery of Thomas Sims in 1852 while serving as a Fugitive Slave Law Commissioner. (See SIMS' CASE.) In 1856 he represented Dred Scott before the United States Supreme Court in DRED SCOTT V. SANDFORD. Curtis wrote numerous legal treatises, three political biographies, and a two-volume *History of the Origin, Formation, and Adoption of the Constitution* (1854–1858)—revised as *Constitutional History of the United States* (1889–1896). This work presents a classic Federalist-Whig interpretation of American political and constitutional history. It was begun at the suggestion of DANIEL WEBSTER and reflects the senator's approach to the Constitution and the Union.

PAUL FINKELMAN

Bibliography

FISH, CARL RUSSELL 1930 George T. Curtis. *Dictionary of American Biography,* Vol. 4:613–614.

CURTISS-WRIGHT EXPORT CORPORATION, UNITED STATES v.
299 U.S. 304 (1936)

Nearly two years after Paraguay and Bolivia went to war in 1932, Congress authorized President FRANKLIN D. ROOSEVELT to embargo American arms shipments to the belligerents if he found that the action might contribute to reestablishing peace. Indicted in January 1936 for conspiring to violate the embargo resolution and Roosevelt's implementing proclamation, Curtiss-Wright Export Corporation demurred on grounds of unconstitutional DELEGATION OF POWER. Recent rulings against New Deal legislation in PANAMA REFINING CO. V. RYAN (1935) and SCHECHTER POULTRY CORP. V. UNITED STATES (1935) lent weight to the company's position, and the district court sustained the demurrer. On appeal, however, the Supreme Court approved the embargo resolution and proclamation with a ringing endorsement of independent presidential authority in the area of FOREIGN AFFAIRS.

For a 7–1 majority, Justice GEORGE SUTHERLAND defended the embargo measures by distinguishing between powers of internal and external SOVEREIGNTY, a distinction the government had not employed in arguing *Curtiss-Wright.* For him, the federal government's domestic authority derived from states having delegated power via the Constitution. External sovereignty had passed, however, from the British Crown to the United Colonies and then to the United States in their collective capacities, with the states severally never possessing it nor delegating it. "Rulers come and go; governments end and forms of government change; but sovereignty survives." In the realm of foreign relations, the authority of the federal government therefore equaled that of any sovereign nation, and the usual constitutional divisions between the President and Congress were largely irrelevant, as was the normal prohibition on delegation of legislative power. Keenly aware of the need for energy and dispatch in the delicate business of conducting foreign relations, the Framers had endorsed this arrangement, Sutherland claimed, and early statesmen put it into practice. Although dissenting, Justice JAMES C. MCREYNOLDS filed no opinion.

Later characterized as dictum-laden, Sutherland's argument made sense within the constitutional climate of the 1930s and in view of his own commitments. The government, for example, had claimed that the 1934 embargo resolution and proclamation met the straited *Panama-Schechter* requirement that delegatory legislation specify the findings of fact the President must make before taking the anticipated action. Such an approach ignored the plausible objection that findings involving diplomatic and military imponderables were no firmer than those already disallowed as "opinion" in *Schechter.* An alternative was simply to rely on judicial precedent and legislative practice regarding delegation in areas cognate to foreign relations. Sutherland did examine earlier embargo, tariff, and kindred measures in which Congress had given latitude to the President, but he did so primarily as a means of showing that his view of external sovereignty had been accepted from the beginning. Neither judicial nor legislative iterations carried the same weight as the original intent and first principles he valued so highly. Perhaps most important, Sutherland himself had broached the external–internal distinction the previous May, in CARTER V. CARTER COAL COMPANY (1936), and had earlier explicated his full theory of sovereignty in his book *Constitutional Power and World Affairs* (1919).

The real weakness of Sutherland's opinion was its faulty history. Scant evidence exists that the Framers held the extraconstitutional understanding of the foreign relations power he attributed to them. Sutherland also misconstrued many of the earlier episodes and commentaries that, he argued, were informed by his theories of sovereignty and plenary executive authority. *Curtiss-Wright* nevertheless had timing on its side. It soon provided a base for upholding EXECUTIVE AGREEMENTS as domestic law in UNITED STATES V. BELMONT (1937) and UNITED STATES V. PINK (1942). More broadly, Sutherland's opinion appealed to proponents of an expanded presidential role as the United States acquired global responsibilities, engaged in nuclear diplomacy, fought undeclared wars, and debated the requirements of internal security.

CHARLES A. LOFGREN

Bibliography

LEVITAN, DAVID M. 1946 The Foreign Relations Power: An Analysis of Mr. Justice Sutherland's Theory. *Yale Law Journal* 55:467–497.

LOFGREN, CHARLES A. 1973 *United States v. Curtiss-Wright Export Corporation:* An Historical Reassessment. *Yale Law Journal* 83:1–32.

CUSHING, WILLIAM
(1732–1810)

William Cushing served on the United States Supreme Court, in an undistinguished manner, for nearly twenty-one years. Born into a politically well-connected, upper middle class Massachusetts family, he graduated from Harvard College, and then studied law; he was admitted to the bar in 1755. He practiced law in Maine, where he represented the interests of large landholders against squatters and debtors. In 1771 he succeeded his father as a judge of the Massachusetts Superior Court. Because many of his family had loyalist leanings and he owed his position to a royal appointment, Cushing expressed his political views cautiously during the 1770s, when colonial resistance to British policies turned into revolution. Although he chose the patriot side in 1776, some ardent

radicals doubted his enthusiasm for independence. Nonetheless he was appointed to the newly created superior court and became chief justice for the state in 1777 when JOHN ADAMS resigned the post. He also served as a member of the convention that wrote the MASSACHUSETTS CONSTITUTION of 1780.

While chief justice, Cushing played an important role in bringing about the end of slavery in Massachusetts, beginning with COMMONWEALTH V. JENNISON (1783). In his charge to the jury, Cushing interpreted the clause of the state constitution that declared that "all men are born free and equal" as abolishing slavery in the state. Unsympathetic to the debtors in western Massachusetts who prevented the collection of taxes and closed the courts during SHAYS' REBELLION, Cushing opposed their activities while riding circuit and presided over the TREASON trial of the leaders; some of his sentences included the death penalty. He advocated RATIFICATION OF THE CONSTITUTION in 1788 and served as vice-president of the state ratifying convention.

GEORGE WASHINGTON appointed Cushing the first associate Justice of the United States Supreme Court in 1789. Despite his extensive judicial experience he did not play a very active role on the Court. Although he participated in many of the most important cases of the 1790s—CHISHOLM V. GEORGIA (1793), WARE V. HYLTON (1796), HYLTON V. UNITED STATES (1796), and CALDER V. BULL (1798)—his opinions tended to be brief, and dealt with narrow legal and procedural questions. Ceremonious in his deportment, Cushing was the last member of the Court to wear a wig. His affability and courtesy enabled him to enforce the Sedition Act with minimal rancor. After 1800, illness, age, and the difficulties of riding circuit caused him considerable hardship. He could no longer adequately perform his duties, and he probably would have retired early if a federal pension had been available. He died, while still a member of the Supreme Court, in 1810.

RICHARD E. ELLIS

Bibliography

JOHNSON, HERBERT ALAN 1969 William Cushing. Pages 57–70 in Leon Friedman and Fred L. Israel, eds., *Justices of the Supreme Court, 1789–1969*, Vol. I. New York: Chelsea House.

CUSHMAN, ROBERT E.
(1889–1969)

Robert Eugene Cushman taught constitutional law for many years at Cornell University. His landmark anthology, *Leading Constitutional Decisions* (1925; 16th ed. by Robert F. Cushman, 1982), quickly established itself as a standard casebook for constitutional law and history courses. Cushman founded and edited the Cornell Studies on Civil Liberty; the contributors to this series of monographs included Robert K. Carr, Milton R. Convitz, Walter Gellhorn, James Morton Smith, and Cushman himself. Cushman described his monograph, *Civil Liberties in the United States* (1956), as "a guide to current problems and experience." A synoptic description of the state of the law and an attempt to chart its future development, it was well-received, although some critics questioned its formalistic approach and its skeletal coverage of various issues. Cushman's major scholarly work, *The Independent Regulatory Commissions* (1941), a byproduct of his service with the President's Committee on Ad-

ministrative Management (1937); prophetically proposed the separation in independent regulatory commissions of the prosecutorial and adjudicative functions. For many years he wrote the *American Political Science Review*'s annual survey of the work of the Supreme Court. From 1958 until his death, Cushman was editor-in-chief of the *Documentary History of the Ratification of the Constitution;* he was succeeded by MERRILL JENSEN.

RICHARD B. BERNSTEIN

CUSTODIAL INTERROGATION

See: Police Interrogation and Confessions

D

DAIRY QUEEN, INC. v. WOOD
369 U.S. 469 (1962)

The owners of the "Dairy Queen" trademark sued a licensee alleging breach of contract and trademark infringement and asking for injunctive relief and an "accounting." Since this was a case in EQUITY, U. S. District Judge Wood denied the defendant's motion for a jury trial.

A unanimous Supreme Court, speaking through Justice HUGO L. BLACK, held that Wood's decision deprived Dairy Queen of its SEVENTH AMENDMENT rights: although the complaint asked for an "accounting," it was really a suit for damages or debt. As Black wrote, "the constitutional right of TRIAL BY JURY cannot be made dependent upon the choice of words used in the pleadings."

DENNIS J. MAHONEY

DALLAS, ALEXANDER J.
(1759–1817)

Admitted to the bar in 1785, Alexander James Dallas practiced law in Philadelphia. He supplemented his income by reporting the opinions of the courts that sat in that city, including the Supreme Court of the United States (1790–1800). From 1801 to 1814 he was United States attorney for eastern Pennsylvania.

As secretary of the treasury under President JAMES MADISON (1814–1816), Dallas secured enactment of the highest federal taxes to that date, restored confi-

dence in the currency, and dictated terms of the second BANK OF THE UNITED STATES ACT (1816). In 1815 he was also acting secretary of war.

DENNIS J. MAHONEY

DAMAGES

From the earliest days of COMMON LAW, courts have ordered the payment of money ("damages") to compensate for legal wrongs. Two related but separable lines of cases shape the availability of damages for violations of constitutional rights. One line of cases involves interpretation of SECTION 1983, TITLE 42, UNITED STATES CODE, and its express provision for "an action at law" to redress deprivations of constitutional rights by state officials. Since the revival of section 1983 in MONROE V. PAPE (1961), it has been understood that damages are available to compensate for constitutional violations by state officials. CAREY V. PIPHUS (1978) reaffirmed this understanding, but held that substantial damages could not be recovered for PROCEDURAL DUE PROCESS violations without proof of injury. *Smith v. Wade* (1983) clarified the standards governing awards of punitive damages under section 1983.

In actions against federal officials, which are not governed by section 1983, the Court, in BIVENS V. SIX UNKNOWN NAMED AGENTS OF THE FEDERAL BUREAU OF NARCOTICS (1971), inferred a damages action based on the FOURTH AMENDMENT. Later cases, such as DAVIS V. PASSMAN (1979), extended the implied constitutional damages action to other constitutional provisions. The *Bivens* line of cases may be viewed as an extension of EX PARTE YOUNG (1908) and other decisions that allowed actions for injunctive relief to be based directly on the Constitution.

THEODORE EISENBERG

Bibliography

NEWMAN, JON O. 1978 Suing the Lawbreakers: Proposals to Strengthen the Section 1983 Damages Remedy for Law Enforcers' Misconduct. *Yale Law Journal* 87:447–467.

DAMES & MOORE v. REGAN
453 U.S. 654 (1981)

The United States hostage crisis was settled by the 1981 Algerian Agreement under which, *inter alia,* the United States undertook to terminate certain litigation by American claimants against Iran and its agencies. Under the agreement, the claims involved were required to be submitted to binding international arbitration. By EXECUTIVE ORDER, President JIMMY CARTER suspended various claims pending in American courts. Certain American claimants challenged this action as exceeding presidential authority. The Supreme Court upheld the President's authority to conclude and implement this part of the agreement on the basis of his constitutional FOREIGN AFFAIRS powers. It relied on congressional acceptance of broad presidential power during crises in foreign affairs, and on Congress's historic acquiescence in the practice of settling American claims by EXECUTIVE AGREEMENT. The Court also held that if the agreement caused a TAKING OF PROPERTY within the scope of the Fifth Amendment, American nationals had a remedy for compensation in the CLAIMS COURT OF THE UNITED STATES.

The decision effectively permitted the President to remove a category of cases from federal court JURISDICTION (although the Court characterized its action as only approving a change in the "applicable substantive law"). And it opened the way to subsequent "takings" litigation over a broad area of foreign economic policy. In both respects the Court went beyond previous decisions involving presidential executive agreement authority, and treated the presidential executive agreement as fully equivalent to a Senate-approved treaty. Accordingly, it seems to be the most sweeping judicial recognition to date of presidential foreign relations power.

PHILLIP R. TRIMBLE

Bibliography

MARKS, LEE R. and GRABOW, JOHN C. 1982 The President's Foreign Economic Powers after Dames & Moore v. Regan: Legislation by Acquiescence. *Cornell Law Review* 68:68–103.

TRIMBLE, PHILLIP R. 1984 Foreign Policy Frustrated—Dames & Moore, Claims Court Jurisdiction and a New Raid on the Treasury. *Columbia Law Review* 84:317–385.

DANDRIDGE v. WILLIAMS
397 U.S. 471 (1970)

Dandridge stifled the infant DOCTRINE, born in cases such as GRIFFIN V. ILLINOIS (1956) and DOUGLAS V. CALIFORNIA (1963), that governmental WEALTH DISCRIMINATION, like RACIAL DISCRIMINATION, demanded strict judicial scrutiny of its justifications. Maryland provided welfare aid to dependent children on the basis of need, partly determined by the number of children in a family. However, payment to any one family was limited to $250 per month, irrespective of the family's size. A 6–3 Supreme Court, speaking through Justice POTTER STEWART, characterized the case as one involving "social and economic" regulation, and applied the RATIONAL BASIS standard of review. Here there were legitimate state interests in encouraging employment and avoiding distinctions between welfare recipients and the working poor. Although some welfare beneficiaries were unemployable, the maximum-grant rule was generally reasonable.

Justice THURGOOD MARSHALL, dissenting, rejected the idea of two separate STANDARDS OF REVIEW, rational basis and STRICT SCRUTINY. He argued for a "sliding scale" of judicial supervision that would demand progressively more state justification as the classification in question bore more heavily on the powerless and in proportion to the importance of the interest at stake. Here, where indigent children were being deprived of basic subsistence as defined by the state's own standards of need, the permissive rational basis standard was inappropriate. Marshall also argued that the maximum-grant rule was invalid even under that permissive standard, given the state's aim of aiding children and the unemployability of a large proportion of welfare recipients.

After *Dandridge*, it became futile to argue to the Supreme Court either that welfare subsistence was a FUNDAMENTAL INTEREST or that wealth discrimination implied a SUSPECT CLASSIFICATION. Since 1970 the Court has regularly shied away from decisions that would place the judiciary in the position of allocating state resources.

KENNETH L. KARST

DANE, NATHAN
(1752–1835)

A loyal graduate of Harvard College, Nathan Dane of Beverly, Massachusetts, became a lawyer, politician, and scholar. In 1787, while representing his state in Congress, he single-handedly composed the NORTHWEST ORDINANCE. Its provision outlawing slavery derived from THOMAS JEFFERSON's LAND ORDINANCE OF 1785, but Dane deserves credit for writing the various other provisions that amounted to the first national BILL OF RIGHTS. It included, too, a precursor of the CONTRACT CLAUSE.

After serving in various state offices, Dane was forced by deafness to retire to his law practice and to legal scholarship as the century ended. Although he attended the HARTFORD CONVENTION, he spent most of his energies on a compendium of American law, published in eight volumes between 1820 and 1829 and known as "Dane's Abridgment." The work earned him the name of "the American Blackstone" and the money that he gave to develop Harvard Law School. Dane Hall was the first building and Dane himself chose the first Dane Professor, Justice JOSEPH STORY.

LEONARD W. LEVY

Bibliography

JOHNSON, ANDREW W. 1986 *The Life and Constitutional Thought of Nathan Dane.* New York: Garland Publishing.

DANIEL, PETER V.
(1784–1860)

Peter Vivian Daniel, a Virginian born in 1784, served as an Associate Justice of the Supreme Court of the United States from 1841 until his death in 1860. His opinions were notable for the extremist positions he adopted on constitutional issues, including the powers of the federal and state governments, the status of corporations, and slavery.

Daniel, a Republican and later a Jacksonian Democrat, served in the Virginia General Assembly, as privy councillor, and as lieutenant governor. President AN-

drew Jackson appointed him to the U. S. District Court in 1836 and President MARTIN VAN BUREN to the Supreme Court in 1841. There the bulk of his work involved cases concerning land titles, procedure, and EQUITY. However, he did participate in most of the major constitutional decisions of the TANEY COURT. But in all instances save one, he spoke either in a concurring or in a dissenting opinion.

Viewing the federal Constitution as a compact among sovereign states, Daniel opposed the extension of federal regulatory authority in COMMERCE CLAUSE cases and extolled the states' POLICE POWER (LICENSE CASES, 1847; PASSENGER CASES, 1849). He concurred in COOLEY V. BOARD OF WARDENS (1851) because he denied that the subject matter of that case (pilotage regulation) was within the federal commerce power at all. In the first *Pennsylvania v. Wheeling Bridge* case (1851), Daniel condemned the use of the commerce power to restrict commerce on navigable rivers. Daniel's hostility to federal ADMIRALTY JURISDICTION sprang from the same source and was buttressed by his insistence on preservation of JURY TRIAL. He dissented in PROPELLER GENESEE CHIEF V. FITZHUGH (1851), one of the few times in which he disagreed with Chief Justice ROGER B. TANEY, opposing the extension of federal admiralty jurisdiction to nontidal waters. In his *Searight v. Stokes* dissent (1845), Daniel insisted that the federal government lacked any power at all to finance INTERNAL IMPROVEMENTS, going far beyond the constitutional doctrine of Jackson's MAYSVILLE ROAD BILL veto (1830).

Daniel was an inveterate foe of banks and corporations, seeking unsuccessfully to deny them access to federal courts as the "Citizens" requisite to Article III jurisdiction (*Rundle v. Delaware and Raritan Canal Co.*, 1852, dissent). In his dissent in *Planters Bank v. Sharp* (1848), he sought to limit the CONTRACT CLAUSE'S scope as a restraint on state regulatory power over corporations. In the only significant constitutional case where he spoke for the Court, WEST RIVER BRIDGE V. DIX (1848), Daniel upheld the state's use of EMINENT DOMAIN and police power to condemn corporate property.

In his later years, Daniel came to despise the institutions and values of the free states. His concurrence in DRED SCOTT V. SANDFORD (1857) was remarkable for its intemperate condemnation of the MISSOURI COMPROMISE and for his insistence that no free blacks could be citizens.

Daniel himself best evaluated his contribution to the work of the Court in his *Genesee Chief* dissent: "My opinions may be deemed to be contracted and antiquated, unsuited to the day in which we live, but they are founded upon deliberate convictions as to the nature and objects of LIMITED GOVERNMENT."

WILLIAM M. WIECEK

Bibliography

FRANK, JOHN P. 1964 *Justice Daniel Dissenting: Peter V. Daniel.* Cambridge, Mass.: Harvard University Press.

DARBY LUMBER COMPANY, UNITED STATES v.
312 U.S. 100 (1941)

This decision held the FAIR LABOR STANDARDS ACT of 1938 to be a valid exercise of federal power under the COMMERCE CLAUSE. That was no surprise after the 1937 decisions upholding the WAGNER (NATIONAL LABOR RELATIONS) ACT and after the retirement of the four Justices who had voted consistently for a narrow interpretation of the commerce clause. The opinion of Justice HARLAN FISKE STONE was nevertheless of great significance. For instead of speaking in terms of such nonconstitutional concepts as "direct" and "indirect," it returned to basic constitutional principles as to the scope of the power of Congress.

The commerce clause itself precluded states with high labor standards from protecting their wage levels by forbidding the entry of goods produced elsewhere at lower wages. This meant that in the absence of federal legislative action, states with the lowest labor standards could drive the standards down throughout the country. In 1916 Congress first sought to meet this problem by barring the interstate transportation of goods produced by children. Although that statute was clearly a regulation of INTERSTATE COMMERCE the Supreme Court held it unconstitutional by a vote of 5–4 in HAMMER V. DAGENHART (1918) because the purpose of the act was to control what occurred during the course of intrastate PRODUCTION. Five years later, in ADKINS V. CHILDREN'S HOSPITAL (1923), the Court ruled, 6–3, that the DUE PROCESS clause forbade the fixing of minimum wages by either federal or state governments.

The downward spiral of prices and wages during the Great Depression of the 1930s forced employers seeking to survive to reduce wages to incredibly low levels. Congress sought to deal with this problem by requiring the codes of fair competition under the NATIONAL INDUSTRIAL RECOVERY ACT to prescribe MAXIMUM HOURS AND MINIMUM WAGES. SCHECHTER POULTRY CORP. V. UNITED STATES (1935), holding the

NRA unconstitutional, brought this program to a halt, and CARTER V. CARTER COAL COMPANY (1936), holding that Congress lacked power to regulate labor conditions and relations in the coal industry, seemed to create an insurmountable impediment. Unpredictably, this lasted for only a year, when *Carter* was in substance overruled in the WAGNER ACT CASES (1937) and *Adkins* was overruled in WEST COAST HOTEL CO. V. PARRISH (1937). The result was passage of the Fair Labor Standards Act in June 1938.

That statute prescribed a minimum wage of twenty-five cents per hour for employees engaged in interstate commerce or in producing goods for such commerce. Payment of fifty percent more for overtime was required for all hours over forty-four per week (to be reduced to forty after two years). The act penalized violation of those standards or interstate shipment of goods produced in violation of them.

The lumber industry was typically afflicted with depressed wage rates; wages ranged from ten to twenty-seven and one-half cents per hour. The annual average wage for all lumber industry employees in Georgia in 1937 was $389. Fred Darby was paying his employees twelve and one-half to seventeen cents per hour; he devised a scheme to continue doing so after the Fair Labor Standards Act became effective, and he was indicted.

Although the other federal lower courts had seen the light after the Labor Board cases and sustained the new statute, the Georgia district judge deemed himself bound to follow HAMMER V. DAGENHART and CARTER until the Supreme Court explicitly overruled them. Accordingly, he dismissed the INDICTMENT as an invalid regulation of manufacture, not interstate commerce, and the government appealed directly to the Supreme Court.

In upholding the statute Justice Stone spoke for a unanimous Court—undoubtedly because Justice JAMES C. MCREYNOLDS had retired three days before. The Court first held that the prohibition against the interstate shipment of goods produced under substandard labor conditions was "indubitably a regulation of [interstate] commerce." And this was none the less so because the motive or purpose may have been to control the "wages and hours of persons engaged in manufacture." The commerce power of Congress, as defined in GIBBONS V. OGDEN (1824), "may be exercised to its utmost extent, and acknowledges no limitations other than are prescribed in the Constitution." "The motive and purpose of a regulation of interstate commerce are matters for the legislative judgment upon which the courts are given no control." The contrary decision in HAMMER V. DAGENHART "by a bare majority of the Court over the powerful and now classic dissent of Mr. Justice [OLIVER WENDELL] HOLMES" was accordingly overruled.

In determining the validity of the regulation of wages and hours for manufacturers, the Court adopted the approach approved in MCCULLOCH V. MARYLAND (1819), the initial pronouncement on the scope of the ENUMERATED POWERS. The test was whether a regulation of intrastate activities was an "appropriate means to the attainment of a legitimate end, the exercise of the granted power of Congress to regulate interstate commerce." The directness or indirectness of the effect on such commerce was not mentioned, although the substantiality of the effect was. (See EFFECTS ON COMMERCE). The Court noted that legislation under other powers had often been sustained "when the means chosen, although not themselves within the granted power, were nevertheless deemed appropriate aids to the accomplishment of some purpose within an admitted power. . . ." The policy of excluding from interstate commerce goods produced under substandard labor conditions could reasonably be effectuated by prohibiting such conditions for manufacturers producing for interstate distribution. That would suppress a method of interstate competition Congress deemed unfair.

The opinion flatly rejected the contention that the TENTH AMENDMENT restricted the enumerated powers. That amendment, which provides that "the powers not delegated to the United States by the Constitution nor prohibited by it to the states are reserved to the states respectively or to the people," did not deprive the federal government of "authority to resort to all means for the exercise of a granted power which are appropriate and plainly adapted to the permitted end." "The amendment states but a truism that all is retained which has not been surrendered."

Darby was followed a year later by WICKARD V. FILBURN in which the Court alluded to the NECESSARY AND PROPER clause, which MCCULLOCH V. MARYLAND had emphasized, as the source of the power of Congress to regulate intrastate transactions. It also identified the cases which *Darby* had disapproved by implication, among others *Hammer*, *Schechter*, and *Carter*. *Darby* and *Wickard* together have provided the foundation for commerce clause interpretation thereafter. They firmly establish that the national economic system is subject to the control of the only entity that can possibly control it, the federal government.

ROBERT L. STERN

Bibliography

DODD, E. MERRICK 1946 The Supreme Court and Fair Labor Standards, 1941–1945. *Harvard Law Review* 59:321–375.

STERN, ROBERT L. 1946 The Commerce Clause and the National Economy, 1933–1946. *Harvard Law Review* 59:645–693, 883–947.

DARNEL'S CASE (FIVE KNIGHTS CASE)

See: Petition of Right

DARTMOUTH COLLEGE v. WOODWARD
4 Wheaton 518 (1819)

The most famous and influential CONTRACT CLAUSE case in our history, *Dartmouth College* was a boon to higher education and to corporate capitalism. The case established the DOCTRINE, never overruled, that a CORPORATION charter or the grant by a state of corporate rights to private interests comes within the protection of the contract clause. Although the case involved a small college in New Hampshire rather than a manufacturing concern, a bank, or a transportation company, the Court seized an opportunity to broaden the contract clause by making all private corporations its beneficiaries. DANIEL WEBSTER, counsel for the college, said that the judgment was a "defense of VESTED RIGHTS against Courts and Sovereignties," and his co-counsel, Joseph Hopkinson, asserted that it would "secure corporations . . . from legislative despotism. . . ." Corporations were still a recent innovation; JAMES KENT, in his *Commentaries on American Law* (1826), remarked that their rapid multiplication and the avidity with which they were sought by charter from the states arose as a result of the power that large, consolidated capital gave them over business of every sort. The Court's decision in the *Dartmouth College* case, Kent said, more than any other act proceeding from the authority of the United States, threw "an impregnable barrier around all rights and franchises derived from the grant of government; and [gave] solidity and inviolability to the literary, charitable, religious, and commercial institutions of our country." Actually, FLETCHER V. PECK (1810) had made the crucial and original extension of the contract clause, construing it to cover public and executed contracts as well as private executory ones. The *Dartmouth College* doctrine was a logical implication.

The college case was a strange vehicle for the doctrine that emerged from it. Dartmouth, having been chartered in 1769 in the name of the crown to christianize and educate Indians, had become a Christian college for whites and a stronghold of the Congregationalist Church, which had benefited most from the laws establishing the Protestant religion in New Hampshire. The college had become embroiled in state politics on the side of the Federalists, who supported the establishment. When in 1815 the trustees removed the president of the college, they loosed a controversy that drew to the ousted president a coalition of Jeffersonians and religious denominations demanding separation of church and state. The reformers having swept the state elections in 1816, the legislature sought to democratize the college by a series of statutes that converted it into a state university under public control, rather than a private college as provided by the original charter. The state supreme court sustained the state acts, reasoning that the institution had been established with public aid for public purposes of an educational and religious nature. The state court held that the contract clause did not limit the state's power over its own public corporations.

On APPEAL, the Supreme Court held that Dartmouth was a private eleemosynary corporation whose VESTED RIGHTS could not be divested without infringing a continuing obligation to respect inviolably the trustees' control of property given to the corporation for the advancement of its objectives. The Court held unconstitutional the state acts subjecting Dartmouth to state control and ordered Woodward, the treasurer of the institution who had sided with the state, to return to the trustees the records, corporate seal, and other corporate property which he held.

At every step of his opinion Chief Justice JOHN MARSHALL misstated the facts about the history of the original charter in order to prove that it established a purely private corporation. That, perhaps, was a matter primarily of interest to the college, which, contrary to Marshall, had received its charter not from George III but from the governor of the colony; moreover, the private donations, which Marshall said had been given to Dartmouth on condition of receiving the charter, had been given unconditionally to an entirely different institution, Moor's Charity School for Indians, and had been transferred to Dartmouth over the donors' objections. Also, the funds of the college, contrary to Marshall, did not consist "entirely of private donations," because the endowment of the college at the time of the issuance of the chapter derived mainly from grants of public lands. Even if the grant of the charter were a contract, as Marshall said it "plainly" was, Parliament could have repealed it at will. The Chief Justice conceded the fact but added that a repeal would have been morally perfidious. If, however, the charter were subject to revocation at the will of the sovereign authority, or the grantor, the "contract" did not bind that party and created no obligation that could be impaired.

Marshall conceded that at the time of Independence, the state suceeded to the power of Parliament and might have repealed or altered the charter at any time before the adoption of the Constitution. The provision in Article I, section 10, preventing states from impairing the obligation of a contract, altered the situation. That clause, Marshall conceded, was not specifically intended to protect charters of incorporation: "It is," he said boldly, "more than possible that the preservation of rights of this description was not particularly in the view of the framers of the constitution," but the clause admitted no exceptions as far as private rights were concerned. "It is not enough to say that this particular case was not in the mind of the convention when the article was framed, nor of the American people when it was adopted." In the absence of proof that the language of the Constitution would have been altered had charters of incorporation been considered, the case came within its injunction against state acts impairing the OBLIGATION OF CONTRACTS.

Although Marshall can be doubted when he said, "It can require no argument to prove that the circumstances of this case constitute a contract," his general doctrine, that any state charter for a private corporation is a constitutionally protected contract, was not far-fetched. The Court must construe the text, not the minds of its framers, and, as he said, "There is no exception in the constitution, no sentiment delivered by its contemporaneous expounders, which would justify us in making it." If a state granted a charter of incorporation to private interests, the charter has "every ingredient of a complete and legitimate contract," should it be made on a valuable consideration for the security and disposition of the property conveyed to the corporation for management by its trustees in perpetuity. Unless, as Justice JOSEPH STORY stressed in his concurring opinion, the government should reserve, in the grant of the charter, a power to alter, modify, or repeal, the rights vested cannot be divested, except by the consent of the incorporators, assuming they have not defaulted. Whether, however, a modification of the charter, as in this case, impairs an obligation, if the charter be executed and by its terms should not specify a term of years for the corporation's existence, is another question. In *Fletcher v. Peck,* however, the Court had brought executed as well as public contracts within the meaning of the contract clause. Marshall construed contract rights sweepingly, state powers narrowly.

Max Lerner's comment on the case, referring to Webster's peroration, is provocative. "Every schoolboy," he wrote, "knows Webster's eloquent plea and how Marshall, whom the Yazoo land scandals had left cold, found his own eyes suffused with tears, as Webster, overcome by the emotion of his words, wept. But few schoolboys know that the case had ultimately less to do with colleges than with business corporations; that sanctity of contract was invoked to give them immunity against legislative control, and that business enterprise in America never had more useful mercenaries than the tears Daniel Webster and John Marshall are reputed to have shed so devotedly that March day in Washington. . . ." In fact, the reserved power to alter or repeal, of which Story spoke, limited corporate immunity from legislative control. Moreover, the protection given by the Court to corporate charters came into play after the legislatures, not the Court, issued these charters, often recklessly and corruptly, without consideration of the public good; Marshall's opinion should have put the legislatures and the public on guard. Finally, the case had a great deal to do with higher education as well as business. *Dartmouth College* is the MAGNA CARTA of private colleges and universities, and, by putting them beyond state control, provided a powerful stimulus, not only to business corporations but also to the chartering of state institutions of higher learning. Unable to make private institutions public ones, the states established state universities.

LEONARD W. LEVY

Bibliography

BEVERIDGE, ALBERT J. 1916–1919 *The Life of John Marshall,* 4 vols. Vol. IV:220–281. Boston: Little, Brown.
HAINES, CHARLES GROVE 1944 *The Role of the Supreme Court in American Government and Politics, 1789–1835.* Pages 378–419. Berkeley: University of California Press.
SHIRLEY, JOHN M. (1879)1971 *The Dartmouth College Causes and the Supreme Court.* New York: Da Capo Press.
STITES, FRANCIS N. 1972 *Private Interest and Public Gain: The Dartmouth College Case, 1819.* Amherst: University of Massachusetts Press.

DAVIS, DAVID
(1815–1883)

David Davis's Supreme Court appointment in 1862 stemmed from his longtime legal and political association with ABRAHAM LINCOLN. Throughout the Civil War, Davis loyally supported the administration in the PRIZE CASES (1863) and EX PARTE VALLANDIGHAM (1864), but he opposed the president regarding emancipation and military trials of civilians. At one point, Davis urged Lincoln to withdraw the EMANCIPATION PROCLAMATION, believing that it would only increase southern resistance and border-state hostility toward the Union. The military trial issue, however, aroused Davis's unrelenting enmity and criticism. Appropriately, Davis delivered the Court's unanimous opinion in EX PARTE MILLIGAN in 1866, holding that civilian trials by presidentially created military commissions were unconstitutional. Davis, joined by the four Democrats on the bench, added that Congress could not authorize such commissions, provoking sharp dissent from Chief Justice SALMON P. CHASE and the other three Republicans.

Democrats and Southerners claimed that the subsequent Republican military reconstruction program was unconstitutional on the basis of *Milligan.* But Davis's opinion really offered little comfort on this point. While he found that the "laws and usages of war" could not apply where civil courts were open, he qualified this conclusion by specifying those "states which have upheld the authority of the government." In his private correspondence, Davis showed that he was disturbed by contemporary interpretations. He noted that there was "not a word said in the opinion about reconstruction, & the power is conceded in insurrectionary states."

Disenchanted with the Republicans, and equally wary of the Democrats, Davis castigated the partisan wrangling that characterized the Reconstruction period. He opposed suffrage for blacks, stating that "the thrusting on them [of] political rights is to their injury." He advocated the preservation of traditional state powers, and he expressed alarm "at the tendency to consolidated Govt manifested by the Republican party." Yet he believed that the military reconstruction program would have been avoided if the Democrats and the South had accepted the FOURTEENTH AMENDMENT. Davis displayed little inclination to have the judiciary thwart the Republican program, however. He was with the majority in TEXAS V. WHITE (1869). He also resisted the attempts of some colleagues to force a decision in EX PARTE McCARDLE

(1868) before Congress repealed the appropriate JU-RISDICTION legislation, thinking "it was unjudicial to run a race with Congress." Finally, he opposed a motion to challenge the Reconstruction Act on property rights grounds in *Mississippi v. Stanton* (1868).

Davis's sense of restraint characterized his votes in most of the other issues involving the Civil War and Reconstruction. Despite the libertarian concerns he had expressed in *Milligan*, he joined the dissenters who favored upholding both federal and state TEST OATHS. He also joined the dissenters who favored sustaining LEGAL TENDERS in *Hepburn v. Griswold* (1870) and then joined the new majority a year later when the decision was reversed. His political conservatism, combined with his notions of JUDICIAL RESTRAINT, best explains his adherence to the majority view in the SLAUGHTERHOUSE CASES (1873).

Davis's literal reading of the compact clause (Article I, section 10), however, led him to dissent in *Virginia v. West Virginia* (1871) when he denied the legality of West Virginia's annexation of two western Virginia counties during the Civil War. And in *Miller v. United States* (1871), a key case testing the CONFISCATION ACT of 1862, he supported the act's constitutionality but found reversible error. In a number of circuit rulings involving confiscation, his insistence on procedural fairness largely masked his distaste for the law.

In the Court's consideration of emerging economic questions in the 1870s, Davis again adopted rather traditional views on federalism and state prerogatives. He dissented, for example, in PHILADELPHIA & READING RAILROAD v. PENNSYLVANIA (the *State Freight Tax Case*, 1873), arguing that a state tax imposed on freight tonnage was simply a business tax and not an interference with INTERSTATE COMMERCE. In a long series of municipal bond cases in the 1860s and 1870s, Davis usually supported Justice SAMUEL F. MILLER's vigorous battle against the Court's attempts to provide bondholders protection from state taxation or repudiation. In his most notable statement on the issue, Davis dissented when the Court held that the interest of nonresident bondholders could not be taxed. In *State Tax on Foreign-Held Bonds* (1873), Davis relied on traditional state statutes requiring taxation of "all mortgages [and] money owned by solvent debtors." Such taxation, he said, did not impair any contractual obligations between creditors and those who issued bonds. A quarter-century later, Davis's views were adopted by a new majority.

Despite his prominence and reputation, Davis produced few noteworthy constitutional opinions beyond his contribution in *Milligan*. In truth, he was mis-

placed as a Supreme Court Justice. He preferred the involvement of political life or trial court work. Davis eagerly sought the presidency and he courted anti-Grant elements within the Republican party in 1872. He finally resigned in 1877 when the Illinois legislature elected him to the Senate. He eventually was elected President *pro tem*, prompting Chief Justice MORRISON R. WAITE, who deplored Davis's political ambitions, to remark that the position was "as near to the Presidency as he can get."

Davis himself offered the most candid and fitting estimate of his judicial career. "[A]s I never did like hard study, the work is not always agreeable," he wrote to his brother-in-law in 1870. "I believe I write the shortest opinions of any one on the bench, & if I had to elaborate opinions & write legal essays as some Judges do, I would quit the concern. I like to hold trial court, but this work on an appellate bench is too much like hard labor."

                                              STANLEY I. KUTLER

(SEE ALSO: *Constitutional History,* 1861–1865 and 1865–1877.)

DAVIS, JEFFERSON
(1808–1889)

A Mississippi planter, Jefferson Davis graduated from West Point, served with distinction in the Mexican War, and was a congressman (1845–1846), senator (1847–1851, 1857–1861) and secretary of war (1853–1857). In 1861 he reluctantly resigned from the Senate when Mississippi left the Union. Davis served as Confederate President (1861–1865) and at the end of the Civil War was indicted for TREASON and jailed but never tried because prosecutors were unsure they could legally convict him. Stripped of his CITIZENSHIP, Davis never returned to politics, but he did write a tedious and defensive two-volume history of SECESSION and his presidency, *The Rise and Fall of the Confederate Government* (1881).

Davis came to national political prominence with his opposition to the COMPROMISE OF 1850. He was one of ten senators who voted against California statehood. Davis supported only the 1850 Fugitive Slave Act, which he thought should be passed and enforced "as a right not to be estimated . . . by the value of the property, but for the principles involved." Unlike JOHN C. CALHOUN, with whom he usually agreed, Davis opposed a constitutional amendment to secure southern rights in all the TERRITORIES. Davis supported extending the MISSOURI COMPROMISE line to California.

After Calhoun's death Davis was the Senate's foremost supporter of southern rights and STATES' RIGHTS. He asserted that secession was constitutional because: the Constitution did not prohibit it nor provide power to coerce a state to remain in the Union; the national government was created by "the states," not "the people," and therefore the states could exist separately from the national government; and the Union "was in the nature of a partnership between individuals without limitation of time" and could be dissolved by the unilateral action of any of the parties.

Davis was ambivalent, however, on whether the theoretical right of secession should be implemented. He opposed secession at the NASHVILLE CONVENTION (1850), arguing that southern rights could be protected within the Union. In 1851 he unsuccessfully sought the Mississippi governorship on a "states' rights" ticket, but later in the decade he opposed states' rights parties because he thought southern interests could best be protected by alliances with sympathetic northern Democrats. In 1860 he attempted to mediate a compromise that would have taken John Bell, JOHN C. BRECKINRIDGE, and STEPHEN A. DOUGLAS out of the presidential contest, in favor of a single Democratic candidate. In 1858 he said publicly that if a Republican were elected "I should deem it your duty to provide for your safety outside the Union." In 1859 he said that the John Brown raid meant that loyalty to the Constitution required secession. Even so, after ABRAHAM LINCOLN's election Davis urged compromise, and served on the Committee of Thirty-Three. Only when this committee failed did he support secession.

Davis was ambivalent in other ways. He believed that blacks were inferior to whites, that congressional prohibition of the African slave trade was unconstitutional, and that the federal government should not interfere with slavery. Yet his plantation was a model, surpassed only by his brother's for treating blacks with compassion and for giving them a great deal of self-government. He opposed reopening the slave trade on moral grounds and in 1865 advocated emancipation to save the Confederacy. He saw secession as a conservative measure to protect the Constitution from tyranny by Lincoln and the national government. But as Confederate president, Davis implemented CONSCRIPTION, suspension of HABEAS CORPUS, and impressment of supplies. A lifelong states' rights man, Davis was vilified by politicians and governors as he sought, unsuccessfully, to create a Confederate national policy.

PAUL FINKELMAN

Bibliography

DODD, WILLIAM E. 1907 *Jefferson Davis.* Philadelphia: George Jacobs.
MCCARDELL, JOHN 1979 *The Idea of a Southern Nation.* New York: Norton.

DAVIS, JOHN W.
(1873–1955)

One of the nation's most celebrated lawyers, John William Davis served as SOLICITOR GENERAL under WOODROW WILSON, winning WILSON V. NEW (1917) and the SELECTIVE DRAFT LAW CASES (1918). In 1924 he was the Democratic candidate for President. He remained prominent at the Supreme Court bar, successfully challenging New Deal legislation, and in 1952 Davis attacked HARRY S. TRUMAN's seizure of the steel mills as a "usurpation" of power "without parallel in American history." (See YOUNGSTOWN SHEET AND TUBE COMPANY V. SAWYER, 1952.) He won that case but would lose his last one: *Briggs v. Elliott* (1954). Arguing this companion case to BROWN V. BOARD OF EDUCATION (1954), Davis dismissed arguments about SEGREGATION's psychological harm and urged the continued validity of the SEPARATE BUT EQUAL rule.

DAVID GORDON

DAVIS v. ALASKA

See: Compulsory Process

DAVIS v. BEASON
130 U.S. 333 (1890)

Davis involved an Idaho territorial statute directed at POLYGAMY. The law required voters to foreswear membership in any organization that "teaches, advocates, counsels or encourages" its members to undertake polygamous relationships. Davis was convicted of swearing falsely.

Justice STEPHEN J. FIELD, speaking for the Supreme Court, saw the case as identical to REYNOLDS V. UNITED STATES (1879). The free exercise clause of the FIRST AMENDMENT protected religious beliefs not acts that prejudiced the health, safety, or good order of society as defined by the legislature operating under its POLICE POWER. Field concluded that if something is a crime, then to teach, advise, or counsel it cannot be protected by evoking religious tenets.

The decision became one of the principal underpinnings of what later came to be called the "secular regulation" approach to the free exercise clause whereby no religious exemptions are required from otherwise valid secular regulations.

RICHARD E. MORGAN

DAVIS v. PASSMAN
442 U.S. 228 (1979)

Congressman Otto Passman fired Davis, a female member of his staff, because "it was essential that the [job] be [held by] a man." Such sex discrimination normally violates Title VII of the CIVIL RIGHTS ACT OF 1964 but Congress had exempted itself from that act's coverage. Davis therefore brought suit directly under the Constitution, alleging that sex discrimination by members of Congress violates the EQUAL PROTECTION guarantees contained in the Fifth Amendment. The Supreme Court, in an opinion by Justice WILLIAM J. BRENNAN and over four dissents, found that Davis had stated a cause of action. The Court extended its holding in BIVENS v. SIX UNKNOWN NAMED AGENTS OF THE FEDERAL BUREAU OF NARCOTICS (1971) to allow direct private damage actions under the Fifth Amendment. The majority did not discuss the SPEECH OR DEBATE CLAUSE's effect, if any, on the action.

THEODORE EISENBERG

DAVIS v. SCHNELL

See: Literacy Test

DAY, WILLIAM R.
(1849–1923)

William Rufus Day was named to the Supreme Court by THEODORE ROOSEVELT in 1903, after WILLIAM HOWARD TAFT had declined the nomination to remain at his post in the Philippines. Coincidentally, Day had replaced Taft on the Sixth Circuit Court of Appeals in 1899 when President WILLIAM MCKINLEY dispatched Taft to the Pacific outpost.

Day's tenure spanned the Progressive era. He generally favored the movement's interventionist thrust, particularly state regulatory actions. Day's decisions relating to federal power, however, were more am-

bivalent, as reflected by his famous opinion in HAMMER V. DAGENHART (1918), which invalidated a congressional attempt to regulate child labor premised on the COMMERCE CLAUSE. Unlike many STATES' RIGHTS advocates, he consistently supported state police regulations.

Justice Day faithfully followed the precedent of UNITED STATES V. E. C. KNIGHT COMPANY (1895), holding that Congress's INTERSTATE COMMERCE power did not extend to PRODUCTION. For example, in *Delaware, Lackawanna and Western Railroad Company v. Yurkonis* (1915) he declined to extend coverage of the federal EMPLOYERS LIABILITY ACT to coal miners even though the coal they produced eventually was used in interstate commerce. Three years later, in the child labor case, Day elaborated his conception of FEDERALISM with an expansive discussion of the TENTH AMENDMENT and its limitations on national power. He found that a congressional law prohibiting the interstate transportation of goods made by child labor unconstitutionally regulated production.

Generally, however, Day supported federal regulation of business. In *Atchison, Topeka and Santa Fe Railway Company v. Robinson* (1914), he wrote an opinion sustaining amendments to the HEPBURN ACT that greatly expanded federal JURISDICTION in railroad regulation, and in *Harriman v. Interstate Commerce Commission* (1908) he vigorously dissented from an opinion by Justice OLIVER WENDELL HOLMES that weakened the commission's SUBPOENA powers. Day also consistently sided with the government in antitrust suits. Soon after his appointment, he provided the decisive vote for the government in NORTHERN SECURITIES COMPANY V. UNITED STATES (1904). Although he acquiesced in the Court's RULE OF REASON doctrine in STANDARD OIL COMPANY V. UNITED STATES and UNITED STATES V. AMERICAN TOBACCO COMPANY (1911), Day expressed reservations toward the doctrine in a number of opinions that strongly supported the SHERMAN ACT. Finally, in UNITED STATES V. UNITED STATES STEEL CORPORATION (1920), he led the dissenters who hotly disputed the Court's approval of the corporation's control of most of the steel industry. Consistently acting as a principled foe of monopoly, Day advocated governmental intervention to destroy concentrated power and insure competition.

Despite Day's views in the child labor case, he supported the concept of a NATIONAL POLICE POWER based on the commerce clause. In *Pittsburgh Melting Company v. Totten* (1918) he sustained the Meat Inspection Act of 1906, and in HOKE V. UNITED STATES

(1913) he offered a classic defense of the police power to uphold the MANN ACT. Congress's control over commerce, he said, was "complete in itself," and Congress might adopt "not only means necessary but convenient to its exercise, and the means may have the quality of police considerations."

Similarly, Day upheld widespread uses of state police powers. He joined Justice JOHN MARSHALL HARLAN's dissent in LOCHNER V. NEW YORK (1905), and he supported the Court's approval of compulsory VACCINATION in JACOBSON V. MASSACHUSETTS (1905). Day consistently rejected the rigid FREEDOM OF CONTRACT dogma of *Lochner*. In *McLean v. Arkansas* (1909) he wrote to sustain state mining safety regulations and deferred to legislative prerogative: "The [state] legislature being familiar with local conditions is, primarily, the judge of the necessity of such enactments." Although the judiciary might have different views of social policy, Day insisted judges had no warrant to interfere. When the Court invalidated a state law prohibiting YELLOW DOG CONTRACTS in COPPAGE V. KANSAS (1915), Day protested against a literalist view of liberty of contract and, ignoring the *Lochner* precedent, he argued that "liberty of contract may be circumscribed in the interest of the State and the welfare of its people."

Day served on the Court until 1922. His opinions, though not memorable, were relatively free from rigid dogma. He contributed significantly to the Court's general approval of the expanded scope of governmental authority, federal and state. In the latter part of his career, that support extended to the prosecution of dissenters and radicals as he consistently sided with the government in the "Red Scare" cases. His 1918 child labor opinion unfortunately has served to obscure his more enduring contributions to constitutional law, such as his support for national regulatory power and an expanded state police power authority.

STANLEY I. KUTLER

Bibliography

MCLEAN, JOSEPH E. 1946 *William Rufus Day: Supreme Court Justice from Ohio.* Baltimore: Johns Hopkins University Press.

DAYTON, JONATHAN
(1760–1824)

Jonathan Dayton, the youngest signer of the Constitution, represented New Jersey at the CONSTITUTIONAL CONVENTION OF 1787. He spoke several times at the Convention in support of small-state positions. He was afterward speaker of the House of Representatives and a senator. In 1807 he was arrested for conspiring with AARON BURR but was not tried.

DENNIS J. MAHONEY

DAYTON BOARD OF EDUCATION v. BRINKMAN

See: *Columbus Board of Education v. Penick*

DAYTON-GOOSE CREEK RAILWAY COMPANY v. UNITED STATES
263 U.S. 456 (1924)

A unanimous Supreme Court here sustained the constitutionality of the recapture provision of the ESCH-CUMMINGS TRANSPORTATION ACT of 1920. The Dayton-Goose Creek Railway earned a return exceeding six percent of its property value, prompting the Interstate Commerce Commission to ask what arrangements it had made to contribute to the fund for which the act had provided. The railroad then sought an INJUNCTION against enforcement of the act, alleging the provision's unconstitutionality. Sixteen railroads, including some of the most powerful of the day, filed AMICUS CURIAE briefs.

Chief Justice WILLIAM HOWARD TAFT asserted that Congress's power over INTERSTATE COMMERCE was not limited to prescribing reasonable rates and voiding unjust ones. Its regulatory power was "intended . . . to foster, protect, and control the commerce with appropriate regard to the welfare of those who are immediately concerned, as well as the public at large, and to promote its growth and insure its safety." Because private railroads offered a public service, Congress might regulate them in order to assure performance of that function. After considering the necessity and justification for the recapture provisions, Taft concluded that the railroad's obligation to serve the public limits it to only "fair or reasonable profit." Reducing a carrier's income to what the Court deemed a FAIR RETURN did not constitute a TAKING OF PROPERTY without compensation because the act made the carrier only a trustee of any "excess." The government was entitled to appropriate that amount for "public uses because the appropriation takes away nothing which equitably belongs either to the shipper or to the carrier."

DAVID GORDON

DEAN MILK COMPANY v. CITY OF MADISON
340 U.S. 349 (1951)

A Madison, Wisconsin, city ordinance that prohibited the sale of milk pasteurized at a plant more than five miles outside city limits provided the basis for clarification of the limits on STATE REGULATION OF COMMERCE. A 6–3 Supreme Court invalidated the law as an "undue burden on INTERSTATE COMMERCE" because it effectively barred the sale of milk from firms in neighboring Illinois. Justice TOM C. CLARK also found a discrimination against outside producers which could not be sustained as an exercise of the state's POLICE POWER when "reasonable nondiscriminatory alternatives" were available, as here.

DAVID GORDON

DEATH PENALTY

See: Capital Punishment

DEBS, IN RE
158 U.S. 564 (1895)

Eugene V. Debs, head of the American Railway Union, petitioned for a writ of HABEAS CORPUS on the ground that he had been imprisoned illegally, for contempt of court, because of his defiance of an INJUNCTION issued by a United States CIRCUIT COURT. That draconian injunction, which became a model for subsequent injunctions in American labor disputes, sought to end the strike by Debs's union against railroads hauling Pullman sleeping cars. The Pullman Company and the managers association of twenty-four railroad CORPORATIONS, according to a later federal investigation, sought to crush the strike and the union rather than accept any peaceable solution. The managers jubilantly described the injunction as a "gatling gun on paper." It prohibited the strikers from attempting to obstruct the movement of mail or INTERSTATE COMMERCE by the struck railroads. It also forbade the use of "persuasion" aimed at preventing workers from doing their jobs.

Justice DAVID J. BREWER, speaking for a unanimous Supreme Court, delivered a breathtakingly broad opinion based not on any statutory authority for the injunction, but on general principles of national supremacy. "The strong arm of the national government," he declared, "may be put forth to brush away all obstructions to the freedom of INTERSTATE COMMERCE or the transportation of the mails. If the emergency arises, the army of the Nation, and all its militia, are at the service of the Nation to compel obedience to its laws." Similarly, Brewer added, the United States might invoke the power of its courts to remove obstructions by injunctions. Brewer's opinion transcended the particular injunction in this case; he failed to examine its terms, though it outlawed persuasion as well as force and assumed that the refusal to work for a railroad is an obstruction of commerce and the mails.

National supremacy, which the Court rendered nearly impotent to cope with obstructions to commerce caused by giant corporations, triumphed against the militant union. The union never recuperated from its defeat in this case and soon disintegrated. *Debs* taught that injunctions could be effective union-smashing devices. They became common afterward. The case also foreshadowed the use of the SHERMAN ANTITRUST ACT against unions. The circuit court had issued the injunction mainly on the ground that the strike was a combination in restraint of interstate commerce. The Supreme Court said that it did not dissent from that conclusion but preferred to rest its judgment on "broader ground."

LEONARD W. LEVY

Bibliography

LINDSEY, ALMONT 1942 *The Pullman Strike.* Chicago: University of Chicago Press.

DEBS v. UNITED STATES
249 U.S. 211 (1919)

During his long and controversial career as a labor leader and radical, Eugene V. Debs twice ran afoul of the federal government, which looked upon his activities as a threat to the nation's economic and political orthodoxy. In 1894 he was sentenced to six months' imprisonment for contempt of court as part of the GROVER CLEVELAND administration's efforts to crush the Pullman boycott in Chicago. In IN RE DEBS (1895) the United States Supreme Court affirmed this conviction and upheld the sweeping labor INJUNCTION which Debs and other leaders of the American Railway Union were alleged to have violated. Two decades later, as the leader of the American Socialist Party and one of the most visible critics of the WOODROW WILSON administration's decision to enter World War I, Debs again found himself in federal court, this time charged with violating the ESPIONAGE ACT of 1917.

Debs was tried and convicted on the basis of a speech he delivered at a socialist, antiwar rally in Canton, Ohio, for inciting insubordination, disloyalty, and mutiny in the armed forces and for obstructing military recruitment. In his oration, Debs praised other imprisoned leaders of the party who had been convicted for aiding and abetting resistance to the draft. In the course of his speech Debs also accused the government of using false testimony to convict another antiwar activist and he labeled the war as a plot by "the predatory capitalist in the United States" against the working class, "who furnish the corpses, having never yet had a voice in declaring war and . . . never yet had a voice in declaring peace." He told the audience that "you need to know that you are fit for something better than slavery and cannon fodder," and he ended by noting: "Don't worry about the charge of TREASON to your masters; but be concerned about the treason that involves yourselves." Debs was sentenced to ten years in prison.

When the *Debs* case reached the Supreme Court, a postwar "red scare" had descended on the nation. CRIMINAL CONSPIRACY trials of leaders of the Industrial Workers of the World were still underway. The Department of Justice had embarked on a large-scale program that would culminate in the PALMER RAIDS and the deportation of hundreds of ALIEN radicals.

Without even a reference to the CLEAR AND PRESENT DANGER test enunciated a week earlier, a unanimous Supreme Court affirmed Debs's conviction in an opinion written by Justice OLIVER WENDELL HOLMES. Although Holmes conceded that "the main theme" of Debs's speech had concerned socialism, its growth, and its eventual triumph, he argued that "if a part of the manifest intent of the more general utterance was to encourage those present to obstruct recruiting . . . the immunity of the general theme may not be enough to protect the speech." As Harry Kalven has remarked, "It is somewhat as though George McGovern had been sent to prison for his criticism of the [Vietnam] war." Holmes saw the case as a routine criminal appeal; in a letter to Sir Frederick Pollock, Holmes referred to the *Debs* case, saying, "there was a lot of jaw about free speech."

Debs remained in federal prison long after the armistice. Although a convicted felon, he received the Socialist Party nomination for President in 1920 and nearly a million votes. President Wilson, in failing health and embittered by the war and its critics, refused to pardon Debs before leaving the White House in 1921. His successor, the Republican conservative WARREN G. HARDING, displayed greater compassion by granting the socialist leader a pardon.

MICHAEL E. PARRISH

Bibliography
FREUND, ERNST 1919 The Debs Case and Freedom of Speech. *The New Republic*, May 3, 1919, p. 13. Reprinted in *University of Chicago Law Review* 40:239–42 (1973).

DECISION

A decision is the final determination by a competent tribunal of matters of law and fact submitted to it in a CASE OR CONTROVERSY. The decision is ordinarily in writing and comprises the JUDGMENT or decree in the case. The decision is not itself law, but only evidence of the law; and the value of a case as precedent derives less from the decision than from the reasoning behind the decision. The term "decision" is one of popular usage and not a technical legal term.

The Supreme Court reaches its decisions in CONFERENCE following the ORAL ARGUMENT of a case. A vote is taken after each Justice has had a chance to state his or her views. The decision is announced by means of a memorandum order or as part of a formal opinion.

In casual usage, the decision is often confounded with the OPINION OF THE COURT, a usage sanctioned by certain law dictionaries and a number of court opinions. In precise usage, however, the decision is the conclusion reached by the court, while the opinion is a statement of the reasoning by which the decision was reached. In the simplest terms, the decision answers the question: who won the case.

DENNIS J. MAHONEY

DECLARATION AND RESOLVES OF FIRST CONTINENTAL CONGRESS

See: First Continental Congress

DECLARATION OF INDEPENDENCE
1 Stat. 1 (July 4, 1776)

America's most fundamental constitutional document was adopted by the United States in Congress on July 4, 1776. The Declaration of Independence may carry little weight in the courts; it may, for all its being placed at the head of the *Statutes at Large* and described in the United States Code as part of the "organic law," have no legally binding force. Yet it is the Declaration that constitutes the American nation. JOHN HANCOCK, president of the Continental Congress, transmitting the Declaration to the several states, described it as "the Ground & Foundation of a future Government." JAMES MADISON, the Father of the Constitution, called it "the fundamental Act of Union of these States."

The Declaration of Independence is the definitive statement for the American policy of the ends of government, of the necessary conditions for the legitimate exercise of political power, and of the SOVEREIGNTY of the people who establish the government and, when circumstances warrant, may alter or abolish it. No mere tract in support of a bygone event, the Declaration was and remains the basic statement of the meaning of the United States as a political entity.

The historical event, the Revolution, provided the occasion for making that statement. RICHARD HENRY LEE, on instructions from the Virginia convention, introduced three resolutions on June 7, 1776: to declare the colonies independent, to establish a confederation, and to seek foreign alliances. Each of the resolutions was referred to a select committee, one of which was charged with preparing "a declaration to the effect of the first resolution." Lee's motion was adopted on July 2, the Declaration two days later.

Although the Congress had appointed for the task a distinguished committee, including JOHN ADAMS of Massachusetts, BENJAMIN FRANKLIN of Pennsylvania, ROGER SHERMAN of Connecticut, and ROBERT LIVINGSTON of New York, THOMAS JEFFERSON of Virginia actually penned the Declaration. So well did Jefferson express the sentiments of the Congress that his committee colleagues made only a few changes in his draft.

Jefferson, by his own account, turned to neither book nor pamphlet for ideas. Nor did he seek to expound a novel political theory. His aim was to set forth the common sense of the American people on the subject of political legitimacy. To be sure, there are ideas, and even phrases, that recall JOHN LOCKE: the Declaration follows Locke in stressing the NATURAL RIGHTS of man as the foundation of the political order. But the concept of man's natural autonomy, modifiable only by his consent to the rule of others in a SOCIAL COMPACT, was long acknowledged in the American colonies; it inhered in congregational church polity, and it was transmitted through such theoretical and legal writers as EMERICH DE VATTEL,

Jean-Jacques Burlamaqui, and Samuel Pufendorf, as well as by the authors of CATO'S LETTERS and other popular works.

The Declaration of Independence has a structure that emphasizes its content. It begins with a preamble, by which the document is addressed not to the king of Great Britain or to the English public, but to the world at large, to the "opinion of mankind." Moreover, the purpose of the document is said explicitly to be to "declare the causes" that impelled the Americans to declare their independence from Britain.

There had been other revolutions in British history, but this one was different. From the barons at Runnymede to the Whigs who drove James II from the throne, British insurgents had appealed to the historic rights of Englishmen. The declarations they extracted—from MAGNA CARTA to the BILL OF RIGHTS—were the assurances of their kings that the ancient laws obtaining in their island would be respected. The preamble of the Declaration of Independence makes clear that this is not the case with the American Revolution. The case of Britain's rule in America was to be held up to a universal standard and exposed as tyrannical before a "candid world." Against the selfsame standard all government everywhere could be measured. Everyone who reads the Declaration with his eyes open must be struck by this fact: the Declaration justifies the independence of the American nation by appeal not to an English or an Anglo-American standard, but to the universal standard of human rights.

There follows next a statement of the ends of government and of the conditions under which obedience to government is proper. "All men are created equal . . . endowed by their Creator with certain unalienable rights . . . among [which] are life, liberty, and the pursuit of happiness." Equality is the condition of men prior to government—logically prior, not chronologically. But that equality is not equality of condition, or even equality of opportunity; certainly it is not equality of intelligence, strength, or skill. The equality that men possess by nature is equality of *right*. There is, among human beings, none with a right to rule the others; God may claim to rule human beings by right, human beings may rule the brutes by right, but no human being has a claim to rule another by right.

The rights with which men are endowed are said to be "unalienable." That is, human rights may be neither usurped nor surrendered, neither taken away nor given up. The Declaration rejects the false doctrine of Thomas Hobbes (more gently echoed by WILLIAM BLACKSTONE) that men on entering society and submitting to government yield their natural rights and retain only "civil" rights, dispensed and revoked at the pleasure of the sovereign.

"To secure these rights, governments are instituted among men." The purpose of government is to protect the natural rights which men possess, but which, in the absence of government, they are not secure enough to enjoy. Government in society is not optional, it is a necessary condition for the enjoyment of natural rights. But the institution of government does not create an independent motive or will in society. All just powers of government derive "from the consent of the governed."

The Declaration asserts that the people retain the right of revolution, the right to substitute new constitutions for old. But it also asserts that the exercise of that right is properly governed by prudence—a prudence that the Americans had shown in the face of great provocation.

The next section of the Declaration is a bill of indictment against George III on the charge of attempted tyranny. The specifications are divided almost evenly between procedural and substantive offenses. The fact that the king—by his representatives in America—assembled the provincial legislatures at places far from their capitals or required persons accused of certain crimes to be transported to England for trial, evinced a tyrannical design by disregard of procedural safeguards. But even when the established procedures were followed, as in giving or withholding assent to legislation, the result could be tyrannical; for example, the suppression of trade, the discouragement of population growth, and the keeping of standing armies in peacetime were acts according to the forms of due process that unjustly deprived the Americans of their liberty. Still other acts, such as making the royal assent conditional on surrender of the right of representation and withholding assent from bills to create provincial courts, were tyrannical in both form and substance.

The most critical charge, the thirteenth, was that the king had conspired with others—the British Parliament—to subject the Americans to a JURISDICTION foreign to their constitution. The Americans had come to see that a compact existed between the British king and each of his American provinces by which the king exercised executive power in each even as he did in the home island, and that the common executive was the sole governmental connection between America and Britain. The imperial constitution, as the Americans had come to understand it, no more permitted the British legislature to regulate the internal affairs of Massachusetts or Virginia than it did the provincial legislatures to regulate the internal affairs of England or Scotland. But the British legislature could not breach the compact between the king and the provinces because Parliament was not a party to that compact. The king, however, by conniving at that usurpation, did breach the compact.

The final five accusations deal with the fact that Britain and America were at war. One charge that Jefferson included, but Congress struck out, accused the king of waging "cruel war against human nature itself" by tolerating the introduction of SLAVERY into the colonies and sanctioning the slave trade. Only two states, Georgia and South Carolina, objected to the passage, but the others acquiesced to preserve unanimity. In any case, the condemnation of slavery was implicit in the opening paragraphs of the Declaration.

The conclusion of the document asserts that the Americans had tried peaceably to resolve their differences with the mother country while remaining within the empire, and in a final paragraph contains the actual declaration that the erstwhile colonies were now independent states.

Whether the colonies became independent collectively or individually was a matter of debate for at least a hundred years. At the CONSTITUTIONAL CONVENTION OF 1787, JAMES WILSON and ALEXANDER HAMILTON advanced the former position, while LUTHER MARTIN maintained the latter position. At least until the Civil War, different THEORIES OF THE UNION arose based on differing interpretations of the act of declaring independence.

Considered as a tract for the times, as a manifesto for the Revolutionary cause, the Declaration marks an important step in American constitutional development. The resistance to British misrule in America had, at least since the French and Indian Wars, been based on an appeal to the British constitution. The Americans had charged that the imposition of taxes by a body in which they were not represented and the extension to them of domestic LEGISLATION by a Parliament to whose authority they had not consented violated the ancient traditions of British government. The constitution, that is, the arrangement of offices and powers within the government and the privileges of the subjects, had been overridden or altered by the British Parliament. Although the differences between the American provinces and the mother country were great, they were differences about, and capable of resolution within, the British constitutional framework. The liberties that the colonists had claimed were based on prescription.

When independence was declared, the British constitution became irrelevant. The liberties claimed in the Declaration are grounded in natural law; they are justified by reason, not by historical use. The American Revolution was, therefore, the first and most revolutionary of modern revolutions. Not the quantity of carnage but the quality of ideas distinguishes the true revolution. In the Declaration was recognized a HIGHER LAW to which every human law—constitution or statute—is answerable. The British constitution, as it then existed, was tried by the standards of that higher law and found guilty of tyranny. As the British constitution, so every constitution, including the American Constitution, may be tried; and on conviction the sentence is that the bonds of allegiance are dissolved.

Much of American constitutional history has revolved around the attempt to reconcile the nation's political practice with the teachings of the Declaration. The gravest problem in our constitutional history was SLAVERY. Although the Congress struck out Jefferson's condemnation of slavery as "cruel war against human nature," the founders clearly understood that slavery was incompatible with the principles of liberty and equality that they espoused.

Chief Justice ROGER B. TANEY, in DRED SCOTT V. SANDFORD (1857), tried to read the black man out of the Declaration. But this was a distortion of the history and the plain meaning of the document. Even JOHN C. CALHOUN had not stooped to this, choosing rather to denounce the Declaration than to pervert its meaning. The antithesis between the Declaration and the existence of chattel slavery was recognized by the slave power in Congress when, during the gag rule controversy, any petition referring to the Declaration of Independence was automatically treated as a petition against slavery and laid on the table.

The intimate connection between the Declaration of Independence (and therefore of antislavery) and the Constitution became the theme of the political career of ABRAHAM LINCOLN. When the slavery question divided the nation, Lincoln, with the voice of an Old Testament prophet, called for rededication to the principles of the Declaration. During Lincoln's presidency, the Civil War, begun as a challenge to the Union, was won as a struggle to vindicate the Declaration of Independence. It was fought to prove that a nation "dedicated to the proposition that all men are created equal" could endure.

The putative antagonism between America's two basic documents, invented by the slave power in the nineteenth century, was revived as a political theme during the Progressive movement. Authors like J. ALLEN SMITH and CHARLES A. BEARD contended that the Constitution's system of FEDERALISM, SEPARATION OF POWERS, CHECKS AND BALANCES, and BICAMERALISM frustrated the unfettered will of the people allegedly set free by the Declaration. Smith and Beard posited a virtually bloodless coup d'état by wealthy conservatives—a "Thermidorian reaction" to the success of the democratic revolution. Thus constitutional forms were attacked as illegitimate, notwithstanding that they were intended to preserve the Declaration's regime of LIMITED GOVERNMENT.

The Beard-Smith thesis remained popular as long as the Constitution seemed to be a barrier to social reform and redistribution of wealth and income by the government. The later twentieth century, however, witnessed another change in the attitude of intellectuals toward the two documents. President FRANKLIN D. ROOSEVELT appointed a sufficient number of Supreme Court Justices to insure that the Court would ratify his policies as constitutional. Later, the WARREN COURT devised a host of new "constitutional" rights and remedies for criminal defendants, ethnic minorities, and political dissenters. The Constitution was transformed into a "living" document, that is, one almost infinitely malleable in the hands of enlightened judges. History, understood as progress, rather than nature thereafter dictated the ends of government. The Declaration of Independence, with its references to "the laws of nature and of nature's God," although revered as a symbol of American nationality, ceased to be regarded as the source of authoritative guidance for American politics.

The Constitution of the United States is sometimes pronounced, by scholars or politicians, to be neutral with respect to political principles. But the Constitution was not framed in a vacuum. It was devised as the Constitution of the nation founded by the Declaration of Independence. The Declaration prescribes the ends and limits of government, and proclaims the illegitimacy of any government that fails to serve those ends or observe those limits. The Constitution is thus ruled by the Declaration. The Constitution provides for the government of the regime created by the Declaration: the regime of equality and liberty.

DENNIS J. MAHONEY

Bibliography

BECKER, CARL L. 1922 *The Declaration of Independence.* Cambridge, Mass.: Harvard University Press.

DIAMOND, MARTIN 1975 The Declaration and the Constitution: Liberty, Democracy and the Founders. *The Public Interest* 42:39–55.

HAWKE, DAVID 1964 *A Transaction of Free Men: The Birth and Course of the Declaration of Independence.* New York: Scribner's.

JAFFA, HARRY V. 1959 The Universal Meaning of the Declaration of Independence. Chap. 14 of *The Crisis of the House Divided.* New York: Doubleday.

WHITE, MORTON 1978 *The Philosophy of the American Revolution.* New York: Oxford University Press.

DECLARATION OF WAR

The Constitution gives Congress the power "to declare War . . ." (Article I, section 8, clause 11). There is no explicit provision for any other exercise by the United States of its sovereign power to make war, although the President is made "COMMANDER IN CHIEF of the Army and Navy of the United States . . ." (Article II, section 2). But the draftsmen were certainly familiar with the concept of undeclared war, usually with limited purposes and theaters of operation, such as the French and Indian War of 1754–1756 and the opening campaign of the Seven Years War between England and France, in which GEORGE WASHINGTON had fought as a lieutenant colonel. Indeed, ALEXANDER HAMILTON observed that "the ceremony of a formal denunciation [*i.e.,* declaration] of war has of late fallen into disuse" (THE FEDERALIST #25). Whether the Framers intended to give Congress the paramount power to wage war against other sovereigns is a question that has ever since been debated but not formally resolved. The problem had not, of course, arisen under the ARTICLES OF CONFEDERATION, when all federal (or confederate) power was vested in the Continental Congress. The records of the CONSTITUTIONAL CONVENTION furnish no clear answer. The draft submitted by the Committee on Detail on August 6, 1787, gave Congress the power "to make war." When it was considered eleven days later, on motion by ELBRIDGE GERRY and JAMES MADISON, "make" was changed to "declare." The brief debate gives no indication of any effect the change was intended to have on the allocation of warmaking power between President and Congress. For what it is worth, some years later Hamilton expressed the view that making war was essentially an executive function, while Madison thought the power belonged primarily to Congress.

Whatever the Framers may have intended, the practice has clearly been in accord with the Hamiltonian view. The United States has fought only five declared wars (the War of 1812, the Mexican War, the Spanish War, and World Wars I and II), but the President has committed the armed forces to combat on more than 150 other occasions, from JOHN ADAMS's undeclared naval war with France in 1798–1799 to the KOREAN WAR and the VIETNAM WAR. (See also POLICE ACTION; STATE OF WAR.) The Civil War was, of course, undeclared, since a declaration would have constituted a recognition of Confederate SOVEREIGNTY, but it was treated as war for the purposes of international law. (See PRIZE CASES, 1863.) As a practical matter, whether a formal declaration of war adds much to the power of the President is doubtful, so long as Congress furnishes the necessary men and money. Thus, during the Vietnam War the lower federal courts held that Congress, by supplying troops and arms, made the President's actions constitutional; and the Supreme Court let their decisions stand. (See MASSACHUSETTS V. LAIRD, 1971.)

Congress has occasionally attempted to assert its primacy in war, but without much success. In 1896, when a group of congressmen proposed to declare war on Spain, GROVER CLEVELAND scotched the project by informing them that as Commander in Chief he had no intention of using the Army and Navy for any such purpose. The WAR POWERS RESOLUTION of 1973, enacted over President RICHARD M. NIXON's veto, provides in substance that before the President can commit the armed forces to actual or potential combat he must first "consult" with Congress and must withdraw the forces within ninety days unless Congress declares war or provides "specific authorization" for their continued employment.

Scholars disagree on the constitutionality of the War Powers Resolution. In any case, it seems unlikely to have much practical effect, as President GERALD R. FORD demonstrated in 1975 when he immediately, and with a minimum of "consultation," used the armed forces to rescue an American vessel, the *Mayaguez,* and its crew, who had been seized by the communist regime in Cambodia. History suggests that it will be politically very difficult for Congress to deny support when the troops are actually fighting. If there is any historical difference between wars declared by Congress and other wars, it seems to be that the former have usually been larger in scale and have had as their goal not some more or less limited objective, such as rescuing American citizens or defending an ally from attack, but the total defeat of the enemy.

JOSEPH W. BISHOP, JR.

Bibliography

CRUDEN, JOHN C. 1975 The War-Making Process. *Military Law Review* 69:35–143.

LOFGREN, CHARLES A. 1972 War-Making Power under the Constitution: The Original Understanding. *Yale Law Journal* 81:672–702.

ROSTOW, EUGENE V. 1972 Great Cases Make Bad Laws: The War Powers Act. *Texas Law Review* 50:833–900.

DECLARATORY JUDGMENT

Until the beginning of the twentieth century, most American courts would entertain lawsuits only when plaintiffs sought redress for harm already suffered or imminently threatened. Except in certain real property actions, the plaintiff was not deemed harmed simply because uncertainty about his or her legal rights made potentially beneficial conduct too risky to undertake. For example, if a manufacturer were uncertain about whether a new product would infringe another's patent, or a would-be demonstrator were uncertain whether the planned demonstration was protected under the FIRST AMENDMENT, the only choices were to refrain from acting or to proceed and wait to be sued or prosecuted.

The declaratory judgment is a judicial remedy that allows the uncertain individual instead to file suit, asking a court to determine the legal rights in question. It reflects the view, long accepted in land title law, that paralysis due to uncertainty is real harm that courts should alleviate.

Over the first decades of the twentieth century, the states and the federal government adopted this remedy by statute. Declaratory judgments came into use not only to eliminate uncertainty but also to provide a similar but less coercive remedy to individuals eligible for injunctive relief.

Under Article III, the life-tenured federal judiciary may not give ADVISORY OPINIONS but may hear only real disputes between adverse, concretely interested parties. Because declaratory judgments are typically sought in advance of liability-causing conduct, there were early doubts that declaratory judgment actions would satisfy this requirement, known as RIPENESS. To allay this concern, the drafters of the federal declaratory judgment statute limited the remedy to "case[s] of actual controversy within [the courts'] JURISDICTION."

The Supreme Court held in *Perez v. Ledesma* (1971) that, for reasons of comity, a person being prosecuted in a state court for violation of a state criminal law may not seek a declaratory judgment in a federal court that the law is unconstitutional. Prior to a state prosecution, however, an individual may obtain a federal declaration of constitutional rights. That individual may have to flirt so dangerously with actual prosecution in order to satisfy the ripeness requirement, however, that the declaratory judgment may not be able to perform its salutary function of encouraging constitutionally protected conduct.

The plaintiff in a declaratory judgment action is frequently the person who would be a defendant in a more traditional lawsuit, and the elements of a complaint for declaratory relief often differ from those of a more traditional complaint. In applying legal doctrines that antedated the declaratory remedy to this new form of litigation, courts sometimes require that the suit be transposed to what it would have been had the declaratory remedy not existed. Thus, in determining whether the right to TRIAL BY JURY exists in a suit for a declaratory judgment, the courts must ascertain whether the claim could have been filed as an action at COMMON LAW had the declaratory judgment not been invented. Similarly, in determining whether a suit arises under federal law within the meaning of the FEDERAL QUESTION statute, the courts must ascertain whether the federal element would have appeared in the plaintiff's *prima facie* case had the suit been brought for a conventional remedy. Unfortunately, there is not always only one conventional alternative to a given declaratory judgment action, and this cumbersome transposition process has been difficult to administer.

CAROLE E. GOLDBERG-AMBROSE

Bibliography

NOTE 1949 Developments in the Law: Declaratory Judgments, 1941–1949. *Harvard Law Review* 62:787–885.

DE FACTO/DE JURE

De facto and de jure are old COMMON LAW terms meaning, respectively, "in fact" and "in law." In older usage, de facto carried at least a hint of reference to illegitimacy or illegality. Thus, a usurper might be called a de facto king, or a corporation whose formation was irregular might be called a de facto corporation. As these examples suggest, the connotation often was that for some legal purposes the person or institution would be treated *as if* there were no irregularity. De jure, on the other hand, carried a suggestion of lawfulness or rightfulness.

In modern constitutional law, these terms have come to be used almost exclusively in the context of racial SEGREGATION, and particularly segregation in the public schools. In this context the connotations concerning lawfulness are reversed. De jure segregation refers to the separation of pupils by race resulting from deliberate action by state officials, such as the legislature or the school board. De facto segregation refers to the racial separation of pupils by other causes, and particularly through the adoption of the "neighborhood school" policy in a community characterized by residential separation of the races. The Supreme Court has held that only de jure segregation violates the Constitution. (See COLUMBUS BOARD OF EDUCATION V. PENICK, 1979; DAYTON BOARD OF EDUCATION V. BRINKMAN, 1977–1979.)

There is some artificiality in this distinction. When a school board's members are aware of racial patterns in residential neighborhoods, and they draw school attendance district lines in ways that do not minimize the racial separation of pupils, it would not do violence to the language to call the results of their action de jure segregation. Yet the courts tend not to "find" the "fact" of de jure segregation in this circumstance.

On the other hand, deliberately segregative actions of the school board in the rather distant past may be held to constitute de jure segregation, so that the school board remains under a continuing obligation to dismantle a "dual" (segregated) system by taking affirmative remedial action, such as the busing of children. The *Columbus* and *Dayton* cases, cited above, exemplify this line of reasoning.

KENNETH L. KARST

(SEE ALSO: *Swann v. Charlotte-Mecklenburg Board of Education*, 1971; *Keyes v. School District No. 1*, 1973; *School Busing*.)

Bibliography

SEDLER, ROBERT ALAN 1979–1980 The Constitution and School Desegregation: An Inquiry into the Nature of the Substantive Right. *Kentucky Law Journal* 68:879–969.

DEFAMATION

See: Libel and the First Amendment

DEFUNIS v. ODEGAARD
416 U.S. 312 (1974)

DeFunis challenged the constitutionality of the University of Washington law school's use of racial preferences in admitting students. The case was expected to be a decisive test for AFFIRMATIVE ACTION programs in higher education. Instead, by a 5–4 vote, the Supreme Court held that the case was moot, be-

cause the law school would graduate DeFunis at the end of the current term, however the case might be decided. Cynics, remembering how the Court had recently dealt with the argument of MOOTNESS in ROE V. WADE (1973), suggested that the majority had been readier to reach the merits of the ABORTION issue in *Roe* than it was to face the problem presented by *DeFunis.*

Justice WILLIAM O. DOUGLAS, who thought the case was not moot, wrote an opinion on the merits. He concluded that the law school had denied DeFunis, a nonminority applicant, the EQUAL PROTECTION OF THE LAWS by awarding a preference solely on the basis of race. Justice Douglas commented that minority applicants should be evaluated specially to avoid cultural bias in admissions, but he did not explain how a school could evaluate minority applicants separately without devising a scale to measure them against other applicants. Such a scale would necessarily involve setting goals for minority representation. *DeFunis* was Justice Douglas's last chance to speak to these issues, which returned to the Court in REGENTS OF UNIVERSITY OF CALIFORNIA V. BAKKE (1978), after his retirement.

KENNETH L. KARST

DE JONGE v. OREGON
299 U.S. 353 (1937)

The Oregon Criminal Syndicalism Law was declared unconstitutional as applied to a person who conducted a meeting of the Communist party at which "neither CRIMINAL SYNDICALISM nor any unlawful conduct was taught or advocated." The Supreme Court held that peaceful speech at a peaceful, open meeting could not be punished constitutionally simply because of party sponsorship even if it were assumed that the party advocated violent overthrow of government. "Peaceable assembly for lawful discussion," declared Chief Justice CHARLES EVANS HUGHES for an 8–0 Court, "cannot be made a crime."

This is one of the early cases "incorporating" the FREEDOM OF SPEECH and FREEDOM OF ASSEMBLY provisions of the FIRST AMENDMENT into the DUE PROCESS clause of the Fourteenth Amendment, thus making them binding on the states. Unlike many other speech cases of the 1920s and 1930s, *De Jonge* rests firmly on freedom of speech rather than on collateral due process grounds such as VAGUENESS. It also foreshadows later, not altogether successful, attempts by the Court to distinguish between those Communist party members and activities devoted to constitutionally protected advocacy and those implicated in incitement to revolutionary violence.

MARTIN SHAPIRO

DELEGATION OF POWER

Early in American constitutional history the Supreme Court announced a rule that Congress could not delegate its power to the President or others. Yet the practical demands of an increasingly complex governmental environment have forced Congress to delegate, often quite broadly. The Court has rationalized all but a few delegations without abandoning the rule of nondelegation. This has been accomplished through successively more permissive formulations of the rule. Though the rule is in a state of desuetude, some revival is possible in the aftermath of the Court's invalidation of a LEGISLATIVE VETO in IMMIGRATION AND NATURALIZATION SERVICE V. CHADHA (1983).

A few commentators call the rule against delegations a judge-made doctrine lacking genuine constitutional status. This suggests the untenable proposition that genuine rules of constitutional law must be explicit in the constitutional document. Building on a COMMON LAW maxim against redelegation of delegated authority and on JOHN LOCKE's observation that only the sovereign people can determine the legitimate location of legislative authority, most commentators have found nondelegation implicit in the SEPARATION OF POWERS and in concepts of representative government and DUE PROCESS OF LAW. The status of the rule thus secured, debate has concentrated on exactly what it prohibits.

As if the rule prohibited all delegations, nineteenth-century judges tried to reconcile it with the practical needs of government by denying that delegations in fact were delegations in law. In *The Brig Aurora* (1813) the Supreme Court held that Congress had not breached the rule by empowering the President to make factual finding on which the application of a previously declared congressional policy—an embargo—was contingent. In *Wayman v. Southard* (1825) the Court permitted a delegation to federal judges for "filling up the details" of part of the Federal Process Act of 1792. Though the rules announced in these cases were modest when stated in the abstract, the delegations themselves were the objects of acrimonious political conflict. By the early 1900s, power to declare facts and fill up details had become the foundation for the delegation of such discretionary authority to the President and administrative agencies as power to decide which grades of tea to exclude from import, to make rules regulating grazing on lands in national forests, and even to vary tariffs on imported goods.

In J. W. HAMPTON & COMPANY V. UNITED STATES (1928) the Court formulated a more realistic delegation doctrine when it acknowledged that transfers of discretionary authority were essential to the effectiveness of Congress's will in modern conditions. The new rule was that congressional delegation is permissible if governed by adequate "legislative standards," a term that now includes statutory specifications of facts to be declared, preambulatory statements of legislative purpose, and even judicial imputations of legislative purpose inferred from legislative and administrative history.

The Court has rarely taken the standards requirement seriously. Illustrative of a pattern that prevails to the present, *Federal Radio Commission v. Nelson Brothers* (1933) found adequate guidance for issuing radio station licenses in what Congress called the "public convenience, interest, and necessity." This pattern was interrupted when the Court unexpectedly used the delegation doctrine against the NATIONAL INDUSTRIAL RECOVERY ACT (1933) in PANAMA REFINING COMPANY V. RYAN (1935) and SCHECHTER POULTRY CORPORATION V. UNITED STATES (1935). But the spirit of these decisions was not to survive, and by the middle of World War II the Court had returned to using the delegation doctrine more for rationalizing than for limiting transfers of congressional power.

As if delegations were not broad enough, the Court in *United States v. Mazurie* (1975) suggested an even more permissive approach. UNITED STATES V. CURTISS-WRIGHT EXPORT CORPORATION (1936) had seemed to hold that because the President had independent powers in the field of FOREIGN AFFAIRS, the standards requirement for congressional delegations to the President could be relaxed in that area. At a time when *Panama* and *Schechter* had recently limited the scope of delegated power, *Curtiss-Wright* was a reasonable move toward flexibility in foreign affairs. But *Curtiss-Wright* featured an unorthodox theory of extraconstitutional or inherent governmental power, and the need for a special approach to foreign affairs delegations disappeared as the Court returned to its old permissiveness toward delegations generally. During the VIETNAM WAR, however, the nondelegation doctrine was raised in opposition to American policy, and, although the Court successfully avoided the issue, government lawyers invoked *Curtiss-*

Wright before congressional committees. One of these lawyers was WILLIAM H. REHNQUIST, who later led the Court to its first reaffirmation of *Curtiss-Wright*'s delegation doctrine in *Mazurie,* a relatively noncontroversial case involving a delegation to the tribal council of an American Indian tribe over liquor sales on a reservation. The tribe's council, said Justice Rehnquist, had "independent authority over tribal life," just as the President had over foreign affairs, and *Curtiss-Wright* was cited for a new rule that the standards requirement is "less stringent in cases where the entity exercising the delegated authority itself possesses independent authority over the subject matter." In light of what "less stringent" can mean today, *Mazurie* has a potential for rationalizing virtual abdications of congressional responsibility, not only to the President but to the states, whose legal claims to "independent authority" are stronger than that of Indian tribal councils.

Since the 1930s and with accelerated frequency after the Vietnam War, Congress used the legislative veto to recapture power lost through broad delegations. To the extent—perhaps modest—that regulatory and political conditions permit, Congress may choose to delegate more narrowly now that the legislative veto is unavailable. And if the Court really has renewed its commitment to the separation of powers, it may honor the standards requirement with something more than mere lip service.

SOTIRIOS A. BARBER

Bibliography

BARBER, SOTIRIOS A. 1975 *The Constitution and the Delegation of Congressional Power.* Chicago: University of Chicago Press.

DAVIS, KENNETH C. 1958 *Administrative Law Treatise.* St. Paul, Minn.: West Publishing Co.

DELIBERATE SPEED

See: All Deliberate Speed

DELIMA v. BIDWELL

See: Insular Cases

DEMEANOR EVIDENCE

See: Confrontation, Right of

DE MINIMIS NON CURAT LEX

(Latin: "The law does not concern itself with trifles.") It is a maxim of the COMMON LAW that the courts will not intervene in disputes where the substance of the controversy is insignificant. For example, a court will not hear a case that turns on an amount less than a dollar or a time period shorter than a day.

DAVID GORDON

(SEE ALSO: *Cases and Controversies.*)

DEMONSTRATION

The FIRST AMENDMENT guarantees the right of persons to congregate peaceably in large numbers in appropriate public spaces in order to communicate ideas or grievances. In *Edwards v. South Carolina* (1963) the Court described an assemblage of 187 protesters on the grounds of a state capitol as "an exercise of . . . basic constitutional rights in their most pristine and classic form." Mass demonstrations cannot be prohibited simply on account of their size or their need to occupy public land.

Constitutional litigation over demonstrations tends to focus on three issues. First is the question of what public spaces must be made available to demonstrators. By virtue of the number of persons involved, mass demonstrations can be disruptive of other activities even when the demonstrators remain peaceable and orderly. When must those other activities give way to the First Amendment claims of persons who wish to engage in a mass demonstration?

The Supreme Court has never given a definitive and comprehensive answer to that question, and probably never could. The Court has indicated, however, that demonstrations in PUBLIC FORUMS such as streets, sidewalks, and parks cannot be subjected to a blanket prohibition. On the other hand, the Court has upheld regulations that entirely prohibited demonstrations in a jailyard and in areas of a military base otherwise open to the public.

Second, the issue has arisen whether a demonstration can be prohibited or postponed on the ground that audience hostility to the demonstrators threatens to produce a BREACH OF THE PEACE. The Court has inveighed against any such "heckler's veto" in OBITER DICTUM, and has reversed disorderly conduct convictions of speakers who continued their orderly protests in the face of potentially threatening crowds. In language quoted many times in the United States Reports, the Court stated in TERMINIELLO V. CHICAGO (1949):

[A] function of free speech under our system of government is to invite dispute. It may indeed best serve its high purpose when it induces a condition of unrest, creates dissatisfaction with conditions as they are, or even stirs people to anger. Speech is often provocative and challenging. It may strike at prejudices and preconceptions and have profound unsettling effects as it presses for acceptance of an idea. That is why freedom of speech . . . is . . . protected against censorship or punishment, unless shown likely to produce a clear and present danger of a serious substantive evil that rises far above public inconvenience, annoyance, or unrest.

Despite strong dicta and case outcomes favorable to speakers, it cannot be said with assurance that a hostile audience can in no circumstances provide a basis for disallowing a demonstration. The Court has yet to decide a case in which the regulatory authority was confined by a narrowly drawn statute and the police could not contain the HOSTILE AUDIENCE by the exercise of due diligence. There is also the unresolved question of whether demonstrators who wish to proceed in the face of a hostile audience have a First Amendment right to do so on repeated occasions, or whether at some point the mounting costs of police protection for the demonstrators might justify a prohibition on the continuation of their expressive activity.

A third set of issues that arise frequently in disputes over demonstrations concerns the doctrine of prior restraint. Demonstrators who wish to assemble in large numbers can be required to obtain permits in advance, despite the general presumption in First Amendment law against licensing. Officials who administer permit systems for marches and rallies are required to rule upon permit requests expeditiously, and to validate denials in court on a strict timetable. Thus, administrative delay is not permitted to serve as an indirect means of prohibiting mass demonstrations. If a permit request is under administrative or judicial consideration by the time a demonstration is scheduled to take place, the demonstrators may be permitted to proceed without a permit and defend against a prosecution on the ground that they exhausted all channels of prior approval and were entitled under the First Amendment to have their permit request granted. However, demonstrators who do not both apply for a permit and pursue all channels of appeal may be prosecuted for holding a march or rally without a permit, despite the fact that had they applied for a permit they would have been entitled under the Constitution to have it issued.

A fourth issue concerning demonstrations that has not generated a great deal of litigation to date but could do so in the future is whether persons who engage in mass demonstrations can be made to pay the costs of municipal services that attend the event. The Court has indicated in dictum that reasonable costs for such services as clean-up, police protection, and the provision of toilets can be assessed against the demonstrators. However, such assessments can be quite large for major events and can be used as a means of discouraging demonstrations. This issue of cost assessment was important in the litigations during the 1970s over the proposed march of American Nazis in the predominantly Jewish community of Skokie, Illinois, and could emerge as a focus of controversy in other cases.

VINCENT BLASI

Bibliography
BAKER, C. EDWIN 1983 Unreasoned Reasonableness: Mandatory Parade Permits and Time, Place, and Manner Regulations. *Northwestern University Law Review* 78:937–1024.
BOLLINGER, LEE C. 1982 The Skokie Legacy: Reflections on an "Easy Case" and Free Speech Theory. *Michigan Law Review* 80:617–633.

DENATURALIZATION

American CITIZENSHIP can be lost in two ways: denaturalization and EXPATRIATION. Denaturalization is the official cancellation, for cause, of a certificate of naturalization. It can be employed only against a person who has secured his citizenship by NATURALIZATION. Once denaturalized, a person is again an ALIEN in the eyes of the law; unlike the expatriate, he is considered never to have been a citizen. As an alien, the denaturalized former citizen is vulnerable to DEPORTATION and, in the case of a denaturalized criminal, to extradition.

Denaturalization, like naturalization, is governed by statute—currently, the Immigration and Nationality Act of 1952. Congress derives the implied power to denaturalize from its express power set forth in Article I, section 8, to "establish a uniform Rule of Naturalization." Congress has provided for denaturalization when a person's citizenship has been "illegally procured" or "procured by concealment of a material fact or by willful misrepresentation."

Denaturalization has been employed against naturalized citizens because of their membership in communist, Nazi, or other organizations espousing doctrines deemed antithetical to American allegiance. In such cases, the ground for denaturalization is that citizenship has been illegally procured because the applicant failed to comply with the statutory condition that he be attached to the principles of the American Constitution for the five years immediately preceding his naturalization. Also under the act, membership in such an organization within five years of naturalization is "prima facie evidence" of a lack of attachment prior to naturalization.

Denaturalization has also been employed against criminals and racketeers (thereby rendering them subject to deportation), on the ground that they obtained their American citizenship by lying about their criminal past. In such a case, even though the courts have held that denaturalization proceedings are suits in EQUITY and are governed by the FEDERAL RULES OF CIVIL PROCEDURE, the government must prove that the naturalized citizen lied about his criminal past, and thus, in effect, must prove the crime. The Supreme Court has stated, however, that the government need not meet the usual standard of proof for criminal guilt, as the defendant is subject not to penal sanctions but only to denaturalization.

Recently denaturalization suits have also been brought against Nazi war criminals. The central issue in these cases has been falsification or concealment of objective facts about the person's past. Although the courts have been unanimous that the alleged misrepresentations must be material, they have disagreed over whether a misrepresentation is sufficiently material if the truth, which by itself would not have been sufficient to bar the granting of citizenship, would nevertheless have provided leads for uncovering facts of the person's past that would have precluded his naturalization.

Litigants sometimes challenge the constitutionality of denaturalization, arguing either that it reduces naturalized citizens to second class status (in that they can be stripped of citizenship on grounds and by procedures that cannot be applied to native-born citizens), or that Congress's power to naturalize does not carry with it the implied power to denaturalize. To date such arguments have proven unsuccessful.

RALPH A. ROSSUM

Bibliography

GORDON, CHARLES and ROSENFIELD, HARRY N. 1984 *Immigration Law and Procedure*, Vol. 3, chap. 20. New York: Matthew Bender.

ROCHE, JOHN P. 1952 Statutory Denaturalization. *University of Pittsburgh Law Review* 13:276–327.

DENNIS v. UNITED STATES
341 U.S. 494 (1951)

Eugene Dennis and other high officials of the Communist party had been convicted of violating the ALIEN REGISTRATION ACT of 1940 (the Smith Act) by conspiring to advocate overthrow of the government by force and violence. LEARNED HAND, writing the Court of Appeals opinion upholding the constitutionality of the act and of the conviction, was caught in a dilemma. He was bound by the Supreme Court's CLEAR AND PRESENT DANGER rule, and the government had presented no evidence that Dennis's activities had created a present danger of communist revolution in the United States. Hand, however, believed that courts had limited authority to enforce the FIRST AMENDMENT. His solution was to restate the danger test as: "whether the gravity of the evil, discounted by its improbability, justifies such invasion of free speech as is necessary to avoid the danger." Because Dennis's conspiracy to advocate was linked to a grave evil, communist revolution, he could be punished despite the remote danger of communist revolution. Hand's restatement allowed a court to pay lip service to the danger rule while upholding nearly any government infringement on speech. If the ultimate threat posed by the speech is great enough, the speaker may be punished even though there is little or no immediate threat.

The Supreme Court upheld Dennis's conviction with only Justices HUGO L. BLACK and WILLIAM O. DOUGLAS dissenting. Chief Justice FRED M. VINSON's plurality opinion adopted Hand's restatement of the danger rule. At least where an organized subversive group was involved, speakers might be punished so long as they intended to bring about overthrow "as speedily as circumstances would permit."

Justice FELIX FRANKFURTER's concurrence openly substituted a BALANCING TEST for the danger rule, arguing that the constitutionality of speech limitations ultimately depended on whether the government had a weighty enough interest. Congress, he said, surely was entitled to conclude that the interest in national security outweighed the speech interests of those advocating violent overthrow.

Decided at the height of the Cold War campaign against communists, *Dennis* allied the Court with anticommunist sentiment. No statute would seem more flatly violative on its face of the First Amendment than one that made "advocacy" a crime. Indeed, in YATES V. UNITED STATES (1957) the Court later sought to distinguish between active urging or incitement to revolution, which was constitutionally punishable "advocacy," and abstract teaching of Marxist doctrine, which was constitutionally protected speech.

Defenders of the clear and present danger rule criticize *Dennis* for abandoning that rule's essential feature, the immediacy requirement. Such commentators see the Court as correcting its *Dennis* error in BRANDENBURG V. OHIO (1969) in which the Court returned to something like "clear and present danger" and placed heavy emphasis on the immediacy requirement. Justices Black and Douglas subsequently treated *Dennis* as a case applying the clear and present danger rule and thus as an illustration of the failure of the rule to provide sufficient protection for speech and of the need to replace it with the more "absolute" free speech protections urged by ALEXANDER MEIKLEJOHN. Proponents of balancing applaud Hand's "discounting" formula as one of the roots of the balancing doctrine, although only the most ardent proponents of judicial self-restraint support Frankfurter's conclusion that Congress, not the Court, should do the final balancing.

It is possible to read *Dennis*, *Yates*, and *Brandenburg* together as supporting the following theory. The clear and present danger rule, including a strong immediacy requirement, applies to street-corner speakers; so long as their speech does not trigger immediate serious harms, others will have the opportunity to respond to it in the marketplace of ideas, and the government will be able to prepare protective measures against violence that may follow. However, where organized, subversive groups engage in covert speech aimed at secret preparations that will suddenly burst forth in revolution, the "as speedily as circumstances will permit" test is substituted for the immediacy requirement. Covert speech cannot easily be rebutted in the marketplace of ideas; by the time underground groups pose a threat of immediate revolution, they may be so strong that a democratic government cannot stop them or can do so only at the cost of many lives.

Whether or not the Communist party of Eugene Dennis constituted such a covert, underground group impervious to the speech of others and posing a real threat of eventual revolution, a theory such as this is probably the reason the Smith Act was never declared unconstitutional and *Dennis* was never overruled although both have been drastically narrowed by subsequent judicial interpretation.

MARTIN SHAPIRO

Bibliography
CORWIN, EDWARD S. 1951 Bowing Out Clear and Present Danger. *Notre Dame Lawyer* 27:325–359.
MENDELSON, WALLACE 1952 Clear and Present Danger—From Schenk to Dennis. *Columbia Law Review* 52:313–333.

DEPARTMENT OF AGRICULTURE v. MORENO

See: *Department of Agriculture v. Murry*

DEPARTMENT OF AGRICULTURE v. MURRY
413 U.S. 508 (1973)
DEPARTMENT OF AGRICULTURE v. MORENO
413 U.S. 528 (1973)

Piqued by the activities of protesting students and members of "hippie communes" during the Vietnam years of agony, Congress in 1971 amended the Food Stamp Act to deny eligibility for food subsidies to two classes of applicants: "unrelated" persons living together and persons claimed by others in the previous year as tax dependents. On the same day the Supreme Court struck down both these amendments. *Moreno*, 7–2, invalidated the "unrelated" limitation on "Fifth Amendment EQUAL PROTECTION" grounds; the amendment was irrelevant to the act's goals of nourishing the needy and aiding agriculture, and harming "hippies" for their unpopularity was not a legitimate legislative purpose. The law thus lacked a RATIONAL BASIS. *Murry*, 5–4, held the "tax dependency" limitation an unconstitutional IRREBUTTABLE PRESUMPTION. A claimant might be needy during the current year although dependent on another during a previous year; yet the law denied any opportunity to qualify for aid by demonstrating need.

KENNETH L. KARST

DEPORTATION

Deportation is the removal of an ALIEN out of the country. Congress has plenary power to deport aliens, even of long residence; its power rests upon the same grounds and is as unqualified as its power to exclude aliens from entering the country. Aliens permitted to enter and reside in the United States remain subject to the power of Congress to order them deported. Congress may direct that all aliens leave the country, or that some leave and others stay, distinguishing between the two by such tests as it thinks appropriate. While aliens cannot be deported without DUE PROCESS OF LAW, guaranteed to them by the Fifth Amendment, they are entitled only to PROCEDURAL DUE PROCESS: NOTICE and a HEARING at which they may seek to show that they do not come within the classification of aliens whose deportation Congress has directed. (A resident of the United States who claims to be a citizen cannot be deported without a judicial trial.)

Initially, deportation was conceived of only as a method for expelling aliens who had entered the country illegally. Soon, however, Congress employed it to remove aliens who had entered legally but had violated conditions attached to continued residence. Thus, for example, the Immigration Act of 1917 provided for the deportation of aliens convicted of crimes involving moral turpitude. Other statutory grounds for deportation, now codified in the Immigration and Nationality Act of 1952, include violation of alien registration requirements, drug trafficking, addiction to narcotics, becoming a public charge within five years after entry, or membership in the Communist party or other subversive organizations.

By its express terms, the Immigration and Nationality Act applies retroactively to any alien belonging to any class enumerated in the statute, notwithstanding that the alien entered the United States prior to the date of the statute or that the facts alleged to justify deportation occurred prior to that date. Because deportation is not considered a punishment, the prohibition of the EX POST FACTO clause of the Constitution does not apply, and retroactive application of provisions specifying grounds for deportation was upheld in *Lehmann v. Carson* (1957).

In *Harisiades v. Shaughnessy* (1952) Justice WILLIAM O. DOUGLAS declared in his dissent that "an alien, who is assimilated in our society, is treated as a citizen so far as his property and his liberty are concerned. . . . If those rights, great as they are, have constitutional protection, I think the more important one—the right to remain here—has a like dignity." To date, this view has not been able to overcome the two basic propositions announced in the Court's seminal deportation case, *Fong Yue Ting v. United States* (1893), that Congress has the INHERENT POWER to order deportation and that deportation is not a criminal punishment.

RALPH A. ROSSUM

Bibliography
GORDON, CHARLES and ROSENFIELD, HARRY N. 1984 *Immigration Law and Procedure*, Vol. 1, chaps. 4–5; Vol. 2, chaps. 6–8. New York: Matthew Bender.
NOTE 1962 Deportation and Exclusion. *Yale Law Journal* 71:760–792.

DESEGREGATION

Freed finally of slavery's shackles, blacks in America began the long quest for racial equality. Desegregation, a generic term used to describe elimination of the SEGREGATION and RACIAL DISCRIMINATION that nonwhites confronted at life's every turn, has been the equivalent of their Holy Grail.

While blacks have attacked barriers based on color across a spectrum that includes VOTING, employment, housing, the administration of justice, access to public facilities, and even sex and marriage, the elimination of discrimination in the public schools has been and remains the most important goal for black Americans in their continuing struggle against racism in this country.

At an early time in the nation's history, blacks hoped an already hostile society might at least share their fear, as a black minister phrased it, "for our rising offspring to see them in ignorance in a land of gospel light." That petition presented in 1787 to the Massachusetts legislature sought a separate school for Boston's black children whose parents had withdrawn them from the harassment and ridicule heaped on them by white teachers and students in some of the new nation's first public schools.

The legislature denied the petition, which reflected fears shared by succeeding generations of black parents who all during the nineteenth century filed dozens of law suits with state courts seeking relief from the racial discrimination they found in the public schools. Depending on the times and the character of the discrimination they faced, black parents have sought equal educational opportunity for their children through the advocacy of either racially separate or integrated schools.

With few exceptions, the courts were no more sympathetic to these petitions than were the school boards whose policies sometimes excluded black children from the public schools entirely and always subjected them to conditions that left little doubt as to which students were deemed members of the superior race. In ROBERTS V. CITY OF BOSTON (1850) a state court rejected a school desegregation petition almost two decades before the adoption of the FOURTEENTH AMENDMENT; three decades after its ratification, the United States Supreme Court concluded in PLESSY V. FERGUSON (1896) that the Fourteenth Amendment did not prohibit state-sanctioned segregation, citing the *Roberts* decision as support for the reasonableness of what it called SEPARATE BUT EQUAL facilities. *Plessy* provided the Constitution's blessing for laws throughout the South that required racial segregation not only in public schools, but in every possible public facility, including cemeteries and houses of prostitution.

The law and much of society enforced the "separate" phase of the *Plessy* standard to the letter, but the promise of "equal" facilities received only the grudging attention of a public whose racial attitudes ranged from apathy to outright hostility. Deep-South states spent far less for the schooling of black children than for whites. Despite a major effort to equalize segregated schools as a means of forestalling the steadily increasing number of CIVIL RIGHTS challenges in the 1950s, the South as a whole expended an average of $165 for every white child, and only $115 for each black in 1954, the year in which segregated schools were ruled unconstitutional.

More than a half century after its *Plessy* decision, the Supreme Court in BROWN V. BOARD OF EDUCATION (1954) reviewed the "separate but equal" DOCTRINE in the light of education's importance for children in a modern society, and concluded that the Fourteenth Amendment's EQUAL PROTECTION clause was violated by segregated schools "even though the physical facilities and other 'tangible" factors may be equal. . . ."

Chief Justice EARL WARREN's ringing rhetoric in the *Brown* opinion condemned racially segregated schooling as "inherently unequal." He found that the separation by the state of children in grade and high schools solely on the basis of race "generates a feeling of inferiority as to their status in the community that may affect their hearts and minds in a way unlikely ever to be undone."

This decision was the result of long years of planning and litigation by the NAACP, and the committed work of lawyers including THURGOOD MARSHALL and Robert L. Carter, social scientists like Kenneth Clark, and hundreds of courageous black parents and their children. The decision, most blacks were convinced, required the elimination of segregated school facilities. Black parents knew that state-mandated black schools were a racial insult, and most hoped that if their children attended schools with whites, they would more likely gain access to the same educational resources as white children.

But the determination of civil rights groups representing an ever-increasing number of black parents seeking to join in school desegregation suits was met by the equally determined and, at least initially, far more powerful resistance of southern whites who strongly opposed sending their children to school with blacks and greatly resented the federal coercion involved in school desegregation orders which they equated with the occupation of the region by Union forces following the Civil War.

Arguably, opposition by southern working class whites could be predicated on the basis that, by invalidating segregation laws, *Brown* betrayed post-Reconstruction promises of white superior status made to them by policymakers in return for political support given during periods when populist movements sought to challenge the monopoly of economic power held by the upper class.

Although the Supreme Court refused to turn the clock back to 1868 to determine whether the framers of the Fourteenth Amendment had intended to condone segregated schools, an examination of post-Reconstruction history shows that policies of segregation reflected a series of political compromises through which working class whites settled their demands for social reform and greater political power. C. Vann Woodward and other historians have shown that segregated schools and facilities were established by legislatures at the insistence of the white working classes who saw color barriers as official confirmation that the society's policymakers would maintain even the poorest whites in a permanent status superior to that designated for blacks.

While not willing to acknowledge that its school desegregation decision would deprive whites of long-held rights of superior status based on race, the Court in *Brown v. Board of Education II* (1955), signaled that it was aware of the major social upheaval its ruling would require. Rejecting the black petitioners' requests for immediate relief, the Court chose a procedure that would permit the individual resolution of administrative and academic problems. It mandated only a "prompt and reasonable start toward full compliance," and returned the cases to the district courts with the admonition that orders and decrees be entered to admit plaintiffs to public schools on a racially nondiscriminatory basis "with ALL DELIBERATE SPEED. . . ."

But the Court's conciliatory efforts did not avoid

and may have encouraged a period of massive resistance by southern elected officials, a rise in the Ku Klux Klan and other white supremacist groups, and a general upswing in economic intimidation and threats of physical violence against blacks deemed responsible for or participants in the civil rights movement. The Court met open resistance in Little Rock, Arkansas, and elsewhere with firm resolve, as in COOPER V. AARON (1958), but for several years condoned pupil placement laws and other procedural devices clearly designed to frustrate any meaningful compliance with the *Brown* mandate.

Federal courts were far less cautious in applying the *Brown* decision as the controlling precedent in cases challenging racial segregation in other public facilities. Thus, in the first half-dozen years following *Brown*, civil rights groups succeeded in desegregating state-operated places of recreation, government buildings, and transportation facilities.

Finally, in 1964, during the height of the SIT-IN protest movement that was bringing an end to "Jim Crow" policies in many hitherto segregated privately owned facilities not covered by the Fourteenth Amendment, the Court indicated that the time for mere deliberate speed had run out, in GRIFFIN V. SCHOOL BOARD OF PRINCE EDWARD COUNTY (1964). But the success of a decade of white resistance to school desegregation was reflected in the statistics. In the eleven states of the old Confederacy, a mere 1.17 percent of black students were attending school with white students by the 1963–1964 school year. The dirgelike progress of school desegregation finally gained momentum through a series of far-reaching lower court orders combined with the federal government's enforcement of Title VI of the CIVIL RIGHTS ACT OF 1964. This provision required the cut-off of federal financial assistance to entities that followed racially discriminatory policies. The federal government's enforcement of Title VI was seldom vigorous, but even the threat of losing the federal monies made available under a host of new antipoverty and educational assistance programs in the late 1960s persuaded hundreds of southern school districts that some form of compliance was in their best interests.

In 1968, the Supreme Court in GREEN V. NEW KENT COUNTY SCHOOL BOARD virtually eliminated the offer by a school board of "freedom of choice" to all children as a sufficient compliance with desegregation requirements. The decision was hailed by civil rights lawyers who believed that the *Brown* mandate could not be implemented unless public schools were rendered nonidentifiable by race. This goal, articulated in the *Green* case by Justice WILLIAM J. BRENnan as requiring school boards to formulate plans that promise "realistically to convert promptly to a system without a 'white' school and a 'Negro' school, but just schools," was furthered when the Court applied the *Green* standard to a large, urban school district in North Carolina in SWANN V. CHARLOTTE-MECKLENBURG BOARD OF EDUCATION (1971). A few years later, the Court held a large northern school district subject to a similar standard in KEYES V. SCHOOL DISTRICT NO. 1 OF DENVER, COLORADO (1973). (See SCHOOL BUSING.)

But while the percentage of children attending desegregated schools increased impressively, opposition to school desegregation remained. Resistance focused on plans like those approved in both *Swann* and *Keyes* requiring the transportation of children in order to achieve a measure of desegregation in each school roughly equivalent to the percentages of white and nonwhite children in the district as a whole. Opponents had gained national political strength, and their support likely played an important role in the election of RICHARD M. NIXON as President in 1968. The Nixon administration adopted policies that had the effect of slowing the federal government's participation in the school desegregation campaign, but the Supreme Court rejected Administration-sponsored delay requests in ALEXANDER V. HOLMES COUNTY BOARD OF EDUCATION (1969) and *Carter v. West Feliciana Parish School Board* (1970), although not without cracks in the solid front of unanimous opinions the Court had handed down in school desegregation cases since *Brown I*.

By 1974, in MILLIKEN V. BRADLEY, an APPEAL from lower court orders requiring the consolidation with the seventy percent black Detroit school system of fifty-three predominantly white suburban school districts, those cracks had grown into a chasm between divergent viewpoints on the appropriateness of school desegregation remedies. The insistence of civil rights lawyers that courts had unlimited discretion to impose racial-balance oriented plans to remedy proven segregation resulted in a significant change in the standards for proving school district liability for violating the Constitution.

In a 5–4 decision, the Court in *Milliken* held that federal courts could not impose multidistrict remedies to cure a single district's segregation absent findings that the other included school districts had failed to operate unitary school systems within their districts, or were responsible for the segregation in the other districts. Proof of this character could be found in few districts without histories of official, state-mandated segregation, and thus plans to desegregate large, urban school districts through metropolitan-wide plans were rendered inoperable.

By the late 1970s, roughly half of all nonwhite children in the nation resided in the country's twenty to thirty largest school districts. Minority children averaged sixty percent of the school population in these districts and close to seventy percent in the ten largest districts. Politically if not physically, desegregation in these districts on the *Green-Swann* model became increasingly difficult.

Lower courts, impressed by detailed prescriptions of racial wrongdoing by urban school boards, continued at the urging of civil rights lawyers to grant relief requiring reassignments and busing to change the racial makeup of schools. But the Supreme Court, now quite divided, set increasingly difficult liability standards in cases from Dayton and Columbus, Ohio; Omaha, Nebraska; Austin, Texas; Milwaukee, Wisconsin; and Indianapolis, Indiana. Plans requiring wholesale reassignment of children in these districts were finally approved, mainly because the proof of past discrimination was so clear. There was little judicial enthusiasm for continued reliance on a remedial process about which there was so much controversy as to its effectiveness even among civil rights proponents.

By this time, a great many black communities were questioning the continued validity of the "neither black schools nor white schools" desegregation approach that had stood as an article of faith since the early post-*Brown* years. Disenchantment was prompted by the hundreds of black schools closed and the scores of black teachers and principals dismissed in the course of the school desegregation process. In addition, black parents were discovering that the sacrifice involved in busing children across town to mainly white schools did not always eliminate racial discrimination. More litigation had to be prosecuted to challenge resegregation tactics as varied as the use of standardized tests to track black students into virtually all-black classrooms, to the exclusion of blacks from extracurricular programs. In most desegregated school systems, black students were far more likely to be suspended and expelled for disciplinary violations than white students. Black parents able to enroll their children in desegregated schools all too often found themselves protesting policies of in-school discrimination quite similar to those that had led their late eighteenth-century predecessors to petition for separate schools.

The NAACP and the few other groups who sponsored most school desegregation litigation remained firm in their belief that identifiably black schools would always be inferior and must be eliminated. But

local black groups in several cities including Atlanta, St. Louis, Detroit, Dallas, Boston, and Portland, Oregon, decided that mainly black schools in black neighborhoods might provide effective schooling for their children if black parents could be involved more closely in faculty hiring, curriculum selection, and other policymaking aspects of these schools.

In 1975, a court of appeals approved in CALHOUN V. COOK, over the vigorous objection of the national NAACP office, a settlement of a twenty-year-old Atlanta school case providing full faculty and employee desegregation but only limited pupil desegregation in exchange for a school board promise to hire a number of blacks in top administrative positions, including a black superintendent of schools.

A few years later, in *Milliken v. Bradley II* (1977), the Supreme Court approved without dissent a Detroit desegregation plan that gave priority to a range of "educational components" while limiting pupil desegregation in the district that was by now more than eighty percent black to a provision that no school be less than thirty percent black. The Court though was unable to decide and left standing a lower court ruling that an almost all-black subdistrict created by the Dallas school desegregation plan met school desegregation standards. The record showed both that housing patterns and geographical conditions would have made desegregation difficult and that much of the black community in the subdistrict supported its retention.

Public resistance to school desegregation continued into the 1980s even though the likelihood of new court orders was lessened by the Supreme Court's application of higher standards of proof even in litigation where metropolitan relief was not sought. For example, California voters approved an amendment to their state constitution barring state courts from ordering racial balance remedies in cases where, absent a finding that the school board was guilty of a specific intent to discriminate, the Fourteenth Amendment would not require racial balance relief. The Supreme Court upheld this provision in *Crawford v. Los Angeles Unified School District* (1982).

Civil rights organizations mobilized to meet such challenges, but local black groups increasingly opted for programs that promised to provide equal educational opportunity in neighborhood schools. At the same time, many black parents either moved to suburban areas or sent their children out of their neighborhoods to enable them to attend predominantly white schools.

The quest for effective schooling in the 1980s mirrors those made by black parents in the 1780s and during all the periods between. They and their children have recognized that neither separate schools nor integrated schools will automatically eliminate racist policies intended to provide priority to white children for scarce educational resources. School desegregation programs mandated by the *Brown* decision, and earnestly sought in hundreds of court cases, have served to slow but have not otherwise much discouraged those policies.

Beyond the real gains made by blacks during the *Brown* years, there remain millions of black and other minority children whose schooling remains both segregated and inferior. For them, there is ample basis for parental fears as they watch their rising offspring grow "in ignorance in a land of gospel light."

DERRICK A. BELL

Bibliography

BELL, DERRICK A. (1973)1980 *Race, Racism and American Law.* Boston: Little, Brown.
KALODNER, HOWARD I. and FISHMAN, JAMES J., EDS. 1978 *Limits of Justice: The Courts' Role in School Desegregation.* Cambridge, Mass.: Ballinger.
KLUGER, RICHARD 1976 *Simple Justice: The History of Brown v. Board of Education and Black America's Struggle for Equality.* New York: Knopf.
WOODWARD, C. VANN (1955)1974 *The Strange Career of Jim Crow.* New York: Oxford University Press.

DEVELOPMENTALLY DISABLED ASSISTANCE AND BILL OF RIGHTS ACT
89 Stat. 486 (1975)

This statute established a grant program under which participating states receive federal financial assistance to aid them in creating programs for the developmentally disabled, a term that refers mainly to the mentally retarded. To qualify for federal funds states must take AFFIRMATIVE ACTION to hire qualified handicapped individuals, submit a plan to evaluate the services provided under the act, have a habitation plan for each person receiving services under a program funded under the act, and have in effect a system to protect and advocate the rights of persons with developmental disabilities. The act's "bill of rights" for the developmentally disabled includes the rights to appropriate treatment in a setting least restrictive of the patient's liberty, to a well-balanced diet, to sufficient medical and dental services, to be free of restraint as punishment, to be free of excessive use of chemical restraints, to be visited by relatives, and to

a safe environment. In PENNHURST STATE SCHOOL AND HOSPITAL V. HALDERMAN (1981) the Supreme Court, in an opinion by Justice WILLIAM H. REHNQUIST and over three dissents, held that the "bill of rights" portion of the act does not confer on the developmentally disabled any substantive rights to appropriate treatment in the least restrictive setting. The act "does no more than express a congressional preference for certain kinds of treatment."

THEODORE EISENBERG

Bibliography

EISENBERG, THEODORE 1981 *Civil Rights Legislation.* Pages 886–887. Charlottesville, Va.: Michie Co.

DIAMOND v. CHAKRABARTY

See: Patents

DICEY, ARTHUR V.

See: Rule of Law

DICKINSON, JOHN
(1732–1808)

The conservative patriot leader John Dickinson, scion of a wealthy Quaker family, was called to the bar at the Middle Temple in London in 1757 and soon after returning to America became one of the most prosperous lawyers in Philadelphia. He served in the colonial legislatures of both Delaware and Pennsylvania, and in 1765 he rose to continental prominence with his pamphlets opposing the Sugar Act and the Stamp Act.

A delegate to the STAMP ACT CONGRESS (1765), Dickinson was the author of that body's Declaration of Rights and Grievances, ostensibly a loyal, even humble, petition to the king. Dickinson's resolutions condemned as unconstitutional the levying of internal taxes upon the colonists by the British Parliament and denounced as subversive of liberty the trial of offenses against tax laws by admiralty courts without juries. Dickinson himself later referred to the Declaration of Rights and Grievances as the first American BILL OF RIGHTS.

After the passage of the TOWNSHEND ACTS in 1767 Dickinson established himself as the preeminent American interpreter of the constitutional relationship between the colonies and Britain. His "Letters from a Farmer in Pennsylvania" (1767–1768), published in all but four American newspapers, advanced an understanding of the British constitution that made Parliament supreme in imperial matters but proscribed all TAXATION WITHOUT REPRESENTATION. Moreover, he abandoned the distinction between external and internal taxes in favor of a distinction based on purpose: if a duty was laid for the purpose of raising revenue, rather than regulating commerce, then it was taxation and fell under the constitutional proscription. The Farmer's Letters counseled petition for repeal of, rather than resistance to, unconstitutional legislation.

By the time he wrote his long essay on "The Constitutional Power of Great Britain" in 1774, Dickinson had come to think of the British Empire as federal—comparable to the Swiss Confederation or the United Netherlands. The British king was king of the American colonies, but "a parliamentary power of internal legislation over these colonies appears . . . equally contradictory to humanity and to the Constitution, and illegal."

In 1774 Dickinson represented Pennsylvania in the First Continental Congress. The petition to the king and the address to the inhabitants of Canada, adopted pursuant to the DECLARATION AND RESOLVES, were products of Dickinson's pen. In 1775, at the Second Continental Congress, he worked with THOMAS JEFFERSON drafting the Declaration of the Causes and Necessity of Taking Up Arms. But Dickinson was still committed to the idea of a resolution of the crisis within the constitutional system of the British Empire. He opposed immediate separation from Britain and refused to sign the DECLARATION OF INDEPENDENCE.

On June 12, 1776, the Congress, anticipating independence, appointed a committee to draft a plan of union. Dickinson was the dominant member of that committee and the principal author of the draft ARTICLES OF CONFEDERATION reported to Congress on July 12. Dickinson's draft called for no mere alliance or league of sovereign states but for a permanent union with a national government. The "United States assembled" was to be heir to those powers of regulation and general legislation legitimately exercised before independence by the British Parliament, while each "colony" retained "sole and exclusive Regulation and Government of its internal police, in all matters that shall not interfere with the Articles of this Confederation." True to the "Farmer's" principles, Dickinson inserted a provision that "the United States assembled shall never impose or levy any Taxes or Duties, except in managing the Post-Office." Dickinson's draft Articles were regarded by many in Congress, especially Southerners, as too centralizing, and even some who favored Dickinson's position despaired of securing ratification. Only after considerably weakening the government to be established by the Articles did Congress finally propose them to the states.

When his stand on independence cost Dickinson his seat in Congress and his colonelcy in the militia, he enlisted in the army as a private soldier. But in November 1776 he was elected to Congress by Delaware, and he was later made a brigadier general in the Delaware militia. In 1779 he signed the Articles of Confederation to signify Delaware's ratification.

Dickinson served as president of Delaware in 1781–1782 and as president of Pennsylvania in 1782–1785. In both states he was recognized as a leader of the conservative party. Although a slaveholder, he favored abolition of SLAVERY, and he opposed its extension into the Northwest Territory.

In 1785 he retired to his estate in Delaware, but he was recalled to public service in 1786 and elected a delegate from Delaware to the ANNAPOLIS CONVENTION. Dickinson was chosen president of the convention, which discussed commercial problems under the Confederation and which issued the first call for a federal constitutional convention.

Notwithstanding his poor health, Dickinson accepted appointment to represent Delaware at the CONSTITUTIONAL CONVENTION OF 1787. Although he was an active and conscientious delegate, his contribution to the work of the convention was not among the most important. A nationalist of long standing, he represented a small state and often had to balance competing interests. He was the first to propose a bicameral congress with equal REPRESENTATION of the states in one house and representation apportioned by population or financial contribution in the other—a proposal that later became the basis of the GREAT COMPROMISE. He favored abolition of the slave trade but acquiesced in the compromise that imposed a twenty-year moratorium on congressional power to accomplish it. He wanted Congress to be the dominant branch of government, with full authority to remove Presidents and judges; and he wanted to limit executive power and to create a council to share the President's appointing power. Forced by illness to leave the convention early, Dickinson authorized a colleague to sign his name to the finished Constitution.

Dickinson wrote a series of nine newspaper essays (signed "Fabius") in support of RATIFICATION OF THE CONSTITUTION; they were influential, especially in

Pennsylvania. He declined appointment as a United States senator from Delaware and never held public office under the new Constitution.

DENNIS J. MAHONEY

Bibliography

FORD, PAUL LEICESTER, ed. 1970 *Political Writings of John Dickinson.* New York: Da Capo.

JACOBSON, D. L. 1965 *John Dickinson and the Revolution in Pennsylvania.* Berkeley: University of California Press.

STILLE, CHARLES J. 1891 *Life and Times of John Dickinson.* Philadelphia: Historical Society of Philadelphia.

DICTA

See: Obiter Dictum

DIES, MARTIN
(1900–1972)

Martin Dies, an anti-New Deal Democrat from Texas, served in the House of Representatives from 1931 to 1945 and from 1953 to 1961. In 1938 he became chairman of the special Committee to Investigate Un-American Activities, forerunner of the HOUSE COMMITTEE ON UN-AMERICAN ACTIVITIES. Dies and his committee attained national prominence through sensational exposés of supposed Fascist, Nazi, and communist activity in government, labor unions, and industry. His published lists of government employees who were "Communists or Communist dupes," the publicity he gave to unsubstantiated accusations, and his disregard of normal CIVIL LIBERTIES foreshadowed the activities of Senator JOSEPH MCCARTHY.

DENNIS J. MAHONEY

DIFRANCESCO, UNITED STATES v.
449 U.S. 117 (1980)

In this case on the DOUBLE JEOPARDY clause of the Fifth Amendment a 5–4 Supreme Court sustained the constitutionality of the ORGANIZED CRIME CONTROL ACT of 1970, which in special instances granted to the United States the right to APPEAL a criminal sentence. Justice HARRY L. BLACKMUN for the majority, rejecting the dissenters' contention that review of a sentence is comparable to the review of a verdict of acquittal, held that a government appeal that suc-

ceeded in increasing a sentence did not constitute double jeopardy.

LEONARD W. LEVY

DILLON, JOHN F.
(1831–1914)

Elected a member of the Iowa Supreme Court at thirty-one, John Forrest Dillon was a leading advocate of the PUBLIC PURPOSE doctrine. In 1869 President ULYSSES S. GRANT appointed Dillon to the Eighth Circuit Court, but after ten years' service Dillon resigned to accept a professorship at Columbia University Law School. Within three years he left that post to enter private practice, and he soon represented major business interests including Jay Gould and the Union Pacific Railroad.

Although Dillon was not an original thinker, his writings and speeches helped establish his tremendous reputation. He served as president of the American Bar Association in 1892 and delivered the prestigious Storrs Lectures at Yale University shortly thereafter. These were published in 1895 as *The Laws and Jurisprudence in England and America,* and in them Dillon claimed that the DUE PROCESS CLAUSE of the FOURTEENTH AMENDMENT "in the most impressive and solemn form places life, liberty, contracts, and property . . . among the fundamental and indestructible rights of all the people of the United States." He endorsed SUBSTANTIVE DUE PROCESS and rhapsodized on the distinction of America's written CONSTITUTIONS: their limitations on government. Restraints such as SEPARATION OF POWERS and CHECKS AND BALANCES were just two of the many means available to prevent "despotism of the many,—of the majority." Dillon also wrote an influential treatise on *Municipal Corporations* (1872).

As a judge, Dillon narrowly construed the public purpose DOCTRINE. He believed that a municipal corporation had the authority to tax to support a public purpose, but incidental public benefits did not justify such taxation. Moreover, he believed that the judiciary could inquire into the legislative purpose and that private enterprises (with the sole exception of railroads) did not qualify under the doctrine. He thus wrote laissez-faire ideas into the law as limitations on legislative power (*Loan Association v. Topeka, Commercial National Bank of Cleveland v. Iola,* both 1873). Dillon appeared frequently before the Supreme Court where, in UNITED STATES V. TRANS-MISSOURI FREIGHT ASSOCIATION (1897) he urged the

Court to adopt the RULE OF REASON whereby the SHERMAN ANTITRUST ACT would be read to prohibit only unreasonable restraints of trade, a position finally adopted in STANDARD OIL COMPANY V. UNITED STATES (1911).

DAVID GORDON

Bibliography

JACOBS, CLYDE E. (1954)1973 *Law Writers and the Courts.* New York: Da Capo Press.

DIONISIO, UNITED STATES v.
410 U.S. 1 (1973)

A gambling suspect refused a federal court's order to provide a voice sample to a GRAND JURY, and was adjudged in civil contempt and committed to custody. The Supreme Court affirmed. The Court rejected, 7–2, a claim that the order violated the suspect's RIGHT AGAINST SELF-INCRIMINATION, saying that the voice sample was to be used only for identification, not for the content of the statements. A 6–3 majority also rejected a claim that the order violated the FOURTH AMENDMENT. Because there was no "seizure" here, there was no need to demonstrate the reasonableness of the grand jury's request.

DAVID GORDON

DIRECT AND INDIRECT TAXES

The Constitution imposes two major limitations on the federal power to tax. Direct taxes can be levied only if allocated among the states according to population. All other taxes (indirect taxes) must be uniform among the United States.

The requirement of apportioning direct taxes apparently was included because the southern states feared that they would bear excessive burdens on land and slaves—a fear demonstrated by the fact that (until the FOURTEENTH AMENDMENT) only three-fifths of slaves were counted in the population. Nobody in the Convention appeared to be very clear, however, on just what was a direct tax that had to be allocated.

The issue first came to the Supreme Court in HYLTON V. UNITED STATES (1796). A duty laid on carriages was challenged as being a direct tax. The Court pointed out the difficulties with direct taxes, particularly the fact that while the total amount allocated to each state related to the population of that state, the individual taxpayers (in this case the owners of carriages) would pay quite different amounts depending not only on population but also on the relative numbers of the taxable subjects within the state. The Court expressed doubt that any taxes other than a capitation tax or a tax on the value of land could be called direct taxes. Over the next century the issue seldom arose, for Congress levied very few taxes beyond customs duties until the Civil War. However, the Court did hold that a tax of ten percent on state-issued currency (VEAZIE BANK V. FENNO, 1869), a tax on the succession to a decedent's property (*Scholey v. Rew,* 1875), and income taxes (*Springer v. United States,* (1881) were all indirect, not direct taxes.

The income tax involved in *Springer* had remained in effect only until 1872. By the 1890s, however, many groups called for a reduction in federal dependence on tariffs for revenue and for an income tax on wealthier persons. In 1894 a statute was passed imposing a tax on all incomes over $4,000. Facing a challenge to this tax, the Supreme Court reversed its earlier stand and in POLLOCK V. FARMERS' LOAN & TRUST Co. (1895) held the tax a direct tax and so invalid because not apportioned. The Court's new position was that taxes on the rents or income of real estate and taxes on personal property or the income from personal property were direct taxes and must be apportioned, though taxes on income from other sources would not be direct taxes.

A few years later there was another attempt to enact an income tax law. More conservative members of Congress countered by presenting a proposal to amend the Constitution to provide that income taxes need not be apportioned. Perhaps to their surprise, the SIXTEENTH AMENDMENT was proposed by Congress in 1909 and secured ratification by three-fourths of the states in 1913. The result, of course, was to open the door to the major federal revenue producer.

During the twentieth century there have been occasional attempts to litigate various taxes as being direct—but never with success. Congress does not impose capitation taxes nor property taxes—and all other kinds of taxes apparently are indirect.

The requirement that indirect taxes be uniform has given little difficulty. In upholding a federal tax on legacies in *Knowlton v. Moore* (1900), the Court said that what is required is geographical uniformity. A tax is uniform when it operates with the same force and effect in every place where the subject of it is found. It does not matter that the subject may exist in some states and not in others so long as the tax is the same. Thus, the Court in *Fernandez v. Wiener* (1945) upheld a federal statute imposing death taxes on community property—even though such property existed in only the few states that had adopted the community property system. In *United States v. Ptasynski* (1983) the Court cast some doubt on the geographical limitation by upholding a provision exempting Alaskan oil from a crude oil windfall profit tax. (See TAXING AND SPENDING POWER.)

EDWARD L. BARRETT, JR.

Bibliography

PAUL, RANDOLPH E. 1954 *Taxation in the United States.* Pages 46–58. Boston: Little, Brown.

DIRECT ELECTIONS

Whenever there has been dissatisfaction with the performance of appointing officials, whether party, legislative, or electoral college, there has been a demand for direct elections. The Progressive Era (1890–1920) marked a heyday for such demands, producing direct election of senators (SEVENTEENTH AMENDMENT), direct nomination of state party candidates (through PRIMARY ELECTIONS), and, in many cities and states, direct legislation through INITIATIVE and REFERENDUM, and direct RECALL of candidates. After most close presidential elections, there has also been talk of direct election of the President in place of the ELECTORAL COLLEGE.

Direct election of the President and direct party primaries have been criticized on policy (but not constitutional) grounds for weakening the two-party system. Initiative and referendum, besides being criticized as "plebiscitary," have been challenged as violative of the GUARANTEE CLAUSE, but such challenges have uniformly been found nonjusticiable. The leading case is *Pacific States Telephone Company v. Oregon* (1912).

WARD E. Y. ELLIOTT

Bibliography

BONFIELD, ARTHUR E. 1962 The Guarantee Clause of Article IV, Section 4: A Study in Constitutional Desuetude. *Minnesota Law Review* 46:513–572.

DIRKSEN, EVERETT M.
(1896–1969)

Everett McKinley Dirksen represented Illinois as a United States congressman (1933–1949) and senator (1951–1969). Despite a previous record as an isolationist in FOREIGN AFFAIRS and a reactionary in domestic affairs, he contributed to the legislative successes of the Democratic Presidents when he was the Republican leader of the Senate in the 1960s. Dirksen was an eccentric—flamboyant in style, florid in oratory, and organ-voiced; he was also a superb parliamentary tactician and a politician who was exceptionally inconsistent in his policies. On matters of constitutional interest, he supported MCCARTHYISM and opposed the censure of Senator Joseph R. McCarthy, and savagely criticized the Supreme Court for opinions he disliked, especially on REAPPORTIONMENT, SEPARATION OF CHURCH AND STATE, and the rights of the criminally accused. Dirksen favored bills to curb the Court's APPELLATE JURISDICTION, proposed a constitutional amendment to allow prayers in public schools, and led a movement that failed by the vote of one state to convene a constitutional convention. Yet the CIVIL RIGHTS ACT OF 1964 and the VOTING RIGHTS ACTS of 1965 would not have been passed without his support.

LEONARD W. LEVY

Bibliography

SCHAPSMEIER, EDWARD L. 1985 *Dirksen of Illinois: Senatorial Statesman.* Urbana: University of Illinois Press.

DISANTO v. PENNSYLVANIA
273 U.S. 34 (1927)

Protection of the public health and welfare temporarily lost ground to the COMMERCE CLAUSE in this case. A Pennsylvania statute required the licensing of persons selling steamship tickets to or from foreign countries. The Court declared the law a "direct" interference with FOREIGN COMMERCE, over the dissents of Justices HARLAN FISKE STONE, OLIVER WENDELL HOLMES, and LOUIS D. BRANDEIS. Stone found the direct/indirect test of EFFECTS ON COMMERCE "too mechanical, too uncertain . . . and too remote . . . to be of value." He proposed a more pragmatic test: "the actual effect on the flow of commerce," a view which prevailed in 1941 when this decision was overruled by CALIFORNIA V. THOMPSON.

DAVID GORDON

(SEE ALSO: *Parker v. Brown, 1943.*)

DISCOVERY

Discovery is a procedure by which one party obtains information from the adverse party in his case. This disclosure of information in criminal proceedings includes statements, documents, test results, reports, and other similar items. Although there is a very broad power to discover items in the exclusive possession of an adverse party in civil proceedings, the Supreme Court stated in *Weatherford v. Bursey* (1977) that "there is no general constitutional right to discovery in a criminal case."

In civil cases, the predominant means for discovery are depositions and interrogatories. In criminal cases, no jurisdiction expressly permits the defense to discover prosecutorial information through interrogatories. Most jurisdictions allow depositions in criminal cases only for the purpose of preserving testimony. Most jurisdictions also have statutes or court rules similar to FEDERAL RULE OF CRIMINAL PROCEDURE 16 governing defense discovery which require the prosecution to disclose items such as: (1) written or recorded statements (including GRAND JURY testimony) of the defendant and, in some states, of any co-defendant; (2) the substance of any oral statement of the defendant (and, in some states, of a co-defendant) that the prosecution intends to use at trial; (3) the defendant's prior criminal record; (4) relevant documents and other tangible objects; and (5) results and reports of physical or mental examinations and of scientific tests or experiments.

The prosecutorial duty to disclose exculpatory information is based on the view that the primary task of the prosecutor is to see justice done and DUE PROCESS upheld through the fair treatment of accused persons. If this duty is breached, the defendant is entitled to a new trial.

The leading modern case on this duty is *Brady v. Maryland* (1963). In separate trials, the petitioner and a companion were convicted of murder and sentenced to death. At his trial, the petitioner admitted participating in the crime but claimed that his companion had done the actual killing. Prior to trial the petitioner's attorney requested the prosecution to allow him to examine all the companion's statements to the police. One such statement, in which the companion admitted the actual killing, was withheld by the prosecution and did not come to the petitioner's attention until after his conviction was affirmed on APPEAL. The Supreme Court held that "the suppression by the prosecution of EVIDENCE favorable to an accused upon request violates due process where the evidence is material either to guilt or to punishment, irrespective of the good faith or bad faith of the prosecution."

In order to determine whether particular information should have been disclosed, courts consider whether the defendant made a specific request for the information at issue or a more general request for exculpatory information. They also consider to what extent the information was material to the outcome of the trial. When a specific request is made, withholding information is seldom excusable. Even when a general request is made or the defense fails to request exculpatory information, withholding clearly material information, such as the fact that particular testimony is perjured, is not permissible. In determining materiality, the test is whether the withheld information creates a reasonable doubt in the mind of the trial judge as to the defendant's guilt.

There is no clear rule as to when exculpatory information must be disclosed, but it would seem that some circumstances would require pretrial disclosure in order to permit the defense adequate time to prepare its case.

Generally, the prosecutor decides what evidence should be disclosed, although the trial court may occasionally decide *in camera* whether a particular piece of evidence is favorable to the defendant and should therefore be disclosed to him.

Finally the Supreme Court indicated in *United States v. Agurs* (1976) and *Smith v. Phillips* (1982) that the focus should be whether the prosecutor's failure to disclose rendered the trial fundamentally unfair, not the extent of prosecutorial culpability.

CHARLES H. WHITEBREAD

Bibliography
SALTZBURG, STEPHEN 1980 *American Criminal Procedure.* St. Paul, Minn.: West Publishing Co.
WHITEBREAD, CHARLES H. 1980 *Criminal Procedure.* Mineola, N.Y.: Foundation Press.

DISCRETE AND INSULAR MINORITIES

The idea of the "discrete and insular minority" originated in the now famous footnote four of the opinion in UNITED STATES V. CAROLENE PRODUCTS COMPANY (1938). Justice HARLAN F. STONE, writing for only a plurality of the Court, queried—without answering the question—"whether prejudice against discrete and insular minorities may be a special condition, which tends seriously to curtail those political processes ordinarily to be relied upon to protect minorities, and which may call for a correspondingly more searching judicial inquiry." In the wake of the Court's about-face in 1937, Justice Stone was serving notice that the Court might not accord the same deference to statutes directed at "discrete and insular minorities" that it would to statutes directed at ECONOMIC REGULATION.

The Court made little use of the concept until the early 1970s, when it began to delineate the class characteristics of such groups. Included were groups that had been "saddled with such disabilities, or subjected to such a history of purposeful unequal treatment, or relegated to such a position of political powerlessness as to command extraordinary protection from the majoritarian political process." Although race, nationality, and alienage seem to have been firmly established as class characteristics of the "discrete and insular minority," the Court has refused to extend such class status to illegitimates, the poor, or conscientious objectors.

REGENTS OF THE UNIVERSITY OF CALIFORNIA V. BAKKE (1978) presented the question of the "discrete and insular minority" in a new light. The question in *Bakke* was whether the same "solicitude" should be applied to test a governmental action designed to benefit rather than injure a "discrete and insular" minority. The university, citing *Carolene Products,* argued that STRICT SCRUTINY was reserved exclusively for "discrete and insular minorities." Four Justices agreed that a white male needed no special protection from the political process that authorized the actions of the university. Justice LEWIS F. POWELL rejected this argument: "the 'rights created by the . . . FOURTEENTH AMENDMENT are, by its terms, guaranteed to the individual. The rights established are personal rights. . . .' The guarantee of EQUAL PROTECTION cannot mean one thing when applied to one individual and something else when applied to a person of another color."

In FULLILOVE V. KLUTZNICK (1980) the Court, for the first time since the JAPANESE AMERICAN CASES (1943–1944), upheld a racial classification that was expressed on the face of a law. *Fullilove* involved a challenge to an act of Congress authorizing federal funds for local public works projects and setting aside ten percent of those funds for employment of businesses owned by Negroes, Hispanics, Orientals, AMERICAN INDIANS, and Aleuts. Chief Justice WARREN E. BURGER, writing for a plurality, called for judicial deference to Congress's power under section 5 of the Fourteenth Amendment, as equivalent to "the broad powers expressed in the NECESSARY AND PROPER CLAUSE. . . ." The irony was that the idea of the "discrete and insular minority" in its inception was designed to curtail such deference when racial classifications were involved.

BENIGN RACIAL CLASSIFICATIONS, it is sometimes said, are justified because they do not involve the stigma of INVIDIOUS DISCRIMINATION. The recipients of the benefits that accrue from the "benign" classification are not branded as members of an "inferior race" as they would be if the classification were an invidious one. This theory erects "stigma" as the standard for equal protection rights. Absent any such stigma the implication is that the Constitution is not offended, even if individuals must bear burdens created by a classification that otherwise would be disallowed by the equal protection clause. As Burger stated in *Fullilove,* " 'a sharing of the burden' by innocent parties is not impermissible." To use the idea of stigma as a racial class concept is, in effect, to translate equal protection rights into class rights.

But the intrusion of class into the Constitution is a dangerous proposition, one that is at odds with the principles of the constitutional regime—principles ultimately derived from the proposition that "all men are created equal." Class considerations explicitly deny this equality because they necessarily abstract from the individual and ascribe to him class characteristics that are different—and necessarily unequal—from those of individuals outside the class. A liberal jurisprudence must disallow all class considerations. When there is a conflict between two different "discrete and insular minorities," which should be accorded preference? No principle can answer this question. And the question is not merely theoretical. The Court has already faced this dilemma in cases such as UNITED JEWISH ORGANIZATIONS V. CAREY (1977) and *Castenada v. Partida* (1977), and in a pluralistic society it is inevitable that many more such cases will arise. Equal protection can be the foundation of a genuine liberal jurisprudence only if it applies to individuals. As Justice JOHN MARSHALL HARLAN remarked in his powerful dissent in PLESSY V. FERGUSON (1896), the case that established the SEPARATE-BUT-EQUAL DOCTRINE, "[o]ur Constitution is colorblind, and neither knows nor tolerates classes among citizens. In respect of CIVIL RIGHTS, all citizens are equal before the law." This is undoubtedly still the essential principle of liberal government.

JAMES MADISON argued, in THE FEDERALIST #10, that in a large, diverse republic with a multiplicity of interests it was unlikely that there would ever be permanent majorities and permanent minorities; thus there would be little probability that "a majority of the whole will have a common motive to invade the rights of other citizens." On this assumption, the majorities that do form will be composed of coalitions of minorities that come together for limited self-interested purposes. The majority will thus never have a sense of its own interest as a majority.

By and large, the solution of the Founders has worked remarkably well. There have been no permanent majorities, and certainly none based exclusively on race. Understanding American politics in terms of monolithic majorities and "discrete and insular minorities"—as the Supreme Court appears to do—precludes the creation of a common interest that transcends racial class considerations. By transforming the Fourteenth Amendment into an instrument of class politics, the Court risks either making a majority faction more likely by heightening the majority's awareness of its class status as a majority, or transforming the liberal constitutional regime into one no longer based on majority rule.

EDWARD J. ERLER

Bibliography

ELY, JOHN H. 1980 *Democracy and Distrust: A Theory of Judicial Review.* Pages 75–77 and 135–179. Cambridge, Mass.: Harvard University Press.

ERLER, EDWARD J. 1982 Equal Protection and Personal Rights: The Regime of the "Discrete and Insular Minority." *Georgia Law Review* 16:407–444.

KARST, KENNETH L. and HOROWITZ, HAROLD W. 1974 Affirmative Action and Equal Protection. *Virginia Law Review* 60:955–974.

DISMISSED TIME

See: Released Time

DISORDERLY CONDUCT

See: Breach of the Peace

DISSENTING OPINION

In cases in which the judges of a multijudge court are divided as to the decision, it is customary for those in the minority to file a dissenting opinion. This practice is followed in the Supreme Court of the United States. In recent years, dissenting opinions have been filed in as many as seventy percent of all cases decided by the Court. In a typical TERM over 150 separate dissenting opinions are filed by Justices who find themselves on the losing side.

The author of a dissenting opinion tries to explain why the Court should have decided the case differently. Often a dissenting Justice will attempt to provide the public with an interpretation of the MAJORITY OPINION in order to narrow its scope or to restrict its impact. A strong dissenting opinion may go far to weaken the decision and may point the way for future litigation.

The OPINION OF THE COURT is written by a Justice on the prevailing side designated by the Chief Justice (or the senior Justice in the majority), and must reflect a consensus of the majority. Dissenters have a freer hand: they can make their point more sharply because they do not need to accommodate colleagues who might balk at aspects of their argument. Before the decision of a case is announced, the draft opinions circulate among the Justices. A well-argued dissent can induce the author of the majority opinion to modify its content, either to retain majority support, as in EVERSON V. BOARD OF EDUCATION (1947), or to respond in kind to a particularly harsh attack, as in DRED SCOTT V. SANDFORD (1857). In an extraordinary case, the dissent may attract enough support actually to become the majority opinion.

Dissents are most common during change in the ideological composition of the Court. For a time the dissents portend an imminent revolution in the tendency of judicial thought and point to the future course of decisions. Once the revolution is perfected there follows a time when the dissents resist the new orientation and recall the old orthodoxy. Two of the Court's great dissenters were Justices JOHN MARSHALL HARLAN (1833–1911) and OLIVER WENDELL HOLMES, each of whom stood against the majority of his day and took positions that much later were adopted by the Court.

CHARLES EVANS HUGHES once wrote that "a dissent in the court of last resort is an appeal to the brooding spirit of the law, to the intelligence of a future day. . . ." Contemporaneously, HARLAN F. STONE wrote that "dissents seldom aid in the right development of the law. They often do harm."

DENNIS J. MAHONEY

DISTRICT OF COLUMBIA

"If any of their officers, or creatures, should attempt to oppress the people, or should actually perpetrate the blackest deed, he has nothing to do but get into the ten miles square. Why was this dangerous power given?" The "dangerous power" to which GEORGE MASON objected so vehemently at the Virginia ratifying convention was that vested in Congress by the seventeenth clause of Article I, section 8, "to exercise exclusive legislation in all cases whatsoever, over such district (not exceeding ten miles square) as may . . . become the seat of the government of the United States." That the power to legislate for the capital district should be controversial was a surprise to JAMES MADISON, who had proposed it in the CONSTITUTIONAL CONVENTION OF 1787. He defended the provision as the means by which the federal government might "be guarded from the influence of particular states, or from insults."

The district was established on the banks of the Potomac River between Maryland and Virginia, at a site chosen by GEORGE WASHINGTON, and Congress assumed JURISDICTION over it on February 27, 1801. The location of the capital was agreed to by northern Federalists in exchange for southern acquiescence in federal assumption of state revolutionary war debts. But that location, south of Mason's and Dixon's line, resulted in the greatest national disgrace before the Civil War, namely, that the federal capital was a bastion of slavery and the home of a flourishing slave market. Not until the COMPROMISE OF 1850 was even abomination of slave trading extinguished.

Originally, the District of Columbia comprised one hundred square miles of land ceded by Virginia and Maryland, and three municipal corporations, Washington, Georgetown, and Alexandria. Alexandria was retroceded to Virginia in 1846, at the request of its inhabitants, and the district has since comprised less than seventy square miles. Since 1871, there has been a single municipal corporation coextensive with the district. The 1980 population of over 600,000 was larger than the populations of each of four states.

During most of its history the district's lawmaking was done directly by Congress. There was a brief period of home rule, under a government like those of the TERRITORIES, from 1871 to 1874, during which the district plunged deeply into debt. From 1878 until 1974 the district was governed by three commissioners appointed by the President. Home rule was restored by passage of the DISTRICT OF COLUMBIA GOVERNMENT REORGANIZATION AND SELF-GOVERNING ACT in 1973 and adoption of a city charter in 1974. Since that time the district has been governed by an elected mayor and council, although Congress must approve the budget and retains a veto over other legislation.

The legal status of residents of the District of Columbia is anomalous. The Framers of the Constitution apparently did not foresee a large permanent population in the district distinct from the population of the surrounding states. Even the CITIZENSHIP of district residents, who were not citizens of any state, was uncertain until adoption of the FOURTEENTH AMENDMENT (1868). At least from *Hepburn v. Ellzey* (1805) until the Supreme Court sustained an amendment to the JUDICIAL CODE in *National Mutual Insurance Company v. Tidewater Transfer Company* (1949), citizens of the district could not sue or be sued in federal court under DIVERSITY JURISDICTION. Moreover, district residents were unable to vote for presidential electors until passage of the TWENTY-THIRD AMENDMENT (1961), and they remain unrepresented in Congress to this day (except, since 1970, by a nonvoting delegate). In 1978, Congress proposed the DISTRICT OF COLUMBIA REPRESENTATION AMENDMENT, which would have given the district a status equivalent to statehood, but the amendment failed of RATIFICATION by the state legislatures.

The district has often been the site of experiments in "model legislation," such as the DISTRICT OF COLUMBIA MINIMUM WAGE ACT (1918) and the District of Columbia Crime Control Act (1970). The district is also the focus of demonstrations, small and great, against government policies, ranging from Coxey's army (1894) and the bonus marchers (1932) to Resurrection City (1968) and the marches against the VIETNAM WAR. The right to carry demands for redress of grievances directly to the seat of government is a unique expression of FREEDOM OF PETITION.

Creation of a capital district outside the jurisdiction of any of the constituent states has been copied by other federal unions, including Australia, Brazil, India, and Mexico. The idea that no one member of the federation should control the conditions under which the central government works has thus become a part of the modern theory of FEDERALISM. The all-too-real practical difficulty is that the conditions come to be controlled instead by those who make up the permanent infrastructure of the government and whose perceived interest is in the perpetual growth of that government. In the United States itself, the District of Columbia remains an anomaly, a city dependent almost entirely upon the public payroll serving as the capital of a republic dedicated to the principle of free private enterprise.

DENNIS J. MAHONEY

DISTRICT OF COLUMBIA MINIMUM WAGE LAW
40 Stat. 960 (1918)

Congress, in its capacity as legislature for the DISTRICT OF COLUMBIA, enacted this minimum wage law for women and minors "to maintain them in good health and to protect their morals." Seeking to ground the act on the POLICE POWER, Congress established a Minimum Wage Board with power to compel testimony and other EVIDENCE. The act authorized the board to investigate wage conditions of women and minors in the District of Columbia and to fix their minimum wages on the basis of adequacy "to supply the necessary cost of living." The act required the board to provide PROCEDURAL DUE PROCESS; it also provided for APPEALS to courts of the District and made violations punishable as MISDEMEANORS. The Supreme Court declared the act unconstitutional in ADKINS V. CHILDREN'S HOSPITAL (1923) as a violation of SUBSTANTIVE DUE PROCESS OF LAW, but when the Court overruled *Adkins* in WEST COAST HOTEL CO. V. PARRISH (1937), Attorney General HOMER CUMMINGS declared that the law was in effect without any need for congressional reenactment.

DAVID GORDON

(SEE ALSO: *Unconstitutionality.*)

DISTRICT OF COLUMBIA REPRESENTATION AMENDMENT
92 Stat. 3795 (1978)

Twenty-three times since 1800, congressional representation for the DISTRICT OF COLUMBIA had been sought, mainly on the grounds that taxation of District residents without REPRESENTATION in Congress was undemocratic. The modern District's predominantly black population is larger than that of each of ten states. In 1978 Congress proposed a constitutional amendment that would treat the district as a state is treated for purposes of congressional and ELECTORAL COLLEGE representation and for participation in presidential elections and RATIFICATION OF CONSTITUTIONAL AMENDMENTS. It would have repealed the TWENTY-THIRD AMENDMENT, which had allowed district residents to vote for President and vice-president, while limiting district representation in the electoral college to that of the least populous state. As with other recent amendments, Congress fixed a seven-year time limit for ratification and provided that it would implement the amendment by legislation at a later date.

Although both houses of Congress passed the proposed amendment enthusiastically, it had slight chance of ratification because it would have added two senators and one representative to Congress, all almost certain to be both black and Democrats. In 1985, the period for ratification expired.

PAUL L. MURPHY

Bibliography

BEST, JUDITH 1983 *National Representation of the District of Columbia.* Frederick, Md.: University Publications of America.

DISTRICT OF COLUMBIA SELF-GOVERNING AND GOVERNMENT REORGANIZATION ACT
87 Stat. 774 (1973)

Limited home rule in the DISTRICT OF COLUMBIA had been a long-time desire of its inhabitants. Since 1874, the President had chosen the city's administrators and Congress had acted as the city's governing council. Washingtonians elected only their school board and a nonvoting delegate to the House of Representatives.

This 1973 act granted the District a council, a mayor, and increased self-government. It provided a charter for local government, subject to approval by a majority of the registered voters. Although Congress sought to avoid day-to-day responsibility for District affairs, it retained ultimate legislative authority as provided in Article I, section 8, including the power to legislate generally for the District and to veto local laws. The city government exercised the functions of several quasi-federal agencies: the Redevelopment Land Agency, the National Capital Housing Authority, and the District of Columbia Manpower Administration. The Act reorganized the National Capital Planning Commission, giving the mayor responsibility for District planning, excepting federal and international projects. Further, it required the President, in appointing judges to the District of Columbia Court of Appeals and the Superior Court, to choose from candidates submitted to him by a newly created District of Columbia Judicial Nomination Commission.

The act, while still denying the District congressional REPRESENTATION, satisfied a number of city residents' demands for local control over city affairs.

PAUL L. MURPHY

DIVERSITY JURISDICTION

Under Article III of the Constitution, the JUDICIAL POWER OF THE UNITED STATES extends to "Controversies between Citizens of different States . . . and between . . . the Citizens [of a State] . . . and foreign . . . Citizens or Subjects." This power is called diversity jurisdiction because its basis is the difference in CITIZENSHIP of the parties.

The accepted justification for diversity jurisdiction has been the need to protect out-of-state citizens against discrimination in state courts. However, the extent of such discrimination as of the time the Constitution was written is uncertain, and there is evidence that financial and commercial interests supported diversity jurisdiction in the hope of finding shelter from state laws and judicial systems favorable to debtors.

In fact, the diversity jurisdiction authorized in Article III is not confined to situations in which out-of-state citizens require protection. For example, a plaintiff may file a diversity action in her home state's federal court if she can obtain personal JURISDICTION over the defendant there. Also, it is constitutionally permissible for Congress to confer diversity jurisdiction even when citizens of the same state are on both sides of the litigation, so long as some out-of-state citizens are also parties. Congress has conferred jurisdiction in just such cases in the federal interpleader statute.

Congress has the power to determine how much of the constitutionally authorized diversity jurisdiction the lower federal courts may exercise. It has enacted a general statute that allows the federal courts to hear some but not all types of diversity cases either originally or on REMOVAL. Examples of excluded cases are those in which less than a required amount is in controversy, those in which there is incomplete diversity (that is, at least one plaintiff is from the same state as at least one defendant), and those which the defendant seeks to remove from his or her home state's court.

In 1946 Congress first provided expressly for diversity jurisdiction over suits involving citizens of the DISTRICT OF COLUMBIA and TERRITORIES. In *National Mutual Insurance Co. v. Tidewater Co.* (1949), the Supreme Court upheld the law because two Justices were willing to declare that the District of Columbia was a "state" within the meaning of the diversity clause of Article III, and three Justices concluded that Congress could confer the jurisdiction even if it were not within the Article III judicial power.

The citizenship of parties for purposes of applying the general diversity statute is not always obvious. Some problems have been solved by statute. For example, problems arising from the Court's 1844 decision that a CORPORATION is a citizen of its state of incorporation were resolved by a congressional declaration that a corporation is a citizen of both the state of its incorporation and of the state where its principal place of business is located. Others have been handled by judicial interpretation, which has held, for example, that an individual is a citizen of the state in which he or she is domiciled at the time suit is filed. Difficult interpretive problems remain, however.

Under the Rules of Decision Act, as interpreted in ERIE RAILROAD V. TOMPKINS (1938), a federal court

hearing a diversity case must apply the substantive law of the state in which it is located. It must also employ that state's CHOICE OF LAW rules and any of the state's procedural rules that have a predictable effect on the outcome of the case and do not conflict with the FEDERAL RULES OF CIVIL PROCEDURE or some overriding federal policy. In cases in which state law is unclear or has not yet been decided, the federal court must strive to resolve the case as the state's highest court would, drawing direction from trends and policies manifest in state judicial opinions at all levels. The state courts are not bound by the federal court's decisions interpreting state law.

It is doubtful that Congress could constitutionally enact a law giving to the federal courts or assuming for itself the power to develop substantive law for diversity cases. Although the *Erie* opinion avoided this constitutional issue, fundamental notions of state sovereignty and the limited role of the federal government dictated the decision's interpretation of the Rules of Decision Act. Notwithstanding these limitations, Congress may enact and has enacted rules of procedure regulating diversity cases, even though the rules also affect substantive rights. And because of the federal interest in the orderly and fair treatment of individuals engaged in multistate transactions, Congress likely could also constitutionally enact a body of federal choice of law rules applicable to diversity actions.

Declining concern over the need to protect out-of-state citizens against discrimination in state courts, coupled with rising distress over the heavy caseload of the federal courts, has spawned proposals to eliminate the federal courts' general diversity jurisdiction. While some continue to praise diversity jurisdiction for the continued acquaintance it offers federal judges with the common law process and the access it offers litigants (albeit selectively) to the often superior federal procedural system, those who support congressional repeal of diversity jurisdiction seem to be approaching success. Eventually it may come to be used only in complex, multistate cases, such as CLASS ACTIONS and interpleaders, in which the federal courts' power to issue process nationwide offers substantial advantages over state jurisdiction.

CAROLE E. GOLDBERG-AMBROSE

Bibliography

ELY, JOHN HART 1974 The Irrepressible Myth of *Erie*. *Harvard Law Review* 87:693–740.
SHAPIRO, DAVID 1977 Federal Diversity Jurisdiction: A Survey and a Proposal. *Harvard Law Review* 91:317–355.

DIVORCE AND THE CONSTITUTION

The constitutional power of the states to prescribe conditions for marriage and divorce went largely unchallenged until the mid-twentieth century. Once Americans became highly mobile, however, new constitutional questions emerged. Divorce might be difficult under some states' laws, and well-nigh impossible under others', but in some places the courthouse doors were open. Could two North Carolinians go to Nevada, stay there for six weeks of "residence," obtain EX PARTE divorces from their respective North Carolina spouses, marry each other, and return to live in North Carolina without being guilty of bigamous cohabitation? In two cases entitled *Williams v. North Carolina* (1942, 1945), the Supreme Court answered that question conditionally. The Nevada divorces were valid, and must be given FULL FAITH AND CREDIT by North Carolina, if the travelers really were domiciled in Nevada when they received their divorces. However, domicile was a jurisdictional requirement for the Nevada courts; North Carolina might constitutionally retry the issue of the previous Nevada domicile, and, if its courts found that domicile lacking, might punish its straying residents.

The *Williams* "solution" soon crumbled. The Court held in 1948 that if both husband and wife entered appearances in the Nevada proceeding, then neither of them could later challenge the Nevada divorce by way of COLLATERAL ATTACK. Nor could a third party attack such a JUDGMENT. Perhaps the "true" domiciliary state might prosecute for bigamy in a case just like *Williams*, but few states had North Carolina's zeal for such prosecutions.

Since mid-century American law in this area has undergone two distinct but related revolutions. First, almost all the states now permit the dissolution of marriage on at least one "no fault" ground. Second, in a variety of contexts the Supreme Court has recognized not only a constitutional right to marry but a broad FREEDOM OF INTIMATE ASSOCIATION. It is doubtful that a state's interest in preserving a marriage against the will of one spouse would be given the same weight today that the Court gave it in the 1940s. In SOSNA V. IOWA (1975) the majority did remark that domicile was still a jurisdictional requirement for divorce, but the Court might take a different view if a latter-day prosecutor were to bring bigamy charges in circumstances closely resembling the *Williams* facts. (See MARRIAGE AND THE CONSTITUTION.)

Sosna itself upheld Iowa's one-year durational RESI-DENCE REQUIREMENT as a condition on access to the state's divorce court, rejecting the argument that this limitation denied the constitutional RIGHT TO TRAVEL with the comment that the state had not denied divorce but only delayed it. Lawyers, including Justices, are experts in rationalizing; each day's delay in getting a divorce is surely a denial of one day's single status and of the right to remarry. The *Sosna* rationalization was aimed at distinguishing the Court's earlier decision in BODDIE V. CONNECTICUT (1971). *Boddie* held, on PROCEDURAL DUE PROCESS grounds, that INDIGENTS could not constitutionally be denied ACCESS TO THE COURTS in divorce cases for inability to pay filing fees. The Court there remarked on the "basic importance" of marriage, and took note that the state had a monopoly over its dissolution—and thus the availability of lawful remarriage.

The Court has not recognized a "right to divorce" analogous to the "right to marry" confirmed in LOVING V. VIRGINIA (1967) and ZABLOCKI V. REDHAIL (1978). However, we are not far from the recognition that the Constitution demands important justification for any significant interference with a spouse's freedom to terminate a marriage. Although the virtual disappearance of highly restrictive divorce laws makes less urgent the recognition of this constitutional liberty, that same change in state law surely alters the climate in which the Justices would evaluate the state's interests urged in opposition to the claim of associational freedom.

The collateral issue of child custody can also raise constitutional issues. Of necessity, a domestic relations court must have wide discretion in awarding custody. Yet because the parent–child relation is itself an intimate association of "fundamental" importance, it is vital that the custody decision not be made arbitrarily. The presumption of custody for the mother over a child of "tender years," for example, raises grave issues concerning SEX DISCRIMINATION. Racial and religious grounds for custody obviously raise constitutional danger signals, as PALMORE V. SIDOTI (1984) shows. And for a court to deny custody to a parent simply because he or she is living with another adult outside marriage, or is involved in a homosexual relationship, would also raise serious problems of associational freedom. Of course, at some level of maturity well below the age of adulthood, the child's preference—his or her own associational freedom—takes on constitutional weight that may dominate the custody decision. The Supreme Court has only begun its exploration of these painful subjects. Surely an early priority for the Court will be the reexamination of its old assumptions about the interests that justify a state's imposing its own preferred family patterns on the individuals who must live in them.

KENNETH L. KARST

Bibliography

GARFIELD, HELEN 1980 The Transitory Divorce Action: Jurisdiction in the No-Fault Era. *Texas Law Review* 58:501–547.
KARST, KENNETH L. 1980 The Freedom of Intimate Association. *Yale Law Journal* 89:624–692.
NOTE 1980 Developments in the Law: The Constitution and the Family. *Harvard Law Review* 93:1156, 1308–1350.

DOCTRINE

In constitutional law as in other pursuits of revelation, initiates commonly refer to "doctrines": bodies of rules or principles either authoritatively declared or systematically advocated. Some such doctrines have been simple; the ORIGINAL PACKAGE DOCTRINE is an example. Others, such as the INCORPORATION DOCTRINE, may become shorthand references to larger and more complex creations of the legal mind. More inclusively, one may speak of a doctrine as the body of principles ruling any branch of law, including constitutional law: the doctrine governing PRIOR RESTRAINTS on speech, for example, or the doctrine governing discrimination based on ILLEGITIMACY. In any such use, "doctrine" refers to a body of judicial interpretations of a particular branch of law.

Even more generally, one may speak of constitutional "doctrine" in the abstract, referring to the whole body of rules and principles resulting from the judicial process of CONSTITUTIONAL INTERPRETATION. Our constitutional law, apart from a few rules explicitly stated in the text of the Constitution (such as the requirement that a senator be thirty years old), consists almost entirely of doctrine made by judges in the tradition of the Anglo-American COMMON LAW. Doctrine thus develops as precedents are made by decisions in particular cases. One branch of constitutional doctrine, in fact, is designed in part to assure that the federal courts' lawmaking is informed by the need to apply doctrine to concrete facts. (See CASES AND CONTROVERSIES.) There is therefore a human quality in nearly every constitutional case; a court's opinion normally begins with a recitation of actual facts touching the lives of named individuals. One danger in an era of CLASS ACTIONS and INSTITUTIONAL LITIGATION is that those techniques carry some risk of squeezing the human flavor out of a case,

with attendant costs to the process of keeping doctrine attuned to life. Yet implied in the idea of doctrine is the elaboration of principles transcending the concerns of particular individuals, to provide guidance—or comfort—to people in the aggregate.

Doctrinal formulas may outlive their usefulness, as the "original package doctrine" has. When they do, they fall into disuse or are explicitly abandoned. One of the paradoxes of law is that it strives to provide the security of enduring rules and principles yet is compelled to adjust to the demands of an evolving human society. Constitutional doctrine is rarely tidy and nearly always susceptible to manipulation; it is full of ambiguity and vagueness; "absolute" rules either give way to interest-balancing or serve as interest-balancing's disguises. Doctrine was ever history's handmaiden.

Yet constitutional doctrine has had generating force of its own. It is hard to imagine what this country would have been like but for the nation-building doctrinal contributions of the MARSHALL COURT. And the doctrinal development begun by BROWN V. BOARD OF EDUCATION (1954) has been a major influence in our twentieth-century social and political life. If constitutional doctrine sometimes seems no more than a chapter in a given era's political story, it is sometimes a chapter that advances the plot.

KENNETH L. KARST

Bibliography

BICKEL, ALEXANDER M. 1962 *The Least Dangerous Branch: The Supreme Court at the Bar of Politics.* Indianapolis: Bobbs-Merrill.

DODGE v. WOOLSEY
18 Howard 331 (1856)

The PIQUA BRANCH BANK V. KNOOP (1854) decision striking down the tax on banks enraged the people of Ohio. They exercised SOVEREIGNTY by amending their state CONSTITUTION to empower and require their legislature to tax all banks, regardless of any tax-immunity or tax-preference clauses in their charters. Woolsey, a stockholder of a bank, sued the bank, as well as the tax collector, in a state court to enjoin the collection of a tax authorized by the state legislature under the new amendment to the state constitution. The Supreme Court, by a vote of 6–3, for the first time sustained its JURISDICTION in a STOCKHOLDER'S SUIT and ruled that the state could no more impair the OBLIGATION OF A CONTRACT, contrary to the CONTRACT CLAUSE, by its constitution than by a statute. Justice JOHN A. CAMPBELL, one of the dissenters, angrily asserted that his brethren had established the DOCTRINE that the final power over public revenues was to be found not in the people "but in the numerical majority of the judges of this court. . . ." Besides his heat, he raised a profound question: "Should it be that a state of this Union had become the victim of vicious legislation, its property alienated, its powers of taxation renounced in favor of chartered associations, and the resources of the body politic cut off, what remedy has the people against the misgovernment?" Chief Justice ROGER B. TANEY answered for the majority by saying that the people govern themselves, wisely or not, and are bound to their contracts by the Constitution. By 1862 the Court handed down five more decisions involving the taxation of Ohio banks. The state finally capitulated, and the Court irrevocably committed itself to the doctrine that a grant of tax privileges could not be repealed for the life of the contract.

LEONARD W. LEVY

DOE, CHARLES
(1830–1896)

Charles Cogswell Doe, associate justice of the New Hampshire Supreme Court from 1859 to 1874, and chief justice from 1876 to 1896, is remembered as one of the country's greatest COMMON LAW judges. He is less renowned for his contributions to constitutional law. One reason may have been his bold originality. During his years on the bench, constitutional law was less tolerant of the unorthodox and less receptive to eccentric genius than was the common law. And Doe was original if not eccentric. The perspective from which he viewed the state constitution is an example. The drafters of the document had adopted words indicating they were writing a SOCIAL COMPACT and Doe insisted it had to be interpreted as a social compact. Under the other types of constitutions—those that were organic laws, not compacts—the government, Doe maintained, possesses INHERENT POWERS limited by certain enumerated provisions (for example, the federal *Bill of Rights*). When the liberty of a citizen is pitted against the authority of the state, the citizen must find specific wording to restrain government. A constitution that is a compact, by contrast, has no place for inherent power. As a result, Doe held in WOOSTER V. PLYMOUTH (1882), CIVIL RIGHTS are not immunities but "privileges which society has engaged to provide in lieu of the natural liberties so given up by individuals" under the "contract." The proposition that the compact made government an agent, and individual rights absolute except when specifically surrendered, permitted Doe to relieve the citizen of the burden of establishing constitutional limits on state authority. The state had to demonstrate that the power it claimed had, by compact, been delegated to it.

The chief constitutional DOCTRINE resulting from the social compact doctrine was equality. "The bill of rights," Doe ruled in STATE V. U.S. & CANADA EXPRESS CO. (1880), "is a bill of their equal, private rights, reserved by the grantors of public power." Equality, he added, is "practically the source and sum of all rights, and the substance of the constitution." Doe sought to make equality the most fundamental civil right protecting nineteenth-century Americans.

The national development in constitutional law most troublesome to Judge Doe was the United States Supreme Court's decision in the SINKING FUND CASES (1879). Fearing that the ruling endangered private property rights, he wrote several opinions hoping to diminish those cases' influence. In *Corbin's Case* (1891) Doe even invented the concept of "constitutional estoppel" to bar the state government from taking an action that in a corporate charter it had expressly reserved the right to take. Doe's particular genius even led him to criticize FLETCHER V. PECK (1810) and DARTMOUTH COLLEGE V. WOODWARD (1819), two decisions most contemporaries thought protected property rights. Doe believed they weakened property rights and increased arbitrary legislative power. Better had they been decided on the SEPARATION OF POWERS principle than on the CONTRACT CLAUSE.

In Doe's hands, the separation of powers principle became a means of enlarging his court's JURISDICTION. His distrust of legislative power resulted in support of laissez-faire principles, but his belief that courts should impose common law tests of reasonableness on business supported a measure of regulation. The supremacy of constitutional limitations was his foremost principle.

JOHN PHILLIP REID

Bibliography

REID, JOHN PHILLIP 1967 *Chief Justice: The Judicial World of Charles Doe.* Cambridge, Mass.: Harvard University Press.

DOE v. BOLTON

See: *Roe v. Wade*

DOMBROWSKI v. PFISTER
380 U.S. 479 (1965)

Dombrowski marks the high point of the Supreme Court's willingness to authorize federal district court interference with pending state criminal proceedings. When decided, *Dombrowski* seemed to suggest that such interference was warranted when the state statutes forming the basis of the prosecution were alleged to violate the FIRST AMENDMENT OVERBREADTH DOCTRINE. The CHILLING EFFECT—a term first used in *Dombrowski*—on First Amendment rights of prosecutions under such statutes derived from the fact of the prosecution, thereby rendering successful defense of the prosecution an inadequate remedy for the chilling effect. *Dombrowski* was "reinterpreted" in YOUNGER V. HARRIS (1971) and has since been of little precedential or practical importance.

THEODORE EISENBERG

DOMESTIC COMMERCE

See: Intrastate Commerce

DOREMUS, UNITED STATES v.
249 U.S. 86 (1919)

Congress moved to suppress illegal drug trafficking in the HARRISON ACT of 1919 by compelling persons dealing in narcotics to register with the federal government. The act further imposed a $1 annual license tax, an exercise of the NATIONAL POLICE POWER. Justice WILLIAM R. DAY, for a 5–4 Supreme Court, sustained the entire act even though the provision at issue was the one requiring the use of federal forms for recording transactions. "The act may not be declared unconstitutional," Day said, "because its effect may be to accomplish another purpose as well as the raising of revenue." He found the tax section closely related to the rest of the act. By ignoring LEGISLATIVE INTENT—and his own recent opinion in HAMMER V. DAGENHART (1918) where such intent had been dispositive—he chose to follow the line of precedents beginning with CHAMPION V. AMES (1903). A single-sentence dissent found that the act overstepped Congress's delegated powers and invaded the states' RESERVED POLICE POWER.

DAVID GORDON

(SEE ALSO: *Drug Regulation; Taxing and Spending Power.*)

DOREMUS v. BOARD OF EDUCATION
342 U.S. (1952)

A New Jersey statute provided for the reading, without comment, of five verses of the Old Testament at the opening of each public school day. This was challenged as an ESTABLISHMENT OF RELIGION by a taxpayer of the town of Hawthorne who had had a child in its school system.

Justice ROBERT H. JACKSON, writing for the Supreme Court, rejected the STANDING of the plaintiff to raise the constitutional question. His child had been graduated from school, so that his claim as a parent suffered from MOOTNESS. Furthermore, because there was no showing that public money was spent on the practice, the plaintiff's taxpayer status gave him no stake in the litigation.

Justice WILLIAM O. DOUGLAS, with whom Justices STANLEY F. REED and HAROLD BURTON agreed, dissented. A taxpayer, Douglas argued, had a general interest in how the schools of the community were managed. The effect of this disposition was to defer for a decade decision on the constitutional merits of religious exercises in public schools.

RICHARD E. MORGAN

DORMANT POWERS

A constitutional power is called dormant if it is granted by the constitution but is not currently being exercised. For a variety of reasons Congress may not see fit to exercise power which it has been granted by the Constitution. These dormant powers may be "awakened" whenever Congress chooses to exercise them.

The federal system of the United States presumes that the states possess the governmental powers not taken away from them by the Constitution. In vesting powers in the federal government, the Constitution grants the national government EXCLUSIVE POWER over some matters of national scope, but CONCURRENT POWERS with the states over other matters. When a power granted to the federal government lies dormant, its effect depends on whether it is an exclusive or concurrent power. When the Supreme Court concludes that the subject matter requires uniform national regulation, then the states are not free to exercise the power even though Congress has not legislated in the area. By its silence Congress is presumed to have decreed that the subject shall remain free of regulation. If, on the other hand, the subject of the power admits of locally diverse regulation, as in COOLEY V. BOARD OF WARDENS (1851), states may legislate until Congress intervenes.

When Congress awakens a dormant power by legislating, its act will preempt inconsistent state laws by force of the SUPREMACY CLAUSE of Article VI. However, the courts do not always hold that Congress has preempted state law simply because it has granted power to a federal administrative agency to regulate an area. If the agency has not exercised the power given to it, then the states may yet be free to regulate the subject just as if the power were still dormant.

GLEN E. THUROW

Bibliography

PRITCHETT, C. HERMAN 1977 *The American Constitution,* 3d ed. Pages 150–216. New York: McGraw-Hill.

DORR v. UNITED STATES

See: Insular Cases

DOUBLE JEOPARDY

Double jeopardy is the most ancient procedural guarantee provided by the American BILL OF RIGHTS. Rooted in Greek, Roman, and canon law, the right not to be put twice in jeopardy may be regarded as essential to a right to TRIAL BY JURY, and is well established in the law of other nations.

The Fifth Amendment of the Constitution includes the simple phrase: "nor shall any person be subject for the same offense to be twice put in jeopardy of life or limb." Yet this phrase, which has been copied in most American state constitutions, conceals a number of complex policy issues, many of which are still unsettled in American law in spite of numerous judicial interpretations since its birth in 1791.

In the course of time American courts abandoned any insistence that the jeopardy required involve a risk of life or limb, even though that had been an important consideration under the harsh criminal law of eighteenth-century England. Thus, the policy underlying the double jeopardy protection does not depend upon the hazard of severe physical punishment or death.

The English COMMON LAW recognizes the pleas of *autrefois acquit* (former acquittal) and *autrefois convict* (former conviction) to preclude retrial of an accused person, but American law has taken a more expansive view of the right. In America a prior accusation without a verdict could result in a successful plea of double jeopardy. The American version of the right is more generous to accused persons in many other respects, making double jeopardy an important potential source of protection.

In *Green v. United States* (1957) Justice HUGO L. BLACK provided a persuasive explanation of the American concept of double jeopardy. He suggested that the guarantee against double jeopardy is aimed primarily at three potential abuses of governmental power: "The underlying idea, one that is deeply ingrained in at least the Anglo-American system of jurisprudence, is that the state with all its resources and power should not be allowed to make repeated attempts to convict an individual for an alleged offense, thereby (1) subjecting him to embarrassment, expense and ordeal and (2) compelling him to live in a continuing state of anxiety and insecurity, as well as (3) enhancing the possibility that even though innocent he may be found guilty."

Double jeopardy policy embodies a conflict between a defendant's interest in "being able once and for all, to conclude his confrontation with society," as the Court said in *United States v. Jorn* (1970), and the public interest in a full and accurate prosecution. To preclude retrial of an accused person on some technical defect in the presentation of the prosecution's case is not in the public interest. Conversely, individuals must be protected against repeated risks of criminal punishment so that they may conclude their confrontation with society in a just manner and resume their normal lives as free citizens.

Surprisingly, it was not until 1969 that the Supreme Court extended the Fifth Amendment's double jeopardy prohibition to state criminal prosecutions. In BENTON V. MARYLAND (1969) the Court finally held "that the double jeopardy prohibition of the Fifth Amendment represents a fundamental ideal in our constitutional heritage." Since then the Court has been deeply involved in reviewing double jeopardy questions, refining and reconsidering many of its earlier interpretations of the clause. Now the Supreme Court is the chief source of policymaking in double jeopardy matters, although some state legislatures have begun to reexamine the DOCTRINE in the process of revising state criminal codes to eliminate overlapping criminal offenses.

Double jeopardy law involves at least four distinct policy questions. The first concerns the time when jeopardy begins or "attaches." Clearly, pretrial proceedings are not covered by double jeopardy, but at some point after a trial opens jeopardy is said to "attach." The second double jeopardy question is the legal significance to be accorded political boundaries such as state/federal, state/municipal, national/international. Third is the problem arising from the numerous definitions of crime which sometimes carve up criminal deeds into small parcels of criminalized behavior. These multiple offense categories could give rise to multiple prosecutions unless bounded by the double jeopardy protection. Finally, there is the issue raised by a criminal appeal (by the defendant or the state) with its potential of a new trial reviving the same risks to the liberty of the defendant.

All these issues are embraced within the American doctrine of double jeopardy and none has been definitively resolved. American double jeopardy law has become one of the most complex areas of JUDICIAL POLICYMAKING. English law on the subject lacks the complexity of American law because it is confined largely to the issue of the effect of a prior final judgment. American law is distinctive in its subtle interplay among the interests of the accused person, the prosecution, and the society at large. However, American double jeopardy law is confused by the judicial failure to separate the strands of double jeopardy and to pursue the essential purposes served by double jeopardy. Indeed, close reading of Supreme Court decisions reveals some conflict among the Justices concerning the goals of double jeopardy policy.

In *Crist v. Betz* (1978) the issue of attachment of double jeopardy was called "the lynchpin for all double jeopardy jurisprudence," but it still is not clearly settled. The federal rule is that jeopardy attaches at the time when the jury is sworn, and this federal rule now extends to state proceedings as well. The rule takes effect when the first witness is sworn in a case tried before a judge. After this point, in the absence of exceptional circumstances, the defendant's jeopardy begins, and it cannot be begun again merely because the prosecution wishes to retry a stronger case at a later time.

However, it is possible for the prosecution to retry a case that has been aborted short of FINAL JUDGMENT if it can bear the heavy burden of showing "manifest necessity" for repetitious proceedings. Courts have wrestled vainly in an effort to define the nature of the "manifest necessity" that justifies reprosecution. Recently the Supreme Court has developed a balancing test to weigh the interests of the prosecution and the defendant. Now, if a mistrial is based upon an error by the state that could be manipulated to strengthen the prosecution's case, a defendant is entitled to immunity from reprosecution if he chooses to oppose the mistrial, but not if he requests it. But

the Supreme Court has wavered in its mistrial decisions, even overruling itself at times.

Attachment doctrines apply to JUVENILE PROCEEDINGS as well as to adult criminal trials, so that jeopardy attaches to an adjudicatory finding in juvenile court, preventing a subsequent trial in the criminal court for the same conduct. However, a closed master's hearing for a juvenile has been treated as a pretrial event, not an attachment of jeopardy.

The clearest interpretation of double jeopardy policy appears in the area of separate prosecutions for the same offense by federal and state governments. According to BARTKUS V. ILLINOIS (1959), double jeopardy is inapplicable when a defendant is charged with having violated the laws of two or more different "sovereigns." Yet, after a barrage of criticism of the Supreme Court ruling, the attorney general adopted a policy of avoiding federal reprosecution of a matter already tried by a state where the state prosecution rested upon the same act or acts. This discretionary policy remains an administrative restraint upon federal prosecution. In 1970 the Supreme Court held in *Waller v. Florida* that a state and its municipalities were not "separate sovereigns" in this sense; successive prosecutions thus were barred by the double jeopardy clause.

The most complex and least settled area of double jeopardy involves the meaning of "same offense" in the Fifth Amendment clause. The basic federal rule does not prohibit imposition of two or more punishments for the same activity. Instead, the Supreme Court has largely left it to the Congress and the state legislatures to carve up a single act or series of acts into an appropriate set of criminal offenses. The possibility of fragmentation of a single act into a number of criminal offenses with separate trials for each generally is not an occasion for judges to invoke the double jeopardy protection, although the Supreme Court has made some limited attempts to do so.

The double jeopardy clause is not a barrier to an APPEAL by the prosecution in a criminal case. The government may appeal decisions in a criminal case only if authorized by statute. Since the ORGANIZED CRIME CONTROL ACT of 1970, which grants the right to appeal a sentence imposed upon a "dangerous special offender," reviews of sentences are available to the federal government. The Supreme Court has held in *United States v. DiFrancesco* (1980) that the increase of a sentence on review under this statute does not constitute multiple punishment in violation of the double jeopardy clause. Whenever a defendant appeals from his own conviction he is usually said to have "waived" his right to plead double jeopardy.

Taken together, double jeopardy doctrines appear still to be somewhat unsettled in the United States. The general contours of double jeopardy have been described since 1969 in increasing detail. Yet inconsistencies and uncertainties continue. This most ancient of American rights is subject to judicial balancing. Increasingly, the balance has been more favorable to the prosecution, contracting the generous scope of double jeopardy evident in earlier years. Since the Supreme Court has been deeply divided on double jeopardy issues we may expect continued developments of policy with changes in judicial personnel. States may have more stringent views of double jeopardy policy under their own double jeopardy provisions. Therefore some states may set higher standards than the Supreme Court for the protection of defendants.

JAY A. SIGLER

Bibliography

FRIEDLAND, MARTIN 1969 *Double Jeopardy.* Oxford: Clarendon Press.
SIGLER, JAY A. 1969 *Double Jeopardy: The Development of a Legal and Social Policy.* Ithaca, N.Y.: Cornell University Press.
WESTIN, PETER and DRUBEL, RICHARD 1979 Toward a General Theory of Double Jeopardy. *Supreme Court Review* 1978:81–169.

DOUGLAS, STEPHEN A.
(1813–1861)

An Illinois lawyer and judge, Stephen Arnold Douglas served in the House of Representatives (1843–1847) and the Senate (1847–1861), where he chaired the powerful committee on the TERRITORIES from 1847 until 1859. Throughout his career Douglas was a strong Democratic partisan who advocated western expansion, railroad development, and compromise on slavery. A major political figure throughout the 1850s, Douglas closed his career with his losing presidential campaign in 1860. When the Civil War began Douglas rallied to the cause of the Union despite his hostility toward Lincoln and his familial and residual political ties to the South.

Throughout his career Douglas attempted to finesse the issue of SLAVERY IN THE TERRITORIES while supporting territorial acquisition and western settlement. Douglas hoped such a policy would lead to a presidential nomination from a united Democratic party. Practical politics dovetailed with Douglas's personal beliefs that blacks were inferior to whites, that slavery was a legitimate institution deserving of constitutional and political protection, and that ABOLITIONISTS were troublemakers or worse.

The key to Douglas's program was POPULAR SOVEREIGNTY, which would allow settlers to decide the slavery issue for themselves, and thus not require Congress, and the national Democratic party, to take a position on slavery in any particular territory. Ultimately, Douglas's position proved costly. Proslavery Democrats eventually demanded federal protection for slavery in the territories and opposed any Democrat who would not support them. On the other hand, Northerners, in Illinois and elsewhere, came to oppose the spread of slavery into the western territories. By 1858 Douglas discovered he could not satisfy the voters at home and remain a viable presidential candidate in the South.

As early as 1844–1845 Douglas had advocated that settlers in the West be allowed to decide for themselves the status of slavery. In Congress he urged the organization of the Oregon Territory without slavery because settlers there did not want slavery. In the House and Senate Douglas enthusiastically supported all American claims in Oregon and the Mexican War, and he opposed the WILMOT PROVISO. As chairman of the Committee on the Territories, Douglas secured the organization of the Oregon and Minnesota territories without slavery. In August 1850, Douglas resurrected the compromise measures of HENRY CLAY's "Omnibus Bill" and adroitly guided them through the Senate, one bill at a time, as the COMPROMISE OF 1850. The Compromise included the infamous Fugitive Slave Law of 1850, the admission of California without slavery, and organization of the rest of the Mexican Cession with slavery. The compromise satisfied few, but it halted a SECESSION movement then building in the South and probably delayed the Civil War by ten years.

In 1854 Douglas supported the KANSAS-NEBRASKA ACT in the expectation that it would stimulate western expansion and set the stage for a transcontinental railroad, which he hoped would begin in Chicago. The act repealed the MISSOURI COMPROMISE, refused "to legislate slavery into any Territory of State, nor to exclude it therefrom," and left the settlers "perfectly free to form and regulate their domestic institutions in their own way." Northern resentment of this sellout to slavery resulted in Democratic electoral defeats and formation of the Republican party, while popular sovereignty in the territories quickly degenerated into "bleeding Kansas." Douglas lost political support throughout the North, but he explained to hostile constituents that popular sovereignty would lead to a free

Kansas. In 1858, however, Kansas petitioned for statehood under the proslavery LECOMPTON CONSTITUTION. Douglas opposed the Lecompton Constitution because it was ratified by fraud, did not represent the majority in Kansas, and thus was not a fair expression of popular sovereignty. For this opposition Douglas was virtually read out of his party. Later that year, in debate with ABRAHAM LINCOLN during the Senate race, Douglas defended the Supreme Court's decision in DRED SCOTT V. SANDFORD (1857) and the Kansas-Nebraska Act by asserting in the FREEPORT DOCTRINE that territorial governments could prevent slavery by denying it police protection or supportive legislation. Despite opposition from the Buchanan wing of his own party, as well as Lincoln, Douglas was reelected to the Senate. In 1859 his party, dominated by Southerners, stripped him of his Territorial Committee chairmanship because of his apostasy on the Lecompton Constitution and his Freeport Doctrine. Openly a presidential candidate since 1852, Douglas led a divided party in 1860. He ran second in popular votes and a distant fourth in electoral votes. Douglas opposed SECESSION and before his death in 1861 urged Lincoln to call out enough troops to defend the Union.

PAUL FINKELMAN

Bibliography

JAFFA, HARRY V. 1959 *Crisis of the House Divided: An Interpretation of the Lincoln-Douglas Debates.* Garden City, N.Y.: Doubleday.

JOHANNSEN, ROBERT W. 1973 *Stephen A. Douglas.* New York: Oxford University Press.

DOUGLAS, WILLIAM O.
(1898–1980)

William Orville Douglas was appointed to the Supreme Court by President FRANKLIN D. ROOSEVELT on April 15, 1939, the youngest appointee since JOSEPH STORY, 128 years earlier. Illness forced his retirement on November 12, 1975, but he had surpassed by nearly two years the record for longevity of service previously held by STEPHEN J. FIELD.

As a child, Douglas contracted polio and overcame the residual weakness in his legs through long solitary hikes. When his father died before Douglas's sixth birthday, his mother was left nearly penniless with three children. Douglas knew grinding poverty and from his childhood, through all of his education, he worked to support himself and his family. Three views that colored his outlook on life emerged from this period and strongly influenced his legal views. Above all an individualist, he believed that, if given enough room by society, one could achieve full potential through self-reliance and hard work. At the same time, he formed a deep sympathetic bond with the outcasts and disadvantaged of society, particularly the poor, racial minorities, and political radicals. Finally, he harbored a lingering resentment of "the establishment," a view that later matured into a distrust of concentrations of power, whether of the private sector, the police, or government generally. A number of Douglas's legal positions trace their origin to these three linked premises, from his populist view of the antitrust laws to his repeated insistence that the function of the BILL OF RIGHTS was to take government off the backs of the people.

Douglas's career prior to his appointment to the Court also explains the hallmarks of his judicial style. (Over the years, even admirers of the Justice's substantive conclusions criticized his opinions for insufficiently explaining the origins of novel legal DOCTRINES, for carelessness in setting out the limits and definitions of the principles announced, and for unnecessary inconsistency in arguments made from one case to another.) Douglas was always a superior student, with an intellect in the genius range, yet from high school through law school, as he explained in his autobiography, "I had been trotting while I learned." His work obligations and his other activities left little time for reflection. Douglas was a quick study.

Douglas described both his initial appointment as a law teacher and his appointment to the Supreme Court as furnishing new leisure for intellectual contemplation. Intellectual habits, however, are not so easily set aside. Douglas was never contemplative. His habit was to analyze swiftly mountains of data, get to the heart of a controversy, and decide. He was impatient with extended discussion as an aid to decision, with long indecision prior to decision, and with excessive concern for peripheral issues. He remained a loner who spent little time trying to proselytize other members of the Court to his own views. In the Court's conferences and in his separate opinions, he was content to state his positions without adapting them to gain greater acceptance from either his brethren or the scholarly community.

Douglas's impatience with traditional legal style in opinions is also easily explained. As a law professor at Columbia and Yale, Douglas was at the center of the realist movement in jurisprudence. (See LEGAL REALISM.) The realists shared the view that traditional judicial opinions obscured rather than explained the reasons for decision. Douglas's own approach to his fields of business organization, securities regulation, and bankruptcy was to study the political, economic, and social institutions with which the law dealt and to shape the law to cope with contemporary problems presented by those institutions. And so it was with his approach to constitutional law. Douglas viewed much of the elaborate argument in standard Court opinions as so much "Harvard fly paper." Indeed, he delighted in sharp criticism of his opinion-writing style, which he viewed as the carping of the conservative legal establishment. He remained a pragmatist who did not try to develop a general theory of constitutional adjudication. Often he was content to let Justices with whom he agreed develop the overarching theories. He was indifferent to scholarly debates about the abstract limits of JUDICIAL ACTIVISM, and he did not have a consistent theory explaining his own pattern of judicial restraint and active judicial intervention.

The substance of Douglas's constitutional jurisprudence can best be explained by contrast with the views of the two other major figures among Roosevelt's appointees to the Court—FELIX FRANKFURTER and HUGO L. BLACK. Between 1937 and 1939, when these three joined the Court, the chief constitutional controversies were still perceived as those of the previous decade—the Court's "economic due process" theory had restrained state ECONOMIC REGULATION, and its "dual federalism" theory had limited federal power to regulate the national economy. The mainstream of constitutional law thought was still preoccupied by the mistakes of the "old Court" in writing its own notions of laissez-faire economics into constitutional limits on state and federal power. All of Roosevelt's appointees shared the opinion that these decisions of the old Court had been erroneous. The major battles surrounding economic due process, and the legitimate scope of federal economic regulatory authority, however, were over before Roosevelt appointed a single Justice to the Court. (See WAGNER ACT CASES; WEST COAST HOTEL V. PARRISH, 1937.)

The early 1940s brought new problems, with personal liberty claims asserted under the FIRST AMENDMENT, and attacks on criminal convictions for procedural irregularities of constitutional dimension. For Frankfurter, the lessons of the Court's previous excesses in second-guessing state and federal economic regulation applied here. It was inappropriate for judges to block decisions of political majorities simply because judges held deep personal views that those decisions were wrong. Issues of personal liberty involved a balance between legitimate interests of government and claims of constitutionally protected liberty. Judges must defer to reasonable governmental accommodations of these competing interests. Moreover, in the case of challenged state laws, interests of FEDERALISM imposed additional constraints.

For a brief initial period, Black and Douglas accepted the Frankfurter position. In *Minersville School District v. Gobitis* (1940), the first of the FLAG SALUTE CASES, Justice Frankfurter wrote for the Court, sustaining a law compelling salute to the flag against a challenge by children of Jehovah's Witnesses, whose religious beliefs forbade their participation. (Only Justice HARLAN FISKE STONE dissented.)

The break with Frankfurter came soon. Black and Douglas shared similar concerns about the rights of minorities and about fair procedures in state and federal criminal trials. In 1942, dissenting in *Jones v. Opelika,* a case sustaining a state license tax applied to the sale of religious literature, they announced that they had recanted their position in *Gobitis. Jones* was overruled a year later in MURDOCK V. PENNSYLVANIA (1943), with Douglas writing for the Court. The same year, West Virginia State Board of Education v. Barnette overruled *Gobitis,* with Black and Douglas joining Justice ROBERT H. JACKSON's opinion.

Even though Black and Douglas often wrote jointly in constitutional cases involving claims of constitutionally protected liberty, it was Black who was the theoretician. Black gradually evolved the views that protection of liberty required the Court to give liberal—and even literal—construction to the Bill of Rights, and that the Bill of Rights restricted not only the national government but also state governments, because, historically, it had been "incorporated" into section one of the FOURTEENTH AMENDMENT. (See INCORPORATION DOCTRINE.) Douglas and Black often clashed with Frankfurter on both issues throughout the 1940s and 1950s.

In ADAMSON V. CALIFORNIA (1947) the Court decided, 5–4, that the RIGHT AGAINST SELF-INCRIMINATION of the Fifth Amendment was inapplicable to the states. Justice Frankfurter, concurring, defended the Court's position that the historic and practical meaning of due process was not contained in the specific provisions of the Bill of Rights, but he also insisted that working out the limits of DUE PROCESS OF LAW required more than personal judgments according to a judge's idiosyncratic sense of justice. Black, joined by Douglas, wrote a lengthy dissent arguing that the Fourteenth Amendment incorporated the "specific" standards of the Bill of Rights.

As time passed, Black, again joined by Douglas, further insisted that the guarantees of the Bill of Rights were specific indeed. Characteristic was their position concerning the First Amendment—that it literally forbade all government restrictions upon the content of "speech," leaving to the government power only to regulate "conduct" (for example, YATES V. UNITED STATES, 1957, separate opinion). Justice Frankfurter predictably insisted that free speech claims involved a balance between competing interests and required deference to legislative choices (BEAUHARNAIS V. ILLINOIS, 1952). During the 1950s, the Frankfurter position usually prevailed. Black and Douglas were often in lonely dissent as the Court sustained a series of state and federal antisubversion measures. With the appointment of Chief Justice EARL WARREN and Justice WILLIAM J. BRENNAN in the mid-1950s, the dissenting group grew to four.

After Frankfurter's retirement in 1962, the substance, if not the rhetoric, of many of the Black and Douglas dissenting opinions prevailed. Although the Court rejected total "incorporation" of the Bill of Rights, a process of "selective incorporation" of "fundamental" provisions applied nearly all of its provisions to state governments (for example, GRIFFIN V. CALIFORNIA, 1965, overruling Adamson v. California). The provisions of the Bill of Rights governing procedure in criminal trials were expansively construed in cases such as MIRANDA V. ARIZONA (1966). And while no other Justice accepted the Black-Douglas theory that the First Amendment literally protected all speech, the Court's cases of the 1960s rejected the Frankfurter position that the First Amendment tolerated all reasonable governmental restriction on speech. (See NEW YORK TIMES V. SULLIVAN, 1964; BRANDENBURG V. OHIO, 1969.)

The 1960s, however, brought new constitutional problems and a noticeable split between Justices Black and Douglas. There was a negative side to Black's theory pinning activist protection of liberty to the literal meaning of the Bill of Rights. For Black, the Bill of Rights defined not only the minimum guarantees of constitutionally protected liberty but also the maximum. As with Frankfurter's approach, the restrictive branch of Black's theory could be traced to the judicial excesses of the past. The "old Court" had used a natural law approach to write into the Constitution laissez-faire economic policies not fairly reflected in the document's history or text. For Black it was equally wrong for judges to import subjective notions of personal liberty into the Constitution. If judges balanced competing interests in interpreting the Constitution, there was danger beyond the certainty that judges would "balance away" constitutional restrictions with which they were unsympathetic. Judges

might also use an open-ended balancing process to create rights according to their subjective predilections.

In Adamson v. California, two other dissenting Justices—FRANK MURPHY and WILEY B. RUTLEDGE—had agreed with Black and Douglas that the Fourteenth Amendment incorporated the Bill of Rights as restrictions on state government. They had disagreed, however, with the contention that the Bill of Rights was the outer limit of constitutionally protected liberty. In their view, the Fourteenth Amendment's conception of due process required "fundamental standards of procedure . . . despite the absence of a specific provision of the Bill of Rights." Black and Douglas, on the other hand, had condemned the "natural law-due process formula" which allowed courts "to roam at large in the broad expanse of policy and morals and to trespass, all too freely, on the legislative domain. . . ."

In the late 1940s and the 1950s Douglas continued to support Black's literalist position. Occasional votes can be identified during this period, however, to suggest that his agreement with Black was only skin deep. In Francis v. Resweber (1947), decided only months before Adamson, the Court permitted a state to electrocute a man after a first attempt at his execution had failed. The vote was again 5–4. This time Black concurred in the result, without opinion. Douglas, along with Murphy and Rutledge, joined Justice HAROLD BURTON's dissent. The same year, another 5–4 vote, in Kotch v. Board of River Pilot Commissioners (1947), sustained a Louisiana law that limited the occupation of river pilots to friends and relatives of incumbents. Black wrote for the Court, but Douglas and Murphy joined Rutledge's dissent.

In the late 1960s, more cases arose testing the negative side of Black's constitutional literalism and the break with Black had become apparent. (Interestingly, Douglas never openly conceded that he had recanted his agreement with Black in the Adamson case. Only in the posthumously published second volume of his autobiography does he admit that the Murphy and Rutledge position was one with which he "in the years to come, was inclined to agree.") The pattern of voting disagreements with Black in the 1960s was no longer episodic but dramatic. Their differences can be seen on a wide range of issues, all centering on Black's consistent rejection of what he called the "natural law" approach to constitutional adjudication and Douglas's growing willingness to go beyond the literal text of the document.

Douglas wrote the Court's opinion in HARPER V. VIRGINIA STATE BOARD OF ELECTIONS (1966), striking down poll taxes in state elections under the EQUAL PROTECTION clause. Black dissented. Douglas also wrote for the Court in LEVY V. LOUISIANA (1968), striking down a state law discriminating against children born out of wedlock. Again, he relied on an expansive interpretation of the equal protection clause. Justice Black was in dissent and, three years later (*Labine v. Vincent*, 1971), wrote an opinion for the Court that seemed at the time to overrule *Levy*. Here, Black emphasized the absence of any "specific constitutional guarantee." Douglas, of course, was in dissent. Douglas endorsed open-ended theories extending the Fourteenth Amendment's restrictions on STATE ACTION to actions by private business. Black disagreed, insisting that in the absence of federal legislation, the Fourteenth Amendment was inapplicable to private conduct. (See BELL V. MARYLAND, 1973.) With reference to limitations on the time, place, or manner of speech activities on public property, Douglas was prepared to balance the need for available avenues of dissent against competing state interests, if the balance favored freedom of expression. Black disagreed. In ADDERLEY V. FLORIDA (1966), a 5–4 decision sustaining a sheriff's order that protesters leave a jail driveway, Black wrote for the Court and Douglas for the dissent. Finally, Douglas was prepared to interpret the Constitution to require government to follow fair criminal, civil, and administrative procedures even where those requirements could not be tied to specific guarantees of the Bill of Rights. Black, of course, disagreed. (See IN RE WINSHIP, 1970; GOLDBERG V. KELLY, 1970.)

The most dramatic clash between the two former judicial allies occurred in GRISWOLD V. CONNECTICUT (1965). Douglas wrote for the Court, striking down a state law forbidding the use of contraceptive devices. In that case, Black's dissent was predictable, since no provision of the Bill of Rights dealt with the issue. Douglas made a valiant attempt in his opinion to maintain the façade of his agreement with Black eighteen years earlier in *Adamson*. The opinion explained that the right of marital privacy was within "penumbras, formed by emanations" of specific guarantees of the Bill of Rights. (See PENUMBRA THEORY.) The façade was thin, particularly as Douglas relied on the NINTH AMENDMENT for the proposition that constitutionally protected liberty was not limited to the specific guarantees of the Bill of Rights. Just how far removed from even the "penumbras" of the Bill of Rights was Douglas's own conception of the constitutional guarantee of privacy became apparent years later in his concurrence in the abortion cases (*Doe v. Bolton* and ROE V. WADE, 1973; see also RIGHT OF PRIVACY.) Here, he explained that the term "liberty" in the Fourteenth Amendment, as he read it, was broader than the Court's conception of a right to freedom of choice in the areas of marriage, divorce, procreation, contraception, and the education and upbringing of children. It included "the freedom to care for one's health and person, freedom from bodily restraint or compulsion, freedom to walk, stroll or loaf." These, too, were rights that he insisted could not be abridged by government absent a COMPELLING STATE INTEREST.

Douglas had come to believe that the excesses of the old Court in the economic due process cases had not been that the judges read personal values into the fabric of the Constitution. The problem was, rather, that the Court's laissez-faire economic values were the wrong values. For Douglas, the "right" values had been clear all along. They required protecting the individual's right to self-fulfillment, protecting the politically powerless from unsympathetic legislative majorities, insulating the individual from excess concentrations of governmental and private power, and insisting that government procedures be fundamentally fair.

These values best explain Douglas's decisions, up until the end. In his own written instructions for his funeral service, conducted in Washington, D.C., in January 1980, Douglas requested that Woody Guthrie's song "This Land is Your Land" be sung. He patiently explained that some had falsely assumed the song to be a hymn to socialism. Quite to the contrary, he said, the song was in praise of the freedom to wander from place to place which had received constitutional protection in his opinion for the Court in *Papachristou v. City of Jacksonville* (1972).

The *Papachristou* decision was a fitting epitaph. Douglas had written for a unanimous Court striking down a local VAGRANCY ordinance under the due process clause of the Fourteenth Amendment. The technical basis for the decision was that the ordinance was unconstitutionally vague. Insofar as activities that were "normally innocent" were made crimes, an unfettered discretion was placed in the hands of the police. But, quoting Walt Whitman, Henry David Thoreau, and Vachel Lindsay, he went on to argue that wandering and strolling were more than merely "innocent" activities. They were "historically part of the amenities of life as we have known them. They are not mentioned in the Constitution or in the Bill of Rights. These unwritten amenities have been in part responsible for giving our people the feeling of independence and self-confidence, the feeling of creativity. These amenities have dignified the right of dissent and have honored the right to be nonconformists and the right to defy submissiveness. They have encouraged lives of high spirits rather than hushed, suffocating silence." The *Papachristou* opinion, in its results, its style, and the values it enshrined, was vintage Douglas.

WILLIAM COHEN

Bibliography

COUNTRYMAN, VERN 1977 *The Douglas Opinions.* New York: Random House.
DOUGLAS, WILLIAM O. 1974 *Go East, Young Man: The Early Years.* New York: Random House.
———— 1980 *The Court Years: 1939–1975.* New York: Random House.
KARST, KENNETH L. 1969 Invidious Discrimination: Justice Douglas and the Return of the "Natural-Law-Due-Process Formula." *UCLA Law Review* 16:716–750.
POWE, L. A., JR. 1974 Evolution to Absolutism: Justice Douglas and the First Amendment. *Columbia Law Review* 74:371–411.
SIMON, JAMES F. 1980 *Independent Journey: The Life of William O. Douglas.* New York: Harper & Row.

DOUGLAS v. CALIFORNIA
372 U.S. 353 (1963)

Douglas, decided the same day as GIDEON V. WAINWRIGHT (1963), established an EQUAL PROTECTION right for INDIGENTS to be supplied counsel by the state, free of charge, to represent them in direct APPEALS from their criminal convictions. Justice WILLIAM O. DOUGLAS, for a 6–3 majority, followed the lead of GRIFFIN V. ILLINOIS (1956): DUE PROCESS might not require the state to offer appellate review of convictions, but once appeals were granted as of right, they must be made *effectively* available for all. The state's procedure, which provided appellate counsel only when the appeals court found such an appointment appropriate, denied "that equality demanded by the FOURTEENTH AMENDMENT."

Justice JOHN MARSHALL HARLAN, dissenting, elaborated on his *Griffin* dissent. The Fourteenth Amendment had enacted no "philosophy of leveling"; the state had no affirmative duty to relieve the poor from the handicaps of poverty. Due process was satisfied by the reasonableness of the state's procedure for appointing counsel.

Douglas appeared to be a major precedent pointing toward strict judicial scrutiny of WEALTH DISCRIMINATION. However, the BURGER COURT ended such speculations, even in the field of criminal justice. (See ROSS V. MOFFITT, 1974; STRICT SCRUTINY.)

KENNETH L. KARST

DOWDELL v. UNITED STATES

See: Insular Cases

DOWLING, NOEL T.
(1885–1969)

Constitutional problems of FEDERALISM were the chief interest of Noel Thomas Dowling, Columbia University's principal teacher of constitutional law for three decades (1926–1956). Joining the Columbia faculty in 1922, Dowling, a gentle Alabamian, moved into constitutional law when the more corrosive THOMAS REED POWELL departed for Harvard. The main sources of Dowling's influence were his casebook, his articles, and his consulting activities.

Dowling's widely used book, *Cases on Constitutional Law,* was first published in 1937, at the height of the New Deal crisis. Its major theme reflected his lifelong concern: "the regulatory power of government, national and state." His teaching stressed the lawyer's role in constitutional litigation. His emphasis on statutes and LEGISLATIVE FACTS reflected his long participation in the work of Columbia's Legislative Drafting Research Fund.

Dowling advised on the drafting of a number of federal and state statutes. PRUDENTIAL INSURANCE CO. V. BENJAMIN (1946), upholding the McCARRAN ACT of 1945 granting congressional permission for continued state regulation of insurance, was a special vindication for Dowling's emphasis on the broad scope of the congressional "consent" power. Similarly, Chief Justice HARLAN F. STONE's "balancing" opinion in SOUTHERN PACIFIC CO. V. ARIZONA (1945) vindicated Dowling's advocacy of a significant judicial role in curbing state intrusions on free trade in the absence of congressional action.

GERALD GUNTHER

Bibliography
SYMPOSIUM 1958 A Tribute to Noel Thomas Dowling. *Columbia Law Review* 58:589–613.

DOWNES v. BIDWELL

See: Insular Cases

DRAFT CARD BURNING

The burning of Selective Service registration certificates—or "draft cards"—was a brief and dramatic episode that punctuated the early opposition to the VIET-

NAM WAR. Many draft registrants, often before television cameras, publicly burned their cards to demonstrate their refusal to participate in the draft. These events attracted wide attention and often served as a rallying point for war protesters.

Congress responded in 1965 by amending the Universal Military Training and Service Act to make it a FELONY when any person "knowingly destroys [or] knowingly mutilates" his registration certificate. This law was challenged by David O'Brien with the aid of the AMERICAN CIVIL LIBERTIES UNION. O'Brien had burned his registration certificate before a sizable Boston crowd, including several FBI agents. He was indicted, tried, convicted, and sentenced to prison in the Massachusetts District Court, but the United States Court of Appeals held that the 1965 law unconstitutionally abridged FREEDOM OF SPEECH because it interfered with O'Brien's "symbolic" protest against the war.

In *United States v. O'Brien* (1968), the Supreme Court in an opinion by Chief Justice EARL WARREN reversed the Court of Appeals and upheld the challenged law and O'Brien's conviction. The Court first ruled that the Government has a "substantial interest in assuring the continued availability" of draft cards—for example, so that the individual can prove he has registered and so communication between registrants and local boards can be facilitated, particularly in an emergency. Second, in a more far-reaching holding, the Court rejected O'Brien's claim that the 1965 amendment was unconstitutional because Congress sought to suppress freedom of speech. The Court did not determine whether that in fact was Congress's purpose. Instead it ruled that such a purpose would not invalidate the law in light of the principle that courts may not "restrain the exercise of lawful [congressional] power on the assumption that a wrongful purpose or motive has caused the power to be exercised." (See MCCRAY V. UNITED STATES, 1903.)

Only Justice WILLIAM O. DOUGLAS dissented from the Court's decision, in an opinion that dwelt less on draft card burning than on the power of Congress to initiate a peacetime draft. The *O'Brien* case led to a sharp curtailment of draft card burning and opponents of the Vietnam War turned to other forms of protest.

NORMAN DORSEN

Bibliography

ALFANGE, DEAN, JR. 1968 Free Speech and Symbolic Conduct: The Draft Card Burning Case. *Supreme Court Review* 1968:1–52.

DRAPER v. UNITED STATES
358 U.S. 307 (1959)

In *Draper* the Supreme Court held that information provided by a previously reliable informer, even though hearsay and not within the personal knowledge of the police, is sufficient to establish PROBABLE CAUSE for an arrest, at least when there is substantial corroboration for the information.

JACOB W. LANDYNSKI

DR. BONHAM'S CASE

See: Bonham's Case

DRED SCOTT v. SANDFORD
19 Howard 393 (1857)

Closely associated with the coming of the Civil War, DRED SCOTT V. SANDFORD remains one of the most famous decisions of the United States Supreme Court. It is certainly the prime historical example of judicial power exercised in the interest of racial subordination, and, as such, it stands in sharp contrast with BROWN V. BOARD OF EDUCATION (1954), handed down almost a century later.

Scott was a Missouri slave owned by an army medical officer named John Emerson, who took him to live at military posts in Illinois and in federal territory north of 36°30′ where SLAVERY had been prohibited by the MISSOURI COMPROMISE. In 1846, Scott brought suit against Emerson's widow in St. Louis, claiming that he had been emancipated by his residence on free soil. Missouri precedent was on his side, and after two trials he won his freedom. In 1852, however, the state supreme court reversed that judgment. By a 2–1 vote and in bitterly sectional language, it declared that the state would no longer enforce the antislavery law of other jurisdictions against Missouri's own citizens. Scott's residence elsewhere, it held, did not change his status as a slave in Missouri.

Normally, the next step should have been an APPEAL to the United States Supreme Court, but a recent decision in the somewhat similar case of STRADER V. GRAHAM (1851) may have persuaded Scott's legal advisers that the Court would refuse to accept JURISDICTION. They decided instead to initiate a brand new suit for freedom in the federal CIRCUIT COURT for Missouri against Mrs. Emerson's brother, John F. A.

Sanford of New York, who had been acting as her agent in the Scott litigation and may even have become the slave's owner. Sanford's New York CITIZEN-SHIP provided the foundation for DIVERSITY JURISDIC-TION. So began the case of *Dred Scott v. Sandford* (with Sanford's name misspelled in the official record).

Up to this point, the principal issue in Scott's suit had been how residence on free soil affected the legal status of a slave. It was a familiar issue that dated back to the noted British case of *Somerset v. Stewart* (1772) and had been dealt with in a number of state court decisions. (See SOMERSET'S CASE.) During the early decades of American independence, a tacit sectional accommodation had prevailed. Southerners accompanied by slaves were generally able to travel and sojourn in free states without interference. At the same time, southern courts joined in upholding the rule that a slave domiciled in a free state became forever free. Beginning in the 1830s, however, this arrangement broke down under antislavery pressure. State after state in the North withdrew the privilege of maintaining slaves while sojourning, and there was growing judicial acceptance of the view that any slave other than a fugitive became free the moment he set foot on free soil. (See COMMONWEALTH V. AVES, 1836.) To Southerners the change meant not only inconvenience but also insult, and by the 1850s they were retaliating in various ways.

Dred Scott v. Sandford raised an additional issue. In order to maintain a suit in federal court, Scott had to aver that he was a citizen of Missouri. Sanford's counsel challenged this assertion with a plea in abatement arguing that Negroes were not citizens and that the Court therefore lacked jurisdiction. The trial judge ruled that any person residing in a state and legally capable of owning property was qualified to bring suit under the diverse-citizenship clauses of the Constitution and the JUDICIARY ACT. On the merits of the case, however, he instructed the jury in favor of the defendant. Like the Missouri Supreme Court in *Scott v. Emerson*, he declared that Scott's status, after returning to Missouri, depended entirely upon the law of that state, without regard to his residence in Illinois and free federal territory. The jury accordingly brought in a verdict for Sanford.

The case then proceeded on WRIT OF ERROR to the United States Supreme Court, whose membership at the time consisted of five southern Democrats, two northern Democrats, one northern Whig, and one Republican. Argument before the Court in February 1856 introduced another new issue. For the first time, Sanford's lawyers maintained that Scott had not be-

come free in federal territory because the law forbidding slavery there was unconstitutional. This, of course, was the issue that had inflamed national politics for the past decade and would continue to do so in the final years of the sectional crisis. With a presidential contest about to begin, the Justices prudently ordered the case to be reargued at the next session. On March 6, 1857, two days after the inauguration of James Buchanan, Chief Justice ROGER B. TANEY finally read the decision of the Court.

Although Taney spoke officially for the Court, every other member had something to say, and only one concurred with him in every particular. The effect of the decision was therefore unclear, except that Dred Scott had certainly lost. Seven Justices concluded that at law he remained a slave. Taney, in reasoning his way to that judgment, also ruled that free blacks were not citizens and that Congress had no power to prohibit SLAVERY IN THE TERRITORIES. But were these declarations authoritative parts of the decision?

According to some contemporary critics and later historians, Taney did not speak for a majority of the Court in excluding Negroes from citizenship. Their conclusion rests upon the assumption that only those Justices expressly agreeing with him can be counted on his side. Yet, since Taney's opinion was the authorized opinion of the Court, it seems more reasonable to regard only those Justices expressly disagreeing with him as constituting the opposition. By this measure, the opinion never encountered dissent from more than two Justices at any major point. Furthermore, five Justices in their opinions spoke of the citizenship question as having been decided by the Court. In other words, the authoritativeness of that part of Taney's opinion was attested to by a majority of the Court itself.

More familiar is the charge that Taney indulged in OBITER DICTUM when he ruled against the constitutionality of the Missouri Compromise restriction after having decided that Scott was not a citizen and so had no right to bring suit in a federal court. "Obiter dictum" was the principal battle cry of the Republicans in their attacks on the decision. By dismissing Taney's ruling against territorial power as illegitimate, they were able to salvage the main plank of their party platform without assuming the role of open rebels against judicial authority. What the argument ignored was Taney's not unreasonable contention that throughout his opinion he was canvassing the question of jurisdiction. Having concluded that Scott could not be a citizen because he was a *Negro*, the Chief Justice elected to fortify the conclusion by demonstrating also that Scott could not be a citizen because he was a *slave.* Such reinforcement was especially appropriate because some of the Justices were convinced that the Court could not properly review the citizenship question.

It therefore appears that none of Taney's major rulings can be pushed aside as unauthoritative. In any case, the long-standing argument over what the Court "really decided" has been largely beside the point; for Taney's opinion was accepted as the opinion of the Court by its critics as well as its defenders. As a matter of historical reality, the *Dred Scott* decision is what he declared it to be.

Taney devoted about forty-four percent of his opinion to the question of Negro citizenship, thirty-eight percent to the territorial question, sixteen percent to various technical issues, and only two percent to the original question of whether residence on free soil had the legal effect of emancipating a slave. Throughout the entire document, he made not a single concession to antislavery feeling but instead committed the JUDICIAL POWER OF THE UNITED STATES totally to the defense of slavery. Behind his mask of judicial propriety, the Chief Justice had become privately a fierce southern sectionalist, seething with anger at "Northern insult and Northern aggression." His flat legal prose does not entirely conceal the intensity of emotion that animated his *Dred Scott* opinion.

The citizenship issue concerned the status of free Negroes only; for everyone agreed that slaves were not citizens. Yet Taney persistently lumped free Negroes and slaves together as one degraded class of beings who "had been subjugated by the dominant race, and, whether emancipated or not, yet remained subject to their authority." Thus all blacks, in his view, stood on the same ground. Emancipation made no difference. Negroes could not have been regarded as citizens by the Framers of the Constitution, he declared, because at the time they "had no rights which the white man was bound to respect." These notorious words were not mere historical commentary as defenders of the Chief Justice have often insisted. Taney also held that the constitutional status of Negroes had not changed at all since 1787, which meant that in 1857 they still had no federal rights that white men were bound to respect. His reasoning excluded blacks not only from citizenship but also from every protection given to *persons* by the Constitution.

Much more forceful in its political impact was Taney's ruling against the constitutionality of the antislavery provision in the Missouri Compromise. He began by dismissing as irrelevant the one clause of the Constitution in which the word "territory" appears, preferring instead to derive the territorial power of Congress by implication from the power to admit new states. No less remarkable is the fact that he never said precisely why the antislavery provision was unconstitutional. Historians have inferred from one brief passage that he based his holding on the DUE PROCESS clause of the Fifth Amendment. Yet there is no explicit statement to that effect, and in the end he did not declare that congressional prohibition of slavery in the territories *violated* any part of the Constitution; he said only that it was "not warranted" by the Constitution, a phrasing that suggests reliance on the principle of strict construction.

Not satisfied with ruling in effect that the Republican party was organized for an illegal purpose, the Chief Justice also struck a hard blow at northern Democrats and the doctrine of POPULAR SOVEREIGNTY. If Congress could not prohibit slavery in a territory, he said, neither could it authorize a territorial legislature to do so. This statement, being on a subject that did not arise in the case, was *dictum.* It exemplified Taney's determination to cover all ground in providing judicial protection for slavery. The dissenting Justices, JOHN MCLEAN and BENJAMIN R. CURTIS, rejected Taney's blanket exclusion of Negroes from citizenship. Having thus affirmed Scott's capacity to bring suit in a federal court, they proceeded to the merits of the case while denying the right of the Court majority to do so. Both men upheld the constitutionality of the Missouri Compromise restriction by interpreting the territory clause, in Republican style, as an express and plenary delegation of power to Congress. They went on to maintain that antislavery law, state or federal, dissolved the legal relationship between any master and slave coming within its purview, thereby working irrevocable emancipation.

Antislavery critics made good use of the dissenting opinions in launching an angry, abusive attack upon the Court majority and its judgment. The influence of the decision on the sectional conflict is difficult to assess. No doubt it contributed significantly to the general accumulation of sectional animosity that made some kind of national crisis increasingly unavoidable. It also aggravated the split in the Democratic party by eliciting STEPHEN A. DOUGLAS's FREEPORT DOCTRINE and inspiring southern demands for a territorial slave code. At the same time, there is reason to doubt that the decision enhanced Republican recruiting or had a critical effect on the election of ABRAHAM LINCOLN.

For the two principals in the case, the verdict of the Court made little difference. John Sanford died in an insane asylum two months after the reading of the decision. Dred Scott was soon manumitted, but he lived only sixteen months as a free man before succumbing to tuberculosis. The constitutional effect of the decision likewise proved to be slight, especially after the outbreak of the Civil War. The wartime Union government treated *Dred Scott v. Sandford* as though it had never been rendered. In June 1862, Congress abolished slavery in all the federal territories. Later the same year, Lincoln's ATTORNEY GENERAL issued an official opinion holding that free men of color born in the United States were citizens of the United States. The THIRTEENTH AMENDMENT (1865) and the FOURTEENTH AMENDMENT (1868) completed the work of overthrowing Taney's decision.

The *Dred Scott* case damaged Taney's reputation but did not seriously weaken the Supreme Court as an institution. Aside from its immediate political effects, the case is significant as the first instance in which a major federal law was ruled unconstitutional. It is accordingly a landmark in the growth of JUDICIAL REVIEW and an early asserton of the policymaking authority that the Court would come to exercise more and more.

DON E. FEHRENBACHER

Bibliography

EHRLICH, WALTER 1979 *They Have No Rights: Dred Scott's Struggle for Freedom.* Westport, Conn.: Greenwood Press.

FEHRENBACHER, DON E. 1978 *The Dred Scott Case: Its Significance in American Law and Politics.* New York: Oxford University Press.

SWISHER, CARL B. 1974 *The Taney Period, 1836–1864,* Volume V of the Oliver Wendell Holmes Devise *History of the Supreme Court of the United States.* New York: Macmillan.

DRUG REGULATION

Congress's power to regulate the manufacture, distribution, and use of narcotic drugs, formerly limited by a considerable body of constitutional DOCTRINE based on the TENTH AMENDMENT, today is regarded as plenary, limited only by the guarantees of the BILL OF RIGHTS.

The Constitution nowhere expressly grants to Congress power to regulate narcotics. Congress's efforts to regulate the area have thus relied on its powers to tax and regulate foreign and interstate commerce, and on its implied power to make laws enforcing treaty obligations. In the early part of this century,

though, the Supreme Court viewed these powers as being constrained by the Tenth Amendment, which, the Court repeatedly held, reserved the POLICE POWER exclusively to the states; federal laws attempting to usurp the police power were void.

Thus, for example, tax statutes were void unless they indicated on their face a revenue purpose rather than an intent to exercise reserved police power. As the Court stated in *United States v. Jin Fuey Moy* (1916), a tax statute would be upheld where it was clearly designed to raise revenue, even though it had "a moral end as well as revenue in view," provided that moral ends were reached "within the limits of a revenue measure." In practice, purported taxes would seldom be voided, but ambiguities in statutory language would be resolved by reference to the purported revenue purpose.

The requirement of a revenue purpose has become less important over time. Congress quickly became adept at structuring tax measures to pass the facial scrutiny of the courts. At the same time, the Court's review of purpose became more cursory. Indeed, at least one lower court expressed the view that a tax purpose is no longer required. In any case, the expansion of the COMMERCE CLAUSE power has made the use of the TAXING POWER unnecessary, and the Comprehensive Drug Abuse Prevention and Control Act of 1970 repealed most prior federal statutes based on the taxing power.

The development of the commerce power largely paralleled that of the taxing power. The Court for many years distinguished sharply between the commerce power granted to the federal government and the police power reserved to the states. The Court's decision in CHAMPION V. AMES (1903), though, established that Congress had the power to ban goods dangerous in themselves from interstate and FOREIGN COMMERCE. Under this power, Congress was free to ban trade in narcotics with foreign countries and between states, but had no power to regulate the intrastate manufacture or sale of narcotics. Thus, prosecution of narcotics violators under federal law required a case-by-case showing that the drugs in question were involved in foreign or interstate commerce, although Congress could create a statutory presumption that drugs of a type normally imported from foreign countries had been so imported.

Now that the courts have sweepingly interpreted the commerce clause, Congress may impose sanctions without showing in each prosecution that the narcotics transaction affected interstate commerce. Challenges to recent federal narcotics regulations have been routinely brushed aside by the courts.

Congress has also occasionally regulated drugs through the TREATY POWER. Thus, a law requiring narcotics addicts to register with customs upon leaving the United States was valid as a measure to carry out the nation's obligations under the Hague Convention of 1912, a treaty ratified by the Senate. With the rise of the commerce power, however, Congress has had little need for the treaty power in regulating narcotics.

Congress's power to regulate narcotics is, of course, limited by the Bill of Rights. In general, these limits are the same in narcotics cases as in other criminal cases; for example, Congress may not authorize unreasonable SEARCHES AND SEIZURES or CRUEL AND UNUSUAL PUNISHMENT of narcotics violators. Nonetheless, the BURGER COURT's contraction of the reach of the Fourth Amendment has led some commentators to speak ironically of a "narcotics exception" to that guarantee.

One issue unique to the narcotics laws, however, has arisen from the FIRST AMENDMENT's guarantee of RELIGIOUS LIBERTY. Several religious groups in the United States use drugs in their observance. The question thus arises whether the federal and state governments may constitutionally forbid the possession and use of drugs for religious purposes. The Supreme Court has held that only a COMPELLING STATE INTEREST can justify substantial infringement of the right to free exercise of religion. This compelling interest must, under the holding in SHERBERT V. VERNER (1963), be "some substantial threat to public safety, peace or order."

Two state courts have found that this standard bars legislative prohibition of the use of peyote by members of the Native American Church in their religious ceremonies. California, indeed, has found that the same ban applies to any person who uses peyote in connection with a bona fide religious practice, even if the person is not a member of any recognized religious group. In a 1964 case involving a "self-styled peyote preacher" the California Supreme Court granted a new trial to determine whether the defendant's professed religious belief was bona fide. Most courts, however, have rejected this view. As of 1983, courts in at least five states have held that the interest of defendants in free exercise of religion is outweighed by the compelling governmental interest in controlling the distribution and use of dangerous drugs.

Whether or not Congress is constitutionally compelled to do so, it has occasionally granted exemptions for the sacramental use of otherwise controlled substances. Just as sacramental wine was exempted from the provisions of the National Prohibition Act (1919), the Controlled Substances Act of 1970 exempted from its prohibitions the sacramental use of peyote. Although the Drug Enforcement Agency has consistently interpreted this exemption as being available only to members of the Native American Church, at least one lower court has held that Congress intended to exempt all bona fide religious groups using peyote for sacramental purposes and regarding the drug as a deity.

Other than this single exemption for peyote, however, the federal narcotics laws have not authorized sacramental use of otherwise forbidden drugs. Nor have the courts yet recognized any religious claims other than those made for peyote. The Supreme Court has not yet spoken on the matter, and constitutional claims for religious exemptions to the narcotics laws cannot be regarded as wholly frivolous. Still, neither the Supreme Court nor the lower courts seem currently to view these claims with favor.

JOHN KAPLAN

Bibliography

BONNIE, RICHARD J. 1980 *Marijuana Use and Criminal Sanctions*. Charlottesville, Va. Michie Co.
KAPLAN, JOHN 1970 *Marijuana: The New Prohibition*. New York: World Publishing Co.
——— 1983 *The Hardest Drug: Heroin and Public Policy*. Chicago: University of Chicago Press.
MOORE, MARK H. and GERSTEIN, DEAN R., EDS. 1981 *Alcohol and Public Policy: Beyond the Shadow of Prohibition*. Washington, D.C.: National Academy Press.
NATIONAL COMMISSION ON MARIHUANA AND DRUG ABUSE 1973 *Drug Use in America: Problem in Perspective*. Washington, D.C.: Government Printing Office.

DUAL FEDERALISM

EDWARD S. CORWIN devised the term "dual federalism" to describe a constitutional theory enunciated by the Supreme Court and by many COMMENTATORS ON THE CONSTITUTION at various times (and to various purposes) in the nation's history—a theory concerning the proper relationships between the national government and the states. This theory, Corwin wrote, embodied four postulates of constitutional interpretation: "1. The national government is one of ENUMERATED POWERS only; 2. Also, the purposes which it may constitutionally promote are few; 3. Within their respective spheres the two centers of government are 'sovereign' and hence 'equal'; 4. The relation of the two centers with each other is one of tension rather than collaboration."

This theory gives enormous importance to the TENTH AMENDMENT, with its declaration that powers not delegated to the national government and not prohibited to the states by the Constitution "are reserved to the States respectively, or the people." (The ARTICLES OF CONFEDERATION had reserved to the states powers that were not "expressly delegated" to Congress.) Confronted with the competing concept of national authority in the Constitution's SUPREMACY CLAUSE, proponents of dual federalism have insisted that the Tenth Amendment holds a superior position. The TANEY COURT, especially in the LICENSE CASES, often portrayed the states' reserved powers as a constitutional limitation on the legitimate authority of Congress. In the post-Civil War period, the Court built another constitutional monument to dual federalism theory in its doctrine of INTERGOVERNMENTAL IMMUNITIES. In the hands of a conservative, property-minded judiciary in the late nineteenth century, dual federalism became a potent instrument for invalidation of federal regulatory measures. In HAMMER V. DAGENHART (1918) the Court's majority took an extreme view of the Tenth Amendment, declaring that it forbade even a federal regulation of interstate commerce when the regulation's purpose was to invade the province of the states' reserved powers.

A series of decisions in the late 1930s, however, put to rest the formal constitutional theory of dual federalism. The Court's revised interpretations of the COMMERCE POWER, the CONTRACT CLAUSE, and the TAXING AND SPENDING POWER all rejected Tenth Amendment limitations on national authority. Meanwhile, the Court also validated the administrative innovations of COOPERATIVE FEDERALISM, in the form of extensive programs of FEDERAL GRANTS-IN-AID to the states.

The only serious reappearance of dual federalism theory in post-New Deal constitutional law has been in NATIONAL LEAGUE OF CITIES V. USERY (1976), in which a concept of inviolable powers and functions of the "states as states" became a limitation on congressional regulatory power, in this instance the power to establish wages and hours for municipal workers.

HARRY N. SCHEIBER

Bibliography

CORWIN, EDWARD S. 1950 The Passing of Dual Federalism. *Virginia Law Review* 36:1–24.
MASON, ALPHEUS THOMAS 1968 Federalism: Historic Questions and Contemporary Meanings. The Role of the Court. In Valerie, Earl, ed., *Federalism: Infinite Variety in Theory and Practice.* Itasca, Ill.: F. E. Peacock Publishers.
SCHEIBER, HARRY N. 1978 American Federalism and the Diffusion of Power. *University of Toledo Law Review* 9:619–680.

DUANE, JAMES
(1733–1797)

James Duane, a wealthy New York lawyer and conservative political leader of the Revolutionary period, served in the Continental Congress (1774–1784) and helped write and secure ratification of the ARTICLES OF CONFEDERATION. As mayor of New York City (1784–1789) he presided over the Mayor's Court case of RUTGERS V. WADDINGTON (1784), a disputed precedent for JUDICIAL REVIEW. Not named, because of his nationalist views, as a delegate to the CONSTITUTIONAL CONVENTION OF 1787, he attended the New York convention and worked for RATIFICATION OF THE CONSTITUTION. He was later the first UNITED STATES DISTRICT COURT judge in New York (1789–1794).

DENNIS J. MAHONEY

DUE PROCESS OF LAW

A 1354 act of Parliament reconfirming MAGNA CARTA paraphrased its chapter 29 as follows: "That no man . . . shall be put out of Land or Tenement, nor taken, nor imprisoned, nor disinherited, nor put to death, without being brought in Answer by due Process of Law." This was the first reference to due process in English legal history. Chapter 29 of the 1225 issue of Magna Carta originally concluded with the phrase "by the LAW OF THE LAND." Very probably the 1354 reconfirmation did not equate "the law of the land" with "due process of law"; the two were not synonymous. Due process in the 1354 enactment, and until the seventeenth century, meant an appropriate COMMON LAW writ.

In the Five Knights Case (see PETITION OF RIGHT), JOHN SELDEN, the great parliamentarian, said in defense of the accused that "No freeman shall be imprisoned without due process of law," meaning that the "law of the land" was an equivalent for "either INDICTMENT or PRESENTMENT." Sir EDWARD COKE, in his commentary on Magna Carta, also equated due process with the law of the land, meaning regularized courses of proceeding in common law prosecutions for crime. Coke's primary claim was that the law of the land was the common law, one of several rival systems of law then prevalent in England. When abolishing the courts of High Commission and Star Chamber, Parliament in 1641 quoted the due process phraseology of the act of 1354 and added that trials by "ordinary Courts of Justice and by the ordinary course of law" protected property right against arbitrary proceedings. JOHN LILBURNE and his Levellers agreed, but they also asserted that due process signified a cluster of procedural protections of the criminally accused, including TRIAL BY JURY, the RIGHT TO COUNSEL, and the RIGHT AGAINST SELF-INCRIMINATION. By the mid-seventeenth century due process and the law of the land referred to PROCEDURAL DUE PROCESS in both civil and criminal cases. The "law of the land" usage, however, was the dominant one, and "due process" continued to be used in the very limited sense of a writ appropriate to a legal proceeding. A century later WILLIAM BLACKSTONE discussed various processes—original, mesne, and final—without discoursing on due process of law per se. After referring to indictment in capital cases and the principle that "no man can be put to death without being brought to answer by due process of law," Blackstone referred to the different writs that summoned an accused to trial in MISDEMEANOR and FELONY cases.

In the American colonies the usage was similar. In deference to Magna Carta, the "law of the land" formulation was by far the most common, although a variety of paraphrases existed. The MASSACHUSETTS BODY OF LIBERTIES (1641) guaranteed that one's life, liberty, and property could not be deprived except by "some expresse law of the Country warranting the same, established by a generall Court and sufficiently published"—that is, by known, standing law. West New Jersey protected the same substantive rights by a clause guaranteeing "due trial and judgment passed by twelve good and lawful men." New York in 1683 sought a charter that incorporated the famous chapter of Magna Carta with a clause requiring "by due course of law." Probably the first American reference to "due process of law" was in a Massachusetts act of 1692 endorsing chapter 29 of Magna Carta.

During the controversy with Great Britain leading to the American Revolution, Americans frequently spoke of trial by jury, FUNDAMENTAL LAW, the law of the land, no TAXATION WITHOUT REPRESENTATION, and a gamut of CIVIL LIBERTIES, but rarely referred to due process of law. Their references to the "law of the land" had no fixed or single meaning.

They meant by it a variety of safeguards against injustice and abuses of CRIMINAL PROCEDURE; they equated it with NOTICE, hearing, indictment, trial by jury, and, more generally, with regular forms of common law procedure and even the fundamental law itself or constitutional limitations on government. The "law of the land" was an omnibus phrase whose content ranged from specific writs to the concept of CONSTITUTIONALISM, and the phrase connoted protection of substantive rights—life, liberty, and property—as well as various precedural rights. Later, due process inherited all the content and connotations of law of the land.

All the first state constitutions used the "law of the land" phraseology, as did the NORTHWEST ORDINANCE of 1787. No state constitution included a due process clause until New York's of 1821, although Mississippi's constitution of 1817 referred to "due course of law." Before the Civil War, only five state constitutions referred to "due process of law." All others had the older "law of the land" equivalent.

The first American constitution to include a due process clause was the Constitution of the United States in its Fifth Amendment, ratified in 1791. The clause reflected JAMES MADISON's preference. For reasons unknown, he recommended that no person should be "deprived of life, liberty, or property without due process of law." The four states which had ratified the Constitution with recommendations for a comprehensive BILL OF RIGHTS urged versions of chapter 29 of Magna Carta, although only one, New York, referred to "due process of law" rather than "law of the land." The due process clause of the Fifth Amendment was ratified without any discussions that illumine its meaning. Although every clause of the Constitution is supposed to have its own independent meaning, rendering no clause tautological, the due process clause was an exception. It pacified public apprehensions, bowed toward Magna Carta, and reinforced specific rights such as trial by jury.

When the Supreme Court construed the due process clause of the Fifth Amendment for the first time in MURRAY V. HOBOKEN LAND COMPANY (1856), it declared that although due process limited all branches of the government, it had only the procedural connotations that derived from the settled usages and modes of proceeding which characterized old English law suited to American conditions. Chief Justice ROGER B. TANEY's opinion in DRED SCOTT V. SANDFORD (1857) passingly employed SUBSTANTIVE DUE PROCESS OF LAW, which had cropped up in some state decisions and in ABOLITIONIST CONSTITUTIONAL THEORY as well as proslavery theory. The

FOURTEENTH AMENDMENT's due process clause, taken verbatim from the Fifth's, proved to be the turning point in the national acceptance of "due process of law" as the common usage rather than the "law of the land" usage. In the last third of the nineteenth century, state constitutions finally substituted "due process" for "law of the land," and judicial decisions, state and federal, as well as legal treatises, expounded "due process of law," making it the most important and influential term in American constitutional law.

LEONARD W. LEVY

Bibliography
HOWARD, A. E. DICK 1968 *The Road from Runnymede: Magna Carta and Constitutionalism in America.* Charlottesville: University Press of Virginia.
JUROW, KEITH 1975 Untimely Thoughts: A Reconsideration of the Origins of Due Process of Law. *American Journal of Legal History* 19:265–279.
MOTT, RODNEY 1926 *Due Process of Law.* Indianapolis: Bobbs-Merrill.

DUE PROCESS OF LAW, PROCEDURAL

See: Procedural Due Process of Law

DUE PROCESS OF LAW, SUBSTANTIVE

See: Substantive Due Process of Law

DULANY, DANIEL
(1722–1797)

Daniel Dulany was a member of the Delaware governor's council (1757–1774) and one of the most prominent lawyers in America. In 1765 he published a pamphlet opposing the Stamp Act and arguing that "there is a clear distinction between an Act imposing a Tax for the single Purpose of raising a Revenue, and those Acts which have been made for Regulation of Trade." He denounced the doctrine of virtual representation as a "cobweb, spread to catch the unwary, and intangle the weak."

Dulany was a delegate to the STAMP ACT CONGRESS but later opposed the American Revolution.

DENNIS J. MAHONEY

DUN & BRADSTREET, INC. v. GREENMOSS BUILDERS, INC.
472 U.S.　(1985)

The PLURALITY OPINION in this case may portend significant changes in the constitutional DOCTRINE governing LIBEL AND THE FIRST AMENDMENT. Dun & Bradstreet, a credit reporting business, falsely and negligently reported to five subscribers that Greenmoss had filed a petition in bankruptcy, and also negligently misrepresented Greenmoss's assets and liabilities. In an action for defamation, Greenmoss recovered substantial compensatory and punitive damages. Vermont's highest court held that the principle of GERTZ V. ROBERT WELCH, INC. (1974) did not apply in actions against defendants who were not part of the press or broadcast media. A fragmented Supreme Court avoided this question but affirmed, 5–4.

Justice LEWIS F. POWELL, for a three-Justice plurality, concluded that *Gertz*—which had held, among other things, that punitive damages could not be awarded against a magazine without proof of knowing or reckless disregard of the falsity of the statement—was applicable only to "expression on a matter of public concern." Justice Powell spoke only generally about the content of the "matter of public concern" standard, but hinted that "media" speech might qualify automatically for protection under *Gertz*. Dun & Bradstreet's report, however, involved "matters of purely private concern." Although such speech is "not wholly unprotected" by the FIRST AMENDMENT, he concluded, it can be the basis of a punitive damages award even absent a showing of reckless disregard of the truth. Chief Justice WARREN E. BURGER and Justice BYRON R. WHITE, in separate CONCURRING OPINIONS, expressed willingness to abandon *Gertz* altogether, but meanwhile agreed with this radical surgery on *Gertz*.

In a footnote pregnant with meaning, Justice Powell remarked that some kinds of constitutionally protected speech are entitled only to "reduced protection"—COMMERCIAL SPEECH, for example. But he did not place Dun & Bradstreet's report in the latter category, and thus raised speculation that the majority may be prepared to adopt a "sliding scale" for the FREEDOM OF SPEECH, with varying (and, as yet, unspecified) degrees of constitutional protection for each kind of speech, depending on the Justices' determinations about the value of the speech and the context in which it is uttered.

Justice WILLIAM J. BRENNAN, for the four dissenters, agreed that credit reports were not central to

First Amendment values, but argued nonetheless that the *Gertz* requirements should apply to this case: credit and bankruptcy information was "of public concern." Justice Brennan noted with satisfaction that six Justices (the dissenters and authors of the concurring opinions) had rejected a distinction between the First Amendment rights of "media defendants" and of others sued for defamation.

KENNETH L. KARST

DUNCAN v. KAHANAMOKU
327 U.S. 304 (1946)

Interpreting the scope of MARTIAL LAW established in Hawaii after the bombing of Pearl Harbor, Justice HUGO L. BLACK, for the Supreme Court, concluded that the Hawaiian Organic Act of 1900 extended constitutional guarantees to that TERRITORY. The creation of military courts empowered to try civilians violated the SIXTH AMENDMENT right to a FAIR TRIAL, thus contravening the intent of Congress. Chief Justice HARLAN FISKE STONE and Justice FRANK MURPHY wrote separate CONCURRING OPINIONS. Stone would have given greater scope to martial law but found the claim of EMERGENCY POWER unjustified here. Murphy joined the Court's opinion but preferred to rest on constitutional grounds, citing EX PARTE MILLIGAN (1866). Justices HAROLD BURTON and FELIX FRANKFURTER, in dissent, argued that the military situation and the conduct of the war, as an executive function, justified the emergency steps taken here.

DAVID GORDON

DUNCAN v. LOUISIANA
391 U.S. 145 (1968)

A 7–2 Supreme Court here overruled several earlier decisions and held that the FOURTEENTH AMENDMENT incorporated the Sixth Amendment right to TRIAL BY JURY. Louisiana tried Duncan for battery, a MISDEMEANOR charge punishable by up to two years' imprisonment. The court denied his request for a jury trial and sentenced him, upon conviction, to sixty days and a $150 fine. On appeal to the Supreme Court, the Justices abandoned the approach used in PALKO V. CONNECTICUT (1937) and ADAMSON V. CALIFORNIA (1947), where the Court had examined the circumstances to determine whether they pre-

served the implicit DUE PROCESS requirement of "fundamental fairness." In his opinion in *Duncan*, Justice BYRON R. WHITE asked instead whether trial by jury was "fundamental to the American scheme of justice" and concluded that history supported an affirmative response. Conceding a court's duty to distinguish between petty and serious offenses to determine which cases warranted this protection, White declined to do so as a general rule. He declared that an offense punishable by more than two years' imprisonment was sufficiently serious to apply the Sixth Amendment guarantee. Penalties involving less than six months' time were not accorded that right. As usual, Justices HUGO L. BLACK and WILLIAM O. DOUGLAS, concurring separately, advocated the total INCORPORATION DOCTRINE. Justices JOHN MARSHALL HARLAN and POTTER STEWART, dissenting, asserted that "the Court's approach and its reading of history are altogether topsy-turvy." Later decisions in WILLIAMS V. FLORIDA (1970) and *Apodaca v. Oregon* (1972) have limited the extent of the right incorporated.

DAVID GORDON

DUNN v. BLUMSTEIN
405 U.S. 330 (1972)

Tennessee restricted voting to persons with one year of residence in the state and three months in the county. The Supreme Court, 6–1, speaking through Justice THURGOOD MARSHALL, held this limitation a denial of the EQUAL PROTECTION OF THE LAWS. The durational RESIDENCE REQUIREMENTS had to pass the test of STRICT SCRUTINY, both because they penalized exercise of the RIGHT TO TRAVEL interstate and because they restricted the FUNDAMENTAL INTEREST in voting. The state's asserted justifications for the requirements were not necessary for achieving COMPELLING STATE INTERESTS. Fraud could be prevented by the LESS RESTRICTIVE MEANS of requiring registration thirty days before an election. The objective of an informed electorate bore only a tenuous relation to length of residence. Chief Justice WARREN E. BURGER dissented. The recently appointed Justices LEWIS F. POWELL and WILLIAM H. REHNQUIST did not participate.

The following year, the Court approved fifty-day residency requirements in *Marston v. Lewis* (1973) and *Burns v. Fortson* (1973).

KENNETH L. KARST

DUPLEX PRINTING PRESS COMPANY v. DEERING
254 U.S. 443 (1921)

In a case that brought the apparently prolabor provisions of the CLAYTON ACT before the Supreme Court, a 6–3 majority held that the act had placed no substantial bar to issuing INJUNCTIONS against labor unions. Section 6 of the act allowed unions to "lawfully [carry] out . . . legitimate objects," and section 20 denied the issuance of injunctions in a labor dispute unless essential to protect property. Duplex sought an injunction against a SECONDARY BOYCOTT which had been brought to force unionization of their open shop, claiming injury to and destruction of INTERSTATE COMMERCE. The Court declared that the boycott, even though peaceful, was not a "lawful method" of achieving the union's ends and thus violated the antitrust laws. According to the Court, section 6 only approved methods not expressly forbidden. Moreover, the majority redefined section 20: "labor dispute" was not meant generically but applied only "to parties standing in proximate relation to a controversy," an unwarranted gloss. They thus confined the section to a mere reflection of precedent, undoing congressional action.

Justice LOUIS D. BRANDEIS, joined by Justices OLIVER WENDELL HOLMES and JOHN H. CLARKE, dissented. Brandeis argued that the defendants shared a "common interest" with the employees, and the majority's denial of the existence of a dispute, within the act's meaning, simply ignored reality. Section 20, said the dissenters, attempted to render both sides equal. Although the Court refused to acknowledge that the Clayton Act had legalized any new methods for labor's use, a similar decision in BEDFORD CUT STONE V. JOURNEYMEN STONECUTTERS (1927) prompted enactment of the NORRIS-LaGUARDIA ACT in 1932, reversing the doctrinal direction.

DAVID GORDON

(SEE ALSO: *Labor and Antitrust Laws.*)

DU PONCEAU, PETER S.
(1760–1844)

Peter S. Du Ponceau arrived in America from France as Baron von Steuben's interpreter. Following service in the Revolution, he became a citizen of Pennsylvania where he was admitted to the bar in 1785. He defended the radical state CONSTITUTION of 1776 and was an Anti-Federalist, but as time passed he became a Jeffersonian Republican. He declined THOMAS JEFFERSON's offer of the chief justiceship of Louisiana. Du Ponceau was a founder and provost of the Law Academy of Pennsylvania. Among his books were *A Dissertation on the Nature and Extent of the Jurisdiction of the Courts of the United States* (1824), in which he advocated a FEDERAL COMMON LAW, and *A Brief View of the Constitution of the United States* (1834), in which he sought a middle course between a consolidated government and STATES' RIGHTS. In general he taught moderate nationalism and the supremacy of the union.

LEONARD W. LEVY

Bibliography

BAUER, ELIZABETH K. 1952 *Commentaries on the Constitution.* Pages 65–78. New York: Columbia University Press.

DUVALL, GABRIEL
(1752–1844)

Although he served as a Justice of the United States Supreme Court for nearly a quarter of a century, Gabriel Duvall had a relatively small impact on the development of American constitutional law. Born into a prominent Maryland Huguenot family, he studied law and was admitted to the bar in 1788. He supported the movement for independence during the 1770s, and held a number of minor posts under the revolutionary government. Following the adoption of the Maryland Constitution of 1777 he served as clerk of the State House of Delegates. In 1782 he was elected to the Maryland State Council and in 1787 to the House of Delegates as a representative from Annapolis. He was selected to be a delegate to the CONSTITUTIONAL CONVENTION, but, for reasons that are unclear, he declined to serve. He supported THOMAS JEFFERSON during the political battles of the 1790s, and was elected as a Democratic-Republican to Congress in 1794. He resigned the position less than two years later to become a judge of the Maryland Supreme Court. He helped to organize Maryland successfully for the Republicans in 1800 and often advised Jefferson and JAMES MADISON on appointments there. In December 1802 Jefferson appointed him to be the first comptroller of the United States Treasury.

In 1811 President Madison appointed Duvall to the United States Supreme Court. On the most important and controversial cases of the period—MARTIN V. HUNTER'S LESSEE (1816), GIBBONS V. OGDEN (1824), and BROWN V. MARYLAND (1827)—Duvall followed the lead of JOSEPH STORY and JOHN MARSHALL, and he even supported the Chief Justice when he dissented in OGDEN V. SAUNDERS (1827). DARTMOUTH COLLEGE V. WOODWARD was the only major case in which he failed to support Marshall, but since he dissented without opinion, it is not possible to determine his reasons. It is clear that Duvall knew and understood the law, and he did write straightforward and creditable opinions for the Court in several minor commercial law and maritime cases: *Archibald Freeland v. Heron, Lenox and Company* (1812); *United States v. January and Patterson* (1813), *Prince v. Bartlett* (1814); and *The Frances and Eliza v. Coates* (1823).

Although no abolitionist, Duvall had definite antislavery leanings. Dissenting from a Supreme Court ruling in *Mina Queen and Child v. Hepburn* (1812), in which HEARSAY evidence had been excluded "from a trial in which two black persons attempted to establish their freedom," he argued, with some force, "It appears to me that the reason for admitting hearsay evidence upon a question of freedom is much stronger than in cases of pedigree or in controversies relative to the boundaries of land. It will be universally admitted that the right to freedom is more important than the right of property." In another case, *LeGrand v. Darnall* (1829), speaking on behalf of the Court, Duvall ruled that a slaveholder's deeding of property to his ten-year-old son by a slave woman implied an intention to free the boy, despite a Maryland law that denied manumission to any slave under forty-five years of age.

As he grew older, Duvall's increasing infirmities and deafness caused numerous problems and considerable embarrassment for the Court. For almost a decade his resignation was expected, but he did not step down until January 1835, when he received assurances that ANDREW JACKSON planned to appoint fellow Marylander ROGER B. TANEY to the bench. Duvall died nine years later at the age of ninety-two.

RICHARD E. ELLIS

Bibliography

DILLARD, IRVING 1969 Gabriel Duvall. Pages 419–429 in Leon Friedman and Fred L. Israel, eds., *Justices of the Supreme Court 1789–1969.* New York: Chelsea House.

EAKIN v. RAUB
12 Sargeant & Rawle 330 (Pa. 1825)

In this otherwise insignificant Pennsylvania case, JOHN BANNISTER GIBSON offered the classic rationale for JUDICIAL RESTRAINT. His opinion is an explicit refutation of JOHN MARSHALL's arguments for JUDICIAL REVIEW in MARBURY V. MADISON (1803), a position which Gibson confessed he had once accepted, but more as "a matter of faith than of reason."

Gibson's major premise was that the judiciary had no right or power to void legislation without express constitutional warrant. Like Marshall, Gibson agreed that under a written CONSTITUTION, no branch of government could claim more than its granted powers. But as the legislature was supreme within the limits of its grant, Gibson argued, the judiciary could not annul those powers without "direct authority" from the constitution, "either in terms or by irresistible implication." While the judiciary might interpret legislation, it had no power to "scan the authority of the lawgiver." The legislature was superior, Gibson concluded, because "the power to will and to command is essentially superior to the power to act and obey."

Legislative indiscretions and abuses severely tested Gibson's fidelity to his principles. In *Norris v. Clymer* (1845) Gibson acknowledged that he had altered his views on judicial review because the Pennsylvania constitutional convention of 1837, by its silence, apparently sanctioned the power, and also "from experience of the necessity of the case." While Gibson undoubtedly moderated his views for some circumstances, he remained generally faithful to the notion of legislative superiority and the wisdom of judicial restraint. The "experience of the necessity of the case" involved legislative private acts that granted equity. The legislature had given substantially complete EQUITY jurisdiction to the courts in 1836, yet continued to act on its own, inevitably provoking clashes with the judiciary. In *Greenough v. Greenough* (1849) Gibson strongly defended an exclusive sphere for judicial power: "[T]he judicial power . . . is . . . so distributed . . . that the legislature cannot exercise any part of it." The next year, in *De Chastellux v. Fairchild,* he struck down an act ordering a new trial in an action of TRESPASS. "The power to order new trials is judicial," he said; "but the power of the legislature is not judicial."

In the *Eakin* opinion Gibson emphasized judicial independence, and he acknowledged legislative sovereignty, but only "within the limit of its powers." Further, he anticipated cases such as *De Chastellux* when he said that a legislative act directing a reversal of a court judgment would be "a usurpation of judicial power." Finally, he declared that when the judiciary was the prescribed organ to execute the constitution, such as in the conduct of trials, the judges were bound to follow the constitution, a legislative act notwithstanding.

Throughout the remainder of his long career, Gibson adhered to the spirit of *Eakin.* He insisted that the legislature's apprehension of public sentiment, not the fear of judicial interposition, offered the most effective barrier to unconstitutional action. With language similar to later opinions by MORRISON R. WAITE and OLIVER WENDELL HOLMES, Gibson declared that the responsibility for overcoming abusive acts rested not with the courts, but with the people, who were "wise, virtuous, and competent to manage their own affairs."

STANLEY I. KUTLER

E.C. KNIGHT CO., UNITED STATES v.

See: *Knight Co., E.C., United States v.*

ECONOMIC ANALYSIS AND THE CONSTITUTION

To what extent do "economic" ideas and concepts better enable us to understand the American Constitution?

One persisting characterization of the Constitution is that it succeeded both in arresting a decline in the American economy occurring under (and because of) the ARTICLES OF CONFEDERATION and in initiating an epoch of great prosperity. In reality, the shape of the economy during the 1780s was not particularly unsatisfactory. Indeed, in 1786 BENJAMIN FRANKLIN was willing to declare that "America was never in higher prosperity." But deflation injured creditors such as farmers, thereby provoking SHAYS' REBELLION in Massachusetts as well as inducing the enactment by the states of DEBTORS' RELIEF LEGISLATION.

The 1789 Constitution authorized the federal government to tax and to regulate commerce and centralized in the national government the power to print money. The long-range economic implications of these particular grants of power have been profound; their short-range consequences, however, may well have been modest. The federal power to tax was lightly exercised for many decades, and the federal power to print money was of limited importance in an era when "monetary policy" had not yet been recognized as a major instrument of national economic policy. The burst of prosperity in the decades following adoption of the Constitution owed largely to a surge in foreign trade, promoted by America's neutrality during the Napoleonic Wars—a neutrality that had been facilitated, to be sure, by the Constitution's recognition of centralized authority over foreign policy.

The first comprehensive "Economic Interpretation of the Constitution" to attract great attention was that of CHARLES A. BEARD in his celebrated 1913 study. Rejecting the popular view of the Constitution as the noble product of patriotic impulses, Beard assessed the Constitution as an "economic document" designed to advance certain economic interests to the detriment of others. In particular, he believed that "personalty" interests—"money, public security, manufacturers, and trade and shipping"—prevailed at the expense of "landed" interests of farmers and others, as well as at the expense of the unpropertied general public. Beard further asserted that the entire constitutional process had been initiated by a small group of men "immediately interested through their personal possessions in the outcome of their labors." In the preface to his 1935 edition, however, Beard denied that he had meant to suggest that the Framers were merely seeking to enrich themselves personally; rather, Beard explained, the Framers' own economic holdings merely made them receptive to the claims of more general economic groups.

The empirical ambitions that Beard displayed in his research remain commendable. But his particular empirical conclusions have been disputed by more recent scholarship. For example, those attending the CONSTITUTIONAL CONVENTION owned more in realty than they owned in securities; and it is not clearly true that creditors as a class supported the Constitution's RATIFICATION. Those portions of the Constitution that Beard singled out as establishing its economic preferences were the Constitution's general system of CHECKS AND BALANCES, which supposedly served to inhibit the unpropertied majorities; Congress's powers over taxation, war, commerce, and public lands; and the prohibitions on state coinage of money and on state impairment of contractual obligations. The DUE PROCESS clause of the FIFTH AMENDMENT Beard barely mentioned—even though the due process clause of the FOURTEENTH AMENDMENT had served as the basis for the Supreme Court's notorious decision in LOCHNER V. NEW YORK (1905) just eight years previously. Much of Beard's analysis of the Constitution now seems badly forced. In particular, his treatment of checks and balances is extraordinarily reductionistic in its failure to acknowledge that they were designed to serve any purpose other than the protection of certain property interests. In all, Beard's economic interpretation—though a major event in constitutional historiography—no longer commands adherents.

Economists have long been concerned with the objective of economic efficiency, and modern economists have developed an elaborate analysis in support of this objective. Might it be that the goal of efficiency has constitutional status? Insofar as original intent is relevant, information is needed on the economic views of the Framers. One philosophy common in eighteenth-century America was classical republicanism, which, in commending community, equality, and public virtue, was capable of disparaging commercial activity. The Framers, however, were also exposed to the newer tradition of Lockean liberalism, which strongly endorsed individualism and commercial activity. Propitiously, Adam Smith's *The Wealth of Nations* was published in 1776, the year of the DECLARATION OF INDEPENDENCE. Consistent with Smith's free market approach, ALEXANDER HAMILTON in THE FEDERALIST #11 espoused the idea of an open national economy: "The veins of commerce in every part will be replenished and will acquire additional motion and vigor from a free circulation of the commodities of every part." Hamilton began that paper with the observation that "the prosperity of commerce" is "a primary object of [enlightened statesmen's] political cares"—an observation that evidently contemplated mercantilist, rather than laissez-faire, policies. In *The Federalist* #10, JAMES MADISON made clear that he was hardly an economic egalitarian. "The first object of government" is to protect "the diversity of faculties of man, from which the rights of property originate." Elsewhere, however, *The Federalist* set forth theories that were imbued with republicanism; and in a 1792 essay Madison recommended policies that would "raise extreme indigence towards a state of comfort." In all, the free market interests of the Framers should neither be ignored nor exaggerated.

From the early nineteenth century on, free-market norms have exerted their most continuing influence upon constitutional doctrine through the negative underside of the COMMERCE CLAUSE. According to Justice ROBERT JACKSON in *H. P. Hood & Sons v. DuMond* (1949), "Our system . . . is that every farmer and every craftsman shall be encouraged to produce by the certainty that he will have free access to every market in the nation, that no home embargoes will withhold his exports, and that no foreign state will by custom duties or regulation exclude them. Likewise, every consumer may look to the free competition from every producing area in the Nation to protect him from exploitation by any." The Supreme Court has frequently endeavored to protect out-of-state sellers, out-of-state buyers, and multistate transportation concerns from discriminatory or excessive burdens imposed by self-interested state governments. In SOUTHERN PACIFIC COMPANY V. ARIZONA

(1945), for example, the Court invalidated an Arizona statute limiting the lengths of trains operating in Arizona: the Court found that the statute's burdens on INTERSTATE COMMERCE were substantial, its safety benefits probably trivial. At times, however, the Court has been reluctant to intervene even when the prospect of Justice Jackson's "exploitation" has seemed keen. If a state enjoys a monopoly on an important natural resource, then the state, by imposing a substantial tax on the extraction of that resource, can "export" its tax burden, enriching its local treasury at the expense of consumers throughout the nation. Yet in *Commonwealth Edison Company v. Montana* (1981) a divided Supreme Court declined to hold that Montana's thirty percent severance tax on coal violated the commerce clause. The Court majority did not clearly disagree with the proposition that an "exported" state tax violates commerce clause ideals if it is not "fairly related to the services provided by the state." But the majority seemed to regard it as beyond the judicial function to assess the incidence of such a tax and to compute the value of those state-provided "services." (See STATE REGULATION OF COMMERCE; STATE TAXATION OF COMMERCE.)

Though the commerce clause imposes some limits on the states, its primary and explicit purpose is to confer powers on the federal Congress. In GIBBONS V. OGDEN (1824) the Court, in expansively interpreting what counts as interstate commerce, upheld a congressional enactment that implicitly abrogated a New York rule creating a steamboat monopoly between certain New York and New Jersey ports. Because this monopoly plainly offended free-market norms, the federal statute in *Gibbons* vindicated what Justice Jackson in *Hood* regarded as the "vision of the Founders." But what would the result have been in *Gibbons* had it been Congress, rather than the state, that had insisted on a monopoly? In exercising its commerce clause powers in the twentieth century, Congress has frequently chosen to restrict rather than enhance the competitive process. What is noteworthy is that the Supreme Court has found this in no way problematic. Justice Jackson's opinion in WICKARD V. FILBURN (1942) was shrewd in its perception of how intra-farm (and hence intrastate) events could have an aggregate impact on interstate economic arrangements. But the opinion was strikingly uninterested in the extent to which the federal statute it was approving brought about the cartelization of the otherwise highly competitive agricultural economy, thereby curtailing production and elevating consumer prices. Perhaps the point is that the "vision of the Founders," as understood by the Court, is not a competitive economy as such, but merely an economy free of anti-competitive restrictions imposed by the states. Besides accounting for the assumed irrelevance of free-market norms to congressional action under the commerce clause, this attribution of purpose can also explain the fact that the negative underside of the commerce clause has never been thought directly applicable to private monopolies that might severely restrict competition. Consider, however, Paul Freund's view that the spirit—though not the letter—of the commerce clause anticipates a "free national market," and that the commerce clause therefore needs to be supplemented by a strong federal antitrust program.

In the first third of the Twentieth Century, the Court did engage in a rather broad-ranging implementation of free-market values. The Court proceeded primarily in the name of the due process clauses of the Fourteenth and Fifth Amendments, clauses which enabled it to review all state and federal legislation, without regard to interstate impacts. During these years, the quite sophisticated approach of an Adam Smith was frequently replaced by the insensitive dogmatism of the Social Darwinist movement, thereby provoking Justice OLIVER WENDELL HOLMES's *Lochner* quip that "the Fourteenth Amendment does not enact Mr. Herbert Spencer's Social Statics." Since 1937, by contrast, the Court has consistently declined to invalidate "economic" legislation on substantive due process grounds and has stubbornly refused to subject that legislation to even minimal review. In WILLIAMSON V. LEE OPTICAL CO. (1955), for example, the Court unanimously and unhesitatingly upheld an Oklahoma statute requiring consumers to employ a licensed doctor merely in order to fit old eyeglass lenses into new frames.

Judicial tolerance of inefficient economic enactments is probably for the best. Economic analysis is an acquired taste; courts should not insist that legislators be educated in basic economic concepts, let alone that they keep abreast of the current literature on externalities and public goods. Moreover, most economists would acknowledge that a legislature might properly choose to sacrifice economic efficiency in order to achieve some desired distribution of wealth among societal groups. Also, even if certain private conduct is economically acceptable, a legislature could properly conclude that the conduct is interpersonally unfair in the particular way it enables A to cause harm to B.

Nevertheless, the argument favoring somewhat greater judicial scrutiny of inefficient legislation is not altogether without merit. In *Lynch v. Household Finance Corp.* (1972), a PROCEDURAL DUE PROCESS case, the Court—drawing on JOHN LOCKE, JOHN ADAMS, and WILLIAM BLACKSTONE—recognized an important connection between property and liberty. In addition, recent "commercial speech" cases such as VIRGINIA STATE BOARD OF PHARMACY V. VIRGINIA CITIZENS CONSUMER COUNCIL, INC. (1976) have attached considerable constitutional significance to marketplace norms. Moreover, aggressive JUDICIAL REVIEW is often defended on the ground of its ability to correct predictable breakdowns in the legislative process. *Southern Pacific* itself relied, for commerce clause purposes, on the Court's idea that out-of-state railroads are likely to be unrepresented in the state's legislative processes. For due process purposes, "consumers" as such are anything but a DISCRETE AND INSULAR MINORITY. But—as an economic analysis of the legislative process lucidly suggests—the very diffusion of consumers throughout society signifies that consumers may fare poorly in the legislature when challenged by producer groups, which are far better able to mobilize themselves in seeking protective legislation.

In any event, given the Supreme Court's position that neither the commerce clause (as a grant of power) nor the due process clause (as a restriction of power) includes any significant free-market content, it appears likely that Congress, if it chooses, could enact socialism (the ultimate rejection of market values) as this country's form of economic organization. It seems hard to deny that Congress could offer a RATIONAL BASIS on behalf of a socialist program that would satisfy the trivial demands of the commerce and due process clauses. To be sure, the takings clause would require that the nationalization of industry achieve a PUBLIC USE. But recent interpretations of the public use doctrine make it doubtful that the doctrine places any limits on Congress's choice of economic philosophy.

It is true that the takings clause would require Congress to afford JUST COMPENSATION to the shareholders of any companies nationalized. As a general matter, the just compensation requirement serves to rule out at least certain legislative efforts to redistribute wealth, whether by socialism or by more modest measures. It should not be forgotten that the progressive federal income tax—a central feature of federal policy during the last forty years—required for its legality a constitutional amendment. Still, the Supreme Court's invalidation of a pre-amendment federal income tax in POLLOCK V. FARMERS LOAN & TRUST COMPANY (1895) rested on a dubious interpretation of the DIRECT TAXES clause. Consider, moreover, a general tax on wealth or property, the proceeds of which are dedicated to financing welfare programs: it seems entirely clear that such a tax would not constitute a prohibited "taking." It appears, then, that wealth redistribution is constitutionally quite acceptable so long as it is both candid and evenhanded.

When a "taking" does occur, the "just compensation" that the takings clause requires has long been defined in terms of "fair market value." This "fair market value" gloss introduces, almost by hypothesis, certain capitalist values into constitutional doctrine. Yet that gloss can also be critiqued precisely from a free-market perspective. Assume a neighborhood of homes which, if individually available for sale, would each yield a price of $100,000. At any one time, however, only a limited number of houses are in fact offered for sale. To state that a homeowner is not interested in selling for $100,000 is to acknowledge that he presently values his ownership of the house at some figure in excess of $100,000. That excess is what economists call "consumer surplus." "Fair market value" provides less than full compensation in that it deprives the homeowner of this consumer surplus. From an ethical perspective, compensation that is less than full is arguably less than "just." Moreover, economic analysis can make clear that a "fair market value" standard for compensation has the practical effects of subsidizing government in its land acquisitions (by negating consumer surplus) and distorting government EMINENT DOMAIN choices (by encouraging government to ignore variations in consumer surplus among property owners).

Yet an economic analysis also verifies that the problem of measuring full compensation resists easy solution. Rendering consumer surplus compensable would not be satisfactory: consumer surplus would be notably difficult to quantify on an individual basis, and compensability would invite owners to dissemble in representing their surpluses' magnitude. Reminded of the difficulties involved in establishing the proper price for an eminent-domain forced sale, an economist might question the very practice of forced sales: he might suggest that the government be deprived of the eminent domain power altogether, thereby remitting the government to the opportunities afforded by the ordinary real estate market for purposes of acquiring land. Yet it is precisely the economist who can explain why this solution, too, would not always be satisfactory. Without the government's power of eminent domain, the owner of the final parcel within a tract of land that the government has otherwise succeeded in acquiring would be in a position—knowing of the government's situation—to extract an excessive monopoly price from the government-buyer. Because

governments engage in tract acquisition more frequently than private parties do (only governments build superhighways, for example), it may make sense to limit the eminent domain power to governmental bodies. Obversely, the fact that the eminent domain power *is* generally limited to governments helps explain why private parties often are not in a good position to initiate large-tract projects.

As suggested above, an economic analysis is at least able to deepen understanding of the implications of constitutional doctrine. Correspondingly, such an analysis can correct what would otherwise be misunderstandings. In SHAPIRO V. THOMPSON (1969), for example, the Supreme Court considered the states' argument that WELFARE BENEFITS can be properly be denied to indigents who move into a state in order to collect higher benefits. Such an argument, the Court suggested, rested on the implicit premise that such welfare applicants are not "deserving"—a premise that the Court then rejected as unsound. But from the economist's useful perspective, the problem is not the grantee's desert but rather the grantor's incentives. States, anticipating an influx of indigents if welfare benefits are increased, may be dissuaded from raising those benefits, a dissuasion that might ill serve whatever the public's preference may be for compassionate welfare programs. Given an economic point of view, *Shapiro* unwittingly reduces the feasibility of state-administered welfare programs, thereby strengthening the argument in favor of the nationalization of welfare.

At the minimum, economic analysis can assist in identifying the costs or inefficiences of any proposed constitutional ruling. It is, of course, for the courts then to determine what weight to accord these costs in interpreting constitutional doctrine. The economist would be disturbed, however, by any disparagement of these costs that seems naive or inadequately considered. In *Shapiro,* for example, there is language stating that administrative inefficiencies, no matter what their magnitude, are automatically "uncompelling" for purposes of STRICT SCRUTINY review. But it is far from clear that the Court really adheres to such a position. In recent procedural due process opinions such as MATHEWS V. ELDRIDGE (1976), the Court has taken the efficiency criterion significantly into account.

In a number of important ways, then, an economic analysis can be clearly beneficial in the process of constitutional analysis. Nevertheless, economics will probably never achieve, in constitutional studies, the influence that it has secured in certain other fields of law. There are too many constitutional doctrines that endorse ideas or values that are largely beyond the economist's jurisdiction. To employ an extreme example, the economist's recognition of people's "taste for discrimination" is of little help in understanding the Constitution's moral assessment that racial discriminations are inherently invidious.

GARY T. SCHWARTZ

Bibliography

BEARD, CHARLES A. (1913)1935 *An Economic Interpretation of the Constitution.* New York: Macmillan.
BROWNLEE, W. ELLIOT (1941)1979 *Dynamics of Ascent.* New York: Knopf.
EPSTEIN, DAVID F. 1984 *The Political Theory of the Federalist.* Chicago: University of Chicago Press.
EPSTEIN, RICHARD A. 1985 *Takings.* Cambridge, Mass.: Harvard University Press.
FREUND, PAUL A. 1961 *The Supreme Court of the United States.* Cleveland, Ohio: World Publishing Co.
GOLDWIN, ROBERT A. and SCHAMBRA, WILLIAM A., EDS. 1982 *How Capitalist Is the American Constitution?* Washington, D.C.: American Enterprise Institute.
LEE, SUSAN P. and PASSELL, PETER 1979 *A New Economic View of American History.* New York: Norton.
MCDONALD, FORREST 1979 *We the People: The Economic Origins of the Constitution.* New York: Samuel Insull.
POSNER, RICHARD A. 1977 *Economic Analysis of Law.* Boston: Little, Brown.
WOOD, GORDON S. 1969 *The Creation of the American Republic, 1776–1787.* Chapel Hill: University of North Carolina Press.
WRIGHT, ESMOND 1978 *Fabric of Freedom 1763–1800.* New York: Hill & Wang.

ECONOMIC LIBERTIES AND THE CONSTITUTION

Contrary to its existing practice, the United States Supreme Court was once a strong guarantor of economic liberties. This was the period (1897–1937) of "economic due process." The Fifth Amendment and FOURTEENTH AMENDMENT provide that neither the federal nor state governments shall deprive any person "of life, liberty, or property, without DUE PROCESS OF LAW." The Court interpreted these prohibitions to mean that government could not, except in specified or extraordinary circumstances, prevent individuals or corporations from freely engaging in the production and distribution of goods and services.

However, since 1936 the Supreme Court has abandoned this interpretation; economic regulations now are subject to a very low level of review pursuant to which they are upheld whenever rationally related to the achievement of legitimate state purposes. Supporters of the more recent policy conclude that as a result, the Court has wisely steered a neutral role in the nation's economic affairs. Another interpretation of this policy, however, is that it has denied many people a fundamental liberty in a society dedicated to liberty—the opportunity to engage in economic activity. Our Constitution, it is argued, was not intended to be neutral in the conflict between liberty and authority, especially in the economic area.

There is little question that the Framers of the Constitution sought to limit greatly the commercial powers of the states. The tariffs and other economic barriers erected by the states against each other were a major source of discontent with the existing confederation. The regulatory abuses of the state legislatures are not so well detailed, but probably were no less responsible for such sentiments. According to ALEXANDER HAMILTON, writing in 1801, "creditors had been ruined or in a very extensive degree, much injured, confidence in pecuniary transactions had been destroyed, and the springs of industry have been proportionately relaxed" because of the failure of the states to safeguard commercial freedoms.

The deterioration of the economy that followed the revolutionary period led the states to what CHARLES EVANS HUGHES once described as "an ignoble array of legislative schemes for the defeat of creditors and invasion of contractual relations." Among other things, the states passed stay laws extending the due dates of notes and installment laws allowing debtors to pay their obligations in installments after they had fallen due. (See DEBTOR RELIEF LEGISLATION.)

JOHN MARSHALL, later Chief Justice, said in Virginia's ratification convention that economy and industry were essential to happiness, but the ARTICLES OF CONFEDERATION took away "the incitement to industry by rendering property insecure and unprotected." The Constitution, on the contrary, would "promote and encourage industry." JAMES MADISON stated that the passage of laws infringing contractual obligations "contributed more to that uneasiness which produced the convention . . . than those which accrued . . . from the inadequacy of the Confederation to its immediate objectives." During the CONSTITUTIONAL CONVENTION OF 1787 Madison said that an important object of the Union was "the necessity of providing more effectively for the security of private rights, and the steady dispensation of justice. . . . Was it to be supposed that Republican liberty could long exist under the abuses of it, practiced in [some of the] states?" ALBERT J. BEVERIDGE, Marshall's biographer, understandably concluded that the "determination of commercial and financial interests to get some plan adopted under which business could be transacted, was the most effective force that brought about [the Philadelphia convention]."

Several provisions of the Constitution appear to have been intended to curtail the economic regulatory authority of government. These are the prohibitions on the passage of EX POST FACTO laws which affect both the state and federal governments, and the ban on state laws impairing the OBLIGATION OF CONTRACTS. At the time the Constitution was framed and ratified, the term "ex post facto law" was applied to both penal and civil retroactive laws. In the criminal law, it was accepted that an ex post facto law was one that rendered an act punishable that was not punishable when it was committed. The term also described civil laws that operated retroactively to the detriment of a private owner of an iterest acquired or existing under prior law. Justice JOSEPH STORY of the MARSHALL COURT asserted that "every statute, which takes away or impairs VESTED RIGHTS acquired under existing laws, or creates a new obligation, imposes a new duty, or attaches a new disability, in respect to the transactions or considerations already passed, must be deemed retrospective."

Newspapers and judges of that period considered that stay and installment laws operated ex post facto. Members of Congress used the term in the broad sense. Some leading constitutional scholars held similar views on the meaning of the clauses. Although accounts of the CONSTITUTIONAL CONVENTION do not disclose precisely how the Framers defined the term, they are consistent with the view that ex post facto included retroactive civil laws. Nevertheless, a 1798 Supreme Court decision, CALDER V. BULL, interpreted the ex post facto clauses as applying solely to penal laws, thereby removing them as an important restraint on the regulatory powers of the federal and state legislatures.

In Chief Justice Marshall's opinion, the CONTRACT CLAUSE was intended to safeguard FREEDOM OF CONTRACT—which made it, under this view, a severe curb on state economic regulation. According to the Chief Justice, if a law limited the written understanding of the parties, it impaired their contractual obligation whether it was enacted before or after execution of the agreement.

However, the Supreme Court, in a 4–3 decision in OGDEN V. SAUNDERS (1827), ruled that the clause did not cover contracts executed subsequent to the adoption of a law: that is, it applied only to retroactive and not to prospective laws. The case involved a New York bankruptcy law, adopted prior to the execution

of the promissory obligation in issue. In his only dissent on a constitutional issue in his thirty-four years as Chief Justice, Marshall vigorously contended that the New York law, although passed before the execution of the note, changed the understanding of the parties, and therefore impaired the obligation of their contract. The majority decision in the case followed a quarter of a century of failure to obtain a national bankruptcy law. Marshall's interpretation would have greatly limited the operation of state bankruptcy laws, and the majority rejected this outcome.

The BILL OF RIGHTS also evidences constitutional concern for material rights. The TAKINGS clause of the Fifth Amendment states that private property shall not be taken for PUBLIC USE without JUST COMPENSATION. The Fifth Amendment also states that no person shall be deprived of life, liberty, or property without due process of law. The SECOND AMENDMENT prohibits the confiscation of arms. The THIRD AMENDMENT restricts the quartering of troops. The FOURTH AMENDMENT prohibits unreasonable SEARCHES AND SEIZURES, and the Eighth Amendment prohibits excessive BAIL and fines.

Those who doubt that the Constitution protects the material rights from infringement by the states should consider section 1 of the Fourteenth Amendment, the second sentence of which reads: "No state shall make or enforce any law which shall abridge the privileges or immunities of citizens of the United States: nor shall any State deprive any person of life, liberty, or property, without due process of law; nor deny to any person within its jurisdiction the equal protection of the law." The framers of this amendment, the Congress of 1866, were concerned about protecting property and economic liberties as well as other personal rights.

While opinion is divergent as to the full meaning of the quoted language, commentators generally agree that it was primarily intended to make constitutional the CIVIL RIGHTS ACT OF 1866, placing it beyond the power of any subsequent Congress to repeal. The chief purpose of this act was to provide federal protection for the freed blacks in the exercise of certain described liberties.

The 1866 law was not confined to the protection of blacks. It was also intended to secure equality of rights for most other citizens. Thus Senator Lyman Trumbull, who wrote the original bill, viewed it as affecting state legislation generally, quoting in his introductory statement from a note to WILLIAM BLACKSTONE's commentaries: "In this definition of civil liberty it ought to be understood, or rather expressed, that the restraints introduced by the law should be equal to all, or as much as the nature of things will admit." The statute emphasized material, and not political or intellectual, considerations. It protected against discriminatory treatment the rights of most native-born citizens "to make and enforce contracts . . . and to inherit, purchase, lease, sell, hold and convey real and personal property."

The debates on section 1 of the Fourteenth Amendment further spell out Congress's commitment to preserving the material rights. Frequently quoted in the debates was Justice BUSHROD WASHINGTON's definition in CORFIELD V. CORYELL (1823), stating that privileges and immunities included "the right to acquire and possess property of every kind." For the thirty-ninth Congress, Sir William Blackstone and Chancellor JAMES KENT were highly authoritative on the powers and purposes of government. Both strongly emphasized the importance of economic and property rights in a free society.

There should be little doubt that the values of foremost importance to the Framers of many provisions of the Constitution encompassed the protection of economic and property rights.

BERNARD H. SIEGAN

Bibliography

CORWIN, EDWARD S.   1948   *Liberty Against Government.* Baton Rouge: Louisiana State University Press.

McCLOSKEY, ROBERT G.   1962   Economic Due Process and the Supreme Court. *Supreme Court Review* 1962:34–62.

SIEGAN, BERNARD H.   1981   *Economic Liberties and the Constitution.* Chicago: University of Chicago Press.

———   1984   The Economic Constitution in Historical Perspective. In Richard M. McKenzie, ed., *Constitutional Economics.* Pages 39–53. Lexington, Mass.: D.C. Heath.

ECONOMIC OPPORTUNITY ACT
78 Stat. 580 (1964)

Moving rapidly to consolidate his control over the administration he inherited from JOHN F. KENNEDY, President LYNDON B. JOHNSON in January 1964 declared "war on poverty" and announced his aim of building a "Great Society." The Economic Opportunity Act of 1964 was the centerpiece of the Johnson program.

Building on a BROAD CONSTRUCTION of the TAXING AND SPENDING POWER, the architects of the act erected a new conception of the role of the federal government. The government was to eliminate the

"culture of poverty" that kept some people in economic distress. The act established several new agencies, the most important of which was the Office of Economic Opportunity (later the Community Services Administration) within the Executive Office of the President. It also created a plethora of new programs: Job Corps, Neighborhood Youth Corps, Head Start, etcetera.

From the beginning the war on poverty faced problems, and no poor person ever benefited from it as much as the bureaucrats who ran it. Funds were targeted on the basis less of economic need than of political patronage. And simultaneous expenditure for the war on poverty and the war in Vietnam depleted the treasury and fueled runaway inflation.

DENNIS J. MAHONEY

ECONOMIC REGULATION

In the field of economic policy, the composite constitutional powers of American governments—federal, state, and local—are extremely broad. Granted that governments may not implement economic policies that would violate the guarantees of the BILL OF RIGHTS or a few other constitutional limitations, within these spacious constraints there is little that governments may not do. But what they must or should do is more complex. As to macroeconomic policy, whose main instruments are monetary and fiscal, powers amount virtually to duties, for government could not function without taxing and borrowing, nor could the economy run at all smoothly if government declined to issue any money or take any steps to control its value. (See BORROWING POWER; MONETARY POWER; TAXING AND SPENDING POWER.) Just how these essential functions should be carried out is a matter of art and of debate, but few contend that the functions need not be carried out at all. However, as to microeconomic policies—those identified by usage as the substance of "economic regulation"—constitutional powers have not been regarded as inescapable duties. Although governments may intervene directly to regulate prices, wages, quality of products, and various other aspects of markets, they need not do so. Wages, for instance, have been regulated at some times but not others, in some occupations but not all, and so as to set minima but not maxima. In short, economic regulation is constitutionally optional.

Nonetheless, American governments have always practiced economic regulation, albeit in varying forms and degrees. Moreover, they have always been considered to possess broad authority to regulate, even if during a relatively short interval at the beginning of this century the federal courts invalidated a few particular forms of economic regulation without, however, casting doubt on the legitimacy of most other forms. This historically continuous practice of economic regulation shows that American governments were never dogmatically addicted to laissez-faire, notwithstanding a broad though sometimes faltering preference for private enterprise, and that the Constitution, as intended, written, and interpreted, is not a manifesto in favor of laissez-faire.

Before the Civil War, the constitutional authority of the states to carry on any and every form of economic regulation was seldom questioned. And this acceptance was not for want of regulations to question. On the contrary, state and local governments set the prices to be charged by wagoners, wood sawyers, chimneysweeps, pawnbrokers, hackney carriages, ferries, wharfs, bridges, and bakers; required licensing of auctioneers, retailers, restaurants, taverns, vendors of lottery tickets, and slaughterhouses; and inspected the quality of timber, shingles, onions, butter, nails, tobacco, salted meat and fish, and bread. This very incomplete list attests to an intention to exercise detailed control over the operation of markets, especially (though not only) those that have since been characterized as providing "public services" and those thought to be morally dubious because of association with usury, betting, intoxication, or excessive jubilation.

In the few instances before the Civil War when such regulations came before its eyes, the Supreme Court roundly affirmed their constitutional propriety, always provided (for so the issues arose) that the state's legislation did not collide with the federal commerce power. So in GIBBONS V. OGDEN (1824) JOHN MARSHALL referred to "the acknowledged power of a state to regulate . . . its domestic trade" and to adopt "inspection laws, quarantine laws, health laws . . . , and those which respect turnpike roads, ferries, etc." In the LICENSE CASES (1847) ROGER B. TANEY defined the STATE POLICE POWER as "nothing more or less than the powers of . . . every sovereignty . . . to govern men and things," including commerce within its domain, powers absolute except as restrained by the Constitution. Again, in COOLEY V. BOARD OF WARDENS (1851) the Court upheld the constitutionality of a state law requiring ships in the port of Philadelphia to employ local pilots, and further regulating the qualifications of pilots and their fees. Only one notable judgment of the time, by the highest court of New York, seems on casual reading to cast doubt on a state's regulatory power. In WYNEHAMER V. PEO-

PLE (1856) that court invalidated a law prohibiting the sale, and even the possession, of hard liquor on the ground that the statute acted retroactively and thus fell afoul of the DUE PROCESS clause in the state's constitution. The Justices agreed that a PROHIBITION law framed to operate prospectively would lie entirely within the legislature's power, and the only Justice who expressed reservations about outright prohibition went on to say: "It is . . . certain that the legislature can regulate trade in property of all kinds." Long and widespread practice throughout the country confirmed that state legislatures can indeed regulate the terms and conditions not only of trade but also of PRODUCTION, as well as entry into various occupations—though courts repeatedly insisted that the states' police powers, broad though they were, must be limited by profound constitutional antipathy to arbitrary action, such as that instanced by Justice SAMUEL CHASE in CALDER V. BULL (1798): "a law that takes property from A. and gives it to B."

Nor was this broad scope of the police power curtailed by decisions following shortly after the ratification of the FOURTEENTH AMENDMENT in 1868. In the SLAUGHTERHOUSE CASES (1873) the majority of the Supreme Court upheld a Louisiana law that closed down all slaughtering inside New Orleans, confined it to a designated area outside the city, and gave a single private company the right to operate a slaughterhouse there, despite the complaint by butchers that the statute, by depriving them of part of their usual trade, violated the PRIVILEGES AND IMMUNITIES and due process clauses of the Fourteenth Amendment. The Court concluded that the police power undoubtedly authorized regulation of slaughtering, and that the prohibitions imposed on the states by the amendment should not be interpreted as a limitation on reasonable exercises of the police power.

A broadly similar view prevailed in *Munn v. Illinois* (1877), which concerned the validity of a statute fixing the maximum charge to be levied by grain elevators in Chicago. Against the defendants' plea that the ceiling thus set on their earnings effectively deprived them of property without due process, Chief Justice MORRISON R. WAITE marshaled the long history of adjudication prior to 1868: "It was not supposed that statutes regulating the use, or even the price of the use, of private property necessarily deprived an owner of his property without due process of law." The word "necessarily" signaled a departure from the majority's blunt assertion in *Slaughterhouse* that due process should not box in the police power. Instead, the Court adopted in *Munn* the pared-down principle that states could, without offending against due process, regulate the prices of some kinds of business, "those AFFECTED WITH A PUBLIC INTEREST" or, as later usage had it, public service businesses. The tempting inference, that ordinary, "private" businesses are immune to economic regulation, though lent plausibility by some hints in the text, is not confirmed by any forthright judicial statement. (See GRANGER CASES.)

The "affectation with a public interest" DOCTRINE, though frequently invoked by courts in support of state regulation of railroads and public utilities, did not always carry the day. The first notable deviation, not only from *Munn* but from the longer previous tradition, took place in ALLGEYER V. LOUISIANA (1897). In question was Allgeyer's right to buy marine insurance from a New York company despite a Louisiana statute prohibiting out of state insurance companies from doing business there without a license. While conceding the state's power to regulate or even to exclude insurance companies domiciled in other states, the Court concentrated on every American citizen's privilege to pursue an "ordinary calling or trade" and, in the course of it, to make such contracts as might be useful and proper. By interfering with a person's exercise of that privilege, the Court unanimously held, Louisiana had abridged the Fourteenth Amendment's guarantee of liberty and property. To believe, however, as the decision's admirers and detractors alike have believed, that the Court thus read a sweeping FREEDOM OF CONTRACT into the Fourteenth Amendment, so as to equate all economic regulation with denial of due process, is to ignore a vital passage in the opinion, where RUFUS PECKHAM declared that the police power of a state "cannot extend to prohibiting a citizen from making contracts . . . outside the limits and JURISDICTION of the State, and which are also to be performed outside of such jurisdiction." Cavalier disregard of that essential qualification has made the *Allgeyer* opinion seem what it was not. If further evidence were needed, it was supplied by the Court's decision one year later in HOLDEN V. HARDY (1898), where the majority of seven upheld an act of Utah regulating the hours of labor in mines and smelters, without any suggestion that mines and smelters are businesses affected with a public interest, and notwithstanding considerable interference with freedom of contract.

Supposedly initiated by *Allgeyer,* the triumph of "economic due process" or SUBSTANTIVE DUE PROCESS—a triumph never fully consummated—was supposedly completed by LOCHNER V. NEW YORK (1905). Inasmuch as the Supreme Court there struck down a statute that limited the work of bakers to sixty hours

a week, the decision could be so represented. But a close reading of the opinions, including the dissents, leads to the sounder conclusion that the statute was invalidated because, while purporting to be a measure for the public health, it adopted means that (in the majority's view) had no reasonable relation to that end, or alternatively because it was really an effort to interfere in the bargaining between master and employee, an effort lying outside the proper scope of the police power as constrained by the due process clause.

That the *Lochner* decision did not undermine economic regulation was demonstrated three years later in MULLER V. OREGON (1908), when the Supreme Court (with only one new member) upheld a restriction on hours of work of women as a reasonable means of achieving the proper end of public health, and was demonstrated again in BUNTING V. OREGON (1917), where the statute applied to men as well as women and to overtime wage rates as well as to hours. In ADKINS V. CHILDREN'S HOSPITAL (1923), however, the Court once again sailed closer to the *Lochner* tack, when it disallowed a minimum wage law. Nevertheless, despite the *Lochner-Adkins* line and reliance on decisions before, during, and after the brief era of laissez-faire activism, many states continued to pass and enforce laws regulating the conditions of labor as well as other economic relations, especially after the onset of the Great Depression.

The older line of interpretation, temporarily obscured but not reversed, was restored to predominance by the Supreme Court's decision in NEBBIA V. NEW YORK (1934). Here, while apparently relying on *Munn v. Illinois* (1877), the Court effectively reversed it by holding "that the private character of a business does not necessarily remove it from the realm of regulation of charges or prices." Indeed, the Court went on to say that it had upheld an extensive variety of economic regulations, a statement the accuracy of which it vindicated by citing some hundred PRECEDENTS that it had laid down during the three or four decades earlier. A further step toward closing the *Lochner* episode was taken in WEST COAST HOTEL V. PARRISH (1937); and the final (at least until the present) bit of punctuation was supplied in UNITED STATES V. CAROLENE PRODUCTS COMPANY (1938) when the Court committed itself not to invalidate regulatory legislation unless the law's irrationality offended against due process or it otherwise contravened specific constitutional guarantees such as those in the Bill of Rights.

Meanwhile, economic regulation by the federal government had been undergoing a roughly parallel development. Substantively it was less extensive, because until about the Civil War economic activity within the several states far outweighed that which crossed the boundaries of any state, because the federal government spent less and did less than state and local governments, and not at all because the federal government was more attached than were state and local governments to laissez-faire. Ample evidence to the contrary is afforded by the protective tariffs so vigorously advocated by ALEXANDER HAMILTON and HENRY CLAY and so widely supported, by the subsidies granted to transportation facilities in the name of INTERNAL IMPROVEMENTS, and by close regulation of ships and sailors involved in interstate and foreign navigation. If nevertheless the federal government did little to implement the COMMERCE CLAUSE during its first century, Congress's latent constitutional power was recognized and approved. When Marshall wrote in GIBBONS V. OGDEN (1824) that the commerce power "is complete in itself, may be exercised to its utmost extent, and acknowledges no limitations, other than are prescribed in the constitution," he prefigured later judicial pronouncements that the commerce power is effectively the NATIONAL POLICE POWER.

As might have been expected, the coexistence of two tiers of police power occasioned increasing collisions when, after the Civil War, the federal government expanded the exercise of its own power. Such collisions might have been resolved by simple-minded recourse to the SUPREMACY CLAUSE, but that solution would not have appealed strongly to judges who remembered that the professed objective of the Civil War had been, on the one side, to protect the autonomy of the states and, on the other side, to preserve a Union (rather than replace it by a unitary state). Recollections of the crisis reinforced the traditional effort to delineate clear boundaries between the domains of the states and that of the federal government.

A striking specimen of this issue arose from the increasing efforts of state governments after the Civil War to regulate railroad rates, and in particular to prohibit what many shippers regarded as iniquitous discrimination. In this instance a railroad had charged a shipper a certain amount for sending goods from one place in Illinois to New York City while charging another shipper less for sending the same sort of goods from another place in Illinois to New York City, though the latter distance was greater than the former. This habitual practice, known as LONG-HAUL–SHORT-HAUL DISCRIMINATION, violated an Illinois statute. In WABASH, ST. LOUIS, PACIFIC RAILWAY V. ILLINOIS (1886) the Supreme Court decided that, although the Illinois courts had confined application of the statute to transportation within the state, the statute was nevertheless invalid as applied to contracts for continous transportation through several states, so "interfering with and seriously embarrassing" interstate commerce. The counterargument, that state statutes of this sort might be permitted to stand until the federal government might occupy the field, became moot when in the following year Congress passed the INTERSTATE COMMERCE ACT, which among other things established the first federal REGULATORY AGENCY, the Interstate Commerce Commission. For twenty-seven years thereafter, until announcement of the SHREVEPORT DOCTRINE, a relatively comfortable equilibrium recognized the exclusive power of states to regulate purely intrastate transportation and of the federal government to regulate purely interstate transportation, though controversy occasionally erupted as to whether some particular regulation by one tier of government materially spilled over into the other's domain.

Concerning enterprises other than transportation, it was harder to draw a neat line between what is a fixture within a state and what though within a state is visiting it as a bird of passage or, according to a habitual metaphor, "flowing" through it. This difficulty was manifested in UNITED STATES V. E. C. KNIGHT CO. (1894), the Supreme Court's first ruling on the SHERMAN ANTITRUST ACT. It arose from a suit asking that the courts invalidate contracts by which the "Sugar Trust" had purchased four independent refineries, so achieving an almost complete monopoly of refining. Considering that the government had attacked the contracts rather than the trust itself, that the contracts concerned factories necessarily installed within a state, and that no proof had been offered to connect the contracts with a scheme to restrain interstate commerce, the Court held that the contracts were not reached by the Sherman Act; as so construed, the act was valid. In dissent, Justice JOHN MARSHALL HARLAN objected that the nub of the case was not the sugar trust's acquisition of the four refineries but its monopolization of interstate commerce. One may suppose that, contrary to Chief Justice MELVILLE W. FULLER's pronouncement that "commerce succeeds to manufacture," Harlan would have preferred to say that manufacture, when ancillary to interstate commerce, falls within federal legislative power.

Similar partitioning of state and federal domains persisted in most such decisions down to 1936, accompanied by judicial reminders that if the reach of the commerce power were excessively widened, the states would be rendered economically otiose. So in HAMMER V. DAGENHART (1918) the Supreme Court, while agreeing that the working hours of children in mines and factories should be regulated (and in fact was regulated by every state), invalidated a federal child labor law on the ground that it would disturb the desirably "harmonious" balance between the police power and the commerce power. Similarly, when ruling in SCHECHTER POULTRY CORPORATION V. UNITED STATES (1935) that poultry slaughterers in New York City could not be reached by federal regulation, Chief Justice CHARLES EVANS HUGHES wrote: "If the commerce clause were construed to reach all enterprises and transactions which could be said to have an indirect effect upon interstate commerce, the Federal authority would embrace practically all the activities of the people and all the authority of the State over its domestic concerns would exist only by sufferance of the Federal Government."

That traditional view was substantially revised by *National Labor Relations Board v. Jones & Laughlin Steel Corporation* (1937), decided while President Franklin D. Roosevelt's Court reorganization plan was being vigorously debated. Technically the turn hinged on the Court's finding that the defendant company, besides owning steel mills and mines, owned and operated interstate railroads and water carriers and sales offices throughout the country; as the company was "a completely integrated enterprise," one in which manufacture and commerce might be said to have been completely unified, its relations with labor unions in its steelworks and mines as well as in its railroads and water carriers were properly subject to federal regulation. On a narrow view, the Court continued to adhere to the principle that state and federal regulation must coexist—as the Court took trouble to emphasize in UNITED STATES V. DARBY LUMBER COMPANY (1941)—and merely found federal power applicable to "national" firms; on a broader view the Court had considerably shifted the dividing line. The virtual obliteration of the line was confirmed by WICKARD V. FILBURN (1942), where the Court upheld federal regulation of wheat farming, by reinterpreting production as well as consumption on the farm, previously understood to be inherently local, as ingredients of an "economic market" which, being national and indeed international, was properly subject to federal regulation.

Rash though it may be to suppose that one can identify historical patterns, it might nevertheless be ventured that economic regulation by the states was never impeded by laissez-faire nor, except briefly and partially, by the doctrine of substantive due process, and that economic regulation by the federal government has expanded, generally though unsteadily, as a proportion of the whole. This summary, assuming it to be accurate, does not of course endorse the logical rigor of CONSTITUTIONAL INTERPRETATION that underlay those tendencies, nor does it prejudge their political desirability. Those who see private enterprise as self-serving and chaotic conclude that extensive economic regulation is a condition of social welfare; whereas minimalists maintain that economic regulation is desirable only in the event of market failure, that is, only in relation to enterprises that give rise to oppressive externalities or to industries that are natural monopolies. The Constitution provides ample scope for the former view but imposes no restrictions corresponding to the latter view. Despite some indications of "deregulation" in legislation and adjudication since 1960, it would be foolhardy to predict whether economic regulation will diminish or increase during the future.

WILLIAM LETWIN

Bibliography

HALE, ROBERT L. 1952 *Freedom Through Law: Public Control of Private Governing Power.* New York: Columbia University Press.
HAMMOND, BRAY 1957 *Banks and Politics in America from the Revolution to the Civil War.* Princeton, N.J.: Princeton University Press.
HANDLIN, OSCAR 1947 *Commonwealth: A Study of the Role of Government in the American Economy.* New York: Oxford University Press.
KOONTZ, HAROLD and GABLE, RICHARD W. 1956 *Public Control of Economic Enterprise.* New York: McGraw-Hill.
LETWIN, WILLIAM 1965 *Law and Economic Policy in America: The Evolution of the Sherman Antitrust Act.* Chicago: University of Chicago Press.
LIEBHOFSKY, H. H. 1971 *American Government and Business.* New York: Wiley.
MORRIS, RICHARD B. 1946 *Government and Labor in Early America.* New York: Columbia University Press.
WILSON, JAMES Q., ED. 1980 *The Politics of Regulation.* New York: Basic Books.

ECONOMIC STABILIZATION ACT
84 Stat. 799 (1970)

This measure authorized the most comprehensive peacetime ECONOMIC REGULATION in American history. The act extended a temporary sweeping DELEGATION OF POWER which authorized the President "to issue such orders and regulations as he may deem appropriate to stabilize prices, rents, wages, and salaries at levels not less than those prevailing on May 25, 1970." It authorized federal courts to issue INJUNCTIONS to enforce the presidential orders and mandated a $5,000 penalty for violation. A Democratic Congress passed the act at a time of persistent inflation; Republicans charged it was an election-year ploy attacking President RICHARD M. NIXON for failure to curtail rising unemployment, high interest rates, and a balance of payments deficit.

Nixon signed the measure but indicated he would have preferred to veto it and had no intention of using its authority. He opposed committing vast regulatory power to presidential discretion; if Congress favored controls, he said, it should "face up to its responsibilities and make such controls mandatory." One year later, amid growing disapproval of his economic policies, Nixon used the act to impose a ninety-day freeze on wages, prices, and rents. The President twice requested and received congressional extension as "in the public interest." The act was allowed to expire in 1974.

PAUL L. MURPHY

Bibliography

SILK, LEONARD 1973 *Nixonomics*. New York: Praeger.

EDELMAN v. JORDAN
415 U.S. 651 (1974)

This decision defines states' ELEVENTH AMENDMENT immunity from suit in federal court. Plaintiffs, alleging that Illinois welfare officials were unconstitutionally administering a welfare program financed by state and federal funds, sought the payments wrongfully withheld. The Supreme Court, in an opinion by Justice WILLIAM H. REHNQUIST, held the Eleventh Amendment to bar the request for retroactive relief but suggested that, as in EX PARTE YOUNG (1908), the Eleventh Amendment would not bar relief requiring the state to pay the costs of future constitutional compliance. In MILLIKEN V. BRADLEY (1977), the Court reconfirmed *Edelman* by requiring a state to pay the costs of future constitutional compliance.

Edelman also developed the principles regulating Congress's power to modify the states' Eleventh Amendment immunity. First, limiting earlier holdings such as *Parden v. Terminal Railway* (1964), *Edelman* held that mere participation by a state in a federal welfare program does not constitute a waiver of the state's Eleventh Amendment protection. It thus confirmed the narrow approach to waiver signaled by

Employees v. Department of Public Health and Welfare (1973). Second, despite Congress's power to abrogate states' Eleventh Amendment immunity, *Edelman* stated that actions brought under SECTION 1983, TITLE 42, UNITED STATES CODE, are limited by the Eleventh Amendment. At the time, the state's protection from section 1983 actions seemed to stem from the Court's holding in MONROE V. PAPE (1961) that Congress had not meant to render cities liable under section 1983. With the overruling of that portion of *Monroe* in MONELL V. DEPARTMENT OF SOCIAL SERVICES (1978), the question whether section 1983 abrogated the states' Eleventh Amendment immunities reemerged. In QUERN V. JORDAN (1979), a sequel to *Edelman*, the Court held that section 1983 was not meant to abrogate the states' Eleventh Amendment protection.

THEODORE EISENBERG

EDUCATION AMENDMENTS OF 1972 (TITLE IX)
86 Stat. 373

Title VI of the CIVIL RIGHTS ACT OF 1964 prohibits discrimination on the ground of race, color, or national origin in programs receiving federal financial assistance. Title IX of the Education Amendments of 1972 extends Title VI's ban to discrimination on the basis of sex in federally assisted education programs. Title IX excludes from its coverage fraternities, sororities, Girl Scouts, Boy Scouts, and similar organizations, and scholarships awarded to beauty contest winners; the act does not require sexually integrated living facilities. Title IX instructs federal departments to implement its provisions through rules or regulations and authorizes termination of funding in cases of noncompliance.

Title IX has played a major role in increasing female athletic opportunities at educational institutions, and *North Haven Board of Education v. Bell* (1982) held that Title IX could reach sexually discriminatory employment practices. In *Cannon v. University of Chicago* (1979) the Supreme Court held that Title IX may be enforced through private civil actions. (See SEX DISCRIMINATION.)

THEODORE EISENBERG

Bibliography

DORSEN, NORMAN; BENDER, PAUL; NEUBORNE, BURT; and LAW, SYLVIA 1979 *Emerson, Haber and Dorsen's Political and Civil Rights in the United States*, 4th ed. Vol. II: 771–774, 883–893. Boston: Little, Brown.

EDUCATION AND THE CONSTITUTION

Basic to any discussion of the role of courts in educational decision making is the primacy of education in American ideology. Americans believe that education is central to the realization of a truly democratic and egalitarian society. It is through education that the skills necessary to exercise the responsibilities of citizenship and to benefit from the opportunities of a free economy will be imparted, no matter how recently arrived or previously disadvantaged the individual. Thus courts are concerned with protecting access to education. Moreover, since decision making by those charged with the administration of public education is seen as one of the most significant areas of law in terms of its effects on the lives of individuals and groups in our society, courts are inevitably drawn into reviewing the legitimacy of those decisions.

Education is primarily a state function in large part delegated to local school districts; the federal government has no direct constitutional responsibility for education. Nevertheless, Congress has enacted laws providing FEDERAL GRANTS-IN-AID to state and local educational agencies, as well as laws protecting the CIVIL RIGHTS of various categories of students. The constitutional authority for these statutes and their implementing regulations comes from Article I, section 8, clause 1, of the Constitution—the TAXING AND SPENDING POWER—which has been interpreted to permit Congress to attach conditions to the receipt of federal funds. Constitutional authority for congressional civil rights mandates governing educational institutions may also lie in section 5 of the FOURTEENTH AMENDMENT.

In the absence of federal legislation, are there constitutional constraints on the extent to which school authorities can control education and regulate the lives of students and teachers? Conversely, do students and teachers have the same constitutional rights as all citizens in our society, or are these rights limited within the school environment? The courts have acknowledged the importance of education to our democratic society and the importance of schools in preserving and transmitting the values—social, moral, or political—on which our society rests. The challenge is to inculcate those values without stifling the exercise of the freedom of expression, the freedom of religion, and other constitutional rights.

Until the middle of the twentieth century, education was almost the sole prerogative of school administrators and local boards of education. There were few legal constraints on school authorities and even fewer legal entitlements for teachers and students. Today various competing groups and individuals seek to control educational decision making—school boards, school administrators, teachers, parents, students, community leaders, minority groups, and federal and state agencies. Their struggles for control have often ended up in the courts. Since BROWN V. BOARD OF EDUCATION (1954), the Supreme Court has decided cases involving nearly every major area of educational policy.

Whether states may constitutionally compel all children to be educated in state-run schools was resolved by the Supreme Court in PIERCE V. SOCIETY OF SISTERS (1925), which held that while the state may compel all children to obtain schooling, parents have a constitutional right to choose between public and private schools. Nearly fifty years after *Pierce*, however, the Court held that there are certain constitutional interests of parents and children that may outweigh the state's interest in compelling children to attend school. The Court, in WISCONSIN V. YODER (1972), emphasized that parental direction of the religious upbringing of their children is an important interest to be protected. Although education is important to our democratic society, the interest of the state in compelling two more years of education beyond the eighth grade was outweighed by the burden on the RELIGIOUS LIBERTY of Amish parents. Only the dissent discussed the possibility that the child's interest might differ from that of the parent. In this perspective, *Yoder* seems not so much a case about the rights of children as a contest between parents and state over the power to inculcate values.

The state has a much greater role to play in selecting the curriculum and regulating what is taught in its own schools than it does in private schools. Education necessarily involves the process of selection; it also requires some degree of order to carry out the educational mission. However, as the Supreme Court noted in TINKER V. DES MOINES INDEPENDENT SCHOOL DISTRICT (1969), students (and teachers) do not "shed their constitutional rights . . . at the schoolhouse gate." Nevertheless, these rights may be circumscribed because of the "special characteristics of the school environment." The constitutional claims made on the courts with regard to schooling have been directed principally toward the protection of individual freedom and the attainment of equality. In the first instance, the countervailing factors are the stability and order of the educational enterprise; in the second instance, they center on differing conceptions of equality and the extent to which the educational enterprise is constitutionally obligated to respond to the equity-based claims of various groups absent a showing of intentional discrimination.

There has been much litigation regarding constitutional limitations on the inculcation of religious, political, and moral values in the public schools. The principal cases resolving the question of the proper place of RELIGION IN THE PUBLIC SCHOOLS were decided in the early 1960s. In ENGEL V. VITALE (1962) the Supreme Court held that a nondenominational prayer written by the New York Board of Regents for use in the public schools violated the FIRST AMENDMENT's prohibition of an ESTABLISHMENT OF RELIGION. A year later, in ABINGTON SCHOOL DISTRICT V. SCHEMPP (1963), the Court struck down the practice of reading verses from the Bible and the recitation of the Lord's Prayer in public schools, holding that the state's obligation to be neutral with regard to religion forbids it to conduct a religious service even with the consent of the majority of those affected. Justice TOM C. CLARK was careful, however, to distinguish between the study of religion or of the Bible "when presented objectively as part of a secular program of education" and religious exercises. In *Stone v. Graham* (1980), the Court held unconstitutional a Kentucky law that required that the Ten Commandments be posted on the walls of public school classrooms. The Court indicated, however, that the case would be different if the Ten Commandments were integrated into the school's curriculum, where the Bible could be studied as history, ethics, or comparative religion.

Although the extent to which religious socialization can be undertaken by school authorities has been sharply limited by the courts, the constitutional limits on political and moral socialization are less clear. *West Virginia State Board of Education v. Barnette* acknowledged the right of school authorities to attempt to foster patriotism in the schools, but held that the Constitution protects the right of nonparticipation in a patriotic ritual that, in effect, coerces an expression of belief. So too, the First Amendment appears to prevent the editing out of particular ideas with a view to prescribing orthodoxy in politics, religion, or other matters of opinion, but the removal of books and curricular materials from the school library may be permitted when it is done for educational reasons. In so holding, the plurality opinion in BOARD OF EDUCATION V. PICO (1982) recognized a limited right of students to receive information, at least in the context of removal of books from a school library, that was protected by the First Amendment.

The reverse side of the coin involves the extent to which parents have a constitutional right to exempt their children from being socialized by public schools to values to which they object. Absent a clear establishment clause claim, it is unlikely that parents can demand, on moral or philosophical grounds, that certain books or courses be excluded from the public school curriculum approved by school authorities. And absent a clear free exercise claim, it is also unlikely that parents can exempt their children from courses to which they may object, particularly as *Pierce* protects the option of sending their children to private schools if they disagree with the values being taught in the public school.

To what extent does the Constitution protect the right of free expression of students and teachers in the school environment? Complete freedom of expression is inconsistent with the schooling enterprise, which requires order and control. In *Tinker v. Des Moines Independent Community School District* (1969) the Court said that although an "undifferentiated fear or apprehension of disturbance is not enough to overcome the right to freedom of expression," school officials could limit expression if they showed that "the forbidden conduct would 'materially and substantially interfere with the requirements of appropriate discipline in the operation of the school.'"

With regard to First Amendment protection for student organizations, the Supreme Court, in *Healy v. James* (1972), held that "associational activities need not be tolerated where they infringe reasonable campus rules, interrupt classes, or substantially interfere with the opportunity of other students to obtain an education." Nevertheless, because the denial of recognition of a student organization is a form of prior restraint, school authorities have a heavy burden of proving the likelihood of disruption. Although the college in the *Healy* case had denied Students for a Democratic Society access to campus facilities, various other student organizations were permitted such access. Thus, *Healy* might be read as concerned with equal treatment—that is, if a college generally permits student organizations access to its facilities, although it could exclude all such organizations, it may not exclude an organization based on the political or social views it espouses. (See also WIDMAR V. VINCENT, 1981.)

May a teacher's right of expression be restricted in light of the special demands of the school environment? This question arises in a variety of contexts. Is the right of the teacher as citizen to free expression circumscribed by being an employee of the school system? Does the teacher as a professional have the right to determine course content, the selection of books, and the ideas and values to be presented in the classroom? Another question, not yet clearly resolved, is whether there is an independent right of ACADEMIC FREEDOM protected by the Constitution or whether that freedom is merely a corollary of the students' RIGHT TO KNOW.

The Supreme Court has never decided a case that squarely dealt with academic freedom in the classroom. Although KEYISHIAN V. BOARD OF REGENTS (1967) noted that academic freedom is "a special concern of the First Amendment" and that "the classroom is peculiarly the 'MARKETPLACE OF IDEAS',", the case involved neither the classroom nor the teacher's right to choose the curriculum or to teach in any particular way. Justice HUGO L. BLACK, in his concurring opinion in EPPERSON V. ARKANSAS (1968), expressed a narrow view of the "academic freedom" protected by the First Amendment: "I am . . . not ready to hold that a person hired to teach school children takes with him into the classroom a constitutional right to teach sociological, economic, political, or religious subjects that the school's managers do not want discussed. . . . I question whether . . . 'academic freedom' permits a teacher to breach his contractual agreement to teach only the subjects designated by the school authorities that hired him."

Although lower court decisions vary significantly as to whether "academic freedom" in the classroom is constitutionally protected, OBITER DICTUM in the plurality opinion in *Pico* suggested that school authorities have unfettered discretion to inculcate community values through the curriculum. If this view prevails, the teacher would appear to have no unilateral right to dictate the lessons (especially value lessons) to which the student will be exposed. If the classroom is the vehicle for imparting values, it cannot also be an open "marketplace of ideas."

Other issues of "academic freedom" actually involve the extent to which the freedom of expression of teachers as citizens, outside the classroom, must be balanced against the interest of the state as employer. For example, the Supreme Court held in *Pickering v. Board of Education* (1968) that, "absent proof of false statements knowingly or recklessly made by him, a teacher's exercise of his right to speak on issues of public importance may not furnish the basis for his dismissal from public employment." However, if the teacher's statements had been shown to have impeded his or her performance in the classroom or otherwise interfered with the regular operation of the schools, the speech might not be protected. And it is not clear whether protection would extend to teachers who voice their criticisms in the classroom.

The extent to which the Constitution constrains school authorities in the manner in which institutional rules and regulations are applied to students and teachers has been extensively litigated. Must certain procedures be followed before a student can be searched for EVIDENCE of the commission of a crime or a violation of a school rule, or before disciplinary action can be taken for failure to comply with institutional rules and norms?

A search made of private property is ordinarily held to be "unreasonable" under the FOURTH AMENDMENT if made without a valid SEARCH WARRANT. Even when the circumstances are such that courts have permitted warrantless searches, however (such as when necessary to prevent concealment or destruction of evidence), such searches usually require a showing of a PROBABLE CAUSE. However, the Supreme Court, in balancing school authorities' "substantial" interest in maintaining discipline against students' legitimate expectations of privacy, has fashioned a less protective standard. In NEW JERSEY V. T.L.O. (1985) the Court held that a search by school authorities is constitutional when there are reasonable grounds for suspecting that the search will turn up evidence, and when "the measures adopted are reasonably related to the objectives of the search and not excessively intrusive in light of the age and sex of the student and the nature of the infraction." Moreover, there is no warrant requirement for school searches.

Important constitutional values are incorporated in our notions of procedural fairness. GOSS V. LOPEZ (1975) held that state-created entitlements to a public education are protected by the due process clause of the Fourteenth Amendment; thus, the right to attend school may not be withdrawn on the ground of misconduct, absent fair procedures for determining whether the misconduct has occurred. However, having decided that some process is due, the procedural requirements in the school environment are minimal. In the case of a ten-day suspension of a student for disciplinary reasons, *Goss* required only that the student be given notice of the charges and an opportunity to explain his or her version of the story. Immediate removal from school may be justified in some cases even before the hearing. The hearing itself may simply be a brief meeting between the student and the administrator minutes after the alleged transgression. More stringent safeguards, however, may be required for deprivations of education significantly longer than the ten-day period involved in *Goss*. Just two years after *Goss*, the Court held, in INGRAHAM V. WRIGHT (1977), that although the administration of corporal punishment for violating school rules implicated a constitutionally protected liberty interest, "the traditional COMMON LAW remedies were fully adequate to afford due process." Thus, no advance procedural safeguards were constitutionally required. Because, according to the Supreme Court in BOARD OF CURATORS V. HOROWITZ (1978), academic grades and evaluations typically involve more subjective and evaluative judgments than do disciplinary decisions, the determination of "what process is due" turns on whether the disputed action is deemed to be academic or disciplinary in nature.

Yet another constitutional constraint on the public schools is embodied in the Fourteenth Amendment's EQUAL PROTECTION clause. The assertion of an entitlement to a minimum educational opportunity, to equal access to the schooling process, or to a specified educational outcome seeks to impose an affirmative obligation upon public schools. The most fully matured and litigated definition of equal educational opportunity is the right of minority students to be free of RACIAL DISCRIMINATION. The principal issues have concerned the requirements for finding that the Constitution has been violated, and the scope of the remedy once a constitutional violation has been established. The courts have held that intentional actions of school authorities constitute de jure SEGREGATION and, in some cases, that intent to segregate can be inferred from actions that have the foreseeable effect of fostering segregation. The courts have also held that the lapse of time between past acts and present segregation does not alone eliminate the presumption of causation and intent. Courts have also coped with the question whether RACIAL QUOTAS or AFFIRMATIVE ACTION to assist minorities who have been handicapped by past discrimination are unconstitutional, what are permissible remedial techniques (such as zoning, pairing of schools, or SCHOOL BUSING), when a systemwide remedy is permissible and what proof is required before a systemwide remedy can be ordered, and whether a court may require that school district boundaries be reorganized in order to devise an effective remedy.

Some students seeking equal educational opportunity are asserting a right to be free of discrimination on the basis of gender. However, most of the case law has developed under Title IX of the EDUCATION AMENDMENTS OF 1972 and its implementing regulations, and few of these cases have been decided on constitutional grounds.

In CRAIG V. BOREN (1976) the Supreme Court indicated that gender would not be treated as a SUSPECT CLASSIFICATION as is race, but as a category requiring an intermediate level of judicial scrutiny. Thus, a gender classification must serve important governmental objectives and must be substantially related to the achievement of those objectives before it can be upheld. MISSISSIPPI UNIVERSITY FOR WOMEN V. HOGAN (1982), involving the exclusion of males from MUW's School of Nursing, held that the state had failed to meet this standard. The state had argued that its single-sex admissions policy was designed to compensate for discrimination against women, but was unable to show that women had suffered discrimination in the field of nursing. For the majority, not only was the policy excluding males from the School of Nursing not compensatory, it tended "to perpetuate the stereotyped view of nursing as an exclusively women's job." The state also failed to show that the gender-based classification was substantially related to its purported compensatory objective. SEPArate but equal educational offerings, if truly equal, and policies that are truly compensary may still be constitutionally permitted in the case of gender.

Equal educational opportunity has sometimes been defined in terms of financial resources. The school finance reform movement of the early 1970s concerned inequalities in educational resources among school districts within a state. The issue in those cases was whether such inequalities were constitutionally impermissible. In SAN ANTONIO INDEPENDENT SCHOOL DISTRICT V. RODRIGUEZ (1973) the Supreme Court held that because Texas's school finance system neither employed a SUSPECT CLASSIFICATION nor touched on a fundamental interest, the financing scheme must be assessed in terms of the RATIONAL BASIS standard of review. The Supreme Court's opinion distinguished differences among school districts from a state "financing system that occasioned an absolute denial of educational opportunities to any of its children." Those statements raise two related questions: First, under what circumstances, if any, is exclusion of a class of children from public schools constitutionally justifiable? Second, if absolute deprivation of an education is unconstitutional, can this principle be extended to certain children who, although attending public schools, are "functionally excluded?" PLYLER V. DOE (1982) raised the first question and LAU V. NICHOLS (1974) the second.

In *Plyler v. Doe* the Court held invalid a state statute that permitted school districts to bar illegal alien children from public schooling. *Lau v. Nichols* involved non-English-speaking children who, even though they had the same access as other children to teachers and books, were "functionally excluded" because they could not understand what went on in the classroom where only English was spoken. The Court struck down this "functional exclusion" of students on statutory grounds.

Although students with limited English proficiency and handicapped students, like minorities or women generally, have sought equal treatment with respect to educational offerings, in some circumstances they have sought to impose affirmative duties on government to remove barriers to their opportunity to obtain an equal education—barriers that were not of the government's making. If they do not receive special treatment, the argument goes, they do not have an opportunity equal to that of others to take advantage of the education the government offers to all. The Supreme Court has not yet held that this latter approach to equal educational opportunity, focusing on an affirmative duty to provide special, additional services for certain groups, is constitutionally dictated; the only cases to come before the Court have been decided on statutory grounds.

Cleburne v. Cleburne Living Center, Inc. (1985) suggested in OBITER DICTUM that the handicapped are entitled only to application of the rational relationship standard to their equal protection claims. However, now that *Plyler v. Doe* has recognized the importance of education, perhaps the handicapped will receive some special solicitude for their claims to education. On the other hand, *Plyler v. Doe* involved the total exclusion of undocumented alien children from public schooling. Even in *Rodriguez,* the Court suggested that the total deprivation of education might be constitutionally impermissible. Thus, arguably, the total exclusion—or perhaps even the functional exclusion—of handicapped children from education would be unconstitutional, but there would be no constitutional violation in a state's failure to provide the special treatment and additional educational resources needed to bring them to the same starting line as other children.

Since Americans view education as of utmost importance to the maintenance of both their political and their economic systems, as well as to the well-being of the individual and his or her family, schooling is compulsory. The school is, on the one hand, the agency of government closest to the day-to-day lives of people and, on the other hand, the most inherently coercive. Thus courts have been concerned with the appropriate balance between individual liberties and societal interests as well as equal access to an education.

BETSY LEVIN

Bibliography

GOLDSTEIN, STEPHEN R. 1976 The Asserted Constitutional Right of Public School Teachers to Determine What They Teach. *University of Pennsylvania Law Review* 124:1293–1357.
HIRSCHOFF, JON 1977 Parents and the Public School Curriculum: Is There a Right to Have One's Child Excused from Objectionable Instruction? *Southern California Law Review* 50:871–959.
LEVIN, BETSY 1977 Current Trends in School Finance Reform Litigation: A Commentary. *Duke Law Journal* 1977:1099–1137.
VAN ALSTYNE, WILLIAM W. 1970 The Constitutional Rights of Teachers and Professors. *Duke Law Journal* 1970:841–879.
YUDOF, MARK G.; KIRP, DAVID L.; VAN GEEL, TYLL; and LEVIN, BETSY 1982 *Educational Policy and the Law.* Berkeley, Calif.: McCutchan.

EDUCATION OF HANDICAPPED CHILDREN ACTS

84 Stat. 175, 88 Stat. 579, 89 Stat. 773, 91 Stat. 230

Title VI of the Elementary and Secondary Education Amendments of 1970, the Education for All Handicapped Children Act of 1975 (EAHCA), and the Education of the Handicapped Amendments of 1974 and 1977 provide funds and a variety of federal programs to assist states in educating and training handicapped individuals. In states receiving federal educational assistance for handicapped children, the acts require a state policy assuring all handicapped children the right to a free appropriate public education, assuring private school education at no cost to parents if children are placed in private schools as the means of fulfilling state responsibilities under the acts, offering an individual educational plan for every handicapped child, and providing education with nonhandicapped children to the "maximum extent appropriate." The acts require substantial procedural safeguards to assure receipt of a free appropriate public education. EAHCA provides a private right of action, after exhaustion of administrative remedies, to compel compliance.

Board of Education v. Rowley (1982), the Supreme Court's first interpretation of EAHCA, held that the statutorily mandated "free appropriate public education" need not provide each child an opportunity to achieve her full potential. The statute mandates only an "adequate" education, one reasonably calculated to enable the child to achieve passing marks and advance from grade to grade.

THEODORE EISENBERG

Bibliography

BURGDORF, ROBERT L., JR. 1980 *The Legal Rights of Handicapped Persons*. Pages 213–245. Baltimore: Paul H. Brookes.

EDWARDS v. ARIZONA
451 U.S. 477 (1981)
OREGON v. BRADSHAW
462 U.S. 1039 (1983)

In *Edwards*, involving application of the MIRANDA RULES, the Court held that when an accused has invoked his right to have counsel present during interrogation, he has not waived that right simply by responding to further POLICE INTERROGATION unless he himself initiated additional communication. In *Bradshaw* the defendant, who had been advised of his rights and had asked for an attorney, later initiated a conversation with an officer who reminded him that he had no obligation to speak to the police. The prisoner said he understood, continued talking, and confessed. A plurality of the Court decided that the conviction in *Bradshaw* involved no breach of the rule of *Edwards*, which was meant to prevent badgering by the police.

LEONARD W. LEVY

EDWARDS v. CALIFORNIA
314 U.S. 160 (1941)

The years of the Great Depression were especially harsh for residents of the Dust Bowl. Many migrated to the West, and particularly California, in conditions of poverty graphically detailed in John Steinbeck's novel, *The Grapes of Wrath* (1939). California's hospitality to this "huge influx of migrants" was reflected in its "Okie law," making it a MISDEMEANOR knowingly to assist an indigent person in entering the state. Edwards, a Californian, went to Texas and drove his indigent brother-in-law back to California. For his troubles, he was given a six-month suspended jail sentence for violating the Okie law.

The Supreme Court unanimously reversed the conviction. Justice JAMES F. BYRNES, for the Court, concluded that the law violated the COMMERCE CLAUSE. The state's concerns with health and the integrity of its welfare funds were insufficient to justify so severe

a burden on INTERSTATE COMMERCE. Justice WILLIAM O. DOUGLAS, concurring, would have rested decision on the PRIVILEGES AND IMMUNITIES clause of the FOURTEENTH AMENDMENT. Interstate travel was a privilege of national CITIZENSHIP, and to deny that privilege to indigents would create an inferior class of citizens. Justices HUGO L. BLACK and FRANK MURPHY joined this opinion.

Justice ROBERT H. JACKSON, concurring, agreed with Justice Douglas but also remarked that indigence was "a neutral fact—constitutionally an irrelevance, like race, creed, or color."

KENNETH L. KARST

(SEE ALSO: *Wealth Discrimination; Equal Protection of the Laws.*)

EFFECTS ON COMMERCE

"At the beginning Chief Justice [JOHN] MARSHALL described the federal commerce power with a breadth never yet exceeded." So said Justice ROBERT H. JACKSON for a unanimous Supreme Court in WICKARD V. FILBURN (1946), in the course of an opinion recognizing the broad sweep of Congress's modern power to regulate the national economy under the COMMERCE CLAUSE. Marshall's opinion in GIBBONS V. OGDEN (1824) read that clause's reference to commerce "among the several States" to mean "that commerce which concerns more States than one."

For the Constitution's first century, however, Congress did little to regulate INTERSTATE COMMERCE. The first major national regulatory laws were the INTERSTATE COMMERCE ACT of 1887, regulating railroads, and the SHERMAN ANTITRUST ACT of 1890. It fell to another Supreme Court to define the scope of congressional power, and at first the Court's definition was narrow. In UNITED STATES V. E. C. KNIGHT Co. (1895) the Court interpreted the Sherman Act, which prohibited monopolizing "any part of the trade or commerce among the several States," to exclude from its coverage a monopoly of sugar refining. Manufacturing was not commerce, said the Court; that "commerce might be indirectly affected" by a manufacturing combination producing ninety-eight percent of the nation's refined sugar was insufficient to bring the combination under the act's terms.

"Direct" effects on commerce, however, were found in a series of Sherman Act cases culminating in SWIFT & CO. V. UNITED STATES (1905). (See also STAFFORD V. WALLACE, 1922). Yet the Court persisted in its assertion that manufacturing was not commerce, even to the extent of holding in HAMMER V. DAGENHART (1918) that a congressional regulation of the interstate transportation of goods made by child labor was invalid because its purpose was to regulate manufacturing.

Meanwhile, the Court was developing quite another view of congressional power to regulate railroads. In HOUSTON, EAST AND WEST TEXAS RAILWAY CO. V. UNITED STATES, the "Shreveport case" (1914), the Court upheld an Interstate Commerce Commission order requiring a railroad to equalize certain interstate and intrastate rates. Such railroads were "common instrumentalities" of interstate and local commerce; the ICC was regulating only the relation between local and interstate rates. Taken seriously, the SHREVEPORT DOCTRINE implies congressional power to regulate intrastate activity because of its effect on interstate commerce.

After two decades of resisting the implications of the Shreveport case, the Court returned to its logic in NATIONAL LABOR RELATIONS BOARD V. JONES & LAUGHLIN STEEL CORPORATION (1937), the most important judicial victory for FRANKLIN ROOSEVELT's New Deal. There the Court upheld the WAGNER ACT's regulation of collective bargaining in application to a large steel manufacturer that obtained its raw materials in interstate commerce, manufactured steel in Pennsylvania, and shipped finished products to many other states. The opinion was written by Chief Justice CHARLES EVANS HUGHES, who had written the Shreveport case's opinion. A strike by manufacturing employees, said Hughes, would "directly" obstruct interstate commerce. "It is the effect upon commerce, not the source of the injury, which is the criterion."

In every succeeding case, the Supreme Court has applied this "effects on commerce" rationale to sustain congressional power. WICKARD V. FILBURN was the culminating case of ECONOMIC REGULATION, upholding congressional control of a small farmer's on-the-farm consumption of wheat, on the theory that Congress had a RATIONAL BASIS for believing that the aggregate of all such farmers' consumption would have "a substantial economic effect" on commerce. More recently the Court has employed similar reasoning to sustain congressional regulations aimed at distinctly noneconomic purposes. (See PEREZ V. UNITED STATES, 1971, extortion through "loan sharking"; HEART OF ATLANTA MOTEL V. UNITED STATES, 1964, racial segregation). Today, the "effects on commerce" rationale effectively allows Congress to be the judge of its own commerce clause powers.

KENNETH L. KARST

Bibliography
STERN, ROBERT L.   1946   The Commerce Clause and the National Economy, 1933–1946. *Harvard Law Review* 59:645–693, 883–947.

EIGHTEENTH AMENDMENT

The Eighteenth Amendment was framed and adopted to give a peacetime constitutional basis to the national PROHIBITION of alcoholic beverages, originally imposed as a war measure. Congress proposed the amendment in December 1917, and ratification was completed thirteen months later. Congress adopted the National Prohibition Act (VOLSTEAD ACT) to provide a mechanism for enforcement and penalties for violation of the prohibition.

The prohibition amendment provided the occasion for several controversies about the character and extent of the amending power. In Ohio, for example, the voters, by REFERENDUM, attempted to rescind their legislature's ratification of the amendment; but the Supreme Court held that procedure unconstitutional in *Hawke v. Smith* (1920). The Court, in the *National Prohibition Cases* (1920), rejected a number of arguments that the amendment was itself unconstitutional because of purported inherent limitations on the AMENDING POWER, including the contention that ordinary legislation cannot be made part of the Constitution and the assertion that the Constitution cannot be amended so as to diminish the residual SOVEREIGNTY of the states. In the same case the Court held that the requirement of a two-thirds vote in each house to propose amendments was met by the vote of two-thirds of the members present and voting and that amendments automatically become part of the Constitution when ratified by three-fourths of the states, whether or not promulgated by Congress or the secretary of state. In UNITED STATES V. SPRAGUE (1931) the Court rejected the argument that the amendment should have been ratified by state conventions rather than by state legislatures, holding that the mode of RATIFICATION OF CONSTITUTIONAL AMENDMENTS was a matter of congressional discretion.

Prohibition, a product of the reforming impulse that characterized PROGRESSIVE CONSTITUTIONAL THOUGHT, proved very difficult to enforce; and the widespread disregard of federal law scarcely tended toward that moral improvement that the authors intended. In 1933, the Eighteenth Amendment became the only constitutional amendment ever to be wholly rescinded when it was repealed by passage of the TWENTY-FIRST AMENDMENT.

DENNIS J. MAHONEY

EIGHTH AMENDMENT

See: Bail; Capital Punishment; Cruel and Unusual Punishment

EISENHOWER, DWIGHT D.
(1890–1969)

The nation has often rewarded its military heroes by electing them to the presidency. General of the Army Dwight David Eisenhower, who had commanded the Allied forces in Europe during World War II, was President from 1953 to 1961. A 1915 graduate of West Point, Eisenhower held no public office—except his military command—before being elected President.

Eisenhower was a "moderate" Republican: conservative on economic matters but often liberal on social issues. Although he privately expressed to Chief Justice EARL WARREN his disapproval of BROWN V. BOARD OF EDUCATION (1954), he proposed, and successfully pressed for passage of, the CIVIL RIGHTS ACTS OF 1957 and 1960, the first such acts since Reconstruction. They expanded VOTING RIGHTS and created the CIVIL RIGHTS COMMISSION. In 1957, when the governor of Arkansas resisted a federal court's SCHOOL DESEGREGATION order (see COOPER V. AARON), the Eisenhower administration obtained an INJUNCTION forbidding the use of the National Guard to prevent INTEGRATION. When anti-integration rioting broke out in Little Rock, and the local authorities proved unable or unwilling to suppress it, Eisenhower ordered regular federal troops to the city.

Perhaps because of his military background Eisenhower was more cautious than some Presidents in exercising his power as COMMANDER-IN-CHIEF. He brought the KOREAN WAR to an end and, thereafter, no American troops were actively engaged in combat during his administration. When Chinese communists bombarded the Nationalist-held islands of Quemoy and Matsu, Eisenhower sought, and obtained, a JOINT RESOLUTION of Congress authorizing American military action, if necessary. In 1958, again authorized by congressional resolution, he ordered Marines to Lebanon to maintain order, but they did no actual fighting.

In foreign affairs, Eisenhower's was an activist administration. During the Eisenhower presidency the mutual defense treaty with Nationalist China and the Southeast Asia (SEATO) Treaty were signed, each committing the United States to the defense of distant—and not necessarily democratic—countries. Under the SEATO pact Eisenhower in 1954 began the American policy of assistance to South Vietnam that continued through the Vietnam War (1965–1973). Eisenhower supported the United Nations campaign of "anticolonialism," opposing America's European allies in Suez and Africa.

Domestically, Eisenhower was criticized for not speaking out forcefully against Senator Joseph R. McCarthy of Wisconsin, whose inquiries into communist influence in government threatened CIVIL LIBERTIES and often involved GUILT BY ASSOCIATION. Eisenhower promulgated EXECUTIVE ORDER 10450, which revamped the existing LOYALTY-SECURITY PROGRAM for federal employees.

During his two terms in the White House Eisenhower suffered three serious illnesses and was, for a time, virtually incapacitated. During those periods, Vice-President RICHARD M. NIXON presided over the cabinet and the National Security Council while routine matters were handled by a powerful White House staff. Eisenhower's illnesses raised questions about PRESIDENTIAL SUCCESSION in case of disability that were not resolved until passage of the TWENTY-FIFTH AMENDMENT.

Eisenhower made four APPOINTMENTS OF SUPREME COURT JUSTICES: Chief Justice EARL WARREN (1953) and Associate Justices JOHN MARSHALL HARLAN (1955), WILLIAM J. BRENNAN (1956), and CHARLES E. WHITTAKER (1957). Ironically, the moderate conservative Eisenhower made his most lasting mark on American constitutional history by appointing Justices who turned the Court toward liberal activism.

DENNIS J. MAHONEY

Bibliography
GREENSTEIN, FRED I. 1982 *The Hidden Hand Presidency: Eisenhower as Leader.* New York: Basic Books.

EISENSTADT v. BAIRD
405 U.S. 438 (1972)

At a BIRTH CONTROL lecture, Baird gave contraceptive foam to a woman presumed to be unmarried. Convicted in a Massachusetts court for distributing a contraceptive device, Baird sought federal HABEAS CORPUS. On appeal the Supreme Court, 6–1, held the conviction unconstitutional. Four Justices, concluding that GRISWOLD V. CONNECTICUT (1965) would bar prosecution for distribution of contraceptives to married persons, held that the EQUAL PROTECTION clause forbade the state to outlaw their distribution to the unmarried. Two Justices relied on *Griswold* alone, saying the record had not shown the recipient to be unmarried. Chief Justice WARREN BURGER dissented.

KENNETH L. KARST

(SEE ALSO: *Right of Privacy; Freedom of Intimate Association.*)

EISNER v. MACOMBER
252 U.S. 189 (1920)

A 5–4 Supreme Court declared that stock dividends did not constitute income subject to taxation under the SIXTEENTH AMENDMENT. Justice MAHLON PITNEY agreed that dividends were a "mere readjustment of the evidence of a capital interest already owned." Justices OLIVER WENDELL HOLMES, WILLIAM R. DAY, and JOHN H. CLARKE joined the DISSENTING OPINION of Louis D. BRANDEIS, who argued that the dividends represented profit (and thus income) and that the power conferred by the amendment ought to be measured by "the substance of the transaction, not its form." The Court subsequently narrowed the DOCTRINE of *Eisner* through a series of exquisite distinctions.

DAVID GORDON

ELASTIC CLAUSE

See: Necessary and Proper Clause

ELECTIONS, REGULATION OF

Defining "democracy," Henry B. Mayo has argued that the "one institutional embodiment . . . universally regarded as indispensable in modern democracies is that of choosing the policy-makers [representatives] at elections held at more or less regular intervals." In addition to their central democratic function of providing a mechanism for popular choice of officials, parties, and policies, elections have also been credited with two other important democratic functions: offering a forum for public participation and education in politics; and legitimizing the state's coercive authority and peacefully resolving social conflicts, because the public will generally accept officials

and policies selected through fair, participative processes.

The Constitution, by its terms, mandates elections only for members of the House of Representatives and of the Senate. Article I, section 2, provides that members of the House shall be elected by the people of the respective states, and the SEVENTEENTH AMENDMENT provides similarly for senators. Persons meeting the qualifications necessary to vote for members of the larger house of the legislature in each state are constitutionally eligible to vote for representatives and senators. The Supreme Court, in WESBERRY V. SANDERS (1964), held also that "as nearly as practicable one man's vote in a congressional election is to be worth as much as another's." Subsequently, the Court has reaffirmed, in *Kirkpatrick v. Preisler* (1969), that in drawing congressional district boundaries states must "make a good-faith effort to achieve precise mathematical equality."

Characterizing its previous decisions, the Supreme Court, in *Rivera-Rodriguez v. Popular Democratic Party* (1982), said that it has "rejected claims that the Constitution compels a fixed method of choosing state or local officers or representatives." The guarantee clause of Article IV, section 4, has been construed to raise only POLITICAL QUESTIONS within the exclusive jurisdiction of Congress and does not, therefore, make state methods for selecting officials subject to constitutional adjudication in the federal courts. Nonetheless, every state employs popular elections to select presidential electors and its governor and legislature. Other state executive, administrative, and judicial officials, and all manner of local officials are also elected. In all, about 540,000 federal, state, and local offices are filled by election. In addition, the prevailing method of selecting political party nominees and of choosing final contenders in nonpartisan elections is the primary election.

Thirty-seven states provide for popular review of policymaking by the use of referenda, and twenty-one states allow popular instigation of policy through initiative elections. Referendum elections are also widely used in local governments throughout the nation, especially to review tax levies and charter revisions; and initiative elections are available in some local jurisdictions.

Although the Constitution prescribes elections only for Congress, virtually all elections have gradually been constitutionalized and therefore in some degree nationalized. The FIFTEENTH AMENDMENT prohibits the states from impairing the franchise on the basis of race, color, or previous condition of servitude. The NINETEENTH AMENDMENT forbids discrimination in electoral qualification based on sex; and the TWENTY-FOURTH AMENDMENT prevents the states from imposing "any poll tax or other tax" as a condition of voting for a candidate for federal office. The TWENTY-SIXTH AMENDMENT effectively grants the right to vote to all eligible citizens at eighteen years of age.

In the modern era, the right to vote has been declared a "fundamental right" under the FOURTEENTH AMENDMENT, in REYNOLDS V. SIMS (1964), because it is "preservative of other basic civil and political rights." The Supreme Court has therefore declared, in KRAMER V. UNION FREE SCHOOL DISTRICT (1969) and HARPER V. VIRGINIA BOARD OF ELECTIONS (1966), that every classification defining the right to vote in elections must be subject to strict judicial scrutiny and can be sustained only by independent judicial examination which finds "important," "compelling," or "overriding" state interests justifying restrictions on voting rights.

Mayo has argued that elections effectively promote democracy only if two conditions obtain. First, there must be "political equality in which [each] person should have one vote . . . and each vote should count equally." Second, citizens must have the "freedom to oppose," consisting of "formal rules . . . of effective choice—secret ballot, freedom to run for office, and freedom to speak, assemble, and organize for political purposes." It is these conditions for effective elections that the Supreme Court has generally promoted by declaring the vote a fundamental right and by rejecting poll taxes, residence requirements of extended duration, race and sex qualifications, limits on campaign spending, wide deviations from the ONE PERSON, ONE VOTE principle, and impediments to candidacy that significantly narrow voters' choices.

DAVID ADAMANY

(SEE ALSO: *Brown v. Socialist Workers '74 Campaign Committee,* 1982.)

Bibliography

MAYO, HENRY B. 1960 *An Introduction to Democratic Theory.* New York: Oxford University Press.
NOTE 1975 Developments in the Law—Elections. *Harvard Law Review* 88:1111–1339.

ELECTORAL COLLEGE

The Electoral College was hurriedly improvised by the Framers to placate all factions, provide a mechanism for electing GEORGE WASHINGTON, and leave hard questions for the states to resolve after Washington's retirement. Yet it turned out, unexpectedly, to be the forming and sustaining mold of the American party system.

At conception, the College was partly democratic and responsive to the large states, partly aristocratic and answerable to small states. It was apportioned mostly by population, with a delegate for each congressman and senator, and a state could select its delegates in any way it pleased. The Framers seem to have expected that, after Washington, the delegates—acting deliberatively or as agents of state legislatures—would normally fail to muster a majority for one candidate, and that most elections would be settled in the House of Representatives, with one vote per state.

This happened only in 1824, when the House chose JOHN QUINCY ADAMS over ANDREW JACKSON, the frontrunner in popular and electoral votes. In 1800 the House also elected THOMAS JEFFERSON, who tied with his running mate AARON BURR in the Electoral College. This deadlock led to the adoption of the TWELFTH AMENDMENT, which separated the votes for President and vice-president and gave the College its essential modern written constitutional constraints.

In the same decades, the College acquired two powerful unwritten constraints: party control and unit vote. Party control originated in congressional nominating caucuses in 1796 and shifted to state and national nominating conventions during the 1830s. It ended the notion of unbound, deliberative delegates seeking "continental" leadership. POLITICAL PARTIES, not delegates, did the deliberation.

The unit vote, chosen by all but one state by 1836, delivered each state's delegation as a unit to the winner of its popular vote. Unit voting already prevailed in the House and in most state elections, but the Electoral College gave it its widest leverage. It is kind to winners, hard on second parties, and almost prohibitive of third parties. It forces competition for shiftable votes, and it rewards inclusive, center-seeking, accommodational parties (and groups) while discouraging narrow, ideological, exclusive ones. Many scholars believe that the American two-party system has its roots in the unit vote and its taproot in the Electoral College.

The College has prompted two complaints, both largely, but not wholly, theoretical. It might elect as President an "unrepresentative" candidate who had won a minority of the popular vote or had been chosen deliberatively by "unfaithful" delegates, or who was chosen by a House manipulated by splinter groups. Or it might favor some voters against others: urban against rural, liberal against conservative, North against South, or large state against small. Yet we have had only two clear minority Presidents (RUTHERFORD B. HAYES and BENJAMIN HARRISON), one House-chosen President (John Quincy Adams), no Presidents chosen by the rare, unfaithful delegate, and no constitutional crisis over any of these contretemps.

The College was once thought to favor "pivotal" large-state over small-state voters, and hence urban, liberal over rural, conservative interests, but political change and closer analysis have qualified this impression. Liberals who defended the College in the 1950s fought unsuccessfully to abolish it, in favor of direct election, in the 1960s and 1970s.

Any of the major reform proposals—direct election, proportional representation by state, and election by congressional district—arguably would change outcomes of close elections. JOHN F. KENNEDY would have lost the 1960 election, with the same votes cast, under the proportional or district systems. But surely the same vote would not have been cast, for any alternative system would have changed voting and campaign strategies. The district system might have given more weight to rural voters, the direct or proportional systems to third parties. Changes in the party system in either case could have been profound.

These complexities may explain why Congress, which considers proposing an amendment to abolish the Electoral College after most close elections, has never actually done so. The Supreme Court has been likewise acquiescent, upholding state delegate allocations against all challenges and refusing, in *Delaware v. New York* (1966), to hear Delaware's complaint that New York voters had 2.3 times better odds of affecting the outcome of a presidential election.

WARD E. Y. ELLIOTT

Bibliography

CEASER, JAMES W. 1979 *Presidential Selection: Theory and Development.* Princeton, N.J.: Princeton University Press.

ELLIOTT, WARD E. Y. 1975 *The Rise of Guardian Democracy: The Supreme Court's Role in Voting Rights Disputes, 1845–1969.* Cambridge, Mass.: Harvard University Press.

PIERCE, NEAL R. 1968 *The People's President: The Electoral College in American History and the Direct-Vote Alternative.* New York: Simon & Schuster.

ELECTRONIC EAVESDROPPING

A Constitution written in the eighteenth century does not easily accommodate events and developments two centuries later. This has been especially true of the FOURTH AMENDMENT guarantee against unreasonable SEARCHES AND SEIZURES. Originally designed to deal with British soldiers breaking into buildings to search for smuggled goods under overly broad GENERAL WARRANTS, in this century it has had to deal with electronic eavesdropping. In 1928 Justice LOUIS D. BRANDEIS, dissenting in OLMSTEAD V. UNITED STATES, observed that "WRITS OF ASSISTANCE and GENERAL WARRANTS are but puny instruments of tyranny and oppression when compared with wiretapping." Today, there are surveillance devices far more penetrating and efficient than wiretapping, such as tiny microphones that catch the softest utterance hundreds of feet away; pen registers that record telephone numbers; "beepers" that trace movements over miles and for days; and electronic intensifiers that permit photography in almost complete darkness. Continuing advances in miniaturization and surveillance technology will produce even more intrusive and undetectable devices.

At first, the Supreme Court refused to apply any of the BILL OF RIGHTS to these technologies. The FIRST AMENDMENT ramifications were emphasized by Justice Brandeis in his *Olmstead* dissent when he pointed out the link between freedom of expression and invasions of personal security, a link established as early as the WILKES CASES (1763–1770), the first great English cases establishing the right of personal security against governmental intrusion. The *Olmstead* majority did not even mention the First Amendment, however, and that silence continues—the First Amendment has played an insignificant role in constitutional analyses of electronic surveillance, although in UNITED STATES V. UNITED STATES DISTRICT COURT (1972) the Supreme Court did address First Amendment considerations relevant to domestic NATIONAL SECURITY intelligence surveillance. In *Olmstead* the Fifth Amendment was explicitly ruled inapplicable, and electronic surveillance was held not to be a form of compelled self-incrimination. That ruling has been reaffirmed in cases such as HOFFA V. UNITED STATES (1966).

It is the Fourth Amendment that has become the primary constitutional instrument for control of electronic surveillance, and even that development was delayed some forty years. In 1928, the Supreme Court ruled in *Olmstead*, over dissents by Justices Brandeis and OLIVER WENDELL HOLMES, that the Fourth Amendment was limited to physical intrusions on property (TRESPASSES) that "seized" material objects, not intangible conversations. *Olmstead* was gradually eroded in the 1950s and 1960s, particularly with respect to conversations. The trespass aspect of *Olm-*

stead remained applicable, however, until 1967, when KATZ V. UNITED STATES extended Fourth Amendment protection to conversations and other things that people reasonably expect to keep private.

During the forty years between *Olmstead* and *Katz*, electronic surveillance was not left completely uncontrolled, however. Although the trespass requirement produced the ruling in GOLDMAN V. UNITED STATES (1942) that a room microphone placed against the outside of a wall did not violate the Fourth Amendment, telephone wiretapping itself was held to be prohibited by section 605 of the COMMUNICATIONS ACT of 1934, and this prohibition was applied to both federal and state law enforcement officers in NARDONE V. UNITED STATES (1937) and *Benanti v. United States* (1955). New York State also established statutory procedures for regulating electronic surveillance.

Empirical studies of wiretapping prior to 1968 showed that the controls established by these laws were ineffective. The Justice Department construed section 605 so narrowly that it was rarely invoked; judicial supervision of state wiretapping was virtually nonexistent. In addition, two forms of wiretapping and bugging remained completely uncontrolled: national security wiretapping, done pursuant to presidential directives; and surveillance with the consent of one of the parties to the conversation.

As to national security surveillances, the Federal Bureau of Investigation installed over 7,000 wiretaps and room microphones during 1940–1960, and one treasury agent additionally admitted to having installed over 10,000 wiretaps and microphones between 1934 and 1948; other federal agencies also did electronic eavesdropping. Although all of these intrusions were purportedly for national security purposes, many were revealed to be for crime control or political purposes, the most notorious of which was the massive electronic surveillance of MARTIN LUTHER KING, JR., between 1963 and 1968 ordered by FBI Director J. EDGAR HOOVER.

Consent surveillance, either on a telephone extension or with informers equipped with secret radio transmitters or recorders, is probably the most widely practiced type of electronic surveillance, although so much of electronic surveillance remains secret that one cannot be certain. The Supreme Court had consistently held, before and after the *Katz* decision, that under both the Constitution and the Communications Act, consent surveillance is free from virtually all constitutional or statutory controls. Leading cases on this point include ON LEE V. UNITED STATES (1952) and UNITED STATES V. WHITE (1971). The only federal restriction prior to 1968 was a very limited rule of the Federal Communications Commission barring secret recordings.

Ever since the 1937 *Nardone* decision, the Justice Department had sought authority for electronic surveillance. This effort gained impetus from Attorney General ROBERT F. KENNEDY's campaign against organized crime in 1961–1963 and the revelation that FBI Director Hoover had illegally installed hundreds of taps and bugs on alleged organized crime figures under the "national security" authority, many of which stayed in place for many years; the disclosure of these surveillances placed scores of convictions in jeopardy. With the Court's decisions in BERGER V. NEW YORK (1967) and *Katz*, the stage was set for congressional action. In these two decisions the Court discarded the "trespass" requirement imposed by *Olmstead*, ruled that electronic surveillance was subject to Fourth Amendment requirements, and set out relatively detailed requirements for a valid statute, including: (1) a specification and detailed description of the place to be searched, the conversations to be overheard, and the crime under investigation; (2) a limit on the period of intrusion; and (3) adequate NOTICE of the eavesdropping to the people overheard.

Six months after *Katz*, Congress passed the OMNIBUS CRIME CONTROL AND SAFE STREETS ACT (1968), Title III of which legitimated electronic surveillance for law enforcement purposes. The statute provides that electronic surveillance of conversations is prohibited, upon pain of a substantial jail sentence and fine, except for: (1) law enforcement surveillance under a court order; (2) certain telephone company monitoring to ensure adequate service or to protect company property; (3) surveillance of a conversation where one participant consents to the surveillance; and (4) national security surveillance insofar as it is within the President's inherent constitutional powers, whatever those may be. Law enforcement surveillance must meet certain procedural requirements, which include: (1) an application by a high ranking prosecutor; (2) surveillance for one of the crimes specified in Title III; (3) PROBABLE CAUSE to believe that a crime has occurred, that the target of the surveillance is involved, and that EVIDENCE of that crime will be obtained by the surveillance; (4) a statement indicating that other investigative procedures are ineffective; and (5) an effort to minimize the interception.

A judge must pass on the application and may issue the order and any extensions if the application meets the statutory requirements. Shortly after the surveillance ends, notice must be given of the surveillance to some or all of the persons affected, as the judge decides, unless he agrees to postpone the notice. Illegally obtained evidence may not be used in any official proceedings, and a suit for damages may be brought for illegal surveillance, though a very strong good faith defense is allowed. In addition, the manufacture, distribution, possession, and advertising of devices for electronic surveillance for private use are prohibited.

The legislation is written in terms of federal officials but it also authorizes state surveillance if a state passes a law modeled on the federal statute, though the state may (as have some states, like Connecticut) impose more stringent requirements. More than half the states plus the DISTRICT OF COLUMBIA have passed such statutes, though many rarely use the authority. State surveillance is concentrated in New York, New Jersey, and Florida, mostly for narcotics and gambling offenses.

Title III raised many constitutional issues but almost all have been resolved in its favor. For example, a common contention is that electronic eavesdropping is inherently uncontrollable and necessarily intrudes on vast numbers of innocent people who use phones or rooms under surveillance, thus violating the particularization requirements of the Fourth Amendment. In order to meet this objection, and to avoid turning the surveillance authorization into a general warrant, Title III requires that interceptions be minimized. The Supreme Court, however, made this requirement very easy to meet by its decision in *Scott v. United States* (1978). The lower courts do not impose sanctions for the failure to minimize interception, partly because minimization is often very difficult to achieve or supervise. One federal judge in a major drug case excused the interception of seventy-three calls between a suspect's babysitter and her friends and classmates with the comment that although these conversations were indeed "teenage trivia . . . the eavesdropper, unless possessed of the prescience of a clairvoyant, could hardly predict when they might become relevant, or when they might be interrupted by an adult with more pressing problems." There are also many cases where police do not minimize interceptions even though they could. For example, some police listen to every conversation, including privileged conversations between lawyers and their clients, but record only those they think appropriate. In one case, it was accidentally revealed that police had recorded all conversations but had prepared a minimized set for use in court. Where room microphones are used, minimizing the interceptions is virtually impossible, especially if the microphones are placed in areas to which the public has access.

The *Berger* case also seemed to require that the interception be limited to specific and quite short time periods. Title III, however, permits thirty-day authorizations on a twenty-four-hour per day basis, with an unlimited number of extensions, and many interceptions remain in continuous operation for many months. The Report on Applications for Orders Authorizing or Approving the Interception of Wire or Oral Communications for 1981, issued by the Administrative Office of the United States Court, indicates that almost half the 106 federal interceptions reported for 1981 lasted thirty or more days.

One of the most significant ways of enforcing Fourth Amendment requirements is by imposing sanctions for their violation. Imposing these sanctions, of course, requires an awareness by the victim that a search has taken place, and of how it was conducted. With a conventional search, such conditions are easy to meet, but electronic surveillance is surreptitious and may never be discovered. The Supreme Court has therefore insisted that notice of the interception be given to the persons named in the application as targets of the surveillance. The statute, however, permits indefinite postponement of this notice, and this provision, too, has been upheld.

Critics have charged that judicial supervision has been minimal and ineffective, particularly on the state level. At hearings before the National Commission for the Review of Federal and State Laws Relating to Electronic Surveillance, many witnesses lamented the inability or unwillingness of state judges to supervise the process closely.

Passage of the statute, while effectively ending the constitutional debate, has not ended the dispute over the value of electronic eavesdropping. Critics have charged that the device is used almost exclusively for minor crimes involving gambling and drugs; is quite useless for major crimes and especially those involving organized crime, the avowed target of the statute; is very expensive; is largely unsupervised by the judiciary; and has invaded the privacy of millions. For support, they rely on the staff studies of the National Commission. Proponents reply that the technique has produced some very useful results, that many of the problems are those attending any new technique, and that more sophisticated use will produce better results. The opposing views were set out in detail in the Report of the National Commission; over a vigorous minority dissent the majority of the commission supported the use of electronic surveillance under the statute, with some modification.

Two types of surveillance remain uncontrolled by Title III: consent intrusions and national security surveillance. Title III totally exempts interceptions by government officials if an official is a party to the conversation of if there is consent by one of the parties; a private interception that is consented to is also exempt, unless the interception is for the purpose of committing a tortious, criminal, or "other injurious act," the meaning of which is not clear. Several states, however, have imposed more stringent requirements on consent surveillance than the federal statute, such as a warrant, either by statute (California, Georgia) or under their own state constitutions (Alaska, Montana). The Supreme Court, however, continues to rule in cases like *United States v. White* (1971) that consent surveillance does not implicate the Fourth Amendment.

National security surveillance continues to pose difficult constitutional questions. Presidents since FRANKLIN D. ROOSEVELT have claimed inherent executive power to use electronic surveillance to obtain intelligence for national security purposes, and have authorized such intrusions on their own, without prior judicial approval. Most courts have upheld such a power, where national security surveillance involving foreign powers and agents is concerned. But where American citizens or groups are targeted for domestic security purposes, the Supreme Court, in *United States v. United States District Court*, ruled unanimously that the President has no INHERENT POWER to use warrantless electronic surveillance. The Court did suggest that Congress could authorize procedures for domestic intelligence gathering that are less stringent than those of Title III for law enforcement, but so far Congress has not done so.

Intelligence gathering for foreign security purposes is now governed by statute. The 1976 Report of the Senate Select Committee to Study Governmental Operations with Respect to the Intelligence Agencies disclosed massive abuses of executive power to tap telephones and bug rooms for national security purposes, often with the approval of the incumbent President. These abuses included taps on the telephones of National Security Agency advisers authorized by President RICHARD M. NIXON in 1969; on the Los Angeles Chamber of Commerce in 1941; on congressmen in the early 1960s in connection with the "sugar lobby"; and FBI taps and bugs on Martin Luther King, Jr., to find "communist" influence. From 1940 to 1975, the FBI alone installed some 10,000 taps and bugs; the National Security Agency, the Central Intelligence Agency, local police, and many other governmental agencies have also engaged in national security surveillance.

These disclosures resulted in the passage in 1978 of the Foreign Intelligence Surveillance Act, which requires approval from a court for national security surveillances of foreign powers or agents. The President is denied extrastatutory inherent or other power to use electronic surveillance for foreign intelligence within the United States—though not outside—and no Americans may be eavesdropped upon unless their activities have some element of criminality about them. The court operates secretly, and there have been very few published rulings and very little public information about it. The constitutionality of this act and its procedures—which are much less demanding than those under Title III for law enforcement purposes—has been sustained.

The courts have also tried to grapple with other forms of electronic surveillance. In *Smith v. Maryland* (1979) pen registers, which record the telephone numbers called, were held outside Title III and not in conflict with the Fourth Amendment; the Supreme Court concluded that the user has no reasonable expectation of privacy in the numbers called. Electronic signaling devices ("beepers") attached to cars to enable their movements to be traced have also been held to be without Fourth Amendment protection because cars are generally traced while on public streets and highways (*United States v. Knotts, 1983*); if the device is attached to a container or other item that is taken into a private area, however, a warrant and probable cause are required (*United States v. Karo, 1984*).

In 1928, after describing the dangers that the emerging modern technology presented to individual liberty, Justice Brandeis asked, "Can it be that the Constitution affords no protection against such invasions of individual security?" Almost a half century later, it is clear that such protection is available—if the nation wants it.

HERMAN SCHWARTZ

Bibliography

ADMINISTRATIVE OFFICE OF THE UNITED STATES COURTS 1968–1982 *Reports on Applications for Orders Authorizing or Approving the Interception of Wire or Oral Communications.* Washington, D.C.: Administrative Office.

AMERICAN BAR ASSOCIATION PROJECT ON STANDARDS FOR CRIMINAL JUSTICE 1974 *Standards Relating to the Administration of Criminal Justice; Electronic Surveillance.* Pages 33–52. New York: Institute of Judicial Administration.

CARR, JAMES G. 1977 (with 1983 supp.) *The Law of Electronic Surveillance.* New York: Clark Boardman.

NATIONAL COMMISSION FOR THE REVIEW OF FEDERAL AND STATE LAW RELATING TO ELECTRONIC SURVEILLANCE 1976 *Report* and *Staff Studies.* Washington, D.C.: Government Printing Office.

SCHWARTZ, HERMAN 1977 *Taps, Bugs, and Fooling the People.* New York: Field Foundation.

———— 1968 The Legitimation of Electronic Eavesdropping: The Politics of "Law and Order." *Michigan Law Review* 67:455–510.

UNITED STATES CONGRESS, SENATE SELECT COMMITTEE TO STUDY GOVERNMENTAL OPERATIONS WITH RESPECT TO INTELLIGENCE ACTIVITIES 1976 *III Final Report.* 94th Congress, 2d session.

ELEMENTARY AND SECONDARY EDUCATION ACT
79 Stat. 27 (1965)

This first general school aid bill in American history broke an impasse that had long stymied legislation to provide federal moneys to elementary and secondary schools. Previous efforts toward such action had foundered on the question whether education was a state, not federal, function; whether segregated school systems should receive federal aid; and whether aid to private as well as public schools would violate the FIRST AMENDMENT's establishment clause. The segregation issue had been settled by the CIVIL RIGHTS ACT OF 1964. The 1964 elections had filled Congress with federal aid advocates untroubled by STATES' RIGHTS issues. The church–state controversy over federal assistance to parochial schools continued but was generally resolved here for the first time.

As passed, the measure, which appealed to the CHILD BENEFIT THEORY, authorized specialized aid to districts with children from low-income families. Private schools would share in aid to some specialized services such as shared-time projects and educational television. The act gave school districts wide discretion in using the federal funds; it required, however, that the funds be used to meet the special needs of educationally deprived children and that private schools be included in any benefit sharing. The act also authorized for five years grants to states for purchase of textbooks and library material, and for funding supplementary community educational services that schools could not provide. It expanded the 1954 Cooperative Research Act, authorizing a five-year program of grants for new research and training in teacher methods, and it provided for grants to strengthen state departments of education.

Despite overwhelming congressional support for the act, critics continued to express constitutional doubts. The use of public funds for books in parochial schools and special educational centers could not be justified, it was argued, because funds would be chan-neled directly to religious schools. The AMERICAN CIVIL LIBERTIES UNION contended that providing instructional materials and supplementary services to church schools was an unconstitutional subversion of the principle of SEPARATION OF CHURCH AND STATE. In FLAST V. COHEN (1968) the measure was challenged on First Amendment grounds, but the Court did not rule on the constitutional issues in the case.

PAUL L. MURPHY

ELEVENTH AMENDMENT

The Eleventh Amendment of the Constitution provides that "the JUDICIAL POWER OF THE UNITED STATES shall not be construed to extend to any suit in law or EQUITY, commenced or prosecuted against one of the United States by citizens of another State, or by citizens or subjects of a foreign State." Congress submitted this amendment, on votes of twenty-three to two in the Senate and eighty-one to nine in the House of Representatives, for ratification in March 1794. By February 1795, the legislatures of three-fourths of the states had ratified, but, because of delays in certification of this action, adoption of the amendment was not proclaimed until 1798.

According to traditional theory the purpose of the amendment was to correct an erroneous interpretation of the Constitution by the Supreme Court. Impetus for the amendment undoubtedly was the unpopular decision in CHISHOLM V. GEORGIA (1793)—one of seven early suits instituted against a state by citizens of other states or by ALIENS. In *Chisholm* the Court, voting 4–1, held that the judicial power of the United States and the JURISDICTION of the Court reached such suits under the provision in Article III extending the federal judicial power to "Controversies between a State and Citizens of another State . . . and between a State . . . and foreign States, Citizens or Subjects."

Although the language of Article III is broad enough to support the *Chisholm* holding, proponents of the theory that the amendment was adopted to correct an error in constitutional interpretation have argued that (1) the doctrine of SOVEREIGN IMMUNITY, exempting the sovereign from unconsented suits, was part of the COMMON LAW heritage at the time the Constitution was adopted, and hence implicitly qualified some delegations of judicial power in Article III; and (2) an understanding to that effect emerged during the ratification debates.

Existence of an implicit common law qualification upon the various delegations of federal judicial power is doubtful, however. While the supposition that the immunity doctrine was already incorporated into American law appears sound, at least some state immunity surely was surrendered under the Constitution. The purpose behind the various delegations of judicial power to the United States was to create a judiciary competent to decide all cases "involving the National peace and harmony." Surrender—rather than retention—of state immunity is consonant with that objective. Nor is the argument that the ratification debates evidenced an understanding that the states would be immune from suit persuasive. While ALEXANDER HAMILTON, JAMES MADISON, and JOHN MARSHALL offered assurances to that effect in reply to Anti-Federalist objections, these objections were not quieted; and other leading Federalists, including EDMUND RANDOLPH and JAMES WILSON—members of the Committee of Detail where most provisions of Article III were drafted—took the contrary view.

While some proponents of the Eleventh Amendment probably understood it to be corrective, the broad support enlisted for its adoption can be better explained in terms of diverse perceptions and objectives. These ranged from the desire of STATES' RIGHTS advocates to repudiate the extravagant nationalism manifested by Federalist justices in their *Chisholm* opinions, to Federalist perceptions that the amendment effected only a relatively insignificant restriction upon part of the DIVERSITY JURISDICTION of the federal judiciary. Experience was accumulating that suit against a state in the Supreme Court was cumbersome and unnecessary for the maintenance of federal supremacy. Moreover, assumption of a major portion of state indebtedness and rapid liquidation of the remainder had allayed a Federalist concern that partially accounted for the original grant of federal judicial power.

Judicial construction of the amendment has been shaped by the view that as a corrective measure, it restored common law sovereign immunity as an implicit qualification upon some grants of judicial power in Article III. As interpreted, the amendment bars any suit against a state, including those raising federal questions, instituted by private plaintiffs, regardless of CITIZENSHIP (*Hans v. Louisiana*, 1890), as well as by foreign states (*Monaco v. Mississippi*, 1934) in federal court. In general, only where another state or the United States is plaintiff, is a state subject to unconsented suit in federal court (*Virginia v. West Virginia*, 1907; (*United States v. Mississippi*, 1965). The amendment does not affect Article III rights of a state to institute suits in federal courts, nor does it preclude appeals by private plaintiffs in actions commenced by a state. (See COHENS V. VIRGINIA, 1821.)

Although the amendment literally limits the federal judicial power—which, by general rule, may not be modified by consent of the parties—as shorthand for the doctrine of sovereign immunity, it has always been interpreted to permit exercises of Article III powers upon a state's waiver of immunity from suit in federal court. Such waivers ordinarily must be explicit (EDELMAN V. JORDAN, 1974); however, implied and imputed waivers, although exceptional, are not unknown (*Parden v. Terminal Railway*, 1964).

The amendment imposes an absolute bar against unconsented suits commenced in federal court by private plaintiffs against state governments and their agencies. To this generalization, there is a single but increasingly important exception. Congress, pursuant to its enforcement powers under the FOURTEENTH AMENDMENT, may create federal causes of action against the states and thereby deprive them of immunity (FITZPATRICK V. BITZER, 1976). Whether such authority can be inferred from other powers delegated to the national government has not been settled.

The exemption from suit enjoyed by the states under the amendment does not extend to their political subdivisions nor, in general, to governmental corporations (*Lincoln County v. Luning*, 1890). Of paramount importance in restricting the impact of the amendment is the availability of relief in suits instituted against state officers for acts performed or threatened under color of unconstitutional state legislation. The issues whether and to what extent the amendment bars suits against state officers for official acts have occasioned more litigation under the amendment than any others, and the course traversed by the Court from OSBORN V. BANK OF THE UNITED STATES (1824) through *In re Ayers* (1887) to EX PARTE YOUNG (1908) was tortuous. In some early cases the amendment was held applicable only to suits in which a state was a defendant of record, but this rule was never firmly established. Later cases turned on whether a suit against a state officer was substantially a suit against the state itself. In *Ayers* the Court held that a suit against a state officer is a suit against the state unless the officer's act, if stripped of its official character, constitutes a private wrong; but this rigorous test was abandoned in *Ex parte Young*, a landmark case which, despite its unpopularity at the time, fixed the law for the future. While adhering to the general rule that a suit against a state officer is barred by the amendment if it is substantially against the state itself, the Court adopted the fiction that mere institution of state judicial proceedings by a state officer pursuant to an allegedly unconstitutional statute is a wrong for which federal equitable relief is available. The theoretical difficulties posed by this formulation are grave and many, but in facilitating direct access to the federal courts to test the validity of state legislation, *Young* is of transcendent importance in maintaining federal supremacy and the RULE OF LAW. Adopted as the instrument of judicial protection of the rights of property and enterprise, the *Young* principle today does the same essential service in the protection of personal rights and liberties. Even so, not every act of a state may be reached through suit against its officers. Where such suits are adjudged to be against the state itself—actions affecting the public treasury for past wrongs and those seeking to dispossess the state of property—the Eleventh Amendment remains a bar (*Edelman v. Jordan*, 1974).

CLYDE E. JACOBS

(SEE ALSO: *Atascadero State Hospital v. Scanlon, 1985; Pennhurst State School v. Halderman, 1981, 1984.*)

Bibliography

JACOBS, CLYDE E.   1972   *The Eleventh Amendment and Sovereign Immunity.* Westport, Conn.: Greenwood Press.

NOWAK, JOHN E.   1975   The Scope of Congressional Power to Create Causes of Action Against State Governments and the History of the Eleventh and Fourteenth Amendments. *Columbia Law Review* 75:1413–1469.

ELFBRANDT v. RUSSELL
384 U.S. 11 (1966)

By a 5–4 vote, the WARREN COURT struck down a section of Arizona's Communist Control Act of 1961, which subjected state employees to perjury prosecutions if they subscribed to a state LOYALTY OATH while members of the Communist party, later joined the party, or joined "any other organization" having for "one of its purposes" the overthrow of the government. For the majority, Justice WILLIAM O. DOUGLAS argued that even knowing membership in the Communist party could not expose one to criminal punishment without proof of specific intent to further the organization's illegal goals of violent revolution. Such a law "infringes unnecessarily on protected freedoms. It rests on the doctrine of 'GUILT BY ASSOCIATION' which has no place here. . . ."

The dissenters were led by Justice BYRON R. WHITE. "If a government may remove from office . . . and . . . criminally punish . . . its employees who engage in certain political activities," White wrote, "it is unsound to hold that it may not, on pain of

criminal penalties, prevent its employees from affiliating with the Communist Party or other organizations prepared to employ violent means to overthrow constitutional government."

MICHAEL E. PARRISH

ELKINS v. UNITED STATES
364 U.S. 206 (1960)

In Elkins the Supreme Court overthrew the SILVER PLATTER DOCTRINE, an exception to the EXCLUSIONARY RULE allowing use in federal prosecutions of evidence seized by state officers in illegal searches. Two changes had undermined the authority of the doctrine since it was formulated in WEEKS V. UNITED STATES (1914). First, the extension of the constitutional prohibition of unreasonable searches to the states in WOLF V. COLORADO (1949) meant that the doctrine now permitted federal courts to admit evidence unconstitutionally seized. Second, the doctrine vitiated the policies of about half the states, which had in the meantime independently adopted an exclusionary rule.

The *Elkins* opinion, in addition, contains the most thorough and convincing analysis in favor of the exclusionary rule to be found in any opinion of the Court; it thus laid the groundwork for imposition of the rule on the states the following year in MAPP V. OHIO (1961).

JACOB W. LANDYNSKI

ELKINS ACT
32 Stat. 847 (1903)

The decisions in INTERSTATE COMMERCE COMMISSION V. CINCINNATI, NEW ORLEANS & TEXAS PACIFIC RAILWAY (1897) and its companion case, *ICC v. Alabama Midland Railway Company*, had stripped the Interstate Commerce Commission of much of its regulatory power. As a result, many of the evils the INTERSTATE COMMERCE ACT had been designed to remedy had revived. One of the most pernicious abuses was the practice of rebating. Federal legislation forbidding the practice would not only save the railroads money but also protect them against demands imposed by the trusts. Sponsored by the railroads, the Elkins Act made any deviation from the published rate schedule (whether a rebate or a general rate reduction) a criminal offense. Although Congress repealed the imprisonment penalty, it quadrupled the fine and directly subjected the corporations to the penalty; no longer could the principal escape punishment for its agents' acts. Anyone who sought or received a rebate (or other rate concession) was equally liable to criminal penalties. Despite the act's significance, further legislation would prove necessary. Charges were now enforced, but the ICC was still powerless to replace discriminatory rates. Congress would expand ICC powers and extend regulatory control over the rails in the HEPBURN and MANN-ELKINS ACTS.

DAVID GORDON

Bibliography

SHARFMAN, ISAIAH L. 1931–1937 *The Interstate Commerce Commission.* Vol. 1. New York: Commonwealth Fund.

ELLSWORTH, OLIVER
(1745–1807)

Oliver Ellsworth played a key role in the creation of the United States Constitution in 1787 and the establishment of a national judiciary during the Constitution's first decade.

Born into a well-established Connecticut family, he entered Yale in 1762, but left after two years to attend the College of New Jersey (Princeton) where he was graduated with a B.A. in 1766. Ellsworth returned to Connecticut and studied theology for about a year, but abandoned it for the law and was admitted to the bar in 1771. One of the ablest lawyers of his day, he built up an extremely lucrative practice. He also entered politics and was elected to the state's General Assembly in 1773. A warm supporter of the patriot cause against Great Britain, he helped supervise the state's military expenditures during the war for independence, was appointed state attorney for Hartford in 1777, a member of the Governor's Council in 1780, and a judge of the Connecticut Supreme Court in 1785. He also served as one of the state's representatives to the Continental Congress for six terms (1777–1783). While in Congress he became a member of the Committee of Appeals which heard appeals from state admiralty courts, and in this capacity he ruled on the important case of Gideon Olmstead and the British sloop *Active* which eventually culminated in UNITED STATES V. PETERS (1809).

In 1787 Connecticut selected him to be one of its three delegates to the federal CONSTITUTIONAL CONVENTION in Philadelphia. He played an active role at the convention and won respect for his orderly mind and his effectiveness as a debater. Ellsworth favored the movement to establish a strong and active federal government with the power to act directly on individuals and to levy taxes, as a substitute for the weak central government created by the ARTICLES OF CONFEDERATION. But he also thought that the VIRGINIA PLAN went too far in a nationalist direction. "The only chance of supporting a general government lies in grafting it on those of the original states," he argued. In particular, he opposed the idea of apportioning representation in both houses of Congress according to population, to the clear advantage of larger states. To resolve the differences between the large and the small states he helped forge the successful GREAT COMPROMISE which apportioned representation in the lower house according to population and in the Senate by a rule of equality, with each state having two senators. Ellsworth also played an active role on the Committee on Detail which produced the basic draft of the United States Constitution.

Following adoption of the Constitution, Connecticut elected Ellsworth to the United States Senate. He recognized that the Constitution as written and ratified was only a basic outline; an actual government had to be created and its powers implemented. He supported ALEXANDER HAMILTON's financial program and was opposed to attempts to ally the United States too closely with France, but his most important contribution was the drafting of the JUDICIARY ACT OF 1789. This law was in many ways an extension of the Constitution itself, for it fleshed out the terse third article of that document which dealt with the nature and powers of the federal judiciary. The Judiciary Act of 1789 specified that the Supreme Court should consist of six Justices, that each state should have a district court, and that there should be three circuit courts consisting of two Supreme Court Justices sitting with a district judge. Under this law the federal courts were given exclusive JURISDICTION in a number of important areas and CONCURRENT JURISDICTION with the state courts in other matters. The act also provided that decisions of the state courts involving the Constitution or laws or treaties of the United States could be appealed to the Supreme Court.

In 1796 President GEORGE WASHINGTON appointed Ellsworth Chief Justice of the United States. He held the post for three years but had little impact. The cases he heard were not very significant, illness limited his participation in the duties of the Court, and a diplomatic mission took him out of the country. Perhaps his most important decision came in *Wiscart v. Dauchy* (1796) in which he examined the relationship of the Supreme Court to the district and circuit courts, established a series of important rules dealing with WRITS OF ERROR, and extended COMMON LAW procedures in APPEALS to EQUITY and ADMIRALTY jurisdiction as well. His opinions tended to be brief, to the point, and nationalist in orientation. In *United States v. La Vengeance* (1796) he expanded the admiralty jurisdiction of the federal courts to inland navigable rivers, the Great Lakes, and other water routes away from the high seas; and while riding circuit in *United States v. Isaac Williams* (1799) he upheld the English common law DOCTRINE that citizens of a country did not have a right to expatriate themselves without their native country's consent.

As Chief Justice, Ellsworth encouraged the practice of the Supreme Court's handing down PER CURIAM opinions, with a single decision representing the will of the entire court, as opposed to having separate SERIATIM opinions by the individual Justices. JOHN MARSHALL, who succeeded Ellsworth as Chief Justice, considered the continuation and further development of this practice all-important in maintaining respect for the authority of the Court when it handed down controversial decisions.

In 1799 Ellsworth, over the protest of some of his closest associates, agreed to a request from President JOHN ADAMS to be part of a special diplomatic mission to resolve the undeclared naval war with France. The mission was a success, but Ellsworth became ill while abroad, resigned the chief justiceship in October 1800, and stayed in England to recuperate. By the time he returned to America the Jeffersonians had triumphed and he retired from public life.

RICHARD E. ELLIS

Bibliography

BROWN, WILLIAM GARROTT 1905 *The Life of Oliver Ellsworth.* New York: Macmillan.

GOEBEL, JULIUS, JR. 1971 *History of the Supreme Court of the United States, Vol. 1: Antecedents and Beginnings to 1801.* New York: Macmillan.

ELLSWORTH COURT

See: Supreme Court, 1789–1801

EMANCIPATION PROCLAMATION
12 Stat. 68 (1863)

ABRAHAM LINCOLN, employing the Constitution's WAR POWERS, announced the Emancipation Proclamation on September 22, 1862. It had its roots in ABOLITIONIST CONSTITUTIONAL THEORY. Although Lincoln's swift rise in the Republican party was due

in part to his outspoken opposition to the extension of slavery, on the outset of the war he was bound by the Constitution (Article IV, section 2) and federal laws on fugitive slaves that required federal officials to return runaways, even to disloyal owners. Politically ambitious Union general George B. McClellan, a conservative would-be Democratic presidential candidate, sternly enforced the 1850 law; generals BENJAMIN F. BUTLER and John Charles Frémont, by contrast, refused to return runaways in their commands and armed some against rebel guerrillas. Lincoln countermanded the latter's orders to dim the issue of arming Negroes and to keep policy in civilians' hands.

Negroes continued to flee to Union lines no matter what orders civilians or generals issued. Awareness grew in the Union army and among bluecoats' families and other correspondents that almost the only trustworthy southerners were blacks. Gradually, sentiment increased that to return runaways was indecent and illogical, for slaves were the South's labor force. In Congress, with few exceptions, Democrats remained uneducable on the runaway issue and damned as unconstitutional any mass emancipation whether by EXECUTIVE ORDER or statute and whether or not involving colonization of freedmen abroad or compensation to loyal owners. Republicans, from Lincoln down, altered their opinions on race matters. Some northern states softened racist BLACK CODE clauses in constitutions and civil and criminal laws; some made laws color-blind. Congress, in addition to the CONFISCATION ACTS and with Lincoln's assent, enacted laws in March, April, and June 1862, respectively, that prohibited military returns of disloyal owners' runaways without requiring a judicial verdict of disloyalty, ended slavery in the DISTRICT OF COLUMBIA with compensation to owners, and forbade slavery in the federal TERRITORIES, thus challenging part of DRED SCOTT V. SANDFORD (1857). In effect, Republicans, retaining their basic view of the Constitution as an adaptable instrument, were adopting aspirations that abolitionist constitutionalists had long advanced.

Fearing conservative gains in the 1862 congressional and state elections, congressional Republicans then marked time. Lincoln did not have this option. He determined to reverse two centuries of race history *if* continued Confederate intransigence forced further changes and *if* the Union won the war.

Therefore, following the Antietam "victory," Lincoln proclaimed that unless slaveowners in still-unoccupied states of the Confederacy (he excluded unseceded slaveholding states) publicly renounced the rebellion by January 1, 1863, their slaves "shall be then, thenceforward, and forever free." All Union military personnel must positively assist, not merely not impede, runaways from slavery. With respect to unseceded slaveholding states, Lincoln encouraged "immediate or gradual" emancipation by state initiative, with compensation to loyal owners and colonization of freedmen abroad.

The Proclamation was not an immediate success. It diminished opinion abroad favoring recognition of the Confederacy. Few southern whites abjured the rebellion before the deadline. Lincoln, on New Year's Day 1863, announced the Proclamation to be in effect. But he had enlarged his horizons, adding an announcement that he would recruit blacks for the Union's armies. Relatively few blacks lived in northern states. Lincoln's new policy, if successful—which meant if Union voters persevered, if enough slaves kept coming into Union lines, and if Union forces occupied enough Confederate areas—could drain the South of its basic labor force and augment the Union's military power.

The policy eventually succeeded. Almost 200,000 black bluecoats, overwhelmingly southern in origin, helped to crush the rebellion. *Dred Scott* was made irrelevant. Though black Union soldiers and sailors suffered inequities in rank, pay, and dignity compared to whites, their military record made it impossible for the nation to consider them again as submen in law, though racists advocated the retrograde view. Compared to their prewar status even in the free states, blacks' legal and constitutional conditions improved as a result of the Proclamation. It initiated also an irreversible revolution in race relationships leading to the WADE-DAVIS BILL, the THIRTEENTH AMENDMENT, and the CIVIL RIGHTS ACT OF 1866. But the eventual consequence of the Emancipation Proclamation was Appomattox; thereby, alternatives forbidden by *Dred Scott*, by the 1861 Crittenden Compromise, and by the aborted Thirteenth Amendment of 1861, became options. This society could be slaveless, biracial, and more decently equal in the constitutions, laws, and customs of the nation and the states.

HAROLD M. HYMAN

Bibliography

BELZ, HERMAN 1978 *Emancipation and Equal Rights: Politics and Constitutionalism in the Civil War Era.* New York: Norton.
HYMAN, HAROLD M. and WIECEK, WILLIAM M. 1982 *Equal Justice under Law: Constitutional Development 1835–1875.* Pages 252–255. New York: Harper & Row.
OATES, STEPHEN B. 1977 *With Malice Toward None: The Life of Abraham Lincoln.* New York: Harper & Row.

VOEGELI, V. JACQUES 1967 *Free But Not Equal: The Midwest and the Negro During the Civil War.* Chicago: University of Chicago Press.

EMBARGO ACTS
(1807–1809)

For fifteen months the United States under President THOMAS JEFFERSON pursued a policy of economic coercion against foreign powers as an alternative to war. In retaliation for attacks on American commerce during the Napoleonic wars, a compliant Congress gave Jefferson everything he requested, including five embargo acts which sought to compel England and France to respect American maritime rights in return for a restoration of American trade. The first three acts, which interdicted that trade, could be constitutionally defended by a doctrine of IMPLIED POWERS that Jefferson once thought inimical to American liberty. In *United States v. The William* (1808) a federal district court invoked a BROAD CONSTRUCTION of the COMMERCE CLAUSE, reinforced by the NECESSARY AND PROPER CLAUSE, to justify a ruling that the power to regulate commerce included the power to prohibit it. Justice WILLIAM JOHNSON of the Supreme Court, a Jefferson appointee, rebuked the President in a circuit case, *Gilchrist v. Collector* (1808), for having exceeded his statutory authority in enforcing the embargo acts, and another Jefferson appointee, Justice BROCKHOLST LIVINGSTON, in *United States v. Hoxie* (1808), scathed the President for insinuating the doctrine of constructive treason into a prosecution for violation of the acts. The draconian fourth embargo act carried the administration to the precipice of unlimited enforcement powers and mocked Republican principles by its concentration of authority in the President, its employment of the navy for enforcement, and its disregard of the FOURTH AMENDMENT's protection against UNREASONABLE SEARCHES and seizures. Unconstitutional military enforcement characterized the fifth embargo act, which rivaled any legislation in American history for its suppressiveness. The embargo acts, having failed their purpose, lapsed when Jefferson left office.

LEONARD W. LEVY

EMERGENCY BANK ACT
48 Stat. 1 (1933)

When FRANKLIN D. ROOSEVELT took office on March 4, 1933, banks had closed in thirty-eight states. The next day Roosevelt declared a national bank holiday, suspended all gold transactions, and called a special session of Congress for March 9. On that day Congress rushed through, and that same evening Roosevelt signed, a bill submitted by the White House aimed at ending the panic that had begun earlier that year. The bill ratified Roosevelt's actions, which he had based on the questionable authority of the 1917 Trading With the Enemy Act. The act gained constitutional significance by thus expanding executive authority. Congress also gave the President discretionary authority over national and Federal Reserve banks. The act provided for calling in all gold and gold certificates in circulation and assessed criminal penalties for hoarding. The government could appoint conservators for the assets of insolvent banks, and the Treasury could license the reopening of sound ones and reorganize the remainder. The act further authorized the emergency issuance of paper notes up to a limit of one hundred percent of the value of government bonds in its member banks.

DAVID GORDON

EMERGENCY COURT OF APPEALS

In the Emergency Price Control Act of 1942, Congress established a comprehensive system of administrative control over prices, as a means of checking the inflation that accompanied this country's entry into World War II. The Act created a temporary Emergency Court of Appeals, staffed by federal judges from the district courts and courts of appeals, with exclusive JURISDICTION to determine the validity of price control regulations. Regulated persons thus could not challenge the administrative regulations' constitutionality or statutory authorization in the ordinary state or federal courts—either in injunctive proceedings or by way of defense to criminal prosecutions for their violation. The only course open was to obey the regulations and challenge their validity in the newly created court.

In a series of decisions, the most important of which was YAKUS V. UNITED STATES (1944), the Supreme Court upheld the validity of this scheme (LOCKERTY V. PHILLIPS, 1943; BOWLES V. WILLINGHAM, 1944; see also JUDICIAL SYSTEM).

A Temporary Emergency Court of Appeals, established in 1971, is similarly staffed by judges from other federal courts. It hears appeals from the district courts in cases arising under various congressional statutes regulating allocation and pricing of certain commodities.

KENNETH L. KARST

Bibliography

BATOR, PAUL M., MISHKIN, PAUL J., SHAPIRO, DAVID L., and WECHSLER, HERBERT, eds. 1973 *Hart and Wechsler's The Federal Courts and the Federal System*, 2nd ed. Pages 317–322. Mineola, N.Y.: Foundation Press.

EMERGENCY POWERS

As justifications for taking emergency action without first receiving legislative authority, chief executives from different countries have relied on "reason of state" (*raison d'état*) and "prerogative." JOHN LOCKE, in the *Second Treatise on Civil Government* (1690), defined prerogative as the power to act "according to discretion for the common good, without the prescription of the law and sometimes even against it. . . ." More concise is the maxim *salus populi suprema lex:* the safety of the people is the supreme law.

The United States Constitution contains few provisions for emergency power. Congress has the power to meet emergencies by passing LEGISLATION. Under Article I, Section 8, Congress may declare war and call forth the militia to suppress insurrections and to repel invasions. Article II authorizes the President to convene Congress "on extraordinary Occasions" for the purpose of enacting emergency legislation.

An exception to this statutory process is implied in the debates at the CONSTITUTIONAL CONVENTION. The Framers recognized that the President might have to begin military operations for defensive purposes before Congress could act. When one of the delegates proposed that Congress be empowered to "make war," it was objected that legislative proceedings might at times be too slow for the safety of the country. "Declare" was substituted for "make," giving Congress the power to declare war but allowing the President discretionary authority "to repel sudden attacks."

For twentieth-century America, the concept of "defensive war" has expanded to include military actions far beyond the nation's borders. The long drawn-out war in Southeast Asia led to the WAR POWERS RESOLUTION of 1973, an effort to reconcile the war-making power of the President with the war-declaring power of Congress. The statute attempts to insure the "collective judgment" of both branches by requiring the President to consult with Congress "in every possible instance," to report to Congress within forty-eight hours after introducing forces into hostilities, and to withdraw those forces unless he receives congressional support within sixty or ninety days. Congress may at any time during this period pass a CON-

CURRENT RESOLUTION (which is not subject to veto) directing the President to remove forces engaged in hostilities. The consultation and reporting provisions have had mixed results. The LEGISLATIVE VETO mechanism in the War Powers Resolution was declared invalid in IMMIGRATION AND NATURALIZATION SERVICE V. CHADHA (1983).

Article I, section 9, permits the suspension of the writ of HABEAS CORPUS "in Cases of Rebellion or Invasion [when] the public Safety may require it." It has never been determined conclusively whether this power resides solely in Congress or is shared with the President. History supports the latter interpretation. In April 1861, while Congress was in recess, President ABRAHAM LINCOLN issued proclamations ordering a number of emergency actions, including the suspension of the writ of habeas corpus. Congress supported his initiatives, as did a sharply divided Supreme Court in the PRIZE CASES (1863).

Although Chief Justice ROGER B. TANEY had earlier placed the power of suspension exclusively with Congress, in *Ex parte Merryman* (1861), Lincoln ignored the court order and continued to exercise emergency powers. His attorney general, EDWARD BATES, argued that the President shared with Congress the power to suspend the writ of habeas corpus. In such cases as EX PARTE MILLIGAN (1866) and DUNCAN V. KAHANAMOKU (1946), the Supreme Court has held illegal the establishment of military tribunals to try civilians in areas where the civil courts are open. In these decisions, however, the Court took care to assert judicial control at the close of, rather than during, hostilities.

The President's emergency power has also grown because of authority delegated to him by Congress. These authorities would sometimes come to life whenever the President issued a proclamation declaring the nation to be in a state of emergency. A report issued by a Senate special committee in 1973 disclosed that four proclamations (issued by FRANKLIN D. ROOSEVELT in 1933, HARRY S. TRUMAN in 1950, and RICHARD M. NIXON in 1970 and 1971) brought to life 470 provisions of federal law. Each statute conferred upon the President some facet of control over the lives and property of American citizens.

The NATIONAL EMERGENCIES ACT of 1976 restricted the use of presidential emergency powers. The statute terminated emergency authorities two years from the date of the bill's enactment (September 14, 1976). For future national emergencies the President must publish a declaration in the *Federal Register*. Congress could terminate the national emergency by passing a concurrent resolution. After the *Chadha* decision, Congress substituted a joint resolution for the concurrent resolution. To prevent "emergencies" from lingering for decades without congressional attention or action, the 1976 statute contained an action-forcing mechanism. No later than six months after the President declares a national emergency, and at least every six months thereafter while the emergency continues, each House of Congress must meet to consider a vote to terminate the emergency.

The 1976 statute exempted certain provisions of law, including section 5(b) of the Trading With the Enemy Act, first enacted in 1917. This section had become a source of presidential authority in peacetime as well as wartime. President Roosevelt, for example, used section 5(b) in 1933 to declare a national emergency. Legislation in 1977 attempted to strengthen congressional control, allowing Congress to terminate an emergency by passing a concurrent resolution (a joint resolution would now be required). It was under the 1977 legislation that President Jimmy Carter seized Iranian assets in 1979, an action upheld by the Supreme Court two years later in DAMES & MOORE V. REGAN (1981).

LOUIS FISHER

Bibliography

ROSSITER, CLINTON 1963 *Constitutional Dictatorship: Crisis Government in the Modern Democracies.* New York: Harcourt, Brace & World.

U.S. CONGRESS 1976 *The National Emergencies Act (Public Law 94–412). Source Book: Legislative History, Texts, and Other Documents.* Senate Committee on Government Operations and Senate Special Committee on National Emergencies and Delegated Emergency Powers. 94th Congress, 2d session.

EMERGENCY PRICE CONTROL ACT
56 Stat. 23 (1942)

The most important independent administrative agency set up during World War II was the Office of Price Administration (OPA). The agency began studying plans for rationing and price fixing in April 1941 without benefit of statutory authority. The Emergency Price Control Act of 1942 gave the OPA official status, with broad powers for price regulation and a price administrator to make the act effective. The administrator was given broad discretion to supervise and fix prices and rent ceilings, combat profiteering and speculation, expedite defense purchases without excessive waste, and place limits on wages and other income from PRODUCTION. From 1942 to

1945, the OPA approached complete regulation of prices and rents. To prevent sellers and landlords from seeking INJUNCTIONS in state or federal courts against enforcement of particular price orders, the statute directed all determinations of the legality of price orders, including their constitutionality, to an EMERGENCY COURT OF APPEALS, established in Washington, D.C.

Unlike most wartime agencies, the OPA was challenged in the courts. The Supreme Court was supportive, upholding in YAKUS V. UNITED STATES (1944) those portions of the EPCA delegating to the OPA power to fix prices; in *Bowles v. Willingham* (1944) the Court upheld an OPA rent-fixing directive. *Yakus* also upheld the channeling of issues of legality to the Emergency Court of Appeals, which had the effect of requiring other courts to enforce price orders irrespective of the question of their lawfulness. In *Steuart and Bros. v. Bowles* (1944), the system of "indirect sanctions," whereby the OPA imposed its controls on the economy without formal resort to the judicial process, was sustained; the Court refused to interfere with the principal coercive device whereby various executive agencies gave practical force to their directives.

PAUL L. MURPHY

Bibliography

United States Office of Temporary Controls   1947   *The Beginnings of OPA*. Washington, D.C.: Office of Temporary Controls.

EMINENT DOMAIN

In his argument as counsel in WEST RIVER BRIDGE COMPANY V. DIX (1848), the first case in which the Supreme Court ruled directly on the constitutionality of the states' power of eminent domain, DANIEL WEBSTER thundered against the whole concept of state discretion in "takings." Only in the past few years, he contended, had this power of eminent domain been recognized in American law. Claims for its legitimacy, moreover, were "adopted from writers on other and arbitrary [civil law] governments," he declared; and eminent domain could easily become an instrument for establishment by the states of "unlimited despotisms over the private citizens." Webster tried, in effect, to get the court to impose Fifth Amendment standards on the states.

Webster was engaged in a failing cause. Besides, his history was inaccurate and his predictions of disaster were simplistic. He was certainly right, however, in seeing the eminent domain power as a formidable threat to VESTED RIGHTS, corporate or individual. He understood that eminent domain condemnations might become a proxy for regulation under the POLICE POWER, undermining the CONTRACT CLAUSE as a bulwark of property rights. He was right in raising the alarm when he did; when *West River Bridge* was argued there had been a vast increase in activity by government and private CORPORATIONS in exercise of eminent domain. The transportation revolution in America was in an expansionary phase; extensive new railroad construction reinforced the effects on property law already felt from canal, turnpike, and bridge enterprises. All these ventures required use of the "taking" power in order to accomplish their purposes.

Contrary to Webster's version of legal history, government's power to expropriate privately owned property for a variety of public purposes had long been an element of Anglo-American law. The power of eminent domain was the power to compel transfers to government or government's assignees. In its constitutional version, even in the 1840s, it was understood as a power that could be exercised legitimately only for a PUBLIC USE or PUBLIC PURPOSE, and that required the payment of JUST COMPENSATION. In English decisions and statutes going back several centuries, in American colonial law, and in the state law of the early republic, this power of taking by governmental authority had been exercised for such purposes as road-building, fortifications, drainage (including the great Fens projects of England in the seventeenth century), navigational improvement on rivers, and construction of bridges and canals. In colonial Massachusetts, statute had extended a variant of the power into the manufacturing sector by authorizing builders of mills to dam up streams, flooding neighboring lands; these "milldam laws" provided for assessment of damages and payment of compensation in cash.

The Fifth Amendment—which the Supreme Court would rule in BARRON V. BALTIMORE (1833) was not applicable to the states—expressed the views and used language already embodied in several of the state constitutions adopted during the Revolutionary era. Thus the amendment's requirement that property could be taken "for public use" and on payment of "just compensation" had been foreshadowed by such documents as the 1780 Massachusetts Declaration of Rights, which declared that "whenever the public exigencies require that the property of any individual should be appropriated to public uses, he shall receive reasonable compensation therefor."

Although several early state constitutions lacked such language, uniformly the state courts, in reviewing takings cases, ruled that general principles of justice, the writings of the natural-law jurists, or the constitutional values reflected in the Fifth Amendment justified imposition by judges of both a "public use" and a "just compensation" limitation upon their legislatures' uses of the eminent domain power. It was a singular feature of legal development in the states, however, that despite the widespread formal adoption of such limitations, in fact only slight constraints were placed on the legislatures. In practice, compensation paid to persons suffering from takings was far below market value (and, because of offsetting benefits commonly calculated against damages, often they were paid nothing in cash); hence, eminent domain became an instrument for the subsidization, through cost reduction, of both governmental enterprises and favored private undertakings. "Public convenience" became, in most states, a legitimate reading of the "public use" requirement; and in practice, the legislatures enjoyed wide discretion in deciding what types of enterprise might be vested with the power to expropriate private property. Ironically, the very bridge and railroad corporations that Webster represented so often were among the greatest beneficiaries of eminent domain devolution in that era.

The Court in *West River Bridge* wholly rejected Webster's contentions, ruling that state eminent domain powers were "paramount to all private rights vested under the government." It left the state courts to decide for themselves whether compensation payments were just in particular cases, or whether DUE PROCESS requirements of state constitutions had been met.

So stood constitutional doctrine until the adoption of the FOURTEENTH AMENDMENT. Under its due process clause, the door was opened to challenges in federal courts of state eminent domain actions. Increasingly, too, in the late nineteenth century, the Supreme Court was called upon to rule upon the constitutionality of regulatory measures that activist state legislatures were enacting. The issue tended to take the form of defining a "taking," with the constitutional requirement it connoted, as opposed to bona fide use of the police power, which did not require compensation. The Court ruled in a succession of cases that the Fourteenth Amendment embodied the requirements of "public use" and "just compensation." It took a broad view, however, of what types of enterprise the states might aid with devolutions of the eminent domain power; in a series of cases on irrigation districts, drainage companies, individual enterprises and corporation activities in other areas such as logging and mining, and the more traditional areas of state

activity, the Court upheld legislative discretion under a permissive "public use" standard.

In MUGLER V. KANSAS (1887), the Court attempted to distinguish between a taking, which required compensation, and uses of the police power, which it defined as laws abating nuisances or limiting uses of property that were harmful to "health, morals, or safety of the community," not compensable. But drawing the police power/eminent domain line proved difficult; indeed, it perplexes the Court to the present day. In *Pennsylvania Coal Company v. Mahon* (1922), Justice OLIVER WENDELL HOLMES argued that the police power and eminent domain power are on a single continuum; differences are a matter of degree, not qualitative. The Court has continued to struggle with the issue, and in modern land-use ZONING cases from EUCLID V. AMBLER REALTY (1926) to *Agins v. Tiburon* (1980) it has sought a firmer ground to replace the distinction Holmes found so appropriate.

The Court has upheld congressional discretion in deciding what purposes of federal eminent domain met the Fifth Amendment's "public use" requirement. In *United States v. Gettysburg Electric Railway Company* (1896), the Court declared acceptable any use "which is legitimate and lies within the scope of the Constitution." In *United States ex rel. Tennessee Valley Authority v. Welch* (1946) the Court carried the doctrine to an extreme, concluding that a congressional decision to authorize expropriation of property "is entitled to deference until it is shown to involve an impossibility." A few years later, *Berman v. Parker* (1954) upheld federal eminent domain takings to conduct an urban redevelopment project in the District of Columbia. Here the end was the public welfare, a "broad and inclusive" concept, the Court declared, that certainly embraced slum clearance and an urban development designed to be "beautiful as well as sanitary." Given the validity of this purpose, it was legitimate to invoke eminent domain, which was only a means. Congress must decide as to the need for the project and its design.

In its quest to develop standards to distinguish takings from legitimate exercise of the police power, the Court has probed to the heart of property concepts. What rights are "vested," how "reasonable expectations" should be defined, what obligations inhere in the ownership of private property—all are questions that come to the surface repeatedly in continuing litigation. Nearly 150 years ago, Chief Justice LEMUEL SHAW of Massachusetts admonished, in *Boston Water Power Company v. Railroad* (1839), that the eminent domain power "must be large and liberal, so as to meet the public exigencies, and it must be so limited and constrained, as to secure effectually the rights of the citizen; and it must depend, in some instances, upon the nature of the exigencies as they arise, and the circumstances of individual cases." Shaw's view may have lacked prescriptive potential, but it has proved remarkably accurate in predicting the direction that the law would take—and the perplexities that would beset the best efforts of lawmakers and judges to produce definitive formulae.

HARRY N. SCHEIBER

(SEE ALSO: *Hawaii Housing Authority v. Midkiff*, 1984.)

Bibliography

DUNHAM, ALLISON 1962 *Griggs v. Allegheny County* in Perspective: Thirty Years of Supreme Court Expropriation Law. *Supreme Court Review* 1962:63–106.
GRANT, J. A. C. 1931 The "Higher Law" Background of the Law of Eminent Domain. *Wisconsin Law Review* 6:67–85.
HURST, JAMES WILLARD 1964 *Law and Economic Growth: The Legal History of the Lumber Industry in Wisconsin, 1836–1915.* Cambridge, Mass.: Harvard University Press.
SCHEIBER, HARRY N. 1971 The Road to *Munn:* Eminent Domain and the Concept of Public Purpose in the State Courts. *Perspectives in American History* 5:327–402.
STOEBUCK, WILLIAM B. 1972 A General Theory of Eminent Domain. *Washington Law Review* 47:553–608.
———— 1980 Police Power, Takings, and Due Process. *Washington and Lee Law Review* 37:1057–1099.

EMPLOYERS' LIABILITY ACTS
34 Stat. 232 (1906)
35 Stat. 65 (1908)

In the first Employers' Liability Act of June 1906, Congress extended nationwide protection to railroad workers against the arsenal of COMMON LAW defenses which employers had so effectively used to defeat personal injury suits. This act rendered every common carrier engaged in INTERSTATE COMMERCE liable to its employees for all damages resulting from negligence. Congress thus discarded the "fellow-servant" rule which had exculpated employers in accidents caused by another workman's negligence. Moreover, contributory negligence would not bar recovery and the law directed juries, not judges, to determine questions of negligence and assess damages proportionally. The act also prohibited the use of insurance or other benefits as a defense against damage suits. When a 5–4 Supreme Court declared this act unconstitutional

because it extended to railroad employees not engaged in interstate commerce, Congress passed a second version of the act in April 1908. Although substantially the same, the new act covered only employees actually working in interstate commerce. Congress also added several sections further protecting employees and extended the period of limitation on actions from one to two years. As it had implied in its first decision, the Court unanimously sustained the act in the second set of EMPLOYERS' LIABILITY CASES (1912).

DAVID GORDON

EMPLOYERS' LIABILITY CASES
207 U.S. 463 (1908)
223 U.S. 1 (1912)

The first EMPLOYERS' LIABILITY ACT, passed in 1906, made a common carrier liable for the on-the-job injury or death of any employee and eliminated the "fellow-servant" rule by which an employer had been relieved of liability for an injury to one worker caused by another's negligence. In the first *Employers' Liability Cases*, a 5–4 Supreme Court held that Congress had exceeded its INTERSTATE COMMERCE power.

Justice EDWARD D. WHITE's opinion for the Court (only Justice WILLIAM R. DAY concurred completely in his opinion) addressed two objections to the act: that Congress had no power to regulate the subject, and that the act regulated things outside the scope of the commerce power. He dismissed the first objection. The COMMERCE CLAUSE set no limits on subjects regulated. Indeed, the Court decided only the extent of Congress's power, not the wisdom of its action. "We fail to perceive any just reason for holding that Congress is without power to regulate the relation of master and servant . . . [as a subject of] interstate commerce." The argument that the act had unconstitutionally regulated INTERSTATE COMMERCE proved more troublesome. Because the act imposed liability on employers "without qualification or restriction as to the business in which the carriers or their employees may be engaged at the time of injury, of necessity [it] includes subjects wholly outside the power of Congress to regulate commerce." White refused to accept the contention that the Court ought to interpret the act as applying solely to interstate commerce even though it did not explicitly say so.

Chief Justice MELVILLE W. FULLER and Justice DAVID J. BREWER concurred in Justice RUFUS PECKHAM's opinion endorsing White's result but retreating from White's statement about Congress's power over master–servant relations. In a lengthy dissent, Justice WILLIAM MOODY argued that the Court was obliged to read the statute so as to preserve its constitutionality. "We think that the act, reasonably and properly interpreted, applies . . . only to cases of interstate commerce . . . and not to domestic commerce."

After Congress enacted another version of the law accommodating the majority's objections, a unanimous Court upheld its constitutionality. Justice WILLIS VAN DEVANTER's opinion broadly asserted the reach of Congress's power over the subject. He disposed of the objection that the act, by discarding COMMON LAW doctrines, had exceeded Congress's power: "A person has no property, no vested interest, in any rule of common law." The act also promoted safety and advanced commerce, and Van Devanter dismissed the contention that it violated the DUE PROCESS CLAUSE's guarantee of FREEDOM OF CONTRACT.

DAVID GORDON

EMPLOYMENT DISCRIMINATION

Employment discrimination on grounds of race, sex, nationality, or religion may be challenged under two acts of Congress. One of the statutes, now codified as Title 42 of the United States Code, Section 1981, is a survivor of the CIVIL RIGHTS ACT OF 1866, enacted for the protection of former slaves. As originally enacted, the statute was not seen as an employment discrimination statute. It conferred upon blacks the right to make and enforce contracts, to sue and to enjoy on a par with whites the protection of laws. The act was passed pursuant to Congress's authority under Section 2 of the THIRTEENTH AMENDMENT, and Congress proposed the FOURTEENTH AMENDMENT in order to assure the act's validity. After the Reconstruction era, however, it and other Reconstruction-era civil rights legislation fell into disuse until the 1960s. Not until *Johnson v. Railway Express Agency, Inc.* (1975) did the United States Supreme Court confirm the application of Section 1981 to RACIAL DISCRIMINATION in private-sector employment. This statute's use in employment discrimination cases has become secondary to reliance on Title VII of the CIVIL RIGHTS ACT OF 1964, which was enacted by Congress as part of a comprehensive statute prohibiting discrimination on grounds of race, sex, religion, or national origin in employment, PUBLIC ACCOMMODATIONS, and federally funded programs.

Enactment of the 1964 Act followed a long period of civil rights DEMONSTRATIONS against the kinds of discrimination the act prohibited. For twenty years preceding the enactment of Title VII, more than 200 fair employment practice bills had been proposed in the Congress, but none had passed. Allegations of a Title VII violation often are accompanied by additional allegations of a Section 1981 violation.

Another survivor of Reconstruction-era legislation now codified as 42 United States Code 1985(c), was originally designed to protect blacks from Ku Klux Klan violence. The Supreme Court, in *Great American Federal Savings and Loan Association v. Novotny* (1979), rejected the view that Section 1985(c) provides an independent remedy for the adjudication of rights protected by Title VII.

The constitutionality of Title VII of the 1964 act was never seriously questioned. The power of Congress to enact Title VII, either under the COMMERCE CLAUSE or to enforce the FOURTEENTH AMENDMENT, seems to have been assumed. In 1972 Congress extended the coverage of Title VII to include employment discrimination by state and local governments. Subsequently, it was argued that back-pay awards and attorneys' fees levied by a federal court against a state under the amended Title VII violated the jurisdictional limitations of the ELEVENTH AMENDMENT. However, in FITZPATRICK V. BITZER (1976) the Supreme Court rejected that argument, holding that the 1972 amendment was a valid exercise of Congress's enforcement power under Section 5 of the FOURTEENTH AMENDMENT.

REGINALD ALLEYNE

Bibliography

COMMENT 1980 Developments in the Law—Section 1981. *Harvard Civil Rights–Civil Liberties Law Review* 15:29–277.

DEAN, JOHN P. 1978 Title VII and Public Employers: Did Congress Exceed Its Powers? *Columbia Law Review* 78:372–408.

HILL, HERBERT 1977 The Equal Employment Opportunity Acts of 1964 and 1972: A Critical Analysis of the Legislative History and Administration of the Law. *Industrial Relations Law Journal* 2:1–96.

EN BANC

(French: "As a bench.") The term often applies to appellate courts, and in particular to the UNITED STATES COURTS OF APPEALS. Commonly only a three-member panel of a federal court of appeals hears a case. When the full membership is sitting—whether by its own choice or at a litigant's request—the case is heard before them *en banc*. In the federal courts of appeals, the decision of a panel is reconsidered *en banc* if a majority of the full court's members agree on such a hearing.

DAVID GORDON

ENDO, EX PARTE

See: Japanese American Cases

ENFORCEMENT ACTS

See: Force Acts

ENGEL v. VITALE
370 U.S. 421 (1962)

The Board of Regents of the State of New York authorized a short prayer for recitation in schools. The Regents were seeking to defuse the emotional issue of religious exercises in the classroom. The matter was taken out of the hands of school boards and teachers, and the blandest sort of invocation of the Deity was provided: "Almighty God, we acknowledge our dependence upon Thee, and beg Thy blessings upon us, our teachers, and our country." School districts in New York did not have to use the prayer, and if they did, no child was required to repeat it. But if there were any prayer in a New York classroom it would have to be this one. The Board of Education of New Hyde Park, New York, chose to use the Regents' Prayer and directed its principals to cause it to be said aloud at the beginning of each school day in every classroom.

Use of the prayer was challenged as an ESTABLISHMENT OF RELIGION. Justice HUGO L. BLACK, writing for the Court, concluded that neither the nondenominational nature of the prayer nor the fact that it was voluntary could save it from unconstitutionality under the establishment clause. By providing the prayer, New York officially approved theistic religion. With his usual generous quotations from JAMES MADISON and THOMAS JEFFERSON, Black found such state support impermissible.

Justice WILLIAM O. DOUGLAS concurred separately. He had more trouble than Black concluding that the prayer established religion "in the strictly historic meaning of these words." What Douglas feared was the divisiveness engendered in a community when government sponsored a religious exercise.

Only Justice POTTER STEWART dissented, concluding that "the Court has misapplied a great constitutional principle." Stewart could not see how a purely voluntary prayer could be held to constitute state adoption of an official religion. For Stewart, an official religion was the only meaning of "establishment of religion." He noted that invocations of the Deity in public ceremonies of all sorts had been a feature of our national life from its outset. Without quite saying so, Stewart asked his brethren how the Regents' Prayer could be anathematized on establishment clause grounds without scraping "In God We Trust" off the pennies.

Engel v. Vitale was the first of a series of cases in which the Court used the establishment clause to extirpate from the public schools the least-common-denominator religious invocations which had been a traditional part of public ceremonies—especially school ceremonies—in America.

The decision proved extremely controversial. It has been widely circumvented and there have been repeated attempts to amend the Constitution to undo the effect of *Engel.*

RICHARD E. MORGAN

Bibliography
BERNS, WALTER 1976 *The First Amendment and the Future of American Democracy.* Pages 33–76. New York: Basic Books.
MUIR, WILLIAM K., JR. 1967 *Prayer in the Public Schools.* Chicago: University of Chicago Press.

ENGLISH BILL OF RIGHTS

See: Bill of Rights (English)

ENGLISH CONSTITUTION

See: British Constitution

ENMUND v. FLORIDA
458 U.S. 782 (1982)

Before this decision, nine states permitted infliction of the death penalty on one who participated in a FELONY resulting in a murder, even if committed by confederates. Earl Enmund drove the getaway car in a robbery at which co-defendants killed the victims when he was not present and had not premeditated murder. A 5–4 Court held that the CRUEL AND UNUSUAL PUNISHMENT clause of the EIGHTH AMENDMENT, which the FOURTEENTH AMENDMENT extended to the states, prevented imposition of the death penalty. Capital punishment was disproportionate to the crime when Enmund had not himself killed, attempted to kill, intended to kill, or even intended the use of lethal force.

LEONARD W. LEVY

ENTANGLEMENT TEST

See: Government Aid to Sectarian Institutions

ENTRAPMENT DEFENSE

The entrapment defense is not constitutionally safeguarded and raises no constitutional issue unless a guilty defendant claims that law enforcement conduct violates the fundamental fairness mandated by DUE PROCESS OF LAW; if such a constitutional defense were to be recognized by the Supreme Court the effect would, like an EXCLUSIONARY RULE, be aimed at deterring unlawful police conduct.

Entrapment is a means of securing evidence to convict by luring a person into the commission of a crime of which he is suspected. Ordinarily the duty of an officer of the law is to deter crime and apprehend those who commit it, not to incite or instigate it. Certain offenses of a clandestine or consensual character, however, are difficult to expose and punish except by some degree of covert government participation. Official deceit is not necessarily illegal or unconstitutional. Undercover police work is particularly effective in uncovering crimes that involve gambling, drugs, prostitution, and official corruption. Nevertheless the government should not fight crime with crime.

When an undercover officer has gained the confidence of a radical organization and encouraged its members to engage in terrorist activities and provided them with the weapons and explosives to do so, he has become an *agent provocateur* who has conceived and procured the commission of a crime that would not have occurred but for him. If an officer posing as an imposter approaches a law-abiding person with no criminal record and induces him to smuggle contraband, the officer has passed the law's tolerance and the smuggler's guilty conduct may be legally excusable. When entrapment goes too far, it creates a legal defense which, like insanity or killing to save one's own life, merits a verdict of not guilty. The question in any case is whether the evidence shows that entrapment is a sufficient defense by a person who has in fact committed the crime charged against him. The mere fact that a government agent provides a favorable opportunity to one willing and ready to break the law is not entrapment for the purpose of making good a defense; if, however, the defendant had no previous intent to commit the offense and did so only because the police induced him, the verdict should be an acquittal.

Entrapment comes before the Supreme Court as a nonconstitutional defense in cases involving federal crimes. The Justices have always divided into two wings: one focuses on the criminal intent or predisposition of the defendant to commit the crime; the other focuses on the conduct of law enforcement officers. The view that has always prevailed, from the first case, *Sorrells v. United States* (1932), to *Hampton v. United States* (1976), is that it is no entrapment for the police merely to instigate the crime; they must also instigate its commission by luring an innocent person with no previous disposition to commit it. The criminal design, as Chief Justice CHARLES EVANS HUGHES said in 1932, must originate with the authorities who implant the predisposition in the mind of an otherwise innocent person and incite him to commit it so that they may prosecute. Thus, in *United States v. Russell* (1973), the Court sustained the conviction of the manufacturer of an illegal drug, who claimed that the government had violated due process when an undercover agent supplied him with an essential chemical ingredient. But the ingredient was harmless, its possession was not illegal, and, above all, the defendant was already engaged in the criminal enterprise. In *Hampton*, however, a government informant supplied an illegal drug and arranged its sale by the defendant to undercover agents. Although the government deliberately set him up, the Court stressed that his previous propensity to commit the crime negated his entrapment defense. He was, in a phrase of Chief Justice EARL WARREN, "an unwary criminal" rather than an "unwary innocent."

Justice WILLIAM H. REHNQUIST wrote the entrapment opinions of the BURGER COURT, from which Justices POTTER STEWART, WILLIAM J. BRENNAN, and THURGOOD MARSHALL dissented. The dissenters insisted that the majority's focus on the criminal's predisposition is "subjective," and they preferred an "objective" test: whether, despite predisposition, police conduct instigated the offense. The objectivity of that view, however, can be deceptive, and it ignores criminal intent. Doubtless, though, the trend of decision has made the entrapment defense nearly useless if a jury does not accept it. If the "outrageousness" of police conduct should pass the threshold of judicial tolerance in some future case, the Court may find a due process basis for the entrapment defense.

LEONARD W. LEVY

Bibliography

DUNHAM, DAN S. 1977 Hampton v. United States: Last Rites for the "Objective" Theory of Entrapment? *Columbia Human Rights Law Review* 9:223–262.

O'CONNER, PETER J. 1978 Entrapment versus Due Process: A Solution to the Problem of the Criminal Conviction Obtained by Law Enforcement Misconduct. *Fordham Urban Law Journal* 7:32–53.

ROSSUM, RALPH A. 1978 The Entrapment Defense and the Teaching of Political Responsibility. *American Journal of Criminal Law* 6:287–306.

ENUMERATED POWERS

Instead of establishing a national government with a general power to do whatever it might deem in the public interest, the Constitution lists the authorized powers of Congress. The chief source of these "enumerated powers" is Article I, section 8, which authorizes Congress to regulate commerce among the several states, tax and spend, raise and support military forces, and so on. This enumeration has been supplemented by other grants, including authority to enforce the Civil War Amendments.

The enumeration of powers has both a negative and a positive implication. Enumerating or specifying powers implies that some of government's ordinary concerns are beyond the constitutional competence of the national government. This implication is made explicit by the TENTH AMENDMENT. Nevertheless, the founding generation wanted to solve such specific problems as commercial hostility among the states and an unpaid war debt. When THE FEDERALIST defended the proposed national powers it cited the desiderata that might be achieved through their successful exercise. The enumeration of powers thus implies affirmative responsibilities as well as limited concerns. These competing implications are associated with competing approaches to constitutional interpretation and different conceptions of the normative character of the Constitution as a whole. As a reminder of a line between national and state powers, the enu-

meration of powers suggests THOMAS JEFFERSON's view of the Constitution as a contract between sovereign states to be construed with an eye to preserving state prerogatives. As a reminder of affirmative responsibilities the enumeration suggests JOHN MARSHALL's view of the Constitution as a charter of government to be construed in ways that permit achievement of the social objectives it envisions. History has not favored the Jeffersonian view.

ALEXANDER HAMILTON, in *The Federalist* #84, cited the enumeration of powers as one reason for opposing a BILL OF RIGHTS. Not only were bills of rights unnecessary in countries whose governments possessed only those powers that their people had expressly granted, specifying rights could undermine the enumeration of powers by suggesting "to men disposed to usurp" that the Constitution authorized all that the bill of rights did not prohibit. The result Hamilton ostensibly feared was achieved through constitutional doctrines that accompanied the nation's progress toward the economically integrated industrial society Hamilton favored. These doctrines included Hamilton's own theories of the SUPREMACY CLAUSE and the NECESSARY AND PROPER CLAUSE, theories that influenced John Marshall's doctrine of IMPLIED POWERS in MCCULLOCH V. MARYLAND (1819).

Marshall's original theory of implied powers was consistent with the idea of enumerated powers because it removed STATES' RIGHTS burdens on national power while insisting that national concerns were limited. In the twentieth century, however, the Supreme Court changed the meaning of implied powers and gave nationalist readings to the general welfare clause and other powers. The aggregate and practical effect of these interpretations was to empower the national government to deal with anything that Congress may perceive as a national problem. This development has all but eliminated the restrictive implication of the enumeration of powers, leaving the Bill of Rights and the Constitution's institutional norms as the principal limitations on national power.

SOTIRIOS A. BARBER

(SEE ALSO: *General Welfare Clause; Tenth Amendment.*)

Bibliography

ALFANGE, DEAN, JR. 1969 Congressional Power and Constitutional Limitations. *Journal of Public Law* 18:103–134.

BARBER, SOTIRIOS A. 1984 *On What the Constitution Means.* Chap. 4. Baltimore: Johns Hopkins University Press.

ENVIRONMENTAL QUALITY IMPROVEMENT ACT

See: Environmental Regulation

ENVIRONMENTAL REGULATION AND THE CONSTITUTION

Indirectly, at least, the Constitution provides the federal government with power to regulate on behalf of environmental quality, but it also sets limits on the power. It sets limits, likewise, on the regulatory power of the states. What it does not do, at present, is grant the "constitutional right to a clean environment" so avidly sought in the heyday of environmental concern, the decade of the 1970s. Thus, the one unique aspect of the general topic considered here has no doctrinal standing; the remaining aspects are matters of doctrine, but they are not unique to environmental regulation. It is quite sufficient, then, merely to illustrate the wide range of constitutional issues that arise in the context of environmental regulation, and to suggest the nature of the debate on the question of a constitutional right to an environment of good quality.

Environmental lawmaking at the national level of government—whether by Congress, the executive, or indeed the federal courts—became important only in the 1970s, but the beginnings reach back well into the nineteenth century, if not farther. This history, especially the strong federal presence of recent years, makes apparent the significant constitutional authority of the central government in regard to the environment. Granting that it is a government of LIMITED POWERS, and mindful of occasional suggestions "that these powers fall short of encompassing the breadth of concerns potentially subject to environmental regulation," one can still conclude, with Philip Soper, "that no conceivable measure reasonably intended to protect the environment is beyond the reach" of federal authority.

The most important source of federal power to regulate in the environmental field is found in the COMMERCE CLAUSE. The clause, especially as it pertains to congressional authority to regulate activities *affecting* commerce, has been so expansively applied by the federal courts as to justify federal control of virtually any problem of environmental pollution. Some pollution sources, such as automobiles and ships, move in INTERSTATE COMMERCE; other sources manufac-

ture products that do so; pollution affects such mainstays of interstate commerce as agricultural commodities, livestock, and many raw materials; pollutants themselves can be seen as products, or at least byproducts, moving "in commerce" across state lines. An imaginative federal district court relied upon this last theory to sustain the Clean Air Act in *United States v. Bishop Processing Company* (D.Md. 1968).

These views lend support not only to the federal air pollution control program but also to programs concerning noise, pesticides, solid waste, toxic substances, and water pollution. Regarding the last especially, Congress can draw on its unquestioned authority over navigable waters, and on the willingness of the federal courts to regard as navigable any waters of a depth sufficient, as someone once said, to float a Supreme Court opinion.

The federal government can draw on other sources of power, at least on a selective basis, to support programs of environmental regulation. The property clause of Article IV, section 3, for example, gives Congress the power to "make all needful Rules and Regulations respecting" the property of the United States. In *Kleppe v. New Mexico* (1976) the clause was relied upon to sustain the Wild Free-Roaming Horses and Burros Act of 1971 as a "needful regulation" "respecting" public lands, against New Mexico's claim that the federal government lacked authority to control the animals unless they were moving in interstate commerce or damaging public lands. It seems clear that under the property clause Congress may regulate the use of its own lands, and perhaps adjacent lands as well, to protect environmental conditions and promote ecological balance on government property.

Other powers relevant to environmental regulation include the TAXING POWER, which presumably would authorize effluent and emission fees to control pollution; perhaps the ADMIRALTY power, as a basis for controlling pollution from ships; and the power to approve INTERSTATE COMPACTS, as an indirect means by which to impose federal environmental standards on compacting states, as the Court suggested in *West Virginia ex rel. Dyer v. Sims* (1951), involving a compact among eight states to control pollution in the Ohio River system. And the Supreme Court may draw on its ORIGINAL JURISDICTION to shape a FEDERAL COMMON LAW of pollution in suits between states or between a state and the citizens of another state.

The TREATY POWER provides yet another basis for federal environmental quality and conservation measures. The leading case here is MISSOURI V. HOLLAND

(1920), sustaining the Migratory Bird Act of 1918. Congress enacted the legislation in question in order to give effect to a treaty between the United States and Great Britain. Missouri, claiming "title" to birds within its borders, sought to prevent a federal game warden from enforcing the Act. The Court, through Justice OLIVER WENDELL HOLMES, rejected the state's contention. Treaties, under the SUPREMACY CLAUSE, are the "supreme Law of the Land"; so too are acts of Congress "NECESSARY AND PROPER for carrying into Execution" the treaty power vested in the president and the Senate. *Missouri v. Holland* is of particular interest because the Court upheld the Migratory Bird Act notwithstanding the fact that a similar act, not based on a treaty, had earlier been invalidated as beyond the scope of congressional power. As Soper remarks, the case "accordingly seems to stand for the proposition that Congress may do by statute and treaty what it has no power to do by statute alone."

The specific basis for the state's claim in *Missouri v. Holland* was the TENTH AMENDMENT, which reserves to the states powers not delegated to the United States by the Constitution. The provision introduces the subject of constitutional limitations (as opposed to powers) that may apply to programs of environmental regulation, and illustrates a limitation applicable only to the federal government, and not to the states.

The Tenth Amendment figured prominently in a series of cases involving the federal Clean Air Act and decided by several courts of appeals in the 1970s. A central question in the cases was whether the amendment foreclosed the federal Environmental Protection Agency from promulgating regulations compelling various implementation and enforcement measures by the states, under threat of fines and imprisonment for recalcitrant state and local officials. The courts of appeals divided on the question, at least one of them intimating a constitutional violation, one explicitly finding no violation, and one interpreting the Clean Air Act in such a way as to sidestep the issue. The Supreme Court granted certiorari and heard argument in several of the cases, but it ultimately declined to reach the merits because counsel for the United States conceded that the regulations in question would have to be rewritten to eliminate requirements that states adopt implementation and enforcement measures. The Court's later decisions in HODEL V. VIRGINIA SURFACE MINING AND RECLAMATION ASSOCIATION (1981) and *Federal Energy Regulatory Commission v. Mississippi* (1982) show that Congress can constitutionally place great pressures on the states to regulate, so long as it uses indirect means for doing so.

Another constitutional limitation operating upon state but not federal environmental protection programs arises from the supremacy clause. The limitation may come into play in two common respects. One of these involves PREEMPTION and is illustrated by BURBANK V. LOCKHEED AIR TERMINAL, INC. (1973), where the Court concluded that federal legislation, including the Noise Control Act of 1972, reflected a congressional intention to "occupy the field" of aircraft noise regulation; hence, Burbank's noise ordinance was held invalid under the supremacy clause. The second application of the clause is illustrated in *Hancock v. Train* (1976) and *Environmental Protection Agency v. State Water Resources Control Board* (1976), in which the Court held that the supremacy clause sheltered federal facilities from permit requirements imposed by state governments pursuant to the Clean Air Act and the Federal Water Pollution Control Act, respectively, absent a clear congressional indication to the contrary.

The remaining constitutional limitations on environmental regulation apply more or less equally to state and federal government alike. We can put aside the general question of state *authority* to regulate on behalf of the environment. States, unlike the federal government, are not creatures of limited powers. It has long been acknowledged that the STATE POLICE POWER justifies the widest range of health and safety measures insofar as the federal Constitution is concerned, absent some conflict with supreme federal law. This generalization stood fairly firm even during the most active period of SUBSTANTIVE DUE PROCESS review by the federal judiciary. And it bears mention, regarding health and safety measures, as the Court said in *Northwestern Laundry v. Des Moines* (1916), that "the harshness of such legislation, or its effect upon business interests, short of a merely arbitrary enactment, are not valid constitutional objections. Nor is there any valid Federal constitutional objection in the fact that the regulation may require the discontinuance of the use of property or subject the occupant to large expense in complying with the terms of the law or ordinance."

The BILL OF RIGHTS may bear on state and federal environmental regulation just as it may bear on regulation generally. Recent cases illustrate the point. Thus the FIRST AMENDMENT came into play in *Metromedia, Inc. v. San Diego* (1981), where a local ordinance controlling billboards and the like for the sake of safety and aesthetics was invalidated insofar as it pertained to noncommercial advertising. In *Air*

Pollution Variance Board of Colorado v. Western Alfalfa Corporation (1974), the issue was whether the FOURTH AMENDMENT prohibition of unreasonable searches and seizures was violated when a health inspector entered the grounds of a pollution source to make an opacity check of smoke coming from a chimney. The Court held the entry lawful under a line of cases sustaining "open field" searches. In *United States v. Ward* (1980), the Court held that civil penalties imposed for violating certain provisions of the Federal Water Pollution Control Act pertaining to oil spills were not "quasi-criminal" so as to implicate the Fifth Amendment RIGHT AGAINST SELF-INCRIMINATION (or, presumably, the Sixth Amendment's procedural restrictions applicable to criminal prosecutions). Similarly, *Atlas Roofing Co. v. Occupational Safety and Health Review Commission* (1976) held that administrative civil penalty provisions of the Occupational Safety and Health Act did not contravene the SEVENTH AMENDMENT right to TRIAL BY JURY.

In principle, the takings clause of the Fifth Amendment might be thought to contain the most significant restriction on state and federal environmental regulation. The clause, which applies to the states through the FOURTEENTH AMENDMENT, provides: "nor shall private property be taken for PUBLIC USE, without JUST COMPENSATION." It is clearly recognized that a government regulation can work a taking, but it is seldom held that it actually does. Most environmental regulations challenged on taking grounds are alleged to reach too far, to reduce value too much, and thus to transgress the bounds drawn by Justice Holmes in one of his most famous—and least informative—generalizations, uttered in *Pennsylvania Coal Co. v. Mahon* (1922): "that while property may be regulated to a certain extent, if regulation goes too far it will be recognized as a taking." The statement suggests that if a regulation reduces property value by a great deal, a taking will be found. In practice, however, the courts tend to look not at value lost but value left. If the regulation leaves significant value intact, then usually it will be upheld. The central case in point is PENN CENTRAL TRANSPORTATION COMPANY V. NEW YORK CITY (1978), upholding New York's historic landmark preservation law as applied to Grand Central Terminal, notwithstanding very large losses to the terminal's owners. In any event, the takings clause has little bite in the context of conventional environmental regulation because control of nuisance-like activities has long escaped takings challenges even if the value of the regulated property is reduced to zero. Because virtually any environmental regulation can be characterized as a nuisance control measure, virtually none is likely to be regarded as a taking.

The state and federal governments, then, may regulate rather freely on behalf of environmental quality, but are they constitutionally obliged to do so? Nothing in the federal Constitution says as much. There are arguments that diligent and imaginative searching would find the right between the lines of text, chiefly in the "penumbra" of the Bill of Rights, or as a fundamental personal right protected by the NINTH Amendment, or as a right "implicit in the concept of ORDERED LIBERTY" and guaranteed by the DUE PROCESS clause. The Supreme Court and all but a few federal district courts have been unmoved by these arguments. Courts generally have displayed an unwillingness to make the difficult business of environmental policy a matter of constitutional principle, a point reflected in state court decisions holding that state constitutional amendments setting out environmental rights are not self-executing but require, rather, legislative implementation. The courts, quite obviously, feel ill-equipped to play a role thought better suited to legislatures. It is not that the environment is somehow less important than other recognized constitutional values, but rather that it is less amenable to adjudication.

Richard B. Stewart summarizes the arguments in this regard: a constitutional right to environmental quality would give courts ultimate responsibilities for making resource allocation decisions beyond their analytic capabilities; for trading off allocative efficiency and distributional equity without any principled means by which to do so; and for engineering and implementing dynamic policies through the clumsy and apolitical means of litigation. Stewart adds:

A familiar justification for constitutional protection of given interests is that they are held by a "discrete and insular" minority or are otherwise chronically undervalued because of basic structural defects in the political process. This rationale has been utilized by advocates of a constitutional right to environmental quality, buttressing it by claims that environmental degradation violates "fundamental" interests in health and human survival and implicates the fate of future generations that are unrepresented in the political process. But the spate of environmental legislation enacted by federal and state governments over the past ten years flatly contradicts the general claim that the political process suffers from structural defects that necessitate a constitutional right to environmental quality [*Development*, 1977: 714–715].

Whether future generations will agree is an open question.

JAMES E. KRIER

Bibliography

SOPER, PHILIP   1974   The Constitutional Framework of Environmental Law. Pages 20–125 in E. Dolgin and T. Guilbert, eds., *Federal Environmental Law*. St. Paul, Minn.: West Publishing Co.

STEWART, RICHARD B.   1977   The Development of Administrative and Quasi-Constitutional Law in Judicial Review of Environmental Decisionmaking: Lessons from the Clean Air Act. *Iowa Law Review* 62:713–769.

——— 1977   Pyramids of Sacrifice? Problems of Federalism in Mandating State Implementation of National Environmental Policy. *Yale Law Journal* 86:1196–1272.

EPPERSON v. ARKANSAS
393 U.S. 97 (1968)

Arkansas prohibited the teaching in its public schools "that mankind ascended or descended from a lower order of animals." In dealing with a challenge to the law based on establishment clause and FREEDOM OF SPEECH grounds, Justice ABE FORTAS, speaking for the Supreme Court, concluded that the Arkansas law violated the establishment clause. "There can be no doubt," he said, "that Arkansas sought to prevent its teachers from discussing the theory of evolution because it is contrary to the beliefs of some that the book of Genesis must be the exclusive source of the doctrine of the origin of man."

Justice HUGO L. BLACK and Justice POTTER STEWART concurred in brief opinions resting on VAGUENESS grounds. The Black opinion raised important GOVERNMENT SPEECH issues that are still unresolved.

RICHARD E. MORGAN

EQUAL EMPLOYMENT OPPORTUNITY COMMISSION (EEOC) v. WYOMING
460 U.S. 226 (1983)

The EEOC sought to enforce the AGE DISCRIMINATION IN EMPLOYMENT ACT (ADEA) against the state of Wyoming in a case involving the involuntary retirement of a fifty-five-year-old game warden. The Supreme Court, 5–4, upheld the ADEA as so applied. Justice WILLIAM J. BRENNAN, for the Court, found congressional power in the COMMERCE CLAUSE, and rejected the state's claim, based on NATIONAL LEAGUE OF CITIES v. USERY (1976), that it was immune to this form of congressional regulation. The majority was composed of the four dissenters in *Usery* plus Justice HARRY A. BLACKMUN.

Wyoming, Brennan said, failed the third part of the formula of *Hodel v. Virginia Surface Mining and Reclamation Association* (1981): the ADEA did not "directly impair" Wyoming's ability to "structure integral operations in areas of traditional governmental functions." Wyoming could use other means to test the fitness of game wardens—or, as the ADEA allowed, justify the necessity of the age limit. The ADEA would affect state finances and state policies only marginally. Chief Justice WARREN E. BURGER, for the four dissenters, employed the same *Hodel* formula and concluded that the ADEA was unconstitutional as applied to a state.

This decision helped set the stage for *Usery's* overruling in GARCIA V. SAN ANTONIO METROPOLITAN TRANSIT AUTHORITY (1984).

KENNETH L. KARST

(SEE ALSO: *Intergovernmental Immunities.*)

EQUAL PROTECTION OF THE LAWS

The ancient political ideal of equality did not find explicit recognition in the text of the Constitution until the FOURTEENTH AMENDMENT was ratified in 1868. Yet equality was an American ideal from the earliest colonial times. There was irony in the expression of the ideal in the DECLARATION OF INDEPENDENCE; the newly independent states generally limited voting to white male property owners, and THOMAS JEFFERSON, the Declaration's author, was the troubled owner of slaves. Even so, one feature of white American society that set it apart from Europe was an egalitarian climate for social relations. The Constitution's ban on TITLES OF NOBILITY symbolized the nation's determination to leave behind the old world's privileges of monarchy and aristocracy.

Jefferson, who believed in an aristocracy of "virtue and talents," understood that equality of opportunity was consistent with wide disparities among individuals' wealth and power. The equality he envisioned was, above all, equality before the law. The principle of universal laws, equally applicable to all citizens, itself provided a foundation for a market economy whose competitive struggles would lead to further inequalities. An equality that was formal, or legal, thus would undermine the "equality of condition" that attracted some of Jefferson's contemporaries. Yet formal equality was something that mattered greatly in the nation's first decades, and it matters greatly today. When Europeans remark, as they still do, on America's relatively high degree of equality, they are referring not to equality of wealth or political power but to equality of social status. With pardonable literary exaggeration, Simone de Beauvoir said it this way: "the rich American has no grandeur; the poor man no servility; human relations in daily life are on a footing of equality. . . ."

The Fourteenth Amendment's wording emphasizes legal equality. A state is forbidden to "deny to any person within its jurisdiction the equal protection of the laws." On its face this language seems to demand no more than even-handed enforcement of laws as they are written. Such a reading, however, would drain all life from the guarantee of equal protection. On this view even a law barring blue-eyed persons from state employment would pass constitutional muster if the state applied it equally, without discrimination, to all applicants, refusing jobs only to those who were blue-eyed. No one has ever seriously argued for so restricted a scope for the equal protection clause. The Supreme Court casually dismissed the idea with a passing comment in YICK WO V. HOPKINS (1886): "the equal protection of the laws is a pledge of the protection of equal laws."

At the other extreme of silliness, the *Yick Wo* statement might be taken literally, interpreting the equal protection clause to forbid the enforcement of any law that imposed any inequality. As Joseph Tussman and JACOBUS TEN BROEK showed nearly forty years ago, so sweeping a reading would convert the clause into a constitutional prohibition on legislation itself. All laws draw lines of classification, applying their rules only to some people (or some transactions or phenomena) and not to others. Furthermore, the very existence of law—that is, of governmental regulation of human behavior—implies inequality, for some individuals must evaluate the behavior of others and enforce the state's norms by imposing sanctions on the recalcitrant. In Ralf Dahrendorf's biting formulation, "all men are equal *before* the law but they are no longer equal *after* it." Given the diverse characteristics of humans, the achievement of equality as to one aspect of life necessarily implies inequalities as to other aspects. And if it were possible to construct a society characterized by total, uncompromising equality, no one would want to live in that society.

Then what kinds of inequality are prohibited by the equal protection clause? The abstraction, equality, cannot resolve cases; the question always remains, equality as to what? To give meaning to the equal protection clause requires identification of the substantive values that are its central concern. The inquiry begins in the history leading to the adoption of the Fourteenth Amendment, but it does not end there. To understand the substantive content of the equal protection clause, we must consider not only what it meant to its framers, but also what it has come to mean to succeeding generations of judges and other citizens.

Just what role the framers had in mind for the equal protection clause remains unclear; the amendment's sketchy "legislative history" has been given widely divergent interpretations. All the interpreters agree, however, that the framers' immediate objective was to provide an unshakable constitutional foundation for the CIVIL RIGHTS ACT OF 1866. That act had been passed over the veto of President ANDREW JOHNSON, who had asserted that it exceeded the powers of Congress.

The 1866 act had declared the CITIZENSHIP of all persons born in the United States and subject to its JURISDICTION. This declaration, later echoed in the text of the Fourteenth Amendment, had been designed to "overrule" the assertion by Chief Justice ROGER B. TANEY in his opinion for the Supreme Court in DRED SCOTT V. SANDFORD (1857) that black persons were incapable of being citizens. Taney had said that blacks—not just slaves but any blacks—were incapable of citizenship, because blacks had not been members of "the People of the United States" identified in the Constitution's PREAMBLE as the body who adopted that document. Blacks has been excluded from membership in the national community, according to Taney, because they were "considered as a subordinate and inferior class of beings, who had been subjugated by the dominant race, and, whether emancipated or not, yet remained subject to their authority. . . ." Discriminatory state legislation in force when the Constitution was adopted, Taney said, negated the conclusion that the states "regarded at that time, as fellow-citizens and members of the sovereignty, a class of beings whom they had thus stigmatized; . . . and upon whom they had impressed such deep and enduring marks of inferiority and degradation. . . ."

This dubious reading of history is beside the point; *Dred Scott's* relevance to our inquiry is that Taney's assumptions about racial inferiority and restricted citizenship were just what the drafters of the 1866 act sought to destroy. There was to be no "dominant race" and no "subordinate and inferior class of beings," but only citizens. Indeed the act's conferral of various CIVIL RIGHTS was aimed at abolishing a new system of serfdom designed to replace SLAVERY in the southern states. That system rested on the BLACK CODES, laws methodically imposing legal disabilities on blacks for the purpose of maintaining them in a state of dependency and inferiority.

The 1866 act, after its declaration of citizenship,

provided that "such citizens, of every race and color [including former slaves], shall have the same right [to contract and sue in court and deal with property, etc.] as is enjoyed by white citizens. . . ." The "civil rights" thus guaranteed were seen as the equal rights of citizens. When President Johnson vetoed the bill, he similarly linked the ideas of citizenship and equality, and argued that the THIRTEENTH AMENDMENT was an insufficient basis for congressional power. Congress overrode Johnson's veto, but from the time of the veto forward, a major purpose of the promoters of the Fourteenth Amendment, then under consideration in Congress, was to secure the constitutional foundations of the 1866 act.

The amendment, like the act, begins with a declaration of citizenship. In the same first section, the amendment goes on to forbid a state to "abridge the PRIVILEGES OR IMMUNITIES of citizens of the United States," to "deprive any person of life, liberty, or property, without DUE PROCESS OF LAW," or to deny a person "the equal protection of the laws." No serious effort was made during the debates on the amendment to identify separate functions for the three clauses that followed the declaration of citizenship. The section as a whole was taken to guarantee the equal enjoyment of the rights of citizens.

Beyond those specific goals, nothing in the consensus of the Fourteenth Amendment's framers would have caused anyone to anticipate what the Supreme Court made of the amendment in the latter half of the twentieth century. Yet the Fourteenth Amendment was not written in the language of specific rights, such as the right to contract or buy or sell property, but was deliberately cast in the most general terms. The broad language of the amendment strongly suggests that its framers were proposing to write into the Constitution not a "laundry list" of specific civil rights but a principle of equal citizenship.

To be a citizen is to enjoy the dignity of membership in the society, to be respected as a person who "belongs." The principle of equal citizenship presumptively forbids the organized society to treat an individual either as a member of an inferior or dependent caste or as a nonparticipant. As Taney recognized in his *Dred Scott* opinion, the stigma of caste is inconsistent with equal citizenship, which demands respect for each individual's humanity. Further, a citizen is a participant in society, a member of a moral community who must be taken into account when community decisions are made. Citizenship also implies obligations to one's fellow citizens. The values of participation and responsibility contribute to the primary citizenship value of respect, but they are also independently significant as aspects of citizenship.

For the first eight decades of the Fourteenth Amendment's existence, its interpretation by the Supreme Court was largely a betrayal of the constitutional ideal of equal citizenship. First by inventing the STATE ACTION limitation on the Fourteenth Amendment in the CIVIL RIGHTS CASES (1883), and then by giving racial SEGREGATION the stamp of constitutional validity in the SEPARATE BUT EQUAL decision of PLESSY V. FERGUSON (1896), the Supreme Court delivered virtually the entire subject of race relations back into the hands of the white South. The equal citizenship principle was left to be articulated in dissenting opinions. Notable among those dissents were the opinions of Justice JOSEPH P. BRADLEY in the SLAUGHTERHOUSE CASES (1873) and of Justice JOHN MARSHALL HARLAN in the *Civil Rights Cases* and *Plessy v. Ferguson*. The latter dissent included a passage that is now famous: "In view of the Constitution, in the eye of the law, there is in this country no superior, dominant, ruling class of citizens. There is no caste here. Our Constitution is color-blind, and neither knows nor tolerates classes among citizens." For half a century, those words expressed not a reality but a hope.

Outside the field of RACIAL DISCRIMINATION, the equal protection clause had little force even during the period when the due process clause of the Fourteenth Amendment was in active use as a defense against various forms of ECONOMIC REGULATION. By the 1920s, Justice OLIVER WENDELL HOLMES could say in BUCK V. BELL (1927), with accuracy if not with compassion, that the equal protection clause was the "usual last resort of constitutional arguments."

Even during the years when Holmes's "last resort" epithet summarized equal protection jurisprudence, the NAACP was pinning its hopes for racial justice on the federal judiciary, and was winning some victories. The Supreme Court had struck down LITERACY TESTS for voting that contained GRANDFATHER CLAUSES exempting most white voters, in GUINN V. UNITED STATES (1915) and *Lane v. Wilson* (1939); the Court had begun the process of holding "white primaries" unconstitutional; and it had invalidated racial zoning in BUCHANAN V. WARLEY (1917). And after the nation had emerged from the Great Depression and World War II, the judicial climate was distinctly more hospitable to equal protection claims.

The Depression had brought to dominance a new political majority, committed to active governmental intervention in economic affairs for the purpose of achieving full employment and major improvements in wages and the conditions of labor. The judiciary's main contribution to those egalitarian goals was to free the legislative process from the close judicial supervision of economic regulation that had attended the flowering of SUBSTANTIVE DUE PROCESS doctrines in the recent past. The war not only ended the Depression; it was a watershed in race relations. The migration of blacks from the rural South to northern and western cities, which had slowed during the Depression, dramatically accelerated, as wartime industry offered jobs that black workers had previously filled only rarely. Urban blacks were soon seen as a potent national political force. By the end of the war, the Army had begun the process of racial integration. Wartime ideology, with its scorn for Nazi racism, had lasting effects on the public mind. Even as the Supreme Court was upholding severe—and racist—wartime restrictions in the JAPANESE AMERICAN CASES (1943–1944), it reflected a new national state of mind in its celebrated OBITER DICTUM in KOREMATSU V. UNITED STATES (1944): "All legal restrictions which curtail the civil rights of a single racial group are immediately suspect. . . . [C]ourts must subject them to the most rigid scrutiny."

In the immediate postwar years the Supreme Court held unconstitutional the judicial enforcement of RESTRICTIVE COVENANTS in SHELLEY V. KRAEMER (1948), and it even ruled that the equal protection clause forbade some forms of segregation in state universities. (See SWEATT V. PAINTER, 1950.) The expected return to economic depression did not materialize. Instead, the country entered a period of unprecedented economic expansion. Good times are the most propitious for egalitarian public policies; it is relatively easy for "haves" to share with "have-nots" when they see their own conditions as steadily improving. The time was ripe, in the 1950s, for important successes in the movement for racial equality.

On the national scene, however, the political branches of government remained disinclined to act. One-party politics in the South had given disproportionate influence in the Congress to Southerners whose seniority gave them chairs of major committees. With President DWIGHT D. EISENHOWER reluctant to intervene, the prospects for effective civil rights legislation seemed dim. Thus was the stage furnished when Eisenhower appointed EARL WARREN to the Chief Justiceship in 1953.

In Warren's first term the Court decided BROWN V. BOARD OF EDUCATION (1954)—still the leading authoritative affirmation that the Constitution forbids

a system of caste—and in so doing began what Philip Kurland has called an "egalitarian revolution" in constitutional law. *Brown* was a major event in modern American history. Race relations in America would never again be what they were on the eve of the decision. The political movement for racial equality took on new vitality, and other egalitarian movements drew encouragement from that example. The constitutional law of equal protection gained powerful momentum, and the doctrinal effects went well beyond the subject of racial equality. If *Brown* itself represented JUDICIAL ACTIVISM, it was no more than a shadow of what was to come. The equal protection clause became the cutting edge of the WARREN COURT's active intervention into realms that previously had been left to legislative choice.

Two doctrinal techniques served these egalitarian ends. First, the Court heightened the STANDARD OF REVIEW used to test the constitutionality of certain laws, insisting on STRICT SCRUTINY by the courts of legislation that employed a SUSPECT CLASSIFICATION or discriminated against the exercise of a FUNDAMENTAL INTEREST. Second, the Court relaxed the "state action" limitation on the Fourteenth Amendment, bringing new forms of private conduct under the amendment's reach. Although the BURGER COURT later revitalized the "state action" limitation and slowed the advance of equal protection into new doctrinal territory, it made its own contributions to the development of the principle of equal citizenship.

Once the Court had firmly fastened the "suspect classification" label to racial discrimination, other forms of discrimination were attacked in the same terms. Some Justices have refused to find any legislative classification other than race to be constitutionally disfavored, but most of them have been receptive to arguments that at least some nonracial discriminations deserve heightened scrutiny. Thus, while only discrimination against ALIENS has been assimilated to the "suspect classifications" category—and even that assimilation is a sometime thing—the Court has announced clearly that judicial scrutiny should be heightened in some significant degree for SEX DISCRIMINATION or legislative classifications based on ILLEGITIMACY. Not only in these opinions but also in opinions refusing to apply similar reasoning to other forms of discrimination, the Court has developed a consensus on two sets of factors that are relevant in determining a classification's degree of "suspectness" or disfavor, and thus the level of justification which courts should demand for it.

The first set of factors emphasizes the equal citizenship value of respect; these factors reflect the judiciary's solicitude for the victims of stigma. A classification on the basis of a trait that is immutable and highly visible—such as race or sex—promotes stereotyping, the automatic assignment of an individual to a general category, often implying inferiority. The second set of factors, emphasizing the equal citizenship value of participation, focuses on the historic disadvantages (especially political disadvantages) of DISCRETE AND INSULAR MINORITIES. Both the phrase and the idea antedate Warren Court activism; they come from Justice HARLAN FISKE STONE's opinion for the Court in UNITED STATES v. CAROLENE PRODUCTS CO. (1938). Legislation that burdens a group likely to be neglected by the legislature is a natural candidate for special judicial scrutiny.

The equal citizenship themes of respect, participation, and responsibility also informed the Warren Court's decisions demanding close examination of the justifications for legislative discrimination against the exercise of "fundamental interests." Those decisions, in theory, might have been rested on grounds of substantive due process rather than equal protection. In fact, the Burger Court, which refused to recognize any new "fundamental" interests in equal protection doctrine, employed similar reasoning under the heading of due process, with corresponding attention to the values of equal citizenship. (See ABORTION AND THE CONSTITUTION; FAMILY AND THE CONSTITUTION; RIGHT OF PRIVACY.) The equal protection cases, however, identify only three clusters of interests as "fundamental": VOTING RIGHTS and related interests in equal access to the electoral process; certain rights of ACCESS TO THE COURTS (which have come to be explained more recently on due process grounds); and rights concerning marriage, procreation, and family relations. (See FREEDOM OF INTIMATE ASSOCIATION.)

Voting, of course, is one of the core responsibilities of citizenship. Perhaps more important, it is the citizen's preeminent symbol of participation as a valued member of the community. Access to the courts, like voting, is instrumentally valuable as a way to protect other interests. But—also like voting—the chance to be heard is an important citizenship symbol. To be listened to, to be treated as a person and not an object of administration, is to be afforded the dignity owed to a citizen. Finally, the marriage and family cases similarly implicate the citizenship values of respect, responsibility, and participation. Marriage and parenthood do not merely define one's legal obligations; they define one's status and social role and self-concept. For the state to deny a person the right and responsibility of choice about such matters is to take away

the presumptive right to be treated as a person, one of equal worth among citizens. None of these "fundamental" interests is entirely immune from state interference; what the principle of equal citizenship requires is that government offer weighty justification before denying their equal enjoyment.

In retrospect the whole apparatus of differential standards of review can be seen as judicial interest-balancing, thinly disguised: the more important the interest in equality, the more justification was required for its invasion by the government. Perhaps the Warren Court's majority chose to clothe its decisions in a "judicial"-sounding system of categories because the Justices were sensitive to the charge that they were writing their own policy preferences into the equal protection clause, and not just "interpreting" it. As a consequence, the Court extended the reach of equal protection without ever explicitly articulating the substantive content of the equal protection clause.

The Warren Court, in its final years, was well on the way to effective abandonment of the "state action" limitation on the Fourteenth Amendment, finding "significant state involvement" in all manner of private racial discriminations that denied their victims full participation in the public life of the community. Once Congress passed the CIVIL RIGHTS ACT OF 1964, however, it became unnecessary for the Court to complete its dismantling job; now there was a federal statutory right of access to PUBLIC ACCOMMODATIONS such as hotels, restaurants, and theaters. When the Court in JONES v. ALFRED H. MAYER CO. (1968) discovered the Thirteenth Amendment as a source of congressional power to forbid most other private racial discrimination, the chief practical motivation for doing away with the "state action" doctrine was removed. In later years, a different majority of Justices has gone far to restore the "state action" limitation to its former status but at the same time it has both reaffirmed the power of Congress to stamp out private racial discrimination and promoted that purpose with an expansive interpretation of existing civil rights acts.

The right to participate in the community's public life—even those portions of public life that are owned and managed by private persons—is an essential ingredient of effective citizenship, part of what it means to be a respected member of society. The "state action" limitation, when the Supreme Court invented it, insulated the "private" choices of the owners of public accommodations and other commercial businesses not only from the direct reach of the Fourteenth Amendment's guarantee of equal protection but also from congressional vindication of the rights of equal citizenship. Although "state action" remains an impediment to the application of the equal protection clause to some private conduct, Congress can protect, and has protected, the most important claims to participation by all citizens in society's public life.

To say that the principle of equal citizenship is the substantive core of the equal protection clause, and that the Supreme Court's recent equal protection jurisprudence has centered on the values of equal citizenship, is not to decide particular cases. Equal citizenship is not a decisional machine but a principle that informs judgment by reference to certain substantive values. Like other constitutional principles, it is inescapably open-ended. The Warren Court's expansion of the content of equal protection doctrine was regularly greeted with the criticism that the Court had not specified exactly how far its egalitarian principles would reach. The critics did no more than echo what Jeremy Bentham had said more than a century earlier: the abstraction, equality, is insatiable; where would it all end?

This "stopping-place" problem is implicit in any constitutional guarantee of equality. Most obviously, it lies at the center of the question of affirmative governmental obligations to reduce inequality. In a few decisions over the past three decades the Supreme Court has imposed on government the duty to compensate for the inability of INDIGENTS to pay various costs or fees required for effective access to the courts. The Burger Court's consciousness of the stopping-place problem produced two types of response. Some claims of access, although accepted, were explained as resting on rights to procedural fairness, and thus on due process rather than equal protection grounds. (See BODDIE V. CONNECTICUT, 1971.) Other access claims were rejected, halting further extension of the demands of equal protection. (See ROSS V. MOFFITT, 1974.) Yet the Court has not been willing to put an end to the notion that some inequalities, although not caused directly by the state, are constitutionally intolerable, requiring governmental action to relieve their victims from some of their consequences.

Similarly, consciousness of the stopping-place problem has influenced the Court's definition of what constitutes a legislative discrimination based on race, or gender, or, presumably, any other disfavored classification. After flirting in some school segregation cases with a view that would equate de facto with de jure segregation, the Court declared in the employment discrimination case of WASHINGTON V. DAVIS (1976) that it was not enough, in making a claim of racial discrimination, to show that legislation had a racially discriminatory impact. To succeed, such a claim must be based on a showing of official discriminatory purpose. (See LEGISLATION.) The "impact" principle, said the Court, "would be far reaching and would raise serious questions about, and perhaps invalidate, a whole range of tax, welfare, public service, regulatory, and licensing statutes that may be more burdensome to the poor and to the average black than to the more affluent white." In other words, where would it all end?

What is needed, in dealing with the stopping-place problem as with any other aspect of equal protection interest-balancing, is the guidance that can be found in the Fourteenth Amendment's substantive values. Some inequalities will invade the core values of equal citizenship, and others will touch them hardly at all. The level of justification required for governmental action—or failure to act—will vary according to the magnitude of that invasion. Some economic inequalities may be so severe as to impose a stigma of caste, but most do not. Part of our tradition of responsible citizenship, after all, is to provide for oneself and one's family. The principle of equal citizenship is not a charter for economic leveling but a presumptive guarantee against those inequalities that dehumanize or seriously impair one's ability to participate as a member of society. To say that such determinations turn on questions of degree is merely to acknowledge that no constitutional principle is a substitute for judicial judgment.

Since the late 1960s a number of governmental and private bodies have voluntarily taken steps to compensate for inequalities that are the legacy of past societal discrimination, and generally to integrate various institutions by race and by gender. These AFFIRMATIVE ACTION programs, sometimes in the form of racial or gender-based quotas for employment or housing or admission to higher education, do not merely equalize. Every equality begets another inequality. Even absent a quota, when a person's race becomes a relevant qualification for a job, all other relevant factors are diminished in weight. To put the matter more concretely, an individual can lose the competition for the job on the basis of his or her race. If affirmative action is constitutionally justified—and the Supreme Court has largely validated it—the reasons lie not in any lack of sympathy for such arguments, but in the weight of countervailing considerations supporting the programs. The Justices' various opinions upholding affirmative action have mainly sounded the theme of remedying past discrimination, but other arguments emphasize the urgency of integrating American institutions in the present generation.

The debate over affirmative action has touched a more general issue: the appropriate role of groups in equal protection analysis. In one view, group membership is simply irrelevant. The text of the equal protection clause provides its guarantees to "any person," and much of our constitutional tradition is individualistic. Yet, inescapably, a claim to equality is a claim made on behalf of a group. If every law draws some line of classification, then it is also true that every individual is potentially classifiable according to an enormous variety of characteristics. Legislative classification implies a selection of certain attributes as the relevant ones—the "merits" that justify conferring a benefit (or "demerits" that justify a burden). Once such a classification is written into law, any individual is classified either with the group of persons who possess the "merits" (or "demerits") or with the group of those who do not. To complain against a classification scheme is not merely to say "I am wronged," but to say "We—the whole group of individuals disadvantaged—are wronged." Indeed, any claim based on a rule of law is intelligible only as a demand to be treated the same as other members of a group, that is, all others who share the relevant "individual" attributes specified by the rule.

The origins of the Fourteenth Amendment strongly suggest that a group, defined by race just as the *Dred Scott* opinion had defined it, was intended to be the amendment's chief beneficiary. If today the equal protection clause prohibits other forms of inequality, there is nothing incongruous about viewing that development in one perspective as the recognition of the claims of groups of people: women, aliens, illegitimate children, homosexuals, the handicapped. When equal citizenship is denied, the denial typically takes a form that affects not merely isolated individuals but classes of people.

The equal protection clause limits only the states; nothing in the constitutional text expressly imposes an analogous limit on the federal government. Yet since BOLLING V. SHARPE (1954) the Supreme Court has consistently interpreted the Fifth Amendment's due process clause to guarantee equal protection against federal denial. This interpretation has roots in the original Constitution's assumption that the new national government would have a direct relationship with individuals. The idea of national citizenship was current long before the Civil Rights Act of 1866. And that citizenship, as Justice Bradley argued in his dissent in the *Slaughterhouse Cases*, implies some measure of equality before the law. *Bolling*, a companion case to *Brown v. Board of Education*, presented a challenge to school segregation in the District of Co-

lumbia. *Brown* held the segregation of state schools unconstitutional, and Chief Justice Warren said it would be "unthinkable" if a similar principle were not applied to the national government. After the Fourteenth Amendment's reaffirmation of national citizenship, such a result would, indeed, have been unthinkable.

The Warren Court's expansion of constitutional guarantees of equality necessarily implied an expansion of the powers of the national government. The Civil War amendments were reinterpreted to give Congress sweeping powers to reach virtually all racial discriminations, public and private. The Fourteenth Amendment's equal protection clause became the basis for intensified intervention by the federal courts into areas previously governed by local law and custom, as a new body of uniform national law replaced local autonomy. As the "state action" limitation was relaxed, the Constitution brought the commands of law to areas previously regulated by private institutional decision. In ALEXANDER BICKEL's phrase, the Warren Court's main themes were "egalitarian, legalitarian, and centralizing."

The desegregation of places of public accommodations in the South is an instructive example. The Supreme Court first held unconstitutional all forms of state-sponsored segregation, including segregation of public beaches, parks, golf courses, and restaurants. Then, cautiously, it began to apply the same reasoning to some privately owned public accommodations, finding "state action" in the most tenuous connections between public policy and the private decision to segregate. Finally, in HEART OF ATLANTA MOTEL CO. V. UNITED STATES (1964) the Court moved swiftly to validate the Civil Rights Act of 1964, which forbade segregation in most public accommodations that mattered. In all these actions the Court promoted the extension of a body of uniform national law to replace the local laws and customs that had long governed southern communities, with an earlier Supreme Court's blessing.

These changes in the law governing racial discrimination in public accommodations were, in one perspective, a repetition of a course of events that had been common in the Western world since the seventeenth century. An older system, basing a person's legal rights on his or her status in a hierarchical structure, came to be replaced by a newer law that applied impersonally to everyone. The abolition of slavery, the 1866 Civil Rights Act, the Civil War amendments—all had been earlier episodes in this same historical line. And the law that liberated individuals from domination based on race, like the law that previously had broken feudal hierarchies and the power of the guilds, was the law of the centralized state. If one were asked to compress three centuries of Western political history into three words, the words might be: "egalitarian, legalitarian, and centralizing."

Justice ROBERT H. JACKSON, concurring in EDWARDS V. CALIFORNIA (1941), remarked that the Fourteenth Amendment's privileges and immunities clause was aimed at making United States citizenship "the dominant and paramount allegiance among us." Whatever the historical warrant for that assertion, it reflects today's social fact. We think of ourselves primarily as citizens of the nation, and only secondarily as citizens of the several states. The Constitution itself has become our pre-eminent symbol of national community, and the judiciary's modern contributions to our sense of community have centered on the principle of equal citizenship.

It is hard to overstate the importance of the ideal of equality as a legitimizing force in American history. For the SOCIAL COMPACT theorists of the eighteenth century whose thinking was well-known to the Framers of the original Constitution, some measure of equality before the law was implicit in the idea of citizenship. DANIEL WEBSTER, speaking of "the LAW OF THE LAND," agreed: "The meaning is, that every citizen shall hold his life, liberty, property, and immunities, under the protection of the general rules which govern society." By Webster's time, support for the principle of equality of opportunity could be found even among the most comfortable Americans, who saw in that principle a way to justify their advantages. More generally, the egalitarian spirit that has promoted a national consciousness has also lent legitimacy to government. There has been just enough truth in the belief that "anyone can grow up to be President" to provide a critical measure of the diffuse loyalty that is an essential ingredient of nationhood.

Never in our history has it been true that *anyone* might aspire to the presidency. Slavery and racial discrimination are only the most obvious and uglier counterexamples; not until our own time have women's aspirations to such high position become realistic. Yet the guarantee of equal protection of the laws, even during the long decades when lawyers deemed it a constitutional trifle, stood as a statement of an important American ideal. Much of the growth in our constitutional law has resulted when the downtrodden have called the rest of us to account, asking whether we intend to live up to the principles we profess. Vindication of the constitutional promise of equal citizenship did not take its rightful place on our judicial agenda for an unconscionably long time, and it remains far

from complete. What is most remarkable, however, is the nourishment that the promise—the promise alone—has provided for a national community.

KENNETH L. KARST

Bibliography

BELL, DERRICK A., JR. 1980 *Race, Racism, and American Law,* 2nd ed. Boston: Little, Brown.
BICKEL, ALEXANDER M. 1970 *The Supreme Court and the Idea of Progress.* New York: Harper & Row.
BLACK, CHARLES L., JR. 1969 *Structure and Relationship in Constitutional Law.* Pages 51–66. Baton Rouge: Louisiana State University Press.
ELY, JOHN HART 1980 *Democracy and Distrust: A Theory of Judicial Review.* Cambridge, Mass.: Harvard University Press.
FISS, OWEN M. 1976 Groups and the Equal Protection Clause. *Philosophy and Public Affairs* 5:107–177.
KARST, KENNETH L. 1977 The Supreme Court, 1976 Term—Foreword: Equal Citizenship under the Fourteenth Amendment. *Harvard Law Review* 91:1–68.
KINOY, ARTHUR 1967 The Constitutional Right of Negro Freedom. *Rutgers Law Review* 21:387–441.
MICHELMAN, FRANK I. 1969 The Supreme Court, 1968 Term—Foreword: On Protecting the Poor Through the Fourteenth Amendment. *Harvard Law Review* 83:7–59.
POLE, J. R. 1978 *The Pursuit of Equality in American History.* Berkeley: University of California Press.
RAE, DOUGLAS 1981 *Equalities.* Cambridge, Mass.: Harvard University Press.
TOCQUEVILLE, ALEXIS DE 1945 *Democracy in America,* P. Bradley, ed., 2 vols. New York: Vintage Books.
TUSSMAN, JOSEPH and TEN BROEK, JACOBUS 1949 The Equal Protection of the Laws. *California Law Review* 37:341–381.
WESTEN, PETER 1982 The Empty Idea of Equality. *Harvard Law Review* 95:537–596.

EQUAL RIGHTS AMENDMENT

In March 1972, Congress proposed an Equal Rights Amendment (ERA) to the United States Constitution. The amendment provided:

Section 1. Equality of rights under the law shall not be denied or abridged by the United States or by any State on account of sex.
Section 2. The Congress shall have the power to enforce, by appropriate legislation, the provisions of this article.
Section 3. The Amendment shall take effect two years after the date of ratification.

In May 1982, the extended deadline for ratification expired without the necessary approval from three-fourths of the states; fifteen had never ratified and five had voted to rescind their ratification. Challenges to the legality of those rescissions and to Congress's extension of the ratification deadline became moot.

Proponents subsequently reintroduced the amendment in Congress, thus continuing a campaign that began a half-century earlier. Some version of an equal rights amendment had surfaced in every congressional term between 1923 and 1972. In the view of most proponents, the text adopted in 1972 was designed to prohibit gender classifications except those concerning personal privacy, physical characteristics, or past discrimination. The rationale was that a constitutional prohibition would avoid piecemeal remedies for various forms of discrimination. Such a mandate would also subject sex-based classifications to a more rigorous standard of review than that prevailing under FOURTEENTH AMENDMENT doctrine, which allows discrimination substantially related to an important state purpose.

Although conceived as a measure to unite women, the amendment has often divided them. Throughout its history, the ERA campaign has triggered fundamental controversies about the meaning of equality and the means to attain it in a society marked by significant disparities in sexual roles. Much debate has centered not on legal entitlements but on cultural aspirations. Dispute has focused on the amendment's effect concerning laws purportedly advantaging women, such as protective labor legislation, marital support requirements, and military service exemptions. Particularly during the earlier part of the century, opponents contended that equality in formal mandates could never secure equality in fact. So long as female wage earners and homemakers were more economically vulnerable than men, a demand for equal rights appeared out of touch with social realities. By contrast, ERA proponents contended that protective legislation had often "protected" women from opportunities for higher paid vocations, and had legitimated stereotypes on which invidious discrimination rested. Supporters also noted that by the time Congress proposed the amendment in 1972, much sex-based regulation had been either invalidated or extended to men, and that which remained could be cast in sex-neutral terms.

So too, much of the discrimination that the amendment was originally designed to redress was, by the 1970s, illegal under various judicial, executive, and legislative mandates. Accordingly, the ERA ratification campaign frequently focused on symbolic rather than legal implications. To proponents, a constitutional mandate would serve as an important affirmation of women's equal status and as a catalyst for change in social practices beyond the scope of legal regulation. For opponents, however, the amendment's symbolic subtext represented an assault less on gender discrimination than on gender differences, and an invitation for further encroachments on states' rights.

In the ratification struggle of the 1970s, ERA supporters lacked the leverage to make their interests felt. But if the equal rights campaign helps inspire and empower women to expand their political influence, then the struggle itself may prove more important than its constitutional consequences.

DEBORAH L. RHODE

Bibliography
BOLES, JANET 1979 *The Politics of the Equal Rights Amendment: Conflict and the Decision Process.* New York: Longmans.
BROWN, BARBARA A.; EMERSON, THOMAS I.; FALK, GAIL; and FREEDMAN, ANN E. 1971 The Equal Rights Amendment: A Constitutional Basis for Equal Rights for Women. *Yale Law Journal* 80:872–985.
RHODE, DEBORAH L. 1983 Equal Rights in Retrospect. *Journal of Law and Inequality* 1:1–72.

EQUITABLE RESTRAINT

See: Abstention Doctrines

EQUITY

First named (in Article III) among the subjects to which the judicial power "shall extend" are "all Cases, in Law and Equity, arising under this Constitution, the Laws of the United States, and Treaties made, or which shall be made, under their authority." The word "equity" has here a technical meaning well comprehended by American lawyers of the eighteenth century, and today still generally familiar to lawyers in all legal systems derived from that of England. The explanation is necessarily historical.

In a development more than well begun in the Middle Ages, and pretty much completed by Stuart times, England developed a unique double system of courts at the national level—the courts of "law," or COMMON LAW courts, and the "court of equity"— or, as it was often called, the "court of chancery."

The common law courts administered a system of law that was radically deficient, first as to remedies available, and, second, as to the breadth of considerations that could be taken into account in the formation of decisions. These courts could in most cases award only damages in money, in many cases a step inadequate to the doing of full justice. The common law courts were also excessively formalistic. If, for example, an error occurred in the transcription of a written contract, the common law courts had no conceptual apparatus for dealing with the mistake. Similarly, they had little capacity for taking into account the problems created by fraud. And the "trust," an institution of great importance, was utterly unknown to the "common law."

During the Middle Ages, suitors who could not get full justice out of the common law courts began to appeal to the Lord Chancellor, a high royal official, for supplementary or corrective help. By Tudor times, this practice had become firmly institutionalized, so that the Lord Chancellor became in some sense a judicial officer, hearing and dealing with such pleas. Little by little, the "chancery" came to be a court. This court had at its disposal a remedy enormously more versatile and efficient than the award of damages—the remedy of the order, or command, that the defendant do or refrain from doing something. The chancery court, in contrast to the courts of common law, knew nothing of the jury; the Chancellor decided all issues of fact and law.

This "court of chancery" opened its eyes, moreover, to many things the common law courts were institutionally disabled from seeing. While a suitor in the common law courts might, for example, get a JUDGMENT in his favor on a written contract procured by fraud on his part, the chancery court might order him to give up the fraudulently procured instrument, or to refrain from suing on it, or even to refrain from collecting on a "law" judgment he had already procured by using it.

Because this chancery court so often intervened in the name of a higher justice or of "conscience," it came to be thought of as (and called) a "court of equity." By the time of the drafting of the Constitution, the doctrines and practices of this kind of "equity" had become well systematized. And most of the new states had borrowed from English practice the two-part system of "law" courts and "chancery" courts, with the doctrines and remedial apparatus of equity available in the latter. It is against this background that the constitutional phrase, "cases in law and equity," is to be understood. "Cases in law" were such cases as would be heard by the common law courts; "cases in equity" were such as would be heard by the Court of Chancery, in England or in a state mirroring the English division.

At the very beginning, the new national government rejected (in the JUDICIARY ACT OF 1789) the idea of totally separate courts of "law" and of "equity."

The lower federal courts combined "legal" and "equitable" JURISDICTION in the same judges. But the ancient division was in some sense continued. Down to 1938, the federal district court had the two separate sides of "law" and "equity," respectively—in addition to such special jurisdictions as admiralty and bankruptcy. Even today, after the formal merger of "law" and "equity" cases under the single name of "civil action," lawyers still refer, for example, to the INJUNCTION (an order to do or not to do something) as "equitable relief."

"Equity" cases, in the language of Article III, are of great importance. The injunction is enormously more flexible and powerful than the remedies—mostly the award of damages—available to the court in a "case at law." Dramatic examples abound. It would have been impossible even to begin thinking about the lower federal courts' desegregating the schools if those courts had not had jurisdiction over "cases in equity" seeking orders to state officials. On this jurisdictional grant, indeed, rests the whole elaborate development of efficacious relief against official action thought to be unconstitutional—ranging from injunctions against the enforcement of unconstitutional laws (as in PIERCE V. SOCIETY OF SISTERS, 1925, enjoining state enforcement of a law requiring all pupils to go to public schools) to the running of state prisons by an Alabama district judge. (See INSTITUTIONAL LITIGATION.) The modern history of practical constitutional safeguards is a history of the use of the "equitable" remedy of injunction, together with the remedy of the DECLARATORY JUDGMENT—a remedy that would probably have been judged outside the "judicial power" were it not for its close analogy to "cases in equity."

Another characteristic of "cases in equity," overpoweringly important in the use of the national judicial power to protect constitutional rights against action of the states, is that the "court of equity" does not use the jury. This, as far as we can tell, is a gift of history; there appears to be no intrinsic reason why a local jury should not find "the facts" in, say, school desegregation cases. Experience shows that local juries will not often convict, for example, in prosecutions for CIVIL RIGHTS crimes, where the jury is constitutionally required. The whole course of development of national protection of human rights against local oppression might have been quite different if it were not for the fact that the "court of equity," the Lord Chancellor's court, sat without a jury—so that the federal judge, wielding the vital weapons in the "equity" remedial armory, does the same.

CHARLES L. BLACK, JR.

Bibliography

FISS, OWEN M. 1972 *Injunctions.* Mineola, N.Y.: Foundation Press.

MCCLINTOCK, HENRY LACY 1948 *Handbook of the Principles of Equity.* St. Paul, Minn.: West Publishing Co.

ERDMAN ACT
30 Stat. 424 (1898)

The report of a commission appointed by President GROVER CLEVELAND to investigate the Pullman strike of 1894 (see IN RE DEBS) prompted this act, one of the earliest federal acts providing for the arbitration of railway labor disputes. The act applied to all railroads and their employees engaged in INTERSTATE COMMERCE and provided mediation of any labor dispute "seriously interrupting or threatening to interrupt" interstate commerce. If mediation failed to resolve the dispute, the parties could turn to an arbitration board whose award would be binding and enforceable through EQUITY proceedings. Neither strikes nor lockouts were permitted during arbitration or ninety days after an award. Section 10 made it a MISDEMEANOR for any employer to require, as a condition of employment, any discriminatory agreements, particularly with regard to union membership. Clearly aimed at outlawing YELLOW DOG CONTRACTS, section 10 fell in ADAIR V. UNITED STATES (1906) as a violation of FREEDOM OF CONTRACT. The act otherwise operated quite successfully, and Congress fortified its mediation provisions in 1913. A bitter nationwide strike in which both sides refused to invoke mediation, however, forced replacement of the act three years later with the ADAMSON EIGHT-HOUR ACT.

DAVID GORDON

Bibliography

TAYLOR, BENJAMIN J. and WITNEY, FRED 1971 *Labor Relations Law,* 2nd ed. Englewood Cliffs, N.J.: Prentice-Hall.

ERIE RAILROAD CO. v. TOMPKINS
304 U.S. 64 (1938)

The Supreme Court in *Erie* posed the question whether the "oft-challenged doctrine of SWIFT V. TYSON (1842) shall now be disapproved," and answered that it should. The Court rejected its earlier construction of the Rules of Decision Act, originally section 34 of the JUDICIARY ACT OF 1789, and held that the "laws of the several states"—which, except as otherwise required by federal law, are to be "regarded as rules of decision" in civil actions in the federal courts "in cases where they apply"—included all of the decisional or COMMON LAW of the states.

Erie, like *Swift,* involved an exercise of the DIVERSITY JURISDICTION of the federal courts. In *Erie,* plaintiff Tompkins brought a federal court suit against the railroad for personal injuries, and the court of appeals upheld a substantial jury verdict in the face of the railroad's claim that it had not violated the limited duty owed to plaintiff under the decisional law of the state where the injury occurred. That court concluded that, in the absence of a state statute, the question of the scope of the railroad's duty was one not of "local" but of "general" law, and under the general law the railroad had a duty of care that the jury could properly find to have been broken.

The Supreme Court, in an opinion by Justice LOUIS D. BRANDEIS, reversed and remanded for application of state law with respect to the scope of the railroad's duty. The Court concluded that (1) the refusal in *Swift* to read the mandate of the Rules of Decision Act as embracing all of the decisional law of the states was based on an incorrect construction of the purpose of that act; (2) the construction in *Swift* had prevented uniformity in the administration of state law and had permitted "grave discrimination by noncitizens [of a state] against citizens"; and (3) the doctrine of *Swift* represented "an unconstitutional assumption of powers by the Courts of the United States." Justices PIERCE BUTLER and JAMES C. MCREYNOLDS dissented; Justice STANLEY F. REED concurred in part, believing it unnecessary to reach the constitutional issue addressed by the Court.

Although the parties in *Erie* had not briefed the question whether *Swift* should be overruled, there had been intimations of the Court's intentions in earlier majority and dissenting opinions. And while the *Erie* result itself still finds general acceptance, the years since the decision have seen much debate about its rationale, scope, and application.

DAVID L. SHAPIRO

(SEE ALSO: *Federal Common Law, Civil.*)

ERNST, MORRIS
(1888–1976)

With his colleague ARTHUR GARFIELD HAYS, Morris Ernst served as general counsel to the AMERICAN CIVIL LIBERTIES UNION from 1929 to 1954. Together with Hays and ROGER BALDWIN, Ernst fought to protect individual rights against government action. Although he excoriated both the Ku Klux Klan and the Communist party, he defended members of both organizations. He was a staunch opponent of government censorship and defended James Joyce's novel against OBSCENITY charges in the ULYSSES trial (1934). Ernst participated in a number of well-known cases, including COMMONWEALTH OF MASSACHUSETTS V. SACCO AND VANZETTI (1921), HAGUE V. C.I.O. (1939), and the *Associated Press v. N.L.R.B.* (1937), one of the WAGNER ACT CASES. He wrote several popular books championing civil liberties.

DAVID GORDON

ERROR, WRIT OF

A writ of error is an order of an appellate court, directing a lower court to transmit the record of a case that it has decided, for review by the appellate court. The JUDICIARY ACT OF 1789 established the writ of error as the means of invoking the APPELLATE JURISDICTION of both the CIRCUIT COURTS and the Supreme Court. For a century, the writ of error was, in practice, virtually the exclusive method of invoking review by the Supreme Court. In the cases specified by law for issuance of the writ, review by the Supreme Court was obligatory. In 1891 Congress reorganized the federal judiciary, establishing the circuit courts of appeals. (See CIRCUIT COURTS OF APPEALS ACT.) In some cases, these courts' decisions were final, unless the courts certified questions for review by the Supreme Court, or the Supreme Court in its discretion granted WRITS OF CERTIORARI to review their decisions. In 1925, in the course of reducing the Supreme Court's obligatory JURISDICTION and expanding the Court's discretionary control of its docket, Congress changed the name of the writ of error; since that time the Supreme Court's theoretically obligatory appellate jurisdiction has been invoked by APPEAL.

KENNETH L. KARST

Bibliography

ROBERTSON, REYNOLDS and KIRKHAM, FRANCIS R. 1951 *Jurisdiction of the Supreme Court of the United States,* ed. Richard F. Wolfson and Philip B. Kurland. Pages 191–196, 756, 806–807. Albany, N.Y.: Matthew Bender.

ERVIN, SAMUEL J.
(1896–1985)

A conservative Democrat who graduated from Harvard Law School in 1922, Samuel J. Ervin described himself as an "ol' country lawyer" from North Carolina, his native state. In 1954 he left that state's supreme court to enter the United States Senate. During his two decades as a senator, he supported business against labor and opposed CIVIL RIGHTS legislation, equal rights for women, voting by eighteen-year-olds, and federal encroachments on STATES' RIGHTS. He also became a strict separationist on church–state issues, and he opposed intrusive searches, computer invasions of privacy, preventive detention, and any other measures he deemed subversive of the Constitution. By 1973 he was respected as the Senate's expert on the Constitution. Central casting destined him to be chairman that year of the Senate's Select Committee on Presidential Campaign Activities—the WATERGATE Committee. As chairman, he was a relentless but fair interrogator who expressed outrage when witnesses equivocated or lied. The televised hearings made him a national celebrity as the watchdog of the Constitution who preached the constitutional responsibilities of those entrusted with public office. Ervin projected a grandfatherly image of a judicious moralist, the very model of integrity when models were in short supply. The public adored "Senator Sam," and he adored the Constitution.

LEONARD W. LEVY

Bibliography

ERVIN, SAMUEL J., JR. 1980 *The Whole Truth: The Watergate Conspiracy.* New York: Random House.

ERZNOZNIK v. CITY OF JACKSONVILLE
422 U.S. 205 (1975)

An ordinance prohibited drive-in movie theaters from showing films containing nudity on screens visible from public streets or places. Conceding that the films were constitutionally protected speech, the city asserted an authority to protect its citizens, particularly minors, against unwilling exposure to offensive materials. The Supreme Court declared the ordinance unconstitutional, holding that people on public streets, unlike people in their homes or people on buses who are a captive audience, have only a limited interest in privacy which does not justify the city's discrimination among movies based solely on content.

KIM MCLANE WARDLAW

(SEE ALSO: *Obscenity*.)

ESCH-CUMMINGS TRANSPORTATION ACT
41 Stat. 456 (1920)

Congress favored the return of the railroads to private ownership and operation after government control during World War I. This act accomplished that objective and altered Congress's regulatory approach. It did not seek to prevent abuses so much as to strengthen the industry and foster the public interest. The act granted the Interstate Commerce Commission extensive new powers including the authority to set minimum rates, oversee fiscal operation of the roads, regulate acquisitions and consolidations, and supervise services. One provision prescribed a rate-making rule to assure "a FAIR RETURN upon the aggregate value of the railroad property," allowing the ICC to determine what constituted such a return. A recapture clause, inserted to protect weaker lines, required that roads earning a return over six percent divide that profit between a reserve fund for their own stability and a general fund (administered by the ICC) to compensate those railroads earning under four and one-half percent. The Supreme Court sustained this clause in DAYTON-GOOSE CREEK RAILWAY V. UNITED STATES (1924). The act also established labor boards with JURISDICTION over a variety of disputes.

DAVID GORDON

Bibliography

SHARFMAN, ISAIAH L. 1931–1937 *The Interstate Commerce Commission*. Vol. 1. New York: Commonwealth Fund.

ESCOBEDO v. ILLINOIS
378 U.S. 478 (1964)

Daniel Escobedo was arrested and taken to the police station for questioning. Over the course of several hours, his repeated requests to see his lawyer were refused and his lawyer sought unsuccessfully to consult with him. The Supreme Court held that Escobedo's subsequent confession was obtained in violation of his Sixth Amendment RIGHT TO COUNSEL. For the first time, the Court spoke of "an absolute constitutional right to remain silent," which the presence of a lawyer would facilitate. *Escobedo* is important also because it presaged MIRANDA V. ARIZONA (1966) in discussing the possibility that warnings about the right to counsel might serve to cure the infirmity of in-custody interrogation.

Although *Escobedo* retains historical significance, the arguments in POLICE INTERROGATION AND CONFESSION cases have largely shifted from the Sixth to the Fifth Amendment with an emphasis on whether warnings were given, and given correctly, and whether the right to remain silent was waived.

The case has lost authority as precedent in another respect. It seemed to establish a practical flexible standard for the time when Sixth Amendment rights would come into play: when "the investigation is no longer a general inquiry into an unresolved crime but has begun to focus on a particular suspect." This approach was specifically abandoned in *Kirby v. Illinois* (1972), when the court limited *Escobedo* to its facts and ruled that the right to counsel does not attach until adversary judicial proceedings have been initiated.

BARBARA ALLEN BABCOCK

ESPIONAGE ACT
40 Stat. 451 (1917)

When on April 2, 1917, President WOODROW WILSON asked Congress to recognize a STATE OF WAR, he included in his indictment of Germany the activities of German agents in the United States. Such activity, he said, should be treated with "a firm hand of stern repression." Nine weeks later, a much discussed and much amended Espionage Act was signed into law.

The initial measure, an amalgamation of seventeen bills prepared in the attorney general's office, was intended to "outlaw spies and subversive activities by foreign agents." Critics, particularly in the American press, quickly complained that the measure was far too restrictive and imposed a type of PRIOR RESTRAINT AND CENSORSHIP potentially destructive to basic American liberties. Thus, despite Wilson's contention that the administration must have authority to censor the press since this was "absolutely necessary to the public safety," the most overt censorship provisions were removed. The belief of a majority of national lawmakers that now the bill could not be used to suppress critical opinion overlooked the fact that two of the twelve titles of the act as passed still bore directly on freedom of expression. One provided punishment for (1) making or conveying false reports for the benefit of the enemy; (2) seeking to cause disobedience in the armed forces; and (3) willfully obstructing the recruiting or enlistment service. Another section closed the mails to any item violating any of the act's provisions.

The constitutional basis of these two provisions rested on a broad interpretation of the federal WAR POWERS and upon the argument that a denial of use of the mails did not constitute censorship, since the federal courts had ruled that the mails constituted an optional federal service. Thus, it was argued, refusal to extend the facility did not deprive anyone of a constitutional right. Further, the measure's supporters argued that FREEDOM OF SPEECH was not absolute and could not protect a person who deliberately sought to obstruct the national war effort.

The difficulty of applying the law, however, was clear from the outset, since the statute sought to punish questionable intent, a difficult factor to measure. With punishment set at a $10,000 fine, imprisonment for up to twenty years, or both, and with its interpretation largely in the hands of patriotic enforcers, many suffered under the measure and its subsequent amendments. The Justice Department prosecuted more than 2,000 cases. At least 1,050 citizens were convicted under its terms, including Industrial Workers of the World leaders, Socialists (especially Eugene V. Debs), and a number of suspect hyphenates, particularly German-Americans, whose verbal criticism of aspects of the war were often brutally repressed. The Supreme Court upheld the constitutionality of the act's prohibitions on causing disobedience in the armed forces and obstructing enlistment in a series of postwar decisions: SCHENCK V. UNITED STATES (1919), FROHWERK V. UNITED STATES (1919); DEBS V. UNITED STATES (1919).

Under the mails provisions, the postmaster general exercised virtually dictatorial authority over the effective circulation of the American press, a power which he used capriciously and subjectively for punitive reasons. In an effort to preserve FIRST AMENDMENT values through the process of statutory construction, Judge LEARNED HAND construed the mails provision narrowly to exclude its application to ordinary criticism of government policies, including war policy. Hand's decision, however, was reversed by the court of appeals. (See MASSES PUBLISHING CO. V. PATTEN, 1917.)

The measure remained on the books through the 1920s and 1930s and was reenacted in March 1940, Congress increasing its penalties for peacetime violation. The Supreme Court narrowed its application in *Hartzel v. United States* (1944) by interpreting its provisions through a literal application of Holmes's clear and present danger test. The government again turned to it in 1971, seeking unsuccessfully to prevent the publication by the *New York Times* of the "Pentagon papers," which the government called harmful to the security of the United States. (See NEW YORK TIMES CO. V. UNITED STATES, 1971.)

PAUL L. MURPHY

Bibliography

CHAFEE, ZECHARIAH 1941 *Free Speech in the United States.* Cambridge, Mass.: Harvard University Press.

MURPHY, PAUL 1979 *World War I and the Origin of Civil Liberties in the United States.* New York: Norton.

ESTABLISHMENT CLAUSE

See: Establishment of Religion; First Amendment; Religious Liberty; Separation of Church and State

ESTABLISHMENT OF RELIGION

The FIRST AMENDMENT begins with the clause, "Congress shall make no law respecting an establishment of religion. . . ." There are two basic interpretations of what the framers meant by this clause. In EVERSON V. BOARD OF EDUCATION (1947), the first decision on the clause, the Supreme Court unanimously adopted the broad interpretation, although the Justices then and thereafter disagreed on its application. (See SEPARATION OF CHURCH AND STATE.) Justice HUGO L. BLACK declared that the clause means not only that government cannot set up a church but also that government cannot aid all religions impartially or levy a tax for the support of any religious activities, institutions, or practices. "In the words of [THOMAS] JEFFERSON," Black said, "the clause against establishment of religion by laws was intended to erect 'a wall of separation between Church and State.'"

EDWARD S. CORWIN, a distinguished constitutional scholar who espoused the narrow view of the clause, asserted that the Court's interpretation was "untrue historically." What the clause does, he wrote, "and all that it does, is to forbid Congress to give any religious faith, sect, or denomination preferred status.

. . . The historical record shows beyond peradventure that the core idea of 'an establishment of religion' comprises the idea of preference; and that any act of public authority favorable to religion in general cannot, without manifest falsification of history, be brought under the ban of that phase" (Corwin, "Supreme Court as National School Board," pp. 10, 20). Justice POTTER STEWART, dissenting in ENGEL V. VITALE (1962), endorsed the narrow view when he noted that a nondenominational school prayer did not confront the Court with "the establishment of a state church" or an "official religion."

The debate in the First Congress, which proposed the First Amendment, provides support for neither the broad nor the narrow interpretation. The history of the drafting of the clause, however, is revealing. Congress carefully considered and rejected various phrasings that embraced the narrow interpretation. At bottom the amendment was an expression of the intention of the Framers of the Constitution to prevent Congress from acting in the field of religion. The "great object" of the BILL OF RIGHTS, JAMES MADISON had said, when introducing his draft of amendments to the House, was to "limit and qualify the powers of Government" for the purpose of making certain that none of the powers granted could be exercised in forbidden fields, including religion. The history of the drafting of the establishment clause does not provide a clear understanding of what was meant by the phrase "an establishment of religion." But the narrow interpretation, which permits government aid to religion in general or on a nonpreferential basis, leads to the impossible conclusion that the First Amendment *added* to Congress's powers. The amendment meant to restrict Congress to the powers that it possessed, and since it had no power to legislate on matters concerning religion, and therefore could not support religion on any basis, Congress would have had no such power even in the absence of the First Amendment. To suppose that an express prohibition on power vests or creates power is capriciously unreasonable. The Bill of Rights, as Madison said, was not framed "to imply powers not meant to be included in the enumeration."

Congress did not define "an establishment of religion" because its members knew from common experience what they meant. At the time of the framing of the amendment, six states maintained or authorized establishments of religion. That amendment denied to Congress the power to do what those states were doing, and since *Everson* the states come under the same ban. An establishment meant to the framers of the amendment what it meant in those states. Thus,

reference to the American experience with establishments at the time of the framing of the Bill of Rights is essential to any understanding of what the clause in question meant.

The narrow interpretation is based on European precedents but the European form of an establishment was not the American form, except in the Southern colonies before the American Revolution, and the European meaning of establishment was not the American meaning. The revolution triggered a pent-up movement for separation of church and state in the nine states that had establishments. Of these nine, North Carolina (1776), New York (1777), and Virginia (1786) separated church and state. Each of the remaining six states made concessions to anti-establishment sentiment by broadening their old establishments. After the Revolution, none maintained a single or exclusive establishment. In all six an establishment of religion was not restricted to a state church or a system of public support of one denomination; in all an establishment meant public support of all denominations and sects on a nonpreferential basis.

Three of these six states were in New England. The MASSACHUSETTS CONSTITUTION (1780) authorized its towns and parishes to levy taxes for the support of Protestant churches, provided that each taxpayer's money go to the support "of his own religious sect or denomination" and added that "no subordination of any one sect or denomination to the other shall ever be established by law." An establishment in Massachusetts meant government support of religion. Congregationalists, for a few decades, benefited the most, because they were the most numerous and resorted to various tricks to fleece non-Congregationalists out of their share of religious taxes. But the fact remains that Massachusetts had a multiple, not a single, establishment under which Baptist, Episcopalian, Methodist, and Unitarian churches were publicly supported until the establishment ended in 1833. In 1784 Connecticut and New Hampshire modeled their multiple establishments after that of Massachusetts, ending them in 1818 and 1819, respectively.

In the South, where the Episcopal Church was the sole established church before the revolution, three states either maintained or permitted establishments of religion, and in each the multiple form was the only legal one. Maryland (1776) permitted its legislature to tax for the support of "the Christian religion," with the proviso that every person had the right to designate the church of his choice, making every Christian church an established church on a nonpreferential basis. The legislature sought to pass an enabling act in 1785, but the nonpreferential system was denounced as an establishment and defeated. The situation in Georgia was the same as in Maryland, and a revised constitution (1789), which was in effect when the First Amendment was adopted, continued the multiple establishment system, allowing each person to support only his own church. South Carolina restricted its multiple nonpreferential establishment to Protestant churches. The last Southern establishment died in 1810. Virginia sought to emulate the Maryland system, but a general assessment bill benefiting all Christian churches failed, thanks to the opposition of most non-Episcopal denominations and to MADISON'S MEMORIAL AND REMONSTRANCE; the VIRGINIA STATUTE OF RELIGIOUS FREEDOM (1786) then separated church and state.

In none of the six states maintaining or allowing establishments at the time of the framing of the First Amendment was any church but a Christian one established. The multiple establishments of that time comprehended the churches of every denomination and sect with a sufficient number of adherents to form a church. Where Protestantism was established it was synonymous with religion; there were either no Jews or no Roman Catholics or too few of them to make a difference. Where Christianity was established, as in Maryland, which had a significant Roman Catholic minority, Jews were scarcely known. To contend that exclusive establishments of one religion existed in each of the six states ignores the novel American experiment with multiple establishments on an impartial basis. Europe knew only single-church establishments. An establishment of religion in the United States at the time of the First Amendment included nonpreferential government recognition, aid, or sponsorship of religion. The framers of the amendment looked to their own experience, not Europe's.

LEONARD W. LEVY

(SEE ALSO: *Grand Rapids School District v. Ball, 1985; Larkin v. Grendel's Den, 1983; Lynch v. Donnelly, 1984; Marsh v. Chambers, 1983; Mueller v. Allen, 1983; Thornton v. Caldor, Inc., 1985; Valley Forge Christian Schools v. Americans United, 1982; Wallace v. Jaffree, 1985; Widmar v. Vincent, 1984.*)

Bibliography

ANTIEAU, CHESTER JAMES, ET AL. 1964 *Freedom from Federal Establishment: Formation and Early History of the First Amendment Religion Clauses.* Milwaukee, Wisc.: Bruce Publishing Co.
COBB, SANFORD H. 1902 *The Rise of Religious Liberty in America.* New York: Macmillan.
CORWIN, EDWARD S. 1949 The Supreme Court as National School Board. *Law and Contemporary Problems* 14:3–22.
LEVY, LEONARD W. 1986 *The Establishment Clause: Religion and the First Amendment.* New York: Macmillan.

ESTELLE v. SMITH
451 U.S. 454 (1981)

A unanimous Supreme Court held that the protection of the MIRANDA RULES applied to every phase of an in-custody prosecution, and that a psychiatrist's testimony introduced at the penalty phase of a capital trial violated the RIGHT AGAINST SELF-INCRIMINATION. At the pretrial interview on which the testimony was based, the defendant had not received the appropriate warnings about his right to silence.

LEONARD W. LEVY

ESTES v. TEXAS
381 U.S. 532 (1965)

The trial of Billy Sol Estes for swindling involved a FREE PRESS/FAIR TRIAL confrontation in which the Supreme Court held that televising trials was inherently prejudicial to a FAIR TRIAL. Circuslike live television and radio broadcasts of Estes's pretrial hearings involved such extensive disruption of the courtroom that many changes were ordered for coverage of the trial. Although live broadcasts of the actual trial were forbidden, excerpts from the proceedings were broadcast regularly.

The Court split 5–4 on the constitutionality of televising the proceedings. Justices HUGO L. BLACK, WILLIAM J. BRENNAN, POTTER STEWART, and BYRON R. WHITE called the practice unwise and dangerous, but not constitutionally objectionable. Chief Justice EARL WARREN and Justices ARTHUR J. GOLDBERG and WILLIAM O. DOUGLAS joined an opinion by Justice TOM C. CLARK seeking to ban television completely from the courts—subject to future developments (see CHANDLER V. FLORIDA, 1981)—as a violation of the right to a fair trial. Both the jury and the witnesses, Clark declared, would be under great pressure and be more self-conscious, aware of a large public audience; prospective witnesses might be influenced by the proceedings. The judge would have additional responsibilities (and temptations), and the defendant would be subject to "a form of mental—if not physical—harassment." Clark said, "A defendant on trial for a specific crime is entitled to his day in court, not in a stadium, or a city or nationwide arena." Justice JOHN MARSHALL HARLAN approved the ban here, but indicated he would do so only in cases of "great notoriety."

DAVID GORDON

EUCLID v. AMBLER REALTY COMPANY
272 U.S. 365 (1926)

This case established the constitutionality of ZONING laws to regulate land use. In *Euclid* a Cleveland suburb sought to preserve an area of single-family dwellings by excluding even two-family dwellings and apartment houses, as well as commercial properties and public buildings. Against claims drawn from supposed deprivations of liberty and property without DUE PROCESS OF LAW and a supposed denial of the EQUAL PROTECTION OF THE LAWS, a 6–3 Supreme Court, speaking through Justice GEORGE SUTHERLAND, sustained the comprehensive zoning ordinance. It was, the Court ruled, a legitimate STATE POLICE POWER measure intended to maintain the residential area and thus protect the community's health, peace, and safety. As a result of this leading decision on comprehensive zoning laws, no argument drawn from the FOURTEENTH AMENDMENT or from the takings clause is likely to survive judicial scrutiny in the absence of an ordinance that is demonstrably unrelated to the improvement of a community.

LEONARD W. LEVY

EUTHANASIA

Euthanasia, or mercy killing, has long engaged the attention of philosophers and others concerned with the morality of offering the incurably ill the dignity of a choice whether to end their lives. Only recently, however, has euthanasia become a subject of constitutional debate. Active assistance to suicide remains a crime throughout the country, and the sort of euthanasia actively practiced on the defective newborn and on some very old persons who are ill beyond hope is also murder. Neither of these forms of euthanasia raises any serious constitutional issue. It is "passive euthanasia"—the withholding of aids to the preservation of life—that has been discussed in constitutional terms. Unfortunately, "the right to die," perhaps because it is so effective a slogan, has beclouded discussion of genuine issues of personal choice.

The Supreme Court has not yet confronted these matters. Undoubtedly, however, there is some constitutional right to refuse medical treatment. Compulsory VACCINATION has been upheld against the claim that it deprived its reluctant beneficiary of liberty without DUE PROCESS OF LAW. A strong governmental interest in protecting public health justified that invasion of an unwilling person's body, however, and no such interest is present in the ordinary case of a person who refuses medical treatment. Even absent any claim to RELIGIOUS LIBERTY, the idea of a right to refuse treatment follows easily from the Supreme Court's modern recognition of constitutional rights to personal autonomy, offered in the name of "privacy." The Court's decisions affirming the right of a woman to have an abortion are cases in point.

In the context of euthanasia, however, the constitutional right to refuse treatment fits awkwardly into the typical dilemma a patient's doctors and relatives face. Even if a person has previously directed her doctors not to use artificial means to prolong life, she will ordinarily be unconscious for a time before dying and thus incapable of forming any present intention to refuse aid. Usually, of course, the problem of passive euthanasia arises in connection with patients in a persistent vegetative state who have given no directions whatever to their doctors. To invoke the concept of a constitutional right to die in such a case, as New Jersey's supreme court did in *Matter of Quinlan* (1976), is to beg the critical question whether someone in such a state can have any rights at all. The decision of the *Quinlan* court authorizing the termination of artificial life supports seems justified, but surely its justification appropriately responds to interests of the patient's relatives, not the patient's constitutional RIGHT OF PRIVACY.

KENNETH L. KARST

Bibliography
SYMPOSIUM 1977 In Re Quinlan. *Rutgers Law Review* 30:243–328.

EVANS v. ABNEY
396 U.S. 435 (1970)

The 1911 will of U.S. Senator Augustus O. Bacon gave land to the city of Macon, Georgia, in trust for use as a park for white persons only. The city's operation of the park on these terms could not survive the Supreme Court's decisions invalidating state-sponsored SEGREGATION, and the city was replaced by private trustees. When the Supreme Court held, in *Evans v. Newton* (1966), that the park must still be open to all races, Bacon's residuary heirs claimed the land, arguing that the trust had failed. The Georgia courts agreed, and the Supreme Court held, 5–2, that this judicial enforcement of Bacon's racially discriminatory disposition of property did not constitute STATE ACTION in violation of the FOURTEENTH AMENDMENT. Justice HUGO L. BLACK, for the majority, distinguished SHELLEY V. KRAEMER (1948), saying that *Abney* involved no RACIAL DISCRIMINATION: the terminated park was unavailable for blacks and whites alike. Justices WILLIAM O. DOUGLAS and WILLIAM J. BRENNAN dissented.

Abney's importance lay in showing that *Shelley* did not stand for a broad principle forbidding judicial enforcement of any and all private racial discrimination. It also began the BURGER COURT's revitalization of the state action limitation as a barrier to enforcement of the Fourteenth Amendment.

KENNETH L. KARST

EVARTS, WILLIAM MAXWELL
(1818–1901)

William Maxwell Evarts, called "the Prince of the American Bar," was probably the most famous, successful, and influential lawyer of his time. He defended ANDREW JOHNSON in the President's IMPEACHMENT trial, and he served as attorney general, secretary of state, and United States senator (Republican, New York). Twice Evarts almost became CHIEF JUSTICE of the United States. His lasting impact on American constitutional law derived from his pathbreaking arguments as counsel and his authorship of the CIRCUIT COURTS OF APPEALS ACT (1891). In the GRANGER CASES (1877) he argued that rate regulation interfered with the management and beneficial use of private property, reducing profits and thereby taking private property without JUST COMPENSATION or DUE PROCESS OF LAW. He lost that case, but his argument was destined for eventual acceptance. IN RE JACOBS (1885) was his greatest constitutional triumph. His argument, which the New York Court of Appeals adopted, advanced SUBSTANTIVE DUE PROCESS OF LAW and the doctrine of FREEDOM OF CONTRACT. Evarts was a stalwart champion of VESTED RIGHTS and an opponent of government regulation. The Circuit Courts of Appeals Act (Evarts Act) created the modern three-tier structure of the federal courts and the discretionary WRIT OF CERTIORARI by which the Supreme Court manages its APPELLATE JURISDICTION.

LEONARD W. LEVY

Bibliography
TWISS, BENJAMIN 1942 *Lawyers and the Constitution.* Pages 93–109. Princeton, N.J.: Princeton University Press.

EVARTS ACT

See: Circuit Courts of Appeals Act (1891)

EVERSON v. BOARD OF EDUCATION
330 U.S. 1 (1947)

A New Jersey statute authorized local school boards to reimburse parents for the cost of public transportation of students to both public and private schools. Such reimbursement for the cost of transportation to church-related schools was challenged as an unconstitutional ESTABLISHMENT OF RELIGION.

Justice HUGO L. BLACK delivered the opinion of a 5–4 Supreme Court. He began with a consideration of the background of the establishment clause, which relied heavily on the writings of JAMES MADISON and THOMAS JEFFERSON, but he had little to say about the actual legislative history of the FIRST AMENDMENT's language in the First Congress. Black concluded that the establishment clause "means at least this":

Neither a state nor the federal government can set up a church. Neither can pass laws which aid one religion, aid all religions or prefer one religion over another. . . . No tax in any amount, large or small, can be levied to support any religious activities or institutions, whatever they may be called, or whatever form they may adopt to teach and practice religion. . . . In the words of Jefferson, the clause against the establishment of religion by law was intended to erect "a wall of separation between church and State."

But after this sweeping separationist pronouncement, Justice Black pirouetted neatly and upheld the New Jersey program on the grounds that the state aid in that case was a public safety measure designed to protect students and could in no way be construed as aid to church-related schools.

Four dissenters were convinced that Justice Black had missed the point. Justice ROBERT H. JACKSON likened Black's MAJORITY OPINION to Byron's Julia who, "whispering I will ne'er consent, consented." What could be more helpful to a school, Jackson asked, than depositing the students at its door? Justice WILEY B. RUTLEDGE, with whom Justices Jackson, FELIX

FRANKFURTER, and HAROLD BURTON joined, also filed a lengthy dissent. Justice Rutledge also made lavish use of the writings of Madison and Jefferson, and argued that the New Jersey program could not be justified as a public safety expenditure.

Everson stands at the entrance to the maze of law and litigation concerning participation by church-related schools in public programs. It was the first major utterance by the Supreme Court on the meaning of the establishment clause. Those favoring strict separation between religious institutions and government were pleased by Black's rhetoric and dismayed by his conclusion; those favoring a policy of flexibility or accommodation in church–state relations reacted the opposite way. That *Everson* satisfied no one and enraged many was portentous.

RICHARD E. MORGAN

Bibliography

JOHNSON, RICHARD M. 1967 *The Dynamics of Compliance.* Evanston, Ill.: Northwestern University Press.

MORGAN, RICHARD E. 1972 *The Supreme Court and Religion.* Pages 76–122. New York: Free Press.

EVIDENCE

Excepting cases that may be decided by applying legal rules to undisputed facts, the determination of disputed factual propositions must be central to adjudicating the rights and liabilities of litigants. As an initial matter, a society might adopt an "inquisitorial" system, under which a public official investigates and decides the facts. In the Anglo-American legal tradition, however, we structure the litigation process so that every dispute has at least two parties, each charged with the primary responsibility for proving its factual propositions and therefore discovering and presenting the evidence to support its version of the facts before an impartial arbiter.

In criminal cases, this adversary system is reinforced by rules that place the BURDEN OF PROOF on the prosecution, presuming that the defendant is innocent, and that grant the defendant a RIGHT AGAINST SELF-INCRIMINATION—thus shielding him from being forced to be a witness against himself, and depriving the prosecution of an obvious source of evidence. The structuring of criminal litigation as a contest between the state as prosecutor and the defendant—with the judge as arbiter—has two major consequences. First, this procedure gives greater weight to the autonomy of the individual litigant. Second, placing responsibility on each party to advance its own cause will, in

general, result in the production of more evidence for the finder of fact than would be produced by disinterested—and perhaps bored and overworked—public officials. Though our prototypical case is the criminal case, we use similar procedures and rules in civil cases.

In both civil and criminal cases, TRIAL BY JURY means that a group of laymen decides issues of disputed fact. A great many of the intricacies of our laws of evidence result from two specific worries about the jury. The first is that the jury may systematically overvalue or undervalue some kinds of evidence, such as HEARSAY. The second is that the ad hoc nature of the jury, which is empaneled to decide a particular case, will produce a verdict at odds with the values of a legal system handling many cases over a long period of time. Often a rule of evidence will keep out testimony not so much because a jury might overweigh it but simply because other policies of the law are entitled to equal weight along with the proper resolution of factual issues. In this category fall the exclusion of reliable evidence because it has been unconstitutionally seized; because it has been obtained in violation of the MIRANDA RULES; because it is a coerced confession (which, though typically unreliable, may in a particular case be thoroughly corroborated); or because its exclusion is necessary to enforce a privilege, such as that protecting confidential communications between the attorney and the client.

Nor is the exclusion of evidence confined to cases where we choose this means of vindicating the rights of the individual. Though it is by no means clear that the rule is of constitutional dimension, every Anglo-American JURISDICTION in civil and (until the passage of California's "Victims' Bill of Rights" initiative) in criminal cases kept from the jury certain evidence of the prior character of the accused—not so much because the jury might overvalue it as out of fear that the jury might succumb to the temptation to be lawless and decide that the defendant was either so bad a person that he should be punished regardless of his fault in the particular case at issue. That kind of jury behavior might appeal to common sense, but it would be at odds with our principles requiring a particular act as a precondition of guilt and requiring fair NOTICE of the charge made against a defendant.

Despite the huge body of statutory and COMMON LAW evidence law, the Constitution nowhere states flatly a rule as to admissibility of evidence and refers to evidence in only one place—the requirement of two witnesses to the same overt act before a conviction of TREASON may be returned. Moreover, apart from the rules as to SEARCH AND SEIZURE and self-incrimination, the rules of evidence have largely escaped the Supreme Court's constitutional supervision. In criminal cases, however, two lines of cases have partially constitutionalized the law of evidence. The first involves the defendant's right to exclude inculpatory hearsay evidence that otherwise would be admitted under one or another of the exceptions to the general rule excluding hearsay; the second involves the defendant's rights to introduce exculpatory evidence notwithstanding common or statutory law purporting to exclude such evidence. Both these lines grow out of the Sixth Amendment. The first grows out of the CONFRONTATION clause, which guarantees that "[i]n all criminal prosecutions, the accused shall enjoy the right . . . to be confronted with the witnesses against him." The second line also stems in part from the Sixth Amendment right of the accused to "COMPULSORY PROCESS for obtaining witnesses in his favor," and in part from the DUE PROCESS clause.

Historically, courts read the confrontation clause as guaranteeing only the right of the accused to be present at his trial and to cross-examine any witnesses testifying there. In the 1960s, however, the Supreme Court began to view the clause as forbidding use in a criminal trial of certain inculpatory hearsay declarations. Thus, the Court held in POINTER V. TEXAS (1965) that the clause rendered inadmissible at a criminal trial a transcript of inculpatory testimony elicited during a preliminary hearing at which the defendant was not represented by counsel from a prosecution witness who was no longer available to testify. Likewise, a codefendant's out-of-court confession that also implicated the accused was held inadmissible in *Bruton v. United States* (1968) when the codefendant invoked his right against self-incrimination and refused to take the stand at the trial. Similarly, in *Barber v. Page* (1968) the Court held that preliminary hearing testimony of an absent witness was inadmissible when the prosecutor had failed to make a good-faith effort to obtain the presence of the witness at the trial. These rulings by the Court threw the validity of inculpatory hearsay evidence into doubt. The Court seemed to be drifting toward a rule that would in effect preclude the use of all such hearsay.

California v. Green (1970) arrested this drift. In *Green*, a prosecution witness testified adversely to the defendant during a preliminary hearing at which the defendant's attorney subjected him to a rigorous cross-examination. At the later trial, however, the witness claimed to have suffered a memory lapse and refused to repeat his testimony. The prosecutor then read into evidence portions of the preliminary hearing testimony. The Court held that, under these circumstances, admission of the hearsay did not violate the confrontation clause. The Court stated that its previous confrontation clause decisions had all rested on the inability of the defendant effectively to cross-examine witnesses, and that where, as here, defendant had once had a full and fair opportunity to cross-examine, there was no constitutional impediment to the hearsay.

Green made it clear that when the declarant was unavailable at the trial, his declaration would be admissible if he had been subject to meaningful cross-examination by defendant's counsel at the time he made the declaration. The meaning of "unavailability" and the nature of "meaningful cross-examination" were left open to interpretation, but clearly where these criteria were met, the evidence was admissible. By the same token, *Green* left little doubt that when the declarant was available at the trial for meaningful cross-examination, evidence of his out-of-court declaration would be admissible even if he had not been subject to cross-examination at the time he made the statement.

Since *Green*, the Court's decisions have withdrawn even further from the constitutionalization of hearsay law. The Court made apparent in *Ohio v. Roberts* (1980) that hearsay evidence of a declarant's out-of-court statements will be admissible, even when the defendant has never had an opportunity to cross-examine the declarant, provided that the declarant is truly unavailable and that the statements bear adequate "indicia of reliability." "Reliability can be inferred without more in a case where the evidence fails within a firmly footed hearsay exception," that is, an exception "rest[ing] upon such solid foundations" that "virtually any evidence within them" will in fact be reliable. Thus, dying declarations are admissible, as are properly administered business and public records. Hearsay evidence is admissible even under less "firmly rooted" exceptions when there is a particularized showing of its trustworthiness under the circumstances. Thus, under some circumstances, at least, declarations against penal interest and party admissions by coconspirators (such as a spontaneous admission by a coconspirator to his prison cellmate) are admissible.

The Court's decisions since *Green* thus have confined the pre-*Green* decisions narrowly to their facts. Apparently, the Court is unlikely to find that evidence admitted under an established hearsay exception offends the confrontation clause, unless, as in *Barber v. Page*, a prosecutor falsely alleges for purposes of the exception that a declarant is unavailable, or, as in *Bruton v. United States*, the hearsay consists of a codefendant's confession which ostensibly is read into evidence against him alone but in fact contains statements inculpating other defendants in the same trial, and the codefendant refuses to take the stand. Moreover, even when a defendant alleges a *Barber* or *Bruton* violation, the Court is unlikely to find that the facts of the case at hand justify reversal. Twice since *Green* the Court has refused to sustain arguments that a prosecutor had failed to make a good-faith effort to find absent declarants, and repeatedly the Court has found even clear and admitted violations of the *Bruton* rule to result in merely HARMLESS ERROR not justifying reversal.

It would seem, then, that the Court has substantially withdrawn from the field of writing hearsay law. While it has not explicitly reverted to the traditional view of the confrontation clause in this area, the manner in which it has analyzed hearsay exceptions in recent cases leaves little doubt of its reluctance significantly to reduce the prosecutor's ability to introduce evidence falling within ancient, recognized exceptions.

The rules of evidence traditionally have been held to bind defendants as well as the state. The first significant developments in the line of cases recognizing defendants' rights to introduce exculpatory evidence despite rules of evidence excluding it grew out of the compulsory process clause. In *Washington v. Texas* (1967) the Court overturned a Texas statute that rendered accomplices incompetent to testify for each other. The Court held that the compulsory process clause forbade the state "arbitrarily [to] den[y defendants] the right to put on the stand a witness who was physically and mentally capable of testifying to events that he had personally observed and whose testimony would have been relevant and material to the defense."

In *Chambers v. Mississippi* (1973) the Court faced a case in which it might have used compulsory process reasoning but used the due process clause instead. In *Chambers* the defendant was charged with murder for shooting a police officer during a crowd incident. Another man, McDonald, who had been in the crowd, had confessed to the shooting, and substantial evidence pointed to the truth of this confession, but McDonald had repudiated the confession and had not been charged in the case. The trial judge allowed Chambers to present two witnesses who claimed actually to have seen McDonald fire the shots, but the judge barred the testimony of witnesses who had not seen the incident but to whom McDonald had made damaging admissions, ruling that this testimony did not fall within any applicable state hearsay exception.

In addition, the judge permitted Chambers to call McDonald to the stand and to read his prior confession into evidence, but when McDonald repudiated the confession on the stand and offered an alibi, the judge refused to allow Chambers to examine McDonald as an "adverse witness," ruling that because McDonald had not actually alleged the defendant's guilt, his testimony was not "adverse" within the meaning of Mississippi's exception to the rule that a party may not impeach his own witness.

The Supreme Court reversed, holding that the trial judge's exclusion of this exculpatory evidence had violated the due process clause of the FOURTEENTH AMENDMENT. The trial judge's refusal to allow Chambers to examine McDonald, who was a "witness against him" even if not an "adverse" witness under Mississippi law, constituted prejudicial error. In addition, the Court held that the trial judge's refusal to allow the exculpatory hearsay testimony of the three witnesses to whom McDonald had confessed violated Chambers's right "to present witnesses in his own defense." Although the language used by the Court in discussing these issues is reminiscent of the confrontation and compulsory process clauses of the Sixth Amendment, the Court did not explicitly rest its decision on these clauses. Rather, the Court announced only that "[t]he right of an accused in a criminal trial to due process is, in essence, the right to a fair opportunity to defend against the State's accusations," and that "under the facts and circumstances of this case the rulings of the trial court deprived Chambers of a fair trial."

The Court has applied *Chambers* in only one other case. In *Green v. Georgia* (1979) the defendant was convicted of rape and murder, and a second trial was then held to decide whether CAPITAL PUNISHMENT would be imposed. At this trial, the defendant sought to introduce a witness who had previously testified for the prosecution at the trial of Moore, the defendant's coconspirator. The witness intended to testify, as he had testified at Moore's trial, that Moore had admitted to him that Moore alone had fired the shots that killed the victim, and that the defendant had not been present when the shots were fired. The trial judge, however, ruled this testimony inadmissible as hearsay. At Moore's trial the witness's repetition of Moore's declaration had fallen within the admission exception to the hearsay rule, but its repetition at Green's trial did not fall within the exception. In a brief opinion, the Supreme Court reversed. It noted that the excluded evidence was highly relevant to a critical issue in the trial and that substantial reasons existed to assume its reliability: it was a statement against Moore's penal interest made spontaneously by him to a close friend and for which there was ample corroborating evidence. Most important, the prosecution had considered the evidence reliable enough to use against Moore at his trial. Under these circumstances, the Court ruled, "the hearsay rule may not be applied mechanistically to defeat the ends of justice."

The future of this line of cases is not easy to foresee. The cases may stand for no more than the proposition that the Court will reverse a conviction when it is convinced that a gross injustice has been done. But they seem to stand for more. They seem to suggest that the Court has begun to read into the Constitution the ethical rule that the state's proper goal is not merely to get a conviction but to get a conviction only if justice demands it. Thus, the cases suggest, the prosecutor may not object to evidence that the defense seeks to introduce on any ground other than that it is wasteful of time, or likely to distract the jury's attention from the real issues of the case. This consideration, always important ethically, rises to constitutional significance when failure to abide by it leads to the exclusion of strongly credible exculpatory evidence that is highly relevant to critical issues in the trial.

JOHN KAPLAN

Bibliography

MAGUIRE, JOHN M. 1947 *Evidence, Common Sense, and Common Law.* Mineola, N.Y.: Foundation Press.

McCORMICK, CHARLES T. 1954 *Handbook of the Law of Evidence.* St. Paul, Minn.: West Publishing Co.

MORGAN, EDMUND M. 1961 *Basic Problems of Evidence.* Philadelphia: American Bar Association.

THAYER, JAMES BRADLEY 1898 *Preliminary Treatise on Evidence at Common Law.* Boston: Little, Brown.

WIGMORE, JOHN HENRY 1961 *Evidence in Trials at Common Law,* rev. by John T. Naughton. Boston: Little, Brown.

EVIDENTIARY PRIVILEGE

To say that a person possesses an evidentiary privilege means that he or she cannot be compelled, as a witness, to disclose certain ("privileged") information. The possessor of the privilege (the privilege "holder") may also be entitled to prevent others who share the privileged information from disclosing it. The holder may waive the privilege by failing to assert it in timely fashion, by explicitly consenting to the disclosure of privileged information, or by engaging in conduct interpreted as consent (for example, voluntarily testify-

ing to a portion of the privileged matter). In state courts, the contours of evidentiary privileges are determined by state law. In federal courts, they are determined by federal law, though at times the federal approach has been to defer to state rules of privilege, as specified, for example, in Federal Rule of Evidence 501.

Unlike most of the evidentiary rules of exclusion (such as those excluding HEARSAY or irrelevant evidence), the testimonial privileges do not exclude EVIDENCE because it is unreliable, prejudicial, or lacking in fact-finding utility. Rather, they exclude it *despite* its potential value; the privileges promote goals other than rational fact-finding. To be aware of these goals is to understand why traditional evidentiary privileges can readily take on constitutional dimensions. The interests served by the privileges are commonly phrased in terms that are uncompromisingly utilitarian. For example, privileges concerned with the protection of confidential communications—such as those between husband and wife, attorney and client, doctor and patient, priest and penitant, parent and child (a developing privilege)—are commonly justified on such reasoning: first, that the free flow of communication is indispensable to these important relationships; second, that confidentiality is essential to their free flow. An alternative perspective would support the claims of confidentiality not for such narrowly instrumental reasons but because confidentiality serves the participants' interest in privacy, whether or not the possibility of compulsory disclosure would hinder free communication.

Similar justifications, both instrumental and noninstrumental, could be generated in support of another kind of privilege, protecting interests other than confidentiality. An example is the phase of the husband–wife privilege permitting one spouse to refuse to testify against another, whether or not the testimony may concern intraspousal communications.

Although these privileges were not in their original conception constitutionally based, today they are often seen as implicating constitutional values. The justifications for many of the privileges could be reformulated in terms of constitutional principles. The attorney–client privilege, invoked by a criminal defendant, could draw support from the RIGHT TO COUNSEL, the RIGHT AGAINST SELF-INCRIMINATION, and the DUE PROCESS clauses of the Constitution. Indeed, if the attorney-client privilege were not a common law privilege, some version of it probably would have to be invented to satisfy constitutional requirements. FIRST AMENDMENT arguments could likewise be mustered in support of the priest–penitent privilege and the REPORTER'S PRIVILEGE (which in some states protects against compelled disclosure of a newsperson's sources of information). And, efforts to pierce the confidentiality of certain communications—such as those between husband and wife, priest and penitent, or psychiatrist and patient—could be challenged as infringements of a constitutionally protected RIGHT OF PRIVACY.

On the other hand, just as evidentiary privileges sometimes draw support from constitutional principles, sometimes their enforcement may prove incompatible with other constitutional requirements. Thus to deny a criminal defendant the use of testimony important to his or her defense, out of respect for a privilege invoked by a witness, might run afoul of the defendant's right of CONFRONTATION, to COMPULSORY PROCESS, or to due process of law; the conflicting constitutional claims of the defendant and the witness would then have to be resolved.

LEON LETWIN

Bibliography
CLEARY, E. 1984 *McCormick on Evidence*, 3rd ed. Pages 170–187. St. Paul, Minn.: West Publishing Co.
NOTE 1985 Developments in the Law—Privileged Communications. *Harvard Law Review* 98:1450–1666.

EVITTS v. LUCEY
469 U.S. (1985)

Interpreting DOUGLAS V. CALIFORNIA (1963), the Supreme Court held, 7–2, in an opinion by Justice WILLIAM J. BRENNAN, that the DUE PROCESS clause of the FOURTEENTH AMENDMENT requires the effective assistance of counsel during a defendant's first appeal, as of right, from a criminal conviction. (The Court had previously held that the RIGHT TO COUNSEL at the trial level comprehended effective assistance.) The procedural posture of this case made it unnecessary to spell out standards for judging the effectiveness of counsel on appeal; the Court thus left those standards for another day. Justice WILLIAM H. REHNQUIST and Chief Justice WARREN E. BURGER dissented, arguing that the trial and appellate levels presented different degrees of need for counsel's assistance, and predicting that the decision would allow convicted defendants to "tie up the courts" with petitions for HABEAS CORPUS based on claims of ineffectiveness of appellate counsel.

KENNETH L. KARST

EXCISE TAX

In its original meaning an excise was a tax on goods manufactured or produced within the taxing country, as opposed to a duty or IMPOST on imports. Undoubtedly, this was the sense in which it was used in the constitutional grant of power to Congress to collect "taxes, duties, imposts and excises." In modern times an excise tax is any tax imposed on the manufacture or sale of a commodity, engaging in an occupation, or enjoying any other privilege. It is distinguished from a direct tax, such as a POLL TAX or an *ad valorem* property tax.

EDWARD L. BARRETT, JR.

(SEE ALSO: *Direct and Indirect Taxes; State Taxation of Commerce.*)

EXCLUSIONARY RULE

When the police obtain evidence by violating the BILL OF RIGHTS, the victim of their misconduct may lack any effective legal remedy. Yet some enforcement mechanism is necessary if several important constitutional guarantees are to be a reality and not merely expressions of hope. The Supreme Court responded to this concern by developing a series of rules that have come to be known in the aggregate as the exclusionary rule. In typical application, the rule is that evidence obtained in violation of a person's constitutional rights cannot be used against that person in his or her trial for a criminal offense. The rule is most frequently applied to exclude evidence produced by SEARCHES OR SEIZURES made in violation of the FOURTH AMENDMENT. However, a coerced confession obtained in violation of the defendant's Fifth Amendment RIGHT AGAINST SELF-INCRIMINATION, or a statement taken from the defendant in violation of his Sixth Amendment's guarantee of the RIGHT TO COUNSEL, would also be inadmissible at his trial.

The term "exclusionary rule" is of modern origin, but even at COMMON LAW a coerced confession was excluded or inadmissible as evidence, because its involuntariness cast serious doubt on its reliability. No one today seriously argues that this long-standing rule of evidence should be abandoned. Other aspects of the exclusionary rule, however, have been the source of major controversy among members of the judiciary, professional commentators, law enforcement officials, and the public.

The controversy did not become intense until the era of the WARREN COURT. But as far back as WEEKS

v. UNITED STATES (1914) the Supreme Court had unanimously held that evidence seized in violation of the Fourth Amendment was inadmissible in a *federal* criminal prosecution. However, even after the Court had held in WOLF V. COLORADO (1949) that the Fourth Amendment's guarantee against unreasonable searches and seizures was applicable to the states, the Court had continued until 1961 to resist the argument that the exclusionary rule should also be extended to *state* prosecutions. In that year, in MAPP v. OHIO, the Warren Court held that the Fourteenth Amendment did, indeed, impose on the states the exclusionary rule derived from the Fourth Amendment. Subsequent decisions broadened the Sixth Amendment guarantee of the right to counsel to govern the procedures for police interrogation and for the use of LINEUPS; each of these developments was accompanied by an extension of the exclusionary rule to state-court proceedings. Since the "FRUIT OF THE POISONOUS TREE" DOCTRINE requires the exclusion not only of evidence immediately obtained by these various forms of constitutional violation but also of other evidence derived from the initial violations, the exclusionary rule in its modern form results in the suppression of many items of evidence of unquestioned reliability and the acquittal of many persons who are guilty.

The primary purpose of the exclusionary rule, as the Supreme Court said in *Elkins v. United States* (1960), "is to deter—to compel respect for the constitutional guaranty in the only effectively available way—by removing the incentive to disregard it." Yet this deterrent function is only part of the exclusionary rule's justification. A court that allows the government to profit from unconstitutional police action sullies the judicial process itself, by becoming an accomplice in an unlawful course of conduct. When the Court first applied the rule in *Mapp* to state-court prosecutions, it said:

There are those who say, as did Justice (then Judge) [BENJAMIN N.] CARDOZO, that under our constitutional exclusionary doctrine "the criminal is to go free because the constable has blundered." . . . In some cases this will undoubtedly be the result. But, . . . "there is another consideration—the imperative of judicial integrity." . . . The criminal goes free, if he must, but it is the law that sets him free. Nothing can destroy a government more quickly than its failure to observe its own laws, or worse, its disregard of the charter of its own existence. As Mr. Justice LOUIS D. BRANDEIS, dissenting, said: . . . "Our government is the potent, the omnipresent teacher. For good or for ill, it teaches the whole people by its example. . . . If the government becomes a lawbreaker, it breeds contempt for law."

The evidence seized in an illegal search—a knife, a packet of heroin, counterfeit plates—is as trustworthy and material as if the search had been lawful. The rule's critics argue that to protect the privacy of the search victim by letting a guilty person escape responsibility for his crime is illogical. It would make more sense, they say, to use the evidence (as do the courts in Great Britain, for example) and provide civil or criminal remedies against the errant police officers. If the rule's purpose is to deter police lawlessness, the critics argue, the rule misses the point: prosecutors, not police officers, feel the immediate effects of the rule. If the rule is designed to maintain respect for the courts, they ask how the public can be expected to respect a system that frees criminals by suppressing trustworthy evidence of their guilt.

How many criminals do go free when the constable blunders? Inadequate studies provide no clear-cut answer, except that opponents of the exclusionary rule grossly exaggerate the number of felons it sets loose, and they tend to dramatize the worst cases. In California, whose supreme court has created the most stringent exclusionary rule in the nation, a study by the National Institute of Justice showed that .78 percent of all accused felons are not prosecuted because of search and seizure problems, and of those released, nearly three-fourths were involved in drug-related cases. The effect of the exclusionary rule is slight in cases involving violent crimes. When the charge is murder, rape, assault, or robbery, prosecutors decide not to proceed in one out of every 2,500 cases. Studies of felony court records in other states reach similar conclusions. Only 0.4 percent of all cases that federal prosecutors decide not to prosecute are rejected because of search problems. At the trial level, motions to suppress illegally seized evidence are rarely granted in cases of violent crime. If the exclusionary rule were abolished, the conviction rate in all felony cases would increase by less than half of one percent. Translated into absolute figures, however, thousands of accused felons are released nationally as a result of the exclusionary rule, most of them in drug and weapons possession cases. Street crime does not flourish, though, because of the exclusionary rule, even though it does protect criminals, as do all constitutional rights. They also protect society and help keep us free.

The rule's effectiveness in deterring illegal searches is hotly debated. The critics point out that some ninety percent of criminal prosecutions do not go to trial but are disposed of by pleas of "guilty." (The figure varies from state to state, and according to the nature of the crime.) Without a trial, there is no evidence for the rule to exclude. In the huge number of cases in which the police make arrests but the persons arrested are not prosecuted, the exclusionary rule has, of course, no immediate application. The rule's proponents reply that the decision whether to prosecute or accept a defendant's "guilty" pleas on a lesser offense may itself be influenced by the prosecutor's estimate of the potential operation of the exclusionary rule if the case should go to trial. (In jurisdictions where separate procedures are established to rule on motions to suppress evidence, the rule normally will have operated in advance of the trial.)

Undeniably, however, the exclusionary rule has no application at all to the cases that cry out most for a remedy: cases of police misconduct against innocent persons, who are never even brought to the prosecutors' attention, and cases of illegal searches and seizures made for purposes other than collecting evidence to support prosecutions. In TERRY V. OHIO (1968) Chief Justice EARL WARREN admitted: "Regardless how effective the rule may be where obtaining conviction is an important objective of the police, it is powerless to deter invasions of constitutionally guaranteed rights where the police either have no interest in prosecuting or are willing to forego successful prosecution in the interest of serving some other goal." The police may deliberately engage in illegal searches and seizures for a number of reasons: to control crimes such as gambling or prostitution; to confiscate weapons or contraband or stolen property; or to maintain high visibility either to deter crime or to satisfy a public clamoring for aggressive police action. In none of these cases will the exclusionary rule inhibit police violations of the Bill of Rights.

The rule does not in fact significantly impede the police, despite contentions from the rule's opponents that it handcuffs the police. A 1984 report prepared for the National Center for State Courts concluded that a properly administered search warrant process can protect constitutional rights without hampering effective law enforcement. Nevertheless, police try when possible to conduct search and seizure under some exception to the warrant requirement. The overwhelming number of searches and seizures are warrantless. In 1980, for example, only about 1,000 warrants were issued in Los Angeles in about 300,000 cases. Police usually try to make CONSENT SEARCHES or searches under what they claim to be EXIGENT CIRCUMSTANCES, or they conduct a search to confiscate contraband or harass criminals, without attempting a prosecution. In the few cases in which they seek warrants, they get them almost as if magistrates rubber-stamp their applications, and almost all warrants

survive in court despite motions to suppress. Motions to suppress are made in about five percent of all cases but are successful in only less than one percent of all cases. Still more important is the fact that only slightly over half of one percent of all cases result in acquittals because of the exclusion of evidence.

Even when the rule does operate to exclude evidence in a criminal trial, it has no direct, personal effect on the police officer whose misconduct caused the rule to be invoked. The rule does not require discipline to be imposed by the officer's superiors, nor does either civil or criminal responsibility follow as a matter of course. Police officers are prosecuted only extremely rarely for their official misdeeds. Suits for damages by victims are inhibited not only by the defense of "good faith" and PROBABLE CAUSE but also by the realization that most officers are neither wealthy nor insured against liability for their official acts. Unsurprisingly, most victims conclude that a lawsuit is not worth its trouble and expense. In the typical case of an illegal search, neither the judge who excludes the fruits of the search from evidence nor the prosecutor whose case is thereby undermined will explain to the officer the error of his ways. The intended educational effect of judicial decisions is also diminished by the time-lag between the police action and its final evaluation by the courts. Even if an officer should hear that a court has excluded the evidence he found in an illegal search some months ago, he will probably have forgotten the details of the event. Incentives and sanctions that might influence the officer's future behavior are not within the exclusionary rule's contemplation. On the other hand, advocates of the rule emphasize that it is meant to have an institutional or systemic effect on law enforcement agencies generally, not necessarily on particular officers.

The officer is apt to respond not to judicial decisions (which he may regard as unrealistic if they impede his work) but to departmental policies and the approval of his colleagues and superiors. One whose main job is the apprehension of criminals and the deterrence of crime will have a low tolerance for what he sees as procedural niceties. He may even shade the truth in making out a report on a search or when testifying in court. It is not unheard of for the police to arrange to make a valid arrest at a place where they can conduct a warrantless SEARCH INCIDENT TO THE ARREST, and thus evade the requirement of a SEARCH WARRANT based on probable cause to believe that evidence of crime is in that place. To the extent that the courts have used the exclusionary rule to educate the police, then, the main things learned seem to have been the techniques for evading the rule.

Summarizing the criticisms of the exclusionary rule, Dallin H. Oaks has said:

The harshest criticism of the rule is that it is ineffective. It is the sole means of enforcing the essential guarantees of freedom from unreasonable arrests and searches and seizures by law enforcement officers, and it is a failure in that vital task.

The use of the exclusionary rule imposes excessive costs on the criminal justice system. It provides no recompense for the innocent and it frees the guilty. It creates the occasion and incentive for large-scale lying by law enforcement officers. It diverts the focus on the criminal prosecution from the guilt or innocence of the defendant to a trial of the police. Only a system with limitless patience with irrationality could tolerate the fact that where there has been one wrong, the defendant's, he will be punished, but where there have been two wrongs, the defendant's and the officer's, both will go free. This would not be an excessive cost for an effective remedy against police misconduct, but it is a prohibitive price to pay for an illusory one.

Despite the severity of criticisms, the exclusionary rule's chief critics have not proposed its total abolition. However, the Supreme Court has limited the rule's application in significant ways. Thus, for the most part, only the victim of an illegal search has standing to claim the benefits of the exclusionary rule; if A's house is searched in violation of the Fourth Amendment, and evidence is found incriminating B, the evidence can be used in B's trial. (State courts are free to extend the exclusionary rule to such cases; some state courts have done so, concluding that the point of the rule is not to protect people against being convicted but to deter the police.) Similarly, in UNITED STATES V. CALANDRA (1974) the Court held that illegally obtained evidence is admissible in grand jury proceedings, and it ruled in HARRIS V. NEW YORK (1971) that it can be used for the purpose of impeaching the testimony of the accused at his trial. Some uses of illegally obtained evidence have been tolerated as HARMLESS ERROR. More important, the GOOD FAITH EXCEPTION to the exclusionary rule allows the use of evidence obtained with a search warrant if the police reasonably believed the warrant to be valid, even though it later proves to be illegal. The rule has also been held inapplicable to collateral proceedings for postconviction relief such as HABEAS CORPUS. The Court's opinions in these cases have repeated the familiar criticisms of the exclusionary rule; their logic would seem to suggest abandonment of the rule altogether.

Yet the exclusionary rule remains, largely because no one has yet suggested an effective alternative means for enforcing the Bill of Rights against police misconduct. A federal statute dating from Reconstruction authorizes the award of damages against state or local officials (including police officers) who violate individuals' constitutional rights. In 1971, the Supreme Court found that the Fourth Amendment itself implicitly authorized similar damages awards against federal officers who violated the Amendment. The future effectiveness of such remedies will depend in part on the Supreme Court itself, as it spells out the victim's BURDEN OF PROOF in these cases and the measure of damages. Partly, however, the civil-damages alternative depends for its effectiveness on legislation to provide for real compensation to victims when the police officers are judgment-proof, and for real punishment of officers for constitutional violations when the payment of damages is unrealistic.

Meanwhile, the Supreme Court has only the exclusionary rule, which everyone agrees is an imperfect deterrent to police misbehavior. The rule survives, then, for want of better alternatives. But it also stands as a symbol that government itself is not above the law.

LEONARD W. LEVY

(SEE ALSO: *Electronic Eavesdropping; New York v. Quarles, 1984; Police Interrogation; Wiretapping; Warrantless Searches.*)

Bibliography

LAFAVE, WAYNE R. 1978 *Search and Seizure: A Treatise on the Fourth Amendment,* 3 vols. St. Paul: West Publishing Co.

OAKS, DALLIN H. 1970 Studying the Exclusionary Rule. *University of Chicago Law Review* 37:665–757.

SCHROEDER, WILLIAM 1981 Deterring Fourth Amendment Violations: Alternatives to the Exclusionary Rule. *Georgetown Law Review* 68:1361–1426.

STEWART, POTTER 1983 The Road to *Mapp v. Ohio* and Beyond: The Origins, Development and Future of the Exclusionary Rule in Search-and-Seizure Cases. *Columbia Law Review* 83:1365–1404.

EXCLUSIVE POWERS

The Constitution divides governmental power in two ways: between the states and the federal government, and among the three branches of the federal government. Some powers are vested exclusively in one authority, and may not be exercised by any other authority.

The exclusive powers of the federal government include not only all power over foreign affairs but also certain domestic powers that affect the whole country. Not all of the powers granted to the federal government by the Constitution are exclusive in character; some may be exercised concurrently and independently by both state and federal governments, or may be exercised by the states until Congress acts.

The Constitution makes clear the exclusive character of some powers by explicitly prohibiting the states from exercising them (such as the treaty power). In some other cases, the courts have held the grant to be exclusive when the subject of the power is national in character or requires one uniform system or plan. In some cases the states, with the express permission of Congress, may exercise an exclusive power of the national government.

The states also possess exclusive powers. Because the Constitution establishes a government of limited powers, any domestic governmental power not granted to the federal government by the Constitution and not prohibited by it to the states remains an exclusive power of the state government.

Within the federal government a power may be possessed exclusively by one of the three branches of government. The separation of powers implies that each branch of government has its exclusive sphere of power, which it can independently exercise and from which the other branches are excluded. In theory the legislative power, executive power, and judicial power each belong exclusively to one branch of government. This exclusive power is compatible with the influence of other branches over some part of its exercise. Only Congress may legislate, but legislation may be affected by the President's veto power and the power of the courts to declare statutes unconstitutional. Powers not explicitly granted to one branch have been found by the courts to belong exclusively to Congress, the President, or the courts when they are in their nature exclusively legislative, executive, or judicial.

Although the complexities of modern government require much sharing of power among governmental authorities, the constitutional principles of federalism and the separation of powers require also the maintenance of the proper exclusive spheres of power.

GLEN E. THUROW

Bibliography

PRITCHETT, C. HERMAN 1977 *The American Constitution*, 3d ed. Pages 150–216. New York: McGraw-Hill.

EXECUTIVE AGREEMENT

Executive agreements—that is, international agreements concluded between heads of state or their representatives, commonly without the necessity of parliamentary approval—are nowhere explicitly authorized in the Constitution. The Constitution is silent about international agreement-making except as it vests in the President, in cooperation with the Senate, the power to make and enter into treaties. Nevertheless the principle has long been established that the capacity of the United States to negotiate and enter into international agreements is not exhausted by the TREATY POWER. This principle has been repeatedly recognized in the actual conduct of United States FOREIGN AFFAIRS since the early days of the Republic. Since the mid-nineteenth century, but especially since World War II, the use of executive agreements in United States practice has exceeded the use of treaties by an increasingly wide margin.

The expression "executive agreement," which is not widely used outside the United States but which has its equivalents abroad, is understood by the Department of State to refer, in general, to any international agreement brought into force relative to the United States without the ADVICE AND CONSENT of the Senate that is constitutionally required for treaties. In particular, it is understood to refer to three kinds of agreements: those made pursuant to, or in accordance with, an existing treaty; those made subject to congressional approval or implementation ("congressional-executive agreements"); and those made under, and in accordance with, the President's constitutional powers ("sole executive agreements"). None of these executive agreements is subject to the formal treaty-making process specified in Article II, section 2, clause 2, of the Constitution.

A treaty-based executive agreement, provided that it is within the intent, scope, and subject matter of the parent treaty, has the same validity and effect as the treaty itself and is subject to the same constitutional limitations. Deriving from one of the elements of "the supreme law of the land," it takes precedence over all inconsistent state laws and follows the customary rule favoring the instrument later in time in case of inconsistency with a federal statute. A conspicuous example of a treaty-based executive agreement is the traditional *compromis* defining the terms of submission to adjudication or arbitration under a basic convention. Another is found in the hundreds of STATUS OF FORCES AGREEMENTS and other agreements required to carry out the NORTH ATLANTIC TREATY, the linchpin of United States policy in Europe since World War II.

A congressional-executive agreement is based on either a prior or a subsequent act of Congress authorizing the making of the agreement or providing general authority for the executive action needed internationally to implement the legislation in question. The scope or subject matter of the agreement is the same whether the congressional act comes before or after the negotiation of the agreement; the act of Congress often takes the form of an authorization to enter into or effectuate an agreement already negotiated. In principle, however, the agreement must reside within the joint powers of Congress and the President in order to have constitutional validity. An agreement outside the legal competence of Congress or the President, authorities generally agree, would be unconstitutional. On the other hand, as the American Law Institute has commented, "the source of authority to make a congressional-executive agreement may be broader even than the sum of the respective powers of Congress and the President," and "in international matters the President and Congress together have all the powers of the United States inherent in its SOVEREIGNTY and nationhood and can therefore make any international agreement on any subject." In any event, partly out of a concern to CHECK AND BALANCE the President in the conduct of foreign affairs, the vast majority of executive agreements entered into by the United States—for example, the Lend-Lease Agreements of World War II and the Trade Expansion Acts of 1934 and 1962—are of this type. Like its treaty-based counterpart, deriving from one of the elements of "the supreme law of the land," the congressional-executive agreement supersedes all inconsistent state law and follows the customary rule favoring the instrument later in time in case of inconsistency with a federal statute.

Sole executive agreements are international agreements entered into by the President without reference to treaty or statutory authority, that is, exclusively on the basis of the President's constitutional powers as chief executive and COMMANDER-IN-CHIEF, responsible for United States foreign relations and military affairs. Department of State records indicate that only a small percentage of executive agreements are of this type and that the great majority have dealt with essentially routine diplomatic and military matters. Accordingly, with relatively minor exception (such as agreements settling pecuniary and personal injury claims of citizens against foreign governments), they have had little direct impact on private interests and therefore have given rise to little domestic litigation. However, in part out of fear that the President might undertake by international agreement what would be unconstitutional by statute, as in fact occurred in MISSOURI V. HOLLAND (1920), such agreements have not been free of controversy. Two issues in particular continue to stand out.

First there is the question, not yet conclusively settled, of whether Congress may legislate to prohibit or otherwise limit sole executive agreements. Although comprehensive limitations on such agreements, including the proposed BRICKER AMENDMENT of 1953–1954, have so far failed to be adopted, Congress has nonetheless occasionally restricted presidential authority in ways that appear to preclude some executive agreements. For example, the War Powers Resolution of 1973, requiring congressional authorization to introduce combat troops into hostile situations, arguably restrains the President from making agreements that would commit United States armed forces to undeclared foreign wars. Similarly, the Arms Control and Disarmament Act of 1961 forbids the limitation or reduction of armaments "except pursuant to the treaty making power . . . or unless authorized by further legislation of the Congress of the United States." The validity of such restrictions upon presidential authority has been challenged by Presidents and has yet to be determined by the Supreme Court.

Second, while it is widely accepted that the President, under the "executive power" clause, has the authority to conclude sole executive agreements that are not inconsistent with legislation in areas where Congress has primary responsibility, there is a question as to whether the President alone may make an agreement inconsistent with an act of Congress or, alternatively, whether a sole executive agreement may supersede earlier inconsistent congressional legislation. The prevailing view, rooted in the belief that it would be unconscionable for an act of a single person—the President—to repeal an act of Congress, is that sole executive agreements are inoperative as law in the United States to the extent that they conflict with a prior act of Congress in an area of congressional competence. This is the position taken by a federal appeals court in *United States v. Guy W. Capps, Inc.* (4th Circuit, 1953) and by the American Law Institute. The Supreme Court has not yet rendered a definitive decision in these respects, however.

The foregoing two issues aside, there is broad agreement about the scope and effect of sole executive agreements as a matter of constitutional law. Like the other two kinds of executive agreements, they are subject to the same limitations applicable to treaties, they are not limited by the TENTH AMENDMENT, and they supersede all inconsistent state law.

In sum, all three categories of executive agreements bespeak a historic trend toward strong executive leadership in foreign affairs. Only three final points need be added. First, the judgment to resort to these agreements in lieu of the treaty alternative is essentially a political one, affected more by surrounding circumstances than by abstract theories of law. Second, once in force, executive agreements are presumptively binding upon the United States and the other parties to them under international law, to the same extent and in the same way as treaties. Third, the international obligations assumed under such agreements survive all subsequent limitations or restrictions in domestic law.

BURNS H. WESTON

Bibliography

AMERICAN LAW INSTITUTE 1965 *Restatement of the Law, Second: Foreign Relations Law of the United States.* Pages 361–448. St. Paul, Minn.: American Law Institute.

_____ 1980 *Restatement of the Law: Foreign Relations Law of the United States (Revised), Tentative Draft No. 1.* Pages 71–144. Philadelphia: American Law Institute.

BERGER, RAOUL 1972 The Presidential Monopoly of Foreign Relations. *Michigan Law Review* 71:1–58.

BORCHARD, EDWIN 1944 Shall the Executive Agreement Replace the Treaty? *Yale Law Journal* 53:664–683.

HENKIN, LOUIS 1972 *Foreign Affairs and the Constitution.* Pages 173–188. Mineola, N.Y.: Foundation Press.

MCDOUGAL, MYRES and LANS, ASHER 1945 Treaties and Congressional-Executive Agreements: Interchangeable Instruments of National Policy. *Yale Law Journal* 54:181–351, 534–615.

EXECUTIVE IMMUNITY

In tracing the development of executive immunity in the United States, one should separate immunity for constitutional violations from immunity for nonconstitutional violations and immunity of federal officials from immunity of state officials. State officials' immunity for nonconstitutional violations is a matter left to each state's laws. At least since enactment in 1871 of SECTION 1983, TITLE 42, UNITED STATES CODE, state officials have been liable for some federal constitutional violations. Until well into the twentieth century, however, their immunity in constitutional cases had not been fully explored because there were relatively few federal constitutional restrictions on state officials' behavior. By the middle of the twentieth century, federal officials, who are not covered by section 1983, seemed immune from actions for both constitutional and nonconstitutional misbehavior. Within a few decades, however, with the exception of the President, no executive official, state or federal, was fully immune from damage actions for constitutional violations.

In the Massachusetts case of *Miller v. Horton* (1891)

Justice OLIVER WENDELL HOLMES, writing for the majority, narrowly restricted state officials' state-law immunity from suit. Even reasonable, good-faith behavior might trigger liability if found to violate the Constitution or some other legal limit. But in *Spaulding v. Vilas* (1896) and other cases, the Supreme Court was more protective of federal executives. And in subsequent years, many states provided their executives with more generous protection from suits in state courts, particularly when their acts were viewed as discretionary rather than ministerial.

Gregoire v. Biddle (1949) highlighted the movement away from *Miller v. Horton*. In an influential opinion by Judge LEARNED HAND for the United States Court of Appeals, *Gregoire* suggested that a federal executive officer's malice would not render him liable for an otherwise lawful act. *Gregoire* was read as conferring broad immunity upon federal officials. *Barr v. Matteo* (1959) accentuated this trend when, in a case generating no majority opinion, the Supreme Court seemed to hold federal officials absolutely immune from defamation suits.

After *Barr*, the Supreme Court paused in its treatment of federal executive immunity to explore the liability, under section 1983, of state officers charged with constitutional violations. In a series of cases, including PIERSON V. RAY (1967), SCHEUER V. RHODES (1974), and WOOD V. STRICKLAND (1975), the Court held that unconstitutional acts by state executive officials would not trigger liability under section 1983 if the officials acted under a reasonable, good-faith belief that their behavior was constitutional. But they enjoyed no absolute immunity. *Scheuer v. Rhodes*, in which a governor was found not to have absolute immunity, dispelled illusions some had entertained about special status for high officials.

This experience with state officials undoubtedly influenced the Court's subsequent treatment of federal officials. In BUTZ V. ECONOMOU (1978), over four dissents, the Supreme Court held that the good-faith defense, and not the rule of *Barr*, applied to damage actions against federal officials for constitutional violations. Prior statements about absolute immunity, and the importance of the ministerial/discretionary dichotomy, in effect were limited to cases involving common law torts. *Harlow v. Fitzgerald* (1982) reaffirmed and modified the limited immunity of high federal executive officials and NIXON V. FITZGERALD (1982) found the federal chief executive, the President, to enjoy the absolute immunity that *Scheuer* had denied to state chief executives.

THEODORE EISENBERG

Bibliography

JAFFE, LOUIS L. 1963 Suits against Governments and Officers: Damage Actions. *Harvard Law Review* 77:209–239.

SCHUCK, PETER H. 1981 Suing Our Servants: The Court, Congress, and the Liability of Public Officials for Damages. *Supreme Court Review* 1980:281–368.

EXECUTIVE ORDER

Executive orders, a class of presidential documents, primarily regulate actions of government officials and agencies. Although most executive orders are issued under specific statutory authorization, some, including President HARRY S. TRUMAN's STEEL SEIZURE order and executive orders affecting CIVIL RIGHTS, are issued on the President's own authority under Article II. Executive orders were not numbered until 1907 and were not required to be published until 1935.

Executive orders have taken on particular importance in times of war and in the field of civil rights. President FRANKLIN D. ROOSEVELT's executive orders played a key role in the World War II Japanese relocation program, sustained in the JAPANESE AMERICAN CASES (1943–1944). Most executive orders concerning civil rights relate to employment by government contractors. Executive Order 8802 (1941), generated by a wartime need for labor, established a Committee on Fair Employment Practices to carry out a policy of nondiscrimination in defense industries. EXECUTIVE ORDERS 9980 AND 9981 (1948) declared a national policy of nondiscrimination in federal employment and sought to foster equality of treatment in the armed services. Executive Order 11603 (1962) attempted to promote nondiscrimination in federally assisted housing. On the more mundane level, executive orders also have been a vehicle through which Presidents promulgate the never-ending plans for reorganizing the executive branch of government.

With the enactment of ANTIDISCRIMINATION LEGISLATION in the 1960s and the expansion of constitutional prohibitions on government discrimination, executive orders prohibiting discrimination became less important. They continue, however, to provide internal authority regulating the federal government's employment and contracting policies. And in requiring employers to take AFFIRMATIVE ACTION to hire minorities and women, EXECUTIVE ORDER 11246 (1965) goes further than fair employment statutes. It has

been a significant factor in pressuring government contractors to hire minority and female workers.

THEODORE EISENBERG

(SEE ALSO: *Presidential Ordinance-Making Power.*)

Bibliography

MORGAN, RUTH P. 1970 *The President and Civil Rights: Policy-Making by Executive Order.* New York: St. Martin's Press.

EXECUTIVE ORDER 9066 AND PUBLIC LAW 503 (1942): JAPANESE AMERICAN RELOCATION

On February 19, 1942, citing the necessity for "every possible protection against espionage and against sabotage," President FRANKLIN D. ROOSEVELT issued an EXECUTIVE ORDER authorizing various military commanders to designate any area in the United States from which "any or all persons may be excluded" at their discretion. Although based on a 1918 WAR POWERS act, the order resulted from vigorous anti-Japanese sentiment on the West Coast. Despite its broad wording, the order was enforced almost exclusively against persons of Japanese ancestry. The order conveyed a remarkably broad DELEGATION OF POWER but failed to distinguish between American citizens and ALIENS or even between loyal and disloyal citizens. To provide for enforcement, the War Department drafted a bill making it a federal crime for a civilian to disobey a military relocation order. The bill passed Congress without dissent and Roosevelt signed it into law on March 21. Few spoke out against the use of these two measures to deprive some 110,000 people (an entire community was relocated in ten "camps") of their CIVIL RIGHTS. The Supreme Court sustained the evacuation and relocation in three JAPANESE AMERICAN CASES (1943–1944), despite a vigorous dissent by Justice FRANK MURPHY objecting to the "legalization of racism."

DAVID GORDON

EXECUTIVE ORDER 10340
(1952)

On April 8, 1952, on the eve of a nationwide strike of steelworkers, President HARRY S. TRUMAN issued Executive Order 10340, directing the secretary of commerce to take possession of and operate the plants and facilities of eighty-seven major steel companies. The order anticipated that the plants would continue to be run by company managers, preserving the rights and obligations of the companies until corporation officials and union leaders settled their dispute. As justification for averting a work stoppage, the order referred to Truman's proclamation of December 16, 1950, declaring the existence of a national emergency and the dispatch of American fighting men to Korea. The order called steel "indispensable" for producing weapons and war materials, for carrying out the programs of the Atomic Energy Commission, and for maintaining the health and vitality of the American economy.

Although Truman based the order on authority under "the Constitution and laws of the United States, and as President of the United States and COMMAND-ER-IN-CHIEF of the armed forces of the United States," the Justice Department later argued in court that Truman had acted solely on inherent executive power without any statutory support. On June 2, 1952, the Supreme Court declared the Executive Order invalid.

LOUIS FISHER

(SEE ALSO: *Youngstown Sheet and Tube Co. v. Sawyer*, 1952; *Steel Seizure Controversy.*)

Bibliography
MARCUS, MAEVA 1977 *Truman and the Steel Seizure Case: The Limits of Presidential Power.* New York: Columbia University Press.

EXECUTIVE ORDER 11246 (1965)

Executive Order 11246 required government contractors to take AFFIRMATIVE ACTION to ensure non-discriminatory employment practices. Employers complying with the order may encounter employees or potential employees who claim that affirmative action violates Title VII of the CIVIL RIGHTS ACT OF 1964 or the Constitution. UNITED STEELWORKERS OF AMERICA V. WEBER (1979), which sustained some affirmative action by private employers, does not foreclose all such claims. Efforts to undermine the order by amending the 1964 act have failed. Part I of the order, which banned discrimination and required affirmative action by the federal government, was superseded by Executive Order 11478 (1969) and by the 1972 extension of the 1964 act to government employees.

THEODORE EISENBERG

EXECUTIVE ORDERS 9835 AND 10450 (1947, 1953)

As a result of domestic political and security pressures after 1945, Presidents HARRY S. TRUMAN and DWIGHT D. EISENHOWER instituted sweeping loyalty investigations of federal workers. Truman's Executive Order 9835, affecting over two million employees, established loyalty review boards in executive departments to evaluate information provided by Federal Bureau of Investigation or Civil Service Commission investigations and informants. The basic standards for dismissal required "reasonable grounds for belief in disloyalty," which included evidence of affiliation with groups on the ATTORNEY GENERAL's LIST of subversive organizations. Critics who alleged widespread subversion nevertheless demanded more stringent measures, and Truman's Executive Order 10241 (April 28, 1951) altered the criterion to one of "reasonable doubt" of loyalty. The change effectively shifted the burden of proof to the accused or suspected employee. Eisenhower, however, later complained that the Truman program reflected "a complacency . . . toward security risks," such as homosexuals and alcoholics, and in April 1953, he issued Executive Order 10450 that made security, not loyalty, the primary concern.

The loyalty probes produced new bureaucracies, with agendas of their own and standards and practices that varied widely in different departments. Between 1947 and 1956, approximately 2,700 employees were dismissed and another 12,000 resigned because of the inquiries. After 1953, the security program provided for immediate suspension without pay, and many employees undoubtedly resigned to avoid the stigma of combating the charges, however flimsy. Then, too, the program's shroud of secrecy, including the use of unknown informants, made challenges difficult.

The Supreme Court responded cautiously to the program. In *Bailey v. Richardson* (1951) an evenly divided bench sustained Bailey's dismissal even though she had been denied an opportunity to confront her accusers. The same day, in JOINT ANTI-FASCIST REFUGEE COMMITTEE V. McGRATH, the Court questioned the procedures for compiling the attorney general's list of subversive organizations, yet did not prevent its continued use. Some individuals successfully challenged their dismissals, but courts carefully avoided broader constitutional issues. In *Peters v. Hobby* (1955) the Supreme Court overturned a medical professor's dismissal because his position was non-sensitive, yet the Justices ignored Peters's challenge against secret informers. Similar reasoning was employed in *Cole v. Young* (1956) to reverse the discharge of an employee who had challenged the use of the attorney general's list as a violation of rights of association. The real turning point came in *Service v. Dulles* (1957) when the Court reversed the dismissal of one of the "China Hands" who had been purged from the State Department. Finally, in *Greene v. McElroy* (1959), Chief Justice EARL WARREN condemned the use of "faceless informers," unknown to the accused. Without determining constitutional issues, the Court held that the government's evidence must be disclosed to the individual to give him an opportunity to refute it.

Although the Court's decisions undoubtedly demonstrated that abusive, illegal governmental actions could be brought to account, such challenges required extraordinary individual persistence and courage as well as financial and emotional cost. For all the government's efforts, the results were dubious. Judith Coplon, convicted of passing Justice Department documents to a Soviet agent, had escaped the program's net. And in 1954, the Civil Service Commission acknowledged that no communist or fellow traveler had been uncovered in its probes.

STANLEY I. KUTLER

Bibliography

HARPER, ALAN D. 1969 *The Politics of Loyalty.* Greenwich, Conn.: Greenwood Press.

EXECUTIVE ORDERS 9980 AND 9981: INTEGRATION OF THE FEDERAL GOVERNMENT
(1948)

When issued by President HARRY S. TRUMAN, Executive Orders 9980 and 9981 were among the most far-reaching federal antidiscrimination measures adopted since Reconstruction. Executive Order 9980 authorized the establishment of review boards within federal executive departments and agencies to which employees claiming racially discriminatory treatment could appeal. It also established a Fair Employment Board to coordinate and supervise executive antidiscrimination policy and to hear appeals from agency and department review boards.

Executive Order 9981 declared it "to be the policy of the President that there shall be equality of treatment and opportunity for all persons in the armed services without regard to race, color, religion or na-

tional origin." To this end, the order established the President's Committee on Equality of Treatment and Opportunity in the Armed Services to study and resolve the problem of SEGREGATION in the armed forces. Issued under pressure from black leaders, and in the midst of a reelection campaign, the order and the committee's recommendations were crucial first steps to desegregating the armed services.

THEODORE EISENBERG

Bibliography

BERMAN, WILLIAM C. 1970 *The Politics of Civil Rights in the Truman Administration.* Pages 116–120. Columbus: Ohio State University Press.

EXECUTIVE PRIVILEGE

Executive privilege refers to a right of the chief executive to refuse to produce documents within his control in response to a demand from either the legislative or judicial departments of the national government. There would seem to be no question that the chief magistrate need not respond to such demands from departments of state governments. Raoul Berger has asserted that "executive privilege is a myth," a creature of the Presidents who have asserted this claim to immunity without foundation in the Constitution. Although the Constitution does provide for legislative privilege, there are no words in the Constitution on which to base any such executive privilege. Nevertheless, the Supreme Court, in UNITED STATES V. NIXON (1974), wrote executive privilege into the Constitution on the grounds that it inheres in the notion of SEPARATION OF POWERS that is immanent in our basic document:

The expectation of a President to the confidentiality of his conversations and correspondence, like the claim of confidentiality of judicial deliberations, for example, has all the values to which we accord deference for the privacy of all citizens and, added to these values, is the necessity for protection of the public interest in candid, objective, and even blunt or harsh opinions in presidential decision-making. A President and those who assist him must be free to explore alternatives in the process of shaping policies and making decisions and to do so in a way many would be unwilling to express except privately. These are the considerations justifying a presumptive privilege for Presidential communications. The privilege is fundamental to the operation of Government and inextricably rooted in the separation of powers under the Constitution.

The privilege as created by the Court in *Nixon* is not, however, an absolute one. Interests of the other branches of government may override the presidential interest in the privilege. And in *Nixon* the executive privilege was held subordinate to the claim of a GRAND JURY for EVIDENCE "that is demonstrably relevant in a criminal trial." Thus, the weight of the privilege to withhold information differs according to its function. It is at its lowest force when it "is based only on the generalized interest in confidentiality." It is at its strongest when the claim is based on the ground of "military or diplomatic secrets."

The Supreme Court's constitutional DOCTRINE of executive privilege is still in its nascency. The Court, in *Nixon*, particularly eschewed passing on "the balance between the President's generalized interest in confidentiality and the need for relevant evidence in civil litigation, [or] with that between the confidentiality interest and congressional demands for information, [or] with the President's interest in preserving state secrets." In the absence of constitutional language, the constitutional meaning of executive privilege depends totally on judicial creation, for "it is the province and duty of this Court 'to say what the law is.'"

Prior to the *Nixon* decision, the question of executive privilege, especially as it related to demands of Congress on the executive branch, was resolved in the political rather than the judicial arena. It was a contest of wills, with each side exerting its own powers and its own claims on public opinion, which was frequently dispositive of the issue. The strongest power of the Congress lies in its control over the purse and its threat to cut off funding from programs as to which Congress makes inquiry and as to which the executive branch declines to produce the documents sought. The greatest force on the side of the executive branch lies in its capacity to delay acquiescence, since most executive privilege questions become moot or stale through the passage of time.

The problem has a long history in this country, going back to the time that President GEORGE WASHINGTON declined to deliver to the House of Representatives documents relating to JAY'S TREATY, on the grounds that it was none of the business of the House to participate in the treaty process and that all relevant information had, indeed, been delivered to the Senate, whose job it was to advise and consent on the content of treaties. When in the *Burr* case JOHN MARSHALL subpoenaed communications in the hands of President THOMAS JEFFERSON, Jefferson decided which he would and which he would not provide. In *Burr* the judiciary proved helpless against the adamancy of the President to withhold documents,

although the Court might have tried to invoke the CONTEMPT POWER.

Since the investigatory or oversight power of Congress is itself an implied rather than a granted power, its claim to access to presidential papers generally rests on as weak a reed as does the President's claim to immunity from producing the information. Both are implicit rather than express constitutional rights. But the case differs where Congress, particularly the House, is investigating the question of misbehavior of executive branch officials. The Congress is particularly charged by the IMPEACHMENT provisions of the Constitution with the duty of "throwing the rascals out." And surely they must have access to relevant information to determine whether an executive official, be it the President himself, has committed "high crimes and misdemeanors" for which he might be impeached and convicted. But the problem of executive privilege has not arisen in the impeachment context. Rather the impeachment power is used to justify a general congressional power of investigation.

It is with regard to Congress's legislative duty to secure knowledge on which to base its laws or to assure itself that the President is, indeed, engaged in the faithful execution of the laws which Congress has enacted that "executive privilege" problems tend to arise. History provides us with no doctrinal answer to the correct meaning of executive privilege here. Most are agreed that the privilege can be claimed only by the President himself or by a government official at the command of the President. It is not to be invoked even by the vice-president or the secretary of state except through the President. There is little other consensus. Impeachable offenses aside, the privilege is strong where, as the Court noted, it is concerned with military or state secrets. Beyond this, history shows only that the balance between the two constitutional claims, Congress's to be able to perform its duties and the President's to perform his own, has been resolved on an ad hoc basis, with the President having the greater ability to manipulate public opinion, and Congress being able to invoke only the time-consuming processes of contempt and fiscal restraints.

Now that the Supreme Court seems to have made the question of executive privilege a judicial rather than a political one, some further elucidation may be forthcoming. But, except in times of crisis such as the Watergate affair, the mills of the courts, like the mills of the gods, grind so very slowly that they may prove inadequate to provide greater definition to the amorphous concept of executive privilege. This is especially the case since the Court recognized the privilege as a conditional one and not an absolute one, requiring balancing by a judicial arbiter without any special competence to perform the task. It may be predicted, however, that where the conflict is between the judicial and executive branches, as it was in the *Nixon* case, the judicial branch is more likely to prevail, at least in a criminal case or one in which the government itself is seeking the information. But, as between Congress and the President, the Court is likely to be found where it is usually found, aligned with the executive branch.

Executive privilege could cover immunities other than the right to reject a demand for information from another branch. In the Nixon period, the question arose, speculatively, whether a President of the United States could be arrested, indicted, and tried for crime while still in office. That a successful impeachment would leave the person charged with no immunity to arrest, INDICTMENT, and trial is made clear by the words of the Constitution itself. On the other hand, it says nothing about executive immunity while in office. Without judicial precedent or judgment, there appeared to be agreement that the President of the United States and only the President must be immune from interruption of his duties while he holds office, subject only to the necessity for responding to impeachment charges. There is no moment when the President is not on duty, even while on vacation. This immunity, whether termed executive privilege or not, derives from the implications of the Constitution much more readily than his right to refuse to produce documents, which need not interrupt his presidential obligations.

One must assume, too, that the President, like everyone in the nation, can claim the RIGHT AGAINST SELF-INCRIMINATION both in Congress and in the courts. The practical effects on the electorate of such a claim make it highly unlikely that it will ever be invoked. And again, the privilege not to incriminate himself is not the executive privilege as that term is generally used.

The contours of executive privilege remain hard to define, and certainty is not likely to come soon, if ever.

PHILIP B. KURLAND

Bibliography

BERGER, RAOUL 1974 *Executive Privilege: A Constitutional Myth.* Cambridge, Mass.: Harvard University Press.

KURLAND, PHILIP B. 1978 *Watergate and the Constitution.* Chicago: University of Chicago Press.

UNITED STATES SENATE, JUDICIARY COMMITTEE, SUBCOMMITTEE ON SEPARATION OF POWERS 1971 *Executive Privilege: The Withholding of Information by the Executive.* 92nd Congress, 1st session. Washington, D.C.: Government Printing Office.

————, SUBCOMMITTEE ON ADMINISTRATIVE PRACTICE AND PROCEDURE AND SEPARATION OF POWERS, AND COMMITTEE ON GOVERNMENT OPERATIONS, SUBCOMMITTEE ON INTERGOVERNMENTAL RELATIONS 1973 *Freedom of Information: Executive Privilege; Secrecy in Government.* 3 Vols. 93rd Congress, 1st session. Washington, D.C.: Government Printing Office.

EXHAUSTION OF REMEDIES

Exhaustion-of-remedies questions arise in at least two areas of constitutional adjudication. Since *Ex parte Royall* (1886), state prisoners have been required to exhaust available, effective state court remedies before seeking federal HABEAS CORPUS relief from allegedly unconstitutional state convictions. Congress codified this result more than half a century later. The exhaustion requirement, which is not constitutionally mandated, is said to reflect the Court's sensitivity to relations between federal and state courts; a federal court is prevented from reviewing a state conviction until state courts have had a chance to correct constitutional errors.

In another class of cases seeking to vindicate constitutional rights, the Supreme Court does not require exhaustion of state judicial remedies. In MONROE V. PAPE (1961) and a series of later cases, the Court has stated that there is no requirement of exhaustion of state judicial remedies before bringing an action against state officials under SECTION 1983, TITLE 42, UNITED STATES CODE. *Patsy v. Board of Regents* (1982) held that litigants bringing section 1983 cases also need not exhaust state administrative remedies and thereby resolved a long-standing conflict among the courts of appeal. In the Civil Rights of Institutionalized Persons Act (1980), Congress imposed an exhaustion-of-administrative-remedies requirement upon certain prisoners bringing actions under section 1983.

The exhaustion requirement in habeas corpus cases, and its absence in section 1983 cases, generates difficulty in deciding whether to require exhaustion in constitutional actions brought by prisoners, many of which may be brought either as habeas actions or as section 1983 cases. In *Preiser v. Rodriguez* (1973) the Court held that exhaustion was required in a case close to "the core of habeas corpus," that is, one attacking the validity of a prisoner's conviction or otherwise challenging the fact or duration of confinement. When the prisoner challenges the conditions of confinement, the Court said, the nonexhaustion rule applicable to section 1983 cases governs. Perhaps inspired in part by the long-standing exhaustion requirement in habeas corpus cases, much modern CIVIL RIGHTS legislation reflects sensitivity to state prerogatives by requiring complainants initially to present claims to state authorities. Title VII of the CIVIL RIGHTS ACT OF 1964 requires resort to state antidiscrimination agencies before the Equal Employment Opportunity Commission may act on a complaint. Title VIII of the CIVIL RIGHTS ACT OF 1968 requires federal administrators to allow state and local housing agencies the first chance at a housing discrimination complaint. But post-Civil War ANTIDISCRIMINATION LEGISLATION, such as the CIVIL RIGHTS ACTS OF 1866 and 1870, reflected no such sensitivity. And the practice is not uniform in modern statutes. The VOTING RIGHTS ACT OF 1965 expressly rejects any requirement of exhaustion of administrative or other remedies before initiation of actions in federal court. Other civil rights statutes simply do not address the issue.

THEODORE EISENBERG

Bibliography

COMMENT 1974 Exhaustion of State Administrative Remedies in Section 1983 Cases. *University of Chicago Law Review* 41:537–556.

NAHMOD, SHELDON H. 1979 *Civil Rights & Civil Liberties Litigation.* Pages 143–148. Colorado Springs, Colo.: Shepard's.

EXIGENT CIRCUMSTANCES SEARCH

Although the Supreme Court has denounced WARRANTLESS SEARCHES as *"per se* unreasonable under the FOURTH AMENDMENT," it has recognized "a few specifically established and well-delineated exceptions" to this rule based on exigent circumstances. A SEARCH WARRANT, which in ordinary circumstances provides constitutional reasonableness for a search, may be dispensed with if the delay involved in obtaining the warrant might defeat the purpose of the search. In fact, far more searches are made without warrants than with them. The warrantless search is "exceptional" only in the sense that exceptional (that is, exigent) circumstances are needed to justify it.

Five types of warrantless searches have thus far received the Court's sanction. In WEEKS V. UNITED STATES (1914) the Court upheld SEARCH INCIDENT TO ARREST of a person—and, in later cases, of the area under the arrestee's control— in order to disarm him and prevent the destruction of EVIDENCE. The search of an automobile on the road is constitutional when there is PROBABLE CAUSE to believe the automobile is transporting contraband. As the Court said in CARROLL V. UNITED STATES (1925), to delay the AUTOMOBILE SEARCH is to risk the escape of driver and vehicle. "Hot pursuit" of a suspected felon into a building was held reasonable in WARDEN V. HAYDEN (1967). Delaying to obtain a warrant might endanger the lives of the pursuing officers and others. Such a search may continue until the suspect is apprehended and his weapons are seized. In SCHMERBER V. CALIFORNIA (1966) the Court permitted the compulsory taking of blood from an individual to determine whether he was intoxicated while driving when there was probable cause to believe that he was. The exigency in such cases is furnished by the fact that the level of alcohol in the blood diminishes after its intake ceases. In TERRY V. OHIO (1968) the Court upheld the practice of stopping a suspect and frisking his outer clothing to discover concealed weapons, even when probable cause for an arrest is lacking, provided that circumstances entitle an officer to believe that a criminal venture is about to be launched and that his safety or that of others is endangered.

The concept of exigent circumstances is an open one. Indeed, in *Mincey v. Arizona* (1978) the Court indicated that officers may enter and search without a warrant upon reasonable belief that there is a "need to protect or preserve life or avoid serious injury. . . ."

JACOB W. LANDYNSKI

Bibliography

LANDYNSKI, JACOB W. 1971 The Supreme Court's Search for Fourth Amendment Standards: The Warrantless Search. *Connecticut Bar Journal* 45:2–39.

EX PARTE

(Latin: "From the part [of]. . . .") A legal proceeding is said to be *ex parte* if it occurs on the application or for the benefit of one party without NOTICE to or contest by an adverse party. In the reports such a case is entitled *"Ex parte . . ."* followed by the name of the party at whose instance the case is heard. A proceeding of which an adverse party has notice, but at which he declines to appear, is not considered *ex parte.* Writs, INJUNCTIONS, etcetera, are said to be *ex parte* when they are issued without prior notice to an affected party.

DENNIS J. MAHONEY

EX PARTE . . .

See under name of party

EXPATRIATION

Expatriation was defined by the Supreme Court in *Perkins v. Elg* (1939) as "the voluntary renunciation or abandonment of nationality and allegiance." It refers to the loss of CITIZENSHIP as a result of voluntary action taken by a citizen, either native-born or naturalized. By expatriation, a citizen becomes an ALIEN; he divests himself of the obligations of citizenship and loses the rights connected with those obligations. In general, he can regain citizenship only by the process of NATURALIZATION.

At COMMON LAW, a person owed perpetual allegiance to the country of his birth and could not expatriate himself without the consent of that country. Initially, there was an inclination in the United States to follow this rule. In 1868, however, Congress explicitly broke with that tradition and declared by statute that "the right of expatriation is a natural and inherent right of all people, indispensable to the enjoyment of the rights of life, liberty, and the pursuit of happiness." Congress did so in order to establish that persons naturalized in the United States did not continue to owe allegiance to foreign governments. Congress seemed to rely on the simple mechanism of formal renunciation to determine whether a citizen actually wished to expatriate himself. Because the statute made expatriation dependent upon the voluntary action of the individual, it raised no constitutional questions about Congress's power over expatriation.

Determination of volition, however, has never been limited to formal renunciation, and through a series of nationality statutes, culminating in the Immigration and Nationality Act of 1952, Congress has identified various actions that indicate a citizen's desire voluntarily to expatriate himself. These actions include obtaining naturalization in a foreign state, taking an oath of allegiance to a foreign state, serving in a foreign army, voting in a foreign election, desertion from the armed forces, TREASON against the United States, assuming public office under the government of a foreign state for which only nationals of that state are eligible, formal renunciation of citizenship either in the United States or abroad, and leaving or remaining outside the United States during either a war or a national emergency for the purpose of evading military service.

Congress's power to declare that such actions constitute voluntary renunciation, even when the individual who so acts claims not to have intended to renounce his citizenship, was rarely challenged by the courts until the 1960s. Nationality laws were shielded from judicial scrutiny because the courts believed it was beyond their competence to examine matters so intimately related to foreign affairs. However, in the landmark decision of AFROYIM V. RUSK (1967), the Supreme Court restored citizenship to a naturalized citizen who was considered by the government to have expatriated himself by voting in an Israeli parliamentary election. The Court held that although Congress can provide a mechanism by which an individual can voluntarily expatriate himself, volition is a judicially ascertainable quality and the government bears the BURDEN OF PROOF that the citizen's renunciation was truly voluntary. Put simply, *Afroyim* made the statutory presumption of volition rebuttable rather than conclusive.

While the BURGER COURT seemed to retreat from these principles in *Rogers v. Bellei* (1971), in *Vance v. Terrazas* (1980) it reaffirmed *Afroyim* and held that the government must prove specific intent to surrender citizenship and not simply the voluntary commission of an expatriating act. At the same time, the Court upheld the rebuttable presumption that an act of expatriation is performed with the specific intention of relinquishing citizenship and held that Congress is free to prescribe as the evidentiary standard for proving this intention the "preponderance-of-the-evidence" standard of proof.

RALPH A. ROSSUM

Bibliography

GORDON, CHARLES and ROSENFIELD, HARRY N. 1984 *Immigration Law and Procedure,* Vol. 3, chap. 20. New York: Matthew Bender.
SCHWARTZ, DAVID F. 1975 American Citizenship after *Afroyim* and *Bellei:* Continuing Controversy. *Hastings Constitutional Law Quarterly* 2:1003–1028.

EXPOSITION AND PROTEST
(1828–1829)

JOHN C. CALHOUN drafted the *Exposition* in 1828. The next year, the legislature of South Carolina published the *Exposition* in amended form along with its own resolution of protest against the TARIFF ACT OF 1828. Like most of the great controversial documents in American politics it took the form of a discourse on the meaning of the Constitution. It argued the case for STRICT CONSTRUCTION of the powers of the federal government and spelled out the doctrine of NULLIFICATION.

Rejecting the argument that a protective tariff was justified by custom and precedent, the *Exposition* declared: "Ours is not a government of precedent. . . . The only safe rule is the Constitution itself." But even the Constitution was not a safe rule if its interpretation were left to Congress and the Supreme Court, which were its creatures. The only authoritative interpreter was the constituent body itself, the people of the states in convention.

According to the *Exposition,* if a convention in any state declared a federal law unconstitutional, the law was null and void in that state until the Constitution was amended to authorize the disputed act. Should an amendment pass the state would have no recourse but SECESSION.

DENNIS J. MAHONEY

Bibliography

FREEHLING, WILLIAM W. 1965 *Prelude to Civil War: The Nullification Controversy in South Carolina, 1816–1865.* New York: Harper & Row.

EX POST FACTO

In THE FEDERALIST #84 ALEXANDER HAMILTON argued that "the creation of crimes after the commission of the fact, or, in other words, the subjecting of men to punishment for things which, when they were done, were breaches of no law" has been "in all ages" one of "the favorite and most formidable instruments of tyranny." Indeed, ex post facto legislation has generally been regarded as a violation of the fundamental DUE PROCESS requirement that there must be fair warning of the conduct which gives rise to criminal penalties. The Framers of the Constitution believed so strongly that ex post facto laws were contrary to the principles of republican government that they proscribed their use in two different provisions of the Constitution: Article I, section 9, as a specific exception to the powers of the United States Congress, and Article I, section 10, as a specific prohibition on the powers of state legislatures.

Justice SAMUEL CHASE in CALDER V. BULL (1798) provided what has since come to be regarded as the authoritative delineation of the kinds of LEGISLATION that fall within the Constitution's prohibition against ex post facto enactments:

1st. Every law that makes an action done before the passing of the law, and which was *innocent* when done, criminal; and punishes such action. 2d. Every law that *aggravates a crime,* or makes it *greater* than it was, when committed. 3d. Every law that *changes the punishment,* and inflicts a *greater punishment,* than the law annexed to the crime, when committed. 4th. Every law that alters the *legal* rules of *evidence,* and received less, or different, testimony, than the law required at the time of the commission of the offence, *in order to convict the offender.*

Although there is some question about the Framers' intent, the Supreme Court has consistently followed Chase's lead in restricting the ex post facto rule to criminal laws. Thus the Court has held that the deportation of ALIENS, the loss of a passport, and the denial of certain benefits do not fall within the ex post facto exception because they are not punishments in a criminal sense even though they may be "burdensome and severe." In the TEST OATH CASES (1867), however, the Court held that oaths that disqualified people from holding certain offices or practicing certain professions constituted ex post facto laws.

The essential ingredient of an ex post facto law is its retrospective character; but not all retrospective laws are ex post facto in the technical meaning of the term. An ex post facto law not only is retrospective but also injures those to whom it is directed by imposing or increasing criminal penalties. For example, *Weaver v. Graham* (1981) invalidated retroactive application to a prisoner of a law reducing "good time" credits against a sentence. Retrospective laws that ameliorate penalties, however, are not ex post facto.

The rights affected by retrospective legislation must be substantial. As the Court held in *Beazell v. Ohio* (1925), statutory changes in trial procedures or rules of EVIDENCE "which do not deprive the accused of a defense and which operate only in a limited and unsubstantial manner to his disadvantage, are not prohibited." Thus, the ex post facto prohibition secures "substantial personal rights against arbitrary and oppressive legislation without limiting legislative control of remedies and procedures that do not affect matters of substance." Of its own weight, the ex post facto prohibition applies only to legislative acts, and not to changes in the law effected by judicial decisions. But where an unforeseeable statutory construction by a court is applied retrospectively in a manner that is tantamount to ex post facto legislation, that construction is barred by the due process clause. Although the particular application of the ex post facto clause has generated much controversy and debate, and involves, on occasion, the most intricate and detailed considerations, there seems to be almost universal agreement that the Constitution's prohibition against ex post facto legislation remains one of the mainstays of constitutional government.

EDWARD J. ERLER

Bibliography

FIELD, OLIVER P. 1922 Ex Post Facto in the Constitution. *Michigan Law Review* 20:315–331.

NOTE 1975 Ex Post Facto Limitations on Legislative Power. *Michigan Law Review* 73:1491–1516.

EXTRADITION

See: Fugitive from Justice

EXTRATERRITORIALITY

Around the turn of the century, the Supreme Court placed strict territorial limits on the application of United States constitutional and statutory law. In the case of *In re Ross* (1891) the Court held that a citizen could be tried by an American consular court, without INDICTMENT by GRAND JURY and without TRIAL BY JURY, for crimes aboard an American ship in Japan. The Court flatly declared that "[t]he Constitution can have no operation in another country." And in *American Banana Co. v. United Fruit Co.* (1909) Justice OLIVER WENDELL HOLMES asserted that "[a]ll legislation is prima facie territorial." Although he acknowledged that exceptions could be found in the case of laws applying on the high seas or in "uncivilized" countries, Holmes said "the general and almost universal rule is that the character of an act as lawful or unlawful must be determined wholly by the law of the country where the act is done." No doubt these sweeping statements, even then, were not literally followed. In any event, today DOCTRINES limiting the extraterritorial application of both the Constitution and statutory law have been abandoned.

In REID V. COVERT (1956) the Court effectively overruled *Ross* and held that Congress could not deprive a citizen of the right to a jury trial in a court-martial abroad where CAPITAL PUNISHMENT was potentially involved. Justice HUGO L. BLACK said: "When the Government reaches out to punish a citizen who is abroad, the shield which the BILL OF RIGHTS and other parts of the Constitution provide to protect his life and liberty should not be stripped away just because he happens to be in another land." This decision signaled the end of territorial limitations on the Constitution.

In *United States v. Toscanino* (2d Cir. 1974) a lower court applied the FOURTH and Fifth AMENDMENTS where American officials instigated enforcement activity by foreign officials that included torture and violated United States treaty obligations. Although other courts have declined to apply CONSTITUTIONAL REMEDIES in the circumstances of particular cases before them, they agree that the Bill of Rights may apply where the United States government instigates conduct that "shocks the conscience." The JUST COMPENSATION clause of the Fifth Amendment has also been held applicable to TAKINGS OF PROPERTY abroad in several lower court cases. As a general rule, therefore, the Constitution now unquestionably applies to acts of government abroad.

At the same time the special circumstances that are invariably present in these cases influence the scope of constitutional protection afforded. Although the court only occasionally confronts these questions, it seems clear that protection against government action abroad is more difficult to obtain than in similar cases without a foreign element. This is especially true when foreign policy or national security interests are at issue, as was the case in UNITED STATES V. CURTISS-WRIGHT EXPORT CORP. (1936). Indeed, in HAIG V. AGEE (1981) the Supreme Court questioned whether the FIRST AMENDMENT would apply at all to government suppression of speech abroad, where the speech threatened American intelligence activity.

Perhaps the most accurate description of the modern approach to extraterritorial application of constitutional law was made by Justice JOHN MARSHALL HARLAN in *Reid v. Covert*. He took exception to the broad suggestion that "every provision of the Constitution must be deemed automatically applicable to American citizens in every part of the world." He believed that "the question is *which* guarantees of the Constitution *should* apply in view of the particular circumstances, the practical necessities, and the possible alternatives which Congress had before it." The Harlan view seems more likely to prevail in a world of increased American involvement and interdependence than the absolutist approach of Justice Black.

A related issue of historical interest was whether the Constitution applied to TERRITORIES acquired by the United States. Constitutional guarantees limiting legislative and executive power were applicable only when Congress, expressly or by clear implication, "incorporated" the acquired territory into the United States. In unincorporated territories only undefined "fundamental" liberties were guaranteed.

Finally, the courts have repeatedly applied federal statutes to conduct abroad, assuming other jurisdictional prerequisites were met. Occasionally limitations on the application of a particular statute have been imposed, but those limitations have normally been based on the presumed intent of Congress or on international comity, not the Constitution.

PHILLIP R. TRIMBLE

Bibliography

COUDERT, FREDERIC R. 1926 The Evolution of the Doctrine of Territorial Incorporation. *Columbia Law Review* 26:823–850; *Iowa State Bar Association Report* 1926:180–228.

HENKIN, LOUIS 1972 *Foreign Affairs and the Constitution.* Pages 266–269. Mineola, N.Y.: Foundation Press.

KAPLAN, STEVEN M. 1977 The Applicability of the Exclusionary Rule in Federal Court to Evidence Seized and Confessions Obtained in Foreign Countries. *Columbia Journal of Transnational Law* 16:495–520.

NOTE 1985 Predictability and Comity: Toward Common Principles of Extraterritorial Jurisdiction. *Harvard Law Review* 98:1310–1330.

FAIR COMMENT

See: Libel and the First Amendment

FAIR HEARING

In numerous contexts the Constitution requires the state to afford its citizens DUE PROCESS, which frequently includes an adversarial voicing of opposed contentions. "Fair hearing" in this broadest sense could thus include both the specific constitutional guarantees that attach to criminal trials and the more general requirement that civil litigation meet minimal standards of fairness. Among lawyers, however, the term more narrowly refers to the procedure that must be afforded to persons involved not in judicial trials but in some less formal dispute with the state. Speaking to that issue, the Supreme Court has asked when the Constitution requires any process and what that process should be. For some time the Court focused on the first question, assuming that if any process was due, it would resemble a formal trial; later decisions emphasized the flexibility of appropriate process.

For due process requirements to attach to any proceedings, they must, by involving governmental action that threatens life, liberty, or property, fall within the requirements of the Fifth and FOURTEENTH AMENDMENTS. Following in the wake of the welfare state, the Court has expanded its definition of property to include entitlements to various government benefits (for example, welfare and disability payments, tenured positions in state employment). Many threatened deprivations of such benefits consequently require due process, and the question becomes what that process must be. The Court has never answered that question in categorical terms, insisting that each situation calls for a rather individualized judgment. It has, however, suggested some minimal criteria and a set of factors to be considered in striking the balance from case to case. In deciding what process is due, one must consider "first, the private interest . . . affected by the official action; second, the risk of an erroneous deprivation of such interest through the procedures used, and the probable value, if any, of additional or substitute procedural safeguards; and finally, the government's interest, including the function involved and the fiscal and administrative burdens that the additional or substitute procedural requirements would entail" (MATHEWS V. ELDRIDGE, 1976). These factors represent an attempt to arrive at conclusions about two aspects of process: timing and elaborateness.

At a minimum, due process requires notice that tells the person threatened with deprivation the reason for the action and how he can challenge its factual and legal bases. Usually notice and such an opportunity must precede the deprivation, but even this proposition is not invariable; thus in a case of a threat to public health or other emergency situation, a seizure could occur first and notice and hearing afterward.

More difficult than the question of the timing of the required process is its nature. Because the Court has been unable to articulate guidelines applicable to all situations, it defines appropriate processes on a case-by-case basis. Consequently one can fully understand the requirements of due process only by sampling a large number of cases. It is, however, possible to suggest some rough guidelines and some distinctions. The first might be the line between situations requiring formal adjudicatory hearings, as for the termination of WELFARE BENEFITS in GOLDBERG V. KELLY (1970), and those that do not: the more serious the deprivation, the more likely the Court is to require a trial-type hearing. Even when such a hearing is not required, one can further differentiate situations according to the formality of the process required: the state must provide a written statement of reasons for ending disability benefits and give the recipient a chance to respond (*Mathews v. Eldridge*), but a school official need engage only in a brief oral conversation before suspending a student, as in GOSS V. LOPEZ (1975). Indeed, the Court has approved procedures that are not even adversarial in the normal sense, for example, an expulsion proceeding in which a medical student has an opportunity to demonstrate her medical skills to several local doctors over several days. (See BOARD OF CURATORS V. HOROWITZ, 1978.)

The consequence of such flexibility is that a constitutionally "fair hearing" need not entail a hearing at all, and even if it does that hearing may occupy various points along a continuum of adjudicatory formality. Such flexibility results from the Court's attempts, once it has concluded that due process attaches, to tailor the process to the situation at hand, taking some account of the stakes for the adversaries and of the goals of process. Some commentators have criticized the Court for the narrowness of its focus, arguing that the goals of process include the dignity of the participants as well as the accuracy of the result; the Court has seemed unpersuaded of this point.

The constitutional focus on fair hearings in administrative law has drawn attention to a number of areas presenting similar profiles—to which, however, due process does not apply, either because the institutions involved are private or because life, liberty, or property is not threatened. Nevertheless, under the influence of the constitutional cases many institutions (such as private schools or trade associations) have adopted processes that resemble those that might be required if due process did apply. Some of these procedures have resulted from legislation or regulation and an occasional judicial decision using COMMON LAW; others have come voluntarily. In either case the consequence has been a softening of the lines between the practices of public and private institutions; there is thus a sense in which one can speak of a fair hearing as a practice (though not a constitutional requirement) of many areas of institutional life.

If fairness does not always require a hearing, it is nevertheless true that the constitutional ideal described by the term has permeated many areas of life where neither fairness nor a hearing is constitutionally required. The result, in a society of large institutions and sometimes uncertain responsibility for decisions, has been a requirement taking many forms but having at its basis the idea that persons about to be adversely affected have the right to know why and to respond.

STEPHEN C. YEAZELL

Bibliography

FRIENDLY, HENRY   1975   Some Kind of Hearing. *University of Pennsylvania Law Review* 123:1267–1317.
MASHAW, JERRY L.   1976   The Supreme Court's Due Process Calculus for Administrative Adjudication in *Mathews v. Eldridge:* Three Factors in Search of a Theory of Value. *University of Chicago Law Review* 44:28–59.
VERKUIL, PAUL   1975   The Ombudsman and the Limits of the Adversary System. *Columbia Law Review* 75:845–861.

FAIR HOUSING LAWS

See: Open Housing Laws

FAIR LABOR STANDARDS ACT
52 Stat. 1060 (1938)

The Fair Labor Standards Act (FLSA), usually called the federal wage and hour law, was adopted in 1938. For all covered employees the act required the payment of a minimum wage (initially 25 cents an hour) and time and one-half for all hours worked over forty a week. Child labor was forbidden under certain circumstances. The act prohibited the shipment in INTERSTATE COMMERCE of goods produced under substandard conditions. There were numerous and complicated exemptions.

The constitutionality of the act under the COMMERCE CLAUSE was sustained by the Supreme Court in UNITED STATES V. DARBY LUMBER CO. (1940). Since then the act has been amended many times, principally to increase periodically the minimum wage, which reached $3.35 an hour in 1981, to expand coverage, and to provide more effective enforcement.

The act originally covered employees engaged in commerce or in the PRODUCTION of goods for commerce. Production was defined to include activities necessary to the actual production.

Coverage based on engagement in commerce includes employees engaged in the actual movement of commerce, such as transportation, shipping, and communications. It also includes employees whose work involves the distribution or receipt of goods across state lines. The Supreme Court upheld application of the act to employees who did construction or repair work on interstate instrumentalities and even to employees who prepared plans and specifications for the construction or repair of interstate instrumentalities.

Under the extended production definition, many fringe activities were found necessary to production. Thus, the Court upheld application to employees of an office building occupied by a corporation which at other locations produced goods for commerce and to employees of an independent contractor washing windows in industrial plants that produced goods for commerce.

These decisions, although they involved statutory construction, demonstrated the enormous scope of the commerce power even under coverage formulas less extensive than that used to describe the constitutional maximum, "affecting" commerce. The breadth of the Court's holdings led Congress in 1949 to amend the statute to confine the extended production definition to activities "closely related" and "directly essential" to production.

The reduced coverage effectuated by this change was largely nullified, however, by a 1961 amendment providing for "enterprise" coverage. Before 1961 coverage was determined for each employee; thus, some employees of an employer could be covered while others were not. "Enterprise" coverage extended to all an employer's employees, if at least two employees were covered individually and the enterprise did a requisite annual dollar volume of business. The constitutionality of "enterprise" coverage was upheld by the Court in *Maryland v. Wirtz* (1967).

Other aspects of the act have also received expansive interpretation. Thus, the term "employee" has been defined in accordance with "economic reality" rather than COMMON LAW rules, and applied to persons who in other contexts would be independent contractors. These cases illustrate the peculiar American phenomenon of defining "employee" differently under various statutes, so that an employee may be covered under one statute and not under another.

What constitutes compensable work time has presented a special problem under the FLSA. In *Armour & Co. v. Wantoch* (1944), involving firefighters, the Court held that inactive waiting time was compensable work time. Time spent in travel between the mine entrance and the underground cutting face was held compensable in *Tennessee Coal, Inc. & Railroad v. Muscoda Local* (1944). Finally, in *Anderson v. Mt. Clemens Pottery Co.* (1946), the Court required payment for time spent by employees walking between the factory gate and their work place. Many lawsuits were promptly filed claiming billions of dollars in back wages. Congress responded by enacting the Portal-to-Portal Act of 1947, which distinguished between an employee's compensable principal activity and noncompensable preliminary and after-working activities. Employers were thus absolved in most cases from liability under the *Mt. Clemens Pottery* decision. The Court held, however, that time spent changing clothes, when necessitated by the nature of the work, is a principal activity and thus compensable.

The FLSA applies on a work week basis. Overtime is required for hours in excess of forty a week. The required time and one-half premium is applied to the employee's "regular rate of pay" which is determined by dividing the total weekly compensation (including straight wages plus all fringe benefits) by the number of hours worked. Because employee pay plans are of great variety, determination of the regular rate of pay frequently is a difficult problem.

Among the principal exemptions from the FLSA are executive, administrative, and professional employees (which terms have special definitions), employees of small retail or service establishments, and some employees engaged in agriculture. Special provision is made for learners, apprentices, students, and the handicapped.

The act is enforced by individual employee suits for back wages, or suits by the secretary of labor seeking an INJUNCTION as well as back wages. Individual suits are preempted by suits by the secretary. Liquidated DAMAGES are authorized. TRIAL BY JURY is available in employee suits, but generally is denied in combined injunction–back-wage suits by the secretary. The FLSA is unique in labor legislation in providing criminal prosecution for willful violators. Such actions are handled by the Justice Department, but have not been a major aspect of the statute's enforcement.

Originally the FLSA applied only to private employment. In 1966 it was extended to employees of state hospitals and schools; this extension was sustained in *Maryland v. Wirtz* (1967). In 1974 Congress extended the FLSA to almost all state and local government employees. In NATIONAL LEAGUE OF CITIES V. USERY (1976) the Court held that the TENTH AMENDMENT protected state sovereign functions against commerce power regulation and overruled *Maryland v. Wirtz*. *Usery* in turn was overruled by GARCIA V. SAN ANTONIO METROPOLITAN TRANSIT

AUTHORITY (1985). Congress responded the same year with legislation authorizing states and cities to reimburse employees for overtime with compensatory time off in lieu of cash payment.

In 1938 the principal purpose of the FLSA was to combat the Depression by increasing the purchasing power in the hands of the lowest-paid workers. Thus, it has been called the original antipoverty law. Fifty years later, the wisdom of the act and its effect on the economy are still debated, but the FLSA survives as a permanent and major piece of American labor legislation.

WILLIAM P. MURPHY

Bibliography

PLAYER, MACK 1975 Enterprise Coverage under the Fair Labor Standards Act: An Assessment of the First Generation. *Vanderbilt Law Review* 28:283–347.

WILLIS, ROBERT N. 1972 The Evolution of the Fair Labor Standards Act. *University of Miami Law Review* 26:607–634.

FAIRNESS DOCTRINE

Born out of a progression of decisions by the Federal Communications Commission (FCC) and then codified by Congress in 1959, the fairness doctrine requires a BROADCASTING license holder "to operate in the public interest and to afford reasonable opportunity for the discussion of conflicting views on issues of public importance." Although the doctrine was upheld against a FIRST AMENDMENT challenge in RED LION BROADCASTING COMPANY V. FCC (1969), it has been perceived increasingly as an intrusive exception to the First Amendment, with diminishing justification.

The doctrine, applicable to radio and television licensees and to some cable operators, requires a licensee that presents a controversial issue to provide a reasonable amount of time for contrasting viewpoints. A less frequently litigated aspect of the doctrine requires affirmative coverage of issues important to the public. Finally, the doctrine assures persons who are disparaged on the airwaves a limited right to respond.

The doctrine reflects a distinction in the way Congress and the courts have conceived of newspapers, on the one hand, and broadcasters on the other. Thus, in MIAMI HERALD V. TORNILLO (1974) the Supreme Court held unconstitutional on First Amendment grounds a Florida statute that required a newspaper to grant a right of reply to persons attacked in its columns. The Court did not distinguish *Red Lion* but ignored it.

Recently a campaign to narrow, if not eliminate, the fairness doctrine has gained momentum. When the fairness doctrine was in full sway, its justification was a supposed scarcity of the channels available for transmission of broadcast signals. Those who wished to communicate by the printed word were not curtailed by government action or the rationing of resources. On the other hand, the number of channels for radio and television transmission was demonstrably limited. Cable television and other new technologies have undermined the "scarcity" justification for regulation by providing abundant new channels.

Some have argued that the spectrum of broadcasting channels is a public resource, and thus that the federal government can insist that a private user of that resource give voice to many speakers. In another perspective, emphasis on the right of the licensee to be an unencumbered editor is misplaced. Expressing this view, in *Red Lion*, the Court said that "it is the right of the viewers and listeners, not the right of broadcasters, which is paramount." (See LISTENERS' RIGHTS.)

Recent commentary has proposed quite a different solution to the "fairness" issue: setting aside segments of broadcast time, or even whole channels, for public access. Owners of broadcasting stations would have no editorial control over these "soapboxes of the air." Broadcasters generally consider the fairness doctrine a badge of second-class citizenship in the ranks of the press. The FCC, in the early 1980s, confined the fairness doctrine's scope and considered its repeal. As an interim measure the FCC announced that asserted violations would not be adjudicated individually, but would be considered when a broadcaster sought renewal of a license. Still, despite these limits, the doctrine continues to influence the culture of television. Producers of national and local television news programs take great care to present at least two sides of important controversial issues.

MONROE E. PRICE

Bibliography

BOLLINGER, LEE 1976 Freedom of the Press and Public Access: Toward a Theory of Partial Regulation of the Mass Media. *University of Michigan Law Review* 75:1–42.

FAIR RETURN ON FAIR VALUE

The DOCTRINE of a fair return on a fair value, which the Supreme Court propounded in SMYTH V. AMES (1898), provided that any government regulation of rate schedules charged by railroads or utilities must allow a reasonable profit or fair rate of return based on a fair valuation of the property. The principal considerations were the original cost of the property, and the cost of reproducing it at the time of the rate regulation. Having entered the business of supervising the details of ratemaking, the Court remained in that business until 1944.

The Court first provided the basis for the doctrine by equating rate regulation with EMINENT DOMAIN: just compensation must accompany a TAKING OF PROPERTY, and to the Court a rate regulation was comparable to a taking. In CHICAGO, MILWAUKEE, AND ST. PAUL RAILWAY COMPANY V. MINNESOTA (1890) the Court declared that the failure to allow a company to charge reasonable rates for the use of its property constituted an unconstitutional taking of property or a violation of SUBSTANTIVE DUE PROCESS OF LAW comparable to a taking. In REAGAN V. FARMERS' LOAN AND TRUST COMPANY (1894) the Court voided rates because they were fixed so low that they virtually took property without compensation. (See GRANGER CASES.) In *Smyth v. Ames* the Court, in a unanimous opinion by Justice JOHN M. HARLAN, proclaimed that a company was entitled to receive a reasonable profit based on the rates it could charge and that a reasonable rate must be determined by the fair value of the property. To ascertain that value, Harlan declared that among the matters to be considered "and given such weight as may be just and right in each case" are the following: "the original cost of construction, the amount expended in permanent improvements, the amount and market value of its bonds and stock, the present as compared with the original cost of construction, the probable earning capacity of the property under particular rates prescribed by statute, and the sum required to meet operating expenses. . . ."

Prior to World War I, the Court usually relied on original costs in determining whether a particular rate schedule yielded a fair return. The Court switched to reproduction costs after the war, when prices and costs rose, thereby challenging more rates. *Smyth's* vague and flexible standards allowed the Court to act as it wished, without restraints. In UNITED RAILWAYS & ELECTRIC COMPANY V. WEST (1930), for example, the Court voided rates allowing a profit of 6.26 percent on the ground that anything less than 7.5 percent was "confiscatory."

Fair value governed fair return standards against the opposition of Justices LOUIS D. BRANDEIS and OLIVER WENDELL HOLMES, who attacked the doctrine as legally and economically unsound. In 1939,

Justices FELIX FRANKFURTER and HUGO L. BLACK called for the rejection of the doctrine, and in 1942 the Court indicated that the determination of property value, although useful, was not indispensable. Finally, in FEDERAL POWER COMMISSION V. HOPE NATURAL GAS (1944), the Court rejected the fair value doctrine. Thereafter the Court permitted government ratemaking bodies to fix rates without judicial interference, on condition that the ratemaking process respected PROCEDURAL DUE PROCESS.

LEONARD W. LEVY

Bibliography
HALE, ROBERT L. 1952 *Freedom through Law.* New York: Columbia University Press.

FAIR TRIAL

The requirement of a fair trial in criminal proceedings has its constitutional source in the due process clause of the Fifth and FOURTEENTH AMENDMENTs, which declares that no person shall be deprived of "life, liberty, or property, without DUE PROCESS OF LAW." Other provisions of the BILL OF RIGHTS deal explicitly with particular aspects of a criminal trial. Historically, the coverage of those provisions has tended to expand, narrowing the application of the more general provision. The "incorporation" of provisions of the Fifth and SIXTH AMENDMENTs into the due process clause of the Fourteenth Amendment is especially noteworthy in this respect, having had the effect of eliminating the need for fair-trial analysis of issues in state cases covered by those provisions. While important elements of a fair trial are thus treated individually, the requirements can be summarized generally as a hearing before a competent, impartial tribunal, at which the prosecutor does not present the government's case inaccurately or unfairly and the defendant has an opportunity to present his case fully and effectively.

Ordinarily, any judge of a court having JURISDICTION is presumed to be competent to hear a criminal case. However, a judge is presumed not to be impartial if he has a substantial personal interest in a verdict against the defendant. The requirement of a fair trial prohibits a judge from sitting in that circumstance. In *Tumey v. Ohio* (1927) the Supreme Court held invalid a local practice assigning the mayor of a village as judge in criminal cases, because the compensation for his judicial services and other income for the village accrued only if the defendant were convicted and a fine imposed. In *In re Murchison* (1955) the Court overturned convictions for criminal contempt following a trial before the same judge who was the defendants' accuser and the principal witness against them.

The Sixth Amendment gives a criminal defendant the right to be tried by an "impartial jury." That provision, which applies to federal and state trials, entitles the defendant to a jury selected from a representative cross-section of the community, without inclusions or exclusions because of sex, nationality, race, or other impermissible classifications. (See JURY DISCRIMINATION.) The jury finally chosen need not have any particular composition or be representative of the community as a whole.

The defendant must have a reasonable opportunity to uncover bias or prejudice of an individual juror. This is afforded by VOIR DIRE, the examination of prospective jurors. The trial judge or the prosecutor and defense counsel question the members of the jury panel to reveal any basis for disqualification in the particular case. The trial judge has broad discretion to direct the conduct and scope of the examination, provided it is adequate to ensure the jurors' impartiality. Counsel for either side may challenge a juror "for cause" if there is a basis for disqualification and then exercise a limited number of "peremptory" challenges without explanation. In an effort to secure an impartial jury, the prosecutor may, under the DOCTRINE of SWAIN V. ALABAMA (1965), exercise peremptory challenges on the basis of group factors such as race or nationality.

However fair the formal means for ensuring an impartial tribunal, a trial conducted in an atmosphere of mob violence or insistent public pressure for conviction does not meet the constitutional standard. (See MOORE V. DEMPSEY, 1923.)

The Sixth Amendment gives a criminal defendant the RIGHT TO BE INFORMED OF THE ACCUSATION. This right, which is essential to a fair trial, requires that the statement of the offense charged identify the criminal conduct and the circumstances of the alleged crime precisely enough for the defendant to prepare his defense.

Although the constitutional guarantee of a fair trial does not ordinarily entitle the defendant to PRETRIAL DISCLOSURE of the EVIDENCE against him, all jurisdictions allow limited pretrial DISCOVERY of evidence and some allow rather full discovery subject only to special exceptions. Whenever evidence against the accused is disclosed, the defendant is entitled to enough time to prepare to meet it; if evidence is not disclosed before trial, the defendant may be entitled to a continuance. Furthermore, as the Court held in

Wardius v. Oregon (1973), the defendant cannot be obliged to disclose evidence before trial unless the prosecution has a reciprocal obligation; fundamental fairness requires that discovery be "a two-way street."

Most of the evidentiary requirements of a fair trial are now subsumed under the CONFRONTATION and COMPULSORY PROCESS clauses of the Sixth Amendment, which, as incorporated into the Fourteenth, are applied to state criminal trials. A defendant has the rights "to be confronted with the witnesses against him" and "to have compulsory process for obtaining witnesses in his favor." As part of his right to hear and challenge the evidence against him, the defendant has a right to be present at the trial. (He may lose this right by absenting himself voluntarily or interfering with the orderly conduct of the trial.) Like other constitutional rights, the right to be present cannot be unnecessarily burdened; accordingly, since *Estelle v. Williams* (1976) a defendant cannot be required to appear at trial in prison clothing. Where jurors have obtained information from a person who did not appear as a witness, some courts have treated the event as a violation of the right to confront witnesses.

The confrontation clause also limits the use of out-of-court statements of persons who are not present in court. With few exceptions, an available witness must testify in person, so that he can be cross-examined by the defense. If a witness is not available, his out-of-court statement can be used as evidence only if there are indications of reliability sufficient to satisfy the purpose of confrontation at trial. (See HEARSAY RULES.)

The right to compulsory process assures the defendant that he will be able to present evidence favorable to his case. On occasion, the Supreme Court has held that the application of a state procedural requirement or the trial judge's conduct of the trial denied the defendant an opportunity to present critical evidence and has reversed the conviction, relying on the compulsory process clause or directly on the due process clause.

The Sixth Amendment gives a defendant the right "to have the assistance of counsel for his defense," which requires that counsel be appointed for an INDIGENT defendant in any case in which a sentence of imprisonment is imposed. Before this provision was made applicable to the states by incorporation into the Fourteenth Amendment, an indigent state defendant had a right to appointed counsel only if counsel were necessary to a fair trial. The appointment of counsel was required for defendants who were unable to defend themselves effectively because of their ignorance, or illiteracy, or youth, or because the circumstances of the case made professional skills essential; capital cases were invariably deemed to require the appointment of counsel. Since the decisions in GIDEON v. WAINWRIGHT (1963) and ARGERSINGER v. HAMLIN (1972), the RIGHT TO COUNSEL applies alike in federal and state cases. It is possible although unlikely that in a minor case in which the Sixth Amendment's provision was inapplicable, the defense would be so difficult and complex that counsel would be required for a fair trial.

The requirements of a fair trial embodied in the due process clause continue to govern the conduct of the prosecution, which is not the subject of another, particular provision of the Bill of Rights. Although the prosecution is responsible for the presentation of the case against the defendant, its concern must be, as the Court said in BERGER v. NEW YORK (1967), "not that it shall win a case, but that justice shall be done. . . . It is as much [the prosecutor's] duty to refrain from improper methods calculated to produce a wrongful conviction as it is to use every legitimate means to bring about a just one."

The prosecutor's obligation of fairness requires him to avoid conduct calculated or likely to mislead the jury. The knowing use of false evidence, including testimony of a witness, is ground for reversal of a conviction. If the prosecutor knows that a witness has testified falsely about a material fact, he must take steps to correct the falsehood. The obligation not to use false evidence extends to the government as a whole; even if the prosecutor at trial is unaware that evidence is false, a blameworthy failure of the police or others in the prosecutor's office or elsewhere in the government to avoid or remedy the falsehood is a denial of a fair trial.

The prosecutor has a parallel obligation to disclose evidence favorable to the defendant if, as the Court said in *United States v. Agurs* (1976), the "evidence is obviously of such substantial value that elementary fairness requires it." The constitutional obligation of fairness does not require the prosecution to disclose all evidence that might possibly be helpful to the defense. The test following a conviction is whether the undisclosed evidence "creates a REASONABLE DOUBT that did not otherwise exist." The duty to disclose evidence in response to a specific request by the defense is greater; if the evidence is material at all the prosecutor must either honor the request or inform the court of his refusal.

Aside from his obligation to present the evidence fully, the prosecutor must avoid arguments or conduct before the jury that might mislead it or prejudice it against the defendant. In his opening and closing arguments as well as his questioning of witnesses, the prosecutor is expected not to depart from the evidence or to lead the jury away from a dispassionate judgment based on the evidence. Isolated improper remarks of a prosecutor usually are not deemed to have denied a fair trial, especially if they do not appear to have been a deliberate violation and the trial judge has taken corrective action such as instructing the jury to disregard the remarks. In order to determine whether the standard of fair trial has been met, the prosecutor's conduct is examined in the context of the whole trial.

In a number of situations, the demands of a fair trial are opposed by conflicting demands based on the FIRST AMENDMENT's protection of FREEDOM OF THE PRESS. Pretrial publicity of a case may make it more difficult or impossible to impanel an impartial jury. A fair trial does not require that jurors have been entirely ignorant of the facts of a case but only that, having in mind the news coverage and atmosphere of the community, they be able to decide according to the evidence. The Supreme Court has occasionally reversed a conviction because members of the jury were presumed to have, or acknowledged that they had, strong preconceptions of the defendant's guilt because of extensive coverage of the case in local news media.

A similar problem has sometimes arisen during trial. In *Sheppard v. Maxwell* (1966) the Supreme Court concluded that prejudicial pretrial publicity in the news media as well as the "carnival atmosphere" created by the media in and around the courtroom during trial had denied the defendant a fair trial. In ESTES v. TEXAS (1965) the Court concluded that television coverage of portions of a sensational trial that had also been the subject of massive pretrial publicity was impermissible. There is, however, no absolute constitutional prohibition against radio, television, or photographic coverage of a trial, which may, as the Court held in CHANDLER v. FLORIDA (1981), be allowed if it is conducted in a manner consistent with a fair trial.

The Supreme Court held, in RICHMOND NEWSPAPERS, INC. v. VIRGINIA (1980), that the First Amendment protects the right of the public to attend criminal trials. (In contrast, the right to a PUBLIC TRIAL in the Sixth Amendment is a right of the defendant alone.) Therefore, all other measures for ensuring a fair trial, such as sequestration of witnesses or jurors, must be considered before the public can be excluded, whether or not the defendant asks for exclusion. The Court has indicated strongly that a trial court should exercise its authority in whatever manner will afford a fair trial without closing it to the public.

Unlike some of the more particular provisions of the Bill of Rights that have to do with criminal process, the requirement of a fair trial retains the flexibility of a general standard and is not susceptible to precise definition by a set of rules. While important aspects of a fair trial are covered by other constitutional provisions, some remain within the ambit of the general standard. Jurisprudentially, the principal difference is that, unlike some particular constitutional rules, the general standard does not invalidate a conviction for a single instance of prejudicial error or unfairness. Rather it is set in the context of the whole trial, and a conviction will be reversed only if the trial as a whole was unfair. The standard of a fair trial also serves as a reminder of the government's relationship with an individual even when it seeks to convict him of a crime and as the repository of changing or enlarged conceptions of what fairness in the criminal process requires.

LLOYD L. WEINREB

Bibliography

AMERICAN BAR ASSOCIATION 1968 *Standards Relating to Fair Trial and Free Press.* New York: Institute of Judicial Administration.
FELLMAN, DAVID 1976 *The Defendant's Rights Today.* Madison: University of Wisconsin Press.
KAMISAR, YALE; LAFAVE, WAYNE R.; and ISRAEL, JEROLD H. (1965)1986 *Modern Criminal Procedure.* St. Paul, Minn.: West Publishing Co.
LEVY, LEONARD W. 1974 *Against the Law.* New York: Harper & Row.
WEINREB, LLOYD L. (1969)1987 *Criminal Process.* Mineola, N.Y.: Foundation Press.

FAMILY AND THE CONSTITUTION

Family relations have an uncertain, even ambivalent constitutional status in Supreme Court decisions. If the Constitution protects the family against external interference, it also permits the establishment of public moral standards to regulate social relations among adults and to protect children from apparently harmful parental conduct.

This ambivalence appeared early. In MEYER V. NEBRASKA (1923) the Supreme Court opined that FOURTEENTH AMENDMENT "liberty" included the right "to marry, establish a home and bring up children." The Court did not explain, however, why this right stopped short at monogamy. In REYNOLDS V. UNITED STATES (1878) it had upheld Congress's power to forbid POLYGAMY in the TERRITORIES notwithstanding the religiously grounded objections of Mormon settlers. Nor did the Court subsequently explain how the right "to bring up children" was consistent with the compulsory STERILIZATION of a woman considered retarded by state authorities upheld in BUCK V. BELL (1927). One discernible principle did unify these early cases: the Constitution protects only family relations that judges consider "normal" and "wholesome." This principle might occasionally lead judges to substitute their views of normality for legislative impositions (as in *Meyer* where the state had forbidden schoolroom teaching of children in any language but English); it hardly serves, however, as a MAGNA CARTA for the protection from state interference of family sanctity and autonomy.

The prospect that constitutional doctrine might be elevated to serve this broader protective purpose emerged in the 1960s, as cases involving family relations began to appear in unprecedented numbers on the Supreme Court's docket. But in fact the decided cases exemplify the same conflicting strains as before. The first of the modern cases was GRISWOLD V. CONNECTICUT (1965), striking down a state law that prohibited anyone including married couples from using contraceptives. The Court spoke of marriage as "intimate to the degree of being sacred" and found a constitutionally protected "RIGHT OF PRIVACY surrounding the marriage relationship." In subsequent cases, however, the Court has been reluctant to extend this familial privacy right beyond the conventionally conceived marriage bond. Although EISENSTADT V. BAIRD (1972) recognized the right of unmarried persons to practice contraception, in *Doe v. Commonwealth's Attorney* (1976) the Court summarily affirmed a lower court's rejection of a constitutional attack on a state law criminally proscribing homosexual relations even among consenting adults in private. Similarly in *Belle Terre v. Boraas* (1974) the Court upheld a municipal ZONING restriction excluding communal families unless they were "related by blood, adoption or marriage"; and yet in MOORE V. CITY OF EAST CLEVELAND (1977) the Court struck down zoning restrictions that limited residence to nuclear families and excluded multigenerational families with blood ties. The theme that runs through these two zoning cases and through *Griswold* and *Doe* is that the Constitution protects "families" when they reflect conventional social definitions of decency and morality.

The Court does not unquestioningly defer to legislative conceptions of appropriately conventional family relations. The Court has struck down familial regulations reflecting RACIAL DISCRIMINATION as in LOVING V. VIRGINIA (1967), or SEX DISCRIMINATION regarding alimony entitlements as in *Orr v. Orr* (1979), or required consent for adoptive placement as in *Caban v. Mahammed* (1979). But even in these cases the Justices appear guided more by their own conceptions of appropriate social conventions for family relations than by any principle of protection of individuals against state interference with their autonomous choices in family matters.

The constitutional status of parent–child relations is the result of similar conflicting impulses. In the adult relations cases, the underlying conflict is essentially between principles of individual autonomy and of community, between the individual's FREEDOM OF INTIMATE ASSOCIATION and the right of a group to define and enforce common standards of conduct on every group member. For state regulation of parent–child relations, these same conflicting principles are at stake, but the conflict extends even into these principles' very definition.

Thus the state can plausibly claim that it must restrict parental conduct to protect and enhance the child's developing capacity for individual autonomy. The claim is implicit in compulsory education laws, in laws permitting state intervention to override parental directives in disputes between parent and child (particularly adolescent children), and in laws proscribing child abuse or neglect. Parents, however, can plausibly claim that a child's capacity to develop as an autonomous individual is impaired by state impositions on parental conduct beyond the most minimal standards to protect the child's physical integrity. Thus even if constitutional DOCTRINE should give priority to individual autonomy over communitarian claims in adult relations, this priority does not resolve disputes regarding state regulation of parental conduct when both the state and the parents can plausibly claim to speak for the child's developing capacity for individual autonomy.

These disputes have occurred in three different contexts: claims by state authorities that parents' conduct was harmful to children; claims by parents that their children were harmed by state conduct, particularly in public schools; and claims by children, particularly older children, that state authorities should take their sides in disputes with their parents. In none of these contexts do the decided cases yield consistent constitutional principles.

The unresolved tension between competing principles was particularly evident in two Supreme Court decisions in successive terms that considered the application of constitutional norms to state abuse and neglect statutes. In SANTOSKY V. KRAMER (1982) the Court held that states must meet a higher burden of proof than the ordinary civil standard before the parent–child relationship could be terminated on grounds of harmful parental conduct; but in *Lassiter v. Department of Social Services* (1981) the Court had held that the parental relationship was not of sufficient constitutional weight to require the appointment of counsel to give indigent parents effective assistance against state actions for termination.

A similar if less blatant inconsistency is evident in the Court's rulings regarding the rights of parents to constrain state impositions on their children in public schools. Thus in INGRAHAM V. WRIGHT (1977) the Court ruled that school officials were free to inflict corporal punishment on students notwithstanding parental objections that the punishment was physically and psychologically harmful to their children; but in WISCONSIN V. YODER (1972) the Court had ruled that school officials could not require Amish children to attend secondary schools in the face of their parents' objections that this imposition was harmful to the children and inconsistent with the parents' views on proper child-rearing practices.

In the Amish case, the Court emphasized the religious basis for the parents' claims, a factor that might serve to distinguish the parents' claim in the corporal punishment case. But parental claims to preclude state interference in their decisions regarding children were not similarly honored, notwithstanding the religious grounding of such claims, in PLANNED PARENTHOOD V. DANFORTH (1976) where the parents objected to their unmarried pregnant daughters' wish to obtain an abortion. The minors' abortion and the Amish case might be distinguished on the ground that the pregnant minors openly disagreed with their parents while the Amish students apparently concurred with theirs. But this view of the abortion case—that the Constitution not only permits but requires state intervention to protect the autonomous wishes of older children from being overridden by their parents—cannot readily be squared with the Court's subsequent ruling in PARHAM V. J. R. (1979) essentially upholding parents' authority to confine their adolescent children in psychiatric institutions, notwithstanding the children's objections and claims for independent judicial protection.

These decisions raise at least the suspicion that the same guiding principle is at work in these parent–child–state cases as appeared in the cases regarding state regulation of adult familial relations—the principle that the Justices are not prepared to find constitutional protection for family status as such but only for those families whose conduct meets the Justices' particular approval. This principle could explain the Court's deference to Amish parents who generally succeed in imposing rigid behavioral controls on their children, as the Court repeatedly stressed in *Yoder*, or its deference to parents' wishes to confine their socially disruptive children in psychiatric institutions. A judicial preference for such behavior controls might also explain the Court's refusal to defer to parents' objections to school corporal punishment or to parents' resistance to abortions when they had failed effectively to constrain their unmarried daughters' indulgence in sexual relations.

The Court has not been unanimous in these cases, and no Justice has explicitly defended this particular child-rearing principle as a constitutional norm. Yet the logical plausibility of this harmonizing principle does suggest that current constitutional doctrine gives no special status to family relations as such, either between parents and child or among adults. The occasional rhetorical flourishes in Supreme Court opinions about the "constitutional sanctity" of the family does not yet reflect any consistent constitutional principle.

ROBERT A. BURT

Bibliography

BURT, ROBERT A. 1979 The Constitution of the Family. *The Supreme Court Review* 1979:329–395.
GOLDSTEIN, J.; FREUD, A.; and SOLNIT, A. 1973 *Beyond the Best Interests of the Child*. New York: Free Press.
———— 1979 *Before the Best Interests of the Child*. New York: Free Press.
KARST, KENNETH L. 1980 The Freedom of Intimate Association. *Yale Law Journal* 89:624–692.

FARETTA v. CALIFORNIA
422 U.S. 806 (1975)

In *Faretta* the Supreme Court reversed the conviction of a defendant forced to accept the services of a public defender in a FELONY case, holding that the Sixth Amendment guarantees the right to self-representation when a defendant "knowingly and intelligently" requests it.

This is a major decision about the WAIVER OF CONSTITUTIONAL RIGHTS because the argument of the state and the dissent was that society has an interest in a FAIR TRIAL, independent of the defendant's desires. Recognition of such an interest would necessar-

ily mean that the trial judge must have discretion to reject even a knowing and intelligent waiver of the RIGHT TO COUNSEL.

Standby counsel may be appointed over the defendant's objection to aid him should he request help at the trial, or to intervene if the termination of self-representation becomes necessary.

BARBARA ALLEN BABCOCK

FARRAND, MAX
(1869–1945)

Anyone who cares seriously to study the work of the CONSTITUTIONAL CONVENTION OF 1787 owes a debt to Max Farrand. Farrand, professor of history at Stanford (1901–1908) and Yale (1908–1925) Universities and later director of research at the Huntington Library, compiled and edited all the known *Records of the Federal Convention* (1911, revised 1937). That work was more influential than his narrative history books, which were intended for undergraduate or popular audiences.

DENNIS J. MAHONEY

FAY v. NOIA
372 U.S. 391 (1963)

The Great Writ of HABEAS CORPUS allows state prisoners to seek federal court review of constitutional errors made at their trials, but the JUDICIAL CODE requires EXHAUSTION OF REMEDIES in state court, in order to preserve comity between state and federal courts. Charles Noia's 1942 murder conviction was based solely on a coerced confession procured in violation of his FOURTEENTH AMENDMENT rights to DUE PROCESS. He chose not to file a state APPEAL, however, because he feared that a new trial might end in a death sentence. Years later, he sought review of his due process claim in state courts, but they held that his original failure to appeal was a procedural default that barred further review. In *Fay*, a 6–3 Supreme Court held that his failure was not a "deliberate bypass" of state procedures and thus no bar to habeas corpus relief.

Justice WILLIAM J. BRENNAN, speaking for the majority, posited a "manifest federal policy" that liberty rights should not be denied without the fullest opportunity for federal JUDICIAL REVIEW. The concept of comity could not justify denying habeas corpus relief for failure to exhaust a remedy no longer available.

As for the state's interests in insuring finality of criminal judgments, or exacting compliance with its procedures through default rules, these could not outweigh the "ideal of fair procedure" and the historic habeas corpus policy favoring the free exercise of federal judicial power to enforce this ideal. Finally, the state's rejection of Noia's claim could not be treated as an ADEQUATE STATE GROUND, for this jurisdictional deference would unduly burden the vindication of federal rights. Only when a defendant deliberately evaded state adjudication would FEDERALISM concerns justify the denial of habeas corpus review.

As dissenting Justice JOHN MARSHALL HARLAN noted, *Fay* marked a dramatic expansion of federal power to supervise state criminal justice. The concepts of exhaustion and adequate state grounds were modified to make room for a generous view that excused defendants from uncalculated WAIVER OF CONSTITUTIONAL RIGHTS in state proceedings. The "deliberately bypassing" defendant was a rare one, and *Fay*'s scope freed most defendants from forfeiting their rights through procedural defaults of every kind. Simultaneously, the WARREN COURT's application of the Fourth, Fifth, and Sixth Amendments to the states codified a BILL OF RIGHTS for criminal defendants. *Fay* insured a broad federal path of enforcement for these new guarantees, in an era when the state path of review was not always open or receptive to constitutional claims.

The BURGER COURT era brought a less hospitable federal climate for criminal defendants and, not surprisingly, also brought a corresponding change in the habeas corpus barometer, emerging clearly in WAINRIGHT V. SYKES (1977). *Fay*'s deliberate bypass rule did not endure as an exclusive measure of federalism interests, because a new "manifest" federal policy came to elevate the state's interest in finality above the ideal of fair procedure. With this new federalism, the whole point of habeas corpus review was transformed from the protection of constitutional rights to the protection of those with a claim to innocence.

CATHERINE HANCOCK

Bibliography

COVER, ROBERT M. and ALEINIKOFF, T. ALEXANDER 1977 Dialectical Federalism: Habeas Corpus and the Court. *Yale Law Journal* 86:1035–1102.

FEDERAL . . . ACT

See also under word following "Federal"

FEDERAL COMMON LAW, CIVIL

In the English legal tradition to which this country is heir, judge-made COMMON LAW—law developed by courts in the absence of applicable LEGISLATION—has played a critical role in the determination of rights, duties, and remedies. But because our federal government is one of limited, delegated powers, the questions whether and under what circumstances the federal courts are empowered to formulate federal common law have been the subject of much debate. Although it is now settled that the federal courts do have such authority in civil matters, the debate continues over the sources of that authority and the proper scope of its exercise.

The Supreme Court's decision in ERIE RAILROAD CO. V. TOMPKINS (1938) marks a watershed in the evolution of this problem. Prior to that decision, the federal courts did not strive to develop a federal, or national, common law binding on the states and indeed on occasion denied that it existed (*Wheaton v. Peters*, 1834; *Smith v. Alabama*, 1888). Yet the Supreme Court, in SWIFT V. TYSON (1842), upheld the authority of the federal courts, in cases within the DIVERSITY JURISDICTION, to determine certain controversies on the basis of "general principles and doctrines" of jurisprudence and without regard to the common law decisions of the state courts. Thus, during the reign of *Swift v. Tyson*, the federal courts exercised considerable common law authority over a variety of disputes, ultimately extending well beyond the interstate commercial controversy involved in *Swift* itself and involving matters apparently not subject to federal legislative power. The decisions rendered in these cases, however, did not purport to bind the state courts, and the result was often the parallel existence of two different rules of law applicable to the same controversy, with the governing rule dependent on the forum in which the controversy was adjudicated.

Historians disagree on the justification—statutory and constitutional—of the *Swift* decision. In one view, the decision was not rooted in contemporary understanding of the nature of the common law but instead represented the use of judicial power to aid in the redistribution of wealth to promote commercial and industrial growth. A contrasting position is that the decision was fully consistent with the perception of the time that the common law of commercial transactions was not the command of the sovereign but rather was both the embodiment of prevailing customs and a process of applying them to the case at hand.

There is general agreement, however, that the

Court expanded *Swift* well beyond its originally intended scope and that its OVERRULING, in *Erie*, reflected a very different perception of the proper role of the federal courts. The Court in *Erie*, speaking through Justice LOUIS D. BRANDEIS, concluded that there was no "general" federal common law—that the Rules of Decision Act, originally section 34 of the JUDICIARY ACT OF 1789, required adherence to state decisional or common law in controversies such as *Erie* itself, a case that fell within federal JURISDICTION solely on the basis of the parties' diversity of citizenship.

But the *Erie* decision helped bring to the surface the existence of what has been called a "specialized" federal common law, operating in those areas where the application of federal law seems warranted even though no federal constitutional or legislative provision points the way to a governing rule. Indeed, on the very day that *Erie* was decided, the Court in *Hinderlider v. La Plata River & Cherry Creek Ditch Co.* (1938), again speaking through Justice Brandeis, said that "whether the water of an interstate stream must be apportioned between the two States is a question of 'federal common law' upon which neither the statutes nor the decisions of either State can be conclusive."

What is the source of the authority to formulate federal common law—law that, unlike decisions rendered pursuant to *Swift*, binds state and federal courts alike? To some extent, the source may be traced to specific constitutional provisions, such as the grant of ADMIRALTY AND MARITIME JURISDICTION in Article III, or the prohibition of unreasonable SEARCHES AND SEIZURES in the FOURTH AMENDMENT. (See BIVENS v. SIX UNKNOWN NAMED AGENTS (1971), declaring the existence of a damage remedy for a Fourth Amendment violation.) But the line between CONSTITUTIONAL INTERPRETATION, on the one hand, and the exercise of common law authority, on the other, is indistinct, and there is often disagreement among both judges and commentators about the function the courts are performing. The significance of this disagreement is more than semantic, for the ability of the legislative branch to modify or reject a Supreme Court ruling is plainly more circumscribed if the ruling is seen to be required by the Constitution than if the ruling is a common law one authorized but not compelled by the FUNDAMENTAL LAW.

In other instances, the source of judicial authority may be found in a particular federal statute. Infrequently, the congressional command is explicit, as in the mandate in Rule 501 of the Federal Rules of Evidence that in certain cases questions of evidentiary privilege "shall be governed by the principles of the common law as they may be interpreted by the courts of the United States in the light of reason and experience." More often, the legislative direction is, at best, implicit and the judicial role may be viewed as that of implementing federal legislative policy by filling the gaps left by the legislation itself. Once again, the line between statutory construction and the exercise of common law authority is not easily drawn.

In a significant number of cases, the exercise of authority to formulate federal common law is difficult to trace to a specific provision in the Constitution or in a statute. In such cases, the authority may be attributed more broadly to the nature of the judicial process, to the structure of our federal constitutional system, and to the relationships created by it. The authority, in other words, may be rooted in necessity. As Justice ROBERT H. JACKSON put it, concurring in *D'Oench Duhme & Co. v. F.D.I.C.* (1942): "Were we bereft of the common law, our federal system would be impotent. This follows from the recognized futility of attempting all-complete statutory codes and is apparent from the terms of the Constitution itself."

Some examples of the exercise of this authority may help to clarify its scope. Perhaps most important is the category of those interstate or international disputes that, in the words of the Supreme Court, "implicate conflicting rights of States or our foreign relations" (*Texas Industries, Inc. v. Radcliff Materials, Inc.*, 1981). Such disputes do not always fall within the specific jurisdictional grants of Article III applicable to certain interstate or international controversies. In any event, the existence of a conflict between the interests of two states may make it inappropriate for the law of either to govern of its own force. And controversies affecting our relations as sovereign with foreign nations may require a single federal response rather than a cacophony of responses rooted in varying state laws. (See ACT OF STATE DOCTRINE.)

Another leading instance of the exercise of common law authority embraces controversies involving the rights, obligations, or proprietary interests of the United States. In such controversies, especially those arising in the administration of nationwide programs, formulation of federal common law may be warranted by the need for uniform treatment of the activities of the federal government or, more modestly, for some degree of federal supervision of the application of state law to those activities.

The amorphous origins and uncertain scope of the federal common law power underscore the need to recognize certain limitations that are anchored in the concerns of FEDERALISM and of SEPARATION OF POW-

ERS. The first of these concerns focuses on the interests of the states in preserving a measure of autonomy on matters properly within their sphere—interests reflected in the TENTH AMENDMENT. Because federal law is often interstitial in character—written against a background of state laws governing basic human affairs—the concern for federalism supports a presumption that state law ought not to be displaced in the absence of a clear legislative direction, a sharp conflict between the state law and federal program, or the existence of a uniquely federal interest requiring protection. To some extent, this presumption is supported by and reflected in the provision of the Rules of Decision Act that state laws shall constitute the rules of decision except where otherwise required by the Constitution or by federal treaty or statute. But the last phrase of that act—limiting its command to "cases where they (the rules of decision) apply"—gives the provision a circularity that affords little guidance to the resolution of particular problems of potential conflict between federal and state authority.

Even when the exercise of federal authority is warranted, a careful balancing of state and federal interests may lead to the adoption of state laws rather than to the imposition of a uniform federal rule, so long as the state laws in question are compatible with federal interests. Such results were reached, for example, in *De Sylva v. Ballentine* (1955), involving a definition of "children" under the Federal Copyright Act, and *United States v. Kimbell Foods, Inc.* (1979), dealing with the priority of federal government liens arising from federal lending programs.

The second concern—that of separation of powers—springs from the belief that the primary responsibility for lawmaking should rest with the democratically elected representatives in the legislative branch. At a time when the common law function was seen in terms primarily of the application of established customs and usages, the concern for the proper separation and allocation of federal powers had less force than it does today, when there is more emphasis on the creative potential of the common law. Moreover, the separation of powers question is not unrelated to the regard for state interests, since the bicameral federal legislature is structured in such a way as to protect the states against action that might be taken by a legislature apportioned solely on the basis of population.

Concern that the courts not usurp a function that is properly legislative has led to an emphasis on LEGISLATIVE INTENT in many instances in which the federal courts have been asked to articulate new rights or develop new remedies not specifically provided for

by statute. Moreover, the Supreme Court has stressed the ability of Congress to displace federal common law with statutory regulations, even in some instances in which the source of authority is the Constitution itself.

The problems inherent in the exercise of common law power have been highlighted in the Supreme Court's struggle with the question of implied remedies for federal constitutional or statutory violations. Since BIVENS V. SIX UNKNOWN NAMED AGENTS (1971), the Court has generally been willing to allow a person harmed by unconstitutional action to sue for damages, despite the lack of any constitutional or statutory provision for suit. But persons harmed by violations of federal statutes have frequently been held unable to obtain relief in the absence of an express statutory remedy or strong evidence of legislative intent to permit such a remedy.

In both types of cases the Supreme Court has perhaps too readily yielded its authority to exercise a principled discretion in determining whether traditional common law remedies should be available to implement federal policy. The tendency toward formalistic insistence on a remedy for every wrong in cases involving constitutional violations, and toward ritualistic invocation of legislative intent in order to deny a remedy in cases of statutory infractions, suggests a relinquishment of the judicial responsibility that lies at the heart of our common law heritage.

DAVID L. SHAPIRO

Bibliography

BATOR, PAUL; MISHKIN, PAUL J.; SHAPIRO, DAVID L.; and WECHSLER, HERBERT (1953) 1973 and 1981 Supp. *Hart and Wechsler's The Federal Courts and the Federal System.* Pages 691–832. Mineola, N.Y.: Foundation Press.

BRIDWELL, RANDALL and WHITTEN, RALPH U. 1977 *The Constitution and the Common Law.* Lexington, Mass.: Lexington Books.

FIELD, MARTHA A. 1986 Sources of Law: The Scope of Federal Common Law. *Harvard Law Review* 99:883–984.

FRIENDLY, HENRY J. 1964 In Praise of Erie—And of the New Federal Common Law. *New York University Law Review* 39:383–422.

FREYER, TONY ALLAN 1979 *Forums of Order: The Federal Courts and Business in American History.* Greenwich, Conn.: JAI Press, Inc.

HILL, ALFRED 1967 The Law-Making Power of the Federal Courts: Constitutional Preemption. *Columbia Law Review* 67:1024–1081.

HORWITZ, MORTON J. 1977 *The Transformation of American Law, 1780–1860.* Pages 211–252. Cambridge, Mass.: Harvard University Press.

REDISH, MARTIN H. 1980 *Federal Jurisdiction: Tensions*

in the Allocation of Judicial Power. Pages 79–107. Indianapolis: Bobbs-Merrill.

FEDERAL COMMON LAW OF CRIMES

One of the leading Jeffersonian jurists, ST. GEORGE TUCKER, noted with alarm that Chief Justice OLIVER ELLSWORTH and Justice BUSHROD WASHINGTON had laid down the general rule that the COMMON LAW was the unwritten law of the United States government. The question whether the Constitution adopted the common law, Tucker wrote,

is of very great importance, not only as it regards the limits of the JURISDICTION of the *federal courts;* but also, as it relates to the extent of the powers vested in the *federal government.* For, if it be true that the common law of England has been adopted by the United States in their national, or federal capacity, the jurisdiction of the *federal courts* must be co-extensive with it; or, in other words, *unlimited:* so also, must be the jurisdiction, and authority of the *other branches* of the federal government [Tucker, *Blackstone's Commentaries,* 1803, I, 380].

Tucker's answer to the question was that the JUDICIAL POWER OF THE UNITED STATES under Article III was limited to the subjects of congressional legislative power and that common law did not give jurisdiction in any case where jurisdiction was not expressly given by the Constitution. Tucker's view eventually prevailed, but it was probably not the view of the Constitution's Framers.

Article III extends the judicial power of the United States to all cases in law and EQUITY arising under the Constitution, treaties, and "Laws of the United States." The latter phrase could include common law crimes. At the CONSTITUTIONAL CONVENTION OF 1787, the Committee of Detail reported a draft declaring that the Supreme Court's jurisdiction extended to "all Cases arising under the Laws passed by the Legislature of the United States." The Convention without dissenting vote adopted a motion striking out the words "passed by the Legislature." That deletion suggests that "the Laws of the United States" comprehended the common law of crimes, as well as other nonstatutory law.

The legislative history of the JUDICIARY ACT OF 1789 suggests a similar conclusion. A draft of that statute relating to the jurisdiction of both the federal district and federal circuit courts (sections nine and eleven as enacted) gave these courts "cognizance of all crimes and offenses that shall be cognizable under the authority of the United States and *defined by the laws of the same.* " The italicized phrase, deleted from the act's final text, might have restricted criminal jurisdiction to statutory crimes. Whether a federal court was to apply a federal common law of crimes or apply the common law of the state in which a crime was committed is not clear.

What is clear is that the first generation of federal judges assumed jurisdiction in cases of nonstatutory crimes. Justice JAMES WILSON, an influential Framer of the Constitution, at his state's ratifying convention had endorsed federal prosecutions at common law for criminal libels against the United States. In 1793 he instructed a federal GRAND JURY on the virtues of the common law, which included, he said, the law of nations. The grand jury indicted Gideon Henfield for breaching American neutrality by assisting a French privateer in the capture of a British ship; the INDICTMENT referred to "violation of the laws of nations, against the laws and constitution of the United States and against the peace and dignity of the United States." ALEXANDER HAMILTON prepared the indictment, which Attorney General EDMUND RANDOLPH (another Framer) helped prosecute. Justice Wilson, joined by Justice JAMES IREDELL and Judge RICHARD PETERS, constituted the federal CIRCUIT COURT that tried Henfield's nonstatutory offense. Henfield, having been at sea when President GEORGE WASHINGTON proclaimed American neutrality, pleaded ignorance. Secretary of State THOMAS JEFFERSON, who had urged Henfield's prosecution and endorsed Wilson's opinion as to the indictability of the offense, explained that the jury acquitted because the crime was not knowingly committed. JOHN MARSHALL, in his *Life of Washington,* described the prosecution as having been based on an offense "indictable at common law, for disturbing the peace of the United States."

Subsequent common law prosecutions were not so fuzzy. In 1793 a federal grand jury indicted Joseph Ravara, a consul from Genoa, for attempting to extort money from a British diplomat. Justice Wilson, joined by Peters, ruled that the circuit court had jurisdiction, although Congress had passed no law against extortion. Justice Iredell argued that the defendant's diplomatic status brought him within the exclusive ORIGINAL JURISDICTION of the Supreme Court. Ravara was tried in 1794 by a circuit court consisting of Jay and Peters, who instructed the jury that the offense was indictable at common law, part of the LAW OF THE LAND. The jury convicted. In 1795 a federal court in New York, at the instigation of Attorney General Randolph, indicted Greenleaf, the editor of the *New-York Journal,* for criminal libel, a common law crime. The case was dropped, but in 1797 the editor was again indicted for the same crime and convicted by a court presided over by Chief Justice Oliver Ellsworth, an influential Framer and chief author of the Judiciary Act of 1789. In Massachusetts in 1797 Ellsworth ruled that the federal circuit court possessed jurisdiction over crimes against the common law, which the laws of the United States included, and therefore might try persons indicted for counterfeiting notes of the Bank of the United States (not then a statutory offense).

In the same year a federal grand jury followed Justice Iredell's charge and indicted a congressman, Samuel J. Cabell, for the common law crime of SEDITIOUS LIBEL, but the prosecution was aborted for political reasons. In 1798, before Congress passed the Sedition Act, prosecutions for seditious libel were begun against Benjamin Bache, who soon died, and John Burke, who fled the country before Justice WILLIAM PATERSON could try him. In 1799 Ellsworth and Iredell, in separate cases, told federal grand juries that the federal courts had common law jurisdiction over seditious libel and, in Ellsworth's words, over "acts manifestly subversive of the national government." He added that an indictable offense need be defined only by common law, not statute.

The sole dissenting voice in this line of decision was that of Justice SAMUEL CHASE in *Worrall's Case* (1798), where the common law indictment was for attempted bribery of a federal official. Judge Peters disagreed with Chase's argument that no federal common law of crimes existed, and the jury convicted. Chase, however, changed his opinion in *United States v. Sylvester* (1799), when he presided over a common law prosecution for counterfeiting. Thus, Chief Justices Jay and Ellsworth and Justices Wilson, Paterson, Iredell, and Chase endorsed federal court jurisdiction over common law crimes. The Jeffersonians, by then, vehemently opposed such views, arguing that only the state courts could try common law crimes. When Jefferson was President, however, Judge Pierpont Edwards, whom he had appointed to the federal district court in Connecticut, sought and received common law indictments against several persons for seditious libel against the President and the government. Jefferson knew of the common law prosecutions by the federal court and did not criticize them or take any actions to halt them, until he learned that one of the defendants could prove the truth of his accusation that the President had once engaged in a sexual indiscretion. The prosecutions were dropped except for those against Hudson and Goodwin, editors of Hartford's *Connecticut Courant*, who challenged the jurisdiction of the federal court.

By this time the administration had a stake in a ruling against federal jurisdiction over common law crimes. After much government stalling until a majority of Jeffersonian appointees controlled the Supreme Court, UNITED STATES V. HUDSON AND GOODWIN was finally decided in 1812. Without hearing ORAL ARGUMENTS and against all the precedents, a bare majority of the Court, in a brief opinion by Justice WILLIAM JOHNSON, ruled that the question whether the federal courts "can exercise a common law jurisdiction in criminal cases" has been "settled in public opinion," which opposed such jurisdiction. Moreover, the Constitution had not expressly delegated to the federal courts authority over common law crimes. "The legislative authority of the Union must first make an act a crime, affix a punishment to it, and declare the Court that shall have jurisdiction of the offense."

Justice JOSEPH STORY, who had not made known his dissent at the time, did so in a circuit opinion in 1813 and forced a reconsideration of the rule of *Hudson and Goodwin*. In UNITED STATES V. COOLIDGE (1816), decided without argument, Johnson, noting that the Court was still divided (Marshall and Washington probably supported Story), refused to review the 1812 decision in the absence of "solemn argument." Thus the great question was resolved without reasoned consideration, to the enormous detriment of the power of the United States courts to define criminal acts.

Although "judge-made" or nonstatutory federal crimes disappeared after the *Coolidge* decision, federal courts continued to exercise common law powers to enforce law and order within their own precincts (see CONTEMPT POWER) and continued to employ a variety of common law techniques, forms, and writs in the enforcement of congressionally defined crimes. The FEDERAL RULES OF CRIMINAL PROCEDURE reflect that fact, as does *Marshall v. United States* (1959). By its "supervisory powers" over lower federal courts and, through them, over federal law enforcement officers, the Supreme Court can still be said, loosely, to exercise an interstitial common law authority with respect to federal crimes.

LEONARD W. LEVY

Bibliography

CROSSKEY, WILLIAM W. 1953 *Politics and the Constitution in the History of the United States*, 2 vols. Chaps. 20–24. Chicago: University of Chicago Press.

GOEBEL, JULIUS, JR. 1971—*Antecedents and Beginnings to 1801*. Volume 1 of Freund, Paul, ed., *The Oliver Wendell Holmes Devise History of the Supreme Court*. New York: Macmillan.

PRESSER, STEPHEN B. 1978 "A Tale of Two Judges: Richard Peters, Samuel Chase, and the Broken Promise of Federalist Jurisprudence." *Northwestern Law Review* 73:26–111.

TUCKER, ST. GEORGE 1803 *Blackstone's Commentaries, with Notes of Reference to the Constitution and Laws of the Federal Government of the United States and of the Commonwealth of Virginia,* 5 vols. Philadelphia: Young & Small.

WARREN, CHARLES 1923 "New Light on the History of the Federal Judiciary Act of 1789." *Harvard Law Review* 37:49–132.

WHARTON, FRANCIS, ed. 1849(1970) *State Trials of the United States During the Administrations of Washington and Adams.* New York: Burt Franklin.

FEDERAL COMMUNICATIONS COMMISSION

See: Broadcasting; Communications Act; Regulatory Commissions

FEDERAL COMMUNICATIONS COMMISSION v. LEAGUE OF WOMEN VOTERS

See: Government Speech

FEDERAL COMMUNICATIONS COMMISSION v. PACIFICA FOUNDATION
438 U.S. 726 (1978)

In *FCC v. Pacifica Foundation* the Court held that limited civil sanctions could constitutionally be invoked against a radio broadcast containing many vulgar words. The Court stressed that its holding was limited to the particular context, that is, to civil sanctions applied to indecent speech in an afternoon radio broadcast when, the Court assumed, children were in the audience. The opinion did not address criminal sanctions for televised or closed circuit broadcasts or late evening presentations, nor did it illuminate the concept of indecent speech except to suggest that occasional expletives and Elizabethan comedies may be decent enough even in the early afternoon.

STEVEN SHIFFRIN

FEDERAL COURTS IMPROVEMENT ACT
96 Stat. 25 (1982)

This act reorganized several specialized federal courts. It merged the former COURT OF CLAIMS and COURT OF CUSTOMS AND PATENT APPEALS into a

new UNITED STATES COURT OF APPEALS FOR THE FEDERAL CIRCUIT, transferring to the new court the former courts' JURISDICTION, and staffing it with the judges of the superseded courts. The Federal Circuit is a CONSTITUTIONAL COURT, staffed by twelve judges with life terms.

The act also created a new CLAIMS COURT to handle the trial functions formerly performed by commissioners (later called trial judges) of the old Court of Claims. The Claims Court is a LEGISLATIVE COURT; its sixteen judges serve for fifteen-year terms. Appeals go to the Federal Circuit.

KENNETH L. KARST

Bibliography

SYMPOSIUM 1983/1984 The Federal Courts Improvement Act. *Cleveland State Law Review* 32:1–116.

FEDERAL ELECTION CAMPAIGN ACTS
Presidential Election Campaign Fund Act 85 Stat. 497 (1971)
Federal Election Campaign Act 86 Stat. 3 (1971)
Federal Election Campaign Act 88 Stat. 1263 (1974)

The success of constitutional democracy depends upon the integrity and autonomy of the electoral process. But whether that integrity is threatened more seriously by wealthy individuals and organizations than by regulations that prevent individuals and organizations from using their resources to promote candidates and policies is a matter for debate. During the 1970s several attempts at campaign finance "reform" were enacted, resulting in an almost complete switch from private to public financing at least of the presidential general election campaigns.

Two reform statutes were enacted in 1971: the Federal Election Campaign Act (FECA) and the Presidential Election Campaign Fund Act. The former required any committee receiving or spending more than $1,000 in a campaign for federal office to register with the federal government and publish reports of contributions and expenditures. It also prohibited contributions under names other than that of the actual donor and limited total expenditures on campaign advertising. The second statute created a fund of public money to replace private contributions in financing presidential election campaigns. By means of a "check-off" device, taxpayers would nominally designate one dollar of their annual federal income tax payment for the election campaign fund. Acceptance of these public funds precluded a party or campaign committee from accepting any private contributions.

The FECA of 1974 was an extremely comprehensive effort to regulate the "time, place, and manner" of electing federal officials. Among the provisions of the 1974 act were: maximum spending limits for presidential nominating and general election campaigns; federal matching funds for qualifying candidates in major party nominating campaigns; complete federal funding of major party candidates in the general election campaign; limits on contributions of individuals, organizations, and political action committees to campaigns for Congress and for the presidential nominations; limits on campaign spending per state in presidential nomination campaigns; and rigorous accounting and reporting requirements for campaign finance committees. In addition, the 1974 act created a six-member Federal Elections Commission to enforce the other provisions of the act; the commission was to comprise members appointed by the President, the speaker of the House of Representatives, and the president pro tempore of the Senate.

The Supreme Court heard major constitutional challenges to the 1974 act even as the first campaign was being conducted under it. In BUCKLEY V. VALEO (1976) the Court held unconstitutional the method of appointment of the commission (because the Constitution grants to the President alone the power to appoint federal officers) and all the spending limitations imposed other than as a condition for receiving federal matching funds. The rationale for the latter holding was that the commitment of funds in support of a candidate or cause was a form of expression protected under the FIRST AMENDMENT.

The tendency toward public financing of electoral campaigns, with accompanying regulation, works to the advantage of incumbents and to the disadvantage of challengers, who usually need to spend more than their opponents to overcome the advantages of incumbency. The scheme for financing and regulating the presidential election campaigns serves to insulate the two major parties from challenges by third parties or independent candidates. While claiming to protect the people from the "fat cats," federal politicians have taken steps to protect themselves from the people.

DENNIS J. MAHONEY

Bibliography

ALEXANDER, HERBERT E. 1980 *Financing Politics: Money, Elections and Political Reform.* Washington, D.C.: Congressional Quarterly.

FEDERAL ENERGY AGENCY v. ALGONQUIN SNG, INC.
426 U.S. 548 (1976)

A unanimous Supreme Court, through Justice WILLIAM J. BRENNAN, upheld the constitutionality of oil import licensing fees imposed under the Trade Expansion Act (1962) and the Trade Act (1974). Under those statutes the President was authorized to "adjust" imports of commodities if the importation was in such quantities or under such conditions as to threaten national security. This was not an improper DELEGATION OF POWER, as the laws established preconditions for and limits upon its exercise. Furthermore, the court ruled, license fees were as acceptable a means of adjusting levels of importation as quotas.

DENNIS J. MAHONEY

FEDERAL GRANTS-IN-AID

Federal grants-in-aid are subventions to state or local governments, private institutions, or individuals in support of a wide variety of undertakings. Early in the nineteenth century, governmental transfers of land were used to support road construction and agricultural education. Cash grants to states for diverse functions, such as vocational EDUCATION, forest fire prevention, and maternal health, came of age in the decades preceding the New Deal. The public welfare programs established in 1935 greatly expanded the federal role in state finances. But it is the proliferation of categorical grants since 1960 that has rendered them the principal instrument of federal influence over social services and urban affairs. This recent extraordinary growth reflects an unplanned series of fragmented national responses to state fiscal inadequacy in the face of increased demand for collective goods.

Most of the current 500 or so national grant programs are intergovernmental, and federal monies under them constitute about one-quarter of the annual expenditures of both state and local governments. Notwithstanding federalism-inspired movements toward less directive federal grants, known as REVENUE SHARING and block grants, most aid programs remain categorical, with narrowly defined undertakings and detailed conditions imposed on the receiving agencies.

Grants are made pursuant to Congress's broad discretion to spend for the GENERAL WELFARE and common defense. Like other national powers, grant-making authority rests on permissive and expansive constitutional principles established during the post-New Deal era of judicial reaction and retreat, typified by such cases as STEWARD MACHINE CO. V. DAVIS (1937) and *Oklahoma v. Civil Service Commission* (1947). The recurrent use of grant conditions to impose national solutions on traditionally local issues suggests that the political safeguard of FEDERALISM constraining Congress in the use of national regulatory power is less operative in the exercise of grant-making authority. (See TAXING AND SPENDING POWER.)

For many years intergovernmental relationships in grant programs were understood to be administrative, cooperative, professional, and donative. Consequently, federal judges declined to intervene in grievances founded on grant programs. This aloofness markedly changed with the advent of antipoverty litigation in the late 1960s, when courts acknowledged that private beneficiaries of public WELFARE BENEFITS were entitled to relief against state and local laws and practices inconsistent with federal grant conditions. Litigation over grants soon became a staple of federal court dockets, with suits by federal grantor agencies and local government grantees as well as by private parties. The judicial decisions, while providing a novel and potent injunctive remedy, broadly construed and uniformly validated federal goals and conditions. Federal courts thus placed their stamp of approval on Congress's expansive use of federal grants.

Grants differ from regulation in that they entail expenditures, not direct commands and sanctions, as the inducement for conforming activity. Because of this difference, courts maintain that state and local governmental participation in grant-in-aid programs is voluntary, not coerced. They consequently reject attacks on grant conditions, on the ground that onerous or intrusive requirements can be avoided by the "simple expedient" of not yielding and of refusing the grant. This choice of the state or city is largely fictional in light of citizen-industry mobility and the competition among states for resources. But courts cannot intelligibly resolve the question of whether federal grants have overborne the "free will" of government units.

On several recent occasions Congress has further reduced the difference between grants and regulation through the creation of new grant-in-aid directives without additional federal funding. Instead of monetary inducements, Congress has chosen to condition continuation of eligibility under well-established, and usually large, aid programs on conformity with its new requirements. This tying arrangement has the look

of regulation, but its validity seems beyond question so long as there is a plausible relationship between the new program or condition and the national purposes of the older one.

For example, states may be required to supplement or to provide welfare payments in order to remain eligible for large Medicaid health care grants; the justification is that income maintenance and health-care support once were within a single grant program, and, more fundamentally, that subsistence payments significantly affect the health of the impoverished. Similarly Congress has tied the availability of federally insured mortgages to state participation in a flood control program; has tied the entire portmanteau of federal health dollars to state adoption of an elaborate apparatus for health systems planning and cost control; and has tied highway grants to state regulation of billboards, state enforcement of a federal speed limit, and state adoption of a national minimum age for drinking. There may be constitutional limits on tying new conditions to older grant programs, but the limits remain unenforced and unexplored.

The basic constitutional constraint on grant conditions is that they must be relevant to the purpose of a grant program. Here, as elsewhere, Congress has an exceedingly large discretion to determine relationships between means and goals. Fair treatment of private beneficiaries and efficiency are the two primary categories of relatedness, and they obviously can carry a good deal of baggage. In addition, Congress of late has established a web of elaborate "cross-cutting" conditions applicable to all or most grant-in-aid programs concerning, for example, the handicapped, environmental impacts, labor and procurement standards, citizen participation, merit hiring, and CIVIL RIGHTS. Administrative enforcement of grant conditions played a major role in the DESEGREGATION of southern schools. To be sure, many of these restrictions would fall within congressional powers under the COMMERCE CLAUSE and the FOURTEENTH AMENDMENT, but there is significance in Congress's casting them as grant-in-aid conditions. The judicial assumption that states have the option not to accept the grants apparently makes it easier for Congress to impose new and controversial obligations on the states.

The TENTH AMENDMENT limit established in NATIONAL LEAGUE OF CITIES V. USERY (1976) has not been applied to grants founded on the spending power, no doubt because such a ruling would eviscerate the current system of federal grants. Numerous federal grant conditions directly affect the structure and operation of state and local governments. Grant programs not only pervasively alter the spending priorities of governmental units, but, through the imposition of conditions, also allocate power between state and local governments (and occasionally between governors and legislatures), dictate hiring practices and employment benefits, and, by barring partisan political activity, limit the occasions on which officials administering departments having grants may be elected.

There is, finally, the Supreme Court's assimilation of grant programs to regulatory ones in its holding that state laws inconsistent with the terms of federal grants are invalid under the SUPREMACY CLAUSE. Although not fully explicated, this theory has been used repeatedly to warrant injunctive relief against grantee noncomplicance with national conditions. Traditionally, federal administrative enforcement of grant conditions had been exceptionally lax, perhaps designedly so. Third-party suits for injunctive relief have altered this convention, while enlarging the role of federal courts in monitoring and enforcing grant programs. As a consequence, there is now more law and less discretion defining and governing the relationships under national grants.

LEE A. ALBERT

Bibliography

LAPIERRE, D. BRUCE 1983 The Political Safeguards of Federalism Redux. *Washington University Law Quarterly* 60:779–1056.

MAXWELL, J. and ARONSON, J. R. (1965)1977 *Financing State and Local Government.* Washington, D.C.: Brookings Institution.

FEDERAL IMMUNITY ACT
68 Stat. 745 (1954)

The growing tendency in the early 1950s of witnesses before congressional committees to refuse to testify by relying on the Fifth Amendment's RIGHT AGAINST SELF-INCRIMINATION led Congress in 1954 to amend previous statutes and provide revised immunity arrangements. The purpose of the measure was to bypass the Fifth Amendment by giving Congress the power to grant a reluctant witness immunity from prosecution and compel the individual to testify. Either house of Congress by majority vote or a congressional committee by a two-thirds vote could grant immunity from prosecution to a witness in a national security investigation, provided an order was first obtained from a United States District Court judge. The statute required the attorney general to be given advance notification and an opportunity to offer objec-

tions. The law also permitted UNITED STATES DISTRICT COURTS to grant immunity to witnesses before courts or GRAND JURIES. Witnesses thus immunized faced the choice of testifying or going to jail. The Fifth Amendment could not be raised as a barrier to compulsory testimony.

In ULLMAN V. UNITED STATES (1956) the Supreme Court sustained its constitutionality.

PAUL L. MURPHY

(SEE ALSO: *Immunity Grant.*)

FEDERALISM
(History)

Reflecting on the achievements of the CONSTITUTIONAL CONVENTION, JAMES MADISON wrote in 1831 that the Framers had lacked even "technical terms or phrases" to describe accurately the governmental system they designed. Prior to 1787, the term "federal" had been used to signify confederation, a system in which SOVEREIGNTY remained with the constituent states that ceded certain elements of authority to a central government—and in which the central authority's legislature merely could propose measures to the states for approval. By contrast, in what was known as "consolidated" government, typical of the modern European nation-state, the central authority was the repository of sovereignty and the power of the locally based units of government depended entirely upon it. The Founders departed from all the historical precedents in both these modes, Madison declared, to produce a system that was "a novelty and a compound." It is this system that we know as American federalism, with its combination of features associated with both the consolidated (or unitary) nation-state and the old-style confederational form of government.

Nearly two centuries of colonial history in North America had afforded only rare examples of cooperation and coordination that presaged even in a remote way the system devised in 1787. In 1643, Plymouth, Massachusetts, Connecticut, and New Haven formed a league called the United Colonies of New-England. Commissioners appointed by the four governments dealt with boundary questions, missions to the Indians, and even coordination of military operations in the Indian war of 1675–1676; but the organization soon faded into obscurity. The only serious effort at united action after that time and involving surrender of any colonial powers was the abortive Albany Plan of Union of 1754. Designed by BENJAMIN FRANKLIN and

THOMAS HUTCHINSON, the plan would have created a council of the colonies and an executive appointed by the Crown. In addition to being empowered to declare war, conclude treaties with the Indian nations, and regulate territories outside the existing colonial boundaries, the council would have been given authority to impose taxes. But the plan foundered, with not a single colonial assembly giving assent to the proposal.

Certain qualities of the British colonial system itself had foreshadowed American federalism. Although formal authority remained squarely in the hands of the British government, still the colonies were given significant latitude in governing their own affairs. The sudden centralization of power after 1763, when the British decided to tighten the reins and impose new taxes and administrative reforms, precipitated the Revolutionary crisis. Even the exigencies of newly declared independence and armed conflict with Britain had not induced the American states, however, to surrender claims to sovereignty in the interest of national unity. Indeed, the ARTICLES OF CONFEDERATION specifically provided that each state would retain "its sovereignty, freedom, and independence, and every power, JURISDICTION and right, which is not by this confederation expressly delegated to the United States, in Congress assembled." Article III, moreover, described the government only as "a firm league of friendship." The notorious weaknesses of government under the Articles, leading to demands for basic reform by 1786–1787, derived from precisely this perpetuation of the states' prerogatives.

What the Convention sought to create in 1787 was a system in which some measure of sovereignty would be retained for the states; but the national government would be given powers ample enough to govern effectively, operate directly upon the citizens, and establish the nation as a credible presence in international affairs. The continued existence of the states as separate legal entities was an essential component of the original understanding embodied in the Constitution. Structural features that assured the states of great influence included the system of REPRESENTATION in Congress (including equal representation for each state in the Senate), the AMENDING PROCESS, and the voting by state in the House of Representatives in presidential elections not resolved in the ELECTORAL COLLEGE.

Equally important was the concept of enumerated powers. The jurisdiction of the proposed national government, wrote Madison in THE FEDERALIST #39, extended "to certain enumerated objects only, and [left] to the several states a residuary and inviolable sovereignty over all other objects." The "general principle" underlying enumeration of the central government's powers, as JAMES WILSON later wrote, was "that whatever object was confined in its nature and operation to a particular State ought to be subject to the separate government of the States; but whatever in its nature and operation extended beyond a particular State, ought to be comprehended within the federal jurisdiction." On this principle was designed Article I, section 8, with its enumeration of the specific powers of Congress, including control over foreign and INTERSTATE COMMERCE, coinage, and the military and naval forces; the power to establish roads and post offices, inferior federal courts, and an organized militia; and authority as well to declare war and conclude treaties, to create a federal district as the seat of government, and to govern TERRITORIES and regulate property of the United States. Specific limitations were also embraced in the original document of 1787: the prohibition against import and export taxes, grants of TITLES OF NOBILITY, BILLS OF ATTAINDER, suspension of HABEAS CORPUS except during rebellions or invasions, or congressional interference with the slave trade for a period of twenty years. Demarcating the boundaries of the states' authority were provisions in Article I, section 10, that prohibited the states from enactment of EX POST FACTO LAWS, bills of attainder, or laws impairing the OBLIGATION OF CONTRACT. The Constitution also forbade the states from entering into treaties or imposing duties or tonnage fees without permission of Congress.

The seeds of controversy over the proper reach of the bounds of national power were to be found, however, in the GENERAL WELFARE CLAUSE and in the NECESSARY AND PROPER CLAUSE. Article VI, moreover, included the SUPREMACY CLAUSE, holding that all laws and treaties made under the Constitution "shall be the supreme Law of the Land." Opponents of the Constitution cited all these provisions as evidence that the Constitution could easily justify a dangerous centralization of power, overwhelming the states and rendering their alleged residual sovereignty a nugatory matter. A new tyranny, according to this view, could easily be the result of consolidated, unitary government.

Anticipating exactly such objections, the Framers built into the federal design a guarantee of a REPUBLICAN FORM OF GOVERNMENT to each state. The FULL FAITH AND CREDIT, FUGITIVE SLAVE, PRIVILEGES AND IMMUNITIES, and extradition provisions further buttressed state authority. The most important consequence of concern about the centralization of power and potential tyranny, however, was the movement for a BILL OF RIGHTS. The first nine amendments, together with the original provisions of the Constitution prohibiting the states from enacting bills of attainder or abrogating contracts, represented an effort to establish national ideals of justice—defining boundaries beyond which government must respect the rights of individual citizens. The Bill of Rights served to reinforce federalism itself as a bulwark of defense for liberty against concentrated governmental power.

What values were intended to be served by this new system of federalism, a system described by a New York judge in 1819 as a "complex and peculiar structure" that permitted the states and the national government to move "in different spheres but occupying the same territorial space, operating upon and for the benefit of the same people"? The first value, designed to protect liberty and to give republican principles full play, was maintenance of government "close to the people." The champions of the Constitution contended that by giving a continuing—and vital—role to the states, popular oversight of governmental operations would be effective and there would be a high degree of participation in public affairs. These same contentions have been heard ever since in the arguments for a federal division of powers in American government.

A second value given a high place in the rationale for federalism was diversity itself. Regional differences in cultural values and local preferences on matters of law and policy would be permitted and find expression when important powers of government remained with the states. Providing in this manner for diversity meant, as Justice LOUIS D. BRANDEIS argued in NEW STATE ICE COMPANY V. LIEBMANN (1932), that "a single courageous state may, if its citizens choose, serve as a laboratory, and try novel social and economic experiments without risk to the rest of the country."

Efficiency was another value intended to be promoted by federalism. Loading all the functions of government upon authority at the center is not only potentially dangerous to liberty; it is also potentially the cause of congestion, complexity, and ineffectiveness. Even unitary, consolidated governments find it necessary to devolve certain functions on subnational or local authority. As Madison wrote in *The Federalist* #14, even if the states were to be abolished, "the general government would be compelled, by the principle of self-preservation, to reinstate them in their proper jurisdiction." What distinguishes a system founded on the principles of federalism from a consolidated system, however, is that federalism recognizes the legitimacy of exclusive state claims to some meaningful autonomy in important areas of law and policy. Power to control at least some of the things that really matter, in the regulation of society's affairs, must be left to the states.

A notable distinguishing feature of American federalism, consistent with the effective pursuit of these values, is the provision for constitutional amendment. What seemed a rational division of authority in the largely agrarian-commercial nation of 1787 will not be rational (or even minimally workable) two hundred years later in an integrated industrial nation with over fifty times the population of 1787. Most of the major changes in the American federal system, both in formal doctrine and in actual governmental practice, have occurred in response to that problem. By a remarkable insight of the Framers, expressed through the amendment process explicitly and the judicial processes by implication, they provided mechanisms for successful adaptation to changing circumstances and national values.

The principles of a federal system require that major changes in the boundaries of authority between the states and the national government should be accomplished by the prescribed amendment process. Such fundamental change should not occur through a process of ordinary legislation or mere administrative innovations in policy. The actual operation of the American system has sometimes conformed to this ideal: fundamental change in the structure of powers within the system were initiated, for example, by the Civil War and Reconstruction amendments. Yet at other times basic changes in federal–state relationships were effected without resort to the amendment process. Even the THIRTEENTH, FOURTEENTH, and FIFTEENTH AMENDMENTS, for example, ratified decisions already made on the bloody battlefields of the Civil War. The doctrine of IMPLIED POWERS was a judicial invention in McCULLOCH V. MARYLAND (1819). The dramatic swing in antebellum interpretation of the COMMERCE CLAUSE—first the MARSHALL COURT's nationalistic interpretation; then, the TANEY COURT's assertion of DUAL FEDERALISM and concurrent powers—came about by judicial innovations in doctrine. Vast changes in law and policy, not least the abandonment of economic due process and the emergence of new presidential EMERGENCY and WAR POWERS, have occurred since 1933 without benefit of constitutional amendments.

Provisions for accommodating new states in the course of national expansion is another important feature of the federal scheme. The thirteen original states took the chance, in effect, that they would be confronted by new sectional alignments and powerful interests hostile in some measure to their own. It was a certainty that each new state taken into the Union would significantly dilute the power of the original states in the Senate, and, as population grew in newer areas, would dilute even more their power in the House of Representatives and in the Electoral College. This provision for the admission of new states underlined the values fundamental to the original understanding: government close to the people, diversity, and efficiency.

A legacy of the Founders not easily separated from their creation of a federal system is the "federal creed" that has been as influential in shaping political behavior as constitutional provisions have been in shaping the dynamics of government. By "federal creed" is meant habitual skepticism with regard to centralized power. It was expressed vividly in Walt Whitman's *Leaves of Grass:*

To the States or any of them or any city of the States,
Resist much, obey little.
Once unquestioning obedient, once fully enslaved, no nation state, city of this earth, ever afterward resumes its liberty.

These lines express a political reality of the nineteenth century, namely, that whenever a policy was considered, debate typically centered not only on the wisdom of the policy itself but also on the cognate question: what level of government—the states or Washington—ought legitimately to have responsibility? It was the enduring popular commitment to the values of federalism, some historians contend, that kept the nation from accepting full-scale reorganization as a consolidated, unitary government in the Civil War years. Instead, despite such centralizing measures as the wartime banking laws and the postwar adoption of the Fourteenth Amendment, there remained a strong faith in the desirability of a meaningful "state sovereignty." The culture of federalism was expressed in the enigmatic pronouncement of the Supreme Court in TEXAS V. WHITE (1869) that "the Constitution in all its provisions looks to an indestructible Union composed of indestructible states." Similar convictions about the states' continuing importance found voice in COLLECTOR V. DAY, two years later, when the Court asserted that surviving aspects of state sovereignty made the states "as independent of the general government as [it] is independent of the states."

Opponents of centralized power appealed to such convictions in the late nineteenth century and early twentieth century, when they argued for narrow construction of the commerce clause and found in the due process clause of the Fifth Amendment authority for declaring unconstitutional congressional regulatory measures. The same federal creed led many reformers in the Progressive era to prefer uniform state codes to outright imposition of uniformity in law by congressional action. In the New Deal years and down to the present day, moreover, opponents of the welfare and regulatory features of modern policy have expressed their views in terms that extolled state sovereignty and deplored the centralizing of power in Washington as contrary to the Framers' intent.

The variety and ingenuity of such arguments have led many commentators to conclude that the federal creed is a convenient, all-purpose shield behind which to advocate special-interest positions. The most egregious example in the nation's history has been the invocation of STATES' RIGHTS as a justification for policies of RACIAL DISCRIMINATION. Conservative jurists also created a constitutional void within which neither the national government nor the states could legislate to regulate economic interests; federalism became the handmaiden of laissez-faire. Inconsistency in the application of federal principles in the 1920s led THOMAS REED POWELL to remark that "the sacred slogan of states' rights is easily forgotten when employers wish their laborers sober but unctuously invoked when they wish them young" (a reference to southern opposition to child-labor laws and support of national prohibition). In the post-World War II era, moreover, some of the most outspoken champions of "small government" and states' rights, and opponents of the nationalization of economic and social policy, have also been most consistently in favor of massive increases in the size of the national armed forces and even of federal surveillance of political activists and other infringements on CIVIL LIBERTIES.

Even if one concedes that federalism can be a smokescreen behind which special interests can pursue selfish aims or hide inconsistencies, the prominence of the traditional values of federalism in political rhetoric indicates that such arguments are regarded as effective. They are, in effect, appeals to the values of a "federal" political culture: American political consciousness retains inherited and much-reiterated notions that certain important values are best served by decentralization of power.

Some prominent contemporary students of American federalism claim that the abstract concept of separate governments (state and national), with separate responsibilities and constituencies, is—and indeed always has been—a fiction. According to this view, despite the "fiction" of ENUMERATED POWERS there has always been an overlap of responsibilities and a significant measure of federal–state sharing of power. "Dual federalism"—the concept of state and national governments occupying distinct, separate spheres of authority—is in this version of our history only a myth. Contrary to this view is another that contends that until 1861 the federal system in actuality functioned much as the model of "dual federalism" prescribed, and after the Civil War, there began a progressive centralization of power which continued until the 1980s.

The evaluation of such contending views depends upon analysis not only of doctrinal development but also of the system's practical operation. How has government actually behaved, and to what extent has power been centralized or decentralized in important areas of policy, at different stages of the nation's history? In fact, the story of American federalism is one of progressive centralization. Except for the overarching continuity infusing the whole record—the progressive centralization of power, step by step—distinct stages in the history of federalism indicate fundamental discontinuities.

The first stage was the period from the founding, in 1787–1789, to the Civil War. In this period, a remarkable array of governmental functions were exclusively, or nearly so, in the hands of the states. Power was diffused, and what "sharing" was found tended to be confined to the most superficial types of cooperation between state and national governments. Criminal law, definition of the requirements of due process, prison management, and criminal punishment were all state functions. So was the definition of property rights, confined only by the contract clause decisions of the Supreme Court. The power of EMINENT DOMAIN was exercised by the states virtually without a check by federal authority. Public education and labor relations, even slavery, were state matters. The states controlled the content of commercial law, family law, and such COMMON LAW matters as the rules of torts, nuisance, and liability. Also decentralized were CORPORATION law, most of taxation policy, and the design and control of the nation's transport system. At no other time after 1861 were the theoretical maxims of dual federalism so closely approximated by government in action.

The decentralization of real power before 1861 persisted even though the Marshall Court was handing down a series of landmark "nationalizing" decisions that lay the doctrinal groundwork for centralization. Even the Marshall Court left the door open for robust state regulatory activity. By the late 1830s, moreover, the Taney Court had begun to develop the doctrine of "concurrent powers," and it had shored up the STATE POLICE POWER with its decision

in CHARLES RIVER BRIDGE V. WARREN BRIDGE (1837). Congress simply abstained from acting in many areas of policy that had been left open to it by the Marshall Court's doctrines. The state governments, therefore, held the reins in many vital areas of policy; the structure and dynamics of power were decentralized. One consequence of this decentralization was significant state-to-state variation in the substantive content of law in property, labor, family, and criminal law. The differences between law in slave states and free states were only the most dramatic illustration of such diversity.

The period from 1861 to 1890 was the second stage in the development of American federalism. Formal constitutional change came with the Civil War and had transforming doctrinal and practical consequences, deriving from the Thirteenth, Fourteenth, and Fifteenth Amendments. Meanwhile, Congress in the 1860s was enacting CIVIL RIGHTS laws, instituting an income tax (terminated after the war), inaugurating a national banking system, subsidizing transcontinental railroad projects, and expanding the size and reach of the federal bureaucracy generally. Thus power was centralized at an entirely unprecedented level, both in control of the economy and in protection of individual rights. Laws expanding the jurisdiction of the federal courts further concentrated power in the national government. In 1887, the INTERSTATE COMMERCE ACT inaugurated federal ADMINISTRATIVE LAW and centralized the regulation of the railroads. In 1890, the SHERMAN ACT marked the beginning of federal business law. Although such measures continued the centralizing trend in the distribution of real power, nonetheless elements of dual federalism persisted: property law, criminal justice, family relations, labor law, and most of an infant system of business regulation all remained nearly exclusively with the states.

The third stage of American federalism occupied the years 1890–1933. It was an era of accelerating centralization of policy responsibilities—although diversity persisted and the states did continue to exercise a wide-ranging discretionary authority, without substantial federal interference or direction, in many areas of law. Large-scale aid for irrigation in the West commenced with the Carey Act of 1894; and the Newlands Act of 1902 established an even larger national policy presence in that area. The PURE FOOD AND DRUG ACT (1906) signaled a trend toward exercise of the NATIONAL POLICE POWER, augmenting controls imposed through use of the TAXING AND SPENDING POWER, POSTAL POWER, and commerce power. Both the Federal Reserve Act of 1913 and the CLAYTON

ANTITRUST ACT of 1914 greatly extended federal administrative law, displacing state regulatory powers. Over the next seventy years, one of the most influential changes was the SIXTEENTH AMENDMENT, which set the stage for the national government's use of income taxes as a major source of revenues. Midway in this period, moreover, came the dramatic temporary expansion of centralized power occasioned by World War I. Although the conservative dominance of Congress in the Republican 1920s slowed the centralizing trend, even in that decade new responsibilities were assumed or expanded by the national government. They included the institution of FEDERAL GRANTS-IN-AID to the states for infant and maternity care, and expansion of the federal roads program, established earlier. The 1920 Transportation Act and the Federal Power Act of the same year also enlarged the regulatory powers of the federal government.

Ironically, these expansions of centralized power occurred in counterpoint with recurrent expressions of dual federalism and LIMITED GOVERNMENT doctrines by the Supreme Court. The most important initiatives of Congress struck down by the Court were the income tax instituted in 1893 and the 1916 KEATING-OWENS CHILD LABOR ACT. Matters such as labor relations were "entrusted to local authority" by the Constitution, the Court asserted in HAMMER V. DAGENHART (1918); child labor was "a purely local matter in which federal authority does not extend," and to permit Congress to regulate child labor risked permitting "our system of government [to] be practically destroyed"! Yet the same judges who subscribed to such doctrines of federalism also adhered to the doctrine of economic due process. Hence, when the Court reviewed regulatory and welfare legislation enacted by the states, it frequently struck down such laws under the Fourteenth Amendment. The Court thus immunized many business interests against regulation by either the state or the national government. The federal judiciary's activism in the cause of laissez-faire and dual federalism, ironically, was evidence of a negative type of centralization: the Supreme Court stood as censor of the states in vital social and economic matters.

Against this background of mixed constitutional doctrine and new centralizing initiatives, intergovernmental relations in the modern "sharing" mode emerged. Its most important feature was grants of cash aid to the states. Congress often tied strings to such aid, requiring planning of state programs and some degree of auditing by federal officers. By 1920, eleven programs were paying $30 million annually to the states—about 2.5 per cent of state revenues, or about a tenth the proportion paid by such grants-in-aid in the early 1980s—with most of the payments representing highway construction funds.

In the field of civil rights, the Court made only a small dent in the solid shield of states' rights behind which Jim Crow legislation, disfranchisement of blacks, and control of racial violence remained the exclusive responsibility of state governments. In the South, white supremacy reigned. In the area of FREEDOM OF SPEECH and FREEDOM OF THE PRESS, however, there was some movement by the Court toward applying Fourteenth Amendment constraints on state action.

The fourth stage of American federalism's development embraced the New Deal and World War II years, from 1933 to 1945. This period witnessed the wholesale centralization of policy responsibilities, a movement spurred by the worst economic depression in the nation's history and by four years of total mobilization for war. In the wake of centralizing initiatives by Congress came a dramatic shift in constitutional doctrine by the Supreme Court. To be sure, the Court initially erected doctrinal barriers to the innovations of FRANKLIN D. ROOSEVELT's New Deal administration; but by 1937–1938 a modern "constitutional revolution" had occurred without benefit of formal constitutional amendment. The Court discarded the doctrine of economic due process, and it adopted an interpretation of the commerce clause that validated unprecedented expansion of federal interventions in the economy and of social welfare and relief programs.

One policy area after another that previously had been in the states' hands came into the domain of federal action. Congress made agriculture a managed sector beginning in 1933; and the NATIONAL INDUSTRIAL RECOVERY ACT had much the same effect in the manufacturing sector from 1933 to 1935. The TENNESSEE VALLEY AUTHORITY ACT inaugurated regional development under federal auspices, and national programs proliferated in the conservation and reclamation fields. The WAGNER ACT of 1935 established a comprehensive federal policy of collective bargaining in labor relations, instituting national administrative law in the labor field; and by 1938 wages and hours legislation had augmented the basic labor law by setting uniform national standards. Congress authorized massive federal relief and subsidized work programs; and the SOCIAL SECURITY ACT and unemployment-compensation legislation of 1935 marked a new era of nationally sponsored and directed welfare policy. The net of federal regulatory power was thrown over many areas of industry formerly controlled, if at all, by the states: BROADCASTING, trucking, waterways, the securities exchanges, and previously unregulated segments of the banking industry. Meanwhile grants-in-aid—and the model of COOPERATIVE FEDERALISM of which they were an essential component—began to dominate federal–state relationships. True "sharing," in which the bulk of funding came from Congress, thus became a prominent feature of the working federal system; yet decisions tended to be made at the center, both as to policy and as to funding, with the states exercising administrative functions and serving as conduits for federal money.

Still, except for the three and a half years of war, when emergency powers extended to the national control of virtually every feature of the nation's life, the states remained a source of diversity in the American system of government. Yet the number and the significance of policy areas under their control had been so reduced that a new-modeled federal system had clearly become dominant.

The final stage in the history of federalism dates from 1945 to the present day. Its main feature, at least until the administration of RONALD REAGAN beginning in 1981, was a continued trend toward centralization. Four characteristics of this centralization movement are particularly important. First is the permanent status of large-scale standing military forces, their support taking as much as half of the federal government's operating expenses—something without precedent in peacetime prior to 1940. Second is the tendency toward stronger federal guarantees of civil rights. All three branches of government contributed to the civil rights expansion. The executive branch enforced racial integration of the armed forces and required AFFIRMATIVE ACTION programs of firms taking government contracts. Congress defined new guarantees of rights in areas such as VOTING, PUBLIC ACCOMMODATIONS, and employment; it also enacted legislation under which executive departments instituted affirmative action and equal opportunity policies in labor relations, education, and other areas. The judiciary played a leading role, with the line of DESEGREGATION cases elaborating the principles of BROWN V. BOARD OF EDUCATION (1954). The Court also carved out new areas of federal constitutional rights, such as the RIGHT OF PRIVACY and rights against SEX DISCRIMINATION.

The third major characteristic of centralization since 1945 is the rapid growth in the 1960s and 1970s, and the continued importance since then, of federal grants-in-aid to the states. The design and initiation of new grant programs, especially those associated

with the "Great Society" measures of the LYNDON B. JOHNSON administration, led some analysts to speak of a "near monopolization of innovation by the central government" as a novel form of primary centralization. A fourth characteristic of post-1945 centralization is the continued enlargement of the scope of congressional regulatory concerns. Congress instituted far-reaching controls over air and water pollution, occupational health and safety, food and drug quality, and energy resources. Despite a strong movement in the Jimmy Carter and especially the Reagan years toward "deregulation," the federal regulatory presence in the mid-1980s remained far greater than that of the 1950s.

The Supreme Court seldom has stood in the way of such trends. Indeed, its role has been that of leader in the REAPPORTIONMENT and civil rights areas. In reviewing regulatory measures, only once since 1937 has the Court invoked states' rights or the commerce clause in such a way as to limit congressional power; that one exception was NATIONAL LEAGUE OF CITIES V. USERY (1976), a decision of limited application although notable for its assertion of the rights of the states "as states." Some state activities, the Court held, were beyond the reach of national wage and hour standards. Yet the Court has validated all other federal regulatory measures.

The scores of modern grant-in-aid programs have included many that bypassed the state governments: federal funds were awarded directly to cities and local special-purpose districts. Another hallmark of recent intergovernmental relations is what may be termed "managerialism," taking the form of program realignments, reliance on new budgeting concepts, oversight of programs by regional-level federal offices, and increased attention by Congress to the quality of governmental services at all levels. In 1958, Congress created the Advisory Commission on Intergovernmental Relations, which became a major proponent of reforms in aid programs and also an exemplar of the new-style managerialism in action.

Successive Presidents have championed the realignment of powers and policy responsibilities, as between the nation and the states. Thus Lyndon Johnson called for a "creative federalism" that would involve private-sector institutions as well as all levels of government in jointly administered programs. Some of Johnson's Great Society program complicated intergovernmental relations by permitting community organizations to challenge the existing governmental and political establishments. A reaction to the Johnson-era programs and politics was embodied in RICHARD M. NIXON's call for a "new federalism." His proposals took the form of combining increased executive power with increasing reliance on REVENUE SHARING and "block grants" instead of categorical or conditional grants-in-aid. Although during Jimmy Carter's administration general revenue sharing was continued, the President sought to reemphasize the problems of major urban centers and depressed minority populations; he also sought to impose tighter control on grants-in-aid, to assure the realization of congressional objectives.

Ronald Reagan announced his own brand of "new federalism" on taking office in 1981. Both in his rhetoric and by administrative actions, he sought to turn the clock back dramatically on many features of modern federalism. National political dialogue was infused, for the first time in many years, with an orthodox small-government, anticentralist ideology little heeded since New Deal days. Previous Republican Presidents—DWIGHT EISENHOWER, Nixon, and GERALD R. FORD—had all accepted in varying degrees, and even expanded in some respects, the permanent legacy of the New Deal. But in the 1980s, Reagan led a much more deeply rooted challenge to some of the welfare state and regulatory state foundations of the modern federal system. At the same time, he endorsed legislation designed to curb the authority of the federal courts, especially in the civil rights and CRIMINAL PROCEDURE areas; and he gave his support to constitutional amendments designed to permit school prayer in public schools, to require balanced BUDGETS, and to permit the states to prohibit abortions. Reagan's programs underlined his admiration for the constitutional doctrines and policies of federalism dominant in Republican circles in the 1920s.

Once again, therefore, in the Reagan years, federalism was at the center of political debate in America; and once again, the values of federalism were being invoked for purposes that transcended the mere reordering of federal–state relationships. The classic concerns of federalism in theory—diffusion of power, diversity, liberty, efficiency—remained in the forefront of public attention. How to square the ideals expressed in the original understanding with the social and economic realities of the late twentieth century remained a profoundly important issue.

HARRY N. SCHEIBER

Bibliography

BEER, SAMUEL 1973 The Modernization of American Federalism. *Publius* 3:49–95.
DAVIS, RUFUS 1978 *The Federal Principle: A Journey through Time in Quest of Meaning.* Berkeley: University of California Press.
GRODZINS, MORTON 1966 *The American System: A New View of Government in the United States,* ed. Daniel Elazar. Chicago: Rand, McNally.
MACMAHON, ARTHUR W., ED. 1955 *Federalism: Mature and Emergent.* New York: Columbia University Press.
PATTERSON, JAMES 1969 *The New Deal and the States: Federalism in Transition.* Princeton, N.J.: Princeton University Press.
SCHEIBER, HARRY N. 1975 Federalism and the American Economic Order, 1789–1910. *Law & Society Review* 10:57–118.
———— 1978 American Federalism and the Diffusion of Power. *University of Toledo Law Review* 9:619–680.
WALKER, DAVID 1981 *Toward a Functioning Federalism.* Cambridge, Mass.: Winthrop.
WRIGHT, DEIL 1978 *Understanding Intergovernmental Relations.* North Scituate, Mass.: Duxbury Press.

FEDERALISM
(Theory)

The American federal system came into existence when the United States declared its independence in 1776. Indeed, the very process of declaring independence involved a series of reciprocal initiatives and actions on the part of the colonies; the CONTINENTAL CONGRESS declared independence for all thirteen colonies in one act, federal to the extent that the declaration itself was a culmination of this interplay and was undertaken by delegates from the states, each state speaking with one voice.

The foundation of the United States was a federal act par excellence, involving a consistent and protracted interplay between the colonies (later states) and the Congress, which they created as a single, national body to speak in their collective name. In the year that the representatives of the people of the colonies collectively declared the independence of the United States, other representatives of the same people were reconstituting the colonies themselves as states. Four colonies—New Hampshire, South Carolina, Virginia, and New Jersey—adopted state CONSTITUTIONS in 1776 before the adoption of the DECLARATION OF INDEPENDENCE, and four more —Pennsylvania, Maryland, Delaware, and North Carolina—did likewise before the year was out. Within sixteen months, all the former colonies except Massachusetts had adopted constitutions.

At one time this fact was used to argue that considerable disagreement existed over whether the states preceded the Union. Today it is generally agreed that both came into existence simultaneously—in the original federal act of the United States as such. In sum, all of the ambiguities of diversity in unity endemic to federalism were present at the creation. Even local governments (in this case the towns and counties) participated in the constitutional drafting and ratifying processes.

As Americans moved westward, they created new states "from scratch," in virtually every case establishing local and territorial institutions under the aegis of the federal government, but generally as a result of local initiatives. Ultimately, these new polities, with their new populations, would be admitted to the federation as states, fully equal to their sisters under the Constitution. Thus the American federation expanded from the Atlantic to the Pacific by settling what were, to white Americans, empty lands and organizing them politically.

The last of the forty-eight contiguous states was admitted in 1912; and Alaska and Hawaii, the two noncontiguous states, were added in 1959 and 1960, respectively, after relatively long periods of territorial status. In the same decade, the United States embarked upon a new experiment in federalism by creating a category of commonwealth or "free associated state," whose people, as American citizens, voted to associate their polity with the United States under a special charter. This new arrangement was devised for Puerto Rico, which became the first "free associated state" in 1952. In 1976 a similar arrangement was made with the Northern Mariana Islands. In both cases small, populated TERRITORIES sought that status to increase their autonomy, not to diminish it. (See COMMONWEALTH STATUS.)

Historically, then, the United States model is that of a political entity that was federal from its founding. The American states did not have to find a common cultural denominator because they had one from the first. All of their regimes were of the same character and their level of economic development was roughly equal. No plan for intercolonial union was ever put forth that was not federal in character. The American colonial period, indeed, had been a period of incubation for a uniquely American approach to governance, which properly can be termed "federal democracy."

Federal democracy is the authentic American contribution to democratic thought and republican government. Its conception represents a synthesis of the Puritan idea of the covenant relationship as the foundation of all proper human society and the constitutional ideas of the English natural rights school of the seventeenth and early eighteenth centuries. Contractual noncentralization—the structured dispersion of power among many centers whose legitimate authority is constitutionally guaranteed—is the key to the widespread and entrenched diffusion of power that remains the principal characteristic of and argument for federal democracy.

Federal democracy is a composite notion that includes a strong religious component. The religious expression of federalism was brought to the United States through the theology of the Puritans, who viewed the world as organized through the covenants that God had made with mankind, binding God and man into a lasting union and partnership to work for the redemption of the world, but in such a way that both parties were free, as partners must be, to preserve their respective integrities. Implicit in the Puritan view is the understanding that God relinquished some of His own omnipotence to enable men to be free to compact with Him.

According to federal theology, all social and political relationships are derived from that original covenant. This theological perspective found its counterpart in congregationalism as the basis of church polity and the town meeting as the basis of the civil polity. Thus, communities of believers were required to organize themselves by covenant into congregations just as communities of citizens were required to organize themselves by covenant into towns. The entire structure of religious and political organization in New England reflected this application of a theological principle to social and political life.

Even after the eighteenth-century secularization of the covenant idea, the behavioral pattern resurfaced on every frontier, whether in the miners' camps of southwestern Missouri, central Colorado, and the mother lode country of California, in the agricultural settlements of the upper Midwest, or in the wagon trains that crossed the plains, whose members compacted together to provide for their internal governance during the long trek westward.

It should not be surprising that Americans early became socialized into a kind of federalistic individualism that recognized the subtle bonds of partnership linking individuals even as they preserved their individual integrities. William James was later to write about the federal character of these subtle bonds in his prescription for a pluralistic universe as a "republic of republics."

In strictly governmental terms, federalism is a form of political organization that unites separate polities within an overarching political system, enabling all to maintain their fundamental political integrity and distributing power among general and constituent governments so that they all share in the system's decision-making and executing processes. In a larger sense, federalism represents the linking of free people and their communities through lasting but limited political arrangements to protect certain rights or liberties and to achieve specific common ends while preserving their respective integrities. To reverse the order, federalism has to do, first and foremost, with a relationship among entities, and then with the structure that embodies that relationship and provides the means for sustaining it. Originally federalism was most widely recognized as a relationship to which structural questions were incidental; but since the creation of the American federal system, in which a new structure was invented to accommodate that relationship, federalism has become increasingly identified in structural terms. This usage in turn has contributed to a certain emphasis on legal and administrative relations between the units and to a neglect of the larger question of the relationships federalism is designed to foster throughout the polity.

Although, in a strictly constitutional sense, American federalism is a means by which the national government shares authority and power with the states, the influence of federal principles actually extends far beyond the institutional relationships that link the federal, state, and local governments. The idea of the federal commonwealth as a partnership is a key principle of federalism and the basis of its integrative powers. Like all partnerships, the commonwealth is bound by a compact—the Constitution—that sets the basic terms of the partnership to insure, among other things, the preservation and continued political viability of its basic political units.

The principle of partnership has been extended far beyond its simple sense of a relationship between the federal and state governments. It has come to serve as the guiding principle in most of the political relationships that tie institutions, groups, interests, and individuals together in the American system. The term "partnership" describes a relationship that allows the participants freedom of action while acknowledging the ties that require them to function in partnership.

Partnership implies the distribution of power among several centers that must negotiate cooperative arrangements with one another in order to achieve common goals. Although the basic forms of the partnership are set forth in the United States Constitution, the actual character of the federal system is delineated, maintained, and made functional only partly by constitutional devices. The role of the Constitution (and of its primary interpreters, the courts) should not be minimized; yet equally important is the way in which the institutions and purposes of federalism are maintained through the political process.

The political process, as it affects the federal–state–local relationship most directly, is made manifest through four basic political devices: territorial democracy, the dual system of laws and courts, the POLITICAL PARTY system, and the system of public–private "complexes."

The basic pattern of political organization in the United States is territorial. That is to say, American politics is formally organized around units of territory rather than economic or ethnic groups, social classes, or the like. The nation is divided into states, and the states are divided into counties, and the counties are divided into townships or cities or special districts, and the whole country is divided into election districts of varying sizes. This organization means that people and their interests gain political identity and formal representation through their location in particular places and their ability to capture political control of territorial political units.

A second basic device is the multiple system of laws and courts tied to the federal division of powers. In the nation as a whole, state law is the basic law. Federal law is essentially designed to fill in the gaps left by the existence of fifty different legal systems. Thus both state and federal courts are bound by state-made law unless it is superseded by the Constitution or by federal statutory law. The complexity of this system is compounded by the nature of the dual court structure, with each state and the federal government having its own complete court system. The federal courts have asserted extensive superiority in interpreting the manner in which the United States Constitution protects the rights of American citizens (who, of course, are also citizens of their states). Led by the United States Supreme Court, which is constitutionally placed at the apex of both court systems, the federal courts interpret federal law, review the work of the state courts, and enforce the laws of the states in which they are located in cases that come under federal JURISDICTION.

The third basic political channel is the party system. The Democratic and Republican parties represent two broad confederations of otherwise largely independent state party organizations that unite on the national plane primarily to gain public office. Despite the greater public attention given to the national parties, the real centers of party organization, finance, and power are on the state and local planes. This noncentralization of the parties helps to maintain generally noncentralized governments and to perpetuate a high degree of local control even in the face of "big government." Thus the party system is of great importance in maintaining the basic structure of

American politics and basic American political values, including those of federalism.

The fourth political device, the system of public–private "complexes," is partly reflected in the character of interest group activity. The partnership system extends outward to include private elements as well as governments—both public nongovernmental bodies, such as civic, philanthropic, educational, health, and welfare associations, and private profit-making bodies. These private associations and bodies often work so closely with their governmental allies that it is difficult to distinguish where the public interest ends and the private interest begins.

As a federation, the United States differs from a confederation of essentially separate political systems where the overarching authority is deliberately weak. At the same time, in the noncentralized American system, there is no central government with absolute authority over the states, but there is a strong national or general government coupled with strong state and local governments that share authority and power, constitutionally and practically.

The first important feature of a federation, following the American pattern, is the fundamental role and importance of the federal constitution as an organic law. The American Constitution reflects a federal approach to political SOVEREIGNTY, rejecting the idea that states or governments are sovereign as such, and holding that the people are the ultimate repositories of sovereignty and that governments have only "powers," delegated to them by the people. That approach precludes any notion of INHERENT POWERS. Under the Constitution, all powers possessed by the federal government are delegated to it by the people. The federal government has no inherent powers, although, as a result of those delegated, it gains some inherent extensions of its power. So, for example, because the people have delegated to the federal government the power to conduct some aspects of FOREIGN AFFAIRS, the President is understood to have acquired certain IMPLIED POWERS to negotiate with foreign governments. Once the people delegated the principal power, the implied power flowed automatically, but the second is theoretically dependent upon the first. From time to time, Presidents have claimed that they have inherent powers in the fields of foreign affairs and defense that are not subject to constitutional limitations but, rather, flow from the status of the United States as a sovereign state. Although the United States Supreme Court has recognized the existence of inherent powers, it has clearly limited them. This approach has been possible in the United States because of the dual character of the American founding, which enabled Americans to avoid confronting the issue of sovereignty head on.

Accordingly, as ANDREW C. MCLAUGHLIN suggested, the American federal system was designed to provide for the government of a large civil society without reliance upon hierarchical principles. In its original form, the American political system was designed as a matrix of polities, an indefinite number of structured political arenas linked to one another within the framework provided by the national and state constitutions. These arenas were to be distinguished from one another not on the basis of being "higher" or "lower" in importance but on the basis of the relative size of the constituencies they served. It was further assumed that the arenas were essentially equal, because size, of itself, was no measure of importance. Tasks were designed to be assumed or shared within the matrix on the assumption that sometimes a smaller arena is more appropriate than a larger one and that sometimes the reverse is true. The federal government was constitutionally mandated to serve the largest arena and to maintain the entire structure by assuring the continuity of the matrix itself. The role of the state governments in serving the basic divisions in the matrix was affirmed in the constitutional arrangement, and the states established local governments to serve the smallest arenas. Today the matrix consists of thousands of local arenas within the national framework, divided into fifty basic units—the states of the federal Union.

The American system has increasingly emphasized COOPERATIVE FEDERALISM rather than DUAL FEDERALISM as the basis of its operations. The American pattern of federalism has been cooperative since its beginnings, because since its inception most powers and competences have been treated as concurrent, shared by the various planes of government. In Morton Grodzins's terms, it is not a layer cake but a marble cake. Therefore, in the American polity, it is especially difficult to define what is exclusively in the federal sphere of competence, or in the state sphere, or in the local sphere.

The American federal system is at once extraordinarily simple and unusually complex. The simplicity of the federal system lies in a formal structure of federal, state, and local governments and in the outline of formal relationships between them. The complexity of the system lies in the myriad relationships that have developed between the governments and those who make them work. People often tend to take it for granted that national problems are handled in Washington; state problems in the state capital; and local problems at city hall or in the county courthouse. But, although it is easy to say that this is how things should be, it is well-nigh impossible to take a specific issue or function and to determine that it is exclusively national, state, or local.

The constitutional place of the states in the federal system is determined by four elements: the provisions in the federal and state constitutions that either limit or guarantee the powers of the states vis-à-vis the federal government; the provisions in the federal Constitution that give the states a role in the composition of the national government; the subsequent interpretations of both sets of provisions by the courts (particularly the United States Supreme Court); and the unwritten constitutional traditions that have evolved informally and have only later been formally recognized through the first three, directly or indirectly. The federal constitutional provisions outlining the general position of the states must always be taken into consideration even if some of them can be transcended through politics in specific situations. The specific limitations and guarantees of state powers fall into four basic categories: general concern for the integrity of the states as well as their subordination to the Union; some brief provisions ensuring the states a role in the common defense; a delineation of the role of the states in the two central areas of positive governmental activity at home, management of commerce and raising of revenues; and a description of state responsibilities in the administration of justice.

The procedure by which the basic status of the Union may be revised is found in Article V of the United States Constitution.

Similar procedures are found in most federal constitutions in the world. They underline one of the paramount characteristics of a federation: the revision of the basic status of the union is not totally dependent on the member states. Individual states have no right to veto changes adopted through the accepted procedure. When they oppose an amendment to the constitution—or demand an amendment—they are not sure to win.

One of the most important features of American federalism lies in the impossibility of the member states to abandon the federation. As the Civil War dramatically affirmed, there is no right of SECESSION. The United States Supreme Court, responding to that war, set down the accepted definition of the American federation in TEXAS V. WHITE (1869): "The Constitution in all its provisions, looks to an indestructible Union, composed of indestructible States."

Another characteristic of federalism in the United States is the existence of federal norms, whether legal, administrative, or judicial, that bear directly upon the federation citizens, without any need of intervention of the member states. The architects of the American system recognized that a successful federal system, something more than a loose confederation of states, required that both the national and the state governments be given substantial autonomy. They also recognized that each had to have some way to influence the other from within as well as through direct negotiation. The federal government has the power to deal directly with the public, that is to say, with the citizenry of the states. The states, in turn, have a major role in determining the composition of the federal government and the selection of those who make it work.

DANIEL J. ELAZAR

Bibliography

ELAZAR, DANIEL J. 1962 *The American Partnership: Intergovernmental Cooperation in the Nineteenth Century United States.* Chicago: University of Chicago Press.
——— 1984 *American Federalism: A View from the States.* New York: Harper & Row.
GRODZINS, MORTON 1966 *The American System: A New View of Government in the United States.* Chicago: Rand McNally.
HART, HENRY and WECHSLER, HERBERT 1953 *The Federal Courts and the Federal System.* Mineola, N.Y.: Foundation Press.
MCLAUGHLIN, ANDREW C. (1932)1972 *The Foundations of American Constitutionalism.* Gloucester, Mass.: Peter Smith.
OSTROM, VINCENT 1971 *The Political Theory of the Compound Republic.* Blacksburg: Virginia Polytechnic Institute, Center for the Study of Public Choice.
VILE, M. J. C. 1961 *The Structure of American Federalism.* Oxford: Oxford University Press.
WRIGHT, DEIL S. 1978 *Understanding Intergovernmental Relations.* North Scituate, Mass.: Duxbury Press.

FEDERALIST, THE

In the eight months following the adjournment of the CONSTITUTIONAL CONVENTION OF 1787, ALEXANDER HAMILTON, JAMES MADISON, and JOHN JAY wrote a series of eighty-five essays in support of the proposed Constitution. These essays were published in newspapers and as a two-volume book under the title *The Federalist.* This work was intended to influence voters electing delegates to the ratifying conventions and the delegates themselves; and the length, detail, and subtlety of its argument suggest an additional intention of enlightening later generations. While some contemporaries thought other, simpler and briefer, writings better calculated to influence the decision of 1787–1788, *The Federalist* was regarded as a work of enduring value by THOMAS JEFFERSON ("the best commentary on the principles of government which ever was written"), GEORGE WASHINGTON, and others. It has remained the most comprehensive and profound defense ever written of the American form of government; and it has been, as Chief Justice JOHN MARSHALL wrote in MCCULLOCH V. MARYLAND (1819), "justly supposed to be entitled to great respect" by courts engaged in "expounding the constitution."

The first section of *The Federalist* (#2 through #14) explains the advantages of a union as compared to independent American states. A large country is better suited than small countries to avoid or win wars, to pursue profitable commercial arrangements, and to raise revenue. Moreover, a large country's relative freedom from fear of war makes it more likely to preserve a free government. (Small countries facing frequent wars eventually accept the risk of being less free in order to be more safe.) Most novel was *The Federalist*'s claim that a popular form of government would be more likely in a large country than in a small country to secure private rights and the public good. MONTESQUIEU and the Anti-Federalist writers who quoted him acknowledged that large countries ruled by monarchs enjoyed certain advantages in FOREIGN AFFAIRS, but insisted that only small republics could enjoy the internal advantages of a patriotic citizenry ruling itself for its own good. In the famous *Federalist* #10 Madison argued that even in the smallest republic the citizenry is not an "it" but a collection of diverse individuals. Those individuals' rights deserve protection, but their passions and interests can unite them in groups that oppose the rights of others or the public good. Madison offered a twofold defense of a large republic. First, the diversity of a large country makes it less likely that any single group will constitute a majority of the voters and therefore be able to oppress other groups by virtue of the republican principle of majority rule. Second, in a large republic elections will be more likely to choose "fit characters" who will pursue the public good. The conclusion that republican government was possible, indeed better, in a large country served to reconcile the unpleasant necessities that seem to require largeness with the deep-rooted desire to have a popular government.

Essays #15 through #36 explain the necessity of "energetic" government. Although the national government has limited purposes, it must be able to tax and raise armies. Under the ARTICLES OF CONFEDERATION, Congress could demand the necessary money

and men but had to address its demands to the state governments, whose disobedience could not be punished and whose compliance therefore could not be counted on. The decisive innovation of the new Constitution was the government's ability to address its commands to individual citizens, each of whose inability to contemplate forcible resistance made him respectful of "the arm of the ordinary magistrate." By defending this innovation in the name of FEDERALISM, *The Federalist* transformed the meaning of that term. Whereas others regarded true federalism as requiring what Montesquieu called a "society of societies"—that is, a union composed of and ruling over political communities rather than individuals—*The Federalist* regarded that as a prescription for disunion, thus deserving the name "antifederal" for its inevitable tendency.

The prospect that the new government would be able to exercise its nominal powers and coerce citizens raised the question of how such an energetic government could be confined to its proper purposes and restrained from oppression. *The Federalist* did not look to a careful enumeration of granted or excluded powers to control the government, because mere "parchment" would do little by itself and because certain formidable powers (for example, taxation) could not be excluded or even limited in their extent. The government could only be controlled by being "well modeled," by having a "general genius" and "internal structure" that made it trustworthy. This meant first of all that the government was "wholly popular"; its whole power was entrusted to the representatives of the people, and could therefore be controlled by the people in elections. *The Federalist* #37 through #84 explains the "conformity of the proposed Constitution to the true principles of republican government."

The fact that popular elections permit the people to "oblige the government to control itself" exhausts neither *The Federalist*'s prescription for a well-modeled government nor its argument for popular government. For one thing, the people are vulnerable to rulers who deceive them, misuse their powers between elections, or cancel elections. "A dependence on the people is no doubt the primary control on the government; but experience has taught mankind the necessity of auxiliary precautions." The auxiliary precautions are of various sorts, but all are designed to make ambition counteract ambition, so that no ruler's love of power is given free rein. A SEPARATION OF POWERS, legislative, executive, and judicial, insures that the people will be ruled in accordance with known laws that are enforced even against those who adopt them. The executive's VETO POWER both preserves this functional separation and, together with the legislature's BICAMERALISM, inhibits hasty law-making. The judiciary enjoys a tenure of GOOD BEHAVIOR to fortify judges in their task of preventing illegal executive acts and unconstitutional legislative acts. This last activity, now known as JUDICIAL REVIEW, was given its first sustained intellectual defense by Hamilton in *The Federalist* #78. Hamilton insisted on the court's duty to enforce the Constitution as law and indeed, because it was solemnly and authoritatively adopted by the people, as superior to the laws passed by the legislature, even if the legislature's laws were supported or instigated by the people themselves. The legislature's power of IMPEACHMENT provided a remedy against abuse of this judicial authority, or of the President's formidable powers. And the existence of state and national governments with independent powers to serve their own distinct objects gives each a platform and a motive to expose the other's encroachments.

The Federalist defended such auxiliary precautions (that is, precautions in addition to the people's electoral power) as reducing the chance that the government would betray and oppress the people as a whole. A more difficult problem, already explained in *The Federalist* #10, was that the people are not a whole, and that rulers elected by the majority might oppress the rights of minorities. The longer terms of senators, Presidents, and judges enabled them to oppose sudden and transient unjust impulses of the majority. A grateful people might reward such service once the heat of passion had cooled, or an excellent ruler might do his duty without reward; but the Constitution's institutions could not defend against an enduring majority's unjust passion or interest—hence the importance of a large country's diversity in making such majorities less likely.

The Federalist defends the "particular structure" of the Constitution not only as discouraging oppression but as encouraging good government. The task of a good national government is to secure the nation against foreign and domestic violence and to regulate its commerce so as to promote the general welfare. These activities in turn serve the most fundamental object of government, which is justice, meaning the protection of each individual's right to exercise his own faculties in the acquisition of property and in other activities. Thus an important accomplishment for any government is that it not itself be a source of injustice, that it achieve "the negative merit of not doing harm."

Further, positive merit of doing some good is encouraged by the Constitution's creation of offices in relatively small numbers and with relatively long terms, so as to encourage more capable candidates to seek office and to be elected and (more important) to put those elected in a situation in which they feel a personal motive to do some good. The experience officials could gain in office would help them devise means to promote the public good; and the distance of the people from direct rule would enable them to judge dispassionately and retrospectively the merit of their officials' policies according to their experience of the apparent effects of those policies. In the best case, officials moved by "the love of fame, the ruling passion of the noblest minds" would have an opportunity to "undertake extensive and arduous enterprises for the public benefit." Even in more ordinary cases, a durable senate would tend to foster stability in the laws and a single executive would be able to enforce them energetically.

The Federalist's defense of these institutions does not, however, deduce them entirely from the requirements of safe and good government. By those standards, *The Federalist* would not have found indefensible the "mixed" government of England, whose popularly elected House of Commons permits the people to restrain the government from oppression, whose king is an energetic executive, and whose House of Lords provides a source of stability and of protection for the rights of a minority. *The Federalist* emphatically defends the "strictly republican," "wholly popular" character of the American Constitution, which is made necessary by "that honorable determination, which animates every votary of freedom, to rest all our political experiments on the capacity of mankind for self-government." Not a knowledge of human fitness for self-government but an assertion of that fitness, or a knowledge of the human impulse to assert that fitness, justifies popular government. To protect the faculties of men requires protecting their faculty of passionately defending their own opinions, respecting their "pretension" to rule. *The Federalist* defended the American Constitution not only for its likely service of the interests of Americans but also for its tendency to "vindicate the honor of the human race."

The Federalist remains America's most important political book because it offers an explanation and defense of our form of government written by men who could not take the goodness or permanence of that regime for granted. Americans who study *The Federalist* today may find not only new reasons to appreciate the Constitution they inherit but also an account of government somewhat different from that assumed in contemporary opinion. For example, to *The Feder-*

alist justice means impartial protection of the right to exercise one's faculties, not equal provision for the satisfaction of one's needs or desires. CONSTITUTION-ALISM means that the people's solemn choice of their own form of government can be overridden only by a new, deliberate popular choice, not silently and gradually improved by judges trying to make the Constitution a living document. And REPRESENTATION is an arrangement that allows an opinionated people to select capable rulers and periodically pass formal judgment on their service of the public good, not an imperfect simulation of ancient direct democracy or a primitive version of modern opinion polling. *The Federalist* is thus both a source of understanding and appreciation of the American Constitution and a guide to reflection on its subsequent development.

DAVID F. EPSTEIN

Bibliography

ADAIR, DOUGLASS 1974 *Fame and the Founding Fathers.* New York: Norton.
DIAMOND, MARTIN (1963)1972 The Federalist. Pages 631–651 in Leo Strauss and Joseph Cropsey, eds., *History of Political Philosophy.* Chicago: Rand McNally.
EPSTEIN, DAVID F. 1984 *The Political Theory of The Federalist.* Chicago: University of Chicago Press.

FEDERAL POWER COMMISSION

See: Regulatory Agencies

FEDERAL POWER COMMISSION v. HOPE NATURAL GAS COMPANY
320 U.S. 591 (1944)

In SMYTH V. AMES (1898) the Supreme Court saddled state REGULATORY COMMISSIONS with a specious DUE PROCESS rule for setting public utility rates. Forty-six years later the Justices repudiated the rule of a FAIR RETURN ON FAIR VALUE. Prior to *Hope,* the Court relied primarily on original construction costs and reproduction costs as a means of determining property value.

Justice WILLIAM O. DOUGLAS, speaking for a 5–3 Court, based rate regulation on the POLICE POWER. Douglas declared: "In so far as the power to regulate involves the power to reduce net earnings, it must involve the power to destroy." He adhered to the recent trend of decisions which removed the Court from such determinations. Without mentioning *Smyth,* Douglas accorded regulatory commissions broad power to choose methods of evaluating property: "The Constitution does not bind rate-making bodies to the service of any single formula or combination of formulas." Henceforth, the determination of the reasonableness of a rate would be made by looking to the "end result" or "total effect." This pragmatic approach returned the burden of decision to the commissions because a rate order was "the product of expert judgment," carrying a presumption of validity. Even the dissenters did not feel bound to adhere to *Smyth;* they disagreed over the applicable statutory standard. In *Hope,* the Court eliminated judicial obstruction to effective administrative rate regulation.

DAVID GORDON

FEDERAL PROTECTION OF CIVIL RIGHTS

Although the story of federal protection of CIVIL RIGHTS is most conveniently told chronologically, two themes warrant separate mention. First, federal protection of civil rights has a paradoxical relationship with STATES' RIGHTS. All civil rights legislation has been opposed or limited in response to the argument that the federal government ought not involve itself in areas of state responsibility. The Supreme Court repeatedly has voiced this concern and, in the past, invalidated civil rights legislation partly on this ground. Deference to state law enforcement prerogatives always has been a centerpiece of Justice Department civil rights enforcement policy. And for many years Congress repeatedly rebuffed so basic a measure as antilynching legislation in the name of states' rights. Yet the original federal civil rights statutes, and their underlying constitutional amendments, were responses to outrages by states or to private outrages that states failed to ameliorate. Given the origins of the need for federal protection of civil rights, states' interests may have received undue weight in shaping federal civil rights policy.

Second, there is a seedy underside to the topic of federal protection of civil rights. For many years the federal government was more involved with denying blacks' rights than with protecting them. Well into the twentieth century federal employment policy included racial SEGREGATION and exclusion. DE JURE segregation in Washington, D.C., and the armed forces, government participation in segregated and racially isolated housing projects, racially prejudiced federal judges, and other circumstances demonstrate the depth of federal involvement in discrimination.

Since the 1940s, however, there has been a trend toward increased federal protection of civil rights.

The Bureau of Refugees, Freedmen, and Abandoned Lands (the FREEDMEN'S BUREAU), created near the end of the Civil War, may be viewed as the federal government's initial civil rights enforcement effort. The Bureau's statutory charge, "the control of all subjects relating to refugees and freedmen from rebel states," enabled it to perform a variety of social welfare functions. But this first effort to assist blacks was tainted by, among other factors, the Bureau's role in establishing the oppressive system of southern labor contracts. Although Bureau agents invalidated particularly harsh terms, such as those providing for corporal punishment, much depended on the local agent's views. The Bureau and the Union Army, no less than southern legislatures, felt most comfortable when blacks were on plantations under contract and not seeking their fortune in urban areas.

With few exceptions, federal protection of blacks via the Freedmen's Bureau terminated in 1868. Congress's other Reconstruction legislation employed a variety of techniques to protect civil rights. The CIVIL RIGHTS ACT OF 1866 and the FORCE ACT of 1870 imposed penalties on those who enforced discriminatory features of the southern BLACK CODES, and the 1870 act made it a crime to conspire to hinder a citizen's exercise of federal rights. The 1870 act also provided special protection for black VOTING RIGHTS and the Force Act of 1871 went further by providing for the appointment of federal supervisors to scrutinize voter registration and election practices. The Civil Rights Act of 1871 authorized civil actions and additional criminal penalties against those who violated constitutional rights and authorized the president to use federal forces to suppress insurrections or conspiracies to deprive "any portion or class of . . . people" of federal rights. The CIVIL RIGHTS ACT OF 1875, the culmination of the Reconstruction period civil rights program, imposed civil and criminal sanctions for discrimination in PUBLIC ACCOMMODATIONS, public conveyances, and places of amusement.

Armed with the criminal provisions of the civil rights program, federal prosecutors brought thousands of cases in southern federal courts and established criminal actions as the primary vehicle through which the federal government protected civil rights. This burst of protective activity, along with the rest of Reconstruction, disintegrated with the COMPROMISE OF 1877 and the attendant withdrawal of federal troops from the South. In 1878, only twenty-five federal criminal civil rights prosecutions were brought in southern federal courts.

There are many reasons why federal criminal prosecutions were and are ineffective to protect civil rights. First, shortly after enactment of the post-Civil War ANTIDISCRIMINATION LEGISLATION, the Supreme Court limited Congress's power to protect civil rights. UNITED STATES V. REESE (1876) and JAMES V. BOWMAN (1903) invalidated portions of the 1870 act. UNITED STATES V. HARRIS (1883) and *Baldwin v. Franks* (1887) struck down the CRIMINAL CONSPIRACY section of the 1871 act and the CIVIL RIGHTS CASES (1883) found the 1875 act to be unconstitutional. These and other cases, including the SLAUGHTERHOUSE CASES (1873) and UNITED STATES V. CRUIKSHANK (1876), also narrowly construed constitutional provisions and statutory provisions that were not struck down. The entire federal statutory civil rights program therefore depended upon those provisions that, almost by happenstance, survived judicial scrutiny. And some of these were eliminated by the CIVIL RIGHTS REPEAL ACT of 1894 and a reorganization of federal law in 1909.

The principal criminal provisions that survived, now sections 241 and 242 of Title 18, United States Code, are not well suited to protecting civil rights. They always have been plagued by doubts about the particular rights they protect and the conduct they reach, and more generally by doubt about the federal government's role in law enforcement. Similar difficulties characterized federal civil remedies to protect civil rights. Finally, southern juries, until recently all white, have rarely convicted whites for violating the rights of blacks.

From the Compromise of 1877 until about 1940, reference to federal "protection" of civil rights would be misleading. Racism in America peaked in the early twentieth century, a fact reflected in the federal government's attitude toward blacks. THEODORE ROOSEVELT's lunch with Booker T. Washington summarized his administration's concern with civil rights. Roosevelt's successor, WILLIAM HOWARD TAFT, did not even lunch with Washington, and under Taft and WOODROW WILSON segregation in federal employment was adopted. Neither Warren Harding nor Calvin Coolidge showed any inclination to rise above the worst racial attitudes of their times. As secretary of commerce, HERBERT HOOVER did desegregate the Census Bureau.

Attorney General FRANK MURPHY's decision in 1939 to establish a CIVIL RIGHTS DIVISION within the Department of Justice represented a noticeable shift in federal enforcement activity. The new section studied the dormant post-Civil War statutes and adopted an enforcement program that led to such important decisions as UNITED STATES V. CLASSIC (1941) and SCREWS V. UNITED STATES (1945). Federal criminal civil rights prosecutions, however, did not grow beyond several dozen cases a year. But two decades later, in MONROE V. PAPE (1961), these cases served as precedents in establishing private enforcement of civil rights through SECTION 1983, TITLE 42, UNITED STATES CODE.

Creation of the Civil Rights Division combined with other events to generate pressure for progress in the civil rights field. In June 1941, President FRANKLIN D. ROOSEVELT issued an EXECUTIVE ORDER creating a Fair Employment Practices Committee (FEPC). A response to defense needs and black political pressure, the executive order prohibited discriminatory employment practices on account of race, color, creed, or national origin in government service, in defense industries, and by trade unions. The order, administered by the FEPC, helped many northern blacks to obtain defense jobs and encouraged many southern blacks to move north.

But the nation was not ready for an aggressive federal civil rights program. Roosevelt himself was reluctant to propose or endorse civil rights legislation. In the 1930s, he even refused to endorse an antilynching bill pending in Congress. And where Roosevelt did act, Congress balked. Until 1944, the President's Emergency Fund financed the FEPC. Congress then required congressional approval for all executive expenditures. In 1946, the FEPC expired for lack of funds and subsequent efforts to establish a statutory FEPC failed.

The end of World War II seemed to trigger or coincide with renewed violence against blacks. Following a Democratic party defeat in the 1946 congressional elections, President HARRY S. TRUMAN, in Executive Order 9008, created a presidential civil rights committee to conduct inquiries and to recommend civil rights programs. In its report, *To Secure These Rights*, the committee made far-reaching recommendations in the areas of voting, employment, and federally assisted programs, many of which would be enacted in the 1960s. Although President Truman recommended legislation based on the commission's report, his administration's civil rights accomplishments were to be on other fronts.

Truman, like other presidents, fostered civil rights most effectively in areas not requiring legislative action. Southern political power in Congress precluded significant civil rights legislation. In 1947, under black and liberal pressure, Truman authorized the Justice Department to submit an amicus curiae brief opposing judicial enforcement of racially RESTRICTIVE COVENANTS. Some believe this brief to have been influential in the Supreme Court's decision in SHELLEY V. KRAEMER (1948), which rendered racially restrictive housing covenants judicially unenforceable. From 1948 through 1951, Truman issued a series of executive orders which prohibited discrimination by defense contractors, established a committee to study compliance with government contract provisions prohibiting discrimination, provided processes for handling EMPLOYMENT DISCRIMINATION complaints in federal departments and agencies, and called for equality of treatment and opportunity in the armed services.

Civil rights enforcement received little attention early in the administration of DWIGHT D. EISENHOWER, but there were important exceptions to this pattern. Executive Order 10479 (1953) extended the antidiscrimination provisions previously required in defense contracts to all government procurement contracts. And after BROWN V. BOARD OF EDUCATION (1954), Eisenhower could not avoid civil rights issues. Southern recalcitrance in the face of *Brown* led to a federal–state confrontation in Little Rock, Arkansas, which was settled through the presence of federal troops. (See COOPER V. AARON, 1958.) But Little Rock marked no general turning point in the administration's enforcement efforts. Even when armed with increased authority to investigate denials of voting rights by the CIVIL RIGHTS ACT OF 1957, the Justice Department brought few cases.

JOHN F. KENNEDY's administration also began with little impetus toward substantial civil rights achievement. But the rising tide of civil rights activity, increased public awareness, and continued southern resistance to DESEGREGATION made new federal–state confrontations inevitable. In May 1961, federal marshals were employed to protect freedom-riders. In September 1962, in connection with efforts to integrate the University of Mississippi, heavily outnumbered federal marshals and federalized National Guard troops withstood an assault by segregationists. Only the arrival of thousands of federal troops restored order. In the Birmingham crisis of 1963, which gained notoriety for the brutal treatment of demonstrators by state and local law enforcement officers, the federal government tried to act as a mediator. The administration's inability under federal law to deal forcefully with situations like that in Birmingham led Kennedy to propose further federal civil rights legislation.

Within the executive branch, the Interstate Commerce Commission, at the administration's request, promulgated stringent rules against discrimination in terminals. Armed with the CIVIL RIGHTS ACTS OF 1957 and 1960, the Civil Rights Division established by the 1957 Act conducted massive voter registration suits but secured only token improvements in black registration. Sometimes the judges blocking progress were Kennedy appointees. In November 1962 President Kennedy issued an executive order prohibiting discrimination in public housing projects and in projects covered by direct, guaranteed federal loans. And in executive orders in 1961 and 1963 Kennedy both required AFFIRMATIVE ACTION by government contractors and extended the executive branch's antidiscrimination program in federal procurement contracts to all federally assisted construction projects.

Soon after LYNDON B. JOHNSON succeeded to the presidency, he publicly endorsed Kennedy's civil rights legislation. Due in part to his direct support, Congress enacted the CIVIL RIGHTS ACT OF 1964, the most comprehensive civil rights measure in American history. The act outlaws discrimination in public accommodations, in federally assisted programs, or by large private employers, and it extends federal power to deal with voting discrimination. Title VII of the act created a substantial new federal bureaucracy to enforce antidiscrimination provisions pertaining to employment. The 1964 act also marked the first time that the Senate voted cloture against an anti-civil rights filibuster.

Despite the efforts of the Kennedy and Johnson Justice Departments, the Civil Rights Acts of 1957, 1960, and 1964 proved inadequate to protect black VOTING RIGHTS. Marches and protests to secure voting rights led to violence, including an infamous, widely reported confrontation in Selma, Alabama, in which marchers were beaten. In March 1965, President Johnson requested new voting rights legislation. He included in his speech to the nation and a joint session of Congress the words of the song of the civil rights movement, "We shall overcome," thus emphasizing the depth of the new federal involvement in civil rights. By August, the VOTING RIGHTS ACT OF 1965 was in place. Within ten years of its passage many more than a million new black voters were registered without great fanfare, with corresponding gains in the number of black elected officials. In 1968, after the assassination of Martin Luther King, Jr., Congress enacted a fair housing law as part of the CIVIL RIGHTS ACT OF 1968.

Unlike the Reconstruction civil rights program, Congress's 1960s civil rights legislation survived judicial scrutiny. In a series of cases from 1964 to 1976, the Supreme Court both sustained the new civil rights program and revived the Reconstruction-era laws. In *Katzenbach v. McClung* (1964) and HEART OF ATLANTA MOTEL V. UNITED STATES (1964) the Court rejected constitutional attacks on the public accommodations provisions of the 1964 act. In SOUTH CAROLINA V. KATZENBACH (1966) and KATZENBACH V. MORGAN (1966) the Court rebuffed state challenges to the Voting Rights Act of 1965. And in JONES V. ALFRED H. MAYER CO. (1968) and RUNYON V. MCCRARY (1976) the Court interpreted the Civil Rights Act of 1866 to fill important gaps in the coverage of the 1964 and 1968 acts.

With the passage and sustaining of the 1964, 1965, and 1968 acts and the revival of the 1866 act, the legal battle against RACIAL DISCRIMINATION at least formally was won. The federal civil rights program encompassed nearly all public and private purposeful racial discrimination in public accommodations, housing, employment, education, and voting. Future civil rights progress would have to come through vigorous enforcement, through programs aimed at relieving poverty, through affirmative action, and through laws benefiting groups other than blacks.

Just as the civil rights movement was running out of traditional civil rights laws to support, two other issues brought federal civil rights protection near its outer limits. The comprehensive coverage of federal civil rights laws did not eliminate the inferior status of blacks in American society. Pressure mounted for assistance in the form of affirmative action programs. But these programs divided even the liberal community traditionally supportive of civil rights enforcement. Affirmative action, unlike antidiscrimination standards, meant black progress at the expense of what many believed to be legitimate opportunities of innocent individuals. In its most important aspects affirmative action survived the initial series of statutory and constitutional attacks.

In the 1970s, civil rights enforcement became engulfed in another controversy: whether to bus school children for purposes of desegregation. (See SCHOOL BUSING.) President RICHARD M. NIXON's 1968 "Southern strategy" included campaigning against busing. Within six months of Nixon's inaugural, the Justice Department for the first time opposed the NAACP LEGAL DEFENSE AND EDUCATION FUND in a desegregation case. But under the pressure of Supreme Court decisions, and given the momentum of the prior administration's civil rights efforts, the Nixon administration did help promote new levels of southern integration. The administration, however, continued to lash out at "forced busing."

School desegregation also triggered a legislative backlash. In the 1970s the Internal Revenue Service, under the pressure of court decisions, sought to foster integration by denying tax benefits to private segregated academies and their benefactors. Congress, however, intervened to limit the Service's use of funds for such purposes. Similarly, Congress restrained executive authority to seek busing as a remedy for school segregation.

In the 1960s and 1970s, federal protection of civil rights reached beyond race. In the Age Discrimination in Employment Act, the AGE DISCRIMINATION ACT OF 1975, the REHABILITATION ACT OF 1973, and other measures, Congress acted to protect the aged and the handicapped. And the Equal Pay Act of 1963, the Civil Rights Act of 1964, and the EDUCATION AMENDMENTS OF 1972 increased federal protection against sex discrimination. In each of these areas, attachment of antidiscrimination conditions to federal disbursements became a significant vehicle for civil rights enforcement.

THEODORE EISENBERG

Bibliography

BERMAN, WILLIAM C. 1970 *The Politics of Civil Rights in the Truman Administration.* Columbus: Ohio State University Press.
BRAUER, CARL M. 1977 *John F. Kennedy and the Second Reconstruction.* New York: Columbia University Press.
CARR, ROBERT K. 1947 *Federal Protection of Civil Rights: Quest for a Sword.* Ithaca, N.Y.: Cornell University Press.
GRESSMAN, EUGENE 1952 The Unhappy History of Civil Rights Legislation. *Michigan Law Review* 50:1323–1358.
HARVEY, JAMES C. 1973 *Black Civil Rights During the Johnson Administration.* Jackson: University and College Press of Missouri.
KONVITZ, MILTON R. 1961 *A Century of Civil Rights.* New York: Columbia University Press.
LITWACK, LEON F. 1979 *Been in the Storm So Long: The Aftermath of Slavery.* New York: Knopf.

FEDERAL QUESTION JURISDICTION

Article III of the Constitution provides that the JUDICIAL POWER OF THE UNITED STATES shall extend to all "Cases . . . arising under this Constitution, the laws of the United States, and Treaties. . . ." This power is called federal question jurisdiction, because typically it entails the construction, application, or enforcement of federal law, including federal COMMON LAW. Performance of this function includes interpretation of the Constitution itself; thus federal question jurisdiction provides the jurisdictional basis for the federal courts' important power of JUDICIAL REVIEW. It is also the means by which Congress can secure a sympathetic and uniform interpretation of federal laws.

Although Congress has the power to make exceptions to the Supreme Court's APPELLATE JURISDICTION over federal questions, it currently makes few of them. A few federal trial court decisions, such as those remanding cases to state court following removal, are unreviewable. The Supreme Court reviews state court decisions only when they are FINAL JUDGMENTS that have been rendered by the highest state court in which judgment is available. Such a judgment will not be reviewed if it rests on an independent and ADEQUATE STATE GROUND or if it lacks a substantial federal question (for example, raises only a federal issue already resolved in an earlier case).

Apart from these restrictions, the appellate federal question jurisdiction extends to every federal issue, factual or legal, part of the plaintiff's case or part of a defense, in either a civil or a criminal case. Even if federal law appears in a case solely because a state statute refers to and incorporates it, the Supreme Court may exercise its federal question jurisdiction if it finds an independent federal interest in assuring proper interpretation of the incorporated federal matter.

In contrast, when Congress first created the lower federal courts in 1789, it authorized them to hear only a few federal question cases of special importance, such as PATENT suits and suits involving treaty rights. After the Civil War, Congress realized that state courts would be reluctant to enforce newly created federal CIVIL RIGHTS, and authorized the federal courts to hear the enforcement actions. Then, in 1875, Congress used almost the exact language of Article III to empower federal courts to hear "all suits of a civil nature . . . arising under the Constitution or laws of the United States, or treaties made. . . ." The 1875 act, known as the general federal question statute, required that at least $500 be in controversy in the suit, a requirement that was increased gradually over time.

Notwithstanding the breadth of the general federal question statute, Congress has continued to enact more limited laws authorizing federal jurisdiction over particular kinds of federal questions. These laws, designed to aid in enforcing the vast array of federal rights created in recent decades, have not required any amount in controversy. The range of these specialized federal question statutes is so great that by 1970 few federal question cases drew only upon the general statute. In 1976 Congress eliminated the amount in controversy requirement for the only remaining significant group of such cases, suits alleging unconstitutional conduct by federal officers; and in 1980, it repealed the requirement altogether.

Because Congress's legislative powers are enumerated and limited, a complaint filed in federal court frequently invokes a combination of state and federal law. The issue then arises whether the federal element warrants labeling the case one that "arises under" federal law. For a federal court to have federal question jurisdiction, this inquiry must be determined affirmatively, both under Article III and under the general federal question statute.

Although some Supreme Court decisions, notably Justice BENJAMIM N. CARDOZO's opinion in *Gully v. First National Bank* (1936), have announced an equally demanding construction for both the Constitution and the statute, the currently accepted view is that the statute should be construed more narrowly than Article III despite the near identity of their language. In other words, Congress has a broad power but is assumed not to have exercised all of it. Interpretations of Article III have required that the plaintiff invoke some federal law to support a part of the claim for relief, whether or not the federal right is actually disputed by the defendant. (See OSBORN V. BANK OF UNITED STATES, 1824.) In a theory known as "protective jurisdiction," some judges and scholars have advanced the view that Congress should have the power to confer federal question jurisdiction even over a case arising under state law, when the claim implicates a strong, legitimate federal interest. The Supreme Court has not yet been required to decide whether Article III extends this far, although in some fields, such as BANKRUPTCY, the Court has approved federal question jurisdiction over suits involving only minor elements of federal law.

The Supreme Court has struggled to develop a narrower interpretive principle for the general federal question statute, seeking to allow adequate implementation of federal policy while avoiding an unnecessary deluge of cases into federal courts. For example, the statute is read to require the plaintiff's reliance on federal law to be revealed in the complaint according to traditional rules of pleading. It also appears that if plaintiff's reliance on federal law is not at the forefront of the claim, as when there is a dispute over present property rights that at some remote time had

their source in federal law, jurisdiction will be denied under the general statute even though Congress could constitutionally confer it more specifically. Also, if the plaintiff relies on, refers to, and incorporates state law, the Court may refuse to allow the claim into federal court under the general statute because federal law will not be sufficiently at issue.

No single principle explains all the cases interpreting the general federal question statute. Despite this confusion, most types of cases have been classified either within or outside the federal question jurisdiction. To determine whether a new type of case combining federal and state elements falls within the statute's scope, the courts pragmatically assess the degree of federal interest in the subject matter of the litigation, the relative prominence of state and federal issues, and the likely burden on the federal judicial system of accepting jurisdiction in cases of that type.

The federal question jurisdiction authorized in Article III encompasses cases removed from state to federal court upon the defendant's assertion of a federal defense. Congress has not, however, conferred such broad federal question removal jurisdiction upon the federal courts. With a few exceptions, it has limited removal to cases that fall within original federal question jurisdiction under the general statute.

CAROLE E. GOLDBERG-AMBROSE

Bibliography

COHEN, WILLIAM 1967 The Broken Compass: The Requirement That a Case Arise "Directly" under Federal Law. *University of Pennsylvania Law Review* 115:890–916.
MISHKIN, PAUL J. 1953 The Federal "Question" in the District Courts. *Columbia Law Review* 53:157–196.

FEDERAL RULES OF CIVIL PROCEDURE

Article I of the Constitution empowers Congress to "constitute" lower federal courts and thus, by conventional assumption, to regulate practice and procedure in the cases heard in those courts. When the lower federal courts were first created in 1789, Congress enacted a law, known as the Conformity Act, that required each federal trial court to follow, in civil actions at law, the procedural rules of the state in which it was situated. By contrast, Congress directed the Supreme Court to promulgate federal procedures for federal admiralty and EQUITY cases respectively.

Under the Conformity Act, hypertechnical and arbitrary state procedures hampered the federal courts.

Also, uniform procedures were not available for administration of federal law nationwide under the general FEDERAL QUESTION JURISDICTION first conferred on the federal courts in 1875. Finally, in 1934, Congress adopted the Rules Enabling Act, which authorized the Supreme Court to promulgate federal procedural rules, subject to a congressional veto. Both Congress's power to delegate this authority and the Supreme Court's power to exercise it, consistent with the CASE OR CONTROVERSY requirement of Article III, have been upheld.

In accordance with the Act, the Supreme Court issued the Federal Rules of Civil Procedure in 1938. Congress declined to veto them. The new rules combined law and equity into a single form of action while preserving the SEVENTH AMENDMENT right to TRIAL BY JURY on any issue that would have been so tried before the merger. While they incorporated state law with respect to some matters, such as provisional remedies, the rules also made important innovations, such as simplified pleading, liberal joinder of claims and parties, and greater emphasis on pretrial discovery of facts. Many state procedures have come to resemble the Federal Rules. And the new joinder rules have resulted in enlargement of the definition of a "case" for purposes of determining ANCILLARY and PENDENT JURISDICTION in the federal courts. In 1966, admiralty actions were made subject to the Federal Rules of Civil Procedure, as amended to retain a few specialized rules for suits designated as admiralty actions in the pleadings.

Special constitutional problems have arisen when the Federal Rules have been employed in diversity actions. Congress and the federal courts do not have general substantive lawmaking power over cases simply because they are within the DIVERSITY JURISDICTION. Thus, when a Federal Rule of Civil Procedure differs from the procedural rule that would be applied in state court, and the difference in rules could affect the outcome of the case, the question arises whether the Federal Rule exceeds federal lawmaking authority and impermissibly intrudes on reserved state power. In Hanna v. Plumer (1963) the Supreme Court held that so long as a rule is "rationally capable of classification" as procedural, it is an appropriate subject of legislation under Congress's Article I power to create and regulate the lower federal courts, even though the rule may also affect substantive rights. It is unlikely that the Supreme Court, which promulgates the rules of civil procedure, would decide that those rules are not rationally classifiable as "procedural."

CAROLE E. GOLDBERG-AMBROSE

Bibliography
WRIGHT, C. 1976 Federal Courts, 3rd ed. St. Paul, Minn.: West Publishing Co.

FEDERAL RULES OF CRIMINAL PROCEDURE

After the FEDERAL RULES OF CIVIL PROCEDURE (1938) established a uniform set of procedures for the trial of civil cases in federal courts, Congress authorized the SUPREME COURT to make rules for the trial of federal criminal cases as well. With two Justices dissenting, the Supreme Court adopted the rules in 1944 and submitted them to Congress, which, by silence, approved them.

Before adoption of the rules, the trial of federal criminal cases was regulated by a varying and uncertain mixture of state and federal rules. The first achievement of the Federal Rules was simplification and clarification. The second was uniformity: the same rules would govern the major aspects of federal criminal trials all over the country. The federal appellate courts would now need to know only one body of procedural law, and all federal defendants would now enjoy similar rights and bear similar burdens.

Certain of the changes worked by the rules—for example, the substitution of a simplified complaint for the old, highly technical forms of INDICTMENT, and the consolidation of defense motions under a single heading—were clear gains by any measure. But probably the most significant achievement of the rules was to focus national attention on the regulation of the criminal process, which has consumed an enormous amount of professional and public attention ever since. Surely it was no accident that McNabb v. United States (1943), holding inadmissible a statement obtained from a suspect whom federal officers illegally detained, was decided while the rules were being considered; nor that McNabb was later reaffirmed in Mallory v. United States (1957) on the basis of Rule 5. (See MCNABB-MALLORY RULE.)

The rules have played a significant part in the expansion and clarification of defendants' rights: as an independent source of law, as a model for constitutional judgments, and as a means by which constitutional judgments could be elaborated. Two examples are illustrative. Rule 11, governing guilty pleas, was used as a guide in constitutional decision making and was itself amended to reflect and to elaborate case law. Rule 41, governing SEARCH WARRANTS, has likewise been modified to elaborate Supreme Court holdings, with respect, for example, to the permissible objects of search, and has also been used as a guide by the Court.

The administration, amendment, and interpretation of the Federal Rules have been heavily charged with constitutional significance, especially in a time of fundamental rethinking of the relation between government and the accused. For the most part this process has been carried on in a public and open-minded way, largely immune from politically motivated oversimplifications.

JAMES BOYD WHITE

Bibliography

MOORE, JAMES WILLIAM and WAXNER, MARVIN 1985 *Rules of Criminal Procedure.* Volume 8 of *Moore's Federal Practice,* 2nd ed. New York: Matthew Bender.

FEDERAL TEST ACTS
12 Stat. 430 (1862)
12 Stat. 502 (1862)
13 Stat. 424 (1865)
23 Stat. 21 (1868)

Early in the Civil War northern state and federal officials on an ad hoc basis administered oaths of allegiance to civilians suspected of disloyalty. In June 1862 Congress enacted the "jurors' test oath" which required persons sitting on federal GRAND and PETIT JURIES to swear to future loyalty and that they had not, in the past, voluntarily supported or given "aid or comfort" to the rebellion. The "Ironclad Test Oath" statute, enacted by Congress in July 1862, required all federal officeholders, except the President and vice-president, to swear they had "never voluntarily borne arms against the United States," aided the rebellion, nor "sought nor accepted nor attempted to exercise" any office under the Confederacy. In 1864 the United States Senate required that its members take this oath. In 1865 the "ironclad oath" was extended to attorneys practicing in federal courts, but in *Ex parte Garland* (1867) (one of the TEST OATH CASES) this extension was declared unconstitutional. From 1864 until 1868 the "ironclad oath" kept former Confederates from holding federal offices or being seated in Congress. After 1868 the Republican-dominated Congress allowed exceptions for members of their party (and later Democrats) who had served the Confederacy. The "jurors' oath" was used to prevent former Confederates from serving on juries until the repeal of all test oaths in 1884.

PAUL FINKELMAN

Bibliography

HYMAN, HAROLD M. 1954 *Era of The Oath: Northern Loyalty Tests During the Civil War and Reconstruction.* Philadelphia: University of Pennsylvania Press.

FEDERAL TORT CLAIMS ACT
60 Stat. 842 (1946)

The Federal Tort Claims Act, enacted in 1946, relinquished an important part of the SOVEREIGN IMMUNITY of the United States and was part of a larger twentieth-century trend toward relaxing absolute barriers to suits against governments and officials. By this act, the United States consented to be sued for its agents' torts when private persons would be liable for such torts under the law of the place where the tort occurred. But the act fell short of imposing liability for all torts of United States agents. Generally, the tort must be compensable under state law. In addition, the act excluded liability for a vague category of behavior known as "discretionary functions." As originally enacted, the act also excluded liability for many torts that might arise in the context of law enforcement, including assault, battery, false imprisonment, and false arrest. In 1974, however, the Intentional Tort Amendment Act expanded government liability to include these and other torts. The act continues to exclude liability for defamation, misrepresentation, deceit, and interference with contract rights.

THEODORE EISENBERG

Bibliography

SCHUCK, PETER H. 1983 *Suing Government: Citizen Remedies for Official Wrongs.* New Haven, Conn.: Yale University Press.

FEDERAL TRADE COMMISSION

See: Regulatory Agencies

FEDERAL TRADE COMMISSION v. GRATZ
253 U.S. 421 (1920)

Section 5 of the FEDERAL TRADE COMMISSION (FTC) ACT outlawed, but did not define, "unfair methods of competition." Justice JAMES MCREYNOLDS, for a 7–2 Supreme Court, upheld a contract exclusively binding customers to one supplier. Confining FTC orders against unfair methods to those previously found illegal (a HOLDING reversed in 1934), the courts, not the commission, were henceforth to determine what section 5 meant. Justice LOUIS D. BRANDEIS, joined by Justice JOHN H. CLARKE, dissented. They would have voided this practice, contending that "the Act left the determination to the Commission." They agreed that courts might determine whether—based on FTC findings—a practice was unfair, but they cautioned against overturning commission decisions without substantial reason.

DAVID GORDON

(SEE ALSO: *Regulatory Commissions; Economic Regulation and the Constitution.*)

FEDERAL TRADE COMMISSION ACT
38 Stat. 717 (1914)

When the decisions in STANDARD OIL COMPANY V. UNITED STATES (1911) and *United States v. American Tobacco* (1911) demonstrated that trusts could be dissolved, public calls for a policy regulating combinations and monopolies increased. Responding to President WOODROW WILSON's appeal, Congress created the Federal Trade Commission (FTC) on September 26, 1914. The act created no criminal offenses; the commission would advise business on how to conform to a policy of competition. Congress vested the commission with broad powers of investigation and recommendation regarding enforcement of the ANTITRUST laws, but the act did not cover banks or common carriers. (See INTERSTATE COMMERCE ACT.) Consisting of five commissioners, the FTC is a quasi-judicial tribunal whose findings of fact, if supported by testimony, are binding on the courts and whose decisions are reviewable there.

In furtherance of its goal of fostering competition, section 5 stated that "unfair methods of competition in commerce and unfair or deceptive acts or practices in commerce are hereby declared illegal." Intentionally vague, this provision relied on judicial decisions and experience to give it meaning. By outlawing methods, it improved upon earlier statutes which prohibited only specific acts. Other sections (6 and 9) granted the commission power to require compliance: it could require written responses to inquiries, secure access to corporate books and records, and subpoena witnesses.

DAVID GORDON

(SEE ALSO: *Federal Trade Commission v. Gratz, 1920.*)

FEINER v. NEW YORK
340 U.S. 315 (1951)

Feiner was convicted of BREACH OF THE PEACE for derogatory remarks concerning President HARRY S. TRUMAN which provoked hostility and some threats from a "restless" crowd. Two police officers, fearing violence, ordered Feiner to stop. When he refused, they arrested him. Feiner marked the post-1920s Court's first use of the CLEAR AND PRESENT DANGER rule to uphold the conviction of a speaker. Chief Justice FRED M. VINSON spoke for the majority. JUSTICE FELIX FRANKFURTER'S concurrence urged a balancing approach to replace the danger rule. This case, like TERMINIELLO V. CHICAGO (1949), raised the HOSTILE AUDIENCE problem.

MARTIN SHAPIRO

FELONY

The most common classification of crimes is between MISDEMEANORS and felonies. The Constitution does not control the definitions of felony and misdemeanor; the distinction usually is made by a state statute, or, in a few instances, by state constitution. Federal statutes define the scope of federal felonies and misdemeanors.

A state statute commonly will define a felony as a crime for which a person may be imprisoned in a state penitentiary (rather than a local jail) or as an offense for which a person may be imprisoned for a minimum length of time (such as six months or one year). The distinction between a felony and a misdemeanor may determine whether a police officer had statutory authority to arrest a person without a warrant, which state court has jurisdiction over a criminal charge, or whether the defendant will be subject to punishment under a habitual criminal statute which provides for increased punishment after conviction for several felonies.

Although the distinction between felonies and misdemeanors is an important one under state law, it is not significant for constitutional law purposes. There are three constitutional provisions, applicable to the prosecution of criminal cases, whose meaning or impact is dependent in part upon the seriousness of the crime charged, not upon the felony–misdemeanor distinction. These provisions are the Fifth Amendment GRAND JURY clause, the Sixth Amendment RIGHT TO COUNSEL, and the Sixth Amendment right to TRIAL BY JURY.

The Supreme Court has held that the FOURTEENTH AMENDMENT does not incorporate the Fifth Amendment's grand jury clause; that clause, therefore, is not applicable to state or local criminal prosecutions. In *Ex parte Wilson* (1885) the Supreme Court defined the federal crimes to which the grand jury clause applied as those "punishable by imprisonment at hard labor" in a federal penitentiary. Federal statutes and the FEDERAL RULES OF CRIMINAL PROCEDURE define a federal felony as any federal offense punishable by imprisonment for a term exceeding one year. A federal felony prosecution must be initiated by a grand jury indictment. Someone charged with a federal misdemeanor may be prosecuted based on either an INFORMATION filed by the federal prosecutor or a grand jury indictment.

The Sixth Amendment guarantee of a right to counsel in all criminal prosecutions applies to the states through the Fourteenth Amendment. The Supreme Court has held that the Sixth Amendment also gives an INDIGENT defendant the right to have the government provide him with an attorney in some, but not all, criminal cases. A defendant convicted of a crime cannot be sentenced to imprisonment for even one day unless he has had the opportunity to be represented by counsel at his trial. The government, however, need not appoint attorneys for indigent persons who are convicted of crimes that in fact are not punished by imprisonment. The determination whether the state is required to appoint counsel to represent an indigent defendant is not based on a felony–misdemeanor distinction. A state is not required to provide counsel to an indigent defendant charged with a serious crime so long as the conviction in fact does not result in imprisonment. Any right to an attorney in a case in which incarceration is not imposed would be based upon a case-by-case DUE PROCESS analysis.

The Sixth Amendment also provides that an accused person has a right to "an impartial jury." The jury trial provision of the Sixth Amendment has been incorporated into the Fourteenth Amendment; it governs both state and federal prosecutions. Although the Sixth Amendment refers to the right to a jury trial in "all criminal prosecutions," the Supreme Court has ruled that the accused has a right to a jury trial, rather than a trial before a judge, only when he is charged with an offense that is not "petty." The Court has held that any offense punishable by incarceration for more than six months cannot be deemed "petty." Thus, regardless of the sentence a defendant actually receives, if the defendant is accused of an offense for which there is a possible sentence of more than six months of incarceration, he has a Sixth Amendment

right to a trial by jury. The Supreme Court has not explained how courts are to distinguish between "petty" and "nonpetty" offenses where the crime is punishable by no more than six months' imprisonment.

JOHN E. NOWAK

Bibliography
LaFave, Wayne, and Israel, Jerold 1984 *Criminal Procedure.* St. Paul, Minn.: West Publishing Co.

FERGUSON v. SKRUPA
372 U.S. 726 (1963)

This decision is often cited as a leading modern example of the Supreme Court's permissive attitude toward ECONOMIC REGULATION challenged as a violation of SUBSTANTIVE DUE PROCESS.

Kansas prohibited "the business of debt adjusting" except as an incident of the practice of law. The Court unanimously upheld this statute against a challenge to its constitutionality. Justice HUGO L. BLACK wrote for the Court. Any argument that the business of debt adjusting had social utility should be addressed to the legislature, not the courts. "We refuse to sit as a 'super legislature to weigh the wisdom of legislation.'" The Court had given up the practice, common during the years before WEST COAST HOTEL CO. V. PARRISH (1937), of using "the 'vague contours' of the Due Process Clause to nullify laws which a majority of the Court believed to be economically unwise." Justice Black, unlike many of his brethren, carried this same view of the judicial function into other areas of CONSTITUTIONAL INTERPRETATION; see his dissents in GRISWOLD V. CONNECTICUT (1965) and HARPER V. VIRGINIA BOARD OF ELECTIONS (1966).

In *Ferguson* Justice JOHN MARSHALL HARLAN concurred separately on the ground that the law bore "a rational relation to a constitutionally permissible objective." Apparently Justice Harlan wanted to maintain some level of judicial scrutiny of economic regulations, even if it were only the relaxed RATIONAL BASIS standard, and thought the Black opinion suggested a complete abdication of the judicial role in such cases.

KENNETH L. KARST

FESSENDEN, WILLIAM PITT
(1806–1869)

A Maine lawyer, congressman (1841–1843; 1853–1854), senator (1854–1864; 1865–1869), and secretary of the treasury (1864–1865), William Pitt Fessenden chaired the Senate Finance Committee during the Civil War and later the Joint Committee on Reconstruction. Although sympathetic to many radical goals, Fessenden always demanded strict adherence to constitutional principles. Thus, he opposed aspects of the EMANCIPATION PROCLAMATION, the legal tender acts, the CONFISCATION ACTS, and the TENURE OF OFFICE ACT. Although Senate majority leader, he voted to acquit ANDREW JOHNSON in his 1867 IMPEACHMENT trial, because he did not believe the President had committed an impeachable offense within the meaning of the Constitution.

PAUL FINKELMAN

Bibliography

JELLISON, CHARLES ALBERT 1962 Fessenden of Maine, Civil War Senator. Syracuse, N.Y.: Syracuse University Press.

FEW, WILLIAM
(1748–1828)

William Few represented Georgia at the CONSTITUTIONAL CONVENTION OF 1787 and signed the Constitution. He attended the Convention irregularly (leaving to attend Congress), spoke infrequently, and served on only one committee. He afterward served as a senator and federal judge.

DENNIS J. MAHONEY

FIELD, DAVID D.
(1805–1894)

David Dudley Field, older brother of Justice STEPHEN J. FIELD, won a number of important cases before the Supreme Court in his career as a highly successful lawyer, EX PARTE MILLIGAN (1866), Cummings v. Missouri (1867), and UNITED STATES V. CRUIKSHANK (1876) among them. His appearance on behalf of Jay Gould and Jim Fisk in the celebrated Erie Railroad scandal brought him popular criticism and charges of misconduct from his peers. He would later represent the Tweed Ring when his free services were rejected by the prosecution. As one biographer remarked, Field "was essentially a protestant, an originator, a breaker of precedents."

Field devoted his last decades to codification of municipal and international law. He also played a fundamental role in reforming the substantive and procedural codes of New York State; those codes would serve as models for many other states. He served as president of the American Bar Association, 1888–1889.

DAVID GORDON

FIELD, STEPHEN J.
(1816–1899)

Stephen Johnson Field is a massive figure in the history of the United States SUPREME COURT. Appointed by ABRAHAM LINCOLN in 1863 following six years of distinguished service on the California Supreme Court, Field remained on the bench until 1897 and established a record for length of tenure since surpassed only by WILLIAM O. DOUGLAS. For two generations he preached a radically new gospel of constitutional interpretation that fused natural law concepts, a theory of adjudication based on formally bounded categories of public power and private right, and a designing foresight about the Court's unique capacity to shape American public life. Field's contributions to American constitutional development are conventionally summed up in the phrase laissez-faire CONSTITUTIONALISM. But his profound impact on the institutional character of the Court outlasted his doctrinal formulations. Field was arguably the Court's first self-conscious "activist," and he was certainly the first Justice to describe judicial protection of substantive rights as a democratic endeavor. "As I look back over the more than a third of a century that I have sat on this bench," Field wrote in his valedictory letter, "I am more and more impressed with the immeasurable importance of this court. Now and then we hear it spoken of as an aristocratic feature of a Republican government. But it is the most Democratic of all. Senators represent their states, and Representatives their constituents, but this court stands for the whole country, and as such it is truly 'of the people, by the people, and for the people.'" It was this fundamentally new conception of the Court's position in the American system of government and the manifold ways Field acted upon it during his long career that prompted EDWARD S. CORWIN to describe him as "the pioneer and prophet of our modern constitutional law."

Field's jurisprudence was essentially a constitutional version of the equal rights creed expounded by ANDREW JACKSON in his veto of the bill rechartering the Second Bank of the United States. Field understood democracy in terms of "the natural equal rights of the citizen," particularly equality in the marketplace; he was quick to distinguish the common good of the whole people from the focused demands of interest seekers that sometimes generated legislation favoring some and discriminating against others. Since the Court, like the President, represented "the whole country" rather than a narrow constituency, Field claimed that JUDICIAL REVIEW of legislation was at once the moral equivalent of the executive veto and a consummately democratic power. His two most famous opinions resonated with the substantive concerns of antebellum Jacksonians. The first was designed to protect the rights of the many against legal privileges granted to a few. Dissenting in the SLAUGHTERHOUSE CASES (1873) Field denounced the "odious monopoly" produced by legislative skulduggery in Louisiana and claimed that the newly adopted FOURTEENTH AMENDMENT would become "a vain and idle enactment, which accomplished nothing" if the Court continued to permit state legislatures "to farm out the ordinary avocations of life" to favored corporations. In the second, POLLOCK V. FARMERS LOAN & TRUST CO. (1895), Field resisted a statute that, in his view, was designed to enable the many to steal from the few under color of law. There he attacked the mildly progressive federal tax on incomes as an "assault on capital . . . the stepping stone to others, larger and more sweeping, till our political contests . . . become a war of the poor against the rich; a war constantly growing in intensity and bitterness." If Field had been successful in persuading his colleagues to conceptualize the case as he did, the income tax would have been invalidated not because it was a DIRECT TAX but on the ground that its graduated rates violated the Constitution's requirement that "all duties, imposts and excises shall be uniform throughout the United States." For Field, uniformity mandated equal treatment; the chief defect of the statute was that it created a different rule for rich and poor, thereby violating the first principle of republicanism articulated by his Jacksonian mentors.

Field's penchant for pouring his ideological predispositions into open-ended textual phrases such as "uniform" and "due process" was apparent to colleagues throughout his career. Many were alarmed by his expansive conception of the judicial function; some regarded him as a dangerous man. DAVID DAVIS called him a "damned rascal" in 1866 and HORACE GRAY likened him to a "wild bull" three decades later. HENRY B. BROWN said he was "a man of great determination and indomitable courage, though lacking in judicial temperament." Yet it was impossible to ignore him. What made Field so formidable was his skill in translating the featureless generalities of the Constitution into a coherent system of principled standards.

He had an uncanny ability to diagnose recurrent problems almost immediately and to frame rules derived from the COMMON LAW or the structure of the federal system that accommodated his value-laden premises. He anticipated future controversies and supplied mutually consistent solutions to all of them. For Field, these solutions were neither contingent nor variable; they were "true."

Few of the twenty-eight men with whom Field sat on the bench perceived the whole truth in precisely the way he did. But every Justice shared at least some of his premises, and most were willing to articulate one or more of his pet doctrinal formulations in an opinion for the Court. With each new handhold Field secured, however, his colleagues found it increasingly difficult to resist the entire array of rules he had proposed at the outset. The analogies linking each component of his system to the others were very compelling. As late as 1890, Field remained confident that the whole truth, as he understood it, would eventually be embraced by the Court. "[A]ny grave departure from the purposes of the Constitution . . . will not fit harmoniously with other rulings," he explained at the Centennial Celebration of the Organization of the Federal Judiciary. "[I]t will collide with them, and thus compel explanations and qualifications until the error is eliminated. . . . [T]ruth alone is immortal, and in the end will assert its rightful supremacy."

The system of rules Field proposed for integrating the Fourteenth Amendment into the existing corpus of constitutional law was breathtaking in scope. It also had a deceptively simple and, in its day, alluring structure. First, he called for a clear and immutable boundary between the public and private spheres in order to forestall legislation that emptied one pocket only to fill another. Here the operable phrase in the amendment was not due process so much as "take property." Beginning in the *Slaughterhouse Cases,* Field claimed that some businesses were purely private while others were public in "use." Firms that necessarily "held franchises of a public character appertaining to government," such as those that exercised the EMINENT DOMAIN power or occupied the public rivers or public streets, were public in "use." Consequently government might confer monopoly privileges on such firms, subsidize their operations with tax funds, and regulate their rates of charge. But manufacturers, food processors, warehouse operators, and other businesses that did not need to exercise public franchises were purely private. Those businesses had to be open to all entrants as a matter of common right and their operations could be subject neither to price regulations nor to public subsidy. In the GRANGER CASES

(1877) Field added one corollary to this scheme. When government regulated the rates of firms public in "use," he asserted, the prices fixed must be subject to judicial review in order to ensure that service to the public was not "required without reward, or upon conditions amounting to the TAKING OF PROPERTY for PUBLIC USE without compensation." The Court's duty, he said, was "to draw the line between regulation and confiscation."

Field repeatedly claimed that judicial application of these doctrines required no great departure in constitutional interpretation. All the Court had to do was constitutionalize under the Fourteenth Amendment and apply in a systematic fashion the principles of "general constitutional law" articulated by SAMUEL F. MILLER in *Pumpelly v. Green Bay Co.* (1872) and LOAN ASSOCIATION V. TOPEKA (1874). There the Court proscribed exercises of the eminent domain and tax powers that amounted to "robbery," in the one case by designating irreparable injury to property as a taking and in the other by barring public spending "for purposes of private interest instead of public use." When the Court refused to apply the same principles to the POLICE POWER under the Fourteenth Amendment in the *Granger Cases,* Field dissented. "Of what avail is the constitutional provision that no State shall deprive any person of property except by DUE PROCESS OF LAW," he asked, "if the State can, by fixing the compensation which he may receive for its use, take from him all that is valuable in the property?" Beginning in STONE V. FARMER'S LOAN AND TRUST CO. (1886), however, the majority made one concession after another to Field's position. By 1898 only the doctrine of business AFFECTED WITH A PUBLIC INTEREST, which Field considered dangerously protean, remained to be pulled down before "the truth . . . asserted its rightful supremacy."

The second component of Field's Fourteenth Amendment system dealt with intergovernmental relations. His general theory was based on the Jacksonian principle of DUAL FEDERALISM: "a national government for national purposes, local governments for local purposes," and each "sovereign" within its assigned sphere such that neither was dependent upon or subordinate to the other nor, indeed, capable of clashing with it as long as the powers of each were properly defined. Thus Field eagerly joined majorities that imposed implied limitations on Congress's MONETARY POWER in *Lane County v. Oregon* (1869), its taxing power in COLLECTOR V. DAY (1871), and its commerce power in UNITED STATES V. E. C. KNIGHT CO. (1895). Beginning in *Tarble's Case* (1871) he also developed implied limitations on the states' authority

to impair the national government's independent energy in the exercise of its "acknowledged powers." Yet Miller, speaking for the majority in the *Slaughterhouse Cases,* claimed that the Fourteenth Amendment threatened to unravel these "main features of the federal system." What frightened Miller most was the assumption that if the Court had JURISDICTION to protect FUNDAMENTAL RIGHTS under the amendment's first section, Congress must have jurisdiction to enact statutes affecting the same rights under the fifth section vesting it with power "to enforce, by appropriate legislation" the amendment's substantive provisions. One reason the majority gutted the PRIVILEGES OR IMMUNITIES clause, then, was to avoid articulating doctrine that might ultimately "fetter and degrade the State governments by subjecting them to the control of Congress."

In Field's view, the *Slaughterhouse* majority was afraid of a phantom, for a STATE ACTION doctrine could stay the hand of Congress without disturbing the Court's jurisdiction. Here the operable phrase in the text was: "No State shall make or enforce any law." The Fourteenth Amendment, he asserted in dissent, only "ordains that [fundamental rights] shall not be abridged by State legislation." "The exercise of these rights . . . and the degree of enjoyment received from such exercise," he added in anticipation of UNITED STATES V. CRUIKSHANK (1876), "are always more or less affected by the condition and the local institutions of the State, or city, or town where he resides." These rights had never been a concern of the United States and the amendment did not make them one. The enabling clause in the fifth section, whatever its meaning, could not constitutionally enlarge the modest accretion to national authority envisioned by the first section. Because the amendment was not a grant of power but a series of limitations on state legislation, moreover, the Court could readily distinguish between national remedies for prohibited state action (laws that were not "true" exercises of the eminent domain, taxing, and police powers reserved to the states) and inappropriate acts of Congress invading the sphere of state authority. In practical application, the amendment would affect the federal system in a way comparable to the clauses of the Constitution forbidding the states from passing BILLS OF ATTAINDER, EX POST FACTO laws, and laws impairing the obligation of contracts.

The WAITE COURT tentatively endorsed the state action doctrine in *Cruikshank,* and invoked it with a vengeance in UNITED STATES V. HARRIS (1883) and the CIVIL RIGHTS CASES (1883). These decisions not only assuaged previous doubts about Congress's authority to use the Fourteenth Amendment as a grant of power but also prompted the Court to reconsider Field's blueprint for judicial intervention in government–business relations. Meanwhile, Field elaborated the third component of his Fourteenth Amendment theory. It addressed what he called INVIDIOUS DISCRIMINATION. Here Field was a singularly important pioneer, for he decided the federal case of first impression on circuit. At issue in *Ho Ah Kow v. Nunan* (1879) was the San Francisco "queue ordinance" requiring county prisoners to have their hair cropped. As it was "universally understood" that the regulation had been designed "to be enforced only against [the Chinese] race," Field explained, the ordinance violated the equal protection clause. This decision, along with Field's 1882 opinion striking down an anti-Chinese laundry ordinance, supplied the conceptual foundations for the Court's ringing proclamation of the antidiscrimination principle in YICK WO V. HOPKINS (1886).

Yet Field's understanding of "invidious discrimination" did not compel state governments to be colorblind. Dissenting in STRAUDER V. WEST VIRGINIA (1880), where the Court invalidated a statute that limited jury service to whites, Field claimed that the equal protection clause dealt only with the CIVIL RIGHTS described in *Ho Ah Kow*. It "leaves political rights . . . and social rights . . . as they stood previous to its adoption." "Civil rights," he explained, "are absolute and personal and [a]ll persons within the jurisdiction of the State, whether permanent residents or temporary sojourners, whether young or old, male or female, are to be equally protected." But nobody in the *Strauder* majority was prepared to hold that the Fourteenth Amendment forbade the states from excluding Chinese aliens, women, or children from the jury box. The conclusion was inescapable that jury service could not be regarded as a "civil right," for which the amendment mandated "universality of the [equal] protection secured," but only as a "political right . . . conditioned and dependent upon the discretion of the elective or appointing power, whether that be the People acting through the ballot, or one of the departments of their government." The "social rights" to which Field only alluded in the *Strauder* stood on a similar footing. The capacity of individuals to marry or to have access to public goods such as libraries and schools had always been regulated by law on the basis of age, sex, race, and citizenship. "Such legislation is not obnoxious to the [equal protection] clause of the 14th Amendment," he said, "if all persons subject to it are treated alike under similar circumstances and conditions."

The *Strauder* majority flatly rejected the classification of rights that Field proposed. "The Fourteenth Amendment makes no attempt to enumerate the rights it is designed to protect," WILLIAM STRONG declared for the Court. "It speaks in general terms, and those are as comprehensive as possible." But once again a Field dissent proved to be prophetic. Three years later, speaking for a unanimous Court in PACE V. ALABAMA (1883), Field held that antimiscegenation laws were not forbidden by the Fourteenth Amendment as long as both parties received the same punishment for their crimes. Equal protection mandated equal treatment, not freedom of choice; antimiscegenation laws restricted the liberty of blacks and whites alike. Underlying this ruling was an unarticulated premise of enormous importance: the legal classification "Negro" was not suspect per se. The doctrine of SEPARATE BUT EQUAL enunciated in PLESSY V. FERGUSON (1896) followed almost as a matter of course, especially after the Court had distinguished "civil rights" from "social rights" under the THIRTEENTH AMENDMENT in the *Civil Rights Cases*. Even Field's distinction between "civil rights" and "political rights" eventually got incorporated into the Court's Fourteenth Amendment jurisprudence, albeit in a form substantially different from what he proposed in *Strauder*. The Waite Court conceded from the outset that jury selection officials might constitutionally employ facially neutral yet impossibly vague tests of good character, sound judgment, and the like. In the absence of state laws expressly restricting participation to whites, JOHN MARSHALL HARLAN explained in *Bush v. Kentucky* (1883), the Court had no choice but to presume that jury commissioners had acted properly. When the "civil right" of equal opportunity to pursue an "ordinary trade" was at issue in *Yick Wo*, however, the Court unanimously invalidated the law not only because it had been administered with "an evil eye and an unequal hand" but also because it lacked adequate standards for controlling the discretion of public officials authorized to license the regulated trade.

Simply to sketch the basic contours of Field's jurisprudence is to suggest the degree to which his views, forged into a coherent system at an astonishingly early date and reiterated with great force throughout his record-shattering tenure on the Court, shaped the course of American constitutional law. His associates resisted the whole "truth," as Field understood it, to the very end, and Harlan predicted that he would spend even the final days with "his face towards the setting sun, wondering . . . whether the Munn case or the eternal principles of right and justice will ultimately prevail." Yet appellate judging in America is inherently a collective enterprise. The remarkable thing about Field's career is not that he failed to win every battle but that he eventually celebrated so many victories when the stakes were so very high. What endured was his claim that the Court was "the most [d]emocratic of all" governmental institutions. By acting on that belief Field not only transformed the character of judicial power in America but also influenced debate on the Court's legitimate role long after the structure of doctrine he helped to forge had been annihilated.

CHARLES W. MCCURDY

Bibliography

CORWIN, EDWARD S. 1909 The Supreme Court and the Fourteenth Amendment. *Michigan Law Review* 7:643–672.

GRAHAM, HOWARD J. 1968 *Everyman's Constitution: Historical Essays in the Fourteenth Amendment, the "Conspiracy Theory," and American Constitutionalism.* Madison: State Historical Society of Wisconsin.

MCCURDY, CHARLES W. 1975 Justice Field and the Jurisprudence of Government–Business Relations. *Journal of American History* 61:970–1005.

SWISHER, CARL B. 1930 *Stephen J. Field: Craftsman of the Law.* Washington, D.C.: Brookings Institution.

FIELD v. CLARK
143 U.S. 649 (1892)

This is a leading case on the subject of DELEGATION OF POWER. The Tariff Act of 1890 authorized the President to suspend its free-trade provisions indefinitely as to countries discriminating against American products. The Supreme Court held, 7–2, that though the act invested the President with discretion, it did not invest him with "legislative power"; Congress had fixed adequate standards for his guidance.

Field is also often cited as a POLITICAL QUESTION precedent. Appellants argued that the enrolled act contained one section that the House of Representatives had not passed. The Court refused to examine this question; the act's transmission by the congressional leadership and its enrollment by the secretary of state conclusively established its content.

LEONARD W. LEVY

FIFTEENTH AMENDMENT
(Framing and Ratification)

In January 1869 adult black males could vote in only twenty states. Blacks had received the franchise in ten states of the South under the Reconstruction Act of March 1867 as part of the price of readmission to the Union set by the Republicans in Congress. Because Republicans also controlled the state government of Tennessee, blacks were enfranchised there. But many lived in the ex-slave border states that had been loyal to the Union, and they were not enfranchised. In the North, most blacks did not have the right to vote; however, there were minor exceptions in those states where the black population was small. The New England states except Connecticut allowed black suffrage, as did four midwestern states, Wisconsin, Nebraska, Minnesota, and Iowa. But especially in the lower North, where most northern blacks lived, white voters in REFERENDUM after referendum had rejected their unrestricted enfranchisement. Indeed in 1868 the issue of black suffrage was thought to be so dangerous and debilitating to the Republican party that at the party's national convention the framers of the platform devised a double standard by endorsing black voting in the South while trying not to antagonize white voters in the North: thus each northern state could decide black suffrage without federal interference, but southern states must accept black voting as a matter of national policy.

In the presidential election of 1868 Republican candidate ULYSSES S. GRANT captured most of the electoral vote and the Republicans retained control of Congress. But beneath the surface the situation was not reassuring. Grant's electoral victory was much greater than his popular vote (only 52 percent). Without the southern black voter Grant would have lost the popular, though not the electoral, vote. In state after state Grant squeaked by with narrow margins. Indeed, a switch of a mere 29,862 votes out of the 5,717,246 cast for the two major party candidates (.52 percent) would have made the Democratic candidate president. Moreover, the Democrats gained seats in the House of Representatives in Washington. And Republican majorities in state after state were slim indeed. Finally, Republican politicians throughout the South reported that little reliance could be placed on the southern black voter in the long run because of strong white influence and intimidation and because of black poverty, illiteracy, and inexperience. Danger signals in the South, defeats in state referenda in the North, and a narrow escape from defeat in the presidential election of 1868 taught the Republicans that their platform pledge to the North had to be ignored. Something must be done by the final session of the Fortieth Congress before the Democrats arrived in force.

The Republicans decided it was necessary to augment their strength by enfranchising more blacks, who could be expected to vote Republican en masse. Although egalitarians had begun the advocacy of black enfranchisement, politicians had made its achievement possible. Two years before, Congress had enfranchised blacks in the South because the Republicans then needed southern black votes to counter southern white votes. Now the Republicans also needed the support of northern and border blacks, especially in closely balanced states, and were willing to run limited risks and promote political reform in order to maintain power.

Therefore, during early 1869 the Republicans in the lame-duck Congress pressed for a constitutional amendment to secure impartial manhood suffrage in every state, thereby avoiding further popular rejection in state referenda. They opted for the usual but more indirect method of having Republican state legislatures that were still in session ratify the amendment. Thus they avoided the risk of possible rejection by special conventions.

The amendment finally passed Congress in late February 1869 after a number of compromises. To secure enough moderate votes, the sponsors had to omit a clause that would have outlawed property qualifications and LITERACY TESTS. Such a clause was dispensable because the tests would affect more Negroes in the South than in the North, and because the proponents of the amendment were intent primarily upon securing the northern Negro voter for the Republican party. For the same reasons, they omitted any provision banning RACIAL DISCRIMINATION in qualifications for officeholding. A provision for federal authority over voter qualifications was defeated, and so the potential for evasion in the southern and border states was left wide open.

The legislative history of the Fifteenth Amendment indicated no triumph of radical idealism but rather served to demonstrate its failure—a fact underscored by the fury and frustration of that band of radicals who had favored idealistic and uncompromising reforms. A moderate measure, the amendment had the support of those who understood the limits of party power and who had practical goals in mind; they took into account the possible difficulties of ratification. Time was short, the pressures were great, and the options were limited.

The primary objective—the enfranchisement of blacks in the northern and border states—was clearly understood, stated, and believed by the politicians, the press, and the people during the time when the amendment was framed and then considered by the state legislatures. As the abolitionist organ, the *National Anti-Slavery Standard,* declared, "evenly as

parties are now divided in the North, it needs but the final ratification of the pending Fifteenth Amendment, to assure . . . the balance of power in national affairs." A black newspaper, the Washington *New National Era,* predicted the same for the border states. Indeed, most newspapers both in the North and in the South during 1869 and 1870 unequivocally, incontrovertibly, and repeatedly spoke of the Republican objective of ensuring party hegemony by means of the Fifteenth Amendment. Moreover, congressmen and state legislators, in arguing for passage and ratification, referred again and again to the partisan need for those votes. The southern black, already a voter, was not irrelevant; an important secondary purpose of the amendment was to assure the continuance of black suffrage in the South by forbidding racial discrimination as to the franchise in a virtually unrepealable amendment to the federal Constitution. Still, the anticipated importance of the black electorate in the North and in the borderland was clearly the overriding concern.

To be sure, the political motives of many Republican politicians were not incompatible with a sincere moral concern. The idealistic motive reinforced the pragmatic one: there was no conflict at the outset between the ideal and the practical or between the interests of the black electorate and those of the Republican party. A radical Republican congressman declared, "party expediency and exact justice coincide for once." A black clergyman from Pittsburgh observed that "the Republican Party had done the negro good but they were doing themselves good at the same time." Indeed, the amendment as framed was both bold and prudent: bold in enfranchising blacks despite concerted opposition and in ordering change by establishing constitutional guidelines; prudent in adapting methods to circumstances so that the amendment would not only pass Congress but also be ratified by the states.

Although the struggle over ratification lasted only thirteen months, it was hard going and the outcome was uncertain until the very end. To be sure, ratification was easy in safe Republican territory (New England and most of the Middle West) and in the South where Republican legislators did their duty. But the fight was especially close in the Middle Atlantic states and in Indiana and Ohio, where the parties were competitive and a black electorate had the potential for deciding victory or defeat. In the Democratic border states and on the Pacific Coast, where racial feeling ran high, Republicans feared that pushing the amendment would lose them votes; so they refrained from pressing for ratification in these regions. Nevertheless, in clear-cut conflicts of interest between state and national Republican party organizations, the national party was everywhere victorious. Mutinies in Rhode Island and Georgia were suppressed. The amendment had the backing of the Grant administration, with its rich patronage. By endorsing the amendment in his inaugural address, Grant placed the indispensable prestige of the presidency behind it; he then went beyond pronouncements by swinging Nebraska to ratify it. Those Republican politicians who held or aspired to hold national office added the weight of their influence. As one Ohioan advised, "By hook or by crook you must get the 15th amendment through or we are gone up."

The Fifteenth Amendment became law on March 30, 1870. Republican euphoria followed the hard battle for ratification. Grant, in his message to Congress, wrote that the amendment "completes the greatest civil change and constitutes the most important event that has occurred since the nation came to life." Blacks everywhere celebrated; they regarded the Fifteenth Amendment as political salvation, as a solemn written guarantee that would never be abridged. They now felt secure, protected by both the vote and the "long strong arm of the Government." Whites believed that since the Negro was now a citizen and a voter, he could take care of himself. Antislavery societies throughout the country disbanded, now confident that equality before the law was sufficient and that in any event, "no power ever permanently wronged a voting class without its own consent." But subsequent events made a mockery of such predictions in the South where Democrats denied blacks the franchise for almost a century.

WILLIAM GILLETTE

Bibliography
GILLETTE, WILLIAM (1979)1981 *Retreat from Reconstruction, 1869–1879.* Baton Rouge: Louisiana State University Press.
———— (1965)1969 *The Right to Vote: Politics and the Passage of the Fifteenth Amendment.* Baltimore: Johns Hopkins University Press.
MITTRICK, ROBERT 1985 *A History of Negro Voting in Pennsylvania during the Nineteenth Century.* Unpublished Ph.D. dissertation, Rutgers University, chap. 5.

FIFTEENTH AMENDMENT
(Judicial Interpretation)

The judicial interpretation of the Fifteenth Amendment has been closely intertwined with that of the FOURTEENTH AMENDMENT, largely in a Southern context. Within a year of ratification (1870) Congress passed three FORCE ACTS forbidding both public and private interference with voting on the basis of race or color. Federal officials tried hard at first to enforce these laws, but they were daunted by hostility in the South and growing indifference in Congress and the Supreme Court. Prosecutions dropped sharply in 1874; Reconstruction ended in 1877; the Jim Crow era of systematic SEGREGATION began around 1890; and the conspiracy provisions of the Force Acts were dropped in 1894.

From Reconstruction to World War I the Supreme Court showed more ingenuity in voiding VOTING RIGHTS actions than in upholding them. Although it was willing, under Article I, section 4, to uphold convictions and damage awards for ballot box fraud in federal elections, as in EX PARTE YARBROUGH (1884), it would not allow INDICTMENTS for conspiracy to bribe, even in federal elections as in JAMES V. BOWMAN (1903). It steadfastly refused to uphold convictions for private interference with voting rights in state or local elections in UNITED STATES V. REESE (1875) and UNITED STATES V. CRUIKSHANK (1876), or to uphold civil actions for a state official's refusal to register blacks, in *Giles v. Teasley* (1904).

The Court did shrug off arguments in *Myers v. Anderson* (1915) that the Fifteenth Amendment was itself void for diluting the votes of enfranchised whites and thereby depriving their states of equal suffrage in the Senate without their consent. But it did almost nothing to thwart the new franchise restrictions of the Jim Crow era—literacy, property, POLL TAX, residence, character, and understanding tests—designed to cull black and upcountry white voters. (See WILLIAMS V. MISSISSIPPI, 1898.) Only in GUINN V. UNITED STATES (1915) did it strike down a GRANDFATHER CLAUSE exempting descendants of 1867 voters from Oklahoma's LITERACY TEST—without, however, striking down the test itself. *Guinn* had no practical impact on voting registration, but it was important for serving notice that the Fifteenth Amendment bars subtle as well as blatant discrimination.

The Court moved against white PRIMARY ELECTIONS with more deliberation than speed. Party primary elections emerged in response to the regional party monopolies, Republican in the North, Democratic in the South, which followed the "realigning" election of 1896. By World War I, primaries were universal. The dominant party's nomination became the choice that counted, and general elections merely rubber-stamped the dominant party's nominee. This trend was earliest and most pronounced in the South. It weakened party discipline, lowered turnout drastically in general elections, strengthened the dominance of plantation whites, and froze out blacks almost completely.

Blacks challenged this exclusion in a famous series of Texas cases. In NIXON V. HERNDON (1927) and NIXON V. CONDON (1932) NAACP attorneys successfully attacked statutes barring blacks, and letting the parties bar blacks, from voting in primary elections. Counsel for both sides in *Herndon* argued the Fifteenth Amendment, but Justice OLIVER WENDELL HOLMES, speaking for a unanimous Court, found the statute instead a "direct and obvious infringement of the Fourteenth." The Court followed this precedent in *Condon*.

In attacking the discriminatory law under the Fourteenth, rather than the denial of a voting right under the Fifteenth, the Court ignored its earlier view that the pertinent section of the Fourteenth was not intended to protect voting rights. (See MINOR V. HAPPERSETT, 1875.) It also left Texas free to repeal the *Condon* statute, while permitting the Democrats to exclude blacks legally through their own "private" action. (See GROVEY V. TOWNSEND, 1935.)

The Court returned to the Fifteenth Amendment to overrule *Grovey* in SMITH V. ALLWRIGHT (1944), finding STATE ACTION in laws governing the timing and conduct of primary elections and by the "fusing [in UNITED STATES V. CLASSIC (1941)] of primary and general elections into a single instrumentality for the choice of officers." Later, in TERRY V. ADAMS (1953), the Court extended this concept of "fusion into a single instrumentality" to invalidate a whites-only "pre-primary" election used by the Jaybird party since 1889 to capture Democratic nominations in a Texas county.

Without the white primary, segregationist whites had only franchise restrictions to block black votes. These restrictions had reduced black registrations by a third in the nineteenth century, but they had only limited and temporary effect by the 1950s. Black literacy was up, and only three of the eleven Southern states—Alabama, Mississippi, and Louisiana—retained blatantly discriminatory literacy tests. These the Court struck down, along with nondiscriminatory tests where blacks had been segregated in inferior schools.

Congress greatly aided in expanding the black vote with judicial protection in the CIVIL RIGHTS ACTS OF 1957, 1960, and 1964, and especially with the VOTING RIGHTS ACT OF 1965, which authorized suspension of state literacy and character tests and provision of federal examiners to register blacks where discrimination was found. In 1970, Congress wholly forbade literacy tests as a condition on voting in state elections.

Though the Court took almost seventy-five years

to give the Fifteenth Amendment much practical effect, its interventions since World War II have greatly changed both the constitutional and political landscapes. *Smith v. Allwright,* with its broad reading of the Fifteenth Amendment looking through form to substance foreshadowed such great Fourteenth Amendment cases as SHELLEY V. KRAEMER (1948) and BROWN V. BOARD OF EDUCATION (1954). GOMILLION V. LIGHTFOOT (1960), which struck down a racial GERRYMANDER under the Fifteenth Amendment, was a bridge to BAKER V. CARR (1962).

Opening the primaries and the franchise to blacks brought them out of political exile. Black registration in the South, only five percent in 1940, grew to twenty-eight percent in 1960 and sixty-three percent in 1976, narrowing the gap between black and white registrations from forty-four percent to five percent. Black elected officials in the South increased from fewer than 100 to more than 1,000. White politicians stopped waving ax handles, standing in the doorways of segregated schools, and using terms like "burrhead" in public debate. The Court's enforcement of the Fifteenth Amendment may properly be described as late, but not little.

WARD E. Y. ELLIOTT

Bibliography

ELLIOTT, WARD E. Y. 1975 *The Rise of Guardian Democracy: The Supreme Court's Role in Voting Rights Disputes, 1845–1969.* Cambridge, Mass.: Harvard University Press.

KEY, V. O., JR. 1949 *Southern Politics.* New York: Knopf.

KOUSSER, J. MORGAN 1974 *The Shaping of Southern Politics: Suffrage Restriction and the Establishment of the One-Party South, 1880–1910.* New Haven, Conn.: Yale University Press.

LAWSON, STEVEN F. 1976 *Black Ballots: Voting Rights in the South, 1944–1969.* New York: Columbia University Press.

FIFTH AMENDMENT

See: Double Jeopardy; Due Process of Law; Eminent Domain; Right Against Self-Incrimination; Taking of Property

FIGHTING WORDS

In CHAPLINSKY V. NEW HAMPSHIRE (1942) the Supreme Court upheld the conviction of a Jehovah's Witness who called a policeman "a God damned racketeer" and "a damned Fascist," holding that "fighting words"—face-to-face words plainly likely to provoke the average addressee to fight—were not protected by constitutional free speech guarantees. Viewed narrowly, the fighting words doctrine can be seen as a per se rule effectuating the CLEAR AND PRESENT DANGER principle, relieving the government of proving an actual INCITEMENT by taking the words themselves as decisive. Taken broadly, *Chaplinsky* strips "four-letter words" of free speech protection. "It has been well observed," Justice FRANK MURPHY said, "that such utterances are no essential part of any exposition of ideas, and are of such slight social value as a step to the truth that any benefit that may be derived from them is clearly outweighed by the social interest in order and morality."

The modern tendency of the Court has been to extend partial FIRST AMENDMENT protection to even the "excluded" areas of speech. To the extent that *Chaplinsky* refuses protection to four-letter words because they offend against taste or morality, it has been limited by recent decisions such as COHEN V. CALIFORNIA (1971), *Gooding v. Wilson* (1972), and *Rosenfeld v. New Jersey* (1972). The Justices appear to have been engaging in ad hoc analysis of what persons in what situations are entitled to a measure of protection from the shock to their sensibilities generated by words that, in the language of *Chaplinsky*, "by their very utterances inflict injury."

The shock aspect of four-letter words is obviously related to the shock element in OBSCENITY. In FCC V. PACIFICA FOUNDATION (1978) the Court upheld FCC regulation of "indecent" broadcasting that involved "patently offensive" four-letter words but was not obscene. While admitting that the words in question would warrant constitutional protection under certain circumstances, the Court held that in view of their capacity to offend, their slight social value in the conveying of ideas, and the intrusive character of speech broadcast into the home, their repeated use might constitutionally be banned at least in time slots and programming contexts when children might be listening.

The recent decisions suggest that outside the direct incitement to violence context the Court is prepared to balance PRIVACY against speech interests where four-letter words are at issue. Where statutes go beyond prohibiting incitement to violence, and also bar cursing or reviling, or using opprobrious, indecent, lascivious, or offensive language, they are likely to be held unconstitutionally vague or overbroad. (See *Lewis v. New Orleans*, 1974.)

MARTIN SHAPIRO

(SEE ALSO: *Freedom of Speech; Balancing Test.*)

Bibliography

KONVITZ, MILTON 1978 *Fundamental Liberties of a Free People.* Chap. 17. Westport, Conn.: Greenwood Press.
SHEA, THOMAS 1975 Fighting Words and the First Amendment. *Kentucky Law Journal* 63:1–22.

FILLMORE, MILLARD
(1800–1874)

A Buffalo, New York, lawyer and Whig politician, Millard Fillmore was elected vice-president in 1848 and became President when ZACHARY TAYLOR died in 1850. Unlike Taylor, Fillmore enthusiastically supported passage of the COMPROMISE OF 1850 which he believed necessary to preserve the Union. His administration was particularly vigorous in enforcing the Fugitive Slave Law through the Christiana Treason Trials, and prosecutions of those involved in the Shadrach Rescue, the Jerry Rescue, and the abortive Sims Rescue. Fillmore was not renominated by the Whigs in 1852 and ran unsuccessfully as a Know-Nothing in 1856.

PAUL FINKELMAN

Bibliography

RAYBACK, ROBERT J. 1959 *Millard Fillmore: Biography of a President.* Buffalo, N.Y.: Buffalo Historical Society.

FINAL JUDGMENT RULE

By congressional statute the federal courts of appeals are permitted, in the usual case, to exercise their APPELLATE JURISDICTION only over final judgments of the district courts. An additional provision authorizes review of district court orders granting, denying, or otherwise dealing with INJUNCTIONS, and of certain other INTERLOCUTORY orders less frequently given. Furthermore, a district judge may certify an interlocutory order for review by the court of appeals, and that court can, in its discretion, review such a nonfinal order. The Supreme Court's appellate jurisdiction over cases coming from the state courts also is limited to final judgments of those courts. (The Supreme Court is not limited by this final judgment rule in hearing cases coming to it from a federal court of appeals; it can grant CERTIORARI in any case "in" the court of appeals.)

The final judgment rule, which aims at avoiding piecemeal appellate review, has so many judge-made exceptions that it has aptly been called "a permeable screen." Thus, a "collateral" order, unrelated to the merits of the case, may be reviewed if it presents an issue that might never be decided if the final judgment rule were strictly applied. Similarly, if rigorous application of the rule would do irreparable injury to some important federal policy, the Supreme Court has held that a nonfinal order can be reviewed. And in UNITED STATES v. NIXON (1974) the Court permitted review of a nonfinal order of a district court ordering the President of the United States to turn over the "Watergate tapes," in order to avoid putting the President to the "unseemly" choice between obeying the order and refusing and being cited for contempt. It is hard to avoid the conclusion that the final judgment "rule" has been made into a technique for allowing review of those interlocutory orders the Supreme Court thinks should be reviewed even though they are not final.

KENNETH L. KARST

Bibliography

WRIGHT, CHARLES ALAN 1983 *The Law of Federal Courts,* 4th ed. Pages 697–717, 739–743. St. Paul, Minn.: West Publishing Co.

FIREFIGHTERS LOCAL UNION NO. 1784 v. STOTTS
467 U.S. 561 (1984)

The City of Memphis, Tennessee, laid off white firefighters with more seniority to protect the positions of less senior blacks who had been employed under a "race conscious" AFFIRMATIVE ACTION plan. The white firefighters sued, alleging that their seniority rights were explicitly protected by the CIVIL RIGHTS ACT OF 1964.

Justice BYRON R. WHITE, writing for the Supreme Court's majority, agreed, noting that "mere membership in the disadvantaged class is insufficient to warrant a seniority award; each individual must prove that the discriminatory practice had an impact on him." White thus affirmed the proposition, which is explicit from the plain language of Title VII, that rights vest in the individual and not in the racial class, and that this fact demands a close fit between injuries and remedies. White's opinion raises some doubt about the power of courts to fashion classwide remedies where, as in race-conscious affirmative action plans, benefited individuals are not required to demonstrate individual injury. This case signals an important move toward the restoration of the principle that rests at the core of liberal jurisprudence—that rights

adhere to the individual, and not to the racial class that one happens to inhabit.

EDWARD J. ERLER

FIRST AMENDMENT

The First Amendment today protects the overlapping realms of the spirit—of belief, emotion, and reason—and of political activity against intrusion by government. The amendment directly forbids federal violation of the individual's RELIGIOUS LIBERTY, freedom of expression, FREEDOM OF ASSEMBLY, and associated political liberties. The amendment indirectly forbids state violation because it is held to be incorporated into the FOURTEENTH AMENDMENT's restrictions upon the powers of the states. The body of law presently defining First Amendment liberties has been shaped not so much by the words or intent of the original sponsors as by the actors and events of much later history. The story is one of the continual expansion of individual freedom of expression, of the FREEDOM OF THE PRESS, and, until 1980, of widening SEPARATION OF CHURCH AND STATE.

The CONSTITUTIONAL CONVENTION OF 1787 saw no need to include guarantees of religious liberty, FREEDOM OF SPEECH, or other human rights. Most of the Framers believed in some such rights but supposed that the powers proposed for the new federal government were so severely limited by specific enumeration as to leave scant opportunity for either Congress or President to threaten individual liberty. The threats would come from state law and state governments. For protection against these, the Framers looked to the constitutions of the individual states. In the struggle for RATIFICATION OF THE CONSTITUTION, however, those who feared abuse of federal power exacted an undertaking that if the proposed Constitution were ratified by the states, the first Congress would be asked to propose amendments constituting a BILL OF RIGHTS. The First Amendment is thus the first and most far-reaching of the ten articles of amendment submitted by JAMES MADISON, proposed by Congress, and ratified by three-quarters of the states in 1791 solely as restrictions upon the new federal government, the powers of which were already severely limited.

The assumption that the amendment would have only a narrow function made it possible to ignore fundamental differences that would produce deep divisions more than a century later, after the amendment had been extended to the several states. The colonists held a variety of religious beliefs, though nearly all were Christian and a majority were Protestant. Whatever the limits of their tolerance back home in their respective states where one church was often dominant, they had reason to understand that the coherence of the federal union could be fixed only if the new federal government were required to respect the free exercise of religion. The men of South Carolina with their state-established religion and of Massachusetts with religion appurtenant to their state government could therefore support a prohibition against any *federal* ESTABLISHMENT OF RELIGION shoulder to shoulder with the deist THOMAS JEFFERSON and other eighteenth-century rationalists who opposed any link between church and state. Similarly, in applying ROGER WILLIAMS's vision of "the hedge or wall of separation between the garden of the church and the wilderness of the world," there was originally no need to choose between his concept of protection for the church against the encroachments of worldly society and Jefferson's concept of protection for the state against the encroachments of religion.

The conditions and political assumptions of 1791 also made it easy to guarantee "the freedom of speech or of the press" without accepting or rejecting the Blackstonian view that these guarantees bar only licensing and other previous restraints upon publication, leaving the government free to punish SEDITIOUS LIBELS and like unlawful utterances. Because the original amendment left the states unhampered in making and applying the general body of civil and criminal law, except as the people of each state might put restrictions into its own constitution, there was no need to consider how the First Amendment would affect the law of LIBEL and slander, the power of the judges to punish CONTEMPT of court, or the operation of laws punishing words and demonstrations carrying a threat to the public peace, order, or morality. Such questions could and would arise only after the First Amendment was extended to the states.

The fulcrum for extending the First Amendment to the states was set in place in 1868 by the adoption of the Fourteenth Amendment, which provides in part: ". . . nor shall any State deprive any person of life, liberty or property without DUE PROCESS OF LAW."

The effects of the new amendment upon religious and political liberty and upon freedom of expression were slow to develop. As late as 1922 the Court declared in *Prudential Insurance Co. v. Cheek* that "neither the Fourteenth Amendment nor any other provision of the Constitution of the United States imposes upon the States any restrictions about 'freedom of speech.'" Within another decade, however, the First

Amendment's guarantee of freedom of expression had been incorporated into the Fourteenth by judicial interpretation. INCORPORATION of the other clauses, including the prohibition against laws "respecting an establishment of religion," followed somewhat later. Today the First Amendment restricts both state and federal governments to the same extent and in the same fashion.

Yet the historic sequence is important. Many questions of First Amendment law cannot be resolved truly in terms of the original intention because the questions could not arise while the original assumption held. Resolution of the issues was thus postponed until the middle decades of the twentieth century, an era in which liberalism, secularism, and individualism dominated American jurisprudence.

Disparate strains of thought were merged even in the writing of the First Amendment. Subsequent events, including current controversies, have poured new meaning into the words, yet the juxtaposition of the key phrases still tells a good deal about the chief strains in the philosophy underpinning and binding together guarantees of several particular rights.

The Framers put first the prohibition against any law "respecting an establishment of religion or prohibiting the free exercise thereof." The sequence attests the primacy ascribed to religion. The colonists belonged to diverse churches. Many had fled to the New World to escape religious oppression. Rigid though some might be in their own orthodoxy, probably a majority rejected the imposition of belief or the use of government to stamp out heresy. Certainly, they rejected use of federal power.

It was natural for the authors of the amendment to link "the freedom of speech, or of the press" with freedom of religious belief and worship. The one church was breaking up in late sixteenth- and seventeenth-century Britain. New faiths were emerging based upon individual study of the Holy Word. The man or woman who has discovered the road to salvation has a need, even feels a duty, to bring the gospel to others. Liberty of expression benefits more than the speaker. Suppression would deny the opportunity to hear and read the word of God, and thus to discover the road to salvation. Modern legal analysis recognizes the importance of the hearers' and readers' access to information and ideas in cases in which the author's interest lacks constitutional standing or would, if alone involved, be subject to regulation. (See LISTENERS' RIGHTS.)

Concern for a broader spiritual liberty expanded from the religious core. The thinking man or woman, the man or woman of feeling, the novelist, the poet or dramatist, and the artist, like the evangelist, can experience no greater affront to his or her humanity than denial of freedom of expression. The hearer and reader suffer violation of their spiritual liberty if they are denied access to the ideas of others. The denial thwarts the development of the human potential, the power and responsibility of choice. Although concerned chiefly with religion, John Milton stated the broader concern in *Areopagitica* (1644), the single most influential plea, known to the Framers, for unlicensed access to the printing press.

The Enlightenment gave the argument a broader, more rationalistic flavor. Thomas Jefferson and other children of the Enlightenment believed above all else in the power of reason, in the search for truth, in progress, and in the ultimate perfectibility of man. Freedom of inquiry and liberty of expression were deemed essential to the discovery and spread of truth, for only by the endless testing of debate could error be exposed, truth emerge, and men enjoy the opportunities for human progress.

After John Stuart Mill one should perhaps speak only of the ability to progress *toward truth,* and of the value of the process of searching. The compleat liberal posits that he has not reached, and probably can never reach, the ultimate truth. He hopes by constant search—by constant open debate, by trial and error—to do a little better. Meanwhile he supposes that the process of searching has inestimable value because the lessons of the search—the readiness to learn, the striving to understand the minds and hearts and needs of other men, the effort to weigh their interests with his own—exemplify the only foundation upon which men can live and grow together.

It was not chance that America's most eloquent spokesman for freedom of speech, OLIVER WENDELL HOLMES, was also a profound skeptic. Dissenting in ABRAMS V. UNITED STATES (1919), he wrote:

When men have realized that time has upset many fighting faiths, they may come to believe even more than they believe the very foundations of their own conduct that the ultimate good desired is better reached by free trade in ideas—that the best test of truth is the power of the thought to get itself accepted in the competition of the market, and that truth is the only ground upon which their wishes safely can be carried out. That at any rate is the theory of our Constitution.

On the far side of the First Amendment's guarantee of freedom of speech and of the press one finds the political rights "peaceably to assemble, and to petition the Government for a redress of grievances." (See FREEDOM OF PETITION; FREEDOM OF ASSEMBLY AND ASSOCIATION.) The juxtaposition recalls that freedom of speech and of the press have a political as well as a spiritual foundation; and that the First Amendment protects political activity as part of and in addition to the world of the spirit. American thought, especially in Supreme Court opinions, puts the greater emphasis on the political function of free expression. In GARRISON V. LOUISIANA (1964), for example, the Court explained that "speech is more than self-expression; it is the essence of self-government." ALEXANDER MEIKLEJOHN, perhaps the foremost American philosopher of freedom of expression, argued that whereas other constitutional guarantees are restrictions protecting the citizens against abuse of the powers delegated to government, the guarantees of freedom of speech and of the press hold an absolute, preferred position because they are measures adopted by the people as the ultimate rulers in order to retain control over the government, the people's legislative and executive agents. James Madison, the author of the First Amendment, expressed a similar thought in a speech in 1794. "If we advert to the nature of Republican Government, we shall find that the censorial power is in the people over the Government, and not in the Government over the people."

Despite the eloquence of Justice Holmes, most of us reject the notion that the ability of an idea to get itself accepted in free competition is the best test of its truth. Some propositions seem true or false beyond rational debate. Some false and harmful, political and religious doctrines gain wide public acceptance. Adolf Hitler's brutal theory of a "master race" is sufficient example. We tolerate such foolish and sometimes dangerous appeals not because they may prove true but because freedom of speech is indivisible. The liberty cannot be denied to some persons and extended to others. It cannot be denied to some ideas and saved for others. The reason is plain enough: no man, no committee, and surely no government, has the infinite wisdom and disinterestedness accurately and unselfishly to separate what is true from what is debatable, and both from what is false. To license one to impose his truth upon dissenters is to give the same license to all others who have, but fear to lose, power. The judgment that the risks of suppression are greater than the harm done by bad ideas rests upon faith in the ultimate good sense and decency of free people.

Constitutional law has been remarkably faithful to this philosophy in dealing with both religious and political ideas. In the prosecution of the leader of a strange religious cult for obtaining money by false pretenses, as in UNITED STATES V. BALLARD (1963), the truth or falsity of the leader's claims of miraculous religious experiences is legally irrelevant; conviction depends upon proof that the defendant did not believe his own pretenses. Similarly, although distaste for political ideology may have influenced some of the decisions in the 1920s affirming the convictions of anarchists and communists for advocacy of the overthrow of the government by force and violence, the social, political, or religious activists seeking changes that frighten or annoy all "right-minded" people receive wide protection in their resort to the SIT-INS, PICKETING, marches, mass demonstrations, coarse expletives, affronts to personal and public sensibilities, and other unorthodox vehicles that are so often their most effective means of expression. Such methods of expression may prejudice opposing public and private interests because of the time, place, or manner of communication, regardless of the content of the message; therefore, the amendment allows regulation of particular forms of expression, or of expression at a particular time or place, regardless of content, provided that the restriction protects important interests that cannot be secured by less restrictive means. The courts have typically scrutinized such restrictions, however, with an eye zealous to condemn as unconstitutional any statute or ordinance ostensibly designed to protect the public peace and order but phrased in such loose words as either to deter constitutionally protected expression or to invite discrimination by police, public prosecutors, or judges against radical "troublemakers" and other unpopular minorities. Thus, the American Nazis were secured the right to parade in uniform with swastikas in an overwhelmingly Jewish community many of whose residents had fled the Holocaust.

Distrust of official evaluation of the worth of ideas may also lie behind the decisions barring regulation of political debate in the interest of "fairness" or equality of opportunity. In BUCKLEY V. VALEO (1976), holding that the freedom of speech clause bars laws restricting the dollars that may be spent in a political campaign, the Court observed: "The concept that government may restrict the speech of some elements of our society in order to enhance the relative voice of others is wholly foreign to the First Amendment." Similarly, in MIAMI HERALD V. TORNILLO (1974) the Court held a state law granting a political candidate a right of space in which to reply to a newspaper's attacks upon his or her record to be unconstitutional interference with the editorial freedom of the newspaper. Only in the area of BROADCASTING has the Court thus far recognized that realization of the ideal of free competition of ideas may be irreconcilable with total freedom from regulation in an era in which the public's chief sources of ideas and information are ex-

pensive media of mass communication, which are often under monopolistic control. Federal statutes and regulations subject radio and television broadcasters to loosely defined duties to present public issues fairly and to give a degree of access to political candidates and parties.

Although only deliberately false religious or political representations fall wholly outside the First Amendment, the law is more willing to try to separate the worthless from the valuable in the field of literature and the arts. The amendment gives no protection to "obscene" publications. For many years the definition of OBSCENITY was broad enough to cover works containing individual words or short passages that would tend to excite lustful thoughts in a particularly susceptible person. This standard condemned *Lady Chatterley's Lover, An American Tragedy,* and *Black Boy.* From 1930 to 1973 the legal definition of obscenity was gradually narrowed so tightly that many jurists concluded that the First Amendment would protect the most prurient of matter unless it was "utterly without redeeming social value." After 1973 changes in the composition of the Court led to a somewhat less permissive formulation. A work is obscene if a person applying contemporary community standards would find that it appeals to the prurient interest; if it represents or describes ultimate sexual acts, excretory functions, or the genitals in a patently lewd or offensive manner; and if it lacks serious literary, artistic, political, or scientific value. YOUNG V. AMERICAN MINI THEATRES (1976) suggests that explicity sexual books and motion pictures, even when not obscene, may be regulated as to the places and perhaps the time and manner of their distribution in ways that are forbidden for other materials.

These exceptions from the principle that bars any branch of government, including the judiciary, from judging the value of ideas and sensations seem attributable partly to the emphasis that American law puts upon the political values of the First Amendment, partly to the diminishing but still traditional concern of government for public morals, and partly to the actual or supposed links between producers and distributors of commercial pornography and the criminal underworld.

So long as one is dealing with beliefs and expressions separable from conduct harmful to other individuals or the community, the essential unity of the philosophical core of the First Amendment makes it unnecessary to distinguish for legal purposes among religious beliefs, political ideologies, and other equally sincere convictions. In upholding the First Amendment privilege of Jehovah's Witnesses to refuse to join other school children in a daily salute to the United States flag, the Court pointedly refrained from specifying whether the privilege arose under the free exercise clause or the guarantee of freedom of speech: ". . . compelling the flag salute and pledge . . . invades the sphere of intellect and spirit which it is the purpose of the First Amendment to reserve from all official control." (See FLAG SALUTE CASES, 1940, 1943.) Test oaths, like particular beliefs, cannot be required for holding public office or receiving public grants. In upholding the conviction of a Mormon for POLYGAMY in REYNOLDS V. UNITED STATES (1879), despite his plea that the free exercise clause protected him in obeying his religious duty, the Supreme Court sought to erect this distinction between the realm of ideas and the world of material action into a constitutional principle: "Congress was deprived of all legislative power over mere opinion, but was left free to reach actions which were in violation of social duties or subversive of good order."

As the guarantees of the freedoms of speech and press and of free exercise of religion seek to bar hostile governmental intrusion from the realm of the spirit, so do modern interpretations of the establishment clause bar state sponsorship of, or material assistance to, religion. In the beginning religion and established churches were dominant forces in American life. Nearly all men and women were Christians; Protestants were predominant. In South Carolina the Constitution of 1778 declared the "Protestant religion to be the established religion of this State." Church and state were intertwined in Massachusetts. Where there was no official connection, both the laws and practices of government bore evidence of benevolent cooperation with the prevailing creeds. SUNDAY CLOSING LAWS were universal. Oaths were often required of state officials. Legislative sessions began with prayer. The crier in the United States Supreme Court still begins each session by invoking divine blessing. The coinage states, "In God We Trust." Church property was and remains exempt from taxation. As public education spread, prayers and Bible-reading became the first order of each school day.

These traditional links between church and state were challenged after incorporation of the First Amendment into the Fourteenth Amendment, not only by anticlerical secularists but also by religious minorities whose members were set apart by official involvement in religious practices and who were fearful that their isolation would hamper full assimilation into all aspects of American life and might stimulate INVIDIOUS DISCRIMINATION. The Supreme Court was then forced to choose among the competing strains of religious and political philosophy whose adherents had agreed only that the federal government, but not the States, should be barred from "an establishment of religion." The majority's inclination during the years 1945–1980 toward Jefferson's strongly secular, anticlerical view of the wall of separation between church and state led to two important lines of decision.

One line bars both state and federal governments from giving direct financial aid to sectarian primary and secondary schools even though the same or greater aid is given to the public schools maintained by government. The decisions leave somewhat greater latitude not only for aid to parents but also to include religious institutions in making grants for higher education. (See GOVERNMENT AID TO SECTARIAN INSTITUTIONS.)

The second important line of decisions required discontinuance of the widespread and traditional practice of starting each day in the public schools with some form of religious exercise, such as saying an ecumenical prayer or reading from the Bible. The latter decisions provoked such emotional controversy that in the 1980s, more than two decades after the decisions were rendered, fundamentalist groups were actively pressing for legislation abolishing the Supreme Court's JURISDICTION to enforce the establishment clause in cases involving school prayer, thus leaving interpretation of the clause to the vagaries of judges in individual states. (See RELIGION IN PUBLIC SCHOOLS.)

Even though the line between the realm of the spirit and the world of material conduct subject to government regulation is fundamental to the jurisprudence of the First Amendment, the simple line between belief and conduct drawn in the polygamy cases was too inflexible to survive as a complete constitutional formula. Religious duties too often conflict with the commands of civil authority. Conversely, the public has compelling interests in the world of conduct that sometimes cannot be secured without interference with the expression of ideas.

Two cases suggest the line limiting constitutional protection for religious disobedience to the commands of the state. In WISCONSIN V. YODER (1972) the Supreme Court held that the free exercise clause secured Amish parents the privilege of holding fourteen- and fifteen-year-old children out of high school contrary to a state compulsory attendance law but pursuant to their religious conviction that salvation requires simple life in a church community apart from the world and worldly influence. The Court's constitutional, judicial duty—the Court said—required balancing the importance of the interests served by the state law against the importance to believers of adherence to the religious practice in question. Striking such a balance, the Court held in NEGRE V. LARSEN (1971) that a faithful Roman Catholic's belief that the "unjust" nature of the war in Vietnam required him to refuse to participate did not excuse his refusal to be inducted into the armed forces.

When belief is invoked to justify otherwise unlawful conduct, it may become significant that the First Amendment speaks of the free exercise of "religion," but not of other kinds of belief held with equal sincerity. In UNITED STATES V. SEEGER (1965) the Court skirted establishment clause questions by refusing to make any distinction between the teachings of religion and other moral convictions for the purposes of the Selective Service Act. That act exempted from military service CONSCIENTIOUS OBJECTORS opposed to war in any form by reason of their "religious training and belief" and defined such belief as one "in relation to a Supreme Being involving duties superior to those arising from any human relation." A majority held that, despite the references to religion and a belief in a Supreme Being, the exemption extended "to any belief that occupies a place in the life of its possessor parallel to that filled by the orthodox belief in God of one who clearly qualifies for the exemption." In the *Yoder* case, on the other hand, the opinion of the Court by Chief Justice WARREN E. BURGER, calling upon the example of Henry D. Thoreau, stated that a "philosophical and personal" belief "does not rise to the demands of the Religion Clauses." Perhaps this declaration of orthodoxy puts an end to the question, but in an age of subjectivism it is likely to press for fuller debate and deliberation.

Where religious objectors seek exemption from laws of general application, both federal and state governments must walk a narrow line. On the one hand, the free execise clause may require exception. On the other hand, excepting religious groups from laws of general application may be an unconstitutional "establishment of religion." Here again the decisions call for ad hoc balancing of the individual and public interests affected by the particular legislative act.

The requirement of self-preservation exerts the strongest pressures upon government to violate the realm of the spirit by suppressing the publication of ideas and information. Here, as in other areas, judicial elaboration of the First Amendment has been increasingly favorable to freedom of expression.

The expansion of the freedom by interpretation began within a decade from ratification. WILLIAM BLACKSTONE had taught that the freedoms of speech and press were freedoms from PRIOR RESTRAINTS, such as licensing, and did not bar subsequent liability or punishment for unlawful words, including seditious libels. Dispute arose when Congress enacted a Sedition Act and the Federalist party then in office prosecuted the editors of journals supporting their political opponents, the Jeffersonian Republicans, for publishing false, scandalous, and malicious writings exciting the hatred of the people. (See ALIEN AND SEDITION ACTS.) Thomas Jefferson and James Madison led the attack upon the constitutionality of the Sedition Act by drafting the VIRGINIA AND KENTUCKY RESOLUTIONS declaring that the act violated the First Amendment. The lower federal courts followed the orthodox teaching of Blackstone, upheld the act, and convicted the Republican editors. Jefferson pardoned them after his election to the presidency. Still later, Congress appropriated funds to repay their fines. Events thus gave the speech and press clauses an interpretation extending the guarantees beyond mere prohibition of previous restraints. The Supreme Court subsequently ratified the teaching of history.

The modern law defining freedom of expression began to develop shortly after World War I when pacifists and socialists who made speeches and published pamphlets urging refusal to submit to conscription for the armed forces were prosecuted for such offenses as willfully obstructing the recruiting or enlistment service of the United States. In affirming the conviction in SCHENCK V. UNITED STATES (1919), Justice Holmes coined the famous CLEAR AND PRESENT DANGER test: "The question in every case is whether the words used are of such a nature as to create a clear and present danger that they will bring about the substantive evils that Congress has a right to prevent." When Justice Holmes wrote these words, they gave little protection to propaganda held subversive by dominant opinion. Speaking or circulating a paper, the Justice held, is not protected by the First Amendment if the "tendency" of the words and the intent with which they are uttered are to produce an unlawful act. Later, after Justice Holmes's sensitivity to the dangers of prosecution for words alone had been increased by the prosecution of tiny groups of anarchists and communists for holding meetings and distributing political pamphlets in time of peace, criticizing the government, and preaching its overthrow by force and violence, he and Justice LOUIS D. BRANDEIS in a series of dissenting opinions tightened their definition of "clear and present danger" and laid the emotional and philosophical foundation for the next generation's expansion of the First Amendment guarantees. Justice Brandeis's eloquent opinion in WHITNEY V. CALIFORNIA (1927) is illustrative:

Those who won our independence by revolution were not cowards. They did not fear political liberty. To courageous, self-reliant men, with confidence in the power of free and fearless reasoning applied through the processes of popular government, no danger flowing from speech can be deemed clear and present, unless the incidence of the evil apprehended is so imminent that it may befall before there is opportunity for full discussion. If there be time to expose through discussion the falsehood and fallacies, to avert the evil by the processes of education, the remedy to be applied is more speech, not enforced silence. Only an emergency can justify repression. Such must be the rule if authority is to be reconciled with freedom. Such, in my opinion, is the command of the Constitution. It is, therefore, always open to Americans to challenge a law abridging free speech and assembly by showing that there was no emergency justifying it.

Moreover, even imminent danger cannot justify resort to prohibition of these functions essential to effective democracy, unless the evil apprehended is relatively serious. . . . There must be the probability of serious injury to the state. Among freemen, the deterrents ordinarily to be applied to prevent crime are education and punishment for violations of the law, not abridgement of the rights of free speech and assembly.

In the 1920s a majority of the Justices consistently rejected the views expressed by Justices Holmes and Brandeis. GITLOW v. NEW YORK (1925) held that (1) a state, despite the First Amendment, may punish utterances inimical to the public welfare; (2) a legislative finding that a class of utterances is inimical to the public welfare will be accepted by the Court unless the finding is arbitrary or capricious; (3) the Court could not set aside as arbitrary or capricious a legislative finding that teaching the overthrow of the government by force or violence involves danger to the peace and security of the State because the spark of the utterance "may kindle a fire that, smoldering for a time, may burst into a sweeping and destructive conflagration"; and (4) the Court would not consider the kind or degree of evil threatened by a particular utterance if it fell within a class of utterances found by the legislature to be dangerous to the state.

Ironically, in the very years in which the Court was deferential to legislative restrictions upon radical political expression, the Court was going behind legislative judgment to invalidate minimum wage laws, the regulation of prices and other restrictions upon FREEDOM OF CONTRACT. Beginning in 1937, however, a philosophy of judicial self-restraint became dominant among the Justices. "We have returned to the original proposition that courts do not substitute their social and economic beliefs for the judgment of legislative bodies, who are elected to pass laws," the Court

declared in FERGUSON v. SKRUPA (1963). (See JUDICIAL ACTIVISM AND JUDICIAL RESTRAINT.)

Such sweeping denigration of JUDICIAL REVIEW put civil libertarians in a dilemma. On the one hand, the need for consistency of institutional theory cautioned against activist judicial ventures even under the First Amendment. On the other hand, self-restraint would leave much CIVIL LIBERTY at the mercy of executive or legislative oppression. The only logical escape was to elevate civil liberties to a "preferred position" justifying standards of judicial review stricter than those used in judging economic regulations. The dissenting opinions by Justices Holmes and Brandeis seemed to point the way. Three rationales were offered:

(i) In a famous footnote in UNITED STATES v. CAROLENE PRODUCTS COMPANY (1938), Justice HARLAN FISKE STONE suggested that legislation restricting the dissemination of information or interfering with political activity "may be subject to more exacting judicial scrutiny . . . than most other types of legislation" where the legislation "restricts those political processes which can ordinarily be expected to bring about the repeal of undesirable legislation." The rationale fails to justify STRICT SCRUTINY in cases involving religious liberty, freedom of expression in literature, entertainment, and the arts, and other nonpolitical, personal liberties.

(ii) "Personal liberties" deserve more stringent protection than "property rights." The rationale does not explain why holding property is not a preferred "personal" liberty.

(iii) Stricter review is appropriate in applying the First Amendment, and the First when incorporated into the Fourteenth, because the guarantees of the First Amendment are more specific than the general constitutional prohibitions against deprivation of life, liberty, or property without due process of law. The difference in specificity is considerable, but its relevance is less obvious. Justice HUGO L. BLACK stood almost alone in the supposition that the language of the First Amendment could be read literally. (See ABSOLUTISM.) Perhaps the most that can be said is that the Bill of Rights marks particular spheres of human activity for which the Framers deemed it essential to provide judicially enforced protection against legislative and executive oppression. During the debate in Congress, James Madison observed: "If they [the Amendments] are incorporated into the Constitution, independent tribunals of justice will consider themselves in a peculiar manner the guardian of those rights; they will be an impenetrable bulwark against every assumption of power in the Legislative or Executive. . . ."

At bottom all the rationales assert that the ultimate protection for minorities, for spiritual liberty, and for freedom of expression, political activity, and other personal liberties comes rightfully from the judiciary. In this realm the political process, filled with arbitrary compromises and responsive, as in some degree it must be, to short-run pressures, is deemed inadequate to enforce the long-range enduring values that often bespeak a people's aspirations instead of merely reflecting their practices.

Propelled by this judicial philosophy, the Court greatly expanded the First Amendment guarantees of freedom of expression. The Court avowedly adopted the strict Holmes-Brandeis "clear and present danger" test for judging whether prosecution for a subversive utterance is justified by its proximity to activities the government has a right to prevent. The amendment bars restrictions upon the publication of information or ideas relating to public affairs because of harm which the government asserts will result from the impact of the message unless the government shows pressing necessity to avoid an immediate public disaster. The case of the Pentagon Papers (1971) illustrates the principle. (See NEW YORK TIMES V. UNITED STATES.) A consultant to the Department of Defense, cleared for access to classified information, gave copies of highly secret papers describing military operations and decision making to newspapers for publication. The Department of Justice upon instructions from the President asked the courts to enjoin publication, making strong representations that the risks of injury to national interests included "the death of the soldiers, the destruction of alliances, the greatly increased difficulty of negotiation with our enemies, the inability of our diplomats to negotiate . . . and the prolongation of the war." All the weight of these executive representations was insufficient to induce the Court to bar disclosure.

After 1940 the PREFERRED FREEDOMS theory coupled with the incorporation of the First Amendment into the Fourteenth led to Supreme Court review and invalidation or modification of many familiar state statutes and well-established COMMON LAW doctrines restricting or penalizing sundry forms of expression: libel and slander, contempt of court, obscenity, BREACH OF THE PEACE, and laws limiting access to the streets, parks, or other public places for the purposes of expression. A short reference to the law of contempt will illustrate the trend.

The interest in the impartial disposition of judicial business solely upon the evidence and arguments presented in court often conflicts with the interest in free discussion of public affairs. Newspaper editorials and like public pressures upon a judge may improperly influence or seem to influence the disposition of a pending judicial proceeding. In English and early American law such publications were enjoinable and punishable as contempt of court. Today the First Amendment is held to protect such expression. Similarly, the English law and some American decisions treated the pretrial publication of EVIDENCE as contempt of court where, as in a notorious criminal case, the publicity might reach actual or prospective jurors and serve to make it difficult to assure the accused a FAIR TRIAL and a jury verdict based solely upon the evidence presented in the court room. The Supreme Court has now set its face firmly against GAG ORDERS forbidding newspapers to print or broadcast or publicize confessions or other damaging evidence before their admissibility has been determined and they have been received in court.

The heavy emphasis that constitutional law puts upon the role of the First Amendment in the operation of representative government has led some commentators to ascribe special significance to the amendment's particular mention of "the freedom of the press" in addition to the more general guarantee of "the freedom of speech." In a crowded society, newspapers, radio, and television not only are the most effective vehicles for disseminating ideas and information but also have by far the best, if not the only, adequate resources for gathering information concerning the conduct of public affairs by the vast and omnipresent agencies of government. Starting from this premise, proponents of a "structural view" of the First Amendment argue that the special functions of the "fourth estate" entitle its members to special protection. Some of the claims to exemption from laws of general applicability have been patently excessive, such as the claims to exemption from antitrust laws, labor relations laws, and wage and hour regulation. With much greater force but scarcely greater success, the media have claimed that the First Amendment protects reporters in refusal to disclose their sources or give unpublished information to a court or GRAND JURY in compliance with the general testimonial obligation of all citizens. (See REPORTER'S PRIVILEGE.) On the other hand, the near-immunity from liability for libels upon public figures which the Court has granted to the press under the First Amendment has not yet been extended by that Court to other writers and publishers.

The words of the First Amendment move from religion to speech and press and then to the purely political rights of free assembly and petition for redress of grievances. Denials of the rights of assembly and petition have been infrequent. The express mention of a "right of the people peaceably to assemble" is also taken, however, to symbolize the much broader freedom of association that the amendment is held to secure.

The freedom of association thus far held to be protected by the First Amendment, while broad, is narrower than the freedom of individuals to associate themselves for all purposes in which they may be interested, the right debated by Thomas Hobbes and Jean-Jacques Rousseau, on one side, and, on the other side, by JOHN LOCKE. The enactment of labor relations acts securing employees the right to form, join, and assist labor unions made it unnecessary for workers to appeal to a constitutional right of freedom of association. Only the antitrust laws barring unreasonable restraints on competition impose substantial restrictions upon business combinations. In consequence, the decisional law treats association as a necessary and therefore protected incident of other First Amendment liberties: speech, political action, and religious purposes. Associations formed to provide legal services in litigation have been treated as "political" not only in the plausible instances of suits to establish civil liberties and CIVIL RIGHTS but also in the incongruous instances of actions for damages for personal injuries.

Legislative efforts to outlaw associations formed for religious or political purposes have been infrequent, except in the case of the Communist party. A decision in 1961 sustained the power of Congress to require the party to register and disclose its membership as a foreign-dominated organization dedicated to subversion of the government, but the sanctions directed at members, for example, denial of passports and employment in defense facilities, were held unconstitutional. Associations and their members have had more occasion to complain of coerced disclosure under disclosure laws and in LEGISLATIVE INVESTIGATIONS. Prima facie the First Amendment protects privacy of association. Governmentally compelled disclosure must be justified by a showing of important public purpose. Where the unpopularity of the association makes it likely that disclosure will result in reprisals, an even stronger justification may be required. Similarly, a state must justify by a strong public purpose any interference with the conduct of a religious organization's or political party's internal affairs.

Any pressure for substantial new growth in First Amendment interpretation will probably come in three areas. First, the amendment was intended and has nearly always been construed as a prohibition against active government interference. Today government has a near-monopoly upon much information essential to informed self-government. Although FREEDOM OF INFORMATION ACTS may at least partially satisfy the need, there is likely to be pressure to read into the First Amendment's explicit verbal barrier to abridgment affirmative governmental duties to provide access to official proceedings and even to supply otherwise inaccessible information in the government's possession.

Second, in the crowded modern world broadcasters, newspapers, and other media of mass communication dominate the dissemination of information and formation of public opinion. New technologies make prediction hazardous, but the concentration of control over the most influential media appears to be increasing. In this context the old assumption, that the widest dissemination of information and freest competition of ideas can be secured by forcing government to keep hands off, is open to doubt. Such questions as whether the First Amendment permits government regulation to secure fair access to the mass media and whether the amendment itself secures a right of access to media licensed by government may well multiply and intensify.

Third, the electoral influence of political advertising through the mass media, coupled with its high cost, gives great political power to the individuals and organizations that can raise and spend the largest sums of money in political campaigns. Even though decisions already rendered tend to accord political expenditures the same protection as speech, important future litigation over legislative power to limit the use and power of money in elections seems assured. (See CAMPAIGN FINANCING.)

The First Amendment secures the people of the United States greater freedom against governmental interference in the realms of the spirit, intellect, and political activity than exists in any other country. The future may bring shifts of boundary lines and emphasis. A threat to national survival could revive earlier restrictions. Generally speaking, however, the modern First Amendment appears to meet the nation's needs.

ARCHIBALD COX

Bibliography

ABERNATHY, GLENN 1961 *The Right of Assembly and Association.* Columbia: University of South Carolina Press.

CHAFEE, ZECHARIAH, JR. 1948 *Free Speech in the United States.* Cambridge, Mass.: Harvard University Press.

Cox, Archibald 1981 *Freedom of Speech in the Burger Court.* Cambridge, Mass.: Harvard University Press.

Emerson, Thomas I. 1970 *The System of Freedom of Expression.* New York: Random House.

Howe, Mark DeWolfe 1965 *The Garden and the Wilderness.* Chicago: University of Chicago Press.

Konvitz, Milton 1957 *Fundamental Liberties of a Free People: Religion, Speech, Press, Assembly.* Ithaca, N.Y.: Cornell University Press.

Levy, Leonard W. 1963 *Freedom of Speech and Press in Early American History: Legacy of Suppression.* New York: Harper & Row.

——— 1972 "No Establishment of Religion: The Original Understanding." Pages 169–224 in *Judgments: Essays in American Constitutional History.* Chicago: Quadrangle.

Meiklejohn, Alexander 1960 *Political Freedom: The Constitutional Powers of the People.* New York: Harper & Bros.

Pfeffer, Leo 1967 *Church, State, and Freedom.* Rev. ed. Boston: Beacon Press.

Stokes, Anson Phelps 1950 *Church and State in the United States.* 3 Vols. New York: Harper & Bros.

——— 1964 *Church and State in the United States.* Rev. ed., with Leo Pfeffer. New York: Harper & Row.

FIRST CONTINENTAL CONGRESS, DECLARATIONS AND RESOLVES OF

(October 1, 1774)

The Coercive or Intolerable Acts, passed by Parliament in 1774, threatened colonial self-government. The Boston Port Act sought to starve Boston into paying a tax on tea and making reparations for the "Boston Tea Party." The Massachusetts Government Act altered the charter of the colony: it stripped the lower house of power to choose the upper house, which became the creature of the royal governor; it took from the town meetings the power to choose jurors and vested that power in sheriffs appointed by the governor; and it banned all town meetings not approved by the governor. The Administration of Justice Act allowed the governor to transfer to England trials involving the enforcement of revenue acts. The Quartering Act and the Quebec Act also contained provisions deemed reprehensible by many colonists.

To decide on measures for the recovery of American liberties, delegates from all colonies but Georgia assembled in Philadelphia. After defeating the plan of union proposed by Joseph Galloway, the congress adopted a statement that defined the American constitutional position on the controversies with Parliament. Congress grasped a rudimentary principle of FEDERALISM, asserted various American rights, and condemned as "unconstitutional" the Coercive Acts and all the acts by which Parliament sought to raise a revenue in America. Rejecting Parliament's claim of unlimited power to legislate for America, the congress repudiated TAXATION WITHOUT REPRESENTATION and any parliamentary governance over "internal polity" but recognized Parliament's power to regulate "external commerce." Congress also grounded American rights, for the first time, in "the immutable laws of nature" as well as the British CONSTITUTION and COLONIAL CHARTERS. Among the rights claimed were free government by one's own representatives, TRIAL BY A JURY of the VICINAGE according to the COMMON LAW, FREEDOM OF ASSEMBLY and petition (holding town meetings), freedom from standing armies in time of peace, and, generally, the rights to life, liberty, property, and all the liberties of English subjects. The document was a forerunner of the first state bills of rights. (See PENNSYLVANIA CONSTITUTION and VIRGINIA CONSTITUTION.)

LEONARD W. LEVY

Bibliography

Burnett, Edmund Cody 1941 *The First Continental Congress.* Pages 33–59. New York: Macmillan.

FIRST NATIONAL BANK OF BOSTON v. BELLOTTI
435 U.S. 765 (1978)

Although the Supreme Court had extended FIRST AMENDMENT protections to newspapers that were organized as CORPORATIONS, this was the first case to hold explicitly that the FREEDOM OF SPEECH was not a "purely personal" right such as the RIGHT AGAINST SELF-INCRIMINATION and so might be claimed by corporations. In this case and in VIRGINIA STATE BOARD OF PHARMACY v. VIRGINIA CITY CONSUMER COUNCIL (1976), the Justices adopted the position that where there is a willing speaker, he may be protected by the First Amendment not so much because of his own speech interest but because of the societal interest in maximizing the stock of information upon which the public may draw. Thus a banking corporation was held to have speech rights because limiting its speech would limit the electorate's access to vital information.

After defeat of a REFERENDUM authorizing a personal income tax, which was attributed by some to corporation-funded advertising, Massachusetts adopted a statute forbidding a corporation to spend money for the purpose of influencing the vote on referenda not directly affecting the corporation, including referenda on individual income taxation. In the face of this obvious attempt of protax legislators to muzzle their opponents, Justice LEWIS F. POWELL for the Court had little trouble concluding under a BALANCING TEST that the asserted state interests in preserving the integrity of the electoral process were not compelling and that the statute was not narrowly drawn to protect the interests of stockholders.

The dissent by Justices BYRON R. WHITE, WILLIAM J. BRENNAN, and THURGOOD MARSHALL sounds the theme of a legitimate state interest in limiting the influence of money on elections raised in BUCKLEY V. VALEO (1976). Justice WILLIAM H. REHNQUIST dissented alone on STATES' RIGHTS grounds.

With the recognition of corporate speech rights and the recognition of some First Amendment protection for COMMERCIAL SPEECH, the Court set the stage for a whole new area of freedom-of-speech jurisprudence, particularly in the light of the high levels of corporate institutional and issue advertising engendered by environmental, energy, and deregulation policies. Among the difficult problems are the rights of stockholders who oppose advertised corporate stances and the extent to which laws against false and misleading advertising constitutionally can be applied to advertisements that do more than offer a product for sale.

MARTIN SHAPIRO

FISHER, SYDNEY GEORGE

See: Commentators on the Constitution

FISKE, JOHN
(1842–1901)

A conservative Yankee educated at Harvard, where he later taught, John Fiske was a man of letters who published about a book a year, as many on science, philosophy, and religion as on history. He was essentially a great popularizer. His books were captivatingly written, bold in interpretation, and widely read. His most influential work as a historian was *The Critical Period in American History, 1783–1789* (1888), which vividly depicted the weaknesses and deficiencies of the United States under the ARTICLES OF CONFEDERATION. For Fiske the Constitution was "a Fifth Symphony of statesmanship" that saved the nation from Balkanizing into petty states.

LEONARD W. LEVY

FITZPATRICK v. BITZER
427 U.S. 445 (1976)

This case concerned Congress's power to modify states' ELEVENTH AMENDMENT immunity from suit in federal court. In the 1972 amendments to Title VII of the CIVIL RIGHTS ACT OF 1964, Congress extended Title VII to forbid employment discrimination by state employers. In *Fitzpatrick,* in an opinion by Justice WILLIAM H. REHNQUIST, the Court held that Congress, in exercising its FOURTEENTH AMENDMENT powers, and despite the Eleventh Amendment, could subject states to suit in federal courts for discriminatory behavior. *Fitzpatrick* was an important counterpoint to *Employees v. Department of Public Health and Welfare* (1973) and EDELMAN V. JORDAN (1974), cases that had held that other federal statutes were not meant to abrogate the states' Eleventh Amendment immunity.

THEODORE EISENBERG

FITZSIMONS, THOMAS
(1741–1811)

An Irish-born Roman Catholic and a successful merchant, Thomas FitzSimons signed the Constitution as a Pennsylvania delegate to the CONSTITUTIONAL CONVENTION OF 1787. He spoke infrequently and always in favor of a strong national government to foster and regulate commerce. He served in the first three Congresses under the Constitution, where he supported ALEXANDER HAMILTON's policies.

DENNIS J. MAHONEY

FIVE KNIGHTS' CASE (DARNEL'S CASE)

See: Petition of Right

FLAG DESECRATION

The American flag, as a unique symbol embodying national pride and patriotism, evidences the unity and diversity which the country represents, and the varying ideals and hopes of its people. By the same token, the flag has frequently been used by those who wish to communicate opposition to—or even ridicule of—government policies.

Congress has enacted statutes that prescribe how

the flag may be displayed and disposed of, and how and for what purposes it may be used. Many state laws prohibit flag "desecration" (casting "contempt" on a flag by "mutilating, defacing, defiling, burning or trampling upon" it) and "improper use" of flags (placing on a flag "any word, figure, mark, picture, design, drawing or advertisement").

In *Halter v. Nebraska* (1907) the Supreme Court upheld a state statute prohibiting flag desecration and use of the flag for advertising purposes. But that decision was rendered twenty years before the Court applied the FIRST AMENDMENT to the States, and it was not dispositive when protesters later challenged the constitutionality of flag desecration statutes.

In *Smith v. Gorguen* (1973), the Court reversed a conviction for wearing an American flag on the seat of the pants, ruling that the Massachusetts flag desecration statute was void for VAGUENESS. In *Spence v. Washington* (1974) the Court invalidated a Washington statute prohibiting the affixing of a symbol to the flag, holding that the display of a flag with a peace symbol superimposed on it was protected free expression. The *Spence* decision was consistent with other cases in which the Supreme Court recognized SYMBOLIC SPEECH as a form of activity protected by the First Amendment. On the other hand, the Court has upheld statutes forbidding flag burning, concluding as in *Sutherland v. Illinois* (1976) that they rested on a "valid governmental interest unrelated to expression—that is, the prevention of breaches of the peace and the preservation of public order."

NORMAN DORSEN

FLAGG BROS., INC. v. BROOKS
436 U.S. 149 (1978)

Brooks is one of a series of BURGER COURT decisions reestablishing the STATE ACTION limitation as a barrier to judicial enforcement of FOURTEENTH AMENDMENT rights against private persons acting under state authority. The Uniform Commercial Code, as adopted in New York, authorizes a warehouse operator to sell goods stored in order to pay overdue warehousing charges. This notion of a "warehouseman's lien" is an ancient COMMON LAW remedy. When Brooks and her family were evicted from their apartment, a city marshal had her goods stored with Flagg Bros. Ten weeks later, Flagg Bros. wrote to Brooks, demanding payment of storage charges and threatening to sell her goods to satisfy the charges accrued. Brooks

brought a CLASS ACTION against Flagg Bros. for damages and injunctive relief under federal CIVIL RIGHTS laws claiming DUE PROCESS and EQUAL PROTECTION violations. (See INJUNCTION.) The Supreme Court held, 5–3, that the proposed sale did not amount to state action; thus there had been no constitutional violation.

Justice WILLIAM H. REHNQUIST wrote for the majority, as he had done in other recent cases strengthening the state action limitation. The proposed sale did not fit the "public function" DOCTRINE of state action (here renamed the "sovereign function" doctrine), because the function of dispute resolution historically had not been the exclusive province of the states. Nor had the state authorized or encouraged the use of this creditor's remedy in such a way as to take responsibility for its exercise. The Uniform Commercial Code "permits but does not compel" a warehouse operator's threat to sell goods stored and merely announces the circumstances in which the state will not intervene with that private sale.

Justice WILLIAM J. BRENNAN did not participate in the decision. Justice JOHN PAUL STEVENS dissented, joined by Justices BYRON R. WHITE and THURGOOD MARSHALL. The distinction between state permission and state compulsion was untenable, Stevens argued; on the Court's theory, for example, the state could "announce" its intention not to intervene when a finance company entered a private home to repossess property, with no finding of state action. He also argued persuasively that the "exclusive sovereign function" notion had no basis in the Court's prior decisions. What the state had done here was to "order binding, nonconsensual resolution of a conflict between debtor and creditor"—which is "exactly the sort of power with which the Due Process Clause is concerned."

KENNETH L. KARST

FLAG SALUTE CASES
MINERSVILLE SCHOOL DISTRICT v. GOBITIS
310 U.S. 586 (1940)
WEST VIRGINIA BOARD OF EDUCATION v. BARNETT
319 U.S. 624 (1943)

The Supreme Court's encounter in the early 1940s with the issue of compulsory flag salute exercises in the public schools was one of the turning points in American constitutional history. It presaged the civil libertarian activism that culminated in the WARREN COURT of the 1960s.

The flag salute ceremony developed in the latter half of the nineteenth century. In the original ceremony the participants faced the flag and pledged "allegiance to my flag and the republic for which it stands, one nation indivisible, with liberty and justice for all." While repeating the words "to my flag" the right hand was extended palm up toward the flag. Over the years the ceremony evolved slightly, with minor changes of wording and with the extended arm salute dropped in 1942 because of its similarity to the Nazi salute. At this point in its evolution, however, the salute had official standing; Congress had prescribed the form of words and substituted the right hand over the heart for the extended arm.

Beginning in 1898 with New York, some states began requiring the ceremony as part of the opening exercise of the school day. The early state flag salute laws did not make the ceremony compulsory for individual pupils, but many local school boards insisted on participation. Many patriotic and fraternal organizations backed the flag salute; opposition came from civil libertarians and some small religious groups. The principal opponents of the compulsory school flag salute were the Jehovah's Witnesses, a tightly knit evangelical sect whose religious beliefs commanded them not to salute the flag as a "graven image."

The Witnesses were blessed with legal talent. "Judge" Joseph Franklin Rutherford, who had become head of the sect, brought in Hayden Covington, who, as chief counsel for the Witnesses in the *Gobitis* litigation and in many other cases influenced the development of First Amendment doctrine.

The first flag salute case to reach the Supreme Court came out of Minersville, a small community in northwest Pennsylvania. Because of Rutherford's bitter opposition to required flag salute exercises, Lillian and William Gobitis stopped participating in the ceremony in their school and were expelled.

The argument for the Gobitis children was that requiring them to salute the flag, an act repugnant to them on religious grounds, denied that free exercise of religion protected against state action by the DUE PROCESS clause of the FOURTEENTH AMENDMENT. Arguments for the Minersville School Board relied on REYNOLDS V. UNITED STATES (1878), JACOBSON V. MASSACHUSETTS (1905), and the doctrine that a religious objection did not relieve an individual from the responsibility of complying with an otherwise valid secular regulation. The Gobitis children won in the lower federal courts, but the Supreme Court granted CERTIORARI.

The Court in the spring of 1940 had a very different cast from that which had survived FRANKLIN D. ROOSEVELT's effort to "pack" it three years before. Of the hard-core, pre-1937 conservatives only Justice JAMES C. MCREYNOLDS remained. Chief Justice CHARLES EVANS HUGHES and Justices HARLAN F. STONE and OWEN J. ROBERTS also remained. With them, however, were five Roosevelt appointees: FELIX FRANKFURTER, HUGO L. BLACK, WILLIAM O. DOUGLAS, STANLEY F. REED, and FRANK MURPHY. On three previous occasions the Court had sustained compulsory flag salutes against religious objection in PER CURIAM opinions. Whether because of the extraordinary persistence of the Jehovah's Witnesses or because of the nonconformance of the lower federal courts in this case, the Justices now gave the matter full dress consideration.

Speaking for the majority Justice Frankfurter concluded that "conscientious scruples have not, in the course of the long struggle for religious toleration, relieved the individual from obedience to a general law not aimed at the persecution or a restriction of religious beliefs."

To Justice Stone, dissenting, the crucial issue was that the Gobitis children were forced to bear false witness to their religion. The flag salute compelled the expression of a belief, and "where that expression violate[d] religious convictions," the free exercise clause provided protection.

The reaction to the decision in the law reviews was negative. In the popular press the reaction was mixed but criticism predominated. Most important, the decision seems to have produced a wave of persecution of Jehovah's Witnesses which swept through the country. *Gobitis* emboldened some school authorities. The State Board of Education of West Virginia in January 1942 made the salute to the flag mandatory in the classrooms of that state.

Meanwhile, new decisions of the Supreme Court, notably the 5–4 division of the Justices in *Jones v. Opelika*, raised the hopes of opponents of the mandatory flag salute. Hayden Covington sought an INJUNCTION barring enforcement of West Virginia's new rule against Walter Barnett and other Jehovah's Witness plaintiffs. After a three-judge District Court issued an injunction, the State Board of Education appealed to the Supreme Court.

The case was argued on March 11, 1943, and the decision came down on June 14. Justice ROBERT H. JACKSON, who had joined the Court after *Gobitis*, wrote for a 6–3 majority, overruling the prior decision. Chief Justice Stone was with Jackson, as were Justices Douglas, Black, and Murphy, who had changed their minds. Justice Frankfurter, the author of *Gobitis*, wrote a long and impassioned dissent.

For Justice Jackson and the majority the crucial point was that West Virginia's action, while not intended either to impose or to anathematize a particular religious belief, did involve a required affirmation of belief: "If there is any fixed star in our constitutional constellation, it is that no official, high or petty, can prescribe what shall be orthodox in politics, nationalism, religion, or other matters of opinion or force citizens to confess by word or act their faith therein." West Virginia was pursuing the legitimate end of enhancing patriotism, but had not borne the heavy burden of justifying its use of coercive power.

Justice Frankfurter began his dissent by noting that were the matter one of personal choice he would oppose compulsory flag salutes. But it was not for the Court to decide what was and was not an effective means of inculcating patriotism. West Virginia had neither prohibited nor imposed any religious belief. For Frankfurter this fact was controlling, and he reminded his brethren that a liberal spirit cannot be "enforced by judicial invalidation of illiberal legislation."

Barnett was a landmark decision in the strict sense of that overworked word. By 1943 the Roosevelt Court had largely completed its task of dismantling the edifice of SUBSTANTIVE DUE PROCESS erected by its predecessors to protect economic liberty. Now the Court set out on the path to a new form of JUDICIAL ACTIVISM in the service of individual rights. *Barnett* was the first long step on that path.

Barnett had doctrinal significance both for FREEDOM OF SPEECH and for RELIGIOUS LIBERTY. Jackson's opinion suggested that there were significant limitations on the kinds of patriotic affirmations that government might require, and the decision also moved away from the "secular regulation" rule that had dominated free exercise doctrine.

Barnett also had a significant effect on the Supreme Court. Justice Frankfurter was deeply offended by the majority's treatment of his *Gobitis* opinion and even more alarmed at what he regarded as a misuse of judicial power. The split between the activist disposition of Justices Black and Douglas and the judicial self-restraint championed by Frankfurter date from *Barnett*.

RICHARD E. MORGAN

Bibliography

MANWARING, DAVID R. 1962 *Render unto Caesar: The Flag Salute Controversy.* Chicago: University of Chicago Press.

FLAST v. COHEN
392 U.S. 83 (1968)

A WARREN COURT landmark regarding the JUDICIAL POWER OF THE UNITED STATES, *Flast* upheld taxpayer STANDING to complain that disbursements of federal funds to religious schools violate the FIRST AMENDMENT prohibition of an ESTABLISHMENT OF RELIGION. The decision carved an exception from, but did not overturn, the rule of FROTHINGHAM V. MELLON (1923) that federal taxpayers lack a sufficiently individual or direct interest in spending programs to be allowed to attack them in federal court. To Justice JOHN MARSHALL HARLAN's dissenting chagrin, the Court so ruled knowing that Congress, cognizant of *Frothingham*, had decided against granting taxpayers a right to JUDICIAL REVIEW of federal support for religious education.

The Court was unanimous on one fundamental point: the taxpayers in *Flast* presented an Article III "case." (See CASES AND CONTROVERSIES.) For the majority, Chief Justice EARL WARREN reaffirmed the traditional Article III requirement of a "personal stake in the outcome of the controversy," but deemed that requirement satisfied whenever a taxpayer claims that Congress exercised its TAXING AND SPENDING POWER in derogation of specific constitutional limits on that power. The Court found the establishment clause a specific limit, because, historically, the clause was designed to block taxation to support religion.

Dissenting, Justice Harlan could not agree that taxpayers challenging spending, rather than their tax liability, had a personal stake. They had no financial stake, because victory would only change how the government's general revenues are spent—not their tax bill. Nor was the Court's exception tailored to the requirement of a personal stake. A taxpayer's interests did not vary with the power Congress exercised in appropriating funds or with the constitutional provision ("specific" or not) invoked to oppose the expenditures. For Harlan, the taxpayer's interest in government spending was not personal but public—a citizen's concern that official behavior be constitutional. Nonetheless, he thought the "public action" would satisfy Article III, apparently because the parties were sufficiently adversary. But because "public actions" would press judicial authority vis-à-vis the representative branches to the limit, he concluded the Court should not entertain them without congressional authorization.

The bearing of SEPARATION OF POWERS on taxpayer standing was the pivotal dividing point in *Flast*.

Justice WILLIAM O. DOUGLAS, too, thought *Flast* a public action, the attempt to distinguish *Frothingham* a failure, and the requirements of Article III met. But he found *Frothingham* deficient, not *Flast*, for he perceived the judicial role as enforcement of basic rights against majoritarian control without awaiting congressional authorization—even in "public actions." Chief Justice Warren's view fell between the Harlan and Douglas poles by disavowing the connection between standing and the separation of powers. JUSTICIABILITY requires that a suit be appropriate in form for judicial resolution and implicates separation of powers, said Warren, but standing, with its focus on the party suing, not the issues raised, looks only to form.

Under the BURGER COURT, separation of powers considerations have resurfaced in TAXPAYER SUITS, stunting the potential growth of *Flast* into the mature "public action." Typical of the Burger Court approach was VALLEY FORGE CHRISTIAN COLLEGE v. AMERICANS UNITED FOR SEPARATION OF CHURCH AND STATE (1982). The *Flast* landmark has become a historical marker.

JONATHAN D. VARAT

FLETCHER v. PECK
6 Cranch 87 (1810)

Fletcher was the Court's point of departure for converting the CONTRACT CLAUSE into the chief link between the Constitution and capitalism. The case arose from the Yazoo land scandal, the greatest corrupt real estate deal in American history. Georgia claimed the territory within her latitude lines westward to the Mississippi, and in 1795 the state legislature passed a bill selling about two-thirds of that so-called Yazoo territory, some 35,000,000 acres of remote wilderness comprising a good part of the present states of Alabama and Mississippi. Four land companies, having bribed every voting member of the state legislature but one, bought the Yazoo territory at a penny and a half an acre. Speculation in land values was a leading form of capitalist enterprise at that time, provoking an English visitor to characterize the United States as "the land of speculation." Respectable citizens engaged in the practice; the piratical companies that bought the Yazoo included two United States senators, some governors and congressmen, and Justice JAMES WILSON. In a year, one of the four companies sold its Yazoo holdings at a 650 percent profit, and the buyers, in the frenzy of speculation that followed, re-

sold at a profit. But in 1796 the voters of Georgia elected a "clean" legislature which voided the bill of sale and publicly burned all records of it but did not return the $500,000 purchase price. In 1802 Georgia sold its western territories to the United States for $1,250,000. In 1814 a Yazooist lobby finally succeeded in persuading Congress to pass a $5,000,000 compensation bill, indemnifying holders of Yazoo land titles.

Fletcher v. Peck was part of a twenty-year process of legal and political shenanigans related to the Yazoo land scandal. Georgia's nullification of the original sale imperiled the entire chain of Yazoo land speculations, but the ELEVENTH AMENDMENT made Georgia immune to a suit. A feigned case was arranged. Peck of Massachusetts sold 15,000 acres of Yazoo land to Fletcher of New Hampshire. Fletcher promptly sued Peck for recovery of his $3,000, claiming that Georgia's nullification of the sale had destroyed Peck's title: the acreage was not his to sell. Actually, both parties shared the same interest in seeking a judicial decision against Georgia's nullification of the land titles—the repeal act of 1796. Thus, by a collusive suit based on DIVERSITY OF CITIZENSHIP, a case involving the repeal act got into the federal courts and ultimately reached the Supreme Court. The Court's opinion, by Chief Justice JOHN MARSHALL, followed the contours of Justice WILLIAM PATERSON's charge in VAN HORNE'S LESSEE v. DORRANCE (1795).

Although the fraud that infected the original land grants was the greatest scandal of the time, the Court refused to make an exception to the principle that the judiciary could not properly investigate the motives of a legislative body. (See LEGISLATION.) The Court also justifiably held that "innocent" third parties should not suffer an annihilation of their property rights as a result of the original fraud. The importance of the case derives from the Court's resolution of the constitutionality of the repeal act.

Alternating in his reasoning between extraconstitutional or HIGHER LAW principles and constitutional or textual ones, Marshall said that the repealer was invalid. Before reaching the question whether a contract existed that the Constitution protected, he announced this doctrine: "When, then, a law is in its nature a contract, when absolute rights have been vested under that contract, a repeal of the law cannot devest those rights. . . ." In the next sentence he asserted that "the nature of society and of government" limits legislative power. This higher law doctrine of judicially inferred limitations protecting vested rights was the sole basis of Justice WILLIAM JOHNSON's concurring opinion. A state has no power to revoke its grants, he declared, resting his case "on a general principle, on the reason and nature of things: a principle which will impose laws even on the Deity." Explicitly Johnson stated that his opinion was not founded on the Constitution's provision against state impairment of the OBLIGATION OF CONTRACTS. The difficulty, he thought, arose from the word "obligation," which ceased once a grant of lands had been executed.

The difficulty with Marshall's contract clause theory was greater than even Johnson made out. The clause was intended to prevent state impairment of executory contracts between private individuals; it had been modeled on the provision of the NORTHWEST ORDINANCE, which had referred to "private contracts, or engagements *bona fide,* and without fraud previously formed." What was the contract in this case? If there was one, did its obligation still exist at the time of the repeal bill? Was it a contract protected by the contract clause, given that it was a land grant to which the state was a party? If the land grant was a contract, it was a public executed one, not a private executory one. The duties that the parties had assumed toward each other had been fulfilled, the deal consummated. That is why Johnson could find no continuing obligation. Moreover, the obligation of a contract is a creature of state law, and the state in this instance, sustained by its courts, had recognized no obligation.

Marshall overcame all difficulties by employing slippery reasoning. A contract, he observed, is either executory or executed; if executed, its object has been performed. The contract between the state and the Yazoo land buyers had been executed by the grant. But, he added, an executed contract, as well as an executory one, "contains obligations binding on the parties." The grant had extinguished the right of the grantor in the title to the lands and "implies a contract not to reassert that right." Moreover, the Constitution uses only the term "contract, without distinguishing between those which are executory and those which are executed." Having inferred from the higher law that a grant carried a continuing obligation not to repossess, he declined to make a distinction that, he said, the Constitution had not made. Similarly he concluded that the language of the contract clause, referring generally to "contracts," protected public as well as private contracts. Marshall apparently realized that the disembodied or abstract higher law doctrine on which Johnson relied would provide an insecure bastion for property holders and a nebulous precedent for courts to follow. So he found a home for the VESTED RIGHTS doctrine in the text of the Constitution.

Marshall seemed, however, to be unsure of the text, because he flirted with the bans on BILLS OF ATTAINDER and EX POST FACTO laws, giving the impression that Georgia's repeal act somehow ran afoul of those bans, too, although the suit was a civil one. Marshall's uncertainty emerged in his conclusion. He had no doubt that the repeal act was invalid, but his ambiguous summation referred to both extraconstitutional principles and the text: Georgia "was restrained, either by general principles which are common to our free institutions, or by the particular provisions of the Constitution. . . ." He did not, in the end, specify the particular provisions.

In the first contract clause decision by the Court, that clause became a repository of the higher law DOCTRINE of vested rights and operated to cover even public, executed contracts. The Court had found a constitutional shield for vested rights. And, by expanding the protection offered by the contract clause, the Court invited more cases to be brought before the judiciary, expanding opportunities for judicial review against state legislation.

LEONARD W. LEVY

Bibliography

MAGRATH, C. PETER 1966 *Yazoo: Law and Politics in the New Republic, The Case of Fletcher v. Peck.* Providence, R.I.: Brown University Press.

FOLEY v. CONNELIE
435 U.S. 291 (1978)

New York excluded ALIENS from employment as state troopers. In an opinion by Chief Justice WARREN E. BURGER, the Supreme Court held, 6–3, that this discrimination did not violate the EQUAL PROTECTION clause of the FOURTEENTH AMENDMENT. The Court took its cue from OBITER DICTA in SUGARMAN V. DOUGALL (1973) concerning "political community." Although the admission of aliens for permanent residence showed congressional intent to grant them full participation in earning a livelihood and receiving such state benefits as welfare and education, the "right to govern" could be limited to citizens. Police officers, like high executive officials, exercise discretionary governmental power, whose abuse can have "serious impact on individuals." (The Chief Justice may have had a vision of an alien trooper inviting a citizen to spreadeagle over the hood of a car.)

Justices THURGOOD MARSHALL, WILLIAM J. BRENNAN, and JOHN PAUL STEVENS dissented: the "execution of broad public policy" mentioned in *Sugarman* had not included the day-to-day execution of the law but the formulation of broad policy. The disloyalty of aliens could not be conclusively presumed.

KENNETH L. KARST

FOOD, DRUG, AND COSMETIC ACT
52 Stat. 1040 (1938)

Grounded on the COMMERCE CLAUSE, this act was a sweeping revision of the PURE FOOD AND DRUG ACT of 1906. It passed Congress after a five-year struggle and then only because of an uproar caused by nearly one hundred deaths from a new drug. Despite extensive compromise, this act substantially strengthened earlier legislation, affording greater consumer protection. Different chapters of the law dealt at length with food, drugs, and cosmetics, expanding coverage and increasing penalties. The act prohibited shipment in INTERSTATE COMMERCE of adulterated or misbranded products and broadened the definition of these terms. Indicative of the act's thrust, one section authorized the secretary of agriculture to establish standards of quality for foods to "promote honesty and fair dealing in the interest of consumers." Misbranding received special attention: imitations were to be clearly marked, flavoring or coloring additives noted, and the use of habit-forming ingredients was to be indicated on the label. Drugs had to meet federal formulations or disclose the differences. New drugs would have to pass rigorous tests. Congress partly remedied one of the act's weaknesses, a less stringent control over false advertising, in the Wheeler-Lea Act of the same year. The Supreme Court sustained the act in UNITED STATES V. SULLIVAN (1947).

DAVID GORDON

FORCE ACT
4 Stat. 632 (1833)

Restive over the threat to slavery that they saw implicit in the growth of federal power, South Carolinians devised doctrines of NULLIFICATION and SECESSION in response to the Tariff Act of 1828. When the Tariff of 1832 failed to satisfy their demands for reduction, a special convention adopted an Ordinance of Nullification (1832), nullifying the tariff. President ANDREW JACKSON responded with his PROCLAMATION TO THE PEOPLE OF SOUTH CAROLINA (1832), denouncing the theory of secession, and with a request to Congress to enact legislation that would simultaneously avoid a military clash with the state over the collection of duties and permit a more prompt resort to federal force if confrontation could not be evaded.

Congress responded with the Force Act (Act of 2 March 1833), reaffirming the power of the President to use federal military and naval force to suppress resistance to the enforcement of federal laws, even if the source of resistance was the state itself. The act empowered him to call up states' militias after issuing a proclamation calling on those obstructing to disperse. It also permitted him to revise the procedure for collecting customs duties. Though South Carolina subsequently nullified the Force Act, federal authority had been vindicated.

WILLIAM M. WIECEK

Bibliography

FREEHLING, WILLIAM W. 1966 *Prelude to Civil War: The Nullification Controversy in South Carolina, 1816–1836.* New York: Harper & Row.

FORCE ACTS
16 Stat. 140 (1870)
16 Stat. 433 (1871)
17 Stat. 13 (1871)

Congress enacted three statutes in 1870 and 1871 to protect the right of blacks to vote in the southern states and to suppress anti-Reconstruction terrorism. They are sometimes called the Enforcement Acts. The Act of May 31, 1870, prohibited all forms of infringement of the RIGHT TO VOTE, not merely the exclusion prohibited by the FIFTEENTH AMENDMENT, and made nightriding a federal FELONY. The Act of February 28, 1871, provided for federal supervision of voter registration and congressional elections to prohibit ballot-box frauds and intimidation of black voters. The Act of April 20, 1871, commonly called the Ku Klux Klan Act, provided civil remedies to persons deprived of rights and privileges secured by the federal Constitution; prohibited violent resistance to federal authority, in order to protect civilian and military officials enforcing Reconstruction measures; authorized the President to use militia and federal military force to suppress insurrections and domestic violence when a state was unable to do so; defined "rebellion" against the federal government; and provided that when the president proclaimed that a rebellion exists, he could suspend the writ of HABEAS CORPUS in the rebellious district. Under authority of the Klan Act, President ULYSSES S. GRANT proclaimed nine counties in South Carolina to be in rebellion during October 1871, suspended the writ of habeas corpus, and used federal troops to suppress violence there and elsewhere in the South. The Klan Act was instrumental in breaking the power of the Klans and other terrorist organizations for the time being.

In UNITED STATES V. REESE (1876), the Supreme Court held sections of the 1870 Act unconstitutional on the grounds that "the Fifteenth Amendment does not confer the right of suffrage upon any one." The Court anticipated its later STATE ACTION doctrine in UNITED STATES V. CRUIKSHANK (1876), voiding IN-DICTMENTS under the Klan Act on the grounds that the FOURTEENTH AMENDMENT "adds nothing to the rights of one citizen as against another. It simply furnishes a federal guaranty against any encroachment by the States." The Court held parts of the Klan Act unconstitutional in UNITED STATES V. HARRIS (1883) because they were directed at the actions of private persons, not at the states or their officers. (These decisions have lost most of their force today. See UNITED STATES V. GUEST, 1966.) Later Congresses in 1894 and 1909, hostile to the goals of Reconstruction, repealed most of the 1870 Act and the Klan Act, but the prohibitions of conspiracies and nightriding survive today in the United States Code, and the civil remedies provided by the Klan Act are today the foundation for an overwhelming majority of federal court lawsuits challenging the constitutionality of actions of state officers. (See SECTION 1983, TITLE 42, UNITED STATES CODE.)

WILLIAM M. WIECEK

Bibliography

HYMAN, HAROLD M. 1973 *A More Perfect Union: The Impact of the Civil War and Reconstruction on the Constitution.* New York: Knopf.

FORD, GERALD R.
(1913–)

Gerald Rudolph Ford, Jr., a graduate of the University of Michigan and Yale University Law School, served in the House of Representatives from 1949 to 1973. A moderately conservative Republican who opposed most social welfare legislation but supported all of the CIVIL RIGHTS ACTS, Ford was his party's floor leader in the House from 1965 to 1973. Among his more controversial undertakings in that capacity was his attempt to secure the IMPEACHMENT of Supreme Court Justice WILLIAM O. DOUGLAS in 1970.

President RICHARD M. NIXON appointed Ford vice-president of the United States when the office fell vacant in 1973; this was the first application of proce-dures set forth in the Twenty-Fifth Amendment. When Nixon resigned the presidency in August 1974, Ford succeeded him, thereby becoming the first President to serve without winning a national election. In September 1974 Ford granted Nixon a full pardon for any offense against the United States that he might have committed while in office. (See WATERGATE AND THE CONSTITUTION.)

As President, Ford used the VETO POWER extensively, disapproving some forty-eight bills. In 1974, after Congress failed to act, Ford granted conditional AMNESTY to VIETNAM WAR deserters and draft evaders, exercising the presidential PARDONING POWER. His dispatch of Marines to free the freighter *Mayaguez* from Cambodia in May 1975 demonstrated that the "consultation" provisions of the WAR POWERS RESOLUTION OF 1973 did not prevent the COMMAND-ER-IN-CHIEF from taking decisive action in an emergency. Ford sought election in his own right in 1976 but was narrowly defeated by JIMMY CARTER.

DENNIS J. MAHONEY

FOREIGN AFFAIRS

The words "foreign affairs" are not to be found in the United States Constitution. There are scattered references to "commerce with foreign nations," to TREATIES and ambassadors, to the law of nations, but there is nothing to suggest that the relations of the United States with other nations form a significantly discrete constitutional category. Yet every major theme of constitutional jurisprudence is played differently in respect of foreign affairs. Foreign affairs provide a unique exception to the dogma that the federal government has only the powers expressly enumerated in the Constitution. For the relations of the United States with other countries, FEDERALISM is virtually irrelevant and the United States is essentially a unitary state. The separation and allocation of authority among the branches of the federal government for conducting foreign affairs are different from what they are in respect to domestic matters. Individual rights, strongly safeguarded by the Constitution in the internal life of the country, bow quite readily before the foreign interests of the United States. In this and in other respects foreign affairs discourage JUDICIAL REVIEW and intervention, the hallmark of United States constitutionalism.

The Constitution vests some foreign affairs powers in the federal government in the same manner in which it vests domestic powers, by bestowing them on one or another of the three branches of that government. Thus, Congress in Article I, section 8, is given the power to regulate commerce with foreign nations, to define offenses against the law of nations, and to declare war. The President has the power under Article II, section 2, to appoint ambassadors and make treaties (with the ADVICE AND CONSENT of the Senate). The JUDICIAL POWER OF THE UNITED STATES extends, according to Article III, section 2, to cases arising under treaties, and to certain controversies involving foreign states, their public ministers, or their citizens. Many powers of government relating to foreign affairs, however, are not mentioned: for example, the power to control IMMIGRATION, to regulate ALIENS in the United States or United States nationals abroad, to assert the rights of the United States and to respond to claims by other governments, to participate in the international process of developing customary law, to make international agreements other than treaties, to recognize states and governments, or generally to determine national policy and attitudes on friendship and intercourse with other nations. While some missing powers can plausibly be inferred from ENUMERATED POWERS, others cannot, and, under general principles, powers not enumerated and not fairly to be inferred from expressed powers were not granted to the federal government: the legislative powers of Congress are limited to those "herein granted" (Article I, section 1), and the powers not delegated to the United States are reserved to the states or to the people by the TENTH AMENDMENT. Yet the federal government has exercised all these foreign affairs powers and others from the beginning, and no one has doubted that the federal government had that authority, and that the states did not.

In foreign affairs, then, the principle that the federal government has only the enumerated powers does not apply. All foreign affairs are delegated to the federal government as though that were expressly provided. A hundred years ago the Supreme Court, in CHAE CHAN PING V. UNITED STATES (1889), held, for example, that Congress has the power to regulate immigration because the power to exclude or admit aliens is inherent in the nationhood and SOVEREIGNTY of the United States. In UNITED STATES V. CURTISS-WRIGHT EXPORT CORP. (1936) the Supreme Court expounded a special constitutional principle:

The broad statement that the federal government can exercise no powers except those specifically enumerated in the Constitution, and such implied powers as are NECESSARY AND PROPER to carry into effect the enumerated powers, is categorically true only in respect of our internal affairs. In that field, the primary purpose of the Constitution was to carve from the general mass of legislative powers *then possessed by the states* such portions as it was thought desirable to vest in the federal government, leaving those not included in the enumeration still in the states. . . . And since the states severally never possessed international powers, such powers could not have been carved from the mass of state powers but obviously were transmitted to the United States from some other source. . . .

As a result of the separation from Great Britain by the Colonies acting as a unit, the powers of external sovereignty passed from the Crown not to the colonies severally, but to the colonies in their collective and corporate capacity as the United States of America. . . .

The Union existed before the Constitution, which was ordained and established among other things to form "a more perfect Union." Prior to that event, it is clear that the Union, declared by the ARTICLES OF CONFEDERATION to be 'perpetual,' was the sole possessor of external sovereignty and in the Union it remained without change save in so far as the Constitution in express terms qualified its exercise. The Framers' Convention was called and exerted its powers upon the irrefutable postulate that though the states were several their people in respect of foreign affairs were one. . . .

It results that the investment of the federal government with the powers of external sovereignty did not depend upon the affirmative grants of the Constitution. The powers to declare and wage war, to conclude peace, to make treaties, to maintain diplomatic relations with other sovereignties, if they had never been mentioned in the Constitution, would have vested in the federal government as necessary concomitants of nationality. . . . As a member of the family of nations, the right and power of the United States in that field are equal to the right and power of the other members of the international family. Otherwise, the United States is not completely sovereign. The power to acquire territory by discovery and occupation . . . the power to expel undesirable aliens . . . the power to make such international agreements as do not constitute treaties in the constitutional sense . . . , none of which is expressly affirmed by the Constitution, nevertheless exist as inherently inseparable from the conception of nationality. This the court recognized, and . . . found the warrant for its conclusions not in the provisions of the Constitution, but in the law of nations.

Although the theory underlying *Curtiss-Wright* has been criticized, it has never been questioned by the Supreme Court. In any event, the DOCTRINE resulting from the theory—plenary power of the federal government in matters relating to foreign affairs, beyond those explicitly granted in the Constitution—is firmly established. The Supreme Court has not often found it necessary to resort to "sovereignty" or "nationhood" as a source of power for the federal government. In large part, the foreign activities of the federal government that have come to court are amply supported by enumerated powers of Congress or the President, by powers reasonably implied in enumerated powers, or by construction of the Constitution as a whole. But sovereignty, nationhood, and their implications in international law and in the practice of other nations are ever available as a source of authority to supply any lack of enumerated power for the federal government in matters relating to foreign affairs. The network of regulation of immigration and of aliens in the United States, for a principal example, rests ultimately on United States sovereignty, and other exercises of authority not easily rooted in enumerated powers have been supported as exercises of "the foreign affairs powers" of Congress, with citations to *Curtiss-Wright.*

The powers expressly conferred upon branches of the federal government, and those additional powers implied in sovereignty, give the federal government full authority to act in the United States and for the United States in respect to its foreign affairs. Since plenary power has been delegated, state authority, STATES' RIGHTS, even state immunity (except in remote, hypothetical respects) do not limit federal authority in foreign affairs. When the federal government acts, its action is supreme, superseding any inconsistent state law. Federal action may also preempt, "occupy a field," excluding state action even if it is not inconsistent.

Some state actions in foreign affairs are excluded by Article I, section 10, even when the federal government has not acted. A state may not make a treaty. It may enter into an "Agreement or Compact" with a foreign nation only with the consent of Congress. Although here, as for other purposes, the difference between a treaty and another international agreement is uncertain, presumably if Congress should consent to an agreement by a state with a foreign government the agreement would not be successfully challenged as being a treaty to which Congress could not consent. An agreement requiring the consent of Congress may be formal or informal, even tacit. But, by analogy to doctrine that has developed in cases such as *Virginia v. Tennessee* (1893), with respect to compacts between states of the United States, probably a state may make a compact with a foreign government without congressional consent if the agreement does not tend to "the increase of political power in the states, which may encroach upon or interfere with the just supremacy of the United States."

The states are limited also by implication of the grant to Congress of power "to regulate commerce with foreign Nations and among the several States." Although that doctrine of implied limitations developed principally in respect of INTERSTATE COMMERCE it applies in essentially the same way to FOREIGN COMMERCE. The COMMERCE CLAUSE bars regulation by the states that excludes or discriminates against foreign commerce, or burdens such commerce unduly, as determined by weighing the local against the national interest. The courts continue to monitor such state regulations.

A single case, *Zschernig v. Miller* (1968), has held, more broadly, that even if the federal government has not acted, and even if there is no undue burden on foreign commerce, a state may not intrude on the federal monopoly in foreign affairs. In that case Oregon law required state courts to deny an inheritance to an alien unless the court were satisfied that the government of the alien's state of nationality would allow a United States national to inherit in reciprocal circumstances, and that the alien would be allowed to enjoy his inheritance without confiscation. That state law, the Supreme Court ruled, was impermissible under the Constitution because it involved the state courts in sitting in judgment on the policies of foreign governments. No other case has been decided on that principle.

"In respect of foreign relations generally, State lines disappear. As to such purpose the State . . . does not exist," the Supreme Court said in UNITED STATES V. BELMONT (1937). But while federal authority in foreign affairs is plenary, it is not exclusive. Federal law generally is superimposed on a network of state law; state law of property and contract, state tort and criminal law, state corporate law, tax law, and estate law govern activities and interests that implicate or impinge on foreign trade and other foreign relations of the United States. If in principle all of that state law could be superseded or excluded by federal statute or treaty, it has not been and could not effectively be done in fact, and foreign relations continue to be greatly affected by state law. State influence is reflected also in the system of selection of the national government—the President, the Senate, and the House of Representatives—and particular state interests weigh heavily in the determination of national interest by every branch of the federal government. Increasingly, states have also entered, independently if informally, on the international scene by commercial missions to promote local produce and industry abroad, and by participation in international cultural activities.

The principal field of constitutional uncertainty and the focus of constitutional controversy in foreign affairs have been the respective powers and authority of President and Congress.

The Framers of the Constitution, reflecting the painful lessons of the early years of independence, created the office of President and vested it with "executive power." They gave the President authority to appoint ambassadors and to make treaties but required that he obtain the advice and consent of the Senate. They designated the President the COMMAND-ER-IN-CHIEF of the army and navy. At the same time the Framers gave Congress the power to impose tariffs and otherwise regulate commerce with foreign nations; to define and punish piracy and other offenses against the law of nations; and to declare war. Other general powers given to Congress reach to foreign as well as domestic matters: the powers to tax and spend, to borrow and regulate the value of money, to establish post offices, to authorize and appropriate funds, to create and regulate a federal bureaucracy, and to make other laws necessary and proper to carry out the power of Congress and other federal powers.

Both Congress and the presidency have developed and changed, the President in particular now exercising his constitutional authority through a huge bureaucracy. The enumerated powers of each branch have grown as the United States has grown and achieved its large place in a transformed world. But the division of authority between President and Congress remains today essentially as it was expressly prescribed by the Framers. Although the President may propose, and his proposals weigh heavily, Congress exercises its expressed powers as they have developed. Congress decides whether the United States shall be at war or at peace, and passes the laws necessary to prepare for war, and to wage war successfully, and to deal with the consequences of war. Congress regulates "commerce with foreign nations"—trade, transportation, communication, and other intercourse—in its innumerable forms. Congress enacts laws to effectuate the powers of the federal government deriving from the sovereignty and nationhood of the United States. It passes laws constituting national policy toward other nations, for example, laws fixing the rights of their nationals in the United States or in our coastal waters. It also passes laws regulating our relations with other nations, for example, the 1976 statute determining the immunity of foreign governments in American courts. Congress enacts the laws—including any federal criminal law—necessary and proper for carrying out its own foreign affairs powers, the country's treaty obligations, and the foreign affairs powers of the President, including laws protecting the processes for making foreign policy or conducting foreign relations, *e.g.*, statutes protecting classified documents, or forbidding the harassment of foreign diplomats or the picketing of foreign embassies. Congress also uses its general lawmaking powers for foreign as for domestic affairs.

Congress decides how much to spend for defense, and how much for foreign aid and to which countries. Its power to borrow money and to regulate the value of money (of the United States and that of other countries) has major transnational applications and implications. By its authority to establish post offices Congress has approved American participation in an international postal system; it has used its authority over PATENTS and COPYRIGHTS to authorize dealing with them by international arrangements. Congress appropriates money for the BUDGET of the State Department, or to pay our obligations to the United Nations. Congress creates and regulates the Foreign Service. It investigates so that it can legislate (or not legislate).

For his part, the President (not Congress) makes treaties and appoints ambassadors (with the consent of the Senate) and receives ambassadors. Only the President acts as commander-in-chief of the armed forces; only he can take care that the laws are faithfully executed. A few powers have been inferred from those listed: for example, only the President speaks for the United States to other nations and only the President negotiates with other nations. The President recognizes governments, enters into diplomatic relations with them or terminates these relations, and gives his ambassadors their instructions and receives their reports.

There is more to foreign affairs, however, than is accounted for in the express allocations of the Constitution, and issues have arisen as to matters not clearly implied in those allocations or where argument can support allocation to one of the political branches as plausibly as to the other. The President makes treaties, but who can terminate them on behalf of the United States? Congress declares war, but who can decide to terminate a war? Who can make international agreements other than treaties, or otherwise commit the power and resources of the United States? Who can deploy forces for purposes short of war? Who can determine those general principles, guidelines, and attitudes that go to make up "foreign policy?"

There is no ready principle of allocation of authority between Congress and President, or of CONSTITUTIONAL INTERPRETATION generally, to determine to whom these unmentioned yet clearly federal powers are assigned. In domestic affairs the principle of allocation of authority between Congress and the President is reasonably clear: Congress makes the law; the President executes the law. In foreign affairs that principle of allocation did not obtain even in the original conception, and surely it does not as the two branches have developed. Clearly, the President has substantial authority to "legislate," to determine national policy, as well as to execute it. The President makes foreign policy when he makes treaties and other international agreements; he also makes law, since international agreements create international law, and some treaties and agreements have domestic effect and are the LAW OF THE LAND under the SUPREMACY CLAUSE. The President makes foreign policy also in representing the United States in the international arena—by recognizing states or governments and deciding on the character of relations with them; by making or responding to international claims; by declaring the attitudes of the United States, many of which he can implement or reflect in actions on his own authority. Inevitably, the President makes foreign policy also by the manner in which he conducts foreign relations.

The President and Congress have asserted opposing principles of constitutional jurisprudence to determine allocation of the unallocated federal powers in foreign affairs. The President has claimed a source of plenary authority in that he is the "sole organ of the United States in its international relations." He has argued that Article II, section 2, of the Constitution vests in him not only the power to execute laws but the whole "executive power" of the United States. It is urged that the Framers understood the executive power to include the whole of foreign relations, except insofar as the Constitution expressly limits the President's authority (as by requiring that he obtain the consent of the Senate to appoint ambassadors or to make treaties), or has expressly given some foreign affairs power to Congress, such as the power to regulate foreign commerce or to declare war. Congress, on the other hand, has claimed that its constitutional authority over foreign "commerce" includes all aspects of intercourse with foreign nations; by that authority, and by its control of war and peace, it has been claimed, Congress is the principal political organ of the nation and has all the authority of the United States in international relations except that expressly given to the President.

The competing constitutional doctrines have rarely come to court and the issue remains largely unresolved in principle. Constitutional history, however, has supplied some of the answers that constitutional law has left unanswered. From the beginning, many powers not expressly delegated by the Constitution have flowed to the President and have made his the predominant part in the foreign policy process. Presidential authority grew early and steadily by a kind of "accretion." Even when United States diplomatic missions abroad were few and United States international relations simple and minimal, the conduct of foreign affairs was a continuing process, and it raised issues every day. These came to the President, through his ambassadors and his secretary of state; Congress did not hear of them unless the President saw necessary or fit to tell Congress. The early issues— whether to declare our neutrality in European wars, or send a misbehaving French minister home—were not matters which the Constitution expressly left to Congress or expressly denied to the President. They did not call for general policy best reflected in formal legislation or resolution, but for ad hoc judgment and particular measures tailored to the case. Sometimes decision was urgent, and the President was always "in session" while Congress was not, and could readily or easily be informed and convened, especially in the conditions of communications and transportation of the early days. The President could act quickly and informally, often discreetly or secretly, while action by Congress would have been public and formal, slow and sometimes unduly dramatic. Often, unless the President acted, the United States could not act at all.

And so President GEORGE WASHINGTON declared neutrality, President JAMES MONROE his famous doctrine; later Presidents opened Japan, traded in China, intervened in Latin America. Presidents appointed "agents" (without Senate consent), concluded EXECUTIVE AGREEMENTS (without consent of Congress or the Senate), sent troops abroad, expanded intelligence and "covert activities," acted in the world arena for the United States, making its policies, committing its honor and credit. What early Presidents did became precedents for their successors to do likewise or to exceed. What successive Presidents did became the basis for assertions of authority to do them, supported in constitutional terms in the President's "foreign affairs power" often implemented by his power as commander-in-chief.

Congress contributed to the steady growth of presidential power. Congress early recognized and confirmed the President's control of daily foreign intercourse, and the resulting monopoly of information and experience promoted the President's claim of expertise and Congress's sense of inadequacy. A growing practice of informal consultations between the President and congressional leaders disarmed them as well as members of Congress generally, and helped confirm presidential authority to act without formal congressional participation. Often Congress later ratified or confirmed what the President had done, as in the KOREAN WAR. And repeatedly it delegated its own huge powers to the President in broad terms, so that he could later claim to act under the authority of Congress as well as his own, as in the VIETNAM WAR.

Congress has never formally conceded all these unspecified powers to the President. At most Congress has silently acquiesced in his power to act. Frequently, Congress asserted authority for itself to act in areas where the President also claimed authority. For example, although in 1945, President HARRY S. TRUMAN, without congressional participation, claimed for the United States the resources of its continental shelf, Congress in 1976 acted to declare an exclusive 200-mile fishing zone for the United States, and did so against the wishes of the executive branch. At times, Congress has also insisted on its authority to preclude, supersede, or control presidential action. In foreign affairs, as elsewhere, it has insisted that the President must execute the laws that Congress enacts and must spend (not impound) money that Congress appropriates. In foreign as in domestic affairs Congress has repudiated EXECUTIVE PRIVILEGE when its committees have sought information or documents. In foreign affairs, too, Congress has provided for LEGISLATIVE VETO to recoup delegation of authority and to oversee executive execution of the law. Whether the general invalidation of the legislative veto (IMMIGRATION AND NATURALIZATION SERVICE V. CHADHA, 1983) will totally bar its use in foreign affairs legislation as well is yet to be determined.

A principal unresolved issue between President and Congress has been the claimed authority of the President to deploy the armed forces of the United States. The issue has not been about the WAR POWERS, expressed in the Constitution. The power to decide for war or peace is indisputably with Congress: Congress can declare war or authorize it by other resolution; it can decide for limited war, and though Presidents have claimed plenary authority as commanders-in-chief, theoretically Congress can probably regulate the conduct of war in general though perhaps not in detail. Wars apart, Presidents have claimed authority to deploy the armed forces for political ends and have done so on numerous occasions, sometimes engaging them in hostilities short of war. In Korea in 1950–1952 troops were engaged in war, President Truman claiming authority to act under a treaty— the UNITED NATIONS CHARTER—and Congress soon acquiesced in and ratified his action. In Vietnam, Congress gave two Presidents blanket authority to engage in hostilities. Members of Congress have often challenged the President's authority, although Congress has rarely done so formally. After Vietnam, however, in the WAR POWERS RESOLUTION adopted over President RICHARD M. NIXON's veto, Congress purported to regulate the power of the President to deploy armed forces in circumstances where they are or might be engaged in hostilities. Although Presidents have questioned the resolution's constitutionality, they have acquiesced in principle, but in several instances they may not have respected the resolution in fact.

The power that Presidents have claimed to enter into international agreements or otherwise commit the United States has also been an unresolved subject of controversy. Again, it is not the treaty power, expressed in the Constitution, that has raised serious issues. The President can make a treaty if the Senate consents, and the Senate can ask for changes and impose other relevant conditions upon its consent. The power to terminate treaties has been exercised by the President, often on his own authority. A challenge to the President's authority to terminate the treaty with the Republic of China (Taiwan) in 1979 did not prevail, although the Supreme Court did not decide the merits of the controversy in GOLDWATER V. CARTER (1980).

Since the beginnings of the nation, Presidents have made many international agreements other than by treaty. An agreement authorized or approved by resolution of Congress, by majority vote in both Houses (rather than by consent of two-thirds of the Senate to a treaty), is the equivalent of a treaty for virtually all purposes. But Presidents have also made agreements on their own authority. Some authority to do so is conceded. It is not disputed that the President can make agreements as commander-in-chief during war (for example, an armistice). He can make agreements also to implement his established foreign affairs power, for example, agreements incidental to recognizing a foreign government, as in the Litvinov agreements with the Union of Soviet Socialist Republics in 1933. (See *United States v. Belmont*, 1937; UNITED STATES V. PINK, 1942). At least some other international agreements have been held to be within his authority, for example, the Iranian Hostages Agreement, since, the Supreme Court said, in DAMES & MOORE V. REGAN (1981), the President's exercise of authority to resolve international claims had been acquiesced in by Congress. On the other hand, some agreements clearly require Senate consent (to a treaty) or congressional approval. There has been no authoritative determination, nor any accepted guidelines, as to which agreements the President can make on his own authority and which he cannot. The suggestion that "important" agreements cannot be made by the President alone is not self-defining, and Presidents have in fact made "important" agreements alone, especially when they desired to keep them confidential. The Senate has expressed its sense that the President cannot commit the forces or resources of the United States except by treaty or pursuant to act of Congress. Congress has considered numerous bills to regulate international agreements by the President on his own authority. But it has legislated only a limited measure, requiring the executive branch to transmit any executive agreement to Congress, if only to a congressional committee in confidence.

In general, Presidents and Congress have worked together even when Congress is not controlled by the President's POLITICAL PARTY. That party politics "stop at the water's edge" and do not trouble American foreign relations is not wholly true, and in the view of many would not be desirable. But throughout most of our national history the dominant voices in the two major parties have not differed sharply in foreign policy, and Congress has more or less willingly followed the President's lead, while Presidents have tried to lead chiefly where Congress would not be too reluctant to follow.

The respective authority of the political branches apart, there have been other constitutional issues relating to treaties and other international agreements. Some early issues have been resolved. Treaties and other international agreements, like other acts of the United States government, are subject to the BILL OF RIGHTS and other constitutional limitations. There are no limitations on the subject matter of such agreements other than those implied in the fact that there must be a bona fide agreement between the United States and one or more other nations in a matter related to foreign policy interests of the United States. A treaty or other agreement may deal with matters that might otherwise be regulated by the states or by congressional statute.

Treaties and international agreements have their own place in constitutional law. Some treaties or agreements are "self-executing": they are intended to be enforced by the executive or applied by the courts without waiting for implementation by Congress. Whether a treaty is self-executing is a matter of interpretation of the agreement, usually determined by the intent of the United States government in the matter. If a treaty or other agreement is self-executing it will be treated like a federal law, supreme over state law and superseding any earlier, inconsistent federal law. But the treaty is not superior to later federal law, and although the courts will interpret a statute, where fairly possible, consistently with international obligations of the United States, when Congress passes a law clearly inconsistent with a pre-existing treaty, the courts will apply the later statute, in effect putting the United States in default on its international obligation.

The role of the courts in foreign affairs is not essentially different from their role in domestic affairs. The JURISDICTION OF THE FEDERAL COURTS under Article III of the Constitution extends to cases arising under treaties of the United States as well as those arising under other international agreements of the United States or under customary international law. Foreign affairs may be implicated also in cases arising under the Constitution and various laws of the United States. The federal courts have jurisdiction also over "cases affecting Ambassadors, other public ministers and consuls," and over controversies between a foreign state or foreign citizen and a state or citizen of the United States, but such controversies have not loomed large in the history of the Constitution or of our foreign relations.

Thanks to both political and institutional limitations, the judicial prerogative of invalidating acts of the political branches has not troubled United States foreign affairs. Most constitutional issues in foreign affairs, including some big issues of competition between President and Congress, rarely come to court because in general there is not the required CASE OR CONTROVERSY and there is no one with the necessary STANDING to raise the issue. Challenge to an exercise of national authority in foreign affairs on grounds of "states' rights" is generally futile in view of the established monopoly of the federal government. Foreign affairs have also been a principal source of the POLITICAL QUESTION DOCTRINE, under which the courts have declared some foreign affairs issues "political" and therefore not justiciable. Federalism does provide the court a role relevant to foreign affairs when they scrutinize state activities that, a private party claims, unduly burden foreign commerce or that may be inconsistent with or preempted by congressional policy.

The courts exercise their usual lawmaking function in foreign affairs also. In addition to interpreting the Constitution and laws, the courts have determined and developed the maritime law which remains largely judge-made. They have also developed rules, if only for their own guidance, such as the "ACT OF STATE" DOCTRINE, that courts will not sit in judgment on the acts of a foreign state in its own territory, as in *Banco Nacional de Cuba v. Sabbatino* (1964). Courts also make foreign relations law when they determine and apply customary international law. "International law is part of our law, and must be ascertained and administered by the courts of justice of appropriate jurisdiction, as often as questions of right depending on it are duly presented for their determination," the Court said in *The Paquete Habana* (1900).

Nothing in the Constitution suggests that the rights of individuals in respect of foreign affairs are different from what they are in relation to other exercises of governmental power. But although arguments that individual rights and protections are fewer and narrower in foreign affairs than elsewhere have not prevailed in principle, constitutional guarantees sometimes look different and afford less protection.

In principle, constitutional safeguards apply in foreign as in domestic affairs and apply to governmental activities abroad as at home. The Bill of Rights limits the Congress and the President, foreign affairs legislation as well as treaties and other international agreements. Even temporary or unauthorized aliens in the United States are entitled to the protections of the Bill of Rights, for example, the safeguards for those accused of crime. But where an individual right is not absolute but might be outweighed by an important public interest, national interests in war and peace, and even lesser concerns of foreign relations, would have important weight in the balance. So, for example, courts have upheld prohibitions on picketing near embassies (*Frend v. United States*, 1938), or the cancellation of a passport of someone engaged in systematically identifying U.S. intelligence agents abroad (AGEE V. HAIG, 1981).

In regard to foreign relations as to other matters, DUE PROCESS OF LAW requires fair procedures, and that requirement applies to aliens as to citizens, in the United States or abroad. Trial under the authority of the United States, at least in time of peace, must provide a jury, RIGHT TO COUNSEL, and other constitutional safeguards for those accused of crime. An alien in the United States, subject to DEPORTATION on grounds prescribed by law, is entitled to a FAIR HEARING, and the government must prove by clear, unequivocal, and convincing evidence that the alien is deportable on the grounds provided by Congress. But an alien seeking admission to the United States is due no process beyond consideration and decision by the designated administrative officer.

Due process also limits the substance of what government can do, requiring that it not be "unreasonable, arbitrary or capricious, and [that] the means selected have real and substantial relation to the object sought to be attained," as the Court said in NEBBIA v. New York (1934). Courts have long refrained, however, from invalidating economic and social regulations, and they are even less likely to do so in matters affecting foreign relations. But SUBSTANTIVE DUE PROCESS protects also a person's liberty, and here the constitutional limitation has been greater, and judicial deference to the political branches far less. The Supreme Court declared in KENT V. DULLES (1955) that the RIGHT TO TRAVEL abroad is "a part of the liberty of which the citizen cannot be deprived without due process of law." In AFROYIM V. RUSK (1967) the Court invalidated a statutory provision making it a crime for members of certain communist organizations to obtain or use a passport, because the law "too broadly and indiscriminately restricts the right to travel and thereby abridges the liberty guaranteed by the Fifth Amendment." However, in *Agee v. Haig* the Court upheld withdrawal of a passport from one who systematically exposed the identity of United States intelligence agents. And to date the courts have held that even an alien lawfully admitted and long resident in the United States can be deported for whatever reasons commend themselves to Congress.

The EQUAL PROTECTION OF THE LAWS is required in foreign affairs matters as elsewhere. States cannot discriminate against aliens to deny them WELFARE BENEFITS, EDUCATION, access to the general civil service, or the right to practice their profession. States may not deny educational opportunities even to "undocumented" alien children, not lawfully admitted to the United States (*Plyer v. Doe*, 1982). But a state may reserve for citizens jobs as teachers, policemen, other "peace officers" (including deputy probation officers), and others involved in "the political function of governing." (See FOLEY V. CONNELIE, 1978; AMBACH V. NORWICK, 1979.) Some state discriminations against aliens are invalid because inconsistent with, or preempted by, the immigration laws or other acts of Congress (HINES V. DAVIDOWITZ, 1941; TAKAHASHI V. FISH & GAME COMMISSION, 1948). Unlike the states, however, Congress can limit the federal Civil Service to citizens, and may discriminate against aliens in other respects that do not infringe their basic rights. An act of Congress or treaty may give some rights to aliens on the basis of reciprocity, *i.e.*, that the country of which the alien is a national give such benefits to United States citizens.

Aliens may be denied the right to acquire some kinds of property or invest in some kinds of enterprises in the United States. But an alien (other than an enemy alien in time of war) may not be deprived of his property without due process of law, and it cannot be taken for public use without JUST COMPENSATION.

The constitutional provision that property not be taken for public use without just compensation may have special application in foreign affairs. The United States has frequently in its history entered into an agreement with another government to settle claims of United States citizens against that government. Although the settlements sometimes did not have authorization or approval by the individual claimants, and often gave them only partial recovery, the courts have upheld such agreements as within the authority of the President to make, and have rejected claims that the agreements deprived the claimants of property without just compensation. But where private claims are sacrificed by the United States in settlement of other national interests, as was apparently the case in the early French spoliation cases, and as was claimed in the Iranian Hostages Agreement, the courts may yet find that there has been a taking of the claims requiring compensation.

There is much uncertainty in the constitutional law of foreign relations but it should not be exaggerated. The abiding uncertainties lie principally—almost wholly—in the separation, distribution, and fragmentation of powers between the President and Congress (or between President and Senate), a division different from those prevailing in domestic affairs. Some of the uncertainties and conflicts arise out of different constitutional interpretations, which might in theory be resolved but are not likely to be resolved soon, for courts are reluctant to step into intense confrontation between President and Congress or inhibit either when the other does not object. If the courts do speak to such "separation" issues occasionally, they are likely to reach for the narrowest ground, resolving as little as possible.

Much of the controversy in the conduct of foreign affairs, moreover, does not stem from constitutional uncertainty, but rather reflects what the Framers intended, or were willing to accept, when they separated powers and subdivided functions. If Congress refuses to authorize an anti-ballistic missile program requested by the President, if the President vetoes a tariff adopted by Congress, if the Senate refuses consent to a human rights treaty negotiated by the President, the controversy does not involve competition for constitutional power but the kind of conflict "prescribed" by the Constitution. There is no constitutional issue when the complaint is not that the Constitution has been violated but that it is not working to taste. For a contemporary example, the real complaint in the national crisis over Vietnam was not that the President usurped constitutional power, but that, acting within his powers, he virtually compelled Congress to go along. That is a complaint against the Constitution.

That under a less-than-certain and less-than-happy constitutional arrangement, the conduct of foreign relations continues to function with reasonable effectiveness owes in substantial part to extraconstitutional arrangements, including varieties of congressional committees and staff that have become integral to the foreign policy process. But the Framers thought they had good reasons for prescribing limits to cooperation, even some conflict. If effective government, in foreign relations as elsewhere, requires cooperation, democratic government, in foreign relations as elsewhere, abhors congressional abdication, and even enjoins it to provide legal opposition. The President provides initiative and efficiency, but Congress is the more representative branch and brings to bear the influence of public opinion, diversity, concern for local and individual rights. At its best, there is a counterpoint of presidential expertise and some inexpert congressional wisdom producing foreign policy and foreign relations not always efficient but supporting larger, deeper national interests.

LOUIS HENKIN

Bibliography

CORWIN, EDWARD S.   1957   *The President: Office and Powers.* 4th rev. ed. New York: New York University Press.

HENKIN, LOUIS   1972   *Foreign Affairs and the Constitution.* Mineola, N.Y.: Foundation Press.

LOFGREN, CHARLES A.   1972   War-Making Power Under the Constitution: The Original Understanding. *Yale Law Journal* 81:672–797.

MCDOUGAL, MYRES S. and LANS, ASHER   1954   Treaties and Congressional-Executive or Presidential Agreements: Interchangeable Instruments of National Policy. *Yale Law Journal* 54:181–351, 534–615.

Report of the Commission on the Organization of the Government for the Conduct of Foreign Policy, and Appendices. 1975.

SOFAER, ABRAHAM D.   1976   *War, Foreign Affairs and Constitutional Power.* Cambridge, Mass.: Ballinger Publishing Co.

WRIGHT, QUINCY   1922   *The Control of American Foreign Relations.* New York: Macmillan.

FOREIGN COMMERCE

The Constitution grants to Congress the power "To regulate Commerce with foreign Nations, and among the several States. . . ." A few cases in the 1800s indicated that the power to regulate foreign commerce was the same as the power to regulate INTERSTATE COMMERCE. Later, in *Brolan v. United States* (1915), the Supreme Court indicated that the power given Congress to regulate foreign commerce was so complete that it was limited only by other portions of the Constitution. So the Court upheld Congress in its regulating, prohibiting, and taxing commerce with other nations while sometimes restricting its power to regulate interstate commerce.

Today the issue is of no significance. The power of Congress to regulate interstate commerce is so great as to make any distinctions meaningless. Congress need only concern itself with the specific constitutional restrictions on the foreign commercial power: those preventing the taxation of exports and giving any preference to the ports of one state over those of another state.

In *Japan Line, Ltd. v. Los Angeles* (1979), however, the Court held that the foreign COMMERCE CLAUSE may serve to limit state taxation in cases in which the interstate commerce clause would not. The Court held invalid a nondiscriminatory, apportioned, state property tax on the value of shipping containers belonging to a Japanese shipping company. The Court said that the tax would have been valid if it had been applied to interstate shipments, but was not here because the containers were taxed on full value in Japan and the Court had no authority to require apportioned taxation in foreign lands. The Court said that state taxes on foreign commerce had to meet all the tests for interstate commerce; in addition, the Court must inquire whether even with apportionment a substantial risk of international multiple taxation persists, and whether the tax prevents the federal government from speaking with one voice when regulating commerce with foreign governments.

EDWARD L. BARRETT, JR.

(SEE ALSO: *State Regulation of Commerce; State Taxation of Commerce.*)

Bibliography

HENKIN, LOUIS 1972 *Foreign Affairs and the Constitution.* Pages 69–71. Mineola, N.Y.: Foundation Press.
NOWAK, JOHN E.; ROTUNDA, RONALD D.; and YOUNG, NELSON J. 1980 *Handbook on Constitutional Law.* Pages 129–131. St. Paul, Minn.: West Publishing Co.

FORTAS, ABE
(1910–1982)

Abe Fortas of Tennessee, a graduate of Yale Law School, became a New Deal lawyer. As undersecretary of state, he opposed the removal and internment of Japanese Americans. In 1946 Fortas cofounded a Washington law firm whose corporate clients made him rich and influential, but he contributed his time to defending the rights of underdogs and alleged security risks. One client, LYNDON B. JOHNSON, became a close friend. Fortas continued as his adviser after Johnson became President, and Johnson later appointed Fortas to the Supreme Court.

Justice Fortas served for less than four years, from October 4, 1965, to May 14, 1969. In 1968, President Johnson nominated him to serve as Chief Justice of the United States, succeeding EARL WARREN, but a Senate delay in confirming him, initiated primarily by Republicans eager to save the appointment in case a Republican was victorious in November, caused Fortas to withdraw from consideration before the 1968 Supreme Court Term opened. Before that term was over, Justice Fortas had resigned his seat because of revelations of alleged improprieties in his financial activities.

Four years away from practice is a very brief period in which to develop an overall judicial philosophy. Nevertheless, Fortas developed a distinctive style, notable for flowery prose, the artful phrase, and emphasis on the underlying facts of the particular case. He also developed distinctive positions on particular issues.

Fortas's FIRST AMENDMENT analysis was the most well-developed aspect of his constitutional theory. He disparaged the speech-conduct distinction adhered to by Justice HUGO L. BLACK and others; Fortas thought both speech and conduct could warrant First Amendment protection. But while he gave full protection in cases like TINKER V. DES MOINES INDEPENDENT COMMUNITY SCHOOL DISTRICT (1969) to nonviolent, nondisruptive speech and conduct, he believed, as he said in BARKER V. HARDWAY (1969), that speech or conduct that is "violent and destructive interference with the rights of others" falls outside the scope of First Amendment protections. In drawing this line in individual cases, Fortas focused tightly on the specific facts of the case. For instance, in BROWN V. LOUISIANA (1966), the arrest of demonstrators for conducting a SIT-IN in a segregated public library was unconstitutional because the particular sit-in was "neither loud, boisterous, obstreperous, indecorous, nor impolite."

Those who disagreed with Fortas's approach asked, as in ADDERLEY V. FLORIDA (1966), whether the *type* of demonstration at issue could be disruptive and so was legitimately subject to state prohibition. Fortas reached opposite conclusions by weighing the potential for violence only of the *particular* demonstration involved. He thus gave greater protection to expression in cases the Supreme Court reviewed. But his opinions gave little guidance, simply reporting his own reactions to the facts of the case. Moreover, Fortas occasionally strayed from this approach. Dissenting in STREET V. NEW YORK (1969), he was willing to affirm a conviction under a state FLAG DESECRATION statute, not because the particular flag-burning threatened disorder but because a government seeking to avoid fire hazards could have prohibited all public burning. There, Fortas stated "action, even if clearly for serious protest purposes, is not entitled to the pervasive protection that is given to speech alone." Seemingly, it again was reaction to the particular factual situation that stirred Fortas, but he was unable to articulate persuasively the reasons for the particular sanctity he attached to the American flag.

When appointed, Fortas already was well-known as the victorious attorney in GIDEON V. WAINWRIGHT (1963), establishing indigents' RIGHT TO COUNSEL in criminal cases. As a Justice, he continued to stress procedural regularity and the need for law enforcement officers to obey the law. He was not afraid to extend protections further than the WARREN COURT majority, as he urged in ALDERMAN V. UNITED STATES (1969) and DESIST V. UNITED STATES (1969). One example is the Fifth Amendment RIGHT AGAINST SELF-INCRIMINATION which the majority limited to evidence of a testimonial or communicative nature in SCHMERBER V. CALIFORNIA (1966) and UNITED STATES V. WADE (1967). Fortas disagreed, saying it violated the privilege to subject a defendant to blood tests, or to make him repeat words uttered by the perpetrator of the crime, or to give a handwriting sample. His principle was that the privilege forbade compelling any evidence the gathering of which requires "affirmative, volitional action" on the part of the defendant. He applied that test in a somewhat conclusory fashion, however, maintaining that the accused could be made to stand in a LINEUP, "an incident of the state's power to ARREST, and a reasonable and justifiable aspect of the state's custody resulting from the arrest."

In EPPERSON V. ARKANSAS (1968) Fortas, for the Court, struck down an Arkansas statute that prohibited teaching evolution. *Epperson* suggests that the fact that a prohibition owes its existence to a particular religious dogma or religious campaign may be sufficient to invalidate it under the ESTABLISHMENT OF RELIGION clause—a position that Fortas might have preferred as an explanation for the invalidity of antiabortion legislation, had he remained on the Court to decide that issue. That case and those in which

Fortas championed the rights of children, such as *Tinker* and his landmark opinion IN RE GAULT (1967), or suggested the desirability of parents making some important decisions with their children rather than having a state-prescribed rule, such as GINSBURG V. NEW YORK (1968) (dissent), foreshadowed themes that have since proved important in other contexts (health services, EDUCATION, contraception, and abortion, for example). They suggest that Fortas would have had much to contribute to the Court had his service not been so limited in duration.

MARTHA A. FIELD

Bibliography

GRAHAM, FRED 1969 Abe Fortas. Pages 3015–3027 in Leon Friedman and Fred L. Israel, eds., *The Justices of the United States Supreme Court, 1789–1969.* New York: Chelsea House.

MASSARO, JOHN 1982–1983 LBJ and the Fortas Nomination for Chief Justice. *Political Science Quarterly* 97:603–621.

SHOGAN, ROBERT 1972 *A Question of Judgment: The Fortas Case and the Struggle for the Supreme Court.* Indianapolis: Bobbs-Merrill.

FOURTEENTH AMENDMENT
(Framing)

The Fourteenth Amendment to the United States Constitution consists of a variety of provisions addressed to several problems that arose when the Civil War and the abolition of slavery transformed the American political order. One sentence—"No State shall make or enforce any law which shall abridge the PRIVILEGES OR IMMUNITIES of citizens of the United States; nor shall any State deprive any person of life, liberty, or property without DUE PROCESS OF LAW; nor deny to any person within its jurisdiction the EQUAL PROTECTION OF THE LAWS"—has become the text upon which most twentieth-century constitutional law is a gloss. But this sentence may not have been the most important part of the amendment as it was conceived by its framers, adopted by Congress, and ratified by the states between 1865 and 1868.

The sentence was addressed most pointedly to one of the lesser problems that Congress faced in the winter of 1865–1866. During that winter congressional legislation protecting the CIVIL RIGHTS of former slaves had been vetoed by President ANDREW JOHNSON in part, he contended, because the Constitution entrusted the protection of civil rights to the states.

The Republican proponents of the CIVIL RIGHTS ACT OF 1866 mustered the necessary two-thirds vote to override the veto, but doubt remained about the power of the federal government to protect civil rights. The quoted sentence in section 1 of the Fourteenth Amendment was written, at least in part, to resolve that doubt.

Another concern of some Northerners in the winter of 1865–1866 was that some future Congress might repudiate the debt that the federal government had amassed during the Civil War or might undertake to pay the Confederate debt or compensate former slaveholders for the loss of their slaves. Section 4 of the amendment guaranteed the national debt, prohibited the payment of the Confederate debt, and barred compensation to slaveholders.

However, the most urgent task that the Thirty-ninth Congress confronted when it began its first session in December 1865 was to establish governments in the South that would be loyal to the Union and send loyal representatives to Congress. The problem was compounded by the ratification of the THIRTEENTH AMENDMENT, which not only abolished slavery but also put an end to the original Constitution's THREE-FIFTHS CLAUSE. With the abolition of slavery, the former slaves would be fully counted as part of the population of the former Confederate states; as a result those states would have more power in Congress and the ELECTORAL COLLEGE than they had had before the Civil War. Something had to be done to insure that the war did not increase the political power of the disloyal groups that had brought the war about.

Three solutions were advanced to prevent those who had lost the Civil War from enhancing their power as a result of it. One was to confer the franchise on Southern blacks, whose votes were expected to bring about the election of loyal candidates. A second solution was to deny political rights—both the right to vote and the right to hold office—to some or all who had participated in the rebellion against national authority. This scheme would increase the number of districts in which Union loyalists had a majority or at least some power to tip the electoral balance in favor of loyal candidates.

A third solution was to alter the basis of representation: to base a state's number of representatives in the House and hence its votes in the Electoral College not on total population but on the number of people eligible to vote. Thus, if a state excluded blacks from the right to vote, they would not be counted in determining its representation in Congress and its vote in the Electoral College. Thus the abolition of slavery and the end of the three-fifths compromise would reduce Southern political power in Congress unless Southern states gave blacks the right to vote and hence a share in that power.

The JOINT COMMITTEE ON RECONSTRUCTION, established by CONCURRENT RESOLUTIONS of the House and Senate in the opening days of the Congress, sought to put the possible solutions into some sort of order. Four members of this fifteen-man committee were most prominent in its activities: JOHN A. BINGHAM and THADDEUS STEVENS from the House and WILLIAM PITT FESSENDEN and JACOB M. HOWARD from the Senate.

At the third meeting of the Joint Committee on January 12, 1866, Bingham proposed a constitutional amendment that would give Congress "power to make all laws necessary and proper to secure to all persons in every State within this Union equal protection in their rights of life, liberty and property." The proposal was referred to a subcommittee which eight days later returned it to the Joint Committee in the following form: "Congress shall have power to make all laws necessary and proper to secure to all citizens of the United States, in every State, the same political rights and privileges; and to all persons in every State equal protection in the enjoyment of life, liberty, and property." In this form the proposal addressed two of the problems then pending, because it gave Congress power to protect civil rights and to legislate VOTING RIGHTS for blacks. This proposal, however, was never presented to Congress. The committee spent two weeks debating its language, finally agreeing on February 3 to the following: "The Congress shall have power to make all laws which shall be necessary and proper to secure to citizens of each State all privileges and immunities of citizens in the several States [Art. IV, Sec. 2]; and to all persons in the several States equal protection in the rights of life, liberty and property [5th Amendment]." A key issue that subsequent judges and scholars have long debated is whether this change in language was meant to deprive Congress of power to legislate black suffrage or merely to put that power into more acceptable language.

On the same day that the subcommittee submitted the early version of the amendment to the Joint Committee, it also submitted a proposal basing representation on population, but further providing "[t]hat whenever the elective franchise shall be denied or abridged in any State on account of race or color, all persons of such race or color shall be excluded from the basis of representation." Thus, the total package as of January 20 not only gave Congress power to legislate civil rights and black suffrage—power which Congress might or might not exercise—but also deprived a state of representation based on its black population if blacks were not given suffrage either by Congress or by the state. The package, as altered by the language change of February 3, was submitted to the full House as two separate constitutional amendments.

On February 28, the House postponed consideration of the Bingham amendment conferring legislative power on Congress, and never again considered that amendment as a separate entity. Earlier it had passed and sent to the Senate the amendment depriving states of representation if blacks were denied the right to vote. The Senate, however, never acted on the proposal. Thus, by the end of February 1866, the two forerunners of the Fourteenth Amendment had come to nought.

Both reappeared in slightly different language, however, in the omnibus measure which the Joint Committee presented to both houses of Congress on April 30, 1866. Section 1 of the measure was the sentence containing today's privilege and immunities, due process, and equal clauses, while section 2 reduced the representation of states who denied the right to vote to males over the age of twenty-one. Section 3 deprived all persons who had voluntarily supported the Confederate cause of the right to vote in federal elections prior to 1870, while section 4 dealt with the war debt. Section 5 gave Congress power to enforce the other four sections.

The omnibus amendment passed the House as proposed, but it faced difficulties in the Senate. When it emerged from the Senate on June 8, it had been changed in two significant respects. One of the changes added to section 1 a definition of CITIZENSHIP. The Senate also weakened section 3; instead of disfranchising those who had supported the Confederacy, it merely barred from federal office those Confederate supporters who prior to the Civil War had taken an oath to support the Constitution.

After the House had concurred on June 13 in the Senate's changes, the amendment was sent to the states. Twelve days later, on June 25, Connecticut became the first state to ratify. Five additional states ratified the amendment in 1866, and eleven added their RATIFICATIONS in January 1867. By June of 1867, one year after the amendment had been sent to the states, a total of twenty-two had ratified it.

Ratification by six more states was needed, however, and that did not occur until July 1868. By that time two of the states that had previously ratified the amendment, New Jersey and Ohio, had voted to withdraw their assent. Nonetheless Congress ruled that their ratifications survived the subsequent efforts at withdrawal and remained valid. On July 28, 1868, Secretary of State WILLIAM SEWARD accordingly proclaimed the Fourteenth Amendment part of the Constitution of the United States.

In recent decades, historians and judges have extensively debated three questions about the meaning which the Thirty-Ninth Congress and the ratifying states attached to the Fourteenth Amendment, especially to section 1. First, does section 1 give Congress power to protect voting rights? Second, does section 1 overrule BARRON V. BALTIMORE (1833) and require the states to abide by the provisions of the BILL OF RIGHTS? Third, does section 1 prohibit compulsory racial SEGREGATION?

Did section 1 of the Fourteenth Amendment give Congress power to protect voting rights? The Justices of the Supreme Court have been divided in their answer to this question, although the weight of historical scholarship leans toward the view that section 1 was not concerned with voting rights. As the above summary of the progress of the amendment in Congress suggests, resolution of the issue depends on whether the privileges and immunities language in section 1 was meant to alter the substance or only the form of an earlier version of the section, which explicitly gave Congress power to secure to all citizens in every state "equal political rights and privileges." The question can never be answered definitively, for the substitution was made in committee and the committee left no record of its reasoning. The record of congressional debates is equally ambiguous. When the present language of section 1 was on the floor, some congressmen suggested that the section gave Congress power to protect voting rights, but others disagreed. Similarly, some congressmen claimed after the amendment had been adopted that it gave them power to legislate protection of voting rights—and again others disagreed.

Was section 1 meant to overrule *Barron v. Baltimore* and compel the states to abide by the provisions of the Bill of Rights? Justice HUGO L. BLACK, relying on explicit statements during congressional debates that the section would accomplish that end, declared in a dissenting opinion in ADAMSON V. CALIFORNIA (1947) that the Fourteenth Amendment did incorporate the Bill of Rights and apply it to the states. Some scholars have supported Black's position. However, two years after *Adamson* Charles Fairman wrote an article challenging Black. Fairman noted that many states in the 1860s did not follow procedures mandated by the Bill of Rights, but that no one during state ratification proceedings seemed concerned that adoption of the Fourteenth Amendment would require changes in state practice. He thought it probable that, if the states were concerned that the amendment, through INCORPORATION of the Bill of Rights, would require changes in their practices, they would at least have discussed the issue. He concluded from the lack of discussion that the amendment had no such purpose. The view of several recent scholars has been that, in light of the conflicting and insubstantial evidence, the question raised by Justice Black can never be conclusively answered.

Finally, there is the question whether section 1 was intended to prohibit racial segregation. After asking the litigants in BROWN V. BOARD OF EDUCATION (1954) to address this question, the Court concluded that the historical evidence was too ambiguous to permit an answer. Some scholars, however, have been more confident. Raoul Berger concluded that the framers of the amendment did not intend to prohibit racial segregation. On the other hand, ALEXANDER BICKEL had argued some years earlier that the framers had consciously framed section 1 in broad, open-ended language that would permit people in the future to interpret it as prohibiting the practice of segregation. The historical record itself is sparse. During the debates in Congress on the amendment, little was said about segregation. Earlier, however, Congress had engaged in lengthy debates about the legality of segregation on DISTRICT OF COLUMBIA streetcars. Moreover, school segregation was opposed by some members of Congress, notably CHARLES SUMNER who had been counsel in ROBERTS V. CITY OF BOSTON, an 1849 school desegregation case. In the 1860s, however, Congress was permitting racially segregated schools to exist in the District of Columbia.

Questions about whether the Thirty-Ninth Congress and the states that ratified the Fourteenth Amendment intended it to protect voting rights, make the Bill of Rights binding on the states, or outlaw segregation can never be answered confidently. All that the person who inquires into the historical record in search of an answer can do is make a guess—a guess more likely to reflect his political beliefs than to reflect the state of the historical record. The questions that judges and historians have asked about the original meaning of the Fourteenth Amendment are simply the wrong ones, because they do not address the issues that Congress and the ratifying states in fact debated and decided during the era of Reconstruction.

On one point of political philosophy, nearly all Americans of the 1860s agreed. President Andrew Johnson stated the point in his 1865 State of the Union address: "Monopolies, perpetuities, and class legislation are contrary to the genius of free government, and ought not to be allowed. Here there is no room for favored classes or monopolies; the principle of our Government is that of equal laws. . . . We shall but fulfill our duties as legislators by according 'equal and exact justice to all men,' special privileges to none." Innumerable Republicans argued that the purpose of section 1 of the Fourteenth Amendment was to enact this political principle into law. John A. Bingham, the draftsman of section 1, said what others repeated: that he proposed "by amending the Constitution, to provide for the efficient enforcement, by law, of these 'equal rights of every man' "—of "the absolute equality of all men before the law." Even Democrats from former slave states accepted the principle that the law should treat all persons equally. There was neither division nor sustained debate in the Thirty-Ninth Congress over the contrary principle that people who are in fact the same should receive equal treatment before the law and that people who are different may be treated differently. The issue on which Republicans and Democrats divided was whether black people, in essence, were equal to white people or inherently inferior.

Garrett Davis, a Democratic senator from Kentucky, used typical racist rhetoric. During an 1866 debate on the question whether blacks should be permitted to vote in the District of Columbia, Davis said:

[T]he proposition that a nation of a superior race should allow an inferior race resident in large numbers among them to take part in their Government, in shaping, and controlling their destinies, is refuted by its mere statement. And the further proposition that a nation composed of the Caucasian race, the highest type of man, having resident in it more than four million negroes, the lowest type, of which race no nation or tribe, from the first dawning of history to the present day, has ever established a polity that could be denominated a Government, or has elaborated for itself any science or literature or arts or even an alphabet, or characters to represent numbers, or been capable of preserving those achievements of intellect when it has received them from the superior race; such a proposition is, on examination, revolting to reason, and in its practical operation would be productive of incalculable mischief.

Republicans responded to this "prejudice," which "belong[ed] to an age of darkness and violence, and is a poisonous, dangerous exotic when suffered to grow in the midst of republican institutions." Jacob M. Howard, a key member of the Joint Committee, told the Senate:

For weal or for woe, the destiny of the colored race in this country is wrapped up with our own; they are to remain in our midst, and here spend their years and here bury their fathers and finally repose themselves. We may regret it. It may not be entirely compatible with our taste that they should live in our midst. We cannot help it. Our forefathers introduced them, and their destiny is to continue among us; and the practical question which now presents itself to us is as to the best mode of getting along with them.

Justin Morrill of Vermont added: "We have put aside the creed of the despot, the monarchist, the aristocrat, and have affirmed the right and capacity of the people to govern themselves, and have staked the national life on the issue to make it good in practice. . . . To deny any portion of the American people civil or political rights common to the citizen upon pretense of race or color, is to ignore the fundamental principles of republicanism." The only proper policy for the Government, according to Lyman Trumbull, chairman of the Senate Judiciary Committee, was "to legislate in the interest of freedom. Now, our laws are to be enacted with a view to educate, improve, enlighten, and Christianize the negro; to make him an independent man; to teach him to think and to reason; to improve that principle which the great Author of all has implanted in every human breast, which is susceptible of the highest cultivation, and destined to go on enlarging and expanding through the endless ages of eternity."

Trumbull and his fellow Republicans understood that God had created blacks as the equals of whites and that, if the law gave blacks an opportunity, they would demonstrate their equality. The Republicans made this equalitarian faith the basis of the Fourteenth Amendment. Although the faith was forgotten within a decade of the Fourteenth Amendment's ratification, it still offers a perspective from which to begin analysis of the issues of Fourteenth Amendment jurisprudence that confront us today.

WILLIAM E. NELSON

(SEE ALSO: *Abolitionist Constitutional Theory*.)

Bibliography

BERGER, RAOUL 1977 *Government by Judiciary: The Transformation of the Fourteenth Amendment.* Cambridge, Mass.: Harvard University Press.

BICKEL, ALEXANDER M. 1955 The Original Understanding and the Segregation Decision. *Harvard Law Review* 69:1–65.

FAIRMAN, CHARLES 1949 Does the Fourteenth Amendment Incorporate the Bill of Rights? The Original Understanding. *Stanford Law Review* 2:5–173.

HYMAN, HAROLD M. and WIECEK, WILLIAM M. 1982 *Equal Justice under Law: Constitutional Development 1835–1875.* New York: Harper & Row.

JAMES, JOSEPH B. 1956 *The Framing of the Fourteenth Amendment.* Urbana: University of Illinois Press.

TEN BROEK, JACOBUS 1951 *The Antislavery Origins of the Fourteenth Amendment.* Berkeley: University of California Press.

FOURTH AMENDMENT
(Historical Origins)

Appended to the United States Constitution as part of the BILL OF RIGHTS in 1789, the Fourth Amendment declares that "The right of the people to be secure in their persons, houses, papers and effects against UNREASONABLE SEARCHES and seizures shall not be violated, and no warrants shall issue but upon PROBABLE CAUSE, supported by oath or affirmation, and particularly describing the place to be searched and the persons or things to be seized." In identifying the "specific" warrant as its orthodox method of search, the amendment constitutionally repudiated its antithesis, the GENERAL WARRANT.

The general warrant did not confine its reach to a particular person, place, or object but allowed its bearer to arrest, search, and seize as his suspicions directed. In 1763, a typical warrant by the British secretaries of state commanded "diligent search" for the unidentified author, printer, and publisher of a satirical journal, *The North Briton, No. 45,* and the seizure of their papers. At least five houses were consequently searched, forty-nine (mostly innocent) persons arrested, and thousands of books and papers confiscated. Resentment against such invasions ultimately generated an antidote in the Fourth Amendment and is crucial to its understanding.

General warrants and general searches without warrant had a lengthy pedigree. In 1662, a statute codified WRITS OF ASSISTANCE that allowed searching all suspected places for goods concealed in violation of the customs laws. Such writs had been used since at least 1621 and themselves absorbed the language of royal commissions that had for centuries authorized general searches without warrant. Similarly promiscuous searches had existed for numerous applications: the pursuit of felons, suppression of political and religious deviance, regulation of printing, medieval craft guilds, naval and military impressment, counterfeiting, bankruptcy, excise and land taxes, vagrancy, game poaching, sumptuary behavior, and even the recovery of stolen personal items.

Colonial America copied Britain's machinery of search but varied its applications. Most jurisdictions instituted general searches to collect taxes, discourage poaching, capture felons, or find stolen merchandise. In the southernmost colonies, general searches without warrant blossomed into a comprehensive system of social regulation of the civilian population by quasi-military "slave patrols."

Although general warrants were the basic method of search, numerous restraints qualified their operation. Writs of assistance were invalid at night; certain areas of legislation touching the guilds and excises confined the general searches involved to the persons vocationally concerned. Yet such measures were not a comprehensive guarantee, systematically applied. Moreover, social philosophy outweighed civil libertarianism as a motive for the most conspicuous restraints, for while general "privy searches" plagued the poor, the elite enjoyed immunity from whole classes of similar searches. Covered by a thin veneer of restraints different from the specific warrant, the centrality of the general search remained starkly visible. Conversely, although specific warrants existed in legal manuals, they were rare before 1750, thereby indicating that they were not the intended constitutional successor to the general warrant.

English legal thinkers, however, expressed far greater hostility to the general warrant than did the law itself. As early as 1589 Robert Beale charged that the general search warrants used by the "High Commission" against Puritans violated MAGNA CARTA (1215). In the next two centuries, such titans of English law as Sir EDWARD COKE, Sir Matthew Hale, and Sir WILLIAM BLACKSTONE embellished similar themes with citations from the COMMON LAW.

Such evidence, however, was more embroidery than substance. Magna Carta was a profoundly feudal document that said nothing on the intersection of searches, houses, and warrants. The master case usually cited against the general warrant, *Semayne's Case* (1602, 1604), actually drew a rigid line exempting the Crown from the protections elsewhere extended against invasion of the dwelling by private citizens. Unlike later scholars, the court had there emphasized that a man's house was *not* his castle against the government.

Like legal theorists, ordinary critics of the general search did not identify the specific warrant as its solution. Those whose houses were searched were more likely to execrate being searched than the generality of the authorizing warrant. Indignation that the victim of a general search was a member of the nobility deflected hostility from the search process and implied that it could properly be inflicted on the overwhelming majority who were not nobles. Ubiquitous laments that pregnant wives had miscarried during violent searches simply substituted appeals to the reader's sympathy for criticism of the absence of the concrete laws against such actions. Yet these very mythologies provided legitimacy and impulse for a right against unreasonable SEARCH AND SEIZURE. Although the Magna Carta of the thirteenth century said nothing against general searches, that of the eighteenth century had swollen into a formidable ideological weapon against them.

The movement against general warrants accelerated from 1761 to 1787. The *North Briton* controversy culminated in dozens of trials and in resolutions by the House of Commons against the use of those warrants. In *Wilkes v. Wood* (1763) and *Huckle v. Money* (1763–1765), CHARLES PRATT (Lord Camden) and WILLIAM MURRAY (Lord Mansfield), the chief justices of the Courts of Common Pleas and King's Bench, respectively, condemned the general warrants of search and arrest used by the secretaries of state as incompatible with statute, natural justice, the common law, and Magna Carta. A dozen derivative cases surrounding *Entick v. Carrington* ended in decisions against the seizure of personal papers. (See WILKES CASES.)

Writs of assistance came under attack in the American colonial courts. JAMES OTIS, a fiery young Massachusetts attorney, made a brilliant "higher law" assault on the writs in PAXTON'S CASE (1761). Although Otis lost, most colonial courts refused to issue such writs when requuired to do so by the Townshend Act of 1767, and a series of pamphlets beginning with JOHN DICKINSON's *Farmer's Letters* joined in the assault. Eight states inserted some guarantee against general warrants in their constitutions of 1776–1784. Finally, four state conventions urged a corresponding restraint on searches by the new national government in ratifying the federal Constitution of 1787. JAMES MADISON of Virginia duly responded by including what became the Fourth Amendment among the Bill of Rights which he proposed to Congress on June 8, 1789.

Neither Britain nor the separate American states, however, immediately abolished general searches. Rhetorical implications notwithstanding, the British abandoned only the isolated form of general warrants issued by state secretaries. Writs of assistance and other kinds of statutory general SEARCH WARRANTS survived, for no comprehensive statute to the contrary ever emerged from the House of Commons. Despite their constitutions, the American states retained general search warrants not only as devices for [prosecuting the American Revolution] but also for a wide range of other purposes into the 1780s.

Although the right against unreasonable search and seizure has lengthy British roots, its cornerstone, the confinement of all searches, seizures, and arrests by warrant to the particular place, persons, and objects enumerated, derives from Massachusetts. A cluster of Massachusetts statutes and court decisions from 1756 to 1766, the third stage in a century-long process, uniformly restrained searches and arrests to the person or location designated in the warrant. Legislation in the 1780s extended this specificity to the objects of seizure. The Fourth Amendment is thus the marriage of an ancient British right and a new, colonial interpretation that vastly extended its meaning.

WILLIAM J. CUDDIHY

Bibliography

CUDDIHY, WILLIAM and HARDY, B. CARMON 1980 A Man's House Was Not His Castle: Origins of the Fourth Amendment to the United States Constitution. *William and Mary Quarterly* 3:371–400.

LASSON, NELSON 1937 *The History . . . of the Fourth Amendment.* Baltimore: Johns Hopkins University Press.

FRAENKEL, OSMOND K.
(1888–1981)

Trained at Columbia University Law School, Osmond Kessler Fraenkel made his mark on American constitutional law as a CIVIL LIBERTIES advocate. He was counsel for the New York Civil Liberties Union from 1934 to 1955 and for the AMERICAN CIVIL LIBERTIES UNION from 1955 to 1977. During most of that time he was also an official of the National Lawyers Guild. In addition to being involved in much of the important civil liberties litigation of his time, Fraenkel wrote four books, including *Our Civil Liberties* (1945) and *The Supreme Court and Civil Liberties* (1960), as well as many law review articles.

DENNIS J. MAHONEY

FRANK, JEROME N.
(1889–1957)

Jerome Frank held important positions in FRANKLIN D. ROOSEVELT's New Deal, pioneered American legal realism, taught at Yale Law School, and served on the United States Court of Appeals for the Second Circuit from 1941 until his death in 1957. During this period the Second Circuit was one of the most illustrious courts in the nation's history. On the court Frank developed a highly refined concept of his role as intermediate appellate judge. His decisions greatly influenced the United States Supreme Court by crystallizing and focusing legal issues and by articulating major considerations of precedent and policy. His opinions, even if written as concurrences or dissents, frequently became the law of the land when the Supreme Court followed Jerome Frank's lead. When the VINSON COURT and WARREN COURT protected CIVIL LIBERTIES, they often relied on the spadework of lower federal judges, prominently including Jerome Frank.

In his opinions Frank frequently addressed the Supreme Court as an advocate—urging, persuading, coaxing, and cajoling the Court to move in desired directions. At the same time, he recognized the limits imposed by his subordinate position, and he gracefully accepted those bounds. Frank faithfully followed Supreme Court precedent, but, if a rule seemed misguided, he would criticize the DOCTRINE and urge the Supreme Court to reexamine it. *United States v. Roth* (1956) illustrates Frank's technique. Although he considered a federal OBSCENITY statute unconstitutional, several Supreme Court decisions had assumed the statute's validity without squarely facing the issue. In a new challenge to the law, Frank did not dodge these earlier rulings by describing them as OBITER DICTA. Rather, he followed them and voted to uphold the convictions. At the same time, in a concurrence, he analyzed the serious constitutional issues with a coherence and lucidity that has not yet been surpassed. Frank's seminal effort anticipated many later Supreme Court cases which, over the next two decades, relied on Frank's opinion and reasoning. (See *Roth v. United States,* 1957.)

Protection for civil liberties was a persistent theme in Frank's judicial opinions. He believed that republican government maximized free choice and affirmed the dignity of the individual. On the Second Circuit he struggled to protect this vision. He regularly challenged the Supreme Court to expand the definition of, and protection for, civil liberties. For instance, he tried valiantly to humanize IMMIGRATION and DEPORTATION laws which perennially had treated ALIENS cavalierly. Frank wrote his most passionate opinions in the area of criminal law and procedure. He considered ELECTRONIC EAVESDROPPING a dangerous invasion of privacy which should be limited by the FOURTH AMENDMENT's prohibition on UNREASONABLE SEARCHES and seizures. His skepticism about the accuracy of the law's fact-finding processes led him to believe that courts wrongly convicted many innocent persons. He thought that police investigation practices frequently degenerated into brutal "third degree" tactics which coerced confessions in violation of the Fifth and Sixth Amendments. Following in Frank's path, the Supreme Court moved to curb prolonged POLICE INTERROGATIONS and to control offensive police practices. The progressive constitutionalization of American criminal process secured by the Vinson and Warren Courts reflected not merely the judgment of a majority of the Supreme Court but rather a broader legal movement led prominently by Jerome Frank.

ROBERT JEROME GLENNON

Bibliography

GLENNON, ROBERT JEROME 1985 *The Iconoclast as Reformer: Jerome Frank's Impact on American Law.* Ithaca, N.Y.: Cornell University Press.

FRANK v. MANGUM
237 U.S. 309 (1915)

Vicious anti-Semitism and bitter resentment against encroaching industrialization joined in Atlanta, Georgia, in the spring of 1913. Leo Frank, a young Jewish businessman from the North, was arrested and convicted of murdering a thirteen-year-old girl in a factory he superintended. Prejudice, disorder, and blatant public hostility characterized the trial and its coverage. The Georgia Supreme Court denied Frank a new trial, 4–2, dismissing claims of procedural errors, irregularities, and the trial judge's stated doubts about Frank's guilt.

Justices JOSEPH R. LAMAR and OLIVER WENDELL HOLMES each turned down requests for WRITS OF ERROR on procedural grounds (though Holmes was not convinced that Frank had received DUE PROCESS), as did the entire Supreme Court, without opinion. Frank then petitioned for a writ of HABEAS CORPUS because mob domination had effectively denied him PROCEDURAL DUE PROCESS. The Court likewise denied this relief, 7–2. Justice MAHLON PITNEY declared that habeas corpus could not be substituted for a writ of error to review procedural irregularities. Further, when Frank neglected to object during the trial, he effectively waived the right to claim a denial of due process later. Justices Holmes and CHARLES EVANS HUGHES dissented, pointing to the lack of a FAIR TRIAL: "Mob law does not become due process of law by securing the assent of a terrorized jury." Less than two months after the Georgia governor commuted his death sentence to life imprisonment, Frank was kidnapped from prison and lynched. That he was innocent of the crime for which he was convicted is no longer doubted.

The Supreme Court subsequently embarked on a series of decisions insuring the observance of the constitutional safeguards of procedural due process. In MOORE V. DEMPSEY (1923), the turning point, Holmes wrote for the Court, permitting the use of habeas corpus as a means of preserving criminal defendants' rights. *Frank*'s rule of forfeiture through failure to object, however, returned with only slight modification in WAINWRIGHT V. SYKES (1977).

In 1982 a witness came forward and stated that shortly after the murder he had seen another man carrying the victim's body. In 1986 the governor of Georgia posthumously pardoned Leo Frank.

DAVID GORDON

Bibliography

DINNERSTEIN, LEONARD 1968 *The Leo Frank Case.* New York: Columbia University Press.

FRANKFURTER, FELIX
(1882–1965)

The immigrant son of Austrian Jews, Felix Frankfurter acquired a legendary reputation as a lawyer, law professor, intellectual gadfly, and presidential adviser even before President FRANKLIN D. ROOSEVELT named him to the Supreme Court in 1939. Unable to speak or write a word of English when he entered the public schools of New York City in the 1890s, he was graduated with honors from City College of New York and compiled a distinguished record at the Harvard Law School, where he fell under the influence of Dean James Barr Ames's historical methods, absorbed the constitutional theories of JAMES BRADLEY THAYER, and generally adopted the social and cultural trappings of the New England Brahmins, without their intellectual boorishness or political conservatism.

As a law professor at Harvard, Frankfurter introduced several generations of students to constitutional and ADMINISTRATIVE LAW, and invented a new field of study: the JURISDICTION of the federal courts. His students and protégés, including Dean Acheson, JAMES LANDIS, David Lilienthal, and Tom Corcoran, populated the federal bureaucracy from the days of WOODROW WILSON to those of JOHN F. KENNEDY. His 1917 report on the deportation of striking miners from Arizona by local vigilantes and his severe criticism of the procedural unfairness of the COMMONWEALTH V. SACCO & VANZETTI (1921) showed his deep concern for CIVIL LIBERTIES and political reform. That he should come to be known, at the end of his judicial career, as a conservative on many of these issues reflected not a weakening of personal convictions, but a strongly held view about the proper limits of the judicial function.

Frankfurter served on the Court between the two great periods of JUDICIAL ACTIVISM in this century. He arrived on the bench two years after the HUGHES COURT, retreating from its activism of 1935–1936, laid to rest the DUE PROCESS clause and the COMMERCE CLAUSE as instruments of judicial control over legislative ECONOMIC REGULATION. His retirement and replacement in 1962 by ARTHUR J. GOLDBERG permitted the Warren Court to enter its most activist phase through the expansion of due process and EQUAL PROTECTION to provide Americans with extensive new CONSTITUTIONAL REMEDIES against governmental encroachments upon personal liberties.

Frankfurter deplored both the conservative activism of the Hughes years and the liberal activism of the Warren era. From 1939 until 1962, he attempted to discover some middle ground for the Court to occupy that would be intellectually respectable, politically defensible, and morally satisfying. Although his ultimate posture of institutional self-restraint won him few plaudits from liberals and captured the fancy of only a minority among the legal intelligentsia, it had the virtue of predictability.

He rejected the PREFERRED FREEDOMS doctrine articulated by Justice HARLAN FISKE STONE in UNITED STATES V. CAROLENE PRODUCTS CO. (1938), where the latter urged the Court to adopt a two-tiered system of JUDICIAL REVIEW that would take the justices out of the business of shaping economic policy at large but expand their role as the arbiters of civil liberties, race relations, and criminal justice. When passing upon all constitutional questions, Frankfurter responded, the Justices should always act with restraint, avoid ultimate issues of power, and insist only upon a RATIONAL BASIS test for legislation, whether the challenged law concerned filled milk, labor relations, FREEDOM OF SPEECH, or CRIMINAL PROCEDURE. This judicial posture led Frankfurter to uphold a broad range of social and economic measures adopted by the states and the federal government after 1940, but it also earned him the enmity of constitutional liberals when he applied the same tolerant standards to less enlightened manifestations of the political process, including the SMITH ACT, the McCarran Act (see INTERNAL SECURITY ACT), a GROUP LIBEL statute, and the investigative techniques of the HOUSE COMMITTEE ON UN-AMERICAN ACTIVITIES.

Frankfurter also spurned Justice HUGO L. BLACK's arguments for incorporating the BILL OF RIGHTS into the FOURTEENTH AMENDMENT's due process clause. Like Frankfurter, the Alabama-born justice wished to chain the arbitrary power of judges in the wake of the Great Depression's constitutional crisis, and he urged the Court to replace "the vague contours of due process" with the specific prohibitions and guarantees of the first nine amendments. But beneath Black's façade of positivistic neutrality, Frankfurter suspected, there beat the heart of a judicial fundamentalist, moved by the plight of the poor and the oppressed but no less unbending than PIERCE BUTLER's or GEORGE SUTHERLAND's. Frankfurter eschewed mechanical formulas such as Black's, and he believed that the INCORPORATION DOCTRINE lacked any historical basis in the Fourteenth Amendment. Incorporation, he feared, would encourage the Supreme Court to impose a single code of criminal procedure upon the states and would establish a more rigid judicial tyranny than even the conservative "Four Horsemen" had espoused during the 1930s.

From BETTS V. BRADY (1942) to MAPP V. OHIO in 1961, he insisted that the framers of the Fourteenth Amendment had not intended to subject state criminal proceedings to the precise requirements of the federal Bill of Rights. That amendment, he argued in ADAMSON V. CALIFORNIA (1947), was "not the basis of a uniform code of criminal procedure federally imposed. . . . In a federal system it would be a function debilitating to the responsibility of state and local agencies."

But this did not mean for Frankfurter that the Supreme Court of the United States had no obligation to review state criminal convictions under the due process clause. That clause, he believed, represented no explicit commands, but a requirement of fairness and reasonableness, above all, a prohibition against official conduct that "shocked the conscience" or offended contemporary standards of civilized behavior. Within this broad, subjective framework, the states had flexibility to manage their own affairs in the realm of criminal justice. Police officers could not, in the absence of friends or counsel, interrogate a suspect for days and claim that his confession had been voluntary; they could not recover physical evidence with the aid of a stomach pump (as in ROCHIN V. CALIFORNIA, 1952); or place a listening device in a suspect's bedroom (as in IRVINE V. CALIFORNIA, 1953, dissenting opinion). But due process did not require, in Frankfurter's judgment, that the state provide legal counsel in all felony cases; exclude evidence seized illegally by the police; or refrain from executing a person after a first attempt had failed, although he had strong personal objections to all of these practices

(*Louisiana ex rel. Francis v. Resweber,* 1947, concurring opinion; *Mapp v. Ohio,* 1961, dissenting).

An early high point of Frankfurter's doctrinal influence came in the summer of 1940, when, over Stone's lone dissent, the Justices rejected a FIRST AMENDMENT–due process attack on the mandatory flag salute in the public schools of West Virginia. Within a year of that decision, however, Frankfurter's majority disintegrated. (See FLAG SALUTE CASES, 1940–1943.) Led by Black and WILLIAM O. DOUGLAS, a coalition of from five to six Justices carved out a generous area of constitutional protection for both religious and political minorities under the First Amendment and the due process clause. This same majority also began to impose sharp limitations upon the conduct of state criminal trials and local police methods and to afford state prisoners greater ACCESS to federal courts by means of HABEAS CORPUS proceedings.

Throughout his judicial career, Frankfurter remained skeptical of absolutes. He preached a gospel of relativism and "balancing" that usually encouraged judicial modesty and retrenchment, yet, he too could be a fundamentalist on many constitutional questions. Few Justices took more literally the First Amendment's prohibition against an ESTABLISHMENT OF RELIGION, and his views in EVERSON V. BOARD OF EDUCATION (1947) and MCCOLLUM V. BOARD OF EDUCATION (1948) remained as uncompromising as Black's on freedom of speech. He abhorred CAPITAL PUNISHMENT and used every weapon in his considerable legal arsenal to set aside convictions that carried the death penalty.

Moreover, he consistently championed the FOURTH AMENDMENT by refusing to bend its language to accommodate SEARCHES AND SEIZURES made without a valid warrant or PROBABLE CAUSE as demonstrated by his dissenting opinion in UNITED STATES V. RABINOWITZ (1950). Finally, although he resisted the extension of the EXCLUSIONARY RULE to the states via the due process clause, he expected federal judges, prosecutors, and law enforcement officials to follow a strict code of fairness and decency when confronting persons accused or suspected of crimes (*McNabb v. United States,* 1943, see MCNABB-MALLORY RULE; *Nye v. United States,* 1941; *Rosenberg v. United States,* 1953, dissenting opinion).

In addition to institutional self-restraint, Frankfurter found in FEDERALISM—perhaps the oldest of our constitutional values—a major, articulate premise of his jurisprudence. His concern for maintaining the vitality of local governmental units distinguished him sharply from most other post-1937 Justices. "The states," he wrote, nine years before joining the Court,

"need the amplest scope for energy and individuality in dealing with the myriad problems created by our complex industrial civilization. . . . For government means experimentation. To be sure, constitutional limitations confine the area of experiment. But these limitations are not self-defining and were intended to permit government. Opportunity must be allowed for vindicating reasonable belief by experience. The very notion of our federalism calls for the free play of local diversity in dealing with local problems." From 1939 until 1962, he attempted to apply these convictions.

A great many of Frankfurter's conflicts with other Justices, often viewed as disputes over civil liberties or judicial self-restraint, actually focused for him upon questions of federalism. A good example is the famous 1941 case of BRIDGES V. CALIFORNIA, which, many scholars agree, marked a turning point in his relationship with Justice Black and remains a landmark in the Court's post-1937 concern for civil liberties. In *Bridges,* speaking through Black, the Court reversed contempt sentences imposed by California judges upon a militant union leader and the Los Angeles *Times* for out-of-court publications that the local courts believed had disrupted pending cases. Unless such statements represented a CLEAR AND PRESENT DANGER to the orderly administration of justice, Black wrote, the due process clause (incorporating the First Amendment's protection of speech and press) prohibited judicial punishment of this kind.

Frankfurter took issue with Black on several points, but the heart of his dissenting opinion reflected powerful federalist concerns for the independence and autonomy of local courts. "We are, after all," he noted, "sitting over three thousand miles away from a great state, without intimate knowledge of its habits and its needs, in matters which do not cut across the affirmative powers of the national government. . . . How are we to know whether an easy-going or stiffer view of what affects the actual administration of justice is appropriate to local circumstances?" Nine months earlier, in a similar contempt case that did not raise the problem of a direct conflict with state courts, Frankfurter had no difficulty in joining an opinion by Justice Douglas in *Nye v. United States* (1941) that sharply curtailed the power of federal judges to punish disruptive litigants. For Frankfurter, what distinguished *Nye* from *Bridges* was not the First Amendment, "the clear and present danger" test, or the degree of judicial misconduct involved, but the simple matter of the constitution's limited reach into the processes of state courts.

A passionate New Dealer, Frankfurter consistently

upheld the power of Congress, acting under the commerce clause, to regulate the nation's economic affairs, even when these regulations touched activities within the traditional domain of the states. He sustained, for example, the judgment of the National Labor Relations Board that local newspaper boys, employed by the Hearst chain, were "employees" within the coverage of the WAGNER (NATIONAL LABOR RELATIONS) ACT, and he agreed that the administrator of the FAIR LABOR STANDARDS ACT could entirely prohibit homework in the embroidery industry as a reasonable means to enforce minimum wage decrees.

At the same time, he tended to read congressional regulation of commerce as permitting complementary state legislation, except where the national legislature acted with clarity to preempt local regulations. He insisted that Congress speak with precision on this matter, and he abhorred judicial expansion of congressional intentions, especially where the results limited local authority. In *Cornell Steamboat Co. v. United States* (1944), for instance, he rejected Black's interpretation of the 1940 Transportation Act that gave the Interstate Commerce Commission authority to fix the rates of tugboats operating on the Hudson River, where ninety-five percent of their business took place between New York ports, but where they passed briefly over the territorial waters of New Jersey. He rejected the idea that Congress had intended in the Wagner Act to exempt union officials from state regulation that did not touch directly upon the employee–employer relationship. In close cases, he often supported a solution that expanded federal authority the least.

In commerce clause cases, despite his concern for maintaining local authority, he refused to endorse the extreme views of Justice Black and others, who mechanically endorsed state economic regulations in the absence of specific federal legislation preempting certain fields. He voted to overturn, for example, Arizona's Train Limit Law and he likewise objected to a local milk ordinance that discriminated against competing products pasteurized beyond five miles of the city. On the other hand, he often allowed the states considerable latitude when they attempted to tax or regulate other aspects of interstate commerce, and he did not support wholeheartedly the economic nationalism of Justice ROBERT H. JACKSON, with whom he disagreed in cases such as *Duckworth v. Arkansas* (1941); *Northwest Airlines v. Minnesota* (1944); and *H. P. Hood & Sons v. DuMond* (1949; dissenting).

Frankfurter believed that federalism required the national judiciary, above all the Supreme Court, to respect the autonomy, sagacity, and integrity of state courts. He was a strong supporter of Justice LOUIS D. BRANDEIS's views (which had become law in ERIE V. TOMPKINS, 1938) that required federal judges to apply state law in cases involving diversity of state citizenship, and he often voted to restrict the role of federal courts in this area. (See DIVERSITY JURISDICTION.) State courts, he believed, could efficiently and honestly protect the interests of nonresidents. The Supreme Court should not construe federal statutes in such a manner as to preempt local judicial procedures unless that construction seemed inescapable. For instance, he rejected the idea that Congress intended in the federal bankruptcy laws to strip local courts of their control over their own procedures. "The state courts belong to the States," he wrote. "They are not subject to the control of Congress though of course state law may in words or by implication make the federal rule for conducting litigation the rule that should govern suits to enforce federal rights in the state courts."

America's continuing racial ordeal probably tested the limits of his deference to state authority more severely than did any other constitutional issue. An early member of the NAACP and the first Justice to hire a black clerk, he detested racial discrimination in all of its forms. Yet he refused to interpret the Reconstruction-era CIVIL RIGHTS ACTS to impose criminal and civil penalties on local officials who abused their authority and acted in a hostile manner against minorities. In SCREWS V. UNITED STATES (1945), Frankfurter, dissenting, argued that Congress had intended in the Reconstruction statute to attack only discrimination sanctioned by positive state laws, not the abuse of authority by local officials. "We should leave to the States," he said, "the enforcement of their criminal law, and not relieve States of the responsibility for vindicating wrongdoing that is essentially local or weaken the habits of local law enforcement by tempting reliance on federal authority for an occasional unpleasant task of local enforcement."

Two decades later, Frankfurter still reaffirmed these views in MONROE V. PAPE (1961), when the Court sustained a civil action against several Chicago police officers who invaded a black family's home and illegally arrested a member of the household without a SEARCH WARRANT. The conduct of the police infuriated him, but in Frankfurter's judgment they had not acted with the approval of state law and therefore they could not be sued under the federal statute for damages. "To be sure," he wrote, "this leaves certain cases unprotected. . . . But the cost of ignoring the distinction in order to cover those cases—the cost, that is, of providing a federal judicial remedy for every constitutional violation—involves preemption by the National Government . . . of matters of intimate concern to state and local government."

History treated neither Justice Frankfurter nor his federalism kindly. By means of the commerce clause and its TAXING AND SPENDING POWERS, the federal government continued to absorb more and more authority at the expense of the states, usually with the Supreme Court's approval. Horrified by local police brutality and by the failure of local political elites to eradicate racial SEGREGATION, the federal judiciary became a powerful instrument of social reform in the decade after Frankfurter left the bench. Even during his tenure, American society was not usually prepared to pay the price of his attachment to federalism. As the *Screws* and *Monroe* cases demonstrated, the price could be very high: the inability of the national government to correct glaring denials of constitutional rights that the states themselves refused to correct, and the failure of the states to correct local ills of a kind already eliminated in the conduct of the national government.

From the perspective of many of his colleagues, Frankfurter too often sacrificed efficiency, uniformity, and morality on behalf of an archaic devotion to localism. They hoped to create a new world of prodigious economic growth and humanitarian social policy, where the enlightened judiciary helped to sweep away the provincial forces of commercial and political reaction. For Justice Frankfurter, however, federalism remained both a constitutional command as well as a viable method for ordering American life through the slower process of self-education and social experimentation.

Frankfurter enlivened American politics and immeasurably enriched the nation's legal literature for a half-century. "There is some talk here of replacing him on the Supreme Court," James Reston wrote when he retired in 1962, "but this is as silly as the doctor's bulletins. They may eventually put somebody in his place, but they won't replace him."

MICHAEL E. PARRISH

Bibliography

FREEDMAN, MAX, ED. 1967 *Roosevelt and Frankfurter: Their Correspondence, 1928–1945.* Boston: Little, Brown.

HIRSCH, HARRY N. 1981 *The Enigma of Felix Frankfurter.* New York: Basic Books.

LASH, JOSEPH P. 1975 *From the Diaries of Felix Frankfurter.* New York: Norton.

PARRISH, MICHAEL E. 1982 *Felix Frankfurter and His Times.* Volume One. New York: Macmillan.

PHILLIPS, HARLAN B., ED. 1960 *Felix Frankfurter Reminisces.* New York: Reynal & Co.

FRANKLIN, BENJAMIN
(1706–1790)

Benjamin Franklin, president of Pennsylvania, was the oldest delegate to the CONSTITUTIONAL CONVENTION OF 1787. A beloved elder statesman of the young Republic, Franklin lent prestige to the Convention by his presence. His signature on the new Constitution was a symbol of the continuity of revolutionary principles and a warranty of the democratic character of the document.

Franklin's public career began in 1736, when he was appointed clerk of the Pennsylvania Assembly, and lasted for more than half a century. He served as a member of the assembly and as postmaster of British North America even while pursuing a private career as a printer and inventor.

In 1754, as a delegate to the Albany Congress, Franklin proposed the "Albany Plan" of colonial union. Under his plan, the British Crown would have appointed a president-general and the colonial legislatures would have chosen delegates to a Grand Council with power to raise an army and navy, to make war and peace with the Indian tribes, to control commerce with the Indians, and to levy taxes and customs duties to pay the expenses of the union. The plan, one of the earliest moves toward American FEDERALISM, was too consolidated to find support in the colonies and too democratic to be acceptable in England.

From 1757 to 1762, and again from 1766 to 1775, Franklin was the agent in England of Pennsylvania and several other colonies. In that capacity he explained to Parliament American opposition to the Stamp Act, that is, to TAXATION WITHOUT REPRESENTATION, and persuaded WILLIAM PITT to propose a plan of colonial union within the British Empire.

Returning to Pennsylvania in 1775, Franklin was named a delegate to the Second Continental Congress, where, in July, he proposed ARTICLES OF CONFEDERATION establishing a "league of friendship" among the colonies with a Congress that would exercise considerable legislative power. The following year he served on the committee that drafted the DECLARATION OF INDEPENDENCE.

From 1776 to 1785, Franklin served as minister of the United States to France (and was accredited to several other European governments as well). He negotiated the French military and financial assistance that was crucial to the success of the Revolution, and he carried out a propaganda campaign to win European support for the American cause. In

1781 he was named a commissioner to the peace negotiations that resulted in the Treaty of Paris and formal British recognition of American independence.

At the Constitutional Convention, Franklin was a conciliator and mediator. Although, at eighty-one, he was in failing health and had to have his speeches read by fellow delegate JAMES WILSON, Franklin attended almost all sessions. Such proposals as he put forward (for example, unicameral legislature, plural executive, elected judges, unpaid officials) were too radical to attract much support; but Franklin, with his humorous anecdotes and his commitment to the Union, served the Convention well by cooling tempers and encouraging compromise.

According to a legend, which serves as a warning still, Franklin, emerging from the Convention, was asked, "What have you given us?" "A republic," he replied, "if you can keep it."

DENNIS J. MAHONEY

Bibliography

VAN DOREN, CARL 1938 *Benjamin Franklin.* New York: Viking.

FRAZIER-LEMKE ACTS
Federal Farm Bankruptcy Act
48 Stat. 1289 (1934)
Farm Mortgage Moratorium Act
49 Stat. 942 (1935)

Congress passed the Federal Farm Bankruptcy Act in June 1934 in an effort to stem the flow of foreclosures caused by the Depression. Enacted as an amendment to a general bankruptcy act of 1898, the first Frazier-Lemke Act allowed bankrupt farmers two choices. Under the first, court-appointed appraisers would assess the "fair and reasonable value, not necessarily the market value" of the property, which the debtor could then repurchase within six years according to a graduated scale of interest. Alternatively, a court could halt all proceedings for five years, during which time the debtor would retain possession "provided he pays a reasonable rent annually," preserving the right to buy it after five years.

Within a year a unanimous Supreme Court struck down the act as a TAKING OF PROPERTY belonging to the creditor without JUST COMPENSATION in LOUISVILLE JOINT STOCK LAND BANK v. RADFORD (1935). Congress passed a second Frazier-Lemke (Farm Mort-

gage Moratorium) Act in August 1935, effectively similar legislation to which they added a declaration of emergency and a discretionary provision allowing courts to shorten the stay of proceedings during which time the creditor retained a lien on the property. This act received the Court's approval in WRIGHT V. VINTON BRANCH OF MOUNTAIN TRUST BANK OF ROANOKE (1937).

DAVID GORDON

FREEDMAN v. MARYLAND
380 U.S. 51 (1965)

Although the Supreme Court often remarks that the FIRST AMENDMENT imposes a heavy presumption against the validity of any system of PRIOR RESTRAINT on expression, the Court has tolerated state censorship of motion pictures through advance licensing. Typically, such a law authorizes a censorship board to deny a license to a film on the ground of OBSCENITY. Other substantive standards ("immoral," "tending to corrupt morals") have been held invalid for VAGUENESS. In addition, the Court insists that the licensing system's procedures follow strict guidelines designed to avoid the chief evils of censorship. *Freedman* is the leading decision establishing these guidelines.

In a test case, a Baltimore theater owner showed a concededly innocuous film without submitting it to the state censorship board, and he was convicted of a violation of state law. The Supreme Court unanimously reversed the conviction. The *Freedman* opinion, by Justice WILLIAM J. BRENNAN, set three procedural requirements for film censorship. First, the censor must have the burden of proving that the film is "unprotected expression" (for example, obscenity). Second, while the state may insist that all films be submitted for advance screening, the censor's determination cannot be given the effect of finality; a judicial determination is required. Thus the censor must, "within a specified brief period, either issue a license or go to court to restrain showing of the film." Advance restraint, before the issue gets to court, must be of the minimum duration consistent with orderly employment of the judicial machinery. Third, the court's decision itself must be prompt. Maryland's statute failed all three parts of this test and accordingly was an unconstitutional prior restraint. Justices WILLIAM O. DOUGLAS and HUGO L. BLACK, concurring, would have held any advance censorship impermissible.

KENNETH L. KARST

FREEDMEN'S BUREAU

Congress created the Bureau of Refugees, Freedmen, and Abandoned Lands in March 1865, assigning it the disposition of rebels' lands and distribution of emergency relief to freed blacks and refugees of both races uprooted by the war. Though the Freedmen's Bureau was the first federal human-services organization, its establishment reflected Congress's resistance to constitutional innovation, combined with the pervasive nineteenth-century belief that relief and welfare were beyond the constitutional authority of the federal government. Hence the Bureau was a public–private hybrid, drawing its personnel from the army, assisted by volunteers from the various private relief and welfare organizations working with blacks and soldiers in the South.

The 1865 Act provided that the agency would expire a year after cessation of hostilities. In February 1866, Congress enacted a bill to extend the Bureau's life indefinitely. The bill permitted the President "to extend military protection and jurisdiction over all cases" in which blacks were denied CIVIL RIGHTS enjoyed by whites or were punished in ways whites were not. This provision reflected Republicans' resentment at the de jure and de facto discrimination against blacks in the South, especially that authorized by the BLACK CODES. Democrats and other conservatives denounced trials before military commissions or "courts" composed of Freedmen's Bureau agents, citing the absence of guarantees of INDICTMENT or PRESENTMENT as violative of the prohibition against military trials of civilians implied in the Fifth Amendment. Republicans countered that the bill was authorized by the enforcement clause (section 2) of the recently ratified THIRTEENTH AMENDMENT. The bill thus provided the first opportunity to explore the meaning and extent of this new provision. President ANDREW JOHNSON vetoed the bill, charging its Republican sponsors with racial favoritism and a disregard of FEDERALISM. Congress narrowly sustained the veto, but a similar bill became law four months later over his veto.

In existence until 1874, the Bureau helped blacks to adjust to freedom in the turbulent conditions of the postwar South.

WILLIAM M. WIECEK

Bibliography

NIEMAN, DONALD G. 1979 *To Set the Law in Motion: The Freedmen's Bureau and the Legal Rights of Blacks, 1865–1868.* Milwood, N.Y.: KTO Press.

FREEDOM OF . . .

See also under Right . . .

FREEDOM OF ASSEMBLY AND ASSOCIATION

The FIRST AMENDMENT's "right of the people peaceably to assemble" and the FOURTEENTH AMENDMENT have supplied a basis for federal protection of undefined FUNDAMENTAL RIGHTS from violation by the states. In the landmark case of UNITED STATES v. CRUIKSHANK (1876), the Supreme Court, in the course of allowing some lynchers to escape federal prosecution, said by way of OBITER DICTUM that the right peaceably to assemble was an attribute of CITIZENSHIP under a free government that antedated the Constitution, and that it was a privilege of national citizenship provided that the assembly in question concerned matters relating to the national government. (See PRIVILEGES AND IMMUNITIES.)

With respect to STATE ACTION, the right of peaceable assembly is now regarded as a Fourteenth Amendment DUE PROCESS right. Thus, in DEJONGE v. OREGON (1937), the Supreme Court reversed a conviction for CRIMINAL SYNDICALISM under an Oregon statute of a man who had participated in a peaceful meeting called by the Communist party for a lawful purpose, on the grounds that the due process clause of the Fourteenth Amendment had been violated. Chief Justice CHARLES EVANS HUGHES wrote for a unanimous Court: "The right of peaceable assembly is a right cognate to those of free speech and free press and is equally fundamental," and "peaceable assembly for lawful discussion cannot be made a crime," no matter under whose auspices the meeting is held.

In addition, the rights of assembly and petition are mentioned in rather standardized language in all but two of the fifty state CONSTITUTIONS. The first such statement appeared in the North Carolina constitution of 1776, and the New Hampshire constitution of 1784 began the practice of adding the word "peaceable" to the right of assembly guarantee. Furthermore, the constitutions of Missouri, New Jersey, and New York specifically guarantee a particular form of association, the right of employees to bargain collectively through representatives of their own choosing; the North Carolina constitution forbids "secret political societies" as being "dangerous to the liberties of a free people"; and there is a declaration in the Georgia constitution, of dubious validity, that "freedom from compulsory association at all levels of public education shall be preserved inviolate."

The right of assembly, like nearly all other rights, is not and cannot be regarded as without limit. As Justice LOUIS D. BRANDEIS wrote in 1927, concurring in WHITNEY V. CALIFORNIA, "although the rights of free speech and assembly are fundamental, they are not in their nature absolute. Their exercise is subject to restriction, if the particular restriction proposed is required in order to protect the State from destruction or from serious injury, political, economic or moral." The right of assembly does not protect an unlawful assembly, usually defined in American law as a gathering of three or more people for the purpose of committing acts that will give firm and courageous people in the neighborhood grounds to apprehend a BREACH OF THE PEACE. It must be shown that those who assembled intended to do an unlawful act or a lawful act in a violent, boisterous, or tumultuous manner. Thus the right to engage in peaceful PICKETING is protected by the Constitution, but picketing in a context of violence or having the purpose of achieving unlawful objectives, may be forbidden.

In American law the right of assembly extends to meetings held in such PUBLIC FORUMS as the streets and parks. This point was first spelled out in HAGUE V. C.I.O. (1939), extending constitutional protection to street meetings since, in the words of Justice OWEN J. ROBERTS, streets "have immemorially been held in trust for the use of the public and, time out of mind, have been used for purposes of assembly, communicating thoughts between citizens, and discussing public questions." Public authorities may be given the power to license parades or processions on the public streets as to time, place, and manner, provided that the licensing law does not confer an arbitrary or unbridled administrative discretion upon them. (See PRIOR RESTRAINT.) In addition, Justice Roberts wrote in CANTWELL V. CONNECTICUT (1940) that "When a CLEAR AND PRESENT DANGER of riot, disorder, interference with traffic upon the public streets, or other immediate threat to public safety, peace, or order, appears, the power of the State to prevent or punish is obvious." Thus, a leading decision has upheld the right to assemble on the grounds of a state house, but the Court has drawn the line at the picketing of a courthouse or holding a demonstration on jail grounds. The Court extended the concept of the right of assembly in RICHMOND NEWSPAPERS, INC. V. VIRGINIA (1980) by ruling invalid a state judge's order barring all members of the public and the press from the courtroom where a murder case was being tried,

on the grounds that the First Amendment rights of speech, press, and assembly were violated.

Although the right of association is not mentioned specifically either in the United States Constitution or in the state constitutions, it is now recognized through judicial interpretation of various constitutional clauses, particularly those dealing with the rights of assembly and petition, the right of free press, and the privileges and immunities of citizens. The first forthright recognition by a majority of the Supreme Court that due process embraces the right to freedom of association, as distinguished from the more limited concept of assembly, came in NAACP V. ALABAMA (1958), although the idea had been advanced in several earlier minority opinions. In the *Alabama* case, the Court unanimously held unconstitutional a statute that required the NAACP to give to the state's attorney general the names and addresses of all its members, reasoning that such compelled disclosure of affiliation could constitute an effective restraint on freedom of association. Justice JOHN MARSHALL HARLAN wrote: "Effective advocacy of both public and private points of view, particularly controversial ones, is undeniably enhanced by group association, as this Court has more than once recognized by remarking upon the close nexus between the freedoms of speech and assembly. . . . Of course, it is immaterial whether the beliefs sought to be advanced by association pertain to political, economic, religious or cultural matters, and state action which may have the effect of curtailing the freedom to associate is subject to the closest scrutiny." In later years the Supreme Court, in a series of decisions, protected the NAACP's associational rights from various forms of harassment, subtle as well as heavy-handed, by local authorities.

A leading case involving education was SHELTON V. TUCKER (1960), where the Supreme Court, by a 5–4 vote, declared unconstitutional an Arkansas statute requiring every teacher in the public schools to file annually an affidavit listing all organizations to which the teacher belonged or contributed money during the preceding five years, because disclosure of every associational tie undoubtedly impaired the teacher's right of free association. Furthermore, in HEALY V. JAMES (1972), the Court upheld the right of a student association to receive university recognition, including access to various campus facilities, even though the president of the college regarded the group's philosophy as abhorrent; the Court added that the university might lawfully require the group to agree to obey reasonable rules relating to student conduct.

The Court took an even more generous view of

the right of association in GRISWOLD V. CONNECTICUT (1965), in which a state anticontraceptive statute was held unconstitutional. Justice WILLIAM O. DOUGLAS reasoned that the statute operated directly on the intimate relationship of husband and wife, thus invading the right of association broadly construed. In his opinion there was a first suggestion that although the right of association grows out of the PENUMBRA of the First Amendment, its scope is larger and extends to the marriage relationship. (See FREEDOM OF INTIMATE ASSOCIATION.)

The right of association, however vital it may be in a society committed to maximum freedom of speech and action, is not absolute but is subject to reasonable limitations required by substantial public interests. For example, the right of workers to organize and bargain collectively through representatives of their own choosing is firmly established in statute and judge-made law. But trade unions are not free to organize or participate in SECONDARY BOYCOTTS, since Congress did not intend "to immunize labor unions who aid and abet manufacturers and traders in violating the SHERMAN ACT. . . ." (See ALLEN BRADLEY CO. V. LOCAL UNION #3, 1945.) On the other hand, the Court has ruled that a labor leader cannot be required to secure a license to give a speech soliciting new members.

The right to form or engage in the activities of POLITICAL PARTIES is protected by the constitutional right of association. "The First Amendment," the Supreme Court said in BUCKLEY V. VALEO (1976), "protects political association as well as political expression." In that case the Court upheld a federal statute imposing limitations on contributions to political parties, on the theory that the limitations were designed to prevent corruption and the appearance of corruption, and to open up the political system to candidates who lacked access to large amounts of money. In addition, the right of political association extends to members of minor parties as well as to the two major parties. Many cases hold that government may protect the right to vote in party primaries, and ensure that voters cast ballots of approximately equal weight, but the two large parties are not obliged to apportion national convention delegates among the states according to the ONE-PERSON, ONE-VOTE concept, because party strength varies from state to state, and the parties must have the freedom to operate effectively. Similarly, the Supreme Court has ruled that a national party convention is not bound by state law and state judicial power in deciding which of two slates of delegates from a state should be seated. A state does have the power to decide upon the strength

a party must demonstrate in order to get a place on the election ballot, but such a statute may not impose a rigid and arbitrary formula that applies equally to sparsely settled and populous counties, and unreasonably large signature requirements will not be permitted. Furthermore, the Supreme Court has conceded that, in order to protect the integrity of the electoral process, states may require some sort of party registration during a reasonable period before a primary election is held. Similarly, a state may require that candidates for party nominations pay filing fees, but the fees must not be so excessive as to be patently exclusionary.

Finally, in the unusual case of ELROD V. BURNS (1976), a bare majority of the Court read something new into party membership by holding that in discharging persons in non-civil service positions because they were Republicans, the newly elected Democratic sheriff of Cook County was placing an unconstitutional restraint on freedom of belief and association. This ruling does not apply, however, to persons holding policymaking positions involving broad functions and goals.

Membership in the Communist party or subversive organizations has for some years posed complex issues of constitutional law. (See SUBVERSIVE ACTIVITIES AND THE CONSTITUTION.) In AMERICAN COMMUNICATIONS ASSOCIATION V. DOUDS (1950), the Court upheld a section of the TAFT-HARTLEY ACT of 1947 which denied access to the facilities of the National Labor Relations Board to any union whose officers were members of the Communist party. The Court reasoned that the act validly protected INTERSTATE COMMERCE from the obstruction caused by political strikes and applied only to those who believed in the violent overthrow of the government as a concrete objective and not merely as a prophecy. Similarly, in SCALES V. UNITED STATES (1961), the Court upheld the clause in the SMITH ACT of 1940 making membership in any organization advocating the overthrow of government by force or violence (in that instance, membership in the Communist party) a criminal offense. But the Court stressed that it was reading the statute to mean that the Smith Act did not proscribe mere membership in the Communist party as such but only membership of an individual who knew of the party's unlawful purposes and specifically intended to further those purposes; the proscribed membership must be active and not nominal, passive, or merely theoretical. This construction of the Smith Act was fully consistent with the position the Court had taken in YATES V. UNITED STATES (1957). The distinction between INCITEMENT and abstract teaching was underscored by the Court in the important case of BRANDENBURG V. OHIO (1969), which held the Ohio Criminal Syndicalism Act unconstitutional. Thus, mere membership in the Communist party, without more, cannot be made a predicate for the denial of a passport, or a job in a defense facility, or of public employment. The Court has recognized that membership may be innocent, and that groups may change their positions from time to time.

Whether unions or other associations may engage the services of such regulated professionals as doctors and lawyers has been the subject of much recent litigation. Because the practice of medicine is subject to comprehensive and detailed regulation by the state under its POLICE POWER for compelling reasons, a state statute prohibiting laymen from forming CORPORATIONS for the delivery of medical care has been upheld on the theory that limiting the formation of such corporations to licensed physicians tends to preserve important doctor–patient relationships and prevents possible abuses which may result from lay control.

The constitutionality of regulation of lawyers presents more complex issues. The Supreme Court has ruled that a state may lawfully compel all lawyers in the state to belong to an integrated bar, and a state bar association may be authorized to discipline a lawyer for personally soliciting clients for pecuniary gain, although the Court ruled in BATES V. STATE BAR OF ARIZONA (1977) that a state, through its bar association, may not forbid lawyers to engage in truthful advertising of routine legal services. Furthermore, the Court held in KONIGSBERG V. STATE BAR OF CALIFORNIA (1961) that a state may refuse to admit to the practice of law a candidate who refuses to reply to questions regarding membership in the Communist party, although the Court has also ruled that there must be a showing of knowing, active membership before an applicant can be excluded on this ground.

The Supreme Court has decided that such associations as trade unions, the NAACP, and the AMERICAN CIVIL LIBERTIES UNION may employ lawyers to provide legal services for their members. In BROTHERHOOD OF RAILROAD TRAINMEN V. VIRGINIA EX REL. VIRGINIA STATE BAR (1964), the Court held that a union has an associational right to advise injured members to use the services of specific approved lawyers. Moreover, a labor union is constitutionally entitled to employ a licensed attorney on a salary basis to represent any of its members who desire his services in prosecuting workers' compensation claims. In NAACP V. BUTTON (1963), the Court upheld the right of this association to finance certain types of litigation

through its own staff of lawyers. The Court noted that NAACP litigation is not a mere technique for resolving private differences but a means of achieving the lawful objective of legal equality. Similarly, the Court has affirmed the right of the American Civil Liberties Union to employ attorneys in the pursuit of its objectives.

The right of association has been explored in a wide variety of other situations. Many years ago, in WAUGH V. BOARD OF TRUSTEES OF THE UNIVERSITY OF MISSISSIPPI (1915), the Supreme Court held constitutional a Mississippi statute prohibiting Greek-letter fraternities and other secret societies in all public educational institutions of the state, on the theory that this was a reasonable moral and disciplinary regulation which the legislature might believe would save the students from harmful distraction. Several state appellate courts have sustained the validity of such regulations as applied to high schools. In NEW YORK EX REL. BRYANT V. ZIMMERMAN (1928), the Supreme Court upheld a state statute, aimed at the Ku Klux Klan, which required all secret oath-bound organizations having over twenty members to supply to a designated public official a roster of its members and a list of its officers. In NAACP V. ALABAMA (1958), holding unconstitutional a similar disclosure requirement of the NAACP, the Court noted that the *Zimmerman* decision "was based on the particular character of the Klan's activities, involving acts of unlawful intimidation and violence, which the Court assumed was before the state legislature when it enacted the statute, and of which the Court itself took judicial notice." (See COMMUNIST PARTY V. SUBVERSIVE ACTIVITIES CONTROL BOARD, 1961.) On the other hand, in LANZETTA V. NEW JERSEY (1939), the Court ruled unconstitutional a state statute that purported to make it illegal to associate with gangsters, on the ground that the key words in the statute were so vague, indefinite, and uncertain that it lacked the specificity required of penal enactments.

Although the right of association as such is not mentioned in the Constitution, it holds a firm, indeed expanding, place in American constitutional law. This right is partly an emanation from the First Amendment's cognate guarantees of freedom of speech and assembly, partly a privilege or immunity of citizenship, and partly a by-product of democratic voting and representative government. However the right of association is tied to the text of the Constitution, it is regarded by the judges as such a fundamental right that doubts are resolved in favor of protecting the right of association from governmental restraints.

DAVID FELLMAN

Bibliography

ABERNATHY, GLEN 1961 *The Right of Assembly and Association.* Columbia: University of South Carolina Press.

FELLMAN, DAVID 1963 *The Constitutional Right of Association.* Chicago: University of Chicago Press.

HORN, ROBERT A. 1956 *Groups and the Constitution.* Stanford, Calif.: Stanford University Press.

KALVEN, HARRY, JR. 1965 The Concept of the Public Forum. *Supreme Court Review* 1965:1–32.

RAGGI, REENA 1977 An Independent Right to Freedom of Association. *Harvard Civil Rights-Civil Liberties Law Review* 12:1–30.

FREEDOM OF CONTRACT

Freedom of contract in the United States means that the law accepts and protects broad scope for private individuals and business firms to decide the uses of economic resources in seeking profits. Through the country's history, sharp controversies have centered on exercise of freedom of contract as it has affected concerns for the worth of individuals, the vitality of private markets, the natural and social environment, and the structure of practical as well as formal legal power in the society. Few other concepts touch as many dimensions of the history of American public policy and constitutional law.

The law's attention to freedom of contract has centered on fostering and sustaining the private market as a major institution of social control (ranking in importance with the law itself). Even the assessment of the interactions of freedom of contract and other values, not defined in market, has typically resulted from community reactions to the effects of market operations. Thus, to examine the place of freedom of contract in constitutional law entails examining the roles and working character of the market.

Law and public policy have historically responded to four salient characteristics of private contract activity in market, carrying both constructive and damaging aspects. These responses have provided the institutional setting within which the substantive legal/constitutional meaning of freedom of contract has emerged.

(1) Under the protection of the law of contract, private contract activity seeking profit in market energizes private will in producing and distributing goods and services. This activity promises efficiency in allocating limited resources, partly because the actors are motivated to obtain the most output for the least input, and partly because market bargaining allows flexibility in coordinating a great volume and diversity of private decisions. In the country's constitutional tradition, social and political values also favor freedom of contract. Proponents argue that individuals gain self-respect from the initiatives of will they exercise in markets, as well as courage to participate in and criticize government because their means of livelihood are not dependent on official favor. The law reflects this appraisal of positive values by presuming the legality of private contracts until a challenger demonstrates their unlawfulness, and by casting some constitutional protections around private contract activity and the property interests it produces. (See CONTRACT CLAUSE; SUBSTANTIVE DUE PROCESS; TAKING OF PROPERTY; ECONOMIC REGULATION AND THE CONSTITUTION.) But the driving dynamic of private contract activity is the focused self-interest of the bargainers. We value this dynamic because it counters the inertia prevalent in social relationships, but it largely ignores the impact of bargains on people other than the bargainers. A factory producing to meet its contractual obligations may deposit in a handy stream industrial wastes harmful to the public's interest in pure drinking water or recreational opportunities. The law responds to this narrow focus of the market with ENVIRONMENTAL REGULATIONS, the constitutionality of which may or may not be challenged.

(2) Large-scale markets cannot operate by barter but require use of money (including money-measured credit). Law responds to this need by regulating the money supply. But the money calculus required by extended contract activity carries dangers of a bias in identifying and weighing matters of public interest. Public opinion, public policymakers (including judges), and market-oriented pressure groups seeking to influence legislators and other public officers tend to identify interests deserving law's promotion or protection only with interests readily calculable in dollar terms. Thus, nineteenth-century COMMON LAW readily gave JUDGMENT for money damages if a factory failed to deliver promised goods to a buyer but was grudging in recognizing a community right to redress for more diffuse detriments—hard to measure in dollars—caused by the factory's deposit of industrial waste in a nearby stream. Today's public policy, with the blessings of today's constitutional law, increasingly seeks to offset the bias injected by a monetized calculus of interests by legislating to protect diffuse values and establishing administrative agencies to implement them.

(3) Whether tailored to particular transactions or standardized as in such commercial instruments as promissory notes or warehouse receipts, private contracts can be multiplied to any number of dealings

and varied to shifting conditions of supply and demand. Contracts and the market thus permit flexible adaptation to changes in the conditions of the economy and the parties. Public policy recognizes the value of this adaptability in the law's readiness to enforce such terms of dealing as the parties choose and in legal/constitutional doctrine protecting the play of market competition. However, when change proceeds in this manner, its increments are so small that even the parties, let alone the environing society, may not be aware that the accumulation of relatively limited incremental shifts is producing basic alterations in the social context which no one has predicted, assessed, or chosen to bring about.

(4) Private contracting parties and the markets in which they operate typically work within the distribution of wealth and income in society as they find it. Contract and property law reinforce this distribution; only in rare hard cases will courts set aside a bargain as unconscionable, and normally they will not examine the adequacy of the consideration a party accepted in return for what he promised to perform. But underlying the social utility of freedom of contract and the resource-allocations role of markets lies an assumption: that private bargainers enjoy a considerable range of practical and legal options in dealing with each other. Great inequalities of wealth may grossly distort some bargaining relations, so that freedom of contract becomes illusory and markets sharply accentuate inequalities of bargaining power. While constitutional law only rarely addresses such inequalities (see INDIGENTS; WEALTH DISTRIBUTION), it consistently validates legislation to this end. (See SUBSTANTIVE DUE PROCESS; ECONOMIC REGULATION; COMMERCE CLAUSE.) Sometimes lawmakers seek to encourage private organization of countervailing power, as in the law regarding COLLECTIVE BARGAINING between management and LABOR. Sometimes they interpose between focused centers of private market power and diffused bodies of customers a public bargaining agency, as in the law of public utilities. Such legal interventions and their constitutional underpinnings depart from an abstract model of freedom of contract in order to promote more real freedom of bargaining.

The span from the 1880s through the 1920s witnessed increased resort to state and national law to correct imperfections of private contract activity in market. In this period opponents of government intervention made "freedom of contract" a code phrase for imposing constitutional and other limits on legal regulation. This emphasis has been so prominent in past policy debate that there is danger of equating the idea of freedom of contract with limitations on

the use of law. In fact, law operates at least as much to promote market activity as to regulate it. A realistic assessment of the relation of constitutional law to freedom of contract must recognize the range of such promotional roles of legal processes.

By the late eighteenth century, in this country of abundant land, the law of land titles made land fully transferable and thus readily marketable—thus promoting private contract activity. By the mid-nineteenth century, common law had established a strong presumption in favor of the legality of private agreements for market dealing. By the second half of the nineteenth century, state legislatures were actively removing the common law disability of married women to make binding contracts. The married women's property acts may have responded more to the wish of the husband's creditors to acquire effective pledge of the wife's assets to secure her husband's debts than to any concern for sex equality. Still, these statutes enlarged the potential scope for contract activity in market.

Legal development, often supported by constitutional law, has consistently fostered entrepreneurial energy. Contract law legitimized and standardized a growing range of trade documents and instruments for capital investment. In three respects law especially promoted increased reach and pervasive effect of private contract activity. Though often inefficiently, law provided a money supply to facilitate increased volumes of trade. Particularly under the commerce clause of the national Constitution, Congress and the Supreme Court protected markets of sectional or national scope against intrusion of state parochial interest. (See STATE REGULATION OF COMMERCE; STATE TAXATION OF COMMERCE.) With increasing liberality lawmakers made the device of incorporation available for the general run of business, providing means for mustering and directing otherwise scattered assets. (See CORPORATIONS AND THE CONSTITUTION.)

Many individuals had only their labor to offer in market, and only their wages to spend. For them law gave other positive promotion to freedom of contract. In the nineteenth century, statutes created mechanics' liens, exempted workers' tools from creditors' execution, and abolished imprisonment for debt. In the twentieth century, legislation created administrative agencies to implement laws designed to help consumers get money's worth for their purchases. The most dramatic expansion of freedom of contract for labor was the abolition of SLAVERY. Fulfillment of the substance of that policy through the THIRTEENTH AMENDMENT and the supplementary provisions of the FOURTEENTH AMENDMENT and the CIVIL RIGHTS

ACT OF 1866 had a long and tortured history, but the general line of policy was clear. In the 1960s, CIVIL RIGHTS legislation gave that policy additional impetus, placing the affirmative support of law behind opening markets for labor, goods, and services free of barriers raised on grounds of race, sex, or religion. (See FEDERAL PROTECTION OF CIVIL RIGHTS; EMPLOYMENT DISCRIMINATION.)

Granted that law plays positive, promotional roles in fostering markets, freedom of contract also insists that law protect a substantial area of autonomy for private contract and market activity, to allow operative room for the efficiency criteria which legitimize private contract and market functions. Threats of invasion of this zone come from both private and official power. Accordingly the autonomy that public policy provides for private contract and private markets has two dimensions, relating to private and to official action.

The law protects market autonomy against private interference not only by enforcing contractual obligations through damages or other relief against breach of contract but also by providing sanctions against interference by outsiders with the performance of those obligations. Furthermore, an elaborate body of statutory, judge-made, and ADMINISTRATIVE LAW offers criminal and civil sanctions against efforts to defeat market bargaining by achieving monopoly, or by fixing prices or other terms of trade, or by engaging in such predatory forms of competition as geographical price discriminations so as to limit or destroy competition. (See ANTITRUST AND THE CONSTITUTION.)

More controversy has surrounded the creation of legal/constitutional protections of limited autonomy for private contract activity in market as against interventions by government. Experience shows two quite different sources of concern. Some battles over legal regulation are fought on claims that one set of private interests seeks to handicap another by persuading a legislature to create barriers to free competition as when producers of dairy products obtained laws regulating the sale of oleomargarine. Other battles are fought on claims that in pursuing nonmarket objectives, such as protecting public health, lawmakers impose unreasonable costs on market-measured profit-seeking—as when environmental regulations are opposed on the ground that they hamper "productivity" (meaning that they limit money-measured gains of regulated firms). Common to both types of concern is the objection that law is used in ways that interfere with economic efficiency defined according to the profit and loss calculus of the immediate bargainers

in a competitive private market. "Efficiency" in this sense and freedom of contract are the same thing.

Common law imposes some limits on freedom of bargainers to set terms for which they may invoke the law's support and sets the standards for determining what constitutes an enforceable contract. Generally, however, the courts presume that private bargains are valid. The principal legal battlegrounds for defending freedom of contract against official invasion lie in constitutional law. Both national and state constitutions limit legislative restrictions on the freedom of private contract.

The national and state constitutions forbid government to take private property for PUBLIC USE without JUST COMPENSATION. These guarantees primarily protect property titles rather than contracts not yet performed. However, they help safeguard private contract activity; contracts that call for performance over time are likely to require commitments of assets which bargainers will not make if they do not consider the commitments secure against government appropriation. Some uncertainty attends the definition of what public action amounts to a "taking." However, these guarantees do not require government to pay all costs incurred by those subjected to laws regulating economic affairs. Particularly, when government intervenes in a situation where some detriment will in fact occur to either of two competing private interests whether government acts or not, there is no "taking" requiring compensation when the law determines which interest must bear the burden. (See TAKING OF PROPERTY.)

The national Constitution forbids any state to make a law that impairs the OBLIGATION OF CONTRACTS. This clause limits only retroactive state legislation; it does not affect state laws that operate only on future events. No comparable clause limits the Congress, and the Supreme Court applies a presumption of constitutionality to federal statutes of retroactive impact. (See RETROACTIVITY OF LEGISLATION.) The CONTRACT CLAUSE has not figured in so much litigation as the constitutional guarantees of DUE PROCESS and EQUAL PROTECTION OF THE LAWS. Where litigants invoke the clause, however, judges generally give it firm application in the types of situation that most directly challenge respect for outstanding private agreements in market—that is, where a retroactive state statute undertakes to readjust the terms of a contract or its legal context in order to give one party what the legislature in hindsight sees as a socially more acceptable exchange. The usual case of this kind has arisen when a legislature intervenes to relieve distressed debtors of the full measure of claims or remedies afforded their creditors. Moreover, the Supreme Court requires a state to enforce a contract between the state itself and a private party when the retroactive change has given the state an economic advantage not conferred by the original terms. On the other hand, the Supreme Court treats the contract clause more flexibly when the prime object of the challenged legislation appears to be not to alter terms of dealing between the bargaining parties but to protect public interests in a healthy social context without which private contracts have no meaning. Care for social context may include care for preserving the market itself. Thus the Supreme Court upheld a state statute that imposed a limited moratorium on foreclosing mortgages contracted before the statute was passed, where the Court was persuaded that the legislature reasonably believed the moratorium necessary not mainly to benefit mortgagors but to save the general economy from destruction by averting distress sales of land that would undermine the financial integrity of the banking and insurance systems of the state. (See HOME BUILDING AND LOAN ASSOCIATION V. BLAISDELL, 1934.) The Court has taken a like approach where the challenged legislation seeks to safeguard other than market interests; thus it has sustained against contract clause challenges retroactive legislation that, in the interest of public morals, abrogated an earlier statutory charter for a lottery and that, to protect public health, abrogated an earlier statutory charter for a slaughterhouse.

Another relatively specific constitutional limit on state legislation affecting freedom of contract developed under the COMMERCE CLAUSE of the national Constitution. The core purpose of granting Congress authority to regulate INTERSTATE COMMERCE was to use national law to protect from parochial state legislation contract activity that ranged over state lines into markets of interstate scope. Congress has used this authority notably to provide uniform national regulation of the terms on which private business provides interstate transportation and communication services. Most often, however, the commerce clause has operated to limit state interference with interstate contract activity through the United States Supreme Court. In the Court's construction, the commerce clause of its own force authorizes judges to rule invalid state legislation that discriminates against or unduly burdens interstate transactions. The Court most strictly limits state laws that in their terms or by their practical effect lay legal or economic burdens on dealings in an interstate market that they do not impose on intrastate transactions. Here the Court puts on the supporter of a challenged state statute a heavy burden

of persuading the Court that some overriding local public interest warrants legislation that thus singles out interstate dealing for special regulation. But if a nondiscriminatory state statute affects interstate transactions for a nonmarket purpose, such as protecting public safety on the highways, it enjoys the benefit of a presumption of constitutionality, so that the challenger must persuade the Court that local interests are insufficient to warrant the regulation.

Constitutional guarantees of due process and equal protection are the protections most often invoked on behalf of substantial autonomy of private contract activity in market, as against government intervention. At the threshold of any examination of this body of constitutional law stands an issue of institutional legitimacy. Anglo-American political tradition includes high regard for public policy that favors initiatives of private will in the economy. JOHN LOCKE gave this tradition classic expression in seventeenth-century England, asserting that the individual normally needs no official license before he may make productive use of natural resources. Locke recognized that legislation might properly care for "commonwealth" interests, and particularly that the elected legislature might exercise the power to tax for public purposes. But the legislative authority, he said, was held in "trust," permitting the legislature to act only for the public interest (foreshadowing the Supreme Court's later standard of SUBSTANTIVE DUE PROCESS) and by equal laws. Of course, this English inheritance did not provide authority for judges to hold invalid legislation that infringed standards of public interest and equal protection. When judges in the United States asserted that authority—with some limited warrant in the history of adoption of the national Constitution—it was another, long step for them to conclude that the guarantee of due process of law included judicial protection of some extent of private contract autonomy. In its origins, "due process of law" meant assurance of fair procedures for applying law, not authority of courts to set limits on the substantive content of the policy legislatures might adopt. And the core historic meaning of the equal protection standard referred to application of law rather than to its substantive classifications. However, by the mid-twentieth century, some seventy-five years of Supreme Court practice had outweighed historic doubts; the live issue in the twentieth century is, rather, how the Court will use the authority it has staked out for itself. The fact that judges were able to extend their power of review beyond historic foundations attests to the strength of values which conservative opinion in the past has put on freedom of contract in market. On the other hand, the doubt which history has cast on the political legitimacy of the expanded judicial role correspondingly helps account for the limits set by the Court since the 1930s on its exercise of JUDICIAL REVIEW of economic regulations challenged as violations of due process and equal protection.

Early in the development of the doctrine of substantive due process, in *Powell v. Pennsylvania* (1888), the Court set sharp limits on the scope of judicial review. There a state had banned the sale of oleomargarine, for the declared goals of protecting public health and preventing fraud on consumers. The Court ruled that it would uphold the statute unless the challenger showed beyond a reasonable doubt that the legislature could not reasonably find that the act was an appropriate means to serve some public interest. Nonetheless, in some cases judges, especially state courts interpreting state constitutions, will enforce respect for some degree of autonomy of private contract activity in market. In some cases parties have successfully rebutted the strong presumption of constitutionality by showing that one set of business interests has won the law's favor simply in order to obtain a legal advantage against other socially useful competitors. Such resort to law violates the social justification of legally protected freedom of contract: the promotion of efficient allocation of limited resources through market competition. Thus, in a later case, where the challenger demonstrated that an anti-oleomargarine statute had no reasonable basis in protecting health or preventing fraud, the Wisconsin court held, in *John F. Jelke Co. v. Emery* (1927), that the act violated constitutional standards of due process and equal protection.

In counterpoint with the pattern of judicial self-restraint indicated by *Powell v. Pennsylvania*, over the span from about 1890 into the mid-1930s the Supreme Court developed three other interrelated doctrinal lines which promoted aggressive judicial protection of private contract autonomy.

First, the Court identified freedom of private contract as a key component of the "liberty" protected by the due process and equal protection clauses. The founding decision was ALLGEYER V. LOUISIANA (1897). There the Court held unconstitutional a Louisiana statute forbidding performance of a contract to insure property in the state with a company not licensed to do business there. The Court ruled that in denying the parties the liberty to make the contract the statute violated limits that the due process clause put on the substantive policies which the legislature might enact into law.

Second, in the standard of substantive due process the Court found warrant for a judicial veto over legislative goals. Judicial scrutiny of these goals had two aspects. One concerned the relationship between private contract and the social context in which the contracting went on. Even in decisions most restrictive of legislative power, the Supreme Court did not deny that legislation might properly pay some regard to the impact of private contract activity on the lives and concerns of individuals or groups other than the contracting parties. However, the Court often spoke of legislative authority as the sum of a limited, closed number of categories of goals traditionally recognized as serving public interest, notably protection of health, safety, or morals. (See STATE POLICE POWER; NATIONAL POLICE POWER). The indication was that a statute would violate substantive due process if its objective did not fit handily under one of these familiar designations. Conspicuous in this approach were ADAIR V. UNITED STATES (1908), COPPAGE V. KANSAS (1915), and WOLFF PACKING COMPANY V. COURT OF INDUSTRIAL RELATIONS (1923). These rulings refused to recognize promotion of peace in management–labor relations as a sufficient public-interest goal to sustain statutes that outlawed employment contracts binding employees not to join a union or providing for compulsory arbitration of labor disputes.

The third aspect of heightened judicial scrutiny of statutory goals was more specific. Substantive due process demanded that legislation serve what the Court regarded as the general welfare. A statute might appear to serve one of the judicially approved public-interest goals, such as protection of health. But also, it might have the purpose or likely effect of bringing about a different distribution of gains and costs among private bargainers than might result if bargainers operated simply within the frame of common law contract and property law. Between about 1890 and the mid-1930s many decisions treated the presence of a purpose or effect to alter the distribution of gains and costs among private bargainers as enough to show that a challenged statute did not meet the due process standard of serving the public interest; the redistributive character of such a statute made it "class legislation" or an effort, forbidden by constitutional law, to "take property from A and give it to B." Judges would accept statutes that protected groups commonly recognized as subject to exceptional hazards or weaknesses in bargaining power. Thus, in HOLDEN V. HARDY (1898), the Supreme Court upheld a statutory limit on working hours of men mining coal underground, emphasizing the well-known special hazards of the occupation and the accepted fact that in practice the employers fixed the terms of the employment contracts. So, too, in MULLER V. OREGON (1908), the Court sustained a working hours limit for women, to protect a class which the judges saw as peculiarly dependent. But where a statute apparently sought to offset the weak bargaining power of workers in situations not conventionally regarded as deserving law's special care, the fact that the statute would confer particular benefit on labor was taken as enough to show a lack of justifying public interest. Such was the Court's approach in LOCHNER V. NEW YORK (1905), which held invalid a statutory limit on working hours of bakers. Of similar character was Court doctrine that confined statutory regulation of prices and services of private contractors to what judges regarded as businesses AFFECTED WITH A PUBLIC INTEREST— those conventionally deemed public utilities. On this basis, in TYSON V. BANTON (1927) and in RIBNIK V. MCBRIDE (1928), the Court held invalid statutes regulating resale prices of theater tickets and fees of employment agencies.

There was unreconciled tension between many of these decisions and the approach taken in *Powell v. Pennsylvania*. In *Powell*, the fact that the statutory ban on selling oleomargarine might serve both the private, competitive interest of sellers of butter and the public interest in health was held insufficient to invalidate the regulation. In *Powell*, the favored private interest was that of one set of businessmen, the sellers of butter. In *Lochner* and in *Ribnik*, the interest the statutes immediately protected was that of labor. So, also, in *Adair, Coppage,* and *Wolff Packing,* the interest of labor suffered when the challenged legislation was upset. The pattern suggested a definite bias of policy.

Between 1890 and the mid-1930s the Supreme Court also usually required a positive showing of a "real and substantial" relation between the legislature's goal and the means it provided to reach the goal. That the Court could conceive of other, less burdensome means of achieving the desired result was likely, as in *Lochner v. New York*, to be treated as a distinct and sufficient basis for invalidating the statute. The climax of both lines of doctrine—regarding challenges to the end or to the means adopted by the legislature—came in ADKINS V. CHILDREN'S HOSPITAL (1923), when the Supreme Court held unconstitutional legislation setting minimum wages for women workers. There a Court majority in effect repudiated the presumption of constitutionality by declaring that "Freedom of contract is . . . the general rule and restraint the exception; and the exercise of legislative authority to abridge it can be justified only by the existence of exceptional circumstances." As late as

MOREHEAD V. NEW YORK EX REL. TIPALDO (1936), a Court majority in effect reaffirmed the *Adkins* approach, but a new alignment of Justices repudiated that approach in WEST COAST HOTEL V. PARRISH (1937).

The Court's readiness through some forty years after 1890 to upset legislation limiting freedom of contract had serious implications for the role of legislatures and the interests legislatures sought to advance or protect. But we should not exaggerate the impact of judicial review. One inventory counts 197 cases between 1899 and 1937 in which the Supreme Court invalidated state or federal regulations under the standard of substantive due process, but another estimate notes that between 1889 and 1918 the Court upheld some 369 challenged statutes enacted under the state police power. Other tallies emphasize the more vigorous use of the judicial veto in the later years of the forty-year span; one count finds fifty-three state police power acts held invalid between 1889 and 1918, while another shows almost 140 laws held unconstitutional between 1920 and 1930. All such inventories must be seen in a wider perspective; a great bulk of economic regulatory legislation never came under constitutional challenge in lawsuits.

However, in a sharp turnabout beginning in the mid-1930s, the Court disavowed these enlargements of judicial protection for autonomy of private contract in market. In NEBBIA V. NEW YORK (1934) it ruled that a legislature might regulate pricing practices outside the field of traditional public utilities if legislators could reasonably find that regulation would serve a public interest. In UNITED STATES V. CAROLENE PRODUCTS COMPANY (1938), it ruled that no particular sanctity attached to the "liberty" or "property" interests involved in private contract activity; all regulatory legislation affecting ordinary commercial transactions enjoyed the presumption of constitutionality. *Nebbia* also made clear that there is no closed category of public interests to which legislatures may extend protection; even if a statute intervenes in private contract activity for a purpose not within familiar concerns with public health, safety, or morals, it is valid unless the judges determine that no reasonable legislators could find justification for it. Finally, in WEST COAST HOTEL COMPANY V. PARRISH (1937), the Court expressly overruled the formula declared in *Adkins;* that a statute limits freedom of contract does not cast on its supporter a burden of justifying it; rather, the general presumption of constitutionality applies.

The Court's permissive modern doctrine leaves the autonomy of private contract activity mostly in the hands of the legislature. Given the realities of the legislative process, in two respects this outcome implies a lessening of the preferred status of the private market. Statute law tends to speak more and more for interests of the general social context, as in regulation of burdens—such as air or water pollution—which private contract activity otherwise may place on parties outside the bargaining circle. Less appealing is the practical operation of the presumption of constitutionality to allow special interest lobbies to obtain legal favors, protected by plausible arguments of action taken for a presumed public interest. But this increased scope for lobby influence seems an inescapable cost of a proper division of functions between legislatures and courts in the area of economic regulation. In a more favorable light, the presumption of constitutionality as the Supreme Court defines it means that a statute is not invalid merely because in serving some public interest it may operate concurrently to provide special gain to some private interest. This result seems appropriate. Concurrence of public and private gain from legislation is so common in this society of diverse, interweaving interests that judges would substantially abrogate the legislative function if they held that such parallel effects alone made a statute unconstitutional.

Finally, we should recall that constitutional law is by no means the whole of what determines the realities of freedom of contract. In the second half of the twentieth century several factors other than direct legal regulation work to reduce, or at least realign, the operation of the freedom of contract. One element is the growth in relative economic importance of large-scale business corporations. In a big corporate organization many decisions that once would have been made by private bargains over supply of goods and services now occur through relations of hierarchy, as boards of directors instruct managers and managers plan and instruct subordinates. Thus, much resource allocation is done through internal discipline of firms, rather than by transactions in market. This internalizing of decisions has generated new concerns about the balance of power among affected interests. Such concerns have prompted new government regulation, as in the WAGNER (NATIONAL LABOR RELATIONS) ACT, in legislation governing corporate finance and administered by the Securities and Exchange Commission, and in the regulation of workplace safety under state and federal laws.

Statutes and administrative regulations now standardize many areas of contract dealing, sometimes providing optional standard forms, sometimes requiring adherence to forms fixed by law. Thus, large areas which are still governed by contract, in the sense that parties enter into relationships only by exchange of consents, are nonetheless areas in which individuals and firms no longer bargain out the details of their transactions. Such is the case with most contracts of insurance, contract relations between corporate stockholders and their corporations, collective bargaining contracts for the supply of labor, and lending contracts.

From the 1930s on, national monetary and fiscal policy has greatly affected the practical scope of freedom of private contract. Government's roles in providing and regulating the money supply are not neutral ones; the qualities of public monetary policy affecting rates of deflation or inflation profoundly affect the extent to which people can control their affairs by private bargains. Similarly, as government enlarges the reach of its TAXING AND SPENDING POWERS, it enlarges or restricts practical freedom of private contract. Government-induced transfer payments—payment of interest on public debt, or payments of Social Security allowances or of unemployment compensation—shift purchasing power among groups. Government spending on goods or services for its own needs removes some proportion of material or labor from the field of private contract in market. In the late twentieth century the cumulative effects of public monetary and fiscal programs spell substantial complication of the patterns of private contract activity and public resource allocation, in comparison with the patterns that existed from the late eighteenth century to the end of the nineteenth century. Freedom of contract in the United States continues to stand for important propositions concerning the structure and working procedures of society, but the content of the idea has undergone significant change from the vision of society held by John Locke or by the Justices of the Supreme Court who spoke for strict judicial review of economic regulations between the 1890s and the middle 1930s.

JAMES WILLARD HURST

Bibliography

CHANDLER, ALFRED D., JR. 1977 *The Visible Hand.* Cambridge, Mass.: Belknap Press of Harvard University Press.

FRIEDMAN, LAWRENCE M. 1973 *A History of American Law.* New York: Simon & Schuster.

HORWITZ, MORTON J. 1977 *The Transformation of American Law, 1760–1860.* Cambridge, Mass.: Harvard University Press.

HURST, JAMES WILLARD 1982 *Law and Markets in United States History.* Madison: University of Wisconsin Press.

JACOBS, CLYDE 1954 *Law Writers and the Courts.* Berkeley: University of California Press.

MACAULAY, STEWART 1963 Non-Contractual Relations in Business: A Preliminary Study. *American Sociological Review* 28:55–67.

PAUL, ARNOLD M. 1960 *Conservative Crisis and the Rule of Law: Attitudes of Bar and Bench, 1887–1895.* Ithaca, N.Y.: Cornell University Press.

POUND, ROSCOE 1909 Liberty of Contract. *Yale Law Journal* 18:454–487.

TRIBE, LAURENCE H. 1978 *American Constitutional Law.* Chap. 8. Mineola, N.Y.: Foundation Press.

TWISS, BENJAMIN R. 1942 *Lawyers and the Constitution: How Laissez Faire Came to the Supreme Court.* Princeton, N.J.: Princeton University Press.

FREEDOM OF INFORMATION ACT
80 Stat. 378 (1966)

The Freedom of Information Act of 1966 establishes a public disclosure policy for information in the custody of the executive branch of the federal government. It authorizes public access to government records and provides administrative and judicial APPEAL of decisions to withhold them. The law mandates that unreleased executive branch records be made available on request; however, it permits the withholding of information in nine categories upon government justification. Among them are classified national security information, information protected by other statutes, internal advisory memoranda, invasions of privacy, certain law enforcement records, and certain confidential business information.

The idea of a freedom of information law was first championed by journalists concerned with the effects of government censorship and discretionary bureaucratic secrecy on FREEDOM OF THE PRESS and the accountability of public officials. After eleven years of congressional hearings, the Freedom of Information Act was passed in 1966, amending the Administrative Procedures Act which had allowed the withholding of almost all government records. Initial compliance with the new law fell short of congressional expectations, and effectuating amendments were passed over a presidential veto in 1974.

As the keystone of "open government" legislation, the act was the first of several statutes that subject certain records and activities of the federal government to public scrutiny. These include the Federal Advisory Committee Act of 1972, the PRIVACY ACT of 1974, the Government in the Sunshine Act of 1976, and the Presidential Records Act of 1978.

The freedom of information policy established by the law does not flow from an express, constitutional RIGHT TO KNOW. Some controversy surrounds the question of whether a public right to know is merely political rhetoric or is an unenumerated constitutional right protected by the NINTH AMENDMENT. A majority of the Justices of the Supreme Court concluded, in RICHMOND NEWSPAPERS, INC. v. VIRGINIA (1980), that the FIRST AMENDMENT gave the public a right of access to criminal trials, which rests on the traditional importance of citizen scrutiny of the judicial trial process. In a separate opinion, Justice WILLIAM J. BRENNAN argued that the theory of citizen participation in self-government also supports the right, and that this logic is not confined to access to courtrooms. In another CONCURRING OPINION, Justice JOHN PAUL STEVENS pointed out that in this case the Court recognized for the first time a protected right of access to important government information.

EXECUTIVE PRIVILEGE is embodied in several exemptions to the 1966 Act. Although the scope of the privilege remains in dispute, the Supreme Court in OBITER DICTUM in UNITED STATES v. NIXON (1974) recognized the authority to withhold military and diplomatic national security information, as well as internal memoranda that are advisory and not factual in nature. Later that year, in his veto message returning the 1974 amendments to Congress, President Ford declared that the provision for judicial review of executive branch determinations as to national security classification violates constitutional principles. However, the government has never pressed that argument in litigation.

Individuals have found the act useful for obtaining business information and as an alternative to judicial discovery. Open government policies have affected administrative behavior. Federal law enforcement practices were somewhat restrained after dubious covert investigative activities were disclosed. A government study following the 1974 amendments found that attitudes in the bureaucracy had become more positive toward the release of information and that the quality of some government work had improved because of public scrutiny.

EVERETT E. MANN, JR.

Bibliography

MANN, EVERETT E. 1984 The Public Right to Know Government Information: Its Affirmation and Abridgment. Ph.D. dissertation, Claremont Graduate School.

FREEDOM OF INTIMATE ASSOCIATION

Since the 1960s the Supreme Court has decided scores of cases dealing with marriage and divorce, family relationships, the choice whether to procreate, and various forms of intimate association outside the traditional family structure. Although the factual settings of these cases and their opinions' doctrinal explanations have been diverse, in the aggregate they represent the emergence of a constitutional freedom of intimate association.

The Court had asserted as early as MEYER V. NEBRASKA (1923) and PIERCE V. SOCIETY OF SISTERS (1925) that the Constitution protected the freedom to marry and raise one's children, and SKINNER V. OKLAHOMA (1942) had subjected a compulsory STERILIZATION law to STRICT SCRUTINY. But the modern beginning for the freedom of intimate association was Justice WILLIAM O. DOUGLAS's opinion for the Court in GRISWOLD V. CONNECTICUT (1965). Although that case involved a prosecution of the operators of a BIRTH CONTROL clinic for dispensing advice on contraception and the means to achieve it, the focus of the opinion was a married couple's right to use contraceptive devices. Justice Douglas located that right in a "zone of privacy," created by "penumbras" of various specific guarantees in the BILL OF RIGHTS. He did not specify the scope of the new RIGHT OF PRIVACY, and one product of *Griswold* has been a distinguished body of literature rich with suggested approaches to that issue. In *Griswold* itself, however, the chief object of constitutional protection was the marital relationship.

Griswold has become a major precedent for several lines of doctrinal development. The right to marry has been recognized as a SUBSTANTIVE DUE PROCESS right in LOVING V. VIRGINIA (1967) and ZABLOCKI V. REDHAIL (1978). The right to use contraceptives has been extended to unmarried persons in EISENSTADT V. BAIRD (1972) on an EQUAL PROTECTION theory, and even the right to advertise and sell them has been defended in CAREY V. POPULATION SERVICES INTERNATIONAL (1977) on the basis of the FIRST AMENDMENT and the privacy right of potential buyers, married or not. These protections of intimate relationships outside marriage have been complemented by heightened scrutiny of legislative classifications visiting disadvantage on the status of ILLEGITIMACY. *Griswold*'s most famous doctrinal outgrowth was ROE V. WADE (1973), which squarely placed the new constitutional right of privacy within the liberty protected by substantive due process, and held that the right included a woman's freedom to choose to have an ABORTION.

Here as elsewhere, constitutional doctrine has followed in the wake of social change. After World War II the movement for racial equality accelerated, bringing new awareness and new acceptance of a cultural diversity extending well beyond differences based on race. By the 1970s the feminist movement had succeeded in engaging the nation's attention and changing attitudes of both men and women toward questions of "woman's role," and in particular toward marriage and the family. The white, middle-class "housewife marriage," with the father working and the mother and children at home in a one-family suburban house, may still be the image most often called to mind by general references to "the family." The image, however, represents less than half of America's population. The "wife economy" is now obsolete; increased longevity will place further strains on lifetime marriage; women now know they can choose marriage without motherhood, or motherhood without marriage; racial and ethnic minorities will not again accept the idea that the diversity of their forms of intimate association is merely pathological. Indeed, large numbers of middle-class white couples are openly living together without marrying. What has changed is not so much the fact of diversity as the range of the acceptable in intimate association.

A strong egalitarian theme runs through our society's collective recognition of these changes; it is natural that both due process and equal protection have provided doctrinal underpinnings for the freedom of intimate association. As abstractions, "liberty" and "equality" may sometimes be in tension, but here they have nourished each other. As the civil rights movement sought to advance equality under the banner of "freedom," so the abortion rights movement has sought a new status for women under the banner of "choice."

Taking account of doctrinal development in this area, the Supreme Court, in its opinion in *Roberts v. United States Jaycees* (1984), referred for the first time to a "freedom of intimate association." "[C]ertain kinds of highly personal relationships," said the Court, had been afforded substantial constitutional protection: "marriage; childbirth; the raising and education of children; and cohabitation with one's relatives." The Court noted that these relationships tended to involve relatively small numbers of persons; a high degree of selectivity in beginning and maintaining the affiliations; and "seclusion from others in critical aspects of the relationship." Their constitutional protection reflected "the realization that individuals draw much of their emotional enrichment from close ties with others. Protecting these relationships from unwarranted state interference therefore safeguards the ability independently to define one's identity that is central to any concept of liberty."

For half a century the Court has performed much of its judicial interest-balancing by adjusting the STANDARDS OF REVIEW of the constitutionality of legislation. As the *Jaycees* opinion noted, heightened judicial scrutiny results when the Court perceives the importance of the values or interests impaired when government restricts freedom or imposes inequality. The Court has spoken of procreation as a "basic" right, and has labeled "fundamental" both the right to marry and the freedom of choice "whether to bear or beget a child." To understand what these characterizations may imply for the constitutional status of other forms of intimate association, it is necessary to ask why REPRODUCTIVE AUTONOMY and the freedom to marry are so important. To answer that question requires analysis of the substantive values that may be at stake in intimate associations.

The term "intimate association" is used here to mean a close and familiar personal relationship with another that is in some significant way comparable to a marriage or family relationship. Its connecting links may take the form of living together in the same quarters, or sexual intimacy, or blood ties, or a formal relationship, or some mixtures of these, but in principle the idea of intimate association also includes close friendship, with or without any such links. The values of intimate association are undeniably elusive; they are not readily reducible to items on a list. Yet such an exercise is implicit in any attempt to illuminate the principle underlying the decisions on marriage and reproductive choice. The potential values in intimate associations can be grouped in four clusters: society, caring and commitment, intimacy, and self-identification.

Intimate association implies some expectation of access of one person to another's physical presence, some opportunity for face-to-face encounter. A couple's claim of the right to live together, with or without a sexual relationship, directly implicates this interest in another's society; so does a divorced parent's claim of a right of access to a child in a former spouse's custody, or a prison rule wholly denying visitation rights. Other impairments of the interest in an intimate's society are indirect, as when welfare aid to a mother's family is terminated because she is living with a man. The latter case offers opportunity for manipulation; it might be characterized as a denial of

no more than a money payment, or as a denial of the society of an intimate. To allow a claim of constitutional right to turn on such question-begging seems intolerable; yet that is just what the Supreme Court typically does in cases of indirect interference with the values of intimate association. Concededly, not every impairment of the freedom to enjoy an intimate's society requires the same degree of justification, but there is little to be said for distracting attention from substantive interest-balancing by engaging in definitional legerdemain.

For most people, mutual caring and commitment are the chief values of intimate association. Caring implies commitment, for it requires an effort to know another, trust another, hope for another, and help another develop. The commitment in question is not a legal commitment enforceable by law, but a personal commitment, the sense that one is pledged to care for another and intends to keep the pledge. It is possible to be committed to an association one has not chosen; a young child exercises no choice in forming an association with her family and yet may feel wholly committed to them. Still, the value of commitment is usually heightened for the partners to an intimate association when they know there is real and continuing choice to maintain the association. The caring partner continually reaffirms her autonomy and responsibility by choosing the commitment, and the cared-for partner gains in self-respect by seeing himself through his partner's eyes as one who is worth being cared for. Furthermore, although commitment means an expectation of constancy over time, it is not paradoxical to say that effective legal shelter for this value must offer protection to casual intimate associations as well as lasting ones. Such a casual association may ripen into a durable one, and the value of commitment is fully realizable only in an atmosphere of freedom to choose whether a particular association will be fleeting or enduring. Finally, to limit the law's protection to lasting intimate associations would require intolerable inquiries into private behavior and private intentions.

Intimacy, in the context of intimate associations, is more than privacy in its ordinary sense of nondisclosure. When we speak of intimate friends, or of persons who share an intimate relationship, we refer to the intimacy of a close and enduring association, that is, intimacy in the context of caring and commitment. This sort of intimacy is something that a person can share with only a limited number of others, for it requires time and effort to know another and deal with her as a whole person.

Intimate associations are powerful influences over

the development of most people's personalities. Not only do these associations give an individual his best chance to be seen (and thus to see himself) as a whole person rather than an aggregate of social roles; they also serve as statements to others. As the legal consequences of cohabitation come to approximate those of marriage, and as divorce becomes more readily available, marriage itself takes on a special significance for its expressive content as a statement that the couple wish to identify with each other. The decision whether to have a child is also a major occasion for self-identification. To become a parent is to assume a new status in the eyes of oneself and others. Plainly the freedom to choose one's intimate associations is at the heart of this notion of association-as-statement. And, just as the freedom of political nonassociation is properly recognized as a FIRST AMENDMENT right, the freedom not to form an intimate association is similarly linked to the freedom of expression.

These four sets of intimate associational values—society, caring and commitment, intimacy, and self-identification—coalesce in an area of the human psyche that is awkward to discuss in lawyers' language. Yet even before the *Jaycees* opinion the Supreme Court had occasionally suggested its awareness of the reasons why such values are important. In *Eisenstadt,* for example, Justice WILLIAM J. BRENNAN spoke of "unwarranted governmental intrusion into matters so fundamentally affecting a PERSON as the decision whether to bear or beget a child." Although the word "person" usually is no more than a prosaic reference to an individual, its use in this passage resonates in the registers of matters personal and the human personality. If freedoms relating to marriage and family and reproductive choice are "fundamental," the reason is that these concerns lie close to the center of one's sense of self.

Not all governmental restrictions on associational freedom are intrusive in the same degree on the values of intimate association. The constitutional freedom of intimate association is not a rule for decision but an organizing principle, demanding justification for governmental intrusions on close personal relationships in proportion to the magnitude of invasion of intimate associational values. One complicating feature of this interest-balancing is that the law's interference with the freedom of intimate association usually is not direct. Instead, government typically conditions some material benefit (employment, inheritance, welfare payments, Social Security) on the candidate's associations in fact or formal associational status.

In DANDRIDGE V. WILLIAMS (1970), for example,

a state proportioned welfare benefits to family size but set an absolute limit on aid to any one family. The Supreme Court, treating the law as a restriction on money payments and ignoring its potential effects on family size, subjected it only to RATIONAL BASIS scrutiny. In CLEVELAND BOARD OF EDUCATION V. LAFLEUR (1974), however, pregnant school teachers were required to take a long maternity leave. The Court, emphasizing the right to procreate, rigorously scrutinized the law under the IRREBUTTABLE PRESUMPTIONS doctrine. This sort of question-begging without explanation, far from being aberrational, has been the norm for the Court's treatment of indirect restrictions on intimate association. It is not unusual for the Court to conceal its interest-balancing behind definitional assumptions.

When a state conditions a benefit on a formal associational status such as marriage or legitimacy of parentage, a further analytical complication arises. The state controls entry into the status as well as its legal consequences. Judicial evaluation of such a restriction on benefits must take into account the ease of entry. Alternatively, a law restricting entry into a formal associational status must be evaluated partly on the basis of the consequences of the status, including eligibility for benefits. The opportunities for circular reasoning are evident; only close attention to the associational values at stake will permit noncircular resolutions. The formal status of marriage, for example, must be seen not merely as a bureaucratic hurdle on the road to material benefits but also as a statement of the partners' commitment and self-identification.

In protecting the freedom of intimate association the Supreme Court has followed several different doctrinal paths. The *Griswold* opinion drew on the First Amendment's freedom of political association partly by way of analogy and partly in support of the Court's "zone of privacy" theory. Later decisions have both extended *Griswold*'s results in the name of equal protection and recharacterized its right of privacy as a substantive due process right. For a brief time in the 1970s the Court even used the rhetoric of PROCEDURAL DUE PROCESS and irrebuttable presumptions to defend the freedom of intimate association—a development which some Justices called a disguised form of equal protection or substantive due process. Today the freedom's most secure doctrinal base is substantive due process; yet both the First Amendment and the equal protection clause counsel judicial sensitivity to the need to protect intimate associations that are unconventional or that may offend majoritarian morality. In a society that expresses its cultural diversity in a rich variety of family forms and other personal relationships, these constitutional claims of freedom and equality will overlap.

Whatever its doctrinal context, a claim to freedom of intimate association depends on the nature and magnitude of the intrusion into the substantive values of intimate association, weighed against the governmental interests asserted to justify the intrusion. To give life to this abstraction it is necessary to examine the freedom of intimate association in operation as an organizing principle in particular subject areas. The Supreme Court's decisions can be grouped in seven overlapping categories: marriage and husband–wife relations; divorce; nonmarital relationships; procreation; illegitimacy; family autonomy; and homosexual relationships.

The Supreme Court's clear recognition of a constitutional right to marry by no means forecloses a state from regulating entry into marriage. Some restrictions, in fact, promote the principle of associational choice: minimum age requirements, for example, or requirements demanding minimum competency to understand the nature of marriage. Other restrictions aimed at promoting public health, such as mandatory blood tests, also seem likely to pass the test of strict judicial scrutiny. It is less clear that the balance of state interests against the freedom of associational choice should uphold a prohibition against POLYGAMY, or a refusal to allow homosexuals a status comparable to marriage, or a prohibition on marriage between first cousins. Yet it is safe to predict that homosexual marriage will not gain judicial blessing in the immediate future, and that the constitutionality of incest and polygamy laws will not be questioned seriously in any future now foreseeable. The Supreme Court, after all, is an instrument of government in a human society. Still, in theory, any direct state prohibition of marriage must pass the test of strict scrutiny, and indirect restriction on the right to marry requires justification proportioned to the restriction's likely practical effects as a prohibition.

The freedom of intimate association speaks not only to state interference with the right to marry but also to state intrusion into the relations between husband and wife. A marriage is more than a list of contractual duties; the partners deal with each other on many levels, both practical and emotional, and their relations are necessarily diffuse rather than particularized, exploratory rather than fixed. Spouses who are committed to stay together in an intimacy characterized by caring need to heal their relationship for the future, not settle old scores. Long before *Griswold* recognized a married couple's constitutional right to autonomy over the intimacies of their relationship, our non-

constitutional law largely maintained a "hands-off" attitude toward interspousal disputes. This tradition once supported a system of patriarchy now discredited; today the values of intimate association counsel the state to leave the partners to an ongoing marriage alone and let them work out their own differences—or, if they cannot, to terminate the marriage with a minimum of state interference.

Although the Supreme Court has not formally recognized a constitutional "right to divorce" comparable to the right to marry, both in principle and in practical effect such a right can be derived from the Court's decisions. The freedom of intimate association demands significant justification for state restrictions on exit from a marriage. The relevance to divorce of the associational value of self-identification is evident. Even the value of commitment bears on such a case, and not merely because divorce is the legal key to remarriage. For those who choose to stay married, their commitment is heightened by the knowledge that it is freely chosen. The Constitution apart, state laws setting conditions for divorce have virtually eliminated the requirement of a showing of one partner's fault. The restrictions that remain concern ACCESS TO THE COURTS, and involve limitations such as filing fees, as in BODDIE V. CONNECTICUT (1971), or RESIDENCE REQUIREMENTS, as in SOSNA V. IOWA (1975).

When a marriage terminates, nothing in the principle of associational choice militates against judicial enforcement of interspousal contracts governing the division of property. Once the union is dissolved, application of the usual rules of contract law to postdissolution obligations threatens none of the values of intimate association and demands no special justification. (Issues of child custody, which do require careful balancing of associational values, are discussed along with other parent–child questions.)

When a couple live together in a sexual relationship without marrying, the associational values of society, caring, and intimacy are all present in important degrees. Although the couple's association may not be so definitive a statement of self-identification as marriage would be, such a statement it surely is. Even the commitment implicit in such a union, although it may be tentative, usually is not trivial. If the couple see the union as a trial marriage, it takes on the instrumental quality that the *Griswold* court saw in sexual privacy. The Supreme Court's decisions on contraception and abortion have extended that right of privacy to unmarried persons. In 1968 the Court construed federal welfare legislation to prevent a state from terminating a mother's benefits merely because she had a man, not her husband, living in the house; Justice Douglas, concurring, would have held the state's attempted regulation of the mother's morals a denial of equal protection, by analogy to the Court's then recent decisions on illegitimacy. Some classifications based on marital status plainly are unconstitutional.

It seems no more than a matter of time before the Court, recognizing the expansion of the boundaries of the acceptable in intimate association, follows the logic of the contraception cases and holds invalid state laws forbidding fornication and unmarried cohabitation. Many lower courts have reached similar results, typically without addressing constitutional issues. Most of the cases have involved the claims of unmarried women denied employment, or child custody, or admission to the bar because they were living with men. The freedom of intimate association is, in important part, a product of the movement for equality between the sexes.

So are the Supreme Court's decisions on reproductive choice. "Birth control is woman's problem," said Margaret Sanger in 1920; it still is. The right to procreate, which another generation's Court called "one of the basic civil rights to man," is now matched with the constitutional right of man and woman alike to practice contraception and with a woman's right to have an abortion, even over her husband's objection. Although the right to choose "whether to bear or beget a child" is not reducible to an aspect of the freedom of intimate association, it is in part an associational choice. Given today's facility of contraception and abortion, generally one can choose whether to be a parent. The *Skinner* opinion properly connected marriage and procreation. An unmarried couple living together recognize this linkage when they decide to marry because they "want to have a family." Children are valued not only for themselves and the associations they bring but also as living expressions of their parents' caring for—and commitment to—each other. The decision whether to have a child is, in part, a choice of social identification and self-concept; it ranks in importance with any other a person may make in a lifetime.

Not only the right to be a parent, protected in *Skinner,* but also the right to choose to defer parenthood or to avoid it altogether implicates the core values of intimate association. *Griswold* and its successor decisions, defending these values in the context of nonassociation, protect men and women—but particularly women—against the enforced intimate society of unwanted children, against an unchosen commitment and a caring stained by reluctance, against a compelled identification with the social role of parent.

Coerced intimate association in the shape of forced child-bearing or parenthood is no less serious an invasion of the sense of self than is forced marriage.

Griswold and its successors also protect the autonomy of a couple's association, whether it be a marriage or an association of unmarried intimates. The point was explicitly made in the *Griswold* opinion concerning marital autonomy, and *Eisenstadt v. Baird* (1972) effectively gave unmarried couples the same power to govern the intimacies of their association. What emerges from these decisions, along with *Skinner* and *LaFleur,* is not an absolute rule but a requirement of appropriate justification when the state burdens the decision whether to procreate.

The Supreme Court has focused on equal protection in dealing with the constitutionality of laws defining the incidents of illegitimacy. There is obvious unfairness in visiting unequal treatment on an illegitimate child in order to express the state's disapproval of her parents. Yet the freedom of intimate association suggests an additional perspective: the unfairness of state-imposed inequality between persons in traditional marriage/family relationships and those in other comparable forms of intimate association. In particular, the illegitimacy laws discriminate against unmarried women and their children—as, indeed, such laws have done from their medieval beginnings. The principle of legitimacy of parentage assumes not only that a child needs a male link to the rest of the community but also that the claim of the child's mother to social position depends on her being granted the status of formal marriage. In historical origin and in modern application, the chief function of the law of illegitimacy is to assure male control over the transmission of wealth and status. Deviance from the principle of legitimacy is most likely in subgroups whose fathers lack wealth and status; it is no accident that the incidence of illegitimacy in our society is highest among the nonwhite poor.

As increased numbers of middle-class couples live together without marrying, surely there will be changes in the legal status of unmarried mothers and their children. In the perspective of the freedom of intimate association, the constitutional basis for the whole system of illegitimacy appears shaky. If the informal union of an unmarried couple is constitutionally protected, the relationship between that union's children and their parents is also protected. Significant impairment of the substantive values of such an intimate association must find justification, in proportion to the impairment, in state interests that cannot be achieved by other less intrusive means.

Ever since *Meyer v. Nebraska* (1923) and *Pierce*

v. Society of Sisters (1925) judges and commentators have assumed that the Constitution protects the autonomy of the traditional family against excessive state interference. Those two decisions rested on substantive due process grounds, and they have been cited often by the Supreme Court during the modern revival of substantive due process as a guarantee of personal liberty. When a family is united concerning such matters as the children's education, only a COMPELLING STATE INTEREST will justify state interference with the family's choice.

When a family is not united, however, the constitutional principle of family autonomy is an imperfect guide. Generally, the law assumes that children prosper under their parents' control. For very young children, this assumption is little more than a corollary of the family autonomy principle. As children mature, however, it becomes sensible to speak of the continuing family relationship as a matter of choice. Within the family that stays together, parent–child relations are, from some point in a child's teenage years forward, a matter of intrafamily agreement. Even when parental discipline is the rule, it rests on the child's consent, once the child is capable of making an independent life. Not surprisingly, the Supreme Court held invalid a state law giving an unmarried minor female's parents the right to veto her decision to have an abortion. (See PLANNED PARENTHOOD OF MISSOURI V. DANFORTH, 1976.)

The freedom of intimate association thus counsels severe restrictions on the state's power to intervene either to enforce parental authority or to oppose it— just as considerations of intramarital associational choice and harmony dictate that state intervention into the husband–wife relationship be limited to cases of urgent necessity, such as wife abuse. Conceding that most children want and need parental discipline, it remains true that invoking the state's police officers and juvenile halls to enforce that discipline is destructive of the values of intimate association. For mature children, those values depend on their willingness to identify with their parents and to be committed to maintaining a caring intimacy with them. In cases of a parent's incapacity or serious neglect, state intervention into the zone of family autonomy may be constitutionally justified. Yet removals of children from parental custody and terminations of parental rights are extreme measures, intruding deeply into the values of intimate association—not only for parents but also for children. The most compelling justification is therefore required for so drastic a state intervention, justification found in the child's needs, not any interest the state may have in punishing parental

misbehavior. The Supreme Court's refusal in LASSITER V. DEPARTMENT OF SOCIAL SERVICES (1981) to extend the full reach of the RIGHT TO COUNSEL to indigent parents in termination proceedings seems an unstable precedent.

While a marriage lasts, the law is no more likely to interfere in interspousal disputes over child-rearing than it is in other controversies between husband and wife. When a marriage ends, an agreement between the separating parents over child custody usually will prevail, absent some overriding factor such as the associational choice of a mature child. A custody contest upon divorce, involving competing claims of rights of association, demands discretionary, whole-person evaluations rather than application of specific rules of law. The Constitution comes to bear on such decisions only marginally, as appellate courts seek to assure that trial judges do, in fact, consider the whole persons before them and do not disqualify parents from custody by informally substituting unconstitutional "rules" for the discretion that is appropriate. Such a "rule," for example, might disqualify on the basis of a parent's race—or, as in PALMORE V. SIDOTI (1984), the race of the parent's spouse—or religion, or unmarried cohabitation, or sexual preference. *Stanley v. Illinois* (1972) is an instructive analogy; there the Supreme Court held that a law disqualifying a natural father from custody of his illegitimate child upon the mother's death was an unconstitutional irrebuttable presumption of unfitness.

It is now established beyond question that the "liberty" protected by the two due process clauses protects "freedom of personal choice in matters of marriage and family life"—Justice POTTER STEWART's words, concurring in *Zablocki v. Redhail* (1978). If the logic of that freedom extends beyond formal marriage and beyond the nuclear family, the reason is that the human family is a social artifact, not an entity defined in nature. In MOORE V. CITY OF EAST CLEVELAND (1977) a plurality of four Justices admitted the traditional "extended family" into the circle of due process protection, and that opinion is now regularly cited as if it were an OPINION OF THE COURT. The freedom Justice Stewart described is comprehensible only in the light of intimate associational values that are also found in families that depart significantly from traditional models. One result of the movement for women's liberation has been the increased adoption of alternative living arrangements: couples living together outside marriage; single mothers with children, sometimes combining with other similar families. Other groupings such as communes for the young and the old are responses to what their members see as the failings of traditional arrangements. These people do not risk prosecution under cohabitation laws or other "morals" statutes; they may, however, risk the loss of material benefits.

Any governmental intrusion on personal choice of living arrangements requires substantial justification, in proportion to its likely influence in coercing people out of one form of intimate association and into another. In DEPARTMENT OF AGRICULTURE V. MORENO (1973) the Supreme Court demanded such justification for a law denying food stamps to households composed of "unrelated" persons, and found it lacking. Yet in *Village of Belle Terre v. Boraas* (1974) the Court made no search for justification beyond minimum rationality, and upheld a ZONING ordinance designed to screen out nontraditional families and applied to exclude occupancy of a home by six unrelated students. In design, the *Belle Terre* ordinance was a direct assault on the freedom of intimate association, an attempt to stamp out forms of personal association departing from a vision of family life that no longer fit a large proportion of the population. *Belle Terre*'s standing as a precedent surely will weaken as the Court comes to take seriously its own rhetoric about "family" values in nontraditional families. One occasion for such rhetoric was the opinion in *Smith v. Organization of Foster Families* (1977), recognizing the values of intimate association in a foster family.

Laws prohibiting homosexual conduct are only rarely enforced against private consensual behavior. The middle-class homosexual couple thus have each other's society, including whatever sort of intimacy they want; they care for each other and are committed to each other in the degree they choose. What government chiefly denies them is the dignity of self-identification as equal citizens, along with certain forms of employment and other material benefits that may be reserved for partners to a formal marriage.

Whatever may have been the original purpose of laws forbidding homosexual sex, today one of their chief supports is a wish to regulate the content of messages about sexual preference. One fear is that the state, by repealing its restrictions, will be seen as approving homosexual conduct. The selective enforcement of these laws is itself evidence that one of the main policies being pursued is the suppression of expression; the laws are enforced mainly against those who openly advertise their sexual preferences. The immediate practical effect of this enforcement pattern is to penalize public self-identification and expression, some of which is political expression in support of "gay liberation." Even thoroughgoing enforcement would severely impair expression, along with

the values of caring and intimacy. For a homosexual, a violation of these laws is the principal form that a sexual expression of love can take.

The denial of the status of marriage, or some comparable status, does not merely limit homosexuals' opportunities for expressive self-identification; material benefits also are frequently conditioned on marriage. Some commentators argue that a state's refusal to recognize homosexual marriage raises a problem of sex discrimination, and others contend that homosexuality should be regarded as a SUSPECT CLASSIFICATION for equal protection purposes. In any case, the heart of the constitutional problem lies in the freedom of intimate association. Although the denial of formal recognition of a homosexual couple's union may not demand the same compelling justification that would be required by a total prohibition of homosexual relations, it nonetheless seems unlikely that government could meet any requirement of justification that was not wholly permissive.

The burden of justification is of critical importance in the area of regulation of homosexual conduct, precisely because most such regulations are the product of folklore and fantasy rather than evidence of real risk of harm. If, for example, the state had to prove that a lesbian mother, by virtue of that status alone, was unfit to have custody of her child, the effort surely would demonstrate that the operative factor in the disqualification was not risk of harm, but stigma. The results of serious constitutional inquiry into harms and justifications in such cases are easy to predict. First, however, that serious inquiry must be made, and the Supreme Court showed in *Doe v. Commonwealth's District Attorney* (1976) that it was not eager to embark on that course.

The freedom of intimate association serves as an organizing principle mainly by focusing attention on substantive associational values. In a given case, the impairment of those values is matched against the asserted justifications for governmental regulation. Those justifications are hard to discuss systematically, for they can be asserted on the basis of a range of interests as broad as the public welfare. One cluster of justifications, however, deserves attention: the promotion of a political majority's view of morality. The state may claim a role in socializing its citizens, and especially the young, to traditional values. When a legislature prohibits unmarried cohabitation or homosexual relations or other disapproved forms of intimate association, it does so primarily to promote a moral view and to protect the sensibilities of those who share that view. The freedom of intimate association does not wholly disable government from seeking these ends; however, as *Griswold* and its successor decisions show, neither can the state defeat every claim to the freedom of intimate association simply by invoking conventional morality.

The judicial interest-balancing appropriate to the evolution of many claims of freedom of intimate association thus must consider not only degrees of impairment of associational values but also questions of the kind raised by GOVERNMENT SPEECH cases involving official promotion of particular points of view. There is a difference, for example, between a "baby bonus" designed to assist parents with child-rearing and a state's offer of cash to any woman entering an abortion clinic, conditioned on her agreement to forgo an abortion. To say that the difference is one of degree is to remind ourselves that the judicial function in constitutional cases is one of judgment. The freedom of intimate association is not a machine that, once set in motion, must run to all conceivable logical conclusions. It is instead a constitutional principle, requiring significant justification when the state seeks to lay hands on life-defining intimate associational choices.

KENNETH L. KARST

Bibliography

BURT, ROBERT A. 1979 The Constitution of the Family. *Supreme Court Review* 1979:329–395.
Developments in the Law—The Constitution and the Family 1980 *Harvard Law Review* 93:1156–1383.
GERETY, TOM 1977 Redefining Privacy. *Harvard Civil Rights-Civil Liberties Law Review* 12:233–296.
GLENDON, MARY ANN 1977 *State, Law and Family.* New York: North-Holland Publishing Company.
KARST, KENNETH L. 1980 The Freedom of Intimate Association. *Yale Law Journal* 89:624–692.
SYMPOSIUM 1975 Children and the Law. *Law and Contemporary Problems* 39, no. 3:1–293.
SYMPOSIUM 1979 Children and the Law. *University of California, Davis Law Review* 12:207–898.
SYMPOSIUM 1985 The Legal System and Homosexuality—Approbation, Accommodation, or Reprobation? *University of Dayton Law Review* 10:445–813.
TRIBE, LAURENCE H. 1978 *American Constitutional Law.* Chap. 15. Mineola, N.Y.: Foundation Press.
WILKINSON, J. HARVIE, III and WHITE, G. EDWARD 1977 Constitutional Protection for Personal Lifestyles. *Cornell Law Review* 62:563–625.

FREEDOM OF PETITION

The freedom to petition the government for redress of grievances was recognized in MAGNA CARTA in 1215 and was well established in English law before the American Revolution. The king would summon Parliament to supply funds for the running of government and Parliament developed the habit of petitioning for a redress of grievances as the condition of supplying the money. The growing recognition of the right of subjects as well as of Parliament to petition the Crown culminated in the explicit affirmation in the English BILL OF RIGHTS of 1689 "That it is the right of the subjects to petition the King and all commitments and prosecutions for such petitioning are illegal."

In the United States Constitution, the FIRST AMENDMENT protects "the right of the people peaceably to assemble, and to petition the Government for a redress of grievances." Historically, the FREEDOM OF ASSEMBLY was regarded as ancillary to the right of petition, as if the amendment guaranteed the right to assemble *in order to* petition the government. This view was expressed by the Supreme Court in UNITED STATES V. CRUIKSHANK (1876). Today, however, the right of assembly has independent significance equal to that of the FREEDOMS OF SPEECH, PRESS, and religion. (See DEJONGE V. OREGON, 1937.) The right to petition has received less judicial attention than the other First Amendment rights. Nevertheless, it is one of the freedoms protected by the DUE PROCESS clause of the FOURTEENTH AMENDMENT against infringement by the states. (See HAGUE V. C.I.O., 1939.) Comparable protections of the right of petition are found, expressly or by clear implication, in the constitutions of all the states. And the right to petition Congress for redress of grievances has been recognized as one of the privileges of national CITIZENSHIP protected against state infringement by the PRIVILEGES OR IMMUNITIES clause of the Fourteenth Amendment. (See TWINING V. NEW JERSEY, 1908.)

The right of petition includes the right not only to approach public officials directly with requests for redress of grievances but also to circulate petitions for signature so as to generate mass pressure on the Congress and other public bodies. It is in this context that the right of petition may have its greatest contemporary significance. For the exercise of the right of petition involves the exercise of other First Amendment rights, including not only the right of expression but the right of other people to be exposed to the ideas expressed in the petition. The act of preparing and circulating a petition is itself an exercise of the freedom to associate with others for the expression of political and other opinions. Justice WILLIAM J. BRENNAN, dissenting in BOSTON V. GLINES (1980), remarked: "The petition is especially suited for the exercise of all these rights: It serves as a vehicle of communication; as a classic means of individual affiliation with ideas or opinions; and as a peaceful yet effective method of amplifying the views of the individual signers." As with other First Amendment rights, the freedom of petition cannot be infringed in the absence of a compelling governmental interest justifying the infringement; the right of petition is an essential component of the political liberties protected by the First Amendment.

CHARLES E. RICE

FREEDOM OF RELIGION

See: Religious Liberty

FREEDOM OF SPEECH

Freedom of speech is guaranteed in the American Constitution by the FIRST AMENDMENT. Adopted in 1791 as the first provision of the BILL OF RIGHTS, the First Amendment reads (excluding the clauses on religion): "Congress shall make no law . . . abridging the freedom of speech, or of the press, or the right of the people peaceably to assemble, and to petition the Government for a redress of grievances." Although the provision names four specific rights—freedom of speech, FREEDOM OF THE PRESS, FREEDOM OF ASSEMBLY, and FREEDOM OF PETITION—the several guarantees have never been clearly differentiated; rather the First Amendment has been construed as guaranteeing a composite right to freedom of expression. The term "freedom of speech," therefore, in popular usuage as well as in legal doctrine, has been considered roughly coextensive with the whole of the First Amendment.

The precise intentions of the framers of the First Amendment have never been entirely clear. The debates in Congress when the amendment was proposed do not throw much light upon the subject. The right to freedom of speech derives from English law and tradition. And it is agreed that the English law of the time, following the lapse of the censorship laws at the end of the seventeenth century, did not authorize advance censorship of publication. The English law of SEDITIOUS LIBEL, however, did provide punishment, after publication, for speech that criticized the government, its policies or its officials, or tended to bring them into contempt or disrepute. These features of English law were under severe attack, both in England and in the American colonies, but whether the First Amendment was meant to abolish or change

them has been a matter of dispute. Similarly, the application of the First Amendment to other aspects of free speech, such as civil libel, BLASPHEMY, OBSCENITY, and the like, remained obscure.

Passage of the ALIEN AND SEDITION ACTS in 1798, which incorporated much of the English law of seditious libel, stimulated public discussion of the meaning of the First Amendment. The constitutional issues, however, never reached the Supreme Court. Nor, despite widespread suppression of speech at certain times in our history, such as took place during the abolitionist movement, the Civil War, and the beginnings of the labor movement, did the Supreme Court have or take the occasion to address in any major way the development of First Amendment doctrine. The reason for this failure of the constitutional guarantee to be translated into legal action seems to lie partly in the fact that the Bill of Rights had been construed by the Court to apply only to action of the federal government, not to state or local governments; partly in the fact that, insofar as suppression emanated from federal sources, it was the executive not the legislature that was involved; and partly in the fact that the role of the courts in protecting CIVIL LIBERTIES had not matured to the point it has reached today.

In any event this state of affairs ended at the time of World War I. Legislation enacted by Congress in 1917 and 1918, designed to prohibit interference with the war effort, raised clear-cut issues under the First Amendment. Beginning in 1919, a series of cases challenging the wartime legislation came before the Supreme Court. These were followed by cases arising out of the Red scare of the early 1920s. In 1925, in GITLOW v. UNITED STATES, the Court accepted the argument that the First Amendment was applicable to the state and local governments as a "liberty" that could not be denied without DUE PROCESS OF LAW under the FOURTEENTH AMENDMENT. It also became clear that, while the First Amendment literally refers only to "Congress," its provisions extend not only to the legislature but to the executive and judicial branches of government as well. As the First Amendment has come to be applied to more and newer problems growing out of the operation of a modern technological society, there has developed an extensive network of principles, legal rules, implementing decisions, and institutional practices which expand and refine the constitutional guarantee.

The fundamental values underlying the concept of freedom of speech, and the functions that principle serves in a democratic society, are widely accepted. They have been summarized in the following form:

First, freedom of speech is essential to the development of the individual personality. The right to express oneself and to communicate with others is central to the realization of one's character and potentiality as a human being. Conversely, suppression of thought or opinion is an affront to a person's dignity and integrity. In this respect freedom of speech is an end in itself, not simply an instrument to attain other ends. As such it is not necessarily subordinate to other goals of the society.

Second, freedom of speech is vital to the attainment and advancement of knowledge. As John Stuart Mill pointed out, an enlightened judgment is possible only if one is willing to consider all facts and ideas, from whatever source, and to test one's conclusion against opposing views. Even speech that conveys false information or maligns ideas has value, for it compels us to retest and rethink accepted positions and thereby promotes greater understanding. From this function of free speech it follows that the right to express oneself does not depend upon whether society judges the communication to be true or false, good or bad, socially useful or harmful. All points of view, even a minority of one, are entitled to be heard. The MARKETPLACE OF IDEAS should be open to all sellers and all buyers.

Third, freedom of speech is a necessary part of our system of self-government. ALEXANDER MEIKLEJOHN, the leading exponent of this view of the First Amendment, stressed that under our Constitution, sovereignty resides in the people; in other words, the people are the masters and the government is their servant. If the people are to perform their role as sovereign and instruct their government, they must have access to all information, ideas, and points of view. This right of free speech is crucial not only in determining policy but in checking the government in its implementation of policy. The implication of this position is that the government has no authority to determine what may be said or heard by the citizens of the community. The servant cannot tell the master how to make up its mind.

Fourth, freedom of speech is vital to the process of peaceful social change. It allows ideas to be tested in advance before action is taken, it legitimizes the decision reached, and it permits adaptation to new conditions without the use of force. It does not eliminate conflict in a society, but it does direct conflict into more rational, less violent, channels. From this it follows, in the words of Justice WILLIAM J. BRENNAN in NEW YORK TIMES V. SULLIVAN (1964), that speech will often be "uninhibited, robust, and wide-open."

There is also general agreement that speech is entitled to special protection against abridgment by the state. Freedom of thought and communication are central to any system of individual rights. Most other rights of the person against the collective flow from and are dependent upon that source. Moreover, speech is considered to have less harmful effects upon the community—to be less coercive—than other forms of conduct. And, as a general proposition, the state possesses sufficient power to achieve social goals without suppressing beliefs, opinions, or communication of ideas. Hence, in constitutional terms, freedom of speech occupies a "preferred position."

One further background factor should be noted. Toleration of the speech of others does not come easily to many people, especially those in positions of power. As Justice OLIVER WENDELL HOLMES remarked in ABRAMS V. UNITED STATES (1919), "If you have no doubt of your premises or your powers and want a certain result with all your heart you naturally express your wishes in law and sweep away all opposition." Hence the pressures leading to suppression of speech are widespread and powerful in our society. The mechanisms for protecting freedom of speech, therefore, must rely heavily upon an independent judiciary, standing somewhat outside the fray, and upon the creation of legal DOCTRINES that are precise and realistic.

The principal controversies that have engaged our system of freedom of speech have concerned the formulation of these implementing rules. In general the issues have centered on two basic questions. The first is what kind of conduct is to be considered "speech" entitled to special protection under the First Amendment. The second concerns what degree of protection, or encouragement, must be given that speech under the constitutional mandate.

As to the first question—the issue of coverage—it has been argued from time to time that certain categories of speech are totally outside the purview of the First Amendment. Thus it has been contended that totalitarian and racist groups should not be permitted to advance antidemocratic ideas. The argument has been that political groups that would destroy democratic institutions if they came to power should not be entitled to take advantage of these institutions in order to promote their cause; only those who adhere to the rules of the game should be allowed to participate. Similarly it has been urged that racist speech violates the dignity and integrity of fellow persons in the community, performs no social function, and should not be tolerated in a civilized society dedicated to human rights.

While this position has been strongly urged it has not prevailed in the United States. For both theoretical and practical reasons the concept of freedom of speech has been interpreted to mean that all persons should be allowed to express their beliefs and opinions regardless of how obnoxious or "fraught with death" those ideas may be. As a matter of principle, all ideas must be open to challenge; even totalitarian and racist speech serves a useful purpose in forcing a society to defend and thereby better comprehend its own basic values. Moreover, groups that promote totalitarian or racist ideas do not operate in a political vacuum. Their speech reflects fears, grievances, or other conditions which society should be aware of and in some cases take action to deal with. Suppression of such speech simply increases hostility, diverts attention from underlying problems, and ultimately weakens the society.

In practical terms, experience has shown that it is difficult or impossible to suppress any set of ideas without endangering the whole fabric of free speech. The dividing line between totalitarian and racist speech, on the one hand, and "acceptable" speech, on the other, cannot be clearly drawn and thus is open to manipulation. The apparatus necessary to suppress a political movement—involving government investigation into beliefs and opinions, the compiling of dossiers, the employment of agents and informers—inevitably creates an atmosphere damaging freedom of all speech. Frequently actions ostensibly directed against the outlawed group are merely a pretext for harassment of unwanted political opposition. Most important, once the dike has been broken all unorthodox or minority opinion is in danger. The only safe course is to afford protection to all who wish to speak.

The Supreme Court, accepting the prevailing view, has consistently taken the position that antidemocratic forms of speech are within the coverage of the First Amendment. Thus, while upholding the conviction of the Communist party leaders under the Smith Act for advocating overthrow of the government by force and violence in DENNIS V. UNITED STATES (1951), the Court never suggested that the defendants were not entitled to the protection of the First Amendment. Likewise in BRANDENBURG V. OHIO (1969) racist speech by members of the Ku Klux Klan was given full First Amendment protection. The viewpoint taken by the Court was perhaps most dramatically formulated by Justice Holmes when he said in *Gitlow v. New York:* "If in the long run the beliefs expressed in proletarian dictatorship are destined to be accepted by the dominant forces of the country, the only meaning of free speech is that they should be given their chance and have their way."

It has also been contended that the coverage of the First Amendment should be limited to speech that relates to "political issues." Meiklejohn, who emphasized the role of the First Amendment in the process of self-government, advocated this interpretation, although he ultimately reached a broad definition of "political speech." Other commentators, arguing for a similar limitation, have adopted a far more restrictive concept of "political speech." The position has not, however, been accepted. For one thing, the proposed restriction has no inner logic; virtually all speech has political overtones or ramifications. In any event, there is no convincing reason for restricting the coverage of the First Amendment in this way. Speech concerned with literature, music, art, science, entertainment, ethics, and a host of other matters serves the functions sought by the First Amendment and should be equally entitled to its protection. The Supreme Court has consistently so held.

Other, narrower, categories of speech have also been said to be excluded from First Amendment coverage. In CHAPLINSKY V. NEW HAMPSHIRE (1942) the Supreme Court observed that restrictions on speech that was obscene, profane, libelous, or involved FIGHTING WORDS had "never been thought to raise any Constitutional problem." But this OBITER DICTUM has been eroded in the course of time. Obscenity is still, in theory, excluded from First Amendment protection; but in formulating the definition of "obscenity" the Court has brought constitutional considerations back into the decision. The exception for profanity has been disregarded. The dictum concerning libel has been expressly overruled. And the "fighting words" exemption, which has been narrowly construed to apply only to face-to-face encounters, turns more on the proposition that "fighting words" are not really speech at all than upon a concept of exclusion from First Amendment protection. Thus virtually all conduct that can be considered "speech" falls within the coverage of the First Amendment.

There are certain areas of speech where, although the First Amendment is applicable, the governing rules afford somewhat less protection than in the case of speech generally. These areas include speech in military institutions, which are not structured according to democratic principles, and speech by or addressed to children, who are "not possessed of that full capacity for individual choice which is the presupposition of First Amendment guarantees." COMMERCIAL SPEECH, that is, speech concerned solely with buying or selling goods or services for a profit, was at one time excluded from First Amendment protection. It is now covered by the First Amendment but is entitled to less stringent safeguards than noncommercial speech.

The most controversial aspect of the coverage question concerns not whether conduct that is recognized as speech is exempted from First Amendment protection but what conduct is to be considered speech and what is to be held non-speech, or "action," and hence not protected by the First Amendment. The resolution of this problem poses obvious difficulties. Clearly some verbal conduct, such as words exchanged in planning a CRIMINAL CONSPIRACY, does not constitute "speech" within the intention of the First Amendment. Likewise some nonverbal conduct, such as operating a printing press, is an integral part of the speech which it is the purpose of the First Amendment to protect. Some conduct, such as PICKETING, combines elements of speech and action.

Two approaches to this dilemma are possible. One is to attempt to define "speech" or "action" in light of the values and functions served by the First Amendment. The other is to abandon any effort at a sharp definition of "speech" and to hold that any conduct containing an "expressive element" is within the coverage of the First Amendment. The advantage of the first approach is that it allows the development of more clear-cut rules for protecting conduct found to be "speech," that is, all "speech" or most "speech" could be fully protected without the need for devising elaborate qualifications difficult to apply. The advantage of the second approach is that it avoids the necessity of making refined, and in some cases unpersuasive, distinctions between "speech" and "action." The Supreme Court has, on the whole, tended to follow the second path of analysis. However, in the overwhelming majority of cases where First Amendment protection is invoked, there is no serious question but that the conduct involved is properly classified as "speech."

The second major problem in interpreting and applying the First Amendment is the determination of what degree of protection from government interference, or encouragement by government, is to be afforded "speech." Most of the controversy over the meaning of the First Amendment has involved this issue. The Supreme Court has varied its approach from time to time and no consistent or comprehensive theory has emerged. The question arises in a great variety of situations, and only a brief summary of some of the principal results is possible.

The starting point is that, as a general proposition, the government cannot prohibit or interfere with speech because it objects to the content of the communication. Legitimate government interests must be achieved by methods other than the control of speech. Thus speech that is critical of the government or its officials, that interferes with government efficiency, that makes the attainment of consensus in the society more difficult, that urges radical change, or that affects similar societal interests cannot be abridged.

Somewhat less stringent rules have been applied where the speech is of such a character as to lead to concern that it will provoke violence or other violation of a valid law. Many of the Supreme Court decisions have involved issues of this nature, and a series of legal doctrines emerged. In the earlier cases, mostly growing out of legislation designed to prevent interference with the conduct of World War I or to suppress emerging radical political parties, the Court adopted a BAD TENDENCY TEST under which any speech that had a tendency to cause a violation of law could be punished. Such a test, of course, gives very little protection to nonconforming speech. Subsequently, on the initiative of Justices Holmes and LOUIS D. BRANDEIS, the Court accepted the CLEAR AND PRESENT DANGER TEST. Under this doctrine speech could be penalized only when it created a clear and present danger of some significant evil that the government had a right to prevent. In some cases the Court has used an ad hoc BALANCING TEST, by which the interest in freedom of speech is balanced against the social interest in maintaining order. Ultimately the Court appears to have settled upon the so-called *Brandenburg* test. "[T]he constitutional guarantees of free speech and free press," the Court said in *Brandenburg v. Ohio*, "do not permit a State to forbid or proscribe advocacy of the use of force or of law violation except where such advocacy is directed to inciting or producing imminent lawless action and is likely to incite or produce such action." An approach which attempts to separate "speech" from "action" and gives full protection to speech has never appealed to a majority of the Justices. But the Court has progressively tightened the originally loose restrictions on the government's power to punish militant political rhetoric.

In recent years the question has been posed in various forms whether or not speech can be curtailed where it may cause injury to NATIONAL SECURITY. The term "national security" has never been precisely defined and could of course include virtually every aspect of national life. Generally speaking it is clear that the usual First Amendment principles apply in national security cases; the society must seek to achieve national security by methods that do not abridge freedom of speech. Nevertheless, qualifications of the general rule have been urged with increasing vigor. The chief issues have involved publication of information alleged to jeopardize national security and the conduct of intelligence agencies seeking to acquire information relating to national security matters.

The Supreme Court in NEW YORK TIMES V. UNITED STATES (1971) (the Pentagon Papers case), a landmark decision in this area, rejected attempts by the government to enjoin the *New York Times* and the *Washington Post* from publishing a secret classified history of the VIETNAM WAR obtained illicitly by a former government employee, despite government claims that publication would cause "grave and irreparable injury" to the national security. The decision rested on the ground that the government had not met the "heavy burden of showing justification for the imposition of [a PRIOR] RESTRAINT." The majority were unable to agree, however, upon a single theory of the case. Three Justices thought that an INJUNCTION against publication of information should never, or virtually never, be allowed, but others, including the dissenters, would have accepted less rigorous standards. In UNITED STATES V. UNITED STATES DISTRICT COURT (1972), another critical decision in the national security area, the Court ruled that government intelligence agencies were bound to adhere to constitutional limitations (in that case the FOURTH AMENDMENT) in gathering information pertaining to national security, but it expressed no opinion as to "the issues which may be involved with respect to activities of foreign powers or their agents." The degree to which the Supreme Court will accept claims to national security as ground for qualifying First Amendment rights thus remains uncertain.

Cases where the exercise of free-speech rights runs into conflict with other social or individual interests frequently come before the Supreme Court. Interests invoked as ground for limiting speech have included the right of an accused person to obtain a FAIR TRIAL free from prejudice caused by adverse newspaper publicity; the interest of society in assuring fair elections through regulation of contributions and expenditures in political campaigns; the patriotic interest of the community in protecting the American flag against desecration by political dissenters; the aesthetic interests of the public in maintaining certain areas free from unsightly billboards; and many others. Where the countervailing interest is an appealing one the Court has tended to apply a balancing test: individual and social interests in freedom of speech are balanced against the opposing interests at stake. Likewise, where a government regulation is ostensibly directed at some other objective but has the effect of restricting speech, as in the case of government LOYALTY-SECURITY PROGRAMS or LEGISLATIVE INVESTIGATIONS, the balancing test is usually employed.

The balancing test has come to assume various forms. When most protective of free speech it requires that the government (1) has the burden of justifying any restriction on speech (2) by demonstrating "compelling" reasons and (3) showing that less intrusive means for advancing the government interest are not available. On the other hand, in some cases the balancing test is applied without giving any special weight to First Amendment considerations. The consequence of using a balancing test is that the outcome in any particular case is difficult to predict. Thus in BUCKLEY V. VALEO (1976) the Supreme Court held, in substance, that limitations on the amount of funds that can be contributed to a candidate in a political campaign are permissible but limitations on expenditures are not. Moreover, the balancing test is such a loose standard that, in times of stress, it might afford very little protection to freedom of speech. Thus far, however, the balances struck by the Court have given a substantial degree of support to free-speech rights.

Special rules for measuring the protection accorded speech have evolved in several areas. With respect to laws punishing obscene publications the Supreme Court, as noted above, still adheres to the theoretical position that obscenity is not covered by the First Amendment but it does take constitutional factors into account in determining whether or not a particular publication is obscene. As set forth in MILLER V. CALIFORNIA (1972), the current definition of obscenity is "(a) whether the average person, applying contemporary community standards, would find that the work, taken as a whole, appeals to the prurient interest; (b) whether the work depicts or describes, in a patently offensive way, sexual conduct specifically defined by the applicable state law; and (c) whether the work, taken as a whole, lacks serious literary, artistic, political, or scientific value." In practical application, as nearly as it can be articulated, the *Miller* test allows regulation only of "hard-core pornography."

The Supreme Court has also imposed substantive limitations upon actions for libel. Criminal libel laws have been narrowly construed and, although a GROUP LIBEL law was upheld in BEAUHARNAIS V. ILLINOIS (1952), subsequent developments have cast doubt upon the present validity of that decision. In the field of civil libel the Supreme Court held, in *New York Times v. Sullivan*, that public officials could maintain a suit for libel only when they can establish that a damaging statement about them was not only false but was made with "actual malice," that is, "with knowledge that it was false or with reckless disregard of whether it was false or not." Later the "actual malice" rule was extended to "public figures." As to others, namely "private individuals," the Court has held that the state or federal government could adopt any rule respecting libel so long as it required at least a showing of negligence on the part of the defendant. Although the Court in recent years has tended to take a narrow view of who is a "public figure," and the costs of defending libel actions frequently operate as a restraint upon speech, the curtailment of public discussion through libel laws has been somewhat held in check.

Constitutional doctrine for reconciling the right to freedom of speech with the RIGHT OF PRIVACY remains unformed. In most respects the two constitutional rights do not clash but rather supplement each other. Conflict may arise, however, at several points, such as where a communication contains information that is true, and hence is not covered by the libel laws, but relates to the intimate details of an individual's personal life that are not relevant to any issue of public concern. The scope of the constitutional right of privacy has never been clearly delineated. Nor has the Supreme Court ever held that the right of privacy prevails over the right to freedom of speech. Nevertheless the issue is a recurring one and sooner or later an accommodation between the two constitutional rights will have to be formulated.

The degree of protection afforded speech under the First Amendment may also hinge on various other factors. Where the physical facilities for communication are limited, and the government is therefore forced to allocate available facilities among those seeking to use them, the government has the power, indeed the obligation, to lay down certain conditions in order to assure that the scarce facilities will be used in the public interest. This is the situation with respect to radio and television BROADCASTING where, at least at the present time, the number of broadcast channels is limited. On this theory, government regulations such as the FAIRNESS DOCTRINE, requiring that broadcasting stations give adequate coverage to public issues and that such coverage be fair in accurately reflecting opposing views, have been upheld by the Supreme Court. Such regulatory powers, however, extend only to what might be termed a "macro level" of intervention. The government may require that a broadcasting station devote a certain proportion of its time to public interest programs, but it may not

censor or determine the content of particular programs, that is, it may not exercise control at the "micro level."

Likewise special considerations enter when a person seeking to exercise rights to freedom of speech is an employee of the government or is confined in a government institution such as a mental hospital or a prison. Here the relationship of the individual to the government is somewhat different from the relationship of the ordinary citizen to the general community; the goals and interests of the particular institution involved are entitled to more immediate recognition. The Supreme Court has dealt with these issues by applying a balancing test, but the weights have been cast largely on the government side of the scales.

One further aspect of government attempts to regulate the content of speech should be noted. The letter and spirit of the EQUAL PROTECTION clause have had an important bearing upon the right to freedom of speech. The equal protection element guarantees the universality of the rules protecting the right to speak. It means that the government cannot differentiate, at least without a compelling reason, between speakers on the basis of the content of their communications. Hence if the government allows a patriotic organization to march down the main street of town it must grant equal opportunity to unpopular or radical organizations. If it grants the use of a public building for a meeting to a group of one political persuasion it must grant the same use to all political groups. This combination of the First Amendment and the equal protection clause thus helps to assure that unorthodox speech will receive the same treatment as conventional speech.

Apart from attempts to control the content of speech, government regulation has also dealt with various issues in the administration of the free speech system. Thus the requirement of a permit to hold a meeting in a public building, or to conduct a demonstration that may interfere with traffic, clearly constitutes a justifiable regulation. Likewise, a municipal ordinance may legitimately keep soundtrucks from operating in a residential area during certain hours of the night. It is frequently said that "time, place, and manner" restrictions on speech are permissible so long as they are "reasonable." Such generalizations, however, are overbroad. In many situations, "time, place, and manner" restrictions can be used to curtail freedom of speech to the same degree as content regulations. And to accord them all validity would be inconsistent with the basic premise that the right of free speech is entitled to a preferential position among competing interests. A more precise statement of the applicable legal doctrine would be to say that administrative regulations dealing with physical incompatibilities between the exercise of free speech rights and other interests are permissible. Thus government could validly allocate use of the streets between those seeking to hold a demonstration and those using the streets for passage. And the physical intrusion of noises from soundtrucks would also be subject to control. The principle for resolving such physical conflicts is not mere "reasonableness" but a fair accommodation between the competing interests.

Other legal doctrines play an important role in maintaining the system of freedom of speech. Thus the courts have held that the rules against undue VAGUENESS or OVERBREADTH in legislation or administrative regulation will be applied with special rigor where First Amendment rights are affected. And the prohibition in the Fourth Amendment against UNREASONABLE SEARCHES and seizures is given added force when invoked to protect freedom of speech. Perhaps the most significant supportive doctrine of this nature is the rule against prior restraint. Attempts by the government to prevent publication in advance, through a system of censorship, an injunction, or similar measures, are presumptively invalid and rarely allowed. Thus the silencing of speech before it is uttered—a particularly effective form of suppression—is normally not available as a method of control.

The constitutional doctrines thus far discussed have been of a negative character in that they have been directed against government interference with freedom of speech. In recent years, however, increasing attention has been given to questions relating to the affirmative side of the constitutional guarantee: to what extent does the First Amendment allow or require the government to encourage or promote a more effective system of free speech? These issues are important because of growing distortions within the system. More and more, as the mass media have become concentrated in fewer hands and have tended to express a single economic, social, and political point of view, the concept of a marketplace of diverse ideas has failed to conform to original expectations. The problems are difficult to solve because they involve using the government to expand freedom of speech while at the same time continuing to prohibit the government from controlling or inhibiting speech.

Not only does government itself engage in speech, for example, through schools and libraries and the statements of officials (see GOVERNMENT SPEECH), but government also promotes the freedom of speech in many ways. One of the most significant involves assuring access to the means of communication. The courts have gone some distance in recognizing the obligation of government to make facilities for communication available. Thus the courts have held that the streets, parks, and other public places must be open for meetings, parades, demonstrations, canvassing, and similar activities. Other public facilities have likewise been considered PUBLIC FORUMS and available, to the extent compatible with other uses, for free speech purposes. At one time the Supreme Court ruled that SHOPPING CENTERS and malls, privately owned but open to the public, could not exclude persons seeking to engage in speech activities. However, the Court later withdrew from this position. A very limited right of access to radio and television, justified by the scarcity principle, has been upheld. On the other hand, the Court has refused to allow a right of access to the columns of privately owned newspapers, on the grounds that intervention of this nature would destroy the independence of the publisher. Expansion of a right of access, without jeopardizing the rights of those already using the facilities of communication, remains a critical problem, the solution to which appears to depend more upon legislative than judicial action.

Affirmative governmental promotion of speech also takes the form of subsidies. Government contributions to educational, cultural, research, and other speech activities are widespread. Most of these subsidies have gone unchallenged in the courts. In *Buckley v. Valeo*, however, the Supreme Court did consider the constitutionality of legislation providing for the public financing of presidential election campaigns, upholding that measure upon the grounds that the use of "public money to facilitate and enlarge public discussion . . . furthers, not abridges, pertinent First Amendment values." The decision apparently accepts the basic validity of all government funding that can be found to promote public discussion. Nevertheless certain limitations on the power of government to finance nongovernment speech would seem to be clear. Thus government subsidy of religious speech would certainly be prohibited under the religion clauses of the First Amendment. And although the government would be free to choose at the "macro" level of intervention, that is, to determine the nature of the speech activity to be subsidized, it would have no power to intervene at the "micro" level, that is, to control the content of a particular communication. Likewise some rules against INVIDIOUS DISCRIMINATION, though giving government more leeway than when it is undertaking to regulate speech, would certainly apply. Development of these and other limiting principles, however, remains for the future.

Further support for affirmative promotion of speech rests on the constitutional doctrine of the RIGHT TO KNOW. The concept of a right to know includes not only the right of listeners and viewers to receive communications but also the right of those wishing to communicate to obtain information from the government. In earlier decisions the Supreme Court rejected right-to-know arguments that news reporters had a constitutional right to be admitted to prisons in order to observe conditions and interview inmates. But in RICHMOND NEWSPAPERS V. VIRGINIA (1980) the Court, changing directions, ruled that the public and the press could not be excluded from criminal trials, thereby holding for the first time that some right to obtain information from the government existed. How much further the Court will go in compelling the government to disclose information remains to be seen. Most likely the right of would-be speakers to obtain information from the government will continue to rest primarily upon FREEDOM OF INFORMATION and sunshine laws.

Efforts to expand and improve the system of free speech by affirmative governmental action, although they incur serious risks, remain essential to the continued vitality of the system. Major progress in this area will probably depend, however, more on legislative than judicial action.

The right to freedom of speech embodied in the First Amendment has expanded into an elaborate constitutional structure. This theoretical framework has some weaknesses. At some points it does not extend sufficient protection to speech, and at other places loosely formulated doctrine may not stand up in a crisis. On the whole, however, the legal structure provides the foundation for a workable system. The extent to which freedom of speech is actually realized in practice depends, of course, upon additional factors. The underlying political, economic, and social conditions must be favorable. Above all, freedom of speech, a sophisticated concept, must rest on public interest and understanding.

THOMAS I. EMERSON

Bibliography

CHAFEE, ZECHARIAH, JR. (1920)1941 *Free Speech in the United States.* Cambridge, Mass.: Harvard University Press.

DORSEN, NORMAN; BENDER, PAUL; and NEUBORNE, BURT 1976 Emerson, Haber and Dorsen's *Political and Civil Rights in the United States,* 4th ed. Vol. 1. Boston: Little, Brown.

EMERSON, THOMAS I. 1970 *The System of Freedom of Expression.* New York: Random House.

HAIMAN, FRANKLYN S. 1981 *Speech and Law in a Free Society.* Chicago: University of Chicago Press.

HUDON, EDWARD G. 1963 *Freedom of Speech and Press in America.* Washington, D.C.: Public Affairs Press.

LEVY, LEONARD W. 1960 *Legacy of Suppression.* Cambridge, Mass.: Harvard University Press.

MEIKLEJOHN, ALEXANDER (1948)1960 *Political Freedom.* New York: Harper.

MILL, JOHN STUART 1859 *On Liberty,* R. B. McCallum, ed., London: Oxford University Press.

NIMMER, MELVILLE B. 1984 *Nimmer on Freedom of Speech.* New York: Mathew Bender.

REDISH, MARTIN H. 1984 *Freedom of Expression: A Critical Analysis.* Charlottesville, Va.: Michie Co.

FREEDOM OF SPEECH, LEGISLATOR'S

See: Legislative Immunity; Speech or Debate Clause

FREEDOM OF THE PRESS

The constitutional basis for freedom of the press in the United States is the FIRST AMENDMENT, which provides: "Congress shall make no law . . . abridging the FREEDOM OF SPEECH, or of the press, or the right of the people peaceably to assemble, and to petition the Government for a redress of grievances." In a constitutional interpretation the separate rights enumerated in the First Amendment are merged into a composite right to freedom of expression. Within this general system freedom of the press focuses on the right to publish. Originally concerned with the product of printing presses—newspapers, periodicals, books, pamphlets, and broadsides—the term "press" now includes the electronic media. In general the constitutional issues involving freedom of the press are similar to those pertaining to other aspects of freedom of expression. However, certain areas are of special interest to the press, particularly to the mass media.

Freedom of the press has its roots in English history. When printing presses were introduced into England at the end of the fifteenth century they were quickly brought under total official control. Through a series of royal proclamations, Parliamentary enactments, and Star Chamber decrees a rigid system of censorship was established. No material could be printed unless it was first approved by a state or ecclesiastical official.

Further, no book could be imported or sold without a license; all printing presses were required to be registered; the number of master printers was limited; and sweeping powers to search for contraband printed matter were exercised. (See PRIOR RESTRAINT AND CENSORSHIP.)

In 1695, when the then current licensing law expired, it was not renewed and the system of advance censorship was abandoned. The laws against SEDITIOUS LIBEL remained in effect, however. Under the libel law any criticism of the government or its officials, or circulation of information that reflected adversely upon the government, regardless of truth or falsity, was punishable by severe criminal penalties. Sir WILLIAM BLACKSTONE, summarizing the English law as it existed when he published his *Commentaries* in 1769, put it in these terms: "The liberty of the press is indeed essential to the nature of a free state; but this consists in laying no *previous* restraints upon public actions, and not in freedom from censure for criminal matter when published. Every free man has an undoubted right to lay what sentiments he pleases before the public; to forbid this, is to destroy the freedom of the press; but if he publishes what is improper, mischievous or illegal, he must take the consequences of his own temerity."

Developments in the American colonies followed those in England. Censorship laws existed in some of the colonies well into the eighteenth century. Likewise, prosecutions for seditious libel were not uncommon. in both England and America, however, there was strong opposition to the seditious libel laws. Thus in the famous ZENGER'S CASE, where the publisher of a newspaper was prosecuted for printing satirical ballads reflecting upon the governor of New York and his council, the defense argued vigorously (but unsuccessfully) that truth should be a defense, and urged the jury (successfully) to give a general verdict of not guilty.

The law was in this state of flux when the First Amendment, with its guarantee of freedom of the press, was added to the Constitution in 1791. The specific intention of the Framers was never made explicit. It is generally agreed that the First Amendment was designed to make unconstitutional any system of advance censorship of the press, or "prior restraint," but its impact upon the law of seditious libel has been the subject of controversy. The latter issue was brought into sharp focus when the ALIEN AND SEDITION ACTS, which did include a modified seditious libel law, were enacted by Congress in 1798. Prosecutions under the Sedition Act were directed largely at editors of the press. The constitutionality

was upheld by a number of trial judges, including some members of the Supreme Court sitting on circuit, but the issues never reached the Supreme Court. The lapse of the Alien and Sedition Acts after two years ended public attention to the problem for the time being.

For well over a century, although freedom of the press was at times not realized in practice, the constitutional issues did not come before the Supreme Court in any major decision. This situation changed abruptly after World War I as the Court confronted a series of First Amendment problems. Two of these early cases were of paramount importance for freedom of the press. In NEAR V. MINNESOTA (1931) the Court considered the validity of the so-called Minnesota Gag Law. This statute provided that any person "engaged in the business" of regularly publishing or circulating an "obscene, lewd and lascivious" or a "malicious, scandalous and defamatory" newspaper or periodical was "guilty of a nuisance," and could be enjoined from further committing or maintaining such a nuisance. The Court held that the statutory scheme constituted a "prior restraint" and hence was invalid under the First Amendment. The Court thus established as a constitutional principle the doctrine that, with some narrow exceptions, the government could not censor or otherwise prohibit a publication in advance, even though the communication might be punishable after publication in a criminal or other proceeding. In a second decision, GROSJEAN V. AMERICAN PRESS CO. (1936), the Court struck down a Louisiana statute, passed to advance the political interest of Senator Huey Long, that imposed a two percent tax on the gross receipts of newspapers and periodicals with circulations in excess of 20,000 a week. The *Grosjean* decision assured the press that it could not be subjected to any burden, in the guise of ECONOMIC REGULATION, that was not imposed generally upon other enterprises.

In the years since *Near* and *Grosjean* an elaborate body of legal doctrine, interpreting and applying the First Amendment right to freedom of the press in a variety of situations, has emerged. Before we turn to a survey of this constitutional structure, two preliminary matters need to be considered.

First, the functions that freedom of the press performs in a democratic society are, in general, the same as those served by the system of freedom of expression as a whole. Freedom of the press enhances the opportunity to achieve individual fulfillment, advances knowledge and the search for understanding, is vital to the process of self-government, and facilitates social change by the peaceful interchange of ideas. More particularly the press has been conceived as playing a special role in informing the public and in monitoring the performance of government. Often referred to as the "fourth estate," or the fourth branch of government, an independent press is one of the principal institutions in our society that possesses the resources and the capacity to confront the government and other centers of established authority. This concept of a free press was forcefully set forth by Justice HUGO L. BLACK in his opinion in NEW YORK TIMES CO. V. UNITED STATES (1971) (the Pentagon Papers case): "In the First Amendment the Founding Fathers gave the free press the protection it must have to fulfill its essential role in our democracy. The press was to serve the governed, not the governors. The Government's power to censor the press was abolished so that the press would remain forever free to censure the Government. The press was protected so that it could bare the secrets of government and inform the people. Only a free and unrestrained press can effectively expose deception in government."

A second preliminary issue is whether the fact that the First Amendment specifically refers to freedom "of the press," in addition to "freedom of speech," means that the press is entitled to a special status, or special protection, different from that accorded other speakers. It has been suggested that the First Amendment should be so construed. Thus Justice POTTER STEWART has argued that the Framers of the Constitution intended to recognize "the organized press," that is, "the daily newspapers and other established news media," as "a fourth institution outside the Government," serving as "an additional check on the three official branches." As such an institution, he suggested, the press was entitled to enjoy not only "freedom of speech," available to all, but an additional right to "freedom of the press." Some commentators have echoed Justice Stewart's argument.

There are obvious drawbacks to according a special status to the "organized press." It is difficult to draw a line between "the press" and others seeking to communicate through the written or spoken word, such as scholars, pamphleteers, or publishers of "underground" newspapers. Nor are there persuasive reasons for affording the one greater advantages than the other. Any attempt to differentiate would merely tend to reduce the protection given the "nonorganized" publisher. In any event the Supreme Court has never accepted the distinction.

However, there are some situations where the capacities and functions of the "organized press" are taken into account. Thus where there are physical limitations on access to the sources of information,

as where a courtroom has only a limited number of seats, or only a limited number of reporters can ride on the President's airplane, representatives of the "organized press" may legitimately be chosen to convey the news to the general public. Beyond this point, however, the rights of the "organized press" to freedom of expression are the same as those of any writer or speaker.

The constitutional issues that have been of most concern to the press fall into two major categories. One involves the constraints that may be placed upon the publication of material by the press. The other relates to the rights of the press in gathering information.

On the whole the press has won its battle against the law of seditious libel. The Sedition Act of 1798 has never been revived. In NEW YORK TIMES CO. V. SULLIVAN (1964) the Supreme Court, declaring that the Sedition Act violated the central meaning of the First Amendment, said: "Although the Sedition Act was never tested in this Court, the attack upon its validity has carried the day in the court of history." Many states still retain criminal libel laws upon the books, but they have been so limited by the Supreme Court as to be largely inoperative. Even vigorous attacks upon the courts for their conduct in pending cases, traditionally a sensitive matter, are not punishable unless they present a CLEAR AND PRESENT DANGER to the administration of justice. (See CONTEMPT POWER.) Only the civil libel laws impose restrictions. The result is that the press is free to criticize the government, its policies, and its officials, no matter how harsh, vituperative, or unfair such criticism may be. Likewise it is free to publish information about governmental matters, even though incorrect, subject only to civil liability for false statements knowingly or recklessly made.

The extent to which the press can be prevented from publishing material claimed to be injurious to NATIONAL SECURITY has become a matter of controversy in recent years. The issues are crucial to the operation of a democratic system. Clearly there are some areas, particularly those relating to tactical military operations, where government secrecy is justified. On the other hand, the process of self-government cannot go on unless the public is fully informed about matters pending decision. Moreover, the very concept of "national security," or "national defense," is virtually open-ended, capable of covering a vast area of crucial information. Hence any constitutional doctrine allowing the government to restrict the flow of information alleged to harm national security would be virtually without limits. In addition, claims of danger to national security can be, and have been, employed to hide incompetence, mistaken judgments, and even corruption on the part of government officials in power.

For these reasons no general statutory ban on the publication of material deemed to have an adverse effect upon national security has ever been enacted by Congress. Laws directed at traditional espionage do, of course, exist. And Congress has passed legislation, thus far untested, instituting controls in certain very narrow areas. Thus the Intelligence Identities Protection Act (1982) forbids disclosure of any information that identifies an individual as the covert agent of an agency engaged in foreign intelligence. Beyond this, however, statutory controls on freedom of the press in the national security area have never been attempted. Even during wartime, censorship of press reporting on information pertaining to military operations has taken place only on a voluntary basis.

The constitutional authority of the government to restrict the publication of national security information was considered by the Supreme Court in the Pentagon Papers case. There the government sought an INJUNCTION against the *New York Times* and the *Washington Post* to prevent the publication of a government-prepared history of United States involvement in the Vietnam War. The documents had been classified as secret but were furnished to the newspapers by a former government employee who had copied them. The government contended that publication of the Pentagon Papers would result in "grave and irreparable injury" to the United States.

The Supreme Court ruled, 6–3, that the attempt at prior restraint could not stand, concluding that the government had not met "the heavy burden of showing justification for the imposition of such a restraint." Several theories of the right of the government to prohibit the publication of national security information emerged, none of which commanded a majority of the Court. At one end of the spectrum Justices Black and WILLIAM O. DOUGLAS thought that the government possessed no power to "make laws enjoining publication of current news and abridging freedom of the press in the name of 'national security.'" Justice WILLIAM J. BRENNAN held the same view, except that he would have allowed the government to stop publication of information that "must inevitably, directly and immediately cause the occurrence of an event kindred to imperiling the safety of a transport already at sea." Justices Stewart and BYRON WHITE believed that a prior restraint was permissible if the government could demonstrate "direct, immediate, and irreparable damage to our Nation or

its people," a showing they concluded had not been made in the case before them. Justice THURGOOD MARSHALL, not passing on the First Amendment issues, took the position that, in the absence of express statutory authority, the government had no power to invoke the JURISDICTION OF THE FEDERAL COURTS to prevent the publication of national security information. At the other end of the spectrum Chief Justice WARREN E. BURGER and Justices JOHN M. HARLAN and HARRY L. BLACKMUN, the dissenters, urged that the function of the judiciary in reviewing the actions of the executive branch in the area of FOREIGN AFFAIRS should be narrowly restricted and that in such situations the Court should not attempt "to redetermine for itself the probable impact of disclosure on national security."

The result in the Pentagon Papers case was a significant victory for the press. Had the decision gone the other way the road would have been open for the government to prevent publication of any material when it could plausibly assert that national security was significantly injured. Yet the failure of the Court to agree upon a constitutional doctrine to govern in national security cases left the press vulnerable in future situations. Moreover, the issues were limited to an effort by the government to impose a prior restraint. The Justices did not address the question whether, if appropriate legislation were enacted, a criminal penalty or other subsequent punishment for publication of national security information would be valid.

In two subsequent cases the Supreme Court revealed some reluctance to restrict the executive branch in its efforts to control the publication of information relating to foreign intelligence. In SNEPP V. UNITED STATES (1980) the Court upheld an injunction to enforce an agreement, which the Central Intelligence Agency required each of its employees to sign, that the employee would not publish any information or material relating to the agency, either during or after employment, without the advance approval of the agency. The Court treated the issue primarily as one of private contract law; it dealt with First Amendment questions only in a footnote, saying that the government has "a compelling interest in protecting both the secrecy of information important to our national security and the appearance of confidentiality so essential to effective operation of our foreign intelligence service." Likewise in HAIG V. AGEE (1981) the Court upheld the action of the secretary of state in revoking the passport of a former CIA employee traveling abroad, on the grounds that he was causing "serious damage to the national security [and] foreign policy of the United States" by exposing the names of undercover CIA officers and agents. The constitutional RIGHT TO TRAVEL abroad, said the majority opinion, is "subordinate to national security and foreign policy considerations," adding that [m]atters intimately related to foreign policy and national security are rarely proper subjects for judicial intervention." Unless these later decisions are limited to their somewhat unusual facts, the right of the press to publish national security information that the government wishes to keep secret could be sharply curtailed.

Civil libel laws have also been a matter of paramount concern to the press. For many years it was assumed that the First Amendment was not intended to restrict the right of any person, under COMMON LAW or statute, to bring a suit for damages to reputation arising out of false and defamatory statements. In its well-known OBITER DICTUM in CHAPLINSKY V. NEW HAMPSHIRE (1942) the Supreme Court had declared that there were "certain well-defined and narrowly limited classes of speech," including the "libelous," which had never been thought to raise any constitutional problem.

In time it became clear, however, that libel laws could be used to impair freedom of the press and other First Amendment rights. In 1964 the issue came before the Supreme Court in *New York Times Co. v. Sullivan*. In that case the commissioner of public affairs in Montgomery, Alabama, sued the *New York Times* for publication of an advertisement, paid for by a New York group called the Committee to Defend Martin Luther King, which criticized certain actions of the police in dealing with CIVIL RIGHTS activity in Montgomery. Some of the statements in the advertisement were not factually correct. The Alabama state courts, after a jury trial, awarded the police commissioner $500,000 in damages. The majority opinion of the Court, stating that "libel can claim no talismanic immunity from constitutional limitations," went on to say: "Thus we consider this case against the background of a profound national commitment to the principle that debate on public issues should be uninhibited, robust, and wide-open, and that it may well include vehement, caustic, and sometimes unpleasantly sharp attacks on government and public officials." The Court ruled that public officials could recover damages in a libel action only if they could prove that a false and defamatory statement was made with "actual malice," that is, "with knowledge that it was false or with reckless disregard of whether it was false or not." Three Justices would have gone further and given the press full protection against libel suits regardless of proof of actual malice.

The "actual malice" rule for reconciling First Amendment rights with the libel laws was extended in 1967 to suits brought by "public figures," and in 1971 to all suits involving matters "of public or general interest." At this point it appeared that, although a majority of the Supreme Court had not gone the full distance, the press did have substantial protection against harassing libel suits. Weaknesses in the press position, however, soon developed. In 1974 the Court, changing directions, held that, apart from cases involving "public officials" and "public figures," libel laws would be deemed to conform to First Amendment standards so long as they did not impose liability in the absence of negligence. Moreover, the Court greatly narrowed the definition of "public figure," holding in one case that a person convicted of contempt of court for refusing to appear before a GRAND JURY investigating espionage was not a "public figure." In addition, juries in some cases began to award large sums in damages, legal expenses skyrocketed, and the costs in time and money of defending libel suits, even where the defense was successful, often became a heavy burden. By the same token, persons or organizations without substantial resources found it difficult to finance libel actions.

Efforts to dispose of unjustified libel suits at an early stage by motions to dismiss received a setback from the Supreme Court in HERBERT V. LANDO (1979). Lieutenant Colonel Anthony Herbert brought a libel suit against Columbia Broadcasting System because of a program on "60 Minutes" which suggested that Herbert had falsely accused his superior officers of covering up war crimes. Conceding he was a "public figure" and had to show "actual malice," Herbert sought in DISCOVERY proceedings to inquire into the mental states and editorial processes of the CBS officials who were responsible for the program. The Court held that, despite the CHILLING EFFECT of such probing and the resulting protraction of libel proceedings, the right to make such inquiries was inherent in the "actual malice" rule. The result of the *Herbert* case has been to diminish substantially the value to the press of the "actual malice" doctrine.

Because of these considerations, sections of the press as well as some commentators have urged that libel laws are incompatible with the First Amendment and should be abolished, at least where matters of public interest are under discussion. The courts, however, have shown no disposition to follow this course. The solution most in accord with First Amendment principles would be to provide for a right of reply by the person aggrieved. Yet this poses other difficulties. The press argues, with considerable justification, that it would be impossible for the government to supervise and enforce an effective right of reply system without sacrificing the independence of the media in the process. Federal Communication Commission regulations now grant a limited right of reply where "personal attacks" are made over radio or television and, because of the pervasive governmental controls already in place, such regulation probably does not appreciably reduce existing freedoms of the electronic media. But any broad extension to the printed press or to other forms of communication would almost certainly be seriously inhibiting. Indeed in MIAMI HERALD PUBLISHING CO. V. TORNILLO (1974) the Supreme Court unanimously invalidated a state statute requiring a newspaper to grant equal space for a political candidate attacked in its columns to reply. Moreover, practical difficulties, such as finding a suitable forum, would greatly limit the effectiveness of any attempt to substitute a right of reply for an action for damages. Thus the tension between the libel laws and freedom of the press is likely to continue.

A similar tension exists between freedom of the press and the RIGHT OF PRIVACY. Common law and statutory actions for invasion of privacy are permitted in most states. Moreover, the Supreme Court has recognized a constitutional right of privacy, running against the government, which would seem to impose restrictions upon disclosure to the press of certain information in the government's possession. The Supreme Court has held that the publication of material already in the public domain, such as the name of a rape victim which is available from public records, cannot be prohibited. However, it has never ruled upon the broad issue whether publication of information that is true but is alleged to invade the privacy of an individual can under some circumstances be restricted. The press has expressed concern over the possibility that the right of privacy might be used to curtail its freedom to publish. If the right of privacy is not narrowly limited—and there is presently no agreement upon the scope of the right—the chilling effect upon the press could be substantial. Nevertheless, in view of the current power of the press and the relative weakness of persons seeking to preserve privacy, any danger to the independence of the press from recognition of the right of privacy would seem to be remote.

Another conflict between freedom of the press and rights of the individual arises over the publication of news relating to criminal proceedings. The administration of justice is, of course, a matter of great public concern, and the role of the press in informing the public about such matters is crucial to the maintenance of a fair and effective system of justice. In most cases no conflict arises. On the other hand press reporting of occasional sensational crimes can be of such a nature as to prejudice the right of an accused to a FAIR TRIAL guaranteed by the DUE PROCESS clause and the Sixth Amendment. (See FREE PRESS/FAIR TRIAL.)

A number of remedies are available to the courts by which fairness in criminal proceedings can be assured without imposing restrictions upon the conduct of the press. These include change of VENUE, postponement of the trial, careful selection of jurors to weed out those likely to be prejudiced by the publicity, warning instructions to the jury, sequestration of witnesses and jurors, and, as a last resort, reversing a conviction and ordering a new trial. By and large the courts have found the use of these devices adequate. In some cases, however, trial courts have issued "gag" orders prohibiting the press from printing news about crimes or excluding the press from courtrooms.

In NEBRASKA PRESS ASSOCIATION V. STUART (1976) the Supreme Court dealt at some length with the "gag order" device. The majority opinion pointed out that the trial judge's order constituted a prior restraint, "the most serious and least tolerable infringement on First Amendment rights," but declined to hold that the press was entitled to absolute protection against all restrictive orders. The issue, the Court ruled, was whether in each case the newspaper publicity created a serious and likely danger to the fairness of the trial. And that issue in turn depended upon what was shown with respect to "(a) the nature and extent of pretrial news coverage; (b) whether other measures would be likely to mitigate the effects of unrestrained pretrial publicity; and (c) how effectively a restraining order would operate to prevent the threatened danger." The Court's ruling thus left the issue open to separate decision in each instance. The conditions laid down by the Court for issuance of a restrictive order, however, afford little room for use of that device except under rare circumstances. Three Justices urged that a prior restraint upon publication in this situation should never be allowed.

The exclusion of the press from courtrooms in criminal cases has also received the attention of the Supreme Court. Initially the Court rejected the contention that the Sixth Amendment's guarantee of a PUBLIC TRIAL entitled the press and the public to attend criminal trials, holding that the right involved was meant for the benefit of the defendant alone. Subsequently, however, in RICHMOND NEWSPAPERS, INC. V. VIRGINIA (1980) the Court recognized that the First Amendment extended some protection against exclusion from criminal trials. The Court again refused to hold that the First Amendment right was absolute, but it did not spell out the nature of any exceptions. Because it is always possible in a criminal trial for the judge to sequester the jury, few occasions for closing trials are likely to arise. On the other hand, the right of the press to attend pretrial hearings, where opportunity for sequestration does not exist, was left uncertain.

For many years the press has urged the courts to permit the use of radio, television, and photographic equipment in courtrooms. The courts have been reluctant to allow such forms of reporting. And in 1964 the Supreme Court overturned the conviction of Billie Sol Estes, accused of a notorious swindle, on the grounds that the broadcasting of parts of the trial by radio and television had been conducted in such a manner as to deprive him of a fair trial. Recently the courts have been more willing to open the courtroom to the electronic media and many of them have done so. The movement received the sanction of the Supreme Court in CHANDLER V. FLORIDA (1981) when an experimental program in Florida, which allowed broadcast and photographic coverage of trials subject to certain guidelines and under the control of the trial judge, was upheld by a unanimous vote.

The right of the press to gather news, as distinct from its right to publish the news, raises somewhat different issues. Freedom of the press implies in some degree a right to obtain information free of governmental interference. Indeed the Supreme Court in BRANZBURG V. HAYES (1972) expressly recognized that news-gathering did "qualify for First Amendment protection," saying that "without some protection for seeking out the news, freedom of the press could be eviscerated." But the limits of the constitutional right are difficult to define and remain undeveloped. The issue has arisen in three principal areas: REPORTER'S PRIVILEGE, the application of the FOURTH AMENDMENT to the press, and the right of the press to obtain information from the government.

The press has consistently asserted a right to refuse to disclose the sources of information obtained under a pledge of confidentiality—a claim known as "reporters' privilege." From the point of view of the press the right to honor a commitment to secrecy is essential to much reporting, particularly investigative reporting into organized crime, government corruption, and similar sensitive areas. On the other hand, under certain circumstances the need to obtain evidence in the possession of a reporter is also pressing, particularly where the information is necessary for defense in a criminal prosecution or to prove malice in a libel suit. Over the years the courts have generally refused to recognize the reporters' privilege, but they have attempted to avoid open conflict with the press. Reporters nevertheless continued to urge their claim, often to the point of going to jail for CONTEMPT OF COURT. A number of states have passed legislation recognizing the privilege in whole or in part, but the courts have tended to construe such statutes in a grudging manner, sometimes invoking constitutional objections.

The question whether reporters could invoke the privilege as a constitutional right under the First Amendment came before the Supreme Court in the *Branzburg* case. The reporters, who had refused to appear before grand juries, did not assert an absolute privilege but claimed they should not be compelled to give testimony unless the government demonstrated substantial grounds for believing they possessed essential information not available from other sources. The Court, in a 5–4 decision, rejected their claims. The majority opinion said that reporters had no greater claims to refuse testimony than other citizens. However, Justice LEWIS F. POWELL, whose vote was necessary to make the majority, expressed a more qualified position in a CONCURRING OPINION: "if the newsman . . . has reason to believe that his testimony implicates confidential source relationships without a legitimate need of law enforcement," the court should strike the "balance of these vital constitutional and societal interests on a case-by-case basis." In practice the courts appear to have accepted the Powell formula. Thus, although reporters cannot count on substantial constitutional protection the courts still prefer to avoid direct confrontation with the press tradition that reporters will not reveal confidential sources.

The First Amendment right to freedom of the press and the Fourth Amendment right to be secure from unreasonable SEARCHES AND SEIZURES have historically been closely linked. It was the GENERAL WARRANTS, used in America to obtain evidence of customs violations (and in England to find seditious publications), that in large part prompted the framing of the Fourth Amendment. At times the Supreme Court has recognized that Fourth Amendment protection extends with particular rigor to governmental intrusions affecting First Amendment rights. In the much discussed case of ZURCHER V. STANFORD DAILY (1978), however, the Court displayed less sympathy for the traditional position. The issue was whether the police could search the offices of a student newspaper for evidence of criminal offenses growing out of a student demonstration, or whether they should be confined to the issuance of a SUBPOENA requiring the newspaper to produce what evidence it had. Despite the vulnerability of the press to police searches tht could result in the ransacking of their news rooms, the Court by a 5–3 vote approved the warrant procedure. The press greeted the decision with strong criticism, mixed with alarm.

The third major issue with respect to operations of the press relates to the right of the press to obtain information from the government. The constitutional basis for such a claim grows out of the broader doctrine of the RIGHT TO KNOW. For many years the Supreme Court has recognized that the First Amendment embraces not only a right to communicate but also a right to receive communications. (See LISTENERS' RIGHTS.) The press has insisted that this feature of the First Amendment includes a right to have access to information in the possession of the government. Because a major purpose of the First Amendment is to facilitate the process of self-government, a strong constitutional argument can be advanced that, apart from a limited area of necessary secrecy, all material relating to operations of the government should be made available to the public. The press urged this position in a series of cases where it sought access to prisons in order to interview inmates and report on conditions inside. The Supreme Court, however, was not receptive. In rejecting the press proposals four of the Justices expressly declared in *Houchins v. KQED* (1978) that "the First and Fourteenth Amendments do not guarantee the public a right of access to information generated or controlled by government."

In 1980, in the Richmond Newspapers case, the Supreme Court shifted its position. In ruling that the press had a First Amendment right to attend criminal trials the majority relied heavily upon the right-to-know doctrine. Moreover, the concurring Justices were plainly willing to carry the right-to-know concept beyond the confines of the particular case before them. As Justice JOHN PAUL STEVENS correctly observed, the decision constituted "a watershed case": "never before has [the Court] squarely held that the acquisition of newsworthy material is entitled to any constitutional protection whatsoever." The full scope of the right to obtain information from the government remains to be seen. The development, however, is potentially one of great significance for the press.

Taken as a whole, freedom of the press in the United States rests upon a relatively firm constitutional footing. The press has not been granted any special status in the First Amendment's structure, but its general right to publish material, regardless of potential impacts on government operations or other features of the national life, has been accepted. There are some weaknesses in the position of the press. The law with respect to publication of national security information is obscure and, in its present form, poses some threat to press freedoms. The press is also vulnerable to libel suits, as the protections thought to have been afforded by the "actual malice" rule have not been altogether realized. Likewise the courts have been reluctant to assist the press in its news-gathering activities. From an overall view, however, constitutional developments have left the press in a position where it is largely free to carry out the functions and promote the values sought by the Framers of the First Amendment.

THOMAS I. EMERSON

Bibliography

ANDERSON, DAVID A. 1983 The Origins of the Press Clause. *University of California at Los Angeles Law Review* 30:455–537.
BARRON, JEROME A. 1973 *Freedom of the Press for Whom?* Bloomington: Indiana University Press.
LEVY, LEONARD W., ED. 1966 *Freedom of the Press from Zenger to Jefferson.* Indianapolis: Bobbs-Merrill.
LOFTON, JOHN 1980 *The Press as Guardian of the First Amendment.* Columbia: University of South Carolina Press.
NELSON, HAROLD L., ED. 1967 *Freedom of the Press from Hamilton to the Warren Court.* Indianapolis: Bobbs-Merrill.
SCHMIDT, BENNO C., JR. 1976 *Freedom of the Press vs. Public Access.* New York: Praeger.
SIEBERT, FREDRICK SEATON 1952 *Freedom of the Press in England 1476–1776.* Urbana: University of Illinois Press.
SYMPOSIUM 1975 First Amendment and the Media. *Hastings Law Journal* 26:631–821.

FREE EXERCISE OF RELIGION

See: Religious Liberty

FREEMAN v. HEWITT
329 U.S. 249 (1946)

Justice FELIX FRANKFURTER, for a 6–3 Supreme Court, here voided an Indiana tax levied on proceeds realized from the sale of securities in another state. Frankfurter struck down the tax as a greater burden than police regulations on INTERSTATE COMMERCE.

Justice WILLIAM O. DOUGLAS, dissenting, denied the existence of any interstate commerce.

DAVID GORDON

FREEPORT DOCTRINE

During the LINCOLN-DOUGLAS DEBATES of 1858, Senator STEPHEN A. DOUGLAS attacked ABRAHAM LINCOLN and the Republicans for their unwillingness to accept the Supreme Court's decision in DRED SCOTT V. SANDFORD (1857), which held that Congress could not proscribe SLAVERY in federal territories. But at the same time, Douglas and the Northern Democrats contended that the issue of slavery was to be decided by the people who lived in each territory, a position for which Douglas appropriated the name POPULAR SOVEREIGNTY. At Freeport, Lincoln asked Douglas: "Can the people of a United States territory, in any lawful way, . . . exclude slavery from its limits prior to the formation of a state constitution?"

Douglas's reply is known as the "Freeport Doctrine." It was that "slavery cannot exist a day or an hour anywhere, unless it is supported by local police regulation." In other words, a territorial legislature could exclude slavery by "unfriendly legislation" or simply by failing to pass the laws necessary to enforce slaveholding. The Freeport Doctrine appeared intended to neutralize the *Dred Scott* decision, and it effectively cut Douglas off from the slaveholding interests and divided the Democratic party.

DENNIS J. MAHONEY

Bibliography

JAFFA, HARRY V. 1959 *Crisis of the House Divided: An Interpretation of the Issues in the Lincoln–Douglas Debates.* Garden City, N.Y.: Doubleday.

FREE PRESS/FAIR TRIAL

Although press coverage has challenged the fairness and dignity of criminal proceedings throughout American history, intensive consideration of free press/fair trial issues by the Supreme Court has mainly been a product of recent decades. The first free press/fair trial issue to receive significant attention was the extent of press freedom from judges' attempts to hold editors and authors in contempt for criticizing or pressuring judicial conduct in criminal proceedings. The next category of decisions to receive attention, reversals of convictions to protect defendants from pretrial publicity, began rather gingerly in 1959, but in the

years following the 1964 Warren Commission Report the Supreme Court reversed convictions more readily and dealt in considerable detail with the appropriate treatment of the interests of both the press and defendants when those interests were potentially in conflict. More recently, the Court has considered whether the press can be enjoined from publishing prejudicial material, and whether the press can be excluded from judicial proceedings.

In view of the large number of free press/fair trial decisions handed down over the years by the Supreme Court, this particular corner of the law of FREEDOM OF THE PRESS is probably the best developed of any, and offers a particularly instructive model of how the Supreme Court seeks to accommodate colliding interests of constitutional dimension. Overall, the Court has sought a balance that respects Justice HUGO L. BLACK's OBITER DICTUM in the seminal case of BRIDGES V. CALIFORNIA (1941) that "free speech and fair trial are two of the most cherished policies of our civilization, and it would be a trying task to choose between them."

In one of our history's pivotal FIRST AMENDMENT cases, the Supreme Court in 1941 sharply restricted the power of state judges to hold persons in contempt for publishing material that attacked or attempted to influence judicial decisions. By a 5–4 vote in *Bridges* the Supreme Court struck down two contempt citations, one against a newspaper based on an editorial that stated that a judge would "make a serious mistake" if he granted probation to two labor "goons," the second against a union leader who had sent a public telegram to the secretary of labor criticizing a judge's decision against his union and threatening to strike if the decision was enforced. Black's majority opinion held that the First Amendment protected these expressions unless they created a CLEAR AND PRESENT DANGER of interfering with judicial impartiality. From the start, this test as applied to contempt by publication has been virtually impossible to satisfy. Black insisted that "the substantive evil must be extremely serious and the degree of imminence extremely high before utterances can be punished," and, in order to remove predictions about the likelihood of interference from the ken of lower courts, the Court reinforced the strictness of this standard by using an apparently IRREBUTTABLE PRESUMPTION that judges would not be swayed by adverse commentary. "[T]he law of contempt," wrote Justice WILLIAM O. DOUGLAS in *Craig v. Harney* (1947), echoing a position taken in *Bridges*, "is not made for the protection of judges who may be sensitive to the winds of public opinion. Judges are supposed to be men of fortitude, able to thrive in a hardy climate." Under these decisions, it seems doubtful that anything short of a direct and credible physical threat against a judge would justify punishment for contempt.

For general First Amendment theory and more specifically for the rights of the press in free press/fair trial contexts, the chief significance of the contempt cases is the emergence of a positive conception of protected expression under the First Amendment. As Black put it in *Bridges*, "it is a prized American privilege to speak one's mind, although not always with perfect good taste, on all public questions." Drawing upon the decisions in NEAR V. MINNESOTA (1931) and DE JONGE V. OREGON (1937), which stressed the Madisonian conception of free expression as essential to political democracy, opinions in the contempt cases shifted the clear and present danger rule toward a promise of constitutional immunity for criticism of government. The contempt cases are thus the primary doctrinal bridge between the Court's unsympathetic approach to political dissent during and after World War I and the grand conception of NEW YORK TIMES CO. V. SULLIVAN (1964) that the central meaning of the First Amendment is "the right of free discussion of the stewardship of public officials." Beyond this, the contempt cases make it clear that protecting expressions about judges and courts is itself a core function of the First Amendment. Douglas put it this way in *Craig*, in words that have echoed in later free press/fair trial cases: "A trial is a public event. What transpires in the court room is public property. . . . There is no special perquisite of the judiciary which enables it, as distinguished from other institutions of democratic government, to suppress, edit, or censor events which transpire in proceedings before it."

Although the contempt cases focused on the rights of the press and others who sought to publicize information about trials, the next set of free press/fair trial cases, without dealing with the right to publish, looked with a sympathetic eye toward defendants who might have been convicted because of prejudice caused by such publications. Although individual Justices had objected bitterly to the prejudicial effects of media coverage on jurors, not until 1959 did the Supreme Court reverse a federal conviction because of prejudicial publicity. The first reversal of a state court conviction followed two years later in IRVIN V. DOWD (1961), where 268 of 430 prospective jurors said during their VOIR DIRE examination that they had a fixed belief in the defendant's guilt, and 370 entertained some opinion of guilt. News media had made the trial a "cause célèbre of this small community," the Court noted, as the press had reported the defendant's prior criminal record, offers to plead guilty, confessions, and a flood of other prejudicial items.

In 1963, the special problems of television were introduced into the pretrial publicity fray by *Rideau v. Louisiana*, producing another reversal by the Supreme Court of a state conviction. A jailed murder suspect was filmed in the act of answering various questions and of confessing to the local sheriff, and the film was televised repeatedly in the community that tried and convicted him. The Supreme Court held that "[a]ny subsequent court proceedings in a community so pervasively exposed to such a spectacle could be but a hollow formality." Two years later, in ESTES V. TEXAS (1965), a narrowly divided Court held that, at least in a notorious case, the presence of television in the courtroom could generate pressures that added up to a denial of due process.

In the mid-1960s the Court took a more categorical and more aggressive stance against prejudicial publicity. The shift was consistent with the WARREN COURT'S growing impatience toward ad hoc evaluations of fairness in its review of state criminal cases. This period of heightened concern for the defendant was triggered by the disgraceful media circus that surrounded the murder trial of Dr. Sam Sheppard. Before Sheppard's trial, most of the print and broadcast media in the Cleveland area joined in an intense publicity barrage proclaiming Sheppard's guilt. During the trial, journalists swarmed over the courtroom in a manner that impressed upon everyone the spectacular notoriety of the case. "The fact is," wrote Justice TOM C. CLARK in his most memorable opinion for the Court, "that bedlam reigned at the courthouse during the trial and newsmen took over practically the entire courtroom, hounding most of the participants in the trial, especially Sheppard." The deluge of publicity outside the courtroom, and the disruptive behavior of journalists inside, combined to make the trial a " 'Roman holiday' for the news media" that "inflamed and prejudiced the public."

In *Sheppard v. Maxwell* (1966) Clark adumbrated the techniques by which trial judges may control prejudicial publicity and disruptions of the judicial process by the press. The opinion is a virtual manual for trial judges, suggesting proper procedures initially by listing the particular errors in the case: that Sheppard was not granted a continuance or a change of VENUE, that the jury was not sequestered, that the judge merely requested jurors not to follow media commentary on the case rather than directing them not to, that the judge failed "to insulate" the jurors from reporters and photographers, and that reporters invaded the space within the bar of the courtroom reserved for counsel, created distractions and commotion, and hounded people throughout the courthouse.

But the *Sheppard* opinion went beyond these essentially traditional judicial methods for coping with publicity and the press. The Court identified the trial judge's "fundamental error" as his view that he "lacked power to control the publicity about the trial" and insisted that "the cure lies in those remedial measures that will prevent the prejudice at its inception." Specifically, Clark admonished trial judges to insulate witnesses from press interviews, to "impos[e] control over the statements made to the news media by counsel, witnesses, and especially the Coroner and police officers," and to "proscrib[e] extrajudicial statements by any lawyer, party, witness, or court official which divulged prejudicial matters. . . ."

Sheppard left open the central question whether the courts could impose direct restrictions on the press by INJUNCTIONS that would bar publications that might prejudice an accused. In NEBRASKA PRESS ASSOCIATION V. STUART (1976) the Supreme Court, unanimous as to result though divided in rationale, answered this question with a seemingly definitive No. The Nebraska state courts had ordered the press and broadcasters not to publish confessions or other information prejudicial to an accused in a pending murder prosecution. Some of the information covered by the injunction had been revealed in an open, public preliminary hearing, and the Supreme Court made clear that a state could in no event bar the publication of matters disclosed in open judicial proceedings. As to other information barred from publication by the state courts, Chief Justice WARREN E. BURGER's majority opinion went by a curious and circuitous route to the conclusion that the impact of prejudicial publicity on prospective jurors was "of necessity speculative, dealing . . . with factors unknown and unknowable." Thus, the adverse effect on the fairness of the subsequent criminal proceeding "was not demonstrated with the degree of certainty our cases on PRIOR RESTRAINT require." Burger's opinion made much of the fact that the state court had not determined explicitly that the protections against prejudicial publicity set out in *Sheppard* would not suffice to guarantee fairness, as if trial court findings to this effect might make a difference in judging the validity of a prior restraint against publication. And Burger said again and again that he was dealing with a particular case and not laying down a general rule. But because

Burger termed the evils of prejudicial publicity "of necessity speculative," and viewed the prior restraint precedents as requiring a degree of certainty about the evils of expression before a prior restraint should be tolerated, his opinion for the Court seems to be, in the guise of a narrow and particularistic holding, a categorical rejection of prior restraints on pretrial publicity. Lower courts have read the decision as an absolute bar to judicial injunctions against the press forbidding the publication of possibly prejudicial matters about pending criminal proceedings.

Beyond its rejection of prior restraints against the press to control pretrial publicity, the *Nebraska Press Association* decision emphatically affirmed all the methods of control set out in *Sheppard*, including the validity of judicial orders of silence directed to parties, lawyers, witnesses, court officers, and the like not to reveal information about pending cases to the press. Such orders, indeed, have flourished in the lower courts since the *Nebraska Press Association* decision.

The free press/fair trial conundrum has also presented the Supreme Court with the only occasion it has accepted to shed light on the very murky question whether the First Amendment protects the right to gather information, as against the right to publish or refuse to publish. No doubt in response to the Supreme Court's rejection of direct controls on press publication, either by injunctions or by the CONTEMPT POWER, several lower courts excluded news reporters and the public from preliminary hearings and even from trials themselves to prevent the press from gathering information whose publication might be prejudicial to current or later judicial proceedings. Initially, in GANNETT CO. V. DE PASQUALE (1979), reviewing a closing of a preliminary hearing dealing with the suppression of EVIDENCE, the Supreme Court found no guarantee in the Sixth Amendment of public and press presence. The decision produced an outcry against secret judicial proceedings, and only a year later, in one of the most precipitous and awkward reversals in its history, the Court held in RICHMOND NEWSPAPERS V. VIRGINIA (1980) that the First Amendment barred excluding the public and the press from criminal trials except where special considerations calling for secrecy, such as privacy or national security, obtained. The decision marks the first and only occasion to date in which the Court has recognized a First Amendment right of access for purposes of news gathering, and the Court was careful to limit its holding by resting on the long tradition of open judicial proceedings in English and American law. One year later, in *Chandler v. Florida* (1981), the

Court held that televising a criminal trial was not invariably a denial of due process, thus removing *Estes* as an absolute bar to television in the courtroom.

The pattern of constitutional law formed by the free press/fair trial decisions has several striking aspects. While direct judicial controls on the right of publication have been firmly rejected, the courts have proclaimed extensive power to gag sources of information. (See GAG ORDERS.) Participants in the process can be restrained from talking, but the press cannot be restrained from publishing. However, the broad power to impose secrecy on sources does not go so far as to justify closing judicial proceedings, absent unusual circumstances. The interests of freedom of expression and control over information to enhance the fairness of criminal trials are accommodated not by creating balanced principles of general application but rather by letting each interest reign supreme in competing aspects of the problem. Moreover, the principles fashioned in the cases tend to be sweeping, as if the Supreme Court were acting with special confidence in fashioning First Amendment standards to govern the familiar ground of the judicial process. And in dealing with its own bailiwick, the judicial process, the Supreme Court has acted not defensively but with a powerful commitment to freedom of expression.

BENNO C. SCHMIDT, JR.

Bibliography

FRIENDLY, ALFRED and GOLDFARB, RONALD 1967 *Crime and Publicity.* New York: Twentieth Century Fund.

JAFFE, LOUIS 1965 Trial by Newspaper. *New York University Law Review* 40:504–524.

LEWIS, ANTHONY 1980 A Public Right to Know about Public Institutions: The First Amendment as Sword. *Supreme Court Law Review* 1980:1–25.

SCHMIDT, BENNO C., JR. 1977 Nebraska Press Association: An Expansion of Freedom and Contraction of Theory. *Stanford Law Review* 29:431–476.

TAYLOR, TELFORD 1969 *Two Studies in Constitutional Interpretation.* Evanston, Ill.: Northwestern University Press.

FREUND, ERNST
(1864–1932)

Ernst Freund, professor of law at the University of Chicago, is best remembered today for his huge and immensely influential *Police Power: Public Policy and Constitutional Rights* (1904), the first systematic exposition of its subject. POLICE POWER, said Freund,

was the "power of promoting the public welfare by restraining and regulating the use of liberty and property." Because Freund saw the power "not as a fixed quantity, but as the expression of social, economic, and political conditions," he praised that elasticity which helped adapt the law to changing circumstances. This endorsement, along with only minimal approval of laissez-faire doctrines such as FREEDOM OF CONTRACT, helped provide support for the Progressive movement. His views strongly contrasted with those of CHRISTOPHER TIEDEMAN, a vigorous and authoritative exponent of laissez-faire who decried the use of the police power. In *Standards of American Legislation* (1917), Freund attempted to formulate positive principles to guide legislators and to give DUE PROCESS OF LAW a more definite meaning.

DAVID GORDON

FRIES' REBELLION

In 1798 Congress levied a tax on houses, land, and slaves, to finance a possible war with France. There was considerable resistance to the tax and, in February 1799, an armed band led by John Fries rescued tax resisters from the United States marshal at Bethlehem, Pennsylvania. President JOHN ADAMS ordered the army and militia to suppress the uprising.

Fries and his followers were arrested and some seventy-two insurrectionists were tried for various offenses relating to the incident. Fries and two companions were tried before Justice SAMUEL CHASE and Judge RICHARD PETERS and were convicted of TREASON, the prosecution arguing that armed resistance to the enforcement of federal law amounted to levying war against the United States. President Adams, against the advice of his cabinet, subsequently granted a general pardon to all participants in the "rebellion."

DENNIS J. MAHONEY

FROHWERK v. UNITED STATES
249 U.S. 204 (1919)

In the second major test of the wartime ESPIONAGE ACT to reach the Supreme Court, the Justices unanimously affirmed the conviction of the publisher of a pro-German publication for conspiring to obstruct military recruitment through publication of antidraft articles. Justice OLIVER WENDELL HOLMES invoked the CLEAR AND PRESENT DANGER test. "We do not lose our right to condemn either measures or men because the Country is at war," he wrote, "But . . . it is impossible to say that it might not have been found that the circulation of the paper was in quarters where a little breath would be enough to kindle a flame. . . ." Holmes and his brethren declined to inquire themselves into the degree or probability of the danger represented by the publication.

MICHAEL E. PARRISH

FRONTIERO v. RICHARDSON
411 U.S. 677 (1973)

In *Reed v. Reed* (1971) a unanimous Supreme Court had invalidated a state law preferring the appointment of men, rather than women, as administrators of decedents' estates. The Court had used the rhetoric of the RATIONAL BASIS standard of review but had in fact employed a more rigorous standard of JUDICIAL REVIEW. Conceding the rationality of eliminating one type of contest between would-be administrators, the Court had concluded that the preference for men was an "arbitrary legislative choice" that denied women the EQUAL PROTECTION OF THE LAW.

In *Frontiero*, two years later, the Court came within one vote of radically restructuring the constitutional doctrine governing SEX DISCRIMINATION. Under federal law, a woman member of the armed forces could claim her husband as a "dependent" entitled to certain benefits only if he was, in fact, dependent on her for more than half his support; a serviceman could claim "dependent" status for his wife irrespective of actual dependency. Eight Justices agreed that this discrimination violated the Fifth Amendment's equal protection guarantee, but they divided 4–4 as to their reasoning.

Justice WILLIAM J. BRENNAN, for four Justices, concluded that sex, like race, was a SUSPECT CLASSIFICATION demanding STRICT SCRUTINY of its justifications. Four other Justices merely rested on the precedent of *Reed*. Justice LEWIS F. POWELL, writing for three of them, added that it would be inappropriate for the Court to hold that gender was a suspect classification while debate over ratification of the EQUAL RIGHTS AMENDMENT was still pending. Justice WILLIAM H. REHNQUIST dissented.

The confusion in the wake of *Frontiero* ended three years later, in CRAIG V. BOREN (1976), when the Justices compromised on an intermediate STANDARD OF REVIEW.

KENNETH L. KARST

FROTHINGHAM v. MELLON
MASSACHUSETTS v. MELLON
262 U.S. 447 (1923)

In the SHEPPARD-TOWNER MATERNITY ACT of 1921, a predecessor of modern FEDERAL GRANTS-IN-AID, Congress authorized federal funding of state programs "to reduce maternal and infant mortality." These companion cases involved suits to halt federal expenditures under the act, challenging it as a deprivation of property without DUE PROCESS OF LAW and a violation of the TENTH AMENDMENT. Justice GEORGE SUTHERLAND, for a unanimous Supreme Court, dismissed the *Massachusetts* case for failing to present a justiciable controversy. The state's suit in its own behalf presented a POLITICAL QUESTION calling on the Court to adjudicate "abstract questions of political power," not rights of property or even "quasi-sovereign rights actually invaded or threatened." The state was under no obligation to accept federal monies. The state also lacked STANDING to represent its citizens, who were also citizens of the United States.

Frothingham's due process argument relied on the premise that spending under the act would increase her tax liability. Sutherland concluded that she, too, lacked standing to sue. Any personal interest in federal tax monies "is comparatively minute and indeterminable; and the effect upon future taxation, of any payment out of the funds, so remote, fluctuating and uncertain, that no basis is afforded for an appeal." Because Frothingham could not demonstrate direct injury, her suit must fail. An OBITER DICTUM implying the constitutionality of grants-in-aid was the Court's only pronouncement on such programs until approved in STEWARD MACHINE COMPANY V. DAVIS (1937).

DAVID GORDON

FRUIT OF THE POISONOUS TREE

No doctrine in constitutional CRIMINAL PROCEDURE has created more confusion than the disarmingly simple proposition that when the state has violated FUNDAMENTAL RIGHTS, it may receive no benefit from the violation. The "poisonous tree" is the violation, an illegal search for instance, in which the key to a safe deposit is found. Clearly under the EXCLUSIONARY RULE the government may not use as EVIDENCE the discovery of the key; but neither may it use whatever incriminating items are in the safe deposit box. These are the "fruits."

The existence of a "poisonous tree," however, does not mean that all that is discovered after the tree sprouts is automatically a "fruit." The issue in its classic though grammatically inelegant formulation is: "whether, granting establishment of the primary illegality, [the evidence] has been come at by exploitation of that illegality or instead by means sufficiently distinguishable to be purged of the primary taint" (WONG SUN V. UNITED STATES, 1963). Many exceptions to the fruits doctrine have evolved from these words and have been variously named by courts and commentators, although the basic question is always how far from the tree the fruit has fallen.

The exception used most often is "attenuation": too much has intervened between the primary illegality and the gathering of the fruit. In *Wong Sun* itself, a confession made after an illegal ARREST was found not to be a fruit because of the passage of time between the arrest and confession, during which the accused was free on BAIL. Another exception is labeled "independent source"; the idea is that although the evidence could have been a fruit, it was actually uncovered by means distinguishable from the primary illegality. Closely allied to the independent source exception is that of "inevitable discovery," which the Supreme Court endorsed in NIX V. WILLIAMS (1984). Although the body of the deceased was discovered through a blatant violation of the defendant's Sixth Amendment RIGHT TO COUNSEL, the Court held that it would have been found through other proper investigative techniques that the police were employing at the time that the primary illegality was committed. The burden is on the government to show that the discovery would have been "inevitable." Finally, while refusing to establish an across-the-board rule that eyewitness testimony could never be a fruit, the Supreme Court has indicated that the free will of a witness expressed in the desire to testify would, in virtually every case, attenuate the taint, even when the witness would never have been found without the primary illegality.

As can be seen from the number and nature of the exceptions, the fruit of the poisonous tree doctrine is subject to much interpretation. For instance, in *Harrison v. United States* (1968) the Court held that the defendant's testimony at trial was a fruit of illegally obtained confessions introduced into evidence. Two years later, in *McMann v. Richardson* (1970), the Court found that a guilty plea entered after an arguably illegal confession was not induced by the prospect of the admission of the confessions. These cases can be reconciled by applying the attenuation exception—the defendant's decision to plead guilty was an inter-

vening event that dissipated the poison. But this is hardly a satisfying distinction.

The case that most strikingly reveals the difficulties with the fruits doctrine and is also the key to future interpretation is *United States v. Crews* (1980). In connection with his illegal arrest, the police obtained Crews's photograph which would not otherwise have been available. They showed it in an array of pictures to the victims who made an immediate identification. Next, Crews was placed in a fair LINEUP where the victims also identified him. The first question was whether testimony about the pretrial identifications was fruit; this was easily resolved because the prosecution conceded that it was. The harder issue was whether the victim's identification at trial of Crews must be suppressed. In the metaphoric language that seizes courts when dealing with this doctrine, the Court concluded that: "At trial, [the victim] retrieved the [mental image of her assailant], compared it to the figure of the defendant, and positively identified him as the robber. No part of this process was affected by respondent's illegal arrest. . . . [T]he toxin in this case was injected only after the evidentiary bud had blossomed; the fruit served at trial was not poisoned."

The Court in *Crews* went on to say that there could be cases where the victim's in-court identification was a result of the primary illegality—in other words, that the photograph and lineup identifications had led to the ability to point to the defendant at trial. In finding that this was not such a case the Court implicitly emphasized that the analysis of whether evidence is the fruit of the poisonous tree will continue in a case-by-case, highly pragmatic, and utterly unpredictable vein.

BARBARA ALLEN BABCOCK

Bibliography

LAFAVE, WAYNE R. 1978 *Search and Seizure: A Treatise on the Fourth Amendment.* Vol. 3:621–681. St. Paul, Minn.: West Publishing Co.

FUGITIVE FROM JUSTICE

The second clause of Article IV, section 2, of the Constitution provides that a person charged with a crime in one state, who has fled to another to escape justice, "shall, on demand of the executive authority of the state from which he fled, be delivered up. . . ." The clause makes rendition (or extradition) of fugitives from justice a duty of state officials.

Although extradition of escaped felons from one political JURISDICTION to another was long recognized as an obligation of comity in international law, the process is not automatic. Between sovereign nations, extradition normally occurs only when there is a treaty providing for it. Permanent extradition arrangements were not common before the nineteenth century.

Among the earliest standing arrangements for extradition of accused criminals was the one embodied in the articles of the New England Confederation (1643), which provided for the surrender of a fugitive to the colony from which he had fled when demand was made by two magistrates of that colony. Interstate extradition has been from the first, therefore, a feature of American FEDERALISM. The ARTICLES OF CONFEDERATION contained a provision identical to that in the Constitution. The Constitution's fugitive from justice clause was proposed in the CONSTITUTIONAL CONVENTION as part of the New Jersey Plan and was given its present form by the committee of detail.

EDMUND RANDOLPH, the first attorney general, issued an opinion that the fugitive from justice clause was not self-executing, that is, the Constitution did not specify what official was to render fugitives or establish enforcible procedures. Congress therefore, in 1793, passed a law imposing the duty of rendition on state governors.

The first test of the clause in the Supreme Court was in *Kentucky v. Dennison* (1861). The governor of Ohio had refused to honor Kentucky's demand that he render a fugitive wanted in Kentucky for aiding the escape of a slave. Chief Justice ROGER B. TANEY, for the Court, rejected Ohio's contention that the crime in question was not one contemplated by the Framers of the Constitution as within the scope of the clause; the clause extends to any act defined as a crime in the place where it was committed. The Court held that rendition of a fugitive was a MINISTERIAL ACT, one which a state governor has a duty to perform and not one over which he has any discretion. However, the Court also held that there was no power in the federal courts to compel compliance with the duty. Subsequently, governors have occasionally refused, for various reasons, to deliver fugitives to the states in which they were wanted.

Fugitives' careers are complicated by other factors. In 1934, Congress made it a federal crime to travel in INTERSTATE COMMERCE with the intent to avoid prosecution or confinement. The federal crime must be tried in the state from which the fugitive fled, and one practical effect of the statute is to return fugitives to the states in which they are wanted, facilitating arrest on state charges. Interstate rendition has also been facilitated by INTERSTATE COMPACTS and by adoption in most states of the Uniform Criminal Extradition Act.

DENNIS J. MAHONEY

FUGITIVE SLAVERY

The problem of runaways plagued American slave societies since the seventeenth century and was not solved until the abolition of slavery itself during the Civil War. Statutes of the colonial period dealing with indentured servants and slaves contained extensive provisions providing for punishment of runaways. Those relating to black slaves became increasingly severe over time, culminating in various eighteenth-century provisions permitting death, whipping, branding, outlawry, castration, dismemberment, and ear-slitting for runaways and compensation by the colony to masters of "outlying" slaves who were killed.

Provisions for interjurisdictional rendition of fugitives began with the fugitive-servant provisions of the New England Confederation (1643), but until 1787 rendition was a matter of comity between the colonies/states. The NORTHWEST ORDINANCE (1787) contained a fugitive slave/servant clause. The Constitution contained a clause providing that a "Person held to Service or Labour" shall not be freed when he absconds into another state, "but shall be delivered up." The use of the passive voice and the location of the clause in Article IV blurred responsibility for its enforcement, which caused protracted constitutional controversies in the 1840s and 1850s.

In 1793, Congress enacted the first Fugitive Slave Act, which provided that any slave holder or his "agent or attorney" could seize an alleged runaway, take him before a federal judge or local magistrate, prove title to the slave by affidavit or oral testimony, and get a certificate of rendition entitling him to take the slave back to the master's domicile. The constitutionality of the statute was repeatedly upheld by eminent authority: implicitly in JOSEPH STORY's *Commentaries on the Constitution of the United States* (1833); explicitly by Chief Justice William Tilghman of the Pennsylvania Supreme Court in *Wright v. Deacon* (1819) and Chief Justice Isaac Parker of the Massachusetts Supreme Judicial Court in *Commonwealth v. Griffin* (1823). Early abolitionist societies worked to prevent free blacks from being kidnapped through the instrumentality of the 1793 act and provided counsel to alleged fugitives. Abolitionists challenged the statute on the grounds that Congress exceeded its powers in forcing state officials to participate in federal rendition proceedings, in permitting rendition from TERRITORIES as well as states, and in interfering with the rights of the states to protect their free citizens.

Before 1843, a few states enacted PERSONAL LIBERTY LAWS that provided various procedural safeguards, such as HABEAS CORPUS or TRIAL BY JURY, to alleged fugitives. The slave states resented these and challenged their constitutionality in PRIGG V. PENNSYLVANIA (1842). Speaking for a majority of the Court, Justice Joseph Story held that: the fugitive slave clause of the Constitution was an essential compromise necessary to ratification of the Constitution by the southern states; the 1793 act was constitutional; the master had a right of recapture of a runaway slave, derived either from the COMMON LAW or from the fugitive slave clause; and the Pennsylvania personal liberty law was unconstitutional because it infringed on masters' rights protected by the federal statute. In an OBITER DICTUM, Story stated that the federal government could not constitutionally oblige state officials to participate in enforcement of the act.

Insubstantial as this suggestion was, northern states after 1842 enacted new personal liberty laws prohibiting state officials from participating in enforcement of the federal statute and prohibiting the use of state facilities such as jails for detaining runaways. Abolitionists then mounted a more sophisticated, wide-ranging attack on the constitutionality of the 1793 statute, alleging that it violated the Fifth Amendment's DUE PROCESS clause and the FOURTH AMENDMENT's SEARCHES AND SEIZURES clause.

Congress, as part of the COMPROMISE OF 1850, enacted a new Fugitive Slave Act, which was an extension of the 1793 Act, not a replacement for it. It contained these novel features: owners and agents were authorized to seize alleged fugitives with or without legal process; certificates of rendition could be granted by federal commissioners as well as federal judges; any adult male could be drafted into a posse to assist in capture and rendition; obstruction of the act was punishable by a fine of $1,000; the commissioner's fee was $5 if he determined that the black was not a runaway, but $10 if he awarded the certificate of rendition, prompting an abolitionist's remark that the statute set the price of a Carolina Negro at $1,000 and a Yankee soul at $5.

Residents of the free states objected vehemently to the new statute. Throughout the 1850s, dramatic rescues and recaptures of runaways provided real-life drama to accompany the sensational success of the serialized, book, and stage versions of *Uncle Tom's Cabin*, with its melodramatic runaway scene. Federal authorities and northern conservatives responded to abolitionist challenges and to rescues of fugitives by affirming the constitutionality of the 1850 Act (Chief Justice LEMUEL SHAW of the Massachusetts Supreme Judicial Court in IN RE SIMS, 1851) and by demanding that resistance to enforcement of the measure be prosecuted as treason. Two efforts at doing so, however (resulting from the Jerry rescue, Syracuse, New York, 1851, and the Oberlin-Wellington rescue, northern Ohio, 1858), ended in inglorious failure for the prosecution. In general, however, the northern states attempted to comply with the statute, and most blacks seized as fugitives under the act were sent into slavery.

In a dictum in ABLEMAN V. BOOTH (1859) Chief Justice ROGER B. TANEY declared the 1850 statute constitutional, but the question was soon to be mooted. After the outbreak of the Civil War, the policies of some Union commanders discouraged the return of runaways who fled behind Union lines. Congress partially repealed the Fugitive Slave Acts in 1862 and then fully in 1864. The whole issue, and the fugitive slave clause of the Constitution, became dead letters with the abolition of slavery in 1864–1865.

WILLIAM M. WIECEK

Bibliography

CAMPBELL, STANLEY W. 1968 *The Slave Catchers: Enforcement of the Fugitive Slave Law, 1850–1860.* Chapel Hill: University of North Carolina Press.
DUMOND, DWIGHT L. 1961 *Antislavery: The Crusade for Freedom in America.* Ann Arbor: University of Michigan Press.
HYMAN, HAROLD M. and WIECEK, WILLIAM M. 1982 *Equal Justice under Law: Constitutional Development, 1835–1875.* New York: Harper & Row.

FULL EMPLOYMENT ACT
60 Stat. 23 (1946)

Despite the post-World War II desire to shake off wartime economic controls, Congress passed a Full Employment Act in February 1946, establishing a new concept of the relation of the government to the national economy. The measure declared officially that it was the responsibility of the national government to insure effective operation of the country's economic system and maintain maximum employment, production, and purchasing power. Through a newly created three-person Presidential Council of Economic Advisors, the nation's economic patterns were studied and analyzed with the government responsible for evolving new controls essential to the nation's economic security. These included: tax rates designed to produce a predetermined deficit or surplus based on whether the administration sought to stimulate or cool off the economy; controlling the ease or tightness of credit; raising or lowering public spending levels; and maintaining wage and price guidelines. Such use of deficit financing, public works, and economic controls might alleviate the negative effects of the business cycle and avoid another major economic depression.

The measure was a constitutional landmark. It formally rejected the concept that the government's main role in the economic sphere was negative: to maintain a free enterprise system by preserving, through laws and court decisions, a hands-off policy toward American economic activities.

PAUL L. MURPHY

Bibliography

BAILEY, STEPHEN K. 1950 *Congress Makes a Law: The Story Behind the Employment Act of 1946*. New York: Columbia University Press.

FULLER, MELVILLE W.
(1833–1910)

Melville Weston Fuller, eighth Chief Justice of the United States, was appointed by GROVER CLEVELAND in 1888 and presided over the Court until his death on July 4, 1910. Fuller's twenty-two-year tenure as Chief Justice, the longest during the Court's second century, spanned one of the most significant periods of constitutional development in American history. Fuller and his associates circumscribed the rights of state criminal defendants under the FOURTEENTH AMENDMENT, established an inferior legal status for residents of the new overseas colonies, articulated the infamous SEPARATE BUT EQUAL DOCTRINE, and devised a spate of other juristic strategies for avoiding interventions on behalf of black petitioners in the fields of education and VOTING RIGHTS. At the same time the FULLER COURT made so many new departures in decisions affecting the economic order that one scholar has described its work as "the new judicialism." Fuller and his colleagues invalidated the federal income tax, emasculated the Interstate Commerce Commission, put the Court's imprimatur on the labor INJUNCTION, construed the commerce clause so that the SHERMAN ANTITRUST ACT frustrated the activities of labor unions yet failed to impede the fusion of manufacturing corporations, and elaborated the concept of SUBSTANTIVE DUE PROCESS as a guarantor of VESTED RIGHTS and LIBERTY OF CONTRACT.

The vast bulk of the Fuller Court's work in constitutional law reflected the Chief Justice's constitutional understanding, the contours of which had been firmly fixed before Fuller came to the bench. Beginning in 1856, when he left his native Maine and settled in Chicago, Fuller was an active stump speaker and essayist for the Illinois Democratic party; he styled himself a disciple of Thomas Hart Benton and STEPHEN A. DOUGLAS long after both were dead. Fuller spoke often in favor of free trade, hard money, and equal opportunity in the market. "Paternalism, with its constant intermeddling with individual freedom," he wrote in 1880, "has no place in a system which rests for its strength upon the self-reliant energies of the people." But Fuller's version of the equal rights creed had no place for blacks. An exponent of a conservative naturalism that stressed the importance of homogeneous communities and local autonomy in American public life, Fuller believed that union and republican liberty were possible only if the federal government acquiesced in local racial arrangements on the same ground that it acquiesced in state laws regulating the status of women. He objected to the EMANCIPATION PROCLAMATION on the ground that it was "predicated upon the idea that the President may annul the constitutions and laws of sovereign states." He claimed that the THIRTEENTH AMENDMENT and Fourteenth Amendment protected only the "common rights" of individuals against discriminatory classification. And he never ceased to insist that Congress's powers to regulate persons or property were limited, derivable only from specific grants and not from any assumption of an underlying national SOVEREIGNTY. Fuller's longest, most plaintive dissents came in the INSULAR CASES (1901), where he denied Congress's power to levy tariffs on the products of colonial possessions, and in CHAMPION V. AMES (1903), where he contended that Congress could not exercise police powers on the pretense of regulating commerce.

Fuller did not grapple with the Court's role in the American system of government following his appointment as Chief Justice. For Fuller, as for Benton, Douglas, and Cleveland, the Constitution was more than a text that allocated specific powers and secured particular rights against government. The Constitution was significant above all as the repository of values so integral to the existence of republicanism that any public official who failed to protect and defend them was guilty of a breach of trust. Consequently, Fuller conceptualized the judicial function in terms of duty rather than in terms of role; his approach to judging was instinctive rather than ratiocinative. Since he had long associated the Constitution with the Democratic party's mid-nineteenth-century dogmas, Fuller impulsively enforced those dogmas as the law of the land. It was no accident that JAMES BRADLEY THAYER published his path-breaking assessment of "The Origins and Scope of the American Doctrine of Constitutional Law" five years after Fuller's appointment or that a school of jurisprudence dedicated to "judicial self-restraint" grew increasingly large and vocal during his tenure. Other critics accused his Court of aiding the rich and powerful at the expense of the poor and helpless in the name of judicial neutrality. But Fuller neither replied to them nor sought to persuade others to do so. He simply hoped it would always be said of him, as he said of Cleveland in a 1909 eulogy, that "he trod unswervingly the path of duty, undeterred by doubts, single-minded and straight-forward."

The Chief Justice's constitutional understanding may have been "single-minded and straight-forward," but the Fuller era abounds with anomalies all the same. First there is the matter of Fuller's reputation. Until EARL WARREN's day, no Court was subjected to more strident criticism for a more sustained period of time than Fuller's. Yet when Fuller died the press concurred that none of his predecessors had been so successful in earning the respect and confidence of the country. Even THEODORE ROOSEVELT's *Outlook* conceded that Fuller was "perhaps the most popular" though "not the strongest or most famous Chief Justice." Perceptions of Fuller's capacity for judicial leadership were equally anomalous. The Chief Justice voted with the majority in virtually every leading case decided during his tenure. If STEPHEN J. FIELD is to be believed, moreover, Fuller was effective in setting the tenor of conference discussion. "Field told me on the bench this morning," Fuller informed his wife in 1891, "that in the conference I was almost invariably right. He said I was remarkably quick in seizing the best point." Yet contemporary observers invariably described him as a weak Chief Justice who neither led his Court nor exerted a substantial influence on its outlook.

The greatest anomaly of the Fuller era was the doctrinal structure of "the new judicialism." When Fuller contemplated the future of the republic in a centennial address on GEORGE WASHINGTON, two fears loomed especially large. One was that "the drift toward the exertion of the national will" might ultimately result in "consolidation," which in turn would impair the "vital importance" of the states and undermine self-government by extending the sphere of legislative authority to such a degree that the people no longer controlled it. The other was "the drift . . .

towards increased interference by the State in the attempt to alleviate inequality of conditions." Fuller admitted that "[s]o long as that interference is . . . protective only," it was not only legitimate but necessary. "But," he added, "the rights to life, to use one's faculties in all lawful ways, and to acquire and enjoy property, are morally fundamental rights antecedent to constitutions, which do not create, but secure and protect them." It was imperative, he said, that Americans never grow "unmindful of the fact that it is the duty of the people to support the government and not of the government to support the people." Each of these concerns soon reappeared as major premises in the Court's construction of Congress's COMMERCE POWER and in its articulation of the liberty of contract protected by the Fifth and Fourteenth Amendments. But the Chief Justice directed a cacophonous band, not an orchestra. Decisions which, in Fuller's view, were consistent with one another looked antithetical to other observers because different Justices expressed the Court's opinions in different language.

Fuller regarded the liberty of contract doctrine as a juristic device for distinguishing between "paternalism," which he thought was unconstitutional, and legislation that "is protective only." Thus the maximum hours law for miners at issue in HOLDEN V. HARDY (1898) was valid because it protected the health and safety of workers employed in an inherently dangerous occupation. But the maximum hours law for bakery workers invalidated in LOCHNER V. NEW YORK (1905) and the ERDMAN ACT of Congress prohibiting discrimination against union members were unconstitutional because neither statute was "protective only." In Fuller's view, government had no authority to redress inequalities in the bargaining relation. "The employer and the employee have equality of right," JOHN MARSHALL HARLAN explained for the Court in ADAIR V. UNITED STATES (1908), "and any legislation that disturbs that equality is an arbitrary interference with liberty of contract, which no government can legally justify in a free land." Yet in *Holden* HENRY BROWN spoke at length about the inequality of bargaining power between employees and employers; he also implied that the worker's inability to contract for fair terms provided a legitimate rationale for government intervention. Although Brown apparently retreated from that position when he joined the *Lochner* majority seven years later, the language he used in *Holden* was never expressly disapproved.

The disparity between Fuller's constitutional understanding and the language used by colleagues in opinions he assigned was even more pronounced in the commerce field. Speaking for the Court in UNITED STATES V. E. C. KNIGHT CO. (1895), Fuller held that the Sherman Act could not be constitutionally construed to require the dissolution of manufacturing corporations when the transactions deemed unlawful in the government's complaint involved neither interstate transportation nor interstate sales. "Commerce succeeds to manufacturing," he explained, "and is not part of it." Underlying this distinction were three assumptions which Fuller elaborated with varying degrees of clarity. Congress could not regulate manufacturing combinations under the commerce clause, he said, for if that were permitted there was nothing to prevent Congress from regulating "every branch of human activity." Fuller also contended that that line between manufacturing and commerce was readily ascertainable. In a spate of recent dormant commerce clause decisions the Court had invalidated state tax laws and police regulations that burdened interstate transactions yet had sustained such legislation when it burdened the production process. With the exception of state laws that burdened commerce "indirectly" and might therefore be sustained under the rule of COOLEY V. BOARD OF WARDENS (1851), then, Congress could regulate only what the states could not and vice versa. Finally, Fuller made it clear that when manufacturing firms made "contracts to buy, sell, or exchange goods to be transported among the several states," the federal government had a duty to intervene under the Sherman Act if those contracts, or agreements pursuant to them, were in restraint of trade. In *Robbins v. Shelby County Taxing District* (1887), a leading dormant commerce clause case, the Court had held that "the negotiation of sales of goods which are in another state . . . is INTERSTATE COMMERCE."

Fuller believed that his construction of Congress's powers under the Sherman Act had two important virtues. It forestalled "consolidation" and it was easy to apply. Congress could certainly reach the agreement at issue in *Addyston Pipe & Steel Co. v. United States* (1899), for there a pool had been devised to allocate the interstate distribution of goods among the cooperating firms. And in LOEWE V. LAWLOR (1908) the hatter's union had not only gone on strike, thus disrupting the production process, but had engaged in a secondary boycott to prevent the sale of hats in interstate commerce. SWIFT & CO. V. UNITED STATES (1905) posed equally simple issues for Fuller. Some thirty firms had agreed to refrain from bidding against one another when livestock was auctioned prior to its delivery for slaughter at the Chicago packinghouses. Clearly, as the Court explained, "the subject-matter [was] sales and the very point of the combination . . . to restrain and monopolize commerce among the states in respect to such sales." But Fuller had designated OLIVER WENDELL HOLMES to speak for the Court in *Swift*, and Holmes had a great deal more to say. Holmes remarked that "commerce among the States is not a technical legal conception, but a practical one, drawn from the course of business." He spoke metaphorically about a current of commerce, suggesting that local production and interstate marketing were not distinct processes so much as parts of a single, undifferentiated process. (See STREAM OF COMMERCE DOCTRINE.) And he cast a pall of doubt on the idea, implicit in Fuller's *Knight* opinion, "that the rule which marks the point at which State taxation or regulation becomes permissible necessarily is beyond the scope of interference by Congress in cases where such interference is deemed necessary for the protection of commerce among the States."

Each of the anomalies of the Fuller years is attributable to the personality of the Chief Justice and his conception of the office. Fuller was a self-effacing, amiable man who was gracious and courteous, even deferential, to his colleagues. He made every effort to secure harmonious relations among the Justices. Fuller inaugurated the custom, still followed today, that each Justice greet and shake hands with every other Justice each morning. And he used his authority to assign opinions when in the majority not to enhance his own reputation or to elaborate favorite doctrines but to cultivate the good will of his associates. The opinion in a leading case ordinarily went to the colleague who, in Fuller's judgment, was most likely to want to speak for the Court. Cases involving questions of JURISDICTION and practice or mundane matters of private law Fuller kept to himself. Thus he let Field deliver the Court's opinions in *Georgia Banking & Railroad Co. v. Smith* (1889), a rate regulation case, and *Chae Chan Ping v. United States* (1889), the Chinese Exclusion Case. Both controversies raised issues of enormous importance to Field; for that very reason Fuller's predecessor had been disinclined to permit Field to address them for the Court.

Fuller also assumed that Brown would consider *Holden* a plum, for he had recently addressed the American Bar Association on the labor question. RUFUS PECKHAM had earned the right to speak for the majority in *Lochner* by dissenting without opinion in every previous case involving legislative regulation of the labor contract. The *Adair* decision provided Fuller with an opportunity to elaborate his own liberty of contract views in a systematic fashion, but he gave the opinion to Harlan instead. Harlan had dissented in *Lochner* on the grounds that the Court had no authority to reject the legislature's reasonable claim that long hours affected the health and safety of bakery workers. In *Adair* the government advanced no such claim and Harlan's opinion barely noticed the Court's prior liberty of contract rulings. Holmes was the logical choice for *Swift,* for the opinion would show Roosevelt that the administration had drawn spurious conclusions about Holmes's antitrust views from NORTHERN SECURITIES CO. V. UNITED STATES (1904).

The Chief Justice's obsession with courtesy also accounts for the striking differences between his own views and the Court's language in opinions which he assigned. He stubbornly defended his convictions in conference and, if necessary, in dissent. But once he had voted with the majority and had authorized an associate to speak for the Court, Fuller never criticized the work produced by a colleague. Good will among the Justices might be lost forever because of a single quarrel; incongruities of DOCTRINE could always be repaired later. Fuller let it be known that forthright yet polite concurring opinions were preferable to postconference haggling over doctrine, and silent acquiescence in the opinion of the Court was more preferable still. Fuller's own behavior set high standards for his associates; he wrote only seven concurring opinions in twenty-two years.

Underlying Fuller's management of the Court was a belief that the Chief Justice's primary duty was to convey to the public the impression that in the Court, more than in any other institution of government, reason triumphed over partisanship and statesmanship prevailed over pettiness. Fuller's success in achieving that goal while rarely speaking for the Court in landmark cases accounts for misperceptions of his capacity for intellectual leadership and for his great popularity despite persistent criticism of his Court's work. But Fuller's winning personality and the apparent anomalies it produced should not overshadow the relationship between his convictions and the new principles of law his Court articulated. Not since JOHN MARSHALL's day had the constitutional understanding of the Chief Justice been more at odds with that of voters and party leaders for such a prolonged period of time. Nevertheless, Fuller presided over a Court that made fundamentally new departures in constitutional interpretation which, in the main, incorporated the values he had imbibed during the party battles of a bygone era in American public life. Although Fuller hoped that eulogists would compare him with

Cleveland, it might be more appropriate to analogize his career with that of another charming nineteenth-century Democrat. Like MARTIN VAN BUREN, he rowed to his objectives with muffled oars.

CHARLES W. McCURDY

Bibliography

FULLER, MELVILLE 1890 *Address in Commemoration of the Inauguration of George Washington as First President of the United States, Delivered Before the Two Houses of Congress, December 11, 1889.* New York: Banks & Brothers.

KING, WILLARD L. 1950 *Melville Weston Fuller: Chief Justice of the United States, 1888–1910.* Chicago: University of Chicago Press.

PAUL, ARNOLD M. 1959 *Conservative Crisis and the Rule of Law: Attitudes of Bar and Bench, 1887–1895.* Ithaca, N.Y.: Cornell University Press.

FULLER COURT
(1888–1910)

MELVILLE W. FULLER was Chief Justice of the United States from 1888 to 1910. Lawyers and historians know the period, and its significance for constitutional law, but do not generally identify it with Fuller's name—and for good reason. He was no leader. Fuller discharged his administrative duties effectively, and in "good humor," to borrow a phrase from OLIVER WENDELL HOLMES, one of his admirers, but he was not an important source of the ideas and vision that shaped the work of the Court.

The year of Fuller's appointment, 1888, was nonetheless an important date in the life of the Court because it marked the beginning of a period of rapid turnover. From 1888 to 1895 there were a considerable number of vacancies, and the two Presidents then in office, GROVER CLEVELAND, a Democrat, and BENJAMIN HARRISON, a Republican—whose politics were conservative and largely indistinguishable—appointed six of the Justices. One was Fuller himself. At the time of his appointment he was a respected Chicago lawyer and, perhaps more significantly, a friend of Cleveland's. The others were DAVID J. BREWER, a federal circuit judge in Kansas; HENRY BILLINGS BROWN, a federal district judge in Detroit; RUFUS PECKHAM, a judge on the New York Court of Appeals; GEORGE SHIRAS, a lawyer from Pittsburgh; and EDWARD D. WHITE, a senator from Louisiana. (LUCIUS Q. C. LAMAR and HOWELL JACKSON were also appointed during this period, but served for relatively short periods.) The intellectual leaders of this group of six were Brewer and Peckham. They appeared in their written opinions as the most powerful and most eloquent, and the Chief Justice usually turned to one or the other to write for the Court in the major cases.

In constructing their majorities, Brewer and Peckham could usually count on the support of STEPHEN J. FIELD (Brewer's uncle), who earlier had achieved his fame by protesting various forms of government regulation in the SLAUGHTERHOUSE CASES and the GRANGER CASES. In the late 1890s Field was replaced by JOSEPH MCKENNA, who was chosen by WILLIAM MCKINLEY, a President who continued in the conservative tradition of Cleveland and Harrison. Another ally of this Cleveland-Harrison group, though perhaps not so steadfast as Field or McKenna, was HORACE GRAY. Gray was appointed in 1881 by President CHESTER A. ARTHUR and served until 1902.

As a result of these appointments, the Court over which Fuller presided was perhaps one of the most homogeneous in the history of the Supreme Court. Even more striking, its composition did not significantly change for most of Fuller's tenure. Fuller died in July 1910, just months after Brewer and Peckham. It was almost as though he could not go on without them. Brown resigned in 1906 and Shiras in 1903, but their replacements—WILLIAM H. MOODY and WILLIAM R. DAY—did not radically alter the balance of power. The only important break with the past came when THEODORE ROOSEVELT appointed Oliver Wendell Holmes, Jr., to replace Gray.

At the time of his appointment, Holmes was the Chief Justice of the Supreme Judicial Court of Massachusetts and had already written a number of the classics of American jurisprudence. Brown described Holmes's appointment as a "topping off." On the Court, however, Holmes played a different role, for he had no taste for either the method of analysis or general philosophical outlook of the Cleveland-Harrison appointees. His stance was fully captured by his quip in LOCHNER V. NEW YORK (1905) that "The FOURTEENTH AMENDMENT does not enact Mr. Herbert Spencer's Social Statics." In this remark Holmes was finally vindicated in 1937 with the constitutional triumph of the New Deal, but in the early 1900s he spoke mostly for himself, at least on the bench, and had no appreciable impact on the course of decisions. No other Justice joined his *Lochner* dissent.

The other significant presence on the Court at the turn of the century was JOHN MARSHALL HARLAN. He was originally appointed by President RUTHERFORD B. HAYES in 1877 and served until 1911. He is greatly admired today for his views on the rights of the newly freed slaves and on the power of the national government. But, like Holmes, Harlan suffered the fate of a prophet: He was a loner. He had his own agenda, and though he sometimes spoke for the Cleveland-Harrison group, Harlan seemed most comfortable playing the role of "the great dissenter."

At the turn of the century, as in many other periods of our history, the Court was principally concerned with the excesses of democracy and the danger of tyranny of the majority. In one instance, the people in Chicago took to the streets and, through a mass strike, tied up the rail system of the nation and threatened the public order. President Cleveland responded by sending the army, and the judiciary helped by issuing an INJUNCTION. In IN RE DEBS (1895) Brewer, writing for a unanimous Court, upheld the contempt conviction of the leader of the union, and legitimated the use of the federal injunctive power to prevent forcible obstructions of INTERSTATE COMMERCE. For the most part, however, the people fought their battles in the legislative halls, and presented the Court with a number of statutes regulating economic relationships. The question posed time and time again was whether these exercises of state power were consistent with the limitations the Constitution imposed upon popular majorities. Sometimes the question was answered in the affirmative, but the Court over which Fuller presided is largely remembered for its negative responses. It stands as a monument to the idea of limited government.

The most important such response consists of POLLOCK V. FARMERS' LOAN & TRUST CO. when, in the spring of 1895, the Court invalidated the first federal income tax enacted in peacetime. The statute imposed a 2 percent tax on all annual incomes above $4,000, and it was estimated that, due to the exemption, the tax actually fell on less than 2 percent of the population, the wealthy few who resided in a few northeastern states. The tax was denounced by JOSEPH CHOATE, in arguments before the Supreme Court, as an incident in the "communistic march," but the Court chose not to base its decision on a rule that would protect the wealthy few from redistribution. The Court instead largely relied upon that provision of the Constitution linking REPRESENTATION and taxation and requiring the apportionment among the states according to population of all DIRECT TAXES.

The Constitution identified a POLL TAX as an example of a direct tax. It was also assumed by all that a real estate tax would be another example of a direct tax, and the Court first decided that a tax upon the income from real estate is a direct tax. This ruling resulted in the invalidation of the statute as applied to rents (since the tax was not apportioned according to population), but on all other issues the Court was evenly divided, 4–4. The ninth justice, Howell Jackson, was sick at the time. A second argument was held and then the Court continued along the path it had started. Just as a tax on income from real property was deemed a direct tax, so was the tax on income from personal property (such as dividends). This still left unresolved the question whether a tax on wages was a direct tax, but the majority held that the portions of the statute taxing rents and dividends were not severable and that as a result the whole statute would fall. As Fuller reasoned, writing for the majority, if the provision on wages were severable, and it alone sustained, the statute would be transformed, for "what was intended as a tax on capital would remain in substance a tax on occupations and labors."

A decision of the Court invalidating the work of a coordinate branch of government is always problematic. *Pollock* seemed especially so, however, because the Court was sharply divided (5–4), and even more so because one of the Justices (whose identity is still unknown) seems to have switched sides after the reargument. The Justice who did not participate the first time (Jackson) voted to uphold the statute, yet the side he joined lost. It was no surprise, therefore, that *Pollock*, like *Debs*, became an issue in the presidential campaign of 1896, when William Jennings Bryan—a sponsor of the income tax in Congress—wrested control of the Democratic Party from the traditional, conservative elements and fused it with the emerging populist movement. Bryan lost the election, but remained the leader of the party for the next decade or so, during which the political elements critical of the Court grew in number and persuasiveness. By 1913 a constitutional amendment—the first since Reconstruction—was adopted. The SIXTEENTH AMENDMENT did not directly confront the egalitarian issue, any more than did the Court, but simply declared that an income tax did not have to be apportioned.

The Court's first encounter with the SHERMAN ACT of 1890 was negative and thus bore some resemblance to *Pollock*. In UNITED STATES V. E. C. KNIGHT COMPANY, also announced in 1895, just months before *Debs* and *Pollock*, the Court refused to read the Sherman Act to bar the acquisition of a sugar refinery even though it resulted in a firm that controlled 98 percent of the market and aptly was described (by Harlan in dissent) as a "stupendous combination." The Court reasoned that manufacturing was not within the reach of Congress's power over "commerce." The difference with *Pollock*, however, lay in the fact that this decision (written by Fuller) was in accord with long-standing interpretations of the COMMERCE CLAUSE, which equated "commerce" with the transportation of goods and services across state lines. And this decision was not denounced by the populists; they had no desire whatsoever to have the federal government assume jurisdiction over productive activities such as agriculture. In any event, by the end of Fuller's Chief Justiceship, *E. C. Knight* was in effect eradicated by the Court itself. The Court fully indicated that it was prepared to apply the act to manufacturing enterprises, provided the challenged conduct impeded or affected the flow of goods across state lines.

In the late 1890s, almost immediately after *E. C. Knight*, the Court, speaking through Peckham, applied the Sherman Act to prohibit open price-fixing arrangements by a number of railroads. There was little issue in these cases about the reach of the commerce power, because they involved transportation, but the Court was sharply divided over an issue that was presented by these early antitrust cases, namely, whether such an interference with what was then perceived as ordinary or accepted business practices (supposedly aimed at preventing "ruinous competition") was an abridgment of FREEDOM OF CONTRACT. At first the argument about freedom of contract was presented as a constitutional defense of the application of the Sherman Act, wholly based on the DUE PROCESS clause, but starting with Brewer's separate concurrence in UNITED STATES V. NORTHERN SECURITIES COMPANY (1903) and then again in White's opinions for a near-unanimous Court in the STANDARD OIL COMPANY V. UNITED STATES (1911) and UNITED STATES V. AMERICAN TOBACCO COMPANY (1911), the liberty issue dissolved into a question of statutory interpretation. The Sherman Act was read to prohibit not all but only "unreasonable" restraints of trade, and if a business practice was "unreasonable," then it was, almost by definition, the proper subject of government regulation.

In the late 1890s and early 1900s, antitrust sentiments were the principal cause of the growing Progressive movement. While populists extolled cooperative activity, progressives tried to use the legislative power to preserve the market and the liberties that it implied. They condemned activities (such as mergers or price fixing) that stemmed from the ruthless pursuit of self-interest but that, if carried to their logical extreme, would destroy the social mechanism that both legitimates and is supposed to control such self-interested activity. Progressives were also concerned, however, with stopping certain practices that did not threaten the existence of the market, but rather offended some standard of "fairness" or "decency" that had a wholly independent source. And they used the legislative power for this end.

The Justices were not unmoved by the moralistic concerns that fueled the progressives, but they were also determined—as they had been in *Pollock*—to make certain that the majorities were not using the legislative power to redistribute wealth or power in their favor. In some instances the Court allowed redistributive measures that benefited some group that was especially disadvantaged and thus could be deemed a ward of the state. On that theory, the Court, in a unanimous opinion by Brewer, upheld in MULLER V. OREGON (1908) a statute creating a sixty-hour maximum work week for women employed in factories or laundries. More generally, however, the Court voiced the same fears that had animated *Pollock* and insisted that there be a "direct" connection between the legislative rule and an acceptable (that is, nonredistributive) end such as health. The statute at issue in *Lochner v. New York*, for example, was defended on the ground that a work week for bakers in excess of sixty hours would endanger their health. Justice Peckham's opinion for the majority acknowledged that there might be some connection between a maximum work week and health, but suspected redistributive purposes and argued that if, in the case of bakers, this connection with health were deemed sufficient— that is, direct—the same could be said for virtually every occupation or profession: "No trade, no occupation, no mode of earning one's living, could escape this all-pervading power."

Just as it was fearful of state intervention to control the terms of employment, the Court was also wary of legislation regulating consumer prices—a practice initiated by the Granger movement of the 1870s but continued by the populists and progressives in the 1890s and the early 1900s. In this instance the Court feared that the customers would enrich themselves at the expense of the investors. The danger was, as Brewer formulated it, one of legalized theft. In contrast to cases like *Lochner*, however, the Court took up this issue with a viable and highly visible precedent on the books, namely, *Munn v. Illinois* (1877). Some consideration was given to OVERRULING the decision (there was no limit to the daring of some of the Justices), but the Court finally settled upon a more modest strategy—of cabining *Munn*.

For one thing, the *Munn* formula for determining which industries would be regulated—a formula that allowed the state to reach "any industry AFFECTED WITH A PUBLIC INTEREST"—was narrowed. In *Budd v. New York* (1892) the Court upheld the power of the legislature to regulate the rates of grain operators, but placed no reliance on the *Munn* public interest formula. Instead, it stressed the presence of monopoly power and the place of the grain operation in the transportation system. Second, the Court began to surround the rate-settling power with procedural guarantees. Legislatures were now delegating the power of setting prices to administrative bodies, such as railroad commissions, and the Court, in CHICAGO, MILWAUKEE & ST. PAUL RAILWAY CO. V. MINNESOTA (1890), required agencies of that type to afford investors a full, quasi-judicial hearing prior to setting rates. Finally, the Court ended the tradition of judicial deference initiated by *Munn* by authorizing judicial review of the rate actually set. The purpose was to insure against confiscation and to this end Brewer articulated in REAGAN V. FARMERS' LOAN & TRUST (1894) a right of FAIR RETURN ON FAIR VALUE. In that case the rate was set so low as to deny the investors any return at all. In the next case, SMYTH V. AMES (1898), there was some return to the investors, but the Court simply concluded that the rate was "too low."

Reagan v. Farmers' Loan & Trust and *Smyth v. Ames* were both unanimous and thrust the federal judiciary into the business of policing state rate regulations. A particularly momentous and divisive exercise of this supervisory jurisdiction occurred when a federal judge in Minnesota enjoined the attorney general of that state from enforcing a state statute that set maximum railroad rates. The attorney general disobeyed the injunction and was held in criminal contempt. Peckham wrote the opinion for the Court in EX PARTE YOUNG (1908) affirming the contempt conviction, and in doing so, constructed a theory that, notwithstanding the ELEVENTH AMENDMENT, provided access to the federal EQUITY courts to test the constitutionality of state statutes—an avenue of recourse that was to become critical for the CIVIL RIGHTS movement of the 1960s. Ironically, Harlan, who, by dissenting in the CIVIL RIGHTS CASES (1883) and in PLESSY V. FERGUSON (1896), had already earned for himself an honored place in the history of civil rights, bitterly dissented in *Ex parte Young*, because, he argued, the Court was opening the doors of federal courts to test the validity of all state statutes.

The confrontations between the Court and political branches in economic matters such as antitrust, maximum hours, and rate regulation were considerable— *Northern Securities*, *Lochner*, and *Ex Parte Young* were important public events of their day. Some of these decisions were denounced by political forces, particularly by the Progressive movement, which had begun to dominate national politics. Roosevelt made his disappointment with Holmes's performance in *Northern Securities* well known ("I could carve out of a banana a judge with more backbone than that"—a comment that seems only to have either amused or pleased Holmes) and finished his presidency in 1908 with a speech to Congress sharply critical of the Court. By 1912 the Supreme Court and its work were once again the subject of debate in a presidential election, as it had been in the election of 1896. It was as though the body politic was scoring the Court over which Fuller had presided for the past twenty years. Now the critical voices were more respected and covered a wider political spectrum than in 1896, but the results were mixed.

In the 1912 election the Democratic candidate, Woodrow Wilson, beat the incumbent WILLIAM HOW-ARD TAFT, who was generally seen as the defender, indeed the embodiment, of the judicial power. On the other hand, Wilson was less critical of the Court than Roosevelt, who ran as a Progressive. The legislation of this period also was two-sided. The CLAYTON ACT of 1914, for example, exempted labor from antitrust legislation (thus reversing the *Danbury Hatters* decision of 1908), and also imposed procedural limits on the use of the labor injunction (thus revising *Debs*), but it did not in fact have as critical an edge as the Sixteenth Amendment of 1913. The Clayton Act did not repudiate the idea of the labor injunction altogether nor did it repudiate the rule of reason in antitrust cases. Similarly, although Congress reacted in 1910 to *Ex Parte Young*, it did so only in a trivial, near-cosmetic way, by requiring three judges (as opposed to one) to issue an injunction against the enforcement of state statutes.

In attempting to construct limits on the power of the political branches, and to guard against the tyranny of the majority as it did in *Pollock*, *Ex Parte Young*, and *Lochner*, the Court assumed an activist posture. The Justices were prepared to use their power to frustrate what appeared popular sentiments. The activist posture was, however, mostly confined to economic reforms—redistributing income, regulating prices, controlling the terms of employment—as though the constitutional conception of liberty were structured by an overriding commitment to capitalism and the market. This characterization of their work, voiced in a critical spirit in their day and in ours, is strengthened when a view is taken of the Justices' overall receptiveness to the antitrust program of the progressives, and even more when account is taken of the pattern of decisions outside the economic domain, respecting human rights as opposed to property rights. The Justices were passive about human rights—by and large willing to let majorities have their way.

A particularly striking instance of this passivity consists of their reaction to the treatment of Chinese residents. Ever since the Civil War the Chinese were by statute denied the right to become naturalized citizens, but in the late 1880s and the early 1900s their situation worsened. The doors of the nation were closed to any further IMMIGRATION, and Congress (in the Geary Act of 1892) created an oppressive regime for those who had previously been admitted. Chinese residents were required to carry passes, and failure to have the passes subjected them to DEPORTATION proceedings that were to be conducted by commissioners (rather than judges or juries) and that put them to the task of producing "at least one credible white witness." YICK WO V. HOPKINS (1886), which invalidated, on EQUAL PROTECTION grounds, a San Francisco laundry ordinance that had disadvantaged the Chinese, was already on the books. But neither it nor the passionate dissent of Brewer ("In view of this enactment of the highest legislative body of the foremost Christian nation, may not the thoughtful Chinese disciple of Confucius fairly ask, why do they send missionaries here?") was of much avail. The Court sustained the Geary Act in *Fong Yue Ting v. United States* (1893) in virtually all its particulars.

A few years later the Court held in UNITED STATES V. WONG KIM ARK (1898) that Chinese children born here were, by virtue of the FOURTEENTH AMENDMENT, citizens of the United States. But this decision sharply divided the Court, despite the straightforward language of the amendment ("All persons born . . . in the United States and subject to the jurisdiction thereof are citizens of the United States"), and did not materially improve the quality of the process the Chinese received. There was, by virtue of *Wong Kim Ark*, a chance that a Chinese person whom the government was trying to deport was a natural born citizen, yet the Court did not even require that this claim of CITIZENSHIP be tried by a judge. Holmes wrote the opinion in these cases, *United States v. Sing Tuck* (1904) and *United States v. Ju Toy* (1905), and once again Brewer, now joined by Peckham, dissented with an intensity equal to that he had exhibited in *Fong Yue Ting*.

The same spirit of acquiescence was manifest in the cases involving the civil rights of blacks, though here it was Harlan who kept the nation's conscience. In *Plessy v. Ferguson* (1896) the Court upheld a Louisiana statute requiring racial SEGREGATION of rail cars; Harlan dissented and, borrowing a line from Plessy's lawyer, Albion Tourgee, insisted that "our Constitution is colorblind." In HODGES V. UNITED STATES (1906) the Court dismissed a federal INDICTMENT against a group of white citizens in Arkansas who forced a mill owner to discharge the blacks who had been hired. Brewer, for the majority, said that the power of the federal government under the Civil War-Reconstruction amendments (and thus under the criminal statute in question) extended only to acts by state officials. He reaffirmed the principle of the CIVIL RIGHTS CASES of 1883 by which the Court effectively ceded to the states exclusive jurisdiction to govern the treatment of one citizen by another. In *Hodges,* Harlan, the Union general from Kentucky, replayed his dissent in the *Civil Rights* cases, and denounced this principle as a fundamental distortion of the Thirteenth and Fourteenth Amendments. And in BEREA COLLEGE V. KENTUCKY (1908) the Court, over Harlan's dissent, upheld a state law that prohibited a private educational corporation from conducting its educational programs on an integrated basis.

Berea College was also written by Brewer. He was mindful of the contrast with a case such as *Lochner,* where the judicial power had been used to the utmost to protect the contractual freedom of worker and employer. Accordingly, Brewer stressed the fact that this law was applicable only to CORPORATIONS, which, to pick up a theme he had previously articulated in his concurring opinion in *Northern Securities,* were merely artificial entities created by government, not entitled to the same degree of protection as natural persons. He specifically left open the question of the validity of a similar statute if it regulated the conduct of natural persons. Harlan, in an equally equivocal dissent, said that a different result might follow if the statute regulated public rather than private education. In fact, the distorting impact of public subsidies upon the articulation of civil rights had been implicitly acknowledged some years earlier in *Cumming v. Board of Education* (1899). In that case Harlan dismissed a challenge by black parents to a decision of a local county, which ran its schools on a segregated basis, to close the only black high school and to send the black students out of the county for their education.

In the 1890s and early 1900s blacks, through one scheme or another, were disenfranchised on a grand scale. The FIFTEENTH AMENDMENT was reduced to a nullity, as Jim Crow was becoming more firmly entrenched. On several occasions, the Court was presented with challenges to these electoral practices, yet it was unable to respond with the energy that it had summoned in *Pollock* or *Lochner* or *Reagan* or, even more to the point, *Debs.* Holmes, the spokesman

in these early VOTING RIGHTS cases, saw judicial relief as nothing but an "empty form": "[R]elief from a great political wrong, if done, as alleged, by the people of a State and the State itself, must be given by them or by the legislative and political department of the government of the United States." Harlan dissented, as might be expected, but so did Brewer. They realized that, because the disenfranchisement was the work of state officials, something more was at issue than the allocation of power between states and nation approved in the *Civil Rights Cases.* What was at issue, according to Brewer and Harlan, was nothing less than the integrity of the judicial power and the duty of the judiciary, to borrow a line from *Debs,* to do whatever it could to fulfill the promise of the Constitution.

The principal issue before the Court at the turn of the century was democracy and, more specifically, the determination of what limits should be placed on popular majorities. As was evident in the civil rights cases, however, the Court was also asked to allocate power between the states and the national government. The FEDERALISM issue arose in many contexts, including antitrust, labor, and rate regulation, but the one in which it proved most troublesome was PROHIBITION. By the late 1880s the prohibition movement was an active force in the states, and Fuller began his Chief Justiceship with a set of constitutional decisions that were unstable. In MUGLER V. KANSAS (1887) the Court had held that prohibition was within the STATE POLICE POWER, yet, just weeks before Chief Justice MORRISON R. WAITE's death, the Court in *Bowman v. Iowa* (1888) had also held that the states were without power to prohibit the importation of liquor from other states. The Court seemed to take away in one decision what it gave in the other. Fuller confronted this problem early on in LEISY V. HARDIN (1890), and in probably his most lasting contribution to constitutional law, fashioned an odd response. First, he announced that the commerce clause barred the states from prohibiting the sale of imported liquor (as well as its actual importation). Second, he invited Congress to intervene, and to authorize states to pass laws that would prohibit out-of-state liquor. Congress quickly responded to this invitation, and in the Wilson Act of 1890 authorized states to enact measures aimed at erecting walls to out-of-state liquor.

The state laws in question in *Leisy v. Hardin* were invalidated on the theory that they sought to regulate a matter that required nationwide uniformity. When it came to judging the congressional response, Fuller found the requisite uniformity since it was Congress that had spoken (even though it did no more than allow the states to choose) and on that theory, in *In re Rahrer* (1891), upheld the Wilson Act. In 1898, however, after some change in the composition of the Court and after the responsibility of speaking on this issue had shifted to one of the new appointees, Edward White, a sharply divided Court cut back on the Wilson Act. *Rhodes v. Iowa* (1890) held that the Wilson Act authorized a ban on sales of imported liquor within the state but not a ban on the importation itself. White insisted that any other construction would raise grave constitutional doubts as to the validity of the Wilson Act. Fuller joined White's opinion.

Over the next decade, mail order business in out-of-state liquor grew. The conflict between the Court and the prohibition movement escalated. Then in 1913 Congress, as part of the same era that saw the Sixteenth Amendment and the Clayton Act, passed the WEBB-KENYON ACT to remove any ambiguity over what it sought to accomplish in the Wilson Act. Congress allowed states to bar both the sale and the importation of out-of-state liquor. After considerable struggle and deliberation, the Webb-Kenyon Act was upheld in an opinion by White (then Chief Justice) on the theory (if that is what it can be called) that "liquor is different." For all other goods, the common market was deemed a constitutional necessity.

The federalism issue has recurred throughout the entire history of the Supreme Court. The Court over which Fuller presided did, however, confront one issue pertaining to structure of government that was unique to the times: colonialism. The issue arose from the "splendid little war," as Secretary of State John Hay called the Spanish-American War of 1898, which left the United States with two former Spanish colonies, PUERTO RICO and the Philippines. (Much earlier the United States had purchased Alaska, and in the late 1890s it had also taken possession of Hawaii.) The assumption was that the United States would hold these territories as territories, for an indefinite period, and perhaps ultimately build a colonial empire along the European model. The question posed for the Supreme Court—not just by the litigants but by the nation at large—was whether colonialism was a constitutionally permissible strategy for the United States. Technically, the case involved a challenge to a statute imposing a tariff on goods (sugar) imported from Puerto Rico into the states. The Constitution bars Congress from imposing duties on the importation of goods from one state to another, and so the issue was whether a territory was to be treated the same as a state, or, as phrased in the language of the day, whether the Constitution followed the flag.

Three positions emerged in a series of decisions beginning in 1901 known as the INSULAR CASES. The first, most in keeping with the position of the Court in *Pollock* and the other economic cases, proclaimed the idea of limited government. The government of the United States was formed and established by the Constitution, and thus it was impossible to conceive of a separation of Constitution and government. This was the position taken by Brewer, Peckham, Fuller, and Harlan. At the opposite end of the spectrum was the so-called annexation position. It proclaimed the separation of Constitution and flag, and generally left the government unrestricted in its activities in the territories; whatever restrictions there were flowed from natural law or from a small group of provisions of the Constitution deemed essential (the tariff provision was not one). This position was most congenial to the government and yet at odds with the general jurisprudence of the Court. Only Justice Brown subscribed to it.

The remaining four Justices, in an opinion written by White, put forth what was called the incorporation theory. It tried to chart a middle course, as appeared to be White's trade. It made the Constitution fully applicable to a territory, but only after that territory was incorporated into the United States. (Prior to incorporation the government would be subject only to the restraints of natural law.) Justice White's opinion also made it clear that the decision to incorporate a territory resided in Congress. In the case before it the Court decided that the territory was not incorporated, but White also acknowledged that incorporation could be done by implication and, even more to the point, he reserved for the judiciary the power to determine whether that act of incorporation had taken place.

Ultimately incorporation was adopted as the position of the Court. But this did not occur until 1905, after an insurrection in the Phillipines and other developments in the world (such as the Boer War) had made the idea of a colonial empire seem less attractive, and the danger of further imperial acquisitions seemed to have waned. In fact, incorporation became majority doctrine in *Rassmussen v. United States* (1905) in which the Court held that Alaska had been *implicitly* incorporated and that the United States was bound by the BILL OF RIGHTS in its governance of that territory. The outcome in this case affirmed the idea of limited government and JUDICIAL SUPREMACY, the hallmarks of this Court, and made it possible for Fuller, and perhaps even more significantly, for Brewer and Peckham, to abandon their absolutist position and to support the middle-of-the-road theory of White—perhaps a sign of what was to come in 1910, when Fuller died and Taft, who had once served as the commissioner in the Philippines, replaced him with White.

OWEN M. FISS

Bibliography

DUKER, WILLIAM 1980 Mr. Justice Rufus W. Peckham: The Police Power and the Individual in a Changing World. *Brigham Young University Law Review* 1980:47–67.

———— 1980 Mr. Justice Rufus W. Peckham and the Case of *Ex Parte Young:* Lochnerizing *Munn v. Illinois. Brigham Young University Law Review* 1980:539–558.

GOODWYN, LAWRENCE 1976 *Democratic Promise: The Populist Movement in America.* New York: Oxford University Press.

KING, WILLARD 1967 *Melville Weston Fuller, Chief Justice of the United States, 1888–1910.* Chicago: University of Chicago Press.

KOLKO, GABRIEL 1963 *The Triumph of Conservatism: A Reinterpretation of American History 1900–1916.* New York: Free Press.

PAUL, ARNOLD 1960 *Conservative Crisis and the Rule of Law: Attitudes of Bar and Bench 1887–1895.* Ithaca, N.Y.: Cornell University Press.

PIERCE, CARL 1972 A Vacancy on the Supreme Court: The Politics of Judicial Appointment, 1893–1894. *Tennessee Law Review* 39:555–612.

ROCHE, JOHN 1974 *Sentenced to Life.* New York: Macmillan.

ROGAT, YOSAL 1963 The Judge as Spectator. *University of Chicago Law Review* 31:231–278.

THORELLI, HANS 1954 *The Federal Antitrust Policy: Origination of an American Tradition.* Baltimore: Johns Hopkins University Press.

TWISS, BENJAMIN 1942 *Lawyers and the Constitution: How Laissez Faire Came to the Supreme Court.* Princeton, N.J.: Princeton University Press.

WESTIN, ALAN 1953 The Supreme Court, the Populist Movement and the Campaign of 1896. *Journal of Politics* 15:3–41.

———— 1958 Stephen J. Field and the Headnote to *O'Neil v. Vermont:* A Snapshot of the Fuller Court at Work. *Yale Law Journal* 67:363–383.

WOODWARD, C. VANN 1966 *The Strange Career of Jim Crow,* rev. ed. New York: Oxford University Press.

FULL FAITH AND CREDIT

The full faith and credit clause of the Constitution (Article IV, section 1) provides that: "Full Faith and Credit shall be given in each State to the public Acts, Records and judicial Proceedings of every other State. And the Congress may by general Laws prescribe the Manner in which such Acts, Records and Proceedings shall be proved, and the Effect thereof."

The first sentence of the clause closely tracked language contained in Article IV of the ARTICLES OF CONFEDERATION, the precursor of our present Constitution. The second sentence, which authorizes Congress to enact implementing legislation, was new. "Faith and credit" was a familiar term in English law where it had been used on occasion for some centuries to describe the respect owed to judgments and other public records. Its precise meaning, however, was obscure; it was not clear whether it was concerned only with the admission of public records, including judgments, into evidence or whether it was intended to deal likewise with the effect as RES JUDICATA to which a judgment was entitled. There is similar uncertainty with respect to the meaning which the term was intended to bear in the Articles of Confederation.

The subject of full faith and credit evoked little discussion in the CONSTITUTIONAL CONVENTION, and it seems unlikely that there was any general understanding among the delegates of what the clause was designed to accomplish. In any event, Congress was quick to exercise its power to pass implementing legislation. The initial statute was enacted in 1790 by the First Congress. It provided for the manner of authenticating the acts of the legislatures and of the records and judicial proceedings of the several states and concluded that "the said records and judicial proceedings shall have such faith and credit given to them in every court of the United States, as they have by law or usage in the courts of the State from whence the said records are or shall be taken." The second congressional act, that of 1804, extended the scope of full faith and credit by requiring that the same measure of respect should be given to the records and judicial proceedings of the TERRITORIES of the United States and of the countries subject to its JURISDICTION.

Judicial decisions have now made clear many things that the full faith and credit clause and its implementing statutes left uncertain. The Supreme Court has decided that, provided the requirements of jurisdiction, NOTICE, and opportunity to be heard have been satisfied, a judgment rendered in one state, territory, or possession of the United States shall in general be given the same res judicata effect that it has in the state of its rendition. Exceptions to this rule, if any there be, are few indeed. A state cannot, for example, deny effect to a judgment on the ground that the underlying claim was contrary to its public policy. Initially, some might have wondered whether Congress was empowered to extend the protection of full faith and credit to the records and judicial proceedings of territories and possessions of the United States. The full faith and credit clause itself gives no such authority, but the Supreme Court has held that this is to be found in those provisions of the Constitution that afford the United States with JUDICIAL POWER (Article III), authorize LEGISLATION that is NECESSARY AND PROPER to execute the powers entrusted to the federal government (Article II, section 8), and provide that the Constitution and the laws and treaties of the United States shall be the supreme law of the land (Article VI). Neither the clause nor the implementing statute refer to judgments of the federal courts. The Supreme Court has filled this gap by holding that these judgments are entitled to the same respect that is owed to state judgments.

A sharp distinction must be drawn between the recognition and the enforcement of judgments. With respect to recognition, the Supreme Court has held, as has already been said, that a judgment must be given the same res judicata effect that it enjoys under the law of the state of its rendition. On the other hand, the method of enforcing a judgment is determined by the law of the state where enforcement is sought. It is therefore for this latter law to determine whether a new action in the nature of debt must be brought on the judgment or whether it can be enforced by means of a registration procedure.

Full faith and credit is not owed to the judgments of foreign countries. Each state of the United States determines for itself the measure of respect that such judgments are to receive in its courts. Perhaps because of their experience in giving full faith and credit to federal and sister state judgments, American courts are extremely liberal, perhaps the most liberal in the world, in giving respect to the judgments of other countries.

The intentions of the original Framers may have been obscure. But the Supreme Court has said that the full faith and credit clause should become "a nationally unifying force" by establishing "throughout the federal system the salutary principle of the COMMON LAW that a litigation once pursued to judgment shall be as conclusive of the rights of the parties in every other court as in that where the judgment was rendered."

It will have been noted that whereas the full faith and credit clause speaks of "public Acts, Records and judicial Proceedings," the implementing statutes of 1790 and 1804 required only that full faith and credit be given to records and judicial proceedings. No definite information is available on why public acts were omitted, but it can be surmised that this omission was deliberate and stemmed from the realization that the circumstances, if any, in which one state should be required to apply another's law presented considerations infinitely more complex than those involving the recognition and enforcement of judgments. (See CHOICE OF LAW.) After some years, the Supreme Court held that the clause was self-executing and that there were limited circumstances in which a state was required to apply another's laws. By and large, the Supreme Court has now withdrawn from its earlier opinions and today the command of full faith and credit with respect to public acts is slight indeed. The Supreme Court has, however, held that full faith and credit imposes limitations upon the power of a state to refuse on public policy grounds to entertain suit on a claim arising under the law of a sister state. It can be expected that in due course restrictions will likewise be placed upon a state's power to dismiss a suit on the ground that the claim involved is one for a penalty.

The implementing statute remained substantially unchanged from 1804 to 1948. In the latter year, it was amended as part of a general revision of Title 28 of the United States Code. This revision was not intended to make controversial substantive changes in the law. Nevertheless, the implementing statute was amended to require that full faith and credit be given not only to records and judicial proceedings, as had been the case heretofore, but to acts as well. It seems improbable that this change in wording will lead to any substantial change in the law. No such change was presumably intended by the revisers, and, to date, the amendment has not influenced the decisions of the courts. But, taken literally, the statute, as now worded, requires the same measure of respect for statutes that it does for judgments. There is always the possibility that at some time in the future the courts will seize upon this new language to make substantial changes in what is owed under full faith and credit to the statutes of sister states and of United States territories and possessions.

WILLIS L. M. REESE

Bibliography

AMERICAN LAW INSTITUTE 1971 Restatement of the Law: Conflict of Laws, Second. Chap. 5, pages 271–348. St. Paul, Minn.: American Law Institute Publishers.

NADELMANN, KURT 1957 Full Faith and Credit to Judgments and Public Acts. Michigan Law Review 56:33–88.

WHITTEN, RALPH U. 1981 The Constitutional Limitations on State-Court Jurisdiction: An Historical-Interpretative Reexamination of the Full Faith and Credit and Due Process Clauses. *Creighton Law Review* 14:499–606.

FULLILOVE v. KLUTZNICK
448 U.S. 448 (1980)

The Supreme Court's fragmentation in REGENTS OF UNIVERSITY OF CALIFORNIA V. BAKKE (1978) left open the question of the constitutionality of government-imposed RACIAL QUOTAS or preferences. The following year, in UNITED STEELWORKERS V. WEBER, the Court held that a voluntary AFFIRMATIVE ACTION plan, calling for a racial quota in hiring by a private employer and approved by a union, did not violate Title VII of the CIVIL RIGHTS OF 1964. *Fullilove* reopened *Bakke*'s question: Can government impose a racial quota to remedy the effects of past discrimination?

Congress, in a public works statute aimed at reducing unemployment, provided that ten percent of the funds distributed to each state should be set aside for contracts with "minority business enterprises" (MBE). An MBE was defined as a business at least half owned by persons who are "Negroes, Spanish-speaking, Orientals, Indians, Eskimos and Aleuts." Nonminority contractors challenged this limitation as a denial of the Fifth Amendment's guarantee of EQUAL PROTECTION, as recognized in BOLLING V. SHARPE (1954) and later cases.

The Supreme Court held, 6–3, that the MBE limitation was valid. Three Justices, speaking through Chief Justice WARREN E. BURGER, paid great deference to Congress's judgment that the racial quota was a "limited and properly tailored remedy to cure the effects of past RACIAL DISCRIMINATION." Emphasizing the flexibility provided for the law's administration, they said that the funds could be limited to MBEs that were in fact disadvantaged because of race. The other three majority Justices, speaking through Justice THURGOOD MARSHALL, took the position they had taken in *Bakke,* concluding that the racial quota was "substantially related to . . . the important and congressionally articulated goal of remedying the present effects of past racial discrimination."

Justice POTTER STEWART, joined by Justice WILLIAM H. REHNQUIST, dissented; they would forbid any statutory racial classification, allowing race-conscious remedies only in cases of proven illegal discrimination. Justice JOHN PAUL STEVENS was not prepared

to take so absolute a position but dissented here because Congress had not sufficiently articulated the reasons for its racial quota and tailored its program to those reasons.

KENNETH L. KARST

FUNDAMENTAL INTERESTS

The idea that some interests are fundamental, and thus deserving of a greater measure of constitutional protection than is given to other interests, is an old one. Justice BUSHROD WASHINGTON, sitting on circuit in CORFIELD V. CORYELL (1823), held that the PRIVILEGES AND IMMUNITIES clause of Article IV of the Constitution protected out-of-staters against discriminatory state legislation touching only those privileges that were "in their very nature, fundamental; which belong, of right, to the citizens of all free governments." Washington's list of such interests was limited but significant: free passage through a state; HABEAS CORPUS; the right to sue in state courts; the right to hold and dispose of property; freedom from discriminatory taxation.

Although the *Corfield* doctrine suggested an active role for the federal judiciary in protecting NATURAL RIGHTS against state interference—at least on behalf of citizens of other states—the doctrine was not embraced by the full Supreme Court during Washington's lifetime. If some hoped that the FOURTEENTH AMENDMENT's privileges and immunities clause would breathe new life into the fundamental rights theory, those hopes were disappointed in the SLAUGHTERHOUSE CASES (1873). Rejecting the theory as propounded in two eloquent dissenting opinions, the Court again refused to find any special federal constitutional protection against state invasions of preferred rights.

Within a generation, however, the Court had identified a cluster of preferred rights of property and the FREEDOM OF CONTRACT, to be defended against various forms of ECONOMIC REGULATION. The Court did not use the language of fundamental interests; for doctrinal support it avoided both privileges and immunities clauses, relying instead on a theory of SUBSTANTIVE DUE PROCESS. When this doctrinal development played out in the late 1930s, the Court abandoned its STRICT SCRUTINY of business regulation in favor of a STANDARD OF REVIEW demanding no more than a RATIONAL BASIS for legislative judgments.

Even as the Court adopted its new permissive attitude toward economic regulation, it was laying the groundwork for another round of protections of preferred rights. (See UNITED STATES V. CAROLENE PRODUCTS CO., 1938; SKINNER V. OKLAHOMA, 1942.) When the WARREN COURT set about its expansion of the reach of EQUAL PROTECTION doctrine, it not only followed these precedents but also revived the rhetoric of fundamental interests. A state law discriminating against the exercise of such an interest, the Court held, must be justified as necessary for achieving a COMPELLING STATE INTEREST.

The Warren Court hinted strongly that it would expand the list of fundamental interests demanding strict judicial scrutiny to include all manner of claims to equality. In fact, the Court's holdings placed only a limited number of interests in the "fundamental" category: VOTING RIGHTS and related interests in the electoral process; some limited rights of ACCESS TO THE COURTS; and rights relating to marriage, the family, and other intimate relationships. Even so modest a doctrinal development evoked the strong dissent of Justice JOHN MARSHALL HARLAN: "I know of nothing which entitles this Court to pick out particular human activities, characterize them as 'fundamental,' and give them added protection under an unusually stringent equal protection test."

The BURGER COURT, making Harlan's lament its theme song, called a halt to the expansion of fundamental interests occasioning strict judicial scrutiny under the equal protection clause. However, in cases touching marriage and other close personal relationships, the Court continued to promote the notion of fundamental liberties deserving of special protection—now on a substantive due process theory. (See ABORTION AND THE CONSTITUTION; ILLEGITIMACY; FREEDOM OF INTIMATE ASSOCIATION.) The notion of natural rights as part of our constitutional law is deeply ingrained. Our modern doctrines about fundamental rights are novel only in the particular interests they have termed fundamental.

KENNETH L. KARST

Bibliography

TRIBE, LAURENCE H. 1978 American Constitutional Law. Chaps. 8, 11, 15, and 16. Mineola, N.Y.: Foundation Press. 000 002

FUNDAMENTAL LAW
(History)

The institution of a written CONSTITUTION as fundamental law superior to and limiting ordinary statutory law and government, which we now take for granted, was distinctively American. The concept of fundamental law embodied in a written constitution was one of the most influential and radical ideas to emerge from the American Revolution. It involved a break with the recent English past.

The notion of fundamental law has had a continuing history in Western political thought. Mid-seventeenth century Englishmen anticipated the use of a written constitution as the foundation of government, but the half-hearted experiment did not last. Fundamental law remained an ill-defined and vague term then, standing for the customary constitution as distinguished from revolutionary change. Parliamentarians accused Charles I and James II of attempting by arbitrary acts to subvert the fundamental laws of the realm, especially the traditional rights of liberty and property. Although interest in fundamental law declined in the eighteenth century, the concept never lost its attractiveness for the English. However, the growing acceptance of the omnipotence of Parliament made the idea of a single written instrument creating and limiting the government decidedly obsolete, because no restraints existed on parliamentary power, and for that reason Americans would finally repudiate the unwritten English constitution as less than the embodiment of truly fundamental law.

Reformist ideas about law, current in early seventeenth-century England, influenced the settlers of early America in the creation of their legal systems. The colonists developed a conception of the sources and nature of law that was much more expansive than the traditionally narrow conception of the English COMMON LAW. This broad approach reflected the fundamentally altered state of many aspects of law in the New World. Leaders of the American colonies also assimilated new currents in political thought which led to the conclusion that fundamental or natural law lay behind the civil law of every nation. Fundamental law became equated in their minds with natural law or the law of nature. Many residents of the New World regarded their charters from the crown as a fundamental source for their basic rights as Englishmen.

The revolutionary ferment of the 1760s and 1770s in the American colonies produced the idea of a written constitution embodying fundamental law. Americans regarded as unconstitutional several of Parliament's statutes governing America. In 1761 JAMES OTIS argued that WRITS OF ASSISTANCE were "against the fundamental Principles of Law." Like the English a century earlier, Americans gravitated toward an understanding of a constitution as something antecedent and paramount to all branches of government, including even their legislative representatives. Fundamental law controlled statutory law. A 1760 *Letter to the People of Pennsylvania* noted the relevance to forming a plan of government of "the fundamental laws and rules of the constitution, which ought never to be infringed. . . ." Writing against the authority of Parliament over the colonies in 1774, JOHN ADAMS regarded New Englanders as deriving their laws "not from parliament, not from common law, but from the law of nature and the compact made with the king in our charter. . . . English liberties are but certain rights of nature, reserved to the citizen by the English constitution, which rights cleaved to our ancestors when they crossed the Atlantic. . . ."

The process of state constitution-making that began in 1776 led to eleven written constitutions by 1780, but the basic and largely unchanging nature of such documents was not fully recognized in practice in the first decade, mainly because the first constitutions granted predominant power to the legislatures. Criticisms of excessive legislative activity in the 1780s led to general acceptance of the idea that constitutions should serve as fundamental laws to control legislatures. THOMAS JEFFERSON eagerly sought a Virginia constitution that the legislature could not easily change.

The American states gradually came to regard their written constitutions as fundamental or HIGHER LAWS superior to ordinary legislative acts—which meant restrictions on legislative power, because ordinary courts of law eventually implemented the written constitutions through a process of JUDICIAL REVIEW. The argument in favor of the innovative practice of judicial review was that fundamental laws were predominant. Thus the CONSTITUTIONAL CONVENTION that met in Philadelphia in 1787 accepted the notion that a legislature could not change a constitution without the calling of a special constitutional convention. The recognition of the new federal Constitution as a fundamental law required the calling of special ratifying conventions to avoid disputes about its legitimacy. This process of creating fundamental law through constitution-making was the source of the basic appeal of the American Revolution to continental Europeans.

DAVID H. FLAHERTY

Bibliography

GOUGH, J. W. (1955)1971 *Fundamental Law in English Constitutional History.* Oxford: Clarendon Press.
MULLETT, CHARLES F. (1933)1966 *Fundamental Law and the American Revolution 1760–1776.* New York: Octagon.
WOOD, GORDON S. 1969 *The Creation of the American Republic, 1776–1787.* Chapel Hill: University of North Carolina Press.

FUNDAMENTAL LAW AND THE SUPREME COURT

The DECLARATION OF INDEPENDENCE explicitly invoked the concept of natural justice—a HIGHER LAW, timeless and universal—as a defense against tyranny. By the late eighteenth century there had evolved a conviction that the essence of this fundamental law could at one stroke be captured in a document that would endure for ages to come. Of the original state constitutions several were declared in force without constituent ratification and some made no provision for amendment. By the time of the federal CONSTITUTIONAL CONVENTION OF 1787, these extreme forms of immutability had given way. Article V provided a formalized process of constitutional amendment, while Article VII conditioned adoption on ratification by state conventions. But the concept of written constitutions as the embodiment of fundamental law was central to the federal Constitution and to later state constitutions.

The issue whether fundamental law had other appropriate functions in the American constitutional scheme arose early among Justices of the Supreme Court of the United States, and remains critical at the Constitution's bicentenary. Debate opened in CALDER V. BULL (1798). The Connecticut legislature had set aside a court decree refusing to probate a will, granting a new hearing at which the will was admitted. Denied relief in the state courts, the disappointed heir appealed to the Supreme Court. Outraged at the destruction of the heir's expectancy, Justice SAMUEL CHASE declared "it is against all reason and justice, for a people to intrust a legislature with such powers, and therefore, it cannot be presumed that they have done it." In Chase's view, the fundamental law could not tolerate "a law that takes property from A and gives it to B," even in the absence of constitutional prohibition. Justice JAMES IREDELL challenged this claim of extraconstitutional power to nullify legislation, insisting that if legislation is within constitutional limits "the Court cannot pronounce it to be void, merely because it is, in their judgment, contrary to the principles of natural justice."

Iredell's logic prevailed in *Calder* but in the long run could not hold the line. Chief Justice JOHN MARSHALL hedged on the question in FLETCHER V. PECK (1810), declaring that Georgia's attempt to revoke fraudulent land grants was void "either by general principles which are common to our free institutions, or by the particular provisions of the constitution of the United States. . . ." Similarly, Justice JOSEPH STORY rested the Court's opinion in TERRETT V. TAYLOR (1815) upon several grounds, among them "the principles of natural justice" and "the spirit and letter of the [federal] constitution. . . ." LOAN ASSOCIATION V. TOPEKA (1874), although decided following ratification of the FOURTEENTH AMENDMENT, was grounded by Justice SAMUEL F. MILLER on extraconstitutional principles founded in fundamental law. The taking from A (by taxation) in aid of B (bridge manufacturer not a public utility) was stricken as an "unauthorized invasion of private right." In contrast, DRED SCOTT V. SANDFORD (1857) and HEPBURN V. GRISWOLD (1869) invalidated congressional "takings" under the Fifth Amendment's due process clause.

At the turn of the century the issue of extraconstitutional adjudication intensified with an OBITER DICTUM in ALLGEYER V. LOUISIANA (1897). With LOCHNER V. NEW YORK (1905) and ADAIR V. UNITED STATES (1908), the majority of the court opened a period in which much economic and social legislation was held unconstitutional, ostensibly under the due process clauses. However, the basis given was violation of FREEDOM OF CONTRACT, for which there was no constitutional warrant. Justice OLIVER WENDELL HOLMES, in his celebrated *Lochner* dissent, insisted that the Fourteenth Amendment, properly construed, should accord with "fundamental principles as they have been understood by the traditions of our people and our law." Yet to him that amendment correctly embraced condemnation of governmental expropriation of property from A for B's benefit, as he made clear in PENNSYLVANIA COAL CO. V. MAHON (1922). Justice LOUIS D. BRANDEIS there dissented, but he later invoked the identical principle under both due process clauses: the Fifth Amendment clause in *Wright v. Vinton Branch of Mountain Trust Bank* (1937) upholding a revised moratorium law, and the Fourteenth Amendment clause in *Thompson v. Consolidated Gas Utilities Corp.* (1937). In the latter he declared, "Our law reports present no more glaring instance of the taking of one man's property and giving it to another."

The *Lochner-Adair* venture into noninterpretive constitutionalism was rejected by a split vote in NEBBIA V. NEW YORK (1934), followed by unanimity in LINCOLN FEDERAL LABOR UNION V. NORTHWESTERN IRON & METAL CO. (1949). Yet only two years after categorical repudiation in FERGUSON V. SCRUPA (1963), the seductive appeal of the philosophy of *Lochner* and its progeny was back, this time in the service of noneconomic interests. In GRISWOLD V. CONNECTICUT (1965) the due process clause was used to invalidate an anticontraception law; in HARPER V. VIRGINIA BOARD OF ELECTIONS (1966) the EQUAL PROTECTION clause provided the basis for invalidating the POLL TAX as a condition for exercise of VOTING RIGHTS. In both cases the majority sought to ground decision in constitutional provisions, but Justice HUGO L. BLACK, unpersuaded, accused the Court of invoking "the old 'natural-law–due-process formula,'" which, he declared, "is no less dangerous when used to enforce this Court's views about personal rights than those about economic rights." ROE V. WADE (1973), insulating from governmental intervention a woman's decision to have an abortion during the first trimester of pregnancy, rested upon a doctrine of "personhood" demonstrably beyond the ambit of constitutional text, context, or structure. Reaffirmed in AKRON V. AKRON CENTER FOR REPRODUCTIVE HEALTH, INC. (1983) out of respect for STARE DECISIS, *Roe* highlights the Supreme Court's continuing temptation to give constitutional force to extraconstitutional values it finds lying in the recesses of unwritten fundamental law.

FRANK R. STRONG

Bibliography

GREY, THOMAS 1978 Origins of the Unwritten Constitution: Fundamental Law in American Revolutionary Thought. *Stanford Law Review* 30:843–893.
HAND, LEARNED 1960 *The Spirit of Liberty*, 3rd ed. New York: Knopf.
PERRY, MICHAEL 1982 *The Constitution, the Courts, and Human Rights*, chap. 4. Columbus: Ohio State University Press.

FUNDAMENTAL LAWS OF WEST NEW JERSEY

See: New Jersey, Colonial Charters of

FUNDAMENTAL ORDERS OF CONNECTICUT
(January 14, 1639)

Historians almost invariably refer to this document as a CONSTITUTION, indeed as the first written constitution of the modern world. It was very probably a statute enacted by a provisional legislative body representing the freemen of three towns meeting in Hartford. It was not, however, an ordinary statute, because it described a frame of government, though the statute lacked any explicit provision for amendment. The assembly or "general court" which enacted it, derived its powers from it but could and did alter it.

THOMAS HOOKER, the founder of Hartford and the leading divine of the colony, was probably the principal author of the document. In a 1638 sermon he had declared that the foundation of authority in both state and church was the free consent of the people expressed in a covenant or SOCIAL COMPACT; the people, according to Hooker, had power to appoint officers for their governance and "to set the bounds and limitations of the power and place unto which they call them." But the Fundamental Orders did not impose such limitations or reserve any rights that the government could not abridge.

The preamble stated that the inhabitants of the towns joined together to become "one Public State or Commonwealth" to preserve their churches and be governed according to laws made and administered by the officers described in the document. The people, "all that are admitted inhabitants," chose an assembly or "general court" which in turn annually elected a governor and magistrates, who together exercised the judicial power. The document empowered the general court to make laws, impose taxes, dispose of lands, and admit freemen and deputies from other towns. The general court, "the supreme power of the Commonwealth," consisted of the governor, magistrates, and deputies, who were guaranteed "liberty of speech," probably the progenitor of the SPEECH OR DEBATE CLAUSE in Article I, section 6, of the Constitution.

LEONARD W. LEVY

Bibliography

ANDREWS, CHARLES MCLEAN 1936 *The Colonial Period of American History.* Vol. 2, pages 94–113. New Haven, Conn.: Yale University Press.

FUNDAMENTAL RIGHTS

Inherent in the Anglo-Saxon heritage of DUE PROCESS OF LAW, the concept of fundamental rights defies facile analysis. Yet it constitutes one of those basic features of democracy that are the test of its presence. As defined by Justice FELIX FRANKFURTER, dissenting in *Solesbee v. Balkcom* (1950), it embraces "a system of rights based on moral principles so deeply embedded in the traditions and feelings of our people as to be deemed fundamental to a civilized society. . . ."

The Justice whom Frankfurter succeeded on the high bench, BENJAMIN N. CARDOZO, had spoken in *Snyder v. Massachusetts* (1934) of "principles of justice so rooted in the traditions and conscience of our people as to be deemed fundamental." Three years later, in PALKO V. CONNECTICUT, Cardozo articulated fundamental rights as "implicit in the concept of ORDERED LIBERTY." Because these rights are "fundamental," they have been accorded special protection by the judiciary, which has thus viewed them as PREFERRED FREEDOMS that command particularly STRICT SCRUTINY of their infringement by legislative or executive action. In other words, to pass judicial muster, laws or ordinances affecting fundamental rights must demonstrate a more or less "compelling need," whereas those affecting lesser rights need only be clothed with a RATIONAL BASIS justifying the legislative or executive action at issue.

But which among our rights fall on the "fundamental" and which on the "nonfundamental" side of constitutional protection? The Supreme Court commenced to endeavor to draw a dichotomous line in the turn-of-the-century INSULAR CASES: on the "fundamental" side now fell such rights as those present in the FIRST AMENDMENT (religion, FREEDOMS OF SPEECH, PRESS, ASSEMBLY, and PETITION); on the other side, styled "formal rights," fell such "procedural" rights or guarantees as those embedded in the FOURTH, Fifth, SIXTH, SEVENTH, and Eighth AMENDMENTS, including, for example, TRIAL BY JURY. Justice Cardozo reconfirmed the dichotomy with his *Palko* division, adding to the roster of "fundamental" rights those of assigned counsel to INDIGENT defendants in major criminal trials and the general right to a FAIR TRIAL. He relegated other procedural rights to the nonfundamental sphere, noting that "justice would not perish" in the absence of such "formal rights" at the state level.

Cardozo's dichotomy did not apply to the federal BILL OF RIGHTS, which was wholly enforceable against federal abridgment or denial by the terms of its specific provisions. He used it instead to explain which provisions of the Bill of Rights were, and which were not, made applicable to the states by the FOURTEENTH AMENDMENT. While the "formal" rights, as he explained, do have "value and importance . . . they are not of the essence of a scheme of ordered liberty. To abolish them is not to violate a principle of justice so rooted in the traditions and conscience of our people as to be deemed fundamental. . . . Few would be so narrow as to maintain that a fair and enlightened system of justice would be impossible without them." This dichotomy stood until the 1960s when, through acceleration of the process known as INCORPORATION or "absorption," most of the enumerated safeguards in the Bill of Rights were made applicable to the states by judicial decisions. The Supreme Court's rationale for these decisions was its expanding view of the nature and reach of "fundamental" rights. In practical affect, the incorporation doctrine no longer draws an appreciable distinction between "formal" and "fundamental" rights.

Yet concurrently the WARREN COURT gave new life to the notion that certain fundamental rights should be protected by heightened judicial scrutiny of laws limiting them. This development built on Justice HARLAN FISKE STONE's famed formulation in UNITED STATES v. CAROLENE PRODUCTS CO. (1938). Voting rights and rights concerning marriage, procreation, and family relationships were identified as "fundamental" and clothed with special judicial protection. The Warren Court's other chief category of occasions for strict scrutiny of legislation—that of SUSPECT CLASSIFICATIONS—can also be seen in a similar light. If race is a suspect classification, surely the reason is that no interest in civil society is more fundamental than being treated as a full-fledged member of the community.

In effect, although all but a few of the enumerated rights in the Constitution and its amendments are now regarded as *fundamental,* and thus fully entitled to thorough judicial protection and scrutiny, the Court has embraced a hierarchical or "tiered" formulation. Some fundamental rights thus remain preferred. To what extent that arrangement will stand the test of time and experience will depend chiefly upon the judiciary's perception.

HENRY J. ABRAHAM

Bibliography

ABRAHAM, HENRY J. 1987 *Freedom and the Court: Civil Rights and Liberties in the United States,* 5th ed. New York: Oxford University Press.

CORTNER, RICHARD C. 1981 *The Supreme Court and the Second Bill of Rights.* Madison: University of Wisconsin Press.

GUNTHER, GERALD 1972 The Supreme Court: 1971 Term; In Search of Evolving Doctrines on a Changing Court: A Model for a Newer Equal Protection. *Harvard Law Review* 86:1–48.

FURMAN v. GEORGIA

See: Capital Punishment Cases, 1972

FURNEAUX, PHILIP
(1726–1783)

Philip Furneaux, an English dissenter minister, in 1770 published a volume criticizing WILLIAM BLACKSTONE's exposition of the laws of toleration. Furneaux opposed all restraints on the expression of religious or irreligious opinions. He flatly rejected the BAD TENDENCY TEST, proposing in its place punishment of overt acts only. His book of 1770 was republished in Philadelphia in 1773 under the title *The Palladium of Conscience.* Furneaux influenced THOMAS JEFFERSON and the writing of the VIRGINIA STATUTE OF RELIGIOUS FREEDOM.

LEONARD W. LEVY

GAG ORDER

"Gag order" is the press's pejorative term for a judicial order forbidding public comment, usually about a pending criminal case. Judges issue the order in an effort to prevent publicity that might make it impossible for a criminal defendant to receive a fair trial by an impartial jury. The orders came into use as a result of criticism by the American Bar Association (ABA) and others of press coverage of notorious cases such as the 1932 kidnap-murder of Charles Lindbergh's baby, the murder trial of Dr. Sam Sheppard in 1954, and the assassination of President JOHN F. KENNEDY in 1963. Each of those cases generated a torrent of publicity, much of it prejudicial to the accused's right to a fair trial.

The Supreme Court first discussed gag orders in *Sheppard v. Maxwell* (1966), when it reversed Sheppard's conviction on the ground that he had been denied DUE PROCESS OF LAW. Although the decision turned on the trial judge's failure to control "the carnival atmosphere at trial" rather than prejudicial pretrial publicity, the Court went out of its way to suggest that the judge "should have made some effort to control the release of leads, information, and gossip to the press by police officers, witnesses, and the counsel for both sides."

This *obiter dictum* finally made pretrial publicity a constitutional, rather than merely ethical, issue. In 1968 an ABA committee promulgated new "Standards on Fair Trial and Free Press," endorsing prohibitions against release of information by lawyers and law enforcement officers. Gag orders then came into widespread use, usually over the vehement opposition of the press.

The ABA report distinguished between gag orders directed at lawyers and other trial participants and those directed at the press itself. It did not endorse the latter, fearing that restrictions on the press would violate the FIRST AMENDMENT. This distinction is still widely observed, even though gag orders against lawyers operate as prior restraints on speech just as surely as those against the press.

The constitutionality of gag orders reached the Supreme Court in NEBRASKA PRESS ASSOCIATION V. STUART (1976). In a multiple murder case a state trial judge had forbidden the local press to publish confessions or "other information strongly implicative of the accused as the perpetrator of the slayings." The Supreme Court treated the order as a prior restraint on publication, and held it unconstitutional because there was no showing that less drastic alternatives, such as postponement or sequestration of jurors, would have been insufficient to protect the defendant's right to a fair trial. The Court also doubted the efficacy of the order, because of difficulties in controlling publicity by media beyond the trial judge's jurisdiction and by word of mouth within the community.

The *Stuart* opinion stopped short of saying that all gag orders against the press are unconstitutional, but three members of the Court would have said so, and two others doubted that such orders could ever be justified. Since *Stuart*, gag orders against the press have been rare. The Court reserved judgment on orders against trial participants, however, and these continue to be issued with some frequency. The lower courts generally have upheld narrowly drawn restrictions against lawyers and defendants when judges have determined that they are necessary to prevent a "reasonable likelihood" or "a serious and imminent threat" of interference with a fair trial.

DAVID A. ANDERSON

(SEE ALSO: *Free Press/Fair Trial.*)

Bibliography

BARRON, JEROME A. and DIENES, C. THOMAS 1979 *Handbook of Free Speech and Free Press.* Boston: Little, Brown.

HALLAM, OSCAR 1940 Some Object Lessons on Publicity in Criminal Trials. *Minnesota Law Review* 24:454–508.

PORTMAN, SHELDON 1977 The Defense of Fair Trial from *Sheppard* to *Nebraska Press Association:* Benign Neglect to Affirmative Action and Beyond. *Stanford Law Review* 29:393–410.

GAG RULE

See: Civil Liberties and the Slavery Controversy; Freedom of Petition; Slavery and the Constitution

GALLAGHER v. CROWN KOSHER SUPER MARKET

See: Sunday Closing Laws

GALLATIN, ALBERT
(1761–1849)

Born in Geneva, Switzerland, Albert Gallatin came to America in 1780 and settled in western Pennsylvania. He opposed RATIFICATION OF THE CONSTITUTION because he thought the union too consolidated and the presidency too monarchial. In 1788–1789, as a delegate to the Pennsylvania state CONSTITUTIONAL CONVENTION, Gallatin spoke out for virtually universal suffrage and for popular election of United States senators.

Gallatin served three terms in the Pennsylvania Assembly (1790–1792), where he was leader of the Republican minority. He there advocated public education and INTERNAL IMPROVEMENTS. In 1792 he was secretary of a convention called to denounce ALEXANDER HAMILTON's federal whiskey excise, and he drafted a petition to Congress against the excise; but two years later he publicly opposed the violence of the WHISKEY REBELLION.

Elected to the United States Senate in 1793, Gallatin was denied his seat on the grounds that he had not been a citizen for the requisite nine years. From 1795 until 1801 he served in the House of Representatives, the last four years as Republican floor leader; he rigorously opposed the ALIEN AND SEDITION ACTS.

As secretary of the treasury under Presidents THOMAS JEFFERSON and JAMES MADISON (1801–1814) Gallatin attempted to reorganize public finance on a Republican basis by abolishing both the national debt and all internal taxes and supporting the government by revenue from the tariff and sale of public lands. That design was ultimately frustrated by the War of 1812. During his tenure at the Treasury, Gallatin introduced more efficient statistical accountability and began the practice of issuing annual reports to Congress of revenues and expenditures.

In 1814 Gallatin helped negotiate peace with Great Britain. He continued his diplomatic career as minister to France (1816–1823) and to Britain (1826–1827). He later became a bank president and devoted his leisure to the study of American Indian languages.

DENNIS J. MAHONEY

GALLOWAY, JOSEPH
(1731–1803)

A conservative political leader, Joseph Galloway long sought compromise with England. At the First Continental Congress (1774) he proposed establishment of an "inferior and distinct" branch of Parliament in America. A president-general, chosen by the king, would preside over a "grand council," execute its acts (to which he must assent), and direct all matters concerning more than one colony. Approval by both this council and Parliament would be required for all "general acts," but each colony would retain its own government. Galloway's plan lost by one vote. Although he opposed a parliamentary tax and defended the colonies' right to govern themselves, he accepted parliamentary supremacy and understood English attempts to have the colonies share in the cost of their defense. Galloway's loyalism doomed him to exile after Philadelphia's capture by American forces in 1778.

DAVID GORDON

Bibliography

WERNER, RAYMOND C. 1931 Joseph Galloway. In *Dictionary of American Biography*. New York: Scribner's.

GANNETT CO., INC. v. DEPASQUALE
443 U.S. 368 (1978)

In *Gannett* the trial judge excluded the public, including the press, from a pretrial hearing involving evidence of an involuntary confession in a highly publicized murder case. The Supreme Court rejected arguments that the Sixth Amendment provided a constitutional public right to attend criminal trials. Reasoning that the constitutional guarantee of a public trial is designed to benefit the defendant, not the public, the Court concluded that where the litigants agree to close a pretrial proceeding to protect the defendant's right to a FAIR TRIAL, the Constitution does not require that it remain open to the public. The Court declined to address the corollary issue whether the FIRST AMENDMENT created a right of access to the press to attend criminal trials—a question later answered affirmatively in RICHMOND NEWSPAPERS, INC. V. VIRGINIA (1980).

Justice LEWIS F. POWELL, concurring, conceded that the press had an interest, protected by the First Amendment, in being present at the pretrial hearing, but said that this interest should be balanced against the defendant's right to a fair trial. The order excluding the press from attending the pretrial hearing in *Gannett* was distinguished from the GAG ORDER in NEBRASKA PRESS ASSOCIATION V. STUART (1976) because the press was merely excluded from one source of information; it was not told what it might or might not publish.

Justice HARRY A. BLACKMUN, joined by Justices WILLIAM J. BRENNAN, BYRON R. WHITE, and THURGOOD MARSHALL, also framed the issue as one of access to the judicial proceeding, not one of prior restraint on the press. Blackmun, upon a lengthy historical examination, concluded that the criminally accused did not have a right to compel a private pretrial proceeding or trial. Only in certain circumstances, with appropriate procedural safeguards, might a court give effect to the accused's attempts to waive the right to a public trial.

KIM MCLANE WARDLAW

(SEE ALSO: *Free Press/Fair Trial*.)

GARCIA v. SAN ANTONIO METROPOLITAN TRANSIT AUTHORITY
469 U.S.   (1985)

In NATIONAL LEAGUE OF CITIES V. USERY (1976) a 5–4 majority of the Supreme Court sought to establish a new doctrinal foundation for the concept of STATES' RIGHTS. Overruling its eight-year-old PRECEDENT in *Maryland v. Wirtz* (1968), the Court held unconstitutional the application of the wage and hour provisions of the federal FAIR LABOR STANDARDS ACT to state and local government employees in areas of "traditional governmental functions" such as police and fire protection. After eight more years, *Garcia* followed *Wirtz* and overruled *Usery*—again by 5–4 vote. Justice HARRY A. BLACKMUN, whose change of vote produced this second about-face, wrote the OPINION OF THE COURT.

Lower court decisions following *Usery*, said Justice Blackmun, had failed to establish any principle for determining which governmental functions were "traditional" and essential to state sovereignty, and thus immune from impairment by congressional regulations. Justice Blackmun did not mention his own contribution to the confusion, first in his *Usery* concurrence, which suggested that the reach of Congress's power depended on the importance of the national interests at stake, and later in his votes to uphold congressional power in cases only doubtfully distinguishable from *Usery*, such as *Federal Regulatory Commission v. Mississippi* (1982) and EQUAL EMPLOYMENT OPPORTUNITY COMMISSION V. WYOMING (1983). The reasoning in those opinions—heatedly disputed by the four *Garcia* dissenters—had sapped *Usery*'s strength as a precedent by making the states pass through a doctrinal labyrinth before *Usery* could be applied.

The aspect of the *Garcia* opinion that drew the most fire, from within the Court and from the outside, was its announcement of the Court's virtual abdication from JUDICIAL REVIEW of acts of Congress challenged as invasions of state SOVEREIGNTY. The principal remedy for such potential abuses of congressional power, said Justice Blackmun, is not judicial but political. The constitutional structure assures the states a significant role in the selection of the national government; the influence of the states was demonstrated in the federal government's financial aid to the states and in the numerous exemptions for state activities provided in congressional regulations. The Court's abdication was not complete; Justice Blackmun acknowledged that some "affirmative limits . . . on federal action affecting the States" may remain. Yet he explicitly left to another day the specification of what those limits might be.

Justice LEWIS F. POWELL wrote the main opinion for the four dissenters. He began with a lament for the demise of STARE DECISIS—which he had not mourned when *Usery* overruled *Wirtz*. The *Usery* principle had been "reiterated consistently over the past eight years," he said—not mentioning that those same opinions uniformly had sustained congressional regulations against challenges founded on *Usery*. Justice Powell argued that the majority had abandoned the FEDERALISM envisioned by the Framers, leaving the states' role to "the grace of elected federal officials." In any event, he contended, the "political safeguards of federalism" are not what they used to be. Congressional regulatory techniques have changed, increasingly displacing or commandeering the states' sovereign functions. Furthermore, although the people of the states are represented in the federal government, the state governments as institutions are apt to have little influence on national decision making, in comparison with nationwide interest groups.

Some of the dissenters left no doubt that they expect the *Usery* principle to return when members of the *Garcia* majority are replaced by new Justices more attuned to the symbolism of states' rights. But symbolism may be all that is left of that once vital principle, whatever the future may hold for the *Garcia* precedent. First, Congress can dragoon the state into its regulatory schemes as it did in HODEL V. VIRGINIA SURFACE MINING AND RECLAMATION ASSOCIATION (1981): regulating private conduct directly, but allowing a state to opt out of the federal regulation by adopting its own law under federal guidelines. Furthermore, if Congress wants to buy state sovereignty, it will find willing sellers. By placing conditions on FEDERAL GRANTS-IN-AID—which now amount to about one-fifth of state budgets—Congress can achieve through the spending power virtually anything it might achieve by direct regulation. Even if *Garcia* should be overruled and *Usery* reinstated, Congress can offer subsidies that are vital to local transit authorities or police departments, conditioned on promises to pay transit and police employees the federal minimum wage. The passion of the Justices on both sides may indicate that in these cases the symbolism is what counts.

KENNETH L. KARST

Bibliography

FIELD, MARTHA A. 1985 Garcia v. San Antonio Metropolitan Transit Authority: The Demise of a Misguided Doctrine. *Harvard Law Review* 99:84–118.
VAN ALSTYNE, WILLIAM W. 1985 The Second Death of Federalism. *Michigan Law Review* 83:1709–1733.

GARFIELD, JAMES A.
(1831–1881)

A Civil War general, James Abram Garfield served in Congress from 1863 until 1881, when he became President of the United States. In Congress Garfield was a skilled parliamentarian and self-taught expert on finance. After 1868 he was one of the most powerful Republicans in Congress, and served as minority leader from 1876 until 1880. In a period of pervasive corruption Garfield remained relatively untainted. In 1876 he helped frame the legislation that led to the COMPROMISE OF 1877 that settled the disputed presidential election. He served on the electoral commission, supporting President Rutherford B. Hayes on every issue. In 1880 the Ohio legislature chose him for the United States Senate, for a term beginning in 1881. However, that summer he became a compromise candidate for the presidency, after the Republican convention deadlocked. As President, Garfield attempted to root out corruption in the Post Office Department and the notorious New York customs house. Garfield's insistence that he, as President, should make all appointments, regardless of longstanding notions of senatorial privilege, led ROSCOE CONKLING of New York to resign from the Senate. In July 1881 Garfield was shot and killed by a disappointed office seeker who shouted that he was a party "stalwart" and that now CHESTER A. ARTHUR would be President. In the wake of this tragedy Arthur continued Garfield's investigation of the Post Office and secured the passage of the first civil service reform law, the PENDLETON ACT.

PAUL FINKELMAN

Bibliography

PESKIN, ALAN 1978 *Garfield*. Kent, Ohio: Kent State University Press.

GARLAND, AUGUSTUS H.
(1832–1899)

Augustus Hill Garland, a Whig lawyer, opposed SECESSION in 1861 but represented Arkansas in the Confederate Congress throughout the Civil War. He won readmission to the federal bar in *Ex parte Garland* (1867), one of the TEST OATH CASES; but the same year the United States Senate, to which he had been elected, denied him his seat. He served as governor of Arkansas (1874–1876) and United States senator (1877–1885) before becoming President GROVER CLEVELAND's attorney general (1885–1889). He was later a prominent lawyer practicing in Washington, D.C. He was co-author of a treatise on federal court JURISDICTION.

DENNIS J. MAHONEY

GARLAND, EX PARTE

See: Test Oath Cases

GARRISON, WILLIAM LLOYD
(1805–1879)

William Lloyd Garrison edited America's leading abolitionist newspaper, *The Liberator* (1831–1865), and helped found the New England Anti-Slavery Society (1831) and the American Anti-Slavery Society (1833; president, 1843–1865). Garrison believed pacifism, nonresistance, and moral suasion could end slavery. He argued that the Constitution supported slavery and was "a covenant with death and an agreement with Hell." Thus, he refused to vote or voluntarily support civil government, and after 1843 Garrison and his followers advocated a peaceful dissolution of the Union under the slogan "No Union with Slaveholders." More moderate abolitionists rejected Garrison's analysis of the Constitution, his opposition to antislavery political candidates and parties, and his extreme tactics, such as publicly burning the Constitution and declaring "So perish all compromises with tyranny." Despite his disunionist beliefs, he ultimately gave tacit support to ABRAHAM LINCOLN and the Union during the Civil War.

PAUL FINKELMAN

Bibliography

THOMAS, JOHN L. 1963 *The Liberator*. Boston: Little, Brown.

GARRITY v. NEW JERSEY
385 U.S. 493 (1967)

Justice WILLIAM O. DOUGLAS, for a 6–3 majority, ruled that coercion had tainted confessions exacted from police officers suspected of fixing traffic tickets, when they were made to choose between exercising their RIGHT AGAINST SELF-INCRIMINATION and retaining their jobs. The dissenters argued that the state could require police officers to assist in detecting unlawful activities, that the officers' confessions were not involuntary, and that their constitutional right was not burdened.

LEONARD W. LEVY

GAULT, IN RE
387 U.S. 1 (1967)

In re Gault is the Supreme Court's most important landmark concerning juveniles, both because of its specific requirements for delinquency proceedings and because of its unequivocal declaration of the broad principle that young persons, as individuals, have constitutional rights of their own. Rejecting the informality that had long characterized state juvenile courts, the Supreme Court held that DUE PROCESS OF LAW required four procedural safeguards in the adjudicatory (or guilt-determining) phase of delinquency proceedings: adequate written NOTICE to the juvenile and his parents of the specific charges; notification of the RIGHT TO COUNSEL, with appointed counsel for those who lack the means to retain a lawyer; the right of CONFRONTATION and cross-examination of witnesses; and the notification of the RIGHT AGAINST SELF-INCRIMINATION. For the first time the Supreme Court declared boldly, in a seminal opinion by Justice ABE FORTAS, that "whatever may be their precise impact, neither the FOURTEENTH AMENDMENT nor the BILL OF RIGHTS is for adults alone."

The facts of the case dramatically suggested the risks of procedural informality and "unbridled discretion," which the Court saw as a poor substitute for "principle and procedure." Fifteen-year-old Gerald Gault was found to be a delinquent and was committed for up to six years to the Arizona Industrial School for an offense that would have subjected an adult to a small fine and no more than two months' imprisonment. Neither Gerald nor his parents were ever served with a petition that disclosed the factual basis of the juvenile court proceedings. It was claimed that Gerald and a friend had made an obscene telephone call to a neighbor who never appeared in the proceedings. Although the judge subsequently reported that Gerald had made some sort of admission to him, no transcript was made of what was said at either of Gerald's two appearances before the judge, nor was Gerald offered counsel.

Although a few states had anticipated the Court's rulings in *Gault* by adopting new juvenile justice acts that provided greater safeguards, procedural informality had characterized most juvenile courts since their creation around 1900. This was typically justified on two interrelated grounds. First, the goal of JUVENILE PROCEEDINGS was said to be treatment and rehabilitation, not punishment or deterrence. Second, investigation, diagnosis, and treatment required individualized determinations of what was best for each particular child. Legalistic formalities were seen as inconsistent and counterproductive in a benevolent and paternalistic institution committed to the rehabilitative ideal. State courts had refused to impose safeguards that "restrict the state when it seeks to deprive a person of his liberty," typically with conclusory statements that minors had no interest in liberty (because they would be subject in all events to parental control) or that delinquency proceedings were civil, rather than criminal, because their purpose was not punitive.

Gault rejected these traditional justifications. Pointing to various empirical studies, the *Gault* majority challenged the rehabilitative effectiveness of the juvenile justice system by suggesting that juvenile crime had increased since the establishment of the juvenile courts; questioned the value of procedural informality as a means to shape desirable attitudes about justice in the young people caught up by the system; and disparaged the significance, in terms of loss of liberty, of the difference between detention in a "home" or "school" after a finding of delinquency and incarceration after conviction of a crime. The strength of much of the social science evidence cited by the Court has been subsequently challenged, but the Court's willingness to attach substantial weight to the interest of a young person in avoiding the serious practical consequences of an erroneous determination of delinquency is certainly justified.

The Court did not suggest in *Gault* or in its subsequent decisions that the Constitution requires the state to treat a juvenile accused of delinquency in all respects like an adult accused of a similar act. The Court has extended other procedural safeguards to juveniles in delinquency proceedings—in IN RE WINSHIP (1970) it required proof beyond a REASONABLE DOUBT, for example, and in *Breed v. Jones* (1975) it held that the prohibition against DOUBLE JEOPARDY applied—but it has refused, as in MCKEIVER V. PENNSYLVANIA (1971), to require TRIAL BY JURY in delinquency proceedings. Although the traditional goals of the juvenile courts do not justify the absence of certain safeguards, *Gault* and its progeny suggest that the Constitution does not require abolition of the separate juvenile court system with some distinctive procedural features. Nor does *Gault* require the states to impose identical sanctions on minors and adults after a determination that a criminal statute has been violated. Indeed, by emphasizing that the procedural requirements extended only to the adjudicatory phase, and not to the dispositional phase, of delinquency proceedings, the Court in *Gault* argued that its decision did not threaten the emphasis juvenile courts have traditionally claimed to place on individualized treatment and rehabilitation.

ROBERT H. MNOOKIN

(SEE ALSO: *Children's Rights.*)

Bibliography

STAPLETON, W. VAUGHAN and TEITELBAUM, LEE E. 1972 *In Defense of Youth: A Study of the Role of Counsel in American Juvenile Courts.* New York: Russell Sage Foundation.

GELBARD v. UNITED STATES
408 U.S. 41 (1972)

The Supreme Court held that a witness who refuses to answer a GRAND JURY question derived from illegal electronic surveillance may not be held in CONTEMPT. Title III of the OMNIBUS CRIME CONTROL AND SAFE STREETS ACT excludes from grand jury proceedings any EVIDENCE obtained from illegal surveillance and a witness need not answer a question based on such information.

HERMAN SCHWARTZ

GELPCKE v. DUBUQUE
1 Wallace 175 (1864)

In his introduction to the 1864 reports of the Supreme Court, John Wallace, the Supreme Court reporter, remarked that in *Gelpcke* the Court imposed "high moral duties . . . upon a whole community seeking apparently to violate them." The community was Dubuque, Iowa, which attempted to enhance its property values by issuing municipal bonds, backed by local taxes, to promote railroad development that would put Dubuque on the map. Dubuque acted on authority granted by the Iowa legislature, although the state constitution prevented the legislature from investing in private railroads, as Dubuque did, and from increasing the state's indebtedness as much as the legislature authorized the city to increase its indebtedness. Responding to railroad shenanigans and the objections of taxpayers, Dubuque repudiated its debt, and the Iowa Supreme Court held that the legislature had violated the state constitution when authorizing Dubuque to issue the bonds.

Bondholders, seeking federal relief against default, persuaded the Supreme Court to rule that a contract once valid under state law cannot have its validity or obligation impaired by the subsequent action of a state court. Justice NOAH H. SWAYNE, speaking for all but Justice SAMUEL F. MILLER, who dissented, refused to accept the state supreme court's ruling on a matter of state constitutional law. Swayne took the high ground by declaring, "We shall never immolate truth, justice, and the law, because a state tribunal has erected the altar and decreed the sacrifice." However, the ground of decision was not clear, and the Supreme Court construed a state judicial decision as a "law," contrary to conventional usage.

Justice OLIVER WENDELL HOLMES later remarked that the decision in *Gelpcke* took the Court a good while to explain. In fact, the explanation subsequently provided by the Court was that the state judicial decision had violated the CONTRACT CLAUSE. However construed, *Gelpcke* was a means of the Supreme Court's expansion of its JURISDICTION, either under the doctrine of SWIFT V. TYSON (1842) or under the contract clause, which had previously applied only to statutes, not judicial decisions. And the Court established a basis for curbing municipal repudiation of debts and protecting municipal bondholders.

LEONARD W. LEVY

GENDER DISCRIMINATION

See: Sex Discrimination

GENERAL LAWS AND LIBERTIES OF MASSACHUSETTS

See: Massachusetts General Laws and Liberties

GENERAL WARRANT

General warrants command either apprehension for unstated causes or the arrest, search, or seizure of unspecified persons, places, or objects. Since the *Five Knights Case* (1628) English courts have consistently disallowed the first category of warrant, although its use survived a century later. The general warrant of the second sort, which allowed its bearer to search wherever or seize whomever or whatever he wished, was more common. It existed by the early fourteenth century and found ever growing applications. The Star Chamber and "High Commission" of the Tudor-Stuart period used such warrants vigorously to suffocate political and religious dissent. By the middle of the eighteenth century, general warrants were or had also been used to combat vagrancy, regulate publications, impress persons into the army and navy, pursue felons, collect taxes, and find stolen merchandise. A close relative, the WRIT OF ASSISTANCE, allowed customs officers to search all houses in which they suspected concealed contraband.

Beginning with the WILKES CASES (1763–1770), British courts undermined the use of general SEARCH WARRANTS by secretaries of state. Although they were widely used in colonial and revolutionary America, eight state constitutions of 1776–1784 forbade them, as does the FOURTH AMENDMENT to the federal Constitution.

WILLIAM CUDDIHY

Bibliography
CUDDIHY, WILLIAM and HARDY, B. CARMON 1980 A Man's House Was Not His Castle: Origins of the Fourth Amendment to the United States Constitution. *William and Mary Quarterly* 37:371–400.

GENERAL WELFARE CLAUSE

With no enforceable power to tax under the ARTICLES OF CONFEDERATION, Congress "requisitioned" funds from the states each of which then decided how and whether to raise its share of the confederation's needs. Uneven responses brought resentment among the states and frequent frustration of congressional policies. Dissatisfaction with this system was a leading cause of the failure of the Articles. As a remedy, the CONSTITUTIONAL CONVENTION proposed to empower the new Congress to "lay and collect Taxes, Duties, IMPOSTS, and EXCISES, to pay the Debt and provide for the common Defense and general welfare of the United States." Some Anti-Federalists said this language defeated the principle of ENUMERATED POWERS because it could be read to authorize action for the common defense and general welfare by any legislative means whatever. JAMES MADISON disclaimed this interpretation in THE FEDERALIST #41, saying that the general welfare clause conferred power to tax and spend only for purposes indicated by the enumerated powers that followed in Article

I, section 8. Congress could tax and spend for armies and navies, for example, but not for purposes reserved to the states.

Later, during conflicts with the Jeffersonians over national economic policy, ALEXANDER HAMILTON argued that the enumerated powers did not exhaust the concept of "the general welfare" and that Congress could tax and spend for purposes beyond the enumerated powers, so long as it acted in the general interest. Constitutional history has thus produced three theories of the general welfare clause: as the Anti-Federalists charged, that Congress could claim unrestricted power to act in the general interest; that Congress could tax and spend only for purposes indicated by the enumerated powers, as Madison claimed; and that Congress could tax and spend for purposes beyond the enumerated powers, as Hamilton claimed. In OBITER DICTUM, the Supreme Court adopted the Hamiltonian theory in UNITED STATES V. BUTLER (1936).

In *Butler,* the court voided a federal tax as part of an unconstitutional scheme to use the spending power to invade powers reserved to the states. After first declaring that Congress could tax and spend for purposes beyond the enumerated powers, the Court then ignored the Hamiltonian theory by holding the act unconstitutional as an attempt to invade an area (agricultural production) beyond Congress's enumerated powers. Later decisions that were friendlier to the New Deal effectively reversed this holding and rescued the Hamiltonian theory. The Court enlarged the scope of the COMMERCE CLAUSE by affirming Congress's authority directly to regulate any social or economic activity with an "effect" upon INTERSTATE COMMERCE, regardless of Congress's motives relative to the reserved powers of the states. (See UNITED STATES V. DARBY LUMBER COMPANY, 1941; IMPLIED POWERS.) In SONZINSKY V. UNITED STATES (1937) the Court refused to scrutinize Congress's motives for taxing socially harmful activities so long as the tax produced some revenue. And in STEWARD MACHINE COMPANY V. DAVIS (1937) the Court upheld the taxing scheme that was the foundation of the Social Security system, irrespective of any other enumerated power of Congress.

Such decisions eliminated doubts about the Court's acceptance of the Hamiltonian theory, and the era following World War II saw a great increase in federal regulatory taxes and subsidies conditioned on conformity with policies (such as racial integration) which some state and local governments otherwise would more actively have opposed. The Hamiltonian theory has also supported federal regulatory taxes on narcot-

ics, gambling, and other morally injurious practices. (See UNITED STATES V. KAHRIGER, 1953.) No development has had a more corrosive effect on the old idea that some concerns lay beyond the reach of Congress. Given the broad regulatory uses of the TAXING AND SPENDING POWERS, the triumph of Hamilton's theory vindicated the Anti-Federalists' predictions of what the general welfare clause eventually would become.

SOTIRIOS A. BARBER

(SEE ALSO: *National Police Power.*)

Bibliography

BARBER, SOTIRIOS A. 1984 *On What the Constitution Means.* Baltimore: Johns Hopkins University Press.

GEORGIA v. STANTON

See: *Mississippi v. Johnson*

GERENDE v. BOARD OF SUPERVISORS OF ELECTIONS
341 U.S. 56 (1951)

A Maryland statute barred from public employment or office anyone who belonged to a "subversive" organization. In this unanimous PER CURIAM OPINION, the VINSON COURT sustained the law upon an understanding that the term "subversive" was limited to those somehow engaged in the attempt to overthrow the government by force or violence. The Court assumed that an affidavit negating such activity would satisfy the state's LOYALTY OATH required of those running for office.

MICHAEL E. PARRISH

GERRY, ELBRIDGE
(1744–1814)

A Massachusetts merchant, Elbridge Gerry was particularly active in Revolutionary politics and served as a delegate to the Second Continental Congress. He signed the DECLARATION OF INDEPENDENCE as an early and vigorous supporter of separation from a government and people that he believed had become "corrupt and totally destitute of Virtue."

Gerry devoted most of his life to public service. He represented Massachusetts in Congress from 1779 to 1785, signing the ARTICLES OF CONFEDERATION. As a Massachusetts delegate to the CONSTITUTIONAL

CONVENTION OF 1787, Gerry was, at the outset, a moderate nationalist who favored a strong central government although emphasizing the need for certain "federal features." Gerry opposed democracy— "the evils we experience flow from the excess of democracy"—and he often supported his own business interests. Indeed, he early recognized the need for congressional power "competent to the protection of" FOREIGN COMMERCE in order for Congress to "command reciprocal advantages in trade." A firm believer in republicanism, Gerry insisted on the need for a SEPARATION OF POWERS and the inclusion of additional checks on the national government. He chaired the committee that formulated the GREAT COMPROMISE and helped secure its adoption. The absence of a BILL OF RIGHTS, however, and the concentration of power in the federal government led Gerry to oppose RATIFICATION OF THE CONSTITUTION.

Elected to Congress in 1789, he served for four years as a strong supporter of ALEXANDER HAMILTON's financial program. Gerry retired from Congress in 1793 and was elected Republican governor of Massachusetts in 1810 and 1811. He so opposed the idea of legitimate opposition that his second term saw the passage of a bill radically redistricting the state to assure the Republicans greater representation in the state legislature than their actual strength justified. This political technique was satirized in a cartoon showing one oddly shaped district in the form of a salamander, hence the name GERRYMANDER. JAMES MADISON selected Gerry as his vice-presidential running mate in 1812, and until his death in 1814 Gerry championed Madison's administration.

DAVID GORDON

Bibliography

BILLIAS, GEORGE A. 1976 *Elbridge Gerry, Founding Father and Republican Statesman.* New York: McGraw-Hill.

GERRYMANDER

A gerrymander is a political district drawn to advantage some and disadvantage others: candidates, parties, or interest groups. The name comes from a particularly spectacular partisan apportionment engineered by ELBRIDGE GERRY in 1812. Technically, any winner-take-all district can be called a gerrymander, for district lines inevitably favor some against others. But common usage limits the term to districts deemed unnatural in form or unfair in intent or effect. The Supreme Court boldly and unanimously attacked a blatant racial gerrymander in GOMILLION V. LIGHTFOOT (1960), but it has been almost uniformly acquiescent since then.

Gomillion voided an "uncouth, 28-sided figure" surgically excluding almost all of the blacks in Tuskegee, Alabama, from voting in the city while retaining every white. It cleared the way for BAKER V. CARR (1962) and the REAPPORTIONMENT revolution. But, apart from a few cases of municipal expansion challenged under the VOTING RIGHTS ACT OF 1965, the Court has never since been able or willing to find "cognizable discrimination" in gerrymandering cases.

The leading cases, *Wright v. Rockefeller* (1964) and UNITED JEWISH ORGANIZATIONS V. CAREY (1977), both involved packing of New York black and Puerto Rican voters into what dissenting Justice WILLIAM O. DOUGLAS (in *Wright*) called a "racial borough." Its packed nonwhite majority, if unpacked and spread to adjacent districts, might have formed two or three nonwhite majorities.

But it is difficult to tell clearly what packing does to a group's power, because "wasted" surplus votes in good years can be badly needed in bad years. In *Wright* the black plaintiffs wanted more "effective" black votes through dispersion, while the black incumbent, siding with the defendants, argued for strength through concentration: better one safe seat than two marginal ones. The baffled Court claimed it could find "no evidence of racial discrimination" in the obvious gerrymander, but the Court's real lack was simple rules for making sense of the evidence it had.

It is also impossible to equalize everyone's effective REPRESENTATION, short of ordering proportional representation, which could be a cure worse than the disease. In *UJO v. Carey* the United States attorney general had found the ethnically packed district discriminatory under the Voting Rights Act and ordered the state to create two more districts with nonwhite majority quotas. To do so, the state had to dismember a Hasidic Jewish community, which objected to the explicit RACIAL QUOTAS as a violation of the FOURTEENTH and FIFTEENTH AMENDMENTS. But the Court, ignoring the constitutional attack, argued that the racial quotas served the purposes of the Voting Rights Act by enhancing the black vote and did not involve "cognizable discrimination" against the Jews, who, as "whites in Kings County," might be submerged in their own districts but would have vicarious "fair representation" by white representatives of other districts.

Only in a few cases under the Voting Rights Act, with its heavy statutory burden on the state to prove nondiscrimination, has the Court intervened against racial gerrymandering since _Gomillion._ In constitutional terms, partisan and incumbent-favoring gerrymanders are deemed tolerable, perhaps because political districting is indeed a "mathematical quagmire" ill-suited for resolution with simple rules. The Court all but announced its retreat in _Gaffney v. Cummings_ (1973).

Gerrymandering, largely unregulated, has flourished in reapportionment years. Theoretically, it could give the dominant party a manifold advantage over a numerically equal rival. In practice, it gives a thirty to forty percent advantage to the dominant party in seats per vote, often rewarding a minority of votes with a majority of seats.

Once it was hoped that objective standards—of compactness, contiguity, or competitiveness—or impartial judges or commissioners would curb gerrymandering. But standards have been largely ineffectual and judges and commissioners overwhelmingly partisan. A few states have limited partisan gerrymanders with bipartisan commissions, and roughly half the states have found protection through the happenstance of divided, two-party control of the elected branches. Ironically, despite _Gomillion_ and the reapportionment revolution, the chief protection against gerrymandering has not come from courts but from the "weak" CHECKS AND BALANCES—FEDERALISM, SEPARATION OF POWERS, and multiplication of competing factions—that court intervention was supposed to supplant.

WARD E. Y. ELLIOTT

Bibliography

DIXON, ROBERT G. 1968 _Democratic Representation: Reapportionment in Law and Politics._ New York: Oxford University Press.

ELLIOTT, WARD E. Y. 1975 _The Rise of Guardian Democracy: The Supreme Court's Role in Voting Rights Disputes, 1845–1969._ Cambridge, Mass.: Harvard University Press.

SICKELS, ROBERT J. 1966 "Dragons, Bacon Strips, and Dumbbells—Who's Afraid of Reapportionment?" _Yale Law Journal_ 75:1300–1308.

GERTZ v. ROBERT WELCH, INC.
418 U.S. 323 (1974)

In this major case on LIBEL AND THE FIRST AMENDMENT, the Supreme Court in an opinion by Justice LEWIS F. POWELL held, 5–4, that the rule of NEW YORK TIMES V. SULLIVAN (1964) did not apply when the party seeking damages for libel is not a public official or a public figure. _New York Times_ had applied the rule of "actual malice": the First Amendment bars a public official from recovering damages for a defamatory falsehood relating to his conduct in office unless he proves that the publisher or broadcaster made the statement knowing it to be false or "with reckless disregard of whether it was false or not." The Court had extended that rule in 1967 to PUBLIC FIGURES. In _Rosenbloom v. Metromedia, Inc._ (1971) a plurality ruled that if the defamation concerned a public issue the actual malice rule extended also to private individuals, who were not public figures. In _Gertz_ the Court, abandoning that rule, held that a private plantiff had to prove actual malice only if seeking punitive damages; the FIRST AMENDMENT did not require him to produce such proof merely to recover actual damages for injury to reputation.

Powell reasoned that public officers and public figures had a far greater opportunity to counteract false statements than private persons. Moreover, an official or a candidate for public office knowingly exposes himself to close public scrutiny and criticism, just as public figures knowingly invite attention and comment. The communications media cannot, however, assume that private persons similarly expose themselves to defamation. Powell declared that they "are not only more vulnerable to injury than public officials and public figures; they are also more deserving of recovery." Their only effective redress is resort to a state's libel laws. So long as a state does not permit the press or a broadcaster to be held liable without fault and applies the actual malice rule to requests for punitive damages, the Court held that the First Amendment requires a "less demanding showing than that required by _New York Times_" and that the states may decide for themselves the appropriate standard of liability for media defendants who defame private persons.

Each of the dissenting Justices wrote a separate opinion. The dissents covered a wide spectrum from greater concern for the defamed party to alarm about the majority's supposedly constrictive interpretation of the First Amendment. Chief Justice WARREN E. BURGER worried that the party libeled in this case was a lawyer who ought not to be invidiously identified with his client. Justice WILLIAM O. DOUGLAS thought all libel laws to be unconstitutional. Justice WILLIAM J. BRENNAN preferred the actual malice test to be applied to private individuals in matters of public concern. Justice BYRON R. WHITE, opposing the Court's restriction of the COMMON LAW of libels, condemned the nationalization of so large a part of libel law.

LEONARD W. LEVY

GIBBONS v. OGDEN
9 Wheaton 1 (1824)

Chief Justice JOHN MARSHALL's great disquisition on the COMMERCE CLAUSE in this case is the most influential in our history. *Gibbons* liberated the steamship business and much of American INTERSTATE COMMERCE from the grip of state-created monopolies. More important, Marshall laid the doctrinal basis for the national regulation of the economy that occurred generations later, though at the time his opinion buttressed laissez-faire. He composed that opinion as if statecraft in the interpretation of a constitutional clause could decide whether the United States remained just a federal union or became a nation. The New York act, which the Court voided in *Gibbons*, had closed the ports of the state to steamships not owned or licensed by a monopoly chartered by the state. Other states retaliated in kind. The attorney general of the United States told the *Gibbons* Court that the country faced a commercial "civil war."

The decision produced immediate and dramatic results. Within two weeks, a newspaper jubilantly reported: "Yesterday the Steamboat *United States*, Capt. Bunker, from New Haven, entered New York in triumph, with streamers flying, and a large company of passengers exulting in the decision of the United States Supreme Court against the New York monopoly. She fired a salute which was loudly returned by huzzas from the wharves." Senator MARTIN VAN BUREN (Democrat, New York), who had recently advocated curbing the Court, declared that even those states whose laws had been nullified, including his own, "have submitted to their fate," and the Court now justly attracted "idolatry," its Chief respected as "the ablest Judge now sitting upon any judicial bench in the world." For a Court that had been under vitriolic congressional and state attack, *Gibbons* wedded a novel popularity to its nationalism.

One of the ablest judges who ever sat on an American court, JAMES KENT of New York, whose opinion Marshall repudiated, grumbled in the pages of his *Commentaries on American Law* (1826) that Marshall's "language was too general and comprehensive for the case." Kent was right. The Court held the state act unconstitutional for conflicting with an act of Congress, making Marshall's enduring treatise on the commerce clause unnecessary for the disposition of the case. The conflict between the two statutes, Marshall said, "decides the cause." Kent was also right in stating that "it never occurred to anyone," least of all to the Congress that had passed the Coastal Licensing Act of 1793, which Marshall used to decide the case, that the act could justify national supremacy over state regulations respecting "internal waters or commerce." The act of 1793 had been intended to discriminate against foreign vessels in the American coastal trade by offering preferential tonnage duties to vessels of American registry. Marshall's construction of the statute conformed to his usual tactic of finding narrow grounds for decision after making a grand exposition. He announced "propositions which may have been thought axioms." He "assume[d] nothing," he said, because of the magnitude of the question, the distinction of the judge (Kent) whose opinion he scrapped, and the able arguments, which he rejected, by Thomas Emmett and Thomas Oakely, covering over 125 pages in the report of the case.

Except for the arguments of counsel, the Court had little for guidance. It had never before decided a commerce clause case, and the clause itself is general: "Congress shall have power to regulate commerce with foreign nations and among the several states. . . ." The power to regulate what would later be called "interstate commerce" appears in the same clause touching FOREIGN COMMERCE, the regulation of which is necessarily exclusive, beyond state control. But the clause does not negate state regulatory authority over interstate commerce, and the framers of the Constitution had rejected proposals for a sole or EXCLUSIVE POWER in Congress. Interstate commerce could be, as counsel for the monopoly contended, a subject of CONCURRENT POWER. Marshall had previously acknowledged that although the Constitution vested in Congress bankruptcy and tax powers, the states retained similar powers. THE FEDERALIST #32 recognized the principle of concurrent powers but offered no assistance on the commerce clause. Congress had scarcely used the commerce power except for the EMBARGO ACTS, which had not come before the Supreme Court. Those acts had interpreted the power to "regulate" as a power to prohibit, but they concerned commerce with foreign nations and were an instrument of foreign policy.

Prior to *Gibbons* the prevailing view on the interstate commerce power was narrow and crossed party lines. Kent, a Federalist, differed little from the Jeffersonians. JAMES MADISON, for example, when vetoing a congressional appropriation for INTERNAL IMPROVE-MENTS, had declared in 1817 that "the power to regulate commerce among the several states cannot include a power to construct roads and canals, and to improve the navigation of water courses." In 1821, when JAMES MONROE had vetoed the CUMBERLAND ROAD BILL, whose objective was to extend national authority to turnpikes within the states, he had virtually reduced the commerce power to the enactment of duties and imports, adding that goods and vessels are the only SUBJECTS OF COMMERCE that Congress can regulate. "Commerce," in common usage at the time of *Gibbons,* meant trade in the buying and selling of commodities, not navigation or the transportation of passengers for hire. That was the business of Mr. Gibbons, who operated a steamship in defiance of the monopoly, between Elizabethtown, New Jersey, and New York City, in direct competition with Ogden, a licensee of the monopoly. Had Gibbons operated under sail, he would not have violated New York law; as it was, the state condemned his vessel to fines and forfeiture.

In *Gibbons,* then, the Court confronted a stunted concept of commerce, a STRICT CONSTRUCTION of the commerce power, and an opinion bearing Kent's authority that New York had regulated only "internal" commerce. Kent had also held that the commerce power was a concurrent one and that the test for the constitutionality of a state act should be practical: could the state and national laws coexist without conflicting in their operation? Marshall "assumed nothing" and in his step-by-step "axioms" repudiated any argument based on such premises.

He began with a definition of "commerce." It comprehended navigation as well as buying and selling, because "it is intercourse." This sweeping definition prompted a disgruntled states-rightist to remark, "I shall soon expect to learn that our fornication laws are unconstitutional." That same definition later constitutionally supported an undreamed of expansion of congressional power over the life of the nation's economy. Having defined commerce as every species of commercial intercourse, Marshall, still all-embracing, defined "commerce among the several states" to mean commerce intermingled with or concerning two or more states. Such commerce "cannot stop at the external boundary line of each State, but may be introduced into the interior"—and wherever it went, the power of the United States followed. Marshall did not dispute Kent's view that the "completely internal commerce" of a state (what we call INTRA-STATE COMMERCE) is reserved for state governance.

But that governance extended only to such commerce as was completely within one state, did not "affect" other states, "and with which it is not necessary to interfere, for the purpose of executing some of the general powers of the [United States] government." Marshall's breath-taking exposition of the national commerce power foreshadowed the STREAM OF COMMERCE DOCTRINE and the SHREVEPORT DOCTRINE of the next century. "If Congress has the power to regulate it," he added, "that power must be exercised whenever the subject exists. If it exists within the States . . . then the power of Congress may be exercised within a State."

Having so defined the reach of the commerce power, Marshall, parsing the clause, defined the power to "regulate" as the power "to prescribe the rule by which commerce is to be governed." It is a power that "may be exercised to its utmost extent, and acknowledges no limitations. . . ." In COHENS V. VIRGINIA (1821) he had said that the United States form, for most purposes, one nation: "In war, we are one people. In making peace, we are one people. In all commercial regulations, we are one and the same people," and the government managing that people's interests was the government of the Union. In *Gibbons* he added that because the "sovereignty of Congress" is plenary as to its objects, "the power over commerce with foreign nations, and among the several states, is vested in Congress as absolutely as it would be in a single government. . . ." Were that true, the commerce power would be as exclusive as the TREATY POWER or WAR POWERS and could not be shared concurrently with the states.

Marshall expressly denied that the states possessed a concurrent commerce power; yet he did not expressly declare that Congress possessed an exclusive commerce power, which would prevent the states from exercising a commerce power even in the absence of congressional legislation. That was DANIEL WEBSTER's argument in *Gibbons,* against the monopoly, and Marshall found "great force" in it. Notwithstanding the ambiguity in Marshall's opinion, he implicitly adopted Webster's argument by repeatedly rejecting the theory of concurrent commerce powers. He conceded, however, that the states can reach and regulate some of the same subjects of commerce as Congress, but only by the exercise of powers distinct from an interstate commerce power. Referring to the mass of state regulatory legislation that encompassed inspection laws, health laws, turnpike laws, ferry laws, "etc.," Marshall labeled them the state's "system of police," later called the POLICE POWER. But his jurisprudence-by-label did not distinguish interstate from intrastate commerce powers. Having declared that Congress might regulate a state's "internal" commerce to effectuate a national policy, he allowed the state police power to operate on subjects of interstate commerce, in subordination, of course, to the principle of national supremacy. (See WILLSON V. BLACK-BIRD CREEK MARSH CO., 1829.)

Following his treatise on the commerce clause, Marshall turned to the dispositive question whether the New York monopoly act conflicted with an act of Congress. The pertinent act of 1793 referred to American vessels employed in the "coasting trade." It made no exception for steamships or for vessels that merely transported passengers. The New York act was therefore "in direct collision" with the act of Congress by prohibiting Gibbons's steamship from carrying passengers in and out of the state's ports without a license from the monopoly.

Justice WILLIAM JOHNSON, although an appointee of THOMAS JEFFERSON, was even more nationalistic than Marshall. Webster later boasted that Marshall had taken to his argument as a baby to its mother's milk, but the remark better suited Johnson. Concurring separately, he declared that the commerce clause vested a power in Congress that "must be exclusive." He would have voided the state monopoly act even in the absence of the Federal Coastal Licensing Act: "I cannot overcome the conviction, that if the licensing act was repealed tomorrow, the rights of the appellant to a reversal of the decision complained of, would be as strong as it is under this license." Johnson distinguished the police power laws that operated on subjects of interstate commerce; their "different purposes," he claimed, made all the difference. In fact, the purpose underlying the monopoly act was the legitimate state purpose of encouraging new inventions.

In a case of first impression, neither Marshall nor Johnson could lay down DOCTRINES that settled all conflicts between state and national powers relating to commerce. Not until 1851 did the Court, after much groping, seize upon the doctrine of SELECTIVE EXCLUSIVENESS, which seemed at the time like a litmus paper test. (See COOLEY V. BOARD OF PORT WARDENS OF PHILADELPHIA, 1852.) Yet Gibbons anticipated doctrines concerning the breadth of congressional power that emerged in the next century and still govern. Marshall was as prescient as human ability allows. The Court today cannot construe the commerce clause except in certain state regulation cases without being influenced by Marshall's treatise on it. "At the beginning," Justice ROBERT JACKSON declared in WICKARD V. FILBURN (1941), "Chief Justice Marshall described the federal commerce power with a breadth never exceeded."

LEONARD W. LEVY

Bibliography

BAXTER, MAURICE G. 1972 The Steamboat Monopoly: Gibbons v. Ogden, 1824. New York: Knopf.
BEVERIDGE, ALBERT J. 1916–1919 The Life of John Marshall. 4 vols. Vol. IV:397–460. Boston: Houghton Mifflin.
FRANKFURTER, FELIX 1937 The Commerce Clause under Marshall, Taney and Waite. Pages 1–45. Chapel Hill: University of North Carolina Press.

GIBONEY v. EMPIRE STORAGE & ICE CO.
336 U.S. 490 (1949)

Speaking through Justice HUGO L. BLACK, the Supreme Court unanimously sustained an INJUNCTION issued by a Missouri court against labor pickets who attempted to pressure a supplier of ice not to deal with nonunion peddlers. The pickets claimed that the injunction violated their right to FREEDOM OF SPEECH and also conflicted with THORNHILL V. ALABAMA (1940), where the Justices had protected peaceful PICKETING. The Court rejected these arguments, by pointing out that the dominant purpose of the picketing here was to induce a violation of state law forbidding agreements in RESTRAINT OF TRADE. The FIRST AMENDMENT, Black noted, does not protect speech used as part of conduct that violates a valid state criminal statute.

MICHAEL E. PARRISH

GIBSON, JOHN BANNISTER
(1780–1853)

John Bannister Gibson was a Pennsylvania judge for forty years, thirty-seven of which were spent on the state supreme court. Born in 1780, he studied at Dickinson College and was admitted to the bar in 1803. After a brief legislative experience, the governor appointed him to the Court of Common Pleas in 1813 and three years later elevated him to the state's highest court. In 1827, Gibson became chief justice, a position he retained until 1851 when a constitutional change inaugurated a rotation system. He spent the remaining two years of his life as an associate justice.

Gibson's views on judicial power form the bedrock of his reputation. In particular, his dissent in EAKIN V. RAUB (1825) presented the most important response to JOHN MARSHALL's opinion in MARBURY V. MADISON (1803). Gibson insisted that without specific constitutional authorization, the judiciary had no power to nullify legislative acts. His permissive view of legislative power complemented the "commonwealth idea." For example, he held that state-created monopolies were not constitutionally prohibited and, furthermore, that they were "useful institutions" (*Case of "The Philadelphia and Trenton Railroad Company,"* 1840).

Legislative interference with the judicial process resulted in the only exception to Gibson's temporizing course. The Pennsylvania legislature traditionally had exercised EQUITY powers through private acts. But after the courts were granted substantially complete equity jurisdiction in 1836, Gibson and his colleagues struck down attempts by the legislature to maintain their own practice. When the legislature ordered a new trial in a simple trespass action, Gibson ruled that "the power to order new trials is judicial; but the power of the legislature is not judicial" (*De Chastellux v. Fairchild,* 1850).

Gibson's views of judicial power were eclipsed by the judicial activism of the post-Civil War era. But subsequent demands for judicial restraint in the twentieth century resulted in renewed interest in Gibson and respect for his ideas. ROSCOE POUND ranked him among the ten leading American jurists, and MORRIS R. COHEN praised him as one of the "great creative minds" in American law.

STANLEY I. KUTLER

Bibliography

KUTLER, STANLEY I. 1965 John Bannister Gibson: Judicial Restraint and the "Positive State." *Journal of Public Law* 14:181–197.

GIBSON v. FLORIDA LEGISLATIVE INVESTIGATION COMMITTEE
372 U.S. 539 (1963)

The committee ordered the president of the Miami branch of the NAACP to produce his membership records and refer to them when the committee asked whether specific individuals, suspected of being communists, were NAACP members. Earlier committee attempts to expose the NAACP's entire membership list showed that the communist issue was a screen behind which the state sought to use publicity to weaken a group engaged in activities aimed at racial equality and DESEGREGATION.

The Supreme Court, 5–4, held that Gibson's conviction for contempt for refusal to produce the records infringed the FREEDOM OF ASSOCIATION, which protected associational privacy. The Court, in an opinion by Justice ARTHUR GOLDBERG, was prepared to balance the state interest in legislative investigation against this FIRST AMENDMENT interest, but it held that such an infringement could be constitutional only if "the state convincingly show[s] a substantial relation between the information sought and a subject of overriding and COMPELLING STATE INTEREST," and that Florida had not done so in this instance. Accordingly Gibson's conviction was invalidated.

Gibson and its predecessor, *Bates v. Little Rock* (1960), must be read in conjunction with the BALANCING TEST applied to a congressional investigation into communist activity in BARENBLATT V. UNITED STATES (1959). The later cases may be read narrowly to distinguish *Barenblatt* and provide greater constitutional protection from investigative exposure only for "groups which themselves are neither engaged in subversive or other illegal . . . activities nor demonstrated to have any substantial connections with such activities." Alternatively, *Bates* and *Gibson* can be seen to modify the balancing test of *Barenblatt* to a "preferred position" balancing in which the government must show a compelling interest before it can invade associational privacy.

MARTIN SHAPIRO

GIDEON v. WAINWRIGHT
372 U.S. 335 (1963)

From time to time in constitutional history an obscure individual becomes the symbol of a great movement in legal doctrine. Character and circumstance illuminate a new understanding of the Constitution. So it was in the case of Clarence Earl Gideon.

Gideon was a drifter and petty thief who had served four prison terms when, in 1961, he was charged with breaking and entering the Bay Harbor Poolroom in Panama City, Florida, and stealing a pint of wine and some coins from a cigarette machine. At the age of fifty he had the look of defeat: a gaunt wrinkled face, white hair, a trembling voice. But inside there was still passion—a concern for justice that approached obsession. Through it, in a manner of speaking, Gideon changed the Constitution.

When he went to trial in the Circuit Court of Bay County, Florida, on August 4, 1961, he asked the judge to appoint a lawyer for him because he was too poor to hire one himself. The judge said he was sorry but he could not do that, because the laws of Florida called for appointment of counsel only when a defendant was charged with a capital offense. Gideon said: "The United States Supreme Court says I am entitled to be represented by counsel." When the Florida courts rejected that claim, he went on to the Supreme Court. From prison he submitted a petition, handwritten in pencil, arguing that Florida had ignored a rule laid down by the Supreme Court: "that all citizens tried for a felony crime should have aid of counsel."

Gideon was wrong. The rule applied by the Supreme Court at that time was in fact exactly the opposite. The Constitution, it had held, did *not* guarantee free counsel to all felony defendants unable to retain their own. That was the outcome—the bitterly debated outcome—of a line of cases on the right to counsel.

The Supreme Court first dealt with the issue in 1932, in the Scottsboro Case, POWELL V. ALABAMA. DUE PROCESS OF LAW required at least a "hearing," Justice GEORGE H. SUTHERLAND said, and the presence of counsel was "fundamental" to a meaningful hearing.

But Sutherland said that the Court was not deciding whether poor defendants had a right to free counsel in all circumstances, beyond the aggravated ones of this case: a capital charge, tried in haste and under public pressure.

In JOHNSON V. ZERBST (1938) the Court read the Sixth Amendment to require the appointment of counsel for all indigent *federal* criminal defendants. But in BETTS V. BRADY (1942), when considering the right of poor *state* defendants to free counsel in noncapital cases, the Court came out the other way. Justice OWEN J. ROBERTS said that "the states should not be straitjacketed" by a uniform constitutional rule. Only when particular circumstances showed that want of counsel denied FUNDAMENTAL FAIRNESS, he said, were such convictions invalid.

For twenty years the rule of *Betts v. Brady* applied. Counsel was said to be required only when a defendant suffered from "special circumstances" of disability: illiteracy, youth, mental illness, the complexity of the charges. But during that period criticism of the case mounted. No one could tell, it was said, when the Constitution required counsel. More and more often, too, the Supreme Court found "special circumstances" to require counsel.

That was the situation when Clarence Earl Gideon's petition reached the Court. The Justices seized on the occasion to think again about the Constitution and the right to counsel. Granting review, the Court ordered counsel to discuss: "Should this Court's holding in *Betts v. Brady* be reconsidered?" And then it appointed to represent Gideon, who had had no lawyer at his trial, one of the ablest lawyers in Washington, ABE FORTAS—later to sit on the Supreme Court himself.

On March 18, 1963, the Court overruled *Betts v. Brady.* Justice HUGO L. BLACK, who had dissented in *Betts,* wrote the opinion of the Court: a rare vindication of past dissent. He quoted Justice Sutherland's words on every man's need for the guiding hand of counsel at every step of the proceeding against him. "The right of one charged with crime to counsel may not be deemed fundamental and essential to fair trials in some countries," Justice Black said, "but it is in ours."

The decision in *Gideon v. Wainwright* was an important victory for one side in a general philosophical debate on the Court about whether constitutional protections should apply with the same vigor to state as to federal action: a victory for Justice Black over Jusitce Felix Frankfurter's more deferential view of state power. But on this particular issue changing ideas of due process would have led Justice Frankfurter in 1963 to impose a universal rule; retired and ill, he told a friend that he would have voted to overrule *Betts.* The case thus showed how time may bring a new consensus on the meaning of the Constitution.

And, not least, the *Gideon* case showed that the courts still respond to individuals in a society where most institutions of government seem remote and unresponsive. The least influential of men, riding a wave of legal history, persuaded the Supreme Court to reexamine a premise of justice. The case in fact represented more than an abstract principle. It was a victory for Clarence Earl Gideon. After the Supreme Court decision he was tried again in Bay County, Florida, this time with a lawyer—and the jury acquitted him. Gideon stayed out of prison until he died, on January 18, 1972.

ANTHONY LEWIS

Bibliography

LEWIS, ANTHONY 1964 *Gideon's Trumpet.* New York: Random House.

GILES, WILLIAM B.
(1762–1830)

Virginia Anti-Federalist William Branch Giles served in six of the first seven Congresses and opposed the policies of ALEXANDER HAMILTON, especially the

BANK OF THE UNITED STATES (1791). He opposed the ALIEN AND SEDITION ACTS, endorsed the VIRGINIA AND KENTUCKY RESOLUTIONS, and advocated repeal of the JUDICIARY ACT OF 1801. As a Jeffersonian leader in the Senate (1804–1815) he voted to convict Justice SAMUEL CHASE, arguing that "if the judges of the Supreme Court should . . . declare an act of Congress unconstitutional, . . . it was the undoubted right of the House of Representatives to impeach them, and of the Senate to remove them." After the acquittal of AARON BURR (1807), Giles, at President THOMAS JEFFERSON's behest, introduced a bill to expand the definition of TREASON. In his declining years Giles was an outspoken champion of STATES' RIGHTS.

DENNIS J. MAHONEY

GILMAN, NICHOLAS
(1755–1814)

Nicholas Gilman represented New Hampshire at the CONSTITUTIONAL CONVENTION OF 1787 and signed the Constitution. Gilman was not an active participant in the deliberations or committee work of the Convention. He later served in Congress, first as a Federalist, later as a Republican.

DENNIS J. MAHONEY

GINSBERG v. NEW YORK
390 U.S. 629 (1968)

In *Ginsberg* the Supreme Court upheld the validity under the FIRST AMENDMENT and FOURTEENTH AMENDMENT of a New York criminal statute that prohibited the sale to persons under seventeen years of age of sexually explicit printed materials that would not be obscene for adults. Drawing upon the criteria suggested in ROTH V. UNITED STATES (1957) and MEMOIRS V. MASSACHUSETTS (1966), the New York statute broadly defined sexually explicit descriptions or representations as "harmful to minors" when the material: "(i) predominantly appeals to the prurient, shameful or morbid interest of minors, and (ii) is patently offensive to prevailing standards in the adult community as a whole with respect to what is suitable material for minors, and (iii) is utterly without redeeming social importance for minors." Convicted for selling two "girlie" magazines to a sixteen-year-old, Ginsberg claimed that the statute was unconstitutional because the state was without the power to deny persons younger than seventeen access to materials that were not obscene for adults. Justice WILLIAM J. BRENNAN, for the 6–3 majority, rejected this challenge by introducing the concept of "variable obscenity." According to the majority, the New York statute had "simply adjust[ed] the definition of OBSCENITY to social realities by permitting the appeal of this type of material to be assessed in terms of the sexual interests . . . of such minors."

Although the decision rests on the legitimacy of protecting children from harm, the Court found it unnecessary to decide whether persons under seventeen were caused harm by exposure to materials proscribed by the statute. After suggesting that scientific studies neither proved nor disproved a causal connection, the majority held that it was "not irrational" for the New York legislature to find that "exposure to material condemned by the statute is harmful to minors."

To what extent does a minor's own First Amendment rights constrain the state's power to limit a minor's access to written or pictorial materials? Because of the nature of Ginsberg's challenge to the statute, the Court did not concern itself with the question whether a minor might have the constitutional right to buy "girlie" magazines. In ERZNOZNIK V. JACKSONVILLE (1975) the Court later indicated that while the First Amendment rights of minors are not coextensive with those of adults, "minors are entitled to a significant measure of First Amendment protection" and that under the *Ginsberg* variable obscenity standard "all nudity" in films "cannot be deemed as obscene even as to minors."

ROBERT H. MNOOKIN

(SEE ALSO: *Children's Rights.*)

GINZBURG v. UNITED STATES

See: *Memoirs v. Massachusetts*

GIROUARD v. UNITED STATES
328 U.S. 61 (1946)

An applicant for United States CITIZENSHIP declared that he could take the oath of allegiance ("support and defend the Constitution and laws of the United States against all enemies . . .") only with the reservation that he would not serve in the military in a combatant role.

The Court, speaking through Justice WILLIAM O. DOUGLAS, held that despite UNITED STATES V.

SCHWIMMER (1929), *United States v. MacIntosh* (1931), and *United States v. Bland* (1931), Girouard met the requirements for NATURALIZATION. Justice Douglas argued that Congress had not specifically insisted upon willingness to perform combatant service. Chief Justice HARLAN F. STONE dissented, joined by Justices STANLEY F. REED and FELIX FRANKFURTER.

This case established the eligibility of CONSCIENTIOUS OBJECTORS to be naturalized as citizens of the United States.

RICHARD E. MORGAN

GITLOW v. NEW YORK
268 U.S. 652 (1925)

Gitlow was convicted under a state statute proscribing advocacy of the overthrow of government by force. In a paper called *The Revolutionary Age,* he had published "The Left Wing Manifesto," denouncing moderate socialism and prescribing "Communist revolution." There was no evidence of any effect resulting from the publication. Rejecting the CLEAR AND PRESENT DANGER test which OLIVER WENDELL HOLMES and LOUIS D. BRANDEIS reasserted in their dissent, Justice EDWARD SANFORD for the Court upheld the statute. Enunciating what subsequently came to be called the remote BAD TENDENCY TEST, Sanford declared that the state might "suppress the threatened danger in its incipiency." "It cannot reasonably be required to defer the adoption of measures for its own . . . safety until the revolutionary utterances lead to actual disturbances of the public peace or imminent and immediate danger of its own destruction."

Unwilling to reverse its decision in SCHENCK V. UNITED STATES (1919), the Court limited the clear and present danger test enunciated there to the situation in which a speaker is prosecuted under a statute prohibiting acts and making no reference to language. Under such a statute the legislature has made no judgment of its own as to the danger of any speech, and the unlawfulness of the speech must necessarily depend on whether "its natural tendency and probable effect was to bring about the substantive evil" that the legislature had proscribed. In short, Sanford sought to confine the danger test to its origin in the law of attempts and to strip it of its imminence aspect. He argued that where a legislature itself had determined that a certain category of speech constituted a danger of substantive evil, "every presumption [was] to be indulged in favor of the validity" of such an exercise of the police power.

The PREFERRED FREEDOMS doctrine that became central to the speech cases of the next two decades was largely directed toward undermining the *Gitlow* position that state statutes regulating speech ought to be subject to no more demanding constitutional standards than the reasonableness test applied to state economic regulation.

The *Gitlow* formula was rejected in the 1930s, but the Court returned to some of its reasoning in the 1950s, particularly to the notion that where revolutionary speech is involved, government need not wait until "the spark . . . has enkindled the flame or blazed into the conflagration." Such reasoning, bolstered by the *Gitlow* distinction between advocacy and abstract, academic teaching informed the DENNIS V. UNITED STATES (1951) and YATES V. UNITED STATES (1951) decisions that upheld the Smith Act, a federal statute in part modeled on the New York criminal anarchy statute sustained in *Gitlow*.

The Court's language in *Gitlow* was equivocal, and it provided no rationale. Indeed, *Gitlow* is most often cited today for its dictum, "incorporating" FIRST AMENDMENT free speech guarantees into the DUE PROCESS clause of the FOURTEENTH AMENDMENT, thus rendering the Amendment applicable to the states as well as to Congress. (See INCORPORATION DOCTRINE.)

Holmes's *Gitlow* dissent did not address the question so troublesome to believers in judicial self-restraint: why should courts not defer to the legislature's judgment that a particular kind of speech is too dangerous to tolerate when, in applying the due process clause, they do defer to other legislative judgments? He did attack the majority's distinction between lawful abstract teaching and unlawful INCITEMENT in language that has become famous:

Every idea is an incitement. It offers itself for belief and if believed it is acted on unless some other belief outweighs it. . . . The only difference between the expression of an opinion and an incitement in the narrower sense is the speaker's enthusiasm for the result. . . . If in the long run the beliefs expressed in proletarian dictatorship are destined to be accepted by the dominant forces of the community, the only meaning of free speech is that they should be given their chance and have their way.

MARTIN SHAPIRO

Bibliography
CHAFEE, ZECHARIAH 1941 *Free Speech in the United States.* Cambridge, Mass.: Harvard University Press.

GLIDDEN v. ZDANOK

See: Claims Court; Legislative Court

GLOBE NEWSPAPER COMPANY v. SUPERIOR COURT
457 U.S. 596 (1982)

Writing for a 7–2 Court, Justice WILLIAM J. BRENNAN sweepingly broadened the right of the public and press to attend criminal trials. On FIRST AMENDMENT grounds the Court held unconstitutional a state act intended to protect the juvenile victims of sex crimes by closing the trial proceedings. The exclusion of the press and public rested chiefly on the state's interest in safeguarding those victims from additional trauma and humiliation by not requiring them to testify in open court. The Supreme Court did not find that interest adequately compelling to warrant a mandatory closure rule. The decision created an anomalous condition of law: states can close trials to protect juvenile rapists but not to protect their victims. Chief Justice WARREN E. BURGER and Justice WILLIAM H. REHNQUIST dissented.

LEONARD W. LEVY

GLONA v. AMERICAN GUARANTEE AND LIABILITY INS. CO.

See: *Levy v. Louisiana*

GODCHARLES v. WIGEMAN

See: *Millett v. People*

GODFREY v. GEORGIA
100 S. Ct. 1759 (1980)

This is another case in which the Supreme Court reversed a death sentence because it was imposed under the state's standardless discretion: death for murder "outrageously or wantonly vile, or inhuman." Justice POTTER STEWART for a PLURALITY ruled that those words lacked objectivity and provided no principled basis for distinguishing the few cases in which death is imposed from the many in which it is not. Georgia's standard therefore placed no restraint on arbitrary and capricious infliction of the ultimate penalty. Two Justices argued that the death penalty is always CRUEL AND UNUSUAL. Three found Georgia's standard unobjectionable.

LEONARD W. LEVY

GOESAERT v. CLEARY
335 U.S. 464 (1948)

Goesaert typified the Court's SEX DISCRIMINATION decisions in the century between BRADWELL V. ILLINOIS (1873) and the 1970s. Michigan denied a woman a bartender's license unless she were "the wife or daughter of the male owner" of a licensed establishment. The Supreme Court, 6–3, rejected an EQUAL PROTECTION attack on this limitation. For the majority, Justice FELIX FRANKFURTER applied a RATIONAL BASIS standard of review: the legislature might rationally have believed that the presence of a barmaid's husband or father would help avoid "moral or social problems." Thus the Court could not "give ear to the suggestion that the real impulse behind this legislation was the unchivalrous desire of male bartenders to try to monopolize the calling."

Justice WILEY B. RUTLEDGE, for the dissenters, argued that the law failed to serve these protective ends, because unrelated, nonowner males might be present in some cases, and related male owners might be absent.

KENNETH L. KARST

GOLDBERG, ARTHUR J.
(1908–   )

Arthur Joseph Goldberg's tenure on the Supreme Court was a brief chapter in a long and distinguished career. He served fewer than three years, from October 1, 1962, until he resigned on July 25, 1965, to become the United States ambassador to the United Nations. Goldberg consistently voted with the WARREN COURT majority on CIVIL LIBERTIES and CRIMINAL PROCEDURE issues, although three terms as the Court's junior Justice scarcely gave him enough time to develop a distinctive voice on the major constitutional questions of that active period.

When Goldberg came to the Court, the unanimity of the earlier Warren years had begun to erode. The Court was struggling to give specific content to the broad principles established in the landmark rulings of the 1950s and early 1960s. Goldberg's appointment to replace FELIX FRANKFURTER allowed the flowering of the liberal JUDICIAL ACTIVISM for which the Warren Court is best remembered. Frequently his vote helped to create a bare majority for a FIRST AMENDMENT claim or for the rights of a criminal defendant.

ESCOBEDO V. ILLINOIS (1964), Justice Goldberg's best known opinion for the Court, was such a case. A year before, in GIDEON V. WAINWRIGHT, the Court had ruled unanimously that the state was required to provide counsel for an indigent defendant accused of a serious crime. The question in *Escobedo* was at what stage in the process from arrest through INDICTMENT the Sixth Amendment RIGHT TO COUNSEL attached. Voting 5–4, the Court overturned the murder conviction of a man whose request to consult a lawyer during interrogation by the police had been denied. In his opinion, Goldberg wrote: "The fact that many confessions are obtained during this period points up its critical nature as a 'stage when legal aid and advice' are surely needed. The right to counsel would indeed be hollow if it began at a period when few confessions were obtained." *Escobedo* thus pried open the door for MIRANDA V. ARIZONA (1966).

Goldberg's opinions for the Court also contributed to the growth of the First Amendment's protection of the freedoms of expression and association. COX V. LOUISIANA (1965) promoted the development of the concept of the "public forum." GIBSON V. FLORIDA LEGISLATIVE INVESTIGATION COMMITTEE (1963) remains a major precedent for protecting the privacy of political association. And APTHEKER V. SECRETARY OF STATE (1964) struck down a section of the Subversive Activities Control Act of 1950, which denied passports to members of various communist organizations. The law, Goldberg wrote for the Court, "sweeps too widely and too indiscriminately across the liberty guaranteed in the Fifth Amendment." *Aptheker* was an important stop in the elaboration of the First Amendment doctrine of OVERBREADTH. Goldberg also wrote the opinion for the Court in KENNEDY V. MENDOZA-MARTINEZ (1963), striking down a federal law that automatically revoked the CITIZENSHIP of anyone who left the country during a time of war or national emergency in order to evade the draft.

Goldberg's area of professional expertise was labor law, and he was widely regarded as the nation's most eminent labor lawyer. But because he joined the Court directly from eighteen months as secretary of labor in the cabinet of President JOHN F. KENNEDY, he excused himself from participation in many of the labor cases that reached the Court during his tenure.

Goldberg was born in Chicago on August 8, 1908, and received his law degree from Northwestern University in 1929. He built a labor law practice in Chicago before moving to Washington, D.C., in 1948 to serve as general counsel to both the Congress of Industrial Organizations (CIO) and the United Steelworkers. He was instrumental in the 1957 merger of organized labor's two factions, the CIO and the American Federation of Labor (AFL), and continued to play a key role in AFL-CIO affairs until he joined the Kennedy cabinet in 1961. His appointment to the Supreme Court followed the next year.

In 1965, President LYNDON B. JOHNSON persuaded him to leave the Court to fill the United Nations post made vacant by the death of Ambassador Adlai Stevenson. He resigned his ambassadorship in 1968 and practiced law briefly in New York, where he ran unsuccessfully for governor on the Democratic ticket in 1970. He then returned to Washington, where he continued to practice law and to speak out on civil liberties issues.

LINDA GREENHOUSE

Bibliography

CARMEN, IRA H. 1966 One Civil Libertarian among Many: The Case of Mr. Justice Goldberg. *Michigan Law Review* 65:301–336.

FRIEDMAN, STEPHEN J. 1969 Arthur J. Goldberg. In Leon Friedman and Fred L. Israel, eds., *The Justices of the United States Supreme Court 1789–1969*. New York: Chelsea House.

GOLDBERG v. KELLY
397 U.S. 254 (1970)

Residents of New York receiving WELFARE BENEFITS brought suit challenging the state's procedures authorizing termination of a beneficiary's benefits without a prior hearing on his or her eligibility. The Supreme Court, 6–3, held that these procedures denied PROCEDURAL DUE PROCESS.

For the majority, Justice WILLIAM J. BRENNAN rejected the state's argument that because welfare benefits were a "privilege" and not a "right," their termination could not deprive a beneficiary of "property" within the meaning of the due process clause. Those benefits, said Brennan, were "a matter of statutory entitlement for persons qualified to receive them" and thus qualified as "property" interests whose termination must satisfy the requirements of due process.

These requirements included an evidentiary hearing prior to the termination of welfare benefits, including timely notice of the reasons for the proposed termination, the right to retain counsel, opportunity to confront any adverse witnesses, and opportunity to present the beneficiary's own evidence. The procedural safeguards thus required approximated those available in judicial proceedings; the Court underscored the point by insisting on an impartial decision maker who would "state the reasons for his determination and indicate the evidence he relied on."

Goldberg was the leading decision extending the guarantees of procedural due process in civil proceedings beyond the protection of traditional COMMON LAW property interests to "entitlements" defined by statute, administrative regulation, or contract. It was aptly called the beginning of a "procedural due process revolution." By the mid-1970s, however, the counterrevolution had begun. (See BISHOP V. WOOD, 1976; PAUL V. DAVIS, 1976; MATHEWS V. ELDRIDGE, 1976.)

KENNETH L. KARST

GOLD CLAUSE CASES
Norman v. Baltimore & Ohio Railroad Co.
294 U.S. 240 (1935)
Nortz v. United States
294 U.S. 317 (1935)
Perry v. United States
294 U.S. 330 (1935)

The decisions in these cases were virtually the only Supreme Court opinions upholding congressional New Deal legislation before the judicial "revolution" of 1937. The Depression had caused an emergency in which contracts calling for payment in gold, rather than paper, "obstruct[ed] the power of Congress." So declaring, Congress passed the JOINT RESOLUTION of June 5, 1933, which asserted its regulatory power over gold as an item that "affect[ed] the public interest." Such gold clauses were "against public policy," and henceforth debtors could legally discharge their obligations in any other legal tender. Creditors resisted this action because, in conjunction with earlier legislation that had reduced the gold value of the dollar, it effectively devalued debts by allowing paper to be substituted for gold. Even though these suits involved relatively small amounts, they represented one hundred billion dollars in outstanding gold obligations (three-fourths of which were private debts) at a time when the Treasury had only some four billion dollars in gold reserves.

In *Norman v. Baltimore & Ohio Railroad Company*, the plaintiffs sought to enforce payment of $38.10 in currency, the equivalent of the value of the gold ($22.50) specified in the contract, a sixty-nine percent markup. Chief Justice CHARLES EVANS

HUGHES, for a 5–4 Court, reviewed the MONETARY POWER and, resting on *Knox v. Lee* (1871), insisted on the government's power to void any private OBLIGATION OF CONTRACTS that interfered with the exercise of Congress's power to regulate currency. The majority said that requiring debtors to pay sixty-nine percent more in currency to match the gold value of their debts would cause "dislocation of the domestic economy." The majority opinion, while reaching perhaps the only possible satisfactory result for the stability of the economy, was, in the conventional constitutional wisdom of the time, tenuous. In a spiteful dissent, Justice JAMES MCREYNOLDS attacked Hughes's purely pragmatic approach as a monstrous miscarriage of justice. Delivering his opinion orally, he exclaimed, "This is Nero at his worst. The Constitution is gone!"

In cases involving public obligations, the majority rested on sturdier constitutional ground. In accordance with the EMERGENCY BANK ACT, E. C. Nortz had surrendered his gold certificates after the government refused his demand for payment in gold. He sued for the difference between the currency he received and the value of the gold, over $64,000. Hughes, writing in *Nortz v. United States*, declared that gold certificates were only one form of currency and were thus replaceable by any other valid currency. Because Nortz suffered only "nominal" damages, his suit failed. In so deciding, the Court avoided the question whether gold certificates amounted to a contract with the government. In *Perry v. United States*, however, an 8–1 Court admitted that a government Liberty bond was a contractual obligation. Insofar as the joint resolution abrogated gold clauses in public contracts, it must be unconstitutional. A 5–4 majority quickly moved to destroy the force of this concession, however. Because the rise in gold prices which formed the basis of Perry's suit resulted from government manipulation of monetary values, payment in excess of a simple dollar-for-dollar exchange would constitute "unjust enrichment." Perry, like Nortz, had sustained only minimal damages and his suit likewise failed.

As McReynolds's dissent aptly noted, the majority was more concerned with economic and political consequences than constitutional precedent. ROBERT H. JACKSON, later on the Court himself, wrote that "in the guise of private law suits involving a few dollars, the whole American economy was haled before the Supreme Court." In these cases, by theoretically destroying thousands of obligations, the Court sustained Congress's exercise of the monetary power—

a course it found itself unable to follow when later confronted by other major New Deal legislation.

DAVID GORDON

Bibliography

DAWSON, JOHN P. 1935 Gold Clause Decisions. *Michigan Law Review* 33:647–684.

GOLDFARB v. VIRGINIA STATE BAR
421 U.S. 773 (1975)

By extending antitrust liability to the legal profession, this decision afforded consumers further protection against illegal business practices. The minimum fee schedule of the Fairfax County Bar Association, enforced by the Virginia State Bar, fixed the lowest charge for title searches at one percent of the value of the property involved. A unanimous eight-member Supreme Court, led by Chief Justice WARREN E. BURGER, sustaining a CLASS ACTION against the state and county bars, found violations of the price-fixing provisions of the SHERMAN ANTITRUST ACT as well as restraint of INTERSTATE COMMERCE.

DAVID GORDON

GOLD RESERVE ACT
48 Stat. 337 (1934)

Following the Gold Content Rider of mid-1933, the government sought to stabilize the gold value of the dollar in an effort to raise prices. Congress, fulfilling a request from President FRANKLIN D. ROOSEVELT, passed the Gold Reserve Act on January 30, 1934, under its MONETARY POWER and extended broad authority to establish a sound currency system. The act called in all gold and gold certificates in circulation, with specified exceptions, and granted the Treasury title to all monetary gold. The act also established an Exchange Stabilization Fund with which the secretary of the treasury was empowered to deal in gold in international markets to preserve a favorable balance of exchange and support the dollar. Congress also granted the President authority to regulate the gold content of the dollar. Further sections dealt with silver coinage and retroactively approved actions taken under authority of the EMERGENCY BANK ACT.

On January 31, Roosevelt reduced the gold content of the dollar to just under sixty percent of its former value. By mid-year the absence of circulating gold necessitated a congressional joint resolution abrogating clauses in private contracts and government bonds that called for payment in gold; the Supreme Court sustained this action in the GOLD CLAUSE CASES (1935).

DAVID GORDON

GOLDWATER v. CARTER
444 U.S. 285 (1979)

Members of Congress sued the President for declaratory and injunctive relief, claiming he had exceeded his powers in terminating a treaty with the Republic of China (Taiwan) without any congressional participation. Without briefing or ORAL ARGUMENT, a fragmented Supreme Court held, 6–3, that the case was not justiciable. Justice WILLIAM H. REHNQUIST, for four Justices, concluded that the case presented a POLITICAL QUESTION. Justice LEWIS F. POWELL rejected this argument but concluded that the case lacked RIPENESS because the President and Congress had not reached an impasse. Justice THURGOOD MARSHALL concurred in the result. Justice WILLIAM J. BRENNAN would have affirmed the court of appeals's decision upholding the President's action, and the other dissenting Justices would have set the case for full argument.

KENNETH L. KARST

GOMILLION v. LIGHTFOOT
364 U.S. 339 (1960)

Alabama redrew the boundaries of the city of Tuskegee in "an uncouth twenty-eight-sided figure" that excluded from the city all but a handful of black voters while excluding no whites. The lower federal courts refused to grant any relief from this racial GERRYMANDER, concluding on the basis of COLEGROVE V. GREEN (1946) that municipal boundaries, like legislative districting, presented only POLITICAL QUESTIONS that lacked JUSTICIABILITY.

The Supreme Court unanimously held the case justiciable, and eight Justices, speaking through Justice FELIX FRANKFURTER, concluded that the gerrymander violated the FIFTEENTH AMENDMENT. The effect of the law was so clear as to demonstrate a purpose to deprive blacks of their vote for city officials. Justice CHARLES E. WHITTAKER concurred, on the basis of the EQUAL PROTECTION clause of the FOURTEENTH AMENDMENT.

The door which *Gomillion* pried open was flung wide in BAKER V. CARR (1962), when the Court held that the malapportionment of state legislative districts presented a justiciable controversy under the equal protection clause.

KENNETH L. KARST

GOMPERS v. BUCK'S STOVE & RANGE COMPANY
221 U.S. 418 (1911)

In a decision that presaged the CLAYTON ACT, a unanimous Supreme Court held that an advertisement encouraging a SECONDARY BOYCOTT was unlawful and not protected by the FREEDOM OF SPEECH or of the PRESS. To support a local affiliate, the American Federation of Labor had run a notice in its magazine, the *American Federationist,* which transformed a local dispute into a national boycott by including the firm in a "We Don't Patronize" list. Prompted by a local strike, the company obtained an INJUNCTION prohibiting the AFL, its officers, and the local from obstructing sales or furthering any boycott, including use of the firm's name on the "We Don't Patronize" list. When Samuel Gompers and other union leaders ignored the injunction, they were jailed for contempt. Their APPEAL to the Court maintained that they could lawfully ignore the injunction because it abridged their rights of free speech and press.

Speaking for the Court, Justice JOSEPH R. LAMAR dismissed the free speech claim. Publication might provide a means of continuing an illegal boycott because the printing of words in an unlawful conspiracy might foster actions, thereby "exceeding any possible right of speech which a single individual might have." The resultant "verbal acts" would necessarily be subject to injunction. In this case, the publicity destroyed business and illegally restrained commerce. Here Lamar introduced the analogy of a SHERMAN ANTITRUST ACT violation, an analogy that has misled many authorities to believe that the case found such a violation—which it did not, for the company had not sought such relief. Declaring that the decision in LOEWE V. LAWLOR (1908) extended to any unlawful method of restraint, Lamar asserted that a failure to "hold that the restraint of trade under the Sherman anti-trust act, or on general principles of law, could be enjoined . . . would be to render the law impotent." This was no more than an analogy. Because

the boycott constituted an illegal conspiracy, the Court had the power and the duty to sustain the injunction.

With the effectiveness of the boycott reduced by this decision, labor turned to politics to influence elections and legislation. In a well-intentioned, if ambiguous, attempt to eliminate the confusion over labor's rights and obligations under the Sherman Act, Congress passed the Clayton Act in 1914. Section 20 of this act, ostensibly addressed to the *Gompers* issue, prohibited the issuance of injunctions restraining unions from maintaining secondary boycotts or "from recommending, advising, or persuading others by peaceful and lawful means so to do." Although the Court would virtually divest this section of meaning in DUPLEX PRINTING PRESS COMPANY V. DEERING (1921), Congress had the last word, passing the NORRIS-LaGUARDIA ACT in 1932.

DAVID GORDON

Bibliography

BERMAN, EDWARD (1930)1969 *Labor and the Sherman Act.* New York: Russell & Russell.

GONG LUM v. RICE
275 U.S. 78 (1927)

Classifying a youngster of Chinese ancestry as "colored," thereby compelling her to attend a black school, did not deny her EQUAL PROTECTION under the FOURTEENTH AMENDMENT. By so ruling, a unanimous Supreme Court upheld a Mississippi decision. The Court declined to consider the issue at length; citing ROBERTS V. BOSTON (Massachusetts, 1850) and PLESSY V. FERGUSON (1896), the Court concluded that PRECEDENT had clearly established a state's right to settle such issues of racial SEGREGATION without "intervention of the federal courts."

DAVID GORDON

GOOD BEHAVIOR

Until the late seventeenth century, royal judges held their offices "during the king's good pleasure." After the Glorious Revolution (1688–1689), judges in England (but not in the colonies) were appointed "during good behavior." This was a crucial step toward insuring the independence of the judiciary. The phrase was used in several revolutionary state constitutions, and the CONSTITUTIONAL CONVENTION OF 1787 unanimously adopted it to define the tenure of federal judges. ALEXANDER HAMILTON, in THE FEDERALIST, defended such tenure on the grounds that judicial independence is as necessary in a republic as in a monarchy.

It is by no means certain that a judge deviates from "good behavior" only when he commits "high crimes and misdemeanors"; however, the Constitution provides for no means of removal except IMPEACHMENT.

DENNIS J. MAHONEY

GOOD FAITH EXCEPTION

The good faith exception to the EXCLUSIONARY RULE created to enforce the FOURTH AMENDMENT allows prosecutorial use of illegally seized EVIDENCE if the police made the seizure in good faith reliance on the validity of a SEARCH WARRANT, even though an appellate court later finds that the warrant was unconstitutionally issued. As Justice BYRON R. WHITE for the Supreme Court stated the doctrine in UNITED STATES v. LEON (1984), the Court "modified" the exclusionary rule "so as not to bar the use in the prosecution's case-in-chief of evidence seized on a search warrant issued by a detached and neutral magistrate but ultimately found to be unsupported by PROBABLE CAUSE."

Those who support the good faith exception claim that it does not prevent either the Fourth Amendment or the exclusionary rule from achieving its intended functions. They see the exclusionary rule as a judicially created remedy designed to deter violations of the amendment; and they stress that the substantial costs exacted by the rule often outweigh its benefits. By excluding genuine evidence from the truth-finding process, the rule allows guilty persons to escape punishment and offends basic concepts of criminal justice. These costs can be justified only if the rule deters police misconduct. Advocates of the good faith exception assert, too, that the rule does not lower the probable cause standard and that it loses its deterrent capability when the officer has acted on a good faith belief that he was executing a warrant properly issued by a neutral magistrate and based on probable cause.

Opponents of the exception defend the exclusionary rule as inherent in the Fourth Amendment, preventing law enforcement officials from making any use of evidence obtained through their misconduct or misjudgment. Opponents claim that the amendment itself, not just the rule, makes convictions difficult. They stress that empirical studies show that the social cost of the exclusionary rule in lost prosecutions and acquittals has been exaggerated, and they argue that the rule improves police work by giving real effect to requirements to which law enforcement officials must conform. The good faith exception, on the other hand, places a premium on police ignorance of the law. Although they concede that no individual officer is likely to be deterred from unconstitutional conduct by exclusion of evidence seized in reliance on a defective warrant, the opponents argue that a good faith exception weakens the rule's influence toward a systemic or institutional compliance with the Fourth Amendment. They point out, too, that an objectively reasonable reliance on an UNREASONABLE SEARCH or on a warrant lacking probable cause is *impossible,* because no search and seizure can simultaneously be reasonable and unreasonable. The warrant requirement lies at the heart of the amendment, they contend; and the good faith exception erodes the requirement of probable cause. The Framers of the amendment sought to condition search and seizure on probable cause. They were primarily concerned with illegal warrants—GENERAL WARRANTS and WRITS OF ASSISTANCE. The exception admits illegally seized evidence and in so doing implicates the integrity of the judicial process. The exclusionary rule exists to deter violations of the amendment by all law enforcement agencies, the courts included.

Proponents of the good faith exception regard the courts, including the magistrates who issue warrants, as independent of, not part of, law enforcement agencies. Proponents and opponents of the exception, and of the exclusionary rule, argue from different premises and rarely confront each other's arguments.

LEONARD W. LEVY

Bibliography

KAMISAR, YALE 1984 Gates, "Probable Cause," "Good Faith," and Beyond. *Iowa Law Review* 69:551–615.

GOODNOW, FRANK J.
(1859–1939)

Frank Johnson Goodnow, founding president of the American Political Science Association (1903–1905), professor at Columbia University (1891–1912) and subsequently president of Johns Hopkins University (1914–1929), was one of the leading proponents of PROGRESSIVE CONSTITUTIONAL THOUGHT. Rejecting the traditional doctrine of SEPARATION OF POWERS, he urged a new separation of political decision making from public administration. In *Social Reform and the*

Constitution (1911) he condemned the STRICT CONSTRUCTION of the Constitution that blocked implementation of progressive reforms. He advocated a flexible CONSTITUTIONALISM that would reflect the pace of social change.

DENNIS J. MAHONEY

Bibliography

MAHONEY, DENNIS J. 1984 A New Political Science for a World Made Wholly New: The Doctrine of Progress and the Emergence of American Political Science. Ph.D. dissertation, Claremont Graduate School.

GORDON, THOMAS

See: Cato's Letters

GORHAM, NATHANIEL
(1738–1796)

Nathaniel Gorham, a prominent businessman and political leader, signed the Constitution as a representative of Massachusetts. One of the handful of most active delegates to the CONSTITUTIONAL CONVENTION OF 1787, Gorham presided over the Committee of the Whole, served on several committees, including the Committee on Detail, and spoke frequently. He was a supporter of strong national government.

DENNIS J. MAHONEY

GOSS v. LOPEZ
419 U.S. 565 (1975)

Ohio law authorized a public school principal to suspend a misbehaving student for up to ten days, without a hearing. A 5–4 Supreme Court held that this law violated a student's right to PROCEDURAL DUE PROCESS. For the majority, Justice BYRON R. WHITE found a "property" interest in the state's statute setting out a student's "entitlement" to attend school, and a "liberty" interest in the loss of reputation attending suspension for misconduct. While trivial school discipline might not require any hearing, a ten-day suspension demanded notice of the charges against the student, and, if the charges were denied, an explanation of the EVIDENCE and an opportunity to present his or her story. Justice LEWIS F. POWELL,

a former school board president, led the dissenters. The statute authorizing suspension gave only a conditional entitlement to attend school—as Justice WILLIAM H. REHNQUIST had argued in ARNETT V. KENNEDY (1974)—and the injury to reputation was not serious enough to invade a "liberty" interest. Thus, Powell argued, the school discipline here did "not assume constitutional dimensions."

KENNETH L. KARST

GOUDY, WILLIAM CHARLES
(1824–1893)

The leader of the Chicago bar, William Goudy was a creative constitutional lawyer and railroad counsel who argued many cases before the Supreme Court. He familiarized the Court with the relationship of laissez-faire tenets and constitutional limitations on STATE POLICE POWER. In *Munn v. Illinois* (see GRANGER CASES, (1877), WABASH, ST. LOUIS, AND PACIFIC RAILROAD V. ILLINOIS (1886), and CHICAGO, MILWAUKEE, AND ST. PAUL RAILROAD V. MINNESOTA (1890), he advanced SUBSTANTIVE DUE PROCESS of law in the context of arguments, stressing that the right to property included its unfettered use as well as its title and possession. State regulation of rates, by reducing profits, constituted a TAKING OF PROPERTY without JUST COMPENSATION and a denial of due process, according to Goudy.

LEONARD W. LEVY

Bibliography

TWISS, BENJAMIN 1942 Lawyers and the Constitution. Pages 76–84. Princeton, N.J.: Princeton University Press.

GOVERNMENT AID TO RELIGIOUS INSTITUTIONS

Constitutionality of governmental aid to religious institutions, generally, though not exclusively, in the form of financial subsidies, is most often challenged under the FIRST AMENDMENT's ban on laws respecting an ESTABLISHMENT OF RELIGION. When the purpose of the subsidy is to finance obviously religious activities, such as the erection or repairing of a church building, UNCONSTITUTIONALITY is generally recognized. In large measure the purpose of the establishment clause was to forbid such grants, as is indicated by the Court's opinion and Justice WILEY RUTLEDGE's dissenting opinion in EVERSON V. BOARD OF EDUCATION (1947). On the other hand, where the funds are used for what would generally be considered secular activities, such as maintaining hospitals or providing meals for pupils in church-related (often called parochial) schools, constitutional validity is fairly unanimously assumed.

Constitutional controversy revolves largely around governmental financing of church-related schools that combine the inculcation of religious doctrines and beliefs with what is generally considered the teaching of secular subjects, substantially, though not necessarily entirely, as they are taught in public schools.

In *Everson,* the Court upheld as a valid exercise of the POLICE POWER a state statute financing bus transportation to parochial schools, on the ground that the legislative purpose was not to aid religion by financing the operations of the schools but to help insure the safety of children going to or returning from them. A law having the former purpose would violate the establishment clause, which forbids government to set up a church, aid one or more religions, or prefer one religion over others. "No tax in any amount, large or small," the Court said, "can be levied to support any religious activities or institutions, whatever they may be called, or whatever form they may adopt to teach or practice religion."

The *Everson,* or "no-aid," interpretation of the establishment clause as applied to governmental financing of religious schools next reached the Supreme Court in the case of BOARD OF EDUCATION V. ALLEN (1968). There the Court upheld a New York statute providing for the loan to pupils attending nonpublic schools of secular textbooks authorized for use in public schools. The Court concluded that the statute did not impermissibly aid religious schools within the meaning of *Everson,* nor did it violate the establishment clause ban on laws lacking a secular legislative purpose or having a primary effect that either advances or inhibits religion, as that clause had been interpreted in ABINGTON SCHOOL DISTRICT V. SCHEMPP (1963). In upholding the New York law, the Court recognized that the police power rationale of *Everson* was not readily applicable to textbook laws, but it adjudged that the processes of secular and religious training are not so intertwined that secular textbooks furnished to students by the public are in fact instrumental in the teaching of religion.

It is fairly obvious that the *Allen* rationale could be used to justify state aid to religious schools considerably more extensive than mere financing of transportation or provision of secular textbooks. It could, for example, justify state financing of supplies other than textbooks, costs of maintenance and repair of parochial school premises, and, most important, salaries of instructors who teach the nonreligious subjects, which constitute the major part of the parochial school curriculum.

That this extension was intended by Justice BYRON R. WHITE, the author of the *Allen* opinion, is indicated by the fact that he thereafter dissented in all the decisions barring aid to church-related schools. The first of these decisions came in the companion cases of LEMON V. KURTZMAN and *Earley v. DiCenso* (1973). In *Lemon,* Pennsylvania purchased the services of religious schools in providing secular education to their pupils. In *DiCenso,* Rhode Island paid fifteen percent of the salaries of religious school teachers who taught only secular subjects.

A year earlier, in WALZ V. TAX COMMISSION (1970), the Court had expanded the purpose–effect test by adding a third dimension: a statute violated the establishment clause if it fostered excessive governmental entanglement with religion. The statutes involved in *Lemon* and *DiCenso* violated the clause, the Court held, because in order to insure that the teachers did not inject religion into their secular classes or allow religious values to affect the content of secular instruction, it was necessary to subject the teachers to comprehensive, discriminating, and continuing state surveillance, which would constitute forbidden entanglement of church and state.

In other cases the Court held unconstitutional laws enacted to reimburse religious schools for the cost of preparing, conducting, and grading teacher-prepared tests, of maintaining and repairing school buildings, of transporting students on field trips to museums and concerts as part of secular courses, and of purchasing instructional materials and equipment susceptible of diversion to religious use. The Court also held unconstitutional state tuition assistance to the parents of parochial school pupils, whether by direct grant or through state income tax benefits.

On the other hand, the Court has upheld the constitutionality of reimbursement for noninstructional health and welfare services supplied to parochial school pupils, such as meals, medical and dental care, and diagnostic services relating to speech, hearing, and psychological problems. In COMMITTEE FOR PUBLIC EDUCATION AND RELIGIOUS LIBERTY V. REGAN (1980) the Court allowed reimbursement for the expense of administering state-prepared and mandated objective examinations.

The Court has manifested a considerably more tolerant approach in cases challenging governmental aid to church-related institutions of higher education. While the purpose–effect–entanglement test is in principle equally applicable, the Court held that where a grant is used to finance facilities in colleges and universities used only for secular instruction, the primary effect of the law is not to advance religion. As for entanglement, religion does not necessarily so permeate the secular education provided by church-related colleges nor so seep into the use of their facilities as to require a ruling that in all cases excessive surveillance would be necessary to assure that the facilities were not used for religious purposes. The Court also gave consideration to the skepticism of college students, the nature of college and postgraduate courses, the high degree of academic freedom characterizing many church-related colleges, and their non-local constituencies. For all these reasons, in TILTON v. RICHARDSON (1973) the Court sanctioned substantial governmental financing of church-related institutions of higher education.

In *Walz v. Tax Commission* the Court upheld the constitutionality of tax exemption accorded to property used exclusively for worship or other religious purposes. Exemption, it held, does not entail sponsorship of religion and involves even less entanglement than nonexemption, since it does not require the government to examine the affairs of the church and audit its books or records. The longevity of exemption, dating as it does from the time the Republic was founded, constitutes strong evidence of its constitutionality.

The Court, in *Walz,* did not hold that the free exercise clause would be violated if exemption were disallowed (although it was urged to do so in the AMICUS CURIAE brief submitted by the National Council of Churches). Nor, on the other hand, did it decide to the contrary. As of the present, therefore, it seems that governments, federal or state, have the constitutional option of granting or denying exemption.

LEO PFEFFER

(SEE ALSO: *Separation of Church and State.*)

Bibliography

MORGAN, RICHARD E. 1972 *The Supreme Court and Religion.* New York: Free Press.
PFEFFER, LEO 1967 *Church, State and Freedom.* Rev. ed. Boston: Beacon Press.
———— 1975 *God, Caesar and the Constitution.* Boston: Beacon Press.
TRIBE, LAURENCE 1978 *American Constitutional Law.* Chap. 14. Mineola, N.Y.: Foundation Press.

GOVERNMENT INSTRUMENTALITY

Government instrumentalities are agencies, including government-owned corporations, created by Congress or the state legislatures to carry out public functions or purposes. Since McCULLOCH V. MARYLAND (1819) the doctrine of INTERGOVERNMENTAL IMMUNITY has precluded the state and federal governments from directly taxing one another's governmental instrumentalities.

DENNIS J. MAHONEY

GOVERNMENT REGULATION OF THE ECONOMY

See: Economic Regulation

GOVERNMENT SPEECH

FIRST AMENDMENT commentary has emphasized the danger of government as censor; thus lavish attention has been given to whether government can prevent Nazis from marching in Skokie, Illinois, Communists from advocating revolution, pornographers from selling their wares, or eccentrics from yelling fire in crowded theaters. Much less attention has been paid to the role of government as speaker; yet, one need only notice the ready access of government officials to the mass media, the constant stream of legislative and executive reports and publications, and the massive system of direct grants and indirect subsidies to the communications process (including federal financing of elections) to recognize that speech financed or controlled by government plays an enormous role in the marketplace of ideas. Sometimes the government speaks as government; sometimes it subsidizes speech without purporting to claim that the resulting message is its own. The term "government speech," therefore, includes all forms of state-supported communications: official government messages; statements of public officials at publicly subsidized press conferences; artistic, scientific, or political subsidies; even the classroom communications of public school teachers.

Basic assumptions of First Amendment law are sharply modified when governments speak. A basic canon of First Amendment law is that content distinctions are suspect. Indeed, in POLICE DEPARTMENT

OF CHICAGO V. MOSLEY (1972) the Court insisted that government could not deviate " 'from the neutrality of time, place and circumstances into a concern about content.' This is never permitted." When governments speak, however, content distinctions are the norm. Government does not speak at random; it makes editorial judgments; it decides that some content is appropriate for the occasion and other content is not. The public museum curator makes content distinctions in selecting exhibits; the librarian, in selecting books; the public official, in composing press releases. If government could not make content distinctions, it could not speak effectively.

The government speech problem is to determine the constitutional limits, if any, on the editorial decisions of government. BUCKLEY V. VALEO (1976) squarely presented the issue. Certain minor party candidates argued that their exclusion from the system of public financing of presidential elections violated the First Amendment and the DUE PROCESS CLAUSE of the Fifth Amendment. The Court briskly dismissed the relevance of the First Amendment challenge on the ground that a subsidy "furthers, not abridges, pertinent First Amendment values." This cryptic response has prompted criticism on the ground that it ignores the equality values in the First Amendment. One wonders, for example, how the Court would have reacted if the Congress had funded Democrats but not Republicans. Nonetheless, the Court did consider an equality claim grounded in Fifth Amendment due process, and concluded that the financing scheme was in "furtherance of sufficiently important government interests and has not unfairly or unnecessarily burdened the political opportunity of any party or candidate."

Buckley is important for two reasons. First, it affirms that government subsidies for speech enhance First Amendment values, recognizing that our "statute books are replete with laws providing financial assistance to the exercise of free speech, such as aid to public broadcasting and other forms of educational media . . . and preferential postal rates and antitrust exceptions for newspapers." Second, it seems to recognize that political subsidies are subject to constitutional limits under the equality principle, if not under the principle of free speech.

The First Amendment issues given short shrift in *Buckley* were fully aired in BOARD OF EDUCATION v. PICO (1982). Students alleged that the school board had removed nine books from school libraries because "particular passages in the books offended their social, political and moral tastes and not because the books, taken as a whole, were lacking educational value."

The case produced seven different opinions and no clear resolution of the First Amendment issues. Over the dissent of four Justices, the Court ruled that the students' complaint could survive a summary judgment motion. Four of the Justices in the majority stated that if the allegations of the complaint were vindicated, the First Amendment barred the board's action. The fifth Justice, BYRON R. WHITE, thought that because of unresolved questions of fact the case should proceed to trial; he maintained, however, that discussion of the First Amendment issues was premature.

Most of the eight Justices who did discuss the issues expressed three important notes of agreement. First, they agreed that a major and appropriate purpose of government speech in the public schools is to transmit community values "promoting respect for authority and traditional values be they social, moral, or political." There was substantial disagreement, however, about the relevance of this purpose to book selections for a school library. Second, the Justices agreed that local authorities had wide latitude in making content decisions about library materials. Finally, most agreed that discretion could not be employed in a "narrowly partisan or political manner," such as removing all books written by Republicans. Beyond these agreements, however, the Justices struggled over differences between libraries and classrooms, between lower and higher levels of education, between acquiring books and removing books. *Pico* stands for little more than the proposition that government's broad discretion in subsidizing speech is not entirely unfettered by the First Amendment.

Perhaps the most serious challenges of government speech have surrounded government spending to influence the outcome of election campaigns. In many lower court cases, taxpayers have challenged the constitutionality of spending by cities or administrative agencies to influence the outcome of initiative campaigns. Lower courts have frequently avoided constitutional issues, concluding that state law does not authorize the city or administrative agency to spend the money. At least one question is implicitly resolved by these decisions, however, namely, that cities and administrative agencies do not have First Amendment rights against the state, at least none comparable to the rights of individuals or business corporations. The decisions have left open the question of the extent to which the Constitution permits governments to use their treasuries to help one side in an election campaign.

The establishment clause unquestionably prohibits some forms of religious government speech, and the

EQUAL PROTECTION clause presumably prohibits some forms of racially discriminatory government speech. It remains to be seen what other limits the First Amendment or the equal protection clause may place on government's massive role in subsidizing speech.

STEVEN SHIFFRIN

Bibliography

SHIFFRIN, STEVEN 1983 Government Speech. *UCLA Law Review* 27:565–655.
YUDOF, MARK 1983 *When Government Speaks: Politics, Law, and Government Expression in America.* Berkeley and Los Angeles: University of California Press.

GRACE v. UNITED STATES
461 U.S. 171 (1983)

A federal statute forbids display of any flag or device designed to "bring into public notice any party, organization, or movement" in the United States Supreme Court building or on its grounds. The Supreme Court held this statute invalid, on FIRST AMENDMENT grounds, as applied to lone individuals engaging in expressive activity on the sidewalk adjoining the Court's building. The Court did not address the law's validity as applied to the building or the grounds inside the sidewalk, or to parades or demonstrations on the sidewalk.

KENNETH L. KARST

GRAHAM v. RICHARDSON
403 U.S. 365 (1971)

Arizona denied certain WELFARE BENEFITS to ALIENS who had not lived in the country fifteen years. Pennsylvania denied similar benefits to all aliens. The Supreme Court unanimously held these restrictions unconstitutional. Justice HARRY A. BLACKMUN, for the Court, said that alienage, like race, was a SUSPECT CLASSIFICATION, demanding STRICT SCRUTINY by the Court of its justification. The state argued that its "special public interest" in aiding its own citizens justified discriminating against aliens, but the Court, citing TAKAHASHI V. FISH AND GAME COMMISSION (1948), rejected the argument. The discrimination thus denied aliens the EQUAL PROTECTION OF THE LAWS.

Again citing *Takahashi*, the Court concluded that the two state laws invaded the province of Congress to regulate aliens, encroaching on an area of "exclusive federal power." Justice JOHN MARSHALL HARLAN concurred only as to this FEDERALISM ground, refusing to join in the equal protection ground.

KENNETH L. KARST

GRAMM-RUDMAN-HOLLINGS ACT
99 Stat. 1037 (1985)

The Balanced Budget and Emergency Deficit Control Act of 1985 is better known by the names of its three principal Senate sponsors, Phil Gramm (Republican, Texas), Warren B. Rudman (Republican, New Hampshire), and Ernest Hollings (Democrat, South Carolina). Attached as a rider to the bill that raised the national debt ceiling to $2 trillion, the act amended the CONGRESSIONAL BUDGET AND IMPOUNDMENT CONTROL ACT of 1974. Under the Gramm-Rudman-Hollings Act the maximum budget deficit for fiscal year 1986 was set at $180 billion, and maximum deficits were set for the next four fiscal years, with deficits to be completely eliminated beginning in fiscal year 1991. To enforce the deficit limitation, the act established an automatic mechanism according to which the OFFICE OF MANAGEMENT AND BUDGET (an executive agency) and the Congressional Budget Office (a congressional agency) were required annually to report their estimates of the deficit to the comptroller general (the head of the General Accounting Office, another congressional agency), who was to average the two estimates and report the result to the President. The President would be required to issue an executive order "sequestering" appropriated funds to the extent that the estimated deficit exceeded the deficit authorized by the act. Other provisions of the act divided the sequestration equally between defense appropriations and nondefense domestic programs and exempted from sequestration funds appropriated for Social Security, interest payments on the national debt (the total of previous deficits), and certain other programs.

The constitutionality of some aspects of the act was questioned even before the act was passed by Congress; and President RONALD REAGAN alluded to outstanding constitutional questions even as he signed the act into law. Indeed, the act contained provisions facilitating JUDICIAL REVIEW. It authorized members of Congress to file suit challenging the constitutionality of the act, it provided for challenges to be heard by a special three-judge federal court with direct appeal to the Supreme Court, and it set up an expedited process at each level of the judiciary.

Within hours of President Reagan's signing the act, Representative Michael Synar (Democrat, Oklahoma) filed suit charging that Congress, in the act, unconstitutionally delegated its power to control federal spending and that, even if the DELEGATION OF POWER were constitutional, delegation to the comptroller general, who serves at the pleasure of Congress, was unconstitutional. The latter argument was based on the modern understanding of SEPARATION OF POWERS, exemplified by the Supreme Court's decision in IMMIGRATION AND NATURALIZATION SERVICE V. CHADHA (1983). Should Synar's suit prevail, the deficit limits would be left intact, but the automatic enforcement provisions would be eliminated and imposition of spending controls to meet the limits would depend on the ability of members of Congress to agree to a JOINT RESOLUTION reducing spending. In early 1986, a three-judge federal court in the District of Columbia heard Synar's suit and held that the automatic provisions of the act, insofar as they delegated authority other than to executive branch officials, were unconstitutional.

DENNIS J. MAHONEY

GRANDFATHER CLAUSE

This expression, born of legislative skulduggery, has survived to serve more acceptable purposes. A number of southern states, seeking to circumvent the FIFTEENTH AMENDMENT's prohibition against RACIAL DISCRIMINATION in the field of VOTING RIGHTS, adopted LITERACY TESTS for voter eligibility. These provisions standing alone would have disqualified not only most black registrants but also a large number of whites. Under a typical exception, however, an illiterate might be registered if he had been eligible to vote before some date in 1865 or 1866, or if he were the descendant of a person eligible at that time. The Supreme Court, in GUINN V. UNITED STATES (1915) and *Lane v. Wilson* (1939), held such grandfather clauses invalid.

More recently, the same term has described any legislative exception relieving from regulation a person who has been engaging in a certain practice for a period of time. A new ZONING law, for example, might limit LAND USE in one zone to single-family residences, but contain a grandfather clause allowing the continuation of businesses or apartment houses already operating there. In part, such an exception is designed to avoid constitutional problems that arguably might arise in its absence. (See TAKING OF PROP-ERTY; VESTED RIGHTS; SUBSTANTIVE DUE PROCESS.) But the exception itself may be challenged as unconstitutional. In NEW ORLEANS V. DUKES (1976), the city had prohibited the sale of food from pushcarts in the French Quarter, but had exempted pushcart vendors who had been operating there more than eight years. The Supreme Court unanimously upheld this grandfather clause against an EQUAL PROTECTION attack. Quite properly, the Court omitted mention of *Lane v. Wilson;* it did say, however, that in cases of ECONOMIC REGULATION, "only the INVIDIOUS DISCRIMINATION" was invalid.

KENNETH L. KARST

Bibliography
SCHMIDT, BENNO C., JR. 1982 Principle and Prejudice: The Supreme Court and Race in the Progressive Era. Part 3: Black Disfranchisement from the KKK to the Grandfather Clause. *Columbia Law Review* 82:835–905.

GRAND JURY

Historians date the grand jury to King Henry II's Assize of Clarendon in 1166. That ancient ancestor was markedly different from its American descendants. The Grand Assize, as it was known, was comprised of local gentry, relying on personal knowledge and local rumor to report alleged cases of misconduct. Today's grand jury—surviving in America, but since 1933 abolished in England—normally considers events and people unknown to the grand jurors, who receive fairly formal testimony and other EVIDENCE, presented by prosecutors to decide whether or not alleged wrongdoers ought to be indicted.

Between 1166 and 1791, when the American BILL OF RIGHTS was adopted, the grand jury had come to be viewed as a safeguard for the people rather than an investigative arm of the executive. This is reflected in the portion of the Fifth Amendment that says: "No person shall be held to answer for a capital, or otherwise infamous crime, unless on a PRESENTMENT or INDICTMENT of a Grand Jury, except in cases arising in the land or naval forces, or in the Militia, when in actual service in time of War or public danger."

This means that nobody outside the armed forces may be put to trial for a serious federal crime unless a grand jury has heard enough evidence to satisfy it that there is PROBABLE CAUSE (enough evidence on the prosecution side, largely or wholly ignoring what the defendant may show, to make it reasonable) to issue an indictment. The good sense of the safeguard is the realization that "merely" being brought to trial can be an agonizing, expensive, destructive experience. In this light, the grand jury stands as a shield against arbitrary or wicked or careless prosecutors bringing people to trial on insufficient or improper grounds.

In modern times, this role as bulwark retains an exceedingly limited reality. As a practical matter, grand juries, especially in the busy urban settings where they do the bulk of their work, function largely as the investigative and indicting arms of prosecutorial officials. There could be no other feasible or acceptable way for them to operate. The detection of crime, the decision to investigate, the judgment as to where prosecution resources should be invested are no longer, if they ever were, subjects suitable for amateur, part-time management. Inevitably, then, grand jurors work almost entirely under the guidance and effective control of prosecutors. They consider cases brought to them by the government's lawyers. They tend almost always to indict when they are advised to indict, and not otherwise.

Although this quality of "rubber stamp" is markedly unlike the constitutional ideal, there is no agreeable alternative if we are to keep the grand jury as a body of lay citizens. The grand jury is a potent instrument for invading PRIVACY, threatening reputations, and cutting a swath of terror and anxiety if it proceeds without a prudent awareness of its impact and a deep sense of its duty to be fair and discreet. In the hands of untrained people, it would be an engine of destruction. Such considerations might point in the end to abolishing the grand jury altogether. But while and wherever it survives, the leadership role of professionals is probably desirable as well as inevitable.

The passive character of the grand jury should not, however, be overstated. In strict law, the grand jury is an agency of the court rather than of the prosecution. A judge of the court is required to instruct the jurors concerning their powers and responsibilities. A judge should be available to answer questions and give guidance as the group proceeds with its work. Properly performed, these judicial directions can promote some measure of the independent judgment and common-sense wisdom that grand jurors are in principle expected to supply. Grand jurors do in fact decline now and again to return indictments sought by the prosecution. In far fewer cases "runaway" grand juries may contrive to investigate and indict people whom the prosecutors, for reasons that may be good or bad, do not deem suitable targets. These occur-

rences are, however, rare indeed, and usually happen in circumstances of local disarray and political upset.

In its normal functioning, the grand jury operates as a peculiar variant of the familiar Anglo-American judicial process—in some measure aping courtroom procedures but differing in fundamental respects. The similarity consists mainly in the types of evidence and, partially, in the mode of presentation. Grand juries hear witnesses under oath, proceeding by question and answer in something close to the style of the courtroom, with a prosecuting attorney doing most or all of the interrogation. Similarly, the grand jurors are given documents or other things as "exhibits" to assist in the attempted reconstruction, or partial reconstruction, of the events under inquiry. A critical difference from the courtroom is the one-sidedness of the presentation. In a system that prides itself on being "adversarial"—as distinguished from the so-called inquisitorial system of the European continent and many other countries—the grand jury is more purely inquisitorial and nonadversarial than almost any other criminal law agency anywhere. Subject to some variations among the states, the norm is that only one side, the prosecution, is heard. There is no opposing lawyer to object to questions or answers on grounds of relevance, fairness, privilege, or anything else. Nobody impartial presides; there are no disputes to umpire. In some places a potential defendant may be allowed on request to appear and present evidence that may persuade the grand jurors not to indict. More commonly, the prospective target will be heard only upon being summoned (and duly warned about the RIGHT AGAINST SELF-INCRIMINATION) by the prosecution.

The EX PARTE character of the proceeding means, in most states and in the federal courts, that the trial rules of evidence are not applicable. These rules require for effective operation the presence of an opposing lawyer to object and a judicial officer to rule on objections as the evidentiary record is being made. Free (or deprived) of all that, the grand jury may receive, and base indictments upon, hearsay or other evidence that would be excluded on objection in a trial.

Still more thoroughly ex parte, the grand jury's proceedings, until an indictment is published, are almost totally secret. This aspect accounts for a good part of what is perceived (and not infrequently functions) as fearsome and threatening in the grand jury. The concealed tribunal is by its nature more likely than the open courtroom to be a place where corners are cut and abuses are perpetrated, ranging from the tricking and bullying of witnesses to the misleading of the grand jurors themselves. Still, the received doctrine thought to justify the secrecy retains considerable vitality. As they were summarized in 1958 by the Supreme Court, the reasons are:

(1) To prevent the escape of those whose indictment may be contemplated; (2) to insure the utmost freedom to the grand jury in its deliberations, and to prevent persons subject to indictment or their friends from importuning the grand jurors; (3) to prevent subornation of perjury or tampering with the witnesses who may testify before [the] grand jury and later appear at the trial of those indicted by it; (4) to encourage free and untrammeled disclosures by persons who have information with respect to the commission of crimes; (5) to protect [the] innocent accused who is exonerated from disclosure of the fact that he has been under investigation, and from the expense of standing trial where there was no probability of guilt. [*United States v. Procter & Gamble Company*, 356 U.S. 677, 681 n. 6 (1958).]

Granting these salutary concerns, the concealed proceedings of grand juries are pregnant with grave possibilities of abuse, too often realized in the work of insensitive or malevolent prosecutors. As mentioned, witnesses in the grand jury room face dangers of abuse, oppression, harassment, and entrapment. Judge LEARNED HAND, never tender in enforcing the criminal law, noted this familiar problem in *United States v. Remington* (2d Cir. 1953) where he thought decent bounds had been overstepped: "Save for torture, it would be hard to find a more effective tool of tyranny than the power of unlimited and unchecked ex parte examination."

A grand jury has the power to compel witnesses to testify. (See IMMUNITY GRANTS; BRANZBURG V. HAYES, 1972.) The plight of a grand jury witness is aggravated by the standard rule, in federal and most state courts, barring lawyers from accompanying witnesses to the grand jury room. Abstruse questions of privilege, the ever present dangers of later perjury prosecutions, and problems of relevance or other evidentiary objections must be discerned by the lay witness and somehow handled on the spot or made the subject of hurried consultation with counsel outside the grand jury room, an ungainly procedure that often has witnesses trotting back and forth between lawyer and grand jurors during hours or days of interrogation.

Among other grievances evoked by grand juries is the superficially paradoxical complaint against failures of secrecy. The grand jury "leak" is a familiar and pernicious phenomenon, scarring reputations and threatening the right to a FAIR TRIAL. The problems of preventing and sanctioning leaks remain among the unresolved doubts concerning the grand jury's net worth as an institution. Probably all these criticisms have helped persuade the Supreme Court not to extend the INCORPORATION DOCTRINE, applying the "right" to indictment by grand jury to state felony prosecutions. (See HURTADO V. CALIFORNIA, 1884.)

These unresolved doubts are subjects of ongoing debate. Many distinguished jurists and scholars argue that the grand jury has outlived its usefulness and should be abolished. That is a tall order at the federal level, where it would require amendment of the Fifth Amendment (which would be the first change in any portion of the Bill of Rights since its adoption). On the other hand, over half the states have dispensed with the requirement of grand jury indictment, permitting felonies to be prosecuted by INFORMATION (a written accusation by the prosecutor), and that trend seems likely to continue.

Still, at the federal level and in at least a number of states, total abolition seems highly improbable through at least the remainder of the twentieth century. In this setting, grand jury reform is a recurrently lively topic. Among the proposals (and changes already effected in some states) are provisions that would allow counsel to accompany witnesses before the grand jury; require closer control and supervision by judges; prescribe more detailed accounting by prosecutors and records of grand jury proceedings; better advise and protect prospective defendants; and confine the abuses of leaks and prejudicial publicity by prosecutorial staffs. The prospects for sound reform are greatest when citizens outside the legal profession take an informed interest in the problems.

MARVIN E. FRANKEL

Bibliography

DASH, SAMUEL 1972 The Indicting Grand Jury: A Critical Stage. *American Criminal Law Review* 10:807–828.
FRANKEL, MARVIN E. and NAFTALIS, GARY P. 1975 *The Grand Jury*. New York: Hill & Wang.
NOTE 1961 The Grand Jury as an Investigatory Body. *Harvard Law Review* 74:590–605.
YOUNGER, RICHARD D. 1963 *The People's Panel: The Grand Jury in the United States*. Providence, R.I.: Brown University Press.

GRAND RAPIDS SCHOOL DISTRICT v. BALL

See: *Aguilar v. Felton*

GRANGER CASES
(1877)
Munn v. Illinois, 94 U.S. 113

Chicago, Burlington & Quincy Railroad v. Iowa, 94 U.S. 155

Peik v. Chicago & Northwestern Railway Co., 94 U.S. 164

Chicago, Milwaukee & St. Paul Railroad Co. v. Ackley, 94 U.S. 179

Winona and St. Peter Railroad Co. v. Blake, 94 U.S. 180

Stone v. Wisconsin, 94 U.S. 181

The *Granger Cases,* decided on March 1, 1877, included *Munn v. Illinois,* in which state regulation of grain warehouse and elevator rates and practices was challenged, and five railroad cases in which the companies attacked the validity of state legislatures' imposition of fixed maximum rates. In these decisions, the Supreme Court upheld the state regulations. Conservative, pro-business voices—and Justice STEPHEN J. FIELD, in vigorous dissent in *Munn*—regarded the decisions as a catastrophic surrender of DUE PROCESS values in law and a mortal blow to entrepreneurial liberty. They left legislatures, Field contended, with an unfettered power over private property rights of business firms. To the Court's majority, speaking through Chief Justice MORRISON R. WAITE, however, the issue of state regulation's legitimacy must turn on the difference in nature between business that was purely private and business that was AFFECTED WITH A PUBLIC INTEREST, hence peculiarly subject to regulation.

Laws for the regulation of railroads and grain warehouses, enacted in Illinois, Wisconsin, Iowa, and Minnesota during the period 1871–1874, were at issue in the 1877 decisions. Until recent years, historians and students of constitutional law have tended to accept the view that the Grange and other farm organizations provided the political muscle in the midwestern reform movements that produced those laws. Indeed, it was customary to regard the legislation as radical, antibusiness, and anti-private property in intent and content. Recent research (particularly the work of historian George L. Miller) has shown, however, that there was no general antagonism between agrarian and business interests in the debates over the regulatory laws. Instead, reform was sought by

coalitions, in a pattern of intrastate sectionalism; farmers lined up with commercial interests in some sections that favored regulation, and similar interests joined against regulation in other sections. The division of views depended much more upon calculations of local advantage and disadvantage from regulation than upon political ideology, "agrarian" or otherwise, or even upon political party alignments.

Contrary to another view long held by scholars, the Granger laws did not lack legislative precedent. The charters of early railway companies typically had carried maximum rate provisions and other features that bespoke the state's interest in the efficient provision of transport services. And in the 1850s several states (notably New York and Ohio) had prohibited local discrimination in railroad rate-making and had levied special taxes on railroad companies to offset the effects of rail competition on state-owned canals. The Granger laws may be seen as an extension of a regulatory tradition well established in American railway law.

Still another common error of interpretation concerns the doctrinal basis of the "affectation" doctrine as employed in Waite's majority opinion in *Munn.* The concept of "business affected with a public interest," according to a long-standard view, was a surprising resort to a forgotten antiquity of English COMMON LAW—a concept reintroduced into American law after a lapse of nearly two centuries. In fact, the concept of affectation was well known in American riparian and ADMIRALTY law; and equally familiar was the jurist from whose writings Waite drew the affectation concept for use in *Munn,* for Lord Chief Justice Matthew Hale's tracts on common law had been cited in scores of important American cases in riparian and EMINENT DOMAIN law.

The Court's majority in the *Granger Cases* rejected the contention of railroad counsel that if state legislatures were permitted to mandate fixed, maximum rates, the result would be to deprive business of fair profits, and thus to produce effective "confiscation" of private property. The majority also rejected the view that the EQUAL PROTECTION and due process clauses of the Fourteenth Amendment warranted judicial review of the fairness of rates. Such regulatory power was subject to abuse, Waite conceded, but this was "no argument against its existence. For protection against abuses by legislatures the people must resort to the polls, not to the courts."

Thus the *Granger Cases* decisions held back, at least for a time, the conservative efforts to make the Fourteenth Amendment a fortress for VESTED RIGHTS against the STATE POLICE POWER. The decisions were also of enduring importance in constitutional development for their elaborate formulation of the "affectation with a public interest" doctrine. Relying upon the advice of his colleague Justice JOSEPH P. BRADLEY, who was learned in the English law of common carriers and in admiralty law, Waite explored in his opinion the legitimate reach of the police power in regulation of business. He concluded that modern railroad companies and warehouses played a role in commerce that was analogous to the role played by ferry operators and others who in the seventeenth century had exercised a "virtual monopoly" of vital commercial services, hence were held subject to regulations not ordinarily imposed on other businesses. Thus the Court indicated, by implication at least, that businesses not so affected with a special public interest could not be regulated.

Not long after publication of the decisions, Waite wrote privately: "The great difficulty in the future will be to establish the boundary between that which is private, and that in which the public has an interest. The Elevators furnished an extreme case, and there was no difficulty in determining on which side of the line they properly belonged." This proved an accurate forecast of the Court's future travails, until in *Nebbia v. New York* (1934) the Court finally abandoned the "affectation" doctrine, holding that *all* businesses were subject to state regulation under the police power.

Within fifteen years after the *Granger Cases*, moreover, the Court had begun to invoke both the COMMERCE CLAUSE and the Fourteenth Amendment to strike down state regulations of interstate railroad operations and to review both procedural and substantive aspects of state regulation of business. The drive to establish a new constitutional foundation for vested rights, in sum, for many years relegated the *Granger Cases'* support of a broad legislative discretion to the status of a doctrinal relic.

HARRY N. SCHEIBER

Bibliography
FAIRMAN, CHARLES 1953 "The So-Called Granger Cases, Lord Hale, and Justice Bradley." *Stanford Law Review* 5:587–679.
MAGRATH, C. PETER 1963 *Morrison R. Waite: The Triumph of Character.* New York: Macmillan.
MILLER, GEORGE L. 1971 *Railroads and the Granger Laws.* Madison: University of Wisconsin Press.
SCHEIBER, HARRY N. 1971 The Road to *Munn:* Eminent Domain and the Concept of Public Purpose in the State Courts. *Perspectives in American History* 5:327–402.

GRANT, ULYSSES SIMPSON
(1822–1885)

Next to President ABRAHAM LINCOLN, Ulysses S. Grant was the most important individual in the struggle to maintain the Union and the reconstruction of the nation in the Civil War period. A West Point graduate, Grant left the military in 1854 but returned as a colonel in the Illinois Volunteers in 1861. By 1864 Grant had risen to become America's first lieutenant general since Washington, and commander of all Union forces. Throughout the war Grant understood that victory was synonymous with preserving the Union and the Constitution. He developed strategies that devastated the South, because he believed that only a decisive defeat of the Confederacy, with a military abolition of slavery and an unconditional surrender of southern troops, would remove SECESSION from the American constitutional vocabulary.

In 1866 Grant became America's first full general, and he gradually challenged ANDREW JOHNSON's leadership. Grant accepted an interim appointment as secretary of war, in defiance of the TENURE OF OFFICE ACT, but he relinquished the post to EDWIN M. STANTON, paving the way for Johnson's IMPEACHMENT. As President (1869–1877) Grant supported the FIFTEENTH AMENDMENT (1870), the Ku Klux Klan Act (1871), the CIVIL RIGHTS ACT of 1875, and the creation of a Department of Justice and SOLICITOR GENERAL's office to help enforce these new measures. However, after 1872 Grant gave little support to the freedmen and their white allies. He dismissed his aggressively integrationist attorney general, Amos Akerman, and in 1875–1876 he refused to send federal troops to protect black voters.

Three of Grant's Supreme Court nominees were never confirmed while a fourth, Edwin Stanton, died before he could take office. Apart from JOSEPH BRADLEY, Grant's successful Court appointments to the Court, WILLIAM STRONG, WARD HUNT, and MORRISON WAITE, were lackluster. Grant's administration was scandal-ridden. His secretary of war was impeached and avoided conviction only through resignation.

PAUL FINKELMAN

Bibliography
MCFEELY, WILLIAM S. 1981 *Grant: A Biography.* New York: Norton.

GRANTS-IN-AID

See: Federal Grants-in-Aid

GRAVEL v. UNITED STATES
408 U.S. 606 (1972)

In the midst of efforts by the United States government to enjoin publication of the classified Pentagon Papers (see NEW YORK TIMES CO. V. UNITED STATES, 1971), Senator Mike Gravel (Democrat, Alaska) held a "meeting" of his subcommittee, read extensively from the papers, and placed their entire text in the record. In this case a federal GRAND JURY sought to question Gravel's aide concerning the senator's action and the subsequent private publication of the papers. The Supreme Court, in an opinion by Justice BYRON R. WHITE and over four dissents, confirmed that reading the papers in subcommittee was protected by the SPEECH OR DEBATE CLAUSE. The clause also extended its protection to congressional aides acting as alter egos to members of Congress. But *Gravel* held that dissemination of the papers to a private publisher was not a legislative act, and thus was not protected by the speech or debate clause. Therefore, Gravel's aide could be questioned about the private publication of the papers.

THEODORE EISENBERG

GRAVES v. NEW YORK ex rel. O'KEEFE
306 U.S. 466 (1939)

For practical purposes the decision in *Graves* by a 7–2 Supreme Court toppled an elaborate structure of INTERGOVERNMENTAL TAX IMMUNITIES, which the Justices had erected from assumptions about the federal system. The right of self-preservation immunized the United States and the states from taxation by competing governments within the system. Obviously the United States cannot tax the Commonwealth of Massachusetts or the state capitol in Sacramento, California, any more than the states can tax a congressional investigation. From a sensible assumption first advanced in MCCULLOCH V. MARYLAND (1819) protecting a national instrumentality from state taxation, the Court made progressively sillier decisions that hampered the TAXING POWER of the state and national governments and allowed many commercial activities to escape taxation. COLLECTOR V. DAY (1871) made the salaries of state judges exempt from federal income taxes. In

time the Court held unconstitutional a federal tax on the income of a private corporation leasing state land, and a federal sales tax on a motorcycle sold by a private corporation to city police.

By 1939 the Court had already begun to retrench its doctrines of reciprocal tax immunities enjoyed by "government" instrumentalities. In *Graves,* Justice HARLAN FISKE STONE faced the question whether a state tax on the salary of an employee of a federal instrumentality created by Congress violated the principles of national supremacy. Stone observed that the tax was imposed on an employee's salary, not on the instrumentality itself. Because the Constitution did not mandate tax immunity and such immunity should attach only to a government instrumentality, the Court not only sustained the tax but also overruled *Day* and several related cases. A state may tax the income of officers or employees of the national government, and vice versa. In *New York v. United States* (1946), the Court upheld a national tax on soft drinks bottled by the state. To the extent that government functions cannot be be taxed by another government the core doctrine from *McCulloch* endures.

LEONARD W. LEVY

GRAY, HORACE
(1828–1902)

Horace Gray, Jr., reporter of the Supreme Judicial Court of Massachusetts (1854–1861) and Associate Justice (1864–1873) and Chief Justice (1873–1881) of the same court, was appointed to the United States Supreme Court in 1882 and served until his death twenty years later. Anglo-American legal history was his forte; he was the nation's leading judicial exponent of Harvard-style "legal science" during the second half of the nineteenth century. Like Dean Christopher Columbus Langdell, his Harvard classmate and lifelong friend, Gray viewed the law neither as the changing product of specific historical struggles nor as an imperfect reflection of "the spirit of the age" but rather as an array of immanent principles firmly rooted in a vibrant COMMON LAW tradition. Consequently he insisted on a radical separation of law from politics, linking the former with reason and the latter with will and power. According to John Chipman Gray, his commitment to these central concepts of "legal science" was complete yet unreflexive. "My brother's historical knowledge was confined to a knowledge of legal precedents," he wrote in 1902. "In this sphere he was not only learned, but his treatment of historical matter was strong and broad: but, outside of that, he made and had no pretensions. He was neither a philosophical historian nor a political economist."

Gray's understanding of Anglo-American legal history produced an idiosyncratic style of judging with significant implications for CONSTITUTIONAL INTERPRETATION. His treatise-like opinions were bereft of appeals to public policy or social advantage; because he assumed that the validity of legal rules was unrelated to particular historical contexts, Gray was virtually immune to both historicist and functionalist arguments against the constitutionality of legislation. In WABASH, ST. LOUIS & PACIFIC RAILWAY V. ILLINOIS (1886), *Robbins v. Shelby County Taxing District* (1887), and LEISY V. HARDIN (1890), for example, he dissented when the majority invoked national market imperatives to invalidate state police regulations and tax laws of a sort that had never before run afoul of the COMMERCE CLAUSE. Gray also resisted the majority's contraction of what he regarded as venerable SOVEREIGN IMMUNITY doctrines in *United States v. Lee* (1882) and the *Virginia Coupon Cases* (1885).

Gray's metahistorical approach to judging was especially apparent in Fourteenth Amendment cases. In *Head v. Amoskeag Manufacturing Company* (1884) and *Wurts v. Hoagland* (1885) he conceded that mill acts and drainage laws invariably disturbed valuable rights of property. In each case, however, Gray provided a lengthy digest of statutes to demonstrate that the several states had authorized compulsory flooding or drainage of property for one hundred years or more. It was simply too late, then, for the Court to suggest that such legislation took property either for private use or without JUST COMPENSATION in violation of the DUE PROCESS clause. Similar considerations prompted Gray's dissent in the landmark SUBSTANTIVE DUE PROCESS case of CHICAGO, MILWAUKEE & ST. PAUL RAILWAY V. MINNESOTA (1890). And in *Budd v. New York* (1892), where the Court upheld a New York statute fixing rates of charge for grain storage, he supplied the majority's spokesman with a long memorandum "showing that the prices of necessary articles were controlled by the legislature, in England and America, at the time of the adoption of the State and National Constitutions." His authorities included Hening's statutes of colonial Virginia and a 1709 act of Parliament regulating coal prices.

Gray voted with the majority in every case involving the rights of racial minorities decided during his tenure on the Court. Yet his route to the results often differed substantially from that of his colleagues. If Gray had been assigned PLESSY V. FERGUSON (1896), for example, he would no doubt have supplied a thorough digest of state legislation, as well as acts of Congress pertaining to the DISTRICT OF COLUMBIA, in an attempt to show that racial classifications in "social" contexts had been just as common in American law after ratification of the FOURTEENTH AMENDMENT as before. Legal history, not the conservative sociology that figured so prominently in HENRY B. BROWN's opinion or the natural justice to which JOHN MARSHALL HARLAN appealed in dissent, shaped Gray's construction of minority rights. Thus his associates were not surprised by his opinion in UNITED STATES V. WONG KIM ARK (1898), confirming the CITIZENSHIP claim of a Chinese child born in the United States, even though he had also spoken for the Court in *Elk v. Wilkins* (1884), denying the same claim when filed by an American Indian who had left a government reservation and renounced all privileges of tribal membership. In Gray's view, the anomalous status of Indians as wards of the nation had already been fixed by nine decades of administrative usage. But the status of persons born of unnaturalizable ALIENS was a new question in American law. Consequently he assumed that *Wong Kim Ark* could be decided only after an examination of all the juridical authorities on birthright citizenship running back to CALVIN's CASE (1608).

It is ironic that Gray is best known as the probable "vacillating Justice" in POLLOCK V. FARMER's LOAN & TRUST CO. (1895). We shall never know for certain whether he changed his vote on the validity of the income tax following the second hearing; but, as EDWARD S. CORWIN observed, "the surprising thing would be not that Gray was the last Justice to line up against the act, but that he should have done so at all." Gray's extraordinarily BROAD CONSTRUCTION of Congress's IMPLIED POWERS in *United States v. Jones* (1883), *Juilliard v. Greenman* (1884), and *Fong Yue Ting v. United States* (1893) underscored his constitutional nationalism. Yet he set a face of flint to HOWELL E. JACKSON's claim, in dissent, that *Pollock* was "the most disastrous blow ever struck at the constitutional power of Congress." It is equally astonishing that a self-conscious practitioner of historical method concurred in an opinion that, as Corwin put it, "played ducks and drakes with the precedents." The unkind verdict of modern scholarship is that even Gray, a jurist for whom the separation of law and politics ordinarily served as the very touchstone for judging, succumbed in *Pollock* to the reactionary impulse that gripped the legal profession at large during the turbulent 1890s.

CHARLES W. McCURDY

Bibliography

CORWIN, EDWARD S. 1938 *Court over Constitution.* Princeton, N.J.: Princeton University Press.

FILLER, LOUIS 1969 Horace Gray. Pages 1379–1389 in Leon Friedman and Fred L. Israel, eds., *The Justices of the United States Supreme Court, 1789–1969: Their Lives and Major Opinions.* New York: Chelsea House.

GRAY v. SANDERS
372 U.S. 368 (1963)

Gray, along with WESBERRY V. SANDERS (1964), was a way-station between BAKER V. CARR (1962) (legislative districting presents a justiciable controversy) and REYNOLDS V. SIMS (1964) (the ONE PERSON–ONE VOTE principle governs the issue). In *Gray*, the Supreme Court, 8–1, invalidated Georgia's "county unit system," which weighed rural votes more heavily than urban votes in PRIMARY ELECTIONS for statewide offices. The state, said Justice WILLIAM O. DOUGLAS, was the electoral unit; within that unit, EQUAL PROTECTION demanded the principle of one person, one vote. Justice JOHN MARSHALL HARLAN dissented, drawing an analogy to the ELECTORAL COLLEGE.

KENNETH L. KARST

GREAT ATLANTIC & PACIFIC TEA CO. v. COTTRELL
424 U.S. 366 (1976)

Mississippi allowed the resale of milk from another state only if that state reciprocally accepted Mississippi milk. A. & P. stores were refused a permit to sell Louisiana milk in Mississippi, even though Louisiana milk satisfied all Mississippi quality standards, because Louisiana had not entered a reciprocity agreement with Mississippi. Citing DEAN MILK CO. V. MADISON (1951), the Supreme Court, 8–0, held that the Mississippi law was an unconstitutional STATE REGULATION OF COMMERCE. The law severely burdened INTERSTATE COMMERCE without significantly promoting public health objectives; sales of Louisiana milk would have been allowed in the state if Louisiana had signed a reciprocity agreement. Mississippi could not "use the threat of economic isolation" to force other states into such agreements.

KENNETH L. KARST

GREAT COMPROMISE

The defeat of the NEW JERSEY PLAN provoked the fiercest battle at the CONSTITUTIONAL CONVENTION OF 1787. Small-state nationalists believed that they could not obtain ratification of any constitution that put their states at the political mercy of the large ones. The struggle focused on representation in the bicameral Congress. Small-state delegates, seeking compromise, would accept representation in the lower house based on population, but as to the upper house they would not retreat from the principle of state equality. ROGER SHERMAN of Connecticut declared that he would agree to two houses with "proportional representation in one of them, provided each State have an equal voice in the other." WILLIAM S. JOHNSON of Connecticut explained that in one house "the people ought to be represented, in the other, the States." State representation was essential to a Union "partly national, partly federal," declared OLIVER ELLSWORTH of Connecticut. But the stubbornness of the large state faction resulted in a 5–5 tie vote on what would later be called the "Connecticut Compromise." Its initial defeat brought the convention, in Sherman's words, "to a full stop," and the convention stood at the brink of failure. Concessions were politically necessary. A special committee shrewdly recommended the compromise urged by Connecticut. That recommendation carried by the slimmest majority, averting a breakup of the convention. The principle of state equality having been won, small-state nationalists then supported a motion allowing members of the Senate to vote as individuals, although LUTHER MARTIN objected that individual voting violated "the idea of the *States* being represented."

LEONARD W. LEVY

Bibliography

BRANT, IRVING 1950 *James Madison: Father of the Constitution, 1787–1800.* Pages 79–100. Indianapolis: Bobbs-Merrill.

GREEN v. BIDDLE
8 Wheaton 1 (1823)

This case extended the CONTRACT CLAUSE to INTERSTATE COMPACTS, the obligation of which a state may not impair. The Supreme Court, in an opinion by Justice JOSEPH STORY, voided Kentucky acts that failed to protect property rights guaranteed by that state's compact with Virginia, entered into when Kentucky became an independent state. On reargument, Senator HENRY CLAY defended the state. His Kentucky colleague, Senator Richard Johnson, inveighing against judicial "despotism" and "oligarchy," demanded repeal of section 25 of the JUDICIARY ACT OF 1789, proposed packing the Court, and sought a restriction of JUDICIAL REVIEW. Justice BUSHROD WASHINGTON, grounding the Court's second opinion in the contract clause, declared that "we hold ourselves answerable to God, our consciences and our country . . . be the consequences of the decision what they may." Kentucky passed state-sovereignty resolves, but congressional measures to limit judicial review and to repeal section 25 failed, because the Court's enemies were unable to unite behind one bill. Nevertheless hostility to the Court, further aggravated by OSBORN V. BANK OF THE UNITED STATES (1824), remained intense.

LEONARD W. LEVY

GREEN v. COUNTY SCHOOL BOARD OF NEW KENT COUNTY
391 U.S. 430 (1968)

In states where racial segregation of school children had been commanded or authorized by law, the process of DESEGREGATION following BROWN V. BOARD OF EDUCATION (1954–1955) was impeded by officials' tactics of delay and evasion. One such tactic was the "freedom of choice" plan, which allowed pupils to select their schools. This "freedom" was often restricted by the fear of black parents that sending their children to formerly white schools would be followed by the loss of a job, or by violence and harassment directed at them or their children. In *Green*, the Supreme Court held that a rural Virginia county's "freedom of choice" plan was an insufficient remedy for segregation.

The Court took note of the practical restrictions on the freedom of black parents but did not rest decision on that ground. Instead the Court adopted a doctrinal position that reshaped the course of school desegregation. Justice WILLIAM J. BRENNAN, writing for a unanimous Court, reinterpreted *Brown II* (1955) to require "the dismantling of well-entrenched dual [segregated] systems." A school board had an affirmative duty "to come forward with a plan that . . . promises realistically to work *now*." A "freedom of choice" plan might possibly suffice, but where other alternatives were "more promising" the board must use them. The Court left no doubt that it had in mind the actual integration of black and white children as the index of success in dismantling a dual system.

In a small rural county with no residential segregation, integration would be easily achieved through geographical attendance zones and neighborhood schools. The question remained whether the Court would similarly insist on integrative results in large cities where housing was segregated. That question was answered affirmatively, three years after *Green*. (See SWANN V. CHARLOTTE-MECKLENBURG BOARD OF EDUCATION, 1971; SCHOOL BUSING.)

KENNETH L. KARST

GREEN v. OKLAHOMA

See: Capital Punishment Cases, 1976

GREGG v. GEORGIA

See: Capital Punishment Cases, 1976

GRIER, ROBERT C.
(1794–1870)

The Senate on August 4, 1846, unanimously confirmed Robert Cooper Grier as the thirty-third Justice of the Supreme Court. President JAMES K. POLK nominated Grier because of his STATES' RIGHTS Democratic principles, his position on the FUGITIVE SLAVERY issue, and his familiarity through thirteen years of previous judicial experience with Pennsylvania's unique law of real property. The bar of Pennsylvania thought the last of these particularly important since Grier's duties included presiding over the Third Circuit which included Pennsylvania.

Grier embraced the concept of dual SOVEREIGNTY. He believed that the inherent state police powers included the power to curb the flow of liquor for purposes of public health and morality. (See LICENSE CASES, 1847.) Yet Grier also believed that the states could not interfere in areas of responsibility granted by the COMMERCE CLAUSE to the Congress. Thus, he sided with the narrow majority in the PASSENGER CASES (1849) in striking down taxes levied by two states on ship masters bringing immigrants to the United States.

Grier contributed significantly to the constitutional law of CORPORATIONS and PATENTS. He formulated an important legal fiction in *Marshall v. Baltimore and Ohio Railroad* (1853) by holding that for purposes of establishing federal JURISDICTION federal judges could assume that corporate officers resided in the state of incorporation. The decision aided litigants seeking access to federal courts and prevented a corporation from electing officers in the state of a complaining party in order to avoid a suit in federal court.

Because of his experience with patent litigation in the Third Circuit, Grier spoke for the Court in several important patent cases. He wrote the opinions in *Seymour v. McCormick* (1854) and *McCormick v. Talbot* (1858), which involved the exclusivity of Cyrus McCormick's patent on the reaper. In the 1864 case of *Burr v. Duryee,* the most important patent decision to that time, Grier, writing for the Court, held that the patent clause protected inventors of machinery but did not extend to scientific principles. The decision guaranteed accessibility to technical information in a rapidly expanding economy while protecting manufacturers in recovering the costs of developing new machinery.

Grier staunchly enforced the fugitive slave acts. He regularly charged circuit court juries to find for the rights of masters, even when it meant a hostile public reaction. Contrary to the position of Justice JOSEPH STORY in PRIGG V. PENNSYLVANIA (1842), Grier employed the dual sovereignty theory (in *Moore v. Illinois,* 1852) to assert that state and national governments shared a CONCURRENT POWER of rendition over fugitive slaves so long as the states did not interfere with the performance of federal officers.

Grier compromised his dual sovereignty principles in DRED SCOTT V. SANDFORD (1857). He initially opposed any decision that addressed the issues, and he urged his colleagues to adopt the rule of STRADER V. GRAHAM (1851) that the laws of the state in which a slave resided should prevail. President JAMES BUCHANAN, at the urging of Justice JOHN CATRON, wrote Grier urging him to add bisectional unity to a forceful resolution by the Court of the SLAVERY controversy. Grier succumbed, although he did so equivocally. His one-paragraph opinion concurred in Chief Justice ROGER B. TANEY's holding that the MISSOURI COMPROMISE was unconstitutional and in Justice SAMUEL NELSON's position that the laws of Missouri established Dred Scott's legal status.

Grier's participation in the *Scott* case faded before his loyal unionism. His most notable constitutional contribution while a member of the Court came during the PRIZE CASES (1863). The owners of vessels and cargoes seized as prizes at the beginning of the Civil War argued that President ABRAHAM LINCOLN had imposed an unconstitutional blockade of southern ports, because Congress had not declared war. Grier spoke for a 5–4 majority in holding that Lincoln had acted constitutionally when confronted with hostilities of sizable proportions. The Justice circumvented the constitutional issues of presidential ursurpation

and the definition of the conflict by stressing the President's inherent obligation to preserve the Union.

Grier tarnished his reputation by lingering on the Court after senility had taken its toll. The crisis came when the Justices considered the constitutionality of the Legal Tender Acts. In conference Grier voted in favor of the acts in *Hepburn v. Griswold* (1870), but when the Justices moved to consider the next case involving the same issue Grier's mind wandered. He switched his vote. (See LEGAL TENDER CASES, 1870–1884.) With the prodding of Justice STEPHEN J. FIELD, Grier submitted his resignation in December 1869 and left the Court the following February. Six months later he died at his home in Philadelphia.

KERMIT L. HALL

Bibliography

GATELL, FRANK O. 1969 Robert C. Grier. Pages 873–892 in Leon Friedman and Fred L. Israel, eds., *The Justices of the United States Supreme Court 1789–1969: Their Lives and Major Opinions.* New York: Chelsea House.

GRIFFIN v. BRECKENRIDGE
403 U.S. 88 (1971)

This decision provided a generous construction of section 1985(3) of Title 42 of the United States Code and of Congress's power to reach private deprivations of CIVIL RIGHTS. Casting aside some constitutional considerations that had led to a more constricted reading of section 1985(3) in *Collins v. Hardyman* (1951), and effectively overruling UNITED STATES V. HARRIS (1883), the Court, in an opinion by Justice POTTER STEWART, concluded that section 1985(3) provides a cause of action against private conspiracies to violate constitutional rights. To avoid the "constitutional shoals that would lie in the path of interpreting §1985(3) as a general federal tort law," the Court required that the conspiracy be the product of some racial or other class-based animus.

THEODORE EISENBERG

GRIFFIN v. CALIFORNIA
380 U.S. 609 (1965)

Overruling ADAMSON V. CALIFORNIA (1947) without saying so, the Court, speaking through Justice WILLIAM O. DOUGLAS, held that state laws allowing adverse comment on the failure of a criminal defendant to take the stand and deny or explain evidence of which he had knowledge violated his RIGHT AGAINST SELF-INCRIMINATION. A jury acting on its own might infer what it wished, said Douglas, but what it infers "when the court solemnizes the silence of the accused into evidence against him is quite another thing" and imposes a penalty on the exercise of a constitutional right. Two dissenters argued that adverse comment on the right to silence did not compel the accused to be a witness against himself.

LEONARD W. LEVY

GRIFFIN v. COUNTY SCHOOL BOARD OF PRINCE EDWARD COUNTY
377 U.S. 218 (1964)

Griffin, one of the school segregation cases decided with BROWN V. BOARD OF EDUCATION (1954–1955), arose in Prince Edward County, Virginia. In 1956 Virginia adopted legislation aimed at closing mixed-race schools and providing state aid to private schools. The state courts held much of this "massive resistance" legislation unconstitutional in 1959. The legislature responded by making compulsory school attendance a matter of local option and by authorizing TUITION GRANTS and property tax credits to help support private schools.

Meanwhile, the federal district court in *Griffin* had ordered the commencement of DESEGREGATION in the 1959–1960 year. The county school commissioners refused to levy school taxes for the year, and in the fall of 1959 the public schools of Prince Edward County remained closed. Private schools for white children were established, taking advantage of the state's financial aid. The *Griffin* plaintiffs challenged the constitutionality of this new response to *Brown*, and the case returned to the Supreme Court.

In an opinion by Justice HUGO L. BLACK, the Court held that closing the schools denied EQUAL PROTECTION to black pupils in the county. The Court acknowledged that no general equal protection principle required a state to treat all counties alike. However, the only reason for different treatment of this county's children was to ensure the continuation of racial segregation—an unconstitutional objective. (See LEGISLATION.)

Only the question of remedy divided the Court. All the Justices agreed that the TUITION GRANTS and tax credits should be enjoined while the public schools

remained closed. (A federal court of appeals later enjoined them, irrespective of the closure of the public schools.) But the majority went further, authorizing the district court to order county officials to open the schools and, if necessary, to levy taxes to support them: "the time for mere 'deliberate speed' has run out." Justices TOM C. CLARK and JOHN MARSHALL HARLAN briefly noted their disagreement with the holding that the federal courts had power to order the opening of the county's schools.

Griffin's doctrinal importance is twofold. It is an early suggestion of the state's affirmative obligation to equalize educational opportunity, and it is an early example of federal court intervention deep in the processes of local government. (See INSTITUTIONAL LITIGATION.) In practical terms, the episode also provides a sad example of "white flight." (See DESEGREGATION.) The county's public schools opened, but they were populated almost entirely by black pupils. A whites-only private school flourished, even without the aid of the state's money. Today, while it is true that such "segregation academies" cannot lawfully exclude applicants on account of race (see RUNYON V. MCCRARY, 1976), it is also true that their tuition fees are beyond the reach of most black families. When middle-class white children withdraw from desegregated schools—in Chicago and Los Angeles as well as Prince Edward County—the result is segregation by economic status and the likely continuation of continued racial segregation.

KENNETH L. KARST

GRIFFIN v. ILLINOIS
351 U.S. 12 (1956)

Griffin was the first decision giving constitutional status to an INDIGENT person's claim to invalidate an economic barrier to his or her ACCESS TO THE COURTS.

Illinois normally required persons appealing from their criminal convictions to provide trial transcripts to the appellate courts. The state supplied free transcripts to INDIGENTS appealing in capital cases, but not in other cases. The Supreme Court held, 5–4, that the state must furnish a free transcript to an appellant in a noncapital case.

The opinion of Justice HUGO L. BLACK, for four Justices, rested on both due process and EQUAL PROTECTION grounds, asserting the state's constitutional obligation to provide "equal justice for poor and rich." Justice FELIX FRANKFURTER, concurring, emphasized the irrationality of the capital/noncapital distinction. The dissenters found this distinction reasonable and argued that the state had no affirmative duty to alleviate the consequences of economic inequality.

Griffin, along with DOUGLAS V. CALIFORNIA (1963), raised expectations that the equal protection clause would be interpreted as a broad guarantee against WEALTH DISCRIMINATION, but these decisions are seen today as standing for a more modest proposition: that the right to state criminal appeals must not be foreclosed to the poor because of their poverty. (See ROSS V. MOFFITT, 1974.)

KENNETH L. KARST

GRIFFITHS, IN RE

See: *Sugarman v. Dougall*

GRIGGS v. DUKE POWER CO.
401 U.S. 924 (1971)

Although subject to narrower interpretations, *Griggs* is viewed as establishing that employment selection criteria that disqualify blacks at higher rates than whites may violate Title VII of the CIVIL RIGHTS ACT OF 1964 even if the selection criteria are not chosen for discriminatory purposes. *Griggs* opened the door to vast numbers of Title VII actions seeking to establish violations through statistical analysis of the relative effect of employment criteria on minorities. *Griggs*'s emphasis on effects also influenced non-Title VII cases. Until WASHINGTON V. DAVIS (1976) was decided, many courts and analysts relied in part on *Griggs* to interpret the EQUAL PROTECTION clause to prohibit unequal effects. Even after *Davis*, *Griggs*'s effects test continued to influence litigation under Title VI of the Civil Rights Act of 1964, Title VIII of the CIVIL RIGHTS ACT OF 1968, and other provisions.

THEODORE EISENBERG

(SEE ALSO: *Legislation*.)

GRIMAUD, UNITED STATES v.
220 U.S. 506 (1911)

In 1905, Congress authorized the secretary of agriculture to administer public lands set aside as forest reservations. Varying local conditions had made congressional regulation impractical, so the act designated him to make regulations respecting the use of these lands, violation of which would constitute a criminal offense. A federal district court judge held the act unconstitutional on the grounds that it constituted a delegation of legislative power to the executive and that it empowered the secretary to define federal crimes.

Justice JOSEPH R. LAMAR, speaking for a unanimous Supreme Court, sustained the act. The Court validated the delegation of broad discretion because "the authority to make administrative rules is not a delegation of legislative power." Even the imposition of criminal penalties did not render the regulations legislative. When a statute prescribes the penalty for a violation of administrative regulations, Congress—not the administrative officer—fixes the penalty. The notion, nurtured by this and other cases, that legislative DELEGATION OF POWER had become unimportant received a shock when the Court revived it in 1935 to strike down portions of the NATIONAL INDUSTRIAL RECOVERY ACT. (See PANAMA REFINING COMPANY V. RYAN.)

DAVID GORDON

GRISWOLD v. CONNECTICUT
381 U.S. 479 (1965)

Seen in the perspective of the development of constitutional doctrine, *Griswold* stands among the most influential Supreme Court decisions of the latter part of the twentieth century. A full understanding of its effect on the constitutional future requires a look at *Griswold*'s antecedents. Even seen narrowly, *Griswold* was something of a culmination. The birth control movement had made two previous unsuccessful attempts to get the Court to invalidate Connecticut's law forbidding use of contraceptive devices. In *Tileston v. Ullman* (1943) a doctor was held to lack STANDING to assert his patients' constitutional claims, and in *Poe v. Ullman* (1961), when a doctor and his patients sued in their own rights, the Court again dismissed—this time on jurisdictional grounds that could charitably be called ingenuous. *Griswold* proved to be the charm; operators of a birth control clinic had been prosecuted for aiding married couples to violate the law, furnishing them advice and contraceptive devices. The Supreme Court held the law invalid, 7–2.

Griswold fanned into flames a doctrinal issue that

had smoldered in the Supreme Court for nearly two centuries: the question whether the Constitution protects NATURAL RIGHTS or FUNDAMENTAL INTERESTS beyond those specifically mentioned in its text. (See CALDER V. BULL, 1798; FUNDAMENTAL LAW AND THE SUPREME COURT; HIGHER LAW.) In the modern era, that question of CONSTITUTIONAL INTERPRETATION had focused on Justice HUGO L. BLACK's argument that the FOURTEENTH AMENDMENT fully incorporated the specific guarantees of the BILL OF RIGHTS and made them applicable to the states. Black's dissent in ADAMSON V. CALIFORNIA (1947) had scorned the competing view, limiting the content of the Fourteenth Amendment DUE PROCESS to the fundamentals of ORDERED LIBERTY. This "natural-law–due-process formula," said Black, not only allowed judges to fail to protect rights specifically covered by the Constitution but also permitted them "to roam at large in the broad expanses of policy and morals," trespassing on the legislative domain. In *Adamson* Justice FRANK MURPHY had also dissented; accepting the INCORPORATION DOCTRINE, Murphy argued that other "fundamental" rights, beyond the specific guarantees of the Bill of Rights, were also protected by due process. *Griswold* offered a test of the Black and Murphy views.

Justice WILLIAM O. DOUGLAS, who had agreed with Black in *Adamson*, recognized that the Connecticut birth control law violated no specific guarantee of the Bill of Rights. A number of other guarantees, however, protected various aspects of PRIVACY, and all of them had "penumbras, formed by emanations from those guarantees that [helped] give them life and substance." The *Griswold* case concerned "a relationship lying within the zone of privacy created by several fundamental constitutional guarantees." The NINTH AMENDMENT recognized the existence of other rights outside those specifically mentioned in the Bill of Rights, and the right of marital privacy itself was "older than the Bill of Rights." Enforcement of Connecticut's law would involve intolerable state intrusion into the marital bedroom. The law was invalid in application to married couples, and the birth control clinic operators could not be punished for aiding its violation.

In form, this "penumbras" theory was tied to the specifics of the Bill of Rights; in fact, it embraced the Murphy contention. Justices JOHN MARSHALL HARLAN and BYRON R. WHITE, concurring, candidly rested on SUBSTANTIVE DUE PROCESS grounds. Justice Black, dissenting, expressed distaste for the Connecticut law but could find nothing specific in the Constitution to prevent the state from forbidding the furnishing or the use of contraceptives. He chided the majority for using natural law to "keep the Constitution in tune with the times"—a function that lay beyond the Court's power or duty.

Griswold served as an important precedent eight years later when the Court held, in ROE V. WADE (1973), that the new constitutional right of privacy included a woman's right to have an abortion. (See REPRODUCTIVE AUTONOMY.) The *Roe* opinion, abandoning the shadows of *Griswold's* penumbras, located the right of privacy in the "liberty" protected by Fourteenth Amendment due process. *Griswold* thus provided a bridge from the Murphy view in *Adamson* to the Court's modern revival of substantive due process. Underscoring this transition, later decisions such as EISENSTADT V. BAIRD (1972) and CAREY V. POPULATION SERVICES INTERNATIONAL (1977) have made plain that *Griswold* protected not only marital privacy but also the marital relationship—and, indeed, a FREEDOM OF INTIMATE ASSOCIATION extending to unmarried persons. If substantive due process is a vital part of today's constitutional protections of personal liberty, much of the credit goes to the *Griswold* decision and to Justice Douglas.

KENNETH L. KARST

Bibliography
KAUPER, PAUL G. 1965 Penumbras, Peripheries, Emanations, Things Fundamental and Things Forgotten: The Griswold Case. *Michigan Law Review* 64:235–258.

GROSJEAN v. AMERICAN PRESS CO., INC.
297 U.S. 233 (1936)

In this unique case the Court unanimously held unconstitutional, as abridgments of the FREEDOM OF THE PRESS, any "taxes on knowledge"—a phrase, from British history, used to designate any punitive or discriminatory tax imposed on publications for the purpose of limiting their circulation. Louisiana, under the influence of Governor Huey Long, exacted a license tax (two percent of gross receipts) on newspapers with a circulation exceeding 20,000 copies weekly. By no coincidence the tax fell on thirteen publications, twelve of which were critics of Long's regime, and missed the many smaller papers that supported him. The large publishers sued to enjoin enforcement of the license tax and won a permanent INJUNCTION.

Justice GEORGE SUTHERLAND, writing for the

Court, reviewed the history of taxes on knowledge, concluding that mere exemption from PRIOR RESTRAINT was too narrow a view of the freedom of the press protected by the FIRST and FOURTEENTH AMENDMENTS. In addition to immunity from censorship, that freedom barred any government action that might prevent the discussion of public matters. Sutherland declared that publishers were subject to the ordinary forms of taxation, but the tax here was an extraordinary one with a long British history, known to the framers of the First Amendment, of trammeling the press as a vital source of public information. Similarly, Louisiana's use of the tax showed it to be a deliberate device to fetter a selected group of newspapers. To allow a free press to be fettered, Sutherland said, "is to fetter ourselves." Deciding that the tax abridged the freedom of the press made unnecessary a determination whether it also denied the EQUAL PROTECTION OF THE LAWS. In subsequent cases the Court sustained nondiscriminatory taxes on publishers but extended the principle of *Grosjean* to strike down taxes inhibiting RELIGIOUS LIBERTY.

LEONARD W. LEVY

GROSSCUP, PETER S.
(1852–1921)

Peter Stenger Grosscup served nineteen years in the lower federal courts, the last twelve (1899–1911) on the Seventh Circuit Court of Appeals. Controversy dogged his judicial career. He preached the inevitability of industrial consolidation and the need for reasonable regulation of capital and labor. The judge's numerous critics within the Progressive movement charged that his conception of reasonableness merely disguised a probusiness bias.

Grosscup in 1894 gained national attention during the violent confrontation between Eugene V. Debs's American Railway Union and the Pullman Palace Car Company. The judge's sympathies were clear. Grosscup issued an INJUNCTION ordering the strikers to cease disruption of INTERSTATE COMMERCE and the mails. Grosscup, describing the strikers to a federal GRAND JURY, observed that "neither the torch of the incendiary, or the weapon of the insurrectionist, nor the inflamed tongue of him who incites to fire and sword is the instrument to bring about reform."

Grosscup's pronouncements in favor of reasonable regulation clashed with his advocacy of the abolition of the SHERMAN ANTITRUST ACT and his evanescent

enforcement record. In *United States v. Swift & Co.* (1903) he did hold that since the commerce power included intercourse brought about by sale or exchange, application of the Sherman Act to outlaw price fixing by the Beef Trust was constitutional. However, in *Standard Oil Co. of Indiana v. United States* (1908), he spoke for a unanimous circuit court in reversing a district court fine of $29,240,000 against an oil company valued at $1,000,000. Grosscup testily wrote that the holding company—which could have afforded to pay—had not been on trial. The judge responded with mocking indifference to President THEODORE ROOSEVELT's sharp denunciation of the opinion.

Grosscup was publicly perceived as a tool of the corporations. His involvement as a shareholder and director of several businesses further undermined his judicial credibility. After resigning under pressure, Grosscup successfully defied his critics to prove misconduct.

KERMIT L. HALL

Bibliography

VANCE, JOHN T. 1964 Peter Stenger Grosscup. *Dictionary of American Biography*, Vol. 4:21–22. New York: Scribner's.

GROSSMAN, EX PARTE
267 U.S. 87 (1925)

This opinion, elucidating the scope of the PARDONING POWER, declared executive discretion absolute in the matter. The President had commuted Grossman's sentence, but a court ordered him reimprisoned to serve a sentence for contempt. The Supreme Court, recurring to history, rejected arguments that extension of the pardoning power to criminal contempts would violate judicial independence or the SEPARATION OF POWERS: "Whoever is to make [the pardoning power] useful must have full discretion to exercise it."

DAVID GORDON

GROUNDS OF OPINION

The grounds of opinion are the stated reasons given by a court or a judge for the DECISION (or dissent) in a case. The grounds are the principles, precedents, and logical steps relied upon to support the conclusion. In the OPINION OF THE COURT, the grounds are the RATIO DECIDENDI, as opposed to the OBITER

DICTA. In CONCURRING and DISSENTING OPINIONS, the grounds are, correspondingly, the points necessary to establish the desired result.

DENNIS J. MAHONEY

GROUP LIBEL

Group libel statutes pose uniquely difficult issues, for they produce a clash between two constitutional commitments: to equality and to FREEDOM OF SPEECH. Such laws impose punishments on the defamation of racial, ethnic, or religious groups. Group libel statutes were first enacted following World War II. It was widely believed that the Nazis had come to power in Germany by means of systematic calumny of their opponents and of Jews and other groups that might serve as scapegoats. Group libel statutes were enacted to afford remedies for defamation, to prevent breaches of the peace, and ultimately to protect democracy against totalitarianism. On the other hand, as the Supreme Court stated in NEW YORK TIMES CO. V. SULLIVAN (1964), the FIRST AMENDMENT manifests "a profound national commitment to the principle that debate on public issues should be uninhibited, robust and wide-open." Group libel statutes test that commitment.

The Court purported to settle the question in BEAUHARNAIS V. ILLINOIS (1952). A deeply divided Court upheld an Illinois group libel statute by resort to constitutional premises that have been substantially eroded by subsequent decisions. Although the continuing force of *Beauharnais* as a precedent is subject to serious doubt, it has not been overruled and was cited by the Court with seeming approval in *New York v. Ferber* (1982).

Beauharnais had been convicted for circulating a leaflet calling on officials in Chicago "to halt the further encroachment, harassment and invasion of white people, their property, neighborhoods, and persons, by the Negro." Calling upon white people to unite, Beauharnais's leaflet counseled that "if persuasion and the need to prevent the white race from becoming mongrelized by the Negro will not unite us, then the . . . rapes, robberies, knives, guns and marijuana of the Negro surely will."

One of the dissenting Justices, WILLIAM O. DOUGLAS, found it an easy case. In his view, if the "plain command of the First Amendment was to be overridden, the state was required to show that "the peril of speech" was "clear and present."

Justice FELIX FRANKFURTER, writing for the Court's majority, found it unnecessary to consider any CLEAR AND PRESENT DANGER test; libel, he said, is beneath First Amendment protection. Given the history of racial violence in Illinois, he argued, the legislature was not "without reason" in concluding that expressions like Beauharnais's had contributed to the violence and should be curbed.

In dissent, Justice HUGO L. BLACK challenged the Court's equation of group libel and ordinary libel. He suggested that the limited scope of libel assured that it applied to "nothing more than purely private feuds." The move from libel to group libel, he declared, was a move "to punish discussion of matters of public concern" and "a corresponding invasion of the area dedicated to free expression by the First Amendment."

Although Justice Black's characterization of the law of libel exaggerated its limits, constitutional developments since *Beauharnais* strongly support his general perspective. In *New York Times Co. v. Sullivan* the Court ruled that despite prior history, fresh assessment of the First Amendment yielded the conclusion that some libel was indeed within the scope of First Amendment protection. In a trail of decisions from *Sullivan* to GERTZ V. ROBERT WELCH, INC. (1974), the Court concluded that the First Amendment afforded some protection for a broad range of defamatory material. The driving force behind this constitutionalization of the tort of defamation was *Sullivan's* recognition of the First Amendment's commitment to uninhibited debate; moreover, the profound First Amendment importance of expression on public issues has been echoed in many subsequent opinions.

Sullivan and its successor decisions undermine the premises of *Beauharnais*. No Justice today could write an opinion saying that because libel is beneath First Amendment protection, so is group libel. First, most libel is clearly entitled to some measure of First Amendment protection. Second, putting group libel aside, if some libel remains entirely outside the First Amendment's scope, it would be speech of a private or commercial character. Justice Black's point that the move from libel to group libel is a move from the private sphere to the public sphere describes today's doctrine more accurately than it described the doctrine of 1952.

Another reason to doubt *Beauharnais's* continuing vitality is the Court's statement in *Gertz v. Robert Welch, Inc.* that "under our Constitution, there is no such thing as a false idea." That expression has generally been interpreted to mean that opinions are immune from any imposition of liability based on their asserted falsity. Although the line between fact and opinion is hard to draw, and although some group libel contains false assertions of fact, the sting of most group libel comes from unverifiable opinions. For example, what evidence could have proved the "truth" of Beauharnais's pejorative comments about black Americans? A separate issue is whether it is desirable for American trials to be conducted about the truth or falsity of various pejorative statements about ethnic groups. In the case of religious groups, the legal resolution of such questions could pose serious issues under the religion clauses of the First Amendment.

If group libel statutes are to find constitutional refuge, the necessary constitutional principles will have to be found beyond the defamation decisions. A growing body of opinions resonate with the theme of *Paris Adult Theatre v. Slaton* (1973) pronouncing the right to maintain "a decent society." From *Young v. American-Mini Theatres, Inc.* (1976) to FEDERAL COMMUNICATIONS COMMISSION V. PACIFICA FOUNDATION (1978) and a series of dissents in decisions involving FIGHTING WORDS, there is support for arguments based on concepts of civility, decency, and dignity. Whether or not these arguments succeed in validating group libel statutes, the conflict between public morality and freedom of speech will persist as an abiding theme of constitutional law.

STEVEN SHIFFRIN

Bibliography

ARKES, HADLEY 1974 Civility and the Restriction of Speech: Rediscovering the Defamation of Groups. *Supreme Court Review* 1974:281–335.
KALVEN, HARRY, JR. 1965 *The Negro and the First Amendment.* Columbus: Ohio State University Press.

GROVES v. SLAUGHTER
15 Peters 449 (1841)

Groves was the only case to come before the United States Supreme Court involving the relative powers of the state and federal governments over the interstate slave trade. Mississippi's Constitution forbade the importation of slaves for sale. In suit on a defaulted note given for an imported slave, the Court majority, speaking through Justice SMITH THOMPSON, held that the state constitutional provision was not self-executing and was unenforceable without legislation implementing it. Concurring opinions revealed a wide divergence of opinion among the justices on slavery-related questions. Justice JOHN MCLEAN asserted that slaves were essentially persons, not property. Chief

Justice ROGER B. TANEY insisted that state power over blacks, slave or free, was exclusive and superseded any exercise of federal power under the slave-trade or COMMERCE CLAUSE. Justice HENRY BALDWIN denied that states could exclude the slave trade.

WILLIAM M. WIECEK

GROVEY v. TOWNSEND
295 U.S. 45 (1935)

Following the decision in NIXON V. CONDON (1932), the Texas state convention of the Democratic party adopted a rule limiting voting in PRIMARY ELECTIONS to whites. Grovey, a black, was refused a primary ballot and sued for damages. The Supreme Court unanimously held that the party's rule did not amount to STATE ACTION under the FOURTEENTH or FIFTEENTH AMENDMENT and thus violated no constitutional rights. Grovey was merely denied membership in a private organization. The Court distinguished *Nixon v. Condon* as a case in which the party's executive committee had acted under state authorization. Only nine years later, in SMITH V. ALLWRIGHT (1944), the Court overruled *Grovey*.

KENNETH L. KARST

GUARANTEE CLAUSE

Article IV, section 4, of the Constitution provides that "The United States shall guarantee to every State in this Union a REPUBLICAN FORM OF GOVERNMENT. . . ." Anticipated between 1781 and 1787 in various state and federal legislative requirements that territorial governments be republican, the clause as drafted at the CONSTITUTIONAL CONVENTION embodied the aspirations of republican ideology in the Confederation era. At a minimum, it prohibited regression to monarchical and aristocratic government, but it also incorporated the principles of POPULAR SOVEREIGNTY, representative government, majority rule, SEPARATION OF POWERS, and federal supremacy.

The guarantee clause was first invoked under circumstances JAMES MADISON anticipated in THE FEDERALIST #43: to suppress an insurrectionary challenge to the authority of one of the states (Dorr's Rebellion, Rhode Island, 1842). Then, and in the earlier WHISKEY REBELLION (western Pennsylvania, 1794), it took on a repressive character as a bulwark of extant institutions, affirming GEORGE WASHING-

TON's insistence in his Farewell Address (1796) that "the constitution which at any time exists till changed by . . . the whole people is sacredly obligatory upon all."

In the first significant judicial interpretation of the clause, LUTHER V. BORDEN (1849), Chief Justice ROGER B. TANEY declined to overturn the Rhode Island government established in the aftermath of the Dorr Rebellion. Taney held that the determination of whether a state government was republican rested exclusively with Congress, whose action was binding on the courts. In this case, Taney invoked the POLITICAL QUESTION doctrine, asserting that the issue presented "belonged to the political power and not to the judicial."

The guarantee clause figured prominently in debates on reconstruction of the Union during and after the Civil War. Democrats opposed to effective Reconstruction measures relied on a conservative interpretation of the clause as securing extant, nonmonarchical governments; they extolled self-government but limited it to whites. Republicans rejected the static, backward-looking, and racist implications of the Democratic view. Echoing earlier abolitionist contentions that slavery was incompatible with republican government, Republicans fashioned Reconstruction policies (including military Reconstruction, federal guarantees of blacks' CIVIL RIGHTS, and enfranchisement) that were conceptually derived from Taney's assertion of the exclusive power of Congress to assure republican government in the states. Chief Justice SALMON P. CHASE validated the Republican uses of the clause in TEXAS V. WHITE (1869).

The clause has played a less prominent role in public affairs during the twentieth century. The Supreme Court rejected a conservative interpretation of the clause that would have invalidated the initiative and referendum (*Pacific States Telephone and Telegraph Co. v. Oregon*, 1912). Together with the political question doctrine, the clause became linked with the concept of JUSTICIABILITY (a characteristic of cases requisite to their resolution by judicial tribunals). But the majority opinion of Justice WILLIAM J. BRENNAN in BAKER V. CARR (1962) restricted the scope of the political question doctrine, thus creating the possibility of future judicial, as well as congressional, reliance on the clause to evaluate the republican character of state institutions.

WILLIAM M. WIECEK

Bibliography

WIECEK, WILLIAM M. 1972 *The Guarantee Clause of the U. S. Constitution.* Ithaca, N.Y.: Cornell University Press.

GUEST, UNITED STATES v.
383 U.S. 745 (1966)

This case raised important questions about Congress's power to enforce the FOURTEENTH AMENDMENT and about the scope of section 241 of Title 18 of the United States Code, a federal criminal CIVIL RIGHTS statute deriving from section 6 of the FORCE ACT of 1870. Section 241 outlaws conspiracies to interfere with rights or privileges secured by the Constitution or laws of the United States. A group of whites allegedly murdered Lemuel A. Penn, a black Army officer, while he was driving through Georgia on his way to Washington, D.C. Two of the whites were charged with murder and acquitted by a state court jury. They and others then were indicted under section 241 for conspiracy to deprive blacks of specified constitutional rights by shooting, beating, and otherwise harassing them and by making false criminal accusations causing the blacks to be arrested. The rights allegedly deprived included the right to use state facilities free of RACIAL DISCRIMINATION and the RIGHT TO TRAVEL freely throughout the United States. The Supreme Court held that the alleged conduct constituted a crime under section 241, punishable by Congress under the Fourteenth Amendment.

Guest's principal significance stems from two separate opinions, joined by a total of six Justices, that addressed the question whether the Fourteenth Amendment empowers Congress to outlaw private racially discriminatory behavior. In an opinion concurring in part and dissenting in part, Justice WILLIAM J. BRENNAN, joined by Chief Justice EARL WARREN and Justice WILLIAM O. DOUGLAS, stated that section 5 of the Fourteenth Amendment grants Congress authority to punish individuals, public or private, who interfere with the right to equal use of state facilities. Justice TOM C. CLARK, in a concurring opinion joined by Justices HUGO L. BLACK and ABE FORTAS, in effect agreed with the portion of Justice Brennan's opinion relating to Congress's power. Justice Clark's opinion stated that there could be no doubt about Congress's power to punish all public and private conspiracies that interfere with Fourteenth Amendment rights, "with or without STATE ACTION."

Guest also raised the question whether, in light of the state action doctrine, the defendants, all private persons, were legally capable of depriving others of Fourteenth Amendment rights within the meaning of section 241. Justice POTTER STEWART's opinion for the Court, which, as to this point, Justice Clark's opinion expressly endorsed, avoided the issue by construing the INDICTMENT's allegation that the conspiracy was accomplished in part by "causing the arrest of Negroes by means of false reports that such Negroes had committed criminal acts" to be an allegation of state involvement. Justice Brennan read Justice Stewart's opinion to mean that a conspiracy by private persons to interfere with Fourteenth Amendment rights was not a conspiracy to interfere with a right secured by the Constitution within the meaning of section 241. Justice Brennan rejected this interpretation, arguing that private persons could deprive blacks of rights "secured" by the Constitution "even though only governmental interferences with the exercise of that right are prohibited by the Constitution itself."

Other aspects of *Guest* generated less disagreement among the Justices. The case revived a question addressed in SCREWS V. UNITED STATES (1945) when the Court interpreted section 242 (a remnant of the CIVIL RIGHTS ACT OF 1866). Sections 241 and 242 define proscribed behavior as conduct violating constitutional rights. Since constitutional standards change, defendants argued that the sections were unconstitutionally vague. As in *Screws*, the Court construed the statute to require a specific intent to violate constitutional rights and, therefore, found section 241 not unconstitutionally vague. And the Court found the right to travel throughout the United States to be a basic constitutional right that, like freedom from INVOLUNTARY SERVITUDE, is protected even as against private interference. Only Justice JOHN MARSHALL HARLAN dissented from the HOLDING that the right to travel is protected against private interference.

Both the suggestion by six Justices (through the Brennan and Clark opinions) concerning Congress's power under section 5 of the Fourteenth Amendment and Justice Brennan's views about the scope of section 241 are difficult to reconcile with important nineteenth-century decisions. In UNITED STATES V. CRUIKSHANK (1876), one of the first cases construing Reconstruction-era civil rights legislation, indictments charging violations of section 6 of the FORCE ACT of 1870 were ordered dismissed in part on the ground that Fourteenth Amendment rights could not be violated by private citizens. In UNITED STATES V. HARRIS (1883) the Court held unconstitutional a civil rights statute that punished private conspiracies to interfere with rights of equality. The provision struck down in *Harris*, which stemmed from section 2 of the Civil Rights Act of 1871, was so similar to section 241 that, until *Guest*, it seemed unlikely that section 241 could be applied to private conspiracies to interfere with

rights of equality. And *Guest*'s expansive view of Congress's Fourteenth Amendment powers is difficult to reconcile with the Court's decision in the CIVIL RIGHTS CASES (1883).

Guest thus represents a shift in attitude toward Congress's Fourteenth Amendment power to reach private discrimination. But *Guest* also is part of a larger shift in attitude toward the Civil War amendments. In KATZENBACH V. MORGAN (1966) and SOUTH CAROLINA V. KATZENBACH (1966), cases decided during the same term as *Guest*, the Court for the first time found Congress to have broad powers to interpret and define the content of the Fourteenth and FIFTEENTH AMENDMENTS.

Guest's generous attitude toward Congress's power has had less influence than might have been expected. Prior to *Guest*, HEART OF ATLANTA MOTEL, INC. V. UNITED STATES (1964) and KATZENBACH V. MCCLUNG (1964) already had found Congress to have broad power under the COMMERCE CLAUSE to reach discrimination in facilities affecting INTERSTATE COMMERCE. In JONES V. ALFRED H. MAYER CO. (1968), the Court found Congress to have broad THIRTEENTH AMENDMENT powers to reach private discrimination in all areas. *Jones* and the Commerce Clause cases rendered moot much of the question about Congress's Fourteenth Amendment powers. GRIFFIN V. BRECKENRIDGE (1971), where the Court again faced the question of Congress's power to reach private discriminatory conspiracies, underscores *Guest*'s modest influence. *Griffin* involved a civil statute, section 1985(3), that is similar to section 241. By the time of *Griffin*, however, the Court could rely on Congress's Thirteenth Amendment powers to sustain legislation proscribing private racial conspiracies. *Guest*'s possible implications will be realized only in cases, if any, to which Congress's Thirteenth Amendment and commerce clause powers are inapplicable.

THEODORE EISENBERG

Bibliography

COX, ARCHIBALD 1966 Foreword: Constitutional Adjudication and the Promotion of Human Rights. *Harvard Law Review* 80:91–122.
NOTE 1974 Federal Power to Regulate Private Discrimination: The Revival of the Enforcement Clauses of the Reconstruction Era Amendments. *Columbia Law Review* 74:449–527.
NOTE 1967 Fourteenth Amendment Congressional Power to Legislate Against Private Discrimination: The *Guest* Case. *Cornell Law Quarterly* 52:586–599.
TRIBE, LAURENCE H. 1978 *American Constitutional Law.* Pages 273–275. Mineola, N.Y.: Foundation Press.

GUFFEY-SNYDER (BITUMINOUS COAL CONSERVATION) ACT

See: *Carter v. Carter Coal Company*

GUILT BY ASSOCIATION

The United States Supreme Court frequently proclaims that guilt by association has no place in our constitutional system (for example, *Schneiderman v. United States*, 1943; WIEMAN V. UPDEGRAFF, 1952). Sanctions imposed for membership in a group are said to be characteristic of primitive cultures, or elements of the early COMMON LAW long since eliminated with prohibitions against such punishments as attaint and forfeiture.

In 1920, CHARLES EVANS HUGHES made what is probably still the most famous statement attacking guilt by association as inconsistent with our individualistic legal norms. In protesting the action of the New York Assembly, which had suspended five elected members because they were members of the Socialist Party, Hughes argued: "It is the essence of the institutions of liberty that it be recognized that guilt is personal and cannot be attributed to the holding of opinion or of mere intent in the absence of overt acts."

Other Justices frequently quoted or paraphrased this argument by Hughes, made between the two periods Hughes served on the Court, in decisions invalidating deportations, employment dismissals, and denials of licenses, as well as in criminal prosecutions. It is obvious, however, that frequently ascription of guilt by association is permitted. For example, members of a CRIMINAL CONSPIRACY may be found guilty for actions by their co-conspirators based entirely on their association in the conspiracy. The Supreme Court recognized the potential for abuse in criminal conspiracy in *Krulewitch v. United States* (1949), but convictions of coconspirators still may be upheld without proof of their direct knowledge or participation in the range of crimes committed by other members of the conspiracy.

There are also striking examples of the Court's condoning of government action based on the presumption of guilt by association in constitutional law. These include the JAPANESE AMERICAN CASES (1943–1944), which upheld the internment of West Coast residents of Japanese ancestry during World War II, and numerous decisions during the 1950s, such as AMERICAN COMMUNICATIONS ASSOCIATION V. DOUDS (1950) and BARENBLATT V. UNITED STATES (1959), which allowed sanctions for membership in communist organizations.

Despite reiteration of the unacceptability of punishment premised upon guilt by association, judgments about individuals based upon their membership in groups frequently—perhaps even necessarily—are made in a bureaucratized world in which personal knowledge of others seems increasingly elusive. Nevertheless, the assignment of individual guilt premised on one's associations remains anathema. It is still thought to be an important premise of constitutional law that the government may not use a gross shorthand such as guilt by association to stigmatize or to punish citizens.

Constitutional safeguards derived primarily from the FIRST AMENDMENT and the DUE PROCESS clauses are said to surround FREEDOM OF ASSOCIATION. When the government employs the technique of guilt by association, it endangers this freedom, which the Court proclaimed in DEJONGE V. OREGON (1937) to be among the most fundamental of constitutional protections. Guilt by association also is inconsistent with basic premises of individual responsibility, which lie close to the core of much of America's legal culture.

AVIAM SOIFER

Bibliography

EMERSON, THOMAS I. 1970 *The System of Freedom of Expression.* Pages 105–110, 126–129, 161–204, 235–241. New York: Random House.

O'BRIAN, JOHN L. 1948 Loyalty Tests and Guilt by Association. *Harvard Law Review* 61:592–611.

GUINN v. UNITED STATES
238 U.S. 347 (1915)

In an 8–0 decision, the Supreme Court sustained the conviction of two Oklahoma election officials of conspiracy to deprive blacks of their VOTING RIGHTS. In an opinion by Chief Justice EDWARD D. WHITE, the court held that a state constitutional amendment enacting a GRANDFATHER CLAUSE, which exempted from the literacy test the descendants of persons who had been entitled to vote before 1866, violated the FIFTEENTH AMENDMENT, and that officials could be prosecuted for attempting to enforce it. In a companion case (MYERS V. ANDERSON) the Court held that Maryland officials were liable for civil damages for enforcing that state's grandfather clause.

DENNIS J. MAHONEY

GULF OF TONKIN RESOLUTION
73 Stat. 384 (1964)
84 Stat. 2053 (1971) (repeal)

One criticism of American participation in the VIETNAM WAR was based on the Constitution: half a million troops had been committed to combat without a DECLARATION OF WAR by Congress. In 1964 President LYNDON B. JOHNSON reported that North Vietnamese boats had attacked United States naval vessels in the Gulf of Tonkin. Accepting the truth of these reports, Congress adopted a resolution supporting the President in "taking all necessary measures to repel any armed attack against the forces of the United States and to prevent further aggression." The resolution further approved the use of armed force to defend other nations that had signed the Southeast Asia treaty. Massive escalation of the American involvement in South Vietnam soon followed; the President cited this resolution and successive appropriations measures as evidence of congressional ratification of his actions.

In 1971 Congress repealed the Gulf of Tonkin Resolution. President RICHARD M. NIXON did not oppose the repeal; he asserted that his power as COMMANDER-IN-CHIEF of the armed forces authorized continuation of American participation. After the American troops were withdrawn in 1973, Congress reasserted its authority, adopting the WAR POWERS RESOLUTION over Nixon's veto.

KENNETH L. KARST

GUN CONTROL

See: Second Amendment

GUTHRIE, WILLIAM D.
(1859–1935)

A corporation lawyer and professor of law at Columbia (1913–1922), William D. Guthrie was one of several prominent attorneys who successfully challenged the federal income tax in POLLOCK V. FARMERS' LOAN & TRUST COMPANY (1895). His most famous appearance before the Supreme Court, however, came in a losing cause: CHAMPION V. AMES (1903). In that case, he advocated a doctrine EDWARD S. CORWIN would later call DUAL FEDERALISM (and which the Supreme Court itself would adopt in HAMMER V. DAGENHART, 1918). Drawing on his *Lectures on the Fourteenth Article of Amendment to the Constitution* (1898), Guthrie argued that the suppression of lotteries did not fall under the national commerce power because no commerce was involved. Such regulation belonged solely to the STATE POLICE POWER, to which Guthrie accorded great deference. He also favored the RULE OF REASON in ANTITRUST cases (though he was unable to convince the Court to accept it in UNITED STATES V. TRANS-MISSOURI FREIGHT ASSOCIATION, 1897) and he vigorously opposed the SIXTEENTH AMENDMENT on dual federalism grounds.

DAVID GORDON

HABEAS CORPUS

(Latin: "You shall have the body.") Habeas corpus is the most celebrated of Anglo-American judicial procedures. It has been called the "Great Writ of Liberty" and hailed as a crucial bulwark of a free society. Compared to many encomia, Justice FELIX FRANKFURTER's praise in BROWN V. ALLEN (1953) is measured:

The uniqueness of habeas corpus in the procedural armory of our law cannot be too often emphasized. It differs from all other remedies in that it is available to bring into question the legality of a person's restraint and to require justification for such detention. Of course this does not mean that prison doors may readily be opened. It does mean that explanation may be exacted why they should remain closed. It is not the boasting of empty rhetoric that has treated the writ of *habeas corpus* as the basic safeguard of freedom in the Anglo-American world. "The great writ of habeas corpus has been for centuries esteemed the best and only sufficient defence of personal freedom." Mr. Chief Justice [SALMON P.] CHASE, writing for the Court, in *Ex parte Yerger,* 8 Wall. 85, 95. Its history and function in our legal system and the unavailability of the writ in totalitarian societies are naturally enough regarded as one of the decisively differentiating factors between our democracy and totalitarian governments.

Though even this rhetoric may be a bit overdone, it nonetheless reflects the importance that has come to be attached to habeas corpus. It is a symbol of freedom, as well as an instrument. What is significant in the rhetoric is not the degree of exaggeration but rather the extent of truth.

Habeas corpus is accorded a special place in the Constitution. Article I, section 9, of the basic document, included even before the BILL OF RIGHTS was appended, contains the following provision: "The privilege of the Writ of Habeas Corpus shall not be suspended, unless when in Cases of Rebellion or Invasion the public Safety may require it."

This text of course presumes an understanding of what habeas corpus is. Technically, it is simply a writ, or court order, commanding a person who holds another in custody to demonstrate to the court legal justification for that restraint of personal liberty. The name "habeas corpus" derives from the opening words of the ancient COMMON LAW writ that commanded the recipient to "have the body" of the prisoner present at the court, there to be subject to such disposition as the court should order. A writ of habeas corpus, even one directed to an official custodian, can be obtained routinely by the prisoner or by someone on his behalf. As at common law, the writ that starts proceedings also defines the nature of those proceedings (and lends its name to them and, sometimes, to the final order granting relief). Thus, habeas corpus not only requires the custodian promptly to produce the prisoner in court but also precipitates an inquiry into the justification for the restraint and may result in an order commanding release.

The writ itself is no more than a procedural device that sets in motion a judicial inquiry. Yet the importance attached to habeas corpus necessarily posits that a court will not accept a simple showing of official authority as sufficient justification for imprisonment. Otherwise, the constitutional provision would indeed be much ado about nothing. "The privilege of the

Writ" would hardly be worth guaranteeing if it did not invoke substantial criteria for what are sufficient legal grounds for depriving a person of liberty.

The principle that even an order of the king was not itself sufficient basis had been established in England before the time of our Constitution. In *Darnel's Case* (1627), during the struggle for parliamentary supremacy, a custodian's return to a writ of habeas corpus asserted that the prisoner was held by "special command" of the king, and the court accepted this as sufficient justification. This case precipitated three House of Commons resolutions and a PETITION OF RIGHT, assented to by the king, declaring habeas corpus available to examine the underlying cause of a detention and, if no legitimate cause be shown, to order the prisoner released. But even these actions did not resolve the matter. Finally, two HABEAS CORPUS ACTS, of 1641 and 1679, together established habeas corpus as an effective remedy looking beyond formal authority to examine the sufficiency of the actual cause for holding a prisoner.

Although the Habeas Corpus Acts did not extend to the American colonies, the principle that the sovereign had to show just cause for imprisoning an individual was carried over to the colonies. After the Revolution, the underlying principle was implicitly incorporated in the constitutional provision guaranteeing the regular availability of habeas corpus against suspension by the new central national government.

The broad assumptions underlying the Great Writ have been well articulated by HENRY HART. Speaking in the particular context of PROCEDURAL DUE PROCESS for ALIENS, but with general implications, he wrote of:

the great and generating principle . . . that the Constitution always applies when a court is sitting with JURISDICTION in habeas corpus. For then the Court has always to inquire, not only whether the statutes have observed, but whether the petitioner before it has been "deprived of life, liberty, or property, without due process of law," or injured in any other way in violation of the FUNDAMENTAL LAW. . . .

That principle forbids a CONSTITUTIONAL COURT with JURISDICTION in habeas corpus from ever accepting as an adequate return to the writ the mere statement that what has been done is authorized by act of Congress. The inquiry remains, if MARBURY V. MADISON still stands, whether the act of Congress is consistent with the fundamental law. Only upon such a principle could the Court reject, as it surely would, a return to the writ which informed it that the applicant for admission [to the United States] lay stretched upon a rack with pins driven in behind his fingernails pursuant to authority duly conferred by statute in order to secure the information necessary to determine his admissibility.

The same principle which would justify rejection of this return imposes responsibility to inquire into the adequacy of other returns [Hart, 1953: 1393–1394].

It hardly requires demonstration that an executive directive can provide no more justification than an act of Congress. In fact the Supreme Court very early held in EX PARTE BOLLMAN AND SWARTWOUT (1807) that a President's order was not itself a sufficient basis for a return to a writ of habeas corpus.

The purpose of the habeas corpus clause of Article I, section 9, is to assure availability of the writ, but the provision clearly allows its suspension when necessary in the event of rebellion or invasion. The power to suspend the writ has been rarely invoked. Suspensions were proclaimed during the Civil War; in 1871, to combat the Ku Klux Klan in North Carolina; in 1905, in the Philippines; and in Hawaii during World War II. Furthermore, two of these suspensions were limited by the Supreme Court. In the first case, EX PARTE MILLIGAN (1866), the Supreme Court held that the writ was not suspended in states (*e.g.,* Indiana) where the public safety was not threatened by the Civil War. In the last case, DUNCAN V. KAHANAMOKU (1946), the Supreme Court held that the writ was not suspended in Hawaii eight months after the attack on Pearl Harbor because the public safety was no longer threatened by invasion.

The point is not the rarity with which the power to suspend the writ of habeas corpus has been invoked in this country's history. That can be seen as a function of the relative stability and insulation that the nation has enjoyed. Rather, the significant point is the basic acceptance of the proposition that the courts remain open in habeas corpus proceedings to consider the validity of an attempted suspension of the writ and, if they find it invalid, to examine the validity of the detention. This position has not always been respected by the immediately affected executive or military authorities, and such holdings by the Supreme Court have been handed down after immediate hostilities have ended. Nevertheless, the ultimate verdict of history has upheld the courts' position. The existence of those Supreme Court precedents, and their acceptance and perceived vindication by history, help bolster the likelihood of similar judicial action in response to future emergencies.

The habeas corpus writ described by Article I is not necessarily one issued by a federal court. The Constitution posits the existence of state courts as the basic courts of the nation; it does not require the creation of lower federal courts at all. Thus, the suspension clause was designed to protect habeas corpus in state courts from impairment by the new national government.

The clause may nonetheless have reflected a wider sense of moral duty. The first Congress, in establishing a system of lower federal courts, gave federal judges the power to issue the writ on behalf of prisoners held "under or by colour of the authority of the United States." The federal courts have always retained that habeas corpus jurisdiction, and it has since been much expanded.

Perhaps the most dramatic example of the use of habeas corpus occurred in *Ex parte Milligan*. Milligan, a civilian living in Indiana, was sentenced to death by a court-martial during the Civil War though the local GRAND JURY had refused to indict him. The Supreme Court held that courts-martial do not have jurisdiction to try civilians so long as the civilian courts are open. The Court further held that the writ of habeas corpus was not suspended, despite the general language of a statute purporting to suspend the writ during the Civil War, because the public safety was not threatened in Indiana.

Habeas corpus also provided an effective remedy for challenging an extraordinary extension of military power during World War II. The government relocated Japanese Americans away from their homes on the West Coast to detention camps inland. Although the Supreme Court in *Korematsu v. United States* (1944) held the relocation to be constitutional, the Court on the same day held in a habeas corpus case, *Ex parte Endo* (1944), that the government was not authorized to confine Japanese Americans in the camps against their will. (See JAPANESE AMERICAN CASES, 1943–1944.)

Nor is the availability of habeas corpus to challenge extraordinary military actions limited to American citizens or residents. Even German saboteurs, landed in this country by submarine, were permitted during wartime to challenge the power of a special military commission over them. Though the Court rejected that challenge in EX PARTE QUIRIN (1942), the exercise of military power was drawn into question and examined; the Court denied relief on the merits, holding that the asserted jurisdiction was constitutional.

Habeas corpus is not restricted to testing major or extraordinary extensions of power. Particularly in the last few decades, the writ has provided a means by which federal courts have regularly controlled the reach and exercise of fairly commonplace court-martial jurisdiction. For example, in UNITED STATES EX REL. TOTH V. QUARLES (1955), military police arrested an ex-serviceman in Pennsylvania and flew him to Korea to stand trial in a court-martial on charges related to his time in service. (See MILITARY JUSTICE AND THE CONSTITUTION.) A writ of habeas corpus issued, Toth was returned to the United States, and the civilian court that had issued the writ ordered him released on the ground that he was a civilian not subject to military jurisdiction. More generally and more routinely, habeas proceedings have provided the means to define and enforce constitutional boundaries determining which persons and events may be tried without civilian courts and their procedures. Habeas corpus is a residual font of authority to ensure that the Constitution is not violated whenever individuals are imprisoned.

Indeed, habeas corpus proceedings are not limited to the enforcement of constitutional rights; they also open for scrutiny other issues of basic legal authority. For example, the writ has been used as a means to invoke JUDICIAL REVIEW of individual administrative orders for military CONSCRIPTION or alien DEPORTATION. The issues raised have included questions of statutory authority and the existence of a basis in fact for the official order. Most significant, the federal courts were unwilling to take general language precluding judicial review as barring habeas corpus; habeas corpus proceedings were held to be available even though the applicable statutes expressly provided that the administrative action should be final. Here again that position, insisting on the primacy of habeas corpus, was subsequently vindicated, and indeed, ratified by Congress in statutory revisions. Whether the Constitution entitles an individual to judicial review of military draft or IMMIGRATION orders still has not been authoritatively resolved. One of the strengths of habeas corpus, however, is that it permitted that issue to be finessed. The availability of *habeas corpus* facilitated avoidance of an ultimate confrontation—which might well have resulted in a rejection of the constitutional claim—while securing reaffirmation of the principle that government is subject to the RULE OF LAW as applied in the ordinary courts.

Our focus to this point has been on the writ from a federal court directed to a federal officer or custodian. The matter becomes more complex when the issues involve the relationships between federal and state governments. Seizure of one government's agents by the other, and their release from resulting custody, can be crucial factors in a struggle for political power. It is no accident, then, that the writ has been involved—and had evolved—in jurisdictional battles within or among governments. This involvement was evident, as mentioned earlier, in the battle for parliamentary supremacy over the crown in Britain. The writ has also played an important role in the changing relationships of federal and state governments in this country, and has in turn been shaped by these evolving relationships.

When the first Congress gave the lower federal courts power to issue the writ, it limited the power to federal prisoners and, even as to them, did not provide for exclusive jurisdiction. The state courts, then, had CONCURRENT JURISDICTION to issue habeas corpus for federal prisoners and exclusive *habeas* jurisdiction for state prisoners. The succeeding centuries have witnessed a huge expansion of federal power, including a shift of much power from the states to the central government. As the power of the federal government grew, the federal courts gradually gained the power to issue writs of habeas corpus for state prisoners. At the same time, the power of state courts to issue habeas corpus for federal prisoners has narrowed and today is practically extinguished.

As with many American legal institutions the conflict over slavery figured prominently in the development. The Fugitive Slave Act of 1850, which was enacted as part of the COMPROMISE OF 1850, increased federal power at the expense of the states. Enforcement of the act, which required return of escaped slaves to their owners, met strong resistance in Northern states. State courts would order the arrest of federal officers who attempted to enforce the act and would issue writs of habeas corpus to release individuals charged with violating the act. The federal officers were not helpless, however. Although the federal courts did not have general power to issue writs of habeas corpus for state prisoners, they had been empowered to release state prisoners imprisoned for actions taken pursuant to federal law. Congress had granted this power in 1833 in response to South Carolina's threat to arrest anyone who attempted to collect the federal tariff. The federal courts exercised the power in the 1850s and 1860s to release federal agents arrested for enforcing the Fugitive Slave Act. (See FUGITIVE SLAVERY.)

A more intractable problem was posed by state court writs of habeas corpus releasing individuals convicted in federal court of violating the Fugitive Slave Act. The Supreme Court resolved this problem in ABLEMAN V. BOOTH (1859), holding that state courts did not have the power to release prisoners held pursuant to proceedings in federal court. Otherwise, the laws of the United States could be rendered unenforceable in states whose courts were in opposition. After the Civil War, the Supreme Court went further and held in *Tarble's Case* (1872) that state courts could

not issue habeas corpus to release someone held under authority, or color of authority, of the federal government. A state court may only require the federal officer to inform it of the authority for a prisoner's detention; all further questions as to actions under color of federal authority are to be resolved in the federal courts. Habeas corpus cannot be entirely barred, but so long as the writ is available from the federal courts, state courts are effectively precluded from issuing habeas corpus on behalf of persons held in custody by the federal government.

The power of federal courts to issue habeas corpus for state prisoners followed the opposite course. The JUDICIARY ACT OF 1789 did not give the federal courts any such power and, until after the Civil War, these courts were granted it only in a limited number of circumstances. An example was the release of those seized for enforcing federal law, mentioned earlier. The HABEAS CORPUS ACT OF 1867, however, was general, giving federal courts power to issue the writ "in all cases where any person may be restrained of his or her liberty in violation of the constitution, or of any treaty or law of the United States. . . ." Jurisdiction in essentially these terms continues to the present day.

The precise objectives of the 1867 act were never defined. The act aimed generally at extending the effectiveness of federal authority, particularly against resistance in the former slave states. Its terms extended to prisoners in state custody as to all other persons. Until well into the twentieth century, its thrust was principally against restraints without (or before) trial. Among other reasons, the federal Constitution had not yet been construed to impose any significant requirements for state criminal proceedings. In more recent times, federal habeas corpus has become a forum for challenging state criminal convictions on constitutional grounds. In terms of volume, this is the federal writ's principal use today.

This pattern evolved only sporadically, and only after a number of limiting concepts had been loosened. The first of these was a principle of long standing that habeas corpus was available to persons imprisoned under authority of a court, particularly following criminal trial and conviction, only on the grounds that the court had no jurisdiction to try him. If that court had jurisdiction, all challenges, including constitutional ones, were to be raised there. Trial court decisions were to be reviewable, if at all, by higher courts, not by COLLATERAL ATTACK in other courts of the same level. It was often stated that habeas corpus was not to serve as a substitute for appeal.

The formal doctrine that the habeas corpus court

would not look beyond whether the holding or convicting court had jurisdiction prevailed until near the middle of the twentieth century. Nevertheless, the scope of federal habeas corpus grew substantially even before that time. The concept of "lack of jurisdiction" is not inelastic, and the Supreme Court gradually expanded the meaning of that term to include constitutional violations that might be said to preclude a fair trial.

The first step in this expansion of the meaning of the issue of jurisdiction was to allow habeas corpus relief for a prisoner convicted of violating an unconstitutional law. Unconstitutional laws were null and void, it could be rationalized; thus the state court was without jurisdiction because *no* law authorized the conviction. The next step was to issue habeas corpus to remedy constitutional violations so gross as effectively to deprive the prisoner of a real trial. Such violations were held to be so fundamental that a court, proceeding in those circumstances, lost jurisdiction. Examples included mob-dominated trials and denial to defendants of opportunity to be heard. Reliance on the concept of lack of jurisdiction became more and more attenuated until, in *Waley v. Johnston* (1942), the Supreme Court explicitly abandoned that formal concept as linch-pin. From that time forward, the Court focused on more realistic considerations: whether the constitutional claims being asserted could not have been presented effectively in the original court that tried the case or on direct review of the conviction.

The concerns over the proper "deference" to be accorded by the habeas corpus court to the court that originally tried and convicted a prisoner arose even where both courts were federal. When federal habeas corpus was being sought by a state-convicted prisoner, these concerns were reinforced by further considerations of mutual respect and comity between state and federal systems. In response to these considerations, there developed early two substantial limits on the availability of federal habeas corpus for state prisoners: if the state courts had fully and fairly litigated the prisoner's claim, or if the prisoner failed to exhaust all state remedies, federal habeas corpus would not lie.

The requirement that state remedies be exhausted was established in *Ex parte Royall* (1886). To meet it, the prisoner must first press his claims to be free based on federal law, through the state courts. Thus, the prisoner must appeal his conviction or must seek state habeas corpus or other available postconviction remedy. (See EXHAUSTION OF REMEDIES.) Under the Constitution's SUPREMACY CLAUSE, state courts are required to follow and apply federal constitutional law. Principles of comity—essentially respect for the state courts' responsibility and ability to reach a correct decision—were seen to require that state courts be allowed an opportunity to correct their own errors before federal habeas corpus could be issued. The general exhaustion requirement is now codified in the statute governing habeas corpus.

In view of the exhaustion requirement, it may seem ironic that for many years presentation of the federal claim in state proceedings might mean that it could not thereafter be considered in federal habeas corpus. Federal collateral attack was barred if the state courts had sufficiently considered and passed upon the prisoner's constitutional claim. This is not so perverse as might first appear. Habeas corpus, as a collateral remedy, was to deal with serious constitutional problems involving circumstances outside the record or cognizance of the state courts. It would also serve where appellate consideration was unavailable or ineffective. If the state courts had adjudicated the federal constitutional contention adversely to the prisoner, on full and fair consideration and with effective appellate review, the remedy for error was to seek review in the United States Supreme Court. This was another aspect of the principle that habeas corpus was not to do service as an appeal.

The soundness of this reasoning depends, of course, upon Supreme Court reviews being available and effective. But whatever may once have been true, by the middle of the twentieth century that premise had clearly become unreliable. The Court's docket had grown to the point that it could pass on the merits of no more than a sixth of the cases in which its review was sought. The percentage has become even smaller in recent years. Moreover, even when available, appellate review in particular cases may be innately limited in significant respects because it must be conducted on the basis of a "cold" written record. Tones, attitudes, inflections of voice, and other subtle factors may exert powerful influences on outcomes and yet not be evident on the record. Beyond that, in many criminal proceedings an adequate written record may not even be produced. The significance of these factors in limiting the utility of Supreme Court review is greatly heightened when the applicable federal law is developing rapidly, and particularly if state judges are hostile to or less than entirely sympathetic with the direction of that development. Both of these conditions existed in the 1930s and 1940s and both intensified in the period following World War II, when the Supreme Court greatly expanded the procedural requirements imposed by federal constitutional law in state criminal prosecutions. Many requirements

that previously governed only federal CRIMINAL PRO-
CEDURE were "incorporated" into the FOURTEENTH
AMENDMENT and made applicable in state trials. (See
INCORPORATION DOCTRINE.) Moreover, and surely
of no less import, the Supreme Court was also expansively construing the EQUAL PROTECTION CLAUSE of
the Fourteenth Amendment to heighten prohibitions
against RACIAL DISCRIMINATION. That attitude enhanced federal scrutiny of jury selection and other
elements of state criminal proceedings. Particularly
in the early stages of the development of these growing constitutional demands, there was reason to believe that many state judges might be less than fully
sympathetic, if not directly hostile, to these new federal principles and DOCTRINES.

Under these conditions, direct appellate review by
the Supreme Court could not alone provide reliable
and effective enforcement of federal constitutional
guarantees in the state courts. Indeed, any tendency
toward heel-dragging or resistance might well be encouraged by the knowledge that the statistical probability of federal appellate review was very low.
Moreover, by diverting Supreme Court energy to
enforcement of earlier holdings, resistance might effectively retard further development of the new doctrines.

Habeas corpus from federal courts probing the validity of state convictions could offer an alternative
mode for securing effective enforcement of the new
constitutional rights. Federal judges generally could
be relied upon to be more in tune with Supreme Court
developments than their state counterparts. Because
the entire federal judiciary would be involved, caseload capacity would be much more equal to the task.
Moreover, because trial-type hearings were possible,
habeas corpus had the further advantage that the federal courts need not be dependent upon the state
court record. These gains could, of course, be achieved
only by abandoning the rule that barred consideration
on federal habeas corpus of contentions that had been
adjudicated previously in the state courts. The Supreme Court took that step in 1953 in *Brown v. Allen.*

Brown v. Allen represented a major extension of
the functions of habeas corpus. Its holding, allowing
federal reconsideration of issues previously considered fully by state courts, also effectively opened wide
the range of constitutional contentions that could
serve as sufficient grounds for seeking federal habeas
corpus. From that point forward, it was clear that
at the very least any constitutional claim that could
be said to raise any significant issue of trial fairness
would be open to consideration. That expansion of

the scope of habeas corpus serves important ends,
but it has significant costs.

One of these costs is the adverse reaction of many
state judges. The result of *Brown v. Allen* is that federal courts on habeas corpus may reexamine a state
prisoner's constitutional challenges to his conviction
after a state court has considered and rejected those
same challenges. Because the prisoner must exhaust
his state remedies before federal habeas corpus, normally the federal constitutional claims have been
pressed not only at the state trial but throughout the
state court system, including the state supreme court.
The upshot of the new role of federal habeas corpus,
then, is that a single federal district judge routinely
may review the determination of the highest court
of a state and, if he disagrees with it, overturn the
conviction that the collegial, multimember court had
upheld.

People and state officials in general, and state supreme court justices in particular, long since have
become accustomed to review by the Supreme Court
of the United States. Whatever may have been
thought in their time of the challenges raised and
rejected in MARTIN V. HUNTER'S LESSEE (1816) and
COHENS V. VIRGINIA (1821), the higher authority of
the Supreme Court in matters of federal law has been
fully accepted. There has not been a corresponding
acceptance of the habeas corpus authority of lower
federal court judges. That federal judges may be more
in accord with developing Supreme Court doctrines,
though offered as justification, does not palliate the
felt insult. On the contrary, if state judges are hostile
to those developments, that fact exacerbates it. If the
state court justices see themselves as entirely in accord
with the Supreme Court's developing doctrines, the
routine reexamination by a single district judge may
still be offensive, to some perhaps even more so. On
occasion, state courts have even openly refused to
pass upon a constitutional claim on the grounds that
a federal judge would pass on it anyway. On balance,
the expansion of federal habeas corpus jurisdiction
has almost certainly enhanced even state court enforcement of federal constitutional rights, but the felt
slight to status and the consequent resentment are
real.

At least as important as the resentment of state
judges is the concern that the wide availability of federal habeas corpus may dilute the deterrent effect
of the criminal law. Part of this concern grows out
of the belief that deterrence is enhanced by certainty
of punishment and that the expansion of federal habeas corpus increases the possibility that a conviction

may be overturned. Certainly, the availability of federal habeas corpus, after the full range of state court remedies, does mean that the finality of a conviction is greatly delayed, even when the conviction is ultimately upheld. Moreover, the knowledge that the ultimate decision can always be greatly delayed itself diminishes any general sense in the community that punishment may be swift or certain.

When the conviction is overturned years after the trial and even longer after the alleged crime, these effects are exacerbated. Although the usual habeas corpus remedy is to order release only if the prisoner is not retried and convicted within a reasonable time, retrial after considerable delay may be practically impossible: witnesses may have died or disappeared; memories inevitably fade; other evidence may be lost. In those instances a reversal on procedural grounds amounts to a full release.

In fact, the proportion of habeas corpus proceedings that result in any victory for the prisoner is exceedingly small. But the effect of those few cases may be far greater than their number, particularly if a case was notorious in the community. Each such incident attracts attention and presumably lessens the deterrent effect of the criminal law. It may also be important that each raises questions for the citizenry at large who are already fearful about the capacity of the system to cope with crime.

Finally, the rehabilitative functions of the penal system may be affected. It has been suggested that demonstration of society's deep concern for fair procedure is useful, and even that channeling prisoners' efforts into litigation may be helpful. But it is more likely that the indefinite stringing-out of a conclusion is counterproductive. As Justice LEWIS F. POWELL, concurring in SCHNECKLOTH V. BUSTAMONTE (1973), wrote: "No effective judicial system can afford to concede the continuing theoretical possibility that there is error in every trial and that every incarceration is unfounded. At some point the law must convey to those in custody that a wrong has been committed, that consequent punishment has been imposed, that one should no longer look back with the view to resurrecting every imaginable basis for further litigation but rather should look forward to rehabilitation and to becoming a constructive citizen."

The concerns expressed are real and significant, but they can be accommodated only by restricting the scope of federal habeas corpus. That in turn involves a judgment as to the necessity of having federal judges routinely available to consider particular claims of constitutional violations. Every constitutional claim is important. But the issue here is not whether a constitutional right shall be declared, or whether rights so declared shall be binding on state courts and subject to review and enforcement by the federal Supreme Court. The issue is whether there should be an additional, collateral channel for routine reexamination of every state court rejection of every constitutional claim asserted in a criminal proceeding.

While perhaps in theory all constitutional rights are equal, there are differences among them. For one thing, there may be substantial differences in the justifications for, and consequences of, seeking thoroughgoing enforcement of particular rights in every case where they may be colorably claimed. The Supreme Court has recognized as much in holding that some newly established constitutional rights should be given full retroactive effect (applying to all habeas corpus cases regardless of when the original conviction was obtained) and others should not. In at least one sense it is fair to characterize these decisions as holding some constitutional rights to be more fundamental than others.

Furthermore, constitutional rights serve different sets of purposes. Most procedural requirements in criminal prosecutions are designed to minimize the likelihood of an erroneous conviction, for example, the RIGHT TO COUNSEL or the right to confront prosecution witnesses. (See CONFRONTATION.) Others are designed to protect personal privacy or dignity at trial or in the society; among these are the rules against UNREASONABLE SEARCHES or seizures, and the RIGHT AGAINST SELF-INCRIMINATION. Finally, there may be relevant distinctions between rights and remedies. Thus, the rule excluding evidence obtained by prohibited police actions may be viewed as a means to deter official misconduct rather than an independent right.

These distinctions may be highly relevant in determining the appropriate scope of federal habeas corpus in reexamining state court convictions. Consider, for example, the EXCLUSIONARY RULE that evidence obtained by an unconstitutional search may not be used in a criminal prosecution. State convictions obtained after such evidence has been introduced are invalid and subject to reversal on direct Supreme Court review. (See MAPP V. OHIO, 1961). But if in a particular case the state courts should decide that the search was legal, how important is it that the decision be reviewable on federal habeas corpus—even assuming that the state decision might be wrong and yet not important enough to warrant Supreme Court attention? Illegally seized evidence does not mean actually unreliable evidence; in fact, such evidence is generally highly probative (for example, the drugs themselves in a prosecution for possession or sale of narcotics). The ban on unreasonable searches and the exclusionary rule do not protect against convicting the wrong person; they aim to protect individual privacy and control police conduct. Thus the sole purpose of extending habeas corpus to encompass the exclusionary rule would be to enhance the rule's deterrent effect. But that enhancement would be only marginal, *i.e.*, only to the extent of whatever additional disincentive might be generated by the extra possibility of a conviction, upheld by the state courts, being overturned years later on federal habeas corpus. At the same time, any such gain could be only obtained at the cost of the side effects of habeas corpus already described, including particularly the problems involved in releasing individuals who have been proven to have violated the law.

The Supreme Court has vacillated on precisely this issue. After many years in which federal habeas corpus was held to encompass claims under the exclusionary rule, the Court in STONE V. POWELL (1976) decided that it would not be available to review decisions of SEARCH AND SEIZURE issues reached after full consideration.

That decision stirred much debate. Perhaps as a result of the prominent role of lawyers and judicial review in interpreting the Constitution, there is a tendency to focus attention on the borderlines of case law development. That perspective can be misleading. What is more important than the decision to exclude search and seizure issues is the scope of federal habeas corpus for state prisoners that remains available. Constitutional claims need not be related to ultimate accuracy of conviction in order to be included. Moreover, despite strong suggestions from respected sources that the prisoner's factual innocence ought to be a major element in the availability of habeas corpus relief, the Court has not adopted that position. By any measure, the range of constitutional claims that may be raised and relitigated in federal habeas corpus is far greater than those few precluded—and then only after full and fair state consideration.

Similarly, much of the legal writing concerning habeas corpus today deals with its use to challenge criminal convictions. It is sometimes even suggested that Congress could not constitutionally restrict the scope of that kind of habeas corpus. Related to this, but more generally, it is argued that the provision of Article I, section 9, against the suspension of the privilege of habeas corpus should now be interpreted as prohibiting Congress from suspending or limiting federal habeas corpus—including habeas corpus for state con-

victed prisoners. The argument generally acknowledges that this was not the original intention of the suspension clause. It contends, rather, that in view of subsequent developments and present conditions, the original purpose now calls for extending it to cover habeas corpus from federal courts.

While these arguments, and the general issue of federal habeas corpus for persons held under state court convictions, are important, too exclusive a focus on them risks distorted perspective. Far more significant than the existence of these arguments, or their validity, is their currently academic nature. Despite strenuous objections to the jurisdiction, Congress has not significantly restricted the scope of federal habeas corpus for state prisoners. Moreover, it does not derogate from the importance of this use of habeas corpus to point out that at base the availability of the Great Writ to challenge executive or military actions or other imprisonments without semblance of judicial process is far more vital to the maintenance of liberty. Even the most ardent advocates of collateral attack on judicial convictions are not likely to disagree.

It is surely a measure of the state of liberty in the United States that so much can be taken for granted. Habeas corpus for extraordinary assertions of executive, military, or other nonjudicial authority comes to the fore only rarely—and that is a measure of freedom's health in the nation. Yet it is that general freedom from that kind of arbitrary authority that is most crucial. Habeas corpus has helped to secure that freedom in the past, and its continuing availability helps secure it continually. It is true that liberty is most prevalent when habeas corpus is needed least. It is also true that the effectiveness of the remedy of habeas corpus is dependent upon the substantive criteria that come into play. Yet the existence of the Great Writ, indeed precisely in its taken-for-granted quality, plays a major role in supporting and reinforcing the conditions of freedom.

PAUL J. MISHKIN

Bibliography

BATOR, PAUL M.; MISHKIN, PAUL J.; SHAPIRO, DAVID L.; and WECHSLER, HERBERT 1973 Supplement 1981 Chaps. I, IV, and X in *Hart & Wechsler's The Federal Courts and the Federal System,* 2nd ed. Mineola, N.Y.: Foundation Press.

CHAFEE, ZECHARIAH, JR. 1952 *How Human Rights Got into the Constitution.* Pages 51–74. Boston: Boston University Press.

COVER, ROBERT M. and ALEINIKOFF, T. ALEXANDER 1977 Dialectical Federalism: Habeas Corpus and the Court. *Yale Law Journal* 86:1035–1102.

DUKER, WILLIAM F. 1980 *A Constitutional History of Habeas Corpus.* Westport, Conn.: Greenwood Press.

FRIENDLY, HENRY J. 1970 Is Innocence Irrelevant? Collateral Attack on Criminal Judgments. *University of Chicago Law Review* 38:142–172.

HART, HENRY M. 1953 The Power of Congress to Limit the Jurisdiction of the Federal Courts: An Exercise in Dialectic. *Harvard Law Review* 66:1362–1402.

NOTE 1970 Developments in the Law—Federal Habeas Corpus. *Harvard Law Review* 83:1038–1280.

OAKS, DALLIN H. 1966 Legal History in the High Court —Habeas Corpus. *Michigan Law Review* 64:451–472.

HABEAS CORPUS ACT OF 1679
31 Charles II c.2 (1679)

The right to the writ of HABEAS CORPUS, as ZECHARIAH CHAFEE, JR., said, is "the most important human rights provision in the Constitution" (Article I, section 9) because it safeguards personal liberty, without which other liberties cannot be exercised. This act of Parliament created no new right; the writ was already about a century old as a mechanism by which a prisoner could test in court the legality of his imprisonment. But crown officers knew a variety of stratagems that hamstrung the writ. This statute, which runs on and on in dull detail without a word about the liberty of the subject or any high-sounding principle, sought to seal off every means of circumventing the writ. It is a technical instruction manual—how and what to do in any situation—to make the writ enforceable as a practical remedy for illegal imprisonment. It imposed steep penalties on every officer of government, from the local jailor to the lord high chancellor for breach, evasion, or delay. The only loophole in the statute, a failure to prohibit excessive BAIL, was plugged in 1689 by the BILL OF RIGHTS. Although the statute did not extend to the colonies, it provided a model, and Americans regarded the great writ as a fundamental right protected by COMMON LAW and gave it constitutional status.

LEONARD W. LEVY

Bibliography

PERRY, RICHARD L., ed. 1959 *Sources of Our Liberties.* Pages 189–203. New York: American Bar Foundation.

HABEAS CORPUS ACT OF 1863
12 Stat. 755 (1863)

Justice, before the Civil War and Reconstruction, was overwhelmingly state justice. Under the Constitution's Article III, implemented in the JUDICIARY ACT of 1789, few litigants qualified for federal JURISDICTION. The 1863 Habeas Corpus law lessened this imbalance at least for federal officials who, enforcing EXECUTIVE ORDERS or statutes, were defendants in state courts. After legitimizing Lincoln's HABEAS CORPUS suspensions since 1861 and authorizing future suspensions, Congress, in the Habeas Corpus Act, indemnified federal officials who had been found guilty in state courts of wrongs against civilians. Further, the law authorized a federal officer facing a state court proceeding to remove the case to a federal court. United States attorneys would act for the defendant if the state proceeding were prejudiced against him and if the defendant had been carrying out orders in a proper manner. Though federal proceedings were to flow from state rules, blacks could testify even adversely to whites, and all court officers and jurors were sworn to the TEST OATH. In extending these protections to its officials, the nation bridged, for them at least, ancient interstices in the dual system of courts. Congress exacted a price from the executive, however, by requiring relevant Cabinet department heads to report to federal judges on civilians arrested by soldiers for allegedly violating draft, internal security, emancipation, or trade-control policies. In the HABEAS CORPUS ACT of 1867, Congress further expanded the classes of protected persons who could resort to federal justice.

HAROLD M. HYMAN

Bibliography

DUKER, WILLIAM F. 1980 *A Constitutional History of Habeas Corpus.* Pages 126–224. Westport, Conn.: Greenwood Press.

HABEAS CORPUS ACT OF 1867
14 Stat. 385 (1867)

This act, whose intent one expert has called "unusually murky," fundamentally amended the HABEAS CORPUS provisions of the JUDICIARY ACT OF 1789. Where that act limited availability of the writ to those persons jailed under federal authority, the new act applied "in all cases where any person may be restrained of his or her liberty in violation of the constitution, or of any treaty or law of the United States." Section 1 vested power to issue the writ in all United States courts and judges, established procedures, and authorized APPEALS from inferior courts to CIRCUIT COURTS and to the Supreme Court. A writ could issue at any point in state court proceedings, halting them until the federal habeas corpus action ended. The second section made available WRITS OF ERROR from the Supreme Court in specified instances.

The act gave the Supreme Court JURISDICTION over the appeal of a Mississippi editor who challenged the constitutionality of military reconstruction, but in 1868 Congress withdrew the provisions establishing the Supreme Court's APPELLATE JURISDICTION, and in EX PARTE MCCARDLE (1869) the Court declined to hear the editor's case. The Court nevertheless asserted authority on another statutory basis in *Ex parte Yerger* (1869), and Congress restored the Court's power to hear habeas corpus appeals in 1885.

The federal courts' statutory authority to grant writs of habeas corpus to state prisoners unconstitutionally held in custody continues to this day.

DAVID GORDON

HAGUE v. CONGRESS OF INDUSTRIAL ORGANIZATIONS
307 U.S. 496 (1939)

In separate opinions yielding no majority, over two dissents, and with only seven Justices participating, the Court enjoined enforcement of a local ordinance used to harass labor organizers. Justices OWEN ROBERTS and HUGO L. BLACK and Chief Justice CHARLES EVANS HUGHES deemed the right to organize under and discuss the WAGNER (NATIONAL LABOR RELATIONS) ACT a privilege or immunity of national CITIZENSHIP. Justices HARLAN FISKE STONE and STANLEY F. REED held it a right protected by the FIRST AMENDMENT. Justice Stone's separate opinion, which suggested that SECTION 1983's jurisdictional counterpart authorized federal courts to hear actions involving personal liberty but not to hear actions involving property rights, influenced subsequent CIVIL RIGHTS cases. Some courts accepted the distinction and applied the dichotomy to section 1983 itself. *Lynch v. Household Finance Corp.* (1972) discredited the distinction.

THEODORE EISENBERG

HAIG v. AGEE
453 U.S. 280 (1981)

Philip Agee, a former employee of the Central Intelligence Agency (CIA) who was familiar with its covert intelligence gathering, revealed the identities of its agents and sources, disrupting the intelligence operations of the United States, and exposing CIA opera-

tives to assassination. The secretary of state revoked Agee's passport because his activities abroad damaged national security. Agee objected that revocation of his passport violated his constitutional RIGHT TO TRAVEL, FREEDOM OF SPEECH, and PROCEDURAL DUE PROCESS. An 8–2 SUPREME COURT found his claims meritless, because his freedom to travel abroad was subordinate to national security considerations, his disclosures obstructed intelligence operations and therefore were unprotected by the FIRST AMENDMENT, and his right to due process was satisfied by the opportunity for a prompt hearing after revocation. The dissenters did not rely on constitutional grounds.

LEONARD W. LEVY

HAINES, CHARLES G.
(1879–1948)

Charles Grove Haines was an eminent scholar of American constitutional history who taught political science at the University of California, Los Angeles. In 1939 he was president of the American Political Science Association. His major books continue to be among the best on their subjects. His *Revival of Natural Law Concepts* (1930) is a comparative study of theories of FUNDAMENTAL LAW. *The American Doctrine of Judicial Supremacy* (revised edition, 1932) is the finest book on the history of JUDICIAL REVIEW from the standpoint of a critic of the institution. His *Role of the Supreme Court in American Government and Politics* (volume I, 1944; volume II, posthumous and coauthored by Forest Sherwood, 1957), covering the period 1789 to 1864, is a trenchant history from the viewpoint of a Jeffersonian democrat.

LEONARD W. LEVY

HALL v. DECUIR
95 U.S. 485 (1877)

In 1870 the operator of a steamboat regularly traveling between New Orleans, Louisiana, and Vicksburg, Mississippi, refused a black woman accommodation in the cabin reserved for whites. He thereby violated a Louisiana statute, adopted during the period of MILITARY RECONSTRUCTION, which prohibited RACIAL DISCRIMINATION by common carriers operating within the state. Speaking for the Court, Chief Justice MORRISON R. WAITE sought to avoid the "great inconvenience and unnecessary hardship" which might arise if all states bordering the Mississippi River were to enact divergent and conflicting laws. Waite stressed the importance of uniform regulations and struck down the state act as a "direct burden upon INTERSTATE COMMERCE" in violation of Article I, section 8. Nearly seventy years later, in MORGAN V. VIRGINIA (1946), the Supreme Court struck down a law requiring racial SEGREGATION on buses, on a similar commerce ground. Neither opinion discussed the EQUAL PROTECTION clause.

DAVID GORDON

HAMILTON, ALEXANDER
(1755–1804)

Alexander Hamilton, American statesman, member of the Constitutional Convention (1787), coauthor of THE FEDERALIST, first secretary of the Treasury (1789–1795), and leading member of the Federalist party in New York, was born on the island of Nevis in the British West Indies. He came to New York in 1773 and enrolled in King's College; he served with distinction in the Revolutionary War, from 1777 to 1781 as GEORGE WASHINGTON'S aide-de-camp. Hamilton was a leading member of the New York bar before and after he served in President Washington's cabinet.

During the prelude to independence, Hamilton participated in the pamphlet controversies between American Whigs and supporters of Britain. His most important pamphlet, "The Farmer Refuted" (1775), expressed a conventional natural rights philosophy. He asserted that "nature has distributed an equality of rights to every man." He also upheld the right to resort to first principles above and beyond the "common forms of municipal law." He subscribed to the theory of government as a social compact between ruler and ruled (a model used by WILLIAM BLACKSTONE rather than JOHN LOCKE) and, like JOHN ADAMS and THOMAS JEFFERSON, argued that the British king was "King of America, by virtue of a compact between us and the King of Great Britain."

Hamilton, who by origin was not rooted in any one of the thirteen states, became an early and perhaps the most outspoken advocate of a stronger and more centralized government for the United States. In 1780 he developed a far-reaching program of constitutional reform. First, he pleaded for a vast increase in the power of Congress and asked for a convention for the purpose of framing a confederation, to give Congress complete sovereignty in all matters relating to war, peace, trade, finance, and the management of

FOREIGN AFFAIRS. Second, he called for a more efficient organization of the executive tasks of Congress. Individuals were better suited than boards of administration (with the possible exception of trade matters), because responsibility was then less diffused; "men of the first pretentions" would be more attracted to these tasks if offered individual responsibility. Hamilton developed his plea for strengthening Congress in "The Continentalist" (1781–1782) in which he revealed his future political program by pointing to the need "to create in the interior of each state a mass of influence in favour of the Foederal Government." As a delegate from New York to Congress (1782–1783), Hamilton criticized the ARTICLES OF CONFEDERATION. Only in September 1786 did he succeed having the Annapolis Convention endorse his resolution for calling a convention to meet in Philadelphia in May 1787 "to devise such further provisions as shall appear to them necessary to render the constitution of the Foederal Government adequate to the exigencies of the Union."

Hamilton took a strong stand during that period against New York state legislation discriminating against Loyalists. His "Letters of Phocion" (1784) defended individual rights and the rule of law against "arbitrary acts of legislature," as well as the supremacy of the state constitution over acts of the legislature. As counsel for the defense in the New York case of RUTGERS V. WADDINGTON (1784) Hamilton argued that the New York Trespass Act (1783), which enabled people who had fled New York when British forces occupied the city to recover damages from persons who had held their premises during the occupation, was incompatible with higher law—that of the law of nations, of the peace treaty, and of commands of Congress. The Court did not accept the argument for JUDICIAL REVIEW, but followed another of Hamilton's arguments: that the legislature could not have meant to violate the law of nations.

At the CONSTITUTIONAL CONVENTION OF 1787, Hamilton was somewhat an outsider for two reasons. First, the other two members of the New York delegation, JOHN LANSING and ROBERT YATES, opposed a stronger central government. Second, Hamilton's views, presented to the Convention in a five-hour speech on June 18, were extreme on two counts: he advocated the abolition of states as states, favoring a system that would leave them only subordinate jurisdiction; and he advocated tenure during GOOD BEHAVIOR both for members of the Senate and for the chief executive. He admitted that in his private opinion the British government was "the best in the world." Hamilton's constitutional proposals reflected the idea of "mixed government": the lower house of Congress should be elected on the basis of democratic manhood suffrage, yet the Senate and the President ought to be elected by electors with high property qualifications. A chief reason for Hamilton's "high-toned" constitutional ideas was that "he was much discouraged by the amazing extent of Country"; he feared disruptive tendencies, originating particularly from the larger and more powerful states.

Could his constitutional proposals influenced by the British model still be termed republican? Hamilton held that the standards of republican government were respected as long as "power, mediately, or immediately, is derived from the consent of the people," or as long as all magistrates were appointed by "the people, or a process of election originating with the people." Against later charges of "monarchism," Hamilton replied that his plan submitted at Philadelphia was conformable "with the strict theory of a Government purely republican; the essential criteria of which are that the principal organs of the Executive and Legislative departments be elected by the people and hold their offices by a responsible and temporary or defeasible tenure."

Though Hamilton absented himself during much of the Convention's work, he signed the Constitution on September 17, 1787, as the only member from New York, indicating that he saw only an alternative between anarchy, on the one hand, and "the chance of good to be expected from the plan," on the other.

During the struggle for ratification of the Constitution (1787–1788), Hamilton's two major achievements were the publication of *The Federalist* essays and his part in the New York ratifying convention at Poughkeepsie. He organized and coordinated publication of *The Federalist*, which appeared over the signature of "Publius" from late October 1787, to late May 1788. Of the eighty-five essays, Hamilton wrote fifty-one. In them he developed several major themes, some of which also recurred in his speeches in the New York Ratifying Convention.

Hamilton proved the utility of the union to America's political prosperity chiefly by painting a somber picture of international rivalry, ever ready to exploit dissensions among the states; he raised the specter of a disrupted Confederation, of war between the states, and of the rise of partial confederations, the most likely and most dangerous contingency being the formation of a northern and a southern confederacy. Hamilton then demonstrated the insufficiency of the Confederation to preserve the union by pointing to the necessity that the federal government, to be effective, "carry its agency to the persons of the citizens." He envisaged a broad scope for the powers granted to the federal government. The powers needed to provide for the common defense of the members of the Union "ought to exist without limitation." A vast scope for the federal power to regulate commerce and to provide for the financial needs of the Union, and the maxim that "every POWER ought to be in proportion to its OBJECT," foreshadowed Hamilton's later constructions of the Constitution while he directed the Treasury. The Constitution ought to allow a capacity "to provide for future contingencies," which were illimitable.

Hamilton's most important contribution to the analysis of institutions and procedures is his discussion of the executive branch in *The Federalist* #67–77. Believing that efficient administration was the very core of good government, he supported an individual executive who would be less likely than a plural executive "to conceal faults, and destroy responsibility." The office of chief magistrate, if not shackled by brief duration or restrictions on reeligibility, might attract men imbued with "the love of fame, the ruling passion of the noblest minds" (#72).

Hamilton's analysis of the federal judiciary is best known for the justification of judicial review in *The Federalist* #78. There Hamilton tried to refute the argument presented by the Anti-Federalist "Brutus" that judicial review implied JUDICIAL SUPREMACY. Hamilton invoked the superiority of the will of the people as declared in the Constitution and the duty of the judges to be governed by that will. A constitution "is in fact, and must be regarded by the judges as fundamental law." His statement in *The Federalist* #81 "that the Constitution ought to be the standard of construction for the laws, and that wherever there is an evident opposition, the laws ought to give place to the Constitution" is similarly significant.

Hamilton argued against a federal bill of rights in *The Federalist* #84. His main point that bills of rights were not needed in constitutions founded upon the power of the people is rhetorical; it is contradicted by his own admission that the Constitution as drafted did in fact contain a rudimentary bill of rights, including provisions on habeas corpus, the prohibition of BILLS OF ATTAINDER and EX POST FACTO laws and the guarantee of TRIAL BY JURY in criminal cases.

The office of secretary of the Treasury, coveted by Hamilton more than any other, afforded him the opportunity to initiate policies for strengthening the public support, and particularly the support of the moneyed community, for the federal government. He considered leadership not only as compatible with, but incumbent on, executive office, and once spoke of the "executive impulse." He seems to have considered his office as that of a prime minister on the British model. Hamilton's major effort and achievement was the establishment of public credit for the new federal government. His measures included funding the foreign and domestic debt at par, assumption of the revolutionary state debts, creation of the Bank of the United States, and levying of federal excise taxes; his most important policy papers were his Report on Public Credit (January 1790) and his Report on the National Bank (December 1790). As a program for the future, Hamilton, in the Report on Manufactures (1791), envisaged protective tariffs, aid for agriculture, and INTERNAL IMPROVEMENTS. Increasingly, his policies encountered and provoked opposition from Thomas Jefferson, JAMES MADISON, and the Republican party forming around them.

There were two great constitutional issues on which Hamilton spoke out during his membership in Washington's cabinet: the constitutionality of the proposed Bank of the United States (1791), and the constitutionality of the President's PROCLAMATION OF NEUTRALITY (1793). In the dispute on the bank, both Attorney General EDMUND RANDOLPH and Secretary of State Jefferson denied that the United States had the power to incorporate a bank, this power not being enumerated in the catalogue of powers granted to Congress by the Constitution. Hamilton, in his "Opinion on the Constitutionality of an Act to Establish a Bank," developed the theory of IMPLIED POWERS granted by the Constitution, arguing that implied powers as well as express powers were in fact delegated by the Constitution; he also asserted the existence of such resulting powers as those resulting from the conquest of neighboring territory. Grants of power included means to attain a specified end, the criterion of constitutionality being met if the end was specified in the Constitution. To attain the objective of the "effectual administration of the finances of the United States," there was no "parsimony of power." Also, Hamilton argued that the NECESSARY AND PROPER CLAUSE ought to be construed "to give a liberal latitude to the exercise of specified powers" rather than construing the word "necessary" restrictively, as had Jefferson. These arguments were later adopted by the Supreme Court in McCULLOCH V. MARYLAND (1819), and still guide the interpretation of Congress's legislative powers.

Hamilton's second major constitutional pronouncement concerned the power of the executive to issue a declaration of neutrality. In the first of his "Pacificus" articles justifying the President's action against Jeffersonian criticism, he presented an extremely broad construction of Article II. The grant of "executive power" (singular) as opposed to the "powers" (plural) granted to Congress meant a general grant of power; the enumeration of specific powers of the executive was merely demonstrative, "intended by way of greater caution." Hamilton also argued that the executive conducted the nation's foreign policy and that his duty obligated him to execute the laws including the law of nations.

During the years after his retirement from the Treasury, Hamilton, as leading Federalist politician, yet without federal office except for a brief spell as Inspector of the Army (1798–1800), on several occasions commented on constitutional matters.

Controversy over JAY'S TREATY (1794) involved constitutional issues between the executive and the House of Representatives. Was the President bound to submit papers pertaining to the treaty negotiations to the legislature? Did the treaty power, jointly exercised by President and Senate, oblige the legislature to appropriate the needed funds without any liberty of exercising legislative discretion? Hamilton denied any obligation on the part of the President to transmit papers, arguing that such a transmittal would "tend to destroy" the confidence of foreign governments in the "prudence and delicacy" of the government. He further argued that a treaty could obligate the legislature to appropriate funds.

Representing the federal government in HYLTON V. UNITED STATES (1796), his only appearance as counsel before the Supreme Court, Hamilton argued that a federal tax on carriages (levied by Congress in 1794 on Hamilton's recommendation) was an excise rather than a direct tax, and so did not have to be apportioned among the states according to the census. Hamilton argued that as an excise the tax was constitutional, and the Court upheld his view.

In 1796 Hamilton was approached for a legal opinion on the Yazoo land grant affair in Georgia. An act of the Georgia legislature had repealed an earlier act providing for the sale of vast tracts of land, the repeal having been prompted by charges of fraud in the original transaction and a political changeover in the legislature. Hamilton argued that Article I, section 10, of the Constitution, prohibiting the states from passing any law "impairing the obligation of contracts," applied not merely to contracts between individuals but to contracts between states and individuals as well, and that a land grant was a contract covered by the contract clause. Hamilton's views became the basis of the Supreme Court's decision in FLETCHER V. PECK (1810).

When New York State election results in the spring

of 1800 made it virtually certain that the state legislature would elect presidential electors favoring Jefferson as President, Hamilton suggested that Governor JOHN JAY call the outgoing legislature into special session to elect anti-Jefferson electors. Hamilton believed that it "is easy to sacrifice the substantial interests of society by a strict adherence to ordinary rules." Jay rejected this proposal, which shows Hamilton's readiness to neglect, in cases he considered extraordinary crises or emergencies, "ordinary rules." Hamilton approved, incidentally, the LOUISIANA PURCHASE.

Although not technically concerning the Constitution, Hamilton's defense of freedom of the press in PEOPLE V. CROSWELL (1804) deserves notice. Hamilton was counsel for the appellant before the high court of New York, the appellant having been convicted of LIBEL for publishing an anti-Jefferson piece. Hamilton's two main points, based on the successful plea of Andrew Hamilton in ZENGER'S CASE (1735), were that truth of an alleged libel should be admitted as evidence and that juries, in libel cases, ought to decide both on fact and on law. The Court divided and thus the conviction was allowed to stand, though no sentence was passed. State legislation to give effect to Hamilton's points was enacted soon afterward.

Hamilton's understanding of the federal Constitution was informed by his vision of the United States as one nation rather than thirteen states, and also by his conviction that the United States constituted one nation among many nations in a state of permanent rivalry. In his interpretation of the Constitution, three points stand out: the broad construction of federal powers as opposed to state powers; the broad construction of executive powers; and the doctrine of judicial review.

GERALD STOURZH

Bibliography

COOKE, JACOB ERNEST 1982 Alexander Hamilton. New York: Scribner's.

GOEBEL, JULIUS, JR., et al., eds. 1964–1980 The Law Practice of Alexander Hamilton: Documents and Commentaries. 4 Vols. New York: Columbia University Press.

MITCHELL, BROADUS 1957–1962 Alexander Hamilton. 2 Vols. New York: Macmillan.

ROSSITER, CLINTON 1964 Alexander Hamilton and the Constitution. New York: Harcourt, Brace.

STOURZH, GERALD 1970 Alexander Hamilton and the Idea of Republican Government. Stanford, Calif.: Stanford University Press.

SYRETT, HAROLD E. et al., eds. 1961–1978 The Papers of Alexander Hamilton. 26 Vols. New York: Columbia University Press.

HAMILTON, ANDREW

See: Zenger's Case

HAMILTON, WALTON HALE
(1881–1958)

Although Walton Hale Hamilton never formally studied law, he became an influential member of the faculty of Yale Law School and one of the nation's leading experts on government regulation of the economy. Hamilton's many books discussing the relationship between the government and the economic order include *Prices and Price Policies* (1938), *The Patterns of Competition* (1940), *Patents and Free Trade* (1941), and *The Politics of Industry* (1957). In these and other works, Hamilton criticized as unrealistic the traditional view of the American economy as a self-regulating free market; he pointed out that the government is deeply enmeshed in the economy, often at the urgent request of the private sector. Hamilton's most substantial contribution to constitutional scholarship, *The Power to Govern*, written with Douglass Adair (1937), followed naturally from his other interests. Exploring the intellectual background of the framing of the Constitution, Hamilton and Adair focused on the meaning of the word "commerce"; they concluded that the Framers intended to grant the national government broad powers through the Constitution's COMMERCE CLAUSE to regulate all forms of economic activity resulting in transactions across state lines, thus implicitly supporting the constitutionality of New Deal federal regulation.

RICHARD B. BERNSTEIN

HAMILTON v. BOARD OF REGENTS OF THE UNIVERSITY OF CALIFORNIA
292 U.S. 245 (1934)

This case raised the problem of CONSCIENTIOUS OBJECTION to military service in a state context. California required that male freshman and sophomore state university students enroll in a course of military science. Hamilton, a religious objector, argued that this requirement violated the liberty guaranteed him by the FOURTEENTH AMENDMENT. Justice PIERCE BUTLER spoke for a unanimous Supreme Court, and concluded that nothing in the Constitution relieved a conscientious objector from the obligation to bear arms.

RICHARD E. MORGAN

HAMMER v. DAGENHART
247 U.S. 251 (1918)

From 1903 to 1918, the Supreme Court consistently had approved NATIONAL POLICE POWER regulations enacted under the COMMERCE CLAUSE. But in *Hammer v. Dagenhart*, the Court deviated from this tradition and invalidated the KEATING-OWEN CHILD LABOR ACT, which prohibited the interstate shipment of goods produced by child labor. The Court's restrictive DOCTRINE nevertheless proved vulnerable and the decision itself eventually was overruled.

In CHAMPION V. AMES (1903) the Justices had sustained a congressional prohibition against the interstate shipment of lottery tickets. The ruling actually was quite narrow, holding that such tickets were proper SUBJECTS OF COMMERCE and that Congress could prevent the "pollution" of INTERSTATE COMMERCE. A more general, expansive doctrine seemed to emerge as the Court soon approved similar regulations of the interstate flow of adulterated foods and impure drugs, prostitutes, prize fight films, and liquor. The Court abruptly deviated from this course in the child labor case, perhaps signaling a reaction against some of the Progressive era's social reforms and the Court's prior tendency toward liberal nationalism.

Justice WILLIAM R. DAY, speaking for a 5–4 majority, maintained at the outset that in each of the other cases the Court had acknowledged that the "use of interstate transportation was necessary to the accomplishment of harmful results." But the child labor regulations, Day held, were different because the goods shipped were of themselves harmless in contrast with lottery tickets, impure foods, prize fight films, and liquor. It was an unsound distinction, but one perhaps anticipated by Justice JOHN MARSHALL HARLAN's remarks in the *Lottery Case* that the Court would not allow Congress arbitrarily to exclude every article from interstate commerce.

The Court refuted any suggestions that congressional authority extended to prevent unfair competition among the states, thus enabling it to ignore any discussion of the evils or deleterious effects of child labor. This argument was grounded in the majority's revival of rigid notions of DUAL FEDERALISM. PRODUCTION, Day said, as he resurrected an older, dubious, and arbitrary distinction, was not commerce; the regulation of production was reserved by the TENTH AMENDMENT to the states. "If it were otherwise," Day noted, "all manufacture intended for interstate shipment would be brought under federal control to the practical exclusion of the authority of the States, a result certainly not contemplated by the . . . Constitution." The regulation of child labor, he maintained, not only exceeded congressional authority but also invaded the proper sphere of local power. To allow such a measure, Day concluded, would end "all freedom of commerce," eliminate state control over local matters, and thereby destroy the federal system.

In dissent, Justice OLIVER WENDELL HOLMES uttered his oft-quoted remark that "if there is any matter upon which civilized countries have agreed—far more unanimously than they have with regard to intoxicants and some other matters over which this country is now emotionally aroused—it is the evil of premature and excessive child labor." But Holmes offered more than his customary philosophical discourse on judicial restraint. Congress plainly had the power to regulate interstate shipments, and its motives of doing so were no less legitimate here than they had been in the regulations.

Whether "evil precedes or follows the transportation" was irrelevant, Holmes said; once states transported their goods across their boundaries, they were "no longer within their rights."

The *Hammer* decision did not significantly diminish the Court's willingness or ability to sustain congressional police regulations under the commerce clause. The ruling revealed that the Court seemed less concerned with the evils of child labor than Congress and was more interested in maintaining the purity of the federal system. In BAILEY V. DREXEL FURNITURE (1922), the Justices invalidated a congressional attempt to regulate child labor by using the TAXING POWER, again despite ample precedents justifying national power. But three years later, Chief Justice WILLIAM HOWARD TAFT, who had written the child labor tax opinion, reverted to the Court's earlier POLICE POWER decisions and broadly approved the National Motor Vehicle Act (1919) which made the transportation of stolen automobiles across state lines a federal crime. In *Brooks v. United States* (1925), Taft agreed that Congress could forbid the use of interstate commerce "as an agency to promote immorality, dishonesty or the spread of any evil or harm of other States from the State of origin." *Hammer v. Dagenhart* marred an otherwise consistent pattern in the precedents, but Taft quickly disposed of it by reiterating the distinction that the products of child labor were not harmful. Yet his 1925 opinion refuted such doctrine as he demonstrated that a perceived evil required national action and the question of harmfulness was secondary.

Throughout the 1920s, the Supreme Court, following Taft's strong views, generally approved an ever expanding scope to the commerce clause. There was some retreat during the bitter constitutional struggle over the New Deal, but it proved temporary. After 1937, a number of decisions reaffirmed a broad nationalistic view of the commerce power. Finally, in 1941, the Court specifically overruled *Hammer.* Justice HARLAN FISKE STONE, in UNITED STATES V. DARBY, rebuked the earlier decision as "novel," "unsupported," "a departure," and "exhausted" as a precedent.

The most poignant historical commentary on *Hammer* came from the supposed victor, Reuben Dagenhart, whose father had sued in order to sustain his "freedom" to allow his fourteen-year-old boy to work in a textile mill. Six years later, Reuben, a 105-pound man, recalled that his victory had earned him a soft drink, some automobile rides from his employer, and a salary of one dollar a day; he had also lost his education and his health.

STANLEY I. KUTLER

Bibliography

WOOD, STEPHEN 1968 *Constitutional Politics in the Progressive Era: Child Labor and the Law.* Chicago: University of Chicago Press.

HAMPTON v. MOW SUN WONG
426 U.S. 88 (1976)

In this case the Supreme Court declined to extend to federal government action the constitutional limits it had imposed on the states' discrimination against ALIENS. The Court recognized that "overriding national interests" might justify a limitation of employment in the federal civil service to citizens—as required by the Civil Service Commission (CSC) here—despite the invalidity of a parallel state law. (See SUGARMAN V. DOUGALL, 1973.) But the interests identified by CSC were insufficient: some of them could be asserted only by the President or Congress; others, within CSC's purview, were after-the-fact rationalizations that had not been considered before the regulation was adopted. The regulation thus violated the Fifth Amendment's guarantee of DUE PROCESS OF LAW; that amendment's EQUAL PROTECTION component need not be reached. The vote was 5–4.

Shortly after the Court's decision in *Hampton,* President GERALD R. FORD issued an order embracing the policy of the invalidated CSC rule.

KENNETH L. KARST

HAMPTON & CO. v. UNITED STATES
276 U.S. 394 (1928)

In *J. W. Hampton, Jr., & Co. v. United States,* a unanimous Supreme Court, speaking through Chief Justice WILLIAM HOWARD TAFT, upheld Congress's DELEGATION OF POWER to the President to adjust tariffs in order to protect American business. The delegation was not improper because the law provided an intelligible standard to which tariffs had to conform. The Court also sustained the protective tariff itself, holding that, because its effect was to raise revenue, Congress's motive in enacting it was irrelevant.

DENNIS J. MAHONEY

HAND, AUGUSTUS N.
(1868–1954)

Born in upstate New York to a prominent legal family, Augustus Noble ("Gus") Hand, after graduating from Harvard College and Harvard Law School, practiced law in New York City from 1897 to 1914. President WOODROW WILSON appointed him in 1914 to the UNITED STATES DISTRICT COURT for the Southern District of New York. A defendant in a trial over which Hand presided described him as a judge of such integrity and impartiality that he could have sustained the dignity of the law in a hurricane. In 1927 President CALVIN COOLIDGE, deferring to the acclaim of the bench and bar, promoted Hand, a Democrat, to the UNITED STATES COURT OF APPEALS, Second Circuit, where he joined his famous cousin, LEARNED HAND.

No appellate judge was more austere than Gus Hand, who commanded the respect and influenced the votes of his brethren for a quarter of a century. He preferred judicial self-restraint to JUDICIAL ACTIVISM. A moderate, he once declared that the ignorance of conservatives hardly exceeded the intolerance of liberals obsessed with change. The ardent crusaders who administered New Deal agencies, he declared, should be left to "fry in their own fat" until Congress reformed them.

Hand dissented rarely and cultivated a passionless style, though he could be eloquent. His opinions tended to favor prosecutors in cases involving the rights of the criminally accused and the government in cases involving subversive activities. For example, he sustained the summary contempt conviction of the lawyers who defended the Communist party leaders tried under the SMITH ACT, even though the trial judge who convicted the lawyers gave them no hearing and waited until the trial's end, months after their contemptuous acts. Hand upheld the SEPARATE BUT EQUAL DOCTRINE and ruled that the Army's racially based quota system during World War II did not violate the SELECTIVE SERVICE ACT. But he championed RELIGIOUS LIBERTY and extended the benefits of conscientious objection to persons who founded their claims on philosophical and political considerations as well as purely religious ones. "A mighty oak has fallen," said one of his colleagues on his death.

LEONARD W. LEVY

Bibliography

SCHICK, MARVIN 1970 *Learned Hand's Court.* Baltimore: Johns Hopkins University Press.

HAND, LEARNED
(1872–1961)

Learned Hand is widely viewed, with OLIVER WENDELL HOLMES, LOUIS D. BRANDEIS, and BENJAMIN N. CARDOZO, as among the leading American judges of the twentieth century. His influence on constitutional law stems more from his extrajudicial advocacy of judicial restraint and his modest, yet creative, performance on lower federal courts in fifty-two years of judging than from the relatively few constitutional rulings among his nearly 3,000 decisions.

Christened Billings Learned Hand, the son and grandson of upstate New York lawyers and judges, Hand dropped the Billings after graduating from Harvard Law School in 1896. Hand surrendered to family pressures in turning to law rather than pursuing his interest in philosophy engendered by his Harvard College teachers, including William James, Josiah Royce, and George Santayana. In six years of practice in Albany and seven in New York City, he performed competently but considered himself inadequate. But the young lawyer's associations with New York City intellectuals and reformers prompted President WILLIAM HOWARD TAFT to name the thirty-seven-year-old Hand to the federal trial bench in 1909. President CALVIN COOLIDGE elevated him to the Court of Appeals for the Second Circuit in 1924, where Hand served for the rest of his life.

Hand's persistent belief in judicial restraint antedated his appointment to the bench. He had been strongly influenced by JAMES BRADLEY THAYER at Harvard Law School. His major publication before the judgeship was an article attacking LOCHNER V. NEW YORK (1905). His deepseated skepticism and allergy to absolutes, as well as his devotion to democratic policymaking and his unwillingness to be ruled by a bevy of Platonic Guardians, made him disdainful of judges ready to pour subjective philosophies into vague constitutional phrases. He was unwilling to suppress his hostility to JUDICIAL ACTIVISM, developed in the era of the Nine Old Men and its use of SUBSTANTIVE DUE PROCESS to strike down ECONOMIC REGULATION, in the post-1937 years, when the philosophy of HARLAN FISKE STONE's footnote to UNITED STATES V. CAROLENE PRODUCTS COMPANY (1937), with its preference for personal rather than economic rights, gained ascendancy.

In his early years as a federal judge, Hand participated widely in extrajudicial activities. He was a member of the group that founded *The New Republic* magazine, and he helped draft THEODORE ROOSEVELT's Bull Moose platform in 1912. Indeed, he was so devoted to the Progressive cause that he permitted his name to be entered as that party's candidate for the New York Court of Appeals in 1913.

After World War I, Hand decided that his position precluded extrajudicial involvements in controversial issues. But he had frequent occasion to continue airing his views of the judicial role in papers and addresses, many of which are collected in *The Spirit of Liberty* (1952). Hand's Holmes Lectures, delivered at Harvard three years before his death and published under the title *The Bill of Rights,* were an extreme restatement of Hand's hostility to the *Lochner* interventionist philosophy. The lectures even questioned the judicial enforceability of vague BILL OF RIGHTS provisions.

Hand's judicial reputation rests mainly on his craftsmanlike performance in operating creatively within the confines set by the political branches. His strength is best revealed in the way he handled many small cases in private law and statutory interpretation. He probed deeply to discover underlying questions, rejecting glib formulations and striving for orderly sense amidst the chaos of received legal wisdoms. Although constitutional issues seldom came before his court, he touched upon a wide range of them, from favoring strong enforcement of FOURTH AMENDMENT guarantees in *United States v. Rabinowitz* (1949) to offering innovative views on defining OBSCENITY in *United States v. Kennerley* (1913).

Hand's most important judicial contributions dealt with political speech under the FIRST AMENDMENT. His most enduring impact stems from his controversial decision in MASSES PUBLISHING CO. V. PATTEN

(1917). The ruling, overturned on appeal, protected the mailing of antiwar materials in the midst of national hostility to dissent. Hand's approach shielded all speech falling short of direct INCITEMENT TO UNLAWFUL CONDUCT. Two years later, the Supreme Court, in its first confrontation with the problem, refused to go so far as Hand had. Instead, SCHENCK V. UNITED STATES (1919) launched the CLEAR AND PRESENT DANGER test, under which the protection of speech turned on guesses about its probable impact. In a rare disagreement with his one judicial idol, Oliver Wendell Holmes, Hand criticized Holmes's approach, in ABRAMS V. UNITED STATES (1919) as well as *Schenck*, as an inadequate bulwark against majoritarian passions. With the Supreme Court adhering to Holmes's standard for decades, Hand assumed that his *Masses* approach had failed. But in 1969, Hand's incitement test, combined with the best elements of Holmes's approach, became the modern standard for First Amendment protection, in BRANDENBURG V. OHIO (1969).

Hand is equally well known for recasting and, many believe, diluting the clear and present danger test by affirming convictions of the Communist leaders in UNITED STATES V. DENNIS (1950). This ruling reflected not only Hand's mounting skepticism about judicial protection of fundamental rights but also his consistent obedience to Supreme Court pronouncements. In affirming the *Dennis* convictions, Chief Justice FRED M. VINSON's plurality opinion adopted Hand's reformulation as the proper criterion. Hand, however, remained convinced even in the 1950s that his *Masses* approach offered better protection to dissenters.

The distinctive traits of Hand's model of judging—open-mindedness, impartiality, skepticism, restless probing—came naturally to him. Those traits were ingredients of his personality by the time Hand became a judge. Philosopher and humanist as well as judge, Hand remained intellectually engaged, ever ready to reexamine his own assumptions.

Hand's unmatched capacity to behave according to the model of the modest judge was not wholly a conscious deduction from the theory of judicial restraint instilled by Thayer and confirmed by Hand's early experiences. It was at least as much a product of Hand's temper and personality. The doubting, open-minded human being could not help but act that way as a judge. Hand's major legacy, to constitutional law as well as to all other areas of the law, lies in his demonstration that detached and open-minded judging is within human reach.

GERALD GUNTHER

Bibliography

HAND, LEARNED (1952)1960 *The Spirit of Liberty: Papers and Addresses*, ed. Irving Dilliard. New York: Knopf.
———— 1958 *The Bill of Rights*. Cambridge, Mass.: Harvard University Press.
SHANKS, HERSHEL, ED. 1968 *The Art and Craft of Judging: The Decisions of Judge Learned Hand*. New York: Macmillan.

HARDING, WARREN G.
(1865–1923)

Warren Gamaliel Harding, twenty-ninth President of the United States, served one of the shortest presidential terms, from his inauguration on March 4, 1921, until his death on August 2, 1923. An Ohio newspaperman and politician, and a United States senator (1915–1921), Harding was nominated as a compromise candidate at the deadlocked 1920 Republican party convention and won a landslide victory over his Democratic opponent, James Cox.

Harding's policies flowed from an understanding of the American Constitution very different from that of his predecessor, WOODROW WILSON. His economic policy consisted of tax reduction, economy in government, a higher tariff, and various measures to aid agriculture in its recovery from the postwar depression. His foreign policy consisted of opposition to American participation in the League of Nations (but support for membership in the World Court), reduction of armaments, and refusal to forgive war debts owed to the United States or its citizens.

Harding's presidency was marred by scandals, which were exposed fully only after his death and in which he was not personally implicated. Despite his brief tenure as President, Harding appointed four Supreme Court Justices: WILLIAM HOWARD TAFT, PIERCE BUTLER, GEORGE H. SUTHERLAND, and EDWARD T. SANFORD.

THOMAS B. SILVER

Bibliography

MURRAY, ROBERT K. 1969 *The Harding Era: Warren G. Harding and His Administration*. Minneapolis: University of Minnesota Press.

HARLAN, JOHN MARSHALL
(1833–1911)

Among the Justices of the Supreme Court, few have provoked more diverse reactions from colleagues, contemporaries, and later generations than the first

Justice John Marshall Harlan. Despite a distinguished tenure of over thirty-three years (1877–1911), during which he participated in many cases of constitutional significance and established himself as one of the most productive, independent, and voluble members of the Court, both jurists and historians were inclined to hold Harlan in low esteem from his death in 1911 to the middle of the twentieth century. But two signal events in 1954—the Court's implicit adoption of Harlan's famous solitary dissent in PLESSY V. FERGUSON (1896) in its decision of the public school SEGREGATION cases, BROWN V. BOARD OF EDUCATION and BOLLING V. SHARPE, and President DWIGHT D. EISENHOWER's appointment of his distinguished grandson and namesake to the highest bench—prompted historians to reevaluate the first Justice Harlan. No longer belittled and neglected, Harlan now began to be recast as a great dissenter who had foretold many of the most fundamental developments in later constitutional interpretation: the virtually complete INCORPORATION of the BILL OF RIGHTS into the FOURTEENTH AMENDMENT; the inherent inequality of racial segregation; and the plenary power of Congress under the COMMERCE CLAUSE. How can one account for the wide disparity between the traditional and revisionist interpretations of Mr. Justice Harlan?

Harlan was born in 1833 in Kentucky, the son of a two-term Whig member of the United States House of Representatives. A stern Presbyterian, young Harlan grew up during the worsening estrangement of the South and the Union. Kentucky, as a border state, was sharply divided. Harlan was graduated from Centre College, and, at twenty, completed his law courses at Transylvania University and was admitted to the Kentucky bar.

Harlan participated actively as a moderate in the political struggles that racked the country on the eve of the Civil War. In 1859 he ran for Congress, but was narrowly defeated. A traditional southern gentleman and conservative, he refused to join the Republican party or to support ABRAHAM LINCOLN's 1860 campaign. He supported the Constitutional Union party which sought the peaceful preservation of the status quo.

After the attack on Fort Sumter, Kentucky declined to furnish troops. Harlan volunteered to fight on the northern side and, in the fall of 1861, organized the Tenth Kentucky Volunteer Infantry. Harlan rose rapidly to the rank of colonel and served as acting commander of a brigade until he resigned his military commission in 1863 upon the death of his father.

Shortly after returning to civilian life, Harlan campaigned for the Constitutional Union party and was elected attorney general of Kentucky, a post he held until 1867. Harlan stumped for General George McClellan in the presidential election of 1864, bitterly criticizing the Lincoln administration. He opposed the THIRTEENTH AMENDMENT and continued to hold slaves until forced to free them.

In 1867, however, Harlan changed his party affiliation, becoming the unsuccessful Republican gubernatorial candidate. As a southern slaveholder and Whig he had long sought to support both slavery and a strong national government—a position that grew increasingly difficult in the political environment of *antebellum* Kentucky, where supporters of slavery based their political programs on opposition to the federal government. In the end Harlan resolved his dilemma in favor of the national government. Contending that he would rather be right than consistent, Harlan publicly repudiated his views favoring slavery and defended the civil war amendments as necessary to the reconstruction of the Union. A second try for the Kentucky governorship in 1871 also ended in failure.

At the national level, Harlan supported ULYSSES S. GRANT in the presidential election of 1868 and had attained sufficient prominence by 1872 to have been proposed as a vice-presidential candidate. Four years later Harlan led the Kentucky delegation to the Republican convention. When it became apparent that his friend, Benjamin Bristow, could not win, Harlan threw the Kentucky delegation's support to RUTHERFORD B. HAYES, enabling Hayes narrowly to defeat James G. Blaine and obtain the nomination.

On October 16, 1877, President Hayes nominated Harlan to the Supreme Court, an appointment that was widely regarded as a payment for political services rendered. Until five days before his death on October 15, 1911, for almost thirty-four years, Harlan served on the Court. With the exception of JOHN MARSHALL and JOSEPH STORY, none of its members up to that time had taken part in so many decisions that ultimately so crucially affected the future of American constitutionalism.

Harlan served on the Supreme Court during a period of rapid social and economic change. Although the era of Reconstruction had passed, the effect of the postwar amendments on the federal system remained a topic of bitter constitutional dispute. The Court was also increasingly obliged to rule on constitutional challenges to the validity of state and federal statutes purporting to regulate the economy in the public interest.

Harlan brought to the Court two fundamental convictions drawn from his upbringing and early experiences in Kentucky politics. He believed in a strong national government, especially in the spheres of commerce and economic development. Hence Harlan would view federal laws regulating the economy much more favorably than similar state initiatives. Second, he would ardently support the rights of blacks, although he had developed that posture only late in his political career. While Harlan never wavered in his judicial support for black rights and a strong national economy, the political implications of his Whig principles varied widely during his judicial tenure. When he came to the Court in 1877 Harlan quickly established himself as its foremost defender of private contracts against state regulation since Marshall. Indeed, throughout his long career Harlan closely scrutinized any state law that impinged on private property rights. He often voted to invalidate such statutes under the contract, JUST COMPENSATION, or EQUAL PROTECTION clauses.

After the passage of the INTERSTATE COMMERCE ACT of 1877 and the SHERMAN ANTITRUST ACT of 1890, however, Harlan came to look quite favorably upon national, as opposed to state, regulation of the economy. Harlan's Whig philosophy explains much of his apparent inconsistency in decisions concerning private property rights. Harlan generally upheld national ECONOMIC REGULATION, but often voted to strike down state economic regulations that discriminated against interstate commerce without furthering significantly an important state interest under the POLICE POWER.

During his thirty-four years on the Court, Harlan articulated a broad body of constitutional principles respecting both governmental powers and individual rights. A convinced believer in legislative authority and judgment, he abhorred and denounced what he viewed as "judicial legislation" and advocated a straightforward application of the law as set forth in the Constitution and legislative enactments. But when it came to determining the provisions of a given law, his view was unique: "It is not the words of the law but the internal sense of it that makes the law: the letter is the body; the sense and reason of the law is the soul" (CIVIL RIGHTS CASES, 1883).

Justice Harlan lifted the practice of employing LEGISLATIVE INTENT as a guide to the sound construction of the law to the level of a philosophical principle. In addition, he, above all others, had an all but religious reverence for the Constitution as the fundamental instrument of the ideals of American democracy. A fervent Marshall disciple, he viewed the Court as the ultimate guardian of the Constitution. Harlan also adhered to Marshall's views on the proper distribution of powers within the federal system.

With respect to congressional power under the INTERSTATE COMMERCE clause, Harlan was a liberal national constitutionalist, with an almost slavish devotion to Chief Justice Marshall's opinions in general, and GIBBONS V. OGDEN (1824) in particular. Harlan displayed his broad interpretation of the commerce power most forcefully in opinions construing the Interstate Commerce Act of 1887 and the Sherman Antitrust Act of 1890. He dissented in *Texas & Pacific Railroad Co. v. Interstate Commerce Commission* (1896) and INTERSTATE COMMERCE COMMISSION V. ALABAMA MIDLAND RAILWAY CO. (1897) when the Court interpreted the Interstate Commerce Act as not granting the commission the power either to void discriminatory railroad rates or to set nondiscriminatory rates itself. Harlan believed that these decisions went far "to make that commission a useless body for all practical purposes, and to defeat many of the important objectives designed to be accomplished by the various enactments of Congress relating to interstate commerce. . . ." Congress eventually agreed, amending the Interstate Commerce Act to give the commission the powers for which Harlan had contended in his dissents.

When the Court emasculated the Sherman Antitrust Act, Justice Harlan, again in dissent, registered his strong advocacy of congressional power and the spirit of the law. In UNITED STATES V. E. C. KNIGHT CO. (1895) the Court narrowly interpreted the Sherman Act as applying to monopolies in interstate commerce but not to intrastate monopolies in manufacture of goods; it also stated that Congress lacked power under the commerce clause to regulate manufacturing. In the majority's view, "Commerce succeeds to manufacture, and is not a part of it." Yet Harlan insisted that the statute applied because the goods, although manufactured in one state, entered into interstate commerce. Four decades later, in the WAGNER ACT CASES (1937), Harlan's expansive view of congressional power under the commerce clause would become the generally accepted view.

Although Harlan held to a broad interpretation of national power under the commerce clause, he nonetheless supported some positive uses of STATE POLICE POWER that affected interstate commerce. He believed that, although a state might not—under the guise of inspection laws—discriminate against meat imported from out of state (MINNESOTA V. BARBER, 1890), it might require certain passenger stops of interstate railroad trains unless Congress had superseded local laws. Indeed, Harlan thought that state power should prevail if the statute in question affected interstate commerce "only incidentally" and furthered an important state interest under the police power—as was the case with state laws prohibiting the importation or sale of intoxicating liquor (BOWMAN V. CHICAGO & NORTHWESTERN RAILWAY, 1888). Whether agreeing or dissenting, however, Harlan consistently stood for the freedom of commerce and the rights of citizens of other states. While he upheld state enactments genuinely aiming to protect the public morals, safety, health, or convenience, he strongly expressed his disapproval of those that appeared to have been enacted for the ulterior purpose of discriminating against commerce from other states.

Although fervently opposed to Justice STEPHEN J. FIELD's NATURAL RIGHTS philosophy, Harlan strongly defended the Bill of Rights and, in spite of his border state origin, became a vigorous and eloquent advocate of a nationalistic interpretation of the Thirteenth, Fourteenth, and FIFTEENTH AMENDMENTS. Harlan's most celebrated CIVIL RIGHTS dissent, *Plessy v. Ferguson* (1896), became law in the unanimous Warren Court holding in *Brown v. Board of Education* (1954). It was in *Plessy*, dissenting alone from the Court's decision upholding a Louisiana "Jim Crow" train-segregation statute under the SEPARATE BUT EQUAL doctrine, that Harlan had warned: "The thin disguise of 'equal' accommodations . . . will not mislead anyone, nor atone for the wrong this day done. . . ."

However, it was his dissent in the CIVIL RIGHTS CASES (1883) that Harlan considered as his most notable. There the majority ruled that Congress lacked power under the Fourteenth Amendment to protect blacks against private discrimination; Harlan, in contrast, argued that Congress could prohibit discrimination "by individuals or CORPORATIONS exercising public functions or authority, against any citizen because of his race or previous condition of servitude."

In these and other cases involving racial discrimination, Harlan demonstrated his belief that the Thirteenth Amendment meant more than the mere prohibition of one person's owning another as property. He urged that the framers of the Thirteenth, Fourteenth, and Fifteenth Amendments could not have expected the very states that had held blacks in bondage willingly to protect their new civil rights. Harlan thus championed congressional authority to define and regulate the entire body of civil rights of citizens.

Although Justice Harlan's dissents in racial segregation cases have received widespread attention, some of the most critical questions presented to the Court during his tenure centered on what later came to be termed the INCORPORATION DOCTRINE. Harlan joined the Court after a pattern of decisions had been set. Alone, except for Field, among Justices of his time, Harlan viewed the due process clause of the Fourteenth Amendment as encompassing at least the first eight amendments of the Bill of Rights (for example, HURTADO V. CALIFORNIA, 1884), a stand for which he was still severely castigated more than sixty years later by Justice FELIX FRANKFURTER, in ADAMSON V. CALIFORNIA (1947). The process of "selective incorporation" of Bill of Rights guarantees, which was nearly complete by the end of the Warren Court, vindicated Justice Harlan's position in practice, if not in theory.

Interestingly, the emphasis accorded Harlan's famous dissents in civil rights cases concerning life and liberty interests resulted in a widespread neglect of his staunch defense of property rights. In CONTRACT CLAUSE cases involving states' attempts either to void or alter their obligations to bondholders, or to amend corporate charters without express reservation of the right to do so, Harlan strongly asserted the contractual rights of the individual. Under the equal protection clause Harlan voted to strike down state laws that imposed special contractual duties on corporations without imposing similar obligations on individuals.

More significant, Harlan wrote the opinion in CHICAGO, BURLINGTON & QUINCY RAILROAD CO. V. CHICAGO (1898), frequently cited as the first "incorporation" of a Bill of Rights provision, the Fifth Amendment's just compensation clause, into the Fourteenth Amendment's due process clause. The famous rate case of SMYTH V. AMES (1898) provided an indication of how far Harlan would go in striking down, under SUBSTANTIVE DUE PROCESS principles, an exercise of state police power. Speaking for the Court, he voided a Nebraska statute that pegged intrastate freight rates, on the grounds that the rates were so low as to deprive railroads of property without due process of law. A public utility, asserted Harlan, has a judicially enforceable constitutional right to a "reasonable return" upon the "fair value" of its operating assets. (See FAIR RETURN ON FAIR VALUE.)

Harlan's constitutional doctrines evoked diverse reactions from contemporaries and later generations: patronization, neglect, disdain, and praise. His colleague and friend, Justice DAVID J. BREWER, described Harlan as a simple man who "retired at eight, with one hand on the Constitution and the other on the Bible, safe and happy in perfect faith in justice and righteousness." Justice OLIVER WENDELL

HOLMES patronized him in private as "old Harlan . . . the last of the tobacco-spitting judges." Contemporaneous observers of the Court viewed Harlan as a militant dissenter who was inflexible on civil rights.

How could Harlan's contemporaries and historians in the first half of the twentieth century have held him in such low esteem when the prophetic nature of his many dissents appears so obvious today? Part of the answer is that traditional and revisionist interpreters of Justice Harlan have employed widely different analytical perspectives. Viewed narrowly in comparison with his contemporaries, Harlan was simply an "eccentric exception" on the Court. Many of his most famous dissents were solos. His constitutional doctrines were often "out of tune with the times."

Harlan's eccentricity, however, was principled. In a letter of 1870 Harlan described his conception of the proper role of a Justice as that of "an independent man, with an opportunity to make a *record* that will be remembered long after he is gone." Throughout his tenure on the Court Harlan was constantly concerned with broad questions of the public interest; consequently his opinions often contained extraneous matter, referring to circumstances with no direct bearing on the case at hand.

When the Court in POLLOCK V. FARMERS' LOAN & TRUST COMPANY (1895) decided that a tax on the income from land and personal property constituted DIRECT TAXATION and thereby held unconstitutional the recently enacted Federal Income Tax Act, Harlan vehemently dissented. He correctly warned that the Court's decision would make a constitutional amendment necessary for the imposition of the income tax. Harlan's contemporaries, however, saw his denunciation of judicial legislation and his appeals to practical considerations as ignorance of the principles of legal argumentation.

Recent admirers have perhaps too strongly emphasized Harlan's opinion on civil rights and CIVIL LIBERTIES, recasting him as a Jeffersonian Democrat. Although he strongly defended the Bill of Rights against STATE ACTION and private action clothed in public functions, Harlan viewed himself as a staunch adherent to the views of John Marshall and rejected THOMAS JEFFERSON's states' rights views. Moreover, Harlan was one of the most vigorous defenders of individual property rights ever to sit on the Court, as his opinion in ADAIR V. UNITED STATES (1908) illustrated. His STRICT CONSTRUCTION of the contract and just compensation clauses and his adherence to substantive property protections under the due process clause have been soundly rejected by subsequent Courts.

The composite figure emerging from history is that of a Southern gentlemen of the nineteenth century—absolute confidence in the correctness of his own views; a firm belief that human beings could clearly discern between right and wrong; and an inability to understand, once he had made this distinction, how any reasonable man could disagree with him. An ardent disciple of Chief Justice Marshall's views of the proper judicial role and the nature of the federal system, Harlan was an egalitarian when confronted with questions of civil rights.

But today's distinction between property and liberty interests, with enhanced judicial solicitude for the latter, found no place in Harlan's constitutional philosophy. This antebellum slaveholder applied substantive due process equally to liberty and property interests.

Although Harlan's legacy thus contains elements out of tune with contemporary constitutional fashion, many of his dissents presaged what our nation would become in the second half of the twentieth century. Succeeding generations owe a great debt to this solitary dissenter. Because his philosophy contained a touch of immortality, he will be numbered among the great Justices of the Supreme Court (and he was so voted as one of but twelve "greats" in a 1970 study).

HENRY J. ABRAHAM

Bibliography

ABRAHAM, HENRY J. 1955 John Marshall Harlan: A Justice Neglected. *Virginia Law Review* 41:871–891.

CLARK, FLOYD B. 1915 *The Constitutional Doctrines of John Marshall Harlan.* Baltimore: Johns Hopkins University Press.

FRIEDMAN, LEON and ISRAEL, FRED L. 1969 Pages 1281–1295 in *The Justices of the United States Supreme Court, 1789–1969.* New York: Chelsea House.

WATT, RICHARD F. and ORLIKOFF, RICHARD M. 1953 The Coming Vindication of Mr. Justice Harlan. *Illinois Law Journal* 44:13–40.

WESTIN, ALAN F. 1958 The First Justice Harlan: A Self-Portrait from his Private Papers. *Kentucky Law Journal* 46:321–357.

WHITE, G. EDWARD 1975 John Marshall Harlan I: The Precursor. *American Journal of Legal History* 19:1–21.

HARLAN, JOHN MARSHALL
(1899–1971)

John Marshall Harlan, grandson of the Justice of the same name, served as Associate Justice of the United States Supreme Court from 1955 to 1971. Educated principally at Princeton and Oxford, he enjoyed a highly successful career as a New York trial lawyer, with intervals for military service and in various public positions. Immediately prior to his appointment to the Supreme Court he served briefly on the United States Court of Appeals for the Second Circuit. His work on the Supreme Court was marked by rigorous intellectual honesty, unflagging industry, and an uncommon dedication to judicial craftsmanship. No Justice sought more earnestly to evaluate fairly every relevant fact and authority, and none labored more carefully to decide, not policies or causes, but actual and concrete cases. In the "measured" assessment of Judge Henry Friendly, no other Justice has "so consistently maintained a high quality of performance" or has enjoyed "so nearly uniform respect."

Influenced in his first years on the Court by FELIX FRANKFURTER, Harlan ultimately developed a constitutional philosophy distinctly his own. He combined dignity with an attractive modesty, personal qualities that were reflected in his conception of the judicial function. In REYNOLDS V. SIMS (1964) he emphasized that the Constitution required a "diffusion of governmental authority" within which the Court was assigned a "high" but "limited" function. Rigidly nonpolitical after his appointment to the bench, he believed that the Court could effectively perform its "limited" constitutional role only by studiously respecting the powers variously entrusted to the states, Congress, or the federal executive. He denied that courts are entitled to promote or compel reform whenever others fail to act, and warned that judges should not seek solutions to every social ill in the Constitution.

More than any Justice in recent years, Harlan regarded FEDERALISM as an important limitation upon the Court's authority. He believed, with Justice LOUIS D. BRANDEIS, that the states could serve as laboratories for the solution of social and political issues, and he willingly afforded them freedom to seek such solutions. In FAY V. NOIA (1963), MIRANDA V. ARIZONA (1966), and other cases he resisted the Court's imposition of federal standards upon the conduct of state criminal proceedings, arguing in *Fay* that the federal system would "exist in substance as well as form" only if the states were permitted, within the limits of FUNDAMENTAL FAIRNESS, to devise their own procedures. In HARPER V. VIRGINIA BOARD OF ELECTIONS (1966) he dissented from the Court's invalidation of a state's use of a POLL TAX as a condition on voting, despite his obvious doubts as to the law's wisdom, in part because the issue should be left for decision by the state itself. In ROTH V. UNITED STATES (1957) he urged that the states be permitted greater leeway than the federal government to control "borderline"

PORNOGRAPHY because the risks of nationwide censorship were "far greater." Because the Court could not devise clear rules for regulating OBSCENITY, he saw "no overwhelming danger" if the states were given room to seek their own answers.

Harlan's federalism did not, however, prevent him in appropriate cases from denying the constitutionality of state legislation. In *Poe v. Ullman* (1961) he wrote one of the most important of his opinions, dissenting from the Court's refusal to decide a challenge to a Connecticut statute prohibiting the use of contraceptive devices. Observing that the statute intruded upon "the most intimate details of the marital relation" in order to enforce "a moral judgment," Harlan declared marital privacy to be a "most fundamental" right, any invasion of which requires STRICT SCRUTINY. He defined DUE PROCESS in terms of evolving national traditions and the balance between "liberty and the demands of organized society," and concluded on that basis that the statute was unconstitutional. Four years later, in GRISWOLD V. CONNECTICUT (1965), a majority of the Court reached the same result.

One of the issues most revealing of Harlan's constitutional outlook was the INCORPORATION DOCTRINE, by which large portions of the BILL OF RIGHTS have been held applicable to the states through "incorporation" in the FOURTEENTH AMENDMENT. Harlan vigorously resisted both the "total" incorporation theory advanced by Justice HUGO L. BLACK and the "selective" version adopted by other Justices. In POINTER V. TEXAS (1965), DUNCAN V. LOUISIANA (1968), and other cases he argued that the doctrine lacks historical basis and creates a "constitutional straitjacket" that risks preventing the states from responding to the nation's "increasing experience and evolving conscience." He preferred to test state LEGISLATION and procedures by a standard of fundamental fairness derived from the due process clause of the Fourteenth Amendment, whose generality affords room for future constitutional development. Indeed, in *Griswold* he expressed the fear that the incorporation doctrine might "restrict" the reach of the due process clause, limiting the Court's review of future state actions.

Due process formed the heart of Harlan's constitutional outlook, and two cases illustrate both the breadth of his conception and the restraint with which he employed it. In BODDIE V. CONNECTICUT (1971) Harlan held for the Court that filing and service fees imposed by the state upon persons seeking divorce were denials of due process when applied to INDIGENTS. Carefully avoiding reliance upon the EQUAL PROTECTION clause, whose scope and implications he evidently distrusted, he held that as a matter of fundamental fairness a state could not preempt the right to dissolve marriages unless all its citizens were afforded access to the mechanism prescribed for that purpose. The opinion provoked Justice Black in dissent to reiterate that Harlan's conception of due process permitted judges to determine constitutionality merely by their "sense of fairness." Quoting *Williams v. North Carolina* (1945), Black added that due process afforded judges "a blank sheet of paper" on which to order constitutional change.

The deaths of the two close friends prevented Harlan and Black from continuing their debate after *Boddie*, but part of Harlan's response may be inferred from IN RE GAULT (1967), in which the Court first addressed the constitutional issues presented by state systems of juvenile justice. Such systems often imposed penalties similar to those in criminal cases without the accompanying procedural protections. Harlan's concurring opinion emphasized the novelty of the questions, and urged caution in imposing detailed constitutional requirements. He feared that the hasty adoption of rigid standards might "hamper enlightened development," and found room in the spacious contours of due process to impose only selected procedural requirements. Harlan's caution illustrated his conviction, previously expressed in *Poe v. Ullman*, that the discretion afforded judges by the due process clause must be exercised with "judgment and restraint."

Harlan also made significant contributions to the development of FIRST AMENDMENT principles. In COHEN V. CALIFORNIA (1971) he wrote the opinion for a divided Court overturning the conviction of a man wearing a jacket bearing an antidraft expletive in the halls of a Los Angeles courthouse. Although the protest's form was "distasteful," Harlan explained that "fundamental societal values" are implicated even in "crude" exercises of First Amendment rights. In GINZBURG V. UNITED STATES (1966), he dissented from the affirmance of a federal obscenity conviction in which the Court held that evidence of "commercial exploitation" could tip the balance toward a determination that a publication was obscene. Harlan responded that the Court, by "judicial improvisation," had created a new and impermissibly vague statutory standard, under which "pandering" could justify the censorship of otherwise protected materials. In contrast to his less rigid attitude toward state obscenity prosecutions, he argued that the federal government should be permitted to ban from the mails only hardcore pornography.

The concern for privacy interests expressed in *Poe v. Ullman* was also reflected in Harlan's First Amendment opinions. In NAACP v. ALABAMA (1958) he wrote the Court's opinion overturning an order holding the NAACP in civil contempt for failing to reveal the names of its members and agents in Alabama. He found that such disclosures had previously resulted in threats and reprisals, and explained the "vital relationship" between organizational privacy and freedom of association. Because the contempt order would adversely affect the NAACP's ability to foster beliefs it was constitutionally entitled to advocate, the association's privacy interests overrode the state's regulatory goals. In *Time, Inc. v. Hill* (1967) he argued that where private individuals had by misadventure become involuntary subjects of publicity, the state could constitutionally require the press to conduct a reasonable investigation and to limit itself to fair comment upon the facts. The denial of such state authority, he contended, would create a "severe risk of irremediable harm" to those who had not sought public exposure and were "powerless to protect themselves against it."

Harlan's contributions to constitutional law are not fully measured by the opinions he wrote or conclusions he reached. Time and again, his prodding compelled the Court to revise or reconsider its first assessment of a fact or an issue, drawing from others a higher quality of performance than they might otherwise have achieved. No Justice labored more earnestly to act with care and fairness, and none adhered to a more rigorous standard of judicial integrity. His reassuring example of craftsmanship and rectitude meant much in a period of rapid constitutional change, when the Court and its members were frequently the subject of hostility or question.

CHARLES LISTER

Bibliography

DORSEN, NORMAN 1969 John Marshall Harlan. Pages 2803–2820 in Leon Friedman and Fred L. Israel, eds., *The Justices of the United States Supreme Court 1789–1969.* New York: Chelsea House.

FRIENDLY, HENRY J. 1971 Mr. Justice Harlan, as Seen by a Friend and Judge of an Inferior Court. *Harvard Law Review* 85:382–389.

SHAPIRO, DAVID L. 1969 *The Evolution of a Judicial Philosophy: Selected Opinions and Papers of Justice John M. Harlan.* Cambridge, Mass.: Harvard University Press.

HARLOW v. FITZGERALD

See: *Nixon v. Fitzgerald*

HARMLESS ERROR

Not all denials of a defendant's federal constitutional rights compel reversal of a conviction. The Supreme Court announced in *Chapman v. California* (1967) as a matter of federal constitutional law that, in criminal proceedings, if the beneficiary of the error can prove beyond a REASONABLE DOUBT that the error in no way contributed to the result, the case need not be reversed. This standard applies to state as well as federal proceedings and state rules requiring only a lesser showing of the harmlessness of error are not controlling when federal constitutional error has been shown.

Although the Supreme Court's standard is stricter than that of many state courts (which may adhere to a lesser standard than reasonable doubt or even in some cases shift the BURDEN OF PROOF to the victim of the error), it nevertheless falls short of a per se rule requiring automatic reversal for all violations of federal constitutional rights. Thus, for example, where EVIDENCE obtained through an UNREASONABLE SEARCH in violation of the FOURTH AMENDMENT is improperly admitted into a trial, reversal of a guilty verdict is not always required. The Supreme Court has stated that certain kinds of violations do, indeed, require automatic reversal—such as coerced confessions or unconstitutionally obtained guilty pleas—but these kinds of violation are few in number.

Chapman itself concerned a prosecutor's comments to the jury upon the defendants' failure to testify, in violation of defendants' Fifth Amendment RIGHT AGAINST SELF-INCRIMINATION, and cases involving harmless error doctrine may arise from any part of the Constitution. The bulk of the decided cases, though, have involved application of the EXCLUSIONARY RULE to evidence unconstitutionally seized.

Where illegally obtained evidence is the sole or primary basis for a conviction, of course, the conviction must be reversed. On the other hand, where independent, admissible evidence of defendant's guilt is overwhelming, or illegally obtained evidence is noninflammatory and merely cumulative, reversal is not required. But such a finding will often involve difficult determinations. First, which evidence is actually admissible, and which is a fruit of the federal constitutional error? Second, since the prosecutor in introducing the tainted evidence has represented that it tended to prove guilt, the Supreme Court may look carefully at later claims that the evidence was in fact harmless.

The Court has not yet definitively settled the issue of whether a federal constitutional error can be cured through the trial judge's instructions to the jury. *Chapman* suggests that such instructions may render the error harmless, if they are shown beyond a reasonable doubt to have prevented the error from affecting the jury's verdict. But none of the cases decided by the Court since *Chapman* has found this standard to have been met.

JOHN KAPLAN

Bibliography

SALZBURG, STEPHEN A.   1984   *American Criminal Procedure*, 2nd ed. St. Paul, Minn.: West Publishing Co.

HARPER v. VIRGINIA BOARD OF ELECTIONS
383 U.S. 663 (1966)

Harper epitomizes the WARREN COURT'S expansion of the reach of the EQUAL PROTECTION clause of the FOURTEENTH AMENDMENT. Virginia levied an annual $1.50 POLL TAX on residents over twenty-one, and conditioned voter registration on payment of accrued poll taxes. The Supreme Court, 6–3, overruled BREEDLOVE V. SUTTLES (1937), holding that the condition on registration denied the equal protection of the laws.

The *Harper* opinion, by Justice WILLIAM O. DOUGLAS, played an important part in crystallizing equal protection DOCTRINE by justifying heightened levels of judicial scrutiny. The Court did not quite hold that wealth or indigency was a SUSPECT CLASSIFICATION, saying only that "lines drawn on the basis of wealth of property, like those of race, are traditionally disfavored." It did say, following REYNOLDS V. SIMS (1964), that voting was a FUNDAMENTAL INTEREST, requiring STRICT SCRUTINY of its restriction. The poll tax by itself might be constitutionally unobjectionable; wealth as a condition on voting, however, not only failed the test of strict scrutiny; it was a "capricious or irrelevant factor."

For Justice HUGO L. BLACK, dissenting, *Harper* represented a relapse into judicial subjectivism through a variation on the "natural-law–due-process" formula he had decried in ADAMSON V. CALIFORNIA (1947). The Virginia scheme was not arbitrary; it might increase revenues or ensure an interested electorate. The Court should not substitute its judgment for the Virginia legislature's. Justice JOHN MARSHALL HARLAN also dissented, joined by Justice POTTER STEWART. Harlan, who shared Black's views, added that it was arguable that "people with some property have a deeper stake in community affairs, and are consequently more responsible, more educated, more knowledgeable, more worthy of confidence, than those without means." That this belief was not his own did not matter; it was arguable, and that was all the RATIONAL BASIS standard demanded.

Commentators saw in *Harper* and other contemporary decisions a major shift away from the tradition of minimal judicial scrutiny of laws challenged under the equal protection clause. Invasions of interests of great importance, or discrimination against disadvantaged groups, appeared to call for judicial scrutiny more demanding than that required by the relaxed rational basis standard. Soon the Court found a formula for two levels of review: rational basis for most "social and economic" legislation, and strict scrutiny for laws invading fundamental interests or employing suspect classifications.

The Court has not pursued *Harper's* suggestion that WEALTH DISCRIMINATION is suspect. VOTING RIGHTS, however, are firmly established as interests whose invasion demands strict scrutiny. Implicitly, as in cases involving ALIENS or ILLEGITIMACY, and explicitly, as in cases on SEX DISCRIMINATION, the Court has transformed its two levels of judicial scrutiny into a sliding-scale approach that is interest balancing by another name: the more important the interest invaded, or the more "suspect" the classification, the more the state must justify its legislation. In broad outline this development was portended in *Harper*, which exemplified not only Warren Court egalitarianism but also Justice Douglas's doctrinal leadership.

KENNETH L. KARST

Bibliography

KARST, KENNETH L. 1969 Invidious Discrimination: Justice Douglas and the Return of the "Natural-Law–Due-Process Formula." *UCLA Law Review* 16:716–750.

HARRIS, UNITED STATES v.
106 U.S. 629 (1883)

Harris, like UNITED STATES V. CRUIKSHANK (1876), involved a federal prosecution under a general conspiracy statute, and like *Cruikshank* it was a victory for the Ku Klux Klan. The Supreme Court had gutted the *Cruikshank* statute but allowed it to survive; the *Harris* statute, though similar, did not survive. Section two of the FORCE ACT of 1871 made it a federal crime, punishable by fine and up to six years in prison, for two or more persons to conspire for the purpose of depriving anyone of the EQUAL PROTECTION OF THE LAWS or hindering lawful authorities from securing

equal protection for others. The United States prosecuted Harris who, at the head of an armed lynch mob, had broken into a Tennessee jail and captured four black prisoners, despite the efforts of the sheriff to protect them. The mob had beaten the four, killing one. Could the United States try them under the act of 1871? With Justice JOHN MARSHALL HARLAN dissenting silently, the Court held, in an opinion by Justice WILLIAM WOODS, that the act of Congress was unconstitutional. Woods declared that the FOURTEENTH AMENDMENT merely authorized Congress to take remedial measures against STATE ACTION that violated the amendment; it applied only to acts of the states, not to acts of private individuals. The THIRTEENTH AMENDMENT did not apply to the acts of private individuals, but this statute could apply to conspiracies by whites against whites, a subject having nothing to do with slavery. The statute, therefore, had no constitutional basis.

LEONARD W. LEVY

HARRIS v. MCRAE
448 U.S. 297 (1980)

A 5–4 Supreme Court here sustained a series of restrictions on congressional appropriations for the Medicaid program. The restrictions went beyond the law sustained in MAHER V. ROE (1977) by refusing funding even for medically necessary abortions.

Justice POTTER STEWART'S opinion for the Court relied heavily on *Maher* in rejecting claims based on the SUBSTANTIVE DUE PROCESS right of PRIVACY and on the EQUAL PROTECTION clause. A woman's right to be free from governmental interference with her decision to have an abortion did not imply a right to have government subsidize that decision. Equal protection demanded only a RATIONAL BASIS for the law's discrimination between therapeutic abortions and other medical necessities, and such a basis was found in the protection of potential life. Justice Stewart also rejected a claim that the law amounted to an ESTABLISHMENT OF RELIGION. Opposition to abortion might be a tenet of some religions, but the establishment clause did not forbid governmental action merely because it coincided with religious views.

The *Maher* dissenters were joined in *McRae* by Justice JOHN PAUL STEVENS, who had joined the *Maher* majority. The cases were different, he argued; here an indigent woman was denied a medically necessary abortion for lack of funds, at the same time that the government was funding other medically necessary services. ROE V. WADE (1973), allowing a state to forbid abortions in the later stages of pregnancy, had excepted abortions necessary to preserve pregnant women's lives or health. The government could not create exclusions from an aid program, Justice Stevens argued, solely to promote a governmental interest (preservation of potential life) that was "constitutionally subordinate to the individual interest that the entire program was designed to protect."

KENNETH L. KARST

(SEE ALSO: *Abortion and the Constitution; Reproductive Autonomy.*)

HARRIS v. NEW YORK
401 U.S. 222 (1971)

This case is significant as a limitation on MIRANDA V. ARIZONA (1966). Harris sold narcotics to undercover police officers. The police failed to inform him, after his arrest, that he had a RIGHT TO COUNSEL during a custodial POLICE INTERROGATION and they ignored his request for an attorney. Harris eventually admitted that he had acted as an intermediary, buying heroin for the undercover agent, but he denied selling it to the agent. During the trial Harris contradicted the statement that he had made during interrogation; the judge overruled defense objections that the custodial statement was inadmissible under the MIRANDA RULES because it was made involuntarily and in violation of his rights. The judge instructed the jury that although the statement was unavailable as EVIDENCE OF GUILT, they might consider it in assessing Harris's credibility as a witness.

The Supreme Court, 5–4, upheld Harris's conviction. *Miranda* dissenters JOHN MARSHALL HARLAN, BYRON R. WHITE, and POTTER J. STEWART along with Justice HARRY A. BLACKMUN joined in Chief Justice WARREN E. BURGER's opinion holding that testimony secured without the necessary warnings could nevertheless be used to impeach contradictory testimony at trial. Burger flatly asserted that Harris made "no claim that the unwarned statements were coerced or involuntary"—a statement clearly controverted by the record. Burger also dismissed, as OBITER DICTUM, the assertion in *Miranda* that all such statements were inadmissible for any purpose. The majority relied heavily on *Walder v. United States* (1954), in which evidence secured in an UNREASONABLE SEARCH was admitted to impeach testimony although the EXCLUSIONARY RULE would have prohibited its use as evidence of guilt.

Justice WILLIAM J. BRENNAN, dissenting, said that *Miranda* prohibited the use of any statements obtained in violation of its guarantees and denied the contention that that was obiter dictum. Brennan also distinguished *Walder:* the statement there had no connection to the crime with which the defendant had been charged; in *Harris* the defendant's statements related directly to the crime. Moreover, the evidence there could have been used to assess credibility; here the jury could have misused it as evidence of guilt because the statement provided information about the crime charged.

DAVID GORDON

Bibliography
LEVY, LEONARD W. 1974 *Against the Law: The Nixon Court and Criminal Justice.* New York: Harper & Row.

HARRIS v. UNITED STATES

See: Search Incident to Arrest

HARRISON, BENJAMIN
(1833–1901)

One of a series of "caretaker" Presidents in the last quarter of the nineteenth century, Benjamin Harrison exercised only minimal influence on constitutional issues during his administration from 1889 to 1893. Though Harrison favored civil service reform and a reduction in the labor workday, and opposed southern disenfranchisement of blacks, his philosophy of the executive function limited his actions. Harrison believed his duty lay solely in enforcing the public will, as expressed by Congress.

Although he had called for federal antitrust action in his first message to Congress, claiming that trusts "are dangerous conspiracies against the public good, and should be made the subject of prohibitory and even penal legislation," Harrison's only contribution to the SHERMAN ANTITRUST ACT, passed during his term, was his signature. His administration, moreover, was rather indifferent to the act; of seven cases instituted by the government, only two resulted in a government victory and none was pressed to the Supreme Court. Harrison appointed four Justices to the Court: DAVID J. BREWER, HENRY B. BROWN, GEORGE SHIRAS, and HOWELL E. JACKSON, all conservatives. These appointments indicated Harrison's desire to secure property interests and vested rights against the assaults of reformers.

DAVID GORDON

Bibliography
VOLWILER, ALBERT T. 1932 Harrison, Benjamin. In *Dictionary of American Biography*, Vol. 8, pp. 331–335. New York: Scribner's.

HARRISON ACT
38 Stat. 785 (1914)

Congress passed this act at the behest of the Treasury Department to implement the 1912 Hague Convention banning narcotics trafficking. As with other legislation of the period, the act reflected a belief in the necessity of federal regulation to curb social evils. Although most such acts relied on the COMMERCE CLAUSE, Congress here used the TAXING POWER to establish a complex network of national drug control.

The act required all manufacturers and dealers in certain narcotics to register with the government and to pay a $1 annual license tax. The act also mandated the use of federal forms to complete transactions and ordered these forms kept for two years, accessible to federal inspection. Sale or shipment of specified drugs in INTERSTATE COMMERCE—even their possession by an unregistered person—was illegal. The act exempted physicians and other professionals from filing the federal forms but required them to maintain separate records. A 5–4 Supreme Court sustained the act in UNITED STATES V. DOREMUS (1919). Justice WILLIAM R. DAY asserted Congress's complete discretion to levy taxes, subject merely to the constitutional requirement of geographical uniformity.

DAVID GORDON

HART, HENRY M., JR.
(1904–1969)

At Harvard Law School, Henry Hart was a disciple of FELIX FRANKFURTER. After a clerkship with Justice LOUIS D. BRANDEIS, Hart returned to Harvard as a member of the law faculty, where he remained—with an interruption during World War II—all his life.

Hart was one of a handful of the most authoritative academic lawyers of his time. He was, above all, a teacher; his most important scholarship is embodied in two books designed for law school courses. In *The Federal Courts and the Federal System* (1953), co-authored with Herbert Wechsler, Hart introduced students to a conception of the functions of the federal judiciary that still dominates the thinking of courts and commentators. In *The Legal Process* (1958), co-authored with Albert Sacks, Hart expounded a view of the role of courts in lawmaking focused on "reasoned elaboration" of principle. For a generation that view was so influential that today's critics speak of a "legal process school" as the focus for their attack.

For Hart, reason was "the life of the law." His intellectual integrity was legendary. Nor was the integrity merely intellectual. He was a decent man, as generous and humane in personal dealings as he was formidable in print. During his last illness, he continued to meet his classes until he was physically unable to get to the classroom. To the end, he taught everyone around him.

KENNETH L. KARST

Bibliography
HART, HENRY M., JR. FESTSCHRIFT 1971 *Southern California Law Review* 44:i–x, 305–498.

HARTFORD CONVENTION
(December 15, 1814–January 5, 1815)

The Hartford Convention, called by the Federalists of the Massachusetts legislature, consisted of delegates chosen by the legislatures of Massachusetts, Connecticut, and Rhode Island. The delegates sought to promote the interests and policies of the New England Federalists, who vehemently opposed the War of 1812. Although secessionist sentiment flourished among extremists, moderates—those who opposed a separate New England confederacy and civil war—controlled the convention. The fact that it was held showed a respect for the Constitution, however perverse. Despite the convention's endorsement of theories of state NULLIFICATION and INTERPOSITION similar to those of the VIRGINIA AND KENTUCKY RESOLUTIONS of 1798–1799, the delegates unanimously advocated amendments to the Constitution as a means of curtailing federal powers. After a manifesto assailing the war, American foreign policy, national control of state militias, and the admission of western states, the convention proposed that congressional REPRESENTATION and federal taxation be based on the number of free persons only; embargoes be restricted to sixty days; Congress be prevented from declaring war, restricting foreign trade, or admitting new states except by a two-thirds majority; federal offices be restricted to native-born citizens; and the President be restricted to one term.

The convention had the misfortune of meeting while events were making it irrelevant. As three delegates left for Washington to present its proposals for constitutional amendments, the news arrived of AN-DREW JACKSON's victory at New Orleans, and when the delegates arrived in Washington, the town celebrated peace reports from Ghent. President JAMES MADISON excoriated the convention as a "rebel Parliament" that had engaged in a treasonable conspiracy, and the public ridiculed it. It accomplished nothing, left a bitter heritage, and enhanced the respectability of the doctrine of interposition.

LEONARD W. LEVY

Bibliography

BANNER, JAMES M., JR. 1970 *To the Hartford Convention.* New York: Knopf.

HASTIE, WILLIAM HENRY
(1904–1976)

William Henry Hastie was the first black federal judge. He studied law at Harvard Law School, where he was elected to the *Harvard Law Review.* After graduation in 1930 he pursued a career that included service to the national government, the Howard Law School, and the NAACP.

Hastie in 1939 took the chair of that CIVIL RIGHTS organization's National Legal Committee, a post he used to influence the course of civil rights litigation. He argued successfully with THURGOOD MARSHALL in SMITH V. ALLWRIGHT (1941) that a Texas all-white PRIMARY ELECTION law violated the Fifteenth Amendment. He also joined with Marshall five years later in arguing MORGAN V. VIRGINIA. They persuaded the Court that a Virginia law imposing SEGREGATION on interstate buses unconstitutionally burdened the uniform flow of commerce. *Smith* and *Morgan* were critical victories in the NAACP's attack on the South's dual system of race relations: the former leveled a barrier to black voting; the latter marked the first victory in a transportation case.

Following appointment as judge of the Third Circuit in 1949, Hastie had few judicial opportunities to advance the cause of civil rights. Scarcely two dozen of his 486 opinions dealt with civil rights, and these reveal a commitment to constitutional law rooted in principle and judicial restraint. In *Lynch v. Torquato* (1965) Hastie declined to expand the STATE ACTION theories he had advanced in *Smith.* He held that the EQUAL PROTECTION clause of the FOURTEENTH AMENDMENT did not embrace the management of the internal affairs of the Democratic party. In an article he spurned AFFIRMATIVE ACTION programs that used "race alone as a determinant of eligibility or qualification."

William Hastie stood in the front rank of civil rights leaders. Notably, a strong sense of Madisonian constitutionalism balanced his commitment to legal activism.

KERMIT L. HALL

Bibliography

RUSCH, JONATHAN J. 1978 William H. Hastie and the Vindication of Civil Rights. *Howard Law Journal* 21:749–820.

HATCH ACT
53 Stat. 1147 (1939)
54 Stat. 767 (1940)

The Hatch Act prohibits most federal employees from engaging in any of a broad range of partisan political activities. It was adopted in 1939, but its antecedents go back well into the nineteenth century. The act has twice been challenged on FIRST AMENDMENT, VAGUENESS, and OVERBREADTH grounds, and has twice been upheld: CIVIL SERVICE COMMISSION V. NATIONAL ASSOCIATION OF LETTER CARRIERS (1973) and UNITED PUBLIC WORKERS V. MITCHELL (1947). Similar state legislation was upheld in BROADRICK V. OKLAHOMA (1973).

Although public employee organizations are among the most formidable lobbies in Congress and state legislatures, laws like the Hatch Act severely restrict the individual employee's political activities. These restrictions have been justified as assuring impartiality in public service, preventing the incumbent party from constructing a political machine, and preventing coercion of public employees.

The Hatch Act cases contrast sharply with later BURGER COURT decisions such as BUCKLEY V. VALEO (1976), protecting unlimited campaign spending, and FIRST NATIONAL BANK OF BOSTON V. BELLOTTI (1978), protecting corporate spending in ballot measure campaigns.

These decisions, in combination with the Hatch Act cases, suggest that, in the Burger Court's view, no liberty may be sacrificed to prevent unfair grasping of power by the use of concentrated wealth, but a great deal of liberty may be sacrificed to prevent unfair grasping of power by a mass-based device such as political patronage.

DANIEL H. LOWENSTEIN

Bibliography

COMMISSION ON POLITICAL ACTIVITY OF GOVERNMENT PERSONNEL 1968 *A Commission Report.*

ROSE, HENRY 1962 A Critical Look at the Hatch Act. *Harvard Law Review* 75:510–526.

HAUPT v. UNITED STATES
330 U.S. 1 (1947)

Herbert Haupt, a German-American, infiltrated into the United States during World War II from a German submarine as part of a Nazi plot to sabotage American war industry. His father, Hans Max Haupt, allowed him to stay at the latter's home, bought a car for him, and helped him to get a job in a factory where Norden bomb sights were manufactured. There were at least two witnesses to each of these three acts, and on the basis of that testimony Hans Haupt was convicted of TREASON.

The Supreme Court sustained Haupt's conviction in an 8–1 decision. In an opinion by Justice ROBERT H. JACKSON, the Court held that the overt acts testified to met the test laid down in CRAMER V. UNITED STATES (1945): each constituted the actual giving of aid and comfort to an enemy spy. Unlike Anthony Cramer's public meetings with the saboteurs, Hans Haupt's "harboring and sheltering" of his son were of direct support to the enemy mission.

DENNIS J. MAHONEY

(SEE ALSO: *Ex Parte Quirin, 1942.*)

HAWAII v. MANKICHI

See: Insular Cases

HAWAII HOUSING AUTHORITY v. MIDKIFF
467 U.S. 229 (1984)

The system of feudal land tenure developed under the Hawaiian monarchy had modern consequences. Seventy-two landowners owned forty-seven percent of the land in the state, and the federal and state governments owned forty-nine percent; only four percent of the land was left for other owners. The Hawaii legislature, finding that this system distorted the land market, in 1967 adopted a land reform act. The law authorized use of the state's EMINENT DOMAIN power to condemn residential plots and to transfer ownership to existing tenants. Landowners challenged the law as authorizing TAKINGS OF PROPERTY for private benefit rather than PUBLIC USE. The Supreme Court unanimously rejected this argument, upholding the law's validity. The legislature's purpose to relieve perceived evils of land concentration was legitimately public, and the courts' inquiry need extend no further. Apart from issues of JUST COMPENSATION, the taking of property has virtually ceased to present a judicial question.

KENNETH L. KARST

HAYBURN'S CASE
2 Dallas 409 (1792)

Hayburn's Case was regarded in its time and has been regarded by many historians since as the first case in which a federal court held an act of Congress unconstitutional. Congress in 1791 directed the CIRCUIT COURTS to rule on the validity of pension claims made by disabled Revolutionary War veterans; the findings of the courts were to be reviewable by the secretary of war and by Congress. The circuit court in New York, presided over by Chief Justice JOHN JAY, and the circuit court in North Carolina, presided over by Justice JAMES IREDELL, addressed letters to President GEORGE WASHINGTON explaining why they could not execute the act in their judicial capacities but that out of respect for Congress they would serve voluntarily as pension commissioners.

In the Pennsylvania circuit, Justices JAMES WILSON and JOHN BLAIR, confronted by a petition from one Hayburn, decided not to rule on his petition, and they also explained themselves in a letter to the President. They would have violated the Constitution to have ruled on the petition, they said, because the business directed by the act was not of a judicial nature and did not come within the JUDICIAL POWER OF THE UNITED STATES established by Article III. They objected to the statute because it empowered officers of the legislative and executive branches to review court actions, contrary to the principle of SEPARATION OF POWERS and judicial independence.

Hayburn's Case thus presented no suit, no controversy between parties, and, technically, no "case," and none of the courts rendered judicial decisions; they reported to the President their refusal to decide judicially. (See CASES AND CONTROVERSIES.) Some congressmen thought that *Hayburn's Case* was "the first instance in which a Court of Justice had declared a law of Congress to be unconstitutional," and the same opinion was delightedly trumpeted in anti-administration newspapers, which praised a precedent that they hoped would lead to judicial voiding of Hamiltonian legislation. The "case" reported in 2 Dallas 409 involved a motion for a WRIT OF MANDAMUS to compel the circuit court to grant a pension to Hayburn, but the court held the case over, and Congress revised the statute, providing a different procedure for the relief of pension-seeking veterans.

                                                LEONARD W. LEVY

HAYES, RUTHERFORD B.
(1822–1893)

An Ohio lawyer and Civil War general, Rutherford Birchard Hayes briefly served in Congress and was thrice elected Governor. A compromise Republican presidential candidate in 1876, Hayes received a minority of the popular vote and probably should not have been elected. However, the electoral vote was uncertain because of disputed results in South Carolina, Florida, Louisiana, and Oregon. Claims of vote fraud and threats of civil war led to a crisis which was resolved by the COMPROMISE OF 1876 which gave the election to Hayes on the condition that federal troops would be removed from the South. During his Presidency the rights of the freedmen were severely undermined as Reconstruction came to an end.

                                                PAUL FINKELMAN

Bibliography
KENNETH E. DAVISON 1972 *The Presidency of Rutherford B. Hayes.* Westport, Conn.: Greenwood Press.

HAYNE, ROBERT YOUNG
(1791–1839)

As a United States senator from South Carolina, Robert Young Hayne debated DANIEL WEBSTER of Massachusetts in the famous Webster-Hayne Debate of 1830. The debate began over a bill to slow down the sale of western lands but developed into a heated discussion over slavery, the nature of the Union, and the relationship between the states and the federal government. Hayne argued for the right of states to nullify federal laws. After the debate—which most contemporaries and historians agree was won by Webster—Hayne was a key participant in the South Carolina NULLIFICATION Convention of 1833. The Con-

vention asserted that the federal tariffs of 1828 and 1832 were unconstitutional and null and void in South Carolina. Hayne was then elected governor of the state. In his inaugural address he asserted "we will STAND OR FALL WITH CAROLINA." As governor he organized troops to defend South Carolina's SOVEREIGNTY from the federal government, but he ultimately accepted a compromise that peacefully ended the "Nullification Crisis."

                                                PAUL FINKELMAN

Bibliography
JERVEY, THEODORE D. (1909)1970 *Robert Y. Hayne and His Times.* New York: Da Capo Press.

HAYNES, UNITED STATES v.

See: *Marchetti, United States v.*

HAYNES v. WASHINGTON
373 U.S. 503 (1963)

This was the last of many confessions cases, prior to ESCOBEDO V. ILLINOIS (1964), in which the Supreme Court decided the voluntariness of a confession by a DUE PROCESS standard. In 1944 the Court had held that due process was violated if the police obtained a confession by continuous interogation while the prisoner was held incommunicado in an inherently coercive situation. Thereafter, however, the Court frequently had deferred to a determination of voluntariness by state courts. *Haynes* was the first case since 1944 in which the Court revived the standard of inherent coerciveness where the facts showed incommunicado detention and the prisoner was not allowed to call his lawyer. The case foreshadowed *Escobedo* and MIRANDA V. ARIZONA (1966).

                                                LEONARD W. LEVY

HAYS, ARTHUR GARFIELD
(1881–1954)

A leading defense counsel for and later director of the AMERICAN CIVIL LIBERTIES UNION, Arthur Garfield Hays devoted his career to protecting CIVIL LIBERTIES and FREEDOM OF SPEECH. Two of his books, *Let Freedom Ring* (1928) and *Trial by Prejudice* (1933), recount his participation in the Scottsboro cases (see NORRIS V. ALABAMA, 1935), the Scopes anti-evolution trial in Tennessee with Clarence Darrow (see STATE V. SCOPES, 1925), and on behalf of Sacco and Vanzetti (see COMMONWEALTH V. SACCO AND VANZETTI, 1921). Hays maintained a laissez-faire attitude toward government regulation of business and vigorously championed democracy, positions he elucidated in *Democracy Works* (1939).

DAVID GORDON

HEALTH INSURANCE FOR THE AGED ACT (MEDICARE)
79 Stat. 286 (1965)

The 1965 amendment of the SOCIAL SECURITY ACT establishing a system of health insurance operated by the Social Security Administration culminated thirty years of controversy over the proper role of the federal government in relation to medical care. Medicare provided hospital insurance and a variety of medical benefits for citizens sixty-five years or older. The act was designed to meet the serious problem of providing care for those who faced old age fearful of the financial ravages of illness.

Medicare's two insurance programs operated differently. The Hospital Benefit program automatically covered anyone over sixty-five with no "needs" test. It paid for hospitalization, nursing home care, home visits, and diagnostic services. It was financed by compulsory contributions from the protected persons and their employers and provided benefits as a matter of entitlement. The Supplementary Medical Insurance section created a voluntary individual program subsidized and administered by the government, using private insurance companies to assist in its administration.

Medicare influenced the entire pattern of medical care in the United States. With government financing a growing share of total health care expenditures, its power and role within the American health care system expanded proportionately. Not only administrators but also doctors and nurses adjusted their conduct to comply with newly mandated rules and procedures.

PAUL L. MURPHY

Bibliography
FEDER, JUDITH 1977 *Medicare: The Politics of Federal Hospital Insurance.* Lexington, Mass.: Lexington Books.

HEARING

See: Fair Hearing

HEARSAY RULE

The hearsay rule is a nonconstitutional rule of EVIDENCE which obtains in one form or another in every JURISDICTION in the country. The rule provides that in the absence of explicit exceptions to the contrary, hearsay evidence of a matter in dispute is inadmissible as proof of the matter. Although jurisdictions define "hearsay" in different ways, the various definitions reflect a common principle: evidence that derives its relevance in a case from the belief of a person who is not present in court—and thus not under oath and not subject to cross-examination regarding his credibility—is of questionable probative value.

The Constitution does not explicitly refer to the hearsay rule or implicitly constitutionalize the hearsay rule in civil or criminal cases generally; but it does contain two provisions that share common purposes with the hearsay rule. The TREASON clause of Article III, section 3, prohibits a conviction for treason "unless on the testimony of two witnesses to the same overt act, or on a confession in open court." In CRAMER V. UNITED STATES (1945) the Supreme Court construed this clause to require the federal government to produce witnesses who possessed direct evidence—as opposed to circumstantial evidence—of the same overt act. Although *Cramer* itself did not involve hearsay evidence, its reasoning applies as well to hearsay evidence of overt acts, because hearsay evidence is itself a kind of circumstantial evidence.

The other provision of the Constitution that bears on the hearsay rule is the Sixth Amendment's CONFRONTATION clause, which entitles the accused in a criminal case "to be confronted with the witnesses against him." In contrast to the hearsay rule, the confrontation clause does not treat hearsay evidence as presumptively inadmissible against the accused, and it does not treat traditional exceptions to the hearsay rule as automatically admissible. Nevertheless, the confrontation clause addresses the questionable nature of hearsay evidence by requiring the state to produce at trial the hearsay declarants whose statements it uses against the accused, when it appears that the declarants are available to testify in person and that the defendant could reasonably be expected to wish to examine them in person at the time their hearsay statements are introduced into evidence.

PETER WESTEN

(SEE ALSO: *Compulsory Process.*)

Bibliography
MCCORMICK, CHARLES 1972 *Evidence*, 2nd ed. Pages 579–756. St. Paul, Minn.: West Publishing Co.

HEART OF ATLANTA MOTEL v. UNITED STATES
379 U.S. 241 (1964)
KATZENBACH v. MCCLUNG
379 U.S. 294 (1964)

In these cases the Supreme Court unanimously upheld the portion of the CIVIL RIGHTS ACT of 1964 forbidding RACIAL DISCRIMINATION by hotels, restaurants, theaters, and other PUBLIC ACCOMMODATIONS.

Congressional debates had discussed the appropriate source of congressional power to prohibit private racial discrimination. The COMMERCE CLAUSE was proposed as a safe foundation for the bill; since 1937 the Supreme Court had upheld every congressional regulation of commerce that came before it. Because Congress obviously was seeking to promote racial equality, some thought the commerce clause approach "artificial" and thus "demeaning." They argued for reliance on the power of Congress to enforce the FOURTEENTH AMENDMENT. That amendment's STATE ACTION limitation, however, seemed to obstruct reaching private discrimination. As enacted, the 1964 act's public accommodations provisions were limited to establishments whose operations "affect commerce" or whose racial discrimination is "supported by state action."

The Supreme Court moved swiftly, accelerating decision in these two cases. The majority relied on the commerce power, validating the act in application not only to a large whites-only motel that mainly served out-of-state guests but also to a restaurant with no similar connection to interstate travel. The latter case, *McClung*, illustrates how far the commerce power has been stretched in recent years to allow Congress to legislate on matters of national concern. The restaurant mainly served a local clientele; it served blacks, but only at a take-out counter. Almost half the food used by the restaurant had come from other states, but even the Court recognized that this fact was trivial. More persuasive was the fact, fully documented in congressional hearings, that discrimination in public accommodations severely hindered interstate travel by blacks. Justices WILLIAM O. DOUGLAS and ARTHUR J. GOLDBERG, concurring, argued that both the commerce clause and the Fourteenth Amendment empowered Congress to impose these regulations.

In retrospect the pre-enactment debate over which power Congress should assert seems unimportant, in either institutional or doctrinal terms. Congress need not, after all, specify which of its powers it is using.

And the Supreme Court has not needed to explore the full reach of Congress's Fourteenth Amendment power, because in JONES V. ALFRED H. MAYER CO. (1968) it held that the THIRTEENTH AMENDMENT empowered Congress to prohibit private racial discrimination. (See BADGES OF SERVITUDE.)

KENNETH L. KARST

HEFFRON v. INTERNATIONAL SOCIETY FOR KRISHNA CONSCIOUSNESS , INC.
452 U.S. 640 (1981)

One rule governing the Minnesota State Fair allows the sale or distribution of literature, or the solicitation of funds, only at fixed booths. The International Society for Krishna Consciousness (ISKCON) sued in a state court challenging this rule's validity on its face and as applied. ISKCON contended that the rule violated its FIRST AMENDMENT rights of FREEDOM OF SPEECH and RELIGIOUS LIBERTY. The Minnesota Supreme Court held the law invalid as applied to ISKCON, saying that the state authorities had not shown that exempting ISKCON from the rule would significantly interfere with crowd control at the fair.

The Supreme Court reversed, upholding the rule on its face and as applied to distribution (5–4) and to sales and solicitation (9–0). Justice BYRON R. WHITE wrote for the Court. He concluded that the rule, which made no distinctions based on speech content and allowed no discretion to the licensing authorities, was valid as a regulation of the time, place, and manner of speech. The fair was a PUBLIC FORUM, but differed significantly from a public street. Considerations of safety and crowd control amounted to substantial state interests, justifying the rule restricting sales, distribution, and solicitation to booths. Exempting ISKCON would require exempting all applicants. Other less restrictive means for achieving those interests, such as penalizing disorder or limiting the number of solicitors, were unlikely to deal with the problems posed by large numbers of solicitors roaming the fairgrounds.

Justice WILLIAM J. BRENNAN's partial dissent, joined by two other Justices, argued that the rule was invalid in application to ISKCON's proposed distribution of literature. Such distribution, he argued, was no more disruptive than the making of speeches, or face-to-face proselytizing, both of which were permitted. Justice HARRY A. BLACKMUN also dissented as to the distribution of literature.

KENNETH L. KARST

HELVERING v. DAVIS
301 U.S. 619 (1937)

Plaintiff, a stockholder of an affected CORPORATION, challenged Titles II and VIII of the 1935 SOCIAL SECURITY ACT. Title II creates the old age benefits program, popularly known as "social security," and Title VIII contains the funding mechanism for that program. Under Title VIII, an employer must take a payroll deduction from each employee's wages and pay it, together with an equal amount directly from the employer, to the treasury.

Plaintiff's primary argument was that Congress lacked constitutional power to levy a tax for the purpose of providing old age benefits. Justice BENJAMIN N. CARDOZO, writing an opinion in which six other Justices joined, resoundingly rejected the argument that Congress had transgressed the TENTH AMENDMENT reservation to the states of powers not delegated to the federal government. Only Justices JAMES C. MCREYNOLDS and PIERCE BUTLER dissented. The majority classified the old age benefits program as a legitimate exercise of Congress's power "to lay and collect taxes . . . to . . . provide . . . for the GENERAL WELFARE of the United States." The Court adopted a fluid definition of the general welfare. "Nor is the concept of the general welfare static. Needs that were narrow or parochial a century ago may be interwoven in our day with the well-being of a nation." The Court then examined the effects on older workers of the "purge of nation-wide calamity that began in 1929" and concluded that the problem was national in scope, acute in severity, and intractable without concerted federal effort. State governments were deficient in economic resources and reluctant to finance social programs that would place them at comparative economic disadvantage with competitor states: industry would flee the new taxes and INDIGENTS would flock to any state that provided the new social benefits. (Justice Cardozo's analysis proved prescient. In the 1960s and 1970s a number of socially progressive northeastern and western states experienced these twin problems when they far exceeded national benefit norms in the federal-state cooperative programs of Aid to Families with Dependent Children and Medicaid.) Having determined that the purpose of Title II was well within the scope of the "general welfare" clause, the Court sustained the Title VIII funding provisions.

In its broad, though imprecise, reading of the term "general welfare," *Helvering v. Davis*, even more than its companion case, STEWARD MACHINE CO. v. DAVIS (1937), rejects the view that Congress, in exercising its power to tax for the general welfare, is required by the Tenth Amendment to eschew regulation of matters historically controlled by the states. In so doing, it repudiates that vein of case law, exemplified by UNITED STATES v. BUTLER (1936), that treats the Tenth Amendment as a limitation on the federal TAXING AND SPENDING POWER. Though *Butler* is factually distinguishable, the analysis used by Justice Cardozo in *Steward Machine Co.* and *Helvering v. Davis* would surely have sustained the agricultural price support provisions struck down in *Butler* a year earlier.

GRACE GANZ BLUMBERG

HENRY, PATRICK
(1736–1799)

Unsuccessful as a merchant, Patrick Henry turned to the law. He was admitted to the Virginia bar in 1760 and rose rapidly to prominence and prosperity. In 1765 Henry was elected to the House of Burgesses and, in his first term, won fame and popularity with a series of resolutions opposing the STAMP ACT as an unconstitutional imposition of TAXATION WITHOUT REPRESENTATION. A flamboyant and persuasive orator, Henry became the leader of the radical patriot faction in Virginia. As a delegate to the FIRST CONTINENTAL CONGRESS Henry favored both issuance of a declaration of grievances and formation of the ASSOCIATION. At home, he successfully urged the arming of the militia and served briefly as commander-in-chief of Virginia's forces. He was a member of the convention that, in 1776, adopted the VIRGINIA DECLARATION OF RIGHTS AND CONSTITUTION and instructed the state's congressional delegation to call for a DECLARATION OF INDEPENDENCE. Henry was himself a delegate to Congress but resigned in June 1776 when he was elected first governor of Virginia. In 1776 Governor Henry supported a BILL OF ATTAINDER (written by THOMAS JEFFERSON) against a notorious Tory brigand. When Jefferson and JAMES MADISON proposed to end the ESTABLISHMENT OF RELIGION in Virginia, Henry countered with a plan for general assessment to support all Christian churches and teachers.

Although Henry was a longtime self-proclaimed nationalist and had often called for enlargement of the powers of Congress under the ARTICLES OF CONFED-

ERATION, he declined appointment as a delegate to the CONSTITUTIONAL CONVENTION OF 1787. In the Virginia state convention of 1788 he was the leader of the anti-Federalists and spoke and voted against RATIFICATION OF THE CONSTITUTION. He argued that the document lacked a BILL OF RIGHTS and infringed on state SOVEREIGNTY, and he warned that the new federal Congress might someday abolish SLAVERY.

Henry later converted to the Federalist cause; in 1795 President GEORGE WASHINGTON offered to make Henry secretary of state, but Henry declined. In the 1796 case of WARE V. HYLTON Henry appeared with JOHN MARSHALL as counsel for Virginians who claimed that, the Treaty of Paris notwithstanding, state law precluded their obligation to repay debts due to British subjects. That same year Henry turned down Washington's offer of appointment as Chief Justice of the United States. Like SAMUEL ADAMS of Massachusetts, Henry proved better suited to making a revolution than to erecting a stable constitutional order.

DENNIS J. MAHONEY

HEPBURN ACT
34 Stat. 584 (1906)

A string of adverse decisions by the Supreme Court left the Interstate Commerce Commission (ICC) with few effective powers. Abuses abounded despite the ELKINS ACT of 1903, and in December 1905 THEODORE ROOSEVELT reiterated his earlier calls for corrective legislation. The resulting bill, which met significant opposition only in the Senate, expressly vested the ICC with the power to prescribe "reasonable" maximum rail rates only after current rates and practices had been condemned in a hearing. The bill, which became law on June 29, 1906, nonetheless failed to establish any standards for those rates, thus leaving the Court to apply the FAIR RETURN rule of SMYTH V. AMES (1898). Rates initiated by the ICC were subject to narrow JUDICIAL REVIEW; new rates became effective upon issuance unless challenged in the CIRCUIT COURTS and successfully enjoined, in which case they took effect only when sustained by the courts. The "commodities clause," which forbade carriers from transporting goods produced by railroads or in which they had an interest, was primarily addressed to rail lines serving mining interests. Additional provisions, effective immediately, shifted the burden of APPEALS to the carriers, not the commis-

sion. Congress followed this with the MANN-ELKINS ACT in 1910, further supporting the commission.

DAVID GORDON

(SEE ALSO: *Interstate Commerce Commission v. Illinois Central Railroad,* 1910.)

Bibliography

SHARFMAN, ISAIAH L. 1931–1937 *The Interstate Commerce Commission,* 4 vols. New York: Commonwealth Fund.

HERBERT v. LANDO
441 U.S. 153 (1979)

In *Herbert v. Lando* a majority of the Supreme Court soundly rejected the argument that the constitutional protections afforded journalists should be expanded to bar inquiry into the editorial processes of the press in libel actions. Anthony Herbert, a Vietnam veteran, received widespread media attention when he accused his superior officers of covering up atrocities and other war crimes. Herbert sued for libel when CBS broadcast a report and *The Atlantic Monthly* published an article, both by Barry Lando, about Herbert and his accusations. Herbert conceded that he was a PUBLIC FIGURE required by NEW YORK TIMES V. SULLIVAN (1964) to prove that the media defendants acted with "actual malice." During pretrial discovery, Lando refused to answer questions on the ground that the FIRST AMENDMENT precluded inquiry into the state of mind of those who edit, produce, or publish, and into the editorial process.

The Court recognized that the FIRST AMENDMENT affords substantial protection to media defendants in libel actions, citing specifically the *Sullivan* requirement that public figures and officials must prove knowing or reckless untruth. The Court noted, however, that the Framers did not abolish civil or criminal liability for defamation when adopting the First Amendment. It reasoned that upholding a constitutional privilege that barred inquiry into facts relating directly to the central issue of the defendant's state of mind would effectively deprive plaintiffs of the very evidence necessary to prove their case. That result would substantially eliminate recovery by plaintiffs who were public figures or public officials.

Justice LEWIS F. POWELL separately elaborated upon the majority's admonition that in supervising discovery in libel actions, trial judges should exercise appropriate controls to prevent abuse, noting the courts' duty to consider First Amendment interests along with plaintiffs' private interest. Justice WILLIAM J. BRENNAN, dissenting in part, asserted that the First Amendment provided a qualified editorial privilege which would yield once the plaintiff demonstrated a *prima facie* defamatory falsehood. Separately dissenting, Justice POTTER J. STEWART argued that inquiry into the editorial process is irrelevant, and Justice THURGOOD MARSHALL rejected the majority's balance of the competing First Amendment and private interests.

KIM McLANE WARDLAW

(SEE ALSO: *Balancing Test; Evidence; Freedom of the Press.*)

HERNDON v. LOWRY
301 U.S. 242 (1937)

Herndon was a black organizer convicted of attempting to incite insurrection in violation of a state law. Herndon had sought to induce others to join the Communist party. At the time the party was seeking to organize southern blacks and calling for separate black states in the South. While only indirectly adopting the CLEAR AND PRESENT DANGER test, the Court refused to apply the BAD TENDENCY TEST of GITLOW v. NEW YORK (1925) and stressed the absence of any immediate threat of insurrection. In an opinion by Justice OWEN ROBERTS, a 5–4 Court held (1) that the evidence presented failed "to establish an attempt to incite others to insurrection" even at some indefinite future time; and (2) that the statute was unconstitutionally vague as applied and contrued because "every person who attacks existing conditions, who agitates for a change in the form of government, must take the risk that if a jury should be of opinion he ought to have foreseen that his utterances might contribute in any measure to some future forcible resistance to the existing government he may be convicted of the offense of inciting insurrection." The VAGUENESS DOCTRINE invoked was not specifically articulated as a FIRST AMENDMENT standard; instead, the general criminal standard of "a sufficiently ascertainable standard of guilt" was applied.

The state supreme court believed that a conviction would be justified if the defendant intended that insurrection "should happen at any time within which he might reasonably expect his influence to continue to be directly operative in causing such action by those whom he sought to induce. . . ." This formula, which the Supreme Court found constitutionally infirm, must be compared with its own of the 1950s upholding convictions for conspiracy to advocate overthrow of the government where the intention was that of an organized group to bring about overthrow "as speedily as circumstances would permit."

MARTIN SHAPIRO

HICKLIN v. ORBECK
437 U.S. 518 (1978)

A unanimous court, speaking through Justice WILLIAM J. BRENNAN, held unconstitutional an Alaska law requiring private firms working on oil and gas leases or pipelines to give preference in hiring to Alaska residents. By discriminating against nonresidents, the "Alaska Hire" law violated the PRIVILEGES AND IMMUNITIES clause of Article IV of the Constitution.

DENNIS J. MAHONEY

HIGHER LAW

Americans have never been hesitant to argue that if a law is bad it must be unconstitutional. When no written constitutional provision suggests an interpretation that undermines the law under attack, American lawyers have often looked to the ancient tradition of unwritten higher law for support.

It is worth distinguishing two kinds of unwritten higher law. The first is natural law, conceived by the ancient Stoics as, in Cicero's words, "right reason, harmonious, diffused among all, constant, eternal." The Stoic conception was integrated with Christian theology by the medieval scholastics, and later was reformulated in a secular and individualistic direction by the NATURAL RIGHTS theorists of the Enlightenment. In this latter form, the natural law tradition provided the intellectual background for the American colonists' assertion of "certain inalienable rights" in the DECLARATION OF INDEPENDENCE.

The second kind of unwritten higher law, which we may call FUNDAMENTAL LAW, derives from those conventional and largely unquestioned values and practices that need be neither constant, eternal, nor dictated by reason. The members of a society may see their fundamentals as contingent, peculiar to themselves, and mutable—though, because fundamental, not easily or quickly mutable. On the other hand, those who see their own society's basic conventions as the only possible ones do not accept, perhaps cannot even understand, the distinction between "natural" and "fundamental" law.

In the practice of legal argument either natural or fundamental law can have priority, with the other regarded as ancillary. Thus one can argue that a principle is legally binding because it comports with right reason, as is incidentally confirmed by its acceptance in society; or one can reverse the priorities, leaving reason to confirm what convention and tradition primarily establish. Until about the mid-nineteenth century, American lawyers alternated between these rhetorical strategies, but since the Civil War the fundamental law strand has predominated.

The American idea of fundamental law derived originally from the seventeenth-century English habit of conducting political disputes in terms of an "ancient constitution," unwritten and believed (like the COMMON LAW itself) to be of "immemorial antiquity." Sir EDWARD COKE exemplified this habit when he merged natural with traditional law and both with English common law, and then asserted judicial authority to override legislation in the name of this powerful conglomerate. His declaration in BONHAM'S CASE (1608) that "when an Act of Parliament is against common right and reason . . . the common law will control it, and adjudge such act to be void" supplied a significant argument in the American colonists' struggle with Parliament between 1761 and 1776.

During the prerevolutionary period, the Americans argued for limitations on Parliament's authority over them on the basis of this same conglomerate of reason, common law, and constitutional tradition. Only when they broke with the English crown altogether in 1776—an avowedly revolutionary step—was their justification purely in terms of natural right.

With independence, the new states enacted popularly ratified written constitutions, a process later repeated in the adoption of the federal Constitution. The question then arose whether the new constitutions subsumed the older idea of unwritten constitutional law based on reason or tradition. The classic debate on this question was the exchange of OBITER DICTA between Justices JAMES IREDELL and SAMUEL CHASE of the Supreme Court in CALDER V. BULL (1798). Iredell argued that a law consistent with the applicable written constitutions was immune from further JUDICIAL REVIEW; because the "ablest and the purest minds differ" concerning the requirements of natural justice, judges should assume no special authority to enforce so indeterminate a standard. Chase insisted that "certain vital principles in our free Republican governments" would invalidate inconsistent legislation whether the principle were enacted or not; thus a law that took the property of A and gave it to B could not stand, even if the applicable written constitution did not explicitly protect private property.

Chase's dictum followed the tenor of the NINTH AMENDMENT to the federal Constitution (1791): "The enumeration in the Constitution, of certain rights, shall not be construed to deny or disparage others retained by the people." But the Ninth Amendment does not settle the Chase–Iredell dispute, as it might if it said explicitly whether the unenumerated and retained rights have enforceable constitutional status.

During the first years of the republic, a number of state courts, as in *Ham v. McClaws* (South Carolina, 1789), anticipated Chase by invoking unenacted constitutional law to invalidate legislation. On the other hand, the most influential discussions of judicial review during the early federal period—ALEXANDER HAMILTON's THE FEDERALIST #78 (1787) and JOHN MARSHALL's opinion in MARBURY V. MADISON (1803)—echoed Iredell's view in basing power solely on the judicial authority to construe the written constitution, itself conceived as the expressed will of a fully sovereign people.

On the whole, judicial practice before 1830, particularly in the state courts but in a few federal cases as well, adopted Chase's view while also invoking his natural-law language with its appeal to "general principles of republican government." Marshall himself, in FLETCHER V. PECK (1810), ambiguously justified invalidation of a Georgia statute "either by general principles which are common to our free institutions, or by the particular provisions of the constitution of the United States." The particular provision in question was the CONTRACT CLAUSE, which Marshall heroically stretched to fit the case, perhaps out of reluctance to rest decision solely on "general principles." In a few later cases, such as TERRETT V. TAYLOR (1815), the Supreme Court did invalidate state legislation without reference to constitutional text.

Even during their heyday before 1830, the "general principles" of the unwritten constitution were never regarded as federal constitutional law, binding on the states under the SUPREMACY CLAUSE. Because they did not count as "the Constitution or laws of the United States," unwritten general principles would not support appeal to the Supreme Court from the decision of a state court; federal courts invoked these principles against state legislatures only when acting as substitute state courts under DIVERSITY OF CITIZENSHIP JURISDICTION.

In their content, the unwritten "general principles" applied during this period were largely confined to the protection of traditional vested property rights against retroactive infringement. As such, they were equally well supported by common law tradition and by contemporary ideas of natural justice.

From about 1830 on, judicial assertion of pure unwritten constitutional law became less common, perhaps because of its conflict with Jacksonian ideas of popular sovereignty. The process of stretching the language of vague constitutional provisions to encompass notions of natural or traditional justice continued, however, and there began a historic shift in the favored vague provision from the federal contract clause to the clauses of state constitutions guaranteeing the LAW OF THE LAND and DUE PROCESS OF LAW—phrases that began to be construed to mean more than their originally understood sense as guarantees of customary common law procedures. Thus was born the concept bearing the oxymoronic name of SUBSTANTIVE DUE PROCESS, which ever since has been the main vehicle for the implementation of higher law notions in American constitutional law.

A leading case in this development was *Taylor v. Porter* (New York, 1843), which incorporated in "due process" the prohibition, earlier invoked by Chase as an unwritten general principle, against the state's taking the property of the worthy A only to give it to the undeserving B. In these early substantive due process decisions the language of immutable natural law mixed indiscriminately with talk of historically based common law and tradition; there was no felt conflict between the two rhetorical strands.

By contrast, the discourses of natural justice and of customary practice did conflict in the great constitutional debates over SLAVERY that occurred, largely outside the courts, during the period 1830–1860. Proslavery forces occasionally argued that the natural right of property protected the owners of human as of other chattels. Indeed, in the most notorious of constitutional slavery cases, DRED SCOTT V. SANDFORD (1857), Chief Justice ROGER B. TANEY held that congressional prohibition of SLAVERY IN THE TERRITORIES violated slaveholders' property rights guaranteed by the Fifth Amendment's due process clause. But the legal defenders of slavery did not generally have to rely on unwritten higher law; they could point to the positive guarantees the slave states had insisted on inserting in the federal Constitution.

On the other hand, antislavery lawyers had almost no basis for legal argument except the increasingly widespread conviction that slavery was intolerably unjust. With positive law and custom against them, they tried to translate natural law directly into constitutional doctrine. To this end, they invoked the PRIVILEGES AND IMMUNITIES clause of Article IV; the "liberty" protected by substantive due process; and the proclamation of human equality in the Declaration of Independence, for which they claimed constitutional status. More radical abolitionists opposed these efforts to accommodate the Constitution, the "covenant with Hell," to the antislavery cause; on the other hand, the pre-Civil War courts found the antislavery constitutional arguments unacceptable because too radical. But abolitionist constitutional theory triumphed in larger arenas; it became part of the political program of the Republican party, and thus part of the world view of the politicians who led the war against slavery and afterward framed the Reconstruction amendments.

The language of section 1 of the FOURTEENTH AMENDMENT (1868) directly echoes the old triad of antislavery constitutional arguments in its guarantees of due process, EQUAL PROTECTION OF THE LAW, and the privileges and immunities of national citizenship. These general clauses have ever since provided the main textual basis for the continuation of the higher law tradition in constitutional law.

In the SLAUGHTERHOUSE CASE (1874) the Supreme Court at first by a 5–4 vote rejected the argument that the new amendment constitutionally bound the states to the whole array of unenumerated rights. But by the end of the century, the courts had accepted the arguments of commentators, chief among whom was THOMAS M. COOLEY (*Constitutional Limitations*, 1868), that due process prohibited all legislative intrusions upon basic liberties and property rights that did not reasonably promote the limited ends of public health, safety, or morals. Of the protected liberties, the dearest to the courts of this period was FREEDOM OF CONTRACT, and in a series of decisions epitomized by LOCHNER V. NEW YORK (1905) the courts invalidated economic regulatory laws on the grounds that they unreasonably constrained the terms on which adults could contract with each other.

In developing this doctrine, courts and commentators sometimes echoed the old language of natural law, but the more characteristic note of this aggressive laissez-faire constitutionalism was struck by Justice RUFUS PECKHAM, who condemned a price regulation law as a throwback to the past that ignored "the more correct ideas which an increase of civilization and a fuller knowledge of the fundamental laws of political economy . . . have given us today" (*Budd v. State*, New York, 1889). The notion of evolution had taken hold, and it not only supported the doctrines of Social Darwinism but also promoted the idea that fundamental legal principles evolved—a progress that the courts should accommodate by developing the law of the due process clause through a "gradual process of judicial inclusion and exclusion" (*Davidson v. New Orleans*, 1878). Tradition continued to play a role as well; thus the courts invalidated much new legislation regulating the price charged for goods while accepting old usury laws that regulated the price charged for the use of money, and generally tolerating public regulation of those businesses that had traditionally been treated as AFFECTED WITH A PUBLIC INTEREST.

The legal supporters of Progressive politics fiercely attacked "liberty of contract" and its associated doctrines in the name of popular sovereignty, which they argued required repudiation of the very idea of unwritten constitutional law. When laissez-faire constitutionalism was finally put to rest in the mid-1930s under the combined influence of FRANKLIN D. ROOSEVELT's court-packing plan and more long-run historical forces, it appeared that the higher law tradition might finally have come to the end of its long influence on American constitutionalism.

Only if higher law is given its narrower sense derived from classic natural law has this come to pass. The New Deal and post-New Deal courts found a new active role in the program of correcting for legislative failures sketched by the famous footnote four of the opinion in UNITED STATES V. CAROLENE PRODUCTS (1938). They promoted racial equality and electoral reform while protecting political dissidents, religious deviants, and criminal defendants, a role that reached its peak during the years of the WARREN COURT (1953–1969). The doctrinal vehicles for these projects have been the gradual incorporation within due process of the specific guarantees of the BILL OF RIGHTS and above all the evolutionary interpretation of the equal protection clause as a vehicle of fundamental law.

One of the most effective promoters of these developments, Justice HUGO L. BLACK (1937–1971), did wholly repudiate any invocation of higher law in their support; his characteristic stance was a rigorously exclusive appeal to constitutional text as a source of doctrine. While Justice Black's colleagues did not share his strict constructionist views, they too generally avoided invoking notions of natural or universal human rights, often resting decision on imaginative readings of original intent. Frequently, however, the Justices have openly construed vague constitutional language in light of an evolving fundamental law specific to American history and culture. During these years the Court has said that "notions of what constitutes equal treatment . . . do change" (HARPER V. VIRGINIA BOARD OF ELECTIONS, 1966); that due process requires states to institute criminal procedures that are "fundamental" in the sense of "necessary to

an Anglo-American regime of ordered liberty" (DUNCAN V. LOUISIANA, 1968); and that the prohibition of CRUEL AND UNUSUAL PUNISHMENT is to be construed in the light of "those evolving standards of decency that mark the progress of a maturing society" (*Furman v. Georgia*, 1972).

Its association with laissez-faire constitutionalism had discredited substantive due process as a doctrinal tool during the generation following the New Deal, but beginning with GRISWOLD V. CONNECTICUT (1965) the Court moved toward reviving the use of this old rubric for the protection of substantive liberties. The role once held by "liberty of contract" was now taken by the RIGHT OF PRIVACY, a misleading name for what was at its core a constitutional protection for freedom of REPRODUCTIVE CHOICE, surrounded by a periphery of other doctrines limiting governmental power to regulate the FAMILY. The privacy decisions openly used as precedents substantive due process cases decided before the New Deal. Like those earlier decisions, the privacy cases avoided reference to universal right or natural law in support of their doctrines, with a plurality of Justices stating in MOORE V. EAST CLEVELAND (1977) that "the Constitution protects the sanctity of the family precisely because the institution of the family is deeply rooted in this Nation's history and tradition."

The natural law strand of argument, though much muted in this century, has never entirely disappeared from American constitutional rhetoric. Justice WILLIAM O. DOUGLAS was at times inclined to argue in this vein; before the *Griswold* decision he supported constitutional protection for marriage and procreation on the grounds that they were, as he said in SKINNER V. OKLAHOMA (1945), "basic CIVIL RIGHTS of man." Since the 1970s a number of constitutional commentators have argued for the use of "the methods of moral philosophy" in constitutional decision, referring to philosophical theories that claim universality for their results, and in this sense directly descend from classic natural law approaches. Whether there will be a revival of natural law discourse in constitutional doctrine remains an open question. On the other hand, the broader tradition of an unwritten higher law of the Constitution, encompassing both fundamental and natural law, seems by now too firmly entrenched to be dislodged.

THOMAS C. GREY

Bibliography

CORWIN, EDWARD S. (1928–1929) 1955 *The "Higher Law" Background of American Constitutional Law.* Ithaca, N.Y.: Cornell University Press.

———— 1948 *Liberty Against Government.* Baton Rouge: Louisiana State University Press.

GRAHAM, HOWARD JAY 1968 *Everyman's Constitution.* Madison: State Historical Society of Wisconsin.

HAINES, CHARLES GROVE 1930 *The Revival of Natural Law Concepts.* Cambridge, Mass.: Harvard University Press.

TEN BROEK, JACOBUS (1951)1965 *Equal under Law.* New York: Collier Books.

WRIGHT, BENJAMIN F., JR. 1931 *American Interpretations of Natural Law.* Cambridge, Mass.: Harvard University Press.

HILDRETH, RICHARD
(1807–1865)

A prolific pamphleteer, Richard Hildreth passionately opposed SLAVERY and took a Federalist or Whig stance on most issues. He was also a nationalist and an economic determinist who insisted on free competition. His *History of the United States* (1849–1852), ending in 1821, is meticulous in detail, scrupulously presenting each argument on major issues. His bias is nevertheless apparent in his championing of Federalist legislation; he minimized the effects of the ALIEN AND SEDITION ACTS, stressed the "virulence" of the VIRGINIA AND KENTUCKY RESOLUTIONS, and decried the repeal of the JUDICIARY ACT OF 1801. This six-volume study is still extraordinary for its realism and rejection of nineteenth-century romantic and heroic traditions.

DAVID GORDON

HILLS v. GAUTREAUX
425 U.S. 284 (1976)

Two years after MILLIKEN V. BRADLEY (1974) rejected metropolitan relief for school DESEGREGATION absent a showing of a constitutional violation by both city and suburban districts or by state officials, the Supreme Court encountered a parallel issue in the field of housing discrimination. The United States Department of Housing and Urban Development (HUD) had aided a Chicago city agency in locating low-income housing sites for the purpose of maintaining residential SEGREGATION. HUD, citing *Milliken,* argued that relief should be limited to the city. However, the Court approved the district court's order, which had regulated HUD's conduct beyond Chicago's boundaries. No restructuring or displacement of local government would result here, the Court said.

KENNETH L. KARST

HINES v. DAVIDOWITZ
312 U.S. 52 (1941)

Hines held that under the PREEMPTION doctrine, enforcement of a state alien registration law was barred by the federal ALIEN REGISTRATION ACT. Justice HUGO L. BLACK, for the Court, emphasized the broad power of Congress over ALIENS. Justice HARLAN FISKE STONE, for three dissenters, noted the absence of any conflict between state and federal laws or any express congressional prohibition of state regulation.

KENNETH L. KARST

HIPOLITE EGG COMPANY v. UNITED STATES
220 U.S. 45 (1911)

A unanimous Supreme Court relied on the decision in CHAMPION V. AMES (1903) to sustain the PURE FOOD AND DRUG ACT's prohibition on the interstate transportation of adulterated food. Justice JOSEPH MCKENNA's opinion acknowledged few limits on congressional power over INTERSTATE COMMERCE, declaring that there was no trade "carried on between the states to which it does not extend," and that it was "subject to no limitations except those found in the Constitution." McKenna did not consider the purpose or intent of the act as the Court had previously done in *Champion* and would do so again in HOKE V. UNITED STATES (1913) and HAMMER V. DAGENHART (1918).

DAVID GORDON

HIRABAYASHI v. UNITED STATES

See: Japanese American Cases

HITCHMAN COAL & COKE CO. v. MITCHELL
245 U.S. 229 (1917)

In this case a 6–3 Supreme Court approved use of an INJUNCTION to enforce YELLOW DOG CONTRACTS. The injunction prohibited the union from inducing breach of contract by communicating with employees or potential employees of the company. The majority emphasized that Hitchman had as much right to condition employment contracts on promises not to join a union as the workers had to decline job offers. Indeed, "this is a part of the constitutional right of personal liberty and private property" protected by SUBSTANTIVE DUE PROCESS of law. The Court thus held that these workers were not free because they had signed the yellow dog contracts.

Justice LOUIS D. BRANDEIS dissented, joined by Justices OLIVER WENDELL HOLMES and JOHN H. CLARKE. The union, they said, had merely sought promises to join, and the yellow dog contracts were not genuine contracts because they were not freely entered into by the workers. The Court's hostility to LABOR would not change until 1937. (See HUGHES COURT.)

DAVID GORDON

H. L. v. MATHESON

See: Reproductive Autonomy

HODEL v. VIRGINIA SURFACE MINING AND RECLAMATION ASSOCIATION
452 U.S. 264 (1981)

The *Hodel* opinion provided a formula for interpreting the demands of NATIONAL LEAGUE OF CITIES v. USERY (1976). The Supreme Court unanimously upheld an act of Congress stringently regulating private stripmining operations, but providing for relaxation of the federal regulations when a state undertook to regulate the same activities according to standards set out in the act. Justice THURGOOD MARSHALL, for the Court, wrote that an act of Congress would not be held invalid under the *Usery* principle unless it satisfied three conditions: that the law regulated "the States as States"; that it addressed "matters that are indisputably 'attributes of state SOVEREIGNTY'"; and that it directly impaired the states' ability "to structure integral operations in areas of traditional governmental functions." In *Hodel* itself, the law failed the first part of the test, for it regulated only private parties. All three requirements were taken from the *Usery* opinion; in combination, they proved an insuperable hurdle to states seeking to rely on *Usery* to invalidate federal regulation of state activities, and ultimately led to the overruling of *Usery* in GARCIA v. SAN ANTONIO METROPOLITAN TRANSIT AUTHORITY (1985). Justice WILLIAM H. REHNQUIST, who concurred only in the judgment, wrote separately

to decry the majority's assumptions concerning the breadth of Congress's commerce power.

KENNETH L. KARST

HODGES v. UNITED STATES
203 U.S. 1 (1906)

Black laborers had agreed to work for a lumber firm. Hodges and the other white defendants, all private citizens, ordered the blacks to stop working, assaulted them, and violently drove them from their workplace. The defendants were indicted for violating federal CIVIL RIGHTS laws. In a decision reconfirming much of the CIVIL RIGHTS CASES (1883) opinion, the Supreme Court indicated that the federal prosecution could not be supported under the FOURTEENTH or FIFTEENTH AMENDMENTS because those amendments restrict only STATE ACTION. The THIRTEENTH AMENDMENT did not support a federal prosecution because group violence against blacks was not the equivalent of reducing them to SLAVERY. In JONES v. ALFRED H. MAYER CO. (1968) and GRIFFIN v. BRECKENRIDGE (1971) the Court adopted a more generous attitude towards Congress's Thirteenth Amendment power to prohibit private discrimination.

THEODORE EISENBERG

HODGSON AND THOMPSON v. BOWERBANK
5 Cranch 303 (1809)

Hodgson is a constitutional trivium, of little doctrinal importance. Its interest today is captured in a question: Was *Hodgson* the one occasion between MARBURY v. MADISON (1803) and DRED SCOTT v. SANDFORD (1857) when the Supreme Court held an act of Congress unconstitutional? Various scholars have answered that question differently.

Article III of the Constitution does not explicitly authorize Congress to confer JURISDICTION on federal courts to decide a case in which one ALIEN sues another. The JUDICIARY ACT OF 1789, however, conferred such jurisdiction on the circuit court when "an alien is a party." In *Hodgson*, plaintiffs were British subjects; defendants' CITIZENSHIP was unknown. Chief Justice JOHN MARSHALL, responding to counsel's claim of jurisdiction, was quoted by the reporter, Cranch, as saying only this: "Turn to the article of the constitution of the United States, for the statute cannot extend the jurisdiction beyond the limits of the constitution."

Hodgson plainly holds that Congress cannot constitutionally confer federal court jurisdiction in the alien-versus-alien case. But was Marshall merely limiting the 1789 act's construction to avoid constitutional problems, or was he holding a part of the act's reach unconstitutional? Eighteen decades after the event, the debate goes on.

KENNETH L. KARST

(SEE ALSO: *Unconstitutionality.*)

Bibliography

MAHONEY, DENNIS J. 1982 A Historical Note on *Hodgson v. Bowerbank. University of Chicago Law Review* 49:725–740.

HOFFA v. UNITED STATES
385 U.S. 293 (1966)

Information received from a secret government informer and used to obtain a conviction of James Hoffa, the Teamsters' union leader, did not constitute an illegal search, because the informer was an invited guest; did not violate the RIGHT AGAINST SELF-INCRIMINATION, because compulsion was absent; and did not abridge the RIGHT TO COUNSEL, because the information did not breach the confidential relationship between petitioner and counsel. Hoffa's conviction for jury bribery was sustained.

LEONARD W. LEVY

HOKE v. UNITED STATES
227 U.S. 308 (1913)
CAMINETTI v. UNITED STATES
242 U.S. 470 (1917)

Opinions in CHAMPION V. AMES (1903) and HIPOLITE EGG CO. V. UNITED STATES (1911) laid the foundation for a unanimous decision sustaining the MANN ACT, which prohibited the interstate transportation of women for immoral purposes. Justice JOSEPH MCKENNA, generously construing the power over INTERSTATE COMMERCE, declared in *Hoke* that Congress might exercise means that "may have the quality of police regulations." He denied that the Mann Act violated the TENTH AMENDMENT by usurping the STATE POLICE POWER. In *Caminetti*, the Court held that transportation was illegal under the act, even if not accompanied by financial gain: "To say the contrary would shock the common understanding of what

constitutes an immoral purpose." These cases helped establish a broad basis for the growth of the NATIONAL POLICE POWER.

DAVID GORDON

HOLDEN v. HARDY
169 U.S. 366 (1898)

Utah adopted a maximum hours law fixing an eight-hour day for miners. A mine owner, convicted for working his employees ten hours a day, claimed that the statute violated his FOURTEENTH AMENDMENT rights. For a 7–2 Supreme Court, Justice HENRY B. BROWN declared that the right to FREEDOM OF CONTRACT protected by SUBSTANTIVE DUE PROCESS of law is subject to legitimate POLICE POWER regulations intended to protect the public health. The Court sustained the statute as a reasonable exercise of the police power on the ground that mining is a dangerous occupation that requires an exception to freedom of contract. Brown realistically observed that employees are often induced by fear of discharge to obey management rules that might be detrimental to health. In such cases self-interest is an unsure guide, justifying legislative intervention. Had the Court adhered to this understanding, LOCHNER V. NEW YORK (1905) might have been stillborn.

LEONARD W. LEVY

HOLDING

The holding of a court is the *ratio decidendi* or the ground(s) upon which it bases its decision of a case. The holding, includes all the court's declarations of law necessary to the decision of the case; other pronouncements are OBITER DICTA. The holding in a case establishes a precedent and may be generalized into a DOCTRINE. The term may also be used more narrowly to signify the court's resolution of any particular legal issue or question of constitutional interpretation presented in a case.

DENNIS J. MAHONEY

HOLMES, OLIVER WENDELL, JR.
(1841–1935)

When he was appointed to the Supreme Court in 1902, at the age of sixty-one, he was best known to the general public as the son of a famous poet and man of letters; when he retired, thirty years later, he had been called "the greatest of our age in the domain of jurisprudence, and one of the greatest of the ages." Oliver Wendell Holmes's thirty years on the Supreme Court unquestionably made his reputation, and yet those years, given the aspirations of Holmes's earlier career, were years in which his mood as a judge can best be described as resignation. He was not able to achieve anything like what he thought he could achieve as a judge; regularly he confessed his inability to do anything other than ratify "what the crowd wants." He wryly suggested that on his tombstone should be inscribed "here lies the supple tool of power," and he allegedly told JOHN W. DAVIS that "if my country wants to go to hell, I am here to help it." For these expressions of resignation he was called "distinguished," "mature," and "wise," the "completely adult jurist." The constitutional jurisprudence of Holmes could be called a jurisprudence of detachment, indifference, or even despair; yet it was a jurisprudence in which contemporary commentators reveled.

Holmes's career hardly began with his appointment to the Court. He had previously written *The Common Law,* a comprehensive theoretical organization of private law subjects, taught briefly at Harvard Law School, and served for twenty years as a justice on the Massachusetts Supreme Judicial Court. Although he had not considered many constitutional cases as a state court judge, he had a distinctive philosophy of judging. There was little difficulty in the transition from the Massachusetts court to the Supreme Court; Holmes simply integrated a new set of cases with his preexistent philosophy. That philosophy's chief postulate was that judicial decisions were inescapably policy choices, and that a judge was better off if he did not make his choices appear too openly based on the "sovereign prerogative" of his power.

Arriving at that postulate had been an unexpected process for Holmes. He was convinced, at the time he wrote *The Common Law* (1881), that private law could be arranged in a "philosophically continuous series." His lectures on torts, criminal law, property, and contracts stressed the ability of those subjects to be ordered by general principles and the desirability of having judges ground their decisions in broad predictive rules rather than deferring to the more idiosyncratic and less predictable verdicts of juries. Holmes had accepted a judgeship in part because he believed that he could implement this conception of private law. Academic life was "half-life," he later said, and judging gave him an opportunity to "have a share in the practical struggle of life."

In practice, however, Holmes found that the law resisted being arranged in regular, predictable patterns. Too many factors operated to create dissonance: the need for court majorities to congeal on the scope and language of a decision; the insignificance of many cases, which were best decided by routine adherence to precedent; the very difficult and treacherous policy choices truly significant cases posed, fostering caution and compromise among judges. The result, for Holmes, was that legal DOCTRINE developed not as a general progression toward a philosophically continuous series but rather as an uneven clustering of decisions around opposing "poles" that represented alternative policy judgments. "Two widely divergent cases" suggested "a general distinction," which initially was "a clear one." But "as new cases cluster[ed] around the opposite poles, and beg[a]n to approach each other," the distinction became "more difficult to trace." Eventually an "arbitrary . . . mathematical line" was drawn, based on considerations of policy.

Thus judging was ultimately an exercise in making policy choices, but since the choices were often arbitrary and judges had "a general duty not to change but to work out the principles already sanctioned by the practice of the past," bold declarations of general principles were going to be few and far between. Indeed in many cases whose resolution he thought to turn on "questions of degree," or "nice considerations," or line drawing, Holmes attempted, as a state court judge, to avoid decision. He delegated "questions of degree" to juries where possible; he relied on precedents even where he felt that they had ceased to have a functional justification; he adhered to the findings of trial judges; he resorted to "technicalities" to "determine the precise place of division." And on those relatively few occasions when he was asked to consider the impact of a legislature's involvement, Holmes tended to defer to legislative solutions, especially in close cases. "Most differences," he said in one case, were "only one[s] of degree," and "difference of degree is one of the distinctions by which the right of the legislature to exercise the STATE POLICE POWER is determined." Deference to the legislature was another means of avoiding judicial policy choices.

Holmes thus brought a curious, if consistent, theory of judging with him to the Supreme Court. Although his original aim as a legal scholar had been the derivation of general guiding principles in all areas of law, as a judge he had concluded that principles were not derived in a logical and continuous but in a random and arbitrary fashion, and that in hard cases, where principles competed, policy considerations dictated the outcome. Judges should be sensitive to the fact that cases did involve policy choices, but they should exercise great caution in making them. Hard cases, turning on "questions of degree" or "nice considerations" should be delegated to other lawmaking bodies, such as the jury and the legislature, that were closer to the "instinctive preferences and inarticulate convictions" of the community. What started out as a theory of bold, activist judicial declarations of principle had ended as a theory of deference to lawmakers who were more "at liberty to decide with sole reference . . . to convictions of policy and right." The creative jurist of *The Common Law* had become the apostle of judicial self-restraint.

In his first month on the Supreme Court Holmes wrote to his longtime correspondent Sir Frederick Pollock that he was "absorbed" with the "variety and novelty of the questions." And indeed Holmes's docket was strikingly different from that he had encountered as a Massachusetts state judge: more federal issues, a greater diversity of issues, and far more cases involving the constitutionality of legislative acts. But the new sets of cases did not require Holmes to modify his theory of judging; they merely emphasized his inclination to defer hard policy choices to others. As a Massachusetts state judge Holmes had found only one act of the Massachusetts legislature constitutionally invalid; as a Supreme Court justice he was to continue that pattern. His first opinion, *Otis v. Parker* (1902), sustained a California statute prohibiting sales of stock shares on margin on the ground that although the statute undoubtedly restricted freedom of exchange, that "general proposition" did not "take us far." The question was one of degree: how far could the legislature restrict that freedom? Since the statute's ostensible purpose, to protect persons from being taken advantage of in stock transactions, was arguably rational, Holmes's role was to defer to the legislative judgments.

Otis v. Parker set a pattern for Holmes's decisions in cases testing the constitutionality of economic regulations. Rarely did he find that questions posed by statutes were not ones of "degree"; rarely did he fail to uphold the legislative judgment. He believed that the New York legislature could regulate the hours of bakers (LOCHNER V. NEW YORK, 1905) even though he thought that hours and wages laws merely "shift[ed] the burden to a different point of incidence." He supported PROHIBITION and antitrust legislation notwithstanding his beliefs that "legislation to make people better" was futile and that the SHERMAN ACT was "damned nonsense." His position, in

short, was that "when a State legislature has declared that in its opinion policy requires a certain measure, its actions should not be disturbed by the courts . . . unless they clearly see that there is no fair reason for the law."

Deference for Holmes did not mean absolute passivity. He thought Congress and the states had gone too far in convicting dissidents in a number of war-related speech cases, including ABRAMS V. UNITED STATES (1919) (the case in which he proposed the CLEAR AND PRESENT DANGER test), GITLOW V. NEW YORK (1924), and UNITED STATES V. SCHWIMMER (1928). He invalidated a Pennsylvania statute that regulated mining operations without adequate compensation in *Pennsylvania Coal Company v. Mahon* (1922). He did not think that Congress could constitutionally allow the postmaster general to deny "suspicious" persons access to the mails, and said so in two cases, *Milwaukee Socialist Democratic Publishing Co. v. Burleson* (1920) and *Leach v. Carlile Postmaster* (1921). And he struck down a Texas statute denying blacks eligibility to vote in primary elections in NIXON V. HERNDON (1922), declaring that "states may do a good deal of classifying that it is difficult to believe rational, but there are limits."

Holmes was called, especially in the 1920s, the "Great Dissenter," and some of his dissenting opinions were memorable for the pithiness of their language. In *Lochner v. New York* (1905), Holmes protested against the artificiality of the FREEDOM OF CONTRACT argument used by the majority by saying that "the FOURTEENTH AMENDMENT does not enact Mr. Herbert Spencer's *Social Statics.*" In *Abrams* he said that "the best test of truth is the power of the thought to get itself accepted in the competition of the market," and that "every year . . . we have to wager our salvation upon some prophecy based on imperfect knowledge." And in *Olmstead v. United States* (1928), he decried the use of WIRETAPPING by federal agents: "I think it a less evil that some criminals should escape than that the government should play an ignoble part."

Each of these dissents was subsequently adopted as a majority position by a later Court. Freedom of contract was repudiated as a constitutional doctrine in WEST COAST HOTEL V. PARRISH (1937); Holmes's theory of free speech was ratified by the Court in such decisions as HERNDON V. LOWRY (1937) and YATES V. UNITED STATES (1957); and KATZ V. UNITED STATES (1967) and BERGER V. NEW YORK (1967) overruled the majority decision in *Olmstead.* Despite the eventual triumph of Holmes's position in these cases and despite the rhetorical force of his dissents, "Great Dissenter" is a misnomer by any standard other than a literary one. Holmes did not write an exceptionally large number of dissents, given his long service on the Court, and his positions were not often vindicated.

Holmes's dissents also gave him the reputation among commentators as being a "liberal" justice. But for every Holmes decision protecting CIVIL LIBERTIES one could find a decision restricting them. The same Justice who declared in *Abrams v. United States* (1919) that "we should be eternally vigilant against attempts to check the expression of opinions" held for the Court in BUCK V. BELL (1927) that a state could sterilize mental defectives without their knowing consent. "It is better for all the world, if instead of waiting to execute degenerate offspring for crime, or to let them starve for their imbecility, society can prevent those who are manifestly unfit from continuing their kind," Holmes argued. "Three generations of imbeciles are enough."

Holmes supported the constitutionality of laws prohibiting child labor, defended the right of dissidents to speak, and resisted government efforts to wiretap bootleggers. At the same time he upheld the compulsory teaching of English in public schools, supported the rights of landowners in child trespasser cases, and helped develop a line of decisions giving virtually no constitutional protection to ALIENS. For a time critics ignored these latter cases and followed the *New York Times* in calling Holmes "the chief liberal of the supreme bench for twenty-nine years," but recent commentary has asserted that Holmes was "largely indifferent" to civil liberties.

Holmes's constitutional thought, then, resists ideological characterization and is notable principally for its limited interpretation of the power of JUDICIAL REVIEW. How thus does one explain Holmes's continued stature? In an age where JUDICIAL ACTIVISM, especially on behalf of minority rights, is a commonplace phenomenon, Holmes's interpretation of his office appears outmoded in its circumscription. In an age where the idea of rights against the state has gained in prominence, Holmes's decisions appear to tolerate altogether too much power in legislative majorities. Only in the speech cases does Holmes seem to recognize that the contribution of dissident minorities can prevent a society's attitudes from becoming provincial and stultifying. Elsewhere Holmes's jurisprudence stands for the proposition that the state, as agent of the majority, can do what it likes until some other majority seizes power. That hardly seems a posture inclined to elicit much contemporary applause.

Yet Holmes's reputation remains, on all the modern polls, among the highest of those Justices who have served on the Supreme Court. It is not likely to change for three reasons. First, in an era that was anxious to perpetuate the illusion that judicial decision making was somehow different from other kinds of official decision making, since judges merely "found" or "declared" law, Holmes demonstrated that judging was inescapably an exercise in policymaking. This insight was a breath of fresh air in a stale jurisprudential climate. Against the ponderous intonations of other judges that they were "making no laws, deciding no policy, [and] never entering into the domain of public action," Holmes offered the theory that they were doing all those things. American jurisprudence was never the same again.

Second, Holmes, as a sitting judge, followed through the implications of his insight. If judging was inevitably an exercise in policy choices, if all legal questions eventually became "questions of degree," then there was much to be said for judges' avoiding the arbitrary choice. Other institutions existed whose mandate for representing current community sentiment seemed clearer than the judiciary's; judging could be seen as an art of avoiding decision in cases whose resolution appeared to be the arbitrary drawing of a line. In a jurisprudential climate that was adjusting to the shock of realizing that judges were making law, Holmes's theory of avoidance seemed to make a great deal of sense. Federal judges were not popularly elected officials; if they made the process of lawmaking synonymous with their arbitrary intuitions, the notion of popularly elected government seemed threatened. The wisdom in Holmes's approach to judging seemed so apparent that it took the WARREN COURT to displace it.

These first two contributions of Holmes, however, can be seen as having a historical dimension. To be sure, seeing judges as policymakers was a significant insight, but it is now a commonplace; judicial deference was undoubtedly an influential theory, but it has now been substantially qualified. The enduring quality of Holmes appears to rest on his having a first-class mind and in his unique manner of expression: his style. No judge has been so quotable as Holmes; no judge has come closer to making opinion writing a form of literature. Paradoxically, Holmes's style, which is notable for its capacity to engage the reader's emotions in a manner that transcends time and place, can be seen as a style produced out of indifference. The approach of Holmes to his work as a judge was that of a person more interested in completing his assigned tasks than in anything else. Holmes would be assigned opinions at a Saturday conference and seek to complete them by the following Tuesday; his opinions are notable for their brevity and their assertiveness. The celebrated epigrams in Holmes's opinions were rarely essential to the case; they were efforts to increase the emotional content of opinions whose legal analysis was often cryptic.

Holmes's style of writing was of a piece with his general attitude toward judging. Since judging was essentially an effort in accommodating competing policies, the outcome of a given case was relatively insignificant. Just where the line was drawn or where a given case located itself in a "cluster" of related cases insignificant. One might as well, as a judge, announce one's decision as starkly and vividly as one could. A sense of the delicacy and ultimate insignificance of the process of deciding a case, then, fostered a vivid, emotion-laden, and declarative style.

Thus the legacy of Holmes's constitutional opinions is an unusual one. As contributions to the ordinary mine run of legal doctrine, they are largely insignificant. Their positions are often outmoded, their analyses attenuated, their guidelines for future cases inadequate. One feels, somehow, that Holmes has seen the clash of competing principles at stake in a constitutional law case, but has not probed very far. Once he discovered what was at issue, he either avoided decision or argued for one resolution in a blunt, assertive, and arbitrary manner. One cannot take a Holmes precedent and spin out the resolution of companion cases; one cannot go to Holmes to find the substantive bottomings of an area of law. Holmes's opinions are like a charismatic musical performance: one may be inspired in the viewing but one cannot do much with one's impressions later.

As literary expressions, however, Holmes's opinions probably surpass those of any other Justice. While it begs questions and assumes difficulties away to say that "a policeman may have a constitutional right to talk politics, but he has no constitutional right to be a policeman," the vivid contrast catches one's imagination. While "three generations of imbeciles are enough" was a misstatement of the facts in *Buck v. Bell* and represents an attitude toward mentally retarded persons one might find callous, it engages us, for better or worse. In phrases like these Holmes will continue to speak to subsequent generations; his constitutional opinions, and consequently his constitutional thought, will thus endure. It is ironic that Holmes bequeathed us those vivid phrases because he felt that a more painstaking, balanced approach

to judging was futile. He thought of judging, as he thought of life, as "a job," and he got on with it.

G. EDWARD WHITE

Bibliography

BURTON, DAVID 1980 *Oliver Wendell Holmes, Jr.* Boston: Twayne Publishers.

FRANKFURTER, FELIX 1938 *Mr. Justice Holmes and the Supreme Court.* Cambridge, Mass.: Harvard University Press.

HOWE, MARK DEWOLFE 1957 *Justice Oliver Wendell Holmes: The Shaping Years, 1841–1870.* Cambridge, Mass.: Harvard University Press.

——— 1963 *Justice Oliver Wendell Holmes: The Proving Years, 1870–1882.* Cambridge, Mass.: Harvard University Press.

KONEFSKY, SAMUEL J. 1956 *The Legacy of Holmes and Brandeis: A Study in the Influence of Ideas.* New York: Macmillan.

LERNER, MAX 1943 *The Mind and Faith of Justice Holmes.* Boston: Little, Brown.

ROGAT, YOSEL 1963 Mr. Justice Holmes: A Dissenting Opinion. *Stanford Law Review* 15:3–44, 254–308.

WHITE, G. EDWARD 1971 The Rise and Fall of Justice Holmes. *University of Chicago Law Review* 39:51–77.

——— 1982 The Integrity of Holmes' Jurisprudence. *Hofstra Law Review* 10:633–671.

HOLMES v. WALTON
(New Jersey, 1780)

Decided by the Supreme Court of New Jersey in 1780, this is the first alleged state precedent for JUDICIAL REVIEW. The case, which was unreported, is referred to in *State v. Parkhurst,* 4 Halsted 427, supposedly decided in 1802 but not reported until 1828, where the state court said that in *Holmes* a state act providing for trial by a six-man jury violated the state constitution. In fact, the act, which involved the seizure and forfeiture of goods traded with the enemy, provided for a TRIAL BY JURY. New Jersey employed six-man juries in cases of small amounts (under six pounds) from colonial times to 1844, twelve-man juries in all other cases. The property in *Holmes v. Walton* being valued at $27,000, Holmes had a right to a trial by a twelve-man jury. The trial judge having allowed him only a six-man jury, Holmes contended not that the seizure act was unconstitutional but that the trial judge denied him a twelve-man jury to which he was entitled under the seizure act as well as under the state constitution; the high court so held. The constitutionality of the seizure act was not at issue, and there was no opinion given in which the court discussed, even by OBITER DICTA, its power to void an act for UNCONSTITUTIONALITY. Soon after the decision of the case, which allowed Holmes a new trial by a jury of twelve members, disaffected citizens of the locality alleged in a petition to the state assembly that the high court of the state had held the seizure act unconstitutional. The legislature, however, supported the court by enacting in 1782 that in any suit exceeding six pounds trial by jury meant a jury of twelve. Somehow, a misleading view of the case originated in the 1780s and survived, making *Holmes v. Walton* a "precedent," however inauthentic, for judicial review.

LEONARD W. LEVY

HOME BUILDING & LOAN ASSOCIATION v. BLAISDELL
290 U.S. 398 (1934)

This was the most important CONTRACT CLAUSE case since CHARLES RIVER BRIDGE V. WARREN BRIDGE CO. (1837). The great Depression of the 1930s, by wiping out jobs and savings and savaging the economy, threatened homeowners, farmers, shopkeepers, and others with the loss of their property through foreclosures on mortgages. The states responded by enacting DEBTORS' RELIEF LEGISLATION that postponed the obligations of mortgagors to meet payments. Minnesota's statute authorized a state court, on application from a debtor, to exempt property from final foreclosure for no more than two years, during which time the creditor must be paid a reasonable rental value fixed by the court and the debtor might refinance the mortgage. The Supreme Court's precedents seemed to require a decision that the contract clause was violated by the statute, which operated retroactively on mortgages contracted prior to its enactment and delayed enforcement of the mortgagee's contractual rights.

By a 5–4 vote the Court sustained the statute in an opinion by Chief Justice CHARLES EVANS HUGHES. The prohibition of the contract clause, he declared, "is not an absolute one and is not to be read with literal exactness like a mathematical formula." In times of acute economic distress the states might employ their RESERVED POLICE POWER, "notwithstanding interference with contract," to prevent immediate enforcement of obligations by a temporary and conditional restraint, in order to safeguard the vital public interest in private ownership. As Justice

GEORGE SUTHERLAND, for the dissenters, trenchantly observed, the POLICE POWER, whether reserved or inalienable, had never previously justified impairing the OBLIGATION OF CONTRACT between private parties. Hughes, however, distinguished precedents such as BRONSON V. KINZIE (1843) by saying that they had not, as here, provided for securing the mortgagee the rental value of the property during the extended period. Although the statute affected contracts, it was addressed to a legitimate end of the police power and employed reasonable means to achieve it. The restraint and realism that characterized this opinion and that in NEBBIA V. NEW YORK (1934) of the same term did not dominate the Court's opinions during the next two critical terms, when it confronted New Deal legislation. After *Blaisdell*, however, the contract clause lay almost dormant until the late 1970s.

LEONARD W. LEVY

HOMESTEAD ACT
12 Stat. 392 (1862)

The Homestead Act provided for distribution of public land to settlers who would live on the land and improve it. As enacted in 1862, the act provided for allocation of a quarter section (160 acres) to a homesteader who lived on it for five years and paid a ten dollar fee. The act was sponsored by Speaker of the House Galusha A. Grow (Republican of Pennsylvania), and its passage culminated more than a decade's efforts.

The act bespoke a national commitment to the farmer-freeholder as the prototypical American citizen. The system it established was designed, among other things, to solve the problem of SLAVERY IN THE TERRITORIES by insuring a permanent antislavery majority there; and, for that reason, earlier proposals for a homestead bill were supported by the Liberty and Free Soil parties. The homestead program populated the Midwest and plains with hundreds of thousands of independent farmers, and allowed rapid conversion of wilderness TERRITORIES into STATES.

The act was repealed in 1910, a victim of fraud and inefficiency, as well as of an antipathy during the Progressive era toward distribution of public land. In a little less than half a century, over 100 million acres had been distributed under the act.

DENNIS J. MAHONEY

HOMOSEXUALS' RIGHTS

See: Sexual Preference and the Constitution

HOOKER, THOMAS
(1586–1647)

To escape persecution for his Puritan beliefs, Thomas Hooker fled England in 1633 and settled in Newton, Massachusetts, as its Congregational minister. In 1636 he led most of his congregation to a new settlement at Hartford, thus becoming a founder of Connecticut.

A leader among Puritan clergy, Hooker wrote a major defense of New England Congregationalism and extended his theological convictions into politics. Adopting his flexible stand on formal church affiliation, Connecticut refused to limit the franchise to church members.

In 1639 Hooker's preference for explicit covenants probably prompted Connecticut's leaders to organize the colony's government by drawing up a SOCIAL COMPACT, regarded by some historians as the first written American CONSTITUTION, known as the FUNDAMENTAL ORDERS. This document mirrored Hooker's beliefs that civil government should be a covenant between citizens for the promotion of peace and unity; that political authority should reflect the free choice of the people; that rulers were responsible to those they ruled; that the people, as the source of government's existence, had the right not only to choose magistrates but specifically to limit their powers; and that magistrates should consult with the people on issues involving the common good and heed popular judgment in such matters.

THOMAS CURRY

Bibliography

MILLER, PERRY 1956 *Errand into the Wilderness.* Pages 16–47. Cambridge, Mass.: Harvard University Press.

HOOVER, HERBERT C.
(1874–1964)

Born in Iowa and trained as a mining engineer at Stanford University, Herbert Clark Hoover initially became involved in politics as chairman of the Commission for Relief in Belgium and of the United States Food Administration Board during World War I. After the war, President WOODROW WILSON made Hoover director of European economic relief, and in 1921 President WARREN G. HARDING appointed him secretary of commerce.

Hoover was elected President of the United States on the Republican ticket in 1928. Seven months after his inauguration, the stock market collapsed as the depression that had gripped Europe since the end of the war reached America as well. In the face of the economic crisis Hoover clung to his conservative constitutional principles. He advocated private, voluntary action to spur recovery and expanded relief programs at the state level. He resisted federal government intervention until the election year 1932, when he proposed the Reconstruction Finance Corporation.

Hoover's nominations to the Supreme Court were a mixed lot. He appointed former Justice CHARLES EVANS HUGHES to be Chief Justice in 1930. His nomination of conservative Judge John J. Parker of North Carolina to be an Associate Justice was narrowly rejected by the Senate, but two other appointments were confirmed: moderate OWEN J. ROBERTS of Pennsylvania in 1930 and liberal BENJAMIN N. CARDOZO of New York in 1932.

After FRANKLIN D. ROOSEVELT defeated him in the 1932 election, Hoover retired from public office, but remained influential within the Republican party. He was recalled to public service after World War II to direct food relief programs in Europe, and he served as chairman of two Commissions on the Organization of the Executive Branch. The Hoover Commission Reports of 1949 and 1955 led to greater efficiency in the executive branch, mostly through regrouping of functions and agencies.

DENNIS J. MAHONEY

Bibliography

NASH, GEORGE H. 1983 *The Life of Herbert Hoover.* New York: Norton.

HOOVER, J. EDGAR
(1895–1972)

From his graduation from George Washington University Law School in 1917 until his death in 1972, John Edgar Hoover was continuously employed by the United States Department of Justice. He started as a file reviewer, but in 1919 Hoover became special assistant to Attorney General A. MITCHELL PALMER, with oversight responsibility for the DEPORTATION cases arising out of the PALMER RAIDS. In 1921 Hoover was assigned to the department's Bureau of Investigations, and in 1924 he became its director.

Over the next decade, Hoover transformed his small bureau into a national police agency. As federal criminal law expanded, the bureau expanded with it, acquiring a reputation for professionalism, competence, and efficiency. By the time it was renamed the Federal Bureau of Investigation in 1935, the bureau had established a national fingerprint file, a crime laboratory, and a training academy. The FBI's dual mandate was to investigate violations of federal law and to serve as a domestic, civilian counterintelligence agency. The bureau's success in tracking down bootleggers, gangsters, kidnappers, and spies became legendary.

The FBI was largely Hoover's personal creation, and he ran it autocratically. Although formally supervised by the ATTORNEY GENERAL, Hoover operated with a great deal of independence, gained by tenure, public success, and, reputedly, maintenance of secret dossiers concerning his political superiors. Hoover used the FBI to conduct personal feuds, like that with MARTIN LUTHER KING, JR., and to publicize his own brand of anticommunism. In the end, his apparent indifference to CIVIL LIBERTIES compromised the very professionalism he had worked to instill in the FBI.

DENNIS J. MAHONEY

Bibliography

DE TOLEDANO, RALPH 1973 *J. Edgar Hoover: The Man in His Times.* New Rochelle, N.Y.: Arlington House.

H. P. HOOD & SONS v. UNITED STATES

See: *Wrightwood Dairy, United States v.*

HOSTILE AUDIENCE

Nothing is more antagonistic to the FREEDOM OF SPEECH than a mob shouting a speaker into silence. For state officials to suppress speech merely because the audience is offended by the speaker's message is a violation of the FIRST AMENDMENT. Although some lower courts have experimented with the notion of a heckler's First Amendment right, there is no place in our constitutional order for what HARRY KALVEN called the "heckler veto." The duty of the police, when the audience is hostile, is to protect the speaker so long as that is reasonably possible. Similarly, the potential hostility of an audience—even its potential violence—will not justify denying a license to meet or parade in a PUBLIC FORUM.

When police protection is inadequate, however, and audience hostility poses an immediate threat of violence, the police may constitutionally order a speaker to stop, even though the speech does not amount to INCITEMENT TO UNLAWFUL CONDUCT, and is otherwise protected by the First Amendment. The Supreme Court so held in FEINER V. NEW YORK (1951), a case involving no more than "some pushing, shoving and milling around" in an audience hostile to a speaker in a park. The principle retains vitality, although *Feiner* itself, on its facts, seems an insecure precedent.

The constitutionality of police action requiring someone to stop addressing a hostile audience depends on one form of the CLEAR AND PRESENT DANGER test: the police may not stop the speaker unless the threat of violence is immediate and police resources are inadequate to contain the threatened harm. Thus, if the speaker refuses to stop and is charged with BREACH OF THE PEACE, the court must look beyond the arresting officers' good faith—a point emphasized by the Supreme Court in *Feiner*—to the objective likelihood of violence. Appellate courts, too, in reviewing convictions in such cases, must closely examine lower courts' findings of fact. An important difference between *Feiner* and *Edwards v. South Carolina* (1963), where the Court reversed breach of peace convictions of civil rights demonstrators facing a hostile audience, lay in the *Edwards* Court's willingness to scrutinize the record and reject the state courts' findings of danger.

KENNETH L. KARST

Bibliography

KALVEN, HARRY, JR. 1965 *The Negro and the First Amendment.* Pages 139–145. Columbus: Ohio State University Press.

HOT PURSUIT

See: Exigent Circumstances Search

HOUSE COMMITTEE ON UN-AMERICAN ACTIVITIES

In 1938, because of a growing fear of Nazi and communist activity in the United States, conservative congressmen secured passage of a House Resolution creating a Special Committee on Un-American Activities (HUAC). Under publicity-conscious Texas congressman MARTIN DIES, the Committee set out to expose left-wing groups and individuals whom it considered security risks. After five renewals, by overwhelming votes, the group was made into an unprecedented standing committee of the House in 1945. From then until the mid-1950s, the Committee became a sounding board for ex-radicals, publicity seekers, and critics of the New Deal and the Truman administration. It identified the following tasks for itself: to expose and ferret out communists and their sympathizers in the federal government; to show how communists had won control over vital trade unions; and to investigate communist influences in the press, religious and educational organizations, and the movie industry. The sensational Alger Hiss-Whittaker Chambers hearings, in connection with turning over security information, and the resultant perjury conviction of Hiss, a former New Deal official, added to the Committee's prestige. By 1948, the Committee sponsored legislation against the Communist party, pushing the MUNDT-NIXON BILL.

The activities of HUAC, however, raised important constitutional questions. The Committee's constant probing into political behavior and belief led critics to charge that such forced exposure abridged FREEDOM OF SPEECH and association, and punished citizens for their opinions. Also questioned was the legitimacy of its "exposure for its own sake" approach, when action did not seem to relate to legitimate legislative purpose, and when legislative "trials" violated many aspects of DUE PROCESS including the right to be tried in a court under the protection of constitutional guarantees.

The Supreme Court ultimately dealt with both questions, with contradictory and changing results. In three cases (*Emspack v. United States*, 1955; *Quinn v. United States*, 1955; and WATKINS V. UNITED STATES, 1957) the Court narrowly interpreted the statutory authority for punishing recalcitrant witnesses, and questioned forced exposure of views and activities in light of the FIRST AMENDMENT. Facing sharp criticism, the Court retreated in the cases of BARENBLATT V. UNITED STATES (1958), *Wilkinson v. United States* (1961), and *Braden v. United States* (1961), only to move back again to a more critical position as the 1960s progressed—from 1961 to 1966 reversing almost every contempt conviction which came to it from the Committee. By mid-1966, conservative legislators were condemning the "unseemly spectacles" HUAC chronically elicited. Thus, in 1969, it was rechristened the Internal Security Committee, and although its procedures were modified somewhat in this new form, the committee was eventually abolished by the House in 1975.

                                        PAUL L. MURPHY

Bibliography

GOODMAN, WALTER 1968 *The Committee: The Extraordinary Career of the House Committee on Un-American Activities.* New York: Farrar, Straus.

HOUSTON, CHARLES H.
(1895–1950)

Charles H. Houston was the foremost black CIVIL RIGHTS lawyer before THURGOOD MARSHALL. He was a member of the faculty of Howard Law School and from 1932 to 1935 served as dean. He obtained accreditation and respect for the institution, which trained many civil rights lawyers. From 1935 to 1940 Houston was special counsel for the National Association for the Advancement of Colored People (NAACP). Although he returned to private practice thereafter, he remained active with the NAACP and other civil rights organizations. Marshall later called him "The First Mr. Civil Rights." Houston was of counsel in NIXON V. CONDON (1932), arguing against the white primary, and he assisted in the defense of the Scottsboro Boys. He argued and won MISSOURI EX REL. GAINES V. CANADA (1938), which forced the state to open its law school to black students. He also won from the Supreme Court decisions prohibiting discrimination against black railroad employees. Perhaps his most difficult and greatest victory came in HURD V. HODGE (1948), in which the Court accepted his arguments that the CIVIL RIGHTS ACT OF 1866 outlawed the judicial enforcement of RESTRICTIVE COVENANTS by the courts of the DISTRICT OF COLUMBIA, and that even in the absence of the congressional act, the enforcement of such covenants would violate the public policy of the United States.

                                        LEONARD W. LEVY

Bibliography

MCNEIL, GENNA RAE 1982 *Charles Hamilton Houston and the Struggle for Civil Rights.* Philadelphia: University of Pennsylvania Press.

HOUSTON, EAST & WEST TEXAS RAILWAY CO. v. UNITED STATES (SHREVEPORT RATE CASE)
234 U.S. 342 (1914)

To relieve a competitive inequality in rail rates, the Interstate Commerce Commission (ICC) ordered the Texas Railroad Commission to raise intrastate rates to equal interstate rates. Shreveport, Louisiana, to east

Texas rates, set by the ICC, were higher than west Texas to east Texas rates, fixed by the states, thereby placing INTERSTATE COMMERCE at a competitive disadvantage. With only Justices HORACE LURTON and MAHLON PITNEY dissenting, Justice CHARLES EVANS HUGHES relied on the INTERSTATE COMMERCE ACT and the COMMERCE CLAUSE in upholding the ICC order. Hughes distinguished the MINNESOTA RATE CASES (1913) as neither involving an attempt at federal regulation nor adversely affecting or burdening interstate commerce. Emphasizing Congress's "complete and paramount" power over interstate commerce, he announced the SHREVEPORT DOCTRINE: "Wherever the interstate and intrastate transactions of carriers are so related that the government of the one involves the control of the other, it is Congress and not the state, that is entitled to prescribe the final and dominant rule."

DAVID GORDON

HOWARD, JACOB M.
(1805–1871)

Jacob Merritt Howard was an abolitionist, a champion of CIVIL RIGHTS, and a leading northern politician whose constitutional legacy derived from his advocacy of Radical Republicanism. Born and educated in New England, Howard moved to Detroit where, after admission to the bar, he began his political career as a Whig. In 1854 he helped found the Republican party and framed its resolutions.

In 1862 he became a United States senator, and for a decade he remained in the vanguard of the Radical Republican wing of his party. He advocated black VOTING RIGHTS, served influentially during the Civil War on both the Senate Judiciary Committee and the Committee on Military Affairs, and vigorously supported the FREEDMEN'S BUREAU ACT and the CIVIL RIGHTS ACT OF 1866. Howard was a coauthor of the THIRTEENTH AMENDMENT and, as a ranking Senate Republican on the powerful JOINT COMMITTEE ON RECONSTRUCTION, chaperoned the approval by the Senate of the FOURTEENTH AMENDMENT.

LEONARD W. LEVY

HOWE, MARK DEWOLFE
(1902–1966)

Mark DeWolfe Howe began his legal career as a clerk to Justice OLIVER WENDELL HOLMES, and throughout his life Holmes was the focus of much of Howe's most valuable scholarly work. While professor of law at Har-

vard Law School, Howe prepared definitive editions of Holmes's correspondence with Sir Frederick Pollock (1941) and HAROLD J. LASKI (1953), his Civil War diary and letters (1947), his *Speeches* (1962), and *The Common Law* (1963). Although Howe never lived to complete his biography of Holmes, the two volumes he did publish (1957, 1963) are unparalleled for their illumination of Holmes's intellectual life up to his appointment to the Massachusetts Supreme Judicial Court. A pioneer in the field of American legal history, Howe specialized in the history of freedom of religion. In his last published book, *The Garden and the Wilderness* (1965), Howe criticized the Supreme Court's reading of the history of religion in America, pointing out that the "wall of separation" between church and state was based as much on evangelical theory as Jeffersonian rationalism; Howe suggested that the Constitution recognized a *de facto* ESTABLISHMENT OF RELIGION in American society. An activist as well as a scholar, Howe worked tirelessly for the NAACP LEGAL DEFENSE & EDUCATIONAL FUND, both as a teacher and as a litigator.

RICHARD B. BERNSTEIN

HUDGENS v. NATIONAL LABOR RELATIONS BOARD
424 U.S. 507 (1976)

In terminating its experiment with extending MARSH V. ALABAMA (1946) to privately owned SHOPPING CENTERS, the Supreme Court, 7–2, announced in *Hudgens* that the refusal of owners to permit union picketing did not constitute STATE ACTION and thus did not violate the FIRST AMENDMENT, even though the private property was "open to the public." That vast shopping plazas, which are central features of American culture, are not required by the First Amendment to grant FREEDOM OF SPEECH is a highly significant feature of contemporary constitutional law.

MARTIN SHAPIRO

HUDSON v. PALMER

See: Prisoners' Rights

HUDSON AND GOODWIN, UNITED STATES v.

See: Federal Common Law

HUGHES, CHARLES EVANS
(1862–1948)

The only child of a Baptist minister and a strong-willed, doting mother who hoped their son would become a man of the cloth, Charles Evans Hughes compiled a record of public service unparalleled for its diversity and achievement by any other member of the Supreme Court with the exception of WILLIAM HOWARD TAFT. In addition to pursuing a lucrative career at the bar, Hughes taught law at Cornell, served as a two-term governor of New York, was secretary of state under two Presidents during the 1920s, and served as associate Justice and Chief Justice of the United States. By the narrowest of margins, he lost the electoral votes of California in 1916 and thus the presidency to the incumbent, WOODROW WILSON. Hughes was a man of imposing countenance and intellectual abilities, who left an indelible mark upon the nation's politics, diplomacy, and law.

First appointed to the Court as associate justice by President William Howard Taft, Hughes brought to the bench the social and intellectual outlook of many American progressives, those morally earnest men and women from the urban middle class who wished to purge the nation's politics of corruption, infuse the business world with greater efficiency and concern for the public welfare, and minister to the needs of the poor in the great cities. In an earlier era, such people had found an outlet for their moral energies in religion. By the turn of the twentieth century, they practiced a social gospel and undertook a "search for order" through secular careers in law, medicine, public administration, journalism, engineering, and social welfare.

"We are under a Constitution," Governor Hughes remarked shortly before his appointment to the bench, "but the Constitution is what the judges say it is, and the judiciary is the safeguard of our liberty and of our property under the Constitution." This statement reflected the ambivalence of many progressives about the nation's fundamental charter of government and its judicial expositers on the Supreme Court. On the one hand, Hughes and other progressives clearly recognized that constitutional decision-making was a subjective process, strongly influenced by the temper of the times and by the social biases and objectives of individual jurists. The Constitution, they believed, was flexible enough to accommodate the growing demands for reform that sprang from the manifold desires of businessmen, consumers, farmers, and industrial workers who wished to use government to promote economic security in an increasingly complex, interdependent capitalist economy. Like other progressives, Hughes saw government, both state and federal, as a positive instrument of human welfare that could discipline unruly economic forces, promote moral uplift, and guarantee domestic social peace by protecting the citizen from the worst vicissitudes of the marketplace.

At the same time, Hughes and other middle-class reformers had a morbid fear of socialism and resisted endowing government with excessive power over persons and property. They wanted social change under the rule of law, in conformity with American traditions of individualism, and directed by a disinterested elite of lawyers, administrators, and other experts of enlightened social progress.

By the time Hughes took his seat on the nation's highest court, the Justices had grappled inconclusively for almost five decades with the question of the reach of the constitutional power of the states and the national government to regulate economic activity. One group of Justices, influenced by the Jacksonian legacy of entrepreneurial individualism, equality, and STATES' RIGHTS, had combined an expansive reading of the FOURTEENTH AMENDMENT's DUE PROCESS clause and a narrow interpretation of the COMMERCE CLAUSE and the TAXING AND SPENDING POWER in order to restrict both state and federal regulation of private economic decision making. Another group of Justices, heirs to the radical Republican tradition of moral reform and positive government, had been more receptive to governmental efforts at ECONOMIC REGULATION and redistribution.

Hughes placed his considerable intellectual resources on the side of the economic nationalists and those who refused to read the due process clause as a mechanical limitation upon state regulation of economic affairs. In *Miller v. Wilson* (1915), for example, he wrote for a unanimous bench to sustain California's eight-hour law for women in selected occupations against a challenge that the law violated FREEDOM OF CONTRACT. The liberty protected by the due process clause, he noted, included freedom from arbitrary restraint, but not immunity from regulations designed to protect public health, morals, and welfare.

More significant, he joined the dissenters in COPPAGE V. KANSAS (1915), where six members of the Court, speaking through Justice MAHLON PITNEY, invalidated a Kansas law prohibiting YELLOW DOG CONTRACTS on the ground that the regulation deprived employers of their contractual liberty. Hughes endorsed the dissent by Justice WILLIAM R. DAY which argued that the law attempted only to protect the right of individual workers to join labor unions if they so pleased and represented a legitimate exercise of the STATE POLICE POWER, "not to require one man to employ another against his will, but to put limitations upon the sacrifice of rights which one may exact from another as a condition of employment."

Hughes's views on the federal commerce power were equally generous during this period. He wrote the two leading opinions of the era supporting the authority of Congress and the Interstate Commerce Commission (ICC) to regulate both interstate railroad rates and purely intrastate rates that undermined the efficiency of the nation's transportation network. In the MINNESOTA RATES CASES (1913) he upheld the particular exercise of rate-making by the state, although he and the majority affirmed that the power of Congress "could not be denied or thwarted by the commingling of interstate and intrastate operations" of the railroad. A year later, in the landmark Shreveport Case, HOUSTON, EAST & WEST TEXAS RAILWAY COMPANY V. UNITED STATES (1914), he spoke for all but two Justices in sustaining an order of the ICC that effectively required an increase in intrastate rates in order to bring them into line with those fixed by the commission for interstate carriers over the same territory. The power of Congress to regulate interstate commerce, he wrote, was "complete and paramount"; Congress could "prevent the common instrumentality of interstate and intrastate commercial intercourse from being used in their intrastate operations to the injury of interstate commerce."

Most progressives displayed little sympathy for the plight of either American blacks or the foreign immigrants who entered the country in large numbers during the decades before World War I. Hughes was a striking exception to the usual pattern of collaboration with the forces of racial and ethnic intolerance. He began to speak out in these years against various forms of oppression and bigotry and to lay the foundation for many of his subsequent opinions on CIVIL RIGHTS during the 1930s.

In *McCabe v. Atchison, Topeka & Santa Fe Railroad* (1914), Hughes led a five-Justice majority in striking down a state law that authorized intrastate railroads to provide dining and sleeping cars only for members of the white race. The state and the carriers argued that the statute was reasonable in light of the limited economic demand by black passengers for such services, a point of view that also appealed to Justice OLIVER WENDELL HOLMES. Hughes, however, flatly condemned the law as a violation of the Fourteenth Amendment's EQUAL PROTECTION clause. With support from all but one of the Justices, he also over-

turned, in *Truax v. Raich* (1915), an Arizona law that had limited the employment of ALIENS in the state's principal industries to twenty percent of all workers in firms with five or more employees. Discrimination against such inhabitants "because of their race or nationality," he declared, "clearly falls under the condemnation of the FUNDAMENTAL LAW."

His most impressive effort in this regard came in the famous debt peonage case, BAILEY V. ALABAMA (1911), where he both invalidated the state's draconian statute and gained a notable rhetorical victory over Justice Holmes. Under the Alabama law, as under similar ones in force throughout the South, a person's failure to perform a labor contract without just cause and without paying back money advanced was prima facie evidence of intent to defraud, punishable by fine or imprisonment. The accused, furthermore, could not rebut the presumption with testimony "as to his uncommunicated motives, purposes, or intention." Hughes condemned this "convenient instrument for . . . coercion" as a violation of both the THIRTEENTH AMENDMENT and the Anti-Peonage Act of 1867.

With a few exceptions, the progressives also displayed more concern for the suppression of crime than for the rights of the accused. The due process clause had seldom been invoked successfully against questionable methods of law enforcement and CRIMINAL PROCEDURE on the state level. In this field, too, Hughes attempted to break new ground that anticipated the jurisprudence of a later era. One case in point is FRANK V. MANGUM (1915), arising out of the notorious Leo Frank trial in Georgia. A young Jewish defendant had been convicted of murder and sentenced to death with a mob shouting outside the courtroom, "Hang the Jew, or we'll hang you." Frank and his lawyers had not been present during the reading of the verdict, because the trial judge could not guarantee their safety in the event of an acquittal.

Despite this evidence of intimidation, the Georgia Supreme Court upheld the conviction and sentence; a federal district judge refused Frank's petition for HABEAS CORPUS, which raised a host of due process challenges; and a majority of the Supreme Court affirmed that decision. Hughes joined a powerful dissent written by Holmes, which chastised the majority for its reasoning and called upon the Justices to "declare lynch law as little valid when practiced by a regularly drawn jury as when administered by one elected by a mob intent on death."

Hughes's initial appointment to the Court, following in the wake of his progressive achievements as governor of New York, had been received with almost unanimous acclaim. However, his nomination as Chief

Justice by President HERBERT HOOVER in 1930 sparked furious debate. Twenty-six senators, led by the redoubtable GEORGE NORRIS of Nebraska, voted against his confirmation. Many of them believed, as Norris did, that the former Justice's profitable law practice during the 1920s had turned him into a pliant tool of the "powerful combinations in the political and financial world" and therefore rendered him incapable of fairly deciding the "contests between organized wealth and the ordinary citizen." Events proved Norris to be half right.

Beginning in 1930, Hughes was called upon to pilot the Court through the years of social and economic crisis spawned by the financial collapse of 1929 and the Great Depression. These were the most turbulent years in the Court's history since the decade before the Civil War and the economic crisis of the 1890s—two earlier occasions when the Justices had attempted to hold back the tide of popular revolt against the status quo.

Under Hughes's leadership, the Court majority became aggressively liberal with respect to the protection of CIVIL LIBERTIES and civil rights, often building upon the doctrinal structure erected by the Chief Justice himself during the Progressive Era. In STROMBERG V. CALIFORNIA (1931), NEAR V. MINNESOTA (1931), and DeJONGE V. OREGON (1937) Hughes's distinguished opinions significantly enlarged the scope of FIRST AMENDMENT rights protected against state abridgment via the due process clause. He personally drove the first judicial nail into the coffin of the SEPARATE BUT EQUAL doctrine with his opinion in MISSOURI EX REL. GAINES V. CANADA (1938), holding that a state university's refusal to admit a qualified black resident to its law school constituted a denial of equal protection. He endorsed Justice GEORGE H. SUTHERLAND's opinion in the initial Scottsboro case, POWELL V. ALABAMA (1932), and wrote the second one, NORRIS V. ALABAMA (1935), himself. Both opinions tightened the Supreme Court's supervision over state criminal trials involving the poor and members of racial minorities.

Hughes contributed to Justice HARLAN F. STONE's famous fourth footnote in UNITED STATES V. CAROLENE PRODUCTS COMPANY (1938), where the latter suggested that the Court had a special role to play in defending PREFERRED FREEDOMS, including FREEDOM OF SPEECH, FREEDOM OF THE PRESS, and VOTING RIGHTS, from legislative abridgment and also to protect DISCRETE AND INSULAR MINORITIES from the tyranny of the majority. Under Hughes, finally, the Court broadened the reach of habeas corpus to attack consti-

tutionally defective state criminal convictions, and greatly expanded the IN FORMA PAUPERIS docket which permitted INDIGENT defendants to seek Supreme Court review of their convictions. By any yardstick, Hughes as Chief Justice compiled a civil liberties record of impressive range and impact.

The Hughes who regularly cast his vote on the libertarian side in cases touching civil liberties and civil rights during the 1930s also voted in 1935 and 1936 against many of the social and economic reforms sponsored by the FRANKLIN D. ROOSEVELT administration and state governments in their efforts to cope with the economic crisis of the decade. It is this side of his performance as Chief Justice that has fueled the most controversy—and puzzlement, too, considering Hughes's toleration for many of the early anti-Depression nostrums of both the New Deal and the individual states. It was Hughes, after all, who wrote for the five-Justice majority in HOME BUILDING & LOAN ASSOCIATION V. BLAISDELL (1934), upholding a far-reaching mortgage moratorium law that many observers found to be in flat violation of the Constitution's CONTRACT CLAUSE. He also wrote for the narrow majority in the GOLD CLAUSE CASES, where the Justices sustained the New Deal's monetary experiments over the protests of Justice JAMES C. MCREYNOLDS who declared, "This is Nero at his worst. The Constitution is gone."

The Chief Justice sided as well with Justice OWEN J. ROBERTS's views in NEBBIA V. NEW YORK (1934), which expanded the sphere of business activities subject to state regulation, and he spoke out forcefully against the crabbed interpretation of the federal commerce power in RAILROAD RETIREMENT BOARD V. ALTON RAILROAD COMPANY (1935), where five Justices voted to strike down a mandatory pension plan for railway workers. In 1935 and 1936, however, Hughes began to vote more consistently with Roberts and the Court's four conservatives—Justices McReynolds, PIERCE BUTLER, WILLIS VAN DEVANTER, and Sutherland—against the New Deal and various state reform programs.

Six months later, in the aftermath of Roosevelt's crushing reelection victory and his threats to reorganize the federal judiciary, the Court reversed gears once again when a bare majority of the Justices—including Hughes and Roberts—sustained a minimum wage law in WEST COAST HOTEL COMPANY V. PARRISH (1937) and the New Deal's major labor law in the WAGNER ACT CASES (1937). Hughes wrote both landmark opinions, the first laying to rest "liberty of contract" and the second affording Congress ample latitude to regulate labor–management conflicts under the commerce clause.

Various explanations have been advanced since the 1930s to explain both Hughes's alignment with the conservatives and his eventual return to the progressive fold in 1937. Hughes justified his behavior during the first period by casting blame upon the New Deal's lawyers, who, he complained, wrote vague, unconstitutional statutes. This thesis has some credibility with respect to the controversial NATIONAL INDUSTRIAL RECOVERY ACT which the Court invalidated in SCHECHTER POULTRY CORPORATION V. UNITED STATES (1935), but none at all when one reflects upon the care with which very good lawyers wrote both the AGRICULTURAL ADJUSTMENT ACT and the Guffey Bituminous Coal Act. (See CARTER V. CARTER COAL CO.) Others have suggested that Hughes voted with Roberts and the four conservatives on several occasions in 1935 and 1936 in order to avoid narrow 5–4 decisions that might damage the Court's reputation for constitutional sagacity. But this hypothesis does not explain why he found 5–4 decisions in favor of the New Deal any less injurious to the Court in 1937.

A more plausible explanation may be that Hughes regarded many New Deal regulatory programs and some on the state level as dangerously radical, both to the inherited constitutional system and to the social order, because of their redistributive implications. Other old progressives also fought the New Deal for similar reasons after 1935. Those who resisted the leftward drift of the administration in 1935 hoped that the electorate would repudiate Roosevelt's course of action in the 1936 referendum, but Roosevelt's landslide victory left them with few alternatives but capitulation to the popular will. In bowing to the election returns, Hughes became the leader of the Court's progressive wing once again, salvaged the basic power of JUDICIAL REVIEW, and at the same time administered a fatal blow to the President's misconceived reorganization bill. It was a stunning triumph for the Chief Justice.

Hughes accomplished this feat without serious damage to his intellectual integrity. The Justice who wrote *Miller v. Wilson* in 1915 did not find it too difficult to sustain minimum wage legislation two decades later. And the ideas expressed in *NLRB v. Jones & Laughlin* (1937) had already been given initial shape in the *Minnesota Rates Cases* and the Shreveport Case. For a Justice as brilliant and as crafty as Hughes, leading the constitutional revolution in 1937

was as easy as resisting it a year before, but the latter course assured his place in history.

MICHAEL E. PARRISH

(SEE ALSO: *Constitutional History, 1933–1945.*)

Bibliography
FREUND, PAUL A. 1967 Charles Evan Hughes. *Harvard Law Review* 81:34–48.
HENDEL, SAMUEL 1951 *Charles Evans Hughes and the Supreme Court.* New York: Russell & Russell.
PUSEY, MERLO J. 1951 *Charles Evans Hughes.* 2 Vols. New York: Harper & Row.

HUGHES COURT
(1930–1941)

The years in which Chief Justice CHARLES EVANS HUGHES presided over the Supreme Court of the United States, 1930–1941, are notable for the skillful accomplishment of a revolution in CONSTITUTIONAL INTERPRETATION. The use of the DUE PROCESS clauses of the Fifth Amendment and FOURTEENTH AMENDMENT to protect FREEDOM OF CONTRACT and economic Darwinism against government regulation yielded to legislative supremacy and judicial self-restraint. The prevailing limits on the regulatory powers of Congress under the COMMERCE CLAUSE were swept away. The Hamiltonian view that Congress has power to spend money for any purpose associated with the general welfare was solidified by judicial approval. The Court acquiesced in the delegation of vast law-making power to administrative agencies. The groundwork was laid for expanding the constitutionally guaranteed FREEDOM OF SPEECH and freedom of the press.

Change was all about the Hughes Court. Of the eight Justices who flanked Hughes when he took his seat as Chief Justice, seven left the Court before he retired. The Court moved across the street from the cozy, old Senate Chamber in the Capitol to the gleaming white marble palace and ornate conference room used today. Profounder changes were occurring in the social, economic, and political conditions that give rise to constitutional litigation, that shape the briefs and arguments of counsel, and that the Court's decisions must address.

The preceding era had been marked by the rise to dominance of large-scale business and financial enterprise. Vast aggregations of men and women and material wealth were needed to develop America's resources, to harness the power unleashed by science and technology, and to capture the efficiencies of mass production for mass markets. Unlocking America's agricultural and industrial wealth made for higher standards of living and an extremely mobile society. With the gains had come corruption, hardships, injustices, and pressure for political action; but in the general prosperity of the 1920s the costs were too often ignored.

Yet the farmers were left behind and too much of the wealth was committed to speculation in corporate securities. The bursting of the latter bubble in November 1929 heralded an economic depression of unprecedented length and depth. Ninety percent of the market value of stock in industrial corporations was wiped out in three years. Twenty-five percent of the land in Mississippi was auctioned off in mortgage foreclosure sales. Factory payrolls were cut in half. One out of every four persons seeking employment was without work. The Depression destroyed people's faith in the industrial magnates and financiers, even in the ethic of individual self-reliance. The stability of American institutions seemed uncertain.

The election of FRANKLIN D. ROOSEVELT as President of the United States brought a new, more active political philosophy to government. Government, Roosevelt asserted, should seek to prevent the abuse of superior economic power, to temper the conflicts, and to work out the accommodations and adjustments that a simpler age had supposed could safely be left to individual ability and the free play of economic forces. Government should also meet the basic need for jobs and, in the case of those who could not work, for food, clothing, and shelter. For the most part these responsibilities must be met by the federal government, which alone was capable of dealing with an economy national in scope and complexity.

Roosevelt's "New Deal" not only provided money and jobs for the worst victims of the Depression; it enacted the legislation and established the government agencies upon which national economic policies would rest for at least half a century: the AGRICULTURAL ADJUSTMENT ACTS, the WAGNER NATIONAL LABOR RELATIONS ACT, the FAIR LABOR STANDARDS ACT, THE SOCIAL SECURITY ACT, and the SECURITIES AND EXCHANGE ACT.

JUDICIAL REVIEW permits those who lose battles in the executive and legislative branches to carry the war to the courts. Earlier in the century many courts, including the Supreme Court, had clung to the vision of small government, economic laissez-faire, and unbounded opportunity for self-reliant individuals.

Judges had thus struck down as violations of the due process clauses of the Fifth and Fourteenth Amendments many measures now generally accepted as basic to a modern industrial and urban society: MAXIMUM HOURS AND MINIMUM WAGE LAWS, laws forbidding industrial homework, and laws protecting the organization of labor unions. The critical question for the Supreme Court in the Hughes era would be whether the Court would persevere or change the course of American constitutional law.

The response of Justices WILLIS VAN DEVANTER, JAMES C. MCREYNOLDS, GEORGE SUTHERLAND, and PIERCE BUTLER was predictable: they would vote to preserve the old regime of limited federal government and economic laissez-faire. Three Justices—LOUIS D. BRANDEIS, HARLAN F. STONE, and BENJAMIN N. CARDOZO—could be expected to eschew the use of judicial power to protect economic liberty, and might not condemn broader congressional interpretation of the commerce clause. The balance rested in the hands of Chief Justice HUGHES and Justice OWEN J. ROBERTS.

At first the Court challenged the New Deal. The National Recovery Administration sought to halt the downward spiral in wages and prices by stimulating the negotiation of industry-by-industry and market-by-market codes of "fair competition" fixing minimum prices and wages and outlawing "destructive" competitive practices. In SCHECHTER POULTRY CORPORATION V. UNITED STATES (1935) the Court held the underlying legislation unconstitutional. The major New Deal measure for dealing with the plight of the farmers was held unconstitutional in UNITED STATES V. BUTLER (1936) as "a statutory plan to regulate and control agricultural production, a matter beyond the powers delegated to the federal government." CARTER V. CARTER COAL COMPANY (1936) held that, because production was a purely local activity, Congress lacked power to legislate concerning the wages and hours of bituminous coal miners. In MOREHEAD V. NEW YORK EX REL. TIPALDO (1936) the four conservative Justices, joined by Justice Roberts, reaffirmed the 1923 decision in ADKINS V. CHILDREN'S MEMORIAL HOSPITAL invalidating a law fixing minimum wages for women. These opinions seemed to presage invalidation of such other fundamental New Deal measures as the National Labor Relations Act, a proposed federal wage and hour law, and even the Social Security Act.

President Roosevelt responded with strong criticism. The *Schechter* ruling, he said, was evidence that the Court was still living "in the horse and buggy age." On February 5, 1937, the President sent a special message to Congress urging enactment of a bill to create one new judgeship for every federal judge over the age of seventy who railed to retire. The message spoke of the heavy burden under which the courts—particularly the Supreme Court—were laboring, of the "delicate subject" of "aged or infirm judges," and of the need for "a constant infusion of new blood in the courts." No one doubted Roosevelt's true purpose. Six of the nine Supreme Court Justices were more than seventy years old. Six new Justices would ensure a majority ready to uphold the constitutionality of New Deal legislation. A month later the President addressed the nation more candidly, acknowledging that he hoped "to bring to the decision of social and economic problems younger men who have had personal experience and contact with modern facts and circumstances under which average men have to live and work."

Despite overwhelming popular support for New Deal legislation and despite the President's landslide reelection only a few months earlier, the Court-packing plan was defeated. The President's disingenuous explanation was vulnerable to factual criticism. Justice Brandeis, widely known as a progressive dissenter from his colleagues' conservative philosophy, joined Chief Justice Hughes in a letter to the Senate Judiciary Committee demonstrating that the Court was fully abreast of its docket and would be less efficient if converted into a body of fifteen Justices. Much of the political opposition came from conservative strongholds, but the current ran deeper. The American people had a well-nigh religious attachment to CONSTITUTIONALISM and the Supreme Court. They intuitively realized that packing the Court in order to reverse the course of its decisions would destroy its independence and erode the essence of constitutionalism. Yet no explanation is complete without recalling the contemporary quip: "A switch in time saves nine." The final defeat of the Court-packing plan came after a critical turning in the Court's own interpretation of constitutional limitations.

The shift first became manifest in WEST COAST HOTEL COMPANY V. PARRISH (1937), a 5–4 decision upholding the constitutionality of a state statute authorizing a board to set minimum wages for women. The Chief Justice's opinion overruled the *Adkins* case and markedly loosened the standards of SUBSTANTIVE DUE PROCESS that had previously constricted regulation of contractual relations. To the old STATE POLICE POWER doctrine confining the permissible objectives of government to health, safety, and morals, the Chief Justice added broadly the "welfare of the people" and "the interests of the community." Where the old opin-ions declared as an abstract truth that "The employer and the employee have equality of right and any legislation that disturbs the equality is an arbitrary interference with liberty of contract," the new majority more realistically asserted that a legislature may consider the "relatively weak bargaining power of women" and may "adopt measures to reduce the evils of the 'sweating system.'" There were also hints of greater judicial deference to legislative judgments: "regulation which is reasonable in relation to its subject and is adopted in the interests of the community is due process."

The *West Coast Hotel* case inaugurated a line of decisions sustaining every challenged economic regulation enacted by a state legislature or by the Congress. General minimum wage and maximum hour laws, price regulations, and labor relations acts—all were upheld. Even prior to Hughes's retirement, the trend was intensified by the normal replacement of all but one of the Justices who had sat with Hughes on his first day as Chief Justice. The philosophy of judicial self-restraint gradually became dominant on the Court, in the laws, and throughout the legal profession.

The troublesome problems of constitutional interpretation often call for striking a balance between the opposing ideals of democratic self-government and judicial particularization of majestic but general and undefined constitutional limitations. The philosophy of legislative supremacy and judicial self-restraint that came to dominate constitutional interpretation in the time of the Hughes Court was often asserted and widely accepted as broadly applicable to all constitutional adjudication except the enforcement of clear and specific commands. The Hughes Court thus set the stage for the central constitutional debate of the next major era in constitutional history. As claims to judicial protection of CIVIL LIBERTIES and CIVIL RIGHTS became the focus of attention, JUDICIAL ACTIVISM would be revived by substituting STRICT SCRUTINY for judicial deference in many areas of PREFERRED FREEDOMS and FUNDAMENTAL RIGHTS. Many of the new judicial activists would be liberals or progressives of the same stripe that had pressed for democratic self-government in the days when their political power confronted conservative dominance of the courts. But the opinions of the Hughes Court still mark the end of effective constitutional challenges to legislative regulation of economic activity.

The Hughes Court broke new ground in interpretation of the commerce clause only a few months after the minimum wage decision. In *National Labor Relations Board v. Jones & Laughlin Steel Corporation*

(1937) the Labor Board, under authority delegated by the Wagner Act, had ordered Jones & Laughlin to reinstate four employees discharged from production and maintenance jobs in a basic steel mill because of their union activity. Both Jones & Laughlin's anti-union activities and the order for reinstatement were beyond the reach of federal power as delimited by the old line between production and interstate movement. The lower court had so decided. Led by Chief Justice Hughes, a bare majority of the Supreme Court Justices reversed that decision. Rejecting the old conceptualism that had asked whether the regulated activity had a "legal or logical connection to interstate commerce," the Court appraised the relation by "a practical judgment drawn from experience." Congress could reasonably conclude that an employer's anti-union activities and refusal to bargain collectively might result in strikes, and that a strike at a basic steel mill drawing its raw materials from, and shipping its products to, many states might in fact affect the movement of INTERSTATE COMMERCE. (See WAGNER ACT CASES.)

The *Jones & Laughlin* opinion appeared to retain some judicially enforceable constitutional check upon the congressional power under the commerce clause: "Undoubtedly the scope of this power must be considered in the light of our dual system of government and may not be extended so far as to embrace effects upon interstate commerce so indirect and remote that to embrace them, in view of our complex society, would effectually obliterate the distinction between what is national and what is local and create a completely centralized government." But the check proved illusory. The quoted admonition, while operable as a political principle guiding congressional judgment, yields no rule of law capable of judicial administration. Once the distinctions between interstate movement and production and between "direct" and "indirect" effects upon interstate commerce are rejected, the number of links in the chain of cause and effect becomes irrelevant. Federal power would reach to the local machine shop that repaired the chain saws that cut the trees that yielded the pulp wood that yielded the pulp that made the paper bought by the publisher to print the newspaper that circulated in interstate commerce. The size of the particular establishment or transaction also became irrelevant, for the cumulative effect of many small local activities might have a major impact upon interstate commerce. The new judicial deference, moreover, called for leaving such questions to Congress.

A second doctrinal development accelerated the trend. The Fair Labor Standards Act of 1938 required employers to pay workers engaged in the production of goods for shipment in interstate commerce no less than a specified minimum wage. The act also forbade shipping in interstate commerce any goods produced by workers who had not received the minimum wage. Congress claimed the power to exclude from the pipeline of interstate commerce things that would, in its judgment, do harm in the receiving state. Goods produced at substandard wages and shipped in interstate commerce might depress wages paid in the receiving states, and also in other producing states. The theory had been applied as early as 1903 to uphold a congressional law forbidding the interstate shipment of lottery tickets, but in 1918, under the doctrine barring federal regulation of production, the Court had struck down an act of Congress barring the interstate shipment of goods made with child labor. Having rejected that doctrine in the Labor Board Cases, the Hughes Court readily upheld the constitutionality of the Fair Labor Standards Act upon the theory of the lottery cases. The direct prohibition against paying less than the specified minimum wage was also upheld as a necessary and proper means of preventing goods made under substandard conditions from moving in interstate commerce and doing harm in other states. Years later similar reasoning supported broader decisions upholding the power of Congress to regulate or prohibit the local possession or use of firearms and other articles that have moved in interstate commerce.

Much more than legal logic lay behind the Hughes Court's recognition of virtually unlimited congressional power under the commerce clause. The markets of major firms had become nationwide. A complex and interconnected national economy made widely separated localities interdependent. A century earlier layoffs at the iron foundry in Saugus, Massachusetts, would have had scant visible effect in other states. During the Great Depression no one could miss the fact that layoffs at the steel mills in Pittsburgh, Pennsylvania, reduced the demand for clothing and so caused more layoffs at the textile mills in Charlotte, North Carolina, and Fall River, Massachusetts. Even as the Hughes Court deliberated the Labor Board Cases, a strike at a General Motors automobile assembly plant in Michigan was injuring automobile sales agencies in cities and towns throughout the United States.

The states were incapable of dealing with many of the evils accompanying industrialization. Many states were smaller and less powerful than the giant public utilities and industrial corporations. Massachusetts might forbid the employment of child labor, or fix a minimum wage if the due process clause permitted, but the cost of such measures was the flight of Massachusetts industries to North Carolina or South Carolina. New York might seek to ensure the welfare of its dairy farmers by setting minimum prices that handlers should pay for milk, only to watch the handlers turn to Vermont farmers who could sell at lower prices. The commerce clause barred the states from erecting protective barriers against out-of-state competition.

A shift in intellectual mode was also important. The rise of LEGAL REALISM stimulated by publication of OLIVER WENDELL HOLMES's *The Common Law* in 1881 had made it increasingly difficult for courts to find guidance in such abstractions as the equality of right between employer and employee or in such rhetorical questions as "What possible legal or logical connection is there between an employee's membership in a labor organization and the carrying on of interstate commerce?" The harsh facts of the Depression made both impossible.

The proper division of regulatory activity between the nation and the states is and may always be a much debated question of constitutional dimension. Today the question is nonetheless almost exclusively political. The Hughes Court yielded the final word to Congress.

The enormous expansion of the federal establishment that began in the 1930s and continued for half a century finds a second constitutional source in the power that Article I, Section 8, grants to Congress: "to lay and collect taxes . . . and provide for the common defense and general welfare of the United States." Here, too, the key judicial precedents of the modern era are decisions of the Hughes Court.

The scope of the TAXING AND SPENDING POWER had been disputed from the beginning. Jeffersonian localists argued that the words "general welfare" encompassed only the purposes expressly and somewhat more specifically stated later in Article I. Spending for INTERNAL IMPROVEMENTS gradually became accepted practice in the political branches, but the Supreme Court had had no occasion to adjudicate the issue of constitutional power because no litigant could show that he or she had suffered the kind of particular injury that would sustain a cause of action.

The Roosevelt administration not only spent federal funds on an unprecedented scale in order to relieve unemployment; it also broke new ground in using subsidies to shape the conduct of both state governments and private persons. The Agricultural Adjustment Act of 1933 levied a tax upon processors in order to pay subsidies to farmers who would agree to reduce the acreage sown to crops. The aim was to stabilize the prices of agricultural commodities. Linking the subsidy payments to the processing tax gave the processors STANDING to challenge the tax on the ground that the payments exceeded the limits of the federal spending power. In *United States v. Butler* (1936) the Hughes Court held the act unconstitutional because conditioning the farmer's allotments upon the reduction of his planted acreage made the whole "a statutory plan to regulate and control agricultural production, a matter beyond the power delegated to the federal government."

The decision was a prime target of President Roosevelt's criticism. It aroused fears that the Hughes Court would also invalidate the Social Security Act, a key New Deal measure establishing systems of unemployment and old age and survivors insurance. The title of the act dealing with unemployment levied a federal payroll tax upon all employers of eight or more individuals but gave a credit of up to 90 percent of the federal tax for employer contributions to a state employment fund meeting federal standards specified in the act. Very few states had previously established unemployment insurance, but the act's combination of pressure and inducement proved effective. The combination was attacked as a coercive, unconstitutional invasion of the realm reserved exclusively to the states by the TENTH AMENDMENT, which, if generalized, would enable federal authorities to induce, if not indeed compel, state enactments for any purpose within the realm of state power, and generally to control state administration of state laws. In STEWARD MACHINE COMPANY V. DAVIS (1937) the five-Justice majority answered that offering a choice or even a temptation is not coercion. Spending to relieve the needs of the army of unemployed in a nationwide depression serves the general welfare, the majority continued; the spending power knows no other limitation.

In later decades congressional spending programs would grow in size, spreading from agriculture and social insurance to such areas as housing, highway construction, education, medical care, and local LAW ENFORCEMENT. Many FEDERAL GRANTS-IN-AID to both state and private institutions are conditioned upon observance of federal standards. The balance to be struck between federal standards and state autonomy is sharply debated, but in this area, as under the commerce clause, the question is now almost exclusively left to political discretion as a result of the decisions of the Hughes Court.

Questions concerning the DELEGATION OF POWER gave rise to the fourth major area of constitutional law shaped by the Hughes Court. Congress makes the laws, it is said; the executive carries out the laws; and the judiciary interprets the laws and resolves controversies between executive and legislative officials. Never quite true, this old and simple division of functions proved largely incompatible with the new role established for federal government by the Roosevelt administration. Much law, however denominated, would have to be made by executive departments or new administrative agencies authorized by Congress, such as the Securities and Exchange Commission and the Civil Aeronautics Board. Under the traditional division the new arrangements were subject to attack as unconstitutional attempts to delegate to other agencies part of the legislative power that Congress alone can exercise.

The flow of decisions in the Hughes Court upon this question paralleled the course taken under the due process, commerce, and spending clauses. At first the majority seemed disposed to resist the new political order as in PANAMA REFINING COMPANY V. RYAN (1935) and *Schechter Poultry Corporation v. United States* (1935). Later decisions, however, reversed the initial trend. UNITED STATES V. ROCK ROYAL COOPERATIVE, INC. (1939) is illustrative. The AGRICULTURAL MARKETING AGREEMENT ACT gave the secretary of agriculture broad authority to regulate the marketing of eight agricultural commodities, including milk, with a view to reestablishing the purchasing power of farmers at the level in a base period, usually 1909–1914. In the case of milk, however, if the secretary found the prices so determined to be unreasonable, he was authorized to fix producer prices at a level that would reflect pertinent economic conditions in local milk markets, provide an adequate supply of wholesome milk, and be in the public interest. The purported standards were numerous and broad enough to impose no significant limit upon the secretary's decisions. Nevertheless, the Court upheld the delegation. It was enough that Congress had limited the secretary's power to specified commodities, had specifically contemplated price regulation, and had provided standards by which the secretary's judgment was to be guided after hearing interested parties. The decision set the pattern for all subsequent legislative draftsmen and judicial determinations.

The contributions of the Hughes Court to the law of the FIRST AMENDMENT were less definitive than in the areas of the commerce clause, economic due process, the spending power, and delegation; but they were not less important. The Hughes Court infused the First Amendment with a new and broader vitality

that still drives the expansion of the constitutional protection available to both individual speakers and institutional press.

Apart from the World War I prosecution of pacifists and socialists for speeches and pamphlets alleged to interfere with the production of munitions or conscription for the armed forces, federal law posed few threats to freedom of expression. State laws were more restrictive. The illiberal decisions of the 1920s sustaining the prosecution of leftists under state CRIMINAL SYNDICALISM LAWS assumed that the First Amendment's guarantees against congressional abridgment of freedom of expression are, by virtue of the Fourteenth Amendment, equally applicable to the states. These OBITER DICTA encouraged constitutional attack upon state statutes, municipal ordinances, and judge-made doctrines restricting political and religious expression. In this area Chief Justice Hughes and Justice Roberts quickly allied themselves with the three Justices of established liberal reputation.

Two early opinions highlight the protection that the First and Fourteenth Amendments afford the press against previous restraints. NEAR V. MINNESOTA (1931) was decided upon appeal from a state court's injunction forbidding further publication of *The Saturday Press,* a weekly newspaper, upon the ground that it was "largely devoted to malicious, scandalous and defamatory articles." The newspaper had charged Minneapolis officials with serious offenses in tolerating gambling, bootlegging, and racketeering; the articles were scurrilous and anti-Semitic in tone and content. The decree was authorized by a Minnesota statute. Minnesota had experienced a rash of similar scandal sheets, some of whose publishers were believed to use their journals for blackmail. In an opinion by Chief Justice Hughes, the Supreme Court held that the injunction against publication was an infringement upon the liberty of the press guaranteed by the Fourteenth Amendment regardless of whether the charges were true or false. For any wrong the publisher had committed or might commit, public and private redress might be available; but this PRIOR RESTRAINT was inconsistent with the constitutional liberty.

The law's strong set against previous restraints was underscored a few years later by GROSJEAN V. AMERICAN PRESS COMPANY (1936), where a review of history led the Hughes Court to conclude that the First and Fourteenth Amendments bar not only censorship but also taxes that single out the press and are thus calculated to limit the circulation of information.

The chief danger to freedom or expression by the poor, the unorthodox, and the unpopular lies in state statutes and municipal ordinances that give local authorities wide discretion in preserving the peace and public order. Such laws not only invite suppression of unorthodox ideas by discriminatory enforcement but they also encourage self-censorship in hope of avoiding official interference. The Hughes Court laid the foundations for current constitutional doctrines narrowing the opportunities for abuse.

LOVELL V. CITY OF GRIFFIN (1938) introduced the doctrine that a law requiring a license for the use of the streets or parks for the distribution of leaflets, speeches, parades, or other forms of expression must, explicitly or by prior judicial interpretation, confine the licensing authority to considerations of traffic management, crowd control, or other physical inconvenience or menace to the public. From there it was only a short step to holding in CANTWELL V. CONNECTICUT (1941) that a man may not be punished for words or a street DEMONSTRATION, however offensive to the audience, under a broad, general rubric that invites reprisal for the expression of unorthodox views instead of requiring a narrow judgment concerning the risk of immediate violence. THORNHILL V. ALABAMA (1941), once important for the ruling that peaceful PICKETING in a labor dispute is a form of expression protected by the First Amendment, also introduced the then novel and still controversial doctrine that an individual convicted under a law drawn so broadly as to cover both expression subject to regulation and constitutionally protected expression may challenge the constitutionality of the statute "on its face" even though his own conduct would not be constitutionally protected against punishment under narrower legislation. (See OVERBREADTH DOCTRINE.)

Supreme Court Justices and other constitutionalists still debate the theoretical question how far the First and Fourteenth Amendments secure individuals a right to some PUBLIC FORUM for the purposes of expression. The Hughes Court's decision in HAGUE V. CONGRESS OF INDUSTRIAL ORGANIZATIONS (1939) recognized such a right to the use of streets, parks, and like public places traditionally open for purposes of assembly, communication, and discussion of public questions: "Such use of the streets and public places has, from ancient times, been a part of the privileges, immunities, rights and liberties of citizens. The privilege . . . to use the streets and parks for communication of views on national questions may be regulated in the interest of all; . . . but must not in the guise of regulation be abridged or denied." On this ground *Schneider v. State* (1939) invalidated four city ordinances banning the use of the streets to hand out leaflets. Against this background later Justices would wrestle with the constitutional problems raised by restrictions upon house-to-house canvassing and the use of other government properties for the purpose of expression.

The Hughes Court presided over a revolution in constitutional interpretation. Many conservatives were convinced that in joining the liberal Justices, the Chief Justice and Justice Roberts unconscionably distorted the law to suit the winds of politics. Yet while the revolution is plain, the ground-breaking decisions did appreciably less violence than some reforming decisions of the later WARREN COURT and BURGER COURT to the ideal of a coherent, growing, yet continuing body of law binding the judges as well as the litigants. Doubtless the presence of two competing lines of authority in the Court's earlier decisions often made it easier for the Hughes Court to perform this part of the judicial function. Liberty of contract had never been absolute. The Court had previously sustained, in special contexts, the power of Congress to regulate local activities affecting interstate commerce. Acceptance of the Hughes Court's changes was also the easier because the Hughes Court was diminishing judicial interference with legislative innovations whereas the Warren and Burger Courts pressed far-reaching reforms without legislative support and sometimes against the will expressed by the people's elected representatives. That the old structure and powers of government should be shaped to industrialization, urbanization, and a national economy seemed more inevitable than that public schools should be integrated by busing, that prayer and Bible-reading should be banned from the public schools, or that abortion should be made a matter of personal choice. Yet even when the differences are acknowledged, much of the success of the Hughes Court in managing its revolution in constitutional interpretation seems attributable to the Chief Justice's belief in the value of a coherent, though changing, body of law, to his character, and to his talents combining the perception and sagacity drawn from an earlier, active political life with his extraordinary legal craftsmanship, earlier fine-honed as an Associate Justice.

ARCHIBALD COX

Bibliography

ALSOP, JOSEPH and CATLEDGE, TURNER 1938 *The 168 Days.* Garden City, N.Y.: Doubleday.
JACKSON, ROBERT H. 1941 *The Struggle for Judicial Supremacy.* New York: Knopf.
MURPHY, PAUL 1972 *The Constitution in Crisis Times 1918–1969* New York: Harper & Row.

PUSEY, MERLO J. 1951 *Charles Evans Hughes.* New York: Macmillan.

STERN, ROBERT L. 1946 The Commerce Clause and the National Economy, 1933–1946. *Harvard Law Review* 59:645–693.

SWINDLER, WILLIAM F. 1970 *Court and Constitution in the Twentieth Century,* Part I. Indianapolis: Bobbs-Merrill.

HUMPHREY, HUBERT H.
(1911–1978)

Hubert Horatio Humphrey was the latest in a line of distinguished United States senators whose influence has exceeded that of many Presidents. He served as senator from Minnesota from 1948 to 1964 and from 1972 to his death, during which time he wrote over forty acts of Congress and coauthored considerably more than twice that many on subjects as diverse as children's nutrition, aid to education, nuclear disarmament, full employment, solar energy, and medicare. He led the anticommunist liberal wing of the Democratic party and cofounded its political organ, Americans for Democratic Action, whose constitution barred membership by communists and Fascists. In 1954 Humphrey wrote the COMMUNIST CONTROL ACT; his original version would have made it a crime to be a member of the party. He never spoke against Senator Joseph R. McCarthy in the Senate. Otherwise he was the quintessential liberal, involved in nearly every achievement and failure of American liberalism from the close of World War II until his untimely death. He believed that government existed to serve people, the more service to the larger number of people the better.

Humphrey's finest hours were devoted to CIVIL RIGHTS. In 1948 he became a national celebrity by leading a successful fight for a strong civil rights plank in his party's platform, provoking a walkout of intransigent Southerners who formed the Dixiecrat party. In 1964, when he was party whip, he was floor manager of the battle for the passage of the CIVIL RIGHTS ACT of that year.

As thirty-eighth vice-president, Humphrey was the most unflaggingly active of any in our history. When he was his party's nominee for President in 1968, he lost the election by half a million votes because his strong support of the VIETNAM WAR cost him the allegiance of antiwar voters, and because his civil rights record cost him southern votes that went to a third party candidate.

The pell-mell, all-directions-at-once character of the Great Society mirrored Humphrey as well as President LYNDON B. JOHNSON. Humphrey was not only an effective legislator. He was probably the gabbiest, most exuberant, open-hearted person in American public life.

LEONARD W. LEVY

Bibliography

SOLBERG, CARL 1984 *Hubert Humphrey: A Biography.* New York: Norton.

HUMPHREY'S EXECUTOR v. UNITED STATES
295 U.S. 602 (1935)

This decision probably more than any other contributed to President FRANKLIN D. ROOSEVELT'S animus against the Supreme Court. As Attorney General ROBERT H. JACKSON wrote, the opinion of the unanimous Court by Justice GEORGE SUTHERLAND gave the impression "that the President had flouted the Constitution, rather than that the Court had simply changed its mind within the past ten years." In MYERS V. UNITED STATES (1926) a 6–3 Court had sustained the removal power of the President in a case involving a postmaster. Sutherland had joined the opinion of the Court, including its OBITER DICTUM that the removal power extended even to members of independent REGULATORY COMMISSIONS. Roosevelt, relying on *Myers,* removed from the Federal Trade Commission (FTC) William Humphrey, who had been reappointed for a six-year term in 1931. The FEDERAL TRADE COMMISSION ACT provided for removal for cause, including inefficiency or malfeasance.

Humphrey was a blatantly probusiness, antiadministration official who thwarted the objectives of the FTC. After he died, his executor sued for Humphrey's back pay, raising the question whether a member of an administrative tribunal created by Congress to implement legislative policies can be removed as if he were a member of the executive department. Ruling against the removal power, Sutherland distinguished *Myers,* overruled the dictum, and failed to mention that Roosevelt had acted in good faith when he relied on *Myers.* Liberal Justices joined Sutherland for the reason given privately by Justice LOUIS D. BRANDEIS: if a Huey Long were President and the administration's argument prevailed, the commissions would become compliant agents of the executive.

Despite the Court's unanimity, its strict reliance

on a simplistic SEPARATION OF POWERS theory ignored the fact that the administrative agencies, however mixed their powers, were executive agencies and Congress acknowledged that fact. Moreover, had Roosevelt chosen to remove Humphrey for cause, the Court would not likely have challenged his judgment. The Court followed *Humphrey* in *Wiener v. United States* (1958), ruling that President DWIGHT D. EISENHOWER could not remove a member of a quasi-judicial agency without cause.

LEONARD W. LEVY

(SEE ALSO: *Appointing and Removal Power.*)

HUNT, WARD
(1810–1886)

Ward Hunt, a New York judge, was appointed to the Supreme Court by ULYSSES S. GRANT in late 1872; seven years later, although permanently incapacitated by a stroke, he refused to resign until Congress passed a special retirement act in 1882. His judicial contributions were largely unexceptional and insignificant. He consistently sided with the WAITE COURT majority in supporting bondholders' claims, upholding state regulation under traditional POLICE POWER doctrines, and denying claims for racial equality under the FOURTEENTH AMENDMENT.

Hunt also upheld claims of immunity from federal taxation for states or their instrumentalities. (See INTERGOVERNMENTAL IMMUNITY.) Earlier, in COLLECTOR V. DAY (1871), the Court had exempted state judges from the federal income tax. In one of his first opinions, Hunt treated municipally financed railroads as state agencies and as similarly exempt. "Their operation," he said in *United States v. Railroad Co.* (1873), "may be impeded and may be destroyed, if any interference is permitted." A few years later he dissented from the nationalistic holding in PENSACOLA TELEGRAPH CO. V. WESTERN UNION TELEGRAPH CO. (1877), in which the majority held that states could not interfere with telegraph lines established under federal law. Hunt, however, insisted that federal authority extended only to lands in the public domain.

Hunt usually followed his colleagues in ruling against claims advancing Negro rights. But in UNITED STATES V. REESE (1876) he alone dissented to support the constitutionality of the FORCE ACT (1870) which was designed to implement the FIFTEENTH AMENDMENT. Hunt interpreted the amendment as guaranteeing "the right to vote in its broadest terms" for all citizens, in all elections, state as well as federal. The majority had refused to sanction federal interference against acts of individual state officers who had refused on their own account to allow blacks to vote. For Hunt, it was obvious that such individual acts were tantamount to state action and subject to federal restraint. The word "state" in the Fifteenth Amendment, he maintained, included "the acts of all those who proceed under [a state's] . . . authority." The *Reese* decision reflected the growing national consensus for sectional reconciliation which inevitably meant abandonment of national protection for the freedmen's CIVIL RIGHTS. Hunt acknowledged this mood and he recognized that the majority's decision "brings to an impotent conclusion the vigorous amendments on the subject of slavery." Yet he silently acquiesced later that term in the further emasculation of the Force Act in UNITED STATES V. CRUIKSHANK (1876).

Hunt's fleeting concern for guaranteeing black suffrage did not extend to women. On circuit in 1873, he presided at the trial of Susan B. Anthony, who had voted in the 1872 presidential election in New York despite a state constitutional requirement limiting the franchise to men. Anthony claimed that the state denied her the PRIVILEGES AND IMMUNITIES guaranteed under the Fourteenth Amendment. Hunt flatly denied the argument. He invoked the reasoning of the recent SLAUGHTERHOUSE CASES (1873) and held that such regulations, however unjust, were under the absolute domain of the state. Hunt directed a guilty verdict, refused to poll the jury, and fined Anthony $100. The sentence was not enforced, and there was no APPEAL to the Supreme Court.

Hunt was a hard-working able craftsman during his brief career on the Court (1873–1882) but he had little apparent influence on his brethren or on constitutional law.

STANLEY I. KUTLER

Bibliography

FAIRMAN, CHARLES 1971 *Reconstruction and Reunion, 1864–1888.* Volume 6 of the *Oliver Wendell Holmes Devise History of the Supreme Court of the United States.* New York: Macmillan.

MAGRATH, C. PETER 1963 *Morrison R. Waite: The Triumph of Character.* New York: Macmillan.

HUNTER v. ERICKSON
393 U.S. 385 (1969)

In a perverse application of the EQUAL PROTECTION clause, an 8–1 Supreme Court struck down an amendment to the Akron, Ohio, city charter subjecting any council-passed OPEN HOUSING LAW to a REFERENDUM before it could take effect and requiring a referendum on an open housing law previously enacted.

Six Justices, speaking through BYRON R. WHITE, found in the referendum requirement an "explicitly racial classification," although they conceded that it drew "no distinctions among racial and religious groups." The majority argued that the charter amendment, by making open housing laws harder to enact, "disadvantaged those who would benefit" from such laws—and presumed that the potential beneficiaries were the members of ethnic and religious minorities. The FOURTEENTH AMENDMENT was held to protect minorities against barriers to enactment of favorable legislation.

Justice HUGO L. BLACK dissented, contending that referenda were part of the democratic political process and that advocates of particular types of legislation were not constitutionally disadvantaged merely because they might lose an election.

DENNIS J. MAHONEY

HURD v. HODGE

See: *Shelley v. Kraemer*

HURON PORTLAND CEMENT COMPANY v. DETROIT
362 U.S. 440 (1960)

In a case involving a major COMMERCE CLAUSE issue, a 7–2 Supreme Court sustained Detroit's Smoke Abatement Code. That city sued a Michigan manufacturer operating ships in INTERSTATE COMMERCE for violating its air pollution regulations. The manufacturer stressed its adherence to congressional regulations, claiming that Detroit could not impose stricter standards. Justice POTTER STEWART's opinion, devoted primarily to rejecting claims that federal laws had preempted the field, accorded a high priority to the STATE POLICE POWER. Exercise of that power must stand unless clearly discriminatory or violative of national uniformity, and nothing "suggest[s] the existence of any . . . competing or conflicting local regulations."

DAVID GORDON

HURTADO v. CALIFORNIA
110 U.S. 516 (1884)

DUE PROCESS OF LAW reached a watershed in *Hurtado*. For centuries due process had stood for a cluster of specific procedures associated especially with TRIAL BY JURY. Sir EDWARD COKE, for example, explicitly associated due process with INDICTMENT by GRAND JURY. The BILL OF RIGHTS enumerated many of the rights that the concept of due process spaciously accommodated. The FOURTEENTH AMENDMENT's due process clause was copied verbatim from the Fifth Amendment, where the same clause sat cheek-by-jowl with a number of specific guarantees that due process had embodied as a COMMON LAW concept. The framers of the Fifth Amendment had added the due process clause as an additional assurance, a rhetorical flourish, and a genuflection toward the traditions of MAGNA CARTA. In *Hurtado*, the Supreme Court began to whittle away at the conventional meanings of PROCEDURAL DUE PROCESS and did not pause until MOORE V. DEMPSEY (1923).

California tried and convicted Hurtado on an INFORMATION for murder, filed by his prosecutor. He claimed that because the state had denied him indictment by grand jury, it had violated the due process clause of the Fourteenth Amendment. The Court, sustaining the conviction, 7–1, rejected Hurtado's claim on the ground that "any legal proceeding" that protects "liberty and justice" is due process. Justice STANLEY MATTHEWS, for the Court, reasoned that the Constitution, having been framed for an undefined and expanding future, must recognize new procedures. To hold otherwise, he said, would render the Constitution "incapable of progress and improvement. It would be to stamp upon our jurisprudence the unchangeableness attributed to the Medes and the Persians. . . ." Matthews also argued that no part of the Constitution was superfluous; the fact that the Fifth Amendment included both a guarantee of grand jury proceedings in federal prosecutions and the guarantee of due process showed that the latter did not mean the former.

Justice JOHN MARSHALL HARLAN, dissenting, had history on his side when he found grand jury proceedings to be an indispensable requisite of due process, but whether history should have disposed of the question is a different issue. Harlan did not think that prosecuting individuals for their lives by information inaugurated a new era of progress in the constitutional law of CRIMINAL PROCEDURE. The Court's inexorable logic, he asserted, as if asserting the unthinkable, would lead to the conclusion that due process did not even guarantee the traditional trial by jury. Later cases justified his fears. (See MAXWELL v. DOW, 1900.)

LEONARD W. LEVY

HUTCHINSON, THOMAS
(1711–1780)

Thomas Hutchinson, described by his biographer, Bernard Bailyn, as "the most distinguished, as well as the most loyal, colonial-born official of his time," was the leading exponent of "Tory" constitutional theory at the outbreak of the American Revolution. Hutchinson was not a political theorist, however, but a practical politician who turned to theory in order to justify his actions.

Hutchinson was the leader of the wealthy, interrelated clique that ruled Massachusetts in the eighteenth century. Although he was born in Boston, his loyalty was always to the ministry in England, and he defended his policies by appealing to the most extreme doctrines of royal and parliamentary supremacy. During his career he held every important office in the colony, and at one point (in 1763) he was simultaneously lieutenant governor, chief justice of the Supreme Court, president of the Council, and judge of probate.

In 1761 Hutchinson, as Chief Justice, presided over the PAXTON'S CASE, in which the Superior Court was asked to issue GENERAL WARRANTS to authorize searches by customs officials. He personally opposed the use of WRITS OF ASSISTANCE and as lieutenant governor had argued against their issuance on the governor's authority, but as a judge Hutchinson rejected the argument of JAMES OTIS that such writs were illegal under the COMMON LAW. It was sufficient that writs of assistance were valid in English law and that Parliament had, by statute, authorized their use in the colonies, and so the writs were issued.

Hutchinson became acting governor of Massachusetts in 1769 and governor in 1771. He was temperamentally unsuited for the position in so critical a time. When the policies he pursued became so unpopular that the Assembly would not appropriate money to pay his salary, Hutchinson secured for himself a special salary paid by the British crown. To insure that the courts would remain loyal to the British government he arranged that the judges' salaries, too, should be paid by the crown. These moves, which rendered

the executive and judicial powers independent of the legislature and of the citizens, enraged public opinion.

Responding defiantly, Hutchinson summoned the General Court and, on January 6, 1773, delivered an address that spelled out his understanding of the principles of Anglo-American constitutionalism. The British Empire and Massachusetts's place in it, he argued, required the absolute and indivisible SOVEREIGNTY of the king-in-Parliament. The power of the British Parliament was unlimited and illimitable, but, since Parliament represented all British subjects, both in Britain and in the colonies, that power would necessarily be used benignly and humanely. As the American colonies were too weak to survive without British protection, the freedom of Americans depended upon their acceptance of absolute parliamentary authority. Hutchinson refused to concede the possibility that the General Court of Massachusetts exercised a separate legislative authority. "No line," he argued, "can be drawn between the supreme authority of Parliament and the total independence of the colonies."

If Hutchinson expected the address to quell criticism he was seriously mistaken. The effect was rather to enhance the standing of the most radical leaders of the opposition. The task of preparing the Assembly's response fell to SAMUEL ADAMS, the leader of the popular party and Hutchinson's chief rival. The Assembly adopted a resolution accepting, for argument's sake, Hutchinson's position that there could be no middle ground between absolute parliamentary authority and colonial autonomy. But the conclusion drawn was the opposite of Hutchinson's. The Assembly claimed that Massachusetts was a realm separate from Britain, sharing a common executive—the king—but with its own legislature. Only the General Court, and not Parliament, could legislate for Massachusetts.

Hutchinson was only reluctantly an enemy of his fellow colonists. He opposed many of the measures adopted by the British government, including the SUGAR ACT and the STAMP ACT. But Hutchinson's objections were prudential, not constitutional. He never doubted Parliament's right to legislate for the colonies, however disastrous the exercise of that right, or his own duty to obey and enforce such legislation.

After being forced in 1774 to flee to England, Hutchinson endured the six years until his death as a lonely pensioner of the crown. His career had a deep, if negative, influence on American constitutional thought: it was proof of the evils of plural office-holding and of an executive not dependent on the people's representatives for his pay. His outspoken insistence on the indivisibility of sovereignty helped to impel the formation of American theories of FEDERALISM.

DENNIS J. MAHONEY

Bibliography
BAILYN, BERNARD 1974 *The Ordeal of Thomas Hutchinson.* Cambridge, Mass.: Harvard University Press.
HUTCHINSON, THOMAS 1936 *History of the Colony of Massachusetts Bay.* Cambridge, Mass.: Harvard University Press.

HUTCHINSON v. PROXMIRE
443 U.S. 111 (1979)

This decision reaffirmed a line first drawn in GRAVEL v. UNITED STATES (1972) between official and unofficial communications by members of Congress. Senator William Proxmire gave one Dr. Hutchinson a "Golden Fleece" award for what Proxmire considered to be wasteful government-sponsored research conducted by Dr. Hutchinson. Proxmire publicized the award through a press release and a newsletter to constituents. Under the Supreme Court's interpretation of the SPEECH OR DEBATE CLAUSE, members of Congress are absolutely immune from suit only for legislative acts. In *Hutchinson,* the Court found that Proxmire's communications were not "essential to the deliberations of the Senate" and, therefore, were not legislative acts protected from libel actions by the speech or debate clause.

THEODORE EISENBERG

HYDE AMENDMENT

Beginning in 1976, Congress adopted a series of measures (amendments to appropriation bills, and JOINT RESOLUTIONS) prohibiting the use of any federal funds in the Medicaid program to pay for the costs of ABORTIONS. These provisions were known collectively as the "Hyde Amendment," after their original sponsor, Representative Henry J. Hyde of Illinois.

All versions of the amendment contained exceptions permitting federal funding of an abortion when the woman's pregnancy endangered her life. Some of them also permitted funding of abortions when pregnancies resulted from rape or incest. One version included still another exception when two physicians determined that "severe and long-lasting physical health damage to the mother would result" from a full-term pregnancy.

The Medicaid program was designed to provide federal financial assistance to states that reimbursed needy persons for medical treatment. Funds were provided for reimbursing the expenses of childbirth—at an average cost per recipient around nine times the cost of abortions. Some states continued to provide funds for needy women's abortions. In other states, the effect of the Hyde Amendment was to deny to poor women the financial assistance they needed to exercise the constitutional right recognized in ROE v. WADE (1973): to decide whether to terminate their pregnancies. Critics argued that the amendment was an unconstitutional WEALTH DISCRIMINATION, but the Supreme Court upheld its validity, 5–4, in HARRIS v. McRAE (1980).

KENNETH L. KARST

(SEE ALSO: *Reproductive Autonomy.*)

Bibliography
PERRY, MICHAEL J. 1980 Why the Supreme Court Was Plainly Wrong in the Hyde Amendment Case: A Brief Comment on *Harris v. McRae. Stanford Law Review* 32:1113–1128.

HYLTON v. UNITED STATES
3 Dallas 171 (1796)

The first case in which the Supreme Court passed on the constitutionality of an act of Congress, *Hylton* stands for the principle that the only DIRECT TAXES are taxes on land and CAPITATION TAXES. The Constitution provides that no capitation "or other direct tax" be imposed except in proportion to the population of the states, but that "all duties, IMPOSTS and EXCISES" be levied uniformly, that is, at the same rate. Congress imposed a uniform tax of $16 on all carriages (horse-drawn coaches), despite protests that the tax should have been apportioned among the states according to the census. When Congress levied a direct tax it fixed the total amount of money it intended to raise, so that in a state with ten percent of the nation's population, the parties taxed (carriage-owners) would have paid ten percent of the total. Thus, if a tax on carriages were a direct tax, the amount raised in two states of equal population would be the same, but if one state had twice as many carriages as the other, the tax rate in that state would be twice as great. The contention in this case was that the carriage tax was unconstitutional because it was a direct tax uniformly levied.

The case seems to have been contrived to obtain a Court ruling on the constitutionality of Congress's tax program. To meet the requirement that federal JURISDICTION attached only if the amount in litigation came to $2,000, Hylton deposed that he owned 125 carriages for his private use, each of which was subject to a $16 tax; if he lost the case, however, his debt would be discharged by paying just $16. The United States paid his counsel, ALEXANDER HAMILTON, who defended the tax program he had sponsored as secretary of the treasury. Notwithstanding the farcical aspects of the case, its significance cannot be overesti-mated: if a tax on carriages were indirect and therefore could be uniform, Congress would have the utmost flexibility in determining its tax policies. As Justice SAMUEL CHASE said, "The great object of the Constitution was to give Congress a power to lay taxes adequate to the exigencies of government." Justice WILLIAM PATERSON, having been a member of the CONSTITUTIONAL CONVENTION OF 1787, explained why the rule of apportionment applied only to capitation and land taxes, making all other taxes indirect taxes. The judgment of the Court was unanimous.

LEONARD W. LEVY

ILLEGITIMACY

The Anglo-American law of illegitimacy derives from two interrelated purposes of our institutional progenitors. First, imposing the legal disabilities of illegitimacy on a child was seen as a punishment of the parents for their sin. More importantly, the law of legitimacy supported a system of male control over economic resources. The chief effect of the principle of bastardy-as-punishment was to disable illegitimate children from making claims against their deceased fathers' estates. Similarly, formal marriage was the only basis for a woman's claim to inherit from the man who fathered her children. Thus the punishment was reserved for unmarried women and their children. Unmarried fathers, far from being punished, were strengthened in their power to control the transmission of wealth and status. As the Supreme Court began to recognize in two 1968 decisions, these themes are modern as well as medieval.

The cases were LEVY V. LOUISIANA and *Glona v. American Guarantee & Liability Insurance Co.* On EQUAL PROTECTION grounds, the Court invalidated provisions of Louisiana's wrongful death statute that allowed damages to a surviving child for the death of a parent, and vice versa, only in cases of legitimate parentage. From that time forward, most of the Court's decisions on illegitimacy have dealt with laws regulating inheritance by illegitimate children (especially from their fathers), and laws restricting the right to death damages or benefits in cases of illegitimacy. Both in their results and in their doctrinal explanations, these decisions have pursued a crooked path.

Much of the early doctrinal uncertainty surrounded the question of the appropriate STANDARD OF REVIEW. *Levy* and *Glona* purported to apply the RATIONAL BASIS standard, but in fact they represented a more demanding judicial scrutiny. There were good reasons for categorizing illegitimacy as a SUSPECT CLASSIFICATION that would demand STRICT SCRUTINY of the state's asserted justifications. As the Court has said more than once, it is "illogical and unjust" to burden innocent children because their parents have not married. The status of illegitimacy is out of the child's control. Illegitimates have suffered historic disadvantage. The status has been the centuries-old source of stigma; such legislative classifications are apt to be the result of habit, prejudice, and stereotype rather than serious attention to public needs. After a series of cases characterized by doctrinal instability, in *Mathews v. Lucas* (1976) the Court rejected the assimilation of illegitimacy to the suspect classifications category. The Court did remark, however, that its standard of review in such cases was "not a toothless one."

Part of the reason for the tortuous doctrinal path from *Levy* and *Glona* to *Mathews v. Lucas* was that the Justices were closely divided on the general issue of the Court's approach to illegitimacy as a legislative classification; in these circumstances, trifling factual distinctions tended to affect the decisions of cases. Even after *Mathews v. Lucas* this pattern continued, as TRIMBLE V. GORDON (1977) and LALLI V. LALLI (1978) illustrate—although the Court has identified a verbal formula for its standard of review: An illegitimacy classification must be "substantially related to a permissible state interest." As Justice LEWIS F. POWELL said for a plurality in *Lalli,* the Court's concern for the plight of illegitimates must be measured against a state's interest in "the just and orderly disposition of property at death." A seventeenth century probate lawyer would not be surprised to learn that the justice and order emerging from *Lalli* offered protection for a father's estate against the claims of illegitimate children, even though paternity had been established beyond question.

The Supreme Court has invoked its intermediate standard of review to invalidate state laws imposing severe time restrictions on suits to establish paternity and compel fathers to support children born outside marriage. But if *Lalli* validated an ancient tradition of domination through control over the transmission of wealth and status, *Parham v. Hughes* (1978), just four months later, validated the tradition of the illegitimacy relation as punishment for sin. An illegitimate child and his mother were killed in an automobile accident. State law would have allowed only the mother to sue for wrongful death damages, if she had survived. Given the mother's death, the father would have been entitled to bring the suit if he had formally legitimated the child. Although he had not undertaken formal legitimation proceedings, the father had signed the child's birth certificate, and had supported the child and visited him regularly; the child had taken the father's name. The Court upheld the state's denial of a right to sue, 6–3.

The state court in *Parham* had said the law was a means of "promoting a legitimate family unit" and "setting a standard of morality." The *Parham* dissenters, focusing on SEX DISCRIMINATION, faulted the state for doing its promoting and standard-setting selectively, along lines defined by gender. The decision also intruded seriously on the FREEDOM OF INTIMATE ASSOCIATION. The father–son relationship was complete in every sense but the formal one. Four members of the majority said it was all right, nevertheless, for the state to "express its 'condemnation of irresponsible liaisons beyond the bounds of marriage' " by denying the father the right to damages for the death of his son. In other words, the father should be ashamed of himself.

In *Glona,* the Court had rejected precisely this sort of reasoning. The fact that the legislature was "dealing with sin," the Court said, could not justify so arbitrary a discrimination as the denial of wrongful death damages. *Glona* had involved the claim of a mother, and mothers of illegitimate children have been the historic victims of a system of illegitimacy in a way that fathers have not. But *Parham* involved a man who not only

sired a child but was a father to him. What had been protected in *Glona* was not merely the damages claim of a mother, but the status of the intimate relationship between a mother and her son. The *Parham* law's arbitrariness lay in its assumption that significant incidents of the parent-child relationship should be denied because of the absence of a formal marriage. Seen in this light, the law's discrimination demands some substantial justification for its invasion of the freedom of intimate association. *Glona* teaches that the required justification is not to be found in the state's wish to punish "sin." The Supreme Court plainly is not yet prepared to hold that the status of illegitimacy is itself constitutionally defective. When that day arrives, however, *Glona* will serve as a precedent.

KENNETH L. KARST

Bibliography

PERRY, MICHAEL J. 1979 Modern Equal Protection: A Conceptualization and Reappraisal. *Columbia Law Review* 79:1023–1084.
WALLACH, ALETA and TENOSO, PATRICIA 1974 A Vindication of the Rights of Unmarried Mothers and Their Children: An Analysis of the Institution of Illegitimacy, Equal Protection, and the Uniform Parentage Act. *University of Kansas Law Review* 23:23–90.

ILLINOIS v. GATES
462 U.S. 213 (1983)

This decision revived pre-WARREN COURT law of the FOURTH AMENDMENT concerning SEARCH WARRANTS issued on INFORMANTS' TIPS. Justice WILLIAM H. REHNQUIST for a six-member majority declared, "we . . . abandon the 'two pronged test' established by our decisions in *Aguilar* and *Spinelli.* In its place we reaffirm the totality of circumstances analysis that traditionally had informed PROBABLE CAUSE determination." In AGUILAR V. TEXAS (1962) the Court had developed a test to govern a magistrate's probable cause hearing to determine whether a warrant should issue. Although HEARSAY information (an informer's tip not reflecting the personal knowledge of the police) may underlie an officer's affadavit for a warrant, the officer must also explain his belief that the informant is trustworthy or that his information is reliable. SPINELLI V. UNITED STATES (1969) made the magistrate's hearing a mini-trial controlled by strict rules of EVIDENCE; the Court insisted on a degree of corroboration that proved the truthfulness of a tip apart from any evidence that might subsequently verify it.

In effect the Court had escalated the constitutional requirement of probable cause to reasonably certain cause in order to insure that a magistrate could evaluate all facts and allegations for himself. *Aguilar-Spinelli* meant that although the police secured a warrant based on a tip and their search uncovered evidence of crime, that evidence could be suppressed and a conviction set aside if a court later decided that the magistrate should not have issued the warrant. In *Illinois v. Gates* Rehnquist recalled that probable cause is founded on practical, nontechnical considerations and that magistrates should apply flexible standards based on all circumstances rather than on a rigid set of rules. Justice WILLIAM J. BRENNAN, dissenting, declared that the majority opinion reflected "an overly permissive attitude towards police practices" contrary to Fourth Amendment rights.

LEONARD W. LEVY

IMBLER v. PACHTMAN
424 U.S. 409 (1976)

Imbler established prosecutorial immunity from suit under SECTION 1983, TITLE 42, UNITED STATES CODE, for activities that are integral parts of the judicial process. *Imbler* left open the question whether prosecutors may be civilly liable for administrative or investigative activities. Justice LEWIS F. POWELL, writing for the Supreme Court, indicated in OBITER DICTUM that judges and prosecutors are subject to criminal prosecution for willful deprivations of constitutional rights.

THEODORE EISENBERG

IMMIGRATION

The ambivalence that characterizes today's national policies toward immigration had antecedents in the colonial era. Although the DECLARATION OF INDEPENDENCE complained that the king and Privy Council had tried "to prevent the population of these states," many of the colonies had resisted Roman Catholic immigration, and in 1776 some of them still resounded with expressions of nativist resentment against populations that were non-English. The nation is justly proud of its tradition as a refuge for the oppressed and persecuted. Yet American immigration policy, from colonial times to our own, has been dictated by the "native" majorities' perceptions of self-interest. The perceived need for settlers and workers hangs in precarious balance against the suspicions and hostilities that flow out of cultural differences. Congress decides how the balance shall be struck; in the field of immigration, constitutional law has placed few limits on governmental power.

For almost a century, Congress took little part in the regulation of immigration. Even the ALIEN AND SEDITION ACTS (1798), for all their spirit of partisan nativism, were not conceived as immigration restrictions. An early minimal state regulation of the immigration process survived challenge under the COMMERCE CLAUSE in MAYOR OF NEW YORK V. MILN (1837), but more severe state regulations were held invalid in the PASSENGER CASES (1849). Direct state limits on immigration were held unconstitutional in *Henderson v. New York* (1875), the same year in which Congress adopted the first direct national restriction, forbidding immigration by convicts and prostitutes.

By 1875, Congress's constitutional power to control immigration had come to be seen as one aspect of its power to regulate foreign commerce. Later, the Supreme Court articulated a more sweeping doctrine: the power of the national government to control FOREIGN AFFAIRS was inherent in the idea of nationhood and did not need explicit recognition in the Constitution. That doctrine eventually found its fullest expression in UNITED STATES V. CURTISS-WRIGHT EXPORT CORP. (1936), but it had surfaced half a century earlier in the context of immigration. In CHAE CHAN PING V. UNITED STATES (1889) the Court announced that if Congress "considers the presence of foreigners of a different race in this country, who will not assimilate with us, to be dangerous to its peace and security, . . . its determination is conclusive upon the judiciary." Having cast itself in an acquiescent role, the Court in *Nishimura Eiku v. United States* (1892) justified nearly absolute congressional power over immigration as "inherent in SOVEREIGNTY." An exceedingly inscrutable image of a national community now formally protected Congress's immigration decisions from effective constitutional challenge.

The law upheld in the *Chae Chan Ping* decision was the CHINESE EXCLUSION ACT of 1882. In the years since 1850, some 300,000 Chinese had come to the Pacific Coast, most of them responding to active recruitment of labor for mines and railroad construction in the American West. By the 1860s Chinese had come to compose about nine percent of California's population, and an anti-Chinese crusade was in full cry, fueled by racism and fear. After a long campaign, the Chinese Exclusion Act suspended immigration from China for ten years, made the Chinese ineligible for CITIZENSHIP—not even the strongest congressional supporters of unrestricted immigration could conceive of the Chinese as permanent members of the community—and imposed other restrictions on them.

Although the act was accompanied by unashamedly sinophobic rhetoric, it was ostensibly passed to protect citizen workers. So, too, was the federal legislation of 1882 that added new categories of prohibited immigrants—lunatics, idiots, and persons likely to become public charges—and went on to impose a head tax of fifty cents on each immigrant who entered the United States. Similar justifications were offered for the acts of 1885 and 1887, prohibiting payment for an immigrant's transportation to the United States in return for a promise of labor. This series of laws in the 1880s imposed the first severe restrictions on immigration in the nation's history.

The Supreme Court upheld the head tax, in the *Head Money Cases* (1884), on the basis of Congress's power to regulate foreign commerce—a theory broad enough to sustain the whole series of enactments. However, all the laws were ineffective by design. Congress left border inspections and collection of the head tax to state agencies, which largely ignored the laws. The contract labor laws exempted both skilled workers and domestics, along with foreigners residing temporarily in the country and "coincidentally" working here. The practical effect was to permit a continued disregard for the border and a deepening disrespect for the law, especially among Mexican laborers and the employers who recruited them.

From the 1880s on, a steady trickle of minor immigration restrictions issued from Congress. Paupers and polygamists were excluded, and then epileptics, professional beggars, and anarchists or persons believing in the violent overthrow of the government—the latter provisions a reaction to the assassination of President WILLIAM McKINLEY. Not surprisingly, the next major immigration restrictions accompanied a new surge of nativism associated with a wave of immigration from eastern and southern Europe that began in the 1890s, encouraged by the demand for workers in a growing industrial economy. This nativist impulse was accelerated by World War I and reached a climax in the Red Scare of 1919–1920. Congress adopted a LITERACY TEST for immigrants in 1917, and in the early 1920s set in place a system of immigration quotas based on national origins. The quotas restricted the ethnic proportions of immigration to the ethnic proportions of the nation's population before 1890—that is, before the arrival of large numbers of eastern and southern Europeans. The quota system reflected some of the most respected "scientific" thought of the Pro-

gressive era; the racism that produced the Chinese Exclusion Act had broadened into Anglo-Saxonism, which extended its hostility and its assumptions of superiority beyond race to ethnicity.

The constitutionality of racial and ethnic restrictions on immigration was taken for granted in the 1920s. The *Chae Chan Ping* opinion had placed the whole matter outside the reach of substantive constitutional guarantees such as the EQUAL PROTECTION OF THE LAWS. To say the very least, however, this position is in tension with the Supreme Court's modern treatment of RACIAL DISCRIMINATION. Yet no recent decision has reexamined the premises of *Chae Chan Ping*, and the Court's opinions continue to refer, as in *Fiallo v. Bell* (1977), to "the limited scope of judicial inquiry in immigration litigation." Nonetheless, the modern constitutional climate in race cases seems to have contributed to the abandonment, in 1965, of the national origins quota system. In its place Congress has adopted a single worldwide annual ceiling on immigration, with a system of preferences designed to protect the interests of citizens and of aliens who are already documented residents.

The substantive problem of squaring the nation's constitutional commitment to equal protection with the tradition of judicial deference to Congress on immigration matters has a procedural counterpart. The *Nishimura Eiku* decision held that the DUE PROCESS clause of the Fifth Amendment imposed no limits on the power of Congress to govern procedures for entry into the United States. A few years later, in *Wong Wing v. United States* (1896), the Supreme Court did hold that due process forbade enforcement of the immigration laws by sentencing aliens to hard labor. In the modern era, *Landon v. Plascencia* (1982) has recognized due process rights of a resident alien who was seeking readmission after a short trip to Mexico. But such constitutional limitations are rare; the judicial protection of aliens in the exclusion process mainly has taken the form of interpretations of the immigration statutes.

A notable recent example is *Jean v. Nelson* (1985), in which the Court confronted the practice of long-term detention, without parole, of Haitian aliens who had been taken into custody as they attempted to enter the country without permission. The detention was challenged as unconstitutional discrimination based on race or national origin. Rather than decide that issue, the Court approved a REMAND of the case to determine whether immigration officials were observing the statutes and regulations, which, in the Court's interpretation, required individualized parole decisions without such discrimination. *Jean* appears to reflect an increasing judicial reluctance to keep the exclusion process unfettered by due process considerations. It also strongly suggests that if the Congress were to revive explicit racial exclusions, the PRECEDENT of *Chae Chan Ping* would not prevent judicial examination of their constitutionality.

The interpretation of the United States Constitution concerning immigration has always been influenced by widely shared attitudes concerning the constitution of American society. Today's issues of immigration policy focus on the use of "temporary" workers from other countries. Central to this theme is the story of Mexican labor migration. After 1882 Mexican and Japanese workers, along with immigrants from eastern and southern Europe, were recruited to help fill the void left by the exclusion of the Chinese. When Japanese immigration was effectively closed in 1907, employers in the Southwest intensified the recruitment of Mexicans. Assisted by statutory exemptions and waivers, many employers grew rich on the backs of immigrants who were poor and powerless. When poor whites competed for menial jobs, however—as after the crash of 1929—hundreds of thousands of Mexican workers were deported.

The pattern is repeated, from World War II through the 1942–1964 Bracero Program (admitting temporary workers) and beyond, in a cycle that has not yet ended: Mexican workers are recruited when they serve the needs of domestic employers, and expelled when their usefulness seems to decline. They fill jobs as needed, and at a low wage, but they are not to be allowed to burden local communities. The Bracero Program amounted to an official (but unacknowledged) program of undocumented Mexican migration. At a time when the Border Patrol might have made a real difference in curbing undocumented entry—and thus restricting American growers from employing undocumented workers—the agency's budget was cut. Since 1952, Congress has exempted employers from liability for employing undocumented workers.

The result of all these developments is that the cheapest labor in the United States has become almost exclusively the province of undocumented workers. An entrenched migratory culture now supplies workers from Mexico and other countries to fill low-paying and socially undesirable jobs. If recruitment has become unnecessary, effective enforcement of formal immigration law has become virtually impossible. Very large numbers of undocumented workers are here to stay—and, predictably, America's long-standing ambivalence toward immigration is translated into a paradox of constitutional law. On the one hand, government is to be given the widest powers to seek out and deport undocumented workers, including such far-reaching methods as BORDER SEARCHES and the factory sweeps approved in *Immigration and Naturalization Service v. Delgado* (1984). On the other hand, PLYLER V. DOE (1982), holding it unconstitutional for Texas to deny free public education to children of the undocumented, almost certainly rested on the premise that most of those children are going to remain part of the American community, whether or not Texas chooses to educate them. The *Plyler* decision is one of major potential importance for the definition of the boundaries of that community, and for the recognition and fulfillment of the national community's concrete responsibilities to all its members.

GERALD P. LÓPEZ
KENNETH L. KARST

Bibliography

GORDON, CHARLES AND ROSENFELD, HARRY N. 1985 *Immigration Law and Procedure*, Rev. ed. Vol. 1. New York: Matthew Bender.

LÓPEZ, GERALD P. 1981 Undocumented Mexican Migration: In Search of a Just Immigration Law and Policy. *UCLA Law Review* 28:615–714.

NOTE 1983 Developments in the Law—Immigration and the Rights of Aliens. *Harvard Law Review* 96:1286–1465.

IMMIGRATION AND NATURALIZATION SERVICE v. CHADHA
462 U.S. 919 (1983)

Immigration and Naturalization Service v. Chadha cast serious doubt on the use of the LEGISLATIVE VETO, a device by which Congress seeks to retain control over the use of DELEGATED POWERS. *Chadha* involved a provision in the IMMIGRATION AND NATIONALITY ACT that permitted either house of Congress, by resolution, to overturn orders of the attorney general suspending DEPORTATION of ALIENS.

The Supreme Court held, 7–2, that congressional review of such cases was legislative in character, and was therefore subject to the provisions of Article I requiring the concurrence of both houses and an opportunity for the President to exercise his VETO POWER before the resolution can have the force of law. The majority opinion, by Chief Justice WARREN E. BURGER, declared that the one-house legislative veto violated the constitutional principles of SEPARATION OF POWERS and BICAMERALISM.

Justice BYRON R. WHITE, dissenting, ascribed to

the decision much greater scope than did the majority. White asserted that the *Chadha* decision effectively invalidated every legislative veto provision in federal law. A majority in future cases, however, may choose not to apply the *Chadha* rationale to two-house legislative vetoes or to legislative vetoes of agency actions that are clearly legislative rather than executive or quasi-judicial. It would be curious indeed if administrative agencies promulgating regulations with the force of law were freed from congressional oversight by a Court intent on preserving the separation of powers and bicameralism.

DENNIS J. MAHONEY

IMMIGRATION AND NATURALIZATION SERVICE v. LOPEZ-MENDOZA

See: Deportation

IMMUNITY GRANT (SELF-INCRIMINATION)

"No person," the Fifth Amendment unequivocally states, "shall be . . . compelled in any criminal case to be a witness against himself. . . ." It does not add, "unless such person cannot be prosecuted or punished as a result of his testimony," and it does not refer to self-incrimination. Yet, if the government wants EVIDENCE concerning a crime, it can compel a witness to testify by granting immunity from prosecution. In law, such immunity means that the witness cannot incriminate himself and therefore has suffered no violation of his RIGHT AGAINST SELF-INCRIMINATION. The common sense of the matter is that to "incriminate" means to implicate criminally; in law, however, it means exposure to prosecution or penalties. The law indulges the fiction that when one receives a grant of immunity, removing him from criminal jeopardy, the right not to be a witness against oneself is not violated. If the witness cannot be prosecuted, the penalties do not exist for him, so that his testimony can be compelled without forcing him to incriminate himself or "be a witness against himself."

The first immunity statute in Anglo-American jurisprudence was probably the one enacted by Connecticut in 1698. That act specified that witnesses in criminal cases must give sworn evidence, on pain of punishment for refusal, "always provided that no person required to give testimonie as aforesaid shall be punished for what he doth confess against himself when under oath." Similarly, an act that Parliament passed against gambling in 1710, which some colonies copied, guaranteed that gamblers who confessed their crimes and returned their winnings should be "acquitted, indemnified [immunized] and discharged from any further or other Punishment, Forfeiture, or Penalty which he or they may have incurred by the playing for or winning such Money. . . ." New York in 1758 obtained the king's pardon for certain ship captains in order to compel their testimony against the ships' owners. Although the pardons had eliminated the perils of the criminal law for the captains, they persisted in their claim that the law could not force them to declare anything that might incriminate them. A court fined them for contempt, on grounds that the recalcitrant captains no longer faced criminal jeopardy by giving evidence against themselves.

In modern language these colonial precedents illustrate grants of "transactional" immunity, an absolute guarantee that in return for evidence, the compelled person will not under any circumstances be prosecuted for the transaction or criminal episode concerning which he gives testimony. Absolute or transactional immunity was the price paid by the law for exacting information that would otherwise be actionable criminally. The paradox remained: one could be compelled to be a witness against oneself, but from the law's perspective the immunized witness would stand to the offense as if he had never committed it, or had received AMNESTY or a pardon despite having committed it.

Congress enacted its first immunity statute in 1857, granting freedom from prosecution for any acts or transactions to which a witness offered testimony in an investigation. Reacting against the immunity "baths" that enabled corrupt officials to escape from criminal liability by offering immunized testimony, Congress in 1862 supplanted the act of 1857 with one that offered only "use" immunity. Use immunity guarantees only that the compelled testimony will not be used in a criminal prosecution, but prosecution is possible if based on evidence independent from or unrelated to the compelled testimony. Under a grant of use immunity one might confess to a crime secure in the knowledge that his confession could not be used against him; however, if the prosecution had other evidence to prove his guilt, he might be prosecuted. By 1887 Congress extended the standard of use immunity from congressional investigations to all federal proceedings.

Until 1972 the Supreme Court demanded transactional rather than use immunity as the sole basis for displacing the Fifth Amendment right to remain silent. In COUNSELMAN V. HITCHCOCK (1892) the Court unanimously held unconstitutional a congressional act offering use immunity because use immunity was "not co-extensive with the constitutional provision." The compelled testimony might provide leads to evidence that the prosecution might not otherwise possess. To supplant the constitutional guarantee, an immunity statute must provide "complete protection" from all criminal perils; "in view of the constitutional provision, a statutory enactment, to be valid, must afford absolute immunity against future prosecution for the offense to which the question relates." Congress responded with a statute safeguarding against prosecution, forfeiture, or penalty for any transaction about which one might be compelled to testify. In BROWN V. WALKER (1896) the Court held that transactional immunity "operates as a pardon for the offense to which it relates," thus satisfying the constitutional guarantee. In effect the Court permitted what it had declared was impossible: congressional amendment of the Constitution. By a statute that served as a "substitute," Congress altered the guarantee that no one can be compelled to be a witness against himself criminally.

Until 1970 there were over fifty federal immunity statutes conforming with *Brown*'s transactional immunity standard, which the Court reendorsed in ULLMANN V. UNITED STATES (1956). When the Court scrapped its TWO SOVEREIGNTIES RULE in *Murphy v. Waterfront Commission* (1964), it held that absent an immunity grant, a state witness could not be compelled to testify unless his testimony "and its fruits" could not be used by the federal government. *Murphy* was a technical relaxation of the transactional immunity standard, as ALBERTSON V. SUBVERSIVE ACTIVITIES CONTROL BOARD (1965) proved, because a unanimous Court reconfirmed the transactional immunity standard.

Through the ORGANIZED CRIME CONTROL ACT of 1970, Congress made use immunity and derivative-use immunity the standard for all federal grants of immunity, and most states copied the new standard. No compelled testimony or its "fruits" (information directly or indirectly derived from such testimony) could be used against a witness criminally, except to prove perjury. In KASTIGAR V. UNITED STATES (1972) the Court relied on *Murphy*, ignored or distorted all other precedents, and upheld the narrow standard as coextensive with the Fifth Amendment, which it is not. One who relies on his right to remain silent forces the state to rely wholly on its own evidence to convict him. By remaining silent he gives the state

no way to use his testimony, however indirectly. When he is compelled to be a witness against himself, his admissions assist the state's investigation against him. The burden of proving that the state's evidence derives from sources wholly independent of the compelled testimony lies upon the prosecution. But use immunity permits compulsion without removing criminality.

In *New Jersey v. Portash* (1979) the Court held that a defendant's immunized grand jury testimony could not be introduced to impeach his testimony at his trial. Whether the state may introduce immunized testimony to prove perjury has not been decided. In *Portash*, however, the Court conceded, "Testimony given in response to a grant of legislative immunity is the essence of coerced testimony." The essence of the Fifth Amendment's provision is that testimony against oneself cannot be coerced. Any grant of immunity that compels testimony compels one to be a witness against himself—except, of course, that it is "impossible," as the Court said in *Counselman*, for the constitutional guarantee to mean what it says.

LEONARD W. LEVY

Bibliography

LEVY, LEONARD W. 1974 *Against the Law: The Nixon Court and Criminal Justice.* Pages 165–187. New York: Harper & Row.

IMMUNITY OF GOVERNMENT OFFICIALS

See: Executive Immunity; Judicial Immunity; Legislative Immunity

IMPACT OF SUPREME COURT DECISIONS

The Supreme Court's decisions have regularly embroiled it in controversy. Its rulings have considerable impact. In its early years, the Court, over strenuous objection from the states, shaped our federal system and helped establish the national government's supremacy. The Court also had substantial effects on the economy, aiding in the creation of an American economic common market and providing opportunities for the private sector to develop. The Court's major effects on FEDERALISM and the economy subsided after the 1930s. However, its effect on CIVIL RIGHTS, visible earlier with respect to slavery and its emasculation of Reconstruction civil rights statutes, again became apparent as questions such as school DESEGREGATION came to the fore in the 1950s.

The Supreme Court's impact includes ways in which federal and state agencies and lower federal and state courts carry out the Court's decisions, but it also includes the ways in which the agencies and courts delay, circumvent, misunderstand, and erode them. It includes the response to decisions by different "populations"—those who explain or elaborate its rulings, those supposed to apply or implement them, those for whom the rulings are intended, and the general population. Because the Court, "the least dangerous branch," lacks the capacity to enforce its rulings directly, assistance from those at whom a ruling is directed or from others (legislatures, executive agencies, courts) is required. The Court is now recognized to be a political actor, but one must abandon the tacit assumption held by earlier scholars that Supreme Court decisions are self-executing and recognize that the law is what the judges say it is only after all others have had their say.

Impact and compliance are not identical but are related. Compliance, the process by which individuals accept a decision prior to its impact or effect, cannot occur unless a person knows of the ruling and is required to take or abstain from a certain action. Compliance means an individual's intentionally conforming behavior to the ruling's dictates, that is, doing what the decision commands because of the ruling. Because noncompliance, or refusal to obey, occurs relatively seldom despite the attention it receives, it is important to pay heed to implementation of decisions, the process by which they are put into effect. Short-run resistance may blend into longer-run obedience, as resulted in the aftermath of the REAPPORTIONMENT decisions.

Impact includes all effects, direct and indirect, resulting from a ruling of the Court, regardless of whether those affected knew about the decision; it includes the results of rulings permitting but not requiring the adoption of certain policies. When effects of a ruling indirectly induce behavior congruent with the ruling, that behavior is better viewed as impact than as compliance. Impact encompasses actions neither directly defiant nor clearly obedient, such as attempts at evasion coupled with technical obedience and efforts to anticipate the Court's decisions ("anticipatory compliance"). Impact also includes both short-term and long-run consequences of a decision, for example, massive resistance to school desegregation rulings and the rulings' arguable contribution to "white flight" to the suburbs. There will also be situations in which no response occurs, that is, where there is an absence of obvious impact.

The Supreme Court's effect on the President has generally been one of support and reinforcement. The Court has been least willing to overturn his acts in time of war, when presidential resistance to Court decisions would be most likely. Although limiting somewhat the President's authority to remove certain government employees, the Court, since the New Deal, has sustained DELEGATIONS OF POWER to the President and the executive branch and has generally been deferential to the REGULATORY COMMISSIONS since World War II. Confrontations between Court and President have been relatively infrequent; when the Court invalidates policies the President had espoused, for example, WIRETAPPING, it is not attacking the presidency as an institution. Presidents may have been reluctant to assist in enforcing the Court's decisions, but direct defiance is rare indeed. Both President HARRY S. TRUMAN and President RICHARD M. NIXON complied with orders when their actions (seizure of the steel mills and withholding of tapes) were ruled improper. In those situations, as with IMPOUNDMENT of appropriated funds, the Court insisted that the President follow the law as interpreted by the courts rather than determine for himself whether he should be subject to it; in the case of the STEEL SEIZURE, the Court insisted that he follow a course of action legislated by Congress.

The Court has had considerable impact on Congress's internal processes—its authority to exclude members, LEGISLATIVE INVESTIGATIONS, and the CONTEMPT POWER. Congressional reaction to the Court's decisions has been manifested in a number of ways. After the Court has engaged in statutory interpretation or, less frequently, has invalidated statutes for VAGUENESS, Congress has often rewritten or reenacted the laws to reestablish its "legislative intent," in effect establishing a continuing dialogue between Court and Congress. Congress has also shown negative reaction to the Court's ruling through proposals to eliminate APPELLATE JURISDICTION in particular classes of cases, for example, internal security, abortions, and school prayer, but these attempts have been less frequent and far less successful than those to rewrite statutes. Efforts to overturn the Court's rulings have also resulted in introduction of numerous proposals to amend the Constitution, but most such proposals die. Only a few—the ELEVENTH AMENDMENT, Civil War Amendments, SIXTEENTH AMENDMENT, and TWENTY-SIXTH AMENDMENT—have been both submitted and ratified.

The impact of the Supreme Court's decisions extends well beyond the other branches of the national government. Controversial Supreme Court rulings have affected public opinion and have produced divided editorial reaction on a wide range of decisions. Changes in the public's feelings of trust or confidence in the Court have paralleled changes in feeling about the presidency and Congress but generally have been somewhat more positive. Such ratings have changed rapidly, but shifts in the Court's doctrine on controversial topics (such as CRIMINAL PROCEDURE) in the direction of public opinion usually are not immediately reflected in changed public opinion ratings.

The public generally supports the Court's work. Those giving the Court general (or "diffuse") support, however, outnumber those giving the Court specific support (for particular rulings) by a large ratio. The proportion of the public that feels the Court may legitimately produce structural political change is quite small. Acquiescence in the Court's rulings, which helps produce compliance, has been more common than active approval of the decisions.

The public also has little information about the Court. Even many controversial decisions fail to penetrate the general public's consciousness. The greater the knowledge, however, the greater the *dis*approval, but those reporting negative views on specific cases outnumber those whose general view of the Court is negative. Those with negative views also tend to hold them more intensely, but seldom would most members of the public do more than write letters of protest; demonstrations and other overt protest are atypical. Negative views about the Court are usually accounted for by reactions to the few specific decisions that catch the attention of large proportions of the public. Those salient decisions change with considerable rapidity, shifting in the 1960s from civil rights and school prayer to criminal procedure.

The Supreme Court's impact on the states and local communities is varied. Effectuating many decisions involves little controversy, and implementation may be prompt and complete, particularly if actions of only a few public officials are necessary. Other rulings, such as those on school DESEGREGATION, school prayer, and criminal procedure, produce a disproportionate amount both of resistance or attempts to evade and of critical rhetoric—rhetoric at times not matched by reality. Despite claims that the warnings required by MIRANDA V. ARIZONA (1966) would have a negative impact on police work, suspects and defendants often talk to police after being "read their rights." However, even these criticized rulings have definite impacts,

for example, more professional police work as a result of criminal procedure rulings. Although opponents of the rule that improperly seized evidence should be excluded (the EXCLUSIONARY RULE of MAPP V. OHIO, 1961) have claimed that the rule does not deter illegal seizures and is too costly because guilty defendants are set free, some studies have suggested that the rule might be having some of its intended effect. At least in some cities, few cases were dropped after motions to suppress evidence and a higher proportion of searches conducted after the rule was promulgated were constitutional.

If people are to comply with Supreme Court rulings or if the rulings are to have an impact, they must be communicated to those expected to implement or adhere to them. One cannot, however, assume that effective communication takes place. A ruling may have to be transmitted through several levels, at each of which distortion can be introduced, before reaching its ultimate audience. Lawyers may be accustomed to easy access to the Court's published opinions, but many others, such as police or school officials, often do not receive the opinions or have such direct access to them and must therefore rely on other means of communication through which to learn of them.

The mass media, with the exception of a few newspapers, provide only sketchy information about the Court's decisions. Specialized media, for example, trade publications, provide only erratic coverage even of decisions relevant to the groups for which they are published. Most newspapers and radio and television stations must rely on the wire services for information about Supreme Court rulings. Disproportionate nationwide emphasis is given to decisions the wire services emphasize, with little or no coverage given to other rulings. The media also have different patterns of coverage ("profiles"). Newspapers, for example, give more attention to postdecision events, while the wire services and television pay more attention to cases before they are decided. All the media, however, generally convey much information about immediate reaction to, or impact of, decisions instead of emphasizing the content of, or rationale for, the Court's rulings.

The lower courts do not constitute a bureaucratic structure through which decisions are fully communicated downward. Lawyers thus become particularly important in transmitting the Court's rulings, as they are in transmitting any law. Lower court judges who do not routinely follow the Court's decisions may find out about them only if lawyers arguing cases cite the decisions, which they do not always do accurately.

Lawyers, either individually or through their bar associations, do little to inform the general public about developments in the law. Some state attorneys general and local prosecutors undertake to inform state and local officials of recent rulings affecting their work. The failure of these officials to do so in most locations has led some local agencies, which can afford to do so, to hire their own lawyers, for example, police department "police legal advisers," to monitor the Court's rulings, provide appropriate information to the agency, and arrange for implementation.

Training programs—effective because they combine printed materials with oral presentation—can be particularly important in the transmission of rulings. They are especially necessary because the educational system has generally done little to educate students, later to be members of the general public, about the Court's functioning or its rulings. Training programs are, however, not available to all those expected to be cognizant or familiar with the Court's rulings. Many members of some important occupational groups such as the police do not receive adequate legal training about the Court's decisions. Even if initially well-trained, they are less likely to receive adequate follow-up through in-service training.

The impact of the Court's decisions is, of course, affected by far more than deficiencies and distortions in the lengthy, often convoluted process by which the decisions are communicated. Numerous other factors affect both the communication process, thus indirectly affecting impact, and impact itself. One is the legitimacy attributed to the Court and its work. If a particular audience, for example, the police during the WARREN COURT's "criminal procedure revolution," feels that the Court is not acting fairly or lacks appropriate information on which to base its decisions, that audience will heed the Court's word less carefully even when the opinions are fully communicated. Characteristics of the Court's rulings, such as their relative unanimity and relative clarity or ambiguity, are also important, as both unanimity and clarity are thought to produce greater compliance. In new and sensitive areas of policy such as civil rights and criminal procedure, the lower courts can exercise power over the Supreme Court by their resistance. Rulings by lower court judges applying and extending (or narrowing) the Court's decisions are particularly important in such situations and in those where gaps in doctrinal development—a result of case-by-case development of the law—leave unanswered questions. In many, perhaps most, areas of the law, however, lower court judges enforce Supreme Court rulings because those rulings are a matter of relative personal indifference for the judges, because they have been socialized to follow those rulings, and because they wish to avoid being reversed.

Whether someone follows up a decision, who that "someone" is, and how they act, also affect a decision's impact. Elites' support for a decision may be able to calm negative public reaction. The likelihood that desegregation would be accepted in either the short or long run was decreased because southern elites were not favorably disposed toward either the result of BROWN V. BOARD OF EDUCATION (1954) or the Court's opinion. Because most rulings of the Court are not self-enforcing, follow-up by government agencies is often crucial for effective implementation. Officials not committed to the values in the Court's rulings are less likely to be assiduous in their follow-up; thus the attitudes of individual decision makers, particularly those in key policymaking or enforcement positions, are of considerable importance.

The situation into which a Supreme Court ruling is "injected"—whether in a crisis or in normal times—also affects the ruling's impact. A local community's belief system and its past history both are part of that situation. So are community pressures on the individuals expected to carry out the Court's dictates. Often a wide variety of enforcement mechanisms must be used before compliance is achieved. Incentive systems in organizations can lead individuals either to follow the Court's rulings or to continue existing practices. Because organizations have considerable interest in maintaining such practices, externally imposed penalties may be insufficient to produce required change.

To overcome problems of communicating Supreme Court rulings so that they reach the appropriate audience might seem insuperable. The Court's rulings are, however, often complied with and do have widespread impact. Were it otherwise, we should not hear so much about the problems occurring in particularly sensitive areas of the law such as civil rights and CIVIL LIBERTIES. The difficulties in implementing the Court's decisions to achieve their greatest impact should remind us that, as an active policymaker, the Supreme Court faces many of the same problems faced by other policymaking institutions.

STEPHEN L. WASBY

Bibliography

BECKER, THEODORE L. and FEELEY, MALCOLM, EDS. 1973 *The Impact of Supreme Court Decisions: Empirical Studies*, 2nd ed. New York: Oxford University Press.

JOHNSON, CHARLES A. and CANON, BRADLEY C. 1984 *Judicial Policies: Implementation and Impact.* Washington D.C.: Congressional Quarterly Press.

KRISLOV, SAMUEL, ED. 1972 *Compliance and the Law: A Multidisciplinary Approach.* Beverly Hills, Calif.: Sage Publications.

WASBY, STEPHEN L. 1970 *The Impact of the United States Supreme Court: Some Perspectives.* Homewood, Ill.: Dorsey Press.

IMPEACHMENT

The English Parliament devised impeachment for the removal of ministers of the Crown, the House of Commons serving as prosecutor of charges that the House of Lords adjudged. This, ALEXANDER HAMILTON wrote, was the "model" of the American proceeding—the House of Representatives files and prosecutes charges and the Senate is the trial tribunal. The Framers of the Constitution also adopted the English grounds for removal, "TREASON, bribery, or other high crimes and MISDEMEANORS." They defined "treason" narrowly; "bribery" was a COMMON LAW term of familiar meaning; but the scope of "other high crimes and misdemeanors" remains a subject of continuing debate. Some would confine those terms to indictable crimes. At the other pole, Congressman GERALD FORD, in proposing the impeachment of Justice WILLIAM O. DOUGLAS in 1970, asserted that an impeachable offense is whatever the House, with the concurrence of the Senate, "considers [it] to be." The historical facts indicate, however, that an impeachable offense need not be indictable, but that such offenses have their limits, for which we must look to the English practice the terms expressed.

Advocates of the indictable crime interpretation point to the criminal terminology, for example, "high crimes and misdemeanors." Article III, section 2, of the Constitution provides, "The trial of all Crimes, except in cases of Impeachment, shall be by Jury"; Article II, section 2, confers a power to grant pardons "except in Cases of Impeachment," and pardons relieve from punishment for a crime. In England the House of Lords combined removal and punishment in the impeachment proceeding. But Article I, section 3, clause 7, made an important departure: "Judgment in cases of impeachment shall not extend further than to removal from office, and disqualification to hold and enjoy any [federal] office . . . but the party convicted shall nevertheless be liable and subject to INDICTMENT, trial, judgment and punishment, according to law." The separation of removal from criminal prosecution meant that political passions could no longer sweep an accused to his death, but that he would be tried by a jury of his peers.

In the North Carolina Ratification Convention, JAMES IREDELL explained that if the President "commits any misdemeanor in office, he is impeachable, removable from office. . . . If he commits any crime, he is punishable by the laws of his country," distinguishing an impeachable "misdemeanor" (which has a common law connotation of misconduct in office) from an indictable crime. Hamilton likewise distinguished between "removal from office" and "actual punishment in cases which admit of it," indicating that some impeachable offenses were not criminal. As will appear, some impeachable offenses were not and still are not punishable crimes; nor does the absence of fine and imprisonment, the customary criminal sanctions, comport with the view that impeachment is a criminal proceeding. The doctrine of DOUBLE JEOPARDY also conduces to this conclusion. Although double jeopardy at the framing of the Constitution referred to jeopardy of life, as the Fifth Amendment attests, Congress speedily made treason punishable by death. Impeachment for treason could not, therefore, be regarded as criminal without raising a bar to indictment. Such thinking was carried over to all impeachments by JAMES WILSON: because they "are founded on different principles . . . directed to different objects . . . the trial and punishment of an offense on impeachment, is no bar to a trial of the same offense at common law." Justice JOSEPH STORY deduced from the separation between removal and indictment that "a second trial for the same offense" would not be barred by double jeopardy. Thus double jeopardy requires impeachment to be read in noncriminal terms.

The Sixth Amendment furnishes further confirmation. Earlier Article III, section 2, clause 3, expressly exempted impeachment from the "Trial of all Crimes" by jury. With that exemption before them, the draftsmen of the Sixth Amendment required TRIAL BY JURY in "all criminal prosecutions," thereby canceling the former exception. Since the later Amendment controls, it must be concluded either that the Founders felt no need to exempt impeachment from the Sixth Amendment because they did not consider it a "criminal prosecution" or that jury trial is required if impeachment be in fact a "criminal" prosecution. The latter conclusion is inadmissible. Perhaps the use of criminal terminology is attributable to the fact that words like "offenses," "convict," and "high crimes" had been employed in the English impeachments, and the Framers, engaged in hammering out a charter of government that required major political compromises, could not pause to coin a fresh and different vocabulary for every detail.

Treason and bribery, in contradistinction to crimes against the individual such as murder and robbery, are crimes against the State—political crimes. James Wilson, a chief architect of the Constitution, observed that "impeachments are confined to political characters, to political crimes and misdemeanors." And Justice Story added that they are designed "to secure the state against gross official misdemeanors." By association with "treason, bribery," the phrase "other high crimes and misdemeanors" likewise may be deemed to refer to "political" offenses. "High crimes and misdemeanors" meant "and *high* misdemeanors," not as a matter of grammatical construction but of historical usage. "High misdemeanors" are first met in a 1386 impeachment, long before there was such a crime as a "misdemeanor." At that time FELONIES were coupled with TRESPASSES, private as distinguished from political offenses. It was not until well into the sixteenth century that "misdemeanors" replaced "trespasses" in the general criminal law; and in England "high misdemeanors" remained a term peculiar to impeachment and did not find its way into ordinary criminal law, as is true of American law but for a very few statutory "high misdemeanors." Explaining "high misdemeanors," Sir WILLIAM BLACKSTONE stated that the "first and principal is the *maladministration* of such high officers as are in the public trust and employment. This is usually punished by the method of parliamentary impeachment," which proceeded not under the common law but under the *lex parliamentaria*, the "laws and course of parliament."

Though this arguably left Parliament free to fashion political offenses ad hoc, the Framers took a more restricted view. English impeachments proceeded largely for neglect of duty, abuse of power, betrayal of trust, corruption; and early state constitutions likewise provided for removal for misconduct in office, maladministration, corruption. In the Convention there were proposals for removal upon malpractice, neglect of duty, betrayal of trust, corruption, malversation (misconduct in office). Throughout, the focus was on machinery for removal rather than punishment for misconduct. When the impeachment provision came to the floor of the Convention, it employed "treason or bribery." GEORGE MASON protested that the narrow definition of treason would not reach "many great and dangerous offenses," among them "attempts to subvert the Constitution," which lay at the root of the leading English precedent. He therefore suggested the addition of "maladministration," but Madison objected that "so vague a term will be equivalent to a tenure during the pleasure of the Sen-

ate," whereupon Mason substituted "other high crimes and misdemeanors." Some two weeks earlier RUFUS KING had identified treason "agst. particular States" as "high misdemeanors"; a week before, "high misdemeanor" had been replaced in the extradition provision because it had "a technical meaning too limited." These facts show, first, that "other high crimes and misdemeanors" referred to "high misdemeanors," and second, that the terms were chosen precisely because they were "limited and technical" and would not leave the accused at the "pleasure of the Senate." As with other common law terms employed by the Framers, they expected them to have the meaning ascribed to them under English practice.

Justice Story stated that for the meaning of "high crimes and misdemeanors" resort must be had "to parliamentary practice" or "the whole subject must be left to the arbitrary discretion of the Senate," a "despotism" "incompatible" with "the genius of our institutions," and, it may be added, with the legislative history of the provision. Were impeachment restricted to common law crimes it would founder because there are no FEDERAL COMMON LAW crimes; all federal crimes are creatures of statute. Early on Congress enacted statutes that made treason and bribery crimes; a few statutes made certain minor acts criminal "high misdemeanors." But no statute declared "abuse of power," "neglect of duty," or "subversion of the Constitution" to be criminal, yet the Founders unquestionably regarded these as impeachable offenses. Except for treason and bribery, the "silence of the statute book," said Story, would render the power of impeachment "a complete nullity" and enable the most serious offender to escape removal. It is preferable to regard such silence as a continuing construction by Congress that its impeachment powers are not dependent on a statutory proscription and definition of impeachable offenses, particularly because most of its impeachment proceedings have involved nonindictable offenses. In extrajudicial statements, Chief Justice WILLIAM HOWARD TAFT and Justice CHARLES EVANS HUGHES recognized that such offenses were embraced by "high crimes and misdemeanors."

Another much debated issue is whether impeachment constitutes the sole means for removal of judges. Long before there was mention of impeachment of Justices in the Convention, it conditioned judicial tenure on "GOOD BEHAVIOR." This wording was not, as has been urged, "used simply to describe a life term," but a technical phrase of established meaning: "as long as he shall behave himself well." Hamilton noted that "good behavior tenure" was a "defeasible tenure," copied from the British model. At common law an appointment conditioned on "good behavior" was forfeited on nonperformance of the condition, that is, it terminated on misbehavior. Given a lapse from "good behavior," WILLIAM MURRAY (Lord Mansfield) observed, there must be power to remove the officer lest the formula be impotent. The remedy, Blackstone wrote, was by writ of *scire facias* determinable by the judiciary. Attempts by the Crown to remove a couple of high court judges who enjoyed "good behavior" tenure, Sir John Walter, Chief Baron of the Exchequer, and Sir John Archer, a Justice of Common Pleas, met insistence on removal by *scire facias*. This view was endorsed by Chief Justice Holt, Lord Chancellor Erskine, the future Lord Justice Denman, William Holdsworth, and CHARLES MCILWAIN. When the Framers employed a common law term, they expected it would be given its accepted meaning, as is shown by their redefinition of treason to avoid historic excesses, by JOHN DICKINSON's caution that if EX POST FACTO were to be expanded beyond the Blackstonian association with criminal cases it "would require some further provision," and by assurances in the Virginia Ratification Convention that reference to "trial by jury" included all its attributes, including the right to challenge jurors.

The Framers conceived impeachment as a remedy for misconduct by the President, and throughout the Convention such was its almost exclusive focus. Hamilton explained that "the true light in which it ought to be regarded" is as "a bridle in the hands of the legislative body upon the executive servants of the government." Consequently the Framers placed the provision for impeachment of the President in Article II, the Executive article. Almost at the last minute they amplified it by the addition of the "Vice President, and all civil officers," suggesting it was to apply to officers of the Executive department. The interpretive canon that each provision of an instrument should, if possible, be given effect counsels recognition of judicial removal for breaches of "good behavior," particularly because the standards of "high crimes and misdemeanors" differ from those of "good behavior," so that to insist that impeachment is the sole means for removal of judges is to leave some judicial "misbehavior" beyond remedy.

A number of utterances may seem to require the exclusivity of impeachment; for example, Hamilton stated in THE FEDERALIST #79 that impeachment "is the only provision" for removal of judges found in the Constitution and "consistent with the necessary independence of judges." Yet he had said in *The Federalist* #78 that "the standard of good behavior" is

an "excellent barrier . . . to the encroachments and oppression of the representative body"; independence from Congress, not from judges, was the aim. Hamilton recognized that the "standard of good behavior" created a "defeasible tenure," a tenure terminated by breach of "good behavior." So too, the debate in the First Congress respecting the President's power to remove his subordinates contains tangential references to the protection from removal (chiefly by the President) that "good behavior" tenure afforded judges. Removal of his subordinates by the President made a breach in the "exclusivity" of impeachment, notwithstanding the fact that they squarely fit within "all civil officers" of Article II. It is easier to recognize an "exception" from exclusivity for the forfeiture that was an established concomitant of "good behavior," thus giving effect to that separate provision, than to make an exception for Executive subordinates.

What the First Congress did do with respect to judges further undermines reliance upon such dicta. By the Act of 1790 it provided that upon conviction in court for bribery a judge shall "forever be disqualified to hold an office." Since the impeachment clause provides both for removal and disqualification upon impeachment and conviction, the Act represents a construction that the clause does not exclude other means of disqualification. As with "disqualification," so with "removal," for the two stand on a par in the impeachment clause. The action of the First Congress, whose constitutional constructions carry great weight, when it dealt with judges thus speaks against reliance upon passing remarks in a debate that did not involve their removal. The several remarks, moreover, do not meet the test laid down by Chief Justice JOHN MARSHALL, showing that had "this particular case been suggested"—that is, judicial removal of judges for "misbehavior"—"the language would have been so varied as to exclude it." Well aware of the perils posed to judges by "the gusts of faction which might prevail" in Congress, the Founders were little likely to jettison the time-honored nonpolitical removal trial of judges by the courts in favor of a factional proceeding in Congress. Impeachment could be reserved for the grave situation in which the judiciary neglects to cleanse its own house, exactly as impeachment remains available for removal of a wrong-doing subordinate or "favorite" whom the President fails to remove.

JAMES BRYCE observed that impeachment is so heavy a "piece of artillery" as to "be unfit for ordinary use." The Founders repeatedly stressed that impeachment was meant only for "great injuries"; like Solicitor General, later Lord Chancellor Somers, they were aware that "impeachment ought to be like Goliath's sword, kept in the temple, and used but on great occasions." Hamilton too referred in *The Federalist* #70 to the "awful discretion" of the impeachment tribunal to doom "to infamy the . . . most distinguished characters of the community." Such views do not square with the insistence that the wheels of the nation must grind to a halt so that Congress can oust a venal district judge. Congress is in fact reluctant to undertake the ouster of such judges even, said Senator William McAdoo, "in cases of flagrant misconduct," because an impeachment proceeding draws the Congress away for weeks from weightier tasks. That situation, he stated, constitutes "a standing invitation for judges to abuse their authority with impunity and without fear of removal." To insist that impeachment is the sole means of removal of judges is in practical effect to immunize grave misconduct. In the almost two hundred years since adoption of the Constitution hundreds of complaints have resulted in fifty-five investigations, followed in some cases by censure or resignation. But only nine judges have been impeached and only four convicted and removed.

Some regard the acquittal of Justice SAMUEL P. CHASE in 1805 as a triumph of justice over heated political partisanship. Others view his impeachment as a natural reaction to the gross partisanship of the Federalist judiciary, given to intemperate attacks upon the Republican opposition in harangues to the GRAND JURY, which might be regarded as an "abuse of power" for political ends. Of Chase's trial of James Callender for alleged violations of the ALIEN AND SEDITIONS ACTS, EDWARD S. CORWIN said that Chase came to the case "with the evident disposition to play the hanging judge," and there is evidence that he prejudged the case. Callendar was entitled under the canons of his time to a trial free of "the tyrannical partiality of judges," and Chase was under statutory oath to administer justice impartially. Most students of the era consider that conviction failed of a two-thirds vote because the inept, acid-tongued manager of the impeachment, JOHN RANDOLPH, had alienated many Republicans as well as Federalists.

The *cause célèbre* is the impeachment of President ANDREW JOHNSON in 1868, essentially, as Justice SAMUEL F. MILLER foresaw, "for standing in the way of certain political purposes of the majority in Congress," but ostensibly for discharging his secretary of war, EDWIN M. STANTON, whom Congress had attempted to rivet in place by the TENURE OF OFFICE ACT. Critics of Johnson have noted Stanton's "defective loyalty," his conferences with Republican leaders behind Johnson's back respecting measures that divided Congress from the President. Finally Johnson removed him, presenting the issue whether a President who considered a statute to be an unconstitutional invasion of his prerogative to remove a disloyal subordinate—Stanton himself had advised Johnson that the statute was unconstitutional—and who felt that it was his constitutional duty to exercise his independent judgment, was impeachable. Such differences were contemplated as part of the CHECKS AND BALANCES of the Constitution.

The tone of the proceedings was sounded in BENJAMIN BUTLER's opening statement: "You are bound by no law," "you are a law unto yourselves." THADDEUS STEVENS asserted that Johnson was "standing at bay, surrounded by a cordon of living men, each with the ax of an executioner uplifted for his just punishment." Stevens dared the Senators who had voted for the Tenure of Office Act four times now to vote for acquittal "on the ground of its UNCONSTITUTIONALITY," condemning backsliders to the "gibbet of everlasting obloquy." Senator CHARLES SUMNER dismissed "the quibbles of lawyers" in a trial that "is a battle with slavery." One of the impeachment articles charged that on his "Swing Around the Circle" before the 1866 elections, Johnson attempted to bring Congress into ridicule, disgrace, and contempt. But as Senator John Sherman pointed out, members of Congress themselves had resorted to grossly abusive epithets, so that Johnson was not to be blamed for responding in kind. FREEDOM OF SPEECH, Senator James Patterson cautioned, was not solely for Congress. Current revulsion against Johnson does not overcome the verdict of Samuel Eliot Morison and Eric McKitrick that the impeachment was a "disgraceful episode," "a great act of ill-directed passion." Johnson's conviction failed by one vote. Whatever his faults, Johnson was entitled to a FAIR TRIAL, and that, the record amply discloses, was denied to him. Had Johnson been convicted, a revisionist historian wrote, it would have established a precedent "for the removal of any President refusing persistently to cooperate with Congress."

The failure of that impeachment led another revisionist historian to prophesy in 1973 that impeachment would never again be employed to remove a President. Shortly thereafter the House Judiciary Committee instituted an investigation whether President RICHARD M. NIXON participated in the WATERGATE conspiracy to obstruct justice. Once more the proceedings evidenced that impeachments are swayed by political affiliations; with a few notable exceptions, a Republican phalanx opposed impeachment until the judicially compelled disclosure of the "White House tapes" revealed that Nixon was a participant in the conspiracy. When he learned as a result of that disclosure that he could not count on more than ten votes in the Senate, he resigned from the presidency. In accepting a pardon from his successor, President GERALD FORD stated, he acknowledged his guilt. Fortunate it was for America that the Founders provided "Goliath's sword" for "great occasions."

RAOUL BERGER

Bibliography

BERGER, RAOUL 1979 "Chilling Judicial Independence": A Judicial Scarecrow. *Cornell Law Quarterly* 64:822–854.
_____ 1973 *Impeachment: The Constitutional Problems.* Pages 313–322. Cambridge, Mass.: Harvard University Press.
KAUFMAN, IRVING 1979 Chilling Judicial Independence. *Yale Law Journal* 88:681–716.
KURLAND, PHILIP 1974 Watergate, Impeachment and the Constitution. *Mississippi Law Review* 45:531–600.

IMPLIED CONSTITUTIONAL RIGHTS OF ACTION

One may seek judicial vindication of federal constitutional rights in at least three ways. Constitutional protections may be used as a shield against governmental misbehavior, as for example, when one relies on the Sixth Amendment guarantee of the RIGHT TO COUNSEL to contest a criminal prosecution. Second, one may rely on a constitutional right to enjoin allegedly unconstitutional behavior such as enforcement of an unconstitutional statute. Third, an aggrieved party may seek monetary compensation for past violations of constitutional rights. When invoked without express stautory authorization, the second and third techniques depend upon inferring the existence of implied rights of action to vindicate constitutional rights.

There is disagreement over whether, prior to EX PARTE YOUNG (1908), the offensive assertion of a federal right without a corresponding state-created right was sufficient to invoke a federal court's injunctive power. *Young*, which endorsed a federal INJUNCTION against enforcement of an allegedly unconstitutional state law, became the leading case to suggest that a federal cause of action for injunctive relief was implied merely from the existence of a constitutional right. This result has been a cornerstone of modern litigation contesting statutes and other government behavior. In later years, the Court interpreted SECTION 1983, TITLE 42, UNITED STATES CODE, to supply statutory support for both equitable and monetary relief in constitutional actions against state officials.

By 1971, in light of *Young* and section 1983, only the existence of implied damages actions against federal officials remained open to question. *Bell v. Hood* (1946) suggested that federal courts have JURISDICTION to consider whether alleged Fifth and FOURTH AMENDMENT violations by federal officials give rise to a cause of action for damages but it did not address the question of the cause of action's existence. In BIVENS V. SIX UNKNOWN NAMED AGENTS OF THE FEDERAL BUREAU OF NARCOTICS (1971), however, the Court held that an implied damages action exists for Fourth Amendment violations. DAVIS V. PASSMAN (1979) held that a damages action was implied in the EQUAL PROTECTION guarantee that has been found in the Fifth Amendment and constituted the Court's first extension of *Bivens* beyond Fourth Amendment claims. *Carlson v. Green* (1980), in which plaintiffs were allowed to bring an implied action under the Eighth Amendment, confirmed that *Bivens*-type actions are available under many constitutional provisions. Significantly, the Court has not held that such actions exist against state officials, a holding that would render superfluous much of its section 1983 jurisprudence.

Bivens, Davis, and *Carlson* suggested that Congress has an important role to play in determining the availability and scope of implied damages actions. The Court has left open the possibility of not inferring an implied damages action when defendants demonstrate "special factors counselling hesitation in the absence of affirmative action by Congress," or when, as in *Bush v. Lucas* (1983), Congress provides an effective alternative remedy. But *Davis* and *Carlson v. Green* indicated that the Court does not readily detect a congressional desire to foreclose *Bivens* actions. In *Davis,* Congress had declined to extend federal employment discrimination laws to preclude the behavior for which the Court inferred an implied private right of action. *Carlson* held that the existence of a remedy against the United States under the FEDERAL TORT CLAIMS ACT did not foreclose a *Bivens* action against individual officers alleged to have violated the Constitution.

THEODORE EISENBERG

Bibliography

DELLINGER, WALTER E. 1972 Of Rights and Remedies: The Constitution as a Sword. *Harvard Law Review* 85:1532–1564.
HART, HENRY M., JR. 1954 The Relations between State and Federal Law. *Columbia Law Review* 54:489–542.

IMPLIED POWERS

"Loose and irresponsible use of adjectives colors . . . much legal discussion. . . . 'Inherent' powers, 'implied' powers, 'incidental' powers are used, often interchangeably and without fixed ascertainable meanings." Justice ROBERT H. JACKSON's remark in YOUNGSTOWN SHEET & TUBE COMPANY V. SAWYER (1952) was correct. The vocabulary of "implied powers" is frequently used indiscriminately with other terms. It is associated with not less than six quite different usages.

The original use of "implied powers" was to contrast, rather than to explain, the powers that would vest in the United States. The national government would not automatically possess all the customary attributes of SOVEREIGNTY, but only those expressly provided. As to these, JAMES MADISON declared (in THE FEDERALIST #45): "The powers delegated by the proposed Constitution to the Federal Government, are few and defined. Those which are to remain in the State Governments are numerous and indefinite." Writing for a unanimous Supreme Court in 1804, Chief Justice JOHN MARSHALL, in *United States v. Fisher*, agreed that there were no implied-at-large national powers: "[I]t has been truly said, that under a constitution conferring specific powers, the power contended for must be granted, or it cannot be exercised." And more than a century later, Justice DAVID BREWER in *Kansas v. Colorado* (1907) confirmed the conventional wisdom: "[T]he proposition that there are legislative powers [not] expressed in the grant of powers, is in direct conflict with the doctrine that this is a government of ENUMERATED POWERS."

In this original sense, then, it may be said that the Constitution does not imply a government of general legislative, executive, and judicial powers; it establishes a government of limited, express, enumerated powers alone.

In 1936, in UNITED STATES V. CURTISS-WRIGHT EXPORT CORPORATION, Justice GEORGE SUTHERLAND, in an OBITER DICTUM for the Supreme Court, suggested that the national government need not rely upon any express power to sustain an assertion of executive authority prohibiting American companies from foreign trade which (in the President's view) might compromise the nation's neutral status at international law. Sutherland observed that the United States, as a nation within an international community of sovereign national states possessed "powers of external sovereignty" *apart* from any one or any combination of the Constitution's limited list of powers respecting foreign relations. Accordingly, Sutherland declared:

"The broad statement that the federal government can exercise no powers except those specifically enumerated in the Constitution, and such implied powers as are necessary and proper to carry into effect the enumerated powers, is categorically true only in respect of our internal affairs." Such an extraconstitutional power may informally be described as one derived from the status of being a sovereign nation or as implied by the fact of national sovereignty.

The soundness of this view has been seriously questioned, however, and in fact its acceptance has not been necessary to the outcome of any case. Rather, its principal positive law use has been as a reference in support of very broad interpretations of the several provisions in the Constitution which expressly enumerate executive and congressional powers respecting FOREIGN AFFAIRS. It has also been relied upon to uphold extremely permissive DELEGATIONS OF POWER by Congress to permit the President to determine conditions of trade between American companies and foreign countries, or conditions of American travel and activity abroad.

Not inconsistent with the general view that any claim of implied-at-large national powers is precluded by the text and presuppositions of the Constitution, such specific powers as are conferred by the Constitution have been deemed to carry with them exceedingly wide-ranging implications. Partly this results merely from the doctrine of BROAD CONSTRUCTION that every specific grant of power is to be deferentially interpreted, rather than narrowly construed. For instance, the power vested in Congress to "regulate" commerce among the several states might have been interpreted quite narrowly, in keeping with the principal objectives of enabling Congress to provide for a nationwide free trade zone, as against the tendency of some states to enact discriminatory taxes, and other self-favoring economic barriers. Instead, the power was construed in no such qualified fashion. The power to regulate commerce among the several states is "the power to prescribe the rule by which such commerce shall be governed," which therefore includes the power to limit or to forbid outright such commerce among the states as Congress sees fit to disallow. The result has been that to this extent, the express power to regulate commerce among the states gives to Congress a limited NATIONAL POLICE POWER.

Beyond adopting an attitude of permissive construction respecting each enumerated power, however, the Supreme Court took an additional significant step. It accepted the view that acts of Congress not themselves direct exercises of conferred powers would be deemed authorized by the Constitution if they facilitated the exercise of one or more express powers. An act of Congress establishing a national bank under a corporate charter granted by Congress, vesting authority in its directors to set up branch banks with general banking prerogatives, may arguably facilitate borrowing on the credit of the United States, paying debts incurred by the United States, regulating some aspects of commerce among states, and serving as a place of deposit for funds to meet military payrolls. Each of these *uses* is itself identified as an express, enumerated power vested in Congress although the act establishing such an incorporated national bank may itself not be regarded as legislation that borrows money, pays debts, etc. Nevertheless, insofar as provision for such a bank might usefully serve as an instrument by means of which several expressly enumerated powers could be carried into execution, the Supreme Court unanimously concluded that the congressional power to furnish such a bank was "implied" "incidentally" in those enumerated powers. The opinion by Chief Justice Marshall in MCCULLOCH V. MARYLAND (1819) is crowded with the repeated use of both terms. In tandem with the principle of generous construction, this view of "implied" incidental powers has had a profound influence in assuring to Congress an immense latitude of legislative discretion despite the conventional wisdom that the national government is one of specific, enumerated powers alone. Laws not probably within even a latitudinarian construction of specific grants of power, but nonetheless instrumentally relatable to such grants, are thus deemed to be adequately "implied" by those grants as incidents of grants.

A contemporary example is furnished by WICKARD V. FILBURN (1942). Though some of the "commerce" regulated by the act upheld in that case was not commerce at all (because it was not offered for trade, but was used solely for the farmer's personal consumption), and although the activity regulated was entirely local (growing and consuming wheat on one's own farm), insofar as the regulation of these local matters was nonetheless instrumentally relatable to an act fixing the volume of wheat permitted to be grown for purposes of interstate sale, the power to include local growing and consumption, as part of the larger regulation, was deemed to be implied by the express power to regulate commerce among the several states. The imaginative capacity of Congress to relate the aggregate interstate effects of local activity, thus bringing it within a uniform and integrated national economic policy, has made the principle of incidental implied power at least as important as the principle of broad construction in respect to enumerated national

power. Indeed, the combination of the two doctrines has led Justice WILLIAM H. REHNQUIST, in HODEL V. VIRGINIA SURFACE MINING (1981), to suggest: "It is illuminating for purposes of reflection, if not for argument, to note that one of the greatest "fictions" of our federal system is that the Congress exercises only those powers delegated to it, while the remainder are reserved to the States or to the people. The manner in which this Court has construed the COMMERCE CLAUSE amply illustrates the extent of this fiction." However that may be, the notion that express powers imply an authority to undertake action instrumentally relatable to the use of those powers, albeit action not itself an exercise of any express power, has given to the national government a flexibility and discretion that it would not otherwise possess.

The bank case (*McCulloch*) and the wheat quota case (*Wickard*) are examples of implied powers incidental to *specific* enumerated powers. Each involved acts of Congress establishing an enterprise or furnishing a regulation instrumentally related to one or another express power. Different from this kind of "incidental implied power," but resting on much the same sort of constitutional justification, are implied powers common to each of the three branches of the national government. These powers, sometimes called INHERENT POWERS, are deemed to be implied as reasonably necessary to each department's capacity to discharge effectively its enumerated responsibilities. Because they are regarded as effecting that capacity generally (and not merely in respect to one or another specific enumerated power alone), however, they are generically implied, incidental powers.

A prominent example is the unenumerated (but implied) power of each house of Congress to hold legislative hearings, to subpoena witnesses, and otherwise to compel the submission of information thought useful in determining whether acts of Congress on particular subjects need to be adopted, repealed, or modified. The power to conduct LEGISLATIVE INVESTIGATIONS, nowhere expressly conferred, is deemed to be implied as a reasonable incident of the legislative function. Similarly, a power of federal courts to maintain order in adjudicative proceedings, independent of any act of Congress providing such a power (pursuant to the NECESSARY AND PROPER CLAUSE), rests on the same ground. And although never challenged, presumably the power of the Supreme Court to exclude all but its own members from its private conferences in which discussion is held and votes are taken on pending cases is an example.

A qualified power of EXECUTIVE PRIVILEGE, enabling the President to interdict discovery of advice, memoranda, and other internal executive communications is conceded by the Supreme Court to be implied as an incident of executive necessity and power. The principle common to these several examples was illustrated in a remark by ALEXANDER HAMILTON, in *The Federalist* #74, commenting briefly upon the express power vested in the President by Article II, authorizing the President to "require the opinion in writing of the principal officer in each of the executive departments upon any subject relating to the duties of their respective offices." As to this express provision, Hamilton suggested, "I consider [it] a mere redundancy in the plan; as the right for which it provides would result of itself from the office." And so, undoubtedly, it would, especially as the Supreme Court was subsequently to hold that the President has an implied power to dismiss any executive subordinate at will, though no express clause so provides, and the clause respecting appointment of such officers requires the consent of the Senate.

One may phrase the matter variously, as power "resulting" from the establishment of the executive, legislative, and judicial branches, or as powers "incidental" to their designated powers. The point is the same: instrumental powers deemed reasonably necessary generally to each department's independent capacity to exercise its express, vested powers are treated as generically implied by Articles I, II, and III.

As noted in *McCulloch* an act of Congress establishing a national bank in corporate form may be useful as a means of carrying into execution the several specific fiscal powers of the United States. Equally, a regulation of local commerce may be necessary to keep a regulation of INTERSTATE COMMERCE from frustration. In either case the Court has upheld such exercise of congressional power when instrumentally relatable to the exercise of an express, enumerated power. In neither case, however, is it necessary in fact to describe the power to adopt such instrumentally relatable laws as "implied" power. Rather, all such laws are themselves specifically and expressly authorized by an *enumerated* grant of enabling power vested in Congress: "Congress shall have power to make all laws necessary and proper to carry into execution the foregoing powers, and all other powers vested in the government of the United States or any officer or department thereof." This clause, located at the end of the enumerated powers of Congress in Article I, section 8, is known as the "necessary and proper" clause. Originally, in anticipation of its elasticizing effects, it was known as "the sweeping clause," vesting in Congress discretion to carry into effect its own enumerated powers, and those of the executive and judiciary as well, by means of its own choosing. Consistent with that background, and consistent also with the general doctrine of generous (or loose) construction, the sweeping clause has been construed by the Supreme Court very liberally: "necessary and proper" are regarded as synonymous with "reasonable." Thus, whatever acts of Congress may reasonably relate to a regulation of commerce among the several states are authorized by this clause. Likewise, whatever acts of Congress may reasonably relate to the conduct of the JUDICIAL POWER OF THE UNITED STATES, or the conduct of the executive powers (as described in Article II), as an aid to those departments to carry into execution the executive or judicial powers, are authorized by this clause.

Because of this interpretation of the sweeping clause, it is not clear why the Supreme Court developed the notion of incidental *implied* powers. From one point of view, the latter doctrine is both redundant, because it duplicates a power *already* provided in the Constitution, and illogical because insofar as there is a clause expressly providing for such an instrumental power vested in Congress, to speak of such a power as "implied" rather than as "express" makes little sense. Had there been no necessary and proper clause, the innovation of a doctrine of implied power, incidental to enumerated powers, might be rested on the felt necessity of rendering the national government equal to ultimate growth and needs of the nation. But insofar as the necessary and proper clause was itself construed to provide for such flexibility, no need remained to be filled by the additional innovation of "implied, incidental" power. The doctrine of generous construction (respecting the scope of enumerated power) and the necessary and proper clause (itself generously construed), would in combination grant a vast instrumental latitude to Congress in respect both to its own powers and to those of the executive and the judiciary.

One consequence of this partial redundancy is that there is no particular consistency in the pattern of Supreme Court decisions respecting unsuccessfully challenged acts of Congress. Sometimes they are sustained as but implied incidents of one or more enumerated substantive powers. And sometimes, as happened in *McCulloch*, they are sustained on both grounds at the same time.

Were it not for a related problem, the question whether an exertion of national power not within an express enumerated power (but nonetheless instrumentally relatable to such a power) properly rests on the necessary and proper clause, or instead merely represents an implied power instrumentally incidental to an express power, would be merely academic. But, unfortunately, it is not always so. The necessary and proper clause vests its power in Congress. It implies, by doing so, that if Congress believes it appropriate to facilitate the executive and judicial enumerated powers, it may do so by enacting legislation helpful, albeit not indispensable, to those departments. Merely "helpful" instrumental powers assertable by the executive or by the judiciary will depend, therefore, on whether Congress has, by law, acting pursuant to the necessary and proper clause, provided for them. Correspondingly, the absence of any such act of Congress providing for such incidental executive or judicial powers would be a sufficient basis for a successful challenge to any such unaided assertions of executive or judicial power.

On the other hand, if the mere enumeration of executive and judicial powers (in Articles II and III) are themselves deemed to imply incidentally helpful (but not indispensable) ancillary powers, then the absence of a supportive act of Congress is not fatal to such claims. Thus, in this instance, it does make a difference to resolve the relationship between the necessary and proper clause (addressed solely to what Congress may provide) and the doctrine of implied, incidental powers.

Interestingly, two centuries into the positive law history of the Constitution, this particular question has not been addressed by the Supreme Court. Rather, an uneasy accommodation has been made. Each department of government has been regarded by the Court as possessing a range of incidental powers implied by its express powers, and such assertions of authority have been generally upheld. Nonetheless, insofar as Congress has legislated affirmatively, and by statute has found that such an assertion of incidental executive (or judicial) authority is *not* necessary or proper, the tendency of the Supreme Court is to defer to the authoritative judgment of Congress and, correspondingly, rule against the assertion of "implied" incidental executive power.

The pragmatic accommodation of the doctrine of implied incidental powers and the necessary and proper clause, therefore, has been to treat Congress as *primus inter pares*. Each department of the national government has separate enumerated powers of its own, not subject to abridgment by either of the other two departments. In addition, each may assert implied incidental powers, instrumentally relatable to its enumerated powers albeit not literally within those enumerated powers as even generously construed. But a specific determination by Congress with respect to this latter class of powers is regarded as virtually conclusive of the subject. If the act of Congress confirms such power, it is virtually certain to be sustained. If the act of Congress either expressly or implicitly denies the appropriateness of such incidental executive or judicial power, then that determination also is likely to govern. The case best known for this view is *Youngstown Sheet & Tube Co. v. Sawyer.*

The Constitution enumerates express WAR POWERS and express powers enabling Congress to insure each state against domestic violence. Curiously, however, it has no express clauses directed to the internal security of the national government. Nevertheless, the authority to provide for laws punishing attempts of violent overthrow has been sustained as an implied power of self-preservation. Depending upon how deeply such laws may affect certain freedoms to criticize the government or to bring about fundamental changes in its composition by peaceful means, these acts of Congress may be vulnerable to challenge under the FIRST AMENDMENT or other provisions of the Constitution. Nevertheless, a considerable implied power of self-preservation is deemed to vest in Congress, essentially on the common-sense inference that its express enumerated powers imply a residual existence of the government possessing those powers and thus, of necessity, a power of self-preservation. The Sedition Act of 1798 (see ALIEN AND SEDITION ACTS) was sustained in the lower federal courts partly on this rationale.

Less frequently drawn into litigation, but presumably resting on similar grounds, is the implied power of Congress to provide for incidents of national status. The adoption of a national flag rests on no particular enumerated power. Rather, like other acts of Congress identifying symbols of national status, it is but an implied incident of an expressly established government—of the United States of America.

In sum, the phrase "implied powers" houses a half-dozen quite discrete meanings. They are bound together by but one common element, namely the obviousness of contrast with express powers. Beyond that, however, they speak to distinct (and not always completely reconcilable) propositions. One is an implied residual sovereign power of national self-preservation and the incidental power to adopt ordinary insignia of nationhood. In addition, there are implied powers peculiar to each of the three branches of the national government, incidental to the exercise of all enumerated powers expressly vested in each branch. Such generic implied powers apart, there are also implied cognate powers incidental to each expressly enumerated power, extending the reach of those enumerated powers even beyond what might otherwise be their scope under a doctrine of loose or generous construction. Then, too, although the usage seems inept in reference to an *enumerated* general enabling power, the necessary and proper clause of the Constitution has often been used to anchor the textual source of extensive, instrumental powers. And last, there is also the claim of implied, extraconstitutional power in respect to the external sovereign relations of the United States, standing over and apart from the several enumerations of power provided by the Constitution.

The solidness of the foundations respecting these several varieties of implied powers are not all of a piece, that is, quite plainly they are not all of equally convincing legitimacy. Rather, they but illustrate in still one more way how two centuries of history have operated to show what has followed from Chief Justice Marshall's observation that it is a Constitution we are expounding.

WILLIAM W. VAN ALSTYNE

Bibliography

GUNTHER, GERALD, ED. 1969 *John Marshall's Defense of McCulloch v. Maryland.* Stanford, Calif.: Stanford University Press.

HENKIN, LOUIS 1972 *Foreign Affairs and the Constitution.* St. Paul, Minn.: West Publishing Co.

VAN ALSTYNE, WILLIAM W. 1976 The Role of Congress in Determining Incidental Powers of the President and of the Federal Courts: The Horizontal Effect of the Sweeping Clause. *Law & Contemporary Problems* 1976:102–134.

IMPORT-EXPORT CLAUSE

The Constitution provides: "No State shall . . . lay any IMPOSTS or Duties on Imports or Exports, except what may be absolutely necessary for executing its inspection Laws." It also prohibits the federal government from placing any tax or duty on exports.

The limitation on state taxation of imports came before the Supreme Court in BROWN v. MARYLAND (1827). Chief Justice JOHN MARSHALL pointed out that the clear intention of the Framers was to prohibit the states from levying customs duties. Only Congress was to have this power. He recognized, however, that state power to raise revenues would be unduly restricted if goods that had come from another country could never be subject to taxation along with other goods within the state. He resolved the dilemma by holding that imported goods should be free from state taxation until they have been incorporated into the mass of property in the state. Such incorporation would take place when the importer sold the goods or when he took them out of the original package in which they were imported. Hence was born the ORIGINAL PACKAGE DOCTRINE, which survived as the measure for state taxation of imports until MICHELIN TIRE CORP. v. WAGES (1976).

In *Michelin* the Supreme Court held that the intention of the Framers was only to prevent the states from imposing special taxes on imports. Hence, it concluded that imported goods could, as soon as they came to rest in the taxing state, be subject to nondiscriminatory state property taxes.

The Supreme Court has long held that goods become exports—and thus free from either state or federal taxes—when they have actually commenced the journey to another country. Once the journey has commenced or they have been committed to a common carrier for transport abroad, they may not be taxed.

Application of the import-export clause to those businesses that transport or otherwise handle goods in FOREIGN COMMERCE has posed a separate problem. Recently the Court has held that nondiscriminatory taxes apportioned to cover only values within the taxing state may be imposed upon the instrumentalities of foreign commerce or the business of engaging in such commerce. Thus, in *Department of Revenue of Washington v. Association of Washington Stevedoring Companies* (1978), it upheld a Washington tax on the privilege of engaging in business activities measured by gross receipts as applied to a stevedoring company that confined its activities to the loading and unloading in Washington ports of ships engaged in foreign commerce.

In general, the rules governing state taxation of INTERSTATE COMMERCE now seem to apply to imports and exports.

EDWARD L. BARRETT, JR.

(SEE ALSO: *State Taxation of Commerce.*)

Bibliography

HELLERSTEIN, WALTER 1977 Michelin Tire Corp. v. Wages: Enhanced State Power to Tax Imports. *Supreme Court Review* 1977:99–123.

IMPOST

In its broadest sense the term "impost" refers to any tax or tribute levied by authority. By usage it has come to have the narrower meaning of a tax or duty imposed on imports. The Supreme Court has recently stated that "imposts and duties" as used in the Constitution "are essentially taxes on the commercial privilege of bringing goods into a country."

EDWARD L. BARRETT, JR.

(SEE ALSO: *Excise Taxes; Import-Export Clause; Michelin Tire Corp. v. Wages, 1976; State Taxation of Commerce.*)

IMPOUNDMENT OF FUNDS

Presidents from time to time, and especially beginning with the regime of FRANKLIN D. ROOSEVELT, have asserted a right not to execute the laws or parts thereof, by a decision to "impound" the funds provided by Congress for the effectuation of the law. In effect, this would be an exercise of an item VETO POWER. There is no warrant in the Constitution for the exercise of the power of impoundment. The history of the veto provision in the CONSTITUTIONAL CONVENTION OF 1787 makes clear that the Founders were wary of any veto authority, no less one that would allow the President to rewrite the laws of Congress to suit his predilections. Instead, the Constitution clearly requires that the President "take Care that the Laws be faithfully executed." Only if the provisions of Article II vesting the "executive power" are read to create implicit authority in the President to do as he pleases—what Arthur Schlesinger, Jr., calls a "plebiscitary" presidency—can the impoundment authority be deemed a constitutional one.

This is not to say that a President may not be authorized to exercise the impoundment power. But that authority must derive from legislation and not from the Constitution. Where Congress has mandated the expenditure of funds in support of a legislative program, the President has no choice but to effectuate Congress's will. But legislation may explicitly create discretion in the executive branch as to whether programs are to be carried out in whole or in part. And the courts have suggested that legislation may imply that such presidential power exists. Arguments have also been made that certain general statutes such as those ordering the executive to choose the most economic means of enforcement of the laws, or putting ceilings on the national debt, create a legislative warrant for presidential impoundment. There is little merit in the proposals that these statutes create a general statutory authority for the President to pick and choose among congressional programs.

The President has a veto power. If it is used successfully, the congressional program need not be effected for it is not the law. If the veto be used unsuccessfully, however, it is clear that Congress has mandated the program and it is Congress's will, not the President's, that makes the law of the land. Although there is no item veto, no restriction exists on the veto message explaining that the veto was invoked in response to a particular item in the legislation. If Congress overrides the veto, it will be clear that the portion found objectionable by the President was found desirable by the Congress.

After particularly egregious efforts by President RICHARD M. NIXON to throttle congressional legislation through "impoundment," the CONGRESSIONAL BUDGET AND IMPOUNDMENT CONTROL ACT was enacted (1974). This statute requires the President to inform Congress if he proposes to rescind or defer appropriations. There can be no rescission unless Congress acting through both houses concurs within forty-five days. A deferral can be invalidated by a resolution of disapproval by one house but is valid unless disapproved. The statute is thorny with constitutional issues, but both the legislators and the executive seem willing to accept it as an appropriate accommodation of their respective interests.

The question whether a President may refuse to enforce a law that he deems unconstitutional is not really an "impoundment" question. That issue was mooted but not resolved in the IMPEACHMENT and trial of President ANDREW JOHNSON. Clearly the President can challenge or refuse to defend in the courts any legislation he finds unconstitutional.

PHILIP B. KURLAND

Bibliography

FISHER, LOUIS 1972 *President and Congress: Power and Policy.* New York: Free Press.
GENERAL ACCOUNTING OFFICE 1977 *Review of the Impoundment Control Act of 1974.* Washington, D.C.: Government Printing Office.

INALIENABLE POLICE POWER

THOMAS COOLEY, writing on the STATE POLICE POWER in 1868, concluded that the CONTRACT CLAUSE did not permit a state "under pretense of regulation, [to] take from the CORPORATION any of the essential rights and privileges which the charter confers." Constitutional law changed quickly. In BOSTON BEER CO. v. MASSACHUSETTS (1878), when holding that the RESERVED POLICE POWER allowed a state to revoke the charter of a brewery company, the Supreme Court declared that even in the absence of a reserved power to revoke, the revocation would be valid: the legislature cannot contract away or otherwise alienate the sovereign power to protect the lives, health, safety, or morals of its citizens. A legislature can, however, alienate its tax powers, as NEW JERSEY V. WILSON (1812) and PIQUA BRANCH BANK V. KNOOP (1854) demonstrated. As the Court frequently explained, the tax power is a right of government that the contract clause does not protect; it protects property rights only. That distinction scarcely explains why the power of EMINENT DOMAIN, a government right, cannot be contracted away. Nevertheless, the inalienable police power proved to be an effective rationale for supporting a variety of regulatory legislation against contract clause claims.

In NORTHWESTERN FERTILIZING COMPANY V. HYDE PARK (1878) the Court upheld as a protection of public health an ordinance forcing the removal of a fertilizer plant. In STONE V. MISSISSIPPI (1880) the Court sustained a state act revoking the charter of a lottery company; the contract clause could not limit a power to protect public morality from gambling. Within a few years the Court upheld one state act revoking a monopoly of the slaughterhouse business and another establishing a commission to fix the rates of a railroad company whose charter expressly authorized it to fix its own rates. In the rate case, STONE V. FARMERS' LOAN AND TRUST COMPANY (1886), the fact that the state had not reserved a power to alter or amend the charter made the defeat of the contract clause claim seem kindred to a victory for the inalienable police power. The unreliability of the contract clause, especially in rate cases, led shortly to the acceptance of SUBSTANTIVE DUE PROCESS OF LAW to defeat the police power.

That the inalienable police power was not limited to cases of public health, safety, or morality is shown by the unanimous opinion in *Chicago and Alton Railroad v. Tranbarger* (1915), sustaining a state requirement that railroads construct roadbeds that prevent water damage to private property. Justice MAHLON PITNEY for the Court declared that all contract and property rights are held subject to the exercise of a police power that "is inalienable even by express grant" and is not limited by either the contract clause or the DUE PROCESS clause. Pitney added that the power embraced regulations promoting "public convenience or the GENERAL WELFARE and prosperity" as well as the "public health, morals, or safety." Protection of the "general welfare and prosperity" figured prominently in the Court's decision in HOME BUILDING AND LOAN ASSOCIATION V. BLAISDELL

(1934). In that case the Court referred to the reserved police power but meant the inalienable police power.

LEONARD W. LEVY

Bibliography

WRIGHT, BENJAMIN F.   1938   *The Contract Clause of the Constitution.* Pages 195–213. Cambridge, Mass.: Harvard University Press.

INCITEMENT TO UNLAWFUL CONDUCT

Incitement to unlawful conduct raises a central and difficult issue about the proper boundaries of freedom of expression and of the FIRST AMENDMENT. Many of the Supreme Court's most important FREEDOM OF SPEECH decisions have involved some form of incitement. Though the term incitement sometimes refers to emotionally charged appeals to immediate action, the word is most often used to cover any urging that others commit illegal acts.

The basic problem about incitement is fairly simple, involving a tension between a criminal law perspective and a free speech perspective. Any society seeks to minimize the number of crimes that are committed. Some people commit crimes because others urge them to do so. Although the person who actually commits a crime may usually seem more to blame than someone who encourages him, on other occasions the inciter, because of greater authority, intelligence, or firmness of purpose, may actually be more responsible for what happens than the person who is the instrument of his designs. In any event, because the person who successfully urges another to commit a crime bears some responsibility and because effective restrictions on incitement are likely to reduce the amount of crime to some degree, sound reasons exist for punishing those who incite.

Anglo-American criminal law, like the law of other traditions, has reflected this view. In 1628, EDWARD COKE wrote that "all those that incite . . . any other" to commit a FELONY are guilty of a crime; and, at least by 1801, unsuccessful incitement was recognized as an offense in England. Modern American criminal law generally treats the successful inciter on a par with the person who performs the criminal act; the unsuccessful inciter is guilty of criminal solicitation, treated as a lesser crime than the one he has tried to incite.

From the free speech perspective, the problem of

incitement takes on a different appearance. A basic premise of a liberal society is that people should be allowed to express their views, especially their political views. Some important political views support illegal actions against actual or possible governments. Indeed, one aspect of the political tradition of the United States is that revolutionary overthrow of existing political authority is sometimes justified. Other views deem certain illegal acts justified even when the government is acceptable. Were all encouragements of illegal activity suppressed, an important slice of political and social opinions would be silenced. Further, in the practical administration of such suppression some opinions that did not quite amount to encouragement would be proceeded against and persons would be inhibited from saying things that could possibly be construed as encouragements to commit crimes. Thus, wide restrictions on incitement have been thought to imperil free expression, particularly when statutes penalizing incitement have been specifically directed to "subversive" political ideologies.

The tension between criminal law enforcement and freedom of expression is addressed by both legislatures and courts. Legislatures must initially decide what is a reasonable, and constitutionally permissible, accommodation of the conflicting values. When convictions are challenged, courts must decide whether the statutes that legislatures have adopted and their applications to particular situations pass constitutional muster.

Most states have statutes that make solicitation of a crime illegal. These laws are drawn to protect speech interests to a significant extent. To be convicted of solicitation, one must actually encourage the commission of a specific crime. Therefore, many kinds of statements, such as disinterested advice that committing a crime like draft evasion would be morally justified, approval of present lawbreaking in general, or urging people to prepare themselves for unspecified future revolutionary acts, are beyond the reach of ordinary solicitation statutes.

One convenient way to conceptualize the First Amendment problems about incitement is to ask whether any communications that do amount to ordinary criminal solicitation are constitutionally protected and whether other communications that encourage criminal acts but fall short of criminal solicitation lack constitutional protection.

All major Supreme Court cases on the subject have involved political expression of one kind or another and have arisen under statutes directed at specific kinds of speech. Some of the cases have involved CRIMINAL CONSPIRACY charges, but because the conspiracy has been to incite or advocate, the constitutionality of punishing communications has been the crucial issue. In SCHENCK V. UNITED STATES (1919) the Court sustained a conviction under the 1917 ESPIONAGE ACT, which made criminal attempts to obstruct enlistment. The leaflet that Schenck had helped to publish had urged young men to assert their rights to oppose the draft. Writing the majority opinion that found no constitutional bar to the conviction, Justice OLIVER WENDELL HOLMES penned the famous CLEAR AND PRESENT DANGER test: "The question in every case is whether the words used are used in such circumstances and are of such a nature as to create a clear and present danger that they will bring about the substantive evils that Congress has a right to prevent." Much was unclear about this test as originally formulated and as subsequently developed, but the results in *Schenck* and companion cases show that the Court then did not conceive the standard as providing great protection for speech. During the 1920s, while the majority of Justices ceased using the test, eloquent dissents by Holmes and LOUIS D. BRANDEIS forged it into a principle that was protective of speech, requiring a danger that was both substantial and close in time in order to justify suppressing communication. Even these later opinions, however, did not indicate with clarity whether the test applied to ordinary criminal solicitation or whether an intent to create a clear and present danger would be sufficient for criminal punishment.

During the 1920s, the majority of the Supreme Court was willing to affirm convictions for expression, so long as the expression fell within a statutory prohibition and the statutory prohibition was reasonable. Thus, in GITLOW V. NEW YORK (1925) the Court upheld a conviction under a criminal anarchy statute that forbade teaching the propriety of illegally overthrowing organized government. The Court concluded that the legislature could reasonably anticipate that speech of this type carried the danger of a "revolutionary spark" kindling a fire. The standard applied in *Gitlow* and similar cases would permit suppression of virtually any type of speech that a legislature might consider to create a danger of illegal activity, a category far broader than ordinary criminal solicitation.

In the 1930s the Supreme Court began to render decisions more protective of speech, and in HERNDON V. LOWRY (1937) the Court reversed a conviction for attempting to incite insurrection, when the evidence failed to show that the defendant, a Communist party organizer, had actually urged revolutionary violence.

The majority in *Herndon* referred to the clear and present danger test with approval. In a series of subsequent decisions, that test was employed as an all-purpose standard for First Amendment cases.

In 1951, the Supreme Court reviewed the convictions of eleven leading communists in DENNIS V. UNITED STATES. The defendants had violated the Smith Act by conspiring to advocate the forcible overthrow of the United States government. As in *Gitlow,* the expressions involved (typical communist rhetoric) fell short of inciting to any specific crime. The plurality opinion, representing the views of four Justices, accepted clear and present danger as the appropriate standard, but interpreted the test so that the gravity of the evil was discounted by its improbability. In practice, this formulation meant that if the evil were very great, such as overthrow of the government, communication creating a danger of that evil might be suppressed even though the evil would not occur in the near future and had only a small likelihood that it would ever occur. The dissenters and civil libertarian observers protested that this interpretation undermined the main point of "clear and present" danger. *Dennis* is now viewed by many as a regrettable product of unwarranted fears of successful communist subversion. In subsequent cases, the Court emphasized that the Smith Act reached only advocacy of illegal action, not advocacy of doctrine. In the years since *Dennis* only one conviction under the act has passed this stringent test.

The modern constitutional standard for incitement cases arose out of the conviction of a Ku Klux Klan leader for violating a broad CRIMINAL SYNDICALISM statute, not unlike the statute involved in *Gitlow.* Unsurprisingly, the Court said in BRANDENBURG V. OHIO (1969) that the broad statute was unconstitutional. But it went on to fashion a highly restrictive version of clear and present danger: that a state may not "forbid or proscribe advocacy of the use of force or of law violation except where such advocacy is directed to inciting or producing imminent lawless action and is likely to incite or produce such action." This test requires lawless action that is likely, imminent, and intended by the speaker. Only rarely could such a test possibly be met by speech that does not amount to criminal solicitation, and under this test both solicitation of crimes in the distant future and solicitation unlikely to be acted upon are constitutionally protected. In *Brandenburg,* however, the Court had directly in mind public advocacy; it is unlikely that this stringent test also applies to private solicitations of crime that are made for personal gain. The present law provides significant constitutional protection for political incitements, but how far beyond political speech this protection may extend remains uncertain.

KENT GREENAWALT

Bibliography

AMERICAN LAW INSTITUTE 1985 *Model Penal Code,* Section 5.02 and Commentary. St. Paul, Minn.: West Publishing Co.

GREENAWALT, KENT 1980 Speech and Crime. *American Bar Foundation Research Journal* 1980:647–785.

LINDE, HANS A. 1970 "Clear and Present Danger" Reexamined: Dissonance in the Brandenburg Concerto. *Stanford Law Review* 22:1163–1186.

INCOME TAX CASES

See: *Pollock v. Farmers Loan and Trust Company*

INCORPORATION DOCTRINE

According to the incorporation doctrine the FOURTEENTH AMENDMENT incorporates or absorbs the BILL OF RIGHTS, making its guarantees applicable to the states. Whether the Bill of Rights applied to the states, restricting their powers as it did those of the national government, was a question that arose in connection with the framing and ratification of the Fourteenth Amendment. Before 1868 nothing in the Constitution of the United States prevented a state from imprisoning religious heretics or political dissenters, or from abolishing TRIAL BY JURY, or from torturing suspects to extort confessions of guilt. The Bill of Rights limited only the United States, not the states. JAMES MADISON, who framed the amendments that became the Bill of Rights, had included one providing that "no State shall violate the equal rights of conscience, of the FREEDOM OF THE PRESS, or the trial by jury in criminal cases." The Senate defeated that proposal. History, therefore, was on the side of the Supreme Court when it unanimously decided in BARRON V. BALTIMORE (1833) that "the fifth amendment must be understood as restraining the power of the general government, not as applicable to the States," and said that the other amendments composing the Bill of Rights were equally inapplicable to the States.

Thus, a double standard existed in the nation. The Bill of Rights commanded the national government to refrain from enacting certain laws and to respect certain procedures, but it left the states free to do as they wished in relation to the same matters. State constitutions and COMMON LAW practices, rather than the Constitution of the United States, were the sources of restraints on the states with respect to the subjects of the Bill of Rights.

Whether the Fourteenth Amendment was intended to alter this situation is a matter on which the historical record is complex, confusing, and probably inconclusive. Even if history spoke with a loud, clear, and decisive voice, however, it ought not necessarily control judgment on the question whether the Supreme Court should interpret the amendment as incorporating the Bill of Rights. Whatever the framers of the Fourteenth intended, they did not possess ultimate wisdom as to the meaning of their words for subsequent generations. Moreover, the PRIVILEGES AND IMMUNITIES, due process, and EQUAL PROTECTION clauses of section 1 of the amendment are written in language that blocks fixed meanings. Its text must be read as revelations of general purposes that were to be achieved or as expressions of imperishable principles that are comprehensive in character. The principles and purposes, not their framers' original technical understanding, are what was intended to endure. We cannot avoid the influence of history but are not constitutionally obligated to obey history which is merely a guide. The task of CONSTITUTIONAL INTERPRETATION is one of statecraft: to read the text in the light of changing needs in accordance with the noblest ideals of a democratic society.

The Court has, in fact, proved to be adept at reading into the Constitution the policy values that meet its approval, and its freedom to do so is virtually legislative in scope. Regrettably in its first Fourteenth Amendment decision, in the SLAUGHTERHOUSE CASES (1873), the Court unnecessarily emasculated the privileges and immunities clause by ruling that it protected only the privileges and immunities of national CITIZENSHIP but not the privileges and immunities of state citizenship, which included "nearly every CIVIL RIGHT for the establishment and protection of which organized government is instituted." Among the rights deriving from state, not national, citizenship were those referred to by the Bill of Rights as well as other "fundamental" rights. Justice STEPHEN J. FIELD, dissenting, rightly said that the majority's interpretation had rendered the clause "a vain and idle enactment, which accomplished nothing. . . ." The privileges and immunities clause was central to the incorporation issue because to the extent that any of the framers of the amendment intended incorporation, they relied principally on that clause. Notwithstanding the amendment, *Barron v. Baltimore* remained controlling law. The Court simply opposed the revolution in the federal system which the amendment's text suggested. The privileges and immunities

of national citizenship after *Slaughterhouse* were those that Congress or the Court could have protected, under the SUPREMACY CLAUSE, with or without the new amendment.

In HURTADO V. CALIFORNIA (1884) the Court initiated a long line of decisions that eroded the traditional procedures associated with due process of law. *Hurtado* was not an incorporation case, because the question it posed was not whether the Fourteenth Amendment incorporated the clause of the Fifth guaranteeing INDICTMENT by GRAND JURY but whether the concept of due process necessarily required indictment in a capital case. In cases arising after *Hurtado*, counsel argued that even if the concept of due process did not mean indictment, or freedom from CRUEL AND UNUSUAL PUNISHMENT, or trial by a twelve-member jury, or the RIGHT AGAINST SELF-INCRIMINATION, the provisions of the Bill of Rights applied to the states through the Fourteenth Amendment; that is, the amendment incorporated them either by the privileges and immunities clause, or by the due process clause's protection of "liberty." In *O'Neil v. Vermont* (1892), that argument was accepted for the first time by three Justices, dissenting; however, only one of them, JOHN MARSHALL HARLAN, steadfastly adhered to it in MAXWELL V. DOW (1900) and TWINING V. NEW JERSEY (1908), when all other Justices rejected it. Harlan, dissenting in *Patterson v. Colorado* (1907), stated "that the privilege of free speech and a free press belong to every citizen of the United States, constitute essential parts of every man's liberty, and are protected against violation by that clause of the Fourteenth Amendment forbidding a state to deprive any person of his liberty without due process of law." The Court casually adopted that view in OBITER DICTUM in GITLOW V. NEW YORK (1925).

Before *Gitlow* the Court had done a good deal of property-minded, not liberty-minded, incorporating. As early as *Hepburn v. Griswold* (1870), it had read the protection of the CONTRACT CLAUSE into the Fifth Amendment's due process clause as a limitation on the powers of Congress, a viewpoint repeated in the SINKING FUND CASES (1879). The Court in 1894 had incorporated the Fifth's JUST COMPENSATION clause into the Fourteenth's due process clause and in 1897 it had incorporated the same clause into the Fourteenth's equal protection clause. In the same decade the Court had accepted SUBSTANTIVE DUE PROCESS, incorporating within the Fourteenth a variety of doctrines that secured property, particularly corporate property, against "unreasonable" rate regulations and reformist labor legislation. By 1915, however, PROCEDURAL DUE PROCESS for persons accused of crime

had so shriveled in meaning that Justice OLIVER WEN-
DELL HOLMES, dissenting, was forced to say that "mob
law does not become due process of law by securing
the assent of a terrorized jury."

The word "liberty" in the due process clause had
absorbed all FIRST AMENDMENT guarantees by the
time of the decision in EVERSON V. BOARD OF EDUCA-
TION (1947). Incorporation developed much more
slowly in the field of criminal justice. POWELL V. ALA-
BAMA (1932) applied to the states the SIXTH AMEND-
MENT's RIGHT TO COUNSEL in capital cases, as a "necessary requisite of due process of law." The Court
reached a watershed, however, in PALKO V. CON-
NECTICUT (1937), where it refused to incorporate the
ban on DOUBLE JEOPARDY. Justice BENJAMIN N. CAR-
DOZO sought to provide a "rationalizing principle"
to explain the selective or piecemeal incorporation
process. He repudiated the notion that the Fourteenth
Amendment embraced the entire Bill of Rights, because the rights it guaranteed fell into two categories.
Some were of such a nature that liberty and justice
could not exist if they were sacrificed. These had been
brought "within the Fourteenth Amendment by a
process of absorption" because they were "of the very
essence of a scheme of ORDERED LIBERTY." In short,
they were "fundamental," like the concept of due
process. Other rights, however, were not essential to
a "fair and enlightened system of justice." First
Amendment rights were "the indispensable condition" of nearly every other form of freedom, but jury
trials, indictments, immunity against compulsory self-
incrimination, and double jeopardy "might be lost,
and justice still be done."

The difficulty with *Palko's* rationalizing scheme
was that it was subjective. It offered no principle explaining why some rights were fundamental or essential to ordered liberty and others were not; it measured all rights against some abstract or idealized
system, rather than the Anglo-American accusatory
system of criminal justice. Selective incorporation also
completely lacked historical justification. And it was
logically flawed. The Court read the substantive content of the First Amendment into the "liberty" of
the due process clause, but that clause permitted the
abridgment of liberty with due process of law. On
the other hand, selective incorporation, as contrasted
with total incorporation, allowed the Court to decide
constitutional issues as they arose on a case-by-case
basis, and allowed, too, the exclusion from the incorporation doctrine of some rights whose incorporation
would wreak havoc in state systems of justice. Grand
jury indictment for all felonies and trials by twelve-

member juries in civil suits involving more than
twenty dollars are among Bill of Rights guarantees
that would have that result, if incorporated.

In ADAMSON V. CALIFORNIA (1947) a 5–4 Court
rejected the total incorporation theory advanced by
the dissenters led by Justice HUGO L. BLACK. Black
lambasted the majority's due process standards as
grossly subjective; he argued that only the Justices'
personal idiosyncrasies could give content to "canons
of decency" and "fundamental justice." Black believed that both history and objectivity required resort
to the "specifics" of the Bill of Rights. Justices FRANK
MURPHY and WILEY RUTLEDGE would have gone further. They accepted total incorporation but observed
that due process might require invalidating some state
practices "despite the absence of a specific provision
in the Bill of Rights." Justice FELIX FRANKFURTER,
replying to Black, denied the subjectivity charge and
turned it against the dissenters. Murphy's total-incor-
poration-"plus" was subjective; total incorporation im-
practically fastened the entire Bill of Rights, with
impedimenta, on the states along with the accretions
each right had gathered in the United States courts.
Selective incorporation on the basis of individual Justices' preferences meant "a merely subjective test"
in determining which rights were in and which were
out.

Frankfurter also made a logical point long familiar
in constitutional jurisprudence. The due process
clause of the Fourteenth, which was the vehicle for
incorporation, having been copied from the identical
clause of the Fifth, could not mean one thing in the
latter and something very different in the former. The
Fifth itself included a variety of clauses. To incorporate them into the Fourteenth would mean that those
clauses of the Fifth and in the remainder of the Bill
of Rights were redundant, or the due process clause,
if signifying all the rest, was meaningless or superfluous. The answer to Frankfurter and to those still holding his view is historical, not logical. The history of
due process shows that it did mean trial by jury and
a cluster of traditional rights of accused persons that
the Bill of Rights separately specified. Its framers were
in many respects careless draftsmen. They enumerated particular rights associated with due process and
then added the due process clause partly for political
reasons and partly as a rhetorical flourish—a reinforced guarantee and a genuflection toward traditional usage going back to medieval reenactments of
MAGNA CARTA.

Numerous cases of the 1950s showed that the majority's reliance on the concept of due process rather

than the "specifics" of the Bill of Rights made for unpredictable and unconvincing results. For that reason the Court resumed selective incorporation in the 1960s, beginning with MAPP V. OHIO (1961) and ending with *Benton v. Maryland* (1969). The Warren Court's "revolution in criminal justice" applied against the states the rights of the Fourth through Eighth Amendments, excepting only indictment, twelve-member civil juries, and bail. IN RE WINSHIP (1970) even held that proof of crime beyond a REASONABLE DOUBT, though not a specific provision of the Bill of Rights, was essential to due process, and various decisions have suggested the Court's readiness to extend to the states the Eighth Amendment's provision against excessive bail.

The specifics of the Bill of Rights, however, have proved to offer only an illusion of objectivity, because its most important clauses, including all that have been incorporated, are inherently ambiguous. Indeed, the only truly specific clauses are the ones that have not been incorporated—indictment by grand jury and civil trials by twelve-member juries. The "specific" injunctions of the Bill of Rights do not exclude exceptions, nor are they self-defining. What is "an ESTABLISHMENT OF RELIGION" and what, given libels, pornography, and perjury, is "the freedom of speech" or "of the press"? These freedoms cannot be abridged, but what is an abridgment? Freedom of religion may not be prohibited; may freedom of religion be abridged by a regulation short of prohibition? What is an "UNREASONABLE" SEARCH, "PROBABLE" CAUSE, or "excessive" bail? What punishment is "cruel and unusual"? Is it really true that a person cannot be compelled to be a witness against himself in a criminal case and that the Sixth Amendment extends to "all" criminal prosecutions? What is a "criminal prosecution," a "SPEEDY TRIAL, or an "impartial" jury? Ambiguity cannot be strictly construed. Neutral principles and specifics turn out to be subjective or provoke subjectivity. Moreover, applying to the states the federal standard does not always turn out as expected. After DUNCAN V. LOUISIANA (1968) extended the trial by jury clause of the Sixth Amendment to the states, the Court decided that a criminal jury of less than twelve (but not less than six) would not violate the Fourteenth Amendment, nor would a non-unanimous jury decision. (See JURY SIZE.) Examples can be multiplied to show that the incorporation doctrine has scarcely diminished the need for judgment and that judgment tends to be personal in character.

On the whole, however, the Court has abolished the double standard by nationalizing the Bill of Rights.

The results have been mixed. More than ever justice tends to travel on leaden feet. Swift and certain punishment has always been about as effective a deterrent to crime as our criminal justice system can provide, and the prolongation of the criminal process from arrest to final appeal, which is one result of the incorporation doctrine, adds to the congestion of prosecutorial caseloads and court dockets. However, the fundamental problem is the staggering rise in the number of crimes committed, not the decisions of the Court. Even when the police used truncheons to beat suspects into confessions and searched and seized almost at will, they did not reduce the crime rate. In the long run a democratic society is probably hurt more by lawless conduct on the part of law-enforcement agencies than by the impediments of the incorporation doctrine. In the First Amendment field, the incorporation doctrine has few critics, however vigorously particular First Amendment decisions may be criticized.

LEONARD W. LEVY

Bibliography

ABRAHAM, HENRY J. 1977 *Freedom and the Court*, 3rd ed. Pages 33–105. New York: Oxford University Press.

CORTNER, RICHARD C. 1981 *The Supreme Court and the Second Bill of Rights: The Fourteenth Amendment and the Nationalization of Civil Liberties*. Madison: University of Wisconsin Press.

FRIENDLY, HENRY J. 1967 *Benchmarks*. Pages 235–265. Chicago: University of Chicago Press.

HENKIN, LOUIS 1963 "Selective Incorporation" in the Fourteenth Amendment. *Yale Law Journal* 73:74–88.

NORTH, ARTHUR A. 1966 *The Supreme Court: Judicial Process and Judicial Politics*. Pages 65–133. New York: Appleton-Century-Crofts.

INCORPORATION OF TERRITORIES

Incorporation is the process of formally making a territory part of the United States. Even before the Constitution was written, the United States exercised SOVEREIGNTY over lands not part of any state; but those TERRITORIES were to be organized and prepared for statehood. In the late nineteenth century the United States began to acquire territory outside North America, most of which appeared unsuited for statehood. The Constitution contains no provision for governing a colonial empire, but Congress, under Article IV, section 3, made rules and regulations respecting overseas possessions and dependencies. In the INSULAR CASES (1901–1911) the Supreme Court formulated a DOCTRINE to define the constitutional status of the territories. Those which Congress, expressly or implicitly, intends to make part of the United States are deemed to be incorporated. The people of incorporated territories are United States citizens with all the rights guaranteed by the Constitution. Absent such congressional intent, territories are unincorporated. The residents of unincorporated territories enjoy protection of fundamental NATURAL RIGHTS but not of rights merely procedural or formal—although Congress may, at its discretion, extend United States CITIZENSHIP and full CIVIL RIGHTS to the people of unincorporated territories. There are currently no incorporated territories.

DENNIS J. MAHONEY

INDEPENDENT STATE GROUNDS

See: Adequate State Grounds

INDIANS

See: American Indians and the Constitution

INDICTMENT

An indictment is a formal written accusation charging an individual with a crime. An indictment is issued by a GRAND JURY when, in its view, there is PROBABLE CAUSE to believe that an individual has committed a crime.

Indictments generally arise in two ways. Most commonly, a prosecutor will submit a bill of indictment to the grand jury alleging specific criminal activity by an individual. If the grand jury believes the allegations, the grand jurors will endorse the bill of indictment with the words "a true bill" and thereby officially indict the accused individual. The grand jury can also decide that the accused should not be prosecuted, in which case the bill of indictment will be marked "no true bill" and be dismissed.

An indictment can also originate from a grand jury as a result of the grand jury's own information or as a result of an investigation conducted by a special or investigative grand jury. This type of indictment often arises in cases involving organized crime or political corruption after a secret, lengthy grand jury investigation.

Grand jurors need not be unanimous to indict. The federal grand jury, for example, consists of between sixteen and twenty-three persons, twelve of whom must concur to indict.

The indictment process had its origin in the English grand jury system. Indictments were designed, as the Supreme Court said in *Costello v. United States* (1956), to provide "a fair method for instituting criminal proceedings against persons believed to have committed crimes." Indictment by a grand jury was historically seen as a way of ensuring that citizens were protected against unfounded criminal prosecutions; however, there is now considerable debate as to whether indictment actually fulfills its protective function. Indictments are also designed to inform accused individuals of the charges against them so that they may adequately prepare their defense.

Under the Fifth Amendment an individual has a right to a grand jury indictment in all federal FELONY prosecutions. The Supreme Court, however, held in HURTADO V. CALIFORNIA (1884) that grand jury indictments are not constitutionally required in state criminal prosecutions. Nevertheless, some states, pursuant to their state constitutions, require grand jury indictments in all felony prosecutions.

One recurring question about indictments has been whether they can be based on EVIDENCE that would be inadmissible at trial. The Supreme Court held in CALANDRA V. UNITED STATES (1974) that "an indictment valid on its face is not subject to challenge on the ground that the grand jury acted on the basis of inadequate or incompetent evidence." Indictments can be based even on evidence obtained illegally, which must therefore be excluded at trial.

Furthermore, a grand jury indictment can be based on HEARSAY evidence and other types of evidence that would not be admissible at trial. These decisions rest on the historical view of the grand jury as being a lay body with broad investigative powers that should not be restrained by technical rules of evidence. In addition, the Supreme Court has observed that an indictment is only a formal charge, not an adjudication of guilt or innocence. "In a trial on the merits, defendants are entitled to a strict observance of all the rules designed to bring about a fair verdict," the Court said in *Costello*, so defendants are not prejudiced by indictments based on inadmissible evidence. The prosecutor, therefore, is permitted to find some admissible evidence to support the indictment between the time it comes from the grand jury and the time of trial.

CHARLES H. WHITEBREAD

Bibliography

FRANKEL, MARVIN E. 1977 *The Grand Jury: An Institution on Trial.* New York: Hill & Wang.

INDIGENT

An indigent is a person too poor to provide for certain basic needs. It would be unconstitutional for a state or the national government deliberately to deny benefits or impose burdens on the basis of a person's indigency. To this extent, today's law fulfills Justice ROBERT H. JACKSON's prescription, concurring in EDWARDS V. CALIFORNIA (1941): "The mere state of being without funds is a neutral fact—constitutionally an irrelevance, like race, creed, or color." In a market economy, however, indigency is anything but an irrelevance; unrelieved, it bars access to virtually everything money can buy. Unsurprisingly, therefore, the Supreme Court has found in the Constitution affirmative obligations on government to supply to indigents certain benefits that they cannot afford to buy for themselves. These obligations are few in number; the very idea of a market economy implies de facto WEALTH DISCRIMINATION in the sense of differential access to goods and services, and in no sense has the Court declared capitalism unconstitutional. (See FREEDOM OF CONTRACT.)

The first focus for the Court's egalitarian concerns for relieving the poor from consequences of their poverty was the criminal process. In cases such as GRIFFIN V. ILLINOIS (1956) and DOUGLAS V. CALIFORNIA (1963), one doctrinal vehicle was the EQUAL PROTECTION clause. But the goal of "equal justice for poor and rich, weak and powerful alike" contained no easily discernible place to stop, and it was always clear that the Court would not require the states to make unlimited funds available so that all accused persons could match the spending of the very rich on their criminal defense. The alternative to the equality principle was insistence on minimum standards of criminal justice for everyone, and the Court's post-1950 decisions tightening those standards—not merely in areas such as the RIGHT TO COUNSEL or the setting of BAIL but throughout the criminal process—can be seen in this egalitarian light, reflecting a recognition that the criminal justice system generally bears most heavily on the poor.

A similar approach, setting minimum standards of justice, had characterized the Court's treatment of claims by the poor to access to civil courts and administrative hearings. PROCEDURAL DUE PROCESS, not equal protection, provides the doctrinal foundation for this development. A concern for hardship to the poor surely played an important role in decisions such as BODDIE V. CONNECTICUT (1971) (access to divorce courts for persons unable to afford filing fees), *Sniadach v. Family Finance Corp.* (1969) (prior hearings prerequisite for prejudgment garnishment), and GOLDBERG V. KELLY (1970) (prior hearings prerequisite for termination of WELFARE BENEFITS). But just as the Court has stopped far short of a general principle of equal access to criminal justice, so it has refused to make equality the guiding principle for its decisions on access to civil justice; in LASSITER V. DEPARTMENT OF SOCIAL SERVICES (1981) the Court denied the existence of a right to state-appointed counsel in proceedings to terminate parental rights.

The one area where the equality principle has guided the Supreme Court's treatment of poverty is the electoral process. The development began with HARPER V. VIRGINIA STATE BOARD OF ELECTIONS (1966), which invalidated a POLL TAX as a condition on voting in a state election. Property qualifications to vote, too, were invalidated, except in the elections of special-purpose districts. Not only VOTING RIGHTS but also rights of access to the ballot were secured against financial barriers that would disqualify the poor.

The early 1970s marked a turning point in the constitutional protection of indigents against the consequences of their poverty. Since that time, the Court has drawn one line after another constricting the expansion of either equal protection or due process doctrines to impose on government further affirmative obligations to relieve the burdens of poverty—even when those burdens affect the quality of an indigent's relations with government itself.

KENNETH L. KARST

Bibliography

BRUDNO, BARBARA 1976 *Poverty, Inequality, and the Law.* St. Paul, Minn.: West Publishing Co.

INDIRECT TAXES

See: Direct and Indirect Taxes

INFAMY

Our legal system depends upon the reliability of a person's word—his oath as an officer, his promise as a contractor, his testimony as a witness. Under the COMMON LAW, conviction of certain crimes so diminished a person's credibility that he permanently forfeited certain of his CIVIL RIGHTS, his oath was of no legal value, and he was incompetent to testify in court. Infamy, as this is called, resulted from conviction of TREASON, FELONY, or a crime involving willful falsehood. The Fifth Amendment requires PRESENTMENT or INDICTMENT by a GRAND JURY before a person may be tried in federal court for an infamous crime.

In modern political rhetoric, the term "infamy" often means general harm done to a person's reputation, especially as a result of LEGISLATIVE INVESTIGATIONS or other governmental action.

DENNIS J. MAHONEY

INFLUENCE OF THE AMERICAN CONSTITUTION ABROAD

It can easily be argued that America's most important export has been the Constitution of the United States. It was the first single-document CONSTITUTION. It is the longest-lived. And in only two centuries, virtually every nation has come to accept the inevitability and value of having a constitution. This fact transcends differences of culture, history, and legal heritage. The United States Constitution is perceived as the fundamental point of reference, even by regimes whose philosophical outlook is antidemocratic. Furthermore, nearly every nation has accepted the "Philadelphia formula"—either internally or universally—as the means by which an effective constitution can best be produced.

The international impact of the U.S. Constitution is an ongoing reality: most of the world's constitutions have been written in the last forty years, and constitutions are rewritten and revised all the time. The Constitution of the United States continues to be the guiding pattern, and a wellspring of inspiration and innovation. The fundamental idea behind the U.S. Constitution was the belief that the people of a nation comprise the constituent power. The founders of this country, conceiving of the people as the sovereign, asserted that the people themselves could formulate and promulgate a constitution. The idea of a constitutional convention was the natural expression of this concept, for it literally embodied the SOVEREIGNTY of the people.

Universally influential also have been the American ratification and amending processes. For it was these that gave the U.S. Constitution—and all subsequent constitutions—the essential characteristic of permanence. Prior to the creation of such machinery, any

law could be superseded by another law. Now it is no longer possible. A method had been created for public approbation of the work of the constitution-makers before the constitution could come into effect. And a method had been created for constitutional change to be effected by that public. Every constitution has since copied or been guided by those formulations. Indeed, the very nature of maintaining permanent written constitutions depends upon the creation of these political devices.

The federal structure—the essential product of the U.S. Constitution—innovated a means by which local and central power could be reconciled. The underlying assumption was that the citizenry, and not the government, is sovereign and is the source of derived power. Thus was established a basis for maintaining national unity, and it has been widely adapted.

Australia, Canada, West Germany, Switzerland, Yugoslavia, and, most recently, Nigeria boast of adherence to American concepts in the creation of their own federal structure and so to a lesser extent do Argentina, Brazil, Mexico, and Venezuela.

The United States was the first nation to have an elected head of state called a president. It was a constitutionally created president, described by HAROLD J. LASKI as "both more and less than a king; both more and less than a prime minister." Today more than half the world's nations have presidents as their chief executives, some with even more constitutional power than the American president (France, South Africa), many with only nominal ceremonial powers (India, Zimbabwe).

The American Constitution formalized the concepts required to make such a system work: the SEPARATION OF POWERS and the system of CHECKS AND BALANCES. The result balances leadership and minimizes abuse, encourages stability and obviates tyranny.

It is now universally understood—as it was by a vocal American citizenry that backed the BILL OF RIGHTS 200 years ago—that fundamental freedoms cannot be guaranteed merely by good intentions. The ratifiers of the U.S. Constitution taught that there could be no fundamental law of the land without a separate section listing individual rights. With the adoption of the Canadian Charter of Rights and Freedoms in 1982, the United Kingdom is the only major nation without a constitutional Bill of Rights, although such has been proposed. The belief that liberties require an explicit statement in order to assure their protection animates political endeavors and constitutionalism throughout the world today.

The sheer longevity of America's constitutional experiment illuminates with each passing year a great, yet hidden strength of the U.S. Constitution: It is a device for assuring national dialogue and conflict resolution. The legislative branch, the executive, and especially the judiciary are more than divisions of government. They are America's ongoing constitutional convention. And as much as anything, this aspect of their identities explains why the American constitutional model remains so attractive and thought-provoking at its bicentennial.

Any study of the international influence of the U.S. Constitution must take into account the fact that this influence is both historic and ongoing. And it should consider how American guidelines, practices, and innovations have been improved on by other nations. But more would be accomplished than just a study of the past. A new understanding would be achieved, of what is fundamental to the American Constitution and what is ephemeral, of what is exportable, and even universally applicable.

So pervasive has been the influence of the Constitution of the United States that most nations have followed its lead by adopting one-document constitutions of their own. Beginning in 1791 with Poland and France, the American concept of a constitution to create government speedily became the norm.

Although some nations are under martial rule or have a transitional government with their constitutions in suspension, all but the United Kingdom, New Zealand, and Israel are committed to the concept and principle of the one-document constitution and all have such a document in some stage of preparation or have one in place. Significantly, the act of constitutional suspension has become the most extreme political act of modern government. What makes this American-influenced constitutional universality so historically significant is its short duration on the world stage.

What has made the U.S. Constitution so admired and so imitated? It was not the establishment of a supreme LAW OF THE LAND; that was no innovation. Plato taught in *The Laws* that "some body of law should exist on a permanent basis, on a superior plane—neither subject to individual tyranny nor to raw majority democracy." Historian K. C. Wheare noted that "from the earliest times . . . people had thought it proper or necessary to write down in a document the fundamental principles upon which their government for the future should be established and conducted."

Nor was it the theory of LIMITED GOVERNMENT that intrigued foreign statesmen. Even the notions of establishing a republic or electing a president or the radical concept of POPULAR SOVEREIGNTY were already commonplace—at least in theory. The philosophers of the Enlightenment and their forebears all had written on such subjects and were familiar with each other's works. And there had already existed such governmental documents as the 1579 Act of Union of the United Provinces of the Netherlands, but until the American experience no one had thought of calling their documents "constitutions."

The written constitution is an American innovation. Its genesis can be traced to THOMAS HOOKER's FUNDAMENTAL ORDERS OF CONNECTICUT (1639) which was the first to create a state or governmental entity. This prefigured the state constitutions of Virginia and Pennsylvania, which in turn influenced the French Declaration of the Rights of Man. The U.S. Constitution, however, was the document that influenced and continues to influence foreign constitution-makers. For since that date nationhood was to be achieved via a constitution.

The primary reason for the great influence of the U.S. Constitution abroad is that it institutionalized government based on the sovereignty of the people. Americans also created the machinery to translate constitutional philosophy into constitutional reality. Their main device was the CONSTITUTIONAL CONVENTION or constituent assembly. This device has been the most significant and most followed precedent in constitutional development. For in this way a nation can be formed and gets its "supreme law of the land" (save in those instances where the former colonial power grants independence and bestows a constitution for independence). The constituent assembly institutionalized democracy. It legitimized revolution, enabling men to do what they had not yet been able to do peacefully and legally—to alter or abolish government and institute new governments deriving their authority from the consent of the governed.

By following the United States model, all constitution writers after 1787 could legitimize their revolutions, their independence, their nationhood. In his study of Latin American political institutions, Jacques Lambert wrote: "Here . . . was the worthy model of a constitution that repudiated monarchy and clearly proclaimed the principle of political freedom. . . . The Constitution of the United States lent authority the cloak of democratic respectability. A few countries very shortly adopted constitutions directly inspired by it—Venezuela in 1811, Mexico in 1824, the Central American Federation in 1825, and Argentina in 1826."

Just by being the first, the U.S. Constitution inevitably influenced constitutions abroad. It was the only available national model for the 1791 constitution-makers of Poland who copied its preamble and its impeachment provisions, and in their famous Article V provided Europe's first statement of popular sovereignty.

Another reason for the widespread influence of the United States Constitution abroad is that constitutions are largely written by lawyers, and lawyering normally involves the search for source and precedent. Lawyers have dominated the constituent assemblies and constitutional conventions abroad. The lawyer constitutionalists of America were also proselytizers. They shared the gospel so often proclaimed by THOMAS JEFFERSON. "We feel," he wrote, "that we are acting under obligations not confined to the limits of our own society. It is impossible not to be sensible that we are acting for all mankind."

This message has been well received, starting with France and the men who made the French Revolution. The fact that the constitution consisted of lawyers' ideas contributed to their ready transmittal. Lawyers were popular; the Dantons and Robespierres had sided with the people in their revolt against authority. Jacques Vincent de la Croix, a lawyer, offered a course on the Constitution of the United States at the Lycée de Paris, an institution of free higher education established in 1787. This pattern has continued. The lawyer has been the commoner charged with teaching constitutionalism and translating the needs and aspirations of the people into a legal document. Every constitutional lawyer in the world knows about the U.S. Constitution.

The lawyers who wrote the American constitutions also wrote about them. JOHN ADAMS, author of the MASSACHUSETTS CONSTITUTION and prime "inventor" of the concept of a constitutional convention, could not be in Philadelphia in 1787 as he was then envoy to England. But his *Defence of the Constitutions of Government of the United States of America* was one of the most influential works on constitutionalism, at home and abroad.

Even more influential was THE FEDERALIST, almost immediately translated into French, German, and Spanish to provide constitutional guidelines for a dozen or more nations in Europe and Latin America. Now translated into more than twenty languages, *The Federalist* is still taught in constitutional law classes abroad and new translations are still being published.

The records of the 1848 German constitutional assembly at Frankfurt contain references not only to the U.S. Constitution and *The Federalist* but also to the constitutional commentaries of Justice JOSEPH STORY and Chancellor JAMES KENT. Modern examples abound, with copious references in India's 1947 Constituent Assembly Debates, and, more recently, in the commentaries on the Nigerian Constitution of 1979.

The tradition of the American participant, counsel, or consultant in foreign constitution-making dates from the service of THOMAS PAINE as a member of the 1791 French constitutional assembly. Lawrence Ward Beer wrote of the American role in constitution-making in Asia: "A basic context for American influence has been the *consultation* of American experts on constitutionalism and law during the process of drawing up, applying, interpreting, or amending a national constitution. Concretely, the views of individual American judges and legal scholars have been solicited during visits by Asian constitutionalists to America; American legal literature (including judicial precedent) has been studied, and many Americans have been directly involved in Asian constitution-making."

And the tradition continues. Americans have influenced the writing of constitutions for nations throughout the world, including Liberia, China, Ethiopia, Nigeria, Zimbabwe, Bangladesh, and Peru. ALEXIS DE TOCQUEVILLE was the best known of the foreigners who came to study United States government and who returned home as advocates of the American system. His *Democracy in America*, published in French editions in 1835 and 1840, heightened interest in the United States constitutional system both in Europe and in Latin America.

But Tocqueville was preceded by scores of other Europeans who were attracted by the hope and promise of the new world, most notably Thaddeus Kosciusko, who was later to lead the struggle for democracy in Poland. And Tocqueville was followed by many thousands of scholars in law, government, history, and political science who likewise transported American constitutional ideology. Current manifestations of this development are apparent in the 1982 constitutions of Canada and Honduras and the 1983 constitution of El Salvador.

The United States, a great colonizer, has offered a solution to colonialism. As pointed out by Henry Steele Commager:

No Old World nation had known what to do with colonies except to exploit them for the benefit of the mother country. The new United States was born the largest nation in the Western world and was, from the beginning and throughout the 19th century, a great colonizing power with a hinterland that stretched westward to the Mississippi and, eventually, to the Pacific. [And thence beyond the mainland to Alaska and Hawaii.] By the simple device of transforming colonies into states, and admitting these states into the union on the basis of absolute equality with the original states, the Founding Fathers taught the world a lesson which it has learned only slowly and painfully down to our own day.

This constitutional concept has been studied and followed in France, Portugal, Spain, Yugoslavia, and the Soviet Union, to provide a few examples, but not always with successful results. Algeria is no longer part of Metropolitan France, but French Guiana, Guadeloupe, Martinique, Reunion, and Saint Pierre and Miquelon are. Angola is no longer an integral part of Portugal, but Madeira and the Azores are.

Another reason for the influence of the American Constitution abroad is rooted in military conquest. Although the influence of the Philadelphia experience had been felt in Baden, Bavaria, Frankfurt, and Württemberg before there was a unified Germany, a more general reception of American style constitutionalism attended the preparation of the post-World War II 1949 Basic Law of the Federal Republic. Similarly, the "MacArthur Constitution" influenced—to use an understatement of the greatest order—Japan's 1947 constitution.

Under United States military authority following the Spanish-American War, Cuba's 1901 constitution bears obvious American imprints. And so does the 1904 constitution of Panama, which in Article 136 gave the United States authority to intervene to establish "constitutional order." Haiti's 1918 constitution, putatively the work of then Assistant Secretary of the Navy FRANKLIN D. ROOSEVELT, was based on compromises between existing government forums and the ideologies of the American military forces which had occupied the country since 1915.

American influence was also significant in the preparation of the South Vietnam Constitution of 1967. The Vietnamese actually copied more from the United States model than was appropriate for a nation with a French legal tradition. (The preamble to the North Vietnamese Constitution had been taken directly from Lincoln's Gettysburg Address.)

Most pervasive has been the influence of the U.S. Constitution upon its former colony, the Republic of the Philippines. Under American sovereignty from 1896 until its independence in 1946, the Philippines were given a commonwealth constitution in 1935 which remained virtually unchanged until 1973. And on the eve of the American constitutional bicentennial there was a significant movement to call a new constitutional convention in Manila. A new constitutional

structure will predictably once again follow the Philadelphia model.

ALBERT P. BLAUSTEIN

Bibliography

BEER, LAWRENCE W. 1979 *Constitutionalism in Asia: Asian Views of the American Influence.* Berkeley: University of California Press.
BLAUSTEIN, ALBERT P. 1984 The United States Constitution: A Model in Nation Building. *National Forum* 64:14–17.
BLAUSTEIN, ALBERT P. and FLANZ, GISBERT H., EDS. 1971 *Constitutions of the Countries of the World.* 20 Vols. looseleaf, updated quarterly. Dobbs Ferry, N.Y.: Oceana.
CAPPELLETTI, MAURO 1971 *Judicial Review in the Contemporary World.* Indianapolis: Bobbs-Merrill.
COMMAGER, HENRY STEELE 1977 *The Empire of Reason: How Europe Imagined and America Realized the Enlightenment.* Garden City, N.Y.: Anchor Press/Doubleday.
HAWGOOD, JOHN A. 1939 *Modern Constitutions Since 1787.* New York: Macmillan.
HENDERSON, DAN FENNO, ED. 1968 The Constitution of Japan: Its First Twenty Years, 1947–67. Seattle: University of Washington Press.
PALMER, R. R. 1959 *The Age of the Democratic Revolution: A Political History of Europe and America, 1760–1800.* 2 Vols. Princeton, N.J.: Princeton University Press.
STARCK, CHRISTIAN, ED. 1983 *Main Principles of the German Basic Law.* Baden-Baden: Nomos.

INFORMANT'S TIP

A police officer's own observations may not be required to establish PROBABLE CAUSE for an ARREST WARRANT or SEARCH WARRANT (or for an arrest without warrant). Probable cause may be established by an informant's tip, even if it is hearsay, if there is adequate basis to credit his word. The Supreme Court has, however, been troubled by the criteria necessary to determine an informant's truthfulness.

DRAPER V. UNITED STATES (1959) was the first case to hold that an informant's word, when corroborated, was sufficient to establish probable cause; the informant had previously proved reliable, and his story was later substantially verified by the officer's own observations. AGUILAR V. TEXAS (1964) established a "two-pronged" test, amplified in SPINELLI V. UNITED STATES (1969) and generally followed until 1983: the affidavit (or the officer's personal testimony) must make clear to the magistrate, first, some of the underlying circumstances from which the *informant* concluded that criminal activity was afoot (such as personal observation of the suspect's action), and second, some of the circumstances from which the *officer* concluded that the informant was telling the truth (for example, his previous record of reliability). Failure fully to satisfy either "prong" could be remedied by substituting highly detailed information (even of a nonsuspicious nature) demonstrating that the informant's statement was based neither on rumor nor on the suspect's bad reputation.

In ILLINOIS V. GATES (1983) the Court abandoned the *Aguilar-Spinelli* test in favor of a much looser "totality of the circumstances" approach, which would permit "a balanced assessment of the relative weight of all the various indicia of reliability." Thus, said the Court, the report of an informant who had previously been usually reliable would be acceptable even if it did not explain the basis of his knowledge.

The need to corroborate an informant's statement and demonstrate his reliability arises when the informant has a criminal past; his veracity is naturally suspect. The word of a law enforcement officer who provides information to another officer or that of an honest private citizen without ulterior motive requires no such corroboration according to the decision in *Ventresca v. United States* (1965). Uncorroborated anonymous tips to the police are worthless for establishing probable cause.

In order to prevent reprisals and maintain the future effectiveness of informants, the Court denied in McCRAY V. ILLINOIS (1967) that a defendant has the right to demand the identity of a government informant at a suppression hearing on the question of probable cause. The accuracy of statements, including those of informants, in affidavits for warrants can be challenged at a hearing if the defendant offers proof that the affiant lied or acted with "reckless disregard for the truth" in statements pertinent to the establishment of probable cause. The warrant's legality will not be affected by an informant's misrepresentation, however, if the officer had no reason to doubt the truth of the informant's statement.

JACOB W. LANDYNSKI

Bibliography

LaFave, Wayne R. 1978 *Search and Seizure: A Treatise on the Fourth Amendment.* Vol. 1:489–586. St. Paul, Minn.: West Publishing Co.

IN FORMA PAUPERIS

(Latin: "In the manner of a poor person.") To insure that ACCESS TO THE COURTS is not barred by inability to pay the costs of litigation, poor persons may have fees and some procedural requirements waived and counsel appointed at public expense. In the federal courts this privilege is granted by law to anyone swearing he is without means.

More than half the petitions received by the Supreme Court are filed *in forma pauperis,* often by prisoners seeking review of criminal convictions or of denials of HABEAS CORPUS petitions on constitutional grounds. Probably the most famous case to arise in this way was GIDEON V. WAINWRIGHT (1963).

DENNIS J. MAHONEY

INFORMATION

An information is a formal written accusation against a person for a criminal offense presented under oath by a public officer, usually a prosecutor. An information is used to charge an individual with criminal activity in cases where an INDICTMENT by a GRAND JURY is unnecessary or is waived by the accused. Like an indictment, the filing of an information results in the commencement of a formal prosecution. Thus, the information must be clear and specific in order to give adequate notice to the accused of the charges against him and permit him to prepare his defense.

Most states permit prosecution by information or indictment at the option of the prosecutor. In these states, it is rare for a prosecutor not to use an information because it is easier and less time-consuming than an indictment. Grand jury indictments will be used in these jurisdictions only when the prosecutor wants to use the investigative powers of the grand jury. In other states, indictments are required in all FELONY cases or in all capital cases. However, even in these states, informations are used in MISDEMEANOR cases and in felony cases where the accused has waived his right to a grand jury indictment.

In federal misdemeanor cases, prosecutors have the option under the FEDERAL RULES OF CRIMINAL PROCEDURE to proceed by indictment or information. In federal felony cases, accused individuals have the right to insist on prosecution by indictment, but this right can be waived in all but capital cases.

Most jurisdictions limit the prosecutor's discretion to file an information. Generally, the prosecutor cannot file an information unless the accused has had a preliminary hearing before a magistrate. This requirement is designed to weed out groundless charges, thereby relieving an accused of the burden of preparing a defense. However, the effectiveness of this limitation on prosecutorial abuse in filing informations is undercut in several ways. First, in most jurisdictions, a finding of no PROBABLE CAUSE by one magistrate at a preliminary hearing does not preclude presenting the case to another magistrate. Thus, a prosecutor can "shop around" for a magistrate who will find the requisite probable cause and enable the prosecutor to file an information.

In addition, in filing an information, the prosecutor is not always bound by the findings of the magistrate at the preliminary hearing. Some states permit the prosecutor to charge the accused in the information only with the crimes for which the magistrate decided there was probable cause. In other states, the information can charge the offense for which the accused was bound over at the preliminary hearing and any other offenses supported by the EVIDENCE at the preliminary hearing.

Another problem with using the preliminary hearing as a check on the prosecutor's decision to file an information is that the prosecutor often dominates the magistrate's hearing. Furthermore, in *Gerstein v. Pugh* (1975), the Supreme Court implied that the federal Constitution does not require a preliminary judicial hearing to determine whether there is probable cause for the prosecutor to file an information.

CHARLES H. WHITEBREAD

Bibliography

AMERICAN BAR ASSOCIATION, SECTION OF CRIMINAL JUSTICE 1977 *Policy on the Grand Jury.* Washington, D.C.: ABA Section of Criminal Justice.

INGERSOLL, JARED
(1749–1822)

Jared Ingersoll represented Pennsylvania at the CONSTITUTIONAL CONVENTION OF 1787 and signed the Constitution. Although reputed the best trial lawyer in Philadelphia, he was not a frequent speaker at the convention. He unenthusiastically described the plan proposed by the convention as "all things considered, most eligible."

DENNIS J. MAHONEY

INGRAHAM v. WRIGHT
430 U.S. 651 (1977)

Two Florida junior high school students, disciplined by severe paddling, sued school officials for damages and injunctive relief, claiming that the paddling constituted CRUEL AND UNUSUAL PUNISHMENT. They also claimed that they had been deprived of their right to a prior hearing in violation of their PROCEDURAL DUE PROCESS rights. The lower federal courts denied relief, and the Supreme Court affirmed, 5–4.

For the majority, Justice LEWIS F. POWELL, a former school board president, concluded that the guarantee against cruel and unusual punishment was limited to cases of punishment for criminal offenses and thus had no application to paddling as a means of school discipline. The openness of public schools provided a safeguard against abusive punishments of the kind that might be visited on prisoners. COMMON LAW restraints on the privilege of school officials to administer corporal punishment were sufficient to prevent excesses. As for due process, Powell conceded that the paddling had implicated a "liberty" interest, but he concluded that due process required no hearing, in view of the availability of common law remedies or damages.

For the dissenters, Justice BYRON R. WHITE argued that it was anomalous to conclude that some punishments are "cruel and unusual" when inflicted on convicts but raise no such problem when they are inflicted on children for breaches of school discipline. The relevant inquiry, White argued, was not the label of criminal punishment but the purpose to punish. While some spanking might be permissible in public schools, the majority was wrong in saying "that corporal punishment in the public schools, no matter how barbaric, inhumane, or severe, is never limited by the Eighth Amendment." Here the record showed not just spanking but severe beatings. Furthermore, the risk of erroneous punishment—a crucial aspect of the due process calculus established in MATHEWS V. ELDRIDGE (1976)—demanded at least some informal discussion between student and disciplinarian before paddling was administered. The common law damages remedy offered no redress for punishments mistakenly administered in good faith and obviously could not undo the infliction of pain.

Ingraham seems an unstable precedent. Constitutional law, following social practice, has increasingly insisted that children be treated as persons, as members of the community deserving of respect. (See CHILDREN'S RIGHTS.) The due process right to a hearing rests partly on the premise that the dignity of being heard, before the state takes away one's liberty or property, is one of the differences between being a participating citizen and being an object of administration. The *Ingraham* majority, unmoved by such concerns, reflected nostalgia for a day when children were seen and not heard.

KENNETH L. KARST

INHERENT POWERS

In theory the Constitution establishes the institutions of the national government and vests those institutions with their responsibilities. Such a government is one of delegated powers. Some of these powers are expressed, others are implied. But all powers of the government—expressed and implied—are delegated powers originating in deliberate acts of the sovereign people. This theory cannot successfully deny that the Constitution may in fact succumb to "necessity," or prove inadequate in contingencies beyond human foresight and control. Nor does it deny that the document's terms (like "due process" and "executive power") are open to construction in light of broader ideas and needs. It simply means that to be lawful, a move of the government must fall within a range permitted by arguable interpretations of constitutional language and tradition.

Constitutional theory can admit a notion of "inherent power" in a sense of IMPLIED POWER as in inherent powers of executive privilege and removal of certain administrative appointees. But constitutional theory cannot admit the doctrine of "inherent power" that finds governmental powers beyond those that have been delegated expressly or by implication on the argument that a government must have certain powers before it can be considered a real government. This strong sense of inherent power is the subject here.

A doctrine of inherent power is frequently asserted in connection with a right to national self-preservation, which, as an inherent power, would differ from implied powers, like an implied power of national defense. Looked upon as an implied but still delegated power, a power of national defense can be derived from such expressed constitutional provisions as authorizing Congress to raise, support, and govern military and naval forces, and to declare war. Questions about the scope of an implied power of national defense would have to be answered in ways that would retain its status as part of a greater whole. A constitutionally derived power of national defense would be consistent with the SEPARATION OF POWERS, individual rights, and other provisions, or arguable interpretations thereof. By contrast, inherent powers need not be consistent with other constitutional provisions; asserting them does not require the interpretive adjustments needed to make something fit into a greater whole. A power to suspend elections and declare a dictatorship during a foreign invasion might become a practical necessity, but it could not be considered an implied power of national defense because no plausible interpretation of the Constitution could make room for such a power.

Appeals to inherent power should be distinguished from appeals to HIGHER LAW to which the Constitution might be open. The latter provide arguments for interpreting the Constitution in certain ways. The former propose reasons that might justify violating or suspending the Constitution. Historically, the former usually invoke considerations of "necessity" or "self-preservation" as reasons for ignoring the separation of powers and the BILL OF RIGHTS. These considerations have surfaced in decisions to put innocent Americans in war-time concentration camps and to deny that the government has an obligation to treat ALIENS fairly. They have been used to rationalize congressional abdications of responsibility, especially in FOREIGN AFFAIRS. They therefore imply the supremacy of material safety over constitutional ideals and structures, even over the Constitution itself as a product of deliberative reason.

A strong doctrine of inherent power may have seemed necessary to constitutional theory as a way to circumvent artificially narrow conceptions of national power originating largely in a STATES' RIGHTS parochialism. But this is no longer the problem it used to be. Understanding national powers in terms of the broad ends to which they point—national defense, for example,—reduces the need for a doctrine of inherent power—unless precisely what is sought is justification for ignoring the Constitution.

SOTIRIOS A. BARBER

(SEE ALSO: *Constitutional Reason of State; Delegation of Power; Enumerated Powers; Necessary and Proper Clause; Tenth Amendment.*)

Bibliography

HENKIN, LOUIS 1972 *Foreign Affairs and the Constitution.* Mineola, N.Y.: Foundation Press.
LOFGREN, CHARLES A. 1973 United States v. Curtiss-Wright Export Corp.: An Historical Reassessment. *Yale Law Journal* 83:1–32.

INITIATIVE

Initiative is the practice by which legislation may be proposed and voted on directly by the people (rather than their representatives). Its adoption was an important element of the Progressive era political reform movement. Of some twenty states that now use the initiative all but Alaska adopted it before 1919. Initiative makes possible enactment of legislation that contravenes the class interest of politicians—such as tax reduction and limitation on public expenditure.

Restrictions on the initiative process, such as a requirement for an extraordinary majority to enact housing legislation, have been held to violate the EQUAL PROTECTION clause of the FOURTEENTH AMENDMENT when the Justices were convinced that the intent was to disadvantage racial minorities.

Although the people of a state may reserve a portion of the legislative power, they may not, by initiative, directly exercise powers (for example, RATIFICATION OF AMENDMENTS) conferred on the state legislatures by the federal Constitution.

DENNIS J. MAHONEY

INJUNCTION

In use long before the Constitution, the injunction in the twentieth century came to play one of its most important roles as the enforcer of constitutional and CIVIL RIGHTS. Precisely because it is effective, flexible, and open-ended, the injunction has drawn opposition, and constitutional cases have often included fierce battles over whether the injunction ought to be used as a remedy. These battles have resulted in some complex judicially imposed limitations on the use of injunctions in public law cases.

The injunction rests on a simple idea: that a court may order someone to perform or to cease some action. However simple the idea, it was not a usual feature of the earliest English COMMON LAW. Although it is inaccurate to say that early common law never commanded the performance of an action, by the sixteenth century its typical judgment simply decreed that A, having won the suit, was entitled to "take" some sum of money from B. If B did not cooperate, A could often gain the assistance of the sheriff, but B was subject to no direct order to do anything.

By contrast to the common law courts, the Court of Chancery administered a system of remedies that came to be called EQUITY, vindicated by an order directing someone to do or cease doing something. At an early stage only the imagination of the Chancellor, who presided over the court, limited the precise nature of such orders. Equity has never lost this tradition of flexibility and discretion, but as Chancery developed a sense of precedent, the occasions for such orders began to seem standardized. For example, a court might require a defendant to perform a trust, to convey land, to carry out a contract, or to pay money owed to a business partner. Some orders, typically those forbidding an action (for example, requiring a party to halt a lawsuit or to cease polluting a stream), came to be called injunctions, though the term "injunctive relief" is often used broadly to refer to direct judicial orders of many sorts. Such equitable remedies always remained relatively discretionary: Chancery would not, for example, enter an injunction in all cases; the litigant seeking such an order first had to convince that court that his remedy at law (i.e., from the common law courts) would be "inadequate," a deceptively simple term that over five centuries has taken on some surprising baggage. Because of this requirement a litigant can have a valid legal right for which, however, he cannot obtain injunctive relief.

In America before the civil rights era the injunction saw its most controversial use in labor disputes in which courts, acting on the view that union organizing and strikes were either common law torts or violations of antitrust statutes, frequently enjoined strikes or PICKETING by workers. Such actions engendered great bitterness and led to Congress's withdrawing from federal courts JURISDICTION to enter an injunction in any labor dispute. (See NORRIS-LAGUARDIA ACT.) That withdrawal in turn has bolstered arguments in favor of occasional proposals to withdraw injunctive jurisdiction in other areas in which courts were enforcing unpopular decisions.

In the late twentieth century the injunction has had its most prominent career not as a remedy in tort, contract, and property disputes but as a vindicator of civil rights. That new role flowed largely from EX PARTE YOUNG (1908), which held that although SOVEREIGN IMMUNITY might bar a damage action against a state, it did not bar injunctive relief against a state official acting unconstitutionally. This development meant that even if there was no remedy for past unlawful action, an injunction could halt continuation of that activity. Until the birth of the modern civil rights damage action with MONROE V. PAPE (1961) and the CIVIL RIGHTS ACTS of the 1960s, the injunction served as a primary tool for the enforcement of civil and constitutional rights.

Because the injunction is open-ended, it has the potential for use in a wide variety of contexts. Not only can simple acts be required or forbidden but, more important, elaborate public institutions can be restructured. Probably the most noteworthy and certainly the most controversial use of injunctive relief came in the years following BROWN V. BOARD OF EDUCATION (1954) as the courts ordered school systems to end racial SEGREGATION. Drawing on their experience in complex antitrust and BANKRUPTCY cases, the courts employed the injunction as a tool for the reorganization of the schools. In the case of recalcitrant systems, such desegregation decrees sometimes called forth elaborate and detailed orders concerning the assignment of students and teachers, the curriculum, and other details of the schools' operation. Such orders often engendered resistance and involved the courts in the conduct of the schools over a number of years in particularly intractable cases. Courts have also ordered injunctive relief in INSTITUTIONAL LITIGATION involving PRISONERS' RIGHTS and the rights of mental patients.

Part of what makes the injunction such a powerful and controversial tool is the enforcement power that stands behind it. One disobeying an injunction is subject to CONTEMPT penalties—with the threat of indefinite imprisonment and mounting fines until one obeys the order. Perhaps because the injunction carries with it such a formidable arsenal for enforcement, the Supreme Court has enunciated a series of restrictions on the use of injunctive relief in favor of litigants wishing to challenge official action. Thus a federal court may abstain from deciding the constitutionality of a state practice until the state courts have had an opportunity to clarify the law or practice in question, as in *Railroad Commission of Texas v. Pullman Co.* (1941). Moreover, even if the law or practice is clear, a federal court should refrain from adjudicating the constitutionality of a state statute if the challenger of the statute will have an adequate opportunity to present that challenge in pending litigation to which the state is a party (YOUNGER V. HARRIS, 1971). Both the so-called *Pullman* and *Younger* ABSTENTION doctrines have complexities not hinted at in these summaries; they testify to the power of the injunction and its centrality in much modern constitutional litigation.

STEPHEN C. YEAZELL

Bibliography

FISS, OWEN 1978 *The Civil Rights Injunction.* Bloomington: Indiana University Press.

FRANKFURTER, FELIX and GREENE, NATHAN 1930 *The Labor Injunction.* New York: Macmillan.

IN PERSONAM

(Latin: "Against the person.") A legal action or case is *in personam* if it is directed against a particular individual to enforce an obligation. Cases in EQUITY proceed *in personam.*

DENNIS J. MAHONEY

IN RE

(Latin: "In the matter [of]. . . .") This is a way of titling a case that presents a question to be decided or an action to be taken in the absence of adversary parties.

DENNIS J. MAHONEY

IN RE . . .

See under name of party

IN REM

(Latin: "Against the thing.") A legal action or case is *in rem* if it undertakes to establish the title to or status of a thing with respect to all persons.

DENNIS J. MAHONEY

INSTITUTIONAL LITIGATION

"Institutional litigation" refers to cases in which the courts, responding to allegations that conditions in some institutions violate the Constitution or CIVIL RIGHTS statutes, become involved in supervising the institutions in question. Loosely used, the term might describe any number of lawsuits, ranging from an assertion of discriminatory employment practices in a CORPORATION to an attack by inmates on the conditions at a state prison. What such apparently diverse cases have in common is the possibility that if the plaintiffs convince the court that a violation of the law has occurred and if the institution proves recalcitrant in remedying the violation, the court may become involved in detailed supervision of the institution over long periods. Though details of such complex suits naturally vary widely, it is the combination of continuous judicial scrutiny and detailed substantive involvement that has characterized institutional litigation.

Laws such as those forbidding discrimination in employment apply to both public and private institutions. Many constitutional provisions, however, guarantee rights only against the government and most institutions to which individuals are involuntarily committed are run by the government. Consequently most of the institutions involved have been public: prisons, mental hospitals, school systems, and the like. Moreover, though the Constitution binds both state and federal courts, the latter tribunals have played the most active role in vindicating constitutional rights. The typical institutional case therefore has involved a federal district court supervising the conduct of a state institution, a setting that has raised constitutional concerns beyond those of the particular substantive law of the case.

From a wide perspective one can trace the roots of institutional litigation to earlier classes of cases: nineteenth-century EQUITY receiverships, bankruptcy reorganizations, antitrust decrees requiring the restructuring of a large industry, even to the efforts of fifteenth-century English chancellors to enforce the duties of trustees to establish and supervise the religious and charitable institutions endowed in a will. Modern institutional cases also have more recent origins in the efforts of the federal judiciary to desegregate schools in the 1950s and 1960s. Resistance to simple desegregation decrees forced federal courts to become involved in many details of local school administration. As some school boards adjusted their strategies for resistance, courts delved deeper into school board practices, to the point of displacing some traditional school board functions. In GRIFFIN v. SCHOOL BOARD OF PRINCE EDWARD COUNTY (1964) the Supreme Court even suggested that a federal court could order taxes imposed to raise funds to finance a public school system that officials had closed to avoid desegregation.

At about the same time courts were articulating other constitutional rights, including constitutional limitations on prison and mental hospital conditions. In cases such as *Wyatt v. Stickney* (1971) and *Holt v. Sarver* (1969) lower federal courts combined the procedural aggressiveness of the school desegregation cases with the newly developed constitutional rights, enforcing their decrees against recalcitrant officials with INJUNCTIONS backed by the force of the contempt power. In dozens of institutional cases in the 1970s these same forces triggered widespread court-ordered institutional reform that covered such details of institutional life as cell size, visiting hours, telephone privileges, hygiene, and disciplinary procedures.

Describing institutional litigation and tracing its origins are easier than isolating, much less resolving, the controversies that surround it. Nearly all the issues that arise in public discourse about a federal system and an independent judiciary eventually appear in some discussion of institutional litigation. Perhaps the most central of these issues are questions about the relationship of institutional litigation to (1) the nature of litigation; (2) the judicial capacity to run institutions; (3) the power of the purse; and (4) FEDERALISM.

Some view institutional cases as a form of litigation previously unknown to Anglo-American jurisprudence. In the contrasted traditional vision of litigation, a lawsuit involves two parties who present an isolatable set of facts to a court, which issues a JUDGMENT; the losing party complies with the court's decree, and judicial involvement with the case ends. To the extent that this statement of traditional litigation is accurate, institutional litigation involves a substantial departure. In institutional litigation the set of facts presented to the court often constitutes all of the physical, psychological, and social conditions within the institution. Such widespread allegations prevent the court from addressing any single dispute which, when resolved, will restore the parties to a proper relationship. In several institutional cases, no matter how many disputes the court resolves, additional issues arise with respect to implementation of and compliance with previous orders.

The frequency with which institutional litigation requires courts to address some aspect of institutional life highlights the second central issue—judicial capacity to supervise large public institutions. By training, judges are neither wardens nor hospital administrators. Some critics question whether judges should substitute their judgment about institutional life for that of professional administrators appointed by elected officials. Courts often try to compensate for their inexperience by appointing SPECIAL MASTERS and expert advisory panels and by seeking the views of the defendant administrators. But these tactics may raise further questions about institutional litigation's departure from traditional ideas about litigation. Yet, once a court has concluded that institutional life is constitutionally deficient because of the acts of the regular administrators, it is difficult for courts simply to defer to the judgment of those same persons found to be responsible for the unconstitutional conditions.

In many cases, however, institutional conditions are constitutionally deficient less because of the acts of administrators than because the state has allocated insufficient funds to institutional budgets. Even willing administrators experience difficulty in upgrading conditions at some institutions. A new prison building may be necessary or more staff may need to be hired. When institutional reform may be accomplished only through expenditures of substantial sums, a new issue arises: may courts order the allocation of public funds against the wishes of legislators who presumably reflect their constituents' wishes?

For many observers, this fiscal confrontation reveals the least palatable aspect of institutional litigation—the antimajoritarian judicial usurpation of legislative and executive authority. Courts, self-conscious about express allocative decision making, sometimes disavow authority to order funds raised to carry out institutional reform. And, despite *Griffin*'s OBITER DICTUM about imposing taxes, there is doubt about how far courts may and ought to go in ordering funds raised to satisfy their orders. Yet it is also a commonplace for courts to state that lack of funds is no excuse for failure to comply with the Constitution. Since any public law decision may have important fiscal effects, perhaps institutional cases have been unjustifiably isolated from the rest of the public litigation on this issue. Indeed, if one assumes that, put to the choice between releasing inmates and rectifying the conditions of their institutional confinement, the public and their elected officials would choose the latter, judicially decreed funding may be more in accord with the majority's wishes than any other course of action.

Ironically, institutional cases flourished during the 1970s, while the Supreme Court was emphasizing that federal courts should not interfere with traditional state or local functions. In RIZZO V. GOODE (1976) and O'SHEA V. LITTLETON (1974) the Court rejected systemic attacks on, respectively, a police department and a city's system of criminal justice. In YOUNGER V. HARRIS (1971) and its progeny the Court established prohibitions on federal court interference with state adjudicative proceedings. As a doctrinal matter, the issues in most institutional cases proved distinguishable from the issues in *Rizzo*, *O'Shea*, and *Younger*. Nevertheless the Court's federalism theme could have been viewed as requiring curtailment of judicial receptivity to institutional litigation. Yet during this period of growing deference to states, the lower federal courts, without Supreme Court disapproval, continued to hear and resolve institutional cases.

THEODORE EISENBERG
STEPHEN C. YEAZELL

Bibliography
CHAYES, ABRAM 1976 The Role of the Judge in Public Law Litigation. *Harvard Law Review* 89:1281–1316.
DIVER, COLIN S. 1979 The Judge as Political Powerbroker: Superintending Structural Change in Public Institutions. *Virginia Law Review* 65:43–106.
EISENBERG, THEODORE and YEAZELL, STEPHEN C. 1980 The Ordinary and the Extraordinary in Institutional Litigation. *Harvard Law Review* 93:465–517.
FISS, OWEN M. 1979 The Supreme Court 1978 Term, Foreword: The Forms of Justice. *Harvard Law Review* 93:1–58.

INSULAR CASES

Originally applied to three cases decided in 1901, the term "insular cases" has come to denominate a series of cases decided in the early twentieth century defining the place of overseas TERRITORIES in the American constitutional system. Following the acquisition of PUERTO RICO, the Philippines, Hawaii, and various other island possessions, the Supreme Court was called upon to decide whether, or to what extent, in William Jennings Bryan's phrase, "the Constitution follows the flag." From the insular cases emerged the DOCTRINE of INCORPORATION OF TERRITORIES.

The first three insular cases (*DeLima v. Bidwell, Dooley v. United States, Downes v. Bidwell*) were argued together and decided in 1901. They raised the question whether Puerto Rico was part of the United States within the meaning of the "uniformity clause" for purposes of levying customs duties. In *DeLima* and *Dooley*, the Court held that from the Treaty of Paris (1899), by which Spain ceded Puerto Rico to the United States, until the Foraker Act (1900), by which Congress organized the territorial government, the collection of duties on goods moving between the United States and Puerto Rico was unconstitutional. In the far more important *Downes* case, the court upheld collection of duties after passage of the Foraker Act. The apparent meaning of the three cases was that the constitutional status of overseas possessions is for Congress to determine, but constitutional protection is to be assumed in the absence of congressional action. The Justices divided into three schools of thought: four Justices, led by Chief Justice MELVILLE W. FULLER and Justice JOHN MARSHALL HARLAN, contended that the Constitution applied automatically and completely to any territory under United States SOVEREIGNTY; Justice HENRY B. BROWN, who wrote the lead opinion in all three cases, believed that Congress, under Article IV, section 3, enjoyed plenary power over the territories and could extend to them all, any part, or none of the Constitution, at its discretion; and four Justices, led by Justice EDWARD D. WHITE, argued that the Constitution applied fully to the territories only after positive action by the Congress to incorporate them into the United States.

In 1903 and 1904 the Court decided four cases dealing with CRIMINAL PROCEDURE in Hawaii, Puerto Rico, and the Philippines (*Hawaii v. Mankichi, Crowley v. United States, Kepner v. United States, Dorr v. United States*). The Court made a distinction between fundamental or NATURAL RIGHTS, which are constitutionally protected everywhere, and rights merely procedural or remedial, peculiar to Anglo-American jurisprudence, which do not apply in the territories—at least "until Congress shall see fit to incorporate the . . . territory into the United States." In the former category was protection against DOUBLE JEOPARDY; in the latter were INDICTMENT by GRAND JURY, TRIAL BY JURY, and JURY UNANIMITY. *Dorr* (1904) was the first case in which the incorporation of territories doctrine received the formal assent of a majority of the Court.

In the 1905 case of *Rasmussen v. United States,* the Court unanimously held the jury trial guarantee of the SIXTH AMENDMENT applicable to Alaska. White, writing for himself and six colleagues, demonstrated that Congress had explicitly incorporated Alaska into the United States and thus had brought its residents under complete constitutional protection. Harlan and Brown, in separate CONCURRING OPINIONS, each reiterated his original position on the Constitution and the territories.

In *Trono v. United States* (1905) and *Dowdell v. United States* (1911), the Court sustained Philippine criminal convictions obtained through indigenous procedures which would have violated the Sixth Amendment had the Philippines been incorporated territory. But in WEEMS V. UNITED STATES (1910), the Court ruled that since Congress had extended the protection against CRUEL AND UNUSUAL PUNISHMENT to the Philippines, the protection was identical to that enjoyed by mainlanders under the Eighth Amendment.

The most forceful and consistent opposition to the incorporation doctrine came from Justice Harlan. He argued that all of Congress's power flows from the Constitution, and therefore Congress is bound in its every action by that document's limitations and guarantees. The "occult" doctrine of the insular cases, he said, permitted Congress, contrary to the spirit and genius of the Constitution, to erect a colonial empire and exercise absolute dominion over dependent peoples.

In *Board of Public Utilities Commissioners v. Ynchausti* (1920), White, by then Chief Justice, was able to report the Court's unanimous acceptance of the incorporation of territories doctrine; and in *Balzac v. Porto Rico* (1922), Chief Justice WILLIAM HOWARD TAFT, for a unanimous Court, applied it as the settled law governing the status of territories.

DENNIS J. MAHONEY

Bibliography

BLOOM, JOHN PORTER, ED. 1973 *The American Territorial System.* Athens: Ohio University Press.

COUDERT, FREDERICK R. 1926 The Evolution of the Doctrine of Territorial Incorporation. *Columbia Law Review* 66:823–850.

FUSTER, JAIME B. 1974 Origins of the Doctrine of Territorial Incorporation and Its Implications Regarding the Power of the Commonwealth of Puerto Rico to Regulate Interstate Commerce. *Revista Juridica de la Universidad de Puerto Rico* 43:259–294.

SEMONCHE, JOHN E. 1978 *Charting the Future: The Supreme Court Responds to a Changing Society, 1890–1920.* Chaps 5 and 6. Westport, Conn.: Greenwood Press.

INTEGRATION

See: Desegregation; Segregation

INTEREST GROUP LITIGATION

Interest group litigation is sponsored by organizations whose attorneys typically are less interested in specific legal claims than in the constitutional principles that a litigation represents. In contrast, most court cases are pursued for the benefit of the parties directly involved.

In seeking their clients' immediate interests private attorneys sometimes invoke constitutional arguments, but these are incidental to the specific claims of the parties. A sponsored case, however, is often pursued in the name of a litigant even though it is initiated, financed, and supported by an organization seeking its own constitutional goals. Interest groups are particularly attracted to cases involving constitutional principles because the judicial decisions emerging from such cases are relatively insulated from subsequent attacks by legislators and other public officials.

It is arguable, of course, that group-supported litigation has always been in existence. For example, following the WAGNER (NATIONAL LABOR RELATIONS) ACT and other New Deal legislation, litigation was managed, or otherwise assisted, by labor unions, trade associations, stockholder groups, and other business interests. However, the social and economic ferment of the 1960s and 1970s brought interest group litigation into sharper focus. The CIVIL RIGHTS movement and the Vietnam conflict not only produced federal legislation but also stimulated new constitutional demands by litigious organizations representing women, welfare recipients, consumers, and persons resisting military service.

The strategies and tactics of interest group litigants

are heavily influenced by SOCIOLOGICAL JURISPRU-DENCE and LEGAL REALISM. These philosophies hold that judges, especially Supreme Court Justices, decide controversial cases by choosing among conflicting goals and policies. Such judges do not reach results or write opinions merely by construing statutes, analogizing cases, or analyzing DOCTRINES. Instead, inquiries into judicial decision making have focused on the ways litigation is influenced by the timing of cases and the quality of the constitutional arguments reaching the appellate courts.

Prototypes of interest group litigation are the cases managed by the United States Department of Justice and similar state agencies. Their attorneys select the appropriate government cases to be appealed, and by confessing error or by compromising cases brought against the government, they seek to inhibit the establishment of unfavorable precedents. Also, a federal Legal Service Corporation, independent of the Department of Justice, has become one of the principal sources for funding and supporting litigation aimed at social and economic reform. Consumers, poor people, prisoners, and other low-resource persons have been represented by government-subsidized attorneys in suits against federal and state agencies and private organizations. Besides managing their own cases, government agencies promote private interest group litigation by reimbursing attorneys who participate and intervene for them in administrative proceedings and in court cases involving ADMINISTRATIVE LAW.

Although strategically less favorably situated than government attorneys, those representing private interest groups are also in a position to choose cases for APPEAL and to control the flow of argument in the higher courts. Unlike government litigation, however, the legal requirements for participation in private law suits sometimes prevent an organization from suing on its own, in behalf of its members, or for a similarly situated class of people. This problem has been partially alleviated by Supreme Court decisions liberalizing rules of legal STANDING to permit lawsuits by environmentalists, taxpayers, and other special interests.

Litigation activity by interest groups is visible in constitutional civil cases as well as in the criminal *cause célèbre*. In some of these cases attorneys representing factions of social movements vie for litigation sponsorship. The extensive publicity often connected with such cases, the constitutional issues perceived to be intertwined in the conflict, and the opportunities for fund-raising sometimes result in interest group controversies. For example, in several church–state cases attorneys representing different organizations have quarreled over the management of litigation. In the "Scottsboro" case, involving blacks accused of rape, attorneys representing civil rights organizations and those representing a communist-sponsored legal defense organization disagreed about the use of trial publicity.

Ideological differences among lawyers are occasionally reflected in varying conceptions of litigation strategy. Some attorneys emphasize the importance of a complete trial record raising all possible legal issues while others concentrate on the constitutional issues.

An alternative approach to a single TEST CASE is a litigation program aimed at accumulating a series of favorable decisions changing constitutional law. An incremental approach emphasizes narrow factual issues and specific claims, and groups with large legal staffs and cooperating attorneys are strategically positioned to conduct litigation in this way. Litigation programs of this kind have achieved changes in the constitutional doctrine governing racial SEGREGATION, CRIMINAL PROCEDURE, selective service, religion, and employment.

In politically tinged criminal cases the less provident and unpopular groups are not likely to use incremental litigation; they usually face immediate problems of securing relief for organization leaders and raising money for their causes. For example, in the 1950s when large numbers of cases involving congressional investigations of communism reached the Supreme Court, the lion's share was controlled by lawyers who depended on individual financial contributions to sustain their legal work.

When litigation is controlled by interest groups, constitutional issues are likely to be advanced and developed at the trial level. The "perfecting of a trial record" also gives the adversaries an opportunity to debate broader issues that are likely to be considered on appeal.

The development of a "good" trial record facilitates the preparation of appellate briefs interlaced with statistical and authoritative bibliographical references to social and economic facts supporting particular constitutional arguments. This technique was first used in the early-twentieth-century social legislation cases, and it has been used to illuminate fields ranging from racial equality to abortion. Similar forms of extralegal argument are found in complex court cases involving PUBLIC UTILITY REGULATION and other economic matters. (See BRANDEIS BRIEF.)

Besides expanding the scope of their arguments,

interest group attorneys have become increasingly adept at coordinating litigation by discouraging the appeal of inconsistent cases or those with less developed records. They have also been successful in getting publication of sympathetic views in legal, scholarly, and popular journals. Networks of attorneys and other observers have also emerged to monitor court decisions and keep central clearinghouses informed about promising court cases.

Sometimes the immediate concerns of the litigants may conflict with those of the sponsoring interest group. A litigant's claim may be compromised or settled. Legal issues advanced by the parties may be formulated so as to avoid the constitutional issues raised by the sponsor. Also, the trial and appellate preparation may be a labor of love, or the work-product of an attorney who jealously guards his professional prerogatives.

A failure to control a litigation does not necessarily mean that an interest group lacks influence. When the issues defined in court are narrow, or the litigant's attorney has failed to develop the case's constitutional implications, an interest group attorney can still participate as AMICUS CURIAE (friend of the court). Nowhere has this phenomenon been more visible than in the medical school admission case, REGENTS OF THE UNIVERSITY OF CALIFORNIA V. BAKKE (1978). In this case fifty-seven organizations submitted amicus curiae briefs to the Supreme Court. Although some interest group attorneys will refrain from submitting such briefs when a client's attorney adequately has argued the constitutional issues, the filing of such a brief does serve the political function of announcing the group's support for a constitutional argument. Amicus curiae participation usually requires the consent of both parties or the approval of the court, and the influence of either briefs or ORAL ARGUMENTS as amicus remains debatable.

Even though interest group litigation is growing, part of the increase is attributable to government legal services and private foundation philanthropy. If government support is curtailed and private foundations are subjected to closer tax scrutiny, individual contributions and voluntary legal services will be called upon to fill the gap. Such a decline in government support seems likely since some judges and political leaders have expressed concern about government-sponsored litigation directed against public officials. They also criticize lawyers who represent causes rather than clients and overburden the judicial process. Other factors affecting the growth of interest group litigation are the strictness of enforcement of traditional restrictions on the scope of law suits (see INSTITUTIONAL LITIGATION) and the rules governing the award of attorneys' fees to interest group attorneys.

Finally, no description of interest group litigation would be complete without noting that many highly publicized civil cases and "showcase" criminal trials as well as ordinary law cases are financed and carried forward without the participation of organized interest groups. The constitutional and policy arguments advanced by attorneys in these cases, in many instances, are just as likely to advance the development of legal and constitutional doctrine.

NATHAN HAKMAN

Bibliography

COUNCIL FOR PUBLIC INTEREST LAW 1976 *Balancing the Scales of Justice: Financing Public Interest Law in America.* Washington, D.C.: Council on Public Interest Law.

HAKMAN, NATHAN 1966 Lobbying the Supreme Court: An Appraisal of "Political Science Folklore." *Fordham Law Review* 35:15–50.

——— 1972 Political Trials in the Legal Order: A Political Scientist's Perspective. *Journal of Public Law* 21:73–126.

KIRCHHEIMER, OTTO 1961 *Political Justice: The Use of Legal Procedure for Political Ends.* Princeton, N.J.: Princeton University Press.

VOSE, CLEMENT E. 1972 *Constitutional Change: Amendment Politics and Supreme Court Litigation Since 1900.* Lexington, Mass.: D. C. Heath.

WEISBROD, BURTON A., HANDLER, JOEL F., and KOMESAR, NEIL K. 1978 *Public Interest Law: An Economical and Institutional Analysis.* Berkeley: University of California Press.

INTERGOVERNMENTAL IMMUNITY

Intergovernmental immunities are exemptions of the state and national governments from attempts to interfere with each other's governmental operations. Thus, one government may claim immunity from the other's regulations and taxes. Though immunity claims may invoke specific provisions such as the TENTH AMENDMENT, they reflect deeper assumptions about the institutional structure envisioned by the Constitution as a whole. Immunity problems originate in the tension between the nation's need to acknowledge the supremacy of federal policies while respecting a tradition of indestructible states. Governmental structures are not ends in themselves in constitutional theory; their ultimate status depends on their efficacy in securing what THE FEDERALIST #45 called "the solid happiness of the people." Implying ends, institutions also imply powers. (See NECESSARY AND PROPER CLAUSE.) Grant the supremacy of national powers over state powers, and the erosion of state institutions follows eventually despite talk of indestructible states. Conversely, protection for state institutions will eventually defeat national power in some respects, talk of federal supremacy notwithstanding. On balance, judicial resolutions of this tension have favored national supremacy.

Immunity claims usually occur in the areas of taxation, regulation, and litigation. Most of the latter involve state claims of immunity from suits by private parties in federal court under the ELEVENTH AMENDMENT. The amendment, however, does not extend immunity that would be considered inconsistent with the Constitution's general plan of government, including the principle of national supremacy. The amendment grants no immunity from suits by other states and the national government. It is not a barrier to Supreme Court review of state court decisions involving federal law. Nor does the amendment bar private plaintiffs seeking federal court injunctions to enforce Congress's CIVIL RIGHTS laws or federal constitutional rights. In *Parden v. Terminal Railway* (1964) the Court declined to exclude state-owned railroads from a congressional act authorizing employees' suits for negligence. The Court reasoned that the state had effectively waived immunity by engaging in activity subject to congressional regulation. Though later decisions gave this doctrine of "constructive waiver" a STATES' RIGHTS twist by requiring clear statements of congressional intent, the Court still assumes that Congress can lift state immunity as necessary for national objectives.

The doctrine that one government cannot tax the instrumentalities of the other is sometimes credited to the OBITER DICTUM in MCCULLOCH V. MARYLAND that power to tax is power to destroy. Chief Justice JOHN MARSHALL made this remark in the course of voiding a state tax on the Second Bank of the United States; he was not seeking to protect the states against Congress. But future Courts transformed Marshall's doctrine of federal immunity into a dual-federalist or states' rights doctrine of reciprocal immunity. In COLLECTOR V. DAY (1871) a Court grown fearful of Reconstruction voided a Civil War federal income tax on the salary of a Massachusetts judge, arguing that if immunity was necessary to preserve the federal government, the same held for the states. Laissez-faire Justices later expanded the immunity doctrine to protect both governments. Items held immune to state taxation included the income of lessees of federal oil lands, sales of gasoline to the national government, and royalties from a federal patent. Fewer decisions went against Congress, but the Court did void some federal taxes, including taxes on income from municipal bonds, profits of state oil leases, and motorcycle sales to a municipal police department.

This pattern of decision ended in the late 1930s as the HUGHES COURT began overruling the most important of the earlier decisions, including those conferring tax immunity on the incomes of governmental officials and contractors. Some tax immunity remains, however. On a theory that combines the principle of national supremacy with the argument that states' interests receive more representation in Congress than national interests receive in state legislatures, the modern Court recognizes a narrower tax immunity for the states than for the national government. Dicta identify state property, state revenues, and traditionally essential state activities as immune to federal taxation. These dicta did not prevent a recent decision upholding a federal registration on state police helicopters. As for federal tax immunity, Congress can confer it on federal contractors and others. Where Congress has not done so, the Court recognizes immunity from state taxation only when the tax legally falls on the federal government itself or its closely connected agencies and instrumentalities. This rule offers no protection to a federal government contractor even where, by contract, the economic impact of a state tax is passed on to the government. The Court continues to invalidate state taxes that discriminate against entities doing business with the federal government or that manifest hostility to federal policy.

Although the SUPREMACY CLAUSE protects federal officials and agencies from state attempts to control the performance of their duties, federal personnel are subject to state laws that do not conflict with federal policies. Indeed, under the federal Assimilative Crimes Act, state criminal law applies to persons on federal enclaves where Congress has not provided otherwise. Examples of state regulations held in conflict with federal policies include attempts to regulate liquor sales and milk prices on military bases and to inspect fertilizer distributed in a national soil conservation program. Until 1985 states were immune from direct federal attempts to interfere in the performance of "functions essential to [the states'] separate and independent existence." The Court failed to give a formula for identifying these essential functions, but they included decisions on where to locate a state capital and the hours and wages of certain state employees. (See NATIONAL LEAGUE OF CITIES V. USERY, 1976.) The Court permitted federal regulation of such "nonessential" state functions as state liquor, timber, and railroad operations and it declined to apply the *Usery* rationale against federal policies affecting state agencies in the areas of civil rights, environmental regulation, and energy policy. The Court overruled *Usery* in 1985 and all but eliminated direct regulatory immunity for the states. (See GARCIA V. SAN ANTONIO METROPOLITAN TRANSIT AUTHORITY, 1985.) Massive, though indirect, federal regulatory control of state policy continues through conditional FEDERAL GRANTS-IN-AID to the states. (See GENERAL WELFARE CLAUSE.)

SOTIRIOS A. BARBER

Bibliography
POWELL, THOMAS REED 1940 Intergovernmental Tax Immunities. *George Washington Law Review* 8:1213–1220.
TRIBE, LAURENCE H. 1978 *American Constitutional Law.* Pages 131–143. Mineola, N.Y.: Foundation Press.

INTERLOCUTORY

The term means temporary, not final, provisional. An interlocutory order is one entered by a court before it renders FINAL JUDGMENT—for example, a preliminary INJUNCTION, to preserve conditions during trial.

KENNETH L. KARST

INTERNAL COMMERCE

See: Intrastate Commerce

INTERNAL IMPROVEMENTS

"Internal Improvements" was the name given to large public works programs in the first half of the nineteenth century. State governments engaged in planning, subsidizing, building, and in some instances owning and operating roads, bridges, canals, and railroads. Most had ambitious programs. None was more successful than New York's Erie Canal. Completed in 1825, it had profound effects on American economic development.

Federal support for internal improvements commenced in 1806 when Congress appropriated money for construction of the Cumberland, or National, Road. The policy was not then a serious constitutional issue, although President THOMAS JEFFERSON, proposing a major program, called for a constitutional amendment to place it beyond cavil. It became a serious constitutional issue after the War of 1812. A federal program was advocated on several grounds: to bind the Union together, to lower the cost of transportation, to effect the "home market" of the AMERICAN SYSTEM. HENRY CLAY and others found constitutional warrant for federal assistance in the powers to establish post roads, to provide for the common defense and GENERAL WELFARE, and to regulate INTERSTATE COMMERCE. In 1817 Congress passed the Bonus Bill to create a permanent fund for internal improvements from the bonus paid by the Bank of the United States for its charter and future dividends on government-owned Bank stock. Surprisingly, President JAMES MADISON, in a return to STRICT CONSTRUCTION principles, vetoed the bill and called for an amendment. His successor, JAMES MONROE, at first took the same position. In 1822, however, he conceded the unlimited power of Congress to appropriate money for improvements of national character, though not to build or operate them. Two years later he approved the General Survey Bill, which offered substantial government assistance. Many projects, the greatest of which was the Chesapeake and Ohio Canal, were launched under federal auspices. The movement was then brought to a virtual halt by President ANDREW JACKSON's veto of the MAYSVILLE ROAD BILL in 1830. He, too, asserted strict construction principles and repeated the call, knowing it to be futile, for a constitutional amendment.

MERRILL D. PETERSON

Bibliography
GOODRICH, CARTER 1960 *Government Promotion of American Canals and Railroads, 1800–1890.* New York: Columbia University Press.
HARRISON, JOSEPH HOPSON 1954 The Internal Improvements Issue in the Politics of the Union, 1783–1825. Ph.D., diss., University of Virginia.

INTERNAL SECURITY ACT
64 Stat. 987 (1950)

The Internal Security Act, or McCarran Act, of 1950 was a massive and complex conglomeration of varied security measures as well as many features of the MUNDT-NIXON BILL and an Emergency Detention

Bill, which had been introduced, unsuccessfully, earlier in 1950. Passed over President HARRY S. TRUMAN's veto in September, shortly after the outbreak of hostilities in Korea, the measure went beyond the Truman loyalty program for government employees and attempted to limit the operation of subversive groups in all areas of American life. It also sought to shift the authority for security matters to congressional leadership.

The measure, the most severe since the SEDITION ACT of 1918, was composed of two parts. Title I, known as the Subversive Activities Control Act, required communist organizations to register with the attorney general and furnish complete membership lists and financial statements. Although membership and office holding in a communist organization was not, by the act, a crime, the measure did make it illegal knowingly to conspire to perform any act that would "substantially contribute" to the establishment of a totalitarian dictatorship in the United States. It also forbade employment of communists in defense plants and granting them passports. Finally it established a bipartisan SUBVERSIVE ACTIVITIES CONTROL BOARD to assist the attorney general in exposing subversive organizations. In ALBERTSON V. SUBVERSIVE ACTIVITIES CONTROL BOARD (1965), the Court held the compulsory registration provisions unconstitutional. (See MARCHETTI V. UNITED STATES, 1968.)

Title II provided that when the President declared an internal security emergency, the attorney general was to apprehend persons who were likely to engage in, or conspire with others to engage in, acts of espionage or sabotage and intern them "in such places of detention as may be prescribing by the Attorney General." Congress subsequently authorized funds for special camps for such purposes. (See PREVENTIVE DETENTION.) Other provisions denied entrance to the country to ALIENS who were members of communist organizations or who "advocate[d] the economic, international, and governmental doctrines of any other form of totalitarianism." Naturalized citizens joining communist organizations within five years of acquiring CITIZENSHIP were liable to have it revoked.

The courts subsequently held invalid the passport, registration, and employment sections of the act. Section 103, establishing detention centers for suspected subversives, was repealed in September 1971.

PAUL L. MURPHY

Bibliography

HARPER, ALAN 1969 *The Politics of Loyalty: The White House and the Communist Issue, 1946–1952.* Westport, Conn.: Greenwood Press.

INTERNATIONAL EMERGENCY ECONOMIC POWERS ACT
91 Stat. 1625 (1977)

This act grants the President limited economic powers "to deal with any unusual and extraordinary threat . . . to the national security, foreign policy, or economy of the United States" which arises "in whole or substantial part outside the United States" and which is declared by the President to constitute "a national emergency." The primary purpose of the act, however, was to restrict the Trading With the Enemy Act of 1917, under which the President had come to enjoy large discretionary power during times of declared emergency.

The 1977 act limits the authority created by declaration of a national emergency to an instant threat only and removes the President's authority to exercise during peacetime certain economic powers available in time of war. It also obligates the President to "consult" with Congress, if possible, prior to the declaration of a national emergency, to report on the circumstances said to necessitate the extraordinary measures, and to report to Congress every six months on the exercise of powers under the act.

Although the act permits the termination of a declared national emergency by concurrent resolution of Congress, the decision in IMMIGRATION AND NATURALIZATION SERVICE V. CHADHA (1983), declaring the use of the LEGISLATIVE VETO unconstitutional, places this restraint in doubt. In sum, however much Congress may have intended to restrict presidential EMERGENCY POWERS over international economic transactions, the actual extent of the change is uncertain.

BURNS H. WESTON

(SEE ALSO: *Dames & Moore v. Regan,* 1981; *Foreign Affairs; War Powers; War Powers Resolution.*)

Bibliography

HENKIN, LOUIS 1972 *Foreign Affairs and the Constitution.* Pages 118–123. Mineola, N.Y.: Foundation Press.
NOTE 1978 Presidential Emergency Powers Related to International Economic Transactions: Congressional Recognition of Customary Authority. *Vanderbilt Journal of Transnational Law,* 11:515–534.

INTERPOSITION

State governments have occasionally declared that acts of Congress are unconstitutional and have sought to "interpose" their authority between their citizens and the national government. This interposition has taken several forms, from refusals to cooperate with federal administration to the purported NULLIFICATION of federal acts, SECESSION, and even armed rebellion. JAMES MADISON and THOMAS JEFFERSON lent their prestige to the general notion of interposition when they wrote, respectively, the VIRGINIA AND KENTUCKY RESOLUTIONS in opposition to the ALIEN AND SEDITION ACTS of 1798. New England Federalists claimed powers of interposition in opposition to trade embargoes and the federal use of state militias during the War of 1812. Acting on the state sovereignty theory of JOHN C. CALHOUN in 1832, South Carolina declared two tariff acts "null, void, and no law." Antislavery legislatures enacted PERSONAL LIBERTY LAWS to obstruct federal fugitive slave laws. Long after the Civil War, southern legislatures attempted "massive resistance" to school DESEGREGATION. And in 1970 Massachusetts sought to prohibit the conscription of its citizens for the VIETNAM WAR.

Although these and other attempts express no single constitutional philosophy, interposition is usually associated with the theory that the sole basis of the Union is the written Constitution, not a common culture or other integrative forces; that the people who created the Constitution were members of separate and still sovereign states, not a national community; and that the Constitution is a mere contract among the states for establishing a general government with but few, well-defined objectives. From these premises it was supposed to follow that individual states could interpose to protect their reserved powers. To Calhoun and his followers in the 1830s interposition included nullifying federal laws and, in extreme cases, secession. The nullificationists cited the Virginia and Kentucky Resolutions and presented their position as consistent with the Constitution. Madison, then in his eighties, bitterly opposed and sought to disclaim paternity of any nullificationist theory. He insisted that his original version of interposition sanctioned no more than nonbinding state expression of constitutional opinion as steps toward arousing the public or amending the Constitution. This kind of interposition was fully consistent with national supremacy, the divisibility of sovereignty between nation and states, and a perpetual union. The nullificationists, said Madison, were asserting a RIGHT OF REVOLUTION, not a constitutional right.

Scholars point out that an extended constitutional debate would hardly have been necessary in the 1790s if all that Madison had then contemplated was a state's right to express and invite other states to express nonbinding opinions. But, Madison's candor aside, his final

version of interposition need not have been toothless. The history of interposition shows that the states' role in the AMENDING PROCESS gives even the nonbinding opinions of a small number of states a special potential for awakening public interest in constitutional questions and undermining the perceived legitimacy of national policy. Practiced with sufficient regularity by enough states, the tamest kind of interposition might have had a strong influence on the pace and direction of constitutional change.

SOTIRIOS A. BARBER

(SEE ALSO: *Theories of the Union.*)

Bibliography

CORWIN, EDWARD S. 1912 National Power and State Interposition. *Michigan Law Review* 10:535–551.

KILPATRICK, JAMES JACKSON 1957 *The Sovereign States: Notes of a Citizen of Virginia.* Chicago: Henry Regnery Co.

INTERPRETIVISM

See: Constitutional Interpretation

INTERSTATE COMITY

See: Full Faith and Credit; Privileges and Immunities

INTERSTATE COMMERCE

The term "interstate commerce" does not appear in the Constitution. Nor do the few debates in the CONSTITUTIONAL CONVENTION OF 1787 over the wording of the COMMERCE CLAUSE offer much help in discerning what the Framers meant by granting Congress the power to regulate commerce "among the several states." The absence of expressed specific intent led WILLIAM W. CROSSKEY to examine contemporary usage and to theorize that the national power over commerce was intended to be virtually exclusive and to include not only interstate commerce but INTRASTATE COMMERCE as well. One of the Framers' intentions was to eliminate the destructive conflicts between contradictory state practices under the Confederation government. Chief Justice JOHN MARSHALL so assumed when he defined the term in GIBBONS V. OGDEN (1824), a case that has guided interpretation to this day. Interstate commerce, he wrote, is that "which concerns more states than one" and it even extends "to those internal concerns which affect the states generally." In the nineteenth century the clause was more often applied as a restriction on state powers than as a positive grant of national power, and as EDWARD S. CORWIN remarked, "the word 'commerce,' as designating the thing to be protected against State interference, long came to dominate the clause, while the potential word 'regulate' remained in the background." In HOUSTON, EAST & WEST TEXAS RAILWAY V. UNITED STATES (1914), the Court expanded the reach of congressional power by permitting federal regulation of purely intrastate commerce because, in the railroad case before it, the two were inextricably linked.

The scope of the commerce clause has encouraged the Court to devise a number of tests throughout its history to determine limits to the term, the best known of which is the STREAM OF COMMERCE DOCTRINE. (See also SELECTIVE EXCLUSIVENESS, EFFECTS ON COMMERCE, and SHREVEPORT DOCTRINE). The Supreme Court has thus held that "interstate commerce" means both movement that crosses state lines and movement that does not but that adversely affects interstate commerce. It includes tangible items as well as intangible ones. In *Gibbons*, Marshall defined it as "commercial intercourse," but even this expansive reading has been widened. *Caminetti v. United States* (1917) is only one of many cases in which the Court decided that no commercial motive need be present. Moreover, movement itself is not essential; in WICKARD V. FILBURN (1942), Justice ROBERT H. JACKSON disdained semantic formulas and declared that agricultural PRODUCTION affects interstate commerce. Such a broad view of the commerce power has allowed Congress to regulate not only traditional SUBJECTS OF COMMERCE but also criminal activity, professional sports, antitrust cases, and RACIAL DISCRIMINATION.

DAVID GORDON

Bibliography
STERN, ROBERT L. 1955 The Scope of the Phrase *Interstate Commerce. American Bar Association Journal* 41:823–826, 871–874.

INTERSTATE COMMERCE ACT
24 Stat. 379 (1887)

This act, which initiated federal authority in ECONOMIC REGULATION, created an administrative commission to wield federal power. Congress's approach, in Isaiah Sharfman's words, was "tentative and experi-

mental" because doubts existed whether the government could so act. The legislation nevertheless marked a first attempt to organize an increasingly chaotic field.

Until the 1870s railroads had been free to expand and operate, essentially unregulated, yet encouraged by land grants and public subsidies. As speculation, rate discrimination, and other abuses increased, popular opinion grew correspondingly negative. State legislatures, especially in the Midwest, began setting maximum rail rates and establishing commissions to maintain their reasonableness. Although the Supreme Court sustained such regulation in the GRANGER CASES (1877), it soon retrenched and, in WABASH, ST. LOUIS & PACIFIC RAILWAY V. ILLINOIS (1886) the Court asserted the states' inability to regulate rates even partly interstate. The Court thus created a vacuum—the states could not regulate and Congress had not regulated.

Compromise legislation finally passed Congress in 1887, the outcome of over 150 bills in nearly twenty years. The act applied to "any common carrier or carriers engaged in the [interstate or foreign] transportation of passengers or property," and specifically exempted INTRASTATE COMMERCE. Reiterating the COMMON LAW, the act ordered all charges to be "reasonable and just." The act created the INTERSTATE COMMERCE COMMISSION (ICC), empowered it to set aside unjust rates, but neglected to give it the power to replace them with new ones. The ICC also had authority to investigate complaints; significantly, an individual need not demonstrate direct damage to file a complaint. Several sections forbade devices such as rebates, pooling, and LONG HAUL–SHORT HAUL DISCRIMINATION. The act also required publication of rate schedules, rendering the carriers liable for injuries sustained as a result of any violations. Courts were to consider ICC findings *prima facie* EVIDENCE but commission orders became effective immediately *only* if voluntarily obeyed. Carriers took advantage of this loophole to APPEAL virtually every order, leaving them free to disregard the ICC until a court sustained it. Demanding to hear cases *de novo*, the courts implicitly invited the carriers to withhold evidence from the ICC; courts reversed ICC orders regularly on both legal and policy grounds. As Sharfman noted, the commission's powers were thus "restricted in scope and feeble in effect." In 1897 the Supreme Court dealt the ICC two stunning blows. Even though the act had not expressly granted the ICC rate-setting authority, the commission had assumed the power. In INTERSTATE COMMERCE COMMISSION V. CINCINNATI, NEW ORLEANS & TEXAS PACIFIC RAILWAY, the

Court denied the commission this power. *ICC v. Alabama Midland Railway Co.* (1897) rendered the long haul–short haul clause a dead letter.

In part because of the judicial evisceration of the act, Congress amended it nearly a dozen times by 1925. Among the most important supplementary legislation were the ELKINS ACT, the HEPBURN ACT, and the MANN-ELKINS ACT. The Supreme Court endorsed Congress's efforts in several cases, culminating in INTERSTATE COMMERCE COMMISSION V. ILLINOIS CENTRAL RAILROAD (1910).

DAVID GORDON

Bibliography

HOOGENBOOM, ARI and OLIVE 1976 *A History of the ICC: From Panacea to Palliative.* New York: W. W. Norton.

SHARFMAN, ISAIAH L. 1931 *The Interstate Commerce Commission.* Vol. I. New York: Commonwealth Fund.

INTERSTATE COMMERCE COMMISSION

See: Regulatory Commissions

INTERSTATE COMMERCE COMMISSION v. ALABAMA MIDLAND RAILWAY COMPANY

See: *Interstate Commerce Commission v. Cincinnati, New Orleans & Texas Pacific Ry. Co.*

INTERSTATE COMMERCE COMMISSION v. CINCINNATI, NEW ORLEANS & TEXAS PACIFIC RAILWAY
167 U.S. 479 (1897)
INTERSTATE COMMERCE COMMISSION v. ALABAMA MIDLAND RAILWAY COMPANY
168 U.S. 144 (1897)

As one of Justice JOHN MARSHALL HARLAN's dissents in these cases declared, these decisions stripped the Interstate Commerce Commission (ICC) "of authority to do anything of an effective character." The ICC succeeded in only one APPEAL to the Supreme Court between 1897 and 1906. The INTERSTATE COM-MERCE ACT required "reasonable and just" rates and, although it gave the commission the right to set aside unreasonable rates, it did not expressly grant them power to revise rates. The ICC had operated for a decade on the assumption that it had had such power; without it, the statute's injunction to provide reasonable rates could hardly be accomplished. In *ICC v. Cincinnati, New Orleans & Texas Pacific Railway* (1897) the Court majority insisted that if the act's framers had intended to grant them such powers, they "would have said so." The act provided no explicit authority, however, and the extent of the power militated against "such a grant . . . by mere implication." If the commission exercised such rate-making powers, it would have been making law and it had only the power to "execute and enforce, not to legislate." Such a quasi-legislative DELEGATION OF POWER could not yet secure approval from the Court; denied power to set rates, the commission now had only the right (of questionable use) to void unreasonable rates. Justice Harlan dissented from that decision as well as from Justice GEORGE SHIRAS's opinion in *ICC v. Alabama Midland Railway Company* (1897), decided a few months later. That case nearly destroyed the LONG HAUL–SHORT HAUL provision in the act as well as the commission's fact-finding authority. Despite unequivocal language declaring the ICC findings of fact to be conclusive and binding on courts, Shiras decided that the clause empowering CIRCUIT COURTS to hear appeals necessarily implied a right of the courts to reexamine all the facts; they could not overrule the commission in both law and fact. By not presenting all EVIDENCE until an appeal, the railroads could and soon did mock ICC orders. These decisions severely restricted the commission's usefulness; not until the HEPBURN ACT of 1906 and the MANN-EL-KINS ACT of 1910 would Congress move to revive the commission.

DAVID GORDON

INTERSTATE COMMERCE COMMISSION v. ILLINOIS CENTRAL RAILROAD
215 U.S. 452 (1910)

The HEPBURN ACT of 1906 and a decision by the Supreme Court the following year began reviving the Interstate Commerce Commission (ICC) after a series of devastating decisions. The Court had denied the commission the power to revise rates in INTERSTATE COMMERCE COMMISSION V. CINCINNATI, NEW ORLE-

ANS & TEXAS PACIFIC RAILWAY (1897), and had struck hard at the provision of the INTERSTATE COMMERCE ACT outlawing LONG HAUL–SHORT HAUL DISCRIMINATION in *Interstate Commerce Commission v. Alabama Midland Railway Co.* (1897). The Court reversed ICC orders on both legal and policy grounds at an astonishing rate, and the commission spent nearly the first twenty years of its existence fighting Court-imposed obstacles.

The Interstate Commerce Act had declared that ICC findings were to be considered *prima facie* evidence but until 1907 the Court, in fact, reviewed all evidence *de novo*, thereby allowing the railroads to present previously withheld EVIDENCE on APPEAL. This practice discredited the commission and put the Court in the business of rate regulation. In *Illinois Central Railroad Company v. Interstate Commerce Commission* (1907), the Court declared that it would no longer reexamine the facts of a case on appeal; the commission was a responsible tribunal and its findings of fact would be accorded "probative force."

Because of the passage of the MANN-ELKINS ACT and a favorable 8–1 decision in *Interstate Commerce Commission v. Illinois Central Railroad,* 1910 was a good year for the ICC. In this case the Court indicated its willingness to support the commission, laying down its guidelines for the determination of the validity of ICC orders. The Justices expected to continue to review commission orders, but solely in reference to constitutional issues, statutory construction of "the scope of the delegated authority" under which the ICC issued the order, and the practical "substance" of the order. Nevertheless, the Court henceforth specifically refused "under the guise of exerting judicial power, [to] usurp merely administrative functions by setting aside a lawful administrative order upon our conception as to whether the administrative power has been wisely exercised. Power to make the order and not the mere expediency or wisdom of having made it is the question."

DAVID GORDON

INTERSTATE COMPACT

The Constitution, in Article I, section 10, recognizes the right of the states to enter into compacts and agreements with one another, but provides that the right shall not be exercised without the consent of Congress. In this respect, the Constitution continued the practice that had obtained under the ARTICLES OF CONFEDERATION. The right to enter into compacts and agreements is, as the Supreme Court said in *Hin-*

derlider v. La Plata Company (1938), the survival under the Constitution of "the age-old treaty-making power of independent sovereign nations."

Before 1921, most interstate compacts involved two (or at most three) states, and were either about boundaries or about boundary streams. One notable exception was the Chesapeake and Ohio Canal Compact (1825), involving Virginia, Maryland, Pennsylvania, and the District of Columbia, providing for joint incorporation of the canal company and mutual acceptance of legislation in its favor. Another was the Virginia–West Virginia Compact (1862) by which seceding Virginia agreed to the creation of West Virginia from part of its territory while the latter assumed part of the state debt.

The modern era of interstate compacts began with the New York Port Authority Compact (1921) and the Colorado River Compact (1923). The former created a single commission, jointly appointed by New York and New Jersey, to administer the Port of New York and the surrounding area. The latter was the first true multistate compact, allocating irrigation water among six states drained by the Colorado.

The success of these two agreements led politicians and scholars to see in interstate compacts a great potential for solving multistate problems without national legislation. FELIX FRANKFURTER and JAMES M. LANDIS, in an influential article published in 1925, advocated "imaginative adaptation" of the device to reach a multitude of subjects they deemed beyond the scope of congressional power under the Constitution, such as the generation and distribution of electricity. Buoyed by this public optimism, states proposed open-membership compacts on subjects such as WORKERS' COMPENSATION and child labor. Experience, however, demonstrated that interstate compacts were not a panacea for the ills of FEDERALISM, and, although the number negotiated steadily increased, after the 1930s compacts were confined to more narrowly interstate matters. This is true even of compacts to which all the states are parties, such as the Interstate Compact for Supervision of Parolees and Probationers.

Compacts between states are somewhat more binding than treaties between sovereign nations, because the states are subject to the CONTRACT CLAUSE, and, within the limits of the ELEVENTH AMENDMENT, the obligations imposed by interstate compacts are enforceable in federal courts.

On its face, the Constitution seems to require congressional consent to all interstate compacts and agreements. However, in *Virginia v. Tennessee* (1893) the Supreme Court held that a boundary agreement of 1802 had received Congress's consent through acquiescence because, although it never voted to approve the agreement, Congress followed its terms in such matters as establishing judicial districts. The court reasoned that only compacts touching on the powers of the national government or substantially affecting intergovernmental relationships within the federal system required explicit congressional approval. On the other hand, Congress may veto *any* compact or agreement, even if the states would have been fully competent to act in the absence of the compact.

When explicit approval is required, it may be given either before or after the compact is negotiated by the states. But the failure of Congress to enact a resolution of consent is not equivalent to a denial of consent: it may signify no more than that Congress believes its explicit consent to a particular compact is unnecessary.

DENNIS J. MAHONEY

Bibliography

FRANKFURTER, FELIX and LANDIS, JAMES M. 1925 "The Compact Clause of the Constitution—A Study in Interstate Adjustments." *Yale Law Journal* 34:685–729.

ZIMMERMANN, FREDERICK L. and WENDELL, MITCHELL 1951 *The Interstate Compact Since 1925.* Chicago: Council of State Governments.

———— 1976 *The Law and Use of Interstate Compacts.* Chicago: Council of State Governments.

INTIMATE ASSOCIATION

See: Freedom of Intimate Association

INTOLERABLE ACTS

See: First Continental Congress

INTRASTATE COMMERCE

The CONSTITUTIONAL CONVENTION OF 1787, by listing among Congress's enumerated powers the power to regulate commerce "among the several states" as well as with Indian tribes and foreign countries, appeared to reserve for regulation by each state its own domestic commerce. Indeed, notwithstanding Chief Justice JOHN MARSHALL's dictum that commerce does not stop at the state line but penetrates into the interior, for most of American constitutional history Congress respected and the Supreme Court enforced that division of power over commerce. After WICKARD V. FILBURN (1938), the distinction between intrastate and INTERSTATE COMMERCE effectively ceased to have any significance in constitutional law.

DAVID GORDON

INVALID ON ITS FACE

Legislation may be unconstitutional as applied to all, some, or none of the behavior it addresses. Usually, affected parties challenge a law's constitutionality only as applied to their own behavior. Occasionally, they claim a law is constitutionally invalid on its face—and therefore unenforceable against anyone, including them—because it would be unconstitutional ever to apply it. A penal law is invalid on its face, for example, when it so vaguely describes the conduct outlawed that it cannot give fair warning to anyone, or when every act the law prohibits is constitutionally protected. A challenge to such a law would present no STANDING problem. Sometimes, however, a litigant will assert that, regardless of whether a law is constitutional as applied to him it should be held invalid on its face because its coverage includes unconstitutional regulation of others.

Normally a federal court will deny standing to raise such a facial challenge when the law constitutionally regulates the would-be challenger, for the court perceives the claim as a request to go beyond the case before it. Responding to the request would require the court to decide what other situations the law governs—frequently an unresolved question of statutory interpretation—and then to decide whether some of the law's unapplied coverage would be unconstitutional. If the court should conclude that part of the law is invalid and part valid, it would have to decide whether the legislative framers would want the valid part to stand separately or the whole law to fall. Finally, if the law is constitutional as applied to the litigant, but would be unconstitutional in hypothetical application to others, the court may still have to decide whether to hold the law facially invalid despite a legislative desire to have the law's valid applications stand.

Formidable considerations militate against judicial rulings that laws are facially invalid. JUDICIAL REVIEW originates in the need to apply constitutional law to decide the case before the court, and a corollary principle requires courts to refrain from deciding hypothetical questions. When a court focuses only on the situation before it, it minimizes the need for unnecessary decisions of issues of both statutory and constitutional interpretation, and avoids considering other possible applications of the law in a factual vacuum. Finally, a conclusion of facial invalidity would prevent the valid enforcement of the law against a party whom the legislature intended to regulate. Normally, then, the Supreme Court denies a litigant STANDING to assert the unconstitutionality of legislation as it would be applied to others, except when the most compelling reasons are present.

The reason most often found compelling is the need to protect the freedom of expression of persons not before the court whom the law might inhibit. That was the rationale, for example, of THORNHILL V. ALABAMA (1940). Specifically, the FIRST AMENDMENT doctrines of OVERBREADTH and VAGUENESS sometimes permit one whose conduct the law constitutionally could reach to escape punishment, arguing that the law is invalid on its face because its seeming application to others discourages their protected expression. Intense controversy surrounds these facial challenges, however, largely because of differing perceptions of how inhibiting such laws really are. In areas involving other fundamental freedoms, such as the RIGHT TO TRAVEL, facial challenges have occasionally been successful, as in APTHEKER V. SECRETARY OF STATE (1964), again to protect persons who are never likely to be before a court from having their liberty circumscribed by the seeming applicability of an unconstitutional regulation.

A court will hold a law invalid on its face only in a case of necessity: where the law's very existence may affect the exercise of cherished liberties by nonparties lacking opportunity or willingness to challenge them, and where the inhibiting feature of the law cannot easily be cured by statutory interpretation. Absent such conditions federal courts will not, at the request of one whose behavior may constitutionally be regulated, decide how a law might apply and whether the law's potential application to other situations warrants holding it invalid on its face. The degree to which the Supreme Court permits facial challenges to legislation directly reflects the Justices' collective perception of the Court's institutional role in enforcing the Constitution. Narrow views of that role incline the Court to restrict facial challenges; a broader view commends it to entertain and encourage such a challenge in the interest of assuring the constitutional governance of society beyond the immediate case.

JONATHAN D. VARAT

INVASION OF PRIVACY

See: Right of Privacy

INVERSE CONDEMNATION

The course of action which a property owner may pursue against a governmental defendant to recover the JUST COMPENSATION guaranteed by the Fifth and FOURTEENTH AMENDMENTs when the defendant, without initiating an eminent domain proceeding, "takes" private property is called "inverse condemnation."

The elements of a compensable TAKING OF PROPERTY can occur under many different circumstances. An action to establish inverse condemnation is clearly proper when a governmental entity has destroyed, confiscated, or substantially abridged some right or privilege in the plaintiff's property or when the normal operation of governmental facilities results in a destructive interference with the use of the plaintiff's property by third persons, as by jet aircraft noise. Excessive regulation, resulting in an effective prohibition of substantially all use and value of the interest regulated, may also constitute a taking.

The most intractable issue in inverse condemnation litigation currently relates to regulatory takings. Although government may carry out many types of programs that adversely affect economic values without its actions constituting a taking, in some contexts PO-LICE POWER regulations may be so restrictive in character as to constitute a compensable taking, as in *Pennsylvania Coal Co. v. Mahon* (1922). However, no "set formula" has been developed for determining when a legislative measure has adversely affected property interests to that degree. The relative magnitude of the loss sustained by the property owner is relevant but not controlling. Factors suggestive of a taking, however, include the extent to which the government's actions have impaired legitimate investment-backed expectations of the owner and the fact that the regulation has resulted in an uncompensated acquisition of resources by the public entity. (See PENN CENTRAL TRANSPORTATION CO. V. NEW YORK CITY, 1978.) Factors often relied upon to negate a taking include the existence of widely shared compensating benefits resulting from the restrictions and the reflecting in the regulation of a rational legislative choice between mutually incompatible private interests.

Inverse condemnation jurisprudence is also complicated by uncertainty, so far not resolved by the Supreme Court, as to the scope of the relief available for regulatory takings. In many cases, for example, *Pennsylvania Coal Co.*, the taking rationale has been invoked to invalidate excessive regulatory action; in others, an award of monetary compensation has been granted. In *San Diego Gas & Electric Co. v. City of San Diego* (1981), four Justices, with a supporting dictum from a fifth, intimated that when a taking is enjoined, compensation for interim losses sustained by the property owner should be granted. And when overriding public interest so requires, governmental action that effects a taking may even be declared valid, subject to the payment of just compensation to those persons whose property has thereby been taken. (See DAMES & MOORE V. REGAN, 1981.)

Some commentators have argued, and a few courts have held, that the exclusive remedy for a regulatory taking is invalidation of the offending measure. These decisions generally reflect judicial reluctance to impose onerous burdens that could interfere with orderly fiscal planning by governmental agencies engaged in regulatory functions. They appear to be based on the questionable assumption that invalidation will necessarily be less disruptive to the achievement of public objectives than payment of compensation. As Justice WILLIAM J. BRENNAN suggested in *San Diego Gas & Electric Co.*, a more appropriate remedial posture would permit the governmental entity to choose whether to repeal the offensive regulation with payment of compensation for temporary losses or to retain it in force with payment of full compensation.

ARVO VAN ALSTYNE

Bibliography

MICHELMAN, FRANK I. 1967 Property, Utility, and Fairness: Commentaries on the Ethical Foundations of "Just Compensation Law." *Harvard Law Review* 80:1165–1258.
SAX, JOSEPH L. 1973 Takings and the Police Power. *Yale Law Journal* 74:36–76.

INVESTIGATIVE POWER

See: Legislative Investigations

INVIDIOUS DISCRIMINATION

Justice WILLIAM O. DOUGLAS led the Supreme Court's modern expansion of the guarantee of EQUAL PROTECTION OF THE LAWS. As early as 1942, in SKIN-

NER V. OKLAHOMA, Douglas used the term "invidious discrimination" to differentiate state-imposed inequalities demanding strict judicial scrutiny from other discriminations (particularly economic regulations) that were valid so long as they had a RATIONAL BASIS. The word "invidious," which suggests a tendency to provoke envy or resentment, is an appropriate label for governmental discriminations imposing the stigma of caste, especially RACIAL DISCRIMINATIONS. Fittingly, Douglas used the same label in LEVY V. LOUISIANA (1968) to describe discrimination based on the status of ILLEGITIMACY.

In HARPER V. VIRGINIA STATE BOARD OF ELECTIONS (1966), Douglas termed "invidious" the state's use of a POLL TAX as a condition on voting. As a WEALTH DISCRIMINATION case, *Harper* fit the dictionary definition of "invidious." In another view, however, *Harper* required STRICT SCRUTINY because the state impaired the FUNDAMENTAL INTEREST in voting. In this perspective, "individious discrimination" broadens into a label for the Court's ultimate conclusion on the issue of an equal protection violation. For Justice Douglas, either use of the term was acceptable.

In more recent racial discrimination decisions, the Court has turned the dictionary meaning of "invidious" upside down, using it to denote not the tendency of a discrimination to provoke ill will, but the malevolent purpose of government officials. In WASHINGTON V. DAVIS (1976), for example, the Court held that a law's racially selective impact did not demand strict scrutiny, absent a showing of "invidious discriminatory purpose." The language of constitutional doctrine, like the language of diplomacy, stands ready to serve causes both fair and foul.

KENNETH L. KARST

Bibliography

KARST, KENNETH L. 1969 Invidious Discrimination: Justice Douglas and the Return of the "Natural-Law–Due-Process Formula." *UCLA Law Review* 16:716–750.

INVOLUNTARY SERVITUDE

See: Peonage; Slavery and the Constitution

IREDELL, JAMES
(1751–1799)

James Iredell was one of the most active and important members of the United States Supreme Court during the 1790s. Although he was a strong nationalist and vigorous advocate of judicial power, he also was a political realist who understood, in a way that his contemporaries on the High Court did not, the widespread distrust of centralized government and an independent judiciary that existed in America following the American Revolution.

Iredell was the eldest son of a well-connected but financially troubled merchant from Bristol, England. When his father suffered a paralytic stroke, his mother's family, in 1768, arranged for him to become comptroller of the customs in Edenton, North Carolina. While performing his duties, Iredell studied law with Samuel Johnston, a leading member of the North Carolina bar, whose sister he married in 1773. Although he remained in the service of the king until the spring of 1776, his real sympathies were with the colonists, and after independence he became a firm supporter of the patriot cause. Following the break with England he served on a committee to revise old laws and draft new legislation to make government in North Carolina compatible with republicanism. He also helped create a judiciary system for the state, and reluctantly accepted an appointment as a Superior Court judge, a position from which he resigned after six months because he disliked riding circuit. In 1779 he was appointed attorney general of North Carolina.

In the sharp struggle that took place over the writing of a state constitution, Iredell sided with the more moderate and conservative Whigs who favored as few changes as possible from the old colonial form of government and wanted to see an independent judiciary, a strong executive, and property qualifications for voting. And in the political struggle of the 1780s, Iredell aligned himself with those who favored the enforcement of contracts, opposed debtor relief legislation, and defended the rights of Tories as protected by the Paris Peace Treaty of 1783. He denounced a number of laws adopted in the mid-1780s to confiscate Loyalist property, and in "An Address to the Public" in 1786 expressed his belief in the need for limitations upon the authority of the legislature: "I have no doubt but that the power of the Assembly is limited, and defined by the Constitution. It is the creature of the Constitution." Iredell further elaborated on how unbridled legislative authority could be checked in an August 26, 1787, letter to RICHARD DOBBS SPAIGHT, a delegate to the CONSTITUTIONAL CONVENTION, which contained one of the earliest and clearest theoretical expressions of the doctrine of JUDICIAL REVIEW: "I confess it has ever been my opinion that an act inconsistent with the Constitution was void;

and that the judges consistently with their duties, could not carry it into effect. The Constitution appears to me to be a fundamental law, limiting the powers of the legislative, and with which every exercise of those powers must, necessarily, be compared."

Iredell was a warm proponent of the adoption of the United States Constitution in 1787–1788, even though the opposition to it was particularly intense in North Carolina. In fact, North Carolina at first refused to ratify the Constitution, and did not accept the new government until November 1789, eight months after it had begun operations. During the course of the debate over ratification Iredell published a pamphlet entitled "Answers to Mr. [George] Mason's Objections to the New Constitution," which attracted national attention. In February 1790, President GEORGE WASHINGTON, recognizing Iredell to be a firm friend of the central government, appointed him to the United States Supreme Court.

Although Iredell continually complained about the hardships entailed in riding circuit, he performed his duties conscientiously and participated in almost all the important cases of the 1790s. Despite the fact that his various decisions were knowledgeable in the law, intelligent, and forcefully presented, it is not easy to classify Iredell according to the political and intellectual currents of his day. To be sure, as a Federalist he supported ALEXANDER HAMILTON's financial program, JAY'S TREATY, and the ALIEN AND SEDITION ACTS. Moreover, his opinions in *Penhallow v. Doane's Administrators* (1795) and HYLTON V. UNITED STATES (1796) had strong nationalist implications, and in CALDER V. BULL (1798) he reiterated his belief in judicial review. He also argued in behalf of an independent judiciary by taking strong exception to an attempt by Congress to require the Justices of the United States Supreme Court to serve as pension commissioners. But Iredell's experiences with North Carolina politics made him not only aware of but also sensitive to the jealousy of the states for their rights and the popular hostility that existed toward the federal judiciary. He thus dissented when the Supreme Court ruled against the state of Georgia in a suit brought by a citizen of South Carolina in CHISHOLM V. GEORGIA (1793). Iredell argued that the decision would be viewed as a dangerous assault upon the sovereignty of the states. His fears were well founded, for the protests against the decision were so widespread and intense that the ELEVENTH AMENDMENT to the Constitution was quickly adopted to deny jurisdiction to the federal courts in suits brought against a state by the citizens of another state or by foreigners. He also dissented in WARE V. HYLTON (1796) when the High Court declared invalid a Virginia statute of 1777 sequestering pre-Revolutionary debts of British creditors. Although ultimately upheld and enforced, the decision, as Iredell recognized, was the source of much popular dissatisfaction.

RICHARD E. ELLIS

Bibliography
GOEBEL, JULIUS, JR. 1971 *History of the United States Supreme Court: Antecedents and Beginnings to 1801.* New York: Macmillan.
MCREE, GRIFFITH J., ED. 1857 *Life and Correspondence of James Iredell.* New York: D. Appleton.

IRREBUTTABLE PRESUMPTION

Virtually any statutory classification can be seen as an irrebuttable presumption. A law forbidding automobile driving by anyone under sixteen may be described as a conclusive presumption that younger persons are unfit to drive—a presumption that is not universally true. The irrebuttable presumptions DOCTRINE was never applied to strike down an age classification, but its reasoning would have served: the law arguably denied PROCEDURAL DUE PROCESS by denying an individualized hearing on the fitness to drive of a person under sixteen. For a brief season in the mid-1970s, the Supreme Court was fond of this sort of analysis, but the infatuation soon ended.

The doctrine was foreshadowed in Chief Justice HARLAN FISKE STONE's concurrence in SKINNER V. OKLAHOMA (1942), which invalidated an Oklahoma law requiring the STERILIZATION of three-time felons. The Court rested on the EQUAL PROTECTION clause, but Stone argued that the law denied due process by denying a hearing on the inheritability of the defendant's criminal traits. He might have called the law an irrebuttable presumption of the inheritability of criminal traits of three-time felons. We can speculate that Stone thought the sterilization law was an irrational deprivation of liberty, but he was disinclined to revive SUBSTANTIVE DUE PROCESS so soon after the Court had tried to lay that doctrine to rest.

When, a generation later, the Court explicitly invoked the irrebuttable presumptions theory, one contributing factor surely was a similar wish to avoid resting decision on another theory. In the mid-1970s the Court was struggling with the question whether sex, like race, should be characterized as a SUSPECT CLASSIFICATION for purposes of equal protection analysis. (See FRONTIERO V. RICHARDSON, 1973.) In two cases, the Court avoided that issue by resorting to irrebuttable presumptions analysis. *Stanley v. Illinois* (1972) invalidated a law providing that the children of an unwed father became wards of the state upon the death of the mother. The law was attacked on SEX DISCRIMINATION grounds, but the Court escaped that issue, holding that the law violated due process by denying Stanley an individualized hearing on his fitness as a parent. Similarly, in CLEVELAND BOARD OF EDUCATION V. LAFLEUR (1974), a school board insisted that a pregnant teacher take maternity leave of several months before the expected birth of her child, and the Court avoided the sex discrimination issue by calling the law an irrebuttable presumption of unfitness to teach during the months of mandatory leave. The denial of a teacher's right to a hearing on her individual fitness was held to deny procedural due process.

The Court's strongest articulation of the irrebuttable presumptions doctrine came in VLANDIS V. KLINE (1973), which invalidated a state law conclusively presuming that a person who was a nonresident upon entering a state college remained a nonresident (for tuition purposes) throughout his college career. It violated due process to deny resident tuition rates on the basis of this presumption which was "not necessarily or universally true."

The irrebuttable presumptions doctrine was severely criticized both within and outside the Court. It was accurately seen as an equal protection or substantive due process doctrine in disguise, demanding the strictest sort of STRICT SCRUTINY of the necessity of legislative classifications. The Court plainly could not invalidate all classifications resting on factual assumptions "not necessarily or universally true." By 1975, the Court had had enough. In *Weinberger v. Salfi* (1975) the Court considered an antifraud provision of the SOCIAL SECURITY ACT allowing death benefits to a surviving spouse only when the couple had been married nine months before the decedent's death. A widow claimed benefits even though she had been married a shorter time, noting that her husband had died of a sudden, unexpected heart attack. The law was an excellent candidate for irrebuttable presumptions reasoning, but the Court blandly upheld it on grounds of administrative convenience. The whole doctrinal development had run its course in four terms of court.

KENNETH L. KARST

Bibliography

NOTE 1974 The Irrebuttable Presumption Doctrine in the Supreme Court. *Harvard Law Review* 87:1534–1556.

IRVIN v. DOWD
366 U.S. 717 (1961)

The Supreme Court ordered a new trial for a convicted mass murderer in Indiana on the ground that extensive pretrial coverage of the case by newspapers and radio had made it impossible for him to receive a FAIR TRIAL, even after one change of VENUE to a nearby county. In his opinion for the Court, Justice TOM C. CLARK noted that two-thirds of the jurors had been familiar with the facts of the case and believed Irvin to be guilty of the crimes. Justice FELIX FRANKFURTER used this occasion for one of his patented denunciations of overzealous reporting in criminal cases.

MICHAEL E. PARRISH

IRVINE v. CALIFORNIA
347 U.S. 128 (1954)

California police installed a listening device in a bedroom. Although this action violated fundamental constitutional principles protecting personal security, the Supreme Court held that under WOLF V. COLORADO (1949) the unconstitutionally obtained EVIDENCE could be used; the bedroom microphone did not sufficiently "shock the conscience," under ROCHIN V. CALIFORNIA (1952), to warrant exclusion.

HERMAN SCHWARTZ

ISLAND TREES BOARD OF EDUCATION v. PICO

See: *Board of Education v. Pico*